D1568516

FORTRESS OF THE SOUL

EARLY AMERICA
History, Context, Culture

Jack P. Greene and J. R. Pole,
SERIES FOUNDERS

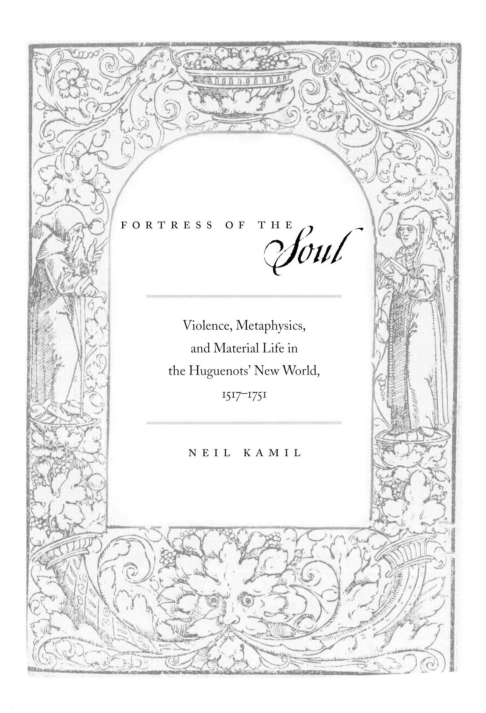

FORTRESS OF THE
Soul

Violence, Metaphysics,
and Material Life in
the Huguenots' New World,
1517–1751

NEIL KAMIL

THE JOHNS HOPKINS UNIVERSITY PRESS
BALTIMORE AND LONDON

*This book was brought to publication with the generous assistance of the Chipstone
Foundation, Milwaukee, Wisconsin, the Cooperative Society of the University of
Texas at Austin, and Oloruntoyin O. Falola, Frances Higginbothom Nalle
Centennial Professor in History at the University of Texas at Austin.*

❦ ❧

The Johns Hopkins University Press
2715 North Charles Street
Baltimore, Maryland 21218-4363
www.press.jhu.edu

Library of Congress Cataloging-in-Publication Data

Kamil, Neil, 1954–
Fortress of the soul : violence, metaphysics, and material life in the Huguenots' new
world, 1517–1751 / Neil Kamil.
p.   cm. — (Early America)
Includes bibliographical references and index.
ISBN 0-8018-7390-8 (hardcover : alk. paper)
1. Huguenots—New York (State)—New York—Intellectual life. 2. Huguenots—
New York (State)—New York—Social conditions. 3. Material culture—New
York (State)—New York—History. 4. Artisans—New York (State)—New York—
History. 5. Decorative arts—Social aspects—New York (State)—New York—
History. 6. New York (State)—History—Colonial period, ca. 1600–1775. 7. New
York (N.Y.)—Intellectual life. 8. Huguenots—France—La Rochelle—History.
9. La Rochelle (France)—Intellectual life. 10. La Rochelle (France)—Religious life
and customs. I. Title. II. Series.
F128.9.H9K36 2004
974.7′00441′0088242—dc21   2003010635

A catalog record for this book is available from the British Library.

Title page illustration: Detail from Martin Luther, *Appellatio* (1520), title page.

IN MEMORY OF

Betty Henry, my little artisan of the spirit,
and Charles Kamil, collector

Contents

PART III ❧ The Secrets of the Craft

❧❧

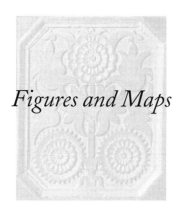

Figures and Maps

❧ Figures ❧

❧ Maps ❧

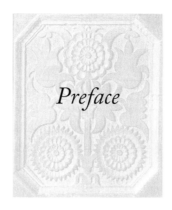

Preface

How were the working relationships between words and things defined in the Huguenots' New World? This is the essential historical question faced by every actor—and myself above all—in *Fortress of the Soul.* Moreover, how were dispersed fragments of spiritual and material life reordered by artisanal experience on the edge of transatlantic memory and perception to embody the substance of everyday life?

These questions emerged at first, from the mystery of a curious old chair. As a graduate student studying material culture made in colonial America, I confronted the puzzle of the New York leather chair for the first time. I was perplexed by this enigmatic thing that tradition had attributed to the hand of some nameless New York "Dutch" craftsman. To my naïve eye, its formal features projected mixed messages, and even these seemed to derive mostly from the ornamental vocabulary of regional French furniture. How did this complex artifactual language remain hidden in plain sight from centuries of antiquarians? My answer is found in chapter 15, a small part of the final project; it seems to me now, however, that *Fortress of the Soul* was inspired by questions about an itinerant culture of artisans that fled to early New York as refugees from demolished bastions of heresy in southwestern France. Once there, they labored in the interstices between concealment and representation to produce an artifact as ambiguous—and as ubiquitous—as their experience in the Atlantic world.

I am an American historian by training, and my research began in New York's colonial archives, which reach back to the Dutch period in New Amsterdam. These revealed the outlines of a transatlantic network of craftsmen and merchants who made and marketed the stylish New York leather chair in the early eighteenth century. Indeed, I discovered a treasure trove of French names from the region of Aunis-Saintonge associated with the luxury trade in upholstered furniture in the cosmopolitan and heterodox city. For, despite being an ethnic minority under both Dutch and English rule that comprised only about 11 percent of New York's total population, the city's most influential artisans were French Calvinist refugees.

This pattern was not surprising. Beginning in the mid sixteenth century, Huguenot refugees—though everywhere a minority—had started to transform the style and structure of artisanry throughout the courts and colonies of international Protestantism. What was surprising however, were the reasons for their mastery over the transformation, production, and consumption of material things. I soon learned that to study Huguenot artisans alone, in isolation from others, would be to disfigure experience. It is precisely their interactional practices that make them compelling for transatlantic historians. To understand refugee culture is also to encounter those people, places and things with which they came into contact. Wherever they went they created new contexts worthy of a kind of total history of material life. This is the subject of *Fortress of the Soul.*

Working my way through the archives back across the Atlantic, I reconstructed New York's French artisans' European origins and migration patterns. My method was the primarily slow and painstaking compilation of family genealogies. Though far from perfect, this is a more reliable indicator of transatlantic networks of interaction than divining cultural heritage from a quick reading of notoriously mutable surnames. Tracing the refugees, I found that their origins converged in southwestern France. Digging deeper into the sometimes grotesquely painful artisanal and religious history of this war-torn region, I came to understand that my initial puzzlement over the form of a New York chair had inadvertently revealed the incubator of a world of secrets.

Southwestern Huguenot artisans were the keepers of these secrets. Their shadow world was, in a social and historical sense, created by clandestine habits acquired over the course of generations of horrific religious violence. Maintenance of a subterranean culture of hiding, silence, and self-effacement became natural. This was especially true of Protestant survivors of the civil wars of religion in Aunis-Saintonge. During the wars, a vanguard of regional craftsmen wrote historical narratives and crafted innovative forms to represent the existence of a new world that had emerged from the ashes of the old in their troubled homeland well *before* they voyaged north into Protestant Europe and west to colonial America. The New World historiography of French refugee artisans in colonial New York was already being written and built on France's Atlantic coast nearly a century before New Amsterdam was settled. Huguenot New World history was perceived by its historian-craftsmen to be permanently fluid and portable. On a metaphysical level, however, craft secrets and the secrets of nature combined to form a powerful nexus in the southwestern Huguenot artisanal cosmos. This too emerged out of a condition of chaotic violence that sparked messianic experience and thoughts of final things, whereby nature, labor, and artisans interacted alchemically through soulish intermediaries capable of moving subtly between organic, bodily, and crafted materials. This artisanal experience of apocalypse reminds us of its definition as an act of unveiling and revelation. Leading Huguenot artisans thus became apocalyptics; they assumed the identity of revealers and interpreters for their communities of knowledge hidden in corrupt natural materials afflicted by the decrepitude of a fallen and aging earth.

The status and identity of skilled artisans during the late medieval and early modern period in general, and in Saintonge in particular, were therefore profoundly altered by alchemic paradigms promulgated by practitioners of the "new" Paracelsian science. Paracelsus celebrated artisans' unique abilities to position themselves as emulators of God's primordial labor in a rustic, fecund, and spiritualized material world. This claim to their special status as soulish reformers of matter was underscored by the widespread phenomenon of artisans' assertions of their role as manual philosophers; that is to say, of their God-given place in privileged territory in between venerable natural, oral, written, and material traditions, including their special hidden knowledge of materials both in and on the earth itself. Theirs was a Neoplatonic universe, in which everything was connected monistically at the most profound level of being and becoming. In this context, inner, soulish knowledge facilitated interdependence of natural and artisanal labor in the production of innovative things that, by virtue of their novelty, were destined to become commercially viable on both sides of the Atlantic. Material things were silent extensions of an entire cosmos of Huguenot artisanal discourse, mediating, like the refugees themselves, among different Protestant groups, as well as vis-à-vis their intractable enemies.

The Huguenot culture of silence and secrecy was commonly amplified by lies, stories, and other creative forms of artisanal representation of self or material goods, when contingency deemed it useful or appropriate. This too was a crucial component of craft skill and of the relation between words and things. Obfuscation was often key to the maintenance of the sort of fictional consensus that kept diverse or heterodox societies—such as Aunis-Saintonge or colonial New York—functioning more or less smoothly, without constant posturing or recourse to chaotic violence. Of course, violent resolution of differences was far more common in southwestern France than in colonial New York, where Old World experience taught that connivance between "enemies" in such tacit understandings should be the rule rather than the exception. Such connivance was over words left unsaid, but also things left unseen. Only if there were breakdowns in those delicate understandings or when renegotiation of new arrangements was necessary, were corrosive Huguenot craft "secrets" exposed to public scrutiny by their hosts. This occurred in early modern Britain when guilds representing native-born English craftsmen accused their Huguenot counterparts of "fraud" and "counterfeit"—forms of alchemic *maleficium*—and again in colonial New York, where Benjamin Faneuil, a refugee from La Rochelle and the foremost merchant of New York leather chairs, was accused of spying for Louis XIV.

Fortress of the Soul considers these phenomena from the perspectives of many disciplines. Much of what follows is intended to engage historians of science as well as historians of religion, technology, art and artisanry, sexuality (and the body), agriculture, human geography, textual criticism, the book, ecology, and, I hope most of all, the colonization of pluralistic New World societies. It is from the latter discipline (my own) that I develop the central questions I pose of the diverse materials, documents, and contexts I examine in this book: What was the relationship between several competing religious and cultural ideologies and the formation of material life? How were Continental and British artisanal paradigms from the Old World transformed in New World settings, and what did these changes mean from several vantage points? Can analysis of material culture address crucial problems in the maintenance and acculturation of colonial identities? What methods can historians use to analyze artifacts for evidence of social interaction, boundaries, and power relationships in pluralistic New World settings? Can our understanding of the Paracelsian worldview of highly mobile Protestant artisans such as the Huguenots of Aunis-Saintonge illuminate understanding of the relationship between skilled refugees and the expansion of a new international religious and political order? How does the interplay of violence, metaphysical experience, and material life help us to elucidate the unique roles that skilled artisans played as agents of change in early modern Atlantic history and culture?

One of the pleasures of completing this book is to acknowledge the enormous amount of help it actually took to get there.

I have been the fortunate recipient of several fellowships and grants, which made the research and writing possible. These included fellowships from the history department of the Johns Hopkins University, where the first part of the book began as a dissertation under the guidance of Professor Jack P. Greene, culminating in a Frederick Jackson Turner Research Fellowship in my final year. Without Professor Greene's support, patience, and especially his openness—ramified by the intellectual intensity of his formidable graduate seminar at Hopkins—this project could not have gotten off the ground. My graduate work was also influenced in many ways by Orest Ranum, whose early belief in material culture as a promising field of study for historians was an indispensable boost to my confidence, and whose awesome knowledge of seventeenth-century France was given generously to this often ill-informed student of early American history. The seminal work of Professors J. G. A. Pocock and Nancy Struever at Hopkins on the pragmatic relationship between language, form, and context in early modern life provided a fertile theoretical foundation, as did participation in Michael Fried's seminar on the phenomenology of perception. Gerard Defaux, Robert Forster, William Freehling, Josue Harrari, Richard Kagan, Vernon Lidke, John Russell-Wood, and Mack Walker were unfailingly helpful as readers, advisors, and teachers.

A Fulbright-Hays Advanced Student Research Fellowship for France facilitated my study in La Rochelle. I lived a wonderful year in the old fortress, where I enjoyed the warm hospitality of today's Rochelais, though most understood that I passed my time searching for traces of people their ancestors had displaced. Françoise Giteau and her staff at the Archives départementales de la Charente-Maritime and Bernard Démay and his staff at the Bibliothèque municipale de La Rochelle cheerfully complied with endless requests for documents and photocopies. The presence of the late Alain Parent, the first *conservateur* of the Musée du Nouveau Monde, a kindred spirit in the study of the transatlantic history of La Rochelle and its material life, and also at that time a newcomer to town, was essential to the success of this project. Alain and I spent many hours driving the backroads of Aunis and Saintonge in search of artifacts from the region's past. His wholehearted support, and the town's strong backing of his new museum with interests in the *outre-mer* similar to mine, encouraged librarians, historians, antiquarians, and collectors to share local knowledge with me. The late Father Bernard Coutant (who, when he discovered my interest in furniture, produced a handwritten manuscript on the subject from decades of work in La Rochelle's notarial registers) was generous with advice on the vagaries of the archives' cataloguing system. Among the local antiquarians who allowed access to their personal collections and shared hands-on experience with the early pottery of La Chapelle-des-Pots, I am particularly grateful to Jean-Pierre Bayeux, Pierre Clion, Jacques Denis, Yvette Gautron, and Florence Laversin. New friends in La Rochelle and Saintes made time away from the archives a great pleasure, as they kindly showed me the parts of their ancient region and its waterways they knew and loved best. Patrick Soulimant and Sylvie Gaud Soulimant opened the doors to their old stone farmhouse at Courcoury, outside Saintes, and joined me whenever I wanted to explore Palissy's old haunts. I also owe a huge debt of gratitude to that great sailor and chef Philippe Lecalve, as well as to his wife, Martine, and all the gang at Le Coquelicot in La Rochelle, for the food and wine and company.

Many fruitful hours were spent as a postdoctoral fellow at the Folger Institute in the Folger Shakespeare Library, where I took part in Owen Hannaway's seminar on *technologia* and natural philosophy in the early modern period. Hannaway's pathbreaking work at Hopkins on the history of alchemy, artisanry, and manual philosophy has informed this project in fundamental ways. His enthusiastic support, friendship, and encouragement have meant more than he can know.

Subsequently, I served as an National Endowment for the Humanities research associate and postdoctoral fellow in early American history at the University of Maryland, College Park, where for two years I worked on the book while administering the Washington Area Seminar in Early American History and Culture, then directed by my friend and colleague John J. McCusker. This experience culminated in a conference that drew its themes from my research and the resulting volume of the same title, *Religion, Popular Culture and Material Life in the Middle Colonies and the Upper South,*

1650–1800, edited by McCusker and myself (College Park, Md.: Maryland Colloquium on Early American History, 1990). I remember my sojourn at College Park fondly, not only because I got to know John, but also because my project benefited from the insights of the famously strong (and strong-minded) group of colonial historians who sat around the table at that seminar. I am speaking, of course, of Lois Carr, Emory Evans, Ron Hoffman, Alison Olson, and Lorena Walsh.

Finally, as its length and numerous photographs will attest, this was an expensive book to publish, and I am happy to gratefully acknowledge generous assistance from the Chipstone Foundation, a personal subvention given by Oloruntoyin O. Falola, Frances Higginbothom Nalle Centennial Professor in History, the University of Texas at Austin, and a University Cooperative Society Subvention Grant, awarded by the University of Texas at Austin.

Research was facilitated by the enthusiastic assistance of the staffs of a number of libraries: among those who were particularly helpful, I thank Neville Thompson of the Winterthur Library; Leo Hershkowitz of the Historical Documents Division, Klapper Library, Queens College, New York; the Interlibrary Loan departments at Eisenhower Library of the Johns Hopkins University and the Perry-Castañeda Library at the University of Texas at Austin; archivists at the New York Historical Society Library, the New York Public Library's Rare Book and Manuscript Room, the New York Genealogical and Biographical Society, and the Friends' Library of New York City; Heidi Hass of the New York Society Library; and Phyllis Barr of the Trinity Church Archives.

Many wonderful days were spent sorting though the collections of museums and historical societies on both sides of the Atlantic. I owe a special debt of gratitude to the unparalleled collections of colonial American furniture and decorative arts at Henry Francis du Pont Winterthur Museum, where, under the guidance of the late Benno M. Forman as my thesis advisor, I first began to ponder problems of influence and form in New York Colony. I am also grateful to the late Marge Sterns and Deborah Waters of the Museum of the City of New York; Joe Butler, Anne Larin, and Kate Eagen Johnson of Historic Hudson Valley; John Scherer of the New York State Museum; Frances Gruber Safford and Peter M. Kenny of the Metropolitan Museum of Art; the late Don Pierce and Diane Pilgrim, formerly of the Brooklyn Museum; Susan Schoelwer of the Connecticut Historical Society; William Hosley, formerly of the Wadsworth Atheneum; Pat Kane and David Barquist of the Yale University Art Gallery; Michael Brown and David Warren of Bayou Bend Museum and Gardens; Roderick Blackburn, formerly of the Albany Institute of History and Art; Mrs. Tennant of the Bowne House Historical Society; Dean Failey, formerly director of the Society for the Preservation of Long Island Antiquities; Mrs. Joan Kindler, Clerk of the Friends' Meetinghouse in Flushing; Mitchell Grubler and Richard Hourahan of the Queens Historical Society; and Luke Beckerdite, whose work at the Chipstone Foundation has reenergized the publication of American furniture history. Chapter 15 has appeared in Chipstone's journal *American Furniture* in a different form and context; I am grateful to its editors for permission to include a new version of that essay here.

The staff at the Musée national céramique de Sèvres in Paris kindly allowed me to view its collection of early Saintongeais pottery although the galleries were closed to visitors. I also benefited from the expertise of Lise Carrier, curator of the Musées d'Or-bigny-Bernon and des Beaux-Arts at La Rochelle; M. le docteur Duguy, curator of the Musée d'histoire naturelle et d'ethnographie de La Rochelle; and Mlle. Olga de Sainte-Affrique, historian and curator of the Musée protestant de La Rochelle. Jean Chapelot, whose archeological scholarship on the pottery and kiln sites in and around La Chapelle-des-Pots has become indispensable to all subsequent work on the subject, helped with advice and encouragement.

A number of friends and colleagues read at least part of the manuscript at various stages, including Bob Abzug, Rudy Binion, Dave Bowman, Sally Clarke, Sam Cohn, David Crew, Susan Deans-Smith, John Demos, Jack P. Greene, Michael G. Hall, Peter Jelavich, Ben Kaplan, Kevin Kenney, Brian Levack, Howard Miller, Martha Newman, Michael O'Brien, Jean Russo, Jim Sidbury, Mark Smith, Pamela H. Smith, Denise Spellberg, Nancy Struever, and Mauricio Tenorio. Elizabeth Hedrick shared her essays and ideas about Sir Kenelm Digby, helping to illuminate the many lives of that obscure yet ubiquitous courtier and alchemist. Bruce Hunt generously placed his encyclopedic knowledge of the history of science at my service too many times to remember. Ann Ramsey's keen insight into expressions of Catholic spirituality in seventeenth-century France was helpful on many occasions, as was Bob Olwell's understanding of the history of French refugees in the South Carolina low country, an early matrix of Huguenot culture in the Deep South. Alan Miller gave freely of his unparalleled knowledge of early woodworking. Bob Brugger at the Johns Hopkins University Press has stood behind this project from the beginning, waiting patiently until I was finally ready to relinquish the manuscript. Peter Dreyer's editing was first-rate. Avi Zakai was a one-man cheering section in Baltimore and Jerusalem. The friendship and moral support of Harvey and Sandy Sussman and John Tongate have been constant, and John Dorfman and Nickie Irvine have helped in so many ways that I can never thank them enough, especially for their generosity of spirit.

Caroline Castiglione, Donna Evergates, Alison Frazier, Janet Meisel, and Anna Taylor helped make sense of my translations of "corrupted" forms of Latin used by artisans and natural philosophers during the sixteenth and seventeenth centuries. Arndt Bohm reviewed some tricky German. But my deepest gratitude in this context is reserved for Marie-Aline Irvine, who spent many hours cheerfully comparing notes on my translations of Bernard Palissy's sometimes intractable Saintongeais French. Translation is a complex and inexact labor at best, but this is especially true of early modern languages. This task was made much less difficult by reference to Randle Cotgrave's great *Dictionarie of the French and English Tongues* (London, 1611), a monument of seventeenth-century translation.

My sister Susan Kamil, a well-known editor, accustomed to refining the work of truly accomplished writers, waded through an early draft of the first part of the book and somehow emerged from the morass with sage advice. My wife, Madeline Irvine, has lived with every word of this book for so long that she tells the story better than I can. She believed in me, and in it, more than I have myself.

I am unable to place this book in the hands of two family members who contributed more to the formation of my historical sensibilities than they ever imagined, but who died before it was finished. For them I reserve the dedication.

FORTRESS OF THE SOUL

Introduction

Fortress of the Soul is the story of a subterranean culture on the move, its membership fragmented by chronic warfare, exclusion, and political instability and actively in search of new modes of security. How, then, was security reinvented as a cultural practice by refugees from religious violence in the early modern transatlantic world?

Beginning with the French civil wars of religion in the 1550s, Huguenot artisans from the southwestern regional culture that supplied the vast majority of French refugee craftsmen and women to New Amsterdam and New York in the seventeenth century mastered an apocalyptic shift from the corporate and militaristic "*place* of security"—epitomized by the massive immobile (and hence militarily vulnerable) medieval fortress system protecting La Rochelle—to a reformed program of protection based on the skillful construction of portable and individualistic modes of personal security, deployed mostly in domestic space. What I call "artisanal security" was based on the rural craftsman's traditional mastery of manual skills and knowledge of natural materials, which were enormously valuable and infinitely transferable in the Atlantic world, particularly in land- and resource-rich but labor-poor British America.

Artisanal security was deeply informed by models of Paracelsian natural philosophy. While Paracelsus believed in prophesy and the power of the stars to control the lives of men and women, at the same time he also believed that chance discoveries in Nature made by mobile individuals with hidden knowledge and skill would enable a few to change fate and resist the tumults and oppressions of history. Paracelsians promoted the secrets of such "rustic" knowledge internationally to technologically minded artisans through a new alchemic program of natural philosophy. This program also promoted natural camouflage through personal and religious dissimulation, inner spiritual knowledge of local earth materials, and socioeconomic and spiritual cooperation across confessions and especially refugee groups exiled by persecution. Paracelsians simultaneously transmuted raw matter and refitted older cultural structures to meet the challenge of New World contexts and encounters. This was inner security without walls. Personal protection and family survival depended on creativity and innovation with available natural materials and commercial markets, exploitation of those materials suffused with hidden (that is, Neoplatonic) soulishness that descended through angelic intermediaries from God, and the ability of mobile craft networks to respond skillfully to almost any contingency. Security depended on the rapidity with which dispersed fragments of Huguenot artisanal and mercantile culture converged on specific New World societies to exploit constantly shifting shortages of skilled labor. One such society was colonial New York, home to religious refugees from European wars from the beginning of its existence as New Amsterdam. Conditioned to quest for personal and economic security by a culture of violence and vulnerability, the Paracelsian material-holiness synthesis, created and diffused in domestic artifacts made by these shadowy New World travelers, is the focal point of the narrative.

The relationship between security, religiosity, and materialism in early American transatlantic history, as an artful product of interaction between written and oral culture, found its impetus in the bloody history of the expansion and persecution of heresy in Reformation and Counter-Reformation Europe during the wars of religion. That is why *Fortress of the Soul* places American colonial history and material life firmly within the larger context of early modern Atlantic history and culture. What I call the "new world" experience of Huguenot artisans in southwestern France began with the mimetic religious violence that exploded between the confessions during the early sixteenth century, continuing through the extended period of emigration to Protestant Europe, as well Latin America and colonial British America. New world historiography was actively written and reconstructed by southwestern Huguenot artisans during the long *désert* ("desert") period in France during which French Protestants were disenfranchised and their churches demolished. This foundational historiography informed and long predated the large-scale emigration of Huguenots to the North American colonies.

This early Huguenot historiographical corpus was vital ideological and material preparation for the ultimate dislocation that occurred over a century later, in 1685, with the Revocation of the Edict of Nantes. This event, played out on a much more familiar political and military terrain, outlawed Reformed religion in France and led to the "dispersion" of the majority of openly practicing Protestants. The Revocation also expedited reconstruction of fragments of Huguenot artisanal culture in colonial British America. While a vanguard of historians of early America has shifted to the study of transatlantic themes, with a few important exceptions, the ever-present European cultural context seldom receives equivalent treatment. Complex and subtle historical patterns have often been reduced to stereotypes, undermining both the European and also the American milieux. This threatens the conceptual balance and unity that remains the great promise of transatlantic projects. In considering the conventionally separated "background" of Europe and the presumably independent historical "foreground" of colonial America together as a single entity, *Fortress of the Soul* devotes equal space and energy to both. By doing so, I hope to underscore the reality of their dynamic and interactional nature in the early modern period.

To follow Huguenot artisans from Aunis-Saintonge in coastal France out into the expanding Atlantic world of international Protestantism is to journey from the great walled city of La Rochelle, whose rebellious citizens experienced the victory of the Reformation in 1568, followed in 1628 by its utter reversal and the annihilation of the fortress and most of its Protestant population by the absolute monarchy to rural artisans' workshops, alchemic laboratories, and clandestine forest conventicles hidden from pursuing Counter-Reformation forces; to the courts, meetinghouses, and marketplaces of Protestant northern Europe and London; and finally to the competitive and diverse commercial and religious milieux that converged in colonial New Amsterdam / New York. In this heterogeneous port town, I explore social, cultural, economic, and spiritual interaction between Huguenot artisanal networks and the many other Protestant, spiritualist, and artisanal traditions that developed similar New World historiographies based on experience of religious violence, enlarging an international process of soulish convergence. Histories of experience of religious violence as an animating force in individual and group identity among the *artisanat* of early America suggest that we try to understand the "confusion" of middle colonial life by using the terms of coherence and unity applied by these fragmented and dispersed groups to their *own* historical conditions and memories, rather than by simply rehearsing conventional historiographical constructs of regional chaos and factionalism.

Combining documentary and artifactual evidence illuminates how the function of sacred violence may be perceived in artisanal adaptations of alchemic processes. Thus certain Huguenot artisans associated the metaphysical and regenerative functions of alchemy with their own experience of religious war. For alchemists, change and material reformation were constants of the natural world; decay, death, and growth were synonymous. The task, therefore, was to control and discipline this fundamental process. Emulating transmutation and change within the hidden recesses of the earth—and by analogy their own bodies—refugee artisans appropriated from Nature innovative and clandestine ways to "build with the destroyer." This brought their personal and corporate history to bear on material life, as ways to survive exile and loss spiritually and finally to prosper materially. Natural artisanal languages were also mute. They functioned as spiritual and material modes of communication under the radar of authority—means for sectarian and heretical groups to supplement voices silenced by military and religious authority.

Conflation of materialism and religiosity had the potential, therefore, to facilitate the social convergence of competing sectarian groups in the heterodox middle colonies. Quiet interaction with and visual perception of natural and hybrid cultural materials (including domestic furniture, pottery, houses, and books) were crucial to alchemical social processes. This, then, is also a history of the practice of spiritualized *perception* among Protestant groups central to the economic, cultural, and political landscape of the middle colonies. New York's Huguenots and Quakers, for example, forged common ground and combined extensive artisanal networks connecting Manhattan and western Long Island. This transpired, in part, by members of both groups privileging similar signifiers in the elemental attributes of available materials. Shared perceptions of natural and crafted materials among craftsmen, patrons, and consumers augmented the potential for communal skill and power through the practice of artisanal security. Common visual vernaculars were created that provided information to some viewers while excluding others. This is perhaps a truism among semioticians, yet it was no coincidence that artisans in New York's Huguenot and Quaker communities were deeply influenced by Germanic spiritualism, understood through the diffusion of Paracelsian texts and intensified by Neoplatonic soulishness under pressure from religious violence. Both shared a messianic sense of visual perception in the natural and man-made worlds, based on the subtle agency of the light of the Holy Spirit in dark and occluded elemental matter.

The seminal figure in the southwestern Huguenot adaptation of the ideas of the German-Swiss alchemist and physician Paracelsus (1493–1541) into the broad program of artisanal security developed by refugees during the civil wars of religion of the mid sixteenth century was the autodidactic potter, natural philosopher, lay preacher, local historian, and self-promoting courtier Bernard Palissy of Saintes (1510–90), the principal town in La Rochelle's agrarian hinterland of Saintonge. Palissy's presence was felt through the diffusion of his books throughout Protestant France, England, and America, as well as his influential ceramic production. Palissy's voice reverberates throughout my narrative, helping to link the story together on both sides of the Atlantic. The potter's self-proclaimed "rustic" writing and craftsmanship give spiritual, scientific, ideological, and material coherence to the practice of artisanal security. His self-consciously heroic stories resonate with a transatlantic chorus of painful and intensely personal efforts to master the confluence of words and things, spirit and matter, life and death.

Palissy claimed to have "invented" the concept of artisanal security—which he opposed to traditional militaristic principles practiced by the Calvinist nobility of the sword—for his co-religionists in rural Aunis-Saintonge. This claim was elucidated in his essay on the vulnerability of the fortress city (implicitly La Rochelle) written in the war year of 1563 while he was imprisoned for heresy. The potter represented himself as singularly responsible for teaching these naturalistic strategies for survival to local artisans and other refugees from confessional violence. Personal piety, artisanal skill and industriousness, soulish refinement in the sacred fire of persecution, and the traditional mobility of craft culture were all at the core of his program. New ideas about security were incorporated into his ceramic production as well. His pottery featured microcosmic worlds materialized out of the interaction of elemental earth with inner spiritual and psychological life to re-form his historical, millennial, and alchemical experience and that of his patrons. Palissy and his refugee followers displaced fear of violence and anxiety over salvation into mastery of natural materials and the pious manipulation of manual arts.

Palissy devised the miniaturized, skillful empirical science of his security system from natural-philosophical observation of the tiny, vulnerable, and overlooked "artisans" of the Saintongeais salt marshes. He did most of his research on the amphibious flora and fauna that lived in flux around his laboratory, surviving predators by shape-shifting in the interstices of earth, water, and air. The role of the alchemist-artisan who labored to rise to the status of manual philosopher was mastery of the element of fire, to forcibly combine the quintessence of all the other elements.

The emblematic creature in his system was the deceptively simple snail. Palissy observed that the common mollusk constructed a portable fortress from hidden interior resources and carried it everywhere on its back, as did the pious Huguenot artisan his craft knowledge and tools. Snails, alongside a ubiquitous army of earth-hugging, shape-shifting chameleons, snakes, little fishes, frogs, tadpoles, and metamorphosing insects, were the Huguenots of Nature's periphery. These were the adaptable subjects of the potter's art and science; the busy, if imperceptibly small, slow, and silent protagonists of his "art of the earth." Such vulnerable prey animals were chosen by God to survive—singled out in Scripture to lead the natural world into the millennium—precisely because they were the smallest and weakest. As God's favored creatures, they were least corrupted by the Fall. As vulnerable prey animals, they escaped devouring enemies by developing natural skills of dissimulation and camouflage.

Unlike large, powerful predators, God gave snails the skill to craft mobile, secure domestic environments—elegant baroque shell houses—wherein the weak communicated silently with one another through a shared language of material elements, unified by the universal spirit revealed to the smallest members of the microcosm by the light of Nature. By analogy, Huguenot artisans concealed their soulish knowledge of materials from predatory enemies, congregating with other refugees on the rustic periphery, where they imperceptibly built security and continued to ply the trade of social, cultural, and economic survival.

When thou a Dangerous-Way *doſt goe,*
Walke ſurely, *though thy pace be* ſlowe.

ILLVSTR. XIX.

Book. I.

FIGURE I.I. George Wither, *A Collection of Emblemes, Ancient and Moderne: Quickened with metricall illvstrations, both morall and divine* (London: Richard Royston, 1635), fig. 19. Courtesy Harry Ransom Humanities Research Center, The University of Texas at Austin. Wither, a devout Calvinist, recycled emblemata engraved originally by Crispin van de Passe (1565?–1637) for *Nucleus emblematum selectissimorum* by Gabriel Rollenhagen (Utrecht, 1611? and 1613), greatly expanding upon the brief Latin, Greek, or Italian mottoes published in the Dutch edition. Wither used these classical couplets as mere starting points for lengthy exegetical poems following each emblem, arguing the sacred virtues of rustic labor and souls enlarged by bodily self-mastery. Here the slow-moving snail skillfully masters marginal public space negotiating a bridge linking the edges of a busy port town with the solitary woods.

The molluscan fortress and house was not merely defensive. Hidden refugee artisans, now a ubiquitous established feature of the periphery in Old World and New, might expect in God's time to become instruments of his "Just-Vengeance." By 1635, for example, plate 19 of George Wither's influential *Collection of Emblemes, Ancient and Moderne* (an English compendium, much used by artisans, of mostly Continental emblemata) depicted a Palissian snail in the process of negotiating a rustic bridge to safety in the woods; crossing over a dangerous precipice, with a dynamic urban port scene lurking in the chasm below (fig. I.1).[1] "When thou a Dangerous-Way dost goe," the epigram reads, "Walke surely, though thy pace be slowe." Wither explained that time was on the side of the industrious snail, who refused to "trifle" it away, unlike "many Men [who] have sought / With so much *Rashnesse,* those things they desir'd, / . . . And, in the middle of their *Courses,* tir'd." Rash men, "seeing [God] deferres his *Judgements* long," thought "His *Vengeance,* he, forever, would forbeare." But contemplating "the slow-pac'd *Snaile,* . . . we learne," the primary axiom of Paracelsian alchemistry: "that *Perseverance* brings Large Workes to end, though slowly they creepe on; And, that *Continuance* perfects many things, Which seeme, at first, unlikely to be done." Chief among those "Large Workes," for tiny creatures, was "*Just-Vengeance* [which] moveth like a *Snaile,* / and slowly comes; her coming will not faile." God's millennial time paralleled the slow and industrious artisan.

For Palissy and his artisan followers, the failure of frontal resistance to overcome the superior military power of Counter-Reformation forces during the wars of religion signaled the slow advent of final things and the ultimate victory of skill as the power of weakness. Yet millennial expectations merely provided the teleology for mastery of these new forms of security, based on innovation and craftsmanship and adapted from the artisanal emulation of the underground obstetric processes of Nature, to the domestication of an eschatology of waiting. The weak will certainly inherit the earth that they refine continually through the growth of matter in agriculture and artisanry. So they must also develop the skills to produce material life that supported patience and endurance, if only to survive the "end times" when the harvest will be reaped. Huguenots in southwestern France began to reconfigure their world around this paradigm in the 1550s, and artisans used Palissy's artifacts, as well as stories of his life and painful labor, as inspirations, talismans, and guides. Artisanal security allowed refugees, working within the chameleon structures of their homespun Neoplatonic philosophy and subterranean lives to transmute and reconstruct the boundaries of power into permeable materials. With the complicity of their merchant patrons and clients, they insinuated silent mastery over the economic and social structure of host countries' craft networks.

If Palissy's sixteenth-century artisanal ideology resonated through the inner life of rustic workshops, meeting houses, and domestic settings of the Huguenots' New

World, the operatic and transformational historical event in *Fortress of the Soul* is the fall of the Huguenot fortress of La Rochelle to Louis XIII and Cardinal Richelieu in 1628. This resulted from a year-long siege that cost perhaps 20,000 lives, or nearly the entire population of the city. It is impossible to overestimate the effect that this apocalyptic event, and the response in its wake of the Protestant forces, which retreated to colonize the Americas, had on the religious, political, military, and scientific worldview of international Protestantism. Palissy predicted the events of 1628 as early as the 1550s, and encouraged artisans to prepare for events that would take place after his death in "end times" when artisanal security must flourish. The destruction of the fortress led to activation of his security system among survivors in the crafts, now mostly in Palissy's home region of rural Saintonge, who now prepared their escape to northern Europe, England, and, over time, New Amsterdam / New York.

The Christic ordeal and annihilation of La Rochelle—the genocide of its population and the leveling of its iconic walls—was witnessed by the reformed world as an event of enormous cosmological implications. This was true not only in France, but also in England (which shared a long political, economic, and religious history with the city), particularly among what would become the first wave of English Calvinist settlers in colonial America. The fortress's capitulation effectively broke the back of Huguenot military resistance in France's western maritime provinces, with their ties to the large Protestant trading nations of the North Atlantic, thus laying the foundation for the Revocation, which marked the beginning of the final, massive Huguenot exodus to northern Europe and the New World. This event sent shock waves through the fast-growing refugee workshops and alchemic laboratories of London, where all eyes focused on the meaning of "the Rock's" shocking "disintegration into powder." The effects of 1628 were still being felt, remembered, and acted upon in the metropolis, as we shall see, during Hogarth's time.

The most influential British-American witness to the siege of 1627–28 was John Winthrop Jr. The younger Winthrop, the alchemist son of the first governor of the Massachusetts Bay Colony, lobbied his father to accompany the duke of Buckingham's failed expeditionary force. Buckingham's armada was sent by Charles I and Parliament to capture the strategic Île de Ré and use the island as a base of operations to compel Richelieu's forces to lift the siege of La Rochelle. The younger Winthrop and his transatlantic scientific community read deeply from Huguenot science and history during this formative period of colonization. Winthrop possessed at least one of Palissy's two books (his personal copy survives), and so it is plausible that his experience at La Rochelle, and the potter's published views of the weakness of the medieval fortress system and frontal security in this region of France, played a key role in the young military planner's future strategic thinking. This was evident in New World settlements and in international Protestantism's deepening concern with acquiring a practical understanding of the Huguenot adaptation of Paracelsian science to refugee life. Given the victories of the Counter-Reformation at La Rochelle and in the Palatinate, many European Protestants now perceived their own refugee status as an intractable reality of history.

The experience and enduring memory of this singular event was seminal in the younger Winthrop's emergence as early colonial America's leading Paracelsian natural philosopher, physician, alchemist, bibliophile, and military strategist, and in his relatively pluralistic and latitudinarian view of the growing confessional diversity of the Protestant world, so very different from his absolutist father's. This cosmology, and his privileging of skill in New World history, were essential to John Winthrop Jr.'s consuming interest in personal resettlement in the middle colonies, and especially to his long-held, if finally unsuccessful, plan to absorb New Amsterdam into the Connecticut Colony. The linchpin of this plan was control of the Long Island Sound region. The younger Winthrop concluded—after consulting with European colleagues—that this was the American "Mediterranean"; a "middle" gateway to the Northwest Passage, and therefore the philosopher's stone—the ultimate weapon of the skilled elite.

Winthrop did not simply experience the siege as an event fraught with powerful alchemic implications. His presence on the Île de Ré, within sight of the dying La Rochelle, had sanctified him, conveying enormous prestige within the international community of Protestant natural philosophers. He had "been," in person, at the event that led to the catastrophic outcome that Palissy had predicted in the previous century. Following Palissy's example, the younger Winthrop—himself silent, dissimulating, innovative, and industrious in the flexible space he fashioned for himself between Counter-Reformation genocide and his father's notorious practice of orthodoxy—pursued his own "rustic" program of artisanal security on the southern periphery of New England and the northeastern frontier of New Netherlands. He searched for the philosopher's stone in isolation at his new alchemical laboratory and compound on the north shore of Long Island Sound, just across the American "Mediterranean" from heterodox New Netherlands. Having attended the event that many in his religious and scientific community believed marked the death of the orthodox Reformation in Europe, Winthrop was now perfectly positioned to serve as the alchemist of its latitudinarian rebirth in British colonial America.

Winthrop's alchemical experiences, and Palissy's—as well as those of all the mostly obscure philosophers, artisans, and scientists who pass through the pages to follow—are best understood if historians are prepared to enter a murky, monistic universe of mystical connectedness, quite alien to our own. Theirs was an interactive world of macrocosm and microcosm, where well into the Enlightenment and beyond, spirit mixed easily with matter, while apocalyptic time was counted in ages of the earth. The subterranean experiences of refugee artisans must be unearthed *watchfully*, by looking closely at small lives moving in slow motion through shadowy spaces. Our practice of close perception will parallel their own wary ways of seeing and stress points of focus that may sometimes seem marginal or even repulsive to modern eyes. These viewpoints, however, were central to artisanal perception. By custom and training, historians have focused on the written word. Yet to engage the culture of the word in isolation from material life obscures the nature of the Huguenots' New World.

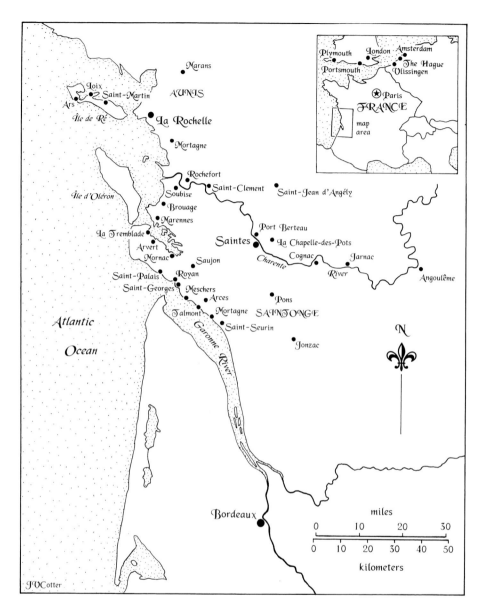

MAP I. Aunis-Saintonge. Drawn by John Cotter.

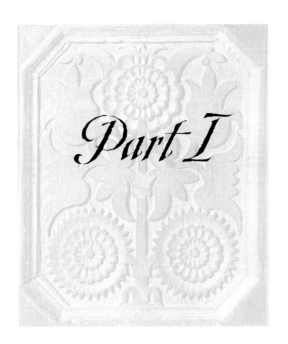

Part I

The Art of the Earth

CHAPTER ONE

A Risky Gift

The Entrance of Charles IX into La Rochelle in 1565

Unfortunate happenings occurred during the king's stay in La Rochelle.
. . . The passions were so fiery and the interests so strong and oppositional
that it was not easy to strike a balance or find some sort of equilibrium. . . .
People were too inflamed to express their grievances with moderation and
to insinuate things [*insinuer les choses*] rather than to express them out loud.
But if it is allowed to complain, it is also required that the complaint must
be expressed with decency in all its forms and especially that the tone be
most respectful and modest. Anyway, the people ignored the fact that the
true Christian was expected to suffer without complaint and even die if
need be.   —LOUIS-ÉTIENNE ARCÈRE,
             Histoire de la ville de La Rochelle et du pays d'Aulnis (1756)

❧ Insecurity and Fear ❧

Let us begin by considering the ramifications for Atlantic history and culture of Louis-
Étienne Arcère's (1698–1782) understated remark that "unfortunate happenings occurred during the king's stay in La Rochelle." These "unfortunate happenings" were
part of a larger story about a civic gift of an elaborately wrought and engraved gold
and silver basin given to Charles IX by "the people" of La Rochelle in 1565. The gift
was presented to the young king during the famous two-year "tour" of principal towns
and cities in France (1564–66) made by Charles and his mother Catherine de Médicis
between wars of religion, immediately after the thirteen-year-old was officially declared of age in the fall of 1563.

The ostensible purpose of the tour was pacification; to use the mystical presence of the young king to reunite discordant religious and political factions, while introducing him to his people. But there was also a strong measure of geopolitical strategy—a quest to master Protestant space—associated with the royal party's southern itinerary. Some Huguenot commentators thus perceived the tour in an ominous light. This would be no simple circuit of the south, especially given Catherine's intended meeting with Philip II of Spain at Bayonne (where some charged, albeit without evidence, that plans for the St. Bartholomew's Day Massacre eight years hence were made). This, it was argued by startled Huguenot commentators and hopeful Catholics alike, was a "hidden" attempt at a "revolution" to alter the map of France; that is, to "turn" the heretical south on its axis and so into a replica of the relatively pacified north. Be that as it may, the procession south from the heart of Paris of a royal retinue nearly 15,000 strong has been likened to a "traveling city," whereby Charles IX and the queen mother virtually brought the center of France to its factional and rebellious periphery.[1]

❧∙❧

The story of Charles IX's traveling city actually begins in March 1562, when religious warfare raged in France in the first of a series of confessional wars that lasted nearly two centuries. The itinerary of the royal tour thus underscored the fact that the violence centered around the predominantly Protestant regions south of the Loire Valley. Officially sanctioned violence may have been punctuated by numerous formal pauses in the fighting—including the one that allowed time for the gift to be given at La Rochelle—but royal edicts of pacification from faraway Paris failed to allay the pervasive fear of both personal and communal danger from religious atrocities as well as economic and political disenfranchisement on the local level. Savage assaults from both sides on individuals, families, and their property (including iconoclasm in churches and cemeteries), vengeful gang violence, opportunistic thuggery, and even full-scale sieges and destruction of fortified châteaux and towns by private armies were not uncommon during these times of ostensible peace.

Horrific acts of confessional violence causing a pervasive sense of terror were constant, as both sides fought to control pockets of regional power in the face of local resistance, but open warfare did not break out officially between the Catholic and Protestant forces until after September 1561, when the queen mother, Catherine de Médicis, was unable to negotiate an accommodation between the leaders of the two "oppositional" factions at the Colloque de Poissy. The first civil war ended officially on March 19, 1563, when the Edict of Amboise was issued by Catherine in the name of her young son Charles IX, then barely thirteen years old. The fragile Valois dynasty, and the queen mother in particular, were under enormous pressure to survive a crisis of succession that began in 1560, when Catherine's eldest son François II died within a year and a half of her husband, Henri II. Given this crisis of succession, Charles IX had become a very vulnerable king at age ten, on December 5, 1560. He was crowned at Reims on May 15, 1561, yet would still not reach his formal majority until the ceremony of attainment was performed at Rouen on August 21, 1563, more than five months after the Edict of Amboise was sealed.[2]

The Valois dynasty's palpable sense of insecurity about its own mortality influenced Catherine's toleration of religious heterodoxy during the 1560s, a position that was particularly remarkable when compared with the reign of the famously intolerant Henri II. The dangerous relation between insecurity and toleration was made clear during the short reign of François II, when the ultra-Catholic Guise family, whose priority was the enforcement of religious uniformity, took control of the government. This action presented a very real threat to the queen mother's power and her dwindling aspirations to dynastic continuity. Though their period of direct rule was brief, the Guises managed to initiate severely intolerant policies that intensified persecution of the Huguenots. The Guises fully intended to extend these aggressive tactics into the reign of the new child-king through the establishment of a Guise regency. Although it was clear that a regency was absolutely necessary, the queen mother thwarted the ambitions of the Guises by establishing herself in the position. Catherine's deep insecurity did not diminish, however, when she failed to remove the Guises as a threat to herself or her young son.[3]

The violently uniformist policies initiated by the Guises under François II still had the force of law under Charles IX, as Catherine searched for a strategy to accommodate their interests without relinquishing her tenuous hold on power. To submit fully to the Guises' project would be to ensure their control over the kingdom's dangerously unstable noble orders, while removing the greatest impediment to their return to domination of the court. And such a submission would inevitably invite violent retaliation from the other end of the political and religious spectrum, where the equally dangerous Huguenot Prince Louis de Condé stood ready to mobilize Protestant forces in pursuit of his own claims to the throne.

Catherine's answer to the triple threat posed to the Valois dynasty by confessional violence, noble factionalism, and the weak instability of the monarchy was to maintain power by pursuing a middle course of religious tolerance for the Huguenot moderates, who responded with measured royalist rhetoric claiming loyalty to the king. Huguenot royalist rhetoric was far from unambiguous; yet Catherine's strategy temporarily kept the violent Guises and warlike Condé at arm's length. In pursuit of a strategy to occupy the middle ground against radical competitors, the Colloquy of Poissy became the first of several extraordinarily conciliatory gestures made toward the Huguenots by the queen mother in the 1560s. Here, Catherine risked accepting Calvin's authoritarian deputy Théodore de Bèze as the Calvinists' spokesman on equal terms with his Catholic counterpart. This was followed in January 1562 by an Edict of Toleration that guaranteed Huguenots the right to maintain their consistorial system and granted freedom of worship in most places.[4]

Such gambits were part of an extremely fluid process and potentially dangerous, despite efforts to play one side off against the other and to neutralize aggression among the factions in an effort to maintain the monarch's (and his regent's) singular authority. To survive, the monarchy was, in effect, reduced to the position of power broker between the magnates. Alliances were formed, dissolved, and then reformed again as authority was negotiated at court, seemingly moment by moment. That is why it is difficult to conclude that Catherine and Charles actually had the power, political support, and resources, at least when the tour began, to "turn" the map in 1564–65. It may have been sufficient that the contending factions—southwestern Huguenot leaders in particular—perceived that they did, and the impressive size of the procession and its formidable military escort could only have added to that desirable perception. Certainly, the tour was intended to shore up the dynasty's faltering position in Paris while "on the move," as was manifestly the case in the ostensibly last-minute decision to change the itinerary and enter La Rochelle in 1565. Even taking Catherine's sometimes desperate attempts at maintaining equilibrium into consideration, however, it was always within the power of the great magnates to force her hand by instigating savage confessional warfare. The duc de Guise did precisely that in March 1562—only two months after Catherine's Edict of Toleration—when he led his private army in the massacre of a Protestant congregation at Vassy, thus provoking the expected response from Condé and precipitating the first civil war of religion.[5]

The massacre at Vassy and the resulting civil war caused deep divisions in the Protestant leadership of La Rochelle. By 1562, the Reformation had succeeded in bringing a Calvinist majority to the fortress, so this new factionalism was not between Protestants and Catholics. Rather, the initiation of full-scale confessional violence in France caused a schism between La Rochelle's moderate leadership, who remained loyal to the crown and favored liberty of conscience for the minority Rochelais (and Aunisian) Catholics, and the rising militant party, who openly supported Condé's subversive political program, which favored the violent suppression of local Catholics and threatened the monarchy.[6] The context in which this internal factionalism between moderates and militants played itself out was La Rochelle's deeply divided Corps de ville,[7] the city's supreme political body, where the presumably common will of its magistrates and municipal officers was, in theory, negotiated in private and ultimately presented to the king as a consensus. In practice, however, this ostensibly united body was a chaotic hotbed of confrontation and power shifts, which began in 1562, when civil war broke out, and ended only in 1568, when the militants finally emerged victorious, having defeated the once-dominant moderates in a move that enabled them to declare the Corps for Condé.[8]

Factional infighting had intensified to the point where, by the time of the 1563 mayoral election, the Corps was so divided that it was impossible to elect one mayor alone. Each candidate led a faction: Michel Guy was the king's man, representing the moderates, opposed by Jean Pierres, representing the militants. Coalition and compromise were subverted by polemics and confrontation. When neither candidate emerged victorious, Amateur Blandin, a lawyer and *lieutenant particulier,* representing the king's interests, decided the election for Guy. The militants refused to accept the outcome, and La Rochelle was led by two mayors until Charles IX intervened personally to oust Pierres. The resulting animosity between the two opposing factions worsened to such an extent that in order to avoid open conflict (and perhaps civil war) between coreligionists in the city, most magistrates simply absented themselves from the meetings. In time, the Corps was unable to mount a quorum and effectively ceased to function altogether. By December 1563, the king was finally forced to give it his official permission to carry on La Rochelle's business without the usual majority.[9] Thus, when Charles IX and Catherine de Médicis confronted the Corps de ville of the powerful Huguenot fortress at its porte de Cougnes in 1565, their agenda, once again, was to exploit divisions between oppositional factions. The primary goal was simply to survive the encounter. Given the ascendancy of the militants, Charles's personal security was not guaranteed. Were he to survive the "unfortunate happenings [that] occurred during the king's stay in La Rochelle," and, as part of that process of survival, perform his dominant role as monarch competently in the series of dramatic rituals from "days of yore" that preceded the giving of the gift, then he would also extend the power of the monarchy deep into the divided heart of the rebellion.

❧ The Spirit of Difference ❧

The civil wars of religion took place nearly two hundred years before the publication of Arcère's magisterial two-volume, 1,400 page *Histoire,* arguably the most influential if also the most self-consciously balanced history of La Rochelle during the time of the troubles. In 1756, however, as local historian of the Oratory of La Rochelle, Arcère surveyed the past from his study in the city's medieval monastery of Sainte-Marguerite.[10] To be sure, this had been contested space during the Reformation, but now Arcère occupied a secure, pacified vantage point, located both literally and metaphorically above the ruins of what zealous predecessors had perceived to be the very core of heresy in France.[11] The siege of 1627–28 had, however, utterly decimated La Rochelle's Protestant population, and most of the remaining Huguenots of rural

Aunis-Saintonge had of necessity either become *nouveaux convertis* Catholics or migrated out of the region into the expanding world of international Protestantism.[12]

Arcère lamented those who still could not forgive La Rochelle for centuries of heresy and treason against church and state. "One must always condemn rebellion," he wrote magnanimously, "and [yet] it is sometimes permitted to pity the rebel."[13] Eighteenth-century royalist academicians and churchmen would resist the unstigmatized absorption of La Rochelle's independent local history into Arcère's new "progressive" master narrative of France's national past. But Arcère and his order were well connected to patronage networks that combined the interwoven bureaucracies of church and state in both La Rochelle and Paris, a fact emphasized by his modest claim that his work had originally been "outlined" by his fellow *érudit* Père Jaillot (1690–1749), a leading light among Oratorians, and that he himself had had only to complete the task after his famous mentor's death. The *Histoire* was published with royal privilege and dedicated to a nobleman of the sword, Count d'Argenson, "ministre et secretaire d'état de la guerre." Arcère commended his patron for the particular care with which he "maintained military readiness through an institution that shapes war heroes," and for his keen understanding that, above all, "history consecrates the actions of the most powerful kings."[14] Arcère knew, of course, that such rhetoric about the replication of the *gloire* of kingship through the entire genealogy of the Bourbon dynasty was the "artisanal" task of the court historians of Louis XV in Arcère's own time, as it certainly was in 1628, when crafted by the court historians of Louis XIII.[15]

Arcère argued from his own vantage point, without a trace of irony, however, that now, 128 years after the last of the "passions . . . fiery and . . . inflamed" had subsided, it was at last possible to write an equitable didactic history of La Rochelle and its central role in the wars. "This city has become an object of [historical] interest above all since the era of the civil wars incited by differences in religion," he wrote.[16] Yet these were fiercely polemical histories, driven by the raw passions of sixteenth-century historians intimately involved with the outcome of events. Unlike Arcère, such historians, whose narratives were "destined" to be "coarse and gothic,"[17] had not perfected rational self-control sufficiently well to master the subtle symmetries of eighteenth-century analysis:

> In working on the history of La Rochelle, one has to contend with difficulties not often found in the historical genre. . . . It is very difficult to describe the wars of religion and the revolutions of a place too well known for its long and obstinate defection. . . . This was born in the spirit of difference in belief . . . the most implacable enemy of history. In matters of pure speculation, the light of reason will ultimately dispel the shadows of ignorance, but . . . in a writer struck with this delirium, the pen will follow the natural disposition of his soul rather than the nature of his subject. . . . The voice of the new reform

was ordinarily doleful and too often audacious. . . . The Catholics on the other side were not much more moderate. It was not often with the sweetness of Christian charity that they defended the truth. "True just like false religious zeal," said a judicious and elegant author, "makes people forget the laws of humanity."[18]

Religious zeal was thus the "implacable enemy" of historical discourse and the lessons history taught about the ethics of social life. Some teaching communities of Oratorians in particular made the militant Church the target of their pedagogy. That is why Jaillot and Arcère chose the historical La Rochelle as the most logical site for this project of retrospective religious pacification and renewal. For progress to be made, rational believers had to analyze the "factual" basis of their grievances with others dispassionately. Most important, since harmony could not always be achieved through analytical discourse, one should learn to "insinuate things" rather than "express them out loud." In the late seventeenth century, some Oratorians were at the forefront of promulgating this program—sometimes awkwardly called "Cartesianism"—in Paris seminaries and universities. In 1682, because this inner-directed aspect of Oratorian teaching was considered to be in conflict with absolutism, Louis XIV tried to suppress the order in Paris by turning the Oratorians' seminaries over to the Jesuits, their ideologically more trustworthy competitors.[19]

When Arcère completed his *Histoire,* however, the Oratorians had achieved a secure pedagogical foothold in the new diocese of La Rochelle, reconstructed as a consequence of the Calvinist defeat in 1628.[20] Between 1604 and 1613, Oratorians were allowed only a tiny presence in the Huguenot-dominated city, and the order was banished altogether by the Corps de ville after another Rochelais military confrontation with the crown in 1621, this time with the young and extremely violent warrior-king Louis XIII.[21] The exiled Oratorians returned in triumph in 1628, however; and in the late 1670s, their "rich benefices" were considered the envy of every other religious order in La Rochelle.[22] It is possible, therefore, to infer that the force of the Oratorians' patronage and prestige, as well as the order's local influence in the schools, lay in the continuing stake of the monarchy and the Rochelais leadership in the absorption and domestication of the vivid memory of civil war religious violence and confrontation with the state that had defined La Rochelle's history. The *Histoire* attempted to demonstrate to the crown that unlike those religious orders during the times of rebellion, La Rochelle's modern Oratorians were moderate, rational, and loyal. Inasmuch as the *Histoire* was published with royal privilege, Louis XV must have thought there were still lessons to be learned from La Rochelle's "various revolutions" during those "unhappy times," not least of which was how to avoid dangerous passions and civil strife among the competing social and political factions that still threatened the status quo in mid-eighteenth-century France. Even as "coarse," "gothic," and "unhappy" local histories were absorbed into the master narrative of a French national history progressing toward the perfection Arcère avidly sought, so too society itself was capable of perfection, defined as both religious and regional unity under the rule of a single rational monarch.

Arcère had access to all the available "ancient" histories of La Rochelle. This was no small accomplishment after 1628, since so many of the most important (and politically sensitive) early manuscripts and archives had been lost, destroyed by royal forces or removed by the censorial and covetous Richelieu after the siege. Not everything had vanished, however; some notarial and consistorial archives survived, and "the Rochelais of old wrote down everything that passed before their eyes." For the entrance of Charles IX in 1565, "the Rochelais of old" was the Huguenot historian Amos Barbot (1566–1625), and Arcère openly acknowledged this debt.[23] Royal patronage also played a crucial role. It would appear that the comte de Matignon, "then governor of the province," had already gathered together what remained of these materials and made them available to Jaillot and ultimately Arcère.[24] Arcère's approach to sources adhered strictly to his eighteenth-century methodology promoting symmetry between warring confessional historians. For the sake of fairness (as in Barbot's case), historians from both religious camps were cited in almost every instance. It followed that Arcère would then mediate confidently, adding a final layer of "rational" (as opposed to "superstitious") interpretation, to forge the required historical synthesis.[25] While "an author isn't always in a position to confirm the truth," he wrote, he could "support the facts"; and to "authenticate the facts," it "is natural" that "these historians are always cited in the margin."[26]

In his narrative of the gift, Arcère observed these rules of citation scrupulously. He cites three historians, two Catholics and Barbot. These accounts of the royal entry of Charles IX into La Rochelle in 1565, and the town's civic gift to France's adolescent king are explicitly interwoven, such that the three, when read together with Arcère's commentary, have come to constitute a dense narrative of the event. Arcère was careful to commend Barbot's manuscript (ca. 1613?), though not without professional reservations. Unlike so many of his "doleful" and "audacious" colleagues, Barbot was one of Arcère's most "impartial" sources:

> Of all of our manuscripts, the most considerable is that of Amos Barbot, Rochelais, *baillif* of the grand fief of Aunis, and one of the *pairs* of the Corps de ville. The writing style of this annalist is simple, but too slipshod. Since he doesn't have the fire to *fondre les matières* [literally, to "found metal," or "synthesize"], he solders pieces together rather coarsely. He copies the public registers too baldly. Sincere and impartial, he narrates with much naïveté; and though he is a completely zealous Protestant, he sometimes disapproves of the conduct of his brethren.[27]

Barbot does indeed underscore divisions within the town's Protestant community, speaking from the privileged vantage point of the Corps de ville (of which, as a *pair,* or *peer,* he was a member), and he also comments extensively on Charles IX's visit in 1565. Arcère quotes virtually all Barbot's observations verbatim, citing him as much in the body of the text as in its margins.[28] The two Catholic historians Arcère cites were eyewitnesses to the gift ceremony as servants of the court. The manuscript by [Philippe] "Caurian[a]," "Catherine de' Medecis' physician," was, he says, "extremely useful." In this analysis, however, Arcère was also able to display the depth of his own rational disinterest by discounting his co-religionist Cauriana's most extreme biases as those of a "zealous royalist."[29]

Arcère depended heavily on the work of the other Catholic historian—and the one indispensable published source for everyday life in Charles IX's court during its two years on tour—Abel Jouan's *Recueil et discours du voyage du roy Charles IX* (Paris, 1566).[30] Jouan, an obscure figure, identifies himself as "one of his Majesty's servants" on the *Recueil*'s title page. He is sometimes referred to as an "orator," "historian," or (least appropriate) a "poet," but Jouan's official title at court was "clerk of the king's larder" ("commis du garde-manger"), an occupation that probably accounts for the scrupulous, quantitative, and almost inventorylike quality of his narrative. It should come as no surprise therefore, that Jouan's typically detailed description of the gift—surviving in lieu of the artifact itself (which is lost)—is compelling in its specificity. No one could ever accuse this court historian of zealousness, except perhaps in compiling lists of basic information about his youthful master's activities. This is both the text's great strength and its great weakness. "Although exhaustive, the *Recueil et discours* is merely a succession of instants, lacking artifice, *mémoire,* or depth; hence, it is in reality the negation of a journey narrative. On the why and how of the narrative, or the social and political practices that it constituted, one must resort to those who were its primary witnesses, above all the actors themselves."[31]

Because his "phlegmatic" methodology separated historians into binary oppositions that privileged the balance of "impartial" witnesses over the instability of "enthusiastic" actors, Arcère would have perceived Jouan as a nearly unimpeachable source.[32] Twenty-first-century readers, instinctively repulsed by the exotic rituals of dominance and savage personal violence of the wars of religion, will find comfort in Arcère's narrative impulse to balance religious passions to achieve a "respectful and modest" decorum. But Arcère would fail to "find some sort of equilibrium" in his critique of the history of emotion without finally acknowledging the "absolute" primacy of fear during the war years. If "the people ignored the fact that the true Christian was expected to suffer without complaint and even die if need be," then it was "fear, the feeling that disturbs our soul so strongly, and that rules over all of the soul's functions like an absolute monarch; fear, [which] commanded them imperiously to disobey, and love of life prevailed over their duty."[33]

If fear was the "absolute monarch" of a sixteenth-century Huguenot's soul, would "moderation" alone move "the people . . . to insinuate things rather than express them out loud"? What style might this mode of insinuation have taken? An analysis of the ambiguous history and discourse of the royal gift of 1565 may suggest some possibilities.

❧ The King's Absence ❧

Arcère's reading of La Rochelle's "chronicles" from the 1560s suggests that if the majority of La Rochelle's divided Huguenot leadership could agree on anything, it was their shared fear of Catherine's well-known tendency to vacillate between factional influences. Every member of the Corps de ville knew that this was a dangerous strategy, which could cut both ways. On some occasions, as with the treaty of Amboise (March 19, 1563), which ended the war, the queen mother might vacillate in the direction of the Protestant factions; on others, such as an ominous decision taken on August 4, 1564—shortly before the gift was given—the pendulum could swing in reverse: "The court took only halfway measures in religious matters. It would make laws and then reverse them. The declaration of August 4, 1564, diminished greatly the advantages given to the Reformed by the Edict of March 19, 1563."[34] Where sixteenth-century commentators saw weakness and confusion in these actions, Arcère perceived balance and reason: "Some writers have suspected that there was not a consistency of views in the government; that it did not produce a coherent policy with which to confront obstacles. This approach, however, must not be underestimated. In effect, during these unhappy times, both gentleness and vigour were equally dangerous . . . it is perhaps this equilibrium that was sought through these variations, but never found."[35]

La Rochelle's Huguenot leadership was far from being of one mind as to how to respond, but some—especially the militant faction in the Corps de ville and, above all, the increasingly militant and influential ministry—were appalled by the reversal of August 1564. Perhaps counting on the court's weakness, certain ministers openly incited "the people" to resist with "vehement speech" rather than quiet insinuation:

> The Protestant party made claims daily and believed they had a right to do so. This caused much dissatisfaction. The ministers of La Rochelle, far from limiting themselves to their functions, dared loudly to censor the conduct of the court. Amos Barbot sincerely believed in such opinions, but he was also a faithful subject and so could not keep himself from chastising the ministers for their excesses. He said that "the ministers—de Lisle [Pierre Richer], Maingault, and de Nord [Odet de Nort]—were carried away with their

zealousness. Their vehement speech criticized the violence and force that was used against those of the [Protestant] religion. In addition to blaming the king and sovereign powers for allowing such license, they spoke out against the king's edicts, saying that the Edicts of Pacification had been broken violently and illegally. Such preaching led the people to resist implementation of the edict's modifications. Because of the actions of these pastors, the inhabitants took various licenses and there were some who spoke slander and invective against the king, the queen, and the council."[36]

"The people's dissatisfaction," Arcère wrote, "was a portent of sedition. This news was reported to the king, who was then in Bordeaux. The king decided to leave for La Rochelle immediately to calm the dangerous unrest there."[37] There is no direct evidence that Charles and Catherine had originally planned a visit to La Rochelle, in part because the court did not wish to appear to give credence to sedition, and also because it was now difficult to guarantee security there. Perhaps they were following the fluid course of events before making a decision on the move. The uprising of militant Protestantism in the city, beginning in earnest in the 1550s, had obviously gained sufficient political and military strength during the civil wars to spark "vehement speech" over the Declaration of August 4, 1564. If well-defended discursive boundaries had been crossed in La Rochelle, then surely the royal person was also in danger there.

These dangers were ultimately outweighed by the realization that the administration of Jarnac, the royal governor of La Rochelle, was losing ground rapidly to radicals in the Protestant party. The governor had barely survived a plot to surrender La Rochelle to Condé in 1563, and the radicals continued to close in on the moderate majority in the Corps. In the governor's desperation, "it seems clear that Jarnac . . . prompted the prince's decision. Jarnac planned to use the royal presence to shore up his administration (which had been faltering since the onset of the most recent troubles) and so gain renewed authority for the office of governor."[38] The king may also have been waiting for an invitation. Arcère reports that "Charles IX communicated his decision to visit La Rochelle to the town's magistrates." These anonymous magistrates must have been associated with moderate factions, since "they, in turn, decided to receive him with all the pomp due the sovereign."[39] Given the lack of consensus in the Corps, it seems reasonable to assume that this decision was not taken lightly, and that many members feared and resented the king's visit. It is also reasonable to assume that his allies in the Corps reported any dissention to Charles as well.

The elaborate spectacles and gifts eventually presented to Charles on his impending visit could have been negotiated and prepared in the approximately two months it took the procession to wind its way the short distance north from Bordeaux to La Rochelle. More probably, however, these magistrates suspected all along that the king could be persuaded to perform his *joyeux avènement* [joyous advent] at La Rochelle, and certain factions—including Jarnac, naturally, but also other moderate Huguenots, as well as the dwindling number of remaining Catholic Rochelais—had planned for such a contingency. This cannot be known for certain, but the hurried preparations must have been stressful and expensive. The question of the invitation does provide circumstantial evidence—Barbot infers as much in his *Histoire*—that the Huguenots' "vehement speech" and apparently united front masked a lack of unanimity within the Protestant community and in the city as a whole. Thus, while La Rochelle tried to mask these differences as its leadership prepared to meet the king, the king was preparing just as industriously to exploit them.

What we do know from the usually terse Jouan is that the court's progress north to La Rochelle from friendly Bordeaux—the fortress's bitter religious and economic rival on the Bay of Biscay and the seat of a zealously repressive Catholic *parlement* (royal court)—through rural, heavily Protestant Saintonge had its tense moments. On his journey to La Rochelle, Charles passed through the governor's ancestral seat of Jarnac, then Cognac, then the king crossed the Charente River at Port Chauveau, "which is the beginning of the country of Xaintonge."[40] Then Charles made a royal entry into Gallo-Roman Saintes, a town with "great and ancient antiquities." Here, Anne de Montmorency, Constable of France, undoubtedly presented his client Bernard Palissy, the famous Huguenot artisan and historian "from Saintes," to his new patron Catherine de Médicis. Presumably, this was when Catherine commissioned Palissy to construct the ceramic grotto in the Tuileries that would make his name. Palissy quickly left for Paris, quite possibly the same year (the evidence suggests that he arrived there no later than 1567), where he set up his new alchemical laboratory and ceramic shop near the Louvre palace.[41]

After two days at Saintes, the tour passed through Corme-Royal, Le Mesnil, and Saint-Just-Luzac, where the inhabitants "all mariners," and "all dressed in their colors, having their ensigns deployed . . . fired their artillery to honor the king."[42] Since the inhabitants of Saint-Just were not only "all mariners" but also almost all recently converted Huguenots, this show of force must have been received as a mixed message, especially by Montmorency, whose job it was to guarantee the king's personal security.

A similar display met the king at Marennes, also in the coastal salt marsh region. Pausing at Marennes, an acknowledged hotbed of heresy in Saintonge, the king witnessed a "magnificent" display of arms carried by "six to seven thousand men . . . from surrounding villages," who passed "before the king's lodgings." If part of the strategy of the tour was to learn the relative military strength of southwestern Protestantism, this display must have been both impressive and frightening. More unsettling perhaps was the bungled naval display at the small but powerful fortress known as Brouage—one of La Rochelle's economic competitors on the Bay of Biscay—where "magnificent" ordinance was again fired, this time from vessels in the harbor. "But," Jouan reports dispassionately, "they did not take care, so they killed two men and wounded several others."[43]

Finally, the king returned to remote Marennes, in the center of the salt marshes, to pass the night. Marennes was perhaps the earliest center of Protestant activity among artisans and mariners in Saintonge, so it was remarkable that "during the day" of Thursday, September 6, 1565, just nine days before his entry to La Rochelle, "there assembled easily eight or nine hundred persons at the church at this place." There the throng—which one might speculate was largely, if not totally Protestant—gathered to make a sacramental expression of fidelity to the old religion as a ritual offering to their king. They waited in vain "to have confession and communion" in Charles's presence. "This was something that could not be done," as Jouan explained, since "the king was absent, because the leaders of this place were of the religion *prétendue réformée,* what we call Huguenots."[44] The king's calculated absence punished the heretics of Marennes by denying these dissimulators his most precious gift of the royal presence. The gift of presence was reserved for loyal subjects alone; that is, those who loved their king transparently and were united in his Church. This humiliating denial of royal reciprocity was a rehearsal for the king's subversion of centuries of ritual at La Rochelle.

❧ At the porte de Cougnes ❧

Early on the morning of September 14, 1565, advance parties for the royal procession arrived at La Rochelle and stood waiting to enter before its famously intimidating limestone walls. This set in motion the first of two dangerous gambles by Charles IX, both of which played with La Rochelle's traditional—that is to say medieval—ritual expectations of the king. The first of these events occurred at a threshold (the royal gateway at the porte de Cougnes); the second concerned the giving of a special civic gift (an elaborate silver-and-gold basin) and turned ultimately on the possible meanings of the gift itself. If La Rochelle's Huguenot leaders noted Charles's strategy of disequilibrium in Saintonge, particularly in relation to their co-religionists at Marennes, then they should have had a premonition of the "unfortunate happenings" to come in the next few days.

The first to arrive at the porte de Cougnes was the formidable Anne de Montmorency, Constable of France, a tough survivor of wars on the battlefield and at court. Montmorency was also a scion of perhaps the wealthiest and most powerful *noblesse d'épée* (nobility of the sword) family in France. By 1565, Montmorency had ties with the then-moderate Catherine (due, in part, to the Constable's role as the king's protector) as well as with her competitors at court, the ultra-Catholic Guises. He also had Protestant nephews in the Châtillon family, whom he did not hesitate to use as brokers with hostile Protestant factions. Montmorency thus communicated across confessional boundaries through family ties if it was advantageous. His patronage of Bernard Palissy (who dedicated his first book, published in La Rochelle in 1563, to the Constable)—and his recommendation of Palissy to Catherine to construct a grotto in the Tuileries gardens—show again that Montmorency was willing to cross confessional lines, because he recognized that the talented, innovative, and fashionable Huguenot artisanal sector was becoming indispensable to the material culture of the Valois court. But the Constable was, above all, France's principal military commander, and his job on March 14, 1565, was to lead the heavily augmented military contingent of 3,000 cavalry and 2,000 infantrymen that accompanied the king to La Rochelle to provide security.[45]

The Constable's first strategic move caught the Rochelais magisterial and especially its military leadership completely off guard. "The Constable of France," Arcère wrote, "who rode ahead to announce the arrival of the king, had the artillery that was placed on top of the ramparts in the place de Château removed, and ordered that it be transported to Maubec Meadow. The Constable's defiance mortified the inhabitants of La Rochelle."[46] In defiance of La Rochelle's military autonomy and political sovereignty, this provocative action not only asserted royal dominance but also demonstrated how fearful Montmorency was for the king's personal safety.

Shortly after this act of royal defiance of local rights, the king, whose mother and sister, Princess Marguerite, would not catch up to the head of the procession for another day, stopped at the suburb of Saint-Eloi, as everything was made ready at the porte de Cougnes. The city fathers had used their limited time well in making the customary preparations for the royal entry:

> First, the magistrates ordered that the bourgeois militias should be adorned with shining parade arms and red and blue uniforms. These were considered appropriate to meet the king. The militia would be led by Jarnac's son and his lieutenant, Jacques du Lyon. The magistrates of La Rochelle had a review stand constructed just outside the town walls, facing the church of Saint-Jean, and had it adorned with a superb drapery. This is where the king and his large entourage of courtiers were to stop to review the troops parading in the king's honor. A triumphal arch decorated with mythological figures was also erected near the porte de Cougnes. [These figures] represented the twelve labors of Hercules and were surmounted by a portrait of the king, with the device *pietate & justitia*, "religion and justice characterizes him." Beneath these words one read *Herculea fortitudo Carolo nono Regi optimo felici auspicio coelo dimittitur alto*, "the Herculean strength is spread from high heaven to Charles IX, the best king, with a favorable omen."[47]

Montmorency's removal of the artillery from the place de Château was obviously to ensure that the appearance of La Rochelle's militia for the ritual at the entrance (he knew that the militia's commander was Jarnac's son) would be no more than colorful ceremony. But the allegory of the eleventh labor of Hercules—in which he bore the earth on his shoulders while Atlas picked the apples of the Hesperides for him—was nonetheless a particularly complex and problematic representation for La Rochelle. Throughout the tour, especially in the majority Catholic cities, this allegory was updated to represent Hercules in the act of forcing the rotation of the earth and stars back to their proper axis, and it became a standard emblem for Charles IX. Ronsard, a member of the ancient Rochelais Chaudrier family (although himself a zealous royalist), made clear in a poem of 1567 that this terrestrial iconography signified that Hercules— like Charles—was on a warlike purification mission to confront heresy and turn back the Protestant revolution in France's southern provinces:

> As Hercules made the earth revolve,
> Monsters waged war on all sides;
> So too you revolve your kingdom, Sire,
> To righteously cleanse your empire
> Of all error, and the monsters
> Are too ashamed to show their face[s].[48]

Given the potentially virulent anti-Protestant message of this allegory—and the implication that La Rochelle's rebels had gone underground, "too ashamed to show their face[s]"—the Rochelais chose to replace warlike terrestrial messages diffused by the court poet Ronsard, with the open, neutral, and negotiable "labors of Hercules" theme. Their program also adopted the moderate and hopeful motto "religion and justice." The transmutation of the allegorical themes of a militant monarchy associated with the tour into more ambiguous language that could be read simultaneously in La Rochelle's favor was central to the fortress's strategy of self-representation. But the king received these mixed messages with disastrous results.

Symbolic catastrophes were to begin for the rebellious leadership of La Rochelle, however, even before Charles had a chance to view himself as Hercules on the triumphal arch erected across the threshold of the porte de Cougnes just *inside* the walls of the church of Saint-Jean. Montmorency's tactics the day before had left the militia and the Corps de ville jittery, but preparations for the ancient ceremony at the gate began routinely enough. However, the king still held back in the suburb of Saint-Eloi, where he awaited the arrival of his mother and sister. In effect, when they left the protection of the fortress to enter the king's distant presence, this meant that representatives of the city's leadership endured demotion in status and a sort of disequilibrium in the symbolically balanced relationship between the monarch and the city that subverted the history of the ritual at the gate even before it began:

At the first news of the arrival of the king, the city deputies came outside the walls to welcome him. It was the task of Jean Blandin, an alderman, to lead the welcoming committee. Some hours later, the militias came out bearing arms, followed by all the different orders of the town. The procession stopped at the suburb of Saint-Eloi. When Charles IX arrived there, he received their homage, as well as the keys to the city, which he immediately placed into the hands of the mayor. That night, however, the prince refused to solemnly enter the town without the queen mother and Princess Marguerite. . . . Instead he slept at Saint-Eloi and awaited their arrival the next day.[49]

The mayor, the fiercely divided two hundred members of the Corps de ville, and the *présidial* of La Rochelle (the city's new, contested sovereign court of no appeal), anxiously stood waiting according to rank outside the twelfth-century porte de Cougnes, for the ceremonial royal entrance of Charles IX. Meanwhile, Charles, Catherine, and Montmorency finally assembled with the king's entourage outside the walls. Everyone knew full well, of course, that La Rochelle was then in the midst of its most important and, from the king's, his regent's and Governor Jarnac's perspective, most dangerous and subversive period of Protestant revival, mass conversion, and politicization. Not only was the Corps virtually dysfunctional, but the *présidial,* despised by La Rochelle's ministry and other Huguenot activists as an attack on the city's independence and corporate sovereignty, had been formed to hear civil cases as a new, *local* tribunal by Henri II in 1551, in an ultimately futile but still highly provocative effort to use a royal court to further the king's cause in La Rochelle. What "vehement speech" emerged from the declaration of August 1564, must have been amplified by the continuance of the *présidial,* which was perceived by the Rochelais Protestant hierarchy as a brazen attack from Paris on local judicial privilege, and it was a very specific question of local privilege that would be decided at the porte de Cougnes.[50]

❧ The End of Privilege ❧

Following Abel Jouan word for word (as the Huguenot Amos Barbot had before him), Arcère set the scene:

> On the next day, the ceremony started in earnest with the march of the militia, which the king reviewed in good order. With Charles IX nearing the first porte de Cougnes, the aldermen and the peers stretched a silk cord across the passage according to ancient custom, as if to stop him with the intent to supplicate and at the same time to have the king swear confirmation of their privileges. The Constable, who was the first to notice this, was surprised and became angry. He asked the magistrates if they meant to refuse entrance to the city to their master. They replied deferentially, quietly giving the reason for this ritual. But

the Constable, unsatisfied, drew his sword and cut the cord, saying that such usage was no longer the fashion.[51]

The insecure young monarch and the intriguing city fathers of the most powerful heretical fortress in France stared through a gateway at each other. The former had only a tenuous hold on power; the latter were trying to complete the fluid process of creating a fully Protestant polity in the face of a strong counterattack by the town's royal governor and his moderate allies on the Corps de ville. The ritualistic aspects of Charles IX's visit thus afforded all actors the opportunity to master their state of flux, if only momentarily, and to construct more permanent identities with which to face their mutable worlds. And because a unique assertion of privilege prompted Charles's visit, here was a chance for the divided Rochelais on one side of the gate, and the monarch on the other, to put themselves on a firmer footing with their respective (or desired) constituencies. The former sought to affirm that the ritual was intended to confirm the endurance of La Rochelle's local privileges given by former kings as permanent rights; the latter, to assert the right of a monarch to subvert the ritual and supersede prior privilege with just cause, because such rights were merely gifts, contingent on loyalty, which monarchs took back at their pleasure.

Thus, one important reason why Charles IX's visit had been in doubt until two months before was that by tradition, the king was expected to come ostensibly to reconfirm La Rochelle's ancient communal privileges, at the start of his young monarchy, as had most of his predecessors since the twelfth century. Indeed, at the beginning of each reign, one method that every new monarch used to announce his accession to the throne was to issue an edict to the different provinces confirming their privileges. But while "privilege was the primary instrument of government and the chief measure of political exchange between state and society . . . [whereby] the monarch tacitly acknowledged the rights of his subjects, who, in turn, implicitly recognized the legitimacy of his claim,"[52] La Rochelle's particular privileges traditionally went far beyond any in the kingdom and, from the perspective of the crown, went right to the heart of the issue of its crimes of heresy and sedition—and its early prominence in the larger world of Atlantic history and culture—even though La Rochelle's privileges long predated the Reformation. As David Parker has observed:

> The privileges about which the Rochelais were so concerned had their origins in the twelfth century. The commune was founded in 1140 by Guillaume, Comte de Poitou; through his daughter Eleanor of Aquitaine it passed first to the French crown and then to Henry II of England, but it was not until it received a charter from King John in 1199 that the corps de ville appeared. . . . In 1371 the Rochelais helped expel the English for the last time from their shore and Charles V rewarded them with a further extension of their

privileges. This included conferment of hereditary nobility on the mayor and echevins and their exemption from taxation. In addition the corps de ville was given complete control over the municipal finances "and all governors, judges and others were forbidden to act in this sphere." Subsequently La Rochelle's military strength enabled the municipality not only to preserve these important rights but to build on them at a time when most towns were experiencing a steady erosion of their franchises.[53]

La Rochelle's privileges as a *commune* not only gave the city unequaled autonomy among municipalities in France until 1628, but, most threatening to those from the kingdom's center, the history of these privileges carried with it the mark of Englishness and the *outre-mer* world. This autonomy was not only political—with the Huguenot Corps de ville maintaining the privilege of independence from the royal governor, Jarnac—but also military and, perhaps most of all, economic. This too had English—and Atlantic—origins, since "the intensity of the town's commercial activity justified its description as a permanent fair," and after "1199 when it was in English hands . . . its development was rapid."[54] Arcère, ever with an eye toward religious conflict, was quick to underscore the linkage in the post-Reformation popular mind between local privileges, La Rochelle's autonomy, Englishness, and Calvinist republicanism, an idea he cavalierly dismissed as "chimerical." Still, Arcère perceived one important reality that could not be dismissed so easily. After the Rochelais expelled the English in 1371, they obtained the first of their great treasure trove of privileges (mostly in the form of valuable tax exemptions) from King Charles V, "in the capacity of *strangers* who entered in submission to France."[55] In the 1560s, the "strangers" in France's midst turned again to their former allies, this time in religious complicity. As late as 1627, this expanded to include a famously failed military alliance, and after accepting the capitulation of the city in 1628, Louis XIII would remind his conquered subjects of what the ancient status of "stranger" had ultimately cost them.

The ceremonial entrance of Charles IX in 1565, was thus the centerpiece in a crucial ritual that would, in effect, symbolize the current state of the delicate power relations between Huguenot La Rochelle, with long-standing cultural, commercial, and religious ties outside of France to international Protestantism and the Atlantic world, and a weakened and dislocated Catholic monarchy with centripetal ambitions that, despite moments of moderation intended to keep its enemies at court off balance, mostly feared and bitterly resented those ties. So here was a grand entrance with a venerable history; but one now fraught with strange uncertainty after nearly five hundred years of catechistic repetition—all the more so because of its unique quality. While each province expected the monarch to confirm its local privileges periodically, the extension of such privileges to La Rochelle seems to have had no exact parallel in ancien régime France.

Rochelais tradition dictated that, first, a silk cord was to be strung across the fortified gateway that opened landward (to the northeast), away from Janus-faced La Rochelle's powerful Atlantic allies, and toward the road to Paris, and the Île de France, the seat of the French monarchy and the Gallican church. The mayor performed his role in the ritual by then asking the king to swear an oath to protect the town's "ancient" privileges *before* entering. In 1565, however, in a theatrical gesture calculated to dramatize the crown's dangerous displeasure at La Rochelle's religious infidelity, and hence ingratitude, which rendered all hope of reciprocity impossible, Montmorency galloped forward with sword drawn, through the porte de Congnes, abruptly severing the ribbon of ceremonial exchange prematurely, with the symbol of kingship, noble power, and violence. The centuries old ritual at the gate —the liminal space par excellence between the fortress and the crown—had been reduced to shambles by this unexpected action and the king's silence. And when Montmorency declared that the ritual at the gateway "was no longer the fashion," he made it absolutely clear who set the style for ritualistic discourse in France. La Rochelle would not dictate terms of symbolic exchange to the king.

Asserting domain over La Rochelle's local rights, custom, and memory, Charles then rode slowly through the porte de Cougnes, without pausing, as was expected of him, to confirm the city's communal privileges:

> All of a sudden, the mayor marched up and stood before his monarch, halting the king's horse by grabbing hold of its reins. The mayor then recalled for His Majesty the memory of what former kings—that is, his predecessors—had done on similar occasions, and asked him to reiterate the confirmation of La Rochelle's privileges by stamping them with the august character of his own hand. The prince replied, "Be faithful and loyal servants and I shall be a good king to you." Then, without responding to the mayor's request, he rode on across the city.[56]

The mayor of La Rochelle made the single most dramatic gesture at the porte de Cougnes, by aggressively "halting the king's horse by grabbing hold of its reins," invoking the memory of the king's predecessors and the customary practice of confirming La Rochelle's privileges, and calling for Charles to play his role as scripted and without deviation. The moment had arrived when violence might follow, but the surprised mayor was caught off balance and let go of the horse's reins. The mayor also failed to command the moment in the ritual when La Rochelle's privileges might have been reaffirmed. Charles made it clear that such privileges were the gift of patronage, contingent on the king's personal experience with his subjects, and not determined by historical precedent. The king took his first gamble at the porte de Cougnes and survived; winning convincingly with Catherine's and Montmorency's carefully scripted guidance. The young king had augmented his personal power at the expense of the most politicized members of the Corps de ville and the ministerial leadership, both of which lost face at court and among competing factions in the city.[57]

Charles was literally chased by the confused and humiliated Huguenot elites as he "rode on across the city." Forced to scramble in Charles's wake after he left them behind at the porte de Cougnes, they were nonetheless still determined to maintain a front of unanimity, equilibrium, and politeness, despite what were now overtly strained relations over fundamental questions of communal memory, reciprocity, privilege, and decorum. The mayor, the Corps de Ville, and the Protestant party had suffered an attack on their authority that called into question their ability to maintain the customary course of communal memory. With fading hopes of future reconciliation resting in the balance, the local authorities had little choice but to try to set things right again, by proceeding with the presentation of marvels prepared at enormous expense for the king's pleasure. Thus, as Charles rode into town ahead of his astonished hosts, he must have felt a real sense of victory when "he beheld a fabulous theater of the streets, strewn with greenery and hung with tapestries in his honor."

In addition to Hercules, Charles also saw representations of himself deployed on numerous theatrical machines and in various tableaux vivants, all of which—far too many to summarize here—were intended to communicate the dual message of the arrival of a new golden age symbolized by the syncretism of pagan deities and Christianity (here, for example, Charles was juxtaposed with Hercules and other mythological heroes; and there, Charles was seated upon a triumphal chariot pulled by allegorical figures signifying Peace, Victory, Justice, and Prudence). As if to mask the botched ritual at the porte de Congnes, and the rise of the seditious Protestant factions in the fortress, representations of enduring fidelity were especially prominent.

Despite such loyalist rhetoric, undoubtedly quite natural and sincere for most Rochelais, who had no other discourse with which to address their king, it seems possible to read at least one of these spectacles in more than one way. Take, for example:

> A theater covered with rich tapestries decorated the crossroads of the Fountain of the Little Benches. There, in the king's presence, another group of children were to convey the feelings of the public with touching shouts of joy. The background of the theater was decorated with a large painting depicting a vast park. Two men standing at one corner of the park stretched nets between them. Cunning birds fluttered and soared freely above, evading capture as if they sensed the snare. In another corner, two shepherds escorted by their dogs and standing in the middle of their flock observed the actions of the bird catchers. They seemed to enjoy the craftiness of the birds, which made sport of the hunters' attempts and outwitted their efforts. The shepherds' feelings were mirrored by words from Solomon's Proverbs ["it is in vain that one throws a net in front of the eyes of those who have wings"].
>
> On still another side, a man playing a flute was trying to force his way into the park.

But another man who was inside got up on the fence to push him back. From the show of anger that manifested itself, one guessed that the man inside repulsed the stranger because he had hidden his true intentions under the lure of a seductive song. The following verse interpreted his thought; *Fistula dulce canit volucrem dum decipit auceps:* "The bird catcher plays while he beguiles the bird with the sweet pipe."[58]

"By these symbolic figures," Amos Barbot interpreted, "the Rochelais wanted to bear witness to the king of their fidelity and vigilance as they protected their town in their obedience. Neither by force nor violence nor seduction would they ever be taken from his service."[59] To be sure, this was the moderates' preferred reading of loyalty, despite religious difference, in the presence of the king. That Barbot chose to supply an appropriate reading is significant, however, stabilizing a text that was meant to be ambiguous and implying different messages to different audiences. While it is true that "shepherd" is a common metaphor for the minister, in this fortresslike enclosed park, shepherds were apparently benign yet potentially seditious. They enjoyed the craft and wit of the hunter's elusive prey. This may be a comment on different Rochelais ministers; one perhaps more militant in his sedition than another, more moderate and loyal pastor. Could parallel readings suggest that, in this instance, the shepherds were also protectors of La Rochelle from the "seductive song" of the king's men? Did they command the actions of the men who now repulsed the "beguiling" stranger? What might the piper's identity be, and was resistance from inside the fence an act of loyalty or subversion? Recall the ninety-first psalm, crucial for the Huguenots in search of refuge during the civil war years, wherein it is said that "the Lord," is "My refuge and my fortress;. . . . For he will deliver you from the snare of the fowler." Surely this psalm had special meaning to the fortress-bound Rochelais, and it is implicit in the tableau. The question remained for a multiple audience: what was the identity of the hunters and of the pious and watchful shepherds? Where is God's authentic place of refuge? "Under" whose "wings," as the psalm reads, will you "find refuge"?

The beauty of this allegory from the perspective of multiple audiences in La Rochelle consisted mainly in its playful openness, birdlike lightness, and overall ambiguity. Or, to borrow Arcère's word, its use as a medium of silent "insinuation," an artful muffling of the "loud" expression of rebellion.

❧ The Gift ❧

"After the king was taken to his apartments," Arcère informs us, "the municipal magistrates came and presented him with a silver basin":

> In the center of the basin rose a rock flanked by two figures representing Charles IX surrounded by undulating waves. The basin was also surmounted by a massive gold heart

covered with fleurs-de-lis. The artist had engraved an explanation of this emblem around the inside of the basin. The verses were so bad that it would be almost more proper to leave them in the shadows (in which Amos Barbot's manuscript shrouded them). However, they shall be shown to the Rochelais because of the feelings that these verses expressed.

> The heart strewn with flowers sitting upon a rock,
> And the portrait of the king engraved on both sides,
> Demonstrate that Mars did not overcome
> your humble Rochelais, faithful without reproach.
> From father to son upon you the royal lily descends,
> They have consecrated to you their firm will:
> By them of yore the proud English were daunted;
> Piety a companion of justice
> Declare that together they have embraced him.
> The rock surrounded by an undulating sea shows the firm constancy of your subjects,
> Whose hearts, goods and spirits are yours, Sire.[60]

Foremost among these representations of Rochelais fidelity was the civic gift—an expected part of the ritual—but this particular object was a marvel of linguistic and material gamesmanship. It was given to Charles IX at the end of the day, ostensibly in exchange for his presumed grant of communal privilege, in fact denied with such masterful theatricality just hours earlier.

Despite the time and thought lavished on the creation and iconography of this gift, however (and the time modern historians—including this one—have spent interpreting its iconography), the materiality of gifts was probably far more important in the eyes of the king and his court than their symbolic language. It may be that most gifts as elaborate as La Rochelle's basin were recirculated among courtiers in exchange for debts or as royal favors, or simply melted down for specie, especially during the civil wars:

> There was usually some sort of gift for the King which had been decided in advance by consultation. This really amounted to a levy and, even in the case of more elaborate gifts created in gold and silver, the weight was the critical factor. One feature which is somewhat surprising is that the King often assigned the gift in advance to a member of the court and then, if he wished to keep it for any reason, he was obliged to give the prospective recipient the equivalent in coin of the realm.[61]

If Charles did in fact assign La Rochelle's gift to a wealthy courtier, this leaves open the slight possibility that the missing artifact may resurface some day among the effects of a noble family. Be that as it may, one can easily imagine that Charles was more concerned with his basin's heft than with the "bad" verses of which Barbot was so ashamed.

If the materiality of the gift rather than its discourse was valued most, then perhaps the awkward verses went completely unnoticed by the king. Still, one should never assume that Charles, Catherine, and Montmorency neglected to read them; particularly because they were so carefully transcribed by court historians.

The verses themselves indicate that it was the intention of the magistrates to use the gift as a representation of the fiction of the town's unity and to assert prematurely the reality of its reformed corporate identity under the new Huguenot regime. The verse proclaimed that certain things were fundamental and unchanging. Despite the recent civil warfare (and "slander and invective"), La Rochelle identified itself as subject to the king, "faithful without reproach." Yet again, however, the gift reminded Charles that it was given in reciprocal exchange for privileges granted "From father to son upon you the royal lily descends / They have consecrated to you their firm will." Only the glorious *end* of La Rochelle's medieval English alliance is recalled—hence, again, the reason for the privileges. La Rochelle's English associations are renounced as past, having taken place in days "of yore." The verse ends with a memorable play on word and image, which simultaneously materialized and initiated the ironic history of the place-name La Rochelle—from the Latin *rupella* (which was engraved defiantly on the fortress's walls), or "The Little Rock"—as a civil war polemical figure:

> This rock surrounded [*entourée*] by an undulating sea
> Shows the firm constancy
> of your subjects
> Whose hearts, possessions, and spirits
> are yours, Sire.

With these supplications contained in the fortresslike shape of the circular walled enceinte (common to other basins that have survived from the period)[62]—and also including puns and double references to the royal progress of pacification (*entourée),* as it enveloped and surrounded France's "frontier" (but given its Atlantic alliances, not La Rochelle's frontier)—the Rochelais hoped that the silver and gold basin would signify a gift of themselves to the new king that was simultaneously intimate and public. Perceived whole, with all of its mixed messages, the gift and the ritual of *avènement* leading up to its presentation crystallized the ambivalence of La Rochelle's religious and political condition in relation to the monarch; that is to say, the *simultaneous* desire of all its factions to serve both the new faith and the old monarchy. Because the unification of faith and kingship was central to the ideology of the French monarchy—and would serve as the core of seventeenth-century absolutism—it should come as no surprise that the loyal discourse of the gift achieved the opposite effect to what was intended. Unmoved by rhetorical and material protestations of civic unity and the Rock's "steadfast constancy" to images of a militant monarchy engraved on the fortress's heart, Charles received the gift without recorded comment. And again, instead of completing the exchange of privileges desired by his frustrated hosts, the king took another gamble.

Charles lent his presence to a meeting of Jarnac's anti-Huguenot faction, which had the effect of accomplishing precisely what both the governor and the king must have wished. Having received extensive knowledge of the internecine feuds of the Corps de ville, the king wisely bet that the Rochelais unified identity as represented on the basin was mere bluff and that, in fact, the disunity of the Corps, combined with the events of the king's entry and visit, had already sent the message of the gift careening out of control. In the end, the king's strategic gambles on his ability to manipulate the rituals of privilege worked to promote further intrigue and discord. Moving quickly to take advantage of this, the crown then struck out forcefully at Rochelais Protestantism:

> Jarnac had persuaded the municipal magistrates to promote his zeal for the good of the city, his caring, and the advantages of his administration to His Majesty. Jarnac promised in return that he would stress to the prince how satisfied he was with their behavior. A lawyer named Jean de Haize spoke to His Majesty in the presence of the Corps de ville to instruct the king on the state of affairs in the town. He sang the praises of the governor, whom he flattered excessively. Suddenly, Jean placed the Rochelais in the role of the odious opposition, speaking out indecently against them. La Rochelle had to suffer the humiliation of seeing itself torn apart at the hands of one of its own children, whose black treason was armed against his patria by a tongue that was supposed to speak in its defense. The discord that reigned among the citizens added to the evil. Those who feared the resentment of the king intrigued behind the scenes to exculpate themselves at the expense of others.[63]

The king had won his gambles by exploiting La Rochelle's contentious politics and the possibilities available to the monarch alone in early modern ritual. Charles took calculated personal risks and called La Rochelle's bluff of Protestant unity to assert his dominance over what was, in reality, an unstable situation. In the end, the monarch's traditional military, hunting, and gaming identity, as "the one who always wins," was far more charismatic and solid, even in this young and insecure king, than the shifting and uncertain civic and political identity of La Rochelle's new Huguenot party. This trope of the victorious king was routinely manifested in the more or less constant martial games and elaborate entertainments that occupied much of Charles IX's and the court's leisure time on tour. In several scenarios staged on the road between towns that seemed to foreshadow events at La Rochelle, Charles performed for the traveling court in the role of the legendary hero. This questing knight, through superior strength and guile, single-handedly entered a mythic evil fortress. Once inside, after claiming a great prize, he fought against overwhelming odds before finally escaping with the treasure unscathed. The uniqueness of the monarch's skill at winning was proven over and over again, particularly by the failure of many other young knights—his would-be competitors—to safely enter the fortress, defeat evil, secure the prize, and attain his *gloire,* which belongs by divine right to the king alone.[64]

As a result of Charles's gamesmanship and its own instability, the Rochelais Huguenot leadership was put on the defensive in 1565, and the town remained without its privileges being officially put in place by the king. Charles was now in control, and he "showed his displeasure with La Rochelle" by issuing an edict forbidding the despised declaration of August 4, 1564, to be changed in any way. In fact, Charles extended its repressive powers. The king censored La Rochelle's Corps de ville and those gift-giving magistrates he considered part of the militant faction, "who," according to Ar-cère, "were ordered to protect the Catholic religion and to move strongly against those pastors who, going beyond the bounds of their ministry, continued to criticize the government publicly. This behavior [caused unrest because it] made the people wish for better days."[65]

Barbot tells us that the royal campaign against the Protestant ministry of La Rochelle actually began in November 1562, under the command of the brutal duc de Montpensier. Montpensier's solution to the growing politicization of the clergy was to order all Rochelais Calvinist churchmen banished from the city within twenty-four hours or to face immediate death by strangulation. By May 1565, however, the leading Rochelais divines—including the charismatic Pierre Richier (called de Lisle), who played a central role in the Calvinist New World histories of Jean de Léry in Brazil and Bernard Palissy in Saintonge, as well as Noel Magnen, Odet de Nort, and Nico-las Folion (called de la Vallee)—had begun an aggressive campaign from the pulpit against the subversion of the edicts of toleration by Charles and Catherine and openly blamed the violence against the Huguenots that resulted on the monarch himself. In response to this extraordinary challenge to his moral authority, as his royal visit to La Rochelle in September ended, Charles ordered the city's ministry never again "to use scandalous or seditious words touching the honor of his majesty," or to suffer the death penalty. As if to underscore the reality of this threat, Nicolas Folion was banished in perpetuity beyond the borders of Aunis, on pain of death if he tried to return or preach anywhere in France.[66]

To demonstrate his displeasure with the Corps de ville, other outspoken bourgeois, and his own placemen who failed to perform their duty, Charles banished Jean Pierres (one would-be mayor who was elected in 1563, the king's *lieutenant-général,* and the lead criminal prosecutor of La Rochelle's ostensibly royalist *présidial*) and placed him under house arrest in Paris. In addition to seditious activities with the Huguenot party, Pierres had not maintained law and order as required by the *présidial,* and he faced the humiliating prospect of having to report personally to the governor of Paris, who reviewed his activities every week and reported them to the king. Far less imaginative banishments were suffered by five additional bourgeois "of less distinguished rank," who were simply dispersed to live in exile in five different cities throughout France.[67] As a final theatrical gesture devised by Anne de Montmorency for the king's security and as a strategy to further humiliate the anxious and threatening Rochelais nobility of the sword, Charles IX boldly refused the obligatory military escort out of town, and made a quick getaway from the fortress, once again through the porte de Cougnes.

❧ "The Rock": 1565 and 1628 ❧

When a now anonymous Rochelais goldsmith was commissioned to engrave honorific supplications of rocklike fidelity in the midst of historical turmoil on the surface of Charles IX's gift of "La Rochelle" in 1565, the communal promise of the gift of self was implicitly contingent upon the king's customary reciprocity with the gift of privilege. But, as the anthropologist Pierre Bourdieu has wisely demonstrated for other contexts, such strategies of gift-giving may evoke effective counterstrategies (though such strategies are sometimes undertaken at risk of violent personal revenge). Holding in abeyance his traditional obligation to grant La Rochelle its privileges *before* crossing the threshold, and therefore extending indefinitely into the future the crucial moment of exchange, Charles subverted the historical power of the gift a priori, while withholding as an instrument of royal power the implied offer of potential symmetry. What the Rochelais had hoped represented their gift to the king in exchange for his privileges already given, had, in effect, had been given unconditionally.[68]

That this moment of symmetry never actually arrived was early evidence of irreconcilable differences between the monarchy and the Huguenot city-state, which could only be reconciled, as the action of Montmorency's sword implied, through separation and violence. It is clear that the crown stubbornly refused to accept La Rochelle's strategy of using the language of gifts to signal fidelity, closure, and love, while practicing heresy, treason, separation, and disaffection. Despite the gratitude, reciprocity, and exchange invited, there would thus be no discursive symmetry—no full dialogue— between the state and local, heretical power. While both sides tried to appropriate the language of the gift for their own ends in the quest for advantage, thus subverting reciprocity and closure in the ritual of exchange, the king made it clear that this represented a far greater risk for the Rochelais. La Rochelle's options during this period of conversion to the international political program of Protestantism were becoming extremely limited.

La Rochelle's response to its estrangement from the monarchy came three years later, in 1568, when the fortress finally unified sufficiently behind Condé to formally enter his rebellious camp—depending on ideological and economic support from the expanding Protestant world of the North Atlantic—and the now "radicalized" Corps de ville and mayor declared the city an independent Huguenot republic on the Genevan model.[69] The term "radical" must be used cautiously, however; here it is used from the perspective of the monarchy. Still, it should be remembered that at the same time, the city refused to relinquish its ancient sense of loyalty to the French monarch and struggled to reconcile the link from "days of yore" with its now virtually unanimous faith in the "new," albeit "primitive," religion. By 1627, the Huguenot leadership continued to maintain that the dissonant fiction of dual loyalties was still useful; but an increasingly militant monarchy, guided by Cardinal Richelieu—that most covetous of Counter-Reformation warrior-priests—was already constructing a new historical narrative for the French state, based on the monistic principles of an absolute monarchy, in which the violent synthesis by the expanding state of La Rochelle's divided loyalties played an essential part.

As for the language of the gift itself, the discourse of the Rock continued to circulate, but with unfortunate consequences for the Rochelais. Listen to this exemplary passage from an oration given on November 1, 1627, three days after the catastrophic rout of English forces under the duke of Buckingham at Île de Ré (ending La Rochelle's hopes of international aid), and sixty-two years after the series of ritualistic posturings and incomplete exchanges at the porte de Cougnes. The speaker was a dedicated inquisitor: first *président* de Gourges of the *parlement* of Bordeaux, which had regional jurisdiction over heresy trials that originated in the region of Saintonge, in La Rochelle's southern hinterland. Among his auditors was Louis XIII, then at his base camp at Aytre, well within sight of the southwestern walls of besieged La Rochelle, which would capitulate to Louis and Richelieu in October 1628. "This *rock*," Gourges punned, "has always been the *heart*, the first to move [*mouvant*], and will be the last to move among the factions and rebellions in your kingdom. It is a *rock* upon which public tranquility has been shipwrecked fourteen times since the beginning of the troubles with the Huguenots."[70]

Gourges's polemical double entendre on "the rock" with a moving heart (a heart he knew was about to stop beating), reactivated—and turned upon itself—language initiated with Charles's gift in 1565, in which geological metaphors were manipulated ironically by the enemies of Protestantism in conjunction with La Rochelle's pivotal role in the civil wars of religion. There are many other prominent examples. The royalist poet François de Malherbe, for one, who was to die in Paris on October 16, 1628, days before the final surrender of La Rochelle, nevertheless still managed to compose a lovely (and often quoted) panegyric as a parting gift to his patron, in anticipation of Louis's triumphant return: "The Rock is dust, its fields deserted / Nothing to see but cemeteries / Where Titans once lived, there they lie buried."[71] Such geological figures fell largely out of fashion in Counter-Reformation texts after 1628. La Rochelle was defeated, its population of Protestant rebels all but decimated or exiled, and its walls leveled. By Richelieu's design, the city was repopulated by a Catholic majority and ceased to be of any real consequence to the propaganda apparatus of the state. Given Charles's disdainful response to the gift of the "rock" with a golden "heart" in 1565, one might assume that the king would have shared Gourges's understanding of the metaphor. Here, even the iconography of the thing itself overtly begged the question of who would control the discourse of the gift—its giver (whose heart could keep rebellious secrets) or the recipient—since, ironically, its metaphoric language called attention to fundamental doubts about loyalty shared by a Catholic king and his heretical subjects. How does one peer into the gift-giver's heart—understood to be the place of his innermost, secret self, his true, hidden identity; his love, friendship, and above all, loyalty—especially when the heart itself is the substance of the gift? What is withheld from the heart that is given? The Rochelais thus appeared to give themselves turned inside-out to their prince in 1565; or rather, the Huguenots insisted that there was no substantive difference between the outward appearance of fidelity made of silver and gold and their innermost feelings.

When a prince peered into his own heart, however, he was also said to see into the hearts, not only of his ancestors, but of all his subjects. The hearts of French kings were symbolically identical and so could never really die. The hearts of kings of the Bourbon dynasty were removed after death and placed in one of two churches—le Val-de-Grâce or Saint-Louis des Jesuites—so that "the royal blood returns to its source and rejoins the heart of Saint Louis. It is always the same blood that runs in the veins of the reigning prince, and it never stops flowing, since the prophesies promise eternity to the sons of Saint Louis."[72] In the best of times, the triumphal entrance of Charles IX in 1565 would have signified precisely the kind of reciprocal exchange of hearts that La Rochelle claimed in its gift. On those occasions, "the goodness, virtue, and majesty of the prince triumph in the hearts of his subjects, and. . . the love, submission, and obedience of his subjects triumph in the heart of the prince."[73] However hard La Rochelle's Huguenots tried to construct a viable discourse of loyalty, Charles, Catherine, and Montmorency—and their followers—understood from both historical and recent experience, that the Rock's disaffected heart did not belong to the kingdom. Despite the language of the gift, La Rochelle had always been seduced by strangers.

❧ A History of Strangers: Louis XIII's "Relation" (1628) ❧

It thus remained for the victorious Louis XIII to sum up the events of 1565 in 1628. The king's (and Richelieu's) historian's incisive and vengeful "Relation du siège de La Rochelle" (1628) makes it clear that the fortress's infidelity was tied directly to its historical "freedom of trade and obsession with strangers, and principally the English, their great friends ... [England] where criminals of *lèse-majesté* ... [go to seek] refuge."[74] Sometimes Louis XIII simply referred to La Rochelle's "adherence to strangers." Not only La Rochelle was accused of infidelity, but the entire borderland region under its foreign sphere of influence; one that Louis mapped—with good reason—along the coast from the Gironde north all the way to the Loire. The totality of southwestern Huguenot culture, then, was condemned as "hidden, secret and not acknowledged by legitimate authority," or "not authentic."

This secret inauthenticity was particularly true of Huguenot religiosity: "the most specious pretext, which always serves as a veil to cover their ambition. We know only too well . . . that certain discordant spirits, under the color of religion, have recourse to strangers." The bodily source of such disloyalty and hidden malice was not a gift of pure constancy, but rather the baneful animus of "rebels who brew poison in their hearts." The gift of such a heart would mean certain death if it were joined—or exchanged—with that of another, especially an unsuspecting monarch. Thus, the "Relation" warned the Huguenots' potential royal hosts in the Atlantic world of their duplicity, particularly Louis's own brother-in-law, England's Charles I, who attempted to break the siege of La Rochelle in 1627 with the failed expedition to Île de Ré. Perhaps that is why Louis reserved his particular scorn for southwestern Huguenot historians in exile. Surveying the ruins of La Rochelle, the "Relation" quoted with delighted sarcasm "one of their historians . . . writing from Geneva . . . [who] said [to the besieged Rochelais], 'know that he who pleases God holds the heart of kings in his hand.'" Louis XIII chided the Huguenots that they would always be strangers in the hearts of their hosts. A chain of events that had begun in 1565 with a thwarted ritual of gift exchange thus ended in 1628 with a ritual of violent military and linguistic overthrow.

That Louis XIII and his interlocutors would choose to devote twenty-four lines of the summation of this all-important document to a frontal attack on a Rochelais Huguenot historian in exile is evidence enough not only that southwestern Huguenot historiography was read in court circles but also of how serious a threat to historical memory the crown took it to be. Clearly, Louis's historians (under the influence of Richelieu's developing mercantilist policies) were writing in 1628 not only for domestic consumption but also for a growing transatlantic audience—particularly in England, Holland, Germany, *and* the rapidly expanding colonial extensions of the former two countries (as well as New France)—which hosted the refugees and might be misled by their historians. Southwestern Huguenot historiography and the history of the dispersion—of which Louis's unnamed historian was surely a part—cannot be considered separately from that of the New World, and particularly, beginning much earlier than the Revocation of the Edict of Nantes in 1685, from that of the colonial American transatlantic experience.

As the French crown clearly understood, historians of southwestern France traditionally wrote their histories with reference to Atlantic history and culture, which is to say bound up with the history of outsiders (or "strangers") and not the French territorial state. This was especially so after 1628, when it fell to the oral and material history of the mainly agrarian and artisanal survivors from the Saintonge hinterlands—along with a few surviving Rochelais mercantile families—to labor to reconstitute memory in the remainder of their world, decimated by war and a culture of reciprocal violence since the sixteenth century. For many, the place where this process of reconstitution took place was ultimately in the New World. Ironically, even while the fortress was destroyed and its population of 27,000 all but exterminated or otherwise depleted in 1628, the structures of escape for survivors in the Saintongeais hinterland to the New World—a strong regional source of refugees for the colonial American dispersion—followed old trade routes to the North Atlantic, set up sometimes centuries earlier by La Rochelle merchants. Moreover, as early as the 1560s, Saintongeais historians began to write histories of the long period of Huguenot military defeat and destruction of the temples, which led to the secret and highly risky assemblies of the *désert,* a sort of internal exile. These texts suggest that the Huguenots of Aunis-Saintonge, sometimes long before the time of their physical dispersion, saw themselves to be standing literally at the nexus of Revelation and Genesis. These strangers in their own land occupied sacred space at the beginning of the end of one world, as harbingers of final things, and at the initiation of another, New World experience, while still in situ in France. Given the reality of the apocalyptic context in Saintonge, and the traditional links between the Protestant southwest and Atlantic history and culture, it should be remembered that these were, for the Huguenots, actual as well as metaphorical spaces.[75] This was especially true of southwestern Huguenot artisans.

❧ Building with the Destroyer ❧

> All those who seek to generate metals by fire wish to build with the destroyer.　　—BERNARD PALISSY, *Discours admirables* (1580)

There is strong archeological evidence—some of it quite recent—that links the beginnings of what I have called the New World historiography of sixteenth-century Saintonge with the complex material life of gifts and gift production, and especially with the Huguenot potter, natural philosopher, alchemist, lay minister, *and* local historian Bernard Palissy of Saintes.[76] We shall see in chapter 2 how Palissy's essay "History of the Church of Saintes" (1563) depicted the "beginnings" of the "Primitive Church" of Saintonge, in both the spiritual and the material senses, as a New World Church. The reader will recall that the progress through the southwest that brought the cortège of Charles IX, the queen mother, and Anne de Montmorency to La Rochelle in 1565 to receive the gift of the fortress's heart, also stopped in Saintes, where Palissy was introduced to his future patron, Catherine de Médicis, the regent. Saintes was an important town on the itinerary, in part because of its evocative Gallo-Roman ruins, but mostly because Montmorency, Palissy's principal patron, was its royal governor.

What were the extraordinarily complex patronage, artisanal, and scientific relationships that linked the fate of the autodidactic Palissy, arguably one of the most prominent and, if his leveler rhetoric is to be believed, anti-aristocratic and anti-Catholic heretics in the region, with the same royal cast of characters that treated the disloyal Rochelais with such complete disdain? As we shall see in subsequent chapters, Palissy's life and work were a masterpiece of the successful use of "insinuation" and of multiple, dissonant allegiances, tactics that the majority of Rochelais were unable (or unwilling) to put into practice systematically in either 1565 or 1627. Palissy managed to engage in precisely the sort of secretive and subversive activities that Louis XIII's "Relation" denounced, but only with the connivance of the court.

In 1562, as the first of eight civil wars of religion between the Catholic majority and followers of the "lutherien et calvinien" heresy consumed southwestern France in a frenzy of confessional violence, Palissy secreted himself inside a fortified laboratory hidden in a tower among the parapets of Saintes, read the German-Swiss natural philosopher and mystical alchemist Paracelsus and the Book of Revelation, and conducted clandestine experiments in his alchemic furnace and pottery kiln. Palissy later claimed, in a narrative of the war in Saintonge, that these panicked experiments resulted in the covert "invention" of ceramic glazes of such astonishing color and translucency that they were mistakenly perceived to have been made in the "bowels" of the earth and not by man. Palissy's life was shaped by the long period of confessional violence that preceded the wars of religion (1562–1598), and then by the wars themselves, which, as we have seen, were sometimes interrupted by short periods of "pacification," when less overt forms of persecution and intolerance were practiced by whatever group of combatants was temporarily in the ascendant in contested regions such as Saintonge. This horrific experience of utter chaos and entropy was shared by everyone who lived in the southwest of France, especially in the valleys of the Charente and Gironde and in the coveted salt marshes along the Atlantic coast of Saintonge. Luther's Germanic critique of the Roman Church resonated powerfully in La Rochelle—the region's metropolis and entrepôt—and tensions peaked throughout the region after 1534, when the Roman Catholic mass was openly denounced by Huguenot polemicists in Paris during the "Affair of the Placards," an event that merged seamlessly with the publication, in 1536, of Calvin's *Institutes of the Christian Religion.* Just five years later, a highly disciplined theocracy was established in Geneva, under Calvin and Théodore de Bèze, to challenge Rome's status as Christ's holy city on earth.[77] Despite having voiced his early conversion to the Huguenot cause—an admission that compelled the local Inquisition to bend dangerously in his direction, nearly taking his life—Palissy's artisanal skills as a self-proclaimed "inventor" of "rustic figures" also caught the attention of the powerful Pons family, leaders of the Protestant nobility of the sword in the coastal province of Saintonge, and ultimately of the Constable of France himself.

Even with such influential patronage from local Protestant leaders, the potter had only a limited degree of personal protection from the Catholic authorities and the *marechaussee* (rural police) in Saintes and Bordeaux. Like so many of his co-religionists in La Rochelle's hinterland, he despaired over his sudden vulnerability. Having seen so many Huguenots die, like the exiled ministers of La Rochelle who preached against the violent attacks on Protestants during times of "pacification," he became consumed with thoughts of violent death and premature endings. From that moment on, the potter had embarked on a lonely and, from his perspective, heroic struggle to decode the sacred meaning of such violence in the materials of his own life and, by extension, in the French Reformation as well.

Nevertheless, shortly thereafter, this particular heretic's unique skills in artisanry and self-promotion gave his life value to certain powerful members of the nobility. In time, Palissy's survival was to become useful to the sometimes equally vulnerable court of Charles IX, then in the process of trying to solidify its unsteady control over the state. The potter's reputation as a maker of "rustic figures" and naturalistic ceramic grottoes had reached Paris through Montmorency. There, his work excited the demand for novelty at this fragile but ambitious court—which found ceramic (and hence cheap) novelties enormously useful as courtly gifts in a patronage system that relied on gift exchange as an indispensable component of political culture—and, ultimately, Palissy managed to achieve a grant of royal protection from the queen mother, Catherine de Médicis, through the offices of Montmorency, thus linking the potter with two of the greatest contemporary producers and consumers of gifts. The Constable used a tiny portion of his store of personal and financial capital in the region of Saintonge and extricated Palissy from a potentially deadly inquest by the *parlement* of Bordeaux in 1563, which enabled the ruthlessly self-interested Catherine to invite the potter to Paris sometime between 1565 and 1567, where Palissy, now in debt for his life to two of the leading anti-Calvinists in France, set up a kiln and alchemical laboratory. Having depended on powerful patrons to survive both the war in Saintonge and the St. Bartholomew's Day Massacre in Paris (which followed Catherine's approval of the assassination in 1572, of the Huguenot leader and New World projector Admiral Gaspard de Coligny), the potter continued his risky double life as a creature of the Catholic nobility and a pious Calvinist. He outlived his resourcefulness as an "inventor" in the late 1590s and finally succumbed to the vicious factionalism of French court politics. Palissy's long life ended in the Bastille at the turn of the seventeenth century; he was an unrepentant old heretic whose religious errors were tolerated while his skills and courtly taste for appropriation of the "rustic" style (with which he was personally identified) lasted in Paris.

Art historians cite Palissy as a major figure in production of innovative ceramics during the French Renaissance. At the same time, he has been of interest to the history of science since at least the nineteenth century, having written two significant (if relatively minor) treatises on artisanry and natural philosophy. Most important for our purposes here, Palissy was concerned with the symbiotic—indeed cosmological—relation he perceived to exist between the universal practices of pottery production and the invention of ceramic glazes in the kiln, agriculture, and the earth's internal production of geological specimens. That is why Palissy's books and artifacts were understood by him to take the form of natural histories of words and things; that is to say, of the mingling of his experience as an artisan, natural philosopher, and Calvinist seeker. They also mapped his pilgrim's path as he wandered through the apocalyptic religious, social, and geological landscape of sixteenth-century Saintonge. As such, they are at once religious allegories and careful archaeological inventories of collections of "artifacts" of God-in-nature, which documented an artisan's search for hidden meanings to make sense of the chaos, instability, and fragmentation that defined his war-torn world.

To varying degrees, both Palissy's *Recepte veritable* (La Rochelle, 1563) and *Discours admirables* (Paris, 1580) shed light on his pilgrimage in search of a personal material-holiness synthesis. In these deeply metaphysical narratives, the potter assumed the duplicitous persona of a learned but humble craftsman, a survivor who struggled heroically with heart and hands against all odds for the sake of faith, work, and the dream of tranquility. The struggle was not only to survive the effects of violence and alienation that history inflicted upon Palissy and the Huguenots of the earliest years of the *désert,* but also to manipulate effects that he perceived to occur simultaneously in Nature into the material basis for new, less vulnerable forms of social, evangelical, and material discourse. These tasks caused the potter to undertake the creation of both written and material texts drawn from his scientific and artisanal explorations of his endangered "rustic" reality at the deepest level as he meditated on the essences of life. As Palissy pursued personal salvation, he proceeded by harnessing himself physically as well as metaphorically to the alchemic process of purification of local earthy matter retrieved on furtive, solitary walks through the isolated tidal salt marshes of the Atlantic coast and the mudflats of the Charente River Valley of Saintonge. Here the potter labored with the specimens unearthed to comprehend his personal history in terms of his alchemical analysis of these fragments of material life and death. Thus, it was his heightened personal understanding of what historians of early modern science now call animate materialism, and of the universality of the individual's place in the natural world, that helped bind together Palissy's identity as a Huguenot artisan and those of his followers in the Protestant communities of Saintonge.

Stigmatized and besieged by Catholics at every level of society as a noted member of France's most highly skilled (and hence most potentially subversive) heretical group, Palissy invented for himself the social role of a manual laborer for the earthly stabilization of the fragmented Huguenot—a kind of metaphysical fixer—amid the ruins of the fallen microcosm of the natural world. He worked to reconstruct the lost prelapsarian purity of his own soul, which, as Paracelsus's mystical writings taught him, was also inextricably linked to a process of destruction and regeneration in the macrocosm. Only after the potter's soul was thus inspired and momentarily purified—uniting microcosm and macrocosm in brief but amazingly productive "flashes" of experimentation and lucidity—could he begin to amplify this process of personal and material cleansing, to reform society and effect historical change in everyday life.

In 1580, when Palissy looked back on his violent past as a pious artisan who struggled to survive and provide a secure context for heterodoxy in Saintonge, he warned that "all those who seek to generate metals by fire wish to build with the destroyer." In so doing, Palissy resigned himself to writing an ambivalent coda for his part in this painful historical process, one that forced open long-dormant millennial space that lay hidden in the "generative" parts of the human and earthly interior. In these secret places in natural bodies, where violence and the sacred combined to form a symbiotic whole, the Huguenot artisan thought he found the raw materials necessary to "invent" and to "build" fundamental spiritual and material change. To precipitate this process, the metals this potter excavated and fired to purify his glazes came from matter already burned and tempered in the scorched earth of sixteenth-century Saintonge. We shall see how the ambiguous meanings Palissy associated with his "rustic figures" were intended to be fluid, subtly coded, and potentially multiple, whatever his royal patrons may have had in mind; like their maker, to survive, they had to be adaptable to new audiences, contexts, and functions.

Palissy addressed a visually sophisticated audience at every level of early modern society, whose symbolic rules and emblematic structures were drawn from a noble culture that assigned great charismatic value to power created by violence. Thus, much of the communicative value of Palissy's work for the Huguenots—as self-proclaimed "victims" of that violence—lay in the artful and holy ways it represented the natural resilience and creativity of life animated by death. Palissy's figures conveyed (and at times prophesied) an artisan's material sense of his spiritual relation to Christ's sacrifice and the millennial primacy of that sacrifice as the ur-ending, which was also a beginning. As we shall see, it was in the construction of Palissy's tiny ceramic figures that the conceptual foundations necessary for the relocation of survivors to the Huguenots' new world lay. In "the *désert*," refugee artisans constructed portable millennial spaces to secure soulish fragments of their own sacred bodies in matter saved from total annihilation by "the destroyer." This alchemical process revealed the inner life of the pious artisan momentarily to God and his chosen community of believers, before he returned to the security of hiding again.[78] Mutable experience such as this, absolutely integral to the Huguenots' mobile nature as a diasporic culture, seemed to defy mapping by simple geographic boundaries. Thus, the Huguenots' New World would be located on both sides of the Atlantic. The basic conditions for the existence of this New World artisanal culture were certainly available to Palissy and his followers in Saintonge by the 1560s, at the same time that the first Huguenot refugees from southwestern France settled in the Western Hemisphere.

I shall now begin to show the process by which Bernard Palissy associated himself and his community of Huguenot craftsmen with a very specific millennial and artisanal epistemology based on practical experience with Nature and agriculture, which he (and other natural philosophers) developed out of a syncretic reading of Scripture, the Apocrypha, and Paracelsus (among much else). Palissy was, in fact, a first-generation French Paracelsian, which led him to present himself to Catherine and the court in Paris as a "rustic artisan without learning" and a producer of marvels. It was in this rhetorical guise—a standard persona of self-effacement adopted by Paracelsian artisans—that Palissy constructed the grotto for Catherine in the Tuileries.

Cultural historians of the Renaissance are familiar with much of Palissy's artisanal production, which goes beyond the famous grottoes to include ewers, platters, and rustic figurines, often "live cast" from natural specimens to give the appearance of having been cut out of the Saintongeais salt marshes; portable earthenware microcosms to house tiny plants and animals captured, undisturbed, in the middle of everyday life. But it was not until 1986 that another facet of Palissy's artisanal life was uncovered, when archaeological excavation of his house, atelier, and furnace beneath the cour du Carrousel in Paris (during construction of the new I. M. Pei entrance to the Louvre Museum) revealed that Palissy was also working—indeed, may have established a sort of factory—to produce numerous ceramic medallions with images of noble patrons cast on their surfaces, such as the one of his patron Anne de Montmorency (fig. 1.1). Are these archeological fragments surviving examples of the ceramic gifts Palissy produced for powerful patrons to circulate among their clientage networks as visible emblems of a creature's belonging and loyalty? Most Renaissance medallions were originally cast in bronze, and indeed virtually every design for Palissy's medallions can be traced to bronze prototypes. But bronze was expensive, so some were cast in cheaper lead. Ultimately, Palissy experimented with enameled clay as the cheapest substitute of all—yet, in this potter's workshop, fired clay was an alchemical material that had already achieved the highest spiritual status, to which base lead could as yet merely aspire.[79] Because he was called to Paris to construct Catherine's grotto in the Tuileries in 1565, and construction was still under way in 1572, his patron spared his life in the St. Bartholomew's Day Massacre, when many of Palissy's artisanal and scientific co-

FIGURE I.I. Bernard Palissy and workshop, lead-glazed earthenware medallion of Constable Anne de Montmorency, Paris, ca. 1565–67. 5.1 cm in diameter. Courtesy Musée national de la Renaissance—Château d'Ecouen.

hort perished. But the self-dramatizing and innovative heretic survived many years after the completion of this commission, in large part, I would argue, on the basis of his ability as a gift-maker. What we know about the pervasiveness, as well as the structure and function of clientage networks, suggests the centrality of the courtly practice of gift-giving. Hence, by extension, gift-*making* was an enormous enterprise, in the *material* sense, in the early modern Atlantic world.[80] Surely it would have been a substantial political and economic asset to possess as one's creature a notable and prolific producer of relatively inexpensive, fashionable gifts, such as Bernard Palissy, that rare artisan whose work was recognized instantly, signifying, with powerful immediacy, the sophisticated "rusticity" of urbane patrons in court circles.[81]

How then, in the end, does one begin to determine the meaning of such gifts as understood by the artisans who made them, as well as the audience that received them, inasmuch as evidence suggests that the southwestern Huguenot culture that survived and whose members dispersed as refugees in the American diaspora was largely arti-sanal? Of the Rochelais maker of Charles's silver and gold basin we know nothing, ex-cept what local historians say about his lost product, and that he was presumably a Huguenot. But, as we shall see, Palissy clearly declared his allegiance to a natural philo-sophical system that stressed hierarchies of meaning encoded in a sort of material lit-eracy: the primacy of a hidden, interior world—the world of the spiritual heart—over the "dead letter" of inanimate appearances. A master of Arcère's art of political insin-uation, Palissy privileged the material basis of craft before its surface iconography. To rephrase as a question an idea borrowed from the anthropologist James C. Scott: how do historians read the "hidden transcripts" that informed Palissy's life and the "inven-tion" (his own word) of his craft in Saintonge?[82] Palissy's ceramic "transcripts" carried messages into the households of patrons. He was above all a master craftsman, but he was also a teacher and a lay evangelist. Other artisans and clients were meant to re-ceive and replicate material messages as well, even in New York, where southwestern Huguenot makers of leather chairs and merchants followed similar artifactual strate-gies.

Palissy was, therefore, an artisan and scientist who used the most portable tools and skills available to survive the violence of the civil wars of religion. His primary tool of survival was his physical and craft mobility, which enabled the potter and many thou-sands of other refugee Huguenot artisans to escape persecution by relocating elsewhere in the Atlantic world. Palissy's written texts and material artifacts tell us in no uncer-tain terms that his understanding of materials and glazes was inextricably intertwined with his historical status as a Huguenot living and working at what to him was the end of time. What millennial messages and personal expectations were contained and cir-culated in Palissy's gift medallions, which were applied as ornaments to other ceramic forms from his workshop, or worn like pendants over the hearts of royalist recipients?[83] The lessons of La Rochelle's exposed heart were not lost on the "humble" potter from Saintes. To craft frontal resistance may have been the strategy of an impregnable stone fortress heading for destruction after its decision to join Condé's military and political alliance in 1568. But Palissy and his artisan followers on the Saintongeais periphery knew that they were too insignificant and vulnerable to adopt Condé's medieval *noblesse d'épée* security program: an outdated and one-dimensional strategy that the potter would dis-credit as unfit and in need of reform. That is why, when Palissy was appropriated to Paris as a refugee from religious violence in Saintonge, in order to enter court life as a gift-maker for the same royal household that, at that exact moment, was subverting rit-ual offerings of fealty made by his brethren in La Rochelle, it seems reasonable to ask: what, in the *material* sense, was this artisan's understanding of the multiple languages of appropriation? In other words, who was appropriating whom?

CHAPTER TWO

Palissy's Fortress

The Construction of Artisanal Security

❧ "De la ville de forteresse" ❧

Rochelais were the first to see Bernard Palissy's brief, but prescient, essay "De la ville de forteresse" ("Of the Fortress Town"), which appeared in bookstalls in France's most powerful fortress in 1563, just two years before Charles IX's contentious visit, printed at La Rochelle by the fledging Huguenot publisher and propagandist Barthélemy Berton as a chapter of the potter's *Recepte véritable* ("True Recipe").[1]

Although Berton's imprint was founded in March 1563 (immediately after the edict of pacification ending the first civil war of religion was signed), his name was well known in the greatly expanding book trade of international Protestantism by the time of his death, which took place during the first unsuccessful royal siege of La Rochelle in 1572–73. (La Rochelle, like many important Huguenot strongholds, was besieged as a consequence of the St. Bartholomew's Day Massacre in 1572.)[2] Barthélemy Berton was an immigrant to La Rochelle. He was born in Limoges, 100 miles east of Saintes, into a family of printers. During the sixteenth century, this town was famous through-out Europe for painted metal enamelware. Palissy thus worked a short distance from Limoges's artisans and their products, and he doubtless learned much from them about the technology of translucent enamelware. This would have been valuable in his in-ventive use of enamels; first on glass (he was apprenticed to a glass stainer) and ulti-mately on ceramics.[3] Palissy and the Bertons may well have known one another per-sonally, or by reputation, long before their paths cross in the historical record.

After his father, Paul Berton, was arrested and brought before the *parlement* of Bordeaux (where, in 1551, he was convicted of the heresy of printing forbidden books and sentenced to "faire amende honorable"), Barthélemy Berton wisely fled to the heterodox publishing center of Lyon, where he took refuge and found work among the large Protestant artisan population. In 1561, however, Barthélemy left town abruptly, carrying the tools of his trade and a case of type on his back (the type used in his books after he relocated to La Rochelle in 1563 is characteristic of work from a Lyonnais press).[4] What caused him to return to the troubled southwest after ten years' of steady employment in Lyon? The utter obscurity of his first destination sheds light on one reason: he headed directly for the remote salt-producing *presqu'île* of Marennes, which is located in the *marais* (or salt marshes) that define coastal Saintonge, giving this maritime region its particular geographic character.

Marennes was the property of the ambitious Antoine de Pons (1510–80), hereditary *sire* of Pons.[5] The town of Pons, near neighbor to Saintes, was the seat of Antoine's *sirerie,* a domain that extended to 52 parishes and 250 noble fiefdoms. Pons was also a fortress town, and was later named one of two dubious *villes de sûreté* in the region in the Edict of Nantes (1598). The other was Saint-Jean d'Angély. La Rochelle remained the only capable fortress in Aunis-Saintonge, however. In Antoine's time, Pons's garrison was notoriously weak, and its walls were ineffectual and easily breached. When Louis XIII led his successful military campaign against these two Protestant strongholds in Saintonge in 1620–21, Pons fell in a matter of hours to a small contingent of soldiers diverted from Saint-Jean d'Angély. Hence, the fortress at Pons retained more symbolic than military significance. As long as perceptions of Antoine's enormous personal and family prestige remained intact, his town's permeable walls were not tested.[6]

Antoine was also count of Marennes, baron of the Île d'Oléron, and seigneur of several valuable salt-cultivating and trading towns on the Saintonge coast. This was the geographic center of heresy in isolated Saintonge. To confirm his hold over the politics and economy of this region, Antoine also served as governor of Saintes and Saintonge. Scion of an extended household, Antoine inherited family property in Périgord, Quercy, Poitou, and Guienne as well.[7] Most important for our purposes here, Antoine de Pons was best known outside his home region for establishment of a "rustic" Huguenot court with strong northern Italian influence in isolated Saintonge. It was to the religious and artistic patronage—and isolated security—afforded by this Huguenot court and rustic academy that both Berton and his friend and co-religionist Bernard Palissy (among many other Huguenot refugees) were drawn during the early 1560s, when the region's confessional violence was at its most dangerous.[8]

The centripetal pull of Pons's court culture originated with the unification of two powerful Saintongeais noble families, both with strong personal links to northern Italy, particularly to the heterodox region around Venice. When Antoine de Pons married

Anne de Parthenay in 1534, he united the house of Pons and its enormous holdings in Saintonge with the family of Anne's land-rich father, Jean Larcevesque-Parthenay, baron de Soubise, and Michelle de Saubonne, her Brittany-born mother. By the date o f his marriage to Anne, Antoine de Pons had already lived for fourteen years in northern Italy, where he acted as a French royal agent in both political and military affairs. Not surprisingly, Antoine was a common presence at the francophile court of Ferrara, just southwest of Venice, on the road to Bologna. But Anne de Parthenay's mother, Michelle de Saubonne, had even deeper connections to the court of Ferrara, where she lived between 1528 and 1536 as the governess of Renée de France, consort of Hercule II d'Este, duke of Ferrara. Renée became a dedicated patron of the earliest Protestant leaders, especially important during their periods of exile in both France and Italy. Risking Rome's displeasure, Renée used status and cash resources to create a dazzling refuge at court in Ferrara—in effect, a humanist academy of Huguenot expatriate learning and performance in poetry, the arts (especially music), theology, and natural philosophy. Not just Huguenots came there, however; Paracelsus himself was a guest. In the early sixteenth century, Renée also extended her court's financial patronage and noble protection to Théodore de Bèze, Jean Calvin, and Clément Marot when they sought refuge in the north of Italy.[9]

The complementary roles played by the republic of Venice in conjunction with this aristocratic French court at Ferrara were essential to the maintenance of a rich and complex (albeit mostly hidden) Protestant presence, noble and commoner, native and foreign, in northern Italy. As John Martin has pointed out in his study of sixteenth-century Italian heterodoxy, even though the "Jesuit order was gaining sway, and the Inquisition had been established," it was by no means certain that "all conditions were antithetical to the goals of the *spirituali*—especially not in Venice, a republic that occupied a special place between Renaissance and Reformation. For in the context of sixteenth-century Italy, Venice stood out as a survivor." In a larger sense, Renée's French academy also survived in Venice's shadow. Martin elucidates "deep affinities between the ideals of Renaissance republicans and those of the evangelicals." Yet, because she was under the influence of Venetian republicanism, Florentine civic humanism as articulated by the Protestant Antonio Brucioli in the Rucellai gardens (when Machiavelli and Guicciardini were present), and the charismatic leadership of the French Reformation in exile at her court, "Duchess Renée of Ferrara, though her power was limited," and standing almost alone among the Italian nobility, "gave her support to the evangelicals."[10]

Noble support crisscrossed the Alps. The marriage of Antoine de Pons and Anne de Parthenay was not arranged at home in Saintonge, but at Ferrara, where the two first met, and where they returned to celebrate their wedding in 1534.[11] This union of noble humanists and spiritual seekers harnessed classical learning to the new evangelical religion. These links ramified in material ways: they expanded their role as patrons of Huguenot artisans of novel "inventions" made in the rustic manner, then fashionable in ceramics, and, above all, the naturalistic (or *rustique*) gardens and subterranean grottoes of northern Italy and southwestern France in which the first of many Protestant religious conversions were known to take place. After Anne's death and his remarriage to Marie de Monchenu, Pons renounced his overt association with Protestantism, yet Palissy nonetheless dedicated his *Discours admirables* to his former patron years later.[12] In his dedication of July 1580 (probably in anticipation of Pons's death), the potter extolled Antoine as a latitudinarian man of science whose mind had been expanded by his formative sojourn at the academy at Ferrara:

> I say it truly and without any flattery: for as much as I had good evidence of the excellence of your mind as early as the time when you returned from Ferrara to your castle of Ponts [that opinion was confirmed] when lately it pleased you to speak to me of various sciences, namely philosophy, astrology, and other arts drawn from mathematics. This, I say, has made me doubly sure of the competence of your marvelous mind, and although age dims the memory of many, yet I have found yours more increased than diminished. This I have learned through your statements to me. And for these reasons I have thought that there is no nobleman in the world to whom my work might [better] be dedicated than to you, knowing well that though it may be esteemed by some as a fable full of lies, by you it will be prized and esteemed a rare thing.[13]

Palissy's opinion of Pons as a singular "nobleman" championed by Protestant polemicists for his "marvelous mind"—in this case buttressed by the spiritual gift of a strong natural-philosophical memory—was articulated in print for the first time by Théodore de Bèze, Pons's colleague at the Ferrara academy and a stubborn defender of Calvin's legacy of authoritarianism. Four years before Antoine renounced his conversion to Calvinism and lifted the protection extended by his court to the Huguenots of Saintonge (he remained a useful intermediary between the state and local Protestants), de Bèze complimented Pons, calling him "an *amateur* of virtue and truth, who had really profited from reading the sacred Scriptures."[14] Perhaps Palissy's call to memory—an arrogant slap from below at noblemen who, unlike Pons, aspired to the status of philosopher yet failed to recognize that Palissy's "manual" and "unlearned" labors should "be prized and esteemed a rare thing"—also offers reconciliation of past conflict through the transcendent joining of philosophical minds. Among most philosophers however, Anne de Parthenay was more celebrated than her husband. She excelled at classical learning in Latin and Greek and mastery of poetic song and theology. As a refugee at Ferrara, Clément Marot composed a "Lost Epistle *au jeu*[,]" after the fashion of madame de Pons" as a gift in verse; a "counterfeit" in the style of his Saintongeais patron, the "Dame de Pons, Nymphe de Parthenay / For you who have learning and sound knowledge."[15] Antoine de Pons and Anne de Parthenay had earned their bona fides as "sound" evangelical humanists and patrons at Ferrara.

Ferrara was also the site of the formal conversion of Antoine de Pons and Anne de Parthenay to Calvinism, although it is possible that Anne had been prepared for conversion earlier by her Huguenot cousin Marguerite de Navarre. In both cases, Calvin himself was an agent of change. De Bèze claimed that Calvin had converted secretly in 1532–33, the year he left his birthplace of Noyon to attend the University of Paris. (Calvin, Palissy, Pons, and Berton were all born in or around the year of 1609–10.) However, the key months with regard to his public acknowledgement of heresy were April 1534 and August 1535 respectively, when Calvin openly declared his personal experience of reformation ("God by a sudden conversion subdued my heart to teachableness"), and the subsequent completion of the manuscript of his *Institutes of the Christian Religion* (the original Latin edition was published in March 1536; Calvin's French translation appeared in France in 1541).[16]

By 1534, Calvin was on the run from the authorities in Paris. He sought refuge in Angoulême (under Marguerite's protection) and then Poitiers, converting local nobles and their extended households in both places. However, when the *Institutes* were about to appear, he was forced to flee France under the pseudonym Charles d'Espeville, and claimed refuge in Ferrara. Calvin converted Anne de Parthenay there, then her mother Michelle de Saubonne; and then, finally, following the enthusiastic example of his wife and mother-in-law, Calvinism was embraced, albeit cautiously, by the politically calculating Antoine de Pons.[17] If, as we shall see, Palissy traced the origins of Protestantism among artisans in coastal Saintonge to itinerant "Lutheran" brethren, influenced by some faraway Germanic order to evangelize the isolated maritime islands, then, not very long before, the cream of the Saintongeais nobility had been converted at Ferrara, and carried the Calvinist heresy home to the courts of southwestern France. This confluence of geography, patronage, and evangelism ensured that Saintongeais Huguenot artisanal and natural-philosophical culture was a hybrid of southwestern French, Germanic, and northern Italian influences by the early sixteenth century.

Upon returning to their court in Saintonge, Antoine and Anne strove to replicate the Protestant paradigm of the humanist academy and place of refuge at Ferrara. Throughout the 1540s and early 1550s, however, the region's maritime islands lacked a printer of any kind, though publishing was considered an essential component of the academy's intellectual and religious project. To be sure, books were exceptionally rare in Saintonge—both in towns and the countryside—during the earliest years of the Reformation. This absence changed radically in 1553, with the sudden appearance of Philibert Hamelin in Saintes and Arvert. The itinerant Hamelin, a Geneva-trained minister and master printer-publisher, originally from Touraine, is best known to historians as Palissy's spiritual mentor, and he is the subject of a key martyrological essay

in the *Recepte*. Hamelin was very open in his dealings and quickly caught the attention of Church authorities for selling bibles and other religious books with his imprint
while traveling the coastal region to evangelize artisans and mariners. Hamelin served
Geneva (and Antoine) in his dual function of artisan-preacher until 1557, when he was
executed. Antoine then recruited Berton from Lyon to fill the void left by Hamelin's
execution.[18]

Nothing at all is known of the production of Berton's press at Marennes, with the
exception of its address, prior to the printer's removal to La Rochelle in 1563. What *is*
known, however, is that he was forced to leave Marennes the same year that Antoine
renounced his conversion and drove heretical practice underground. Despite this set-
back, Berton recruited his first authors for the *imprimerie* of La Rochelle from the tal
ented circle of refugee Huguenot writers and artisans that had gathered at the Pons
academy. This included the potter Palissy, to whom Pons extended protection in 1562–
63 after he was released from the Conciergerie of Bordeaux when Montmorency and
Pons interceded on his behalf, and the minister Yves Rouspeau, for whom Berton published both spiritual and polemical texts.[19] In fact, the first publication printed at
Berton's new press at La Rochelle was a pamphlet by Palissy, dated 1563. This was dedicated to his Catholic savior, the duc de Montmorency, and concerned the potter's
design for a grotto for him.[20] Pons's renunciation forced Berton to print Palissy's
seminal account of the Constable's rustic grotto at La Rochelle, rather than in rural
Marennes; but the project made Palissy's name at Paris's Medician court, because it
signified a novel, natural-philosophical fusion of courtly Italian Neoplatonism, Germanic Paracelsism, and the local and above all rustic material culture of Saintonge,
which fulfilled the monistic hope of cosmological unification behind the Huguenot
academies at Ferrara and Pons. That was one reason why Palissy dedicated the *Discours admirables* to his former rural patron, nearly two decades after Antoine renounced
the Huguenots of Saintonge. The aging potter had chosen not to forget that "the excellence of [Antoine's] mind" and his great memory had been revealed "as early as the
time [he] returned from Ferrara to [his] castle of Ponts."

In 1563, the year Pons banished Berton from Marennes, it was as well known in
Saintonge, as in Paris, that La Rochelle was then undergoing a Protestant revolution.
The fleeing Huguenot printer loaded the contents of his shop onto a boat and headed
north along the coast for the fortress. Berton sought refuge and patronage among the
militant factions formed by the same group of polemical Calvinist churchmen and
bourgeois merchants that would confront Charles IX two years hence. His imprint
was soon valued throughout international Protestantism for its contributions to the
Huguenot corpus. Berton's books were sought after for religious, cultural, and political knowledge about the crucial fortress town and—as a result of the printer's personal
contacts at the Pons academy—La Rochelle's rustic hinterland as well.

On September 3, 1563, Barthélemy Berton signed a contract with the "merchant and bourgeois" François Barbot (from the same La Rochelle family as the moderate Huguenot historian Amos Barbot), who remained a loyal patron of Palissy's even after the potter's removal to Paris, where Barbot continued to lend him money. Their relationship changed for the worse on November 20, 1570, when Barbot took Palissy to court for nonpayment of a loan made in Paris on October 4, 1567.[21] Barbot's 1563 contract with Berton stipulated, however, that he would employ "Berthon, master printer, [and] resident of this city of La Rochelle, [to] make and print well and satisfactorily to the said Barbot . . . a work made by M. Bernard Palissyz, potter [*ouvrier de terre*], living at Sainctes, titled *Recepte veritable,* containing three parts, one called *Recepte veritable,* another called *L'un desseing d'un jardin* ['A Design for a Garden'], and the third, *Le desseing d'une ville imprenable* ['The Design of an Impregnable Town']." Berton's edition of the *Recepte* had a very respectable run of 1,500 copies.[22]

Nevertheless, if Rochelais were the first audience for the *Recepte* after it was made available as a printed text, readers were not necessarily the original audience intended for Palissy's philosophical discourse on the nature of security in Saintonge. Palissy's "design" for his impregnable "Forteresse," conceived and written "from experience" while the potter worked among the rural poor, was communicated as part of his evangelical program for illiterate artisans living in La Rochelle's rustic hinterlands before it appeared in print in the fortress. As Berton's contract indicated, the potter maintained a ceramic workshop, which included a kiln and alchemic laboratory, in Saintes until shortly before his removal to Paris, two years after publication of the *Recepte,* where he reinvented himself as Catherine de Médicis's creature. Indeed, as the third inventory of Anne de Montmorency's art collections in his Paris house in the rue Sainte-Avoye (now du Temple) indicated, by January 14, 1568, Parisian appraisers called Palissy's ceramics "de terre cuicte esmaillee, ouvrage de Xainctes . . . aussi facon de Xaintes [enameled earthenware, workmanship of Saintes . . . also in the fashion of Saintes]." Among the ten items listed in this "fashion" were "an oval basin, two feet long and one and one half feet deep, . . . with diverse animals inside" and "a tree made in the manner of a rock . . . scattered with shells and many animals of all sorts." The other forms inventoried included three vases, a "grand chandelier," one bottle, a ewer, and "two other great basins," all of which were made "of the same stuff and fashion."[23] By the latter part of the sixteenth century, inventory appraisers far from Saintes identified this style with Palissy by name. In 1589, after Catholic *liguers* had destroyed the great Normandy château of the Huguenot Claude II Le Roux, sieur de Bourgtheroulde and Infreville, a room-by-room inventory was taken to assess the damage. Hidden inside a cabinet within a closet in the "girls' bedroom," the appraiser found a "very great number of large basins and vases, [all] vessels of value, of the fashion of messire Bernard Palissy, of diverse exquisite colors, all of these vessels are valued at more than one hundred fifty *escus,* these were stolen or broken so that not one whole piece remains."[24] Was this considered to be vandalism of luxury goods or an act of iconoclasm against Huguenot sacred objects?

✿ Artisanal *Sûreté* ✝

Although ostensibly concerned with innovation and reform of the technology of Huguenot fortress design and construction for a medieval *place de sûreté,* Palissy's "De la ville de forteresse" is significant precisely because of what it failed to deliver outright. Palissy reneged on his promise to provide the expected architectural drawings for the "dessin et pourtrait" of a modern fortress capable of repelling a long siege. This is not to say that readers were left without hope of protection. Instead of providing straightforward plans useful to a military engineer, Palissy recounted a socially constituted, natural-philosophical allegory that elucidated the dissimulating practice of artisanal *sûreté,* based on observation of natural modes of protection, which was arguably more advantageous to "common" Saintongeais Huguenots than to professional soldiers. He formulated sûreté as a Paracelsian artisan's local response to chronic religious violence; it leveled the old walls of distinction and social distance and opposed exposure and vulnerability to warfare in the open countryside, which Palissy identified with "ancient" martial strategies that simultaneously promoted the *gloire* of the *noblesse d'épée* and invited overt confrontation with powerful enemies, while accepting the sacrifice of impoverished rural Huguenots without regret.

Noble (that is to say, *noblesse d'épée*) military strategies based on such theatrical displays of knightly honor and overt use of armored protection for individual bodies and towns had always centered on security provided those soldiers, citizens, or refugees locked safely inside the walled-in enceinte of the fortress town. Following Palissy's comprehensive framework, these "ancient" yet immobile modes of protection were inadequate over the long term for the majority *menu peuple* of Saintes and its rural countryside—mostly heretical farmers, artisans, and mariners—who, like Palissy himself, were suddenly exposed to the fluid and entropic violence of religious civil war, far from the protective shadow of the "impregnable fortress" of La Rochelle. The civil wars focused on southwestern France in large part *because* the fortress was sited there, confronting the monarchy with both an ominous threat and an irresistible invitation to respond with force to its challenge. This dangerous invitation had been taken up many times during Palissy's lifetime, and his "De la ville de forteresse" posited a new paradigm of regional security that would give skilled artisans means of providing new, domestic modes of protection for dispersed Huguenot refugees made vulnerable by what Palissy perceived to be the inevitable destruction—and ultimately the complete *absence*—of the regional fortress town. In analyzing the destruction of Saintes and its countryside by enemies of the Huguenots, Palissy effectively predicted the catastrophic events of 1627–28, the resulting fragmentation of the southwest's medieval fortress culture, and the broad material and metaphysical outlines of the new terms of Protestantism's struggle for refuge and survival. As a consequence, the atomized Huguenot communities of Saintonge were to be abandoned to compensate for the lost unity and walled communal protection of the medieval *place de sûreté*. Artisans would now construct rustic and "subterranean" inversions of the fortress town: mobile, hidden, secret places of security, disguised as if made by "natural," not human, artisans.

"De la ville de forteresse" was published during the period in which the most militant Protestant factions in La Rochelle consolidated their growing power and resistance to the state, based on unshakable belief in the "impregnability" of the artificial structures of the old fortress itself, and it is hard to imagine that the "humble" potter from Saintes—and his Rochelais publisher—could have introduced a more quietly subversive thesis from the "rustic" periphery.

Palissy understood this move from the frontality of walled-in protection to the subtlety of artisanal security as simultaneously a metaphysical and a material shift—strikingly reminiscent of Luther's reactivation of medieval themes of man's "twofold nature" and the carnal body in his famous vernacular *Treatise on Christian Liberty* (1520)—that privileged the hidden inner world of the purified Holy Spirit over the corrupt and exposed outer world of fallen material bodies.[25] To be sure, this was a contradictory and binary conceptual framework, but in context, such thought was neither static nor represented unchanging oppositions. Both Luther and Palissy *experienced* the fragmentation of the spiritual and material as part of a monistic whole; that is, the oppositions were, in fact, interdependent, permeable, and even "married" by a primitive Christian synthesis of violence and the sacred identified with the exquisite pain of Christ's suffering for the redemption of mankind. Change was constant; death and growth were synonymous. Channeled by self-mastery and driven by ceaseless labor and self-mortification, Christ's pure spirit emerged despite the presence of the corrupted body, through the holy mediation of pious suffering. In turn, this focused the inner labor of the industrious artisan's creative soul. In this context, physical pain was purposeful and, in the larger sense, cleansing and providential.

More disturbing, therefore, than the threat to Palissy's bodily self was the spiritual insecurity of being surprised by physical violence and, ultimately, death. In an unprepared condition of body and soul, that is to say, in a chaotic state of disequilibrium between macrocosm and microcosm (spirit and matter), the artisanal benefits caused by the carnal reduction produced by sacred suffering were ultimately disordered, anarchic, and hence unmastered. The animating spirit was thus agitated rather than focused in its God-directed, creative movement between heaven and earth—this meant an ability to pierce through permeable bodily matter—by the chaos and *esmotions* that Palissy and his followers experienced in civil war Saintonge. Théodore Agrippa d'Aubigné, author of a much-quoted martyrology of Palissy—and a leading Protestant theologian, poet, historian, and polemicist, as well as being a military strategist, Henri de Navarre's vice-admiral of Saintonge, and a Huguenot field marshal during the civil wars—defined the complex word *esmotions* as a pejorative. It represented a highly combustible and dangerously visible mixture of the spiritual "motion of the soul," corrupted by its corrosive combination with the carnal matter produced by "public unrest." According to Randle Cotgrave's *Dictionarie of the French and English Tongues* (1611), this led to "emotion, commotion, sudden, or turbulent stirring; an agitation of the spirit, violent motion of the thoughts," causing "a vehement inclination of the mind."[26]

In this suddenly disturbed psychological state, the secrets of craft knowledge still had potential to act as invisible, portable containers of the soul hidden inside the self-mastered body. The justified artisan possessed an internal compass to pinpoint motions of the aspiring spirit searching for openings of light in the midst of occlusion. Discipline was a fire wall against the dark, willful chaos of fallen, fleshy matter. If man's *esmotions* raised internal boundaries to quiet spiritual movement through matter, then metaphysical foundations for artisanal security were effectively raised by a Huguenot artisan's pious self-mastery. Skillful manipulation of the junction of spirit and matter as they intersected in a master artisan's body allowed for the hidden, internal construction of security to begin, based on the subtle, fluid armature of soulish motion.

Throughout the *Recepte* and his later *Discours,* though Palissy represented himself as being in grave personal jeopardy on more than one occasion, he also used language to place himself in self-conscious harmony with the Stoic tradition and, as such, unmoved internally in the face of danger, chaos, and death. Death happened all around him, an everyday occurrence in the violent world of the Saintongeais countryside during the civil wars of religion. Still, the potter dwells on the horror of facing death *unprepared*—like an unarmed soldier unprepared for battle—to achieve mastery over the turbulent personal *esmotions* that violent historical events had instilled as threats to the calm of his immortal soul. A dialectic between appropriate contexts for legitimate "animation" and stoical suppression of bodily pain considered an indication of the health of the aspiring soul—emerged powerfully among religious women, in monastic culture, and during the ritual of pilgrimage in the later Middle Ages. These practices provided sixteenth-century neo-Stoic Protestants, martyrologists, and natural philosophers with a long history of sacred precedents.[27] Personal stoicism vis-à-vis worldly insecurity and the expectation of impending death was a common theme in Renaissance art. In late antiquity and early Christianity, humanists found ample precedents for the virtuous endurance of pain and the veneration of martyrdom as important components of the political performance of resistance.[28] Norbert Elias has claimed, moreover, that beginning in the fifteenth century, stoicism among elites served as an important aspect of "the civilizing process."[29] By extension, stoicism finds its place in Philippe Ariès's general category of "tamed death."[30] Specific to the primitive Calvinist experience, however, was Palissy's deep personal investment in the possession of interior security through arduous preparation of the soul. To be successful, as a mode both of Christian self-protection and social self-identity, this mystical practice had to remain hidden from the weakening effects of corruption spread by outer bodies that operated in the fallen matter of the world. In the white-hot emotional contexts of confessional violence that incubated early modern millennialism, reformed, Platonic, classical, and neo-Stoic texts were commonly read together by commentators. The fundamental connections between such texts were intuited by quietly enthusiastic (albeit unlearned) autodidacts like Palissy and others, who read copiously while living through anarchic experiences of war and suffering.

John Winthrop the Elder's "Experiencia" of 1616–18—turbulent diary entries written in Groton, England, where the future governor of the Massachusetts Bay Colony was mourning the untimely death of his second wife, Thomasine Clopton Winthrop (1583–1616)—contemplated the covert ways he "prepared with a peaceable conscience" for God's "trials," lest they "harm me." Despite the intense "grief" and personal "affliction" that he experienced as a result of Thomasine's death, Winthrop's trials, though eliciting real psychological pain, were contested "not in any grosse manner outwardly, yet seacreatly, togither with a seacrit desire . . . to forsake my first love [of God], whence came much troble and danger."

Winthrop's fear of seduction by "Worldly cares," exhaustion from inner conflicts with "mine owne rebellious wicked hearte yieldinge itselfe to the slaverye of sinne," and survivor's guilt at outliving his pious, "plaine hearted" wife, caused him to contemplate the "desire" for an immediate death, and the option of releasing himself from arduous interior preparations for soulish security. Whether this meant that suicide was considered a viable option or a subject for overt, serious theological debate among predestinarians is very difficult to say. There is good evidence, however, that such morbid desire was discussed quietly on the local level, in both congregations and guild halls. Seventeenth-century English Calvinists like Paul Seaver's morose, deeply pious turner Nehemiah Wallington are known to have attempted suicide to destroy the physical source of spiritual corruption. "Experiencia" may have considered the self-destructive impulses Winthrop knew in himself and saw in others, from the perspective of bitter experience with the emotional effects of death and despair.[31] "It is a better and more safe estate to be prepared to die then to desire deathe," he concluded stoically. "For this commonly hath more selfe love with it than pure love of God: And," he reasoned, "it is a signe of more strength of faithe, and Christian courage, to resolve to fight it out, than to wishe for the victory."[32] How did the pious artisan "prepare to die" and achieve a "more safe estate"?

❧ Luther's "good workman" ❧

The militant Luther of *Christian Liberty* resonated deeply in Winthrop's Calvinist "Experiencia," though the German's ideas about death, law, and liberty were expressed with greater confidence than the bereaved and conflicted Englishman mustered from the vantage point of Reformation England at the beginning of the Thirty Years' War. "So," Luther wrote in 1520, "the heart learns to scoff at death and sin,

> and to say with the Apostle, "O death, where is thy victory? O death, where is thy sting? The sting of death is sin, and the power of sin is the law. But thanks be to God, who gives us the victory through our Lord Jesus Christ" [1 Cor. 15:55–57]. Death is swallowed up not only in the victory of Christ but also by our victory, because through faith his victory has become ours and in that faith we are also conquerors.[33]

Luther's widely read and audited *Christian Liberty* echoed most powerfully in the eclectic discourse of the "unlearned artisans" who found their voices in the mid sixteenth century. This would include Palissy, of course, as well as Protestant "hidden enemies" in Venice, and Menocchio, the overtalkative Friulian miller and woodworker chronicled by Carlo Ginzburg, whose life ended in Rome by decree of the Inquisition. *Christian Liberty* was written in a simple and straightforward manner, in both Latin and German, and was soon published in French, English, and Italian translations: "To make the way smoother for the *unlearned*—for only them I serve . . . ; and I hope that I can discuss it, *if not more elegantly,* certainly more to the point, than *those literalists and subtile disputants have previously done* [emphasis added], who have not even understood what they have written."[34]

That is why the central analogy Luther uses for "unlearned" readers of his influential text, to illustrate his theme that man cannot be justified by works but only by interior faith in soulish communion with the Holy Spirit—an analogy that would also become crucial to Palissy's own contemporaneous concept of skilled labor—was that of the pious artisan and his work. Luther's inside-out formulation of the relationship between faith and works allowed that artisanry may be pious, but only if proven to be an outward manifestation—a material extension—of a workman's hidden, inner purity. Inquiry into the metaphysical value of material culture necessarily began with the interior experience of the artisan.

This mystical inquiry into the nature of material culture was fraught with potential for satanic deception for Lutherans, just as the question of postlapsarian justification was deeply problematic for Calvinist predestinarians, including the Huguenot artisans of Saintonge. "A man must first be good or wicked before he does a good or wicked work," Luther explained to his "unlearned" audience, "and his works do not make him good or wicked, but he himself makes his works good or wicked. Illustrations of the same truth can be seen in all trades:

> A good or a bad house does not make a good or a bad builder; but a good or a bad builder makes a good or a bad house. And in general, the work never makes the workman like himself, but the workman makes the work like himself. So it is with the works of man. As the man is, whether believer or unbeliever, so also is his work—good if it was done in faith, wicked if it was done in unbelief. . . .
>
> . . . It is indeed true that in the sight of men a man is made good or evil by his works; . . . all this remains on the surface, however, and very many have been deceived by this outward appearance. . . . They go their way, always being deceived and deceiving [2 Tim. 3:13], progressing, indeed, but into a worse state, blind leaders of the blind.[35]

If the good "workman makes the work like himself," then the artisan-alchemist's task became to invent processes by which he could see through the blindness and deception of outward appearance for this proof of purity hidden in the interior of animate material bodies. (This problem, fundamental to the history of perception, is discussed at length in chapters 14, 15, and 16.)

Though Calvinist, Palissy, like Luther, posed rhetorically as "unlearned," while attacking the "elegant," "subtile disputants" of scholasticism with "simple" prose that got to "the point." Palissy freely incorporated knowledge of some of the German's texts into his work, due, in part, to local historical context. In his essay "History of the Church of Saintes," the chapter just preceding "De la ville de forteresse" in the *Recepte,* Palissy writes that the Reformation in Saintonge had originated with the appearance of a group of Lutheran "monks." This cell of four "returned" mysteriously from "the east" in the mid 1540s and began to evangelize the coastal islands. Luther and Calvin blended easily in Palissy's work and personal experience. In the same essay, he celebrated the pastoral life and martyrdom of his great friend and mentor Philibert Hamelin, a Calvinist artisan and minister who was the first itinerant to bring Genevan discipline into the region. Palissy's natural philosophy was based on the work of Paracelsus, a German-Swiss and a nominal Catholic whose writings on alchemic medicine and material processes were deeply indebted to Lutheran discourse. So the potter also internalized Germanic theology indirectly.

Palissy habitually conflated Lutheran, Calvinist, and Catholic doctrines, as he combined those aspects of theology that promoted the reformation of "primitive" Christianity. Palissy's primitivism was shared by Luther and Calvin, as well as Paracelsus. All were concerned with mastery of the corrupted body, so that the soul could channel unencumbered through the flesh. Palissy and Winthrop both understood, as Caroline Walker Bynum reminds us in her work on the continuity of the medieval practice of piety that preceded the Protestant project to reconstruct the primitive Church on the foundation of Christ's ecstatic suffering, how "control, discipline, even torture of the flesh" was "not so much a rejection of physicality as the elevation of it—a horrible yet delicious elevation—into a means of access to the divine."[36]

St. Paul built bridges of textual continuity between the painful pleasures of medieval asceticism, and the Reformation discourse of bodily discipline and self-mastery preached by Luther and Calvin and their disciples. "In this life [a man] must control his own body," wrote Luther:

> Here the works begin; here a man cannot enjoy leisure; here he must indeed take care to discipline his body by fastings, watchings, labors, and other reasonable discipline to subject it to the Spirit so that it will obey and conform to the inner man and faith, and not revolt against faith and hinder the inner man, as it is the nature of the body to do if it is not held in check. . . . While he is doing this, behold, he meets a contrary will in his own flesh which strives to serve the world and seeks its own advantage. This the spirit of faith cannot tolerate, but with joyful zeal it attempts to put the body under control and hold it in check, as Paul says in Rom. 7 [22–23], "For I delight in the law of God, in my inmost self, but I see in my members another law at war with the law of my mind and making me captive to the law of sin," and in another place, "But I pommel my body and subdue it, lest after preaching to others I myself should be disqualified" [1 Cor. 9:27], and in Galatians [5:24], "And those who belong to Christ Jesus have crucified the flesh with its passions and desires.[37]

Luther argued that "man has a twofold nature, a spiritual and a bodily one," which were inseparable until "the last day, the day of the resurrection of the dead," when "we [shall become] wholly inner and perfectly spiritual men." Luther's interactive formulation of the play of opposites posited:

> According to the spiritual nature, which men refer to as the soul, he is called a spiritual, inner, new man. According to the bodily nature, which men refer to as flesh, he is called a carnal, outward, or old man, of whom the Apostle writes in II Cor. 4 [16], "Though our outer nature is wasting away, our inner nature is being renewed every day."[38]

This "ecstatic" process of spiritual renewal as our "outer nature is wasting away" from violent mortification of the metaphorically worn and aging body (whether by self-inflicted "pommeling" or the historical violence of religious war and oppression), is perceived through the filter of an intensely sexual Neoplatonic language of soulish intercourse, marriage, and monistic unification:

> in that it unites the soul with Christ as a bride is united with her bridegroom. By this mystery . . . Christ and the soul become one flesh [Eph. 5:31–32]. And if they are one flesh and there is between them a true marriage—indeed the most perfect of all marriages, since

human marriages are but poor examples of this one true marriage—it follows that everything they have they hold in common, the good as well as the evil. Accordingly, the believing soul can boast of and glory in whatever Christ has as though it were its own, and
whatever the soul has Christ claims as his own . . . for if Christ is a bridegroom, he must
take upon himself the things which are his bride's and bestow upon her the things that
are his. If he gives her his body and very self, how shall he not give her all that is his? And
if he takes the body of the bride, how shall he not take all that is hers? . . . the soul which
clings . . . with a firm faith will be so closely united . . . and altogether absorbed . . . that
it . . . will be saturated and intoxicated.[39]

Paracelsians reinterpreted Luther's admonition that "as long as we live in the flesh
we only begin to make some progress in that which shall be perfected in the future life"
in alchemical terms. This presumed that materials of "our outer nature" could be
"wasted away" in the laboratory or workshop, to renew "our inner nature" in the present by replicating natural processes of "the last day," when the dead are resurrected to
become "wholly inner." Palissy's task—to discipline his body, emotional disorder, and
physical pain—also contextualized specific natural-philosophical problems basic to his
artisanal work and his science. Palissy repeated the word *esmotions* in particular situa-
tions that signified the corrupt passage of human history and hence superficial change.
Superficial change occurred as part of what he called *ondoyant* time, which "surged"
like a "wave." The serpentine conceptualization of historical or "diachronic" time
snaked in and out, negotiating the boundaries between macrocosm and microcosm.
The territory of the former was principally synchronic, calm, and unaccidental; and as
the experience of the wave of time moved "down" into the fallen chaos of the microcosm, the perceptual confusion of history and of *esmotions* followed. The simultaneity
of historical experience was understood as a Stoic balance between the waves of time.

Palissy's spiritual preparation for *esmotions* was silence and motionlessness. This
state signified *contained* inward motion, so it also signified scientific preparedness for
achieving the monistic status intrinsic to the practice of Paracelsian and Neoplatonic
artisanry. Deep interiority was preparation for scientific inquiry into the unity behind
diverse earth materials. Pious artisans thus conceptualized their immortal souls in the
process of astral travel. The soul flowed directly into and between macrocosm and microcosm by means of its vehicle, a "chariot": the sidereal but still mortal astral body.[40]
At these mystical moments of harmonic convergence, at the axis of violent history and
sacred time, the inner artisan and natural scientist prepared for elevation to divine
knowledge of the essential nature of materials perceived empirically in the microcosm.

Channeling the entropy of civil war through the self-contained, God-directed motion of a natural-philosophical pilgrimage—where the artisan-scientist sought soulish refuge and essential truths hidden beneath the corrupted "outer body" of natural

materials—was propaedeutic to Palissy's discourses. These personal pilgrimages formed patterns in which several elements interacted: (1) physical movement over geographic space, signifying experience; (2) related fortuitous accidents crucial to Paracelsian experimental science; and (3) unexpected—from the perspective of scholastic Neoplatonism—faith, even joy in the empirical *materiality* of the natural world. Like his fallen body, natural matter laid bare by its inner spirit was also man's potential instrument of personal transformation and salvation amid the apocalyptic rubble. These pilgrimages were ordered and functioned like self-contained, centripetal artifacts, each with a life of its own, yet simultaneously connected to a universal spirit active in the natural world.

Security in Palissy's "De la ville de forteresse" was measured by such mystical standards of artisanal competence in achieving the material-holiness synthesis. These represented basic sociocultural rules, expectations, and behavior that Palissy established in the *Recepte* to characterize local standards for how something was made. Thus, comprehending a builder's competence depended on the outside-in "deconstruction" (or, from the alchemist's perspective, "decay" and "destruction") of an artifact made by a predecessor's "hand" in order to emulate its system of inner rules and procedures. This approximation of original performance facilitated appropriation, interpretation, and ultimately mimesis.

Yet one artisan's deconstruction of another's competence is inevitably confused by the process of creative misreading that has always accompanied interpretation of artifacts of experience over time and in changing sociocultural contexts. Such misreading is an extraordinarily intricate problem, but a useful critical framework has been argued with great subtlety for the study of poetics by Harold Bloom, whose work has implications for the study of historiography, as well as of the reproduction of material life in the pre-"mechanical" era.[41]

This sort of critical analysis implies the convergence of written text and hand-wrought artifact with (for Bloom) the violent "death" of the maker (father) at the hands of the influenced (son). As we shall see in chapter 15, in the Boston leather chair's emulation by Huguenots in New York City during the late seventeenth and early eighteenth centuries, an artifact's intrinsic systems of communication were transformed by the capricious effects of its dissemination (as commodity, booty, or baggage), over which makers or sellers might have little control. Retrospective appropriation of the inferred logic of another artisan's competence to emulate a specific product did not necessarily carry with it complete understanding of the intentionality of either the prototype's maker or the original society and culture that determined his standards of competence.[42]

These daunting problems in retrospective logic represent the creative tension between theory and practice that animated so much Paracelsian thought about artisanry during the early modern period. For Palissy, the faithful student (and emulator) of God in Nature, much was at stake: the artisan whose competence (and intention) was deconstructed, "decayed"—or, to use an appropriately biblical term borrowed from Frank Kermode, "decreated"[43]—in rustic artisanry and empirical natural philosophy was the Genesis (or artisan) God; the context remained entropy associated with the civil wars of religion in Aunis-Saintonge; and the natural "artifacts" of anxious mimetic desire—the pious potter's "art of the earth"—were automatically limited, and in a very real sense *defined,* by local, personal, and spiritual interaction with natural and man-made materials. Palissy believed that though these things "accidentally" fell into his path on walks, such accidents resulted from the providential interaction of God with human experience during each artisan's personal pilgrimage through the serpentine waves of time.

❧ The Critique of Stone Walls: ❧
"One cannot understand the one who knows how to die"

Palissy began "De la ville de forteresse" by questioning the effectiveness of stone walls per se. The young Palissy had made a reputation for himself drawing maps and architectural "*pourtraits*" —a flexible term that could connote both the "image" of an individual and a "counterfeit" of landscape and architecture "drafted" with compass and ruler.[44] Yet, by 1563, Palissy had subverted the received wisdom that an archetypal Huguenot fortress town must be designed in the manner of La Rochelle (exemplar of the traditional paradigm of *sûreté* undermined in "De la ville de forteresse"). This was one reason why permanent ("drawn") plans of a singular military structure, such as La Rochelle, were never provided, as advertised, to accompany the written text of Palissy's essay.

Religious motives supplied another powerful argument for the absence of a reified plan. Luther's critique of Roman Catholic ritual and ceremony devalued human plans as inessential, transitory, and ephemeral. At best, they were merely preliminary. He asserted by analogy that "ceremonies are to be given the same place in the life of a Christian as models and plans have among builders and artisans."

> They are prepared, not as a permanent structure, but because without them nothing could be built or made . . . what we despise is the false estimate of them since no one holds them to be the real and permanent structure. If any man were so flagrantly foolish as to care for nothing all his life long except the most costly, careful, and persistent preparation of plans and models and never to think of the structure itself, and were satisfied with his work in producing such plans as mere aids to work, and boasted of it, would not all men pity his insanity and think that something great might have been built with what he has wasted?

. . . [Such men] seem to wish to build, they make their preparations, and yet they never build. Thus they remain caught in the form . . . and do not attain unto its power [2 Tim. 3:5].[45]

Essential structure versus superficial form and flexibility of natural experience opposed to rigid scholastic plan were also at the core of Palissy's natural philosophy. Hence, Palissy identified the traditional fortress's main design flaw as its inflexible and rigidly artificial surrounding walls, which were based on a standard plan with too simplistic an understanding of geometry's potential to emulate the complexity and adaptability of natural defenses. Walls in medieval fortresses were detached from and *extrinsic* to the domestic housing and inhabitants ("with houses separated from the walls") they were ostensibly built to protect. To reform the *place de sûreté,* a term structurally synonymous with the detached, walled-in fortress in Huguenot political and military discourse, walls and boundaries had to be made *intrinsic* to the social and material fabric; indeed, to the fluid experience of everyday life.

"And why?" the potter asked rhetorically. Palissy offered two specific "proofs," which he claimed, insincerely, were not drawn from plans of prior authorities, or the scholastics, but from the more reliable evidence of his own practical experience: (1) "in times of Peace the walls are useless [and yet] great treasure and labor are expended to build and maintain them"; and, more important, (2) "when the walls are overtaken, the town has no choice but to surrender. It is truly a defective town body [*un pauvre corps de Ville*] when the parts [*les membres*] are unable to unify [*consolider*] and help one another. In brief, all such [fortress] towns are designed badly, considering that their parts are unable to link up with [the whole; that is] the principal body. It is a simple matter to defeat the body if the members do not come to its aid."[46] Given what we know about the events of 1565, the hypothesis that Palissy makes double reference here to the factionalism that afflicted La Rochelle's Corps de ville in the early 1560s makes sense. At the time, a "defective" Corps did lapse into weakness and near "death" as a governing body. The divided Huguenot members were unable to unify to protect the town's privileges from attack by the monarchy. Other recurring themes also emerge here that were central to Palissy's discourse on security. The critique of fragmentation and disunity that prevented "concatenation" of the "principal body" of the town with its outer extremities resonates strongly with both medical and religious discourse of the period. Palissy, a follower of Paracelsus and his reformed model of medical therapy, subscribed to the "new," systemic treatment of illness. Paracelsus argued for the cosmological approach to treatment, whereby the patient's body and spirit were conceptualized as a single unified entity. Instead of fragmenting the body into specific therapy zones in order to act on symptoms alone, Paracelsus and his followers sought "principal" (or "elemental") causes hidden beneath the corrupted flesh. These were always connected in *both* spiritual and material ways. Linking macrocosm and microcosm formed *the* fundamental concatenation with pathology of the spirit—or carnal occlusion of spiritual purity—usually an animating cause of illness in the body. This resonated strongly with the Reformation's reactivation of Augustine's popular analogy of a primitive Christian community united in the suffering body of Christ despite fragmentation of its "members" by warfare and forced migration.

Palissy's remarks are an indication of the religious and political tension that separated the protected core of urban Huguenots living in the fortress of La Rochelle from their vulnerable rural counterparts (or *membres*) struggling to survive the civil wars in its Saintongeais hinterland. Palissy internalized and ultimately inverted this historical and geographic relationship by redefining security from the rustic perspective in "De la ville de forteresse." In so doing, he cast serious doubt on the status, identity, and finally even the spatial location of the new "principal body."

Despite Palissy's rhetorical rejection of all prior textual authorities in the formulation of an unlearned rustic's "natural" critique of the medieval fortress town, he did adapt ideas from a lively international debate on the modern values and strategies of fortification inspired by Machiavelli (1469–1527), which emerged after publication of *The Prince* in 1513. Subsequently, in *The Art of War* (1520), Machiavelli drew up detailed plans to improve the technology of fortress design, applying specific knowledge of the sieges of Pisa and Padua (ca. 1509) to his designs for modern fortifications, which were adjusted, in part, to meet the challenge of gunpowder (the complex geometry of architectural form being less vulnerable to decisive bombardment than the simple inertia of massed stone).

In *The Prince* (and the *Discourses*), however, Machiavelli reconsidered fortification as a total psychological and geopolitical problem rather than a matter of the deployment of stone and mortar as a physical barrier. In so doing, he set plans aside, and questioned the viability of the walled fortress per se, both as an effective instrument of military power and, from the perspective of a prince, as a dominant symbol of noble territorial mastery. Machiavelli's detailed plans for improvement of internal and external defenses of the fortress in *The Art of War* were the most comprehensive ever to appear in print. However, this straightforward technical account of modern siege warfare elicited an astonishingly meager published response. Conversely, his brief theoretical essay in *The Prince*—a harsh critique of the social psychology of fortified walls, and, by extension, of the effect of fortification on a total *culture* of state security—engaged a wide spectrum of commentary. Machiavelli had redefined the subject and made it hotly contested among political theorists, military engineers, theologians, alchemists, and natural philosophers during the wars of religion.[47]

The Machiavellian critique originated with a famous maxim in *The Prince:* "[T]he best fortress that exists is [for the prince] to avoid being hated by the people." Disadvantages of fortifications were enumerated further in the *Discourses*, where J. R. Hale sees "an unyielding prejudice against" them. Thus, Machiavelli claimed that fortifications could be overcome by both violence and famine. And, while a well-defended fortress might buy time for negotiation at the beginning of an invasion, this temporary advantage was lost by two strategic weaknesses that could never be overcome by delay: plain visibility and immobility. "Even if they are so strong that the enemy cannot take them," Machiavelli wrote, "he will march by with his army and leave them in the rear."[48] Far better to depend on human skill and the mobility of a loyal army. In this instance, the lessons of Spartan experience were seen as more compelling than the Roman, as Machiavelli parsed the flawed relation between stone walls and security in classical sources. Spartans rejected both the fortress and the common walled town, "to rely solely upon the valor of their men for their defence, and upon no other means."[49] Security was a matter of natural inner fortitude, not artificial external barriers.

New theories of mobile security extended to extraterritorial theaters as well. Here, Machiavellians followed the model of Roman colonization. It was preferable to insinuate the inner strength of expanding imperial culture by planting colonies as means of foreign conquest, rather than to wall in the natural diffusion of dominance in the form of sedentary marchland fortresses. By the time of the advent of the Commons debates of 1628 following the failure of the English invasion of the Île de Ré, an alarmed Calvinist faction blamed the weakening subversion of a "Machiavellian" "Praetorian Guard" hidden among the kingdom's Catholic and foreign population for the catastrophic defeat.[50] Hence, the effect of an invading colony was viral and poisonous; functioning, as it were, in the Machiavellian shadows of baneful insinuation, interiority, and dissimulation.

Inasmuch as Palissy's reading of the Stoics was refracted through the soulish lens of the Saintongeais Reformation, he could comfortably collapse the Machiavellian critique into that of Pliny the Younger, who argued dismissively: "[T]he unassailable fortress is to have no need for protection. In vain he encircles himself with terror who is not surrounded with love, for arms are roused up by arms."[51] The protective power of fortress walls was relocated to the hidden security of the loving heart. This discursive tradition emerged powerfully in late sixteenth-century Saintonge in the work of Agrippa d'Aubigné, Palissy's co-religionist and contemporary at Pons. In the epic poem *Les Tragiques* (ca. 1574–1600, published in 1616), d'Aubigné's most influential text, a case was made for this act of inner relocation of protection. Interior fortification is represented here as both a reformation of security and a return to primitive virtue lost in the "declining age" of man.

In the section "Misères," d'Aubigné chastises the "shameful, degenerate French" of his age for depending on fortifications, a corruption of the crude protective barriers that "used to be light in the old days," yet had provided better security. In that earlier time, "the foreigner overstepped [these small] barriers / [and the French defenders] disdaining the fortress and frontier bastion: / [so that only after] the enemy entered and fought / [did these French of old] test their courage in the campaign." Now, in witness of "the declining age / . . . our cold hearts need to see themselves walled in / like old people bundled up in [protective] layers / of ramparts, bastions, moats and buttresses." Thus, "our excellent [fortress] designs are nothing but [superficial] orna-ments[52] / from which our forefathers would flee as if they were prisons."[53] To subtract these bastions of ornament—and the protective walls that reduced bodily risk but yielded to the greater risk of shielding an aging, cold heart from the rejuvenation of God's light—appealed to d'Aubigné's unmediated, reformed sensibility.

D'Aubigné and Palissy were, moreover, linked inextricably in Reformation histori-ography by the former's martyrological narrative of Palissy's final hours imprisoned in the Bastille (appropriately, "small fortress"). Here readers encountered the textual ori-gin of the old potter's mythic refusal to abjure heresy and undergo conversion to save himself from execution at the last moment, despite personal pleas from his king, who failed to understand why Palissy would not abjure. D'Aubigné merged this construc-tion of Palissy's stoic performance in his apocryphal final moments with that of a Huguenot Seneca who faced death prepared by his hidden fortitude (a warm heart) and skillful self-mastery. At the end of the story, d'Aubigné's Palissy famously switches roles with the king, assuming the position of spiritual and political dominance, while taking pity on the monarch for his incomprehension of the secret, inner life of mar-tyrs. "You would say," d'Aubigné concludes in a didactic tone, "that [Palissy] had read the verse of Seneca, *Qui mori scit, cogi nescit:* One cannot understand the one who knows how to die."[54] Indeed, Seneca was among the few philosophers "of the ancients," whom Calvin apparently respected in the *Institutes*. "In his own conception very shrewdly," Calvin wrote in chapter 13, Seneca (in *Quaestiones naturales* 1) "said that whatever we see, and whatever we do not see, is God," as "he imagined that the De-ity was diffused through every part of the world."[55]

Although a line of discursive inheritance may be drawn between Machiavelli and the Saintongeais Huguenots d'Aubigné and Palissy on the subject of the debate over fortification, Palissy's influences were never wholly clear, linear, or, for that matter, tex-tual. The language of doubt over the effectiveness of walls when contrasted with the security of the human spirit predated Machiavelli. Only after publication of *The Prince* did such language ramify in learned political, military, and scientific discourse. Indeed, so enduring and deep-seated was the pre-Machiavellian mistrust of mortar that Hale prudently admonishes historians to remember, "there are some ideas whose neatness conceals so complex a suggestiveness that the study of their transmission is the prov-ince of the folklorist rather than the historian."[56] It was in the nexus between folklore and history—between the folkloric "oral culture" of the "rustic" yet literate Huguenot master artisan and learned culture extended by the proliferation of printed texts in the sixteenth century—that Palissy stood. A confluence of influences vied for his attention, demanding innovation in response to the challenge of a culture of horrific religious violence in Saintonge. Palissy constructed the practice of artisanal security in this nexus of orality and literacy.

So Palissy had more at stake in "De la ville de forteresse" than could be understood within the framework of the Machiavellian critique of fortification. To begin, Palissy's critique of the modern fortress town emerged from the potter's clear attempt to assume the humble perspective, despite frequent recourse to the rhetoric of patronage to demonstrate, "the uses and secrets of the said fortress" to "le Roy," and, in a transparently Machiavellian gesture, "le Prince."[57] His agenda was to provide security for the pious if lowly artisan or farmer. Palissy's concern was their self-preservation and the protection of local towns, country farms, artisan shops, families, and churches, rather than the interests of a dominant prince whose concerns were maintenance of political power and construction of his glory through imperial statecraft. The potter was thoroughly engaged in a struggle, common to his entire oeuvre, to discover a practical, even instrumental, middle ground where form, natural philosophy, local folklore, and historical context functioned in reciprocal relation with popular religious belief to achieve the protective power of authentic *sûreté*.

Hence, Palissy's claim that fortress walls, deployed in an enceinte artificially detached from a town's *corps*—its human and natural environments—constituted a financial liability in peacetime that was also dangerously one-dimensional in war.[58] Given the perpetual cycle of warfare, punctuated by brief moments of exhausted calm, that was endemic to confessional violence in Saintonge, Palissy argued that modes of protection must function proportionally, for both individuals and communities, as integral, autochthonous parts of the domestic setting of bodies, houses, and towns. Palissy insisted, it will be recalled, on the bodily analogy serving as the theoretical foundation for secure places: "its members . . . assist each other," he wrote, arguing above all, that members of the *corps* must always "concatenate with the main body." Artisanal production of sûreté must create a built environment capable of overcoming the double weaknesses of visibility and immobility, both flaws of the old-style stone fortress. Creating designs for security based on the experience of natural bodies living without recourse to artificial fortresses, artisanal security encouraged the development of skills and strategies to become unobtrusive and mobile—to repeat, structurally *invisible* (or perceptually *natural*)—parts of the domestic setting.

But where to find an innovative natural design upon which to base the new, truly impregnable "ville de forteresse"? Palissy's argument held that designs inspired by existing fortresses, such as (indeed, especially) La Rochelle's, were inadequate—in effect, dead to the world. So were preexisting plans on paper conceived for other historical moments and contexts. Yet evidence suggests that these were consulted closely by Palissy, including some "made by master Jaques [Androuet] du Cerceau, and many other designers." The potter knew du Cerceau's spiral plans (ca. 1550) for his Ideal Fortified City and the Tower of Babel. He also consulted "plans and drawings of Vitruvius and Sebastian, and other architects," probably including Leonardo da Vinci and Francesco di Giorgio. These "were of no use, for invention of the said fortress town: it was never possible to find a single image, that was helpful in this job." Palissy's visits to "all the most excellent gardens" were just as disappointing as the works of these modern and classical fortress designers. "Some plans based on the labyrinth invented by Dedalus" for Minos in Greece were equally unimpressive. All this revealed the negative information that "it was impossible for me to find anything *that contained my spirit* [qui contenast mon esprit]" (emphasis added).[59] No existing plan had "attain[ed] unto [the] power of the "spirit" (also "soul," "heart")[60] of Palissy's "inner nature," under pressure from the *esmotions* of war. The potter's insecurity over the falseness of a received, ossified plan that did not contain his spirit seemed to signal the pious presence of "the workman [who] makes the work like himself," as an extension of "a spiritual, inner, new man."

Readers were shuttled here and there on the Huguenot artisan's pilgrimage in search of available, if inappropriate, *artificial* prototypes. This was a device that allowed the narrator—now in the pilgrim's obligatory pose of being "nearly beyond all hope" (*esperance*—a play on *esprit*)—to finally reject the products of mere human theory, design, and false labor altogether. Having exhausted all man-made possibilities, and facing the earth beneath his feet with "head lowered," Palissy activated a Paracelsian code that signified that fatigue and mortification born of *expérience*—sloughing off of bits of his "old" carnal outer body—had shifted his empirical perspective "down" to elemental earth. Uncovering *authentic* paradigms at last, Palissy discovered where to clarify his confusion of influences. If Nature's genesis is read together exegetically with the Word to provide insight into the competence of God as Nature's creator, then so, too, Nature's production must logically signify the perfect marriage of the theory and practice of artisanal security. Process in Palissy's empirical discourse was paradoxical in ways that made perfect sense from the monistic perspective of integrated connections. While looking "down" at the rustic earth of Nature and working to emulate and improve it, the pilgrim-researcher simultaneously focused his own internal vision vertically, toward a more perfect understanding of God the artisan. Protestant emblemata that depicted the pious rustic exploited this terrestrial rhetoric. Best known in the transatlantic context was the emblem on the title page of Tieleman Janszoon van Brachts's *Martyrer Spiegel* [Martyrs' Mirror] (fig. 2.1). Originally published in Dutch in 1660, this martyrology was translated into German for a new edition published in 1748, by the press at the Ephrata Cloister in Pennsylvania. Its motto was "Urbeite und

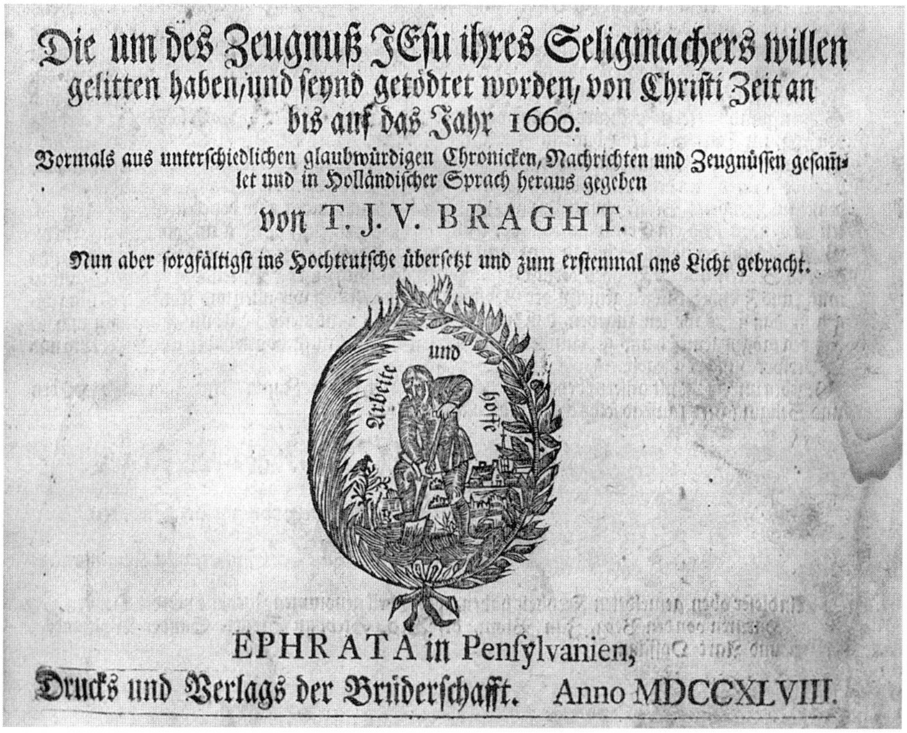
Die um des Zeugnuß JEsu ihres Seligmachers willen gelitten haben, und seynd getödtet worden, von Christi Zeit an bis auf das Jahr 1660.

Vormals aus unterschiedlichen glaubwürdigen Chronicken, Nachrichten und Zeugnüssen gesamlet und in Holländischer Sprach heraus gegeben

von T. J. V. BRAGHT.

Nun aber sorgfältigst ins Hochteutsche übersetzt und zum erstenmal ans Licht gebracht.

Arbeite und hoffe

EPHRATA in Pensylvanien,

Drucks und Verlags der Brüderschafft. Anno MDCCXLVIII.

FIGURE 2.1. Emblem on the title page of Tieleman Janszoon van Brachts's *Martyrer Spiegel* [Martyrs' Mirror] (Ephrata, Pa., 1748), a martyrology of European Anabaptists, translated from the 1660 Dutch edition into German. Private collection. Photo, Neil Kamil. *Martyrer Spiegel,* one of the largest American books (and print runs) during the colonial period, was printed and bound at the Ephrata Cloister. The press at Ephrata was usually devoted to illuminated musical texts, but the Cloister also published the works of Jakob Böhme, some in English translation.

hafte" ("Work and hope"), above an image of a rustic farmer digging in the dirt, with a church steeple over his hunched shoulder. A bird, representing the aspiring spirit, waits and watches, perched in a nearby tree, overlooking the scene of pious labor by an impoverished yet stoic martyr of everyday life.

"Then I began to journey through the woods, mountains and valleys," Palissy wrote urgently, "to see if I could discover some industrious animal, who had constructed an ingenious house of some sort."[61] The text, now disguised further in the potter's rustic style of on-the-road empiricism, proceeds with various descriptions of the domestic arrangements of promising species discovered, as if by accident, while on solitary walks to different geographical and natural contexts, mostly in Saintonge. Newfound rustic creatures were examined scientifically on these peregrinations to decipher the mechanism by which they implemented their innate, inside-out, *natural* strategies of *sûreté.*

Most early modern French artisans were mobile and traveled in gangs of *compagnons* for security; but Palissy walked privately in search of secure things to contemplate, alone with his artisan God.[62] Representation of solitude in heroic quest of new experiences removed from the burden of man's venerable traditions of slavish repetition—whether scholastic or artisanal—was both the necessary precondition for Palissy's personal reformation in the crucible of religious violence and fundamental to his transmutation of ceramic materials in the "art of the earth."

❧ The Snail and Its Enemies ❧

Given Palissy's coastal habitat in Saintonge and historical status as a Huguenot refugee, it should come as no surprise that he focused on tiny, overlooked, and apparently defenseless molluscan "artisans" on these walks. Attentive to the attributes of protection given to such humble species by God, the potter posited that their survival depended on a sort of domestic body armor (the shell) generated of the creatures' own volition and then self-fashioned, seamlessly, from materials *brought inside-out* from within their soft inner bodies. That is, each animal's "fortress" emerged from and functioned as a hidden, primordial element of its own being. Neoplatonic elements in Palissy's natural philosophy were embodied by behavior exhibited by the diminutive artisans he observed for "De la ville de forteresse."[63]

Palissy conceptualized these secreted molluscan fortresses as portable wonders. They held the code to life-saving "inventions" of natural artisanry. He thus came to the conclusion that molluscan bastions were generated in a kind of matrix built on the spiritual and material foundations of a snail's primordial nature, which reached its final material form through interaction with its specific domestic history. The snail's natural defenses are not "opposed" to culture in "De la ville de forteresse," since its domestic domain, although constructed, was simultaneously natural.[64] As a prime example of this dual domestic-defensive capacity in nature, Palissy cited "une jeune limace [a young snail], who *built his house and fortress of his own saliva* [emphasis added]." True to the method of Paracelsian alchemy, this inside-out building process was not achieved immediately but rather as a ripening of slow, steady, organic craftsmanship. As the outside shell of the snail grew, it transmuted imperceptibly from one elemental state (liquid) to another (solid). "And so it was made, little by little," Palissy observed of the formation of the snail's external skeleton, as the result of a subtle process that occurred "over the course of many days." "Once I captured the snail" and examined it closely to master the secrets of its craftsmanship, "I found that the inside edge of his building was still liquid, and the rest hard, and so I learned that it took some time to harden the saliva that the snail had used to build his fort."[65]

Palissy's elucidation of the natural artisanry of molluscan fortress construction in terms of a gradual metamorphosis from liquid to solid material states evokes the hardening of ceramic clay and mineral glazes in the potter's kiln. This analogy is reinforced by philology. The French word for snail (*limace*) is associated with the word for clay (*limon*). The Latin word for snail is *limax,* but the common Latin root is most probably *limus,* meaning mud. This relationship makes sense in terms of the natural history of snails. Since classical times, most mollusks have been classified as filter-feeders, or mud-ingesters. Most snail species are also mud-dwelling burrowers that hide from enemies by digging down into the subterranean mire.[66] The Latin usage of *limax* and *limus* reflected the classical belief that all snails were gestated, born, protected, and matured in the bowels of the earth, in a womb of mud.

Consider, as well, the obscure but provocative connection in Latin philology to *limen,* or "threshold." Both words come into play with some degree of frequency both in the historiography of French Calvinist diasporic culture and in Reformation theology generally. Philologists posit that *limen* is connected to both *limus* and *limes,* with *limus* referring simultaneously to mud and, in the abstract sense, a setting out toward a new beginning. (Is this analogous, perhaps, to the alchemist's mudlike *negrido,* resulting from putrefaction and a material matrix for rebirth?) *Limes* has been interpreted, moreover, not only as a cross path (another sort of threshold), but also as a riverbed (a muddy home for snails) and, indeed, as a fortified boundary path.

Snail shells were famously ubiquitous throughout Palissy's "rustic" pottery production—"scattered," as the appraiser of Anne de Montmorecy's Paris collection noted, across the surface of all his oeuvre in the "façon de Xaintes." Ubiquitousness provided its own natural cover—the camouflage of banality—that was associated with the humble, overlooked thing of little power or significance; like the mud itself, or rocks (recall that Montmorency owned Palissy's "tree made in the manner of a rock," scattered with shells). Made of elemental earth, both stones and mud are trodden thoughtlessly underfoot. Yet snails are also hard to find if camouflaged, even when sought out—especially if settled in between water and earth on the murky edges of riverbeds. Snails sometimes lie hidden in shadow in the watery grottoes of Palissy's pottery, under a leaf or blade of grass (perhaps the same color as their shell)—natural habitats for the *limace* in the Charente River Valley. And inasmuch as the vast majority of mollusks live beneath the surface of the visible world, a scattering of shells represents only the outer skin of a subaquatic and subterranean world teeming with invisible life.

In the sixteenth and seventeenth centuries, *limace* connoted the spiral form as well. Cotgrave reports that while the primary definition was "A Snaile," *limace* was "also, as Volute; anything that winds, or turnes like a Snaile-shell." The verb *limaçonner,* therefore, meant "To twirle, turne, or wind about, like the shell of a Snaile, or as souldiers that cast themselves into a ring."[67] Furniture historians will similarly recognize in this definition, the well-known association of refugee Huguenot turners with the diffusion of so-called spiral or twist turning in baroque woodworking. New York was, in fact, the only settlement in colonial British America that adapted this turning form for commercial use during the late seventeenth century.[68] An arboreal spiral is commonly formed when trees or parasitical woody vines spiral around the immobile limbs of a larger tree, using it as a host to climb to the light.

Modern naturalists also reconstruct the process of molluscan shell formation in formal terms of the coiled development of the exoskeleton into a remarkably specific spiral architecture. The snail's building materials consist of a laminate of thin layers of the mineral calcium carbonate, which is secreted like "saliva" in an organic protein matrix by a cluster of cells located along the growing edge of the shell mantle. The calcium carbonate hardens to protect the animal's soft internal organs from predators. Mollusks of many varieties also build shells covered with a thick, glossy transparent glaze. This intensified underlying colors in ways that gave exotic varieties a prominent place in humanists' cabinets of curiosities and inspired emulation by both alchemists and ceramic artisans during the later Renaissance.[69] As the appraiser in the Normandy château sadly noted of what remained of Palissy's pottery destroyed by *liguers* in 1589, the broken shards were glazed with "diverse colors, most exquisitely." Palissy's "De la ville de forteresse" was not a natural history of the architecture of molluscan shells written simply for the sake of classification. The defensive strategies of the tiny, mostly subterranean life forms were the primary subject of inquiry.

Palissy's empathetic and analogical approach to the life of snails is surprisingly relevant to the sorts of inquiry that some naturalists now make in modern laboratory science. "We can think of shells as houses," writes the influential zoologist and natural historian Geerat J. Vermeij, whose research and fieldwork into the life of snails, like Palissy's inquiry four hundred years ago, considers molluscan building practices from the perspective of the inner and outer lives of the mollusks themselves. Palissy and Vermeij both characterize snails as prey living circumspectly in the dangerous and highly contingent world of marauding predators. As a result, "the shell," Vermeij argues, is best understood as "a complete archive of the builder's life and times." Vermeij's material archive of molluscan domesticity resonates with Palissy's dark and violent—yet also intensely beautiful and deeply creative—world of Huguenot artisanal security. To quote Vermeij:

> Shells are built by animals that live in a world of multiple dangers, limitations, and opportunities. Divorced from their natural surroundings, they are objects of abstract architectural beauty in which form takes precedence over function. Only when we observe shells and their makers in nature do we gain some appreciation for the ecological factors that effect the well-being and reproductive success of molluscs. Shells . . . reflect the ways in which the animals that build shells are adapted to and limited by their surroundings.

Environments and functions vary from place to place. Temperature, water flow, food, predators, [and] competitors . . . vary along gradients of geography and habitat. Shells that work well in one situation may be quite ill-suited to another. The way shells work is, in short, a question of ecology and the adaptive responses of molluscs to it.[70]

Above all, snail shells "reveal just how important enemies are in controlling the lives of molluscs."[71]

The sort of interactive life that necessitated the spiral domestic fortress of the diminutive snail "house," is inextricably entwined with the lives and predatory habits of the builder's many aggressive enemies. Most enemies of mollusks seek their armored prey over great distances. Either visual or chemical "cues" or the faint resonance of a faraway movement can be detectable. Mammalian predators of snails (including humans), birds, octopuses, and most fish use vision exclusively. Sight "works well as long as habitats are exposed to light," Vermeij reasons. Hence, "shallow clear-water habitats such as reefs, sand flats, rocky shores, and lakes are ideal for the use of vision," while "turbid rivers, mud flats, and deep-water environments are not."[72] Palissy's "rustiques figulines" encrusted with snail shells are often contextualized in and around the turbid rivers or the ubiquitous tidal mud flats that occlude the watery environments of the Charente River near Saintes, and the *marais* along the Saintongeais coast. Therefore, the first line of defense for mollusks against mammalian predators is either to inhabit occluded places or camouflage themselves in well-lit environments with cryptic, chameleonlike coloration of the shell, to blend in with the surrounding space and be invisible. Both of these molluscan environments appear in pottery made "in the fashion of Xaintes."

Once detected, a snail has four basic options for self-defense: (1) silent, rapid burrowing; (2) reliance on its shell as a stationary fortress, depending on its thickness, corrugations, and buttresses to resist external pressure; (3) retraction of its vital soft parts deep into the coil and away from the rim of the shell's aperture (or "door"); and (4) help from "intimate associations," or symbiotic relationships with powerful hosts (ecological "patrons," as it were)—including corals, sea anemones, sea fans, jellyfishes, and other creatures equipped with stinging cells ("nematocysts")—that attack predators. Many types of snail survive by hiding in the fronds of certain toxic plants, including varieties of seaweed. Plants also provide camouflage. Snails thus benefit from double protection by "others," obtaining both concealment and "patronage."[73]

By the time readers completed "Forteresse," Palissy had also elucidated these four forms of protection as basic elements of artisanal security, observed in the natural "house and fortress" built by his rustic *limace*, the paradigmatic Saintongeais artisan surrounded by predatory enemies. But Palissy took these analogies generated by experiments with the *limace* and his close observation of molluscan building practices further than Vermeij, as a modern scientist, could sanction. Palissy's personal experience (unlike Vermeij's) revealed that like the snail, dangerous "enemies" had become such an "important" factor in his everyday life and the lives of the Huguenots of Saintonge during the first civil war that, in effect, they constituted a "controlling" influence in Saintongeais Huguenot culture. Here, Palissy's empathy created an identity between his natural analogy and his inner and outer selves under pressure.

For Palissy, the essence of the artisanal security revealed by the *limace*'s self-defense structures was the infinite flexibility of spiral forms to contain and channel the motions of inner and outer bodies in a chaotic world controlled by enemies. The experience of the snail's industrious, self-mastered life, contained in its spiral "house and fortress," gave form to the natural interweaving of symmetries of inner and outer experience. The resulting spiral formed a sort of twisting, mutual conduit between the two bodies, facilitating the contingent motions of the protective and creative spirit through old matter in the "new man," while maintaining tight control over the *esmotions* that corrupted the mystical intercourse of macrocosm and microcosm. This integrated serpentine theater of soulish revelation and concealment was also the place where the potter cultivated noble patronage ("intimate associations") from allies in competing confessions (Antoine de Pons, Montmorency, and Catherine de Médicis). Powerful hosts provided a sort of temporary inoculation against his enemies, just as the spiral hid Palissy's inner self from these same hosts when necessary, camouflaging it behind the coded matter of a courtier's artisanry and theatrical self-fashioning. Still, that this option became available to him clearly resulted from noble demand for his extraordinary artisanal talents. At the same time, however, most Huguenot artisans could rely on the general strategies of artisanal security learned from Palissy himself— or, later, from his book—in which he documented experimental encounters with the dual nature of the simultaneously obfuscating and armored *limace*.

Palissy devoted the final section of "Forteresse" to these *armored* structures of the *limace*. Here, he proposed guidelines for a "new," flexible fortress, based on the natural "house and fortress" of the *limace*. This "natural" *pourtrait* depended on the amorphous snail's inner, mutable flesh, and a mollusk's unique ability, depending on the actions of its enemies, to retreat into the hidden recesses of its spiral outer body. The outer body (or exoskeleton) varied somewhat in the form it revealed to the outside world, but the basic construction of the interior space was always spiral, so an enemy that made its way beyond the shell's aperture would fail to reach its soft inner body by taking a straight route. Palissy discovered that many of the snail's predators, and the garfish in particular, had straight-pointed jawbones. With these they could force their way into the spiral so far as the first turn, but there they were stymied and obliged to extract themselves. In theory, since the *limace* spiraled back to its innermost core by turning its "subtle" inner body in a reverse serpentine motion, presumably only a spiritual creature with a similarly subtle and fluid nature could locate it there.

The exceptions were satanic "demons." In his controversial, widely read book of plates and commentary on the multiple spiritual and material meanings of deformity in Nature *On Monsters and Marvels* (1575), Ambroise Paré (1510–1590), Palissy's acquaintance, fellow Paracelsian writer and researcher, and exact contemporary (they were born and died in the same years), who had been a military surgeon during the civil wars before becoming a highly successful Huguenot courtier and surgeon-physician at the courts of Charles IX and Henri III (and personal physician to the two kings), claimed: "Demons can, in many manners and fashions deceive our earthbound heaviness, by reason of the subtlety of their essence and malice of their will."[74] Having reached the deepest room in the molluscan spiral—the most private epicenter of the little artisan's fortress—shape-shifting creatures with pure inner bodies, free from corruption, entered the sanctum sanctorum in Christian fellowship to share in its protection. But the greatest threat to the construction of artisanal security came from the malicious will of demonic forces. The demon's subtle essence enabled it to enter the hidden heart of protected space (an earthly container of soulish power received from the macrocosm) to corrupt the inner body of the spirit. This effectively sullied the deeply pious, Neoplatonic intercourse between God and weakness that crafted the fortress of faith, and so its material body could not converge, form into being, or maintain coherence. Christians knew that in the human anatomy, this absolute interior— this inviolable space of serpentine protection and convergence—was hidden deeply inside the microcosmic heart of man. Man's heart was a place of secret testing, where spirit and matter flowed together continuously in purity or corruption.

Consider how these forms of security may be signified in the "great oval basins . . . scattered with shells and many animals of all sorts . . . inside" made "in the fashion of Xaintes." Thanks mostly to recent archeological discoveries, several of these works can now be safely attributed to Palissy or his workshop. The art historian Leonard N. Amico, who has done an admirable job of classifying the authenticity of the surviving artifacts based on the new archeological record, takes a particular interest in the form and function of the "oval basins" (fig. 2.2) that are the most famous of Palissy's surviving works. Unfortunately, after this promising start, Amico falls back on conventional iconographical readings to interpret the meaning of both the material and spiritual experiments represented in the works of his anti-conventional subject: "One wonders if Palissy's art, which concentrated almost exclusively on the image of a serpent invading an island and causing fish and other creatures to flee, may have codified for him and his followers the image of 'snakelike traitors' attacking the Elect, represented by the fish, that ancient symbol of Christianity."[75]

FIGURE 2.2. Rustic lead-glazed earthenware basin by a contemporary follower or school of Bernard Palissy, Saintes ca. 1560. 15¾″×19⅝″. Courtesy The Walters Art Museum, Baltimore.

From Palissy's experiential perspective, this art-historical language of iconography would probably represent a scholastic—that is, superficial or "dead letter"—reading. It diverts attention away from the natural-philosophical and artisanal traditions and languages with which he identified and communicated both in print and through his ceramics. Amico, then, reads only the "outer body" of the basin. More appropriate to Palissy's scientific framework was the cosmological tradition, from Ptolemy to Paracelsus to Robert Fludd (fig. 2.3), representing the relationship of man's arts to Nature. *Integrae naturae*—nature imaged whole—was the conjunction of macrocosm and microcosm conceptualized on paper in two dimensions. Cosmologies were common in the natural-philosophical books known to Palissy. From the perspective of the alchemists, Palissy basins were part of a tradition of concentric representations that would invariably include elemental earth and water—with the snake (*anguis*) a part of a standard code from the zodiac that signified elemental earth; snails (*limax*), elemental earth *and* water; and fish (*pisces*), elemental water alone.[76]

That this snake was "invading an island and causing fish and other creatures to flee" cannot be supported by a Palissian reading of these ceramic cosmologies—which depict soulish *coexistence* and harmony between the spheres inhabited by naturally contentious creatures, and not violence or invasion—or even a cursory inventory of serpents' behavior on the islands. Every surviving basin, to be sure, usually includes serpents openly inhabiting a central island (like the coastal islands of Saintonge), but here the snake (or snakes) coexists in a peaceable manner with their natural prey (amphibians, fish, mollusks, and other crustaceans, such as crayfish, as well as lizards and insects). There is no evidence whatever of violence in basins made by Palissy; only in nineteenth-century "revival" pottery made by post-Darwinian followers of Palissy is such behavior displayed.

Following Palissy's "De la ville de forteresse" is it not more plausible to say, with him, that the serpentine snake embodied the wavelike and spiral movements of the spirit of the inner body through the matter of elemental earth (the material of the basin

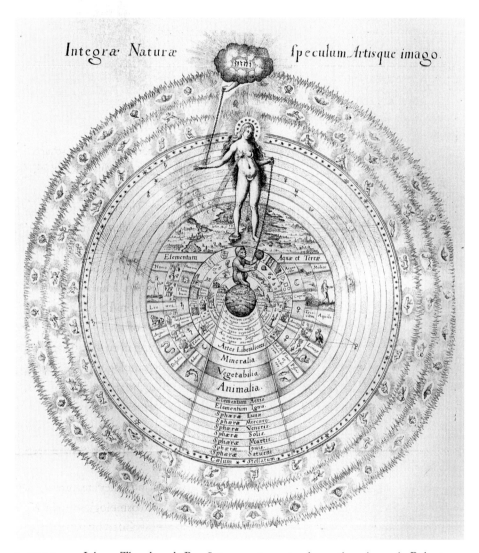

FIGURE 2.3. Johann Theodore de Bry, *Integrae naturae speculum artisque imago*, in Robert Fludd's *Utriusque cosmi majoris scilicet et minoris metaphysica, physica atque technica historia in duo volumina secundum cosmi dfferentiam divisa . . . tomus primus De macrocosmi historia* (Oppenheim, 1617; 2d ed., Frankfurt, 1624). Courtesy Harry Ransom Humanities Research Center, The University of Texas at Austin.

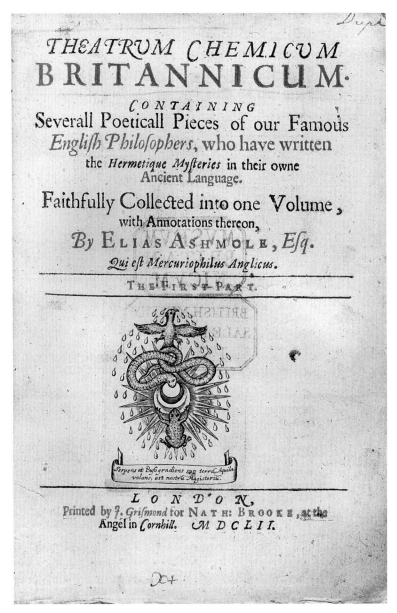

THEATRUM CHEMICUM
BRITANNICUM.
CONTAINING
Severall Poeticall Pieces of our Famous
Englifh Philofophers, who have written
the *Hermetique Myfteries* in their owne
Ancient Language.

Faithfully Collected into one Volume,
with Annotations thereon,
By ELIAS ASHMOLE, *Efq*.
Qui eft Mercuriophilus Anglicus.

THE FIRST PART.

*Serpens et Bufo gradiens fup terrā, Aquila
volans, eft noftrū Magifteriū.*

LONDON,
Printed by J. Grifmond for NATH: BROOKE, at the
Angel in *Cornhill*. ℳ *DCLII*.

FIGURE 2.4. Title page from Elias Ashmole's *Theatrum chemicum* (London, 1652). Courtesy
Harry Ransom Humanities Research Center, The University of Texas at Austin. Like Palissy's
rustic basins, where translucent glazes can redeem and rise above basic earth materials, this
publisher's device uses the combination of a toad and serpent within a matrix of alchemical
symbols to signify the conjunction of macrocosm and microcosm, leading to the goal of unification, metamorphosis, and distillation of formerly dark and corrupted earth materials, shed
like transparent tears from a purified and light "Aquila volans," or flying eagle.

itself)? The basins, like cosmologies that depicted the great synthesis of the macrocosm and microcosm, put diverse outer bodies ("scattered with shells and many animals of all sorts") unified by the one, "fired" inner body (the snake) on display all at
once. These clay serpents did not disperse the inhabitants of Palissy's cosmology, "causing" the "other creatures to flee." On the contrary, they appear to signify the underlying
knot binding a material-holiness synthesis together, at the center of Palissy's artisanal
"forteresse." Consider, for example, the role of the snake in the early modern iconography of alchemic distillation (fig. 2.4). This potter's serpent seems closer to God
reanimating postlapsarian Nature than the devil. Calvin asked Palissy, a reader of Philibert Hamelin's edition of the *Institutes* and "a maker" in his own right, to consider:

> how far men are fallen from that purity which was bestowed upon Adam. And first let it
> be understood that, by his being made of earth and clay, a restraint was laid upon pride;
> since nothing is more absurd than for creatures to glory in their excellence who not only
> inhabit a cottage of clay but who are themselves composed partly of dust and ashes. But
> as God not only deigned to animate the earthen vessel but chose to make it the residence
> of an immortal spirit, Adam might justly glory in so great an instance of the liberality of
> his Maker.[77]

This representation of the synthesis of the pure spirit with fallen matter most closely
approximates the Protestant sacrament of baptism, a visible sign of inward grace. And,
indeed, a sparkling stream of translucent water always runs through or around earth
on which the serpent is coiled. The elements of water and earth are explicit in the
basins, while both fire and air remained implicit in the process of firing the pottery in
the kiln, and in the rustic, outdoors environment, with its flying insects and, above all,
that ubiquitous serpent spiraling between macrocosm and microcosm. It is also suggestive that many sixteenth-century Protestant baptismal fonts were markedly oval in
shape, much like Palissy's basins.[78] Luther had expressly linked this sacrament with
death and rebirth through the baptism of Christ, giving it even greater meaning for
Huguenots during the genocidal civil wars. In his tract of 1520, *The Babylonian Captivity of the Church,* Luther made this relationship his central point: "Baptism, then,
signifies two things—death and resurrection, that is, full and complete justification.
When the minister immerses the child in water it signifies death, and when he draws
it forth again it signifies life." This signification, as such, connoted reconstruction of
the prelapsarian unity of Adamic clay and immortal spirit in elemental fire and water.
For Luther, moreover, baptism was not merely a single brief experience in the Christian's life. Rather, it was a permanent condition, signifying each new man's and
woman's covenant with God. Death fulfilled the ultimate promise by God, made in
baptism, when a Christian's sin was put to death permanently.[79]

This condition of permanence also permeated the green fecundity of Nature in

Palissy's rustic basins. In most, the stream flows in an endless circle of time, while the snakes' serpentine line shifts or conflates synchronic and diachronic time. In some, the alchemist's salamander turns back toward its tail, appearing in the central space. This was a symbol of the crucible with its fire that does not destroy purity in matter but facilitates alchemic rebirth. The confluence of water and fire in these artifactual contexts suggests the symbiosis between death and life that Palissy conceptualized in the natural history of Saintonge and in the artisanal syncretism of alchemy and baptism.[80] Perhaps Amico's reading is an unintended example of Palissy's manipulation of the surface to hide his multiplicity of messages? Did Palissy suggest the ambiguity of corruption and purity in the movement of the spirit? Were the snakes a variation of the snail, emerged outside its shell? Could they therefore embody the hidden potential of the power of weakness to animate both the destructive and the creative force of nature's tiny, industrious creatures. If perceptions of weakness masked strength, and divisiveness and evil obscured the presence of unity and pure goodness, then may we argue that the basins were made to possess a rhetoric that simultaneously concealed and revealed protective strategies based on the spiritual potential contained in the elemental materials that Palissy brought back to life through the fire of his pious artisanry?

"An ignorance of things makes figurative expressions obscure when we are ignorant of the natures of animals, or stones, or plants, or other things which are often used in the Scriptures for purposes of constructing similitudes," Augustine said in *On Christian Doctrine*, perhaps the most influential early text on natural wisdom and spiritual security. "The well known fact that a serpent exposes its whole body in order *to protect* its head from those attacking it illustrates the sense of the Lord's admonition that we be wise like serpents." After adumbrating the exposed Palissian serpent and the Huguenot concept of hiding in plain sight, Augustine concluded that "the same thing is true of stones, or of herbs or of other things that take root. For a knowledge of the carbuncle which shines in the darkness also illuminates many obscure places in books where it is used for similitudes, and an ignorance of beryl as of diamonds frequently closes the doors of understanding."[81]

❧ An Invisible *pourtrait* ❧

One particular "walk," in the course of which he came into possession of the specific species of snail whose shell inspired his invisible *pourtrait* of the newly invented fortress town, is pivotal in Palissy's "De la ville de forteresse."

Like the shape of the snail and the snake, this walk through coastal Saintonge seemed to follow the same serpentine pattern used in the basins. The narrative movement was similar in effect to the ceramic snakes that twisted and spiraled from one edge of the basin to the other. "I took a walk from here to there," Palissy wrote, "from one coast to the other, to see if I might yet learn something about buildings made by animals." "This went on for many months," he said, "and at the same time I always practiced my art of the earth [*mon art de terre*] in order to feed my family."[82] This passing reference to simultaneous practice of natural-philosophical research and artisanry must not be overlooked. Palissy begins to forge basic equivalences here, integrating experiments with the kiln that resulted in his "art de terre," research undertaken with his "head lowered," looking down at the earth floor, and the dual, domestic-military labors of the tiny industrious animals that he pursued so relentlessly. The "rustiques figulines" with surfaces encrusted—figuratively crawling on the basins—with precise models of these creatures (literally duplicates molded from life from the bodies of the animals and plants Palissy collected on these walks)—were used in his "art de terre," natural philosophical studies and writings on the natural history of artisanal security. This was the potter's source material for his "impregnable" fortress town.[83]

The serpentine pattern was primarily vertical (up and down), following steep wilderness terrain: into woods, over hills, and down valleys, where Palissy failed initially to find an appropriate natural artifact of mimetic desire. As in his first encounter with the *limace,* however, God's animated (or soulish) motion provided further clues to fruitful direction after a chastening interval of apparently aimless wandering. Following the hermeneutic structure conventional in pilgrimage narratives, empirical clues, gathered through physical experience and "decreated" for their secrets by artisanal labor, were ultimately turned inward toward the pilgrim himself. Return to self (the inner body), knowledge, and wisdom were achieved using local geographical references as both a literal and metaphorical map; a framework by which to return to the point of embarkation (Saintes) and epiphany. What is most extraordinary about the stages of Palissy's outer and inner journeys of self-transformation is that the walks were harnessed to experience of the movement of his spirit into the matter of the scorched earth of Saintonge. Hence, he documented the process by which "mon art de terre" was sacramentalized by violence.

Experience of spiral movement was the crux of this narrative. Despite numerous pilgrimage studies that followed on his pioneering work, the etymological relationship of *limace* to *limen,* and hence to liminality, makes Victor Turner's comparative work on the sacred structures of pilgrimage particularly apposite here, as Palissy's Saintongeais promenades were constructed in molluscan forms. That Palissy's Saintonge was quintessentially *liminal* territory is crucial to the implications that the long, allusive passages describing his walks have for understanding his texts, written and nonverbal, and of the interplay between structures of societal power and community standards of competence expected from Saintongeais Huguenot artisans during the wars of religion. The folklorist Arnold van Gennep first introduced the term *limen* into the anthropologist's lexicon in 1908. Turner then mapped the relation between liminality, pilgrimage, and performance in a series of ethnologies (his term is "comparative symbologies") in which concepts of liminality serve, in a historical framework, to analyze the progressive marginalization of subcultures and their responses (what Turner calls the innovative and creative "anti-structural" manifestation of *communitas*) under pressure from dominant social orders.[84]

Turner's useful reformulation of Gennep's tripartic processual structure (or "rites of passage")—"that is, separation, *limen* or margin, and reaggregation"—is very well known among historians and requires no lengthy discussion here.[85] Rather, by way of reminder and for future reference, I shall quote Turner's working definition of liminality modified for Christian cultures:

> The state and process of mid-transition in a rite of passage. During the liminal period, the characteristics of *liminars* (the ritual subjects in this phase) are ambiguous, for they pass through a cultural realm that has few or none of the attributes of the past or coming state. Liminars are betwixt and between. The liminal state has frequently been likened to death; to being in the womb; to invisibility, darkness, bisexuality, and the wilderness. Liminars are stripped of status and authority, removed from a social structure maintained and sanctioned by power and force, and leveled to a homogenous social state through discipline and ordeal. Their secular powerlessness may be compensated for by a sacred power, however—the power of the weak, derived on the one hand from the resurgence of nature when structural power is removed, and on the other from the reception of sacred knowledge. Much of what has been bound by social structure is liberated, notably the sense of comradeship and communion, or communitas; while much of what has been dispersed over the many domains of culture and social structure is now bound, or cathected, in the complex semantic systems of pivotal, multivocal symbols and myths, numinous systems which achieve great conjunctive power. In this no-place and no-time that resists classification, the major classifications and categories of culture emerge within the integuments of myth, symbol, and ritual.[86]

Consider for the moment, Palissy's artisan-scientist's status in "De la ville de forteresse" as Huguenot pilgrim *cum* liminar in Turner's sense; and indeed henceforth, the potter consistently recreated this role in precisely those crucial moments strategically located throughout the *Recepte,* when innovative processes specifically related to new artisanal practices were at stake. But unlike with Turner's liminar, it is clear there was a violent context that functioned as a foil for this pilgrim's return, so his situation defies rigid classification as "no-place and no-time." Rather, the empirical *specificity* of Palissy's geographic references to the rocky coast that alternates with the three vast *marais* comprising southwestern Saintonge is striking.

The context of "De la ville de forteresse," written in 1562–63—"some time after that I had considered the horrible dangers of war, from which God had miraculously delivered me"—becomes absolutely crucial to explicating both the force of the text and the magnitude of Palissy's contribution, not only to the historiography of the Reformation in provincial France, but to the historiography of Atlantic history and culture. It is possible to argue that *this* historical moment above all others—even including the massacre on St. Bartholomew's Day in 1572 (which *increased* the flow of Huguenot refugees to the southwest, making it an even larger center of Huguenot culture in regional France)—was the one in which significant elements of the local Saintongeais Huguenot community *initiated* a pervasive discourse of margination for the first time. This was the moment of historical consciousness when Huguenots, especially artisans such as Palissy, began to represent themselves and their community to one another and the outside world *artfully,* as a socially alienated culture—simply put, a "sub" (or "out") culture—still in continuous, albeit necessarily oblique, dialogue with the centralizing power, then beginning the arduous process of systematically consolidating the institutional basis of absolutism. The long history of these complex representations and dialogues, and the extension of the southwestern Huguenot regional subculture to the markets and plantations of colonial America, exemplified by the craft and mercantile network of New York leather chair makers, must therefore begin with this historical moment and with Palissy as its most articulate artisan. Understanding Palissy and his followers, together with his sociocultural milieu, provides insights into the foundation of such New World discourse among coastal Saintongeais Huguenots as early as the late 1550s.

Palissy's pilgrimage in search of the prototype for his New World fortress town was undertaken in response to the turmoil of local confessional violence and the *esmotions* of war—this narrative was about security—but it was also intended to present the authority of scientific evidence to document Palissy's personal experience with animate nature:

After many days of spiritual turmoil [*debat d'esprit*], I decided to travel to the coast and the rocks of the Ocean sea [the Atlantic coast], where I saw such a variety of houses and fortresses made by certain little fish from their own juice and saliva, I then began to think that I could find something there that would suit my project. At that time, I had started to contemplate the industriousness of all these species of fish, to learn something from them, from the biggest to the smallest: *I discovered things that made me feel small* [*tout confus* also connotes "confused" and "ashamed" in this context] when I considered the marvelousness of Divine providence, which took such care with these creatures, to the point that God has endowed the smallest with the greatest industry, but not so the others: I had thought I would find some great industry and excellent knowledge among the large fish, [but] I found nothing industrious about them, which made me consider that they were sufficiently armored, feared, and dreaded, because of their grandeur, that they had no need of other weapons: but *as for the weak, I found that God had given them the industry and know-how to make fortresses marvelously excellent to counteract the intrigues of their enemies* [emphasis added].[87]

Fundamental to Palissy's pilgrimage experience with Nature was his spiritual and material epiphany when "I discovered things that made me feel small in the presence of God's artistry." This was the crucial act of self-transformation—of identity with survivors in nature that most clearly approximated his own experience as a Huguenot artisan in Saintonge during the civil wars—that marked Palissy's inculcation of the power of weakness, the spiritual foundation of industriousness and hence artisanal security. The world had been turned upside down, with power now residing on the earth's floor, at the lowest levels of natural history. Palissy's smallness—his embarrassment and inversion of perception—allowed him to see for the first time that although the largest fish were so obviously well armed, their very "grandeur" had obviated the necessity for creativity and innovation. Big fish had "nothing industrious about them." Grandeur made for uninspired artisanry. God directed the natural philosopher not to look for useful secrets of fortress construction among the well-protected. "As for the weak," Palissy "found that God had given them the industry and know-how to make fortresses marvelously excellent to counteract the intrigues of their enemies." While walking away from violence in molluscan spirals—"where I saw such a variety of houses and fortresses made from [their] own juice and saliva"—to find a prototype upon which to model a new paradigm of security, Palissy transformed himself into a snail.

After some time "walking on the rocks" like the snail he had become in his imagination, "where I saw marvels," Palissy was given "occasion to cry, after the Prophet: 'Not for us, Lord . . . but to your Name is given the honor and the glory.'" The pious artisan paid preliminary homage to the artisan God of Genesis and source of the creative power hidden in his soul. Palissy, overwhelmed by the difficulty of his project of godlike emulation, "began to think to myself that I would never be able to find anything to counsel me best on how to design my fortress town. Then, I took to examining all the fish that were most industrious in architecture, with a goal of taking some counsel from their industry."[88]

Ironically, given the source, a natural paradigm for the new stationary fortress—advertised as an improvement over all previous immobile designs because of its flexibility—was never found among the *rustique rochers* of Saintonge, but was a foreign specimen that was presented to Palissy from inside "The Rock," as a gift from a collector with a suspiciously hermetic name, "a bourgeois from La Rochelle, named l'Hermite":

who presented me with two good-sized snail shells, seeing one was the shell of a *pourpre* [*Purpurellus muricidae*?],[89] and the other was from a *buxine,* these [shells] had been brought in from Guinea [in coastal West Africa], and were both made in the shape of the *limace* with a spiral line; but that of the *buxine* was stronger and bigger than the other. However, considering the statement that I made above, that God had given the most *industry*[90] to the weakest things and not the strongest, I resolved to contemplate the shell of the *pourpre* more closely than that of the *buxine,* because I am secure in the knowledge that God has given it some kind of advantage to compensate for its weakness. And so, having pondered these thoughts for a long while, I observed that on the shell of the *pourpre* there were a number of sufficiently large points ["spires or beads"], which were all around the said shell; I was certain from that moment on that it was not without cause the said horns were formed, and that these were so many sundry little troughs, vessels, and safeguards for the fortress and [places of] refuge for the said *pourpre* [when it withdrew into its shell].[91]

Palissy demonstrated the ways in which "God had given the most industry to the weakest thing"—the smaller *limace*—by presenting a lengthy analysis of the *pourpre*'s enormously complex and varied internal defense system as a model for his fortress. Camouflage seemed infinitely available for industrious Huguenot defenders and their armaments inside the vast labyrinthine spiral of the town, as it turned in upon itself. Defenders counterattacked from places of surveillance hidden in shadow. No one was visible for long enough to absorb the brunt of a full frontal assault. The entire fortress was alive—the inner and outer walls in particular—with furtive eyes and fluid bodies in motion. "You see," Palissy claimed, "that I could find nothing better upon which to frame my fortress town than to use the fortress of the *pourpre* as my precedent to follow":

forthwith, I took up a compass, ruler, and the other tools necessary to make my pourtrait. Firstly, I made a drawing of a large central square; towering around and encompassing this place, I drew a great number of houses, in which I put windows, doors and shops, having every view toward the exterior part of the plan and the streets of the town. And inside one of the corners of this place, I designed a great portal, on which I noted the plan of the house or domicile of the principal governor of this town, so that nothing could enter the said place without his leave. And to put around the base of the tower, I designed certain lean-tos, or lower galleries, to hide the artillery under cover, so that the walls in front of the lower gallery will serve both for defense and as a platform for the battery, they will have several master gunners all around all with their sights set on the center of the square, so that even if enemies enter by undermining the said place, they can all be exterminated at once [by cannon fire].[92]

Accordingly, if enemies managed to penetrate the hidden, innermost square of the fortress by force—not welcomed through the door by the "governor" (or soul?) of the fortress's "heart"—annihilation came instantaneously. Thus, what appeared to be the weakest space in the inner body—the hub where invaders expected to claim victory—was the heart of reversal and secret power. Here the malefactors were destroyed through the pious industry of artisans and the vast, decentralized security system they had created to project invisible power from the depth of shadow.

Continuing to work inside out from the core, as did the pious artisan and the *limace,* Palissy used the compass almost exclusively in order to complete drawings of his fortress, following the spiral constructed by his natural "precedent": "That done, I started at the end of the street, coming out from the said portal, to create a circular plan for the houses that I marked for the outside edges of the [central edifice], wanting to frame my town on the spiral form and line, following the form and industry of the *pourpre.*"[93]

Palissy continued to extend the drawing for his "town and fortress" outward from center in this concentric pattern, plotting a series of spiral streets, most with squares occupied by towers with both domestic space and artillery, having much the same double security function as the central edifice. These "Vitruvian" circled squares were necessary as stages for defenders to counterattack at specific points along the spiral, because Palissy "perceived that the task of the cannon is to fire in straight lines and that, if my town was framed totally on spiral lines, the cannon could not fire on the streets." "That is why," Palissy "thought it prudent," to adapt humanist classical learning to his natural plan, and to "follow the industry of the said *pourpre* only when it would behoove me."[94] The pragmatic pattern of beginning with a natural precedent, subject to adaptation from humanism, or commonsense experience in everyday life, was a hallmark of Palissy's written and material work.

Having "found my invention" of a new fortress that synthesized human learning with the natural arts "exceedingly good and useful," the potter announced a final step that would fully "concatenate the fortress's members with its body." After drawing numerous streets in the "spiral line" emanating out, yet still connected with its hub hidden inside the central tower, Palissy now planned the outermost street of the fortress; the one conventionally located just inside, but always separated from, the freestanding outer walls:

> I found that the said town was big enough and proceeded to set down the houses all around the said street, joining the houses' walls to the town walls, which walls I joined together with the walls of the houses of the street next to them, [and so on, inward, back to the central portal]. Then, having thus completed my design, it seemed to me that my town had made a mockery of all the rest, *because all the walls of the other [fortress] towns are useless in times of peace, and those that I made served all the time for habitation for the same people who practice many trades [arts] to protect and defend the said town* [emphasis added].[95]

Palissy revealed the essential element of artisanal security. Artisans live virtually *inside* the walls of the fortress itself. Inhabiting the seamless, concatenated flesh of the town's inner and outer protective bodies, workmen labor covertly and with devious efficiency, to compensate for their lack of size and ostensible weakness. As their artful construction of platforms and housing and their stealthy manipulation of the deadly artillery hidden in the central tower's shadowy galleries indicates, artisans "practice many trades to protect and defend the said town." Above all, alchemists' workshops, and even alchemic crucibles themselves, were represented as turreted fortress towers (fig. 2.5). In short, these Huguenot artisans have been transformed into the very embodiment of the fortress wall and have assumed its protective function. Unlike the old medieval wall, however, this "natural" wall was alive and vigilant (a synonym for industrious) with the eyes, ears, hands, and souls of its craftsmen. What gave this particular aspect of Palissy's *pourtrait* power and resonance was the knowledge that following representations like the one in figure 2.5, his own pottery workshop and kiln, as well as his alchemical laboratory, were hidden inside a tower of a rampart of Saintes's surrounding walls (fig. 2.6), during the first civil war of religion.[96]

The plan of Saintes in 1560 reproduced in figure 2.6 shows where Palissy installed his workshop (in the large tower situated between D and E). Following convention, almost all domestic housing in Saintes was separated from the defensive walls (and hence plainly visible and vulnerable if the outer defenses were breached). And, from Palissy's vivid description of "reports" of the slaughter of Huguenots in those houses (which he mostly heard from friends in the street or sometimes spied himself from furtive "eyes" in the tower, where he hid until the terror had passed), the decision to build a clandestine living area and workshop-laboratory into the fortress walls saved his life, while simultaneously being a formative natural-philosophical experience. In 1576, eleven years after Palissy left Saintes (and one year after hostilities started up again, to begin the fifth civil war of religion), a certain Bastien de Launay, an artisan whose occupation is not mentioned, petitioned "our Lords the mayor and aldermen of the town of Saintes," to "give and rent the said de Launay the room and tower next to the house of master Bernard Pallicis, for the price and sum of five *sous* rent that the said supplicant had always paid." Before being displaced by the prefect of Saintes to serve Palissy's powerful patron, de Launay's own workshop had occupied the tower. Palissy was long gone now, and de Launay had reason to want his old atelier back:

> for some time he [de Launay] had ceased paying the rent because the said master Bernard occupied the said room and tower to lay out his work . . . that was due to monsieur the Constable [Montmorency], and nevertheless, before occupation by M[aster] Bernard . . . my lord the Prefect, as a provisional measure and until the said work was taken away from the said town [of Saintes] and place occupied, had leased to the supplicant another tower, vulgarly called the executioner's tower, to practice and labor in his art . . . [but] during the troubles, it fell into ruin . . . please allow the said supplicant to pay the old rent and reestablish himself in the tower and room.[97]

FIGURE 2.5. Alchemical furnace in the form of a fortified tower, from Philippus Ulstadius, *Coelum philosophorum* (Strasbourg, 1526). This item is reproduced by permission of The Huntington Library, San Marino, California. RB 483479. An early representation of the fortress as a secure container that internalized, mastered, and diverted powerful forces for man's use in making things, inverting the traditional definition of the fortress as a place of security capable of repelling force and maintaining distance and exclusivity.

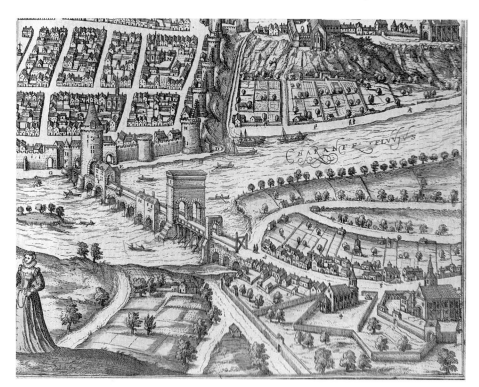

FIGURE 2.6. Detail of the "Pourtrait de la vile et cite de Saintes, Chef de la Comte de Sain-tonge . . . Anno 1560," from George Braun (fl. 1593–1616), Franz Hogenberg (d. 1590), Abra-ham Hogenberg (fl. 1608–53), Simon Novellanus (fl. 1560–90), and Anton Hierat (fl. 1597–1627), *Civitates orbis terrarum* (Cologne, 1572–1618), bk. 5: 17–18. Courtesy Harry Ransom Hu-manities Research Center, The University of Texas at Austin. This detail from Braun's atlas shows the location of Palissy's artisanal workshop, kiln, and alchemical laboratory in 1560. The potter lived and worked in the crenellated central tower in the fortified south wall of Saintes, which overlooked the Charente River, where he went walking in search of solitude and natural specimens. Palissy's personal fortress was situated between E ("port Moucher") and D ("port des freres cordeliers").

Nothing more can be said of Bastien de Launay. His religious affiliation and the state of his prior relationship with Palissy is unknown. Bastien's use of the honorific "Master," in deference to the man who displaced him, and the fact that this "suppli-cant" did not reveal Palissy's hiding place to avid pursuers when Saintes was sacked during the first civil war, suggests a deeper connection to Montmorency and Palissy than the limitations of this document reveal. But it seems perfectly clear that other ar-tisans practiced their trade inside the walls and towers of Saintes before Palissy estab-lished himself in the town. The potter had appropriated and reimagined the material and metaphysical possibilities of a local custom to accommodate the larger natural-philosophical intent of artisanal *sûreté.*

"Having made my *pourtrait*," Palissy expressed satisfaction to have "found that the walls of all the houses also served as so many fortified spurs, and, from whichever side cannon were fired against the said town, it would find the walls extended." And if Palissy's plan had successfully domesticated the fortress wall by joining it with the houses of the town, then the spiral form of the *limace* was the natural answer to the unified defense of the fortress town and its interior even if the individual, yet concatenated, walls were somehow bypassed by invading enemies:

> Therefore, in the town, there will be but one street and one entry, which will always be winding about [in a spiral] and going in from the outer corners to inner corners; this will lead in a curved line until it ends at the square in the center of the town. And in each corner and angle facing the street, there will be a double, turning door, and above each of these, a high battery, or platform, placed in such a way, that from the two angles of each corner, the cannons could fire constantly from one angle to the other, and by means of these turning doors, the cannoneers can also be hidden so that they will not be offensive.[98]

As with the snail, whose "house" was also its fortress, every domestic function in Palissy's impregnable fortress town was a "double door" (or mirror) that literally "turned" into a hidden weapon. Palissy's spiral town of corners and angles was an inverted Trojan Horse, which led enemies to their deaths. If the Trojan Horse dissimulated a benignly natural object, constructed to capture a closed fortress by stealth from the outside in, then Palissy's construction was a Trojan Horse in reverse—in effect, it was turned inside out by artisanal industriousness—and was transformed into an instrument of the fortress's protection.

Palissy's "*pourtrait*, plan, and model of the most impregnable town known to man," a human invention, was built in emulation of Nature, with "knowledge of the art of geometry and architecture," to withstand the assaults of enemies better than any, "excepting those places which God had fortified naturally."[99] He guaranteed that "were a town built according to the specifications of my model and *pourtrait*," it would be impervious to attack, whether "by a multitude of men [and] bombardment; by fire; by a tunnel [that "emerges in the middle of town"]; by scaling; by famine; [or], by undermining [the walls]." And after listing the most common methods of attack from without, Palissy evoked an "interior" danger, surrender "by treason."[100]

How could any formal plan guarantee against treason, a threat from the inner man? In an illuminating coda titled the "Explanation of Certain Articles," Palissy acknowledged that "some may find the article of treason strange." The explanation again lay in decentralization of parts and the interconnection of inner and outer bodies. Palissy's spiritual and anatomical principle of "concatenation" of macrocosm and microcosm was key when combined with the power of small things to resist:

When the ten or twelve parts of the town, and even their governors, conspire with the enemy to surrender the town, it is not in their power to deliver, *provided that there is one small part of the town that resists them* [emphasis added], because the order of the buildings will be so well concatenated that it will be necessary for all the inhabitants to consent to the treason before the town can be surrendered, and such a general conspiracy could never happen . . . [without] warning.[101]

Like the tiny *limace,* small, overlooked elements in the Palissian cosmology were always the essential source of power and virtuous resistance to corruption of the whole. "Even their local governors" were powerless against them.

The secure body was only as powerful as its weakest and most subtle, nearly imperceptible part. Enemies who contrived to spy over the outer walls would only be able to "see up to the pavement of the streets next to the walls" and nothing more. Their view was blocked by design, and they would be unable to aim effectively so as to be able "hurl down their bullets" and other missiles. Only "the street next to the walls" would be affected by such an attack, and its "inhabitants would receive no injuries." If anything, they might suffer from "fear and poisoning by bad fumes." So, too, enemies on ground level, down in the streets, would only be able to see until their sightlines were blocked at the next bend in this town of spirals. Defense was carefully choreographed in a theater of revelation and concealment.[102]

Palissy envisioned artisanal security, both literally and metaphorically, without straight lines. His fortress town would "be built with such subtlety and invention that even children, younger than six years old, could be helpful in its defense . . . ; indeed, without anyone having to shift from his room and domestic dwelling, and without putting anyone in danger of their lives."[103] Here was Palissy's most astonishing claim: that the artisanal defense of his Huguenot fortress involved so "subtle and inventive" a *system* of security that even children, its most innocent and seemingly defenseless members, could play a part in it. A system of household security that obviated the need for a fortress on the model of La Rochelle was necessary, because in this new, apocalyptic world without walls, security had either to be internalized as skill and industriousness or carried by fleeing refugees "on their backs" the way an artisan carried his tools, or the *limace* its portable, inside-out shell.

Palissy ended "De la ville de forteresse"—and indeed the *Recepte veritable*—with an abrupt dialogue of one question and response, returning to complete his thoughts on the subject of the invisible *pourtrait.* Having just finished reading the allusive yet finally unsatisfying essay without seeing the promised plan realized in concrete form, an impatient and exasperated "Demande" complained:

You make a promise above in which you have the temerity to say that with the drawing and plan you will produce, one will easily learn that what you have called the fortress town contains truth. Why, then, have you not put in this book the actual drawing and plan for the said town? Only by seeing the plan would it be possible to judge whether what you say contains truth.[104]

But the "truth" "contained" in the town body of this "forteresse," was unavailable from an exterior plan, but hidden deeply inside the soul-animated rooms of a Huguenot artisan's serpentine interior. Demande demonstrated that he had learned nothing from the text. "Seeing the plan" would never reveal truth. Seeing was not necessarily believing. Visible truth appeared only to uncorrupted eyes that looked beneath the material surface of things to see God's plan in the invisible *pourtrait.* If truth were made plain for even corrupt enemies to see, then where—in which private "room and dwelling"—would Huguenot artisans find the space to "invent" their "subtle" fortresses? The very subtlety invested in Palissy's artisanry lay in the mutability of perception and the potter's "recipe" for the naturalistic camouflage of inner reality. So Palissy proposed an inversion of the plan.

In *Response,* Palissy replied, condescendingly: "You have completely misunderstood my statement; *for I did not tell you that by the plan and drawing you would be able to judge the whole.*" To judge the whole was the philosopher's task. Then, rather abruptly, he diverted the reader's attention from the metaphysical meaning of "the whole" to the material requirements of the marketplace, where artisans sought to extend their search for security. Palissy was in quest of patronage. After all, the metaphysical foundations of his natural philosophy did not stipulate that he had to give his secrets away. Palissy would be pleased to negotiate the value of his labor face-to-face with wealthy patrons:

> With the plan and drawing I have added that it would be required to make a model. Considering that there would be no reason to make one at my own expense, it was sufficient to tell you that the thing merited payment, because it is only proper that those who want the said model should pay for the labor. Now, if there is anybody who wants to have a model of my invention, you may give him my address, which is what I hope you'll do, and I trust he'll be satisfied.[105]

And yet, with the last line of "De la ville de forteresse," Palissy subverted the singular status of his stationary fortress for the Huguenots of Aunis-Saintonge, even as he boldly advertised the availability of his new plan to any noble patron who purchased the *Recepte* from Chez Berton, La Rochelle. "And if you live hereabouts," he wrote in defiance of La Rochelle's very reason for being, "I will pray the Lord God to take you into his protection."[106] No one fortress town of stone and mortar could provide security for Huguenots in the southwest of France. God chose not to give industry to all the faithful. A "poor unlettered artisan" inferred that while La Rochelle (the *buxine* of fortresses) was "sufficiently armored, feared, and dreaded because of [its] grandeur,"

God had not "given [the Rochelais?] industry and know-how to make fortresses . . . to counteract the intrigues of their enemies." The Huguenot potter from Saintes had imagined the unthinkable and "proved" it with science. Palissy predicted the fall of "feared" La Rochelle, and so the relocation of cultural and economic power from the wreckage of a monolithic, enclosed center to the hinterlands—a diversified, fragmented, and open yet "concatenated" haven for "the weak" but "industrious." He found truth and power intertwined in a serpentine spiral, having "discovered things that made me feel small."

CHAPTER THREE

Personal History
and "Spiritual Honor"

Philibert Hamelin's Consideration of Straight Lines
and the Rehabilitation of the Nicodemite
as Huguenot Artisan of Security

❧ Perspectives on Nicodemism ❧

Concealed faith was anathema to Calvin, who condemned it as "Nicodemism," a name derived from Nicodemus, a Pharisee depicted as a hypocrite in the Gospel of John (3:1–21; 7:50–52; 19:39). Those who hid their Protestant convictions, dissimulating what was concealed in their hearts and outwardly adhering to the rituals and social behavior of religious orthodoxy, were branded "Nicodemites."

Calvin assailed Nicodemism in 1544 in a publication entitled *Excuse de Jehan Calvin, à messieurs les Nicodemites, sur la complaincte qu'ilz font de sa trop grand' rigueur* (John Calvin's Justification in Response to the Nicodemites' Complaint About His Excessive Rigor).[1] His unforgiving polemical essay focused on French Nicodemism. Diffused widely in France, it was published twice more in French during Calvin's lifetime, in 1551 and 1558. All three editions were in print long before publication of Palissy's *Recepte véritable* (1563), and they were widely diffused during the French civil wars of religion, a time when Nicodemism was practiced as a defense against confessional violence. Many passages in the *Recepte* make it quite clear that Palissy was completely familiar with Calvin's text.[2]

From the 1550s through the St. Bartholomew's Day Massacre, Calvin's *Excuse . . . à messieurs les Nicodemites* gave rise to numerous propagandistic tracts, of which Jehan Crespin's martyrology, *Actes des martyrs* (1554, 1565, 1619), to which Palissy refers in the *Recepte,* was the most celebrated example on the Continent. Taking their lead from Calvin, martyrologies from Crespin's to the Englishman John Foxe's *Book of Martyrs* (1563), and, later, the Dutchman Tieleman Janszoon van Brachts's *Martyrer Spiegel (Martyr's Mirror)* (1660, 1748) codified the Protestant ideal of the martyr on the model of Christ, who openly confessed heresy to inquisitors. Martyrs in these books relished the pain of execution, to be witnessed by others as a pure, sanctified death and spiritual rebirth.[3] To do otherwise was, for Calvin, to "hide under the robe of Nicodemus," who "came to Jesus Christ at night, in the time of his ignorance."[4] Faith was not hidden under a dissimulating outer garment, but shone brightly from a transparent one, as "we serve God all together, purely." To dissimulate faith did "not follow the soul, but [was] for the good of the body."[5]

Calvin despised, above all other Nicodemites, Paracelsian "adepts," whom he regarded as depraved "half-Christians" who egregiously identified faith and spiritual aspiration with matter,

> both to destroy the immortality of the soul and to deprive God of his right. For, since the soul has organic faculties, they by this pretext bind the soul to the body so that it may not subsist without it, and by praising nature they suppress God's name as far as they can. . . . Some persons, moreover, babble about a secret inspiration that gives life to the whole universe, but what they say is not only weak but completely profane; . . . of what value to beget and nourish godliness in men's hearts is that jejeune speculation about the universal mind which animates and quickens the world![6]

Calvin acquiesced that man was "the loftiest proof of divine wisdom," inasmuch "as all acknowledge, the human body shows itself a composition so ingenious that its Artificer is rightly judged a wonder-worker." Thus, "Certain philosophers" (by this he probably meant Aristotle and, especially, Plato) "accordingly, long ago not ineptly called man a microcosm because he is a rare example of God's power, goodness, and wisdom, and contains within himself enough miracles to occupy our minds, if only we are not irked at paying attention to them."[7]

Yet if "the knowledge of God shines forth in the fashioning of the universe and the continuing governing of it," then the corruption engendered by Adam's fall from prelapsarian grace and purity had assured Calvin that "they entangle themselves in such a huge mass of errors that blind wickedness stifles and finally extinguishes those sparks which once flashed forth to show them God's glory."[8] This mass of errors and blind wickedness willed them to "imagine Platonic ideas in their heads," propound "crazy superstitions," and "consider in private chambers how things were going . . . in secret," before unveiling their hidden belief. "For I would love best if all the human sciences were banished from the earth," wrote Calvin, "if they were the cause of cooling thus the zeal of Christians, and turning them away from God."[9]

The Nicodemites' "hypocrisy and lies" were nothing less than self-idolatry. The perverse adornment of one's own corrupt (albeit "ingenious") "exterior" body to assume a false exterior and the persona of sinfulness for the sake of duplicitous self-protection bought the superficial perception of security at the unacceptable cost of "spiritual honor":

> I must insist upon this point with the greatest vehemence. . . . It is already a great crime to commit an exterior idolatry, to abandon your body, which is the temple of God, to a pollution which the scriptures condemn as much or more than debauchery. And it is not a light offense, to transfer the honor of God to an idol; I call for reverence for the exterior, because it is the sign and witness of spiritual honor.[10]

Luther was arguably more ambiguous on this subject. Pride and honor were common pejoratives in his theology. Yet, while Luther railed against doing the Lord's work "deceitfully," he thought the outer body too corrupt to signify the spirit *openly* (except as its opposite).[11] To drive home this point, however, Calvin began the 1544 edition by quoting from a particularly censorious text: Isaiah 30:9–11. This reappeared later as a coda in the 1551 edition: "For they [the Nicodemites] are a rebellious people, and they are hypocrites; people who will not hear God's Law. Who say to those who see, See not; and to those who consider, Let us not consider things in a straight line, but speak of things that will humor us, and see deceptions."[12]

Palissy's critique of "straight lines" in the *Recepte* can be read in dialogue with Calvin's citation of Isaiah. The potter's canny manipulation of "the exterior" as the "sign and witness of spiritual honor" was linked to events in his own personal history. Thus, he substituted invisibility and artisanal security for the "honor" of frontal resistance ending in the operatic theater of martyrdom. Palissy's mistrust of orthodoxies of all sorts—Roman Catholicism, scholasticism, and Calvinism—was focused by the martyrdom of the master printer and minister Philibert Hamelin, who had been sent by Calvin himself to bring Genevan discipline to Saintonge.

Palissy's sympathy for the hidden style preceded Hamelin's appearance in Saintes. Like the Cathar and Waldensian heretics of pre-Reformation France, Palissy allied himself in his writing with lowly agricultural laborers and country people. It was for their improvement, he said, that the *Recepte* and *Discours* were written. Palissy called his craft the "art of the earth" in part to validate this alliance, as did his "rustic figures." Pottery, made from coarse earth materials by craftsmen one step above common laborers, ranked low in status in the hierarchy of skilled trades. Although he worked within their spheres of influence, Palissy possessed the persona of leveler-artisan-philosopher, not guildsman or citified bourgeois. Palissy considered his art novel and innovative because his creative life developed in the fullest sense in the primitive world, outside of the ancient "scholastic" rules of guild masters. Like Paracelsus, who learned cures from "skilled women" and other unlearned folk healers, Palissy acquired the basics of his trade as an apprentice to the rustic potters of La Chapelle-des-Pots (literally, "Little Church of Pots"), a small artisanal hamlet four kilometers northeast of Saintes. His self-created persona of "paysan de Xaintonge" did not appear in print until after his influential friendship with Hamelin, however.

Though he openly courted wealthy Roman Catholic aristocrats for patronage, he also used heated rhetoric "from below," antithetical to the noble culture he desired to serve. Gerrard Winstanley (b. 1609)—another earth-obsessed Paracelsian natural and political philosopher, with whom Palissy is usefully compared—would have thought him a kindred spirit.[13] Although he worked in Saintes, beginning around 1536–37, and represented himself unambiguously as a "paysan de Xaintonge," Palissy was "a native of Agen in the Agenais," probably born about 1510 (1499 and 1520 are also possible). Agen was a source of refugees to La Rochelle, the isolated coastal island regions of Saintonge during the civil wars, and the Americas as well. Located on the Gironde River in southwestern France, Agen is about seventy-five kilometers southeast of La Rochelle's hinterlands by *pirogue,* or dugout canoe. These long, narrow boats, which reached a length of thirteen meters or more and could be fitted with sails, were the commonest form of river transport in the southwest of France from the early Middle Ages until near the end of the nineteenth century.[14]

Palissy had traveled extensively throughout the southwest years earlier, but it was not until 1536 that he appears in Saintes's town records as an established resident and working artisan.[15] Assuming the public role and professional identity of "paysan de Xaintonge" was thus significant on a number of levels. While Palissy tells us much about his life starting with his arrival at Saintes, he reveals nothing of his early years in Agen and elsewhere. His birthplace is never mentioned; it was learned posthumously (Agen was noted as Palissy's place of birth by his jailers in the Bastille).[16] Willful forgetfulness and elision of his personal history conformed with Palissy's spiritual and artisanal rebirth in Saintonge as a "new man," Reformed natural philosopher, and master potter. While this "new man" identity authenticated Palissy's religious credentials for rusticity, reinventing his personal history would add value to his "rustique figulines," books, and laboratory demonstrations. His scientific performances were paid for by Parisian patrons amused by Nature's "rough," exotic qualities, and were attended by competitors from the international scientific community. Palissy's new identity also had strong religious and political connotations for a large audience of literate co-religionists across France, who identified rural Saintonge with the *rustique* "New World" style of Huguenot culture.

Palissy's artisanal career began in Agen. He worked there as a glass painter, primarily for churches. Palissy hints that he changed trades for economic reasons. Pottery was in demand in Saintonge: there was a growing need for ceramic containers owing to the popularity at home and abroad of eau-de-vie distilled in Cognac.[17] Meanwhile, church construction declined dramatically in the provinces, so demand for stained windows had diminished.

As a glass painter, Palissy spent much of his working life on the road, as did the eighteenth-century glazier Jacques-Louis Ménétra, who worked side by side with the painters to materialize designs into glass. Palissy wrote that demand for traditional glassmaking and painting had diminished in his customary markets in "Périgord, Limousin, Saintonge, Angoulême, Gascogny, Bearn, and Bigorre, where glass[making] became so mechanized that it was sold by street-criers in all the villages, even by street-criers selling drapery and scrap metal, so much so that maker and seller alike had a hard time earning a living."[18] Palissy clearly objected to the "modernization" of his craft.

As an enthusiastic newly converted Protestant, recently accused of iconoclasm, Palissy no longer wished to produce liturgical ornamentation to adorn the same Roman Catholic churches he now sought to destroy. The cross-fertilization of skills also gave him a practical advantage over his competitors in ceramics. Palissy's understanding of the optics of glass and enamel glazes and the construction and operation of highly specialized wood-fired kilns and alchemic crucibles facilitated the innovation of new pottery glazes, the subject of his essay in the *Discours* "On the art of the Earth, its Usefulness, on Enamels and Fire." This was the technical impetus behind his shift to production of new glazes discovered in natural-philosophical experimentation.

Beginning in Agen, before becoming fully engaged in pottery experiments and production at Saintes, Palissy applied his glass-painting skills to survey maps. He called this practice drawing landscape *pourtraits;* hence, maps were related to the fortress *pourtrait.* Like fortress drawings, these geometric renderings were drawn to scale, worked with "my compass and ruler." These two basic drafting tools, emblemata of artisanal competence and control, were very commonly depicted on the maps themselves.[19] Palissy's *pourtraiture* proved a lucrative supplement for glass painting prior to 1536. It also supported him while he learned to make pottery in Saintonge, where he sought patronage for his innovative lead glazes. "People thought I was more skilled in painting than I actually was," he wrote; "this led to my being called upon to make diagrams for litigations. Now, when I had such commissions, I was very well paid, and I also kept up with my glassmaking for a long time, until I was sure I could make a living in the art of clay."[20]

Most commissions for these precise, geometric renderings came from the legal community, one of the few groups in early modern France able to pay in cash. In 1543,

Palissy worked as a court draftsman on litigation involving real estate, when he was chosen by bureaucrats representing François I to serve the state as an official *pour-traitist*, surveyor, and mapmaker. Palissy drew maps for administration of the gabelle, the hotly contested tax on the sea salt cultivated and exported through La Rochelle after it was extracted from the *marais* of coastal Saintonge.[21]

Palissy's maps focused on assigning taxable boundaries to the vast cell structure that honeycombed the great salt flats of Marennes, which had been cultivated on a large scale since the Middle Ages. Palissy's connection with the *gabelle* was a source of personal conflict. By 1543, the marshlands contiguous to Saujon and the Île d'Arvert were quickly becoming centers of Reformed evangelism and conversion, and the inhabitants, already angered by the new tax, added religion to economics as clear reasons they preferred to remain unmapped by the state. Obscurity had always been the key to security for the coastal communities of Saintonge, never more so than now. Yet it was Palissy's task, and that of the tax official and scribe who accompanied him, to map territories along the coast. Palissy's maps were instrumental in instituting the gabelle, which led to violent revolts throughout the coastal region. This galvanized coastal inhabitants politically, making them even more sympathetic to evangelical preaching against the official state religion. The gabelle changed Palissy indirectly as well. Tax rebellions brought Montmorency to Saintonge. In 1548, the Constable suppressed a revolt over the gabelle on the coast, and Palissy met the future patron who changed his life.

At the same time as he mapped their geography, Palissy came into extended contact with inhabitants from the hinterlands outside of Saintes. Many islanders were also skilled artisans who had recently undergone (or were undergoing) their conversion to the embryonic Saintongeais Reformation. When Palissy converted from glassmaker to potter between 1536 and 1543, he simultaneously set out on the path to religious conversion. Following Palissy's conversion experience, adherence to rural Huguenot culture, and return to Saintes from the islands, he was unable to find further employment in the Catholic and royalist courts. He was reduced to poverty and began the search for new patrons, a process that linked him with both Antoine de Pons and Montmorency. At this complex moment of artisanal and religious conversion, and economic reversal, Palissy turned his attention with renewed vigor to research into enamel glazes and pottery production based on what he had learned from folk potters in La-Chapelle-des-Pots. Not only did he learn the basics of his trade from local potters, but also the formula and firing process for translucent lead- (as opposed to the more opaque tin-) glazed earthenware.

Lead was key to Palissy's experiments to perfect translucent glazes from 1536 through the 1550s.[22] Innovative work in his new craft helped Palissy acquire influential local Huguenot *noblesse d'épée* (Pons) and Catholic royal (Montmorency) patronage. This was protection of a much higher order than that of the bourgeois *avocats* and *no-*

blesse de robe judges who rejected him on religious grounds. Ascent in status, both as a rustic artisan and "paysan de Xaintonge" and as a royal *créature* would later save his life when he was arrested by the *parlement* of Bordeaux in 1562 and finally charged with heresy. Catherine made sure her talented Huguenot *paysan*'s life was spared in 1572 as well. He was warned beforehand of the Saint Bartholomew's Day Massacre and was able to escape.

Having carefully cultivated rusticity, it was logical for the potter to adopt the "medieval custom" of the countryside, as Euan Cameron has described the heretical practice of the rural Waldensians. The custom of the countryside was pragmatic: "to deny heresy as far as possible to save one's skin, if one had not first succeeded in escaping capture. In the late sixteenth century, defense and not martyrdom was still the norm."[23] Consider, also, the impressive lineage of Palissy's patrons among the great Protestant nobility of Saintonge. We have seen the network of association of the court of Antoine de Pons and Anne de Parthenay, which reached back through marriage, religious, and patronage ties to Marguerite of Angoulême, sister of François I, queen of Navarre in France, and Renée of Ferrara's court in Italy. These nobles were Protestant sympathizers. Yet they pursued careful, often secret strategies, especially in Italy during the Roman Inquisition, where the spread of Nicodemism found both sympathy and learned theorists. Although Calvin and de Bèze found refuge in Ferrara, after France, Calvin's anti-Nicodemite propaganda targeted Venice in particular, and northern Italy in general.[24]

Palissy focused on Philibert Hamelin's role in the potter's personal history in "my town" of Saintes and "my country" of Saintonge when he recounted how local artisans organized in the earliest years of the Saintongeais Reformation and maintained the faith in Saintonge from 1540 to 1562. Hamelin's story was central to Palissy's "little narration," his "History . . . not of all, but a part of the beginning of the [Reformed] church of Saintes." This chapter was placed just before "De la ville de forteresse" in the *Recepte*. As the only text called overtly a "History" in the *Recepte* or *Discours,* it merits close reading, especially in relation to the final chapter. The word "overtly" is chosen carefully. All Palissy's oeuvre—written and material—is, in effect, a composite of natural, political, and religious history. Unlike his other writing, however, the "little narrative" was specifically intended to contribute to a new Huguenot historiography of the civil wars.

The history of Saintes was to be "put into writing," by Palissy, who actually *experienced* it, "so that it will live in perpetual memory to help those who come after us."[25] Calvin laid the groundwork for Palissy's sentiments in the *Institutes.* He argued that the pure doctrine must be written for posterity and with exactitude, so that "it should neither perish through forgetfulness nor vanish through error nor be corrupted by the audacity of men."[26] Explicit reference to the relation between the act of writing history (*mettre par escrit*) as experienced—following the Paracelsian critique of scholasticism's distancing project—and the fate of individual and collective memory (*perpetuelle memoire*) underscored discursive tensions inherent in Palissy's artisanal project.[27]

This was complicated by the need to write artisanal history simultaneously as family and *oral* history. Here, memory was diffused from master to apprentice, by example and word of mouth, in domestic contexts of familial, face-to-face interaction. But Palissy's compulsion to *write* history was also informed by two competing influences. First, his was a culture in which the widespread diffusion of printed and written materials already began to subvert the authority of traditional memory systems surviving since classical times.[28] Second, Palissy and his artisan *compagnons* had every reason to believe that they would not survive long enough to guarantee dissemination of their stories by word of mouth. The "little narration," then, was intended as a "perpetual" safeguard against the state's demonstrated ability to extinguish local sectarian memory by violence. Palissy was hopeful, however, that his written history of the early beginnings of the Saintongeais Reformation would survive to be disseminated internationally by Protestantism's underground book publishing and distribution network.

Palissy hints that he might have written the "little narration" expecting that it would be included in Crespin's martyrology, a "living," local prosopography of the progress of the Reformation in provincial France during the civil wars. It did not appear in Crespin, however. Given his unorthodox interpretation of the martyrdom of Philibert Hamelin, the tacit support for Nicodemism embodied in his critique of the straight line, and his contentious relationship with the Calvinist hierarchy, the decision to exclude Palissy's text from Crespin's orthodox Genevan martyrology is understandable. Ultimately, Crespin wrote a short biography of Hamelin, which Calvin himself was pleased to recommend to the faithful in a pastoral letter to Saintonge. Hamelin's story also warranted inclusion in de Bèze's *Histoire ecclésiastique des églises reformées au royaume de France*.[29] Did Palissy's implicit critique of Calvin's ideal of martyrdom in the *Recepte* reflect, in part, bitterness at being ignored as the official historian of his great friend and mentor's martyrology? Did he perceive his famously "inelegant, rustic" writing style as the reason for the decision to overlook his authority?

❧ Hamelin's Story ❧

Philibert Hamelin was a native of Chinon, Touraine, who first appeared in Saintonge as early as 1545. Nothing is known of him before that time. Hamelin's story is the second of four contiguous narratives in the "petit narré," which are arranged chronologically, with Hamelin's following the story of the three "Lutheran monks" who evangelized the coastal islands systematically during the 1540s. The three former monastics were the Franciscan René Mace of Gemozac; the shadowy Dominican Hubert Robert (known to Palissy as "frère Robin", "the preacher" of Saint-Denis-d'Oléron); and the Celestine Nicolle Maurel.[30] Chapter 4 will show how the heretical monks evangelized in secret, and carried the charismatic, interior, pietistic style of Germanic Protestant religiosity to the artisans of the coastal islands. This hidden style of worship was reestablished by Palissy as a lay practice after Hamelin's death, and it endured among poor Huguenot artisans in the southwest. The "petit narré" also recorded the captivity and symbolically loaded torture of the three monks and "frère Robin's" mysterious escape from prison in 1546. Robin thus escaped the torture and execution suffered by his colleagues Mace and Maurel.

Philibert Hamelin was ordained a Roman Catholic priest when he arrived in Saintes in the year the three monks were arrested for heresy in the coastal islands, suggesting he may have belonged to the tradition of heretical priests or monks who fled to secluded parts of the region for refuge. Hamelin converted to Protestantism almost immediately, which supports this theory, and he was ordained a Protestant minister in 1545. The hotbed of Reformation activity was then in the islands, and Hamelin soon left the small cadre of Calvinists in Saintes to help evangelize the Île d'Oléron. In 1546, he was arrested for heresy for the first time, with another heretical priest from Arvert and a group of recent converts. Hamelin was taken back to Saintes where he was imprisoned at the *siège episcopal* and threatened with torture. Fearful, he publicly denied having been converted to Protestantism and the crime of heresy, and he was soon set free. By Calvin's definition, Hamelin was thus a failure and a Nicodemite.[31]

By 1547, Hamelin had set up shop as a master printer in Geneva, a status suggesting that he had been trained in this notoriously heretical trade in his native Touraine before arriving in Saintes. Going first to Saintes and then the islands made sense for a master printer under the noble patronage and protection of Antoine de Pons, who sought to fill a need in Saintonge. Hamelin's immediate successor in the trade, Barthélemy Berton, followed the same geographical path under Pons.

In Geneva, Hamelin published four important titles under his own imprint, and probably several more in collaboration with other theological publishers, including Crespin. The most significant of these books was Hamelin's French translation of the Old and New Testaments, which was published in five volumes in 1552, followed by a two-volume edition in 1556.[32] He also published an edition of Calvin's *Commentaires*, as well as the 1554 edition of *L'Institution chrétienne*. If survival is any indication, Hamelin's edition of Clément Marot's psalter, the *Oraisons sainctes*, was his most widely disseminated title.[33] The output of Hamelin's press was distinctive in three ways: first, his titles were published only in French, not in Latin, indicative of his interest in converting the country people of Saintonge, and in popular evangelism generally; second, the books were printed in the smallest practical formats ("petit in-12°" or "petit in-quarto"), to facilitate distribution in rural areas through colportage, which

Hamelin pioneered in Saintonge; and third, Palissy undoubtedly received his copies of these basic texts of Genevan Calvinist orthodoxy directly from Hamelin's hands.[34]

Hamelin had not left Saintes in 1546 to settle in Geneva for the sole purpose of establishing a Calvinist publishing house. Guilty of dissembling his faith to save his skin while under arrest in Saintes, Hamelin sought ideological reindoctrination and repurification in the ways of Calvin's "straight line." He could then return to Saintonge and redeem himself. After the destruction of the Lutheran monastic cell in 1546, Protestants in the islands appealed for Geneva to install a new minister. In 1555, Hamelin returned to take up the ministry and work as an itinerant colporteur of his tiny books. Hamelin and Palissy have been documented as being together in 1555, when the two worked as surveyors on the private estate of Anne de Parthenay's sister, Antoinette d'Aubeterre, the wife of Jean de Parthenay-l'Archevêque, seigneur de Soubise.

Palissy played an essential role in Hamelin's return, augmenting his distinctive status and personal religious authority at every level of local Huguenot society. On the one hand, Palissy functioned as a middleman between Hamelin and local Huguenot noble patrons (with whom the printer had had little direct contact since 1546); and on the other, he was Hamelin's sponsor and organizer among the rural poor, and especially the skilled artisans, who together comprised the vast majority of Hamelin's congregation in Saintonge. This demonstrates the scope of Palissy's networking structure and the strength of his commitment to this fellow Huguenot artisan—like himself an itinerant and a lover of books and of the countryfolk—whom he had met ten years earlier. Palissy walked Saintonge with Hamelin as his close personal friend, protector, fellow artisan, and religious confidant. He was keenly aware of the intense feelings of guilt and desire for self-sacrifice that accompanied Hamelin on his return from Geneva in 1555. He also had a foreboding sense of Hamelin's plans to relinquish the spiral line that had saved his life the first time around. "Because he lived in Geneva for a good long time after his imprisonment," Palissy wrote in the "petit narré":

> and had his faith and doctrine augmented in Geneva, he always had a guilty conscience for having dissimulated in the confession he made in this town [of Saintes], and wanting to make up for his mistake, he strove everywhere he went to incite the people to get ministers and raise some form of church, and he went thus to the country of France, having some servants, who sold Bibles, and other books printed at his printing press, for he . . . was a printer. In doing this, he came sometimes to this town, and went also to Arvert. Now he was so righteous and of such great zeal that, even though he was not a healthy man, he would never ride a horse . . . and . . . he carried no sword in his belt, but only a simple staff in his hand, and he went all alone, without fear.[35]

From 1555 until 1557, Hamelin traveled back and forth between Geneva, Saintes, and Arvert, with a few excursions to Royan and Mornac. He returned to Geneva to restock the books that he and his "servants" carried on their shoulders in colporteur's sacks into La Rochelle's Protestant hinterlands. As printer, minister, and colporteur, Hamelin began to rebuild a Reformed church in "some form" in the islands after the bloodletting of 1546. Hamelin's success was based on his ability to leave the walled enceinte of the town and integrate his preaching into the work rhythms of country artisans and farm laborers. Rather than adopting a tone of sacerdotal distance, Hamelin evangelized in a low-key conversational style, arriving in the fields or workshops during breaks for meals. Palissy followed Hamelin closely in his evangelical style, and he echoes his mentor in the *Recepte* in chiding immobile Huguenot pastors who avoided the countryfolk and stayed in town near their churches. For Hamelin and Palissy, their church was not some specific building but anywhere the Word was heard or read.[36]

From Geneva's perspective, although "the Lutheran heresy" had been flourishing in Saintonge since the 1540s, Hamelin's was the first authentic Reformed church in the region, built on the transparent foundation of the ideological "straight line" of Church discipline by a minister indoctrinated by Calvin himself. De Bèze, writing an official version of Hamelin's experience in his *Histoire ecclésiastique,* proclaimed that the coastal islands of Saintonge were places where neither religion nor culture had ever existed before. Hamelin's task, de Bèze wrote, was to subdue Saintonge's "people of the sea," who were "nearly savage."[37] Yet these people and places created a form of culture and religion that the opportunistic Palissy emulated and further expanded. There, he developed his rustic style of artisanry, writing on security, and natural philosophy. De Bèze's personal distance and cultural alienation from the rural Huguenots of Saintonge was shared in La Rochelle, where corporate identity turned on a different kind of emulation, namely, becoming the little Geneva of France. Conversely, a sense of distance and alienation from the Calvinist orthodoxy of Geneva and La Rochelle pervaded Palissy's "savage and rustic" writings. The dead and exiled Lutheran monks had been his friends, mentors, and fellow artisans. Palissy was careful to include them in his history as Hamelin's predecessors, the revered founders and martyrs of the "primitive" Church of Saintonge, but Crespin and de Bèze did not accord their conventicles the status of Protestant churches, contending that they had operated in secret and their members were "savage."

Hamelin was arrested a second time in 1557. The authorities discovered that he had baptized a child at Arvert, after openly preaching heresy to a large assembly of coastal Huguenots. The official account of Hamelin's arrest in de Bèze's *Histoire* is notably theatrical; in effect, this passion play was represented as an inversion and erasure of Hamelin's "mistaken" dissimulation of 1546.

The inhabitants of Arvert had hurried to hide the minister at the home of a local "gentleman" when the police came to make the arrest. According to de Bèze's story, although well hidden and impossible to find, Hamelin emerged from his hiding place, went out openly "before those who searched for him, and saluted them all in a joyous fashion." Palissy's "little narrative" recalls no such heroic action or speech, only that the "gens-d'armes" trailed Hamelin and captured him at the gentleman's house in Arvert.[38] The two accounts agree that Hamelin was returned to the same prison in Saintes where, eleven years before, he had lamented dissimulating and committing the crime of Nicodemism.

Hamelin did not dissimulate this time. The tribunal at Saintes was composed of six principal judges. They determined that inasmuch as Hamelin was an ordained priest, his prosecution fell under the higher jurisdiction of the *parlement* of Bordeaux. On April 12, 1557, Hamelin was therefore transferred to Bordeaux under an arrest warrant. Once there, he underwent the rigorous tortures reserved for heretical ministers. According to all accounts, Hamelin refused to recant. Finally, Hamelin was marched to the courtyard fronting Bordeaux Cathedral, where he was strangled by an executioner to conclude the public spectacle. His remains were then burned on a pyre.[39]

Palissy was traumatized. The "petit narré" is unsparing in the raw intensity of its author's emotional distress, spiritual confusion, frustration, and anger. Palissy was so distraught that he openly defied his own secretive rules of stoicism at the core of artisanal security. Just before Hamelin was transferred from Saintes to Bordeaux, the potter took the grave risk of bringing his personal association with Hamelin's heretical activities to the attention of the local courts. Thus, Palissy himself stood before the same judges and magistrates at Saintes who brought Palissy to trial five years later to plead Hamelin's case and, in a very real sense, his own:

> I was completely astonished how the men could have sat in judgment of death over him, seeing how they knew him well and had heard his holy conversation; because I was certain, after the truth was told, that he would be released from the prisons of Xaintes, I took the bold step (inasmuch as those were perilous days) to go and remonstrate with six of the principal judges and magistrates of this town of Xaintes that they had imprisoned a prophet, an angel of God, sent to announce his word and pronounce his judgment of condemnation to men at the end times, [and] to assure them that in the eleven years I had known Philibert Hamelin he had lived such a holy life that it seemed to me that other men were devils when viewed next to him. . . . Finally . . . while it is true that they did not actually kill him, no more than Pilate and Judas [did] Jesus Christ, they delivered him into the hands of those who they knew perfectly well would put him to death. And, to better succeed in washing their hands of their burden, they contended that he was a priest of the Roman Church, and for that reason he would be sent to Bordeaux under the good and sure guard of a provost marshal.[40]

Hamelin had returned to Saintes with the intention of taking "the straight road" that Calvin himself commanded he "consider" during Hamelin's ideological rehabilitation in Geneva between 1547 and 1555. Palissy thus witnessed the murder of his dearest friend and mentor; a visible saint whose "works were certain witness that he was a child of God and directly elect."⁴¹ Geneva's command that he make himself visible had thus literally squandered the time on earth of a divine messenger, and the death of this "angel of God" was certain to forestall final judgment. When captured, Philibert Hamelin was caught in the act of preaching "end times" from Revelation. For Palissy, God's "prophet" who returned to open the seals of the apocalypse that "these evil days" of religious war had initiated had been martyred. Now Hamelin's artisan followers in Saintonge waited patiently for another divine messenger, and to find other ways to initiate the cleansing of earthly matter in final things. Indirectly accusing Calvin, de Bèze, and Crespin of complicity in Hamelin's murder, Palissy ends "The Essence of the Mind of Man"—a chapter that precedes the "History of the Church of Saintes"—with lines that lead into, and can be read as his epigram for, the "petit narré" and "De la ville de forteresse" to follow:

> Be warned that if you return to your original simplicity, you can be assured that you will have enemies and be persecuted all the days of your life if, *by direct lines,* you would follow and stand up for the quarrel of God; because these are the promises written originally in the Old and New Testaments. Take refuge therefore in your chief, protector and captain, Our Lord Jesus Christ, who in his own time and place will know very well how to avenge all the injuries that he has suffered, and yours too.⁴²

Following the capture, trial, torture, and execution of Philibert Hamelin in 1557, it seems unclear whom Palissy and other unnamed Saintongeais artisan followers of the "angel of God" loathed and feared more: the Roman Catholic clergy, police, and judges, at both Saintes and Bordeaux, who had carried out the execution, or Calvin, who had set up the guilt-ridden Hamelin to die a martyr's death. For the devastated Palissy, Geneva sacrificed Hamelin's artisanal ingenuity and industriousness in exchange for a show of ideological force that led to an operatic and wasteful death (presaging the fall of La Rochelle seventy years later). This dynamic of ambiguous *esmotions* was directed at both Catholic and Protestant orthodoxies and inscribed in the potter's renderings of the serpentine line in material form.

Palissy failed, "after the truth was told," to return his master's life to the people. "Holy conversation" was strangled. In its place, the pious potter constructed silent martyrologies on crooked paths running throughout everyday life.

❧ The "end times" ❧

Hamelin's death ushered in an artisans' "interregnum" in which Palissy, now acting as Hamelin's apostle, took up the complex role of lay *artisan-prédicateur* in the absence of a formally ordained Genevan minister. The "interregnum" did not genuinely terminate for Hamelin's (now his "apprentice" Palissy's) artisan assembly, when Hamelin's replacement, André de Mazières (also "de la Place") was sent to the region by the Paris Consistory.

Palissy's "narré" complained that Mazières—his competitor from Geneva and not a craftsman—was concerned primarily with the spiritual life of the local Protestant *noblesse*. He was charged with spending far too much time in châteaux and not enough time in Hamelin's preferred places to evangelize: impoverished peasant farmsteads and artisan workshops. The root of the problem with Mazières lay in the poverty of the Reformed church of Saintonge. "It was a pitiful thing," wrote Palissy, "but the power to maintain the ministers was not there; in respect to de La Place, during his time here, he was maintained on the side, paid for by those gentlemen who summoned him often."[43] Palissy was unwilling to relinquish the life-threatening mantel of lay ministerial authority passed down to him by Hamelin, even *after* the *parlement* of Bordeaux executed Mazières later in 1557. Palissy's mistrust of Mazières may have been owing in part to the Parisian's ambiguous role during Hamelin's imprisonment at Bordeaux. Although Mazières was credited with rushing directly to the prison to console and fortify the condemned Hamelin, it is probable that he had received instructions from Geneva to prevent Hamelin from recanting again.[44]

Claude de La Boissière arrived in 1557 to take Mazières's place. Unlike his predecessor, La Boissière was cautiously accepted by Palissy and his followers as a shepherd of the *menu* people. Palissy had acquired a powerful hold on local religious life during the artisanal interregnum following Hamelin's death, however, and he projected his growing lay authority onto La Boissière, imposing a vow of poverty on the newcomer to ensure that he did not follow Mazières's elitist example. "Fearing that this was nothing but a means of corrupting our ministers," Palissy wrote, "*one* counseled Monsieur de La Boissière not to leave town without permission in order to serve the nobility." Claude was forced by his flock to became an anchoritelike ascetic, in Christ's (and Hamelin's) tradition of poverty and humility, to conform with the worldview of his congregation. Palissy distanced La Boissière from Mazières and asserted his control as a kind of spiritual jailer. "By this means," he wrote, "the poor man was shut in like a prisoner; he frequently ate potatoes and drank water for his dinner . . . because there were very few resources from our assembly . . . from which to pay him his wages."[45]

La Boissière's ministry under Palissy's control (or so the potter would have us believe) ushered in a new and flourishing period of Protestant theological and social asceticism and Huguenot artisanal hegemony in Saintonge, extending ultimately to Saintes itself. This process was, as we shall see, roughly simultaneous with that taking place in La Rochelle, the effect of whose Protestant coup d'état resonated outward to the hinterlands, aided by a set of fortuitous political circumstances. At the same time, there were certain personnel changes that weakened the intimidating local apparatus of religious repression. These changes ended by putting Protestantism in Saintes in the ascendant, concurrent with that already established in the islands.

First, two energetic local persecutors of rural Reformed assemblies, the bishop of Saintes, Tristan de Bizet, and the *sénéchal,* Charles Guitard des Brousses, were called to Toulouse, leaving a local power vacuum that the state bureaucracy moved slowly to fill, and that Saintongeais Huguenots quickly exploited. Second, the Édit d'Amboise was instituted in late 1559. This more "liberal" proclamation reversed harsh punishments instituted by the Édits de Compiègne (1557), under which Hamelin had been executed, and of Blois (1559), which specified the death penalty for the state crimes of heresy and illegal religious assembly. The Édit d'Amboise reduced regional tensions (at least from the Protestant perspective) while still allowing core rituals of Reformed theology—including those of assembly, communion, and especially psalmody—to be brought out into the open for the first time, in contact with Catholic-dominated public space. A new golden (or primitive) age was heralded for Saintes's Reformed Church. Palissy wrote that the town had now been largely converted, psalms were heard everywhere in the street, and "in those days, there was prayer in the town of Xaintes every day from one end to the other."[46]

By March 1561, as a result of this confluence of events, the Reformation in Saintes had achieved unprecedented success in terms of numbers and social prestige, as well as military and political power. In recognition, a Huguenot Synod was held in Saintes that month, followed by a national assembly in April. Thirty-eight ministers now led Reformed congregations in the region, and La Boissière wrote Calvin asking for fifty more. Saintongeais divinity students were sent abroad to Geneva or to Protestant academies in La Rochelle and Saumur before returning to take up the many available pulpits.[47]

Such evangelical success did not endure long, according to the dominant pattern presented by French Reformation history, which was distinguished by reversal and mimetic violence, not continuity. Parallel to the process that afflicted Rochelais confessional competition between 1517 and 1628, the Huguenots of Saintonge gratuitously abused their hard-won recent victories by savaging the remnants of the weakened Catholic opposition, making inevitable the state's devastating retaliation. Thus, the Huguenots' success and subsequent abuse of power did not signify victory but instead the beginning of the end. Unlike La Rochelle, where a great fortress and formidable fleet enabled the Rochelais by dint of sheer military power to extend their revolution for more than two generations after the Protestant coup d'état in 1568, Saintonge had no dominant or centralizing *place de sûreté.* Instead, the very success of the Saintongeais Reform made it vulnerable to counterattack and guaranteed its defeat as an overt force.

Protestant military forces completed the work the evangelists had started. By May 1562, they had overwhelmed the last of the Catholic resistance. Huguenot violence in the southwest then began openly and in earnest, starting with acts of iconoclasm in Saintes. In June 1562, Protestant gangs sacked the churches of Saint-Pierre and Saint-Eutrope. Emboldened Huguenots in twenty other towns, including Marennes, Cognac, Agen, and even parts of Bordeaux, seat of the regional *parlement,* committed similar acts of aggression against symbols of Catholicism.

Arrogant attacks on the Roman Church, its ritual instruments, and its priests drove local Catholic officials to an apocalyptic chorus of their own, demanding assistance from Paris. Protestant evangelical and military successes had subverted the Catholic Church's ability to inspire awe and fear, and hence its ability to support itself. Saintongeais peasants and artisans simply ceased paying "the tithes and duties of the Church," without which the already wounded apparatus of Catholicism in Saintes and the countryside—especially the relatively prosperous local clerical hierarchy and monasteries—would be forced to fall back upon their own resources or cease to function altogether. Little did they know, or care, that local Reformed congregations such as Palissy's had also stopped paying their minister's salaries or limited them severely.

Here is a typical complaint to Paris from the regional official M. de Burie, lieutenant-general of Guyenne, in a letter dated June 10, 1561, to the newly crowned Charles IX:

> For it is those from this new sect, Sire, who daily make themselves masters of the principal churches and in most of these places they have torn down the altars, holy-water fonts and baptismal fountains, burned the missals and church ornaments, and prevented, Sire, any services from taking place; they boast that they have already begun, in certain quarters, not to pay the *dixmes* [church tithes] and *droictz de l'Eglise* [church duties], and they boast openly, Sire, that they won't pay any more taxes, nor their debts to *seigneurs,*[48] they endeavor day after day to become the strongest in the towns, and they are determined to steal church bells to melt down for artillery, and the number of these people, Sire, increases every day, to the great sadness of the good and loyal subjects of Your Majesty.[49]

It was during this riotous period that Palissy was accused of an act of iconoclasm, resulting in his arrest on March 24, 1563, after the Catholics finally returned to power. Palissy had come to the attention of the authorities in 1557 when he spoke in defense of Hamelin, and a warrant was issued for his arrest in 1558 for his activities as a lay preacher and organizer during the interregnum, but this was the first time his arrest and imprisonment are officially recorded.[50] In the trial transcript from the *parlement* of Bordeaux, Palissy testified:

> that the day that the pillagers . . . were at the great altar of the church of Xaintes, where they broke and demolished the woodwork and facing, he had gone, [openly], to the place called la Chappelle [*sic*] [des Pots] where he commonly [went] to get his potter's clay, to work and labor at his trade.

That outside of the assemblies that gathered at Xaintes, he did not wish to leave nor did he venture outside of his house because some of the populace yelled at him to take up arms.[51]

After Palissy was captured in Saintes and taken to prison in Bordeaux, his workshop and laboratory were destroyed, by command, he said, of the numerous enemies whom he accused of persecuting him in his brief but profane testimony. With a record of heresy dating back to the 1540s, Palissy would have met Hamelin's fate had it not been for his appeal to Montmorency in a letter from prison. He wrote his patron that work on the Constable's grotto, begun in 1555, was not yet completed and that his workshop and laboratory had been sacked. Wanting his new grotto completed, Montmorency intervened with the help of Antoine de Pons and others to obtain Palissy's release. Palissy's letter shows that he almost certainly lied when he claimed in court that he was at La Chapelle-des-Pots when the acts of iconoclasm took place in Saintes. He refused to deny his involvement to Montmorency, claiming only that he had been justified. Palissy had become a victimizer, though he tried to dissimulate his involvement to save his own skin.[52]

On June 19, 1561, the archbishop of Bordeaux wrote the king to raise an alarm far more likely to motivate a military response from Paris than iconoclasm and the still merely local nonpayment of Church *dixmes*. He reported a virtual military invasion led by the fifty "ministres de l'étranger" requested from Geneva by Claude de La Boissière. The shrewd archbishop threatened implicitly that if local beneficiaries were not paid, neither would Charles IX be:

> The ministers are in great number. They come daily from Geneva and because of all their arms and ammunition, it is no longer within our power to stop them. Sire, most of the beneficiaries [*bénéficiers*] of your said dukedom are despairing that they will ever enjoy any of the benefits that rightly are theirs—because they are withheld for the said ministers and used to support them—which loss they would bear patiently were it not that with this loss they not only see the danger that would befall the monarchy but also the ruin and desolation of the Church of God, so long preserved in your kingdom, and they would be deprived of the means to make any subvention to you and so would be unable to show the obedience that they have in their hearts.[53]

Palissy denounced the controversy surrounding the *dixmes* as an example of the hypocrisy and avariciousness of Roman Catholicism. In the "petit narré," he associated Catholicism with the rich and powerful. The courts were their primary instruments of hypocrisy, thievery, and repression of Palissy's "plowmen," his rustic yeoman of the spirit:

Would you like to really understand, how the Roman churchmen said their so-called prayers hypocritically and maliciously? . . . Most townspeople in those days asked for ministers—from their priests or *fermiers* [tax collectors], or others—or they wouldn't pay the *dixmes:* nothing made the priests more furious than that, and this was very strange. In those days, things happened that could really make you laugh and cry all at once: since some *fermiers* were enemies of the religion [i.e., anti-Protestant], when they saw the reports [of nonpayment], the *fermiers* went to the ministers to beg them to come and exhort the people, where there were *fermiers* [collecting taxes]: in order that the *dixmes* would be paid. When they couldn't get what they wanted from the ministers, they asked the church elders. I never laughed so hard while crying at the same time, as when I heard said that the *procureur* [prosecutor] who was [also] the criminal court clerk, even as he wrote down the charges against those of the religion [Protestant], had prayed just a short time before the church in the parish where he was *fermier* was ransacked: do we know whether, when he was praying, he was a better Christian, than when he wrote accusations against those of the religion [Protestant]: doubtless he was as good a Christian when he wrote out the charges as when he said his prayers, seeing that he did not say them except to mock God and possess the grains and fruits of the plowmen.[54]

The reversal came in October 1562, when Louis II de Bourbon, the duc de Montpensier, was sent by Charles IX to end to the outbreak of heresy, rebellion, and repression of Catholicism. Montpensier defeated Protestant forces in Saintonge, returning the recently victorious sect to its accustomed subordinate status, thus setting the stage for mimetic acts of revenge by Catholics for Huguenot atrocities. Duras's and La Rochefoucault's armies were overwhelmed, and thousands of Protestant troops retreated north to La Rochelle. Saintes, where Palissy was in hiding, and where his home, shop, and laboratory were under the fragile protection of Montmorency, was overrun and looted by the invading Catholic forces. Troops and Catholic clergymen representing the duc de Montpensier entered Saintes to take control and perform the obligatory rituals of atrocity on the town's few remaining Huguenots.

The best account of the "end times" in Saintes is Palissy's "little narrative." Palissy did not blame the Catholic thirst for revenge on the earlier Huguenot atrocities in Saintes (which he elided from the text), but rather on the dissimulating Catholic "gens de bien." These "wicked" hypocrites had been "constrained to act like good men" when the Huguenots were on top. But these were the *true* dissimulators and victimizers of the pious, whose violence was motivated by profit alone, not sacred purification. Palissy's poor and industrious artisans, notwithstanding their participation in well-documented atrocities, were reinvented as innocent victims of demonic possession and murderous materialism, which reversed the process of purification begun in the town by the primitive Huguenots of Saintes's brief golden age:

The fruit of our little Church had grown so well that the wicked were constrained to act like good men [*gens de bien*]: however their hypocrisy has since become amply manifested and well known: for when they were free to do evil, they displayed outwardly what was hidden inside of their miserable breasts: they committed such miserable acts that I shudder at the memory of the times that they rose up to cause dispersion, destruction, loss, and ruin for those of the Reformed Church. To counter [*obvier*] their horrible and accursed tyrannies, I withdrew myself secretly into my house, so as not to see the murders, disavowals, and ransackings that they committed in the countryside: and as I was hidden in my house for about two months, it seemed to me that hell had been split open [*défoncé*] and that all of its diabolical spirits were set loose and entered into the town of Xaintes: whereas in place of the psalms, hymns, and all the decent words of edification and good example that I had heard a short time before, I heard nothing but blasphemies, tirades, threats, tumults, all [sorts of] horrible and dissolute words, [and] wanton and detestable songs, in such a manner that it seemed to me that all the virtue and sanctity of the earth were choked [*estouffée*] and extinguished: for certain young devils emerged from the Château de Taillebourg, who committed more havoc than the devils of old.

They entered into the town, accompanied by certain priests, having drawn swords in their hands, yelling, where are they? They wanted to cut everyone's throat with their own hands, and so they attacked with swords raised, though there was no resistance: because those of the Reformed Church were all gone: however, just to do evil, they found a Parisian in the street, who was thought to have money: they killed him, without resistance, and as was their custom, they stripped him down to his shirt before he was even dead. After that, they went from house to house, stealing, ravaging, taunting, laughing, mocking, and making lascivious merriment and [saying] blasphemous words against God and man . . . they mocked God. . . . In those days, there were certain esteemed people in prison [i.e., the local Huguenot leaders], that when the [church] canons passed by the prison they called out mockingly, the Lord will assist you, and told them, or said to their faces, [Lord] come and get me, take up this quarrel: and many others struck them with a cudgel, saying, the Lord bless you.[55]

This lurid passage is particularly interesting for the subterranean perspective Palissy adopted in recording for posterity the reversal of Saintes's former Edenic place in providential history. How did the "inventor" of "the art of the earth" imagine the end of the earth? Peering out surreptitiously from inside Saintes's hollow stone town walls, which enclosed his workshop and hiding place, Palissy wrote that war's malefactors had split open the earth's exterior shell, unearthing "l'enfer." This violent process unleashed the diabolical evil barely contained underneath ("hidden inside their miserable chests"), disturbingly close to the fragile skin of the town, so "all of its diabolical spirits were set loose and entered into the town of Xaintes." Genesis and Revelation—the story of rustic Adamic virtue corrupted by the Fall and the final battle between virtue and the Beast—were shuffled like a deck of cards. "[I]n the place of the psalms," Palissy "heard nothing but blasphemies." So "it seemed to me that all the virtue and sanctity of the earth," the fundamental element of the microcosm and living material of the potter's art, "were choked and extinguished."

The earth's natural language of virtue, the sounds of which were elemental, mastered, and harmonic ("psalms, hymns, and decent words"), was perverted. Pious sound was overwhelmed and transformed into its infernal opposite, *esmotion* ("blasphemies, tirades, threats, tumults, all [sorts of] horrible and dissolute words"). A corrupt babble drowned out "holy conversation" in the place Palissy called "my country." The natural, harmonic language of Palissy's earth, indeed, "*all* the virtue and sanctity of *the* earth were *choked* and *extinguished* [emphasis added]." The framework of soulish Neoplatonic universals that convinced Paracelsian natural philosophers that difference and plurality were connected to form the harmonies of a monistic cosmos was fragmented. The earth—natural and material "mother" of the potter's art of the earth—was strangled and then burned; martyred in precisely the same way as Philibert Hamelin, Palissy's spiritual and intellectual father.

Harmony, then, was violently displaced by dissonance. But the replacement of "paroles honnestes" by "paroles miserables" did not mean the end of cosmological symmetries. The "little narrative" hinted darkly that such oppositions should be understood as doubles or mirrors of one another. As such, heaven and hell—the spiritual and material essence of light and dark in the macrocosm and microcosm—were intertwined. The nature of purity on (and in) earth, made it subject to corruption, just as the alchemic process could redeem fallen matter.

❧ "Little children" and Their "inheritance" ❧

Palissy's history ended with this atomized representation of man and nature without God. Would irreconcilable dissonance and fragmentation in postlapsarian time remain the only historical outcome possible from Adam's original legacy of difference, which created the "split open" cosmic opposition between the corrupted earth and its divine artisan?

> I was greatly terrified during a respite of two months, seeing how peddlers and base beggars had become lords at the expense of those of the Reformed Church. There wasn't a day that passed that I didn't hear reports [of what went on outside Palissy's studio and hiding place]; the most grievous of which concerned certain little children from the town [of Saintes], who came daily to assemble at a square near the place where I was hiding (meanwhile, I exerted myself every day to make some works of my art), they divided up

into two gangs, and then threw rocks at each other, [at the same time] they swore and blasphemed more execrably than I had ever heard man utter: for they said by the blood of Christ, die, and go to hell, piss-head, double piss-head, triple piss-head, and some blasphemies so horrible, that I am almost too horrified to write them down: and this lasted quite a long time with neither the fathers nor the mothers intervening to bring them under control. This often made me wish to risk my own life, to [go out and] punish them myself; but I said the seventy-ninth psalm in my heart, the one that begins "['O God] the heathen are come into thine inheritance; [thy holy temple have they defiled; they have laid Jerusalem on heaps]."

I know many Historians will discourse on these things at much greater length, however, I have wanted to speak of this matter en passant, because during these evil days, there were precious few people of the Reformed Church in this town.[56]

Geological metaphors are ubiquitous. Having been caught in a wasteland between two bands of implacable enemies, joined on an ambiguous battlefield that the violence of war has wrenched up from a millennia-old subterranean world (the camouflaged location of both natural and historical truths in the "narré"), Palissy peered furtively from the "place where I was hiding," keeping under cover, although "there wasn't a day that passed by that I didn't hear reports." Inside his subterranean hiding place, a small open space created by the fortress walls surrounding his workshop, Palissy discovered how the children of Saintes hurled rocks that had been disgorged from "l'enfer." They hurled oaths at one another at the same time, until words and weapons became interchangeable.

Even as Saintes turned itself inside out, disintegrating into Huguenot apocalyptic historiography, Palissy built himself, *parenthetically,* into the interstices of dissonance. "Meanwhile," as hidden witness to the self-immolating violence of oppositional forces, "I exerted myself every day to make some works of my art." The "walls" of his parenthesis may be likened to the walls of his tower and, inside, to the walls of his potter's kiln and alchemic crucible. The significance of the tiny, pious artisan locating himself in this "recipe" for posterity, in a superficially powerless, silenced, but still creative liminal space cannot be overlooked. Here, Palissy was buffeted between violent binary opposites, exposing himself to action in the matrix at great personal risk ("this often made me wish to risk my own life"). To practice his craft, creating an art of the earth out of its ruins, was the ultimate act of artisanal sacrifice, reform, and alchemic rebirth.

Palissy was reborn as well, baptized as a hybrid of the Calvinist new man and the alchemist's homunculus. He recreated himself spiritually and materially in the historical crucible of war and the scientific crucible of his laboratory. This process was a direct result of the silencing and violent deaths of his spiritual father, Philibert Hamelin, and of the earth of Saintes, his natural-philosophical mother. From these deaths, the potter created a new synthesis. He took Hamelin's place to preach to his orphaned flock, not on the basis of Genevan discipline, but of artisanal security. Hence, the seventy-ninth psalm was recited "in my heart" as an artisan's prayer of self-mastery. "With neither the mothers nor the fathers intervening to bring them under control," Palissy lamented, "the heathen are come into thine inheritance." Yet the potter was comforted that, finally, so too had he. For this was the space Palissy reserved to fashion a secure social self-identity for Huguenot artisans in a world turned inside-out, with its insides atomized. The hidden artisan's task became to reveal and reconcile these dispersed atoms, fragments, and oppositions *materially*, through the labor of "industriousness." Palissy had thus supplemented Hamelin's and the earth's "choked" voices with the silent language of reformed matter.

In the *Recepte*, Palissy dwelled on metaphysical relationships that unified confessional violence and artisanal security with material life. Emulating the model of his tiny, industrious *limace*, Palissy seems less concerned with discovering precise geometric equivalence than with finding the metaphysical power to combine artisanry with the "language" of nature to *compensate* for physical and political limitations and maintain social and cultural equilibrium.

Max Weber has, of course, harnessed industriousness to both Reformation ideology and materialism in *The Protestant Ethic and the Spirit of Capitalism*.[57] Weber posits a paradigm shift in Palissy's time that instigated the disunity of faith and reason, the triumph of positivism, the devolution of spiritual experience into subjectivity, relativism, private acts of self-absorption, and, in the end, modern man's "disenchantment of the world." Fragmented communities without hope of moral reconciliation were permanently alienated from each other and from moribund nature. Modern man was as dead to the mysteries of primitive universal spirits as metaphysics was to viable scientific and philosophical inquiry.

I would suggest that Palissy's project takes precisely the opposite position. His task was to illuminate the underlying cosmological connections of soulish interiority in man and matter as a gateway to empirical reality. Metaphysical knowledge was essential to control of the primordial forces that connected man with Nature's universal soul and made available secret prophesies during end times of trauma and travail. Such primitive knowledge *re*enchanted the fallen world, reformed the primitive Church, reunited the dispersed Huguenots, and reversed the historical process of spiritual, social, and material fragmentation. So metaphysical unity between microcosm and macrocosm was reclaimed by artisanal industriousness. "[S]ecular powerlessness may be compensated for by a sacred power," Victor Turner says of liminality. "The power of the weak," he concludes, was "derived on the one hand from the resurgence of nature when structural power is removed, and on the other from the reception of sacred knowledge."[58]

As Caroline Walker Bynum has reminded historians in her wise critique of Turner, the "power of weakness" had a long tradition in the West, beginning with the primordial Christian concept of *reversal*: "we must never forget the emphasis on reversal which lay at the heart of the Christian tradition. According to Christ and to Paul, the first shall be last and the meek shall inherit the earth." Bynum complicates subsequent readings by insisting weakness was spiritual and bodily—and so material—*practice*. The political practice of weakness lay in manipulation of spiritualized material toward the reconquest of structural power. "Inferiority," Bynum concludes, "would—exactly because it was inferior—be made superior by God."[59] The material of reversal was hidden in the small. That was why Luther warned Leo X of Isaiah's prophesy: "The Lord will make a small and consuming word upon the land . . . [Isa. 10–22]. This is as though he said," Luther continued, "'Faith, which is a small and perfect fulfillment of the law, will fill believers with so great a righteousness that they will need nothing more to become righteous.'" Therefore, "this means nothing else than that 'power is made perfect in weakness.'"[60]

❧ "The Island of Ceylon" in the East Indies ❧

For Palissy the artisan, it followed that the construction of Huguenot power was "made perfect" in its smallness and in the codes of hidden knowledge and perception animating artisanal security. In retrospect, Palissy provided the perfect clue to his agenda in the *Recepte,* en passant, at the beginning of the book, in this short poem that serves as its epigraph:

> TO THE READER,
>
> *salut.*[61]
>
> In a small body great power is often couched,
> This will be learned, reader, by reading this book,
> Which is something novel, come into the open
> So no sots will make a living on error;
> *For it shows plainly to the eye what it must follow*
> *Or reject* [emphasis added], in these admirable sayings;
> In reciting many truthful speeches,
> Cleave to this end that Art, imitating Nature,
> Can accomplish what many esteem fables,
> People without reason and of unjust censure.[62]

Palissy's cryptic epigraph and his natural-philosophical book of "admirable sayings" and "truthful speeches," on "Art, imitating Nature," influenced the painter of a curious manuscript illumination, "The Island of Ceylon," in *Secret de l'histoire naturelle contenant les merveilles et choses memorables du monde* (fig. 3.1).[63] "The Island of Ceylon,"

Car ilz se maintenēt coē bestes mues 2 nōt ne sen' ne raiso' en eulx 2 ne font cōte de lamort. 2 sentretiēt de lē bōne volute Et croiet p ferme oppinio' q quāt ilz sot mors q lē ames sot plº eureuses apχ lamort en lautre monde qsses ne sot en ce monde pxp. Ite quāt lexº enfās sot nouellemēt nes de lexº mexº ilz sot grāt deul 2 demostrēt grāt signe de coxouχ 2 de tristesse 2 diēt q lexº enfās biēnēt en ce mōdx po peine auoir 2 malle meschice. Ite quāt lexº pures 2 amps font mors ilz sen resioissēt 2 en sot molt grāt 2 excessiue feste. Et diēt q quāt lexº amps meurēt q lexº ame entrēt en la grāt ioyx de laut mōdx. Ite dit solin qlz ont vne ordōnāce entreulx q celluy q plº aura eu de femes sxa le plº honoure 2 pxise. Ite dit solin q les femes si marient de lexº pxe etxe 2 volute a lē plaisir sās le xseil 2 xsentemēt de lexº pures 2 amps. Et qnt elle sot belles les maris q lexº veulēt auoir les achxetēt moult chxremēt. Et se vendxt elle mesme au plº offrāt 2 qnt elle sot laideχ 2 maladuenas elle achxetēt lexº maris. 2 p aisi il appt q la bōte 2 honestete dēº pucelleχ 2 dēº femes de ceste txe ē mois pxise 2 honouxe q nest lexº beaulte 2 lexº richesse

rxpvīree d'vne psle q est sitxee bien pxes de Inde la maiō deuexs la pxe de mydy de laquelle psle solin 2 dit q auant q alixandxe

FIGURE 3.1. "The Island of Ceylon," in "Secret de l'histoire naturelle contenant les merveilles et choses memorable du monde" [Secret of Natural History Containing the Marvels and Memorable Things of the World] (Paris: Jehan Kerver, n.d., but probably ca. 1580–1600); Bibliothèque nationale de France, MS Fr. 22791, fol. 60 verso. Given the context in which this "New World" text was published, its author was arguably influenced strongly by Palissy's rustic books and ceramics. The inhabitants of this community of snails are engaged simultaneously in the industrious pursuit of craft and security.

painted to illuminate an alchemical and natural-philosophical text on the exploration of the East Indies, was published later in the sixteenth century than the *Recepte*. The gaze of *Secret*'s readers was dropped in this image from the axiometric perspective applied by the potter to his famous basins, to the terrestrial perspective of the *limace* that inhabited them. In so doing, the promise of Palissy's "De la ville de forteresse" was realized. Like the *limace*, refugees have grown a portable fortress, presumably from their inner juices, for domestic and military purposes. In one shell house and fortress, a refugee housewife prepares wool for spinning; in another, a soldier readies his shield and lance. Another woman peers through a secret window cut in her shell wall to communicate with others, since only the refugees can see one another. Are the two snails in the central foreground, hiding behind the giant rock in the center of a Palissian river basin, true mollusks or Huguenots in disguise? The natural philosophy of "Island of Ceylon," "shows plainly to the eye what it must follow," or so it would seem.

Having instructed refugees to build hidden fortresses from the inside out by imitating the industrious *limace*, Palissy conveyed a desire to internalize his analogy for artisanal security by collapsing it into Reformed being and experience. In so doing, he synthesized the essence of alchemy and artisanry contained in Paracelsus's crucial axiom, "[H]e who carries all things with him needs not the aid of others."[64] This play of independence, autodidacticism, and mobility is particularly appropriate to the final "secret" made available by the natural history of the "Island of Ceylon." The cloven rock rising out of the center of the island in the river basin replicates the famous promontory often used to represent La Rochelle during the wars of religion, particularly in images of its fall (see fig. 9.1).

Did the great fortress hovering high on the plateau in the background suggest the doomed grandeur of La Rochelle from the terrestrial perspective of Palissy's Saintonge? To answer this question we must turn to the centrality of La Rochelle's place in this regional and international dynamic of religiosity, war, and the culture of security.

CHAPTER FOUR

War and *Sûreté*

The Context of Artisanal Enthusiasm in Aunis-Saintonge

Reformation culture in southwestern France cannot be defined regionally by Genevan sacerdotalism or the conservative political and military apparatus of La Rochelle's orthodox Consistory. Just such a monolithic definition of religious practice in southwestern France has resulted in the automatic juxtaposition of conservative urban southwestern French Huguenot culture with the radical rural southeast. Lay religiosity, theatrical mysticism, and militant radicalism were well known in the southeast, and southwestern French Protestantism owed formative debts to the noble military culture and orthodox Genevan theological aspirations of La Rochelle. Yet the evidence suggests a more ambiguous landscape. A complex religious legacy was carried by Huguenot refugees from southwestern France out into the Atlantic world.

Under the pressure of civil war, spatial tensions between the southwest's dispersed rural population and its centralized medieval fortress system limited consistorial control or influence over Protestant culture on La Rochelle's Saintongeais periphery. As Bernard Palissy's artisanal theory of *sûreté* and the history of Saintes demonstrates, rural violence made a decentralized "system" based on the necessity of military, religious, and political autonomy from the La Rochelle core available nearly a century before 1628. When La Rochelle fell, this "rustic" system was flourishing among Huguenots in nearly all the agricultural and artisanal hamlets of the Charente River Valley and the isolated islands and marshlands along the coast. Patterns of autonomy revealed an artisanal outlook on religiosity that was rooted in rustic lay enthusiasm, and combined *sûreté* and animate materialism with local interpretation of the great Reformation writers, led by Luther and Calvin, as well as Paracelsian alchemy and natural philosophy. Saintongeais spiritual experience was informed by Geneva, which sponsored the diffusion of Calvin's reading of biblical exegesis and sacramental history into the region.

"Pure doctrine" was provided directly by an itinerant such as Philibert Hamelin or under the auspices of the La Rochelle Consistory. Yet rustic experience was isolated and so sometimes in tension with Genevan or Rochelais discipline. Rustic autonomy and power provided a structure to ensure the continuity of lay practice *after* 1628 in the absence of consistorial protection, guidance, and interference, and in the face of growing pressure from absolutism's law-enforcement apparatus. Defeat and genocide in 1628 broke the power of the fortress-based Genevan Reformation in Aunis, and for Saintongeais Protestantism, this signified the permanent institution of lay, informal, personal, and clandestine measures of spiritual and material security, adopted in times of confessional violence on the Rochelais' periphery since the 1550s.

❧ Parlement and Consistory in Aunis-Saintonge ❧

Every history of southwestern France must confront 1628. With a few notable exceptions, most Reformation histories that consider the "oppressed" southwestern Huguenots take the dramatic siege of La Rochelle as their starting point. But this is to begin with an ending so overwhelming that the event inevitably obscures both its own significance and the quest to see the process of local cultural adaptation to royal power over time clearly. The year 1628 has come to signify the moment that punctuated and finally defined the region's historical sensibilities. Yet if we look first at the previous century, we find the formative period that suffused this famous event with the power it has come to hold to convey such a prophetic sense of reversal and doom for the future of Protestantism in the early modern transatlantic world.

Étienne Trocmé knew this and was devoted to the reconstruction of La Rochelle's most vibrant period of conversion and Reform before the "end times" that accompanied "its resounding fall in 1628."[1] For Trocmé, 1628 was a vulgar anticlimax to a far more nuanced historical drama. In a seminal article that appeared in 1952 and laid the groundwork for future studies of the Rochelais Reformation before 1628, Trocmé, himself a minister and descendant of seventeenth-century Huguenots, had straightforward archival explanations for the dearth of La Rochelle's history before the siege. Between—and probably during—the two regional catastrophes of 1628 and 1685, substantial sections of the official archive that documented Rochelais society in acts of rebellion was lost. All that remains of the voluminous archives of the Corps de ville, also metaphorically, the "mémoire de ville," are several *registres*. It was no coincidence that the archives of the Consistory of La Rochelle—the ruling body of its independent theocracy—were also reduced to manuscript fragments and "some debris."[2] Additions to the archival record have been found in bits and pieces since Trocmé completed his work, but this abrupt erasure left a gap in the Reformation and Civil War historiography of La Rochelle that paralleled the strangulation of the living voices of oral history in Palissy's region.[3]

Trocmé began the task of circumventing the absence of these elusive materials by supplementing the remaining ones with ancillary archival and other primary documentation—much of this discovered outside the region—for the crucial years 1558 to 1628.[4] Read together with lay (i.e., nonecclesiastical) history that he ignored for lack of interest (he dismissed Palissy as "infantile"), Trocmé's early observations on the Rochelais Consistory and politics have profound implications for assessing regional behavior patterns for Protestant culture in retreat into the Atlantic world both before *and* after 1628. Trocmé did not plead the case for La Rochelle's Huguenots as brave fighters for religious freedom and heroic victims of the voracious statism of Richelieu and Louis XIII, but instead scrupulously reconstructed his Reformation and civil war ancestors as opportunistic victimizers *themselves*. Rochelais Huguenot leaders were intent on systematic and brutally repressive hegemony. Militant Calvinists wrested power from their "mediocre" Catholic opponents and Huguenot supporters of the crown's interest with ruthless political skill.[5]

Until the late 1550s, nearly forty years after Luther's texts were first diffused to Aunis-Saintonge, and seventeen years after Calvin's appeared there, Rochelais Huguenots remained little more than a small if growing minority sect, composed mainly of disaffected intellectuals: low-ranking regular clergy, monastics like Luther (Augustinians in particular), printers and booksellers, and regents as well as the regular faculty of La Rochelle's municipal schools, who taught Protestantism to their students. In La Rochelle, as elsewhere in France, the earliest heretics were from institutions at the core of the old Church scholasticism.[6] At the same time, Protestantism began to attract an inclusive cross-section of social and occupational groups in the fortress. La Rochelle's was neither a proletarian nor a mercantile revolution. Rather, it soon engulfed the entire city. Judith Pugh Meyer's study of La Rochelle's economic status and of the occupational distribution of heresy within the fortress concludes: "Though La Rochelle was not insulated from social and economic change, the Reformation's success in the city was not precipitated by social or economic dislocation. Similarly, political divisions and dissention do not provide an explanation, since the Reformation attracted numerous converts from every occupation involved in internal political conflict."[7]

Yet the contentious story of La Rochelle's municipal gift to Charles IX in 1565 shows that inclusiveness did not mean consensus. Factionalism was endemic well beyond

1568, when La Rochelle allied itself with Prince Louis de Condé's militant Huguenot nationalist cause. Even then, dominance was achieved and maintained through dramatic demographic change. Rochelais Catholics were banished from the fortress or stifled criticism for fear of reprisal. Reformed heterodoxy remained strong despite the ministry's best efforts, and in 1562 and then 1572, the city's population of militant Huguenots was augmented further by a steady influx of refugees from north of the Loire, after having been politicized by violence in the first civil war of religion and the St. Bartholomew's Day Massacre.

There is no doubt however, that the Rochelais Reformation was fostered and maintained through its conflation in the public mind with the ancient tradition of privileges that gave La Rochelle its roiling confluence of civic autonomy and private interest. Rochelais memory of the city's autonomous privileges was grafted over time onto the increasingly coherent body of Protestant belief, which was also based on autonomy from Roman ecclesiastical control, and fed by revivals whenever threats were perceived to La Rochelle's unshakeable identity of historical independence from the monarchy.[8] A threat to La Rochelle's privileges was perceived as early as the 1540s, when the crown began to impose taxes from which the town thought it was exempt. Anger and resentment reached a fever pitch in 1542, when François I established the Gabelle in the Saintonge region. Since Rochelais merchants controlled the trade in salt, the economy of the fortress was directly threatened. Tax revolts followed. The economic component of La Rochelle's anxiety over confirmation of its civic privileges in 1565, stemmed, in part, from this quarrel with the crown.[9] Louis-Étienne Arcère complained that "the people and the bourgeois" had initiated a campaign of "hatred—bitter fruit of civil dissensions that disturbed the harmony of the municipal government. Diverse cabals were formed against the government."[10] Bourgeois and popular disenchantment with authority was directed at the local apparatus of François I's centralization program, which the "cabals" correctly perceived as dangerous threats to communal privileges. Dissension was also heightened when François I reduced the Corps de ville to only twenty *echevins,* while reserving the right to choose to mayor for himself.[11]

François I died in 1547, and it was not until the 1550s that discontent over autonomy was overtly intertwined with religious reform. During the reign of Henri II, the dangerous atmosphere of local dissent over matters of control, authority, and privilege was charged with religious specificity for the first time. In what was an extremely threatening extension of the harsh anti-heresy policy of his *parlement* of Paris, Henri II appropriated the Corps's judicial privileges in 1551, and invested them in the *présidial,* a sovereign tribunal.[12] The threat to local Protestants from judiciary repression within the fortress walls was made palpable in 1552, when the *présidial* ordered the four standard punishments used by the *parlement* of Paris against heretics—strangulation, burning at the stake, public whipping, and banishment—read publicly into Rochelais law.[13]

To understand the enormous negative impact that the presence of the *présidial* had on the growing Rochelais Reform in 1551–52, consider that Henri II intended it to function as a lesser *parlement. Parlements* were very effective in curbing heresy within their local jurisdictions. Philip Benedict explains this pattern in his analysis of Civil War Rouen:

> Rouen was also a major administrative center, the seat of a parlement, and such cities proved in general less receptive to the new religion than those cities where the authorities were a comfortable distance away. Most of the greatest Huguenot strongholds—La Rochelle, Montauban, Nîmes—were situated far from the watchful eyes of the local parlement, while those cities which housed high courts proved almost uniformly to be less heavily Protestant than other major towns in their resort [jurisdiction]. Often, as in the case of Paris and Toulouse, they became great bastions of Catholicism. However creaky the machinery of judicial repression might be, its presence within a city nonetheless seems to have acted as a brake on the development of Protestantism. And so it is not surprising that, no matter what success the movement might attain within Rouen and how menacing it might appear at times, Protestantism would never attain majority status. After a period of dramatic growth, the new faith was to level off in the position of an imposing but decidedly outnumbered minority.[14]

Under the provisions of the Edict of Fontainebleau (June 1, 1540), Aunis was technically in the jurisdiction of the *parlement* of Paris.[15] Yet Paris could not realistically expect to police a jurisdiction that covered nearly one-fourth of the territory of France without delegating authority to subordinate tribunals. In practice, the *direct* authority of Paris to successfully prosecute and enforce judgments against heresy beyond the city itself ended at the northern Loire Valley. Parisian agents seldom initiated "inquiries, searches, and arrests," south of the 100-mile stretch of the Loire between Orléans and Angers.[16] Hence, Paris's intelligence and enforcement apparatus were severely limited geographically. It was forced to rely on the "creaky machinery of repression" assigned to local *parlements.*

Until 1628, the high court for Saintonge was the *parlement* of Bordeaux, whose jurisdiction extended deep into La Rochelle's rural hinterlands. The presence of a *parlement* in the city curtailed heresy in Bordeaux and held the line against the growth of Protestantism in Saintes. Outside Saintes's town walls, however, in rural areas and along the coast, Bordeaux's power to intimidate was limited by distance, isolation, and the lack of reliable paid informants. As Hamelin's experience demonstrated, moreover, in Saintes and other isolated jurisdictions, responsibility for the capture and earliest stages of prosecution for heresy fell on local "provosts and other judges of inferior status." Few magistrates in southwestern France prosecuted heresy with fanatical zeal on a day-to-day basis without military support from Paris. All were susceptible to local social and political pressure, and many succumbed to heresy themselves. In 1565, Charles IX punished a royal jurist on La Rochelle's *présidial* for failing to prevent the spread of heresy.[17]

The need to delegate judicial authority in frontier provinces should not be mistaken for decentralization. The edict of 1540 commanded Protestants of certain ranks convicted in the provincial courts be transported to Paris for final sentencing, or if need be, execution. "By the terms of this edict," Nathanaël Weiss wrote:

> clerics who had not received sacred orders, or lay people suspected of heresy, were prosecuted by the provincial authorities, either by the bishops, their vicars, or the inquisitor of the faith, or the bailiffs, prefects, or their general or particular lieutenants. Usually, the inquisitor of the faith commenced by examining the accused, and if he declared them to be heretics, they were tried first in the original jurisdiction, [but] only up until the point of a definitive sentence or torture. . . . The right to pronounce the final sentence belonged to the *parlement* alone. The accused and their trial transcripts were thus sent to Paris—at the bishop's expense—and a special court was instituted there for the purpose of interrogating them, in order to decide if a new inquest was warranted, and ultimately to pass final judgment without hope of further appeal.[18]

Although Henri charged the *présidial* with powers of judicial repression usually reserved for *parlements,* its installation in La Rochelle did not stem the tide of heresy (as Benedict reports high courts accomplished elsewhere). Rather, the *présidial* had the opposite effect. This innovation from Paris was considered a radical and illegal abridgment of ancient privileges. Municipal anxieties over the corrupting presence of a royal judiciary in the fortress itself were harnessed to a growing desire for the purity of primitive religious autonomy from ecclesiastical interference. Isolated within a hostile community, the *présidial* was undermined by local opposition backed up by La Rochelle's military strength, which was magnified by isolation from the main roads to Paris, a two-week journey on horseback for royal forces had they been sent to intervene.[19] Hence, the *présidial* could not count on timely, sustained enforcement. "Situated at the periphery of the kingdom," Louis Pérouas has observed, "La Rochelle found itself outside the great axis of road traffic." The port was its means of commerce and communication, and "it opened on the Atlantic." The French interior remained sealed against large-scale intervention.[20] The orientation of the fortress changed radically only after the siege. "The secular attachment of the city to its independence practically disappeared with the capitulation," Pérouas writes. "Doleful memory of this event rendered the population docile to royal power."[21] La Rochelle's *présidial* ultimately combined with the *présidiaux* of Poitiers and Angers and consolidated the reach of the *parlement* of Paris into southwestern France.[22]

Much has been written by both European and American historians about the theology of orthodox Calvinism and the association of its leaders with a rigid, patriarchal, and hierarchized social armature. Yet, for Meyer, "the strongest clue to Protestantism's initial attraction comes from the Rochelais' religious and ecclesiastical experience, particularly their strong sense of lay independence from ecclesiastical authority. The Rochelais had worked for centuries to free themselves from ecclesiastical taxes and ecclesiastical influence in municipal affairs."[23]

Kevin C. Robbins' masterful reconstruction of La Rochelle's history from the perspectives of families with conflicting religious, economic, and political interests builds powerfully on Meyer's work. Robbins dismisses the consistory's disciplinary program, arguing the Genevans were disdained as foreigners and overwhelmed by popular religious practice. Hence, more local and factional than Genevan, La Rochelle's was not a conservative Reformation. While lay authority was strong in theory and practice, one must be careful not to overstate the case as the Rochelais Reformation progressed into the late 1550s and the Consistory began to play a more active role inside the walls. Give and take should not be confused with the sort of rustic dominance "from below" that was practiced by Palissy and his lay followers, and described vividly in Saintes's history in the *Recepte.* Lay influence checked abuses of Calvinist sacerdotalism, and La Rochelle's ministers could be harried by challenges from their congregations, but at the same time, the Consistory was dedicated to order and control. It tried, with limited success, to assert a ministerial hierarchy as doctrinaire as—and identical in its social and political interests to—its displaced Catholic predecessors.[24] In the absence of consistorial archives, it is difficult to assess the extent to which discipline had proved effective against Protestant latitudinarianism and heterodoxy. We do know, however, that between the first great period of conversion, beginning in 1558, and the siege of 1627, the Rochelais Consistory pursued its "task as the defender of the pure doctrine" of Calvin. During that time, the Consistory pursued prosecution of Protestant heretics at La Rochelle. The Consistory's perceived intolerance of social leveling, doctrinal dissent, licentiousness, paganism, and other disorders was very well known in the Protestant world, especially when these crimes assumed the dissident forms of heterodoxy or enthusiasm within the Reformed Church itself.[25] Effective or not, La Rochelle's Consistory and defense of Genevan purity became synonymous with the city. As its international fame grew, the city retained its image as a defiant fortress of Protestant orthodoxy.

Reasons for such anxiety over internal disorder were suggested by the publication of a "list of warnings and censures" distributed by the Consistory during the first civil war, in 1562–63. This document showed equal measures of the Consistory's fearfulness over the instability of the laity in wartime, and lack of confidence in its own dominance, as it successfully threatened the disobedient "faithful, all of whom were entirely free to return to Catholicism the next day."[26] While Trocmé tries to moderate this view of an oppressive Consistory by balancing its "severity" against what he calls its "pa-

tience and prudence," as the ministry struggled to consolidate power, Palissian lay enthusiasm lay claim to the hinterlands, where it could flourish (although still at risk from
both the Rochelais Consistory and the *parlement* of Bordeaux). The suppressive impulse of the Rochelais Consistory vis-à-vis unorthodox co-religionists in Saintonge was
structurally analogous to that of its institutional opposite, the *parlement* of Bordeaux.

Palissy is a perfect example of the sort of Protestant against whom both the regional
parlement and the Rochelais Consistory would take severe repressive measures given
the opportunity. Setting aside the content of his written work for the moment, Palissy
was an alternately secretive and bellicose man. He was equally capable of rebelling
against either confession, and he found himself facing Catholic and Protestant authorities on charges of heresy or heterodoxy several times. Palissy's name came before
the *parlements* of Guyenne (1558), Bordeaux (1563), and finally Paris (1587–8). Though
a warrant for his arrest was handed down at Guyenne, there is no record of a trial. However, Palissy was tried twice for heresy, in Bordeaux and Paris. He survived Bordeaux
with the help of Montmorency, but the Paris trial proved fatal, because Catherine de
Médicis, his last great patron and protector, died in Blois on January 6, 1589, just after
Palissy was condemned to death for heresy, but before he was sent to the Bastille.[27]

Meanwhile, after Palissy and his family fled Paris for Sedan in 1572 as refugees from
the St. Bartholomew's Day Massacre, he appeared before Sedan's Protestant Consistory on six occasions on charges ranging from family squabbles to acts of rebelliousness. The most revealing appearances occurred on three occasions in the summer of
1575, when he was charged with creating a "scandal" with "habitual scenes and insolent
behavior." Confrontation escalated to such a degree that the Consistory finally "cut
M[aster] Bernard off from the Lord's Supper for his rebellion, and the cause will be
declared publicly the day of the Lord's Supper during sermon."[28] With his leveler's
attitude of rebelliousness against established authority, it is little wonder that Palissy
did not join the thousands of other refugees who fled to La Rochelle after 1572. History and personal experience with the Rochelais Consistory had taught the potter how
risky rebellious behavior was for outside in the fortress, particularly in wartime.[29] For
its part, the Consistory never welcomed him with open arms. Palissy balanced opportunity against risk and went back to his royal patrons in Paris, where he reestablished
his workshop and laboratory on the left bank in 1576. He decided that returning to a
city purged of Huguenots was preferable to life in either La Rochelle or Sedan.

❧ Jean de Léry, Palissy, and La Rochelle in 1558; ❧ or, A Corrupted New World Fortress

I walked up the Avenida Rio-Branco, once a site occupied by Tupinamba
villages, but in my pocket I carried Jean de Léry, the anthropologist's

breviary. . . . Henceforth, it will be possible to bridge the gap between the two worlds. Time, in an unexpected way, has extended its isthmus between life and myself; twenty years of forgetfulness were required before I could establish communion with my earlier experience, which I had sought the world over without understanding its significance or appreciating its essence.   —CLAUDE LÉVI-STRAUSS, *Tristes tropiques*

Rochelais Protestants were all influenced powerfully by the preaching of Pierre Richier, who had sailed west with Jean de Léry.[30] Now both had returned from their failed expedition to colonize Brazil, a Huguenot experiment to advance a systematic plan for settlement in the Americas. Richier returned to La Rochelle, and Léry migrated to another famously ill-fated Huguenot fortress town—Sancerre—by way of Geneva. Admiral Coligny's colonization project of the 1550s was in retreat, and for many Calvinists, the Huguenot *places de sûreté*—La Rochelle and the less well fortified Sancerre, among others—became the French Reformation's last hopes of surviving the wars of religion. The Huguenots would not be able to colonize the New World in large numbers until the seventeenth century, when Dutch and English settlements in North America served as their hosts.

Although contention over municipal privilege, the history of the city's autonomy, and possession of an impregnable fortress were crucial factors, the Reformation in La Rochelle must be framed as a religious process in which the desire for the militant revival of primitive Christianity was paramount. This was the primary agency of change and conversion for the majority of Huguenots in the fortress. La Rochelle's Protestant Consistory came to power during a religious revival that began in 1558 and was initiated by two Huguenot ministers: the itinerant Charles de Claremont, and the well-traveled Richier, "dit de l'Isle." Trained in Geneva, the latter was both a formidable theologian and a seasoned adventurer. He had returned to take up the pulpit in La Rochelle after surviving the joint Huguenot and Catholic expedition to colonize Brazil, which had unraveled in chaos, violence, and mutual hatred in 1558. The Brazil expedition was made famous by Richier's friend and co-religionist Jean de Léry's account of it. Since Richier was above all associated with the revival of 1558–59 that dismantled the old Catholic order in La Rochelle, how did the Huguenot transatlantic experience inform and contextualize the Rochelais Reformation? Can this process advance our understanding of the concept of artisanal security as a seminal component of New World historiography?[31]

Palissy's syncretism of artisanal and natural philosophy in the rustic cosmology of the "paysan de Xaintonge" is strikingly similar to that of his Burgundian contemporary de Léry (1534–1611). The famous Huguenot ethnographer was also a Geneva-trained minister, New World traveler, the survivor and historian-witness of famine and cannibalism during the royal siege in 1573 of the Protestant fortress at Sancerre and, though the fact is often overlooked, a master shoemaker. As the complete title of de Léry's influential history of Brazil makes clear, a formidable natural philosophical agenda was the primary focus of his *Histoire d'un voyage fait en la terre du Brésil, autrement dite Amérique. Contentant la nauigation, & choses remarquables, veuës sur la mer par l'aucteur: le comportement de Villegagnon, en ce pais la. Les meurs & façons de viure es-tranges des sauuages ameriquains: auec vn colloque de leur langage. Ensemble la description de plusieurs animaux, arbres, herbes, & autres choses singulieres, & du tout inconues par deça.* . . . When the *Histoire* was published in Lyon in 1578—nearly two decades after the Brazil expedition—Palissy's *Recepte* had been in circulation for fifteen years.

The rich historical, cultural, and textual implications of de Léry's artisanal origins are mentioned only by way of passing in recent scholarly readings. This reflects a certain disciplinary bias. Frank Lestringant, a comparative historian who specializes in the literature of the early modern French transatlantic world, devalues the natural philosophical significance of Léry's *History* as wholly derivative of the Franciscan André Thevet, his fierce religious and intellectual rival. Thevet preceded Léry to Brazil, and he was the first to publish a comprehensive ethnography of the Tupinikin Indians of the southern coastal region in *Les Singularitez de la France antarctique, autrement nom-mée Amérique* (1558). Two years later, Thevet expanded upon his early observations in his influential *Cosmographie universelle* (1575). "The interest of Léry's work," Lestringant argues, is not natural-philosophical discourse. It "lies, rather, in the gaze and the con-science that emerge in the face of the other, in the course of an arduous ocean voyage that takes the narrator into the midst of naked and cannibalistic peoples."[32]

No one would dispute the significance of de Léry's contribution to early American ethnography, yet the dismissive reading of de Léry's authorial voice as merely deriva-tive, without fully exploring the meaning of that word, represents a lost opportunity. To pursue debate on this problem is not my task here. I would suggest, however, that this Huguenot's natural-philosophical gaze into the face of America and its aborigi-nal people was deeply textured by his own artisanal experience. De Léry himself un-derscores this point, particularly when his ethnographic curiosity focuses on Tupinikin craftsmanship and materials, an interest that was shared and further elucidated by Claude Lévi-Strauss, who claimed de Léry as his direct emotional and intellectual an-cestor.[33] Thus, while de Léry scholarship has emerged mostly from the perspectives of comparative literature and anthropology, surprisingly, de Léry remains all but invis-ible in the history of science, a fluid discipline that has found intensive textual, biog-raphical, and ethnographic analysis of early modern artisans, artisanry, and artisanal materials—termed "manual philosophy" or the "mechanical arts"—to be a fruitful field of inquiry. Paolo Rossi's observations on the stake of the history of science in the "cul-tural significance of the mechanical arts" summarize the potential. He finds an unprecedented rise in artisanal status and the "fusion" of sixteenth- and seventeenth-century learned and artisanal knowledge:

> Juan Luis Vives in the *Diffusion of Knowledge* (*De tradendis disciplinis,* 1531) makes the statement that scholars would be well advised to study the technical methods of such trades as building, navigation, and weaving; they should, besides, observe the artisan at work and question him on the secrets of his craft. . . . Rabelais, in *The Most Fearsome Life of the Great Gargantua,* numbered among the prerequisites of a complete education the study of the artisans' crafts. . . . This new interest in technical and mechanical methods, based on a belief in their educative powers, is typical of the sixteenth and seventeenth centuries. The accomplishments of artisan, engineer, technician, navigator, and inventor were considered of equal importance to intellectual achievements, and Bacon, Galileo, and Harvey, among others, explicitly acknowledged their debt to the artisan. Sciences such as chemistry, mineralogy, botany, and geology thrived on the fusion of scientific and technical knowledge. Another consequence . . . was the realisation that theories should be tested before they could be accepted.[34]

The work of early modern natural philosophers such as Vives, Bacon, and Palissy, reminds us that although the historiographical outcome of de Léry's voyage to Brazil was one of the first Protestant natural histories of America, this was not his primary project in the New World. In 1554, de Léry was not yet sanctified as a survivor of the siege and cannibalism at the Huguenot fortress at Sancerre, which had occurred in the wake of the St. Bartholomew's Day massacre of 1572. Neither had he written his personal narrative of that experience, the *Histoire memorable du siège de Sancerre* (1573), which resonates powerfully with *Histoire d'un voyage fait en la terre du Brésil* and invites explicit comparison to the New World in comparative analysis of cannibalism and its epigrammatic sonnet, which likens Sancerre's destruction to "l'horreur d'Amérique."[35] In 1573, Sancerre had become an apocalyptic completion; a millennial event foretold by the Huguenots' failure to expand their foothold in America and maintain the security of the fortress at Guanabara. Yet in 1554–55, de Léry was only twenty, and he had still to study theology at Geneva, where he first appears in 1559, upon his return from Brazil. De Léry was merely a colonial Huguenot artisan who, like Palissy, had turned his hand to a specific sort of labor that was at once intensely material and spiritual, with powerful debts to folkloric traditions and the printed word. The pragmatic projectors of the New World settlement were concerned, first and foremost, with recruiting and maximizing scarce colonial labor. Their assessment of de Léry's value was based on an impressive combination of his natural-philosophical learning in "mechanical arts"—valuable in fortress construction and maintenance—devotion to evangelical Calvinism, and competence as the new colony's master shoemaker.[36] De Léry's flight to Sancerre in 1572 may also have been understood as a reaffirmation in dangerous times of his double identity as refugee artisan and now an ordained minister. Sancerre's fame in France for its tanning industry and the leather trades made the fortress a haven for Huguenot shoemakers.[37] A "humble" Huguenot artisan such as de Léry could strive for the exalted status of rustic natural philosopher, and maximize his personal spiritual power, by joining the New World settlement in Brazil. Was de Léry's narrative, wherein he helped sympathetic and pious Tupi artisans build Fort Coligny at Guanabara, based, in part, on naturalistic theories of artisanal security derived from Palissy's essay "De la ville de forteresse," which he did not read until after his return? Was Palissy's text influenced by manuscript (or oral) accounts of fortress building in Brazil that began to circulate in Saintonge in 1558, carried back by Pierre Richier? Perhaps Palissy and de Léry had converged through similar readings of Paracelsus? The rhetoric of the *Histoire d'un voyage fait en la terre du Brésil* pays homage to the Huguenot branch of the Paracelsian artisanal tradition.

An overview of key personnel involved in the Brazil project reveals significant overlaps among pivotal individuals whose names were common to Léry's and Palissy's readership, patronage, and networks of association. If books published by Léry, Theodore de Bry, Philippe du Plessis-Mornay, Urbain Chauveton, and Calvin himself formed the canon of the sixteenth- and early seventeenth-century "Huguenot corpus on America," then it is appropriate to contextualize Palissy and his artisan followers in Saintonge and colonial America within this widely dispersed international community of Protestant artisans, publishers, theologians, and projectors. The civil war vanguard of the Reformation hurried to stake an intellectual claim on the New World, which was becoming a social, scientific, and cultural project of great importance. Calvin sent Richier and three other ministers to evangelize Brazil in 1554, and Léry has documented Geneva's active interest in the colony.[38] The "corpus" was read avidly throughout the Protestant diaspora. Nowhere were close readers more readily available than in the publishing centers of London, Geneva, Amsterdam, Leiden, and Frankfurt. Huguenot refugees fled to the entrepôts of both dispersion and the book trades, where readers actively considered the option of New World colonization.

In the late 1560s, Huguenot New World historiography began to exert profound influence on the British discourse on colonization of North America. Elizabethan projectors, particularly Richard Hakluyt, Walter Ralegh, Francis Drake, and Martin Frobisher had the books of the Huguenot frontier and New World chroniclers in their libraries.[39] Despite differences in state religion, it was evident to both the English and French monarchies that they shared imperial interests in restricting Spanish overseas expansion. The English in particular admired the aggressive policy vis-à-vis the Spaniards of Gaspard de Coligny's Huguenot colonization program. Coligny's initially secret Protestant sympathies emerged clearly when he became the principal backer of the Brazil colony. Huguenot writers tended to devalue the colonization potential of the Saint Lawrence River Valley, focusing instead on the tropics (despite calling Brazil part of "France Antarctique . . . Otherwise Called America"). Staples grown in the tropics were highly valued on the world market. They were also of consuming interest to natural philosophers, as potential materials for the philosopher's stone as well as a source of cash. Coligny's strategy for exciting the interest of the vacillating French monarchy in the resettlement of Huguenot refugees in the Caribbean region was predicated on economic promise and the ability of his colonies to pose a real military threat to Spain's supply of Latin American bullion.

A corollary to the Huguenot program was the colonizers' moral imperative to convert Amerindians to Reformed Christianity, to avoid relinquishing their powerful bodies and fragile souls to corruption by Roman Catholicism, or at least to help the Americans protect their perceived Adamic primitivism from appropriation by the hated Franciscans, if conversion to the true faith proved impossible. In Brazil, the competition for conversion of the Tupi was particularly keen between Protestant and Catholic settlers. Whichever side won an alliance with the Tupi would gain strategic advantages against the other, as well as against Spanish and Portuguese invaders.

At a minimum, grudging respect for natural, if fallen, innocence (at least in the face of the less palatable Catholic alternatives) had an analogue in the rustic "paysan de Xaintonge" and resonated in sixteenth-century French Calvinist theological discourse, which focused primarily on the individual's conversion experience. This posited a powerful relationship between conversion and the rebirth of childlike innocence, which, in turn, would lead inevitably to a general reconstitution of the primitive Church (or, as Léry would have it, "pure religion"), in a truly godly society. While it may be argued that his learned reading of "the beginning of ideology" as a consequence of the pervasive intellectual and emotional tumult experienced during the early years of the French Reformation in the crucible of religious warfare has overstated the radical origins of sixteenth-century reformed religion, Donald R. Kelley does show how "the word 'conversion' has been rich in signification," and is convincing in his insistence on the stake French Calvinists had in both the transformative power of the conversion experience itself and the mythological status assigned its narrative:

> It has encompassed various forms of fundamental change. . . . In individual terms it was associated with Greek ideas of repentance (metanoia) and the turning from evil to good (epistrophe), and as such it was related to the idea of conscience. In the sixteenth century the process of conversion was central to all varieties of reformed faith, for it (and not the mass or any external observance) signified the most direct encounter between humanity and divinity. . . . Not only did conversion represent the pivotal point in the experience of many persons in this age, it suggested also a basic explanation for the turn which history as a whole seemed to be taking. Most generally, in other words, the conversion experience

was connected to the idea of reform itself in its several senses of restoration, renovation, regeneration and resurrection—a vision of lost innocence recaptured. The basic text was the Pauline exhortation not to conform but to be "transformed in the newness of your minds". Like "conscience", then, "conversion" reflected directly and dynamically the psychological aspect of the Reformation and, elaborated in countless works of theology, history and popular literature, became one of the most powerfully transforming myths of modern times.[40]

Huguenot ministers and natural philosophers sensed they need only make the Tupis conscious of the spiritual purity of their childlike innocence—which all but Reformed mankind had lost in the present age—in order to effect a conversion of the Amerindians to their true selves and the simultaneous revivification of the Huguenots' own conversion to "newness." Mystical and symbolic reunification of human relics of the primitive earth's providentially rediscovered naturalistic past with heroic modern men who sought to reform the corrupting artifice of its declining old age was essential to the Huguenot transatlantic project in the 1550s.

This theme was avidly quoted in the large body of Elizabethan colonization literature. Projectors including Hakluyt and Ralegh thought ancient and natural religious affinities existed between Protestant colonists and savage man, and that conversion of the indigenous population of America should result almost spontaneously at initial contact.[41] Unfortunately for Fort Coligny, both Spain and Portugal were alarmed by the French Protestants' overt and arrogant incursions into territory claimed by Spain since 1492. They responded swiftly and with overwhelming force to the threat to assume control of the most profitable regions of the New World. The Brazil colony was lost to the Portuguese in 1560, only six years after it gained a toehold in Rio de Janeiro. De Léry blamed the invidious command of the Catholic villain of his *Histoire,* the chevalier de Villegagnon, who allowed confessional rivalry to subvert a Christian alliance to promote "the pure service of God" in the primitive world. "I will let you judge how Villegagnon, besides rebelling against the Religion [Calvinism] (contrary to his promise, which he had made before leaving France, to establish the pure service of God in that land), by abandoning the fortress to the Portuguese, gave them the occasion to make trophies of the names both of Coligny and of Antarctic France, which had been placed there," de Léry wrote.[42]

Coligny was also the principal name behind the rest of the hugely ambitious Huguenot colonization program between 1554 and 1565. Coligny followed the settlement of Brazil with similar efforts at Charlesfort in South Carolina and La Caroline in Florida. Like Brazil, these too ended in failure. The Florida catastrophe was particularly memorable. On September 20, 1565, when narratives of horrific acts of confessional violence were so commonplace that European readers seldom found news of any one event particularly shocking, the Spanish commander of St. Augustine, Pedro Menendez de Abila, showed he was capable of transcending the known limits of human cruelty. Menendez marched south from his stronghold and proceeded to put a famously brutal end to Coligny's hopes for the Huguenot colonization of North America with the genocidal massacre of over a thousand purportedly sick and unarmed Calvinist colonists under the command of Jean Ribaut at La Caroline. Menendez defended his actions with a marker that claimed the "innocents" massacred at La Caroline were not women and children, only Protestants. Perhaps the notorious Menendez assumed that if given a similar opportunity, his innocent Huguenot victims would surely have perpetrated the same atrocities on their Spanish Catholic murderers.[43] With the end of the colonization program, Coligny returned his attention to France, converted openly to Calvinism, and led successful Huguenot military campaigns during the second and third wars of religion (1567–70).

Coligny's prestige grew after he skillfully negotiated the Peace of St. Germain in 1570, which ended the civil war and gave the Huguenots the right to maintain military garrisons in La Rochelle, as well as in the fortified towns of Montauban, Cognac, and La Cité. Yet Medician court politics (influenced by Philip II) meant that Coligny's skill and prestige made him vulnerable to assassination. On August 24, 1572, the feast of St. Bartholomew's Day, under the personal direction of the Catholic ultra leader Henri, duc de Guise (who had also supervised the massacre of 1,200 Huguenots at Vassy on March 1, 1562), and with the approval of a weak and threatened Catherine de Médicis, Coligny was murdered in Paris, triggering the massacre of the Huguenots, a bloodletting with portentous long-term effects, which quickly took on a bloody life of its own in the streets of Paris and throughout France. Following Coligny's murder, hundreds of Parisian Huguenots were massacred and their bodies thrown into the Seine. Witnesses observed Catholics roast and consume the hearts of their victims. After St. Bartholomew's Day, Pope Gregory III had a commemorative medal struck in Rome to celebrate the massacre.[44] Admiral Coligny was thus international Protestantism's martyr, in part to his own failed experiment to save French Huguenot culture from destruction in civil war by its relocation as a corporate body to the New World. The return of Pierre Richier and Jean de Léry to their respective Old World fortresses was the earliest result of that transatlantic failure. Brazil had fallen as a result of internal religious dissention and external military force.

Beyond the enduring memory of Coligny's martyrdom, the bloody failures of the Huguenot colonization project of the 1550s and 1560s caused cosmological shifts in the Reform movement as it emerged from the first three civil wars in southwestern France. Inhabiting a centrifugal, frontier region with a great naval tradition on the far edge of a mostly landlocked monarchy, La Rochelle's merchant-*armateurs* and the mariners of Saintonge's coastal islands were at the forefront of transatlantic expansion from New

France to the French Antilles and Brazil.[45] The end of Fort Coligny—which came into being as a result of the Huguenot quest for extraterritorial refuge—caused French Protestant artisans and natural philosophers, including the returning de Léry, to reevaluate old security methods and technologies. Palissy's "De la ville de forteresse," read in this context in 1563, provided innovative alternatives to the traditional modes of colonization, at least as it was practiced within the medieval long march and fortress culture in which Coligny, Condé, and the Huguenot noble military leadership had been trained.

The removal of the colonization option meant that southwestern Huguenots would now be forced to become more dependent than ever on this outmoded system of internal fortresses—*places de sûreté*—for personal and corporate security. After the shocking failure of Coligny's military colonies in Brazil and Florida, and with civil war beginning again, the future of the French Reformation was very much in doubt. The development of new modes of security had become a central issue for international Protantism. Exploration of a new sort of settlement in the Atlantic world had to be considered if cultural death were to be avoided, and the discourses on artisanal security in "De la ville de forteresse," which reimagined the Huguenots' new world in "end times," absent medieval fortresses, were thus particularly timely.

Palissy's essay derived from his artisanal experience with manipulation of natural and alchemic material in spiral form. It demonstrated his agenda that French Calvinists must now learn to innovate on the fly, with available materials, to master change on the basis of experience, spirit, industriousness, and dissimulation. Had recent history not shown that it was too risky to follow "ancient" regional traditions by continuing to fashion southwestern Huguenot self-protection based on the survival of a unique eleventh-century fortress at La Rochelle? What had once been the most palpable evidence of the region's autonomy and its power to dissent from both Paris and Rome was redefined by Palissy at the last stages of Coligny's colonization program as a threat to the continued existence of Protestant culture in France and the world. Fort Coligny's failure in Brazil was only the most recent example of the vulnerability of the fortress as a system of security.

Unlike many Calvinist colleagues in the crafts and sciences, Palissy survived the St. Bartholomew's Day massacre unharmed when he escaped to Sedan. He was spared Coligny's fate because he was still Catherine's valued creature, and he remained in her employ at the Tuilleries. Palissy undoubtedly mourned Coligny, as had most Huguenots in the 1570s. But Coligny's reputation was secure long before it was memorialized by martyrologists in 1572, and he was revered by thousands of "common" French Protestants who lived in coastal communities like Aunis-Saintonge and depended on the sea and the admiral's patronage for their livelihoods. There is also reason to believe that Coligny was likely to have been acquainted with Palissy's work—both written and material—either directly or indirectly by citation from other texts. This may be claimed for many reasons, but in particular because Coligny and Palissy were in Paris at the same time and shared a desire to discover a permanent refuge for the Huguenots in rustic or New World environments. With the publication of his first book in La Rochelle in 1563, Palissy became known to the readers of the Huguenot corpus on colonization. This was especially true in Parisian court circles, where Coligny attempted to influence crown politics. In 1565, after his removal from Saintes and the failure of Coligny's transatlantic colonies, Palissy arrived in Paris to construct his rustic grotto and place of refuge for Catherine de Médicis, and subsequently to write and give "lessons" on alchemic and natural philosophical subjects in his now famous rustic persona.

Palissy's demonstrations of adaptation to rural life and arts were well known among the community of Huguenot adepts, physicians, and intellectuals in Paris and would have been attended by anyone as deeply involved in the colonization effort as Coligny. It is reasonable to assume that Coligny knew Palissy's written work and may have visited the potter's laboratory, where Palissy gave public demonstrations "face-to-face" to verify the "truth" of his published experiments. Given strong archaeological evidence that many early modern New World sites built pottery kilns to provide for the settlements' need for ceramic vessels, it is also reasonable to assume that Coligny was interested in Palissy's skills as a rustic potter and builder of his own kiln. Consider, too, Coligny's well-known interest in the development of brazilwood and other tropical staples, in addition to precious minerals, to be exploited for the transatlantic market and carried east on ships owned by Huguenot merchant-*armateurs*. Palissy's natural-philosophical research and experimentation focused on the "formation," through "gestation and growth," of trees and rocks and other mineral formations (including calcified fossils) found "in the bowels of the earth" and "dissected." The potter displayed numerous examples of such living minerals to the public in a cabinet of curiosities at his laboratory in Paris. At the same time that Coligny was concerned with subtropical staple plantation agriculture, Palissy wrote an influential discourse on fertilizer in the *Recepte.* The potter followed this early interest in the *Discours* (1580) with a widely quoted chapter, which he titled in the manner of a transatlantic projector: "How to Find and Know the Earth Called Marl With which barren fields are fertilized, in countries and regions where it is known . . . and in other places where this earth is still unknown."[46] Moreover, de Léry tells us, Coligny set Villegagnon the Palissian task of directing both colonists and Tupi in the construction of a "rustic" fortress in Brazil, an edifice de Léry called, symbiotically, "the building and refuge."[47] Unfortunately, Palissy does not make written reference to Coligny. He published a long "catalogue of . . . witnesses," to "my last lessons of the year 1576" in the *Discours* after returning from Sedan the year before. This was the only time Palissy compiled such a list of erudites and patrons. Since the admiral was killed in 1572, it is impossible to prove that Coligny had once been among them.[48]

De Léry's *History* and Palissy's "De la ville de forteresse" both supported the hidden craftiness of "naturalistic" fortresses. Both argued for dualistic domestic and military sites, which must emerge from the Huguenot craftsman's hand almost organically as experiments in interaction with Nature to revive and improve God's traces and take advantage of local topography to augment artisanal skill and provide strength and concealment. Refugees and colonists would both benefit from available materials and folkloric construction methods learned from local artisans—Saintongeais potters or Tupi builders—with a history of practical manual experience.

De Léry's description of Fort Coligny's topography in Guanabara Bay as he imagined it might be perceived when encountered by suspicious Portuguese sailors for the first time tells us something of how this pious Huguenot craftsman projected the mutability of his own shifting identity onto the psyche of potential adversaries. Also, we glimpse what may have been learned from reading Palissy between de Léry's return to France in 1558 and the publication of his *Histoire* in 1578. Fort Coligny's assets as a place of refuge lay not only in the treacherous approach, which endangered warships sailing into the bay and kept them out of cannon range, but also in the apparent communication of what de Léry represents as its own ambiguous natural discourse, whereby sailors were compelled to read the geology of the Huguenot site in terms of the conflation of "artificial" and "natural" workmanship. De Léry understood that Fort Coligny's fragile sense of security was based on the uncertain perception of liminality, like that of the *limace* and the material culture of the Tupis (which became an integral part of the completed site).

De Léry described the fort as a hybrid that occupied unstable territory and was concealed inside a permeable threshold where the natural and man-made mixed, mingled, and were confused. Do I perceive a "mountain" in the distance, or the cannon tower of a Huguenot stronghold, built like the three limestone towers that guarded the entrance to the harbor of the fortress of La Rochelle? De Léry's assessment of the entrance to Guanabara Bay laid bare the complex, dissimulating power of a shape-shifter that survived challenge by concealing itself in plain sight. Nature was a chameleon made of earth, fire, water, and air, where real strength emerged from a living tableau on the frontier of the New World. Here an enemy's worst fears and expectations were projected and knowledge was acquired experientially on a first come, first served basis.

De Léry demonstrated how reformed natural-philosophical knowledge was a fundamental condition of Huguenot security in the New World. With spiritual insight and mechanical knowledge, the animate qualities of natural material were harnessed, distilled, and redirected by rustic artisans to merge with the mental and material worlds of *both* besiegers and besieged. As in Palissy's paradigm, the fortress becomes more than just a static defensive shell. It comes alive—inextricably entwined with what can only be called an inner life—and so the fortress itself was complicitous in the defense of the newly constructed Huguenot domestic and sacred space inside.

Thus de Léry began a discourse on the history of Guanabara's natural fortress by acknowledging and then dismissing the dead letter scholasticism of Thevet's earlier accounts. Like Palissy, he insisted upon the epistemological primacy of personal, lived experience in a specific place. This allowed de Léry to claim authentic knowledge that was bolstered by the providential parallel he draws between the geography of Guanabara Bay and Lake Geneva (where de Léry lived and trained as a lay minister after his return):

> I will begin without lingering over what others have chosen to write about it, having myself lived in and sailed around this land for about a year . . . with the mainland lying close by on all sides, Guanabara rather resembles [Lake Geneva] in its situation. As you leave the open sea, you must sail alongside three small uninhabitable islands, against which the ships, if they are not, indeed, well handled, will dash and be shattered; so the mouth is rather troublesome. After that, you must pass through a straight that is barely an eighth of a league wide, bounded on the left side as you enter by a mountain, or pyramidal rock; not only is this of an amazing and extraordinary height but also, seeing it from a distance, one would say that it is artificial. And indeed, because it is round, and like a big tower, we French hyperbolically named it "Butter Pot."[49]

Initially, de Villegagnon overlooked these natural defenses. He tried and failed to build a standard provincial European stronghold with a medieval enceinte. The original site was clearly vulnerable to siege, almost by design. The revolution in the technology of gunpowder warfare made the traditional walled city more vulnerable to attack than ever before. This inspired the growing literature against such fortifications, of which Palissy's essay was a part.[50] Medieval fortress architecture was designed to be seen from afar; to stand out on flat, open terrain as a visible marker of conquered territory and the extension of feudal power into the frontier: "A little farther up the bay there is a rather flat rock, perhaps one hundred or one hundred twenty paces around, which we called the 'Ratcatcher,' on which Villegagnon thought to build a fortress, having off-loaded his equipment and artillery there upon his arrival," de Léry goes on.[51] "But," he reported, the tide or "the ebb and flow of the sea drove [de Villegagnon] away" from this rock, so he was forced by practical experience with local conditions to change his plans for the original site of the fortress at Brazil.[52]

For these reasons, de Villegagnon's second choice for a site was, if not the ideal choice according to tradition, far wiser than the first. If well guarded, this site could have allowed the colonists to hold out indefinitely against the Portuguese. De Léry thought it "a superb natural stronghold." His description of the second fortress as a rustic, barely postlapsarian edifice, constructed from unimproved forest materials left behind by the divine artisan for the Tupi, implied that although a refuge was reclaimed by pious artisans from fallen Nature, it must be nurtured and protected by the "pure" religion of the Gospels in order to retain the power to hide, protect, and recreate. Fort Coligny's innate power of exterior protection came from the choice of a specific natural space "built" by God and then adapted (or reanimated) as a millennial refuge by the Huguenots. The Tupis' primitive structures then extended this naturalistic power of refuge, initially provided by that ambiguous entrance at the mountainous outer ring of Guanabara Bay deep *inside* the interior world of Fort Coligny itself.

These artificial and natural structures were man-made, but in "native style," which is to say, they were artlessly made (in the European sense) of unimproved materials from the Brazilian forest ("wooden logs . . . and grasses"). These buildings created a rustic ring around de Villegagnon's "French" house to protect the heart of this hybrid, idiosyncratic fortress. Perhaps he remembered Fort Coligny as kind of Palissian ceramic basin? De Léry thus revealed a Huguenot affinity for primitive and naturalistic "workmanship," expended on the fortress's interior structures by "the savages [who] were their architects":

> A league beyond [Ratcatcher rock] lies the island where we stayed . . . it is only about half a league around, and six times as long as it is wide, surrounded by little rocks that just break the surface of the water and which keep the ships from coming closer than the reach of a cannon shot, it is a superb natural stronghold. And in fact, even with the little boats, we could only land there from the inland side, which is to say from the side opposite to an approach from the open sea; so that if it had been well guarded it would have been impossible to take it by force or in a surprise attack—as the Portuguese, by the fault of whom we left there, have done since our return.
>
> There was a hill at each end of the island, and on each of them Villegagnon had built a little dwelling; on a rock fifty or sixty feet high, at the middle of the island, he had had his own house built. On either side of this rock, we had leveled some small areas on which to build the rooms where we assembled for the sermon and for dining, and some other buildings where all eighty of us, including Villegagnon's men, installed ourselves. *But note* that except for the house on the rock, where there is a little timbered structure, and for some bulwarks where the artillery was placed, and which are covered with some kind of masonry, all the other buildings are huts, which, since the savages were their architects, were built in the native style—that is, of wooden logs, and covered with grasses.
>
> So there you have, in brief, the workmanship of the fort, which Villegagnon named "Coligny in Antarctic France," thinking he would please Messire Gaspard de Coligny, Admiral of France (without whose favor and assistance . . . he would never have had the means to make the voyage, nor to build any fortress in the land of Brazil).[53]

De Léry takes pains to demonstrate that no intrinsic weakness in the elemental materials reformed by the savage artisans and their primitive Huguenot compatriots from the fallen earth, water, and air was responsible for the loss of Coligny's "natural" fortress to the Portuguese governor-general Men de Sá. Because it was simply "impossible"—a fortiori, unnatural—that Fort Coligny be conquered materially from the outside in, de Léry's logic dictated that the purity of its interconnected protective tissues must have been compromised from the inside out. Manichean forces effected an internal corruption of the soul of Fort Coligny.

This bodily corruption had, in fact, emanated from its virtual heart. De Villegagnon himself "was splendidly arrayed" at its precise center,[54] "on a rock fifty or sixty feet high, at the middle of the island, [where] he had his own house built." De Léry and the Huguenot contingent endured "the inconstancy and changeability that I have known in Villegagnon in matters of religion," from the very center of this otherwise pious and natural body, whence "the treatment he offered us under that pretext." The corrupt heart of the fortress was pinpointed as the source of "his disputes and the opportunity he seized to turn away from the Gospel, his habitual demeanor and discourse in that country [and] the inhumanity he showed . . . beating and tormenting his people in his fort."[55] If the "heart" providing the most impenetrable outer shell with the spiritual basis of its material integrity is corrupted, then the natural defenses of the refuge will also be made corrupt and ultimately insecure. Palissy planned for the contingency of a corrupt governor by subdividing his fortress so that even the smallest internal part could resist his corruption. Yet de Léry represented Villegagnon's religious, or interior body—the "inconstancy and changeability" of his core—as an unconquerable evil.

For the Nicodemite who walked a serpentine line, dissimulation as a defensive characteristic of the outer body was perceived to be natural, ethical, and pragmatic. "In matters of religion," however, and so at its metaphorical middle, the fortress at heart, like the heart of the pious body, must remain constant and unchanging in the "pure service of God," to remain a secure refuge and pious space.[56] De Léry assessed the hopeful rise and premature fall of Fort Coligny more unambiguously: Huguenot artisans and natural philosophers must forge personal covenants with both God and Nature to attain mastery over the soul of earthy matter. Only in this way could a place of refuge be provided with sustained abilities to manipulate external appearances against the threat of overwhelming force. Corruption at the center crippled security. Once again, inhabitants of secure places must cleanse inner corruption to maintain religious unity.

While de Léry revered the martyred Coligny, he utterly despised his intellectual and religious rival, the Franciscan friar André Thevet. Thevet had been in Brazil for ten weeks as the colony's chaplain when de Léry arrived with Coligny's expedition in Guanabara and the Huguenots attempted to assert their evangelical reading of "pure religion" over the fragile settlement. Predictably, Thevet left Brazil soon after the arrival of the Huguenot contingent, and he returned to Paris an indefatigable antagonist of Richier, de Léry, and their group.[57] Having a common interest in the polemics of civil war and the natural philosophy of rustic life, Palissy certainly encountered

Thevet in Parisian court circles. The Franciscan had gained similar lofty patronage among the Valois, as Catherine's chaplain and royal cosmographer to Charles IX. Courtly fascination with New World or aboriginal and rustic themes from distant provinces such as Saintonge fed the upward trajectory of Thevet's career, as it did Palissy's. Europeans consumed domesticated exotic fantasies about Brazilian Indians, which court artists and artisans syncretized with the available classical tropes. Thevet made his reputation at court with the publication of the greatly influential *Singularitez de la France antarctique* (1558), which mythologized the colonists' problematic encounters with the Tupis, settled scores with Huguenot colonists (excoriating Coligny, whom Catherine de Médicis had begun to fear), and gained him the heroic literary reputation of a new Jason or Ulysses.[58]

When the fifth civil war had turned much of France into a killing field, and with Coligny removed from the scene, Thevet increased his anti-Huguenot rhetoric with the publication of the polemical *La Cosmographie universelle* (Paris, 1575), which rehearsed much of the same material that had previously appeared in *Singularitez* but also included controversial additions that openly accused Richier and the other three Geneva-trained Huguenot ministers from the Coligny group of causing the colony to fail.[59] De Léry did not read the *Cosmographie* until 1577, and as he wrote a year later with disgust in the complex and vitriolic "Preface" to his *Histoire:*

> I saw that [Thevet] has not only revived and augmented his early errors, but what is more (perhaps supposing that we are all dead, or that if one of us were still alive he would not dare to contradict him), with no other pretext than the desire to backbite and, with false, stinging, and abusive digressions, to slander the ministers and those—of whom I was one—who in 1556 accompanied them to . . . Brazil, he has imputed [crimes to us]. Therefore, in order to refute these falsehoods of Thevet, I have been compelled to set forth a complete report of our voyage.[60]

De Léry's *Histoire* thus entered the publishing battlefield of the New World historiography of the French religious wars. Yet unlike Thevet, personified as his scholastically trained enemy, de Léry was an artisan and natural philosopher. His *Histoire* uses a number of "key words" that suggest that he had read widely in the Paracelsian philosophical method. So his initial rhetorical move was to unmask Thevet's willful misrepresentations of life in Brazil, quoted with theatrical specificity from the Franciscan's polemical narrative, by launching a subversive appeal to the primacy of his own *personal* experience. "And before I go on," de Léry continues archly, "lest you think I am complaining about this new 'cosmographer' without just cause, I will record here the libels that he has put forth against us, contained in Volume II, Book 21, Chapter 2, page 908":

Moreover [says Thevet] I had forgotten to tell you that shortly before, there had been some sedition among the French, brought about by the devisiveness and partiality of the four ministers of the new religion, whom Calvin had sent in order to plant his bloody Gospel. Chief among them was a seditious minister named Richier, who had been a Carmelite and a Doctor of Paris a few years before his voyage. These gallant preachers, who were trying only to get rich and seize whatever they could, created secret leagues and factions, and wove plots which led to the death of some of our men. But some of these mutineers were caught and executed, and their carcasses went to feed the fishes: the others escaped, one of whom was the said Richier, who soon went to be minister at La Rochelle, where I believe he still is. The savages, incensed by such a tragedy, nearly rushed upon us to put to death all who were left.[61]

To this de Léry replied that Thevet "never saw us in America, nor we him." Thus, "I want to show that he has been in this respect a bold-faced liar and a shameless calumniator." It was clear "that his report does not refer to the time when he was in that country, but that he means to be recounting an act that took place since his return." The retrospective logic that corrupted scholasticism had rendered Thevet's work invalid as well. Manipulation or strategic distancing of the truth of lived experience became the basis of de Léry's critique of the authenticity of Franciscan natural history, and of Thevet's lies: "his intention was . . . to have it believed that *he really saw,* in America, the ministers that he speaks of."[62] The polemics of civil war historiography had followed the Huguenots and Paracelsians to the New World and back.

❧ Richier's Return to La Rochelle and the Huguenot Coup d'État ❧

Richier was intent on succeeding in La Rochelle where he had failed at Fort Coligny. There would be no sharing of power or risk of internal corruption of the fortress's security by Catholics. He came back to La Rochelle in 1558 knowing that American colonization was now a lost opportunity, and his stake in the French Reformation in the near future lay of necessity in the militant exclusionary religious culture and walled protection of the Huguenot *place de sûreté.* For him, at least, the rustic fortress as an idealistic setting for the diversity of man and nature and the "pure service of God," was no longer an option. Richier knew this was also the conclusion of Admiral Coligny, his patron on the Brazil expedition. Coligny now worked to guarantee secure places and fortified towns in strategic areas in France, with La Rochelle as his centerpiece, so that Huguenots could survive the civil wars and hope for the eventual installation of an enlightened monarchy. Coligny codified this strategy in the Peace of Saint-Germain (1570) before his murder by militant Catholics.

In November 1558, La Rochelle's Consistory was built around Richer's preaching.

Upon his return, the "seditious minister created secret leagues and factions, and wove plots which led to the death of some of our men" in La Rochelle, just as Thevet said he had done in Brazil. Yet the Rochelais Consistory remained clandestine only until 1559, while gaining in power and followers. In 1561 and 1562, the Consistory grew from eight to twenty-seven members. This shows how the outbreak of the first civil war— like the failure of the Brazilian settlement before it and the St. Bartholomew's Day Massacre afterward—helped build the Rochelais Reformation. The Consistory's growth reflected the moment when the Huguenot factions, bolstered by an influx of politicized refugees, attained a population majority in the fortress. The Roman Catholic churches of Saint-Barthélemy and Saint-Sauveur were first appropriated for Reformed services as well.

On May 30, 1562, Huguenots performed La Rochelle's first open air celebration of the Lord's Supper. That evening, building on this seditious act of public defiance, mobs pillaged the churches, committed iconoclasm on Roman Catholic altars, images, and statues, and massacred thirteen priests in the Tour de la Lantern.[63] These acts continued in response to Barthélemy Berton's 1563 publication of Yves Rouspeau's attack on the mass, *Traitté de la préparation à la saincte Cène de Nostre seul Sauveur et Rédempteur Jésus Christ,* which was dedicated "to the Christian Reader" and called "the most popular religious treatise published in La Rochelle."[64] Rouspeau, Palissy's friend and the minister at Pons and Saintes, wrote with "wonderment," of the recent civil war, "with which in the past year 1562, God so rudely chastised us with plague, war, and famine, in this poor kingdom of France." War provided the apocalyptic context that encouraged him to take up Calvin's attack on transubstantiation.[65]

The combination of iconoclasm, sacred violence against priests, and the enormous popularity of Rouspeau's attack from Saintonge on the primacy of the Mass, when harnessed to La Rochelle's history of autonomy, were turning points in the Rochelais Reformation. "These acts of protest," writes Judith Pugh Meyer:

> robbed religious symbols and sacraments of their inherent power. The attacks demystified and desacramentalized the Catholic religion and reflected definite attitudes about the Catholic clergy and ecclesiastical authority. To deride the sacrament of the Mass was to strike at the heart of both clerical function and authority. By rejecting transubstantiation, Protestants deprived the priest of much of his authority by denying the centrality of his function.[66]

Iconoclasm took place in both Saintes and La Rochelle in 1562. In 1563, Berton published Palissy's and Rouspeau's books together at La Rochelle. Thus, these two rustic Huguenots were tied together by personal and publication histories. It is clear that their messages were intertwined so far as "Christian Readers" in La Rochelle were concerned. Hence it followed, if Rouspeau's book encouraged the desacramentalization of artifacts associated with transubstantiation by act of iconoclasm (as Palissy himself was justifiably accused of committing in the Saintes Cathedral), then, the *Recepte* was intended to promote the sacramentalization of everyday life. For Palissy, this meant the redefinition and reform of attitudes toward the sacred, in a centrifugal process away from the Church out into the material of the microcosm. By decentralizing the materiality of the sacred, Palissy further illuminated his decision to stop painting church windows, replacing them with everyday things made for the domestic setting. Yet these were to remain powerful objects of his spirit. Transubstantiation had diffused beyond the priest's altar, into the souls of Huguenot artisans. The construction of security dispersed outward into the hands of industrious craftsmen as well. What were fortresses if not cathedrals of security?

By January 1568 (a decade after Richier's revival), the Reformed Church took power:

> The coup d'état that threw the city into the Reformed camp in January 1568 sealed the fate of the "Roman" Church: places of worship were confiscated and destroyed shortly thereafter; all religious ceremonies ceased immediately; priests and monks fled or were arrested, many were massacred a short time later by soldiers. Ecclesiastical property was not confiscated, but its administration was consigned to provisional *fermiers* or administrators and the revenue was used to finance the Reformed party during the succession of wars that the latter sustained.[67]

Institution of a Huguenot theocracy in 1568 terminated all royal authority to intervene in local affairs in La Rochelle until 1628. The crown's dissatisfaction with Rochelais autonomy, displayed so dramatically by Charles IX in 1565, peaked in 1568, when Charles threatened to put a royal garrison in the fortress.[68] This served to heighten fear and drive La Rochelle into a national political and military alliance with the formidable Condé, the militant leader of Huguenot separatism. The city had tried to maintain its autonomy from Condé as well as the state, but events in 1568 had threatened both its independence and the majority's Protestant creed, which helped drive Condé's agenda.[69] The city had declared itself an independent, international Reformed republic on the Genevan model. Indeed, by 1614, only Geneva, with an average of eight active ministers, supported a larger permanent ministry than La Rochelle, with seven. Paris, by comparison, could never support more than four at once.[70]

La Rochelle became the safe haven for the most notorious Huguenots of the era: Condé, Coligny, Jeanne d'Albret, her son, Henri de Navarre (the future Henri IV), and La Rochefoucault were among the political, military, and theological leaders who took refuge behind its walls.[71] When mass was finally resumed under the new government, it was officially restricted to the tiny Church of Sainte-Marguérite and even then was held only intermittently.[72] Sanctions and public hostility hounded the remaining five *curés* (representing the five formerly Catholic parishes of La Rochelle, who stayed

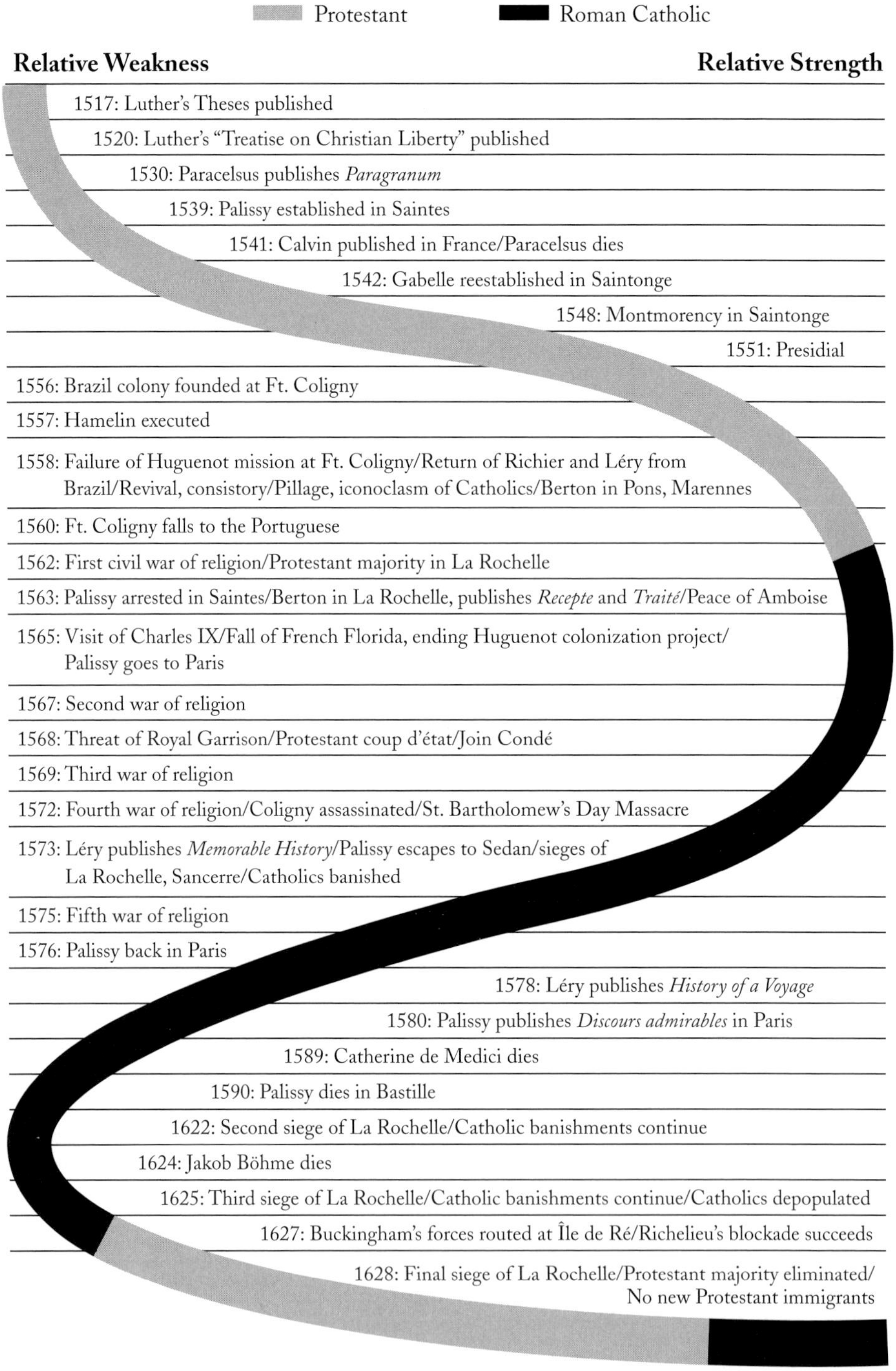

Protestant ▨   Roman Catholic ■

Relative Weakness   **Relative Strength**

1517: Luther's Theses published

1520: Luther's "Treatise on Christian Liberty" published

1530: Paracelsus publishes *Paragranum*

1539: Palissy established in Saintes

1541: Calvin published in France/Paracelsus dies

1542: Gabelle reestablished in Saintonge

1548: Montmorency in Saintonge

1551: Presidial

1556: Brazil colony founded at Ft. Coligny

1557: Hamelin executed

1558: Failure of Huguenot mission at Ft. Coligny/Return of Richier and Léry from Brazil/Revival, consistory/Pillage, iconoclasm of Catholics/Berton in Pons, Marennes

1560: Ft. Coligny falls to the Portuguese

1562: First civil war of religion/Protestant majority in La Rochelle

1563: Palissy arrested in Saintes/Berton in La Rochelle, publishes *Recepte* and *Traité*/Peace of Amboise

1565: Visit of Charles IX/Fall of French Florida, ending Huguenot colonization project/ Palissy goes to Paris

1567: Second war of religion

1568: Threat of Royal Garrison/Protestant coup d'état/Join Condé

1569: Third war of religion

1572: Fourth war of religion/Coligny assassinated/St. Bartholomew's Day Massacre

1573: Léry publishes *Memorable History*/Palissy escapes to Sedan/sieges of La Rochelle, Sancerre/Catholics banished

1575: Fifth war of religion

1576: Palissy back in Paris

1578: Léry publishes *History of a Voyage*

1580: Palissy publishes *Discours admirables* in Paris

1589: Catherine de Medici dies

1590: Palissy dies in Bastille

1622: Second siege of La Rochelle/Catholic banishments continue

1624: Jakob Böhme dies

1625: Third siege of La Rochelle/Catholic banishments continue/Catholics depopulated

1627: Buckingham's forces routed at Île de Ré/Richelieu's blockade succeeds

1628: Final siege of La Rochelle/Protestant majority eliminated/ No new Protestant immigrants

FIGURE 4.1. Power cycles in La Rochelle, 1517–1628.

to maintain Sainte-Marguérite) into nonresidence status at Saintes. In 1599, the bishop of Saintes was forced to recognize their presence and also the decimation of the Rochelais Catholic Church by establishing "a society and small chapter of five priests who were the *curés* of the five parish churches formerly standing at La Rochelle."[73]

Lower-order Rochelais Catholics were restricted from advancing either in the militia (all males were forced to serve) or to master status in the guilds after 1568. Even the *boulangers,* who elsewhere appear to have maintained a substantial Catholic percentage among their number, were mainstays of Protestant political action. Among bourgeois, a few *notaires* and lawyers managed to survive the purge, albeit with their status diminished, probably due to prior professional relationships with influential Huguenot families.[74] Exclusionary behavior at all socioeconomic levels, and indeed crude vengeance, was common in La Rochelle from 1568 to 1628. This was not surprising, as memory of a precisely parallel situation when the Huguenots had been a minority sect under Catholic dominance was still very fresh.[75]

Violent persecution of the Catholic minority was fairly rare, however, with systematic outbursts restricted to wartime. During these frequent periods, Catholics became scapegoats for community tensions and were assaulted, arrested, or banished. La Rochelle was virtually emptied of Catholics by mass exile in 1625–26, and again, for the last time, in 1627–28.[76] This systematic process of wartime exile was also imposed for purposes of simple exchange. For every Catholic ejected, there were dozens of Huguenots fleeing battlegrounds (or billeting) waiting to assume vacated positions of relative *sûreté* inside the walls.

The year 1568, then, precipitated the first astonishing reversal in Rochelais history. Catholics and Protestants exchanged places and hierarchies like mirror images in the social order. Catholicism assumed "the situation of a nonconformist minority," Trocmé writes ironically, "that is to say, in good French, a [minority] sect."[77] This reversal— accompanied by outmigration, conversions, and banishment of Catholics, and massive immigration of Huguenots displaced from other, less hospitable regions—caused a commensurate demographic shift. La Rochelle achieved a Protestant majority by 1562 and, incredibly, a 1618 census indicated that nineteen-twentieths of the population was then Huguenot. By January 1627, on the eve of the siege, 1,000 marginal inhabitants were separated out as nominally Catholic from a total population of 27,000 Rochelais.[78] The fortress at La Rochelle had turned in on itself and became a Protestant monolith, now tied exclusively to the Atlantic world. At the same time, the Reformed Church at Saintes had been destroyed, driven underground to the coastal islands. A flow diagram (fig. 4.1) can illustrate the timing of this reversal, forming a cycle of inverted social and religious hierarchies.

❧ 1628: "true images of death" ❧

The coup d'état of 1568 signified the violent reversal of the Huguenot's former status as a marginalized sect. The victorious militants projected their prior condition onto Rochelais Catholics, who were themselves systematically marginalized and then displaced demographically. By extension, the apocalyptic ending of Huguenot dominance in 1628 must also be understood as itself a reversal—that is to say, a reversal reversed. The awesome completeness of that reversal—in terms of both morbidity and mortality—may also be depicted demographically on a cumulative, month-by-month basis (fig. 4.2).

Working from a census taken on the eve of the siege of 1627, which indicated there were 27,000 people living in the fortress, and extrapolating from cemetery burial archives, hospital records, and eyewitness accounts, it is possible to reconstruct a picture of the demographic fate of Protestant La Rochelle during the year of the final siege.[79] The intractable reality evoked by such demographic evidence—19,800 Huguenots died within nine months; 17,300 in August through October *alone*—makes it nearly impossible not to imagine the fortress transformed into a charnel house during its last days or to dismiss as mere propaganda the apocalyptic images of final things that poured from Protestant printing presses across England and northern Europe in 1627

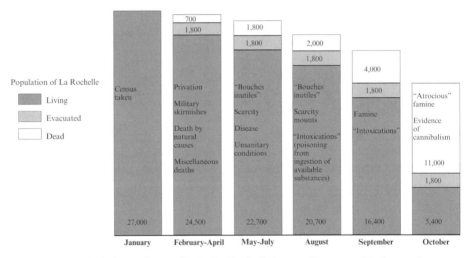

FIGURE 4.2. Morbidity and mortality in La Rochelle in 1628. Demographic figures from Étienne Guibert, "La Rochelle en 1628: État sanitaire des Rochelais et des assiegéants, mortalité, morbidité" (M.D. thesis, Université de Bordeaux II, June 26, 1979), 52–53. Beginning in May the *grand conseil* of La Rochelle ordered "beggar children, orphans, mendicants, and the unknown cast outside the city walls." Such *bouches inutiles* (literally, "useless mouths") strained the city's resources. Most died of starvation or were killed by the soldiers of the two armies.

and 1628. These statistics are compounded and made human by the sometimes grue-some explicitness of clinical knowledge of Rochelais morbidity during the siege year.[80]

Only a miniscule percentage (perhaps 1 percent) of the dead fell in battle. The vast majority died from starvation or the side-effects of bodily deprivation. La Rochelle's food reserves, mostly cereals imported from Saintonge, Poitou, and as far north as Brittany that had been in storage pending transshipment to Spain or Portugal, were depleted rapidly.[81]

Starving inhabitants foraged the city and marshlands outside the walls for wild grasses, insects, and various crustaceans. As the Rochelais ingested toxic plants, cooked leather products, and the flesh of household pets and rodents, they began to suffer from "intoxications," a lethal combination of starvation and poisoning. The symptoms of "intoxications" included disorientation, delirium, and hallucinations, before coma and eventual death. Although there is no recorded evidence of epidemic disease (perhaps because death came too quickly from deprivation), mortality attributed to serious ill-nesses, including *mal de terre* (or "falling sickness"), malaria, dysentery, and typhoid, was extremely high as a result of general weakness and unsanitary conditions.[82]

Yet it was not disease but the inventorylike descriptions of famine victims' decaying *bodies* in the final stages of irreversible malnutrition that drew the attention of contemporary commentators on both sides.

> All you could see everywhere were bodies like skeletons, dry and emaciated, whose bones were covered with skin that was black and shrunken; and one could scarcely tell that they were alive except for a dying man's moan, which you would have thought was coming from someone else, or for a slow and frightful walk. . . .
>
> . . . Left without fat and flesh, having nothing more than skin and bones, men and women could not sustain themselves; their emaciation made their clothing so big on them that it had to be tied around their bodies to keep the rain and cold from penetrating. . . .
>
> . . . their faces were hideous, eyes sunken, teeth sticking out of the mouth.[83]

After Richelieu surveyed the 5,400 survivors, he was able to tell Louis XIII that they represented "true images of death"—a signification probably intended to apply not only to the scene of misery before him but also to genocide both as bodily evidence of corruption caused by the "infection" of Rochelais heresy and of ritual purification caused by the siege.[84] In this "image of death," the victorious Richelieu perceived *transi*—images of corpses in the late stages of physical decay that were a convention of medieval and early modern funerary sculpture. This depiction meant that Richelieu and many Catholic commentators saw in the surviving Rochelais' physical "decomposition the sign of man's failure . . . the worms which devour cadavers do not come from the earth but from within the body, from its natural 'liquors.'"[85] Just as Palissy's pious *limace* was fortified by its natural internal liquids, so too Richelieu's heretics were *destroyed* from within, victims of their own "nature," pride, delusion, and moral failure. "Good and evil are so different and so opposed to each other that they never should be put in competition," wrote Richelieu as advice to Louis XIII in the "Punishments and Rewards" chapter of his Machiavellian *Political Testament.* "If the one is worthy of reward, the other is deserving of punishment."[86]

But how did the *vanquished* perceive the decomposition of their own bodies? By October, the living were too weak to bury the dead, who far outnumbered them in the streets. Richelieu wrote in his *Memoires* of decomposing bodies left to rot wherever they fell, indoors or out. Then, near mid-month, the first of the now famous reports of cannibalism, often in the same family, began to appear:[87]

> [On] October 12, in the house of sieur Superville, the body of a woman was found that
> had had its head removed and was cut up into pieces of meat, which two girls confessed
> having eaten. In the city, they ate dead bodies eight days before the entrance of the king
> [for La Rochelle's formal capitulation], [and] three that ate [the dead] died immediately.
> . . . It was also said that a mother ate her daughter and a niece.[88]

After returning to France from Brazil by way of Geneva, Jean de Léry reported the occurrence of similar taboo practices among besieged Huguenots in his important victim-as-eyewitness account, the *Histoire memorable du siège de Sancerre,* the narrative of which certainly functioned as the antitype for Huguenot histories of La Rochelle's ordeal in 1627–28.[89] De Léry condemned such behavior among these co-religionists, which he compared unfavorably with the cannibalism of the Tupi.[90] "Les Sauvages Ameriquains," unlike the Sancerrois, practiced cannibalism as a ritual of their primitivist culture. As such, it was integral to their history and worldview. Prisoners of war who were to be eaten were treated honorably, and indeed (from de Léry's perspective), participated willingly in the ritual. The prisoner's death was endured stoically, both as vengeance and closure for Tupi killed and eaten in the past. Tupi cannibals and their victims displayed, in fact, the same sort of discipline, mastery, and craftsmanship in these rituals of death, rebirth, and cultural maintenance as skilled Huguenots in constructing artisanal security. Cannibalism was thus a control against the potential for chaos and unrestrained mimetic violence between primitive Americans, to prevent precisely the sort of behavior de Léry had observed on both sides in the civil wars.[91]

However, the cannibalism by starving Huguenots that was observed in Sancerre and later in La Rochelle was not morally equivalent to the barbarous cannibalism that was well known among Catholics in their massacres of the Huguenots. If the people of Sancerre were driven to cannibalize "their kinsmen, neighbors, and compatriots" by the Catholic siege of 1573, what excused the cannibals in the St. Bartholomew's Day massacre? "What I have said is enough to horrify you, indeed, to make your hair stand on end," de Léry wrote of Tupi cannibalism in his *Histoire d'un voyage fait en la terre du Brésil* in 1578:

> Nevertheless, so that those who read these horrible things, practiced daily among these barbarous nations of the land of Brazil, may also think more carefully about the things that go on every day over here, among us: . . . if it comes to brutal action of really (as one says) chewing and devouring human flesh . . . what of France? (I am French, and it grieves me to say it.) During the bloody tragedy that began in Paris on the 24th of August 1572 . . . among other acts too horrible to recount, which were perpetrated at that time throughout the kingdom, the fat of human bodies (which, in ways more barbarous than those of the savages, were butchered at Lyon after being pulled out of the Soane)—was it not publicly sold to the highest bidder? The livers, hearts, and other parts of these bodies—were they not eaten by the furious murderers, of whom Hell itself stands in horror? Likewise, after the wretched massacre of one Coeur de Roy, who professed the Reformed faith in the city of Auxerre—did not those who committed this murder cut his heart to pieces, display it for sale to those who hated him, and finally, after grilling it over coals— glutting their rage like mastiffs—eat of it? . . .
>
> . . . So let us henceforth no longer abhor so very greatly the cruelty of the anthropophagous—that is, man-eating—savages. For since there are some here in our midst even worse and more detestable than those who, as we have seen, attack only enemy nations, while the ones over here have plunged into the blood of their kinsmen, neighbors, and compatriots, one need not go beyond one's own country, nor as far as America, to see such monstrous and prodigious things.[92]

Yet de Léry was able to find divine logic in precedent for the practice of cannibalism under similar historical circumstances in book 6 of Flavius Josephus's *Jewish War*, where cannibalism is reported among the starving victims of Titus's final siege of Jerusalem (March to September 8, A.D. 70), which triggered the diaspora of the Jews.[93] De Léry's *Histoire* found its ideal antitype in Josephus's Jewish *War*, Géralde Nakam argues: "Léry reconstructed, by a nearly instinctive mimeticism, the chronicle of the defeat of Jerusalem. . . . Sancerre, the little community of the Just, was like La Rochelle, the symbol of Jerusalem on earth . . . always in the vertical dimension."[94] The importance of de Léry's seamless "mimeticism" that found a parallel in Jewish history to an anti-Christian war between Christians cannot be overestimated. Moreover, the same mimetic desire for a New Jerusalem rising out of the fragmentation of the aging earth is to be found both in Revelation 21 and in the artisanal work of Palissy and his followers.

This apocalyptic pattern allowed Léry to transform Sancerre's "pitiful history" of war, famine, and cannibalism into a politically charged Neoplatonic allegory of ascetic purification by physical ordeal to cleanse and liberate the soul.[95] The *Histoire mem-orable* was thus also an allegory of the monistic soul's stoical triumph over its corrupt, aging, and fragmented corporeal form (bodily, town, and religious) in the last stages of decay. Old Testament history also harnessed Sancerre's Huguenots to God's chosen in this context. In postlapsarian time, Jewish dislocation from God was represented by the dispersion and a series of punishments and ordeals visited upon the tribes of Israel by the deity, angry that the covenant with his chosen people was continually broken. Punishment and ordeal killed off and distilled the tribes almost to the point of extinction, but in every case—the story of Noah being the most famous example—a small fragment was selected to survive the deluge and begin again. Fragmentary survival was at work in Palissy's triumph of tiny and industrious builders over the large and seemingly complete and this ethos was ultimately redirected into the virtual reenactment of a macabre Eucharist in Sancerre, wherein all the martyred dead served as bodily hosts. As in Jerusalem of old, fallen survivors maintained themselves to begin again in dispersion by eating and drinking from the flesh and blood of martyred dead.

Huguenot historians were well aware that A.D. 70 also marked the beginning of the most influential ascetic tradition among Jews of the dispersion following Jerusalem's fall, a process given its charismatic voice by the revival of the commentaries of Philo of Alexandria (20 B.C.–ca. A.D.45), which thereafter entered into Christian commentary.[96] Philo's task was to incorporate the Neoplatonic dualism he had assimilated from Hellenistic philosophy into Judaic thought: "When we are living, the soul is dead and has been entombed in the body as in a sepulchre; whereas should we die, the soul lives forthwith its proper life, and is released from the body, the baneful corpse to which it was tied."[97]

For Philo, the body was a "source of demonic uncleanness"; the denuded *bones* of pious dead alone remained venerable: "by which I mean the only relics of such a soul as were left behind untouched by corruption and worthy of perpetual memory."[98] Philo extended veneration to incorporate the bodily analogy that would become ubiquitous in his commentaries: bone was to flesh even as the "universal Mind, uncreated and immortal" was to mere sensory perception.[99] Considered a part of this Neoplatonic ascetic dispersion tradition, the emerging bones of the Rochelais dead and dying signified self-knowledge through destruction of the corrupt flesh of the pious to the Huguenot, while Catholic commentators perceived the revelation of vile hidden corruption.

De Léry constructed a dazzling yet unsettling mimetic strategy. His agenda was to seduce readers (including God) into empathy with the Sancerreois as universal victims and chosen people, even while the question of victimization remained open in both Sancerre and La Rochelle. Within the metaphorical confines of Neoplatonic history, "pitiful" Huguenot victims assumed the moral high ground by pleading their passive

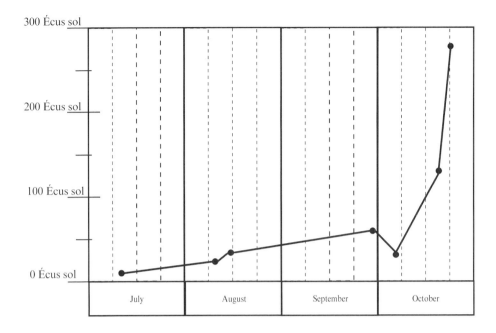

The price of wheat:

About 10 July	average price of 5.3 Écus sol per bushel
About 8 August	20 Écus sol per bushel
About 15 August	33 Écus sol per bushel
29 September	64 Écus sol per bushel
4 October	30 Écus sol per bushel
18 October	133 Écus sol per bushel
21 October	267 Écus sol per bushel

FIGURE 4.3. The price of wheat during the siege of La Rochelle, 1628. Prices from Philippe Vincent, *Le Journal des choses les plus mémorables qui se sont passées au dernier siège de La Rochelle, par Pierre Mervault, rochelois, revu, corrigé et de nouveau augmenté* . . . Rouen: J. Lucas, 1671.

suffering. At the same time, Huguenot historians had disguised another parallel between what happened at Sancerre during the siege of 1573 and at La Rochelle in 1627–28, beyond the pity of famine and cannibalism.

The price of wheat during the siege year (fig. 4.3), reflected the overall price of foodstuffs in the fortress. A combination of dwindling supply due to Richelieu's effective blockade of the port and ruthless profiteering by Huguenot merchants at the expense of their co-religionists, drove up prices approximately 300 percent between July and October 1628. Prices during the siege indicated an unmistakable economy of life and death among Huguenots in both Sancerre and La Rochelle.[100] Writing in *Histoire d'un voyage* with profiteering during the siege of Sancerre fresh in his mind, de Léry compared usury to cannibalism. The pious poor were thus victimized and consumed by physical *and* economic violence:

if you consider in all candor what our big usurers do, sucking blood and marrow, and eating everyone alive—widows, orphans, and other poor people, whose throats it would be better to cut once and for all, than to make them linger in misery—you will say that they are even more cruel than the savages I speak of. And that is why the prophet says [Mic. 3:3] that such men flay the skin of God's people, eat their flesh, break their bones and chop them in pieces as for the pot, and as flesh within the cauldron.[101]

By September 1627, John Winthrop Jr., who had joined the duke of Buckingham's expedition to Saint-Martin, on the Île de Ré, as a clerk and scientific observer, must have shared de Léry's sentiments. The adventuring son found himself short of funds and wrote his worried father (the future governor of Massachusetts), at Groton Manor, in England, that prices were then prohibitive in La Rochelle and on the Île de Ré. "It is a very dear place for strangers," he wrote, "and St. Martins is dearer by reason of our army, and that all we have brought in commeth from Rochell[e]."[102] Prices had risen dramatically in La Rochelle, because Rochelais merchants smuggled supplies to the English relief force and profiteered at the expense of the starving inhabitants of the besieged city as well.

The 5,400 survivors whom Richelieu finally confronted as "true images of death" at La Rochelle's capitulation cannot be considered passive victims in any fundamental sense of the term. Aside from their history of persecution of Catholics in the Rochelais Reformation of the 1560s, which invited acts of revenge, Huguenots survived not by chance but in large part as a result of their high status in the socioeconomic hierarchy and at the expense of compatriots of poor and middling circumstances. The fate of La Rochelle's *bouches inutiles* (that is, "useless mouths"), was remarkably similar to that of the post-1568 Rochelais Catholics who were banished during wartime, and they exemplified the most extreme manifestation of this pattern.[103] Rochelais from the city's *grand conseil* increased their own chances of survival and the available food supply for paying customers by locating and sacrificing marginal groups. In May 1627, the month when food was first becoming scarce, the council ordered that all "beggar children, orphans, mendicants, and the unknown [be] cast outside the city walls." Once outside, exposed individuals died of starvation or were killed by soldiers from either side. Meanwhile, these councilmen underwent their own analogous process of violent marginalization by the expanding state, which culminated in October 1628. Huguenot survivors of the religious wars possessed a very realistic fear of the deadly consequences of marginality.

Absent La Rochelle's death registers, lost for 1628, which would have told us the social status of the dead, and since there is no evidence of epidemics, which would presumably have cut across the social hierarchy, certain conclusions seem self-evident.[104] It is safe to say that the vast majority of the 19,800 Rochelais who died belonged to the lower and middling orders, while the majority of the 5,400 Rochelais who survived derived from elite households. This means that a substantial number of servants attached to elite households may have survived. In addition to ministers and the Consistory, many elite survivors were classified as "gentlemen-merchants." They had access to cash, as well as smuggled goods or foodstuffs stored for transhipment.[105] The most successful profiteers emerged from this powerful group. Indeed, merchants with well-stocked warehouses in early June undoubtedly extracted fortunes from the desperation of compatriots still alive in late October. De Léry and Palissy would have found it difficult to represent these survivors as other than oppressors in the guise of victims; indeed, as both victims and oppressors simultaneously.

After 1628, many *gentilshommes-marchands* abandoned La Rochelle altogether for Paris and lucrative posts as financiers and *fermiers* in the service of the king.[106] Other survivors prefigured the great exodus of La Rochelle's merchants after the Revocation of 1685, by emigrating to the destination points of their cargoes. Even as the dead were buried and rapidly replaced by thousands of opportunistic Catholic immigrants from Poitou and Limousin, many of the merchant families that survived 1628 remained. Some continued to practice Protestantism openly, others were *nouveaux convertis*, or secret Protestants. Together, these families kept dynastic control over commerce in La Rochelle, although now under the watchful eye of intendants and jurists through the unstable era of the Revocation and beyond, into the prosperous eighteenth century.[107]

The most influential of southwestern France's post-1628 urban Huguenot population that migrated to colonial British America were connected by family to these ambiguous, ruthlessly hierarchical, and upwardly mobile Rochelais mercantile elites, who had formerly manipulated the repressive and sacerdotal Rochelais Consistory and eventually found a home in the American Church of England. Colonial "Anglicans" were as ambitious as the Rochelais Calvinists but even less successful in maintaining Church discipline against lay initiatives and heterodoxy.

La Rochelle's lower orders, including its large and militant artisanal sector, were decimated by starvation in the siege. Those who survived 1628 were systematically denied membership in guilds they had once dominated. The vigilant Catholic corporations in La Rochelle perceived a growth in the number of Protestants in town by the late 1650s. Huguenot artisans had reinfiltrated the guilds in particular. A Catholic backlash resulted, and in 1661, a purge was undertaken by the corporations with the police to rid the guilds of Protestant tradesmen. Harsh new restrictions against the making of things were placed on Huguenot artisans. There were no new limits to selling things, however, so many tradesmen became merchants and shopkeepers and followed their crafts secretly, if at all. Hence, the Rochelais Huguenot mercantile sector became even stronger, and its artisans either joined the merchants or left town in 1661 for greener pastures.[108] These demographic and political realities were manifested in colonial America. Some of the 1661 group made their way to New Amsterdam through Holland and contributed to what was to become New York's "old culture" after 1685. But with a few notable exceptions—the Vincent and Coutant craft dynasties were from La Rochelle—the vast majority of all Huguenot artisans in New York, like its turners and leather chair makers, were refugees from Saintonge or the Île de Ré.

Many of La Rochelle's dead were quickly replaced by Catholic outsiders, and the most significant article of Louis XIII's and Richelieu's terms of capitulation forbade the immigration of any new Protestant families into the fortress after 1628. Aided by the massive purge of 1661, this guaranteed that the surviving Rochelais Huguenot families would remain part of an aging minority sect with little or no hope for demographic expansion save conversion to Catholicism or outmigration.[109] It was a formidable first step by the state toward outlawing Protestantism in La Rochelle, though that would not occur until the Reformed religion itself was prohibited in France in 1685. Thus, the Huguenots of La Rochelle were forced to suffer the same devastating social, economic, and religious restrictions the victorious Reformed party had forced on Rochelais Catholics in the 1560s. A decimated "Reformed community in the city found itself transformed overnight from heir to stepchild in a large household with a new head." Yet the economics of mortality in the siege guaranteed that it would remain a very wealthy and influential stepchild indeed.[110]

Despite their tenacity and continued economic success, the power of the merchant oligarchy to determine events independently of the state was effectively eliminated with La Rochelle's military subjugation and the introduction of the intendancy. These changes were effected by Richelieu himself. The cardinal built an enormous financial interest in both Aunis and coastal Saintonge, which was impossible to maximize without the royal subjugation of La Rochelle and the cooperation of leading merchants. In October 1626, Louis XIII awarded possession of all the monarchy's maritime affairs to Richelieu, including lucrative admiralty rights, which he coveted above all else. After that, Richelieu consolidated his control of Brouage and its salt production—also acquired during the 1620s—and made the tiny fort and ancient competitor of La Rochelle his base of operations in the southwestern provinces. From that point on, Richelieu's purchases made him the largest landowner in Aunis-Saintonge, and after 1628, his large business interests dominated La Rochelle's mercantile activity as well. There was far more at stake than reasons of state in his risky promotion of the siege to the mercurial Louis XIII. By the time the full economic impact of the fall of La Rochelle was felt in France's maritime provinces, Richelieu was not only the king's chief minister but his richest subject.[111]

Since Richelieu was an absentee landlord, he needed reliable *fermiers* to administer his growing properties. Such administrators were recruited during the siege itself, when the cardinal was able to assess the capabilities of Catholic leaders from Aunis-

Saintonge under adverse conditions. Henri de Sourdis, archbishop of Bordeaux and Jean Hilayreau, sieur de La Traversière, oversaw his interests in La Rochelle and its hinterlands, effectively becoming a personal intendancy in Aunis-Saintonge, and both entered Richelieu's service during the siege.[112] If the siege almost eliminated La Rochelle's Protestant population, Huguenots still controlled much of the rural landscape of Saintonge, especially the coast. Richelieu's men were directed to replace Protestants on the land and in the salt marshes with docile Catholic immigrants where possible to make collection of rents more reliable.[113] Palissy's "plowmen" were thus forced off the land to become economic refugees, as well as another source for the Atlantic migration prior to 1685.

Key to Richelieu's ambitions in southwestern France, however, was his ability to manipulate and control elements of the surviving mercantile sector of La Rochelle. To maximize profits from rents, and liberate agrarian "income from the unforeseeable accidents of collection, transport and the insolvency of *fermiers*," the cardinal diversified away from his reliance on land, and invested capital in banking and seaborne commerce.[114] This was accomplished through his patronage of a consortium of three Huguenot bankers and financiers, Gedeon Tallemant, Nicolas Rambouillet, and Marc-Antoine Arcère, who signed a ten-year investment contract with Richelieu in April 1632, and again in 1642. Tallemant, the leader of the consortium, was a bourgeois of La Rochelle, where he held office as late as 1620. When the siege began in 1627, Tallemant defected to the crown's side and was accepted into Richelieu's protection. Almost immediately, this Rochelais merchant began financial operations outside the fortress to profit from the ensuing siege of his former allies. Tallement's behavior during the siege certainly fit de Léry's description of "what our big usurers do." Still, the consortium's motive was to acquire Richelieu's protection and patronage more than to profit from him. In fact, it lost money between 1632 and 1642. The "advantages were political rather than financial," Joseph Bergin writes, "a form of insurance which, despite bringing few direct profits, enabled them to make greater profits undisturbed elsewhere."[115]

After 1628, all the merchants of La Rochelle knew that their path to maintaining upwardly mobile status as a subgroup was now serpentine rather than defiant. Success lay in accommodation to the state, or outward assimilation to dominant Catholic norms as *nouveaux convertis*. This was not so easy a process for surviving Rochelais families as it seemed to be for the merchant Tallemant. Religious life inside the once great fortress was now defined by tensions between the necessity for secret devotion and the city's proud history of public witness to Calvinist faith. This tension between revelation and concealment had been resolved for most rustic Saintongeais Huguenots after Philibert Hamelin was executed in 1557.[116]

Indeed, La Rochelle had been stripped of all urbanity and had nearly come to

resemble its hinterland. A traveler named Elie Brakenhoffer who visited the fallen
fortress in 1645, its walls now leveled to the ground, noted sadly in his journal that "it
is deplorable that so beautiful a city has been reduced to barely a burg. From many of
its streets one can see the bare countryside." He was most astonished by the exposed
condition of "the Huguenots [who] are in a bad posture . . . they are now at the south
end of the city, in a dismantled building." He concluded that their state of reduction
was "as bad as possible." In 1646, Philippe Vincent, a minister of the demolished temple whose family emigrated to New Amsterdam / New York, wrote that the siege of
1628, had left "scars [that] will remain imprinted on us always." Yet apocalyptic memory was essential for spiritual survival, and "we should think about it often, so that it
will be a lesson never to fall again into the same sins, by which we attracted this upon
ourselves." After the purge of Rochelais Huguenots in 1661, jeremiads rained down
from the pulpit upon the heads of the dwindling congregation. One such sermon in
particular would surely have attracted Bernard Palissy's attention in 1563. "Each of us
has contributed to the destruction of our Temple, [and yet] we make profession of the
doctrine of the elect," a certain Pastor Flanc preached in March 1662. Flanc had finally
come to realize the essence of "De la ville de forteresse": "One does not transplant trees
except in order to have them produce more fruit," he lamented from the rubble of his
church, open to the countryside, in the fortress without walls. "It must be that God,"
Flanc concluded, "having transplanted us from our Temples into our houses, will give
us more fruit of a holy amendment of life." It is uncertain what his aging congregants,
whose lives and city were defined by the open defiance of kings, thought of Flanc's
sermon of transplantation into the shadows. But by 1680, as the Revocation approached, only 4,750 people still called themselves Protestant in La Rochelle.[117]

   With mostly mercantile elites surviving to bridge its polar revolutionary moments,
La Rochelle's Reformation and Counter-Reformation—and ultimately the events of
1568 and 1628—were in the formal sense symmetrical and interchangeable. What insights did interchangeability, considered within the ancient Christian category of reversal, provide for artisanal process and, above all, material representations of Huguenot cultural identity in the process of formation as it was assaulted during the French
civil wars of religion and, by 1628, the Thirty Years' War in northern Europe? Beyond
that, how was the ambiguity of victimization and of power relations so central to this
process in the Huguenot historiography of both Aunis-Saintonge and colonial British
America transformed into a habitual response in transatlantic religious and material
culture?

   Certain general principles have guided my understanding of La Rochelle 1517–1628:
(1) La Rochelle functioned as a looking-glass culture, animated by Protestant / Catholic (or "Reformed" / "orthodox") mimetic desire, anxiety, and violence; (2) within this
system, and especially among elites, it was sometimes impossible to distinguish victim

from victimizer, or oppressor from oppressed; (3) power was thus exercised within a structure in which difference (and *deference*) was ambiguous; (4) the function of this culture, when animated by violence and threatened with entropy was to perpetuate the logic of these formal requirements; (5) Rochelais Huguenots, however, when in temporary asymmetrical relation to the dominant Catholic order, devised strategies, at risk of revenge, to shift precipitously toward equilibrium through violence or, lacking the power to do so, actively disguised and compensated for personal marginality in ways that made their social disequilibrium endurable (and sometimes profitable). This last category became a permanent condition for Rochelais Huguenots after the fall of their *place de sûreté.* Having experienced two generations of near absolute power followed by total defeat, surviving Rochelais elites were strangers to weakness. Now urban Huguenots in Aunis were forced to converge in matters of security with artisanal practices pioneered by their rustic counterparts in the open countryside of the Saintongeais periphery, in place since the time of Bernard Palissy's artisanal interregnum of the 1560s.

As surviving Rochelais elites devised strategies to maintain their commercial viability and a shadow of their pre-1628 Reformed identity in situ for two generations longer until 1685, the task of Santongeais Huguenot artisans after the fall of La Rochelle was to redouble their rustic effort to build equilibrium through confusion of difference between dominance and marginality. After 1628, their even greater social marginalization required the strong reassertion of Palissy's innovations in a world without fortresses, including his Paracelsian material-holiness synthesis and other metaphysical solutions to the continuity of Protestant culture subjugated by the rise of absolutism under Richelieu and eventually the pressures of dispersion into the networks of the Atlantic diaspora.

The moral questions posed by Palissy and de Léry during the civil wars, and by Catholic enemies of the Huguenots, considered alongside evidence of Huguenot behavior during the siege, suggested a reading of the culture of innovation that illuminated Protestant artisanal discourse in a surprising way. Perhaps such a culture possessed no discrete identity of its own coming out of the wars, having emerged only as a *partial,* chameleonlike entity in violent though symbiotic opposition to some perpetually dominant historical host. Palissy's tiny animal fortresses, after all, had to hide themselves inside of other natural and spiritual forces to remain secure. The Huguenot survivors of 1628—both rural and urban—may have been revealed in their purest form as improvisational parasites needing pluralistic societies to maximize their opportunities to innovate, hybridize, and thrive. This claim is amplified by the overlapping meanings of "parasite" and "Nicodemite" in the seventeenth century.[118] Blatant violence was no longer a viable option. Only in the most oblique domestic, material, and commercial ways could the now perpetually marginal Huguenots hope to maintain the structural capacity to subvert in their historical "oppressors" (or hosts) the defeated aspect of themselves that they simultaneously desired most to emulate and so realize the prophesy of reversal in both everyday life and the millennial future.

❧ The Permanent Interregnum ❧

The emergence of profound urban-rural tensions intrinsic to the regional diffusion of metropolitan Genevan models emanating from Geneva and the La Rochelle Consistory, via its ministerial agents, to the presumably intellectually subordinate Saintongeais laity, laid the groundwork for Palissy's artisanal interregnum in the wake of Philibert Hamelin's execution in 1557. Disruptions, structural dislocation, and an aggressive lay ascendancy resulted in interruption of the flow of face-to-face ministerial discourse, and with it, orthodox doctrinal influence and ideological control, to the fortress's periphery. Yet such regional tensions did not mean complete dichotomy. The ministerial presence of Hamelin and his Genevan followers in Saintonge was essential to the process of diffusion. This was driven by the rural laity and artisan-preachers such as Palissy and his followers, who willfully misread metropolitan models that were deemed too hierarchical or were not inculcated and reinforced fully by catechistic repetition. Such models were therefore subject to manipulation from below and finally even outright appropriation in new forms for local use.

Ultimately, these structural tensions were the result of the same sort of frontier geographical isolation from La Rochelle that the fortress enjoyed in relation to Paris. This was exacerbated by disrupted military organization and practice during wartime, which unmasked La Rochelle's periodic inability to extend its passion for regional centralization to Saintonge. Religious culture was given coherence by the *laity*, whose "free," enthusiastic, and materialist exegesis of biblical text and the "Book of Nature" combined memory of Roman Catholicism and local folklore with primitive Reformation theology. This worried the Rochelais Consistory, concerned with maintaining regional Church unity and tight discipline under strict ministerial control.

Whether the ministers were dispatched by La Rochelle or Geneva to Saintonge, once in the region, the Rochelais Consistory tried to keep them under its influence and protection. Many promising Saintongeais *pasteurs* were in fact eventually called back to serve at La Rochelle after an apprenticeship in the hinterlands.[119] And if we are to judge by the overwhelming number of Rochelais *pasteurs* asked to moderate at the nineteen southwestern regional synods held between 1560 and 1606, then the influence of the Consistory—if not among artisans then among the rural Huguenot elites—was enduring.[120] Indeed, after 1590, the number of ministers of Rochelais origin who served in the province climbed to an average of sixteen.[121]

La Rochelle's ministerial influence and control suggested by these numbers must be considered problematic, however. The large presence of the Rochelais ministry in the hinterlands existed at full capacity *only* under ideal peacetime conditions. These were rarely experienced for long during the civil wars. In practice, centralizing efforts by the Rochelais Consistory were consistently undermined by what Trocmé describes as "a constant phenomenon at La Rochelle" during the war years. When royal armies or the Catholic Sainte Ligue threatened, most *pasteurs* (always the targets of torture and murder) dispatched by La Rochelle or Geneva to Saintonge were sent scurrying north—along with thousands of others in harm's way—to the protection of the fortress.[122] Hence, Saintongeais Huguenots were left to their own intellectual and spiritual devices for increasing periods of time—during the region's most intense era of religious anxiety and innovation—with virtually *no* direct consistorial intervention. What had initially been frequent, temporary, patterns of autonomous sectarian behavior acquired by Saintongeais Huguenots during chronic absences of Genevan and Rochelais ministerial authority in wartime was *institutionalized* during the civil wars and expanded to Aunis with the reduction of the great *place de sûreté* after 1628. Palissy's primitive artisanal church in Saintes signals the origins of this permanent interregnum.

✦ New World Historiography and the Problem with Writing: ✦ "we can declare our secrets to whomever we choose"

And so we conclude with that moment of entropy and violent abandonment in his personal history that occurred four years before the first civil war of religion, when the Genevan minister Philibert Hamelin, Palissy's mentor and friend, was absent from Saintes in the coastal islands and about to be captured and sent to Bordeaux, where he was tortured and executed. At this exact moment, Palissy, Hamelin's main disciple, and his artisan followers, took control of the Reformation in Saintes from below. In so doing, they ushered in the first artisans' interregnum and established a religious and social tradition made permanent in the entire region when events in 1628 turned southwestern France into a *désert* strewn with demolished churches. This tradition extended to the very heart of the periods of escape, dispersion, and the assemblies of the *désert*, which took place in rustic grottoes that were hidden yet still exposed in the natural world. "Natural" subterranean grottoes were thus the stuff of Palissy's material life.

It was at this moment that Palissy's little "History" of "the beginning of the Reformed Church of the town of Xaintes," properly entered into the historiography of the Huguenots' New World:

> the year was 1557. . . . Some time before Philibert was arrested, there was in this town a certain artisan, poor and indigent to an incredible degree, who had so great a desire to spread the word of God that he made it plain to another man, also unlearned, for neither

one knew much: Nevertheless, the first one advised the other that he should employ the most stirring form of exhortation because that would be the most fruitful; and seeing how the second was totally devoid of learning, this gave him heart: and some days later, he assembled one Sunday morning nine or ten people, and because he was unlettered, he had taken some passages from the Old and New Testaments and written them out by hand. And when they were assembled, he read them the passages or authorities and said: For as each one has received the word, so he shall give it to others, and that all trees that bear no fruit will be cut down and thrown into the fire: also he read another authority taken from Deuteronomy, the one that says, You will proclaim my Law in going, and coming, while drinking, and eating, when you sleep, and when you awaken, and when you are sitting in the road; he also propounded for them the parable of the talents and a great number of such authorities, and he was doing that toward two good ends: the first was to show that it is the right of all people to speak about the statutes and ordinances of God, so that one not despise His doctrine because of His abjection [that is, Christ's abject poverty and death—a reference to his crucifixion alongside common criminals]: the second was in order to inspire some of their listeners to follow their example and do the same: for at the same time, there convened together some six among them to give weekly exhortation, so that six of them would each week exhort, meaning that each of the six would take turns preaching every sixth week on Sundays only and because they were getting themselves into something they had not been taught, it was decided that they would write their exhortations and would read them to the assembly, and all these things were done through the good example, advice, and doctrine of Master Philibert Hamelin. This was the beginning of the Reformed Church of the town of Xaintes.[123]

This long passage documents Palissy's understanding of the process of circular diffusion between the ministry of learned Genevan and Rochelais urban Calvinism and the laity of "poor, unlettered artisans" in Saintonge. "A certain artisan, poor and indigent to an incredible degree" was arguably Palissy's description of himself in the seminal role. Those "others," who "got themselves into something they had not been taught" constituted Palissy's first conventicle, an underground group of artisan followers. A warrant of September 1558 issued by the *parlement* of Guyenne for Palissy's arrest, along with the nine other members of his original secret assembly, for an "inquiry on acts of heresy," provides the names of the accused and most of their trades:

> Colete Maudot, wife of Mathurin Seurin, butcher of Xaintes; and likewise . . . Nicolas Veyrel apothecary, Bernard Palisis called the potter, Guillemete Patronne, widow . . . hostess of the public house at the sign of the Noble Vine, André Bodet her son, Mathurin Seurin, butcher, Nicolas the Embroiderer, Joseph the Mason the younger, . . . Master Legier the Mason, [and] Guillaume Girault.[124]

The same arrest warrant also targeted another conventicle of artisan heretics in nearby Saint-Jean d'Angély. This hinted at how widespread the infection was among Saintongeais tradesmen and their wives, many of whom worked in their husbands' shops. This unknown group was smaller than Palissy's, containing only four or five members, and it was led by a glazier, a barber-surgeon, and their wives. All of the members of Palissy's assembly were represented as a community of like thinkers from similar very poor backgrounds. Still, we know nothing more about the lives of Nicolas Veyrel, the apothecary from Saintes, or his co-religionist Cyprien Jousseaulme, the barber-surgeon who lived in Saint-Jean d'Angély. Yet we do know that both of these trades, which used crucibles and distillation by fire—as did Palissy with his pottery glazes and alchemy—were essential to the diffusion of Paracelsian alchemic and manual theory and the practice of experiential natural philosophy that Palissy championed in the *Recepte* and *Discours*. It is self-evident that Veyrel and Palissy had religious insights about Nature in common. However, they may also have perceived the spiritualized transformation of the material world in the same way from closely shared reading, experimental laboratory work, and discussion. Did such religious and artisanal discourse take place in the public house of Guillemete Patronne and her son André Bodet? Publicans were always suspected of harboring heretical artisans and were, for example, targeted for occasional crackdowns by police in La Rochelle after 1628.[125]

Clearly, apart from the Word itself, the group's primary "authority" was Hamelin, and Palissy took great pains to establish that his own authority was derived from the "maistre" himself: "all these things were done through the good example, advice and doctrine of Master Philibert Hamelin." This is made plain in the emphasis on the text and in the transcription of passages directly from (what must have been) Hamelin's own books, carried into the region through colporterage.

Hamelin's "example, advice, and doctrine" is especially evident in Palissy's citation of Deuteronomy [11:19], the book that identifies itself as containing [1:1] "the words that Moses spoke to all Israel beyond the Jordan in the wilderness." Revealing his approach to reading, the potter paraphrased the original lines loosely and simply. Yet when Palissy wrote his advice, as "the first" of the "unlearned," that "You will proclaim my Law in going, and coming, while drinking and eating, when you sleep, and when you awaken, and when you are sitting in the road," he recalled that Hamelin had made preaching an invisible part of the rhythms of everyday life and work. Deuteronomy was also the book of laws, in which the Ten Commandments were given to Moses and the tablets placed in the Ark of the Covenant for the chosen [5:1–21; 10:1–5]. Once given, these laws became "a blessing and a curse" [11:26]. If the covenant was broken, Moses warned: "They shall besiege you in all your towns, until your high and fortified walls, in which you trusted, come down throughout your land; and they shall besiege you in all your towns throughout your land. . . . And you shall eat the offspring of your own body, the flesh of your sons and daughters . . . in the siege and in the distress with which your enemies shall distress you [28:52–53]."

Clearly, here was another archaic source for de Léry's reading of the siege of Sancerre, Palissy's critique of fortresses, the response from both sides to the siege of La Rochelle, and the abiding sense that the popular mistrust of fortresses was older than historical memory.

The Saintongeais laity would obey the discipline of a Genevan minister while in personal contact if it sensed his egalitarianism, as they did in Hamelin's case (but not in the case of his immediate successor). Yet Palissy was concerned here with the problem of spiritual maintenance in the *absence* of the official, learned Calvinist ministry. His choice of Deuteronomy 11 as a focal point was appropriate to this context as well. It not only suggested the mobility of refugee artisans, fragmented and preaching on the open road in the Huguenots' *désert*, but passage 19 also begins by commanding, "you shall teach [the law] to your children."

Palissy described his assembly as analogous to simple children in their religious understanding. The first pair of artisans were childlike, because they were so "unlearned, for neither one knew much." So, like the children in "De la ville de forteresse" who learned to defend themselves and provide for the community's security in time of war, Hamelin's orphaned spiritual children continued in the master's footsteps. Palissy chose to supplement Hamelin's "example and advice" in his own way, as a layman, by teaching how spiritual knowledge was to be diffused by Huguenot artisans who were hidden or limited by their "abjection" and simplicity, and who had no one to teach or lead by example but themselves. "The first one advised the other," Palissy wrote, "that he should employ the most stirring form of exhortation because that would be the most fruitful: and seeing how the second was totally devoid of learning, this gave him heart." This was the doctrine of religious enthusiasm, of speaking from a pious heart and religious experience, if not a learned mind. Promoting rustic security, it was emotional, interior, and natural. Hidden as it was in the domain of the spirit, there was safety in the space between man and God and soulish insight enough to read and interpret Scripture, understanding the natural world without benefit of a university education.

Hence, Hamelin's authority to teach the word was spread from Palissy to the next apparently literate (if unlearned) artisan and then throughout the assembly. Once local artisans gained the confidence to master the "stirring" motion of their inner spirit, they also learned how close they were to Christ himself, as "it was the right of all people to speak about the statutes and ordinances of God, so that one not despise His doctrine because of His abjection." Then they were ready to chart an independent course into the diaspora, for Palissy's plan "was in order to inspire some of their listeners to follow their example and do the same."

Finally, in an attempt to blend oral and written traditions so that unlearned artisans might remember Calvinist doctrine *precisely* as Hamelin had taught it to Palissy, and Palissy to others, text "from the Old and New Testaments" was always written "out by hand" before reading it to the assembly. Calvin originated this advice in order to protect the pure doctrine, and the unlettered Palissy remembered "passages and authorities" that way. Thus, because his followers "were getting themselves into something they had not been taught, it was decided that they would write their exhortation and would read them to the assembly." As each new artisan-preacher led their own secret assembly, he or she presumably read both the text and a Palissian paraphrase of Hamelin's interpretation of the Word aloud. In theory, the strangled Hamelin would "speak" again through a genealogy of hundreds of artisans' mouths and skilled hands preaching in the transatlantic *désert*.

Palissy's dependency on writing "by hand" as a mnemonic device for spreading both the Word and its meaning to the unlettered in the rustic Huguenot *désert* was also one of the few advantages that Jean de Léry found Europeans held unambiguously over the savages of America. Here was a way in which great secrets might be hidden or made public, almost simultaneously. "For while," de Léry wrote in his *Histoire d'un voyage,* savages "can communicate nothing except by the spoken word":

we, on the other hand . . . by means of writing and the letters that we send, we can declare our secrets to whomever we choose, even to the ends of the earth. So even aside from the learning that we acquire from books, of which the savages seem likewise completely destitute, this invention of writing, which we possess and of which they are just as utterly deprived, must be ranked among the singular gifts which men over here have received from God.[126]

De Léry proudly told the story of "when I was first in this country, in order to learn their language I wrote a number of sentences which I then read aloud to them":

Thinking that this was some kind of witchcraft, they said to each other, "Is it not a marvel that this fellow, who yesterday could not have said a single word in our language, can now be understood to us, by virtue of that paper that he is holding and which makes him speak thus?"[127]

It is difficult to share de Léry's confidence that the Tupi sentences he copied down when he first arrived in Brazil said precisely what he thought they did; or, even more slippery, yet to the point, that they elicited the convenient responses he remembered his Tupi hearers saying in a language he did not fully understand. Whether the audience consisted of American savages or childlike and rustic (if literate) Huguenot artisans, attempts to order dissemination of meaning through writing—that is, to orchestrate personal, intimate memory and spiritual understanding—failed from the outset absent strict Genevan discipline. While "we can declare our secrets to whomever we choose," their meaning or application cannot be limited once that declaration has been made. Secrets will have lives of their own. The tiny pieces of paper packed with text that were intended to signify the end of interpretation had marked only its beginning.

CHAPTER FIVE

Scenes of Reading

Rustic Artisans and the Diffusion of Paracelsian Discourses to New Worlds

> To stay in the woods was impossible, for I had been robbed so completely
> of everything that I could no longer subsist there. Nothing was left except
> a few books that lay scattered pell-mell here and there.
> —HANS JAKOB CHRISTOPH VON GRIMMELSHAUSEN,
> *The Adventures of Simplicius Simplicissimus*

❧ Paracelsus in the *désert* ❧

The natural-philosophical paradigm associated with the German-Swiss physician and alchemist Paracelsus, born Philippus Aureolus Theophrastus Bombastus von Hohenheim (1493?–1541), found a particularly receptive audience among early modern Protestant artisans.[1] Paracelsianism operated on at least two levels that Huguenot artisans found compelling during the interminable war years of the sixteenth and seventeenth centuries: one metaphysical, the other (for want of a better word) ideological. Palissy showed that he embraced both completely in his work.[2] The metaphysics of Paracelsianism rested on the Neoplatonic foundation associated with the christianizing Florentine humanist-philosopher Marsilio Ficino (1433–99)—a protégé of the great Renaissance patron Cosimo de' Medici (and his successors)—whose astrological formulations of the infinite movements and aspirations of the universal soul (the "bond and knot" of the cosmos) as it circulated between the complex hierarchies of substances descending from the purity of God to corrupt matter was appropriated by Paracelsus in the early sixteenth century and then adapted to the Germanic context. Above all, the Paracelsians absorbed Ficino's soulish concepts from *Theologia platonica* (1482), *Epistolae* (1495), and his medical and astrological treatise *De vita libri tres* (1489), all of which were commentaries on sacramentality in the natural world and secular material life, through the analogy of the macrocosm and the microcosm.[3]

Ficino's Christianization of Plato, therefore, centered on the subtle operation of aspiring souls in the material world; that is, the corporification of spirit. Plato's system of intelligible reality was superseded by Ficino's monistic universe, given coherence by the soul's quest through matter as it climbed toward God's purity at the apex of the macrocosm. Ficino's metaphysics thus privileged soulish experience by stressing the primacy of hidden realities in everyday life. This resonated deeply with Palissy and other Protestant Paracelsians during the religious wars, because Ficino characterized the essential condition of man's inner life as a melancholy combination of grief, pain, and unrest—a condition, under the sign of Saturn, that exists beneath even the most polished public performance of social interaction or commerce.

Man's external impressions of Nature and history amplified inner sorrow. Because sensible things were fallacious except when viewed by a soul unfettered by corruption in the lower zones of human and natural bodies, all man perceived with bodily (as opposed to soulish) eyes was a shadow world of forms attenuated by chaos, disorder, and obscurity of purpose. Forms thus became more diffuse as they emanated further away from their origin in God. Still, dialectical consciousness of this inner reality of grief and pain led to the soul's aspirations toward the higher realities of divine joy, perfection, and visibility. When the soul was animated by such resonance, whether dissonant or harmonic, it ascended toward love, purity, and light. If man's inner condition of pain and disquietude resonated with similar conditions as the outer world of events and personal experience, then, with discipline, as was the case in Palissy's narrative of his own personal history, it was possible to accelerate the process toward consciousness, soulish epiphany, and synthesis of macrocosm and microcosm. Here was the domain of the philosopher magus: that hidden self-mastery wherein the soul builds a "citadel" to protect the purity of its operations and separates from the corrupting domain of the body, while still remaining within—and controlling—its outer shell.

The soul also possessed potential to overcome the various levels of corruption intrinsic to corporification through inner experience heightened by the contemplative life, extended into the outer world by industriousness in the manual arts. Both disciplines encouraged self-mastery while amplifying soulish knowledge—and hence knowledge of God—and both helped the soul to manipulate, animate, and separate bodily matter. Palissy combined artisanry *and* contemplation to achieve the status of manual philosopher. For him, to follow Paul Oskar Kristeller on Ficino: "the totality of all human life and consciousness thus fills a homogeneous sphere which extends in a straight line from common experience to the highest intuition of God." In this brief, prophetic moment of unity between macrocosm and microcosm, grief and disquiet were replaced by joy and calm; diffuse rays of divine light, once distanced from their source, emanated to suffuse the bodily vessel in flames of revelation; and soulish eyes allowed the mind to perceive universality in the true form of things hidden beneath the shadows of empirical reality. These were to become the subjects of Paracelsian artisanry, moments of linkage between inner experience and external reality made material.[4]

If the Paracelsians received Platonic ideas from Florence via Switzerland, Germany, and Protestant France, it should be remembered that Plato, a "culture-hero of the enemies of school-divinity," had *already* been received, directly or indirectly, by every Christian—in particular, those seekers who favored the reconstitution of the purity of primitive Christianity in early modern times—through St. Augustine's widely venerated text *On the Spirit and the Letter.*[5] The metaphysical foundation for Ficino and Paracelsus was thus laid centuries earlier in Augustine's powerful and universally diffused analysis of justification by faith. Moreover, there are provocative data to suggest that the monastic revival of the tenth century, accompanied by its extensive program of reform, rebuilding, and new building projects in Europe and Britain, was based on architectural systems that relied on plans formulated from Neoplatonic geometry, which "became accepted by the Latin Church in the form of Christian Platonism principally through the influence of Augustine."[6] Hence, Neoplatonic metaphysics informed Christian material life, as "early Christian and non-Christian writers," had "posited a divine Creator bringing into being cosmos out of chaos." In this cosmos, "harmony was maintained by the constituent parts of creation being formed in proportion to each other and to the whole." It has therefore been hypothesized, for example, that "the octagonal shrine stands as an architectural model in which number, geometry, liturgical function and inaugural dedication come together in signifying salvation architecturally." Just as significant for our purposes, is the corollary thesis, that a category of builders—drawn both from monastic founders and also certain masons—used their mastery of such Neoplatonic mathematical and philosophical secrets to set themselves apart as architects or philosophers of godly forms in matter, in much the same manner that Palissy did five hundred years later in Saintonge.[7] Perhaps many Neoplatonic revivals had occurred silently among pre-Reformation Christian artisans when it was perceived that cosmos had to emerge out of chaos.

A lot has been written about the material-holiness synthesis from multidisciplinary perspectives. Briefly stated, it posited a cosmology to encompass man's relation to the universe. This was animated by an active circulation between small and large, low and high, whereby "the body and soul of man are a miniature replica of the body and soul of the world, and that between these two worlds, the great and the little, there are correspondences, sympathies and antipathies, which the philosopher, the *magus,* could understand and control."[8] This framework demonstrated how these "correspondences, sympathies and antipathies" formed a universal system of spiritual and material hierarchies that enveloped the earthly hierarchies of man and that often operated most powerfully in minute elements of Nature. In this system, spiritual reality was virtually invisible to most fallen men; meaning lay hidden *beneath* the appearances of words and things (or, for Palissy, was so tiny as to be overlooked by enemies). Ficino called such blindness the "deception of the senses." The natural philosopher—the *magus* (or adept)—possessed a singular personal power, as he, almost alone, yet beset by vulgar and corrupted seekers after this secret, received the gift of pure inner sight from God. Magi comprehended meanings hidden to others, beneath the surface of materials, through the mystical manipulation and control of the spiritual powers of the macrocosm in everyday life.

Paracelsus's adaptation of Ficino's doctrine of the macrocosm and the microcosm for philosophical medicine was less contemplative than experiential—Paracelsians sought experiences distant from the cloistered spaced of Florentine academic life and then elucidated them in earthy speech intended to sully the rarified language of schoolmen—and alchemic; although dependant on the contexts in which it was practiced, it had social implications that stretched far beyond alchemy. Paracelsus imagined that the macrocosm functioned chemically, like an enormous alchemical crucible. This meant, in effect, that the universe must have been created by God in Genesis as a primordial act of chemical distillation of gigantic proportions. This was conceptualized *materially* in postlapsarian time as the "separation" of pure from impure matter in nature's fallen microcosm.[9] It followed that the human body, centering the microcosm, functioned as an extension of this chemical system, one that should be treated therapeutically by chemical medicine. Hence, Paracelsians assailed the established orthodoxy of the Galenic paradigm, which conceptualized the body as controlled largely by a system of "humours." The two paradigms had coexisted in both university and popular medicine for centuries, but Paracelsus argued that Galen's humoral system was merely based on scholasticism, not actual experience with suffering bodies. Galen was therefore superseded by the three chemical principles of sulfur, mercury, and salt. The chemical triad now represented the subtle materialization of the Holy Trinity in nature. An obsession with the properties and motions of salt, as we shall see, signified Palissy's abiding belief that salt was the "fifth element" animated by the holy spirit. This paradigmatic rift was momentous; in fact, Charles Webster's main claim that "the first major confrontation of the Scientific Revolution was between Paracelsus and Galen, rather than between Copernicus and Ptolemy" is considered axiomatic by most historians of science.[10]

Balancing their emphasis on materiality, however, Paracelsians depended on their performance of spiritual medicine. Most chemical therapy was thus understood to stem from a synthesis of spirit and matter. Building on Luther's fundamental metaphor of the good artisan as the source of good works, Paracelsus reimagined Ficino's universalist framework to signify that God's medical intermediaries achieved material *and* ontological knowledge, but only through practical and manual experience, and then only if the physician and his ailing patient possessed uncorrupted souls and so inner bodies. Illness was an extension, therefore, of spiritual corruption in the microcosm. So therapy had to rely on spiritual remedies hidden in the material world to all but the experienced Paracelsian physician, who manipulated alchemy in order to release cures from the shackles of filth and decay. Separation by fire of purity from impurity—that is, the transmutation of bodily matter with its great implications for manual application—attracted attention from literate artisans working in every material. Potters, glaziers, miners, blacksmiths, and brewers were especially open to experiment, however, as they used furnaces regularly in their work. Protestant artisans were among the most literate and interested in books, and numerous artisan-autodidacts understood the basics of Paracelsian natural philosophy enough to recognize the spiritual and economic potential that a comprehensive material-holiness synthesis had for innovation, and so profits, in their crafts. A philosophical system with a new language thus became available to experimental Huguenot artisans like Palissy. Once mastered and taught to apprentices and spiritual followers through both literary and oral traditions that tended to reinforce one another, this system helped local artisans gain religious, economic, and political authority in their rural towns and the countryside.

Paracelsus and Palissy relied upon folk traditions, biblical exegesis, and experience with nature in their recipes, so this pattern of communication cannot be construed as a trickle-down process. Much of what we now call Paracelsianism was very familiar to rustic artisans, farmers, herdsmen, and midwives, mostly from practical experience, or just intuitive understanding of the process of transformation from the same basic set of sources. Much can be learned about chemical action and fermentation from the belly of a sheep. It is very clear by now that artisans—especially the potters to whom Palissy was apprenticed in Saintonge—practiced alchemy as part of their daily work. There is plenty of evidence that the language of distillation and sublimation was spoken in rural artisans' shops as well as princely courts and university laboratories. Material evidence is especially convincing for Saintonge. Hence, in the wake of the Reformation's earliest teachings on the universal priesthood of Christians who achieved autonomy over their spiritual and material bodies through self-mastery, it makes sense that those who were already master artisans would assert their own experiences in accommodating Paracelsian natural philosophy. And the nearly universal experience of mimetic religious violence was analogous at the most basic level of both scientific and artisanal practice to the alchemical synthesis of spirit and matter in the fire of the crucible.

The "ideological" level at which the new Paracelsian discourse intersected with local artisanry grew directly out of Paracelsus's chemical modification of Ficino's Neoplatonic metaphysics. As Kurt Goldammer explains in his exegetical reading of Paracelsus, when Florentine Neoplatonism was transformed by Paracelsus into chemical principles, it acquired a powerful eschatological force—indeed, an ideological force—when read together, as it usually was, with the appropriate biblical text.[11] Just as Genesis recounted the origin of the universe, so too did the Old Testament Daniel and New Testament Revelation prophesy its finiteness and end. If the creation of the universe was an act of chemical distillation, then it followed that its end would also be chemical. Thus, prophesies could be read and miniature millennial endings brought to fruition by adepts in their studies, workshops and laboratories.

Paracelsus's work was given credence by many because he was also considered one of the greatest prophets of his time. As a result, his prophetic and astrological tracts were immensely popular, and they were his only writings that were published immediately upon completion. Paracelsus contended that prophesy was the highest form of magic. Webster has noted that prophesy was indispensable "in the apocalyptic atmosphere of the Reformation and Radical Reformation," for "there was no sense that creation was a stable entity destined to run its course for an unlimited duration." For Paracelsus, "the instability of history was translated into cosmological terms." The Paracelsian cosmos was a mutable place, beset by trial and impermanence. Halley's Comet was said to have appeared on August 12, 1531, over the town of St. Gallen, in southern Germany, at the same time that Paracelsus visited the town. Meanwhile, St. Gallen was also a center of the growing conflict between Anabaptists, Zwinglians, and Catholics. Soon after these events, Paracelsus famously prophesied: "Each destruction of a monarchy . . . is raised at God's behest, [hence it] is announced by indications and signs, so that everyone will be able to recognize the destruction or ruin, and have forewarnings of such monarchies and their fall or rise." That Ulrich Zwingli was killed subsequently at Kappel was considered positive proof of this prophesy, as were "indications and signs" that appeared in advance of other acts of apocalyptic violence during the religious wars of the sixteenth and seventeenth centuries.[12] Popular representation of ominous portents became a mainstay of early modern—particularly Germanic—iconography. These were read as millennial "signatures." Eschatological interpretations of Paracelsus were particularly alive and compelling to Protestants during the pan-European wars of religion. They had inherited the apocalyptic prophesy of the aging earth, originally devised and disseminated by the twelfth-century Calabrian abbot Joachim of Fiori (1132–1202), from radical friars of the later Middle Ages. Again building on the basic Trinitarian paradigm, Joachim prophesied there were three ascending ages of the world: the age of the Father, the age of the Son, and finally, the age of the Holy Spirit—for enthusiasts, the earth's present age. This age abhorred outer bodies. Its evangelists were thus spiritual brothers of the Lutheran *frères* who "re-turned" the Reformation to Saintonge from the Germanic regions in the 1540s and 1550s. For Joachim, the third and final age of earth would simultaneously herald the return of the prophet Elijah and the coming of the Antichrist. Paracelsus chose to rename Elijah "Elias Artista" (also "Elijah the Artist" and "the Alchemist"), and he prophesied that Elias would appear exactly fifty-eight years after his own death. Eli-jah's role as alchemist of the millennium was to join secretly with the other philo-sophical artisans and alchemists, hidden strategically throughout the shadowy subter-ranean world, who had already begun the process independently. Together, the adepts would complete this long and laborious process of the final transmutation of the earth, which was already undergoing changes associated with geological old age. The al chemical millennium, was "to be not an operatic epiphany or a battle of Armageddon but . . . a chemical act of separation."[13] That was because God worked inside his adepts and helped their cause on earth incrementally through an accumulation of war and violence, which was part of the greater process of the destruction of the corrupt and the renovation of the world.

The Paracelsian millennium was conceptualized, therefore, as an uncharacteristi-cally slow and hidden operation, in contrast to the instantaneous and theatrical results prophesied in Revelation. How such final things would manifest themselves on this grand scale was unclear, because such an operation would be untheatrical, intensely private, and visible—at first—only to adepts. Events would unfold through prophesy, to be sure, but also according to secret internal rhythms of individual *magi* and of enthusiastic artisans, a lesser category of "operators," who were not philosophers, but were also engaged in the alchemic separation of pure from corrupted matter.

Huguenot craftsmen had a specific role. Their province was to use "industriousness" to separate their immediate domestic or fortress environments—and their family, ar-tisanal networks and confessional communities—from the chaos and impurities ram-pant in their part of the world, despite the fact that Huguenots were often compelled to stay in close proximity to corruption among their neighbors. This abhorrence of, yet familiarity, with corruption activated interior, microcosmic building and mainte-nance projects founded on motions of the soul. Such projects would eventually effect a chemical, or, for Saintonge, an artisans' millennium. As we shall see, Palissy aspired to separate himself out and achieve the exalted status of philosopher, in addition to his innovative manual skills as artisan-operator. So in his particular case, the movement that he inspired in Saintonge acquired charisma as his natural philosophy focused on those apocalyptic aspects of the southwestern Huguenot millennial experience that were animated by its tiniest elements, not the grandest or most plainly visible. These *minima*, once refined by the crucible of war—as was Palissy himself—were transmuted into the purest, most uniform "corpuscles" available in the natural world. Reduced by violence, diminutiveness thus intensified purity in the microcosm, and animated the awesome power of the macrocosm, with which the *minima* were inextricably entwined by "sympathies and antipathies." Such hidden, animate power was embodied in Palissy's ceramic basins (or cosmologies) by tiny amphibious creatures.[14]

An artisans' millennium could not promise immediate salvation from the trials and inequities that the children of God had to endure, so proponents of Paracelsian artisanry inculcated patience as their primary virtue and associated it with smallness and an eschatology of industrious waiting. Private refuges of patience were built to function in domestic settings over a long duration of time. Thus, Palissy's tiny, slow-moving snail, its shell industriously crafted from inside out, was a useful metaphor for artisanal *sûreté*. The Saintonge *limace*, having two spiral bodies, used defensive systems that depended on its ability to communicate between them, as would the soulish intermediaries between the macrocosm and the microcosm. The tiny *limace*, like the Saintongeais Huguenot artisan, circulated the eternal and animating light of grace into the light of Nature, which "descended into his soul from the angels via the stars" and moved in a spiral motion from the greater body into the smaller one and back again. The impetus for these deliberate artisanal motions were "imagined" from the heart, the most secret and vulnerable part of the self.[15] This organ was the province of the soul shared only by man and God; it circulated the power of weakness. Such refuges of patient industriousness had potential to provide for individual artisans, families, and communities. At the same time, they housed laboratories and workshops where the slow processes of purification that advanced in secret from macrocosm to microcosm— and from rural localities to other places in the Atlantic world—were invented and reinvented through dissemination by adepts, masters, apprentices, and journeymen, often beset by the chaos of religious war and under threat of personal insecurity and bodily pain.

❧ Palissy's Natural-Philosophical Library ❧

After Palissy arrived in Paris around 1565, he soon exploited the reputation he had earned from the *Recepte* as a rustic practitioner of Paracelsianism. We know this from clear references to books in his scientific library in the *Discours admirables* (Paris, 1580)—instead of veiled ones in the *Recepte*—and evidence that he won an honored position in the scientific and publishing circle of Jacques Gohory, leader of the most influential Paracelsian academy in Paris in the 1570s. Thus, the rustic library Palissy implied he used in rural Saintonge can be reconstructed retrospectively with explicit evidence that he provided for a well-read audience of the most prominent physicians, alchemists, and bibliophiles in Paris.

Gohory's reception and dissemination of Paracelsus reveal much about why Palissy and this Parisian translator and publisher had been drawn together.[16] Gohory developed powerful patronage in the capital and "had a wide circle of friends which included many of the most important scientific and literary figures of his time and country," according to D. P. Walker. Hence, "his championship of the magical tradition of Tritheminus, Agrippa and Paracelsus may therefore have had considerable diffusion and influence by means of personal discussion."[17] Palissy's connections at court, interests, and growing reputation drew him into that "wide circle."

Gohory's main contribution to Parisian science was his ability to recognize and underscore the Neoplatonic impulses in Paracelsus's discourse (also, he must have known, quite strong in Palissy's *Recepte*) and to write (and presumably talk) frequently about Paracelsus in terms of Marsilio Ficino's microcosm/macrocosm paradigm. While Gohory recognized Ficino's fundamental contribution to the Paracelsian project, he privileged Paracelsus, representing the Florentine as overly cautious in that he had failed to perform any great operation of magic as Paracelsus had done. For Gohory and his Paris circle, Ficino's "magic was eminently private, individual, and subjective and hence was nearer to being a religion than a science."[18] It was thus more concerned with theory than practice. Gohory had defined himself as a natural philosopher whose primary interest in alchemy was in the practical aspects of distillation of matter by fire.

Beginning in the *Recepte,* Palissy's artisanry and natural philosophy had itself accentuated his own intensely "private, individual and subjective" alchemical and religious system, which fitted the specific context of security-minded Huguenot artisans in Saintonge. Yet Gohory's main project to further refine and synthesize Ficino and Paracelsus for his scientific community by deemphasizing private and theoretical aspects of Neoplatonism and privileging open practice influenced Palissy's similar rhetoric in the *Discours.* To be sure, furthering practice was a primary legacy of Paracelsianism, but Palissy's move ostensibly from private and individual practice in the 1560s to a public, performance-based one by the 1580s should be considered in part as a function of changing political and geographical context and his continued desire to maintain courtly patronage while belonging to the minority sect. This stance was particularly useful after the St. Bartholomew's Day Massacre in 1572. Gohory may have been trying to detheologize the French Paracelsian movement, distancing his academy from enthusiast involvement. This does not mean that Palissy foreswore his earlier position on the natural-philosophical function of interiority, only that his new public persona, associated with courtly performance and entertainment and so belonging to a scientific network that was sanctioned by the Louvre, had become a requirement.

Palissy's relation to Gohory's vision of Paracelsianism was further explained in the *Discours,* where in the chapter "Treatise on Metals and Alchemy," he remarked that "a book on drinkable gold was printed at Lyon at the time when King Henri III was there on his way back from Poland, in which book it is clearly written that alchemy must be revealed only to the children of philosophy. If they are children of philosophy, they are children of knowledge, and consequently children of God. If that were so, it would be well for all of us to belong to the religion of the alchemists."[19] Palissy's Calvinist understanding of the key role of salvation in the creation of adepts is revealing; moreover, it is very likely that this book, "printed at Lyon," was Alexandre de La Tourette's 1575 *Bref discours des admirable vertus de l'orpotable* . . . (Brief Discourse on the Admirable Virtues of Potable Gold . . .). Potable gold was an alchemical cure famously championed by Paracelsus. La Tourette also promised to augment his discourse with the comprehensive analysis of "the origins and causes of all illness," as well as a lively "defense of the very useful science of Alchemy, against those who condemn it."[20]

Palissy's cryptic allusion to the *Brief Discourse* was arguably prompted by these complex and still largely obscure debates within the Parisian Paracelsian community on the balance between religion and scientific practice, rooted in Ficino's influence over Huguenot natural philosophy, to which Palissy directed much of his attention in the *Recepte* and later *Discours*. Gohory and his circle were without a doubt the focus of La Tourette's vicious attack—he cursed opponents as "counterfeits, thieves, and frauds"— inasmuch as Gohory rushed a reply into print later that year under the polemical title *Discours responsif a celuy d'Alexandre de La Tourete, sur les secrets de l'art Chymique & confection de l'Orpotable* (Discourse Responding to Alexandre de La Tourete's, on the Secrets of the Art of Chemistry and Making Potable Gold).[21] Palissy, a member of the Gohory circle, would have associated his science and artisanry with the "new Paracelsism." Still, it is noteworthy that he expressed sympathy in print for the synthesis of religiosity and natural philosophy he read in La Tourette's treatise. Palissy's statement suggests that he may have tried to hold the middle ground in this debate, thus allowing spiritualism to combine with practice in some definitions of the "new Paracelsism," even in post-1572 Paris. Such a position was certainly true to Paracelsus himself, and it is clear that Palissy was able to parse his position with such care because he had complete access to all the latest Paracelsian treatises and opinion.[22]

In a crucial passage taken from his dedication of the *Discours* to his aging Saintongeais patron Antoine de Pons, Palissy listed a long progression of texts central to his scientific development, while claiming to be a deeply pious autodidact who had taught himself alchemy from the most venerated sources in the medieval medico-alchemical tradition, as well as the books of Paracelsus and his followers:

> I have tried to bring to light the things which it has pleased God to make me understand according to the measure in which he has been pleased to endow me, in order to benefit posterity. And because many men, under beautiful Latin, and other well polished language have left many pernicious talents to delude youth and waste its time: thus a Geber, a Romance of the Rose, and a Raymond Lule, and some disciples of Paracelsus, and many

other alchemists have left books in the study of which many have lost both their time and wealth.[23]

Palissy added the name of Arnald of Villanova (1235–1311) to those of the early ninth-century alchemist Geber and Ramon Llull (1234–1315) to complete his list of medieval writers who had left texts that he read and used but felt compelled to repudiate to establish his personal reputation and the primacy of modern natural language and philosophy.[24] In spite of conventional quarrels with "ancient" predecessors ("Do you think that the men of olden times could not lie?"),[25] his understanding of their "pernicious talents" formed the basis of his early work. When Palissy referred to "ancients," or "men of olden times," his frame of reference seems to have been mostly medieval, a relatively small body of scholastic literature he apparently read more avidly than the classics.

Walter Pagel has established the Gnostic and magical writings of Arnald, Llull, and Geber as fundamental to the natural philosophy of Paracelsus. Like Palissy, Paracelsus absorbed but then claimed to reject his scholastic predecessors' work, for reasons (and in language) similar to those explained in such harsh rhetoric by the potter.[26] William R. Newman, a historian of early modern British-American science who has thought deeply about the relation between the medieval natural philosophers in Palissy's library and the work of Paracelsus and his followers, has argued persuasively that there were two distinct and yet interrelated paradigmatic moments in the history of alchemy (and scientific rhetoric) in the West, which he calls (less persuasively), "revolutions":

> The first revolution occurred directly after the high period of Latin translation in the twelfth century, when the difficult and often intricate works of Arabic alchemy were rendered into the learned language of the West. Certain scholastically oriented alchemists, such as those writing under the names of "Geber," Ramon Llull, and Bernard of Trier, appropriated and transformed the alchemy of the Arabs, making it one with the peripatetic [that is, "Aristotelian"] program for the development of the sciences. The second alchemical revolution occurred when the iconoclastic Swiss physician . . . Paracelsus, revised the doctrines of medieval Latin alchemy and crafted a veritable system of natural philosophy. Paracelsus was the temporal head of a long line of reformers—including Francis Bacon, René Descartes, and Robert Boyle—who felt that the Aristotelianism of the universities could not be discredited without the aid of vituperation.[27]

The essence of the Paracelsian revision—followed closely by Palissy in the sixteenth century—was to focus on what both Geber and Llull, in particular, wrote about the tiny, invisible particles and subtle soulish operations that underlie perceptible chemical changes in elemental matter—that is, "corpuscular science"—as a means to attack the Aristotelian scholastic program, where change was understood to result from the interaction of matter and form. The ninth-century Persian alchemist Jabir ibn Hay-yan, also known as Geber, is accurately called pseudo-Geber, since most of the works published under this name in the West were forgeries. "Geber" was "a sort of 'trade-mark'" representing a particular school of scientific and eschatological thought that began producing texts at least a century after Jabir's death.[28] "The Jabir school assumed," Newman explains, "that every material substance contains its opposite, but in a 'hidden' fashion. Thus every substance has . . . an 'interior' and 'exterior'," which were used interchangeably with "'occult' and 'manifest'. . . 'center' and 'circumference'." The system of Jabirian alchemy and its interior/exterior metaphysics became available in the West with the Latin translation of *Seventy Books*, the school's major work.[29]

The key to Jabirian alchemy therefore lay in the inversion of interior and exterior qualities. This privileged the purity of all inner bodies, for when the hidden qualities of silver were inverted, the alchemist arrived at gold. The motion by which this process of inversion took place was corpuscular and placed particles into tiny but distinct layers of hidden and manifest matter. These tiny, hidden, pure and potent substances were separated and freed alchemically from their elemental corruption by fermentation and/or distillation.

Palissy's version of Jabir's program, by emphasizing geology, agricultural innovation, and the inner working of elemental earths, experimented with such processes in everything from pottery production to manuring, composting, and fertilizing, in particular in championing marl, a white, "fatty earth" consisting of clay and calcium carbonate. Fermentation and distillation, along with other heat-induced actions, including corrosion, by working to dissolve or sublimate, continually refined the freed corpuscles, so that they finally passed airily through the pores in all manifest structure. Actions such as these might purify a base metal into gold, make powerful transmutative elixirs, or reform local history and geography, since all earthly matter is porous and filled with interstices providing hidden access for these tiny agents of purification.

The potential for convergence with Protestant—especially early Lutheran spiritualist or pietist—ideology is self-evident here. It is, moreover, easy to perceive Palissy's rustic basins with tiny metamorphosing creatures filtering in and out of the earth, water, and sky as an artisanal version of Saintongeais Huguenot corpuscularism. This perception may be seen in an even clearer light by considering Palissy's understanding of Llull (or "pseudo–Ramon Lull," as Newman suggests), who in the fourteenth century harnessed alchemy and the quest for the philosopher's stone to the vitalistic, hidden workings of the soul toward salvation. Here was precisely the same soulish framework that inspired Palissy's comment in defense of La Tourette and of vitalistic alchemy in the debate with Gohory.[30]

Llullian texts were profusely emblematic and hence particularly useful to artisans.

Frances Yates demonstrated long ago that the cosmologies were especially sought after. "Most libraries of any size contain one of the sixteenth or early seventeenth-century *Ars Brevis*," Yates found, "with which are often bound a version of the *Ars Magna* and commentaries by Renaissance Lullists."[31] If Palissy was unable to read rudimentary Latin—an unlikely supposition, since there is countervailing circumstantial evidence—he could lay his hands on many French translations available and circulated in the form of unpublished manuscripts. Gohory noted the presence of 500 copies of Llull in French translation at a Paris bookseller in 1561, as well as numerous copies "written by hand."[32] As for the *Roman de la Rose*, it was celebrated by the sixteenth century as one of the oldest surviving poems written in French. Begun sometime around the end of the thirteenth century, probably by Guillaume de Lorris, it was completed by Jehan de Meung, first poet to Philippe-le-Bel. The *Roman* includes two alchemical tracts in verse, both of which weave sexual allegory together with a tale about the philosopher's stone and the transmutation of base metals into gold. This convergence of sexuality and alchemy was a common theme by the fourteenth century, following the works of Bernard of Trier, who understood mineral substances to function sexually and to form from seed. Thus the philosopher's stone was made of liquid mercury, a spermlike seminal liquid. We know well how this reproductive framework influenced Paracelsus, but it also had an impact on Palissy's geology and artisanry. The revival of the *Roman* in Paris was spearheaded by the publication of *De la transformation métallique, trois anciens tractez en rithme françoise* (Paris, 1561). Gohory commented approvingly on the appearance of this volume, which included among its medieval verses "The Remonstrances of Nature to the alchemist errant [see fig. 8.22]: with the response of the said Alchy. by J. de Meung. Together with a tract of his Romant de la Rose, which concerns said art," and noted that sales were brisk.[33]

Gohory's "quite private, informal" academy of new Paracelsian science and revised Ficinian Neoplatonism opened in an apothecary's garden near the Faubourg Saint-Victor in 1571 and was called the "Lycium philosophal San Marcellin."[34] Here, Gohory engaged in his performances of the new science (which he opposed to the "antique" in experiments, or "proofs") and "prepared Paracelsian medicines, did alchemical demonstrations and made occult talismans 'after the opinion of Arnaud de Villeneuve, & de Marsilius Ficinus.'" Gohory also "received learned visitors who admired the rare plants and trees, played skittles, and performed vocal and instrumental music in the 'galerie historiee.'"[35] Palissy was included among Gohory's learned visitors when the Lycium opened six years after his arrival in Paris. Palissy's friend Ambroise Paré, the Huguenot surgeon to Charles IX, was also among the erudites.

Palissy's filial interest in Paré went beyond religion. Both were artisans born in rustic provinces (Paré in Maine) who went on to develop connections to the French court in Ferrara. Paré apprenticed as a *compagnon* barber-surgeon (two brothers were also tradesmen; one a chest maker, the other a barber-surgeon), rose to master status, and was predictably reviled by the schoolmen of Paris for supporting the controversial, largely artisanal project of eliminating the formal boundary between the magisterial physician—who directed the instrumental hand of his artisan assistants—and the surgeon. Galenic physicians never came into contact with patients, a failure for which the followers of Paracelsus and the new science took them to task. Paré argued that surgeons and apothecaries deserved the same status as physicians, since surgeons learn their trade by experience with wounded and diseased bodies. Paracelsians argued that the experience of contact with the ill was preferable to knowledge taken by physicians antiseptically from university lectures or scholastics' books and applied indirectly through a surgeon. Similarly, Paré published his books in French, not Latin, so that the artisanal branches of medicine could read them, a threatening departure from rigid scholastic convention.[36]

Palissy's local method of Saintongeais Paracelsism was formed by personal experience in the religious wars, and so he was keenly interested in Paré's scientific writing on "monsters and marvels," which in large part grew out of Paré's over thirty-year experience on the road as a military surgeon. Paré chronicled this period in *Journies in Diverse Places*, which reflected firsthand knowledge of the local and folkloric in the "excesses" of nature and the martial context of grotesque disfigurement.[37] In his most famous treatise, *Des monstres*—the first of many editions was published in 1573—the surgeon begins with a loaded sentence that Palissy would have appreciated, since the language and conceptual framework are similar to his own: "Monsters are things that *appear* [emphasis added] outside the course of Nature."[38] Monstrosity might thus result from misperceptions of superficial appearance of the abnormal. Natural philosophy was the scientific way to peer beneath the "deception of the senses" to uncover true causes. Indeed, of the thirteen "causes of monsters" that Paré lists in his first chapter, "the first is the glory of God," not sin, degradation or corruption, "in order that the works of God might be magnified."[39]

Huguenots were condemned as monsters whose religion and culture "appear[ed] outside the course of Nature," in particular after the St. Bartholomew's Day Massacre, which had occurred only the year before and should be considered the immediate context for *Des monstres*. Paré divided his subject, in part, into physical and moral monsters; in both cases, most fell victim to a fatal lack of self-discipline and morality that was implicitly opposed to the virtuous qualities of moderation and piety he attributed to Calvinists. Paré's *Des monstres* may thus be compared with de Léry's *Histoire d'un voyage fait en la terre du Brésil*, which asks ironically where the real savages and cannibals are—in Brazil or Paris—after the horrific events of 1572.[40]

The elemental structure of the narrative and subtle politico-religious themes of *Des monstres*, all of which were constructed in the language of natural philosophy, resonated powerfully with many similar impulses in Palissy's *Recepte*. As in Palissy's rustic basins, *Des monstres*'s narrative was carefully divided into four sections on the grotesque and trivial creatures of earth, water, air, and fire: the four elements that structured inquiry in early modern natural philosophy and representation of the tiny and overlooked in Palissy's "art of the earth." Above all, however, as in Palissy's epiphany on artisanal security in experiments with the Saintongeais snail, Paré understood the works of God that appeared to be "outside the course of Nature," not in pathological terms (as monsters), but as evidence of the infinite variety of God's creation and the multiplicity and diversity He encouraged and hence revealed about the world, as well as God's own complex essence. The question thus became one of expanding the definition of what was natural for every area of human experience, religious diversity in particular. Out of their shared experience as Huguenot natural philosophers and artisans during the wars of religion, Palissy and Paré gave impetus to the scientific conception and historical study of pluralism in the Atlantic world. Variety was, for them, a positive sign of emerging inner vitality in material life. *Des monstres* was thereby a "sustained attempt," as Jean Céard has shown, "to 'naturalize' monsters" and to bring "the scandal associated with monsters . . . to a halt."[41]

Gohory died in 1576. By then, Palissy had learned enough about the courtly art of natural-philosophical performance and seen his reputation advance in Paris to the point where he could step into the vacuum and set up a profitable academy of his own, charging an écu entrance fee to each auditor. Paré was among some thirty-five *érudits* listed attending his *cabinet* for lectures "On Rocks." The "birth" of rare, grotesque, or curious earths Palissy conceptualized and explained as "experiencing" the same interior reproductive and obstetric processes as did Paré's "monsters."[42] Palissy also gave lectures and practical workshops in geology in his *cabinet* in Paris twice, in 1575 and 1576, and probably again in 1584. Given the subject of the lectures and the credentials and religious backgrounds of visitors to his academy, it is reasonable to speculate that Palissy sought to reactivate the enthusiastic aspects of Ficino's contributions to Parisian Paracelsianism, which Gohory minimized.

Also in 1576, Francis Bacon left Cambridge for Paris, along with Sir Amyas Paulet, and stayed three years. Bacon certainly attended Palissy's well-known lectures or visited his *cabinet*.[43] What is beyond speculation, however, is the extent to which the potter's efforts to naturalize the monster of religious difference in Paris, and perhaps London as well, were influenced by his personal role in the diffusion of Paracelsism to the rustic Huguenot artisans of Saintonge before 1565. In the southwestern French countryside, after all, the scene of reading was Nature itself.

❧ "I prefer to speak the truth in my rustic language" ❧

The earliest clues revealing Palissy's intellectual debts to Paracelsus's ideas come from the ubiquity of coded Paracelsian language in the *Recepte*. Because of Montmorency's role as a patron and savior, Palissy dedicated the *Recepte* to him in 1563. In his dedication, he described the volume as the work of a simple artisan who was accustomed to earn his living by the "uncorrupted labor" of his hands and so proclaimed his "love of virtue" unconventionally, without benefit of a classical education:

> Monseigneur, the talents, which I consign to you, are, in the first place, many beautiful
> secrets of Nature and Agriculture, which I put in a book, with the goal of provoking all
> the men of the earth to restore their love of virtue and uncorrupted labor. . . . If these
> things are not written with the grace that Your Highness merits, I beg your forgiveness
> . . . [for] I am neither Greek, nor Hebrew, nor Poet, nor Rhetorician, but a simple artisan
> poorly trained in letters: nevertheless, these deficiencies do not make one less virtuous
> than a more eloquent man. I prefer to speak the truth in my rustic language than to lie in
> rhetorical language.[44]

Palissy elaborated this rhetorical attack on rhetoric in the subsequent dedication "to the Reader" with his exorbitant apology for the "smallness and abject condition of the author, as well as his rustic and inelegant language."[45] Attentive readers noted the potter's strategic fascination with the hidden powers of small, overlooked fauna and flora, their connections to the heart of the macrocosm, and their God-given abilities to dissemble for self-mastery and protection. To be sure, Palissy's ubiquitous references to his status as a poor, unlettered artisan have classical precedents in great number, involving purportedly unlettered rustics, whether plowmen or artisans, who proceeded in time to reveal hidden learning disguised beneath crude and unpolished exteriors.

American colonial historians recognize the reemergence of this classical trope in Benjamin Franklin's famous "Poor Richard," or perhaps Washington's self-fashioning after Cincinnatus. Moreover, one common source for classicizing writers on the rustic tradition in Europe, as well as early modern British America, was Tacitus's life of his father-in-law, *De vita Iulii Agricolae*. Religious and political aspects of this influential first-century text were revived extensively during the seventeenth and eighteenth centuries by authors ranging from Calvinist divines like Cotton Mather to English advocates of the "country party ideology" and America's revolutionary elites and pamphleteers during the 1760s.[46] Another important source centered on *Origines* and *De re rustica* by Marcus Porcius Cato (234–149 B.C.). Cato's texts advocated rustic simplicity and self-discipline, which were perceived to be the Stoic keystones of primitive Roman virtue. Cato's influence was particularly strong among French Protestants during the sixteenth century and in eighteenth-century British America, where his name was invoked by a number of polemicists to connote the revolutionaries' repository of primitive English virtue, often styled in the theatrical moral tradition of Joseph Addison (1672–1719).[47]

Still, in what ways can the cultural historian pursue further Palissy's artisanal discourse from the perspective of the *immediate* context and traditions from which Palissy constructed his identity as an "artisan sans lettres," that is, the Paracelsian tradition of Protestant natural philosophy in southwestern France? We have seen how both the religious and cultural foundations for this tradition in Saintonge were prepared initially and diffused along the coastal islands by conventicles of monastic heretics, who were converted in unspecified Germanic regions before returning to evangelize island Huguenots. Shortly thereafter, this tradition was reinforced and synthesized by the Genevan-inspired discipline of Hamelin, further refined by Palissy during the artisans' interregnum, and only then (so far as we know) written down as a history to order its memory. Dissemination was accomplished through available texts, diffused in various oral, written, and material forms, which gave Palissy, as well as other, anonymous artisan reformers and their followers, substantial local control over, and identification with, the rustic style of international Paracelsianism.

Following Palissy's practice of artisanal *sûreté*, which asserted the power of weakness to be its fundamental force, what would appear to be liabilities when performed in interaction with the dominant culture were transformed into lay assets by experienced Huguenot artisans. Therefore, to speak the "natural" truth rather than to "lie" rhetorically was simultaneously to condemn the old Latin scholasticism of the Church and to embrace the experiential science and speculative discourse of the Paracelsians, which devalued prior learning unless proven by physical and spiritual engagement to overcome the corruption of Nature in the human body. Hence, the possibly apocryphal story that before his famous lectures on medicine at the University of Basel in 1526—where he scandalized faculty by speaking German rather than Latin—Paracelsus was said to have overseen a ritual burning of books by Galen and Avicenna, venerated ancients he claimed to supersede. Over a half-century after the Basel lectures, Palissy subscribed to a related ritual when he characterized Paracelsus in the *Discours* as "a personage, who has written more than fifty books on medicine, who was said to be unique, *even a king among physicians.*" This was understood by some of Palissy's sixteenth-century readers as a direct quotation from Paracelsus, revealing Palissy's intellectual kinship with him. Paracelsus famously introduced himself to readers of his own books as "Theophrastus [that is, Philippus Aureolus *Theophrastus* Bombastus von Hohenheim, called Paracelsus], and in addition I am *monarcha medicorum*, monarch of physicians, and I can prove to you what you cannot prove . . . I will not defend my monarchy with empty talk."[48]

By explicitly subscribing to this vernacular framework, the potter concurred that scholastic education was an impediment, an artificial veil that obscured God's truth, which resided only in natural experience, amplified by the enthusiastic lay spiritualism of the Paracelsian natural philosopher. Indeed, the Roman medical writer Celsus, over whom "Paracelsus" declared his dominance through the invention of this sobriquet,[49] was renowned in the Renaissance as the Cicero medicorum— Cicero of physicians— for his elegant style of rhetoric (that is to say, his "empty talk"). It followed that Palissy's apology for using "inelegant" and "natural language" was defiantly ironic. Natural language was the speech of renovation, of empowerment; it was the best hope for the restoration of man's primitive spiritual language. "A more eloquent man" built a Babel of lies to obscure this original foundation. Ciceronian eloquence was therefore the rhetoric of sophistry, the corrupt Roman Catholic Church, royal inquisitors, and ultimately, the Antichrist himself.

Paracelsian discourse enabled Palissy to reverse old scholastic conceptions of both wisdom and beauty. What was *rustique* and *mal orné* embodied beauty and truth, because it contained the wild and the natural. Scholastic artifice was suspect *precisely* because it was overtly and willfully artificial. Every product of human willfulness was harnessed to the corruption of the flesh (and of the earth as well) and hence eloquent artifacts conflated—in fact sullied—the transparent quality of luminosity natural to perfect products of the motions of man's soul unimpeded by flesh. To be covered "with light as with a garment," as the divine craftsman was described in Psalms [104:2], signified absence of material corruption and the beholder's knowledge of God in Nature.[50]

Palissy certainly read Paracelsus in French, or perhaps in German or Latin. This encounter first occurred in Saintonge perhaps, but arguably before. "Have you not seen the book printed long ago," he wrote suggestively in the *Discours,* "which says that Paracelsus, the German physician, has cured a number of lepers with drinkable gold?"[51] Yet even Paracelsus was not above Palissy's reproach. Every figure of authority, Hamelin excepted, was fair game. Predictably, points of contention were often linguistic. "And you who are nothing but a laborer without knowledge of languages, except the one your mother taught you," Palissy wrote playfully in a dialogue in the *Discours*—as Theory needled the potter's alter ego, Practice, for his bold claim to the primacy of experience over knowledge received uncritically from books—"do you really really dare talk against such a personage [as Paracelsus]?"[52]

Unless he could test Paracelsus's claims through experimentation and personal experience, Palissy relegated the master's texts to the lesser category of mere theory. Palissy also tended in his books to downplay overt displays of Paracelsian occultism. This is not to say that Palissy denied magic or the supernatural, only that such theatricality was falsely manipulated by charlatans claiming to be alchemists and adepts to obscure the reality of their inability to perform authentic natural-philosophical tasks. That Palissy found an early audience in England among Paracelsians who were (at least for public consumption) skeptical of the master's occult practices may have been on account of his skeptical tone.

Moreover, there was no shortage of booksellers in La Rochelle. This was a center of Protestant learning with a *grande école,* which aspired to compete with Geneva as a sacred city in the sixteenth century. Great libraries were formed in La Rochelle, only to be dismantled in 1628. The Huguenot population, which focused on male literacy, and emphasized interpretation of God's wisdom through the Scriptures, provided a ready market for printed materials carried from all over Europe, especially Frankfurt and London. The Bertons and several other Protestant publishers flourished. Booksellers peddled polemical tracts from Saumur, Lyon, the Cévennes, and Charenton—the site of the influential Huguenot temple near Paris—among many other strongholds of the Reform. During times of persecution, Huguenots maintained a dedicated network of underground traffic in these printed materials. The conservative Rochelais Consistory, responding to questions raised by the national synods during the religious wars, also entered into the frequent political, military, and theological debates with the publication of tracts and pamphlets of its own. Even more complicated are the old problems of judging book circulation among acquaintances, of reading aloud to the illiterate, and the availability of unpublished manuscripts. But this much seems certain: Palissy had already read widely enough before and during his time in Saintes that when he was prepared to publish the *Recepte* at La Rochelle in 1563, he merited the title of a first-generation "rustic" follower of Paracelsus.[53]

I have maintained that Palissy's narrative functioned as New World historiography in the French civil wars of religion, even as it recounted one French Huguenot artisan's written representation of the social, historical, material, and providential origins of the Saintongeais assemblies of the *désert.* The term *désert* was used by Huguenot refugees of the diaspora to identify themselves during times when congregations became shepherdless flocks, their *pasteur* (or "shepherd") gone, and their churches demolished. With Hamelin's execution, and after the subsequent surrender of Saintes to Catholic forces, Palissy and the remnants of Hamelin's artisans' congregation entered the Saintongeais *désert.* These lay wanderers were left to their own spiritual devices, seeking evidence of God's presence without the protection of an established *place de sûreté* or a pastoral guide in an ambiguously open, contested, and vulnerable liminal space. Located in history between an already (destruction of the visible Church) and a not yet (the millennium), this was an earthly Purgatory dominated by laymen. The geography of such an unstable space was most often conceptualized as wild and uncultured, or even unmapped and unnamed hidden territory.

Palissy had had to labor underground in Saintes, and the *désert* was also typically dominated by enemies. At the same time, however, inhabitants of the *désert,* and the *désert* itself, were transformed in both spiritual and material ways. In Saintes, Palissy gained personal access to spiritual power, which he represented as hidden below the broken skin of the natural world. Sacred violence and the chaos of historical events enveloped and shattered all the outer bodies of refuge, but this served God by revealing the extent of spiritual progress and security growing deep inside the exposed wombs of the refugees' inner bodies. The *désert* was thus a durable metaphor for the instability of psychological and social alienation. Yet it contained eschatological hope for wise and patient craftsmen who were capable of effecting alchemic material transformations, and hence Christian reversal, for the dispossessed and their communities in the diaspora. In this shattered spiritual and material world, pious rebuilders among the lay community gained unprecedented opportunities.[54]

Palissy's rustic library and Hamelin's triple occupation as a printer, minister, and colporteur showed that the *désert* was filled with books.[55] Yet what of the elusive but vital historiographical problem of the diffusion and coherence of lay thought and action in the Saintongeais *désert?* Palissy attempted to position himself at the center of this for Saintes, but if he dropped coded hints from time to time, he systematically obscured sources while assuming the pose that became his credo and public persona. As the subversively rhetorical "poor, simple, and unlettered artisan," whose trove of secrets were the products of piety and rustic experience alone, the potter could claim originality for patrons desiring novelty, while attacking scholasticism with the uncorrupted and sui generis wisdom that grew naturally out of spiritual reading in the open air of the countryside. Meanwhile, Palissy's rhetorical posturing also served as a literary signpost that revealed his rustic library in the form of bona fides shared with fellow adepts, who proved by cracking the bibliographic codes that just as he possessed the appropriate books and understood their secrets, so too his readers had the experience to recognize the validity of his sources.

As we have seen, Palissy's work of the 1560s was responsive to the early publications of both Luther and Calvin. The writings of Calvin, de Bèze, and other "magisterial" Genevan theologians were available locally in new, small-format editions published by Hamelin and distributed in Saintonge by Hamelin and his loyal colporteurs. Although Palissy did not mention his beloved master's books by title, he acknowledged their influence indirectly. Hamelin's interpretations of them, as well as of the text from his tiny Genevan Bible, was inferred, when the potter assumed lay leadership of the artisans' Church and wrote "all these things were done following the good examples, advice and doctrine of Master Philibert Hamelin." Palissy also made it clear that Hamelin put his life in danger by colportage of such books into rural areas of Saintonge without personal protection to distribute the printed word to unlearned country people. For his followers in coastal Saintonge, it would have been nearly impossible to separate the image of the master printer Hamelin walking into their isolated villages from the sack of books slung over his shoulder.

The key texts in Palissy's natural-philosophical library were written by Paracelsus, however. Still, books by Paracelsus and his followers—whether possessed by Palissy in the original form or in translations, reinterpretations, or loose transcriptions—were, in effect, activated by reading Protestant theology and by the conversion experience. As Charles Webster has demonstrated so abundantly and well that he needs no re-hearsal here, Paracelsus's deeply mystical, universal, anti-scholastic, folkloric, and ex-periential science was harnessed by Protestant natural philosophers, alchemists and artisans such as Palissy to Calvin's challenge to reform Catholicism[56]—this despite evidence that Calvin was deeply mistrustful of all Protestant philosophers. Hence, far from being as original as claimed, Palissy is best understood as a creature of his books. His natural-philosophical writings were largely derivative, with the exception of his essay on the relationship between ceramics and alchemy, "On the Art of the Earth," written expressly from Palissy's personal experience as a master glass painter and pot-ter for the *Discours admirables*.

This is not to underestimate Palissy's contribution. Rather, perhaps it is useful to reevaluate the importance of originality in this context and to suggest larger social his-torical implications for the potter's rustic science and artisanry. If Palissy was a cipher for the international book trade in Protestant theology and Paracelsian natural phi-losophy, this fact must be tempered by knowledge that he was also a critical reader in the tradition of enthusiastic seekers, an innovative artisan, and an autodidact. Hamelin and Paracelsus reinforced his inclination to read books and to comprehend the macro-cosm and microcosm though the material and manual senses of artisanal experience. Just as Palissy read Calvin and his attack on Nicodemism from the very local perspec-tive of the civil war history of Saintonge and the martyrdom of Hamelin, so too he read Paracelsus and the Paracelsians from the perspective of its natural and craft history.

So Palissy does not, in a larger sense, provide historians with an opportunity to ex-plore the voice of a unique individual with an original take on the world. Indeed, his writing and even, to a lesser extent, his material production represents one local adap-tation of an international tradition that—due to the uniquely expansive diasporic his-tory of the Huguenots of Aunis-Saintonge—was diffused throughout the Protestant Atlantic world. We can only guess how many other "simple artisans" shared Palissy's association with this international tradition, if not the specificity of his local reading or indeed his artfulness, luck, or talent for self-promotion. How many labored in ob-scurity (except perhaps to neighbors and family members) in the shops, mills, and farms of early modern Europe and the Americas, having self-consciously reinvented themselves in the mode of such "original" Paracelsians? Substantial values within the manual philosophical tradition were derived from the opportunities its rhetoric gave literate artisans to craft personal discourses of innovation, and claim the material and spiritual rewards that attended its mastery and the ability to control the revelation and concealment of its secrets.[57]

Yet, even a detailed genealogy may limit understanding of the diffusion process that illuminates the cosmologies of different artisan networks that operated in the Saintongeais *désert*. Much of what they knew and practiced intuitively or after many centuries of training, had been returned to Huguenot artisans in printed form, as natural philosophy. Paracelsus openly admitted this strategy, acknowledging his closeness to artisanal culture and large debts to venerable folk practices. For their part, artisans such as Palissy claimed that they had known it all along. As Mikhail Bakhtin argued long ago and Carlo Ginzburg and others have reiterated in ways that are now axiomatic, the process of social and cultural diffusion in the early modern period cannot be captured in terms of asymmetry alone, but should rather be viewed as "a circular relationship composed of reciprocal influences, which traveled from low to high as well as from high to low."[58] But even such "firm" categories as high and low should not be accepted complacently. In practice, these were turned inside out as artisans and natural philosophers poached in one another's territory to such an extent that differences became permeable and boundaries notoriously unclear.

In the complex and vague framework of circularity, the whole notion of intellectual responsibility—indeed, artisanal knowledge in the *désert*—remained muddled. In this respect, art reflected life. Bound to the confusion of social action, such an intellectual milieu was as ambiguous as the *désert*. For Palissy, however, ambiguity was useful, convenient, and very much intentional. Consider that Palissy encouraged Huguenot artisans in the *désert* to deploy strategies intended to exploit the communicative potential of such ambiguity—whether oral, written, or material—to maximize the mute voices they suppressed in their choked dialogues with the culture of absolutism and its analogous competitors, Genevan and Rochelais Calvinism.

❧ Touch and Change ❧

Carlo Ginzburg's famous analysis of inquisitorial transcripts from which he reconstructed the cosmology of another sixteenth-century artisan who considered himself a master of originality and innovation—the Friulian miller and carpenter Domenico Scandella, or Menocchio—still provides revealing insights that can supplement what the potter tells us himself about the effect of his library on culture in the Saintongeais *désert:*

> A case such as Menocchio's was made possible by two great historical events: the invention of printing and the Reformation. Printing enabled him to confront books with an

oral tradition in which he had grown up and fed him the words to release that tangle of ideas and fantasies he had within him. The Reformation gave him the courage to express his feelings to the parish priest, to his fellow villagers, to the inquisitors—even if he could not, as he wished, say them in person to the pope, to cardinals, and princes. The enormous rupture resulting from the end of the monopoly on written culture by the educated and on religion by the clergy had created a new and potentially explosive situation.[59]

Precisely the same case can be made for Palissy's written and artisanal texts. But Ginzburg also writes:

> The gulf between the texts read by Menocchio and the way in which he understood them and reported them back to the inquisitors indicates that his ideas cannot be reduced or traced back to any particular book. . . . The roots of his utterances and of his aspirations were sunk in an obscure, almost unfathomable, layer of remote peasant traditions.[60]

The last sentence of this quotation, when read together with Ginzburg's epigraph from Céline for *The Cheese and The Worms:* "Tout ce qui est intéressant se passe dans l'ombre . . . / On ne sait rien de la véritable histoire des hommes" ("All that is interesting happens in the shadows . . . / One knows nothing of men's real history"), disclosed a characteristic fascination with the ineffable. No one can doubt the influence of Menocchio's "peasant traditions" upon his comprehension of what he read. But this is also to underestimate their effect on rustic readers while limiting the methodological potential of circularity. No matter how "obscure, almost unfathomable" Ginzburg perceives those traditions to have been, without further inquiry into practice, it feels impossible to share his confidence that Menocchio's claims "have an original stamp to them."[61]

Certainly Palissy's claims and rhetoric do not. It is folly to attribute the totality of Palissy's discourse to the passive reception of information from one particular book (implicitly and explicitly, he provided titles for many books that influenced him), but it is also impossible to ignore evidence that while the potter was an authentic autodidact, his autodidacticism was deeply informed by his status as a first-generation Protestant reader of Paracelsus. While in fairness Ginzburg did not intend to provide evidence of Menocchio's active awareness of Paracelsus, the miller's language had a lot in common with Palissy and the Germanic Protestant tradition of alchemic and animate materialism. Our sense of their common use of available language suggests bonds that were probably more historical than ineffably folkloric in origin. It is not mere coincidence, as Ginzburg suggests, that when Menocchio was finally executed at the turn of the seventeenth century by order of Pope Clement VIII himself, the great Counter-Reformation show trial of the influential natural philosopher and alchemist Giordano Bruno was also drawing to a violent end in Rome.[62]

All three men were bound by common spiritualist beliefs owing to intensive exposure to German sectarian thought. And all three were skilled artisans (Paracelsus worked in the silver mines) well before they began to use written texts in any public or systematic way to express their ideas. As in Jean de Léry's *History*, because of this conflation of merging artisanal and linguistic skills, one feels engaged with thinkers perceiving, pondering, and elucidating sensations about their worlds as much with their hands—a palpable sense of touch—as with the eye and mind. Artisans like Palissy and Menocchio, both of whom struggled to make the infusion of novel words from the available print culture communicate as eloquently as the potter's wheel or properly maintained mill gears had done, were acutely aware of the importance of their hands and sense of touch—in both the practical *and* spiritual sense—to their crafts, as well as the coherence of their natural-philosophical strategies.

The leading international proponent of the synthesis of man's spiritual and linguistic aspects with manual philosophy, and the true seventeenth-century inheritor and popularizer of the mystical ideas of Paracelsus and Palissy, was a German: the Görlitz shoemaker, and enormously influential Rosicrucian alchemist, Jakob Böhme (1575–1624). Böhme's unabashedly occult program gained prominence in philosophical, scientific, and religious communities throughout northern Europe, and he was a transatlantic force over the course of three hundred years, particularly among Quakers and Continental pietistic groups in Britain and the American middle colonies, from the seventeenth through the late nineteenth century. "*Hands,*" he wrote, possessed the spiritual power to effect change in Nature, through agriculture ("that which is grown) and artisanry ("the work and Being of the whole"), since they "signifie God's Omnipotence: for as God in Nature can *change* all things, and make of them what he pleaseth: so man also can with his Hands *change* all that which is grown in Nature, and can make with his Hands out of them what he pleaseth: he ruleth with his Hands the work and Being of the whole Nature, and so they very well signifie the Omnipotence of God."[63]

An animate sense of touch assumed special primacy—resonating with spiritual powers sometimes ascribed to chiromancy—in Böhme's writing and experience. Inasmuch as touch equated with "feeling," Böhme implied that "touch," in combination with the inner ecstasy of spiritual enthusiasm, caused deep "feeling" to "stir," infusing corresponding feelings in the Trinity. Indeed, Böhme argued that the chemistry of "touching" *preceded,* and so inspired, the harmonic and biological passage—the "tuning, sounding, generating, blossoming, and vegetation or springing"—of rational impulses (or "powers"):

> *Feeling* . . . ariseth also from all the powers of the Body in the Spirit, into the Head . . . if one did not touch the other, nothing would stir *at all,* and so this touching maketh the Holy Ghost *stir* so that he riseth up in all the powers, and touchest all the powers of the

Father, wherein then existeth the heavenly joyfulness of *triumphing;* as also tuning, sounding, generating, blossoming, and vegetation or springing, *all* which, hath its rising from this, that one power *toucheth* the other. . . . Wheresoever one qualifying or fountain-spirit in the divine power is touched or stirred, let the place be where, or thing what, it will, *except* in the Devils and all wicked damned Men; there is the fountain of the divine Birth or Geniture, clearly at hand.[64]

It followed that Behmenist bodies—individual, "joyful," human bodies, the meta-phorical body of the reunited, primitive, "gathered church," in fact, *all* natural bod-ies—were composed of a plurality of resonating "powers," which touched one another along vertical axes, in effect, *reversing* both the flow and authority of emerging Enlightenment models. For Böhme, natural knowledge traveled from bottom to top. It coursed *upward* from the earth itself through the medium of living human tissues by negotiating corpuscular passages unblocked by spiritual ecstasy, generated by "the heavenly joyfulness" of hypersentient religious bodies, through green, vegetal conduits, finally "springing," like a blossom blooming on its fertile stem, "into the head": "Thus *one* power continually toucheth and stirreth the *other* in the whole Body, and all the powers rise up into the head . . . which proveth the stirring of all the powers."[65]

Hence, Böhme's interior, alchemic experience of touching and feeling animated perception of "half-dead nature," reconstituting an edenic state of green rebirth while simultaneously reviving the "dead letter of the word." Paracelsus's relationship with Luther was tense; despite Paracelsus's obvious intellectual debts to the theologian, they remained at arm's length. Luther is celebrated without ambivalence, however, in Böhme's Paracelsian natural-philosophical text on the origin, present history, and coming apocalyptic end of the world, *Aurora* (1612).

Luther's early writing was a key to unlocking Böhme's Neoplatonic sensuality, while "stirring" his spirit's ascent through earth and bodily matter into the mind. Both Paracelsus and Böhme emulated Luther's publication of the seminal *Theologia deutsch* in 1516, his influential compendium of fourteenth-century Germanic folkways and mystical teaching, wherein Luther staked his claim to a theology of spiritualism. Luther did not abandon openness on soulishness until after "Freedom of a Christian." His formative writings deeply influenced the spiritualists, in spite of his famous schism with Böhme's forerunners among the early Anabaptists and pietists. Luther later com-plained bitterly about sectarians in the notorious "Letter of Opposition to the Fanatic Spirit." By then, Luther had publicly condemned enemies of his state Church as *Schwärmer,* a term encompassing both spiritual enthusiasts and religious fanatics.[66]

Yet in 1612, Böhme historicized Luther as foundational to spiritualist natural philosophers and linked him to other soulish reformers—including Böhme himself—who were overlooked by learned men because of their abject poverty, rustic employments, or lack of a classical education. Böhme cobbled together a Paracelsian discursive tradition that privileged the learned layman—with powerful echoes of Palissy's rustic artisan and Anabaptist leveler rhetoric—to the primitive strain of the Lutheran Reformation. "Because I write here of heavenly and Divine things," Böhme informed his readers at the start of chapter 9 of *Aurora*, "which are *altogether strange* to the *corrupted* perished Nature of Man":

> the reader doubtlesse will wonder at the *simplicity* of the Authour, and be offended at it. Because the condition and inclination of the corrupted Nature is, to gaze *onely* on *high* things, like a proud, wild, wanton and *whorish* woman, which alwayes gazeth in her heat or burning Lust after *Handsome* men. . . . Thus also the Proud corrupted perished Nature of Man, it stareth only upon *that*, which is glittering and in *Fashion* in this world, and supposeth, that God hath forgotten the afflicted, and therefore plageth them so, because he mindeth them not. Corrupt Nature imagineth, that the Holy Ghost regardeth onely *high* things, the high Arts and Sciences of *this world*, the profound studies and Great Learning. . . . Therefore I would have the Reader warned, that he read *this Book* with diligence, and not be *offended* at the meannesse or simplicity of the Author, for God looketh *not* at high things, for he *alone* is High: but *he careth for the Lowly,* how to help them.[67]

Having established his core natural-philosophical identity by invoking his place deep in the discourse of Paracelsianism, Böhme effectively harnessed both himself and his scientific tradition to the sacred history of rustic smallness—or, the power of weakness—from Abel to Luther:

> look but back and then you will find the true *Ground: What was* Abel? A Shepherd. *What was* Enoch *and* Noah? plain simple men. *What were* Abraham, Isaac, *and* Jacob? Herdsmen. *What was* Moses, that dear man of God? A Herdsman. *What was* David, when the Mouth of the Lord call'd him? A shepherd. *What were* the Great, and Small Prophets? Vulgar plain and mean People: *some of them* but Countrey people, and Herdsmen, *counted the underlings or footstooles of the world:* men counted them but meer fooles. And though they did Miracles Wonders and shewed great signs, yet *the world* gazed only on high things, and the Holy Ghost must be as the Dust under their feet: for the proud Devil *alwaies endeavoured* to be King in this world. *And how came* Our King JESUS CHRIST into this world? Poor and in great trouble and misery . . . *What were* his Apostles? Poor, dispised, illiterate Fishermen, *and what were* they that believed their preaching? The poorer and meaner sort of the people. The High Priests and Scribes *were the* Executioners of Christ, who *cryed out, Crucifie him, crucifie him,* Luk. 23.21. *What were they* that in all Ages in the Church of Christ stood to it most stoutly and constantly? The poor contemptible despised people, who shed their Bloud for the sake of Christ. *But who were they* that falsified and adulterated the right pure Christian Doctrine, and *alwayes fought* against

and opposed it? *Even* the Learned Doctors and Scribes, Popes, Cardinals, Bishops and great Dons, or Masters and Teachers. *And why did the world* follow after them, and depend on them? But because they had great respect, were in great *authority*, and *power*. . . . *Who was it* that purged the Pope[']s Greedinesse of Money, his Idolatry, Bribery, deceit and Cheating; *out of* the Churches in *Germany?* A poor despised * Monk or Fryer [*Luther* in margin]. *By what* power and might? by the power of God the Father, and by the power and Might of God the Holy Ghost.[68]

For Böhme, as for Paracelsus and Palissy before him, soulish truth "sheweth and declareth" itself to laymen in vernacular form, in "lowly" things. Here, defined as, "The Mother Tongue expounded according to the Language of Nature":

> For understand but thy *Mother Tongue aright;* thou hast as deep a Ground *therein*, as there is, in the *Hebrew,* or *Latine:* Though the Learned elevate themselves therein, like a proud arrogant Bride; it is no great matter, *their* Art is now on the Lees, or Bowed down to the Dust. *The Spirit sheweth and declareth, that yet before the End, many a Layman, will know and understand more, then now the Wittiest or Cunningest Doctors know.*

Reactivating Luther's rhetoric on the marriage of inner and outer bodies, Böhme argued that the process of showing was made visible to the small, because "meeknesse and humility are its proper House or *Habitation . . . for the Gates of Heaven set open themselves; those that do not blind themselves, shall and will see it very well, the Bridegroom Crowneth his Bride.*"[69] The wealthy were seduced by the flesh, "*a very Bath or Lake of hellish Wrath,*" and so were utterly unable to unlock the gates by inner sight. Citing the crucial text on Christ's sacred poverty quoted in the gospels of Matthew [19:24] and Mark [10:25], Böhme sang the rallying cry of all early modern levelers from the Anabaptists to Gerrard Winstanley: "*O Danger upon Danger!* as our King Christ also saith; *It is very hard for a Rich man to enter into the Kingdom of Heaven; a Camel will easier go through the Eye of a Needle, then a Rich man enter into the Kingdom of Heaven.*"[70]

Such subversive language poisoned whatever hope Böhme and his intellectual forebears (or inheritors) harbored for compromise with the magisterial Reformation. Luther's followers, including Philipp Melanchthon, Justus Menius, and Urbanus Rhegius, clearly continued to distribute anti-Anabaptist literature. So did Calvin, who raged against Menno Simons, the great Netherlandish Anabaptist (from whose name "Mennonite" derives), that "nothing could be more conceited than this donkey, nor more impudent than this dog." (Böhme celebrated Luther despite the latter's final turn against the spiritualists, but he criticized Calvin for trivializing both works and free will with predestination.)[71] Catholics attacked claims of revelation and prophesy by enthusiasts as seditious radicalism, challenging them with a fervor equal to that of the reformers. Catholic polemicists claimed spiritualists were an inevitable result of the original Lutheran or Calvinist heresy (both terms were applied indiscriminately to cover Protestant heterodoxy), and yet the Catholic language of condemnation of enthusiasm or unrestrained soulishness was remarkably similar to that of Luther and Calvin.[72] In the end, the competing confessions made common cause to obliterate the brief and violent ascendancy in 1535 of Anabaptism in Münster.

The orthodox reformers' greatest stake in suppression of the Anabaptist movement was threefold: first, the movement rejected the conflation of Church and state, and hence secular control of sacred matters; second, condemnation under Zwingli in Zurich of infant baptism as corrupted undermined the basis of virtually all other Christian ritual practices; and, third, like most Germanic sectarians (and despite their origins in textual literalism), many Anabaptists and their followers regarded communication inspired by spiritual motion to be superior to human interpretation of written text. This contradicted Calvinist orthodoxy, which decreed scriptural text to be the only reliable mode of communication between man and God in modern times (the last bits of holy text had been written in the apostolic era, ending direct communication with the deity). Anabaptism emerged within lay groups when uncompromising "radicals" began to require rigorous qualifications for baptism that were only rarely achieved by adults, making them impossible for infants. These emerged from a practical religion based on works—and thereby *experience* in spiritual, community, and material life—that infants born in sin but without experience could not yet possess.[73] "Infant baptism," Wolfgang Brandhuber argued in his open letter of 1529 to the Lutheran Church in Rattenberg, "is an abomination and the name of mockery of our God, which only John mentions in his revelation, but which shall be further revealed to us, if only we seek the Lord . . . until the end. Then He will reveal it to us, *for interpretation belongs to Him alone.*"[74] Or at least to a soulish reader in hidden communication with God, by private spiritual intercession. Böhme, for one, claimed to have written the *Aurora*, "only *for himselfe,* according to the gift of Gods Spirit."[75]

This emphasis on works and labor was understandably attractive to farmers and artisans, reflecting the basic publishing interests of Palissy and Böhme. Anabaptists were commonly admired in print for improvement and innovation in agriculture and the manual arts. Echoing Böhme, the sociologist Jean Seguy has written that French Anabaptists held convictions that their agricultural practices were a product of spiritual separation and purification. Thus, they were endowed with the ability to see deeply into the mysteries of the inner earth and Nature as the bearers of millennial secrets invisible to others.[76]

Aurora tied Böhme's theory of agricultural production to his critique of Calvinist predestination. Nothing in nature was wholly corrupt or pure, but a mixture of the two—"wrath and love"—at war for dominance until the end of history. "There is still in all things of this world both Love and wrath," Böhme wrote, "*one in another,* and they always wrestle and strive one with another." Here was Palissy's metaphysics again; if Palissy's program was formed out of brutal experience in the French civil wars of religion, Böhme's context was the Thirty Years' War. As alchemists, both men believed that spiritual light was generated from the crucible of battle. Both also argued that corruption was tied to nurture or personal history, what Palissy had called "heritage." "Neither," Böhme argued, "*ought* any man to say":

> that he is generated in the wrath-fire of totall corruption or perdition, *out of Gods predes-*
> *tinate purpose.* No: the corrupted Earth doth not stand, *neither,* in the totall wrath-fire of
> God, but only in its *outward* comprehensibility or palpability wherein it is so hard, dry and
> bitter. Whereby every one may perceive, that this Poison and *fiercenesse* doth not belong
> to the Love of God, in which there is nothing but *Meeknesse.* Yet I do not say this, as if
> every Man were Holy as he cometh from his mother's womb, but as the Tree is, so is the
> Fruit. Yet the Fault is not Gods, if a Mother beareth or bringeth forth a child of the Devil;
> but the Parents wickednesse. But if a wild twigg be planted in a Sweet Soyl, and be *in-*
> *grafted* with some other of a better and sweeter Kind, then there groweth a Mild Tree,
> though the twig were *wild.*
>
> For here all is possible; as soon is the good changed into Evill, as the Evill into Good.
> For every Man is *free,* and is as *a God* to himself; he may *change* and alter himself in this
> life either into wrath or into light: such Cloaths or Garments as a man puts on, such is his
> ornament or lustre: and what manner of Body soever man *soweth* into the earth, such a
> Body also groweth up from it, though in another form clarity and Brightnesse: yet all ac-
> cording to the quality of the *Seed.* For if the Earth were *quite* forsaken of God, then it
> could never bring forth *any* Good Fruit, but meer bad and Evil Fruit. But being the Earth
> standeth yet in Gods Love, therefore his wrath will not burn therein Eternally, but the
> Love *which hath overcome* will spew out the wrath-fire.[77]

The interaction of sacred violence thus inspired Germanic sectarian interest in medicinal plants, alchemy, and homeopathic medicine—all held in common with Paracelsus.[78] In his Anabaptist manifesto, Brandhuber, like Böhme, further claimed that the triumph of love, good works, and products of pious labor would unify the gathered Church into a mutually interdependent body; hence, Anabaptists were also known as the "Family of Love" (pejoratively, the "Familists"):

> If God permits and enables, all things should be held in common, . . . for since we have
> become partakers of Christ in the greatest things (that is in the power of God), why not
> then much more in the smallest, in temporal things. Not that man should therefore carry
> all his possessions to a common collection, for this is not appropriate everywhere. . . .
> [But] even though each laborer should receive his daily wages in accordance with the
> words of Christ that the laborer is worthy of his wages, love should compel him to

contribute faithfully to the common treasury. This should be done because of love. . . . Blessed is the hand which nourishes itself with its work and produces something honest, so that it may be able to give to the needy and thus preserve the whole body. For you know how Paul, in using the natural body as an example, says that no member is concerned only with itself, but all members with the whole body, and none can dispense with the other.[79]

The Anabaptist movement naturally gained avid support within the artisanal fraternities and guilds in urban areas ranging from Strasbourg to Venice. Like Palissy, perhaps, Clement Ziegler of the gardeners' guild of Strasbourg was considered "an indigenous prophet of something between traditional fraternity and Reformation sectarianism."[80] Until the "Tragedy of Münster" humbled them after 1535, Strasbourg was a haven for "all the misfits, intellectual and other, of the German-speaking Reformation."[81] So too was heterodox Venice, its southern counterpart.[82] Yet after Münster, persecution increased dramatically, sending survivors underground, tramping the rural countryside, or into isolated utopian communities. It is not unreasonable to speculate that in this context, some Anabaptist influence—perhaps refugees—reached the western islands of coastal Saintonge. Notions of absolute brotherhood, a leveler ideology in which love shattered social and religious barriers, respect for the pious products of rustic labor, pacifism, the revival of primitive, apostolic Christianity, and the millennialist belief in "end times" by persecuted refugees, inspired by their reading of Revelation, which promised divine vengeance on those who martyred God's saints, found a sympathetic audience among Palissy's Saintongeais Huguenot followers during the wars. To be sure, the language Palissy used to illuminate the religious and social worldviews of his heretical monks suggested their exposure to many elements of the Anabaptist program in "the east." There, to the questing Böhme in 1612, the "Aurora, Dayspring or Morning Rednesse; the lovely *Bright Day*" appeared, "which," he said, "is truly a great WONDER."[83]

This is not to say Saintongeais Huguenots in general, or even Palissy in particular, subscribed fully to Anabaptist notions of Christ as a man like all others—albeit suffused with the Holy Spirit—or that they denied Calvin's predestinarian discipline in favor of a utopian religion based on meritorious works. Still, we have seen that Palissy was not shy about contradicting Calvin's most canonical doctrines when they challenged his notions of moral social order. While he did not openly contest predestination as he did Nicodemism, Palissy focused much of his discourse on the good works of God in Nature, as well as of man in his agricultural and artisanal innovations, as ways to eliminate poverty; geological arguments that the earth was not ossified but constantly engaged in a process of inner and outer change; and that this state of change was conditional, the result of adepts "building with the destroyer."

The alchemic enterprise was, after all, about redemption of that which had remained pure from corrupted matter, using fire and "the work." First-generation rural reformers fell back on traditional Catholic notions of merit more than the Calvinist ministers were willing to admit. Just as the potter filtered Genevan theology through his own personal experience, so too he took what was needed from German spiritualism. Palissy's artisan natural philosophy was, like that of those called Anabaptists, founded on the alchemical emulation of Jesus' redemptive pain and meritorious acts. Above all else, Palissy and his Huguenot followers applied manual labor and skills to reconstruct primitive spiritual security for ordinary Christians who "wrestled" with both corruption and "wrath" in their everyday lives. Here many Protestant groups—especially lay spiritualists—found common cause in some moral tenets of the Anabaptist sects, while at the same time, they prudently maintained a safe distance from the very real danger of open sympathy.

Consider the widely read sentiments of Simplicius Simplicissimus, the poor rustic and refugee in Hans Jakob Christoph von Grimmelshausen's (1625–76) German novel of 1669, set amid the chaotic violence of the Thirty Years' War. Although not openly an Anabaptist himself, the uncharacteristically sober-minded Simplicius treats "their manner of life" with seriousness and respect in Grimmelshausen's "short chapter on the Hungarian Anabaptists," after the bulk of his "adventures" have satirized the cultures of seventeenth-century German wartime experience. First, in a conventional act of distancing for those who may have been sympathizers after Münster, Simplicius says that he "would have joined them" if only "these good people had not become mixed up in, and dedicated to, a false and heretical doctrine contrary to the general Christian church." Still, he compares the Hutterites (one of several Germanic sects pejoratively called Anabaptists) to the Essenes of Galilee, one of the three reformed Jewish sects from which historians surmise that Jesus probably emerged and an appropriate model for primitive Christianity among early modern sectarian reformers.[84] Regarding the Hutterites, he says:

> I considered their life the most blessed on earth, for they appeared to me in their activities very much like the Essenes described by Josephus [*Jewish War* 2.119–61] and others . . . they had treasures laid up and more than enough to eat; yet they wasted nothing. One heard no grumbling or cursing among them, not even unnecessary words. I saw craftsmen working in their shops as if they were paid for piecework. Their schoolmaster taught the children as if they were all his own. . . . If a person got sick, he or she had a special nurse; and there was a doctor and pharmacist for the group, though because of good food and healthy living hardly anyone became ill. I saw many an old person living quietly to extreme old age among them, and that is seldom found elsewhere. They had their appointed hours for eating, for sleeping, for working, but not a single minute for play or for promenading, except for the youngsters. After each meal, for the sake of health, the youngsters went

walking for an hour with their teacher. During this time they also had to pray and sing hymns. There is no anger, no zealotry, no vengefulness, no envy, no enmity, no worry about worldly goods, no pride, no regret. In short, there prevailed such lovely harmony as seemed to purport nothing but the honorable increase of the human race and of God's kingdom. . . . I thought that if I could initiate such a commendable Christian way of life, under the protection of my sovereign, I'd be a second St. Dominic or St. Francis. Oh, if only I could convert the Anabaptists so that they might in turn teach our fellow Christians their way of living, how blessed I would be! Or if only I could persuade my fellow Christians to lead such a (seemingly) Christian and commendable life as do the Anabaptists, what an achievement I would have to my credit![85]

Although he says that "for a long time I went around with such thoughts; I would have been glad to dedicate my farm and my entire fortune to such a Christian association," Simplicius decides in the end that the safest (and cheapest) course of action is to emulate those aspects of their utopian social contract that do not dangerously offend the state Church. He suppresses all talk of infant baptism and direct communication of the spirit and, like Menocchio, Palissy, Böhme, and many other Paracelsians, embraces a personal religion. "[A]mong all the arts and sciences none is better than theology, so long as it teaches a person to love God and serve him," he concludes. Based on this:

> I devised for people a kind of life that could be more angelic than human. A group of married as well as unmarried men and women would have to join together and, under a wise leader, earn their living by manual labor like the Anabaptists; the rest of the time they would exert themselves in the praise of God and the salvation of their souls.[86]

This "kind of life" was both agricultural and artisanal, after the primitive example of the Essenes. In such new worlds, manual labor was privileged and all of its profits were to be shared communally. Craftsmanship, medicine, and education were prized and available to all; language was pure, or silent; there was equality of the sexes; violence and illness were rare, and as a result, so were premature deaths (commonplace in the Thirty Years' War). Members lived by a synthesis of the Ten Commandments, the Gospels, and the golden rule. Consequently, the seven deadly sins were unknown. The real way of Simplicissimus's life, however, was mostly individual, private and noncommunal. His quest for a personal religion to be shared with others remained self-contained and atomized.

Yet Anabaptists, in their militant Christianity and above all the quest for purity, tended toward separation. This practice was manifested later in establishment of the Mennonite and Amish sects in Europe and America. Most other sympathizers, whether sectarians or lay Calvinists like Palissy, tended to adopt discourses of unity rather than separation, despite boundaries or differences.[87] That was why Palissy labored to syncretize his rustic cosmology with the magisterial Reformation and in turn with anti-Huguenot patrons. In artisanal security, Palissy offered an alternative to both militant Christianity and overt separatism, in which Huguenots could work in communities *and* as individuals independent of others.

So too Böhme, who labored to unify the opposition of love and wrath based on the Trinitarian model, as an inseparable plurality in one. Simplicius journeys from place to place to uncover prelapsarian unity beneath the fragmentation of war, from which he has been dispersed as a homeless particle. Although he learns much about "a kind of life that could be more angelic than human," he chooses not to live apart among the Hutterites but to search alone for an independent, individualistic "German hero who will overcome the whole world and make peace among all nations." a hero who can transform Germany into "the land of Cockaigne"—the earthly paradise for laborers—because he "will unite the religions and mold them into one."[88] The quest for unity could therefore be undertaken by heroic individuals in secret and set apart from other like-minded seekers, who were linked by a universal soul. Protestant artisans and natural philosophers in the early modern transatlantic world regarded Paracelsus as their unifying hero and used his legend and writings as models to order their own experience.

"By what means these doctrines were transmitted to the England of the Interregnum, more than a century later, and whether indeed an actual transmission was called for, are difficult questions," John Bossy says of the Anabaptist movement and its diffusion to Britain and the American colonies in the seventeenth century: "Perhaps we should think of them as spores secreted in a Christian culture, guaranteed to produce mushrooms at a certain temperature. In any case, no one who turns from the history of radical Christianity in the Germany of the 1520s and 1530s to the English of the 1640s and 1650s can fail to get the feeling that he has been there before."[89]

Primitivist convergence was key; yet the diffusion of Saintongeais Huguenot refugees to northern Europe, England, and America provides a compelling clue to one specific source for transmission of secret "spores." Perhaps hidden structures took shape in family networks of skilled artisans, refugee cells developed "under a wise leader" such as Palissy. He would claim that these "doctrines," based on manual philosophy, were secreted in material culture. The human geography of this inquiry is more direct for New Amsterdam / New York. The States-General of the Netherlands awarded descendants of refugees from Münster official toleration in 1578. Many of their followers eventually settled in New Amsterdam alongside the refugee Huguenots and Walloons who comprised New York's old French culture. With the Dutch capitulation of 1664, and even before—most famously during Peter Stuyvesant's time—English Quakers and other sectarian groups with Germanic antecedents and traditions of pious artisanry followed them to western Long Island, where they awaited the Huguenot refugee migration from Saintonge following 1685. This process of atomization, migration, and convergence is the subject of Part III of this book. Palissy's history thus introduced the daunting problem of the identification and definition of southwestern French artisans and enthusiasts as they moved through the Atlantic world in search of refuge. That the word "enthusiast" (or *fanatique*) has been used in conjunction with southwestern Huguenot religious practice at all may seem relatively unorthodox to students of early modern France, inasmuch as such language is traditionally used in reference to the far more expressive and theatrically prophetic behavior documented for south*eastern* Huguenot *inspirés*.

Enthusiastic behavior was manifested by different millennial styles. The southwestern Huguenot millennialist style—animate materialist, self-absorbed, disguised, interior, Neoplatonic, quietist (that is to say, closely related to forms of early Quakerism with which many successful southwestern Huguenot artisans would eventually ally themselves in colonial New York)—was a more socially adaptable and enduring alternative for Huguenot refugees in pluralistic colonial settings than the southeastern style, which was defined by open and confrontational theatricality.[90]

✦ Monks Disguised: Wild Men / Green Men / Babblers / Prophets ✦

If there was general agreement that the defining character of spirit was oneness, "the fruits of the spirit appeared to be babel and confusion."[91] Mistrust of "the Enthusiast" was widespread, even among sympathetic Calvinist Neoplatonists. John Smith (1616–1652), representing the influential Cambridge Platonists, said that enthusiastic philosophers made impressive progress toward perfection with an "inward sense of virtue and moral goodness far transcendent to all mere speculative opinions of it." Nevertheless, they also had souls that "heave and swell with a sense of [their] own virtue and knowledge." No doubt this characterized Palissy and Böhme alike, as did "an ill-ferment of self-love, lying at the bottom . . . with pride, arrogance and self-conceit."[92] Willfulness was a powerful signifier of carnality, and critics claimed that this suppressed spiritual communication, making human speech obscure, incomprehensible, or mute. Spiritualists countered, however, that the very insufficiency of human speech signified the active presence of soulish communication.[93]

Paracelsian discourse, steeped in lay rather than clerical rhetoric, was thus deeply—and problematically—pietistic. That is to say, it signified a convergence of natural-philosophical theory and practice that precisely paralleled a shift of focus in the lay religious experience from collective to individual spirituality, as a result of religious warfare and the insecurity of open, communal spirituality. Paracelsism was epitomized by soulish interiority, the secret lives of adepts, and the quest to separate purity from impurity, all—unlike Anabaptism—while remaining engaged therapeutically and commercially with the corrupt outside world. Its common languages were, therefore, multiple: the discourses of heterodoxy, primitive enthusiasm, pious artisanry, leveler politics, economics, rustic naturalism, and experience in civil war. La Rochelle's powerful fortress of Genevan orthodoxy presented one set of problems, eventually overcome by Richelieu's methodical frontal assault. However, this pietist shift toward rustic privatization presented an arguably greater problem of inaccessibility to the state's apparatus of repression.

Mystical writings by Valentin Weigel (1533–88), an influential pietist from Zschopau, Saxony (near Bohemia), were based on his closeted reading of Paracelsus's animate materialism. Böhme studied both Weigel and Paracelsus in nearby Lusatia during his early years. Paracelsus steadfastly refused sectarian alignment, and he was certainly latitudinarian in his beliefs. He had been born Catholic, however, and although his natural philosophy was predicated on the return of Christianity to spiritual unity, represented as being found in the primitive Church, which transcended confessional boundaries, he did accept last rites at his death in 1541. Even if Paracelsus had refused confessional alignment until that time, and although he has usually been associated with the Protestant natural-philosophical tradition, it should not be forgotten that his Catholic experience was present in alchemical reformulations of Trinitarianism and transubstantiation. Yet Paracelsus's books were on the Vatican's Index and his mystical Neoplatonic spiritualism was clearly at the core of the attraction for pietists. The universal soul's power to bind the fragmented confessions together was also fundamental for Protestant scientists in search of harmonization. Writers such as Palissy and Grimmelshausen thus applied Paracelsian discourse with growing frequency during the apocalyptic war years.[94]

Like Palissy, the inwardly mystical and heterodox Weigel was a first-generation Paracelsian. At the same time, Weigel was an outwardly orthodox Lutheran minister, which is why he remained unpublished until after his death in 1588. This strong pietist presence within orthodox Lutheranism parallels Böhme and elements of the tensions in Palissy's relationship to orthodox Calvinism. A shared history of Germanic and Saintongeais Huguenot Paracelsianism, pietism, and outward disguise of an inwardly subversive spirit will help us to understand the significance Palissy accorded the influence of the sectarian "Lutheran monks" who "returned" from Germany to Saintonge to evangelize Saintes and the coastal islands. When Palissy wrote that these monks had returned from "the east," was this simply a generic reference to the Germanic principalities or eastern France? Or was it an allusion to eastern Germany, and to the regions bordering Bohemia, then a hotbed of Paracelsianism among enthusiastic Protestant natural philosophers, such as the hidden Weigel, and ultimately his follower Böhme? Such regional religious foundations might account for the influence of Palissy as a preacher and natural philosopher in Saintonge.

This might also help us to explain why Palissy's religious and craft influences remained strong among Saintongeais artisans after Hamelin's death, Palissy's removal to Paris post-1565, and the latter's own death at the turn of the seventeenth century. Given the isolation of the region and the disruptive influence the wars had on diffusion of formal Genevan Calvinism to the Rochelais hinterland (a situation made permanent by the events of 1628), the naturalistic, pietistic, intensely ascetic artisanal and monastic Lutheranism that traveled west with the monks in the 1540s was probably the single most coherent Reformed religious doctrine and worldview to endure into the periods of the *désert* and dispersion. This was the Germanic sectarian tradition reactivated by Palissy when, in the absence of the fugitive (and doomed) Hamelin, he stepped in (in the role of his anonymous "artisan sans lettres") to preach from the heart and soul and lead other artisans to do the same.

This is not by any means to suggest that Saintongeais artisans rejected formal Calvinism, but simply to say that Germanic pietism may have had a more profound and lasting effect, if only because the Germanic tradition had more of an opportunity to take root in the primitive Church. Its prudent lessons of silence and interiority were more applicable for artisans during wartime than Calvin's denunciations of Nicodemism. Palissy's history indicates that Saintongeais Huguenots took much from Genevan Calvinism and appreciated the presence of Genevan ministry when available, witness his martyrology of Hamelin. But at the same time, the endurance of an early Germanic Protestant and monastic tradition among Saintongeais artisans in part explains Palissy's leveler rhetoric well before such rhetoric appeared in England during the civil wars, as well as his pointed reference to local Huguenot rejection of one Calvinist minister who preferred the nobility in favor of another who lived among the poor, led the ascetic life, and "ate potatoes and drank water for dinner." This regional Germanic tradition makes it much easier, finally, to explain the susceptibility of Palissy and his followers among the *artisanat* to the rapid assimilation of Germanic Paracelsian discourse and alchemic theories of artisanal practice in such a rural and isolated part of the world. It also suggests the syncretism contained in the moment when Hamelin returned to the region for a second time after rehabilitation in Geneva and Palissy engaged in a strategy to assure both the Calvinist minister's local status among the flock and his personal *sûreté*. Palissy helped disguise his mentor in Hamelin's secondary persona as a working artisan—he was, after all, a printer as well as a minister—thus following the Germanic tradition alive in Saintonge from the earliest days of the primitive Church.

This was also the historical context for closer readings of Palissy's narrative of the monks' capture and the state's symbolic response to their acts of heresy with its very specific program of degradation, torture, and execution. With a careful description of the notably well-considered punishments, Palissy reserved pride of place in his Saintongeais "book of Martyrs"—before Hamelin joined them there—for the monks who had founded the artisans' primitive Church in Saintonge on Germanic spiritual principles of interiority and naturalistic dissimulation. These principles were equally well known to enemies. Unfortunately, knowledge alone guaranteed neither access nor control over heterodoxy. Thus, "the cursed Familists do hold," wrote the Englishman John Canne in 1634 (after sectarians emerged as a potent force to challenge his state Church), "that religion standeth not in outward things."[95] "The corrupted earth does not stand in the totall wrath-fire of God," Böhme wrote, "but only in its *outward* comprehensibility . . . hard, dry and bitter." By nature already a lie, the surface of things was the natural place for artisanal dissimulation of earth matter.

Just as Palissy and his followers constructed artisanal *sûreté* in plain sight of the traditional Huguenot *place de sûreté,* so too he narrated his history so that Saintongeais Huguenot craftsmen initially adapted a local version of Germanic sectarianism. This was characterized by the convergence of heresy with dissimulation and craftsmanship with millennial expectation, and it was embodied by new Huguenot leaders who were both lay ministers and pious artisans.[96] This was fertile territory for synthetic visions of the cosmos, a historical foundation combining analogous doctrines uncovered in Paracelsus and in Ficino's Italianate Neoplatonism. That is why Palissy's reading in his little history of end times in Saintonge's primitive Church in 1546 can also be seen as beginning a new transatlantic history of Huguenot spiritual disguise, constructed by pious artisans in material forms. In these contexts, construction spiraled outward from the heretics' Reformed inner bodies, while their corrupted outer bodies—already impure—were dissimulated in response to challenges from external "perils, dangers and great tribulations":

You must understand that the early Church was built on a very small beginning, through perils, dangers and great tribulations, and that on the last days, the difficulty and dangers, pains, labors and afflictions, were great in that country of Xaintonge. . . .

. . . It happened in the year 1546 that some monks, having gone to Germany and then returned, or that some having read books of their doctrine finding that they were misled, dared to secretly uncover some of the abuses, but suddenly the priests and *beneficiers* found out that they were distancing themselves from their deceptions [*coqueilles*] and incited the judges to prosecute them: this the judges did willingly, because none of them owned part of the *benefice,* from which to make a living, and so they were susceptible to bribery. Because of this, these monks were forced to flee [Saintes] into exile, removing their habits, because they worried they would be burned alive. Some became artisans, others became teachers in some of the villages, and because the islands of Oléron, Marennes, and Alvert were far from public roads, a certain number withdrew onto these islands, finding various means of making a living without being recognized: and as they got to know the inhabitants, they risked speaking covertly, [because] they were assured that nobody would say anything.

All this having happened, [the monks'] numbers were greatly reduced, [and yet] they found a way to obtain a pulpit because in those days there was a vicar who favored them tacitly: it therefore ensued that little by little in these regions and islands of Xaintonge, many had their eyes opened, and recognized many of the abuses which they had previously ignored, [and] as a result, many held these preachers in great esteem, so much so that from then on, the abuses were quite thinly veiled.

In those days, the fiscal *procureur* [or collector of tithes, Savary] Collardeau, a perverted man, of bad character, found a means to warn the bishop of Xaintes [Tristan de Bizet], who was then at the court, [and] got him to understand that Xaintes was full of Lutherans, and he asked the bishop to put him in charge of rooting out the Lutherans; not only did Collardeau write to him many times, but he also went to see him. Collardeau tried so hard that he obtained a commission from the bishop and from the *parlement* of Bordeaux, with a hefty sum of money that was given him by the court. This was done for gain and not for religious zeal. This accomplished, he used some judges, on the island of Oléron as well as that of Arvert, and similarly at Gémozac, and had them arrest the preacher of Saint-Denis, which is at the tip of the island of Oléron, by the name of Brother Robin, and took him to the island of Arvert, where they also caught another called Nicole; some days later, they also caught the one in Gémozac, who taught school, and preached on Sundays, and who was well loved by the inhabitants: because of that I think they should be inscribed in the book of martyrs. . . .

. . . These poor people were condemned to be unfrocked and dressed up in *accoutrements* made of greenery, so that the people would think they were fools or mad: and on top of that, because they were upholding God's quarrel in a manly way [*virilement*], they were bridled like horses by Collardeau, before being taken to the scaffold; these bridles each had an iron apple which filled up the whole of their mouths, a hideous thing to behold: and having been thus degraded, they were returned to prison before being sent to Bordeaux, where they would be condemned to death.[97]

Palissy charted trajectories for the pious lives and martyred deaths of these Lutheran heretics who were catalysts and founders of the primitive Church of Saintonge by using the allegorical and historical language of concealment and revelation. He "inscribed," for posterity, the stories of the three martyrs he knew personally: one monk was from the Dominican order and named Hubert Robert ("the preacher of Saint-Denis [-d'Oléron] . . . Brother Robin"); another was a Celestine academic named Nicolle Maurel ("another called Nicole"), who had access to a scientific library at the Collège de Guyenne in Bordeaux; and finally, the Franciscan named René Mace ("the one in Gémozac"). Of the three heretics, only Hubert Robert escaped being burned alive by the authorities. Palissy's mystical tale of this Brother Robin's flight from his captors in effect recycled the story of Peter's miraculous deliverance from Herod Antipas's prison in Jerusalem at the beginning of the early Christian era (Acts 12: 6–10), likewise one of blindness (concealment) and insight (revelation).[98]

Herod had Peter arrested in a roundup of Jews and imprisoned him along with the others. This story drew parallels between Old and New Testament histories of the early Jewish and Christian dispersions, inasmuch as it separated Christ's early disciples from their corrupt Jewish genealogy. An angel visited Peter in prison that night, caused the chains to fall miraculously from his hands and then led the way out of bondage to freedom. As if in a dream, Peter's physical body and angelic protective spirit walked past guards who were either asleep or overlooked them. Peter had been hidden in plain sight under the prophet's own simple "mantle" of faith, which the angel ordered Peter to "wrap . . . around you and follow me." Many paintings confirm the miraculousness of this manipulation of perception, as the eyes of Peter's guards appear wide open yet also covered by an obscuring dross. Brother Robin was likewise saved by an angelic intervention that veiled the corrupt vision of his enemies in order to preserve his tiny fragment of the living word for dispersion into the *désert*.[99]

Such was Palissy's basis for the "very small beginning" of the primitive Church. This was literally true in numerical terms, yet smallness was understood as the container of great spiritual power in the *Recepte*. Here the power was still in a state of potential, however. Paracelsus's generative metaphor of the microcosmic seed that lived in every natural thing and grew after animation by the metaphysical light of nature comes quickly to mind. Consider both the obstetric and the eschatological terms at play in the image of "perils, dangers, and great tribulations" and the potter's choice of words in describing "the last days." During these violent end times, "the difficulty and dangers, pains, labors, and afflictions, were great in that country of Xaintonge." This language provided the natural-philosophical and alchemical context for the birth, decay, death, and rebirth of the primitive Church, constructed by Palissy in subsequent passages. After the seed was planted in the earth of "that country of Xaintonge," it was inseminated by the intervention of God, "through perils, dangers, and great tribulations." Once the seed had germinated, it matured slowly, hidden in this apocalyptic womb during its inside-out *travail* of birth, beset by "pains, labors, and afflictions," until the time for potential to assume prophetic form ripened and it grew *visibly* into its plenitude, up through crevices and holes in the protective shell that mediated the subterranean world that Palissy also constructed in his rustic basins and grottos.

Like Palissy before him, Böhme—claiming that the Holy Spirit would germinate and emerge from the war in matter between wrath and love—internalized this natural philosophy of "perils, dangers, and great tribulations." These dangers were historical and most apparent as social and political chaos, yet they were experienced inwardly, as Böhme "must every day and hour grapple struggle and fight with the Devill who afflicteth me in my corrupted lost Nature, in the fierce or wrathful quality, which is in my flesh . . . *for our life is as a perpetuall warfare with the Devill.*" The desired result of warfare, however, was momentary prelapsarian return and spiritual revelation when the light of Nature, in the Holy Ghost, "riseth up" out of the dead stone of fallen earth like a spark of fire, after being struck by a violent hand:

> This Strife and Battle is about that most High Noble Victorious Garland, till the corrupted perished Adamical Man is killed and dead, in which the Devill hath accesse to Man. . . . For, the Holy Ghost will not be caught held or retained in the sinful flesh; but riseth up like a flash of lightning; even as fire flashes and sparckles [*sic*] out of a stone, when a man strikes fire upon it.[100]

Böhme thus understood convergence of Revelation and alchemy to occur as the hidden inner "Life presseth through Death: the *outermost* Birth is the Death . . . when thou lookest on Earth and Stones . . . Death is therein. . . . [and so] The outward Earth is a bitter stinck, and is dead, and that every man understandeth to be so."[101] This cycle of impermanent, fragmented natural history ended with the millennium, and with it permanence and wholeness (synthesis) was acquired. In the microcosm, a tiny "new Body might continually and constantly be generated out of Death, till time should be accomplished, and the whole [becomes a] new borne Body."[102] Like Palissy's spirit after the first civil war of religion in Saintonge, when he undertook to write his history of the primitive Church of Saintes, Böhme's:

> spirit at this Time of my description and setting it down did *unite* and qualifie or mix with the deepest Birth or Geniture of God; in *that,* I have received my knowledge and from thence it is sucked, not in great Earthly Joy, but in the anxious Birth or Geniture, *perplexity* and Trouble. For what I did hereupon undergo suffer and endure from the Devill and the Hellish quality which as well doth rule in my *outward* Man . . . this thou canst not apprehend, unless thou also *Dancest* in this Round.[103]

"Thou must know," Böhme concluded in this gesture of commonality between Paracelsians and pietists, "that I write not here as a Story or History, as if it were *related* to me from another," but from personal experience of prophesy and revelation in the sacred violence of love and wrath, spirit and matter, hand and tool, word and mouth, pen and paper:

> I must continually stand in that Combat or Battle, and I find it to be full of heavy strivings, wherein I am often *struck down* to the ground, as well as all other Men. But for the sake of the violent fight, and for the sake of the *earnestnesse,* which we have together, this

Revelation hath been given me, and the vehement driving or impulse, to bring it so to passe as to set all this down in *Paper*.[104]

Following these synthetic impulses, Palissy's construction of a Germanic origin for the primitive Church of Saintonge served as the Old Testament antitype of Hamelin's New Testament experience. The common denominator linking the two books—specifically Genesis and Revelation—was the involvement of Palissy himself as an actor, historian, and personal intermediary between beginning and end. He represented himself as the local bridge between Luther and Calvin, Paracelsus and Hamelin, international style and folkloric traditions. The dangers that afflicted the seed in 1546 would grow into the civil wars and ultimately the destruction of Hamelin's Huguenot Church in Saintes, which led to the foundation of his own artisans' Church. Palissy experienced that apocalypse himself, in his secret matrix between the stone-throwing children, who embodied the chaos and corruption of unpurified and unripened matter. At the same time, the potter labored heroically to push other local materials—the earths in his glaze experiments—through death to perfection in his laboratory-workshop.

If Hamelin's mission in Saintonge signaled a Calvinist rebirth of the primitive Germanic Church, then the monks' torture (with mouths gagged with an iron apple to stop heretical speech) was the precursor to Hamelin's death by strangulation. This caused a rebirth of the primitive Church for a third time, led by Palissy, who validated his inheritance as lay leader of the artisans' Church through a genealogy of experience and personal connections with the martyred founders that was reconstructed in his history of Saintes. If the monks and Hamelin both experienced martyrdom, cleansing, and the separation of inner and outer bodies in the executioners' fire, then Palissy survived death as a martyr to the fire in his kiln and alchemic crucible. There he secretly redeemed both himself and the fallen matter of Saintonge through his art of the earth.

For Böhme as well, such inner, secret places of craftsmanship were secure, sacred places for alchemical recreation. "God is in the Center, in the innermost . . . *hiddenly,* [in all the] natural Births," Böhme wrote, "and is not known, but only *in the Spirit of Man;* . . . the outermost Birth in the fruit doth not comprehend . . . *him,* but *he* containeth the outermost Birth of the fruit, and formeth it." Thus in his heroic artisanry, Palissy was protected from enemies and the *esmotions* of blind hatred, seeing all, but able to remain unseen, as the "wrath . . . in this world *cannot* comprehend the Light of God, and therefore the Heart of God is *hidden* and concealed, which however *dwelleth* in all places, and comprehendeth All."[105]

Hence, key roles in Palissy's biblical history were played by heroic artisans. Just as the moment of Revelation was unveiled by Palissy, the last unfallen Adamic artisan in Saintes who was still producing artifacts of purity while hidden inside its ruins, so too

his monastic Adams in a Saintongeais Genesis, midwifed the Reform's local beginnings. These monastics were not quite the prototypical, guileless child-men of Genesis, however. Two of the three mentioned were postlapsarian artisans "sans lettres,"
who were masters of the "art and mystery" of their crafts, as well as dissimulation.
Their wisdom was not obtained from scholasticism—though we know that the third
was in fact a schoolman—but through experience guided by the light of Nature, which
had also taught Palissy the mysteries of artisanal security, revealed by the *limace*'s inner operations.

Palissy's history recorded the monks' appearances in four sets of disguises; three
were of their own devising and one was created by the authorities. Yet these disguises
were not superficial in the way the potter described the priests' corrupt deceptions.
Rather, they signified the continuous stages of a spiritual metamorphosis toward the
goal of a material-holiness synthesis in pious rustic artisans. The first disguise reflected the inner transformations that occurred after the monks' conversion experience
in Germany. In Calvin, this was the disguise of the Nicodemite; thus, the heretics continued to wear monastic robes and outwardly played the false role of Catholic brothers in Saintes.

At the same time however, the monks "dared to secretly uncover [*couvertement, de
descouvrir*] . . . the priests['] and *beneficiers* deceptions [*coquilles*]." Palissy engaged in
delicate wordplay here that recalled his discourse on the *limace*'s inner and outer bodies. He used three words that referred to hidden identity on both sides whose root
meanings also connoted covers or shells on top of a secret body. The monks labored
couvertment (under cover) to *descouvrir* (uncover and lay bare) *coquilles* (snail or scal-
lop shells, as well as the "cheating devises," or deceptions, of Catholicism). When these
two hidden bodies came into contact, the purest had the power to uncover, perceive,
and hence "expose to the world's view" deceptions that obscured abuses of the corrupt
one, even if it had assumed the impenetrable spiral shape.[106] At the same time, however, it was the nature of pure, inner bodies, despite the effectiveness of their outer disguises, to "distance themselves" from all sources of corruption ("books of their doctrine"; "judges . . . susceptible to bribery"). Distancing thereby exposed the monks'
outer bodies to persecution by the corrupt and demonic.

These enemies burned the outer bodies of the pure, thus releasing their inner bodies into spiritual rebirth. To maintain invisibility and stay in disguise, the monks had
to learn to live and work among the corrupt, and not just in "exile," in island sanctu-
aries of the Huguenots, "far from public roads." The monks failed in this, but their fatal inability to find refuge near their enemies was a key innovation of artisanal security. Negotiating access to the heart of corruption as a client of Montmorency, and only
because of that association, he was rescued from the authorities in Saintes in 1563.
Palissy and his family survived the St. Bartholomew's Day Massacre for much the same

reason, because he had become a valued creature near to the household of Catherine de Médicis.

The distinction between the noun *abus* (an abuse, grievance, or misuse) and its verb *abuser* (to deceive, to delude) was significant because Palissy used both forms here and, as was so often the case, worked to project multiple meanings. He implied a world of ethical difference between these Huguenot deceptions as artisanal *sûreté*—as moral instruments of both autonomy and survival in *défense* of an embryonic truth so youthful and vulnerable that, to use a metaphor common to both the *désert* and Paracelsianism, it had to be protected, like the seed of a newly planted fruit tree still nurtured in its arbor—and the deceptions of the Antichrist (by definition, *obfuscation* of truth). Strategies of artisanal *sûreté* drawn from Nature had to be devised if divine truth was to mature sufficiently to grow through violence and pierce the veils of corruption.

Did Palissy seize upon his tiny shelled creature once again as his basic metaphor for this sequence? The dangerous and finally self-exposing process employed to "uncover some of the abuses" was undertaken "secretly" by the monks. "Obscurely" and perhaps also "ambiguously" fit well here, but *couvert* can also be translated materially as ceramic glaze or glazing; this word almost always locates action on the surface (or covers) of things. The process by which the monks (and artisans) undertook to blend superficially with the dominant culture for access to uncover (*descouvrir*) hidden abuses (or deceptions) necessarily began with their *personal* surfaces (representations of public or social self-identity), which were protectively cloaked, and especially those surfaces specific to language (intentionally ambiguous speech) and the body (dress as disguise).

Unfortunately, Palissy's demonic adversaries (clergy fearful for their *bénéfices* and corrupt judges who solicited bribes) penetrated the protective shield of ambiguity out of venality, not faith, to denounce the monks as impostors and heretics. Palissy asserted a dangerous relationship between illicit money (bribery) and the unmasked disguise. He thereby inferred a process of enemies coming to "understand" the nature of the "shell," causing the forces of authority (clergymen, judges) forcibly to remove it (thus exposing its wearer as vulnerable), as at least superficially a function of money. The most carefully constructed *sûreté* could be penetrated "with a hefty sum of money," perhaps a reference to Christ's betrayal by Judas.

Palissy described an economics of penetration and persecution in Saintonge among the local rural bureaucrats of repression, who in many cases were eager—indeed tacitly expected—to supplement their relatively modest incomes with bribes. Hence, the most baneful disguise in Palissy's narrative belonged to the prosecutors, who arrested heretics "for gain and not for religious zeal," as they pretended. On the other hand, he drew a precise symmetry between *couvertement* and *coqueille* and confirmed the relationship proposed in his essay "De la ville de forteresse" between pious dissimulation of purity, and, in both historical and material terms, the potter's notion of artisanal *sûreté.* The monks' disguises were becoming signifiers of *limace* shells; not simply of natural and hence invisible protection of an embryonic or vulnerable personal faith, but of the glaze or container *itself.* In Palissy's rustic forms, a pious vessel displayed the potential *material* of faith *revealed,* artfully and exclusively, to a community of secret believers in the *désert.*

When the monks "were forced to flee into exile," they assumed their second disguise after "removing their habits." They did this "because they worried they would be burned alive," and surely they were. However, double reference to the distilling fire of gehenna in the alchemical crucible, which burned away surface materials (the monks' old Catholic habits), seems equally plausible in this context. On the three coastal islands of Saintonge, most put on an artisan's apron and "became artisans"; some "others became teachers." They "risked speaking covertly" but with the consent of the people (unlike orthodox ministers who did not seek their consent), inasmuch as "they were assured that nobody would say anything." This religion was one of exterior silence; its inner voices expressed in hand craftsmanship.

Yet, theirs were not false disguises. In Palissy's telling, such outward shells were all part of a Paracelsian process of being and becoming. The inwardly pious artisans had followed their trades as faithfully as they did religion (perhaps under the direction of the same Huguenot masters they had themselves converted earlier), as a "means of making a living without being recognized." They blended with the workaday world of their flock—as Hamelin did later—and were further reformed by the humility, piety, and craft practices learned from the same poor, rustic people to whom they had taught Protestant theology. Having become practicing artisans where before they had been men of the spirit alone, these heretical monks reinvented themselves as the embodiment of the material-holiness synthesis and created a Reformed religion founded on manual philosophy. Palissy makes the internal rationale of Saintonge's artisan-led Reformed culture accessible to historians. Despite having discarded their first "shell" to assume a more appropriate alternative disguise in the interest of *sûreté,* these now apparently metamorphosed artisans appeared to act simultaneously, almost *interchangeably,* as skilled artisans *and* subversive churchmen.

Isolation and a reputation as strongholds for heresy were not the only factors leading to the monks' choice of the islands of the coast of Saintonge. The region's large artisanal population, which arguably drew Palissy there as well, was also a pull factor. This vital sector had greatly expanded since the late Middle Ages to supply both containers and transport for traditional local fishing, salt making, and, further inland, wine and eau-de-vie production. Such seasonal enterprises required a steady pool of woodworkers who specialized in blockmaking, shipbuilding, wagon and wheel manufacture (wagons transported sea salt from *marais* to wharf for shipment up the coast to La Rochelle's enormous warehouses and, eventually, transshipment to southern Europe and South America), and cooperage (for salt, fish preserved in salt, oysters, mussels, and wine).

Potters from towns clustered along the Charente River in and around Saintes fired ceramic vessels as containers for wine and Cognac both consumed locally and exported. Much wine produced in the region was exported through the port of La Rochelle, primarily for sale to the upper classes in the British Isles and the Netherlands (where poorer people generally drank beer, at least until the introduction of rum distilled from West Indian sugar in the seventeenth century).[107] Although wine was shipped in barrels, there is good archaeological evidence suggesting that Saintongeais pottery was transported in quantity *alongside* wine barrels to La Rochelle's many agents in Britain, Germany, and the Netherlands. Produced almost exclusively in a cluster of kilns in or around the tiny town of La Chapelle-des-Pots near Saintes, these ceramics were shipped northwest along the Charente River from Port-Berteau to the Atlantic coast in three-man canoes (or *pirogues*), dug out from single logs measuring over forty feet in length, and thence transferred to oceangoing ships, either for the short journey due north to La Rochelle or directly out to sea. Such earthen tableware enabled wine merchants to offer luxury consumers a variety of stylish and (relative to metalware) fairly inexpensive ceramic vessels with which to have servants perform the necessary tasks of carrying the master's wine directly from barrel to table.[108]

Given the economic and occupational milieu of Saintonge, the fugitive Lutherans wisely chose tradesmen's "shells" in which to operate and remain invisible. Yet was their mastery of a trade merely a convenient disguise? Consider that many refugees were skilled craftsmen from the start. Some early modern monasteries were largely self-sufficient communities, supporting a substantial number of highly skilled artisans—from joiners to distillers—in the various orders. During this period, given adherence to master-apprenticeship and guild traditions even in many in rural areas, it is probably unlikely that strangers found a "means of making a living, without being recognized" as skilled artisans if they had not *already* achieved at least the status of journeyman before their arrival. This was certainly the case among early reformers in south-central and southeastern France, where, as Hillel Schwartz asserts, by 1560, "rural artisans had brought Protestant ideas to the most inaccessible parishes of Languedoc."[109] Both Schwartz and Philippe Joutard have shown that the southeastern Huguenot regions—like Palissy's Saintonge— were best able to endure *désert* experiences if initially seeded by an *artisan*'s Reformation. Artisan leaders emerge from the documents as neither simple, instrumental replacements for a decimated but still influential Genevan ministry nor hollow, powerless victims of absolutism. Rather, many were formed by a continuous, oblique dialogue with both of the competing dominant cultures. Meanwhile, they also formed an authentic, self-sufficient—if not autonomous—mobile, parallel, subterranean, and lay religious culture with a coherent leadership (indeed, an artisan elite) and very deep roots in local oral and material folk traditions.[110]

That pious artisans were the earliest leaders of the Reformed movement in coastal Saintonge is also indicative of one specific and local manifestation of a very long-term transformation in Western attitudes regarding the status of artisans and manual labor in general, culminating in the early modern period, which was reflected—if both pinpointed and extolled as virtuous—in Calvin's *Treatises,* but certainly *not* invented by him and his followers. On the contrary, the historian of technology Lynn White Jr. has used a progression of texts and images to argue convincingly that "the spiritual value of hard work was not, as Weber implied, a Calvinist discovery." In White's reconstruction, the Judeo-Christian tradition of virtuous labor and industriousness predated the Reformation and, like much early modern primitivism in general, "was integral to the Christian ascetic tradition going back through the monks to Jewish roots."[111]

White's method is largely philological; he traces the word *labor* from Plato, who "had no respect for labor and no sense of its possible place in the life of the soul," to the later Romans, for whom *labor* connoted "suffering." Yet, for Neoplatonists and Paracelsians such as Palissy and Böhme in the sixteenth and seventeenth centuries, this was precisely the sort of labor that was redeemed by alchemical intervention. In most classical texts, "labor meant Drudgery"; indeed, "in their minds, there was a grave moral defect, comparable to Timidity, Violence, or Fraudulence, in any man who toiled physically." However, the classical stigmatization of *labor* began to ameliorate during the later Middle Ages, initially guided by Benedictine monks who proclaimed widely that *laborare est orare* ("work is worship"); and then by the Franciscans, who perceived in Joseph's vocation as an artisan a commonality with their own monastic interests in Christ's asceticism and humble origins.

The crucial moment of transformation in the meaning of *labor*—and the one that appeared to find great strength in *popular,* not simply scholastic, attitudes—emerged at the beginning of the fifteenth century, with the prominence of the cult of St. Joseph the carpenter. "By the early fifteenth century St. Joseph," White writes, "until recently the complaining, hoodwinked husband, the butt of popular mockery—had been transformed into St. Joseph the strong and kindly *pater familias,* the guardian of the Christ Child and of Our Lady, the hard-working artisan . . . patron of carpenters and cabinetmakers."[112] Joseph was commemorated in the late medieval liturgy and recorded in the popular and humanizing *Golden Legend,* a folkloric handbook of Christ's family and friends that formed the "model and nucleus of the universal community of the redeemed." The *Golden Legend* was particularly important for artisans as a source of themes for "the image-maker, in paint, wood, stone and glass."[113]

Another basic link between Palissy, his artisan followers, and their disciples among the southwestern Huguenots can be located in this popular Judeo-Christian familial and artisanal tradition that anticipated the Reformation. The Lutheran monastic origins of Saintongeais Protestantism supplied a homely language and model of practice—which was reinforced, supplemented, and systematized by Philibert Hamelin and Palissy—to voice and to embody convictions long held among some rural folk and variously practiced in local, especially artisanal, idioms. These cobbled Catholic and pagan notions together with the new Protestant theology to suit local needs. The rehabilitation of Joseph the industrious woodworker in the popular consciousness also paralleled the corresponding rise in the status of the manual laborer, and, moreover, of the potential for virtue in things made by hand. St. Joseph, *paterfamilias,* and his role as provider for the Holy Family of a "human Christ," were, John Bossy has argued, "invented from scratch in the fifteenth century, and promoted by the post-Reformation church."[114] Both the immediate effect and long-term influence of these Protestant monastic artisan-evangelists among the coastal Huguenots and the authority Palissy and his followers inherited from their infiltration of Saintonge suggest an effect of this earlier shift, which was merely amplified by Luther and Calvin.

The third disguise was subsumed inside another transition from the crucible of sacred violence, inasmuch as "all this having happened, [the monks'] numbers were greatly reduced." Hence, a further process of distillation had produced only a very few pious artisans from among the first group of monks who survived the alchemic fire "to obtain a pulpit," with the help of another priestly Nicodemite, a "certain vicar who favored them tacitly." Now "covert" monks who "became" pious artisans were transmuted by fire into Lutheran lay preachers and disguised as what they now were: authentic working artisans, whose mobile pulpits followed the mobility of their trades, ranging from workshops in the *désert* to family conventicles to Huguenot temples. The monks had become—like Palissy—secretive artisan-preachers who found silent followers and knowledge in manual experience with the light of Nature, enthusiastic exegesis of Scripture, and Paracelsian theory and practice. Theirs was a natural Church, founded on the borderlands of the Anglo-French Atlantic, one that sometimes worshipped and practiced heresy in plain sight, protected by dissimulation and privatism and yet integrated by the correspondences between their inner bodies and a universal spirit and the macrocosmic fragments of elemental matter hidden in the bowels of the rustic earth, and dispersed in the ocean and sky.

The Germanic pattern of diffusion of heresy was reenacted in Saintonge. Savary Collardeau, the fiscal *procureur* of Saintes ("a perverted man, of bad character"), had penetrated the protective shell of dissimulation constructed by Huguenot artisan-preachers and warned the bishop that Xaintes was "full of Lutherans," who needed "rooting out." Palissy's use of "Lutherans" specifically is itself significant and indicates the pervasiveness of the Protestant message carried west by the monks from Germany.

This one of the few cases in which the early records of the southwestern Reformation are so specific. Almost from the beginning of the wars of religion, most legal documents show that royal inquisitors tended to address Huguenot defendants generically as either members of the R.P.R. ("religion prétendue réformée"), or, beginning in the 1550s, "adherents" of the "doctrine" of *both* "Luther *and* Calvin."

To borrow an ominous word from absolutist rhetoric, the German "infection" set into the region's body. Despite a long tradition of abuse of such language by early historians, it is difficult to ignore the significance of the biological metaphor in this context. A virus, understood in the modern sense of the word, is an organism that survives in the body of its host, then spreads and grows stronger by disguising its true nature to escape detection by the system's defenses. Palissy's artisans "mingle with the common folk"; they "dare to speak," but again, *couvertement*—only until certain their auditors "would say nothing" that threatened the integrity of the "shell." The fruits of this silent "mingling" began to appear. Conversions grew among the whispers, pulpits were established in the islands because a "grand Vicaire," himself also "infected," favored the Reformation "tacitly." "Eyes [were] opened" by the labors of the artisans— now finally called "these said preachers" as well—and they were "held . . . in great esteem" by the poor as their elite leadership, because they alone had the special sight required to discover "abuses" for all the other faithful who could only perceive deceptions "rather poorly."

Artisan-preachers functioned as magi or adepts able to alter appearances and perceive divine truth in its most mundane forms, and thus to animate an entire community of seekers mostly rendered inert and effectively blinded by earlier deceptions. Herein lies a clue to the mysteries and attractions of Huguenot artisan leadership during the early Reformation, followed by dispersion into the great internal *désert* of Counter-Reformation France and, finally, external exile to the new worlds of international Protestantism. Palissy's history identified a Saintongeais artisanal tradition of evangelical diffusion that did not originate with superficial religious leaders who merely assumed the outer body disguise of a lay preacher or artisan solely for convenience or *sûreté* alone, but as an authentic representation of a dualistic, inextricably intertwined social self-identity. The "Lutheran" founders of Saintongeais Huguenot traditions seem to have been just as independent and self-sufficient and at home in either the material or spiritual world as Palissy and his artisan-preacher followers. It was this dualistic yet inseparable armature that provided the historical foundation for a regional oral, material, and written culture, as well as a way of perceiving reality that laid the basis for the Paracelsian natural-philosophical synthesis on its own terms.

If diffusion of knowledge and culture has been described in terms of circularity, then for Saintonge, the artisan-preacher was at the center of a golden circle. Leadership authority came when the artisan acquired liminal status as an intermediary in a context where the go-between or cultural translator was privileged to serve as a divinely gifted preceptor for others in his network. For adepts, clients dimly perceived and required new understanding to mine the common ground that presumably only they could see, to unmask the myriad disguises that separated supernatural and natural, high and low, oral and written, man-made things and their material properties; indeed, those animate forces of divine being connecting matter and spirit and, ultimately, man and God.

Palissy located himself in that leadership position, in the middle of All, as the local, Saintongeais inheritor of this cosmopolitan historical tradition. Reflecting Menocchio's economic centrality as town miller and leading artisan, Ginzburg's prideful Friulian was motivated by similar artisanal desires to occupy such a position. This was never more apparent than when he continued to jeopardize his life, compulsively interpreting the world for anyone who would listen—including his inquisitors—though he understood and was plainly frightened by the consequences of his actions. These stories should complicate nostalgic interpretations of the role of reforming artisans and the romance of bottom-up formation of leaderless proletarian cultures. On the messy level of social action in Saintonge, all experience of top or bottom, or of spiritual or economic motivation, was too ambiguous to classify in easy categories. Still, we can say that by virtue of their spiritual status, literacy, learning, and innovative use of skills, artisan elites began to acquire greater power as intermediaries, and they found their proper level among poor, often less literate, fellow artisans and other common folk. Palissy's history also showed the qualifications *he* required of artisan leaders in the Saintongeais *désert* and the Huguenots' new world. Not surprisingly, those qualifications were based on the potter's own personal history as both a craftsman and a lay preacher under purifying, creative pressure from internal and external enemies.

Palissy's alchemical theater of the torture and execution of the first leaders of the primitive Church of Saintonge, indicates how would-be local representatives of the state (particularly Collardeau), who imprisoned Palissy pending Montmorency's intercession, responded to the Paracelsian discourses of reformed naturalism, and how Palissy replied in his history to challenge that response for posterity. Therefore, the state's main role in the Palissian narrative, was to overlay its version of their disguises as Saintongeais rustics on the three monks' exposed bodies—and so the force of official interpretation—with a mode of public ridicule, suppression, and ultimately death. A battle was joined to fix this fourth and final disguise as a permanent signifier of the heretics' social identities in official histories, which were countered, in turn, by local histories and legend.

Much was at stake in permanence: Palissy and the authorities vied for control over interpretation and diffusion of symbolic meanings associated with the event, and above all, over the emerging ideology of the Huguenot rustic aesthetic that Palissy had harnessed to the lives of his new Adamic artisan-preachers. This contest over the semiotics of torture and execution was not obscure to early modern audiences—literate or not—inasmuch as it involved the oldest and best-known rustic figure in folklore, mythology, and literature: the "wild man." The key iconographic assertion of the monks' executioners was that Saintonge's Huguenots were in fact wild men. Hence, they were not pure or natural but corrupt or mad. Palissy rightly saw this as a violent attack on the symbolic origins of his system of artisanal security, and so he responded retrospectively to solidify his leadership position and the rational foundation he had constructed for the rustic Reformed movement.

Yet, the ubiquitous image of the wild man had already been the focus of competing aesthetic, religious, and political programs for centuries by 1563. So the story of the monks' martyrdom illustrates the way the very definition of wild man had now entered the vicious transatlantic polemics of the French civil wars of religion. The primary problem at stake in this particular Saintongeais debate over the meaning of an old and culturally ambiguous figure was the conflation of the wild man—with all its corrupt and degenerate associations—and, for want of an appropriate period term, the "green man." This was a generic name for a benign, equally venerable rustic figure (or group of figures) who was always camouflaged by greenery and is usually thought to have pagan roots in Germanic folkloric traditions.[115]

In the British-American variants of this tradition, the green man was most commonly identified with May Day celebrations. These feature the Jack in the Green and his several green man attendants—all covered in foliage to varying degrees—as the central figures in this ritual of Spring. The English legend of Robin Hood, avatar of levelers' narratives, was associated with this tradition as well. Robin and his men dressed in green, lived in the woods and had the ability to watch enemies through the leaves while remaining unseen.[116] In early modern France, analogous figures were known as *la tête de feuilles* (head of leaves), *le masque feuillu* (the leafy mask), or simply *le feuillu* (the leafman). Arnold van Gennep found these three figures formed a dominant motif in rituals located in those parts of France that bordered Germanic regions. This makes its function in an execution of "Lutherans" in Saintonge most provocative. Van Gennep maintained that the leafman was a foreign, specifically German, ritual that was imported into France early in the Middle Ages.[117]

Connections to foreign influences in the French Reformation ran deeper still. One wild man, covered in hair, with leaves to hide his face and groin, and carrying an uprooted tree, was known as the *Wilde Mann* of Basel. This threatening figure was identified strongly with Swiss independence, Protestantism, power, virility, and the drive for freedom from Hapsburg dominance. The *Wilde Mann* exported this ideology, sailing on a raft down the Rhine or crossing the Alps. A drawing for a painting on glass by the German painter Hans Holbein the Younger (1497?–1543), who worked chiefly in

FIGURE 5.1. Hans Holbein the Younger, *A Wild Man Brandishing an Uprooted Tree Trunk,* or *The Wilde Mann of Basel* (ca. 1528). Pen and black ink with gray, brown, and blue washes, on cream laid paper. © Copyright The British Museum. The younger Holbein's design for stained glass was copied throughout the sixteenth century.

England, attests to his importance in the Protestant north, in token of which the Alps loom behind him (fig. 5.1).[118] There were wild or green women as well, and Flora or Demeter, each a female exemplar, presents similar iconography.

Flora or some related figure looms large in an Italianate ceramic plaque, in the Louvre, *Eau* (fig. 5.2), derived from a print by Raphael Sadeler (1560/61–1628/32). There

FIGURE 5.2. Bernard Palissy or a contemporary follower, *Allegory of Water*, 1575–1600; lead-glazed earthenware. Louvre. © Réunion des Musées Nationaux / Art Resource, New York.

is some debate as to whether this object is from Palissy's own hand, but it is generally agreed that it emerged from his large and productive artisanal community in Saintonge or Paris. Here the nymph sits naked by the sea in a blind of greenery, which conceals her fecundity from sight of the town and fortress, small in the distance behind her back. Perhaps referring to La Rochelle itself, a fortress is sited facing out to sea, with dominant towers overlooking the walls. The young woman wears a crown of leaves and releases a flood of what could be called embryonic water; this both frees and sustains denizens of Palissy's rustic basins and grottoes. This female figure is likely an alchemical allegory as well, elemental water, which is akin to the earth mother who gives birth to Nature (*mater* has the same root as matter, meter, and matrix). Four men with similarly verdant headpieces face her, one occupying each of the plaque's corners, positioned like Renaissance allegories of air in the form of the four animating winds. Fire is implied in the production of the glazed ceramic itself. Men in identical headpieces support a large candlestick attributed to Palissy; and a plate revealing distinctive faces of six men with leafy headpieces who peer out of the shadows—each of which expresses different aspects of what could be read as mockery (this was common practice among *les feuillus*)—was also made by a follower early in the generation after Palissy's death.[119]

Typological analysis of several variants of these verdant figures reveals the cross-cultural presence of an archetype harnessed to a coherent rhetoric of materio-spiritual synthesis. "The Green Man," William Anderson writes, "as a composite of leaves and a man's head, symbolises the union of humanity and the vegetable world. He knows and utters the secret laws of Nature." Like the adept, "[he] is the guardian and revealer of mysteries.[120] The synthetic action of the composite and its spiritual reconciliation in the matrix is at the core of the alchemic process, so it is unsurprising that the *feuillu* was harnessed to the same spiritual and material relations exploited by such Paracelsian artisans as Palissy and his Saintongeais Huguenot followers. In this context, perhaps, the equally seductive Minerva, Roman goddess of Wisdom and the mechanical arts (Sophia, in Greek mythology), merged seamlessly with Flora. The Huguenot construction of portable, artisanal Wisdom thus provided security against cruelty, randomness, and war wrought by the chaotic Fortuna.[121]

Composites were thus central to the art of the grotto and the "grotesque" aesthetic, as they are to the carved choir screen in the church of Saint-Étienne on the Île de Ré (figs. 15.38, 15.39), a primary source for the carved work on the "European chair" depicted in figure 15.35, and hence for that on the New York leather chair. Although the subject of the alchemic hybrid or composite will be revisited later, it should be noted that the frontispiece of *Simplicissimus* (fig. 5.3)—related to the Saint-Étienne carvings—is among the most explicitly sociological examples of this genre.[122] The *Simplicissimus* image, unlike most composites, holds a book in its hand. This is held open to two facing pages, picturing weapons and fortifications, to which the grotesque figure—ugly but powerful—slyly points with horned fingers. (Is this a cuckold's sign?) Given this rustic character's preoccupations with security from violence through disguises made by cobbling new identities together out of old forms found by chance among primitives isolated in the forest, it is consistent that a juxtaposition be made between the construction of multiple forms and traditional modes of military security. This message is reinforced by the Palissian smile of Democritus and Heraclitus—a smile and frown at the horrors of the world—and the theatrical masks (not unlike the six mocking faces of *feuillus* on the Saintongeais platter) discarded at the monstrous creature's webbed and hoofed feet, revealing—through events and contingencies in the novel that force on Simplicissimus a survivor's mutability—the painful artisanry behind its composite nature.

Le feuillu was thus traditionally associated with the deepest mysteries of Nature and agriculture, to which natural philosophers and alchemists also aspired in their role as adepts. Indeed, the ourobouros—the serpent devouring its own tail (arguably a source

FIGURE 5.3. The "Phoenix Copperplate," frontispiece of H. J. C. von Grimmelshausen's *Der abentheuerliche Simplicissimus* (literally, "The Adventurous Simplicissimus") (Nuremberg, 1668). Courtesy Beinecke Rare Book and Manuscript Library, Yale University. To paraphrase the poem, like the phoenix, this cruelly deformed and composite creature was born from fire (warfare), yet these very deformities are a source of great power, because they allow him to adapt "safely" to any environment or element in his travels through air and water and over land in search of peace and refuge. As a young man, Grimmelshausen was a refugee from the Thirty Years' War in Germany; he was at the sieges of the fortresses at Magdeburg (1636) and Breisach (1638).

FIGURE 5.4. Tête de feuilles. Tomb of Saint-Abre, Church of Saint-Hilaire-le-Grand, Poitiers, A.D. 400. One of the earliest representations. Drawing by John Cotter.

for Palissy's serpent representing the animate spirit in elemental earth)—and the tree of knowledge, both central to the alchemist's symbolic lexicon, were also synonymous with the green man. He was thought to tap into the primordial knowledge of Nature through wood—the *Wilde Mann*'s weapon is a tree—and is commonly represented as disgorging (or devouring) vegetation, or natural knowledge, just as the alchemical snake devoured its tail. That was why the rhetoric of the *feuillu* was inextricably entwined with rustic cosmologies of death, rebirth, and natural regeneration. This was the basic point of intersection that enabled a pagan icon to syncretize with—or perhaps be appropriated by—Christian iconography, beginning around A.D. 400. The earliest representation of this figure as a disgorger of vegetation known to survive in a Christian context is dated from this period. The ecclesiastical setting is not Germany, as might be expected, but rather the southwest of France. The image is carved on the tomb of Saint-Abre, located in the Church of Saint-Hilaire-le-Grand, at Poitiers (fig. 5.4), no more than a short journey inland from La Rochelle. It appears that the leafy head, mask, or man was used by Christians in this region for more than a thousand years in advance of the monks' execution. In both instances, it signified death and rebirth, though very differently.

The Poitiers *tête de feuilles* is much abraded, but the halo of leaves is clearly visible, as is the emanating vegetation. In this instance, in one of the possible variants, vegetation extrudes from the nose rather than the mouth, culminating in floral rosettes, not the more common leaves. The eyes have disappeared on the Poitiers carving, a significant loss, as is evident from a variant carved and then polychromed for the pulpit of the Elizabethskirche in Marburg around 1340 (fig. 5.5). Here, as in every other surviving example of the image, the eyes are open wide, in reference to the prophetic functions associated with these figures and the sort of inner sight that signified a sacred intelligence that underlay the hidden world of vegetation.

The green man saw the foundations of Nature without being seen, as only an adept, prophet, or perhaps a refuge artisan could. As with the "death's heads" with open eyes

FIGURE 5.5. Tête de feuilles as utterer of the word. Pulpit, Elisabeths-
kirche, Marburg, ca. 1340. Drawing by
John Cotter.

on some New England gravestones, the congregation understood this to mean apocalypse and the hope of future salvation. However, the Marburg carving is particularly
useful for our purposes, since the mouth is carved in the act of uttering the Word. Sacred speech was disgorged simultaneously with natural vegetation. That the carving—
one of many similar leafy heads carved on this German pulpit—was made to hold the
speaker of the Word underscored the importance of the venerable relationship joining the secrets of God and those of Nature, and of the European synthesis of pagan-
Christian naturalism in the Middle Ages. The same may be said for the Reformation.
The elder Lucas Cranach (1472–1553) depicted Luther himself preaching from a similarly carved pulpit (fig. 5.6). The leafy head (again the cornucopia of vegetation is
breathed from the nostrils like the breath of the spirit), also appears on the title page
of Luther's famous *Appellatio* in 1520 (fig. 5.7). As in much of Luther's work from this
period, the *Appellatio* merges the natural piety of the impoverished rustic with that of
the early Christians of the primitive Church as a key element in the rhetoric of Germanic Protestantism.[123]

Palissy made the earth's fecundity in supporting its tiny inhabitants central to dialogues between his natural-philosophical writings and artisanry, and Böhme, too, followed explicitly along the same path of terrestrial growth. However, the German
mined the more overtly Trinitarian and spiritualist vein and embraced Paracelsian occultism. "The Fathers power is all," Böhme wrote in *Aurora*, creating by analogy to the
sun and stars a word picture of his cosmology of the vegetable world:

> in and above all Heavens, and the same power every where generateth the Light. Now
> this ALL-POWER, is, and is called, the all-power of the Father; and the Light which is
> generated out of that all-power, is, and is called the Sonne. But it is therefore called the
> Sonne, in that it is generated out of the Father, so that it is the *Heart* of the Father in his

powers. And being *generated,* so it is another Person, than the Father is: for, the Father is the *power* and the Kingdom, and the Sonne is the Light and Splendor in the Father, and the Holy Ghost is the *moving* or *exit* out of the powers of the Father and of the Sonne, and formeth figureth *frameth* and Imageth all. As the *Ayr* goeth forth from the power of the Sun and Stars, and moveth in this world, and causeth that all creatures are generated, and that the Grasse Herbs and Trees spring and grow; and causeth *all* whatsoever in this world to be: So the Holy Ghost goeth forth from the Father and the Sonne, and moveth or acteth, formeth or frameth and Imageth all that is in the *whole God.* All growing or vegetation and forms in the father arise and spring up moving in the Holy Ghost; therefore there is but ONE only GOD, and three distinct *Persons* in one divine Being, Essense or substance.[124]

In Böhme's Neoplatonic monism of connectedness between vegetation and the highest "all-power" in the macrocosm, hybrid figures like the *feuillu,* having natural knowledge of the underlying secrets of vegetation—that is to say, how "the Grasse Herbs and Trees spring and grow"—knew, *simultaneously,* how "all creatures are generated."

FIGURE 5.6. Lucas Cranach the Elder, *Martin Luther Preaching at Wittenberg,* 1520; large detail of the predella of the altarpiece in the Stadtkirche, Wittenberg. Oil on panel. Photo courtesy the Evangelische Stadtkirchengemeinde, Lutherstadt Wittenberg. The ferocious boar's tail carved on Cranach's representation of Luther's pulpit in his home church spirals into a nearly imperceptible representation of the wild man. Another tiny face appears at its base among eyelike foliate scrollwork that resembles the engraving found on the title page of Luther's *Appellatio* (1520), illustrated in figure 5.7.

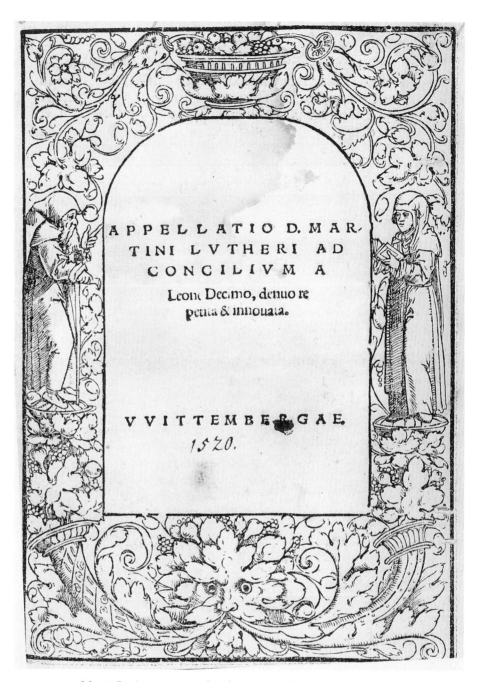

FIGURE 5.7. Martin Luther, *Appellatio* (1520), title page. Courtesy Harry Ransom Humanities Research Center, The University of Texas at Austin. The bottom border nearest the earth is filled completely by a wary, wide-eyed tête de feuilles that recalls figure 5.4.

This was the secret of the creation of life, hidden in the heart of the Trinity, and the key to the philosopher's stone.

If Neoplatonism linked all natural-philosophical practitioners through mutual interest in Paracelsus, crossing boundaries that separated Christian confessions in Italy, Germany, France, and the British archipelago in the sixteenth and seventeenth centuries, earlier Neoplatonic theory had a profound effect on church building in western Europe from the twelfth century on. Chartres was a center of the movement in France, evident among both its schoolmen and stonemasons. Influential Christian Neoplatonists, including Bernard Sylvester and Alan of Lille, likely studied there in the twelfth century. Both elucidated the natural world as the animate and conscious force of the soul, or heavenly wisdom. Meanwhile, although the *tête de feuilles* made an early, isolated appearance in Poitiers, the great north and south transept portals of Chartres display a full program of the iconography of Christian Neoplatonism in the Gothic period. This is magnified powerfully on the royal portal, designed and built by Thierry of Chartres in collaboration with an artisan known only as the "master sculptor." Here, the *feuillu* receives the knowledge of Nature, which radiates directly from the figure of Christ, to which it is clearly linked. This link was reactivated by Ficino and Paracelsus, and subsequently by Palissy and Böhme and their artisan followers, all working out of the same tradition.[125]

Key relationships between the writings of Bernard or Alan and Thierry, or Thierry and the master sculptor, are as hard to measure as any relation of the production of words and things discussed in this book. What is self-evident, however, is the extent to which stone carvers and, especially, woodworking artisans made the *feuillu* their own between the twelfth and seventeenth centuries. Beginning with the appearance of variants of this leafy figure on the portals and pulpits of medieval churches, almost all that we know outside of illuminated manuscripts and title-page borders about the varieties and pervasiveness of the vegetal style in sacred contexts comes from the tools of carvers in wood. That this is so has a lot to do with chance and survival in the vast amount of woodwork that was made for church interiors. Yet the ideology of the *feuillu* did revolve around the hidden knowledge of trees and leaves, as well as the fearsome power of wood, witness the Swiss *Wilde Mann*'s arboreal weapon. Wherever the mighty *Wilde Mann* traveled, he carried the power of the forest with him, as an artisan might carry his tools.

That the *feuillu* was associated with death and rebirth and that the point of syncretism with the Christian tradition was the death and rebirth of Christ—the son of a poor carpenter—would not have been lost on carvers of misericords. Architectural historians have long understood that misericords, along with other seemingly trivial, often overlooked or carefully hidden carved wooden elements in churches, constituted a kind of parallel sacred language—often sexual or fecund, violent, or disfigured in the manner of the Simplicissimus frontispiece—communicated by the carvers themselves. Such artisanal discourse, like the *feuillu,* was drawn from local folk or pagan traditions.[126] Were vegetal and animal carvings understood by late-sixteenth-century woodworkers as analogies in wood to Palissy's tiny, overlooked rustic creatures? Carvers are present in these works, appearing to scuttle about in the shadows in dark churches, eyes everywhere, like the green man, the wise unseen watcher in the wood. Indeed, the arboreal milieu in which these man-made creatures frolicked subversively was amplified by the construction of church interiors. In forest areas, joists and beams in church interiors were joined like trees interlocked in the ancient woods that surrounded them.

This sacred language emerged from oral traditions, exemplified by the emergence of leaves, instead of words, from the mouth of the *feuillu,* who was known as the silent utterer of the natural world. Convergence of natural and textual languages in sacred space by the mid twelfth century was one of the aesthetic, theological, and scientific accomplishments of Christian Neoplatonism. Certainly, there were many interpretations of the carvings understood by both woodworkers and their audiences. Some were probably experienced as ribald entertainments, found by surprise while taking one's seat in a pew; others as private virtuoso performances by a master. There is also the sense of carvers' tiny, idiosyncratic signature pieces, recognizable to others in the guild. Perhaps they were there as Boschian allegories, or to send up the power, wealth, and pomposity of the Church itself. Most may have been ignored or taken for granted as natural elements in churches. Yet this cannot simply be assumed retrospectively by historians. Accomplished carving in this intensive style was time-consuming, particularly when it might have been "commissioned" by the carver himself, to create his own private sacred space.

What is clear, however, is that the production of *feuillu* and related carvings of the hybrid of vegetation and rustic man became an increasingly clandestine operation in churches by the sixteenth and seventeenth centuries, when such creatures rarely appear on portals or pulpits. By then they were not officially associated with the Word or the relationship between travail, death, and rebirth in Nature and Christ's passion. The word "misericord," defined literally as "pity, mercy, and compassion," initially meant a private place in monastic settings where official rules of decorum were relaxed and monks had license to eat and drink as they pleased. By the sixteenth century, the word was used to describe carved wooden supports, usually found hidden under pews or choir stalls.[127] *Feuillu* were found there and in many other furtive and out-of-the-way places in churches.

Then carving was dispersed outside, onto secular artifacts of commerce, such as Palissy's ceramics, but also including metalwork, armor, gunstock carvings, textiles, and furniture in what is commonly called the mannerist style.[128] The wild man's "place in medieval daily life was assured," Richard Bernheimer says, "by the appearance of his image on stove tiles, candlesticks, and drinking cups, and, on a larger scale, on house signs, chimneys, and the projecting beams of frame houses . . . great . . . was the ubiquity of the wild man."[129] These crafts were dominated often by Huguenot craftsmanship both in France and in refuge in the transatlantic world.

The *tête de feuilles* as disgorger of vegetation crossed the Atlantic intact with one group of Huguenots in the late seventeenth century, when it appeared as an unusual motif on two painted chests-of-drawers, attributed to an influential network of French refugee artisans in southern coastal Connecticut, on Long Island Sound, perhaps with connections to the Channel Islands (fig. 5.8). Most of the furniture in this group also displays the rose and thistle, symbolizing the unification of England and Scotland in 1603 under James I. In this insignia, the motif connecting the rose and thistle is the fleur-de-lis, here representing England's medieval claim to rule of France. This played an enormous role in the history of La Rochelle, as we have already seen; however, the hoped-for "reconquest" of France by England in the wake of the Glorious Revolution was also the rallying cry of many Huguenot refugees in England and America, encouraged by the Act of Union of 1707, an appropriate date for the construction of this group of artifacts. Unification and its symbolism clearly projected to multiple audiences in expanding Britain. It follows that the social contexts for the displacement of the *feuillu,* its return to Luther's pulpit in Cranach's painting and the Protestant book trades in the sixteenth century, and finally the pivotal role it plays in Palissy's historical narrative of the primitive Church of Saintonge suggest some ways in which symbolic convergence led to the politicization of this figure over time.[130]

Whereas this ubiquitous and beneficent rhetoric of the *feuillu* was largely derived from oral and artisanal traditions supported by the adaptation of Neoplatonic theory by builders and master craftsmen, the demonization of the "wild man," and ultimately the domestication of his image, was the province of literature and its learned patrons. In some respects, the chronology of this long process indicates that the demonization of wild men—which may have become a pejorative conflated with all *feuillus*—paralleled the complex social and religious dynamics that laid the groundwork for the demonization of witchcraft. Bernheimer charts the perhaps similar downward trajectory of the wild man in literature, who declined from a formidable challenger of kings to the pathetic, degraded, and grotesque figure he had become by the late Middle Ages.[131] Wild men, like *feuillus,* were signified by their appearance. If wild men also always wore vegetation about their heads, more was made of hairiness by commentators. Hence, if the *feuillu* hybridized Nature and man, the wild man was degraded by his status between man and animal, such that it was no longer possible to tell the difference between the wild man and the beast. While the *feuillu* was valorized for deep understanding of hidden secrets of growth in Nature, the wild man was stigmatized as

FIGURE 5.8. Chest of drawers, Long Island Sound region of southern coastal Connecticut, 1707–20. H: 44″, W: 42⅞″, D: 20¼″. Oak, pine, and yellow poplar. Courtesy Wadsworth Atheneum, Hartford. Wallace Nutting Collection Gift of J. Pierpont Morgan. The top two paint-decorated drawer panels of this chest of drawers contain back-to-back images of têtes de feuilles, each uttering a walled garden of flowers from their open mouths. This distinctive painting style has been associated with the Gillam (or Guillaume) family of coastal Connecticut, Westchester, New York City, and western Long Island; this family, as well as this particular type of painting and the construction of certain casepieces in the American group, have been traced to Jersey, one of the Channel Islands off Normandy, a French linguistic domain, where the early furniture is remarkably similar.

deeply stupid. In both literature and the visual arts in the late Middle Ages and early modern period, the wild man's animal status was depicted in terms of inability to walk upright; instead, he is often shown down on all fours. Great stupidity was manifested physically by the loss of the faculties of communication. Most of all, however, wild men were afflicted with aphasia, and their loss of speech was accompanied by incomprehensible sounds or utterances. Was this master narrative a response from the culture of words to the silent utterer of the spirit of Nature and its artisanal representation in sacred space that was increasingly defined by written texts?[132]

Scholastic and theological commentators arrived at a consensus that speechlessness was a sign of insanity among wild men, and as a result, wildness and insanity became interchangeable in the literature. Because of insanity—usually caused by devastating reverses in war or love—wild men shunned all human contact and retreated to the most remote areas of the forest. With their removal to the primordial world of beasts, where mere survival was paramount, wild men were obsessed with personal security. Most lived in grottoes, hiding in holes just under the earth, or crags in rocks, along with serpents, and other amphibious, hybridized, or subterranean creatures. Their natural furtiveness combined with their peltlike hair and masks of vegetation to camouflage wild men in the forests, allowing them to prowl the underbrush in search of raw meat like wolves, to which they were also compared. Similar to that of wolves as well, the wild man's power and aggression toward prey or enemies were as legendary as he was stealthy. Simultaneously hidden and vicious, he struck at victims from under cover of natural materials that made him invisible in the rustic environment, with which he combined without trace or artifice.[133]

Yet for all his naturalness, the wild man was unnatural. Wild men were not made that way by God, in whose image of perfection man is created in Genesis. The wild man had instead degenerated from humanity into madness—descended in corruption manifested by wildness—through historical exigency, misguided causes, willfulness, or personal failure. As a result of his fall from grace, the carnal wild man, unlike the *feuillu*, found himself utterly incapable of spirituality or inner knowledge of God. In the ultimate reversal, the wild man was afflicted with spiritual blindness—a visual corollary to aphasia—that countered the inner sight represented by the *feuillu*'s eyes wide open in eschatological ecstasy. The wild man could neither speak nor see prophetic things and communicated in a babble of confusion. Arguably in reference to the *Wilde Mann* of Basel or earlier Germanic influences, the sources of wildness were often imported from abroad; numerous wild men were tempted to their fate by the lure of the unknown and by foreigners. The wild man was conventionalized as an alien in our midst; as raw, rustic, uncultured, stupid, and foreign. He was the threatening outsider; the invader who corrupted the natural purity of the homeland.[134]

Because the wild man was not by nature degenerate, or insane, or a speechless babbler, but had been made wild by outside forces, it was still possible to reverse the process through violent intervention. Violence was necessary because wild men, reduced to bestiality and conquered by nature and fearfulness, were too irrational to remake themselves in their former image. To exit the woods and return to the core culture was never the choice of wild men, who only returned to civilization when taken captive, and placed in chains. Safely repatriated from desolate isolation, the wild man regained the power of speech and often gained a new sense of grace and even heroic superiority from the experience of a kind of cultural death and rebirth. Many became knights after having received the gift of true cultural memory from the powerful. In gratitude, some used their experience in the woods to serve their newfound patrons as warriors or magicians. Lancelot and Merlin return to Camelot to complete the trajectory of this persona in the Arthurian legends.[135] Did Palissy and his patrons comprehend one another, on some level, as enacting this trope, when, in 1565, the potter was "taken" from Saintes and "brought" to Paris by the Medician court?

Simplicissimus, having emerged from hiding in rustic isolation after his family was slaughtered by marauding soldiers—"to stay in the woods was impossible . . . I could no longer subsist there"—is immediately recognized as a wild man by his captors, two musketeers of the imperial guards, which had just taken Hanau from troops commanded by the Protestant Duke Bernhard of Saxe-Weimar (1604–39). "I must tell the reader about my droll appearance at that time," said Simplicissimus, recalling how he looked when dragged through town:

> for my clothing was very strange and wondrously odd . . . my hair had not been cut in two and a half years . . . it reposed on my head in its natural dishevelment . . . my waxen, pallid face peered out from under it like a hoot owl about to light out at a mouse . . . I wore the hair shirt instead of a cape. . . . My body was girded with iron chains. . . . My shoes were carved from a piece of wood and tied on with ribbons of basswood bark; my feet looked as red as if I was wearing a pair of Spanish red stockings or had colored my skin with brazilwood dye. . . . Well, they led me through town and everybody came out to stare at me like a sea monster and made a big fuss over me. Some thought I was a spy; others, an idiot; still others, a bogey, a ghost, a spook, or an apparition of some kind of evil omen. A few thought I was a fool, and they might have been nearest the mark—if I hadn't had knowledge of God.[136]

When finally led before the governor, Simplicissimus imagines that he could well have been "exhibited" in a cabinet of curiosities as either an Asian or a New World wild man—"a flat-faced Samoyede or a Greenlander"—or like a "red" American Indian.[137] Questioned by an astonished governor, he is, of course, robbed of his speech: "I kept answering I didn't know." After he recovers verbal language, the governor determines that the captive is no longer as dangerous or as stupid as he had thought; he orders that a portrait of Simplicissimus be painted in exotic, imported colors, before allowing him to bathe and dress in clothing appropriate for a court page:

> I was to put my old weeds right back on, for a portrait artist was on his way with the tools of his profession—to wit, minium and cinnabar for my eyelids; lacquer, indigo, and azure for my coral-colored lips, orpiment and yellow lead for my white teeth (which I bared from hunger); and carbon black and umber for my yellow hair, white lead for my ghastly eyes, and lots of other colors for my weather-beaten coat. . . . Now he changed my eyes, now my hair, now hurriedly my nostrils and everything he had not done right the first time, until in the end he had produced the spitting image of Simplicius, and I was quite shocked at my own horrid appearance. Only then was the barber allowed to give me the once-over.[138]

This story about the construction of the wild man aesthetic from the "spitting image of Simplicius"—or "simple rustic"—is complete when the subject fails to recognize his own grotesque and monstrous reinvention by the court artist. After "my rustic dress with its chain and other accessories was put in the museum among other rarities and antiques; my life-size portrait was hung right next to them."[139] Collected and domesticated by aristocrats for voyeuristic entertainment and observation of rustic appearances and cultures, the wild man is thus historicized, reduced to a set of iconographic principles. Fear was transmuted into pleasure by craft. Yet, as Grimmelshausen's seventeenth-century satire shows, this process of transmutation was open to subversive interpretation from the very beginning. Indeed, from the level of his tiny creatures, Palissy's artisan's-eye view called this process into question by suggesting ways in which lay Huguenot craftsmen and historians might make rustic aesthetics the vehicle for extension and revitalization of rural piety from the woods (or *désert*) and churches out into the everyday world of commerce or court politics.

Not coincidentally, of course, the degeneracies attributed to wild men pending the figures' domestication by early modern written culture were simultaneously associated with Huguenot history in the Saintonge region in the sixteenth and seventeenth centuries. Thus, in making his rustic figurines, Palissy constructed his history and martyrology of the beginning of the primitive Church of Saintonge to exploit millennial violence and advance his program for Huguenot artisanal security. While the state made his martyred monks into wild men degraded by foreign influence, Palissy reversed this process alchemically and remade them in his history and ceramics as pious rustic figures from the faraway coastal islands of Saintonge. That is why Palissy refused to acquiesce to the state's assignation of wild man iconography as the fourth or final disguise of "these poor people [who] were condemned to be unfrocked, and dressed up in *accoutrements* made of greenery, so that the people would think they were fools or mad." Camouflage must come from within for the pious artisan; it cannot be applied from extraneous matter that has failed to emerge from the inner body. As Simplicissimus explains to his readers, he would certainly have agreed with the citizens of Hanau, who mocked his appearance as befitting a fool, "if I hadn't had knowledge of God."

In this cruel moment of violent unmasking, Palissy's artisan-preachers were publicly stripped of their disguises and simultaneously remasked by their torturers for posterity before being paraded before "the people" as insane wild men from the woods, not legendary *feuillu* with their hidden knowledge of Nature. Only then were they remanded to the regional *parlement* at Bordeaux for execution. This theatrical instrument of the state's revenge was thus an early document of conflicting interpretations for "common folk" of the meaning of the southwestern Huguenot rustic style, as the figures depicted were derived mostly from folkloric idioms in the process of domestication by centralizing authorities.

For the crime of heresy, the condemned "martyrs" were "degraded" into wild men to confirm what the insane monks had actually done to themselves. The authorities were not the true cause of their deaths; their executions were social suicides, for which the benighted victims had only themselves and barbarous foreign influences to blame. Instruments of state power projected an ideal (if seldom achieved) form of the deferential "society of orders"—essential to any formation of absolutism—where sense of place in the hierarchy was ordered, determining individual and collective social self-identity.[140] In such a hierarchical context, degradation by a state that determined every citizen's place, emanating out from the deified monarch at center, meant being reduced to some level *below* society, stripped of social identity, the sign of godly civility. To degrade meant, ideally, bodily and historical reversal; to devolve from a defined, theoretically unalterable position within an exorbitantly artificial culture characterizing the society of orders to entropy, debasement, or the transgressively natural. That was how the local authorities defined the "primitive beginnings" of Huguenots in Saintonge: not as a genuine reformation or recovery of the lost knowledge and purity of the earliest Church, but as a corruption of and decline from the venerable Roman Church. Neither edenic Adams nor apostolic era prophets, these were postlapsarian wild men, like American savages, who had devolved back into an undeveloped era of benighted primitivism. The builders of an artisan's babel were "fools." Their language was merely material, folkloric, and rustic; degradation stifled their ability to speak, making their every utterance incomprehensible, or simply silent to orthodox ears, while carrying their heretical theology far from the safety of the Word.

Once "condemned to be unfrocked," the prisoners were "dressed up in greenery as objects of ridicule" ("vestus d'accoustremens verds"),[141] to signify—in the eyes of the state—this return to raw, undissembled, authentic appearance. Original Huguenot leaders were represented to "the people," not as legendary *feuillus*, natural philosophers or adepts, but as dumb forest creatures without power, personal security, or spiritual protection. Now wild or uncultured beings in the basest sense, their pretension of being leaders and men of knowledge was a visual joke. Adumbrating Hamelin's courageous but deadly reversal of his initial Nicodemism, the condemned embraced the traditional construction of martyrdom by refusing to submit silently to the ordeal. Unmasked, they articulated resistance to corruption with defiance: "upholding God's quarrel in a manly way." The mouth of heresy again became a primary target of attack, as bodily source of the offending utterances.

Heresy's mouth was a fountain of conflicting prophesy, as well as interpretation—and for the *feuillu*, of spiritual vegetation—in which the Word and the secrets of Nature were syncretized. A confluence of all these patterns was textualized by Ficino and Paracelsus internationally, and by Palissy and his artisan followers locally. By the early seventeenth century, Böhme was explicit on the physiological relation between orality and spirituality. The mouth (including the tongue, gums, teeth, lips), was a primary site of the battle between love and wrath (spirituality and corruption) in an aspiring body. Circulating between the heart, brain, and mouth, every bit of sacred sound was subject to violent conflict with carnal corruption in "this world." The "Voyce of God" was gasped in half-articulated "thrusts" that echoed from the heart yet were returned by blockages in the mouth's fleshy outer body and, by extension, in the microcosm as well:

> the word conceiveth itself in the *Heart,* and goeth forth to the Lips, but there is captivated and goeth back again sounding, till it come to the place where it went forth. And this signifieth now, that the Sound [Voyce of God] went forth from the Heart of *God,* and encompassed the whole place or Extent of this world, but when [the place of this world] was found to be *Evil,* then the Sound returned again to its own place. The word or syllable thrusteth it self out from the Heart and *presseth forth* at the Mouth, and it hath a long following pressure [or murmuring sound]; but when it is spoken forth, then it closeth it self up in the midst or Center of its Seat with the upper Gums, and is *half* without, and *half* within. And this signifieth, that the heart of God had a loathing against the *corruption,* and so thrust away the corrupted Being from himself, but *laid hold* on it again in the midst or Center at the Heart.[142]

So the heart was the holding place for sacred language thwarted by "loathing against the corruption" in its desire to "presseth forth at the Mouth" to "encompass the whole. . . . Extent of this world" with the "Voyce of God."

Still, echoes of sacred speech continued to thrust against the corruption of the world at the mouth's gateway. Sound was only half-occluded with wrath, and it was the nature of love and wrath to assail each other through the senses in quest of the sacred marriage of intercourse, unity, and synthesis. "The Tongue breaketh off or divideth the word or syllable," Böhme reasoned, "and keeps it half without, and half within," until the apocalypse acts as the alchemic furnace that distills all speech, purging the corrupt utterances of Palissy's rock-throwing boys and creating a universal language:

> so the Heart of God would *not wholly* reject . . . [only] the malignity malice and malady of the Devill, and the other part should be re-edified or built again *after* this Time . . . [as] the innermost spirits in the corruption are not *altogether* pure, and therefore they need a sweeping away, *purging*, or consuming of the wrath, in the fire, which *will* be done at the End of this Time.[143]

Yet there were moments of lucidity in historical time when the essence of the Word was freed from the prison of the mouth (where the teeth functioned like bars). Böhme's elucidation of the process by which sacred language manifested itself is remarkably similar to popular depictions of the *tête de feuilles*. Such moments were infinitely small, light, and permeable as "the word conceiveth it self *above* and *under* the Tongue":

> and shutteth the Teeth in the upper and lower gummes, and so presseth it self *close* together, and being held together, and spoken forth again, then it openeth the Mouth again swiftly, like *a Flash*. . . . For the Teeth *retain* the word, letting the spirit go forth *leisurely* between the Teeth: And this signifieth, that the astringent quality [i.e., the wrath] holdeth the Earth and Stones *firmly* and fast together; and yet for all that, *letteth* the spirits of the Earth spring up, grow and bear Blossoms out of the astringent spirit: which signifieth the REGENERATION OR RESTITUTION OF THE SPIRITS OF THE EARTH.[144]

Small flashes of the spirit in matter assumed forms other than words, as inside sacred space, in its "*innermost* Birth or Geniture, [the] word alone by it self is Dumb, and hath no signification or understanding in it alone, but is used only for distinction sake, with some other word." Words were used to make false distinctions, parse differences, build boundaries, and camouflage intentions, as the one unifying foundation of the Word, its animating spirit, lay silent and hidden on the speaker's tongue like the inner body of a Saintonge snail: "it recoils inward at the neather gummes," Böhme imagined, "and *croucheth* as it were before an enemy trembling."[145]

In Palissy's Saintonge, the enemy was distilled by the wars of religion from Böhme's abstracted, natural-philosophical corruption throughout "this world," and personified specifically by Collardeau, the bishop of Saintes, toadies "at the court," and the corrupt judges, all of whom were implicated in condemning the Huguenot martyrs. Collardeau, now the embodiment of corruption, played his natural role in blocking the emanation of sacred utterances by ordering the four pious preacher-artisans to be "bridled like horses," such that "each had an iron apple which filled up the whole of their mouths." In this way, the "wild men" were mastered and domesticated, like dumb beasts, farm animals led to slaughter. The iron apple, a gag as well as an instrument of torture and reference to original sin, served to underscore the insane silence that attended the wild man's iconography, even as it put an end to "manly" defiance.

Yet from the perspective of the spiritualist or natural philosopher, the animated source of motion was reversed. The sacred sound worked from the inside, in order to "thrust away the corrupted Being from himself." Thereupon, the sound returned to its origins in the heart, which "laid hold on it again in the midst or center," where it waited in secret to emerge in material forms other than words that would facilitate spiritual unity not linguistic distinction. The artisan-preachers were able to "speak" mutely before dying. Vines of the *feuillu* would not be allowed to emanate from their suppressed mouths, yet the discourse of nature—red flesh under cloaks of "greenery"—was still evident, even in degradation. This was also the material language of rustic pottery made famous by Palissy and his Saintongeais followers: the "vert et rouge"—green glaze over a red clay body—ceramics, readily identifiable throughout the Western world with the ancient kilns of La Chapelle-des-Pots. These ubiquitous artifacts remained a staple of Atlantic commerce until the nineteenth century.[146]

Palissy perceived a scene transformed into "a hideous thing to behold"—an appropriate reading from the perspective of a Huguenot historian and matryrologist, yet surely also a scene of high comedy for his enemies. To behold the hideous, or comedic, was, of course, a dialogue in the politics of aesthetics, whether articulated by a Protestant maker of grotesque figures or his royal Catholic patron at court. Both sides in this dialogue had defined grotesque as the good, true, and beautiful, though in this context from perspectives that were inversions of a shared reality. Saintongeais authorities delighted in the spectacle of Huguenot wild men, and their heresy of religious difference, as monstrous. The aesthetics of that moment of capture and domestication was a commonplace both of religious warfare and the everyday object of desire and consumption. The molded surface of the grotesque was pleasurable as playful exoticism, but also suggestive of the power and naturalness of the normative forms that held them in check. The appearance of wild and grotesque forms, or composite and fragmented bodies, was thus the embodiment of a failure of the spirit and the potential of the dominant to redeem that failure.

To be sure, Paracelsus often understood disease in these terms, but Palissy and contemporary Huguenot natural philosophers such as Ambroise Paré modified this judgment. The monstrous disfigurement and martyrdom of the artisan-preachers by the authorities was Palissy's metaphor for the experience of inner spiritual beauty and metaphysical unity that operated beneath written official histories. The tiny cell of monastic heretics that carried the Reformation back from Germany to Saintonge were disguised four times during the course of Palissy's narrative, three times voluntarily for *sûreté* and finally by the authorities to expose the monks' "wild" interior to the derision of the people. The first time they were simultaneously Catholic monks and Protestant Nicodemites; the second, working rustic artisans and teachers hiding "in exile" among their fellow Huguenots artisans in the isolated Atlantic islands of Saintonge; the third, artisans and Protestant lay preachers working underground, exactly like their self-appointed historian Bernard Palissy; and fourth, either *feuillus* or "wild men"—depending on the beholder—rustic forest creatures of great age, inextricably entwined with the inner workings and hidden languages of the natural world.

These four disguises represented four composite layers—among many others that were made necessary by the violence and suffering of the religious wars—of the same complex artisanal identity, held together by the shadow history of the soul. In 1705, a scientist in England named John Toland invented the word "pantheist" to describe the inspired naturalism that saw human beings as integral, material parts of Nature that was represented by (and for) the Saintongeais Huguenot artisan-preachers remembered in Palissy's history of the primitive Church.[147] Whether Palissy would have used this word is dubious, although it emerged from a later strain of the Paracelsian tradition owing large very debts to the work of Jacob Böhme. Toland, whose work provided the inspiration for many secret societies fomenting radical republicanism in early eighteenth-century London, would have appreciated and understood the furtiveness of Palissy's program of artisanal security, however.[148]

Thus, these passages taken from the history return us again to Palissy's theory of *sûreté* for the "industrious artisan," and hence to another enduring moment taken from the history of La Rochelle's fall in 1628. The fortress had capitulated, and Louis XIII—at the behest of Cardinal Richelieu—presented one article of victory that permanently altered the landscape of southwestern France. The cannon of La Rochelle were turned upon its own walls from inside. The fortress's enceinte and fortifications (except the three great towers) were razed ("rez-pied-rez-terre") so that: "from all sides, access and entrance to said city can follow freely and easily just as the plow passes through fields of tillage."[149] Louis XIII had thereby "degraded" the signifier par excellence of the southwestern Huguenot martial establishment to the level of an inverted order—noble swords into plowshares; closed fortress into open, husbanded land—by reducing its outer walls to reveal a wholly vulnerable, decaying interior, containing thousands of unburied corpses. An autonomous, defiant, and sacred military *place de sûreté* was plowed under and planted with the seeds of absolutism, sown subsequently over the rest of France.

Eighty years before, Collardeau searched harder to locate the shell of deception constructed between himself and the bodies of an isolated rural community of heretical artisans in La Rochelle's hinterland, far from the protective shadow of the fortress. Once discovered, Collardeau's response was much the same as Louis's and Richelieu's would be. Yet what was exposed inside was as different as La Rochelle from Saintonge (or Geneva from the Germanic regional culture that "returned" the monks to their rustic artisan community). In *their* "degradation," the artisan-preachers' bodily *sûreté* was removed by violence and replaced with garments from "Nature" that were thought to be a mockery of their ethos. Out of these visual dialogues between ambitious executioners and silenced heretics, a new set of clothes was fashioned and worn to punctuate the shared reality of what had been uncovered.

CHAPTER SIX

American Rustic Scenes

Bernard Palissy, John Winthrop the Younger, and Benjamin Franklin

Bernard Palissy's life and work were familiar to colonial British America's two fore-most natural philosophers, both of whom were prominent political figures as well: John Winthrop Jr. (1606–76), the eldest son of the governor of Massachusetts and one of the first governors of Connecticut Colony, and Benjamin Franklin (1706–90).

Though Cotton Mather has acquired a more enduring scientific reputation among colonial historians as a result of his work to develop a technique for smallpox inocu-lation in early New England, John Winthrop Jr. was also internationally known dur-ing his own time and more widely venerated as an alchemist and rustic practitioner of Paracelsian chemical medicine. Indeed, Cotton himself famously eulogized Winthrop as "Hermes Christianus" in 1676.[1] Winthrop's natural philosophy, and his historical connections to Palissy, the fall of La Rochelle, and New York Colony are discussed in subsequent chapters. Yet I think it is particularly appropriate to introduce him here, because he and his "physician's" chair constitute perhaps the earliest verifiable context for a reader of Palissy's books in America.

Winthrop's natural-philosophical reputation was made when he became the first American colonist elected to the Royal Society of London. In 1663, he was listed among the charter members of that stronghold of British Paracelsian science. As his membership in the Royal Society suggests, Winthrop kept up an impressive network of scientific correspondence internationally and was well respected on the Continent and in England. Indeed, despite what European colleagues read as nearly insurmountable wilderness conditions, he maintained a heroic record of scientific research.[2] Just as Palissy's Parisian colleagues were intrigued by the exoticism of his *Recepte véritable,* the author of which was identified as being "from Xaintes," a provincial outpost, the "wilderness" setting only added luster to the sense of primitive authenticity that Winthrop's natural philosophy inspired among London adepts. Londoners surely (with some justice) considered seventeenth-century Connecticut more rustic than Saintes appeared to Parisians. Also, like the Huguenot, Winthrop never hesitated to underscore his isolation from centers of metropolitan learning; a harsh truth, of course, but also an effective way to burnish his own backwoods mythology in Europe.

Winthrop is remembered by historians of science as one of the few colonial scientists who owned Galileo's books and an up to date telescope, which was used to make dramatic—if dubious—observations of Venus, Jupiter, and Saturn. These claims helped his reputation in England, which led, in part, to Winthrop's election to the Royal Society. Above all, however, Winthrop's reputation was built on his status as a Paracelsian physician who managed to accumulate the most advanced, complete, and current alchemical library in seventeenth-century British America. At his death, Winthrop's library was said to contain thousands of British and European titles.

Today, more than 600 volumes on various subjects have been counted among documented survivals. Some 275 of these—almost half—are titles devoted to the study of Paracelsian alchemy, chemistry, and the new chemical medicine.[3] Despite being greatly reduced by attrition, this latter inventory included a cross-section of early modern natural philosophy, from Ramon Llull and many of the leading figures of medieval alchemy, to the complete works of Paracelsus and Winthrop's natural-philosophical contemporaries.

Given his bias toward Germanic alchemical thinking, it is unlikely that Winthrop did not own a copy of Böhme's *Aurora,* but no copy has yet been documented, and neither are the whereabouts known of any copy of Palissy's *Recepte véritable* that he possessed. Winthrop's signed and underlined copy of Palissy's *Discours admirables* (fig. 6.1) is, however, among the 275 surviving alchemical volumes from his library, and it is currently preserved in the New-York Society Library, the repository of many Winthrop books through the largesse of a nineteenth-century New York descendant.[4] So by no later than the 1670s, Palissy's Huguenot artisanal discourse had been diffused far from Saintonge, along Protestant international trade routes, to colonial British America. There, his *Discours admirables* was retrieved from its place on the shelf in Winthrop's New World alchemical library next to the other books of Paracelsian natural philosophy he considered indispensable to understanding the American experience.

The presence of at least one (and originally perhaps both) of Palissy's books in Winthrop's alchemical library signals an extraordinary opportunity in seventeenth-century American cultural history, because here two seemingly disparate artifacts converge in

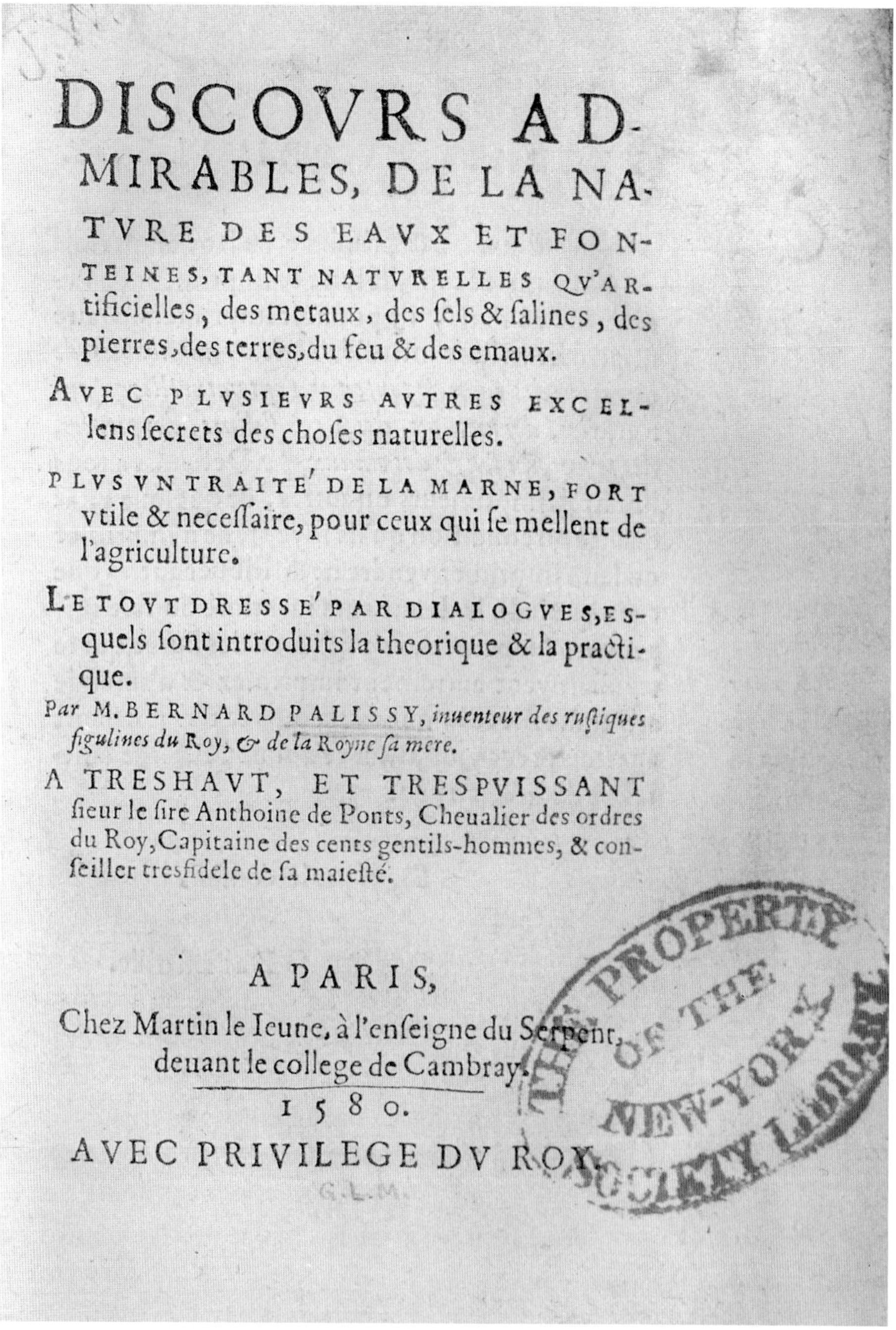

DISCOVRS ADMIRABLES, DE LA NATVRE DES EAVX ET FONTEINES, TANT NATVRELLES QV'ARtificielles, des metaux, des ſels & ſalines, des pierres, des terres, du feu & des emaux.

AVEC PLVSIEVRS AVTRES EXCELlens ſecrets des choſes naturelles.

PLVS VN TRAITÉ DE LA MARNE, FORT vtile & neceſſaire, pour ceux qui ſe mellent de l'agriculture.

LE TOVT DRESSÉ PAR DIALOGVES, ESquels ſont introduits la theorique & la practique.

Par M. BERNARD PALISSY, *inuenteur des ruſtiques figulines du Roy, & de la Royne ſa mere.*

A TRESHAVT, ET TRESPVISSANT ſieur le ſire Anthoine de Ponts, Cheualier des ordres du Roy, Capitaine des cents gentils-hommes, & conſeiller tresfidele de ſa maieſté.

A PARIS,
Chez Martin le Ieune, à l'enſeigne du Serpent, deuant le college de Cambray.
1580.
AVEC PRIVILEGE DV ROY.

FIGURE 6.1. Title page from John Winthrop Jr.'s personal copy of Bernard Palissy's *Discours admirables* (Paris, 1580). Courtesy The New-York Society Library.

FIGURE 6.2. John Winthrop Jr.'s physician's chair, southern coastal Connecticut or Long Island, ca. 1650–60. H: 44½",W: 26½", D: 13⅝". Oak. Courtesy The Connecticut Historical Society, Hartford. The back panel is raised in a Continental manner more common to furniture made in New Amsterdam / New York than early New England. This chair has lost its carved crest rail.

space and time. The joined great chair (fig. 6.2) in which Winthrop presumably sat while reading Palissy's *Discours* in his library (or laboratory) is the *only* known seventeenth-century American-made physician's chair extant, that has been confidently associated with its original owner to help reconstruct at least a significant part of Winthrop's scene of reading; that is to say, the part that held Winthrop's sitting body.

Thanks to its Winthrop provenance and the filial piety with which early New England antiquarians venerated armchairs belonging to a member of the founding oligarchy, the history of this chair, made of American red oak (*Quercus rubra*), and hence reliably a colonial artifact, because red oak was not used in European furniture, is remarkably well preserved for a piece of furniture that was usually mobile. Until it was lost in 1929, a label attached to its seat indicated that the chair had been made for Winthrop's "inaugural" as governor of Connecticut. There were two such events—in 1657, and again in 1659—both appropriate dates for such a chair, although the exact date of its construction was not specified on the label. Winthrop remained governor the second time until his death in 1676 in Boston. He resided in New London, Saybrook, Mystic, and Hartford as well, and the probate inventory taken of Winthrop's Hartford belongings made reference to "1 Timbard bottmd Chayre 00:13:00." This likely denoted the chair in figure 6.2, indicating it was in the governor's household at the time of his death.[5] The chair was to remain in the Winthrop family until about 1836. At that time, the relic was acquired by Wesleyan University for use as the president's ceremonial chair. It remained at Wesleyan until 1964, when it entered the collections of the Connecticut Historical Society.[6]

Leading historians of American furniture have consistently argued, based on tenuous logic, that the makers of Winthrop's chair were Nicholas Disbrowe and Thomas Spencer. Disbrowe, who was born at Saffron Walden in Essex in 1612, emigrated to Dorchester in the Massachusetts Bay Colony sometime before 1635, in which year he was working in Hartford, where he died in 1683. Spencer was also born in England, in 1607, in Stotfold, Bedfordshire; he worked in Hartford as well and died there in 1687.[7] This attribution will not bear close scrutiny, for it is based solely on documentation of Disbrowe and Spencer having worked in Hartford around the time the chair was made.

Moreover, the available evidence must be manipulated heavily to fit this received wisdom. Although Disbrowe has been documented as Hartford's principal joiner at the time, and he could have done the joined and carved work on Winthrop's chair, an extremely detailed inventory of his shop tools reveals that Disbrowe owned neither a lathe nor turner's chisels and hence probably did not possess (or require) the skills necessary to turn the well-regulated columnar posts. On the other hand, the argument goes, Thomas Spencer, who lived just a few yards from Disbrowe in Hartford, was a turner without known joinery skills. But the family alliance of these two interdependent shops was sealed when Spencer's son Obadiah (1639–1712) married Disbrowe's daughter Mary. Working together, the Disbrowe-Spencer shops could, therefore, have joined, carved, and turned Winthrop's chair for his inaugural in 1657 or 1659.[8] A good story, but for the problem that there is no reliable evidence whatever to link the two woodworkers to Winthrop's chair, or, more important in an age of patronage, to Winthrop himself. On the contrary, there is really nothing beyond its appearance in the Hartford inventory of colonial America's most notoriously footloose settler to even suggest that the chair was made in Hartford.

Idiosyncratic formal attributes reveal something other than a variant on the central or southeastern English woodworking styles in which Disbrowe and Spencer trained and that characterize most early Hartford furniture. The chair's dramatic raised (or "tabled"), molded and beveled panel back is an attribute rarely seen on Connecticut work. However, tabled panels were commonplace on oak and other hardwood New Amsterdam furniture and can also be found on a well-known group of furniture from early Rhode Island Colony, as well as on a small quantity of furniture that survives from the seventeenth-century Chesapeake. Most of the Virginia examples were produced in artisans' shops working in the Germanic or Dutch rather than in the British tradition, reflecting the pluralistic settlement patterns of the middle and southern British colonies. Winthrop had invested heavily in real estate and other property on both the Connecticut and the New Netherlands coasts of Long Island Sound by the early 1640s, and he established residence at the mouth of the Mystic River basin in autumn 1646. Consider, then, that the armchair may have been made by an artisan working in those areas bordering New Amsterdam and Rhode Island, places where Winthrop had extensive political and economic interests and patronized local artisans.[9]

There is scant evidence in his huge correspondence of Winthrop's having employed Disbrowe and Spencer, and he was closely associated with other woodworkers from the Long Island Sound coastal region who were more logical choices to make a physician's chair for the American "Hermes Christianus" than the two Hartford men. Among these was "a verry Ingenuous man" called "John Elderkin, the Miller." Elderkin's peripatetic migration from the Boston region south into the Long Island Sound borderlands mirrored Winthrop's own. Having arrived in New England about 1637, Elderkin (b. England, 1616 1687) moved frequently to follow his trade as a builder of meetinghouses, mills, and wharves, as well as ships, interior woodwork, and furniture. Contracts and building receipts record the wanderings of this busy artisan and his family. Between 1641 and 1661, Elderkin lived and worked in Dedham and Lynn in Massachusetts, New London and Norwich in Connecticut, Providence in Rhode Island, and Southold on Long Island. Sometime between 1640 and 1680, Elderkin probably made a singularly idiosyncratic joined, turned, and carved three-posted chair (fig. 6.3) that was long in the possession of the Waldo family of millwrights and carpenters, who lived in Braintree, Charlestown, and Chelmsford, Massachusetts. Its provenance begins with Abigail Elderkin Waldo (b. 1715), not the original owner, but the great-granddaughter of John Elderkin.[10]

While the rigorous inquiry necessary to attribute Winthrop's armchair to Elderkin would be out of place here, some formal, professional, and patronage relationships may reasonably connect these two chairs. Indeed, a casual observer will note only slight differences between the carved arms on both chairs and the closeness of the column under the arms (and above the seat) on the Elderkin chair to the turned front posts on the Winthrop chair. Even if Disbrowe is presumed to have farmed out the turning on the Winthrop chair to Spencer, from Elderkin's detailed construction contracts, it is clear that the highly skilled Elderkin did the joinery as well as the turning and carving. Finally, the backs of both chairs rake back dramatically above the seat, an unusual approach in American armchairs to molding the sitter's posture to provide both comfort and distance. However, this facilitated reading of the carved back panel by visitors: the discourse of the chair was evidently expected to stand in for the sitter when he was absent.

Judging formal attributes can seem tedious or obscure, but they are magnified greatly in significance when seen in light of Winthrop's letters of the 1650s, which clearly refer to his powerful, perhaps bonded, patronage relationship with Elderkin. On August 31, 1651, William Wells of Southold felt compelled to write to Winthrop, not Elderkin, to obtain the latter's services. Winthrop's permission was deemed nec-

FIGURE 6.3. Unique three-posted joined great chair, attributed to that "verry Ingenuous man" John Elderkin, John Winthrop Jr.'s artisan client, who worked as a millwright and woodworker for valued members of Winthrop's patronage network on both sides of the Long Island Sound. H: 42½", W: 22½", D: 19¼". Oak, ash, and cherry. Courtesy Chipstone Foundation, Fox Point, Wisconsin. Photo, Gavin Ashworth. Did Elderkin also make the equally unique and "ingenious" physician's chair in figure 6.2? Compare the arms, as well as the turning, carving and molding patterns.

essary in "grantinge and persuading your Millwright John Elderkin to come a long." Wells wanted Elderkin "to view the ruins of our old water mill; and build us a new." Later that year, Thomas Mayhew of Martha's Vineyard wrote Winthrop: "[W]ee have greate want of a mill and there is one with you that I here is a verry Ingenuous man about such work that is goodman Elderkin, but wee here you have some Ingadgement uppon him. Now these are to intreate you if possible you can disspense a while with him."

The "engagement" to which Mayhew referred was put into writing in March 1652, when Elderkin formally contracted with Winthrop in New London for "one whole yeere beginning the first of April next to worke with him in any Carpentry worke that I can doe and to bueild him a Saw mill and keepe the Corne mill." Meanwhile, probably at the bidding of Winthrop, who was making aggressive forays into Long Island politics and real estate at the time, Elderkin had also accepted the work on offer in Southold, rather than Martha's Vineyard. His contract with Winthrop stipulated that "what time I shall be absent at South hold or upon my own occasions I shall make good."[11]

Elderkin thus contracted to do "any Carpentry worke" to Winthrop's specifications, including millwright's work. Just as plain from the contracts is how broad a definition "carpentry" had in this rural context, where "ingenious" artisans commonly employed multiple skills without guild restrictions. The "Carpentry worke" stipulated in Elderkin's case thus almost certainly included highly elaborate furniture like Winthrop's armchair, made at the end of the decade, and expensive interior finishing joinery of the sort the "Connecticut River God" John Pyncheon Jr. asked Winthrop to facilitate for him. "Sir, I am bold to request that the room in which my wife will be this winter may speedily be made warm," Pyncheon wrote anxiously in October 1654, as the New England winter approached. "I pray let Goodman Elderkin be called on to do it out of hand in regard my wife is but tender and cold will set in quickly." Since any carpenter could clapboard a room's interior, Pyncheon undoubtedly meant that Elderkin should line it with frame-and-panel work like that on joined (or "wainscot") chairs.[12]

This request tells us that Elderkin was still the most highly regarded woodworker in the area, and that Winthrop was still his principal patron, around the end of 1654, less than three years before the earliest date that Winthrop's chair is thought to have been made, and just five years before the latest. Would not his most "ingenious" craftsman and client have been the logical choice to construct the honorific physician's chair? *Ingénieux* was a word Palissy used interchangeably with *expérimenté* and *inventeur* to describe his own craftsmanship of natural-philosophical things. The fact that Elderkin was the Paracelsian Winthrop's client and a venerated millwright suggests that he understood the skilled work of his hands in cosmological terms, based ultimately on the analogy between macrocosm and microcosm. Some sense of the esteem in which Elderkin was held in Winthrop's patronage network (and the level of philosophical discourse in which this artisan engaged) may be gleaned from a greeting conveyed from Elderkin to Winthrop by Roger Williams in a letter from Rhode Island written in October 1650: "Yours by Elderkin (who predicates your just praise in many respects etc.) common, philosophicall, morall virtue, *laudata crescit*." Like the miller Menocchio, he may have perceived the concentric movement of wooden gears in the mills he constructed metaphorically. Of all the artisans in Winthrop's circle, Elderkin embodied the cosmic circles carved into the back of his patron's chair through manual labor. Whether his hands actually made the chair is a subject for future research. Yet the problem of attribution is less important to the overall argument than Elderkin's skills and the indisputable fact that they were available and "engaged" by Winthrop in the Long Island Sound borderlands region.

Despite this symbolically loaded artifact's understandably long historiography, it is surprising that while every publication includes a similar exegesis of Winthrop's chair's history, its attribution to Disbrowe and Spencer and to a lesser degree an inventory of its construction (the continental tabled panel is never discussed), none has analyzed the chair's most noteworthy and historically significant feature: its elaborate carved

back. This is astonishing in light of the fact that the carved back panel was added because of the natural-philosophical and medical identity of the individual whom antiquarians have worked painstakingly to associate with this relic. Of more concern, after
such intensive labor in the archives, is their inability simply to stand back from the
written narrative and *look* at the chair itself; more precisely, to reconsider the chair together with the mental and physical context of the alchemist whose body it was originally built to support.

On the first level of analysis, because the design was unique, the maker was instructed to follow a design to be adapted from one of many books available in Winthrop's Paracelsian medico-alchemical library, to lay out and carve the unusual variant
on the Copernican heliocentric cosmos displayed on the back panel of the chair.
If Winthrop's chair was made no later than 1659, the printed source from which
its maker's template was derived was probably a European book.[13] The Copernican
System had, however, been taught at Harvard as early as 1659, the year of Winthrop's
second inaugural.[14]

Whatever the original source, the relationship between a printed "Copernican System" and the back panel of Winthrop's chair is made plain enough by the woodcut
published in Boston in John Foster's *Almanack* for 1675 (fig. 6.4). The representation
of the sun as an open flower emanating light seems remarkably similar to Foster's more
conventional sun with a smiling face. The central "sun" on Winthrop's chair appears
to have only three orbits revolving around it, despite the information that "*Sol* keeps
his throne, and around him shines / Upon *six* worlds which walk in single lines." Concentric circles were conventional signifiers in the natural-philosophical context for the
emanation of light in and out of matter (here, wood). As is evident in Foster's cosmos,
they were also sometimes used to signify Saturn's rings, which Winthrop reported having seen with his telescope in 1660, and with which he was identified in Europe. To
put Saturn at the center of any cosmology, Copernican or Ptolemaic, was unusual. Still,
it must be considered that the back panel was intended to convey a double meaning;
to imply Winthrop's personal and natural-philosophical associations with both Saturn and Earth. With the availability of simultaneous readings in mind, it is evident
that with only three of the six Copernican rings visible on the chair, the primary text
arguably referred above all to Winthrop's sitting in and preoccupation with the Earth
itself, the third planet in orbit around the sun after Mercury and Venus.

The eight additional "suns," accompanied by small satellite cabochons in "orbit"
around Earth's orbit, are problematical and cannot be explained adequately as representations of Saturn's multiple moons or by the poem's lines "and eight less Globes,
again encompassing / One th' *Earth,* four *Jove,* three *Saturn* with his Ring." These
eight miniature representations are indeed "less[er] Globes" in size, but it is difficult
to read them as the eight Copernican moons encompassing three different planets.

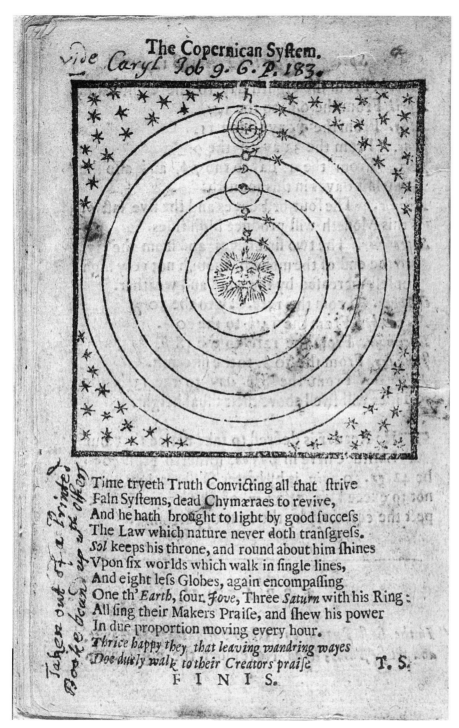

FIGURE 6.4. John Foster, *The Copernican System,* woodcut published in *An Almanack of Coelestial Motions for the Year of the Christian Epocha, 1681* (Boston, 1681). MHS image no. 3627. Courtesy Massachusetts Historical Society. Marginalia were added by the famous Boston diarist Samuel Sewell (1652–1730). Like Winthrop, "Sol keeps his throne."

Rather, the eight flowering celestial bodies revolving in the third orbit around the central "sun" are not eight separate planets, but the earth alone—with its single moon—marked at eight positions as it rotates around the star.

This suggests that the four additional planets in the far corners of the back panel may represent Mars the *next* (or fourth) in orbit from the sun. The carver was constrained by the geometry of the chair's back panel, and was obviously unable to represent the next planet's rotation in a circular fashion as he did Earth, where he had plenty of room to swing his compass. Since Mars was associated with flaming fire (and hence alchemy) but also war and strife, it is possible that these outer four entities signified other planets (perhaps Jupiter) or comets. Winthrop wrote the Royal Society with observations about both. More mundane explanations might be that the four outer shapes served as filler or ambiguous fixed stars (*stellae inerrantes*). Or the outer bodies were simply a standard representation of the boundary between the microcosm and macrocosm, called the *caelum stellatum,* or "the heavens," a convention in seventeenth-century printed cosmologies. Indeed, it is repeated in the Foster woodcut as well.

The motion signified on the panel was heliocentric; Earth's movement around the sun seems clear enough. Yet standard print sources for the Copernican system do not match, so we must begin again with the books in Winthrop's library. Inasmuch as this chair represented its sitter, and Winthrop's fame as a medical practitioner was common knowledge among "rustic" New Englanders and physicians throughout the Atlantic world, it makes sense to turn to his medical treatises for images of physicians' chairs. These were often associated with physicians in early modern representation. The physician was depicted elevated above the stricken body, book in hand, seated enthroned in his impressive chair, directing the manual labors of a lowly chirugeon.

Indeed, a likely pictorial source can be found in Winthrop's library among his remarkably complete collection of books by the influential English Calvinist Paracelsian, alchemist, mystic, and physician Robert Fludd (1574–1637). No fewer than eleven titles by Fludd survive with Winthrop's signature or ex libris mark, reflecting the high regard in which Fludd was held among book collectors and the rising monetary value attending the magnificent illustrations of his books, which always warranted special care and protection. Fludd's cosmologies and medical texts appear in every alchemical library of importance in the Protestant world during the war years of the 1620s and 1630s.[15] So it is unsurprising that Winthrop's copies of Fludd's well-known *Integrum morborum mysterium* (Frankfurt, 1631) and *Katholikon* [Gr.] *medicorum katoptron* [Gr.] (Frankfurt, 1631)—which were bound together in one volume[16]—possessed two engravings concerning Paracelsian medical practice, which reveal that Winthrop's "inaugural chair" was indeed a physician's chair.

A good case can be made that the basic design for the joined back panel was copied directly from *The Circle of Urinary Colours* (fig. 6.5), an anonymous plate from the *In-*

FIGURE 6.5. *The Circle of Urinary Colours.* Anonymous engraving in Robert Fludd, *Integrum morborum mysterium: Sive medicinae catholicae . . .* [and] *Katholikon* [Gr.] *medicorum katoptron* [Gr.] . . . [and] *Pulsus seu nova et arcana pulsuum historia, e sacro fonte radicaliter extracta, nec non medicorum ethnicorum dictis authoritate comprobata,* three works, forming the complete tractate 2 of vol. 1 of the *Medicina catholica* in one vol. (Frankfurt: Wolfgang Hofmann for Willem Fitzer, 1631). Courtesy Yale University, Harvey Cushing / John Hay Whitney Medical Library. The Paracelsian physician in his chair, book open to the appropriate passages, is orbited by vials of different colored urine, which revolve heliocentrically around his seated body like planets in the Copernican system (here, the physician himself, his heart animated by the Holy Spirit, takes the place of the sun, the light of which resides in his heart). Only the alchemical golden color indicated a state of perfect inner health. This image arguably provided the conceptual framework for the carving on the back of the chair in figure 6.2. John Winthrop Jr. acquired a complete set of Flood's titles through his London correspondent Edward Howes.

tegrum, which itself was copied from a fifteenth-century manuscript now in the Bodleian Library at Oxford (the seated physician at center was added later, and distinguishes Fludd's image from the Bodleian manuscript).[17] Here in the "sun" (or central) position on Winthrop's chair sits a physician in his chair, expounding knowledge of urinary colors from a medical book propped open on a small table. Orbiting around

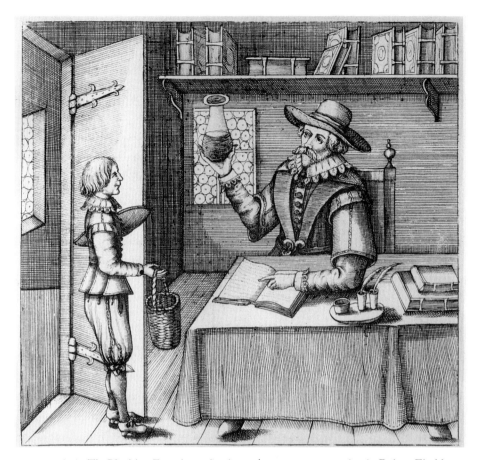

FIGURE 6.6. *The Physician Examines a Specimen,* Anonymous engraving in Robert Fludd, *Integrum morborum mysterium: Sive medicinae catholicae . . .* [and] *Katholikon* [Gr.] *medicorum katoptron* [Gr.] . . . [and] *Pulsus seu nova et arcana pulsuum historia, e sacro fonte radicaliter extracta, nec non medicorum ethnicorum dictis authoritate comprobata,* three works, forming the complete tractate 2 of vol. 1 of the *Medicina catholica* in one vol. (Frankfurt: Wolfgang Hofmann for Willem Fitzer, 1631). Courtesy Yale University Harvey Cushing / John Hay Whitney Medical Library. Color is determined by holding a specimen up to light traveling between the sun and the physician's heart. The pontil glass window forms circles similar to those on the bound books up on the shelves; perhaps the window alludes to the light of grace opening the book of nature?

this central figure are seven spheres filled with text poured into them from urine vials, which read, in a circular pattern beginning from the sphere at top right: "Reds, ranging from a crocus-colour to that of intense fire, signify excesses in the digestion"; with the final sphere of gold and of course perfect health at top left: "Golden colours alone are the sign of a perfect digestion." This engraving of *The Circle of Urinary Colours* was a companion to *The Physician Examines a Specimen* (fig. 6.6) in the *Medicorum.*[18]

The Physician Examines a Specimen was set into the title page of a section of the *Medicorum* Fludd called "Physiological Urinomancy," wherein he devoted five books to diagnosis through the examination of urine. Here the sumptuously dressed physician sits in his chair at a clothed table in his laboratory. He presides over books, pens, and ink, and receives a urine specimen from his young operator or laboratory assistant, who has obtained it from a patient (not pictured). The physician transfers the specimen into a vial (known as a weather-glass) and holds it up to the light to examine its color. The laboratory windows are made of pontil circles from spun glass. This was not uncommon in itself. Still, the circular pieces resonate with the spheres in *The Circle of Urinary Colours* and, at the same time, suggest the corpuscularity of astral light shining down into the alchemist-physician's laboratory, carrying fragmented light split by the duality of fallen Nature and transparent grace through the specimen and on to the open book of natural philosophy on the table.

Images in which the physician's chair played a central role in setting the scene and establishing a practioner's identity show common form, function, and visual grammar when juxtaposed with the carved back panel of Winthrop's chair. Convergence is apparently at hand, and yet why are there only seven orbiting spheres in Fludd, while eight "earths" circle the sun on Winthrop's chair? The answer lies in those carved earths, revolving around the third orbit from the sun. The number seven was commonly used to section a standard color wheel, hence, the same color wheel was transposed onto Fludd's *Circle of Urinary Colours,* with its seven spheres. The number eight in this context was merged with the eight geographical orientation points found on most early modern sundials, signified by an eight-pointed star known as the dial "rose."[19] These composite astrological, geographical, and temporal languages came together in Winthrop's chair. We are confronted, then, with the convergence of pluralist discourse in a dialogue between a much loved relic and its owner's experience. The dialogue was between bibliography and artisanry; geography and temporality; the mystical orders of Paracelsian natural philosophy and a governor's natural and divine right to rule. Convergence speaks, finally, of the meeting of inner and outer geography. How did the accommodation of these multiple discourses, unified in the body of one sitter in his physician's *and* governor's chair, represent John Winthrop the Younger to his local and international constituencies?

The question is ambiguous, but intentionally so, for the issue of pluralism and the willful ambiguity of Winthrop's personal and civic governance in Europe, New England, and New York were central motifs of both his private and his public life. In this way, Winthrop's personal history shared with Palissy's themes of the manipulation of social self-identity as a response to an authoritarian religious regime. Unlike in Palissy's case, however, this was a regime in which Winthrop was ostensibly a part of the ruling order.

Even with no more than speculation about his identity to go on, and lacking a paper trail as rich as Palissy's, we can nevertheless imagine the chair maker's mastery of riven oak and hand tools. Carving the back was not daunting, using compass and rule, the principal tools of joinery and carving (as well as of the millwright, surveyor, and map-maker). Any "ingenious" carver would have found this task relatively routine. These basic scoring tools were analogous to a writer's pen for woodworkers, so the old chair itself will tell us how its carving might have been designed in a dialogue with printed sources in the younger Winthrop's library.

First, a panel of green or partially dried—and therefore soft and workable native red oak—was sawn to measure, held fast or hammered onto the carver's workbench, planed, and "tabled." Taking a ruler in hand, the carver bisected the panel to locate its center. This left a quadripartite rectangle which was again bisected, using the pattern of a St. Andrew's cross, thus subdividing the panel into eight triangles. The original scoring lines are still partially visible to document the process.

Setting aside the rule, a compass was taken in hand. Placing the point carefully at the mark that denoted the panel's center, a circle two and three-quarter inches in diameter was scored, to signify the sun. Extending the compass approximately half an inch each time, three more circles were scored to denote orbits for the three planets closest to the sun, ending with Earth. Taking up a larger compass and placing the point at the panel's center, another larger circle was scored, this one approximately nine inches in diameter, which intersected with those lines ruled previously at eight equidistant points circling the sun.

Then, retrieving the small compass once again (making sure it was still set for a 2¾-inch diameter), eight more 2¾-inch circles were scored at the eight intersecting points of the 9-inch circle. The ruler was retrieved, but this time merely to increase the depth of the previously ruled score marks for reference, for they were then contained in all nine of the 2¾-inch circles. These lines are still visible. Placing the compass point at the endpoint of the single line intersecting with the circle's circumference closest to the panel's corners, another intersecting arc was scored. This provided a center point for the outer stars, perhaps the boundary between the microcosm below and the macrocosm, located at the panel's four corners.

Finally, the small compass point was placed at points located along the circumference of each of the thirteen 2¾-inch circles and a series of intersecting arcs was scored, until all the points were utilized. Ultimately, a final, tiny circle was scored in the center of each one. The pattern that emerged was a basic template to allow a high degree of certainty for carving tools, as the carver now worked freehand with chisels, gouges, and parting tools, and completed his representation of Winthrop's heliocentric system.

The thirteen stylized flowers were then carved with raised stigmas: eight Earths orbiting the sun at the orientation points of the compass star, and four blazing stars in the outer reaches of this earthbound solar system made of wood. Finally, empty peg holes on the crest rail and top of the back stiles of Winthrop's chair, bear witness to the missing carved crest and finials. The absent elements resolved animated motion that emanated out in concentric circles on the back panel as it came to rest at the crest. Following Böhme's logic, impulses absorbed by the physical body from its natural environment eventually moved upward into the head. There they were "proven," but only as an a posteriori effect of action in the soulish heart.

On an existential level, spectators (patients, clients, patrons, citizens) were invited to sense that the entire back panel, with the sun's universal light diffused in speckled patterns completely across, around, and into its surface, was constructed as part of his natural-philosophical and artisanal program, which projected mystical power and significance beyond the immediate physical context of the laboratory. Corpuscular light was perceived to emanate from within or behind the wood, as well as from outside the room. The carver tried to emulate the "stars" represented in the flowery spheres by faceting the wood like a natural crystal or faceted gemstone.

If this chair was painted originally, that surface is long gone, the common fate of chairs that were painted to appear as if they were made of stone, to blend into the subterranean aesthetic of the grotto. When new, the simulated surface of carved stone was itself materially alive, indeed animated, blazing with light and movement. It was animation by the light of grace hidden in the matter of the natural world, so the totality sparkled before the eyes like stars. Light and motion, purity and corruption, eschatological patience and the pressures of personal experience, three of the principal dialectics of Paracelsian science Palissy adapted to his experience, craft, and local history, materialized in this artifact.

Just as earth spun around the sun under God's direction, both driven and constrained simultaneously in his light until end times, so too pulsating circularity was punctuated and ramified by earth's eightfold mimetic repetition on the chair back, with terrestrial moons spinning in, out, and around the moving planet. The implied motion of the carved back panel was designed to command visual perception as the primary point of focus. As stand-in and cosmological pattern for the sitter's inner body absent its habitual occupant, the back's motions became its most specific, *charismatic* scene of reading; following Roland Barthes's "reflections on photography," its *punctum*.[20]

This effect was reinforced further by two separate but interdependent elements of the armchair's internal systems of display. Like that of the New York leather chair, the chair's back hovered above its "timbered bottom" and raked backward rather dramatically, an uncommon feature in seventeenth-century New England joined great chairs. This feature was derived, like so much of Winthrop's library, from European Continental (especially French) prototypes. It effectively forced the tabled panel up into the beholder's field of vision, like a book on a reading stand.

The chair's perceptual field was further transformed into a scene of reading by the strong focal presence of four turned and stacked Doric columns deployed in front, parallel to the sitter's space. These projected aggressively out into the spectator's space as well, appearing on either side of the panel above and below the seat. Furniture historians concerned with colonial America have just begun to address the significance of turned Doric columns in early woodworking. Some would adduce, with good reason, that Winthrop and his chair maker decided to approximate Doric front posts and legs (with academically correct entasis in their profiles) for Winthrop's chair on his lathe, ignoring the other variations he was competent to turn, because the Doric columns indicated that the governor wished to present himself as having inculcated certain desirable values. Winthrop wanted to sit in a chair that reflected the latest international style, refracted through the lens of the turners of metropolitan London. Furniture forms supported or adorned with Doric columns were considered the height of classicizing fashion in mid-seventeenth-century London, and hence were generally found on urban forms in colonial America.[21] This overtly art-historical strategy addresses precedents in the grammar of classicism, beginning with Vitruvius, who associated the Doric order with masculine proportions. Hence, colonial furniture deploying Doric columns signified masculine hegemony.[22]

Certainly, the consideration of metropolitan style diffusion and patriarchy are operative here and are absolutely necessary as preliminary steps in understanding the power of Winthrop's chair. The governor's style-consciousness is self-evident. It is implicit in his elite family and adherence to the latest developments in fashionable Paracelsist science available from the most sophisticated districts of European print culture. To say that the chair is an awesome symbol of patriarchy seems by now redundant: it was made for the "inaugural" of a head of state and had associations back to the thrones of kingship. Even at the level of the poorest family in colonial America that could afford to make or acquire a simple turned armchair, furniture forms with arms were associated by custom with male heads of household. Women and children are usually illustrated sitting on low anonymous forms and stools, which rarely survived, or an available chest.

It is neither style transmission nor iconographical analysis that interests me most in the presence of Doric columns as frontal pendants framing the upturned back panel of Winthrop's chair. Rather, it is their function as a perceptual intermediary and bridge between beholder and text that is most suggestive. The columns direct the spectator-reader specifically to the point of focus—here, the carved back panel that embodied motion and light in the animated material of the wood.

Consider two colonial furniture forms of this period that deployed turned Doric columns in an analogous manner to those on the Winthrop chair: tall-case pendulum-driven clocks and desks. With some notable exceptions, the faces of nearly every early tall-case clock known, where turned elements were involved, employed either free-standing or attached Doric columns, such as the ones on the New York Colony tall-case clock made by Anthony Ward, ca. 1724–30, now in the Bowne House Historical Society in Flushing, New York, the house for which it was originally made. While it is almost impossible to escape the often-repeated analogy between the Copernican system and the face of clockmaking, it is nonetheless instructive to say that Enlightenment notions of a purely mechanistic universe spinning on toward the Apocalypse like a well-oiled clock under God's benign if detached eye, seem a bit naïve or at least premature for the sixteenth and seventeenth centuries. The Paracelsian texts in Winthrop's library—indeed the chair itself—indicate that he did not ascribe to such notions unambiguously when he settled into his "Copernican" armchair. In fact, every American almanac, from the earliest ones published in the seventeenth century to Franklin's *Poor Richard's* in the eighteenth century, published illustrations of both the Ptolemaic and Copernican systems, just as they were mixed in popular consciousness. That heliocentrism was the ascending paradigm does not mean that the earlier one was forgotten; in practice, astronomical structures were absorbed into the stubborn pattern of conservative adaptation of new forms and ultimately cosmological syncretism.

Copernicus was the formal inversion of Ptolemy, yet such cosmological shifts in the monistic universe of spiritualists who believed in the universality of the soul ensured that experience of difference and distance remained ambiguous. Listen first to Böhme's critique of the Ptolemaic system, with the chair's back in mind:

> The SUN hath its own Royall place to itself, and *doth not goe away* from that place, where it came to be at the first; as *some suppose,* that it runneth round about the Globe of the Earth in a Day & a Night, and *some* of the Astrologers also *write so.* . . . This opinion or supposition is *not right,* but the *earth roveth* itself about; and *runneth* with the other Planets, as in a wheele, *round* about the *Sun.* The Earth doth *not* remain *staying* in one Place, but runneth round in a yeare, *once* about the *Sun.*[23]

Following Böhme's Copernican system, however, the sun's "own Royall place" was never fixed or determined at a discrete distance from fallen earth or man, because the sun was not perceived as a body as such, but as made of the same stuff as the infinitely subtle light of God:

> *Planets* are Peculiar Bodys of their own which have a corporeal propertie of themselves, and are *not bound* to any setled or fixed place, but only to their *Circle* Orb or Sphere wherein they runne their course. But the SUN is not such a Body, but only a place or Locality kindled by the *Light* of God. The place, where the SUN is, is such a place, as you may choose or suppose *any where* above the Earth: and if God should kindle the Light by

FIGURE 6.7. Frontispiece by Wenceslaus Hollar from Jakob Böhme's *Aurora* (London, 1656). Courtesy Department of Special Collections, the Sheridan Libraries, Johns Hopkins University. Citations from Revelation explain the imagery: seven torches of fire, "which are the seven spirits of God," burn above the throne of heaven. The throne, shining "under a rainbow that looked like an emerald" and through "a sea of glass, like crystal," is surrounded by four "living creatures" with wings—a lion, ox, a man's face, and a flying eagle—all "full of eyes in front and behind." Before the throne is the Lamb of God with the book of seven seals, broken open. The scene is encompassed by twenty-four elders in white with gold crowns who float above the aurora rising in east. The beast and his minions lurk below in shadow, but finally "the people who walked in darkness have seen a great light" (Isa. 9:2). The postlapsarian veil is dropped at the end of time, and perception is absolute.

the Heat, then the *whole* world would be such a meer SUN; for the same power, wherein the *Sun* standeth, *is everywhere,* all over; and before the time of wrath [the Fall], it was every where all over in the place of *this world,* as Light as the *Sun* is now, but not *so* intollerable. For that heat was not so *great* as in the *Sun,* and therefore the light also was very *meek,* and thus in respect of the horrible fiercenesse of the *Sun,* the *Sun* is differenced or distinguisht from the Meeknesse of God.[24]

The inner and outer sun negated astrological, geographical, and social distance. God's light enabled the sun to exist here, there, and everywhere, ubiquitously. In Winthrop's time, the light of God usually existed only as potential power, to be drawn into the pious body through the veil of postlapsarian corruption by the extension of spiritual heat between macrocosm and microcosm. The application of heat was key to the animation of the spirit, just as it was any alchemical operation. Everything depended on fire in the crucible, as would the ultimate purging of all corruption in the apocalyptic fires. Böhme's frontispiece in *Aurora* (fig. 6.7) considers these themes through a vacant but spiritually complete armchair surrounded by fire, as well as iconography and textual captions from Revelation. The primary text (Rev. 1:4) identifies the chair as God's throne, centering a prophetic vision of the militant Jesus Christ (the Lamb next to the open book of the seven seals) returning to battle the Beast (commanding his dark forces arrayed in deep shadow in the low central foreground): "John to the seven churches that are in Asia: Grace to you and peace from him who is and who was and who is to come, and from the seven spirits who are before his throne."

The title *Aurora* refers implicitly to this text. Böhme's vision of final things takes the form of an aurora, rising radiantly in "the east," the millennial "dawn" (or sunrise) revealing the "seven spirits." These appear as seven flaming urns, which float weightlessly above and "before his throne" in the frontispiece. Several other texts are noted from Revelation, as well as Isaiah and Matthew, which sound themes of God's memory and retribution (Rev. 2:4); whiteness as the elect's "garment" and signifier of purity's conquest over corruption (Rev. 3:4–5); God's light revealing both good and evil hidden in darkness (Isa. 9:2, Matt. 4:16); and, of utmost importance to persecuted Huguenots and other refugees from religious oppression, the ultimate reward of salvation for "you who have kept my word of patient endurance" (Rev. 3:10). The eschatology of waiting patiently was symbolized by worship of God's throne, the savior's place of waiting.

The throne itself descends below the circular vault of heaven (the *caelum stellatum,* boundary between macrocosm and microcosm), ablaze in heat and light. Meanwhile the aurora rises to meet it, reuniting the fragmented heaven and earth for the first time since the Fall. The throne is the conduit for millennial conjunction of the light with the sublunar world, signified by the triangle inside a rectangle on its back. God's chair is pure energy and contained motion. It is the embodiment and channel of Trinitarian forces descending to earth for the penultimate battle between love and wrath. "And this Firmament of Heaven is his throne or footstool," Böhme wrote to describe God's natural position before descending below the arch at the end of time.

Böhme explained postlapsarian astral function further in terms of the Ficinian analogy that overcame the boundary between heaven and earth and promoted soulish unity:

> The qualifying or fountain spirits of his natural Body *rule* in the whole Body of this world, and all is tyed bound or united with them, whatsoever standeth in the Astral Birth in the Part of *Love:* The other part of this world is tyed bound and united with the Devill. . . . Doth not every man in his Astrall qualifying or fountain Spirits *comprehend* the whole place or Body of this world, and the place *comprehendeth man?* It is all but *one Body,* onely there are distinct members.[25]

Such a chair mediated and unified the cosmos through the actions of its occupant, who received and emanated astral light in his heart. Yet Winthrop's physician's chair remained the vehicle of either love or wrath, subject to the sitter's heart and God's leveling impulses. "I have set you upon *Moses* his chair," Böhme wrote (in God's voice) "and entrusted you with my flock; but you mind nothing but the wooll, and mind *not* my sheep, and therewith, you build your great Palaces. But I will set you on *the Stoole of Pestilence.*"[26]

The box that contained the energy of the triangle of air and fire focused readers' perceptions on the back of the throne in the frontispiece, as did the Doric columns that narrowed the field of vision on clock faces, desks, and Winthrop's chair. When perceived from an imagined spectator's perspective on Winthrop's chair, a curious reversal occurred as he approached its front (or back). Perhaps the most resonant deployment of the Doric order occurs on open reading desks such as one mahogany example, ca. 1700 (Fig. 6.8), also from New York colony, in the Brooklyn Museum. Here, as in all similar desks well beyond this period, Doric columns frame and define (in period parlance) the desk's "prospect door." This meant, literally, the door "of perspective view," "of looking forth or out," "of facing or being so situated as to have its front in a specified direction." Until the seventeenth century, "prospect" also meant "point of view."[27] The prospect door flanked by Doric columns also framed the vanishing point in influential design books published by Jean Vredeman de Vries.[28] The governor approaching his physician's chair to reinforce his sense of social and occupational self-identity, or a member of his household standing deferentially or contemptuously to face Winthrop's absent presence in the shape of his unoccupied chair, focused on the available "prospect," as he did while sitting before the prospect door of his desk. His perception had already been conditioned by years of habituation to fo-

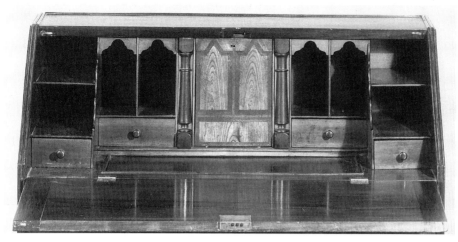

FIGURE 6.8. Detail of desk interior with inlaid prospect door, New York City, ca. 1700. Mahogany, red gum, and ash veneers. Courtesy Brooklyn Museum of Art. The "gothic" inlay between the Doric columns might refer to doors, book boards, towers, or fortress turrets.

cus his eyes on a spot predetermined by the dominant order (in this case by the governor himself) before he began to read.

But such scenes of reading sometimes caused the eye to focus on texts that were more ambiguous than the dominant order might wish. Consider the prospect door of the desk in figure 6.8, made of exotic imported wood, one of the few that survive with architectonic inlay on the prospect door. We know that each of these survivals was probably made by an urban cabinetmaker in the port of New York. At first glance, the old-fashioned gothic-style inlay, a near repetition of the open letter slots with the more contemporary double cyma curve arches on either side of the closed prospect door, resembles an open book on its desk, reading stand, or scriptorium; or perhaps an open book on its stand with pages turning. Indeed, some later desks simulate the spines of well-known books to make it appear as if they are columns guarding the entrance to the prospect door.

Yet the book's image fades back into architecture again when it is remembered that New York City was home to more refugee artisans from the European wars of religion than any other port in the colonies, with the possible exception of Philadelphia. In Europe, many of these artisans had specialized in dovetailed board chests, generically called "Flanders chests" (fig. 6.9). Flanders chests are known by their architectonic "prospects" on the front and were imported into England in large numbers in the sixteenth and seventeenth centuries, a parallel to the wanderings of the refugees.[29] By the seventeenth century, Britain hosted numbers of Dutch, German, Flemish, and French Huguenot woodworkers, especially south of London, and at Ipswich in Suffolk, Norwich in Norfolk, and Aberdeen in northeastern Scotland.[30] Hence, "Flanders chests"

FIGURE 6.9. Flanders chest. England, ca. 1600. H: 23½″,W: 48½″, D: 22¼″. Oak, with marquetry made of sycamore and an unidentified conifer. Courtesy Dedham Historical Society, Dedham, Massachusetts. Gift of Henry Smith, 1887. Such chests were commonly identified with England's continental refugees during the era of the Thirty Years War. This particular example was carried to Dedham, Massachusetts, from Norfolk, England, by the woodworker Michael Metcalfe (1586–1664).

were also produced in Britain and were thought to be among the first board and dovetail furniture forms constructed in great quantities on British soil. Native British craftsmen did not use the dovetail in their guilds until relatively late, depending on often wasteful frame and panel joinery for centuries, even through periods of wood starvation, until they were trained to innovate by masters who were also refugees from the Continent.

For many refugees, the gothic spires inlaid in the board chests in which they carried their belongings recalled some forsaken walled town or fortress near their homes, destroyed in the wars of religion. For the dozen or so southwestern Huguenot woodworking artisans living in New York City by 1700 who were capable of constructing such a desk, the gothic spires that guarded the secrets hidden behind its prospect door read unambiguously as a figure for the two great medieval stone towers that still flank the tiny portal that opens into the inner harbor of what was once the walled fortress of La Rochelle. After all, these towers became so famous by the sixteenth century that Rabelais imagined Gargantua binding up a portion of Pantagruel's body with the giant chain strung between them. And the unknown owner of this desk (perhaps a Rochelais merchant whose family survived 1628) had secrets. The prospect door of these desks usually opens with a key to reveal a small, dark, now empty, space. But it is shallow for the depth of its container. With practiced slight of hand, a hidden, inner lock was slipped, to slide the prospect compartment out from the desk, to be taken away in a moment. Behind the door is a false back hiding a number of tiny, secret drawers: rough-hewn and unfinished; not intended for display. Whatever these obscure little boxes once contained has long since been removed and forgotten.

John Winthrop the Younger thus expanded the material world when taking his seat, perhaps with his tiny copy of Palissy's *Discours admirables* in hand. Of course, until that moment, Winthrop's chair had remained unoccupied, a sort of unstable, asymmetrical text, autonomous yet incomplete. The chair always inferred the presence of its absent intermediary. Winthrop himself had to assume his position for interlocutors, because even a chair as remarkable as this one does not communicate fully until it is occupied by the body for which it was constructed.

Clothing and cow barns, pill boxes or lockets holding a knot of hair preserved from the head of a loved one; a chest of drawers, a grand château, or a pewter spoon resting tenuously on the edge of a simple glazed ceramic dish; nearly every man-made object is essentially a receptacle. Most things were made to serve as an environment for the body or to contain bits of nature and culture that serve to maintain the body. When artisans engaged in maintenance work, the effect could be as primordial (an act of self-preservation) as it was practical. With the exception of garments, or perhaps a bed or coffin, there is no more intimate receptacle for one's body than a chair. Chairs have served in private as "close stools" to function as receptacles for the body's most interior products. Yet, taken together with a sitter's clothing worn at the moment he assumes his seat, there is also no more intimate *public* receptacle for the body than a chair.[31]

When, no later than 1659, Winthrop sat down publicly in his joined great chair for the first time, he was still covered neck to foot with the tight Elizabethan costume members of the colonial elite wore in the seventeenth century. This costume had the effect of defining segments and linkages of the anatomy separately, like military armor, as in figure 6.6. It resembled the costume he wears in one of two surviving portraits. In the second, recently discovered portrait (fig. 6.10), he is still covered neck to foot, but in one of the loose, cloaklike garments that were newly fashionable, which obscured the body.[32] In either case, only the face and some hair were exposed (or, absent gloves, the face, hair, and hands). As Winthrop settled into his seat, each segment of his anatomy, particularly when (as in the 1650s and 1660s) defined by his joined, armorlike clothing, found its corresponding element on the negative space of the joined physician's chair: head to crest (now missing); back to carved back panel; neck, shoulders, and biceps to crest rail and rear stiles framing the back panel; arms and hands to "arms" and grips; buttocks and thighs to "timbered bottom"; and his knees, shins, calves, and shod feet to front legs and "feet." In a very real sense, when Winthrop took his seat, his physician's chair gathered around the back of his torso like a second body.

FIGURE 6.10. *Portrait of Winthrop the Younger,* by an unidentified seventeenth-century artist (school of Lely or Dobson). Oil on canvas. MHS image no. 2015. Courtesy Massachusetts Historical Society.

Or, in Palissy's terms, like the shell of a mollusk. This was clearly the implication of the Netherlandish artist Jacques de Gheyn the Younger's design of 1620, drawn in ink, for a subterranean grotto to be built at the stadholder's house in The Hague (fig. 6.11). Here the wary wild man reappears, sitting in a shell chair, hidden underground in a fortresslike grotto, which appears to be a kind synthesis of Palissy's rustic basins and Winthrop's chair. All Palissy's tiny, overlooked creatures are there with the wild man, crawling in and out of their shells and the holes in the earth, making the subterranean space come alive with motion. The seated rustic rests the arms and hands of his inner body on cosmic wheels that resemble the one carved on the back of Winthrop's chair. The entire scene projects cosmological design, with the crust of the earth arched over this anxious sitter's armored, disguised head, like the arched firmament over the apocalyptic throne in *Aurora*'s frontispiece. At the apex of the grotto, just under the ceiling of earth, hovers a sphere glowing with the light of Nature in the "little world" above. This forms the apex of a Trinitarian triangle as well, with the two wheels in the sitter's hands completing the link.

Hidden inside the elemental earth is a teeming, fecund culture that facilitates growth. At the center sits the natural man, who draws protection and power from the activity around him in the corpuscular labyrinth. This axial position in between the glowing sphere above and the earth below, which merges through his chair, makes this rustic the conduit for the light's creative energy as it enters him, through his shell and chair, and passes, as he sits motionless, into the permeable earth and its tiny creatures. This repeats the motion of the light in God's throne as it descends to earth to merge

FIGURE 6.11. Jacques de Gheyn the Younger, design for a subterranean grotto for the Stadholder's House in the Hague (The Hague, 1620). Ink and wash on paper. © Copyright The British Museum. The silent, wild man armored on his throne of shells, watches and listens for danger. He seems both protected and imprisoned by a permanent need for such modes of security. Fellow denizens of the subterranean world peer from shadowy holes in the rock walls, also depending on camouflage and a highly developed sense of hearing for security. Earlike forms are ubiquitous in the transatlantic visual vocabulary, constituting the "auricular style."

with Böhme's prophesies in *Aurora*. The same motion of heat and light animated Winthrop as he sat still, arms raised parallel to the heart, in his physician's chair.

The parts of Winthrop's anatomy most intimately associated by direct contact with the point of focus of his chair were his chest and back. But the matrix (or *punctum*) of the carved back panel was the sun, at the very center of the Copernican system, which its artisan located by bisecting the panel and scored by piercing the point of his compass precisely into the point of bisection. When seated, Winthrop's body hid that central point of focus, which was now in contact, pulsating simultaneously with his heart.

Imagine Winthrop's heart had heated up, thus activating the celestial order now spinning and shining furiously behind, around, and in him. It was through Winthrop's heart that he was able to draw the heavens (and heavenly knowledge of the healing arts) down to his specific geographical point on earth, located by its orbit on the panel. As if to belie naïve notions that the followers of Copernicus "looked forward rationally" to modern science and the Enlightenment,[33] when mystics and pantheists like Giordano Bruno and other Renaissance *magi* were among the first to embrace heliocentrism, Winthrop's body protected and absorbed the hidden light and motion transmitted from behind his back in the macrocosm, and, with his heart as bridge, both these animating forces entered the microcosm of his body.

Moreover, because the eight earths rotated around the sun like directional points on a compass, Winthrop sat down to position himself, like a gnomon, to refract the light of the sun, no matter where on earth he sat in his chair. Harvey's circulation of the blood, itself tied to great cosmological and political themes, was embedded in the very nature of this physician's chair. If the spheres on the back signified the earth in orbit around the sun, with the sun also the younger Winthrop's metaphorical heart at center, the sphere at center remains identical to the eight in orbit. Thus, there are eight connected hearts circulating at once around Winthrop's physician's heart—the origin of the blood flow—even as earth circulated around the sun.

Winthrop lived and worked by such silent insights of Paracelsian epistemology and experience, which are still communicated by the chair in his absence (to adumbrate a subsequent chapter in which his chair returns to illuminate another scene of reading). The secret heart of man was, for him, at the very center of the microcosm, just as the sun was at the center of the macrocosm. We may surmise this from Winthrop's library, which contained books by Oswald Croll (1560–1609), whose natural-philosophical program merged Calvinist sacramentalism with medical practice. Croll made his name as a Paracelsian philosopher of the medical heart.[34] Listen to Owen Hannaway articulate Croll's systematic understanding of the heart as medium for the astral body in Paracelsian science and medicine:

> It was through [the astral body] that the soul was poured by God into the body of man. The astral body found its principal location in man's heart, from where it spread to all members of his body, having been joined to the spirit in the heart by means of natural heat and thereby diffused throughout the blood. Since the astral body originated in the stars, it kept the same circular course as that of the firmament. Croll presumably believed that the blood circulated in the body on the basis of such analogical reasoning. Thus man had two bodies; his corruptible, visible body of flesh and blood and his invisible, insensible astral body, which was derived from the stars. The astral body, as the source and seat of all vital activity in man, was the "true" body of man, "which moveth, guideth, and performeth all skilful matters." As such, it was the primary locus of Paracelsian physiological and medical theory. . . . The seat of man's knowledge of nature was thus not the mind but the heart, which was the focal point of man's astral spirit, from which it circulated to all the members of the body. The faculty associated with the astral spirit was not reason but the imagination.[35]

Böhme called this convergence of astral heat and light in the pious heart *Barmhertzig-keit,* translated in the popular London edition of the *Aurora* (1656) as "warm-hearted-ness," but also meaning compassion, charity, and mercy.[36] The mystical experience of saying and feeling *Barmhertzigkeit* was an inner process of linguistic, bodily, and cosmic unification:

> Now the word B A R M- [warm] is a dead word, void of understanding, so that no man understands what it meaneth. . . . But when a man saith BARM-HERTZ-, he fetcheth

or presseth the second syllable out from the *Deep* of the Body, out from the Heart, for the *right* Spirit speaketh forth the word HEARTZ, which riseth up aloft from the *heat* of the Heart, in which the Light goeth forth and floweth. . . . The *heat* is the Kernel of the Spirit, out of which the *light* goeth, and kindleth it self in the *midst* or Center . . . and becometh captivated . . . as in the midst or center *wherein* the Sonne of God is generated, and that is the very {*Hertz,* Heart,} of God. And the Lights Flame or Flash; which in the twinkling of an Eye or Moment, shineth into all the powers [of the trinity], even as the Sun doth in the whole world; [it] is the *Holy Ghost,* which goeth forth from the clarity or brightnesse of the Sonne of God, and is the flash of Lightning and sharpnesse.[37]

Without experiencing *Barmhertzigkeit*—as did Winthrop in his physician's chair—facilitating this process of compassionate convergence, it was impossible to comprehend the meaning of Scripture beyond the "dead letter" of the word, or to diagnose and cure illness, or to govern wisely. The inner meaning of all were entwined with the animate soul of the reader.

Hence, when Winthrop took his seat, his physician's chair and body were together transformed by inner and outer body heat and conjoined by light and motion, through warmheartedness, into a unified combination of dualities; the conciliation of opposites between spirit and matter. This was the Neoplatonic resolution that Winthrop's simultaneous reading of Palissy's *Discours* (or his missing copy of the *Recepte*) would have reinforced. Can it be said that Winthrop's "'true' or 'inner' body" is revealed today in the form of his chair? Can this presence be the essence of its metaphysical status as a relic?

I have speculated on how much an artisan such as John Elderkin understood of the Paracelsian system of experience communicated by the younger Winthrop's chair. Dare we presume that he, or some other artisan from close by, understood that the heliocentric system carved into the back panel of the chair was as close to the reality of motion in a carver's compass, the wheel of a great lathe, or the gears in a mill as it was to the heavenly and bodily motion it represented to Winthrop or other natural philosophers at work in their laboratories or studies? This question is made more intriguing in light of Elderkin's role as a courier of alchemical and natural-philosophical books from Winthrop's library to client chemists and laboratory operators on the New England and New York frontier. Surely he read them as well?[38]

Answers may also be supplied by other artisans from different contexts. Quaker joiners and their co-religionist patrons in Chester County, Pennsylvania, suggested some understanding of Winthrop's position from the artisanal perspective. Their sustained, systematic use of heliocentric compass work patterns is to be seen in a very large group of surviving artifacts called "spice boxes" (fig. 6.12); a form that fell out of fashion in the colonies after the seventeenth century everywhere but in Chester

FIGURE 6.12. Detail of a spice box door. Chester County, Pennsylvania, ca. 1730. Walnut, with inlays. Collection of H. L. Chalfant. Photo, George Fistrovich. Chester County spice boxes were usually made by local Quaker craftsmen and descended in Quaker families.

County. It endured there as the region's most identifiable domestic artifact until well into the nineteenth century, or for as long as Quakers remained the dominant religious, cultural, and economic community.[39] Perhaps Quaker artisans, possessed of similar preoccupations with the hidden life of the soul, also reinvented and sustained containers looking very much like freestanding "prospect door" compartments for

FIGURE 6.13. Spice box dated 1676, Essex County, Massachusetts. H: 17¼″, W: 17″, D: 9⅞″. Red oak, soft maple, red cedar, and black walnut. Courtesy Henry Francis du Pont Winterthur Museum, Winterthur, Delaware.

spices and tiny personal effects. Like the spice box drawers they were put into, none of these little things was larger than the palm of one's hand. Evidently, rural Quaker patrons still wanted a heliocentric cosmos scored on a door with compass and rule that opened to a tiny, sometimes playful microcosm of visible and invisible drawers.

The formative role of Quaker patrons as primary customers for such interior artifacts is clear. This was also true of spice boxes with similar decoration made in seventeenth-century New England (fig. 6.13). Intermarried families of Massachusetts Quakers, persecuted by orthodox Calvinists in the late 1650s and 1660s, were the chief users of these earlier spice boxes in New England. Quaker interest in this form peaked during the years of persecution, and spice boxes accompanied refugees as they fled to safety on western Long Island.[40] Some refugee artisans in this migration then founded craft dynasties in New York. Unlike his father, John Winthrop the Younger had quiet sympathy for Quakers in New England, and he subsequently patronized the influential Long Island group. His physician's chair itself suggests shared worldviews.

Hillel Schwartz and Margaret Jacob have made us aware of how much English Quakers and Huguenot refugees had in common in the seventeenth century, when many quietist Huguenots converted to Quakerism. This was especially true among Paracelsian Huguenot artisans, particularly the southwestern Huguenots who emigrated to New York City and western Long Island. It remained for that same group of refugee artisans to remember the hard lessons of their culture of reversals in colonial New York and to effect the profound shift in "imagination" embodied in Winthrop's chair. In New York, the disguised and hidden power of chairs was shifted from the heart of the sitter to its artisans.

❧ Franklin and Palissy ❧

Even as Winthrop's chair exemplified the private, disguised artisanal and occult elements of Palissy's Paracelsianism, Franklin was harnessed to the potter's plainness, egalitarianism, and civic virtue. These two parallel strains of Paracelsianism coexisted in colonial America, though it is prudent to recall that the apparent transparency of Franklin's plainness and public pose is extremely dubious. Still, Franklin's link with Palissy, although distant in time, was more explicit than Winthrop's.

The last edition of Palissy's work in the early modern era, combining the *Recepte* and *Discours* and called the *Oeuvres de Bernard Palissy,* was published in Paris, "Chez Ruault," in 1777. Franklin arrived in France in that year to promote the colonists' revolutionary cause, and to that end he set up a press at Passy. He set to work publishing polemical books and pamphlets, becoming an artisan-hero in France, in particular among those craftsmen who followed the ink trade.[41] The editors at Ruault posited "a great analogy" between Palissy's "method" and that of the "modest" American artisan and scientist, dedicating this new omnibus edition of the Huguenot's writings, "To Monsieur Franklin":

> I offer you the *Works* of Bernard Palissy, to honor the memory of the greatest physician that France produced during a time when natural history was still in its cradle. This profound observer, nearly forgotten for two centuries, could not be restored under worthier conditions that by your auspices. The genius that characterizes him has returned in your work: like him, you announce the greatest truths with the modesty that is the quality of

the true sage; and there is a great analogy between Palissy's method and that which you have used in your discoveries of physical phenomena, so that I cannot offer two names more worthy of the admiration of the learned. But the French philosophe, completely absorbed as he was in uncovering the secrets of Nature, did not penetrate those of political science, which the sages of antiquity cultivated as one of the most important [branches] of philosophy. You have enjoyed all the prizes, Monsieur.[42]

The "great analogy" was a not-so-veiled reference to the practice of Paracelsian natural philosophy shared by the two rustics deemed "worthy of the admiration of the learned," denied in Palissy's era by scholastics. This great analogy was perceived by Franklin as well, inasmuch as publication was "by your auspices," a phrase that connoted Franklin's economic interest and political patronage. The parallels between "Poor Richard," the simple, parsimonious American printer, and the "pauvre artisan sans lettres" were clearly drawn. Robert Darnton has evoked the scientific milieu of the Paris in which Franklin, like his fellow francophile Thomas Jefferson, became a revolutionary symbol to Mesmerists in search of a "new Paracelsus." These occult figures included J. L. Carra who, in his *Esprit du monde et de la philosophie* (Paris, 1777), wrote about the outbreak of the American Revolution in apocalyptic terms. Carra's Neoplatonic explication of natural phenomena prophesied a universal revolution, based on an idiosyncratic reading of Rousseau. According to Carra, all was revealed to him through the physico-moral forces of the universe.[43]

Franklin carefully distanced himself from these "new" Paracelsians. Yet at the same time, he positioned himself alongside Palissy. Following the editors at Ruault, who claim Palissy's "absorption" "in uncovering the secrets of nature" as a precedent for Franklin's ability to "penetrate those of political science," the dedication of Palissy's *Oeuvres* to Franklin during a period of intense political instability in France established that French Paracelsianism had finally come full circle in American revolutionary republicanism and Franklin's "discoveries of Physical phenomena."[44] Palissy had searched shadows for hidden secrets, whereas Franklin triumphed over darkness (with electricity) and "tasted all the prizes." These included, above all, his sense of "political science, which the sages of antiquity cultivated as one of the most important [branches] of philosophy." Ruault's Franklin had reinvented the Paracelsian program for the Enlightenment. He moved natural philosophy into the public scrutiny of Aristotelian civic humanism, suppressing its legacy of clandestine and spiritualist Neoplatonism. Whether such stark distinctions existed in eighteenth-century practice, or in Franklin's life, is debatable.

The same year Franklin's name was linked with the rustic Saintongeais potter's, the American was depicted in a series of French portraits wearing his famous marten-fur cap, acquired on a trip to Canada. The image appears in the 1777 engraving by

FIGURE 6.14. Jean-Baptiste Nini (1717–86). Terra-cotta medallion entitled *B. Franklin Americain*. D. 4½". 1777. Courtesy Nathan Liverant and Son Antiques.

FIGURE 6.15. Reverse of the medallion in figure 6.14.

Augustin de Saint-Aubin, after a Charles Nicolas Cochin drawing. Yet even before the Saint-Aubin print, Franklin in his marten cap was molded for a terra-cotta ceramic medallion by Jean-Baptiste Nini after a drawing by Thomas Walpole, cousin of Horace, which was titled "B. Franklin Americain" (fig. 6.14, fig. 6.15).[45]

Franklin was well aware that Rousseau had been identified with just such a shapeless fur cap when he visited England in 1766, where the French philosophe also wore it in a portrait by Allan Ramsay, which was ultimately engraved and then adapted for a black basalt ceramic medallion by Josiah Wedgwood. Franklin claimed the fur was worn to alleviate a scalp irritation made worse by wigs, though he was enormously pleased by the obvious comparison to Rousseau and the style sensation that his new liberty cap caused in Paris.[46]

The Nini medallion of Franklin was thus the earliest and most successful variant of this image in France, and was widely copied in the eighteenth-century Atlantic world. In fact, the Nini medallion was made a part of a propaganda program hatched by the American faction in Paris. Intent on acquiring war materials for which they had no ready cash through a complex series of speculative ventures, including the sale of future prizes taken at sea, Franklin and his friends decided to have the cheap images made in abundance. "It was necessary for them to establish him as a symbol, to 'sell' him to the public," Charles Sellers writes. "This was the one object of the first Nini medallion and its success is indubitable."[47] Like Palissy, who had pioneered the use of similar ceramic medallions in Paris exactly two centuries before, Franklin, by whose "auspices" the potter's *Oeuvres* were "restored," used ceramic gifts to expand and so-lidify his patronage network. This was clearly the case in the example illustrated in figures 6.14 and 15, which has inscribed on its back: "Presented by his Excellency Doc-tor Franklin to J. L. Austin Paris May 1779." Major Jonathan L. Austin (1748–1826), a Boston merchant and secretary of the Board of War of Massachusetts, was a member of Franklin's revolutionary faction in Paris. Unlike Palissy, however, Franklin's rustic artisan shows his own heroic face on the front of the medal, rather than disguising himself in its materials.

In a letter from Paris written early in 1777, Franklin flirted with his English friend Emma Thompson, then in Lille, saying, "I know you wish you could see me; but you can't, I will describe myself to you. Figure me in your mind [in] . . . a fine Fur Cap, which comes down to my Forehead almost to my spectacles. Think how this must ap-pear among the Powder'd Heads of Paris! . . . Adieu, Madcap."[48] With this playful ri-poste, in which he turned the tables on a *"Hussy,"* the crafty "Americain" linked his costume directly, if ironically, to the *feuillu*/wildman tradition that had once made the Huguenot monks of Palissy's little history appear "so that the people would think they were fools or mad." Franklin contrived to pull the hairy cap down to frame his famous round spectacles. This magnified his eyes to seem as if they were peeping through the fur, recalling medieval prototypes from the forest. This time, however, the amused Franklin consigned the "mad cap" to another rustic in the provinces ("Here the ladies are more civil") and signified his own triumph over—and familiarity with—the hid-den secrets of nature, not their wild furtiveness and dangerous inaccessibility to citi-zens from the metropolis.[49]

Paris embraced Franklin, who was hardly a fool, as a rustic genius of a kind not seen there since Palissy's day. "Everything in him announced the simplicity and innocence of primitive morals," wrote one impressionable nobleman:

> He showed the astonished multitude . . . an erect and vigorous body clad in the simplest garments. His eyes were shadowed by large glasses and in his hand he carried a white cane. He spoke little. He knew how to be impolite without being rude, and his pride seemed to be that of nature. Such a person was made to excite the curiosity of Paris. The people clus-tered around as he passed and asked, "Who is this old peasant who has such a noble air."[50]

Palissy, a skilled heretic, had arrived in Paris from Saintonge two centuries earlier. After barely escaping the St. Bartholomew's Day massacre, he ultimately died a pris-oner in the Bastille, but he was rehabilitated by Benjamin Franklin, who merged the potter's persona with his own as the rustic artisan of the American Revolution. Palissy's costume of heretical concealment had become transparent, noble, polite, and natural.

This moment of convergence also witnessed the rehabilitation of the Huguenot in France, whose "modern" tradition of autonomy and resistance to authority was then nearly three centuries old. Writing in his *Journal de ma vie,* sometime between 1764 and 1803, the glazier Jacques-Louis Ménétra, nominally a Catholic but more accurately a disciple of Rousseau's view that religion was just an excuse for arbitrary abuse of power, expressed admiration and sympathy for persecuted sects, especially Huguenots and Jews: "Ah the Christian religion which they say is tolerant. How can you ministers of the altar act with such cruelty that they [in this instance, the Jews] are forced to hide in doors or alleyways. . . . You don't think that they are our brothers and that they are equal to us in the eyes of the Eternal."[51]

Ménétra's cries of injustice and his pleas to allow the persecuted to step from the shadows into the light came too late. Huguenots had acquired the habit of hiding. Yet it was through strategies of hiding and deception that such heretics as Palissy discovered their identity, their true sense of self. After all, it was scientific and artisanal work done in hiding that inspired Benjamin Franklin and Ruault to retrieve Palissy's memory after two centuries of obscurity and compare him with "B. Franklin Americain." And both Collardeau and Richelieu demonstrated their appreciation for the power that hiding gave southwestern Huguenots. More than for any other reason, it was to deny the Huguenots a place to hide that their artisans' clothing was ripped off the backs of the three Huguenot preachers and the walls of La Rochelle were reduced "par terre." Just as the Rochelais were forced after 1628 to live deceptively in a shadowy subterranean world, based on a century of rustic practice, so too Saintongeais Huguenot artisans continued to labor to construct "second bodies" to extend their quest for refuge above ground.

CHAPTER SEVEN

The River and Nebuchadnezzar's Dream

War, Separation, "the Sound," and the Materiality of Time

Animated by a refugee's impulses to escape and separate, and apocalyptic notions of an aging earth, Palissy took a musical walk along the Charente River, where he was moved to reinterpret the biblical King Nebuchadnezzar's Dream from Daniel (2–5), in language that a potter could understand. In so doing, the artisan separated himself from the aspiring religious enthusiast, whom the Cambridge Platonist John Smith admired yet said had a soul that would "heave and swell with the sense of [its] own virtue and knowledge," puffed up "with pride, arrogance and self-conceit," and began to transform himself, like a butterfly that had finally emerged metamorphosed from a secure cocoon, into "the true metaphysical and contemplative man."[1]

A metaphysical artisan transcended the scholastic definition of manual operator and, by "running and shooting up above his own logical or self-rational life, pierceth into the highest life," in effect, "by universal love and holy affection, abstracting himself from himself." Experience of this arduous transcendental process, "endeavors the nearest union with the Divine essence that may be," like Winthrop in his physician's chair, "knitting his own centre, if he have any, into the centre of the Divine being."[2] Artisanal experience became godlike in itself. Connected universally, the metaphysical artisan's work led simultaneously to the redemption of the corrupt, aging earth. This was particularly true of a Paracelsian potter, like Palissy, whose "art" was "of the earth." Hence, "the socioreligious implications of Paracelsus's concept of alchemy were profound and revolutionary," Owen Hannaway writes:

> Not only was the peasant-artisan elevated to the status of the alchemist, he was allotted a positive role in a great cosmic drama which was nothing less than the redemption of the world. Just as Christ redeemed man the microcosm, who had fallen from grace through the sin of Adam, so man in his turn would redeem the whole of nature, which had fallen with him, by separating the pure from the impure and refocusing the virtues and spiritual powers of nature on himself. . . . Thus the whole of nature would be redeemed—nature through man and man through Christ. This theology of the priesthood of the laborer was at the center of Paracelsus's social and religious challenge to his times.[3]

The martyrs in Palissy's history of the primitive Church of Saintonge had separated themselves and joined the priesthood of the laborer. Now Palissy reconstructed the experience in a form in which he joined them. Like the outcast Ishmael, he alone returned to tell the tale. His story was about the materiality of time.

❧ The River ❧

> I have thus far used simple language, and I cannot boast of any rhetoric or subtleties; I speak in the language of my birth and my country, for I am from Einsiedeln, of Swiss nationality. My writings must not be judged by my language but by my art and experience, which I offer the whole world, and which I hope will be useful to the whole world.
> —PARACELSUS, *Astronomia magna* (1537–38)

> In truth, there are things in my book that it will be hard for ignorant people to believe. Notwithstanding all these considerations, I have not ceased to pursue my undertaking and to counter all calumnies and snares. I have set up a cabinet in which I have placed many and strange things that I have drawn from the bowels of the earth, and that give reliable evidence of what I say, and no one will be found who will not be forced to admit them true after he has seen the things that I have prepared in my cabinet in order to convince all those who otherwise would not wish to believe my writings. —BERNARD PALISSY, *Discours admirables* (1580)

Consider the Paracelsian credos quoted above to suggest a hierarchy of educational "experience" open to the initiate physician. Roughly analogous to Palissy's move from writings to things, this heralded the inversion of the linguistic orders dominated by scholasticism, the scrivener, and the written text:

For many years I studied at the universities of Germany, Italy and France, seeking to discover the foundations of medicine. However, I did not content myself with their teachings and writings and books, but continued my travels to Grenada and Lisbon, through
Spain and England, through Brandenburg, Prussia, Lithuania, Poland, Hungary, Wal-
lachia, Transylvania, Croatia, the Wendian Mark, and yet other countries which there is
no need to mention here, and wherever I went I eagerly and diligently investigated and
sought after the tested and reliable arts of medicine. I went not only to the doctors, but
also to the barbers, bathkeepers, learned physicians, women, and magicians who pursue
the art of healing; I went to alchemists, to monasteries, to nobles and common folk, to
the experts and the simple. . . . I have been criticized for being a wayfarer as though this
made me the less worthy; let no one hold it against me if I defend myself against such allegations. The journeys I have made up until now have been very useful to me because no
man's master grows in his own home, nor has anyone found his teacher behind his stove.
. . . Is there no physician to reveal the lies of the scribes, to denounce their errors and
abuses, to bring them to an end? Will you turn to ridicule the experience that I have acquired with so much diligence. . . . Let me tell you this: every little hair on my neck knows
more than you and all your scribes, and my shoebuckles are more learned than your Galen
and Avicenna, and my beard has more experience than all your high colleges.[4]

Once having arrived at university, the Paracelsian critique argued that the crucial
leap to greater understanding then consisted in a new beginning, an intellectual and
spiritual rebirth from written to oral culture, from the scholastic to the folkloric. These
discursive levels were not mutually exclusive (indeed Paracelsus argued for integration
["I went to . . . the experts and the simple"], as long as medicine is "tested and reliable").
Paracelsus's earliest work suggests that he presented himself as embarking upon a journey of intellectual *devolution,* in which he passed, over the course of his personal history, from a detached philosophical stance to a primordial, experiential one. This physical separation from the centers of learning through journeying enabled him to refute
the scholasticism that identified the Galenic medical tradition with self-purification.
At the same time, it would permit him to proclaim that the most ephemeral bits of his
body ("every little hair on my neck . . . and my beard") had, through communion with
strangers, his personal experience as a healer, and the very animation of travel itself, regained a sensitivity to the outside world lost in the academy.

Paracelsus did not wish his passage from scholasticism to the intuitive to be understood as a mystical retreat from reason. Indeed, the journey was thoroughly reasonable, the result of "many years" of research into the basic *foundations* of medicine,
an undertaking *defined* in the sixteenth century by strict moral and intellectual discipline. Paracelsian discourse cannot be relegated merely to the category of "survivals,
archaisms, the emotional, the irrational." The philosophy of both Paracelsus and

Palissy was strongly rational, although it was not necessarily the same post-Enlightenment secular rationalism with which modern historians identify most easily.[5]

Just as Paracelsus undertook his personal journey in order to construct the foundations of a new medicine, Palissy, who had spent years traveling before settling in Saintonge, made a short pilgrimage away from the tumult of war-torn Saintes to walk along the banks of the Charente River. There he invoked awesome powers of spiritual separation hidden deep in "the bowels of the earth" in order to construct anew the foundations of his innovative and secure Huguenot artisanry. This effort was to be directed toward the erection of a prototypical refuge within a "delectable garden," the central artisanal conception on the model of the snail in the *Recepte,* "where I could *recoil,* and recreate my spirit in times of [violent] separations, plagues, epidemics, and other tribulations, which we are greatly troubled by today."[6]

The Charente was the principal river of commerce in Saintonge, particularly for the many Huguenot potters who worked in and around the river town of La Chapelle-des-Pots. When accused of iconoclasm at Saintes, Palissy testified that he had been at "la Chapelle," where "he usually went to obtain the potter's clay he needed to work at his trade." To conjure the shape of the Charente River, imagine a gigantic shell-less snail, unraveled to meander in a serpentine line down from town to town along the flat grasslands of Saintonge and up through Aunis, ending its long slow journey at La Rochelle. The Charente's form was repeated in Palissy's reptilian rustic basins, and also in his critique of the overt use of straight lines in Calvin's attack on Nicodemites. What better place for Palissy to experience an epiphany?

The river was navigable in wooden, low-riding (and so easily overlooked), locally built pirogues. These canoes built of hollowed-out logs were linked with the coastal Huguenots and New World exploration and they attracted the notice of Theodore de Bry for many illustrations in his *Les Grands Voyages,* although his image of the Charente River shows a gabarot or courpet, also small traditional watercraft (fig. 7.1). Pirogues were thus the main means of commerce as well as of escape for many refugees, who used them to reach Dutch and English ships anchored in the Bay of Biscay with trade goods and refugees.[7] The Charente was, therefore, a lifeline west and north away from religious strife toward La Rochelle and beyond the entrepôt to the larger Protestant world of its trading partners in England, Germany, the Netherlands, and the New World.

Palissy's quest to discover the Neoplatonic origins of the macrocosm and the microcosm and to activate the effects of that doctrine among local artisans began here. It was revealed to his readers in a philosophical dialogue ("to make understanding of the present discourse easier"), which took place between "two Persons": Question, a green apprentice, and Answer, an experienced artisan and natural philosopher infused with God's universal knowledge. Thus we return again to relationships between artisanal

FIGURE 7.1. Theodore de Bry (1528–98), *Sex alia flumina a Gallis observata,* engraving, pl. 3 of Theodore de Bry and Jacques Le Moyne de Morgues (d. 1588), *Brevis narratio eorum quae in Florida Americae provincia Gallis acciderunt* . . . (Frankfurt, 1591). Courtesy Benson Latin American Collection, University of Texas at Austin. Volume 2 of de Bry's series on the Americas contains accounts of the early Huguenot expedition to Florida under Jean Ribaut. Rivers in southwestern France are shown carrying Huguenots in small boats—often mere pirogues— to deep-sea vessels waiting in the Bay of Biscay to transport them to both Protestant Europe and the New World. The Charente appears on the left as one of "six other rivers observed by the French man" that served as primary sources of the migration of refugees from river valleys that flowed west into the Atlantic between the great rival ports of La Rochelle and Bordeaux.

security (serpentine dissimulation) and protection, linked to revelation of the Holy Spirit ("by direct lines"). How does this compare with Palissy's critique of Calvin's straight line?

ANSWER: Some days after all these emotions and the civil wars abated, and it pleased God to send us His peace, I took a stroll one day along the meadow of this town of Saintes, near the Charente River: and while contemplating the horrible dangers from which God had protected me during these past times of horrible tumult, I heard the voices of certain virgins, who were sitting in a grove of trees, singing Psalm 104. And because their voices were soft and well harmonized, I forgot my first thoughts, and stopped to listen to the psalm; setting aside the pleasure of their voices, I began to contemplate the meaning of the psalm, and noted its points; I was in awe [*tout confus en admiration*], of the wisdom of the royal prophet [i.e., David], and said to myself, Oh, divine and admirable goodness of God! That we might have the will to emulate the work of your hands, as the prophet teaches us in his psalm! And then I thought of painting an enormous picture of the beautiful landscapes that the prophet writes about in the psalm: but soon after, I had a change of heart, as paintings do not endure and then I thought of finding a fitting spot to build, if only in part, a garden according to the design, ornament, and excellent beauty, described by the prophet in his psalm, and having created this garden in my spirit, I found that in the same way, I could construct a palace, or amphitheater of refuge next to the garden, to take Christians exiled in times of persecution, which would be a holy pleasure, and an honest occupation of body and spirit.

QUESTION: you say that you would also like to construct an amphitheater of refuge for exiled Christians. This doesn't make sense, considering that we have the peace. Also we hope that soon one will have the liberty to preach throughout France, and not only in France, but also throughout the world: for it is written in Saint Matthew, chapter 24, in which the Lord says that the Gospel of the Kingdom will be preached throughout the world, to be witnessed by all mankind. This makes me say with certainty that it is no longer necessary to seek cities of refuge for Christians.

ANSWER: You have badly misread these passages of the New Testament: for it is written that the children and chosen of God will be persecuted until the end, and hunted and mocked, banished and exiled; and as to that sentence you brought up from Saint Matthew, true it is written, that the Gospel of the Kingdom will be preached throughout the world; but it doesn't say that it will be received by all, but rather that it will be witnessed by all, justify believers, and justly condemn the infidels . . . in conclusion, the perverse and unjust, [the] simoniacs, [the] avaricious, and all sorts of vicious people will always be ready to persecute those who by direct lines would follow the statutes and ordinances of our Lord.[8]

Palissy followed his contemporaries by attributing the musical and magical qualities of Neoplatonism to the Charente River Valley. Twelve years before the publication of the *Recepte,* Jean-Antoine de Baïf—who led a Neoplatonic academy in competition with Gohory's—in his enormously influential *Amours,* a poem in two books dedicated to "Meline" (Paris, 1552), sang the Charente's praises as Nature's incontrovertible witness to his love: "More than me, just as I was / The whole was / On the banks of the Charente. / The Saintongeais bushes / And streams / Bore witness to my song."[9] Here, a crucial transition occurs in the simultaneous coexistence of "I was" and "The whole was"; the Neoplatonic poet becomes part of the All; the monistic universe is activated in de Baïf's metaphorical union of macrocosm and microcosm, just as the union takes place on the banks of a river that is itself metamorphosed to project a voice and a rhetoric beyond mere geographical presence.

Palissy and de Baïf exploited a millennia-old metaphor that became a topos almost with the advent of writing and certainly as early as the Greeks and the epoch of the book of Genesis. By the mid sixteenth century, a rhetoric of rivers had emerged, in which the river, because of the eternal motion of its waters and the specificity of its location, became associated with the *quest* for knowledge and first causes. "A decorum regulates each river's voice," writes W. H. Herendeen, "suiting it to its landscape and local society . . . its language is true, undissembling, and right . . . because, as a unique geographical phenomenon, the river embraces the essential mysteries of nature, and so the rhetoric carried in its current relates first of all to the pursuit of wisdom, and as such it passes freely from the realm of geography into that of language."[10] The language of a river, its particular "rhetoric," must necessarily be local; it is a trope for the flow of a region's history, from its source, the origin. The river is also the centerpiece of regional folklore and topographical literature, hence the obvious site for recovering the secret of man's place in the order of things.

All of the early (and especially pagan) religious traditions associated flowing water—the Egyptian Nile; the Euphrates and the Red Sea (which Moses parts to create an escape route for the Israelites); and the element water and its role in the rivers of the creation myths for the Greeks—with a deity and first creative causes.[11] For Huguenots of the *désert,* Moses was an immensely important figure. Closer to Palissy's Charente, however, was the Stoic tradition inherited by Christianizing Neoplatonists, which held rivers to be the limitless principle element in creation and found its Judeo-Christian counterpart in Genesis 1: parting the waters marked the first act of division separating heaven and earth, the macrocosm and microcosm. Seneca's *Quaestiones naturales,* which was widely read by the humanists, pursued the riverscape as the ideal setting for inquiries into the enigmas of history and humanity and for eloquent expression of ontological insight. Self-knowledge was the Stoic ideal. To know oneself, one sought first causes. But to succeed in the quest, the mind must be freed from the profane weight of the physical body; a key to the classical Christian synthesis. Thus the Senecan river, bisecting two banks, its beginning and end ambiguous, was the earthly place of mind/body bifurcation. And when the mind was freed from the constraints of bodily vices, it could investigate the origin of the river itself. When origins were discovered, so too would absolute knowledge of first causes. Paradoxically, then, bifurcation led to unity.

But perhaps the most crucial aspect of this topos, from Plato to Seneca, Cicero, Pliny, and Palissy, was the synthesis of its metaphoric and metonymic languages. Rivers "speak" simultaneously in the discourses of geography, philosophy, linguistics, eloquence, and, with the advent of the Middle Ages and the Renaissance, magic and, particularly, religion. That was why exegetes, especially natural scientists from Paracelsus to Bacon, regarded the river as the site of the confluence of sacred and profane discourse. Here Scripture and geography were read together and compared. Just as Seneca compared geography with what he read in writings passed down to him from Greek antecedents, Renaissance Paracelsians such as Palissy studied the physical world through an adaptable scheme provided by the Word. Exegetical rivers could be read as tropes for the origins of Genesis, the golden age of Eden, or the fall of Adam, depending on historical context or the experience of the reader. Thus, at its most extreme metaphoric pole, a river might signify an opening or space wherein the desire for the return to prelapsarian unity of spirit and matter might be located. Hence, "the whole was," for de Baïf, where he walked along "the shores of the Charente." Writing his rustic poetry of the river seemed to de Baïf, as Palissy's artisanry did to him, an act of mystical recreation in fallen Nature.

Palissy, too, conceptualized the Charente as the location for the union of macrocosm and microcosm. The river embodied millennia of folklore and mythology, transformed by his spiritual imagination into a metaphorical wilderness; part Eden, part *désert,* to reflect the condition of man after the Fall. Divisions separating sacred and profane were temporarily bridged in his moment of lucidity and now the artisan alone was granted a reprieve from the limitations of sublunar time, the very beginning of which was stigmatized by the failure of humanity to commune with divine knowledge. The reversal of this failure was to become Palissy's alchemical quest—the core of his work—both literary *and* artisanal. More than that, it was his task to achieve communion while still part of the stuff of profane Nature.

The transcendence of corruption by reformed man was to undo what Adam had done, indeed, to neutralize the Adamic act altogether. To negate the Fall was to deny linear history as mere dross: only the light of Nature was direct evidence of God's will. And if, as Plotinus had established, God's reality was in itself a labyrinth with no beginning and no end (and Nature was the ultimate metaphor for that reality), then the act of reading and writing (and artisanry) must follow the form of the centripetal maze—so common in Renaissance gardens—one that attempted to conjoin macrocosm and microcosm so that they coordinated interdependently. This enabled adepts to encompass multiple universes, including the contingencies of everyday life. Analogous to the pilgrim's progress, where every step forward was metaphorically a step backward toward prelapsarian origins, man's cosmological unification was already encompassed in the anatomy of the walker, a "celestial center," and so it remained dormant, awaiting the pilgrim's journey of self-discovery.[12]

In this sense, a powerful symbiosis existed between moral and natural philosophy, and it was clear that a river journey signified the *process* of questing after essence. Thus, natural-philosophical research per se was essential, an act of self-realization or coming into being; the ultimate answers acknowledged by the researcher a priori for process to begin in the first place. The point, then, was less to finish than to endure: to *sustain* the energy of journeying. Historical events became interchangeable, or nearly so, framed and reframed by the actor's own imagination and his experience of the Word. Paracelsian artisans, especially autodidactic Paracelsians, accommodated everything they encountered in the natural world—and rivers in particular—to their own spiritual and material discourse.

Plural classical, Christian, folkloric, and historical languages thus converged at the river. Neoplatonic transformation began at the very moment when the potter, now in the midst of his stroll, was moved to "contemplate" the "horrible dangers" of civil war. Palissy suffered extreme anxiety over the seeming absence of God, and present dangers took precedence. For Palissy, though, the transcendence of history could not proceed without the contingency of violent crisis—that is to say, of tumultuous historical event. This authenticated and thus preceded his insights, as crucifixion preceded the transcendence of Jesus and warfare between love and wrath anchored Jakob Böhme's natural philosophy.

War instigated Palissy's walk and led to contemplation. His stroll separated him physically from society; it spontaneously animated a quasi-sacred space that was removed yet connected to the earth's profane space. Here, Palissy revealed the double consciousness of separation yet contiguity of experience between inner and outer vision. Removal from society into the wilderness coincided with the separation of purity from corruption. Separation was purification from the violent degeneration Palissy associated with the history, past and present, of Saintes. Unlike the communitarian Anabaptists, however, Palissy went alone to the river, and he subsequently returned and rejoined a mixed society with newfound knowledge to further innovation and improve security. Even while the Charente meandered into isolated woods in places, for Palissy, the river remained connected to Saintes, and also to La Chapelle-des-Pots, La Rochelle, and the New World. When he rejoined the milieu of warring Huguenots and Catholics (the sacred and the profane), Palissy returned from a place where he broke through Ficino's deception of the senses, because he stood in the nexus of "the whole" where the macrocosm and microcosm overlapped.

As Palissy contemplated the "times of horrible tumult" of the near-historical past, he "heard the voices of certain virgins, who were sitting in a grove of trees, singing Psalm 104." Thus Palissy documented unity with the macrocosm as his passage through violent chaos, bodily separation, soulish purification, and communion with Nature through the harmonic sound of sacred music. He experienced the inner absorption of contemplation of unity materialized by his mystical sense of nearness to harmonic resonance in Nature, in the pure voices of virgins, which filtered through the corruption of the fallen earth and into an opening in his desiring soul. This grove of trees was Palissy's church in the *désert;* the virgins his choir. In Calvinist sacred music, the soul of the auditor had to be animated "by the pleasure of their voices" in order to transcend the "dead letter" of the text on the page and "contemplate the meaning of the psalm." The pleasure was transitory—and in any event emerged from pain—but much more than the Protestant musical tradition was at work here.[13]

By sixteenth-century convention, the virgins of the glade were a standard trope for the muses. Palissy's Flora (see fig. 5.2) made his spiritual convergence with such figures material. De Baïf's lover heard "les Nymphes Mignonettes" singing along the banks of the Charente, and he ended his *Amours* with a short poem, "To the Muses and to Venus," in which he addressed his devotion to the "Precious Goddesses, [and] Sacred Virgins," in whom he explicitly sublimated his love for the mortal Meline.[14] Pontus de Tyard, like de Baïf a member of the Pléiade, defined the virgins and muses for his academic community, while codifying their use as a metaphor for the universal encyclopedia of knowledge. The Pléiade may have been inspired by Ramon Llull (1232?–1316). If Palissy's walk in the woods invited comparison to the experience of de Baïf's lover in the *Amours,* it also closely resembled a tale from the adventures of Llull's protagonist Felix in his encyclopedia *Libre de meravelles.* The *Libre* remained unpublished until 1750, but it was widely diffused in manuscript form in the sixteenth century.[15]

Felix is also compelled to take a fateful walk. This seems at first to be aimless wandering, until he enters the presence, not of singing virgins, but of a natural philosopher reading in a grove of trees. The philosopher sits beside a beautiful fountain, here the river metaphor of separation and first causes. Felix is still an impressionable novice searching for knowledge, and Palissy had already ascended to the role played by Llull's philosopher. So Palissy locates the muse to spur an already heightened imagination, while Felix discovers a philosopher with whom to play the part of Question. When asked his purpose, the philosopher responds that he is secluded like a recluse in the forest to contemplate the natural order of things and through them understand the mind of their maker. Subsequent explanations initiate Felix (and by extension the reader) into the philosopher's art. Reading in the midst of Nature alludes not only to the "Book of Nature" of which God is the author but also to the rigorous intellectual and moral training Felix undergoes in quest of a unified philosophy of the macrocosm and microcosm.

Most influential of all for Palissy and the French alchemical community on the Neoplatonic sublimation of mortal love into love of God and completion of "the work" was *Hypnerotomachia Poliphili: The Strife of Love in a Dream,* written by the Venetian Dominican monk Francesco Colonna and first published by Aldus Manutius in Venice in 1499. Palissy grapples openly with this text in the *Recepte,* where he chastises critics who think that his design for a "garden is only a dream, and would like to compare it with the dream of Poliphilo."[16] The potter protests that this dream has materialized. An artisan of the earth did not trade in mere fantasies. Still, Palissy depended on the *Hypnerotomachia* for the broad structural outlines of the *Recepte,* and even certain passages in the *Discours,* and was influenced by Colonna more than by any other writer except Paracelsus.

Colonna's text was central to the Venetian Renaissance and was, moreover, profoundly informed by the hermetic, psychic, and Neoplatonic influences of Marsilio Ficino. The Ficinian influence also extended to Colonna's use of nearly inaccessible forms of neolatinate Italian, difficult even for literate Italians to understand. Palissy would have known the *Hypnerotomachia* through his youthful ties with the Pons family and the French Calvinist court in Ferrara. Yet special knowledge was unnecessary in view of the immense popularity and influence of Colonna's dream in early modern France, especially among the artistic and literary communities of sixteenth- and seventeenth-century Paris, which delighted in cryptic images and eroticism and believed they held the key to the philosopher's stone.

Palissy also knew the work through his network of associations. A French translation appeared in Paris under the name of Jean Martin in 1546, but the actual translator was Jacques Gohory, who took enough liberties with its complex Italian to call his translation a paraphrase.[17] Not only the elite but artists and artisans as well were attracted to Colonna's tale. Many of the 174 mystical and quasi-religious woodcuts of classicizing architectural monuments to Poliphilo's dead lovers were copied by craftsmen in various media. Colonna was documented as having been a practicing artisan, as well as a Dominican monk—like the martyred monks in Palissy's history of Saintes. Indeed, some thought he had been as unlearned as the "pauvre artisan sans lettres."[18]

Compare Palissy's walk near the river with the opening of the *Hypnerotomachia,* where the melancholic Poliphilo, a victim of the "strife" of unrequited love, falls into a fitful sleep and dreams that he has wandered onto "a large, plaine, and champion place, all greene and diversely spotted with many sorted flowers." No ordinary plain this, but one absent all signs of faunal life, natural and material: "Here appeareth no humaine creature to my sight, nor sylva beast, flying bird, country house, field tent, or shepheards cote." There are no sounds to be heard, even a "rustikeherdman with Otenpipe making pastorall melodie." Here was a strange Eden before Adam and the naming of the creatures. This plain lacks traces of humanity but also the hellish language of strife and discord that disrupted Palissy's Saintes. It is this silence that draws Poliphilo deeper into the plain, a land of inanimate Nature, stilled by inertia and stagnation until his entrance: "taking the benefit of the place, and quietnesse of the plaine, which assured me to be without feare, I directed my course still forward, regarding on eyther Side the tender leaves and thick grasse, which *rested unstirred, without the beholding of any motion.*"[19]

Polyphilus's aimless wandering animates this stagnant plain. Finally, his "ignorant steppes," which seem to reduce his wandering to movement for its own sake, bring him to an "obscured wood." Terrified because he can locate no path, "eyther to direct me forward, or lead me back againe," Polyphilus sets out to escape the forest. Wandering "now this way, now that way," he circles back on himself. At length, exhausted by his futile attempts to escape and desiring a clue that might "conduct him foorth of the intricite laborinth," Polyphilus finds himself in a sylvan purgatory, caught between the "wish for hated death, or in so dreadful a place to hope for desired life." Nearing the end of his physical resources, our lover, now likening his trials to those of obscure mythological heroes, falls to his knees in Neoplatonic prayer to overcome the blindness and corruption of his outer body. Instantly, a heavenly light appears to guide him from the forest: "glad I was to see the light: as one set at libertie, that had been chayned up in a deepe dungeon and obscure darknesse."[20]

Trailing after the light even as his body is expiring from thirst and injury, he stumbles at last onto "a pleasant spring or head of water. . . from the same did flowe a cleare and chrystalline current streame . . . and trunkes of trees denyed any longer by their roots to be upholden, did cause a Stopping hindrance to their current and wheezing fall, which still augmented by other undissonant torrents, from high and fertlesse mountaines in the plaine, Shewed a beautiful brightnes and Soft passing course."[21] Just as Poliphilo bends to take his first life-saving sip from his cupped hands, he hears "a doricall Songe,"

> with so Sweete and delectable deliverie, with a voyce not terrestriall, with So great a harmonie and incredible a fayning Shrilnesse, and unusuall proportion, and is possible to bee inspired by no tounge Sufficiently to be commended. The Sweetness whereof So greatly delighted me, as thereby I was ravished of my remembrance, and my understanding so taken from me, as I let fall my desired water through the loosened ioynts of my feeble hands.[22]

Having succumbed to a dream of forgetfulness under the spell of a macrocosmic song "with a voyce not terrestriall," Polyphilus loses touch with the reality of historical time. He also loses touch with his body—he forgets to drink the life-sustaining water—only to find himself running, death-driven, toward the siren call of "this inhumane harmonye." The source of this harmony can never quite be found. Instead, Polyphilus finds protection under a mythic tree in the dark forest, the only one with roots still firm in the sacred ground: "my whole bodye trembling and languishinge under the broade and mightye Oke full of Acornes, Standing in the middest of a spatious and large green meade." Under "his thicke and leavie armes," racked by fatigue and the anxiety of "exceeding doubts," Polyphilus dreams that he has succumbed to sleep, only to dream again. His subsequent dream within a dream both animates the rest of his encounters and becomes the structure for an allegory of mortal love stoically displaced into art. The reality of corporeal life is forgotten in sleep, along with history itself, both annihilated by the dream. From this process of sublimation of the physical self arises the pure transcendence of the heart's conjunction between the macrocosm and the microcosm.[23]

The theme of the virgins of the glade maintained textual continuity from the Greeks to Colonna, to de Baïf's Pléiade, up to Gohory and Palissy, and yet there remains a distinct and important difference over time in the nature of their song. Colonna's "doricall Songe" is purely harmonic, whereas Palissy's virgins (whose voices are "soft and well harmonized") sing Psalm 104. Transcription of poetry into measured verse and its ontological interpretation in the new medium was an important enterprise for the sixteenth-century French academies in general and Gohory's *Lycium* and de Baïf's *Academie de poesie et de musique* in particular. From 1565 onward, as a response to Calvin's edict of 1541 to introduce a corpus of Protestant hymns to Geneva, resulting in Clément Marot's ubiquitous reformed Psalter of 1562, de Baïf was occupied with the task of setting the psalms into French measured verse, the centerpiece of his Counter-Reformation efforts in the service of Catherine de Médicis. De Baïf argued that since Huguenots evoked such religious fervor, even political community, with their frequent, public chanting of hymns, then Catholics must also have recourse to their own musical arsenal.[24]

In this early period, there was still hope among some humanists that moderation would close the schism opened up by the religious wars. Musical harmony thus became a prevailing metaphor and recipe for reunification. If heretical song was countered and overwhelmed by music of even greater sacred resonance sung by Catholics as an integral part of their everyday routine like the Huguenot "artisan in his workshop, / With a psalm or canticle, he is comforted in his labor," then discord would dissolve into peaceful harmony.[25] This solution to violent conflict surely seems the epitome of a logic of self-deception and naïve intellectual escapism. Yet in the sixteenth century, alchemists thought the union of measured songs and music to embody very powerful arcana indeed. Theirs was not only the tradition of Orpheus, Amphion, Timotheus, and David, who could reorder the natural world, even create great cities with their music, but the violence of Joshua and Gabriel was there too, and their apocalyptic songs. Combining classical and biblical mythologies was at the very core of the entire Renaissance Neoplatonic program. To induce personal mystical experience to further political and social agendas through Plato's dicta that "songs are spells for souls," the Renaissance Platonists competed to reactivate the power of ancient rhythmic song.

The magic of a "doctrine of effects," extending forward from Plato, captured the moment of perfect symmetry between poetry and music when, by the power of harmonic balance, the auditor's body was arrested, his mind purified and thus cleansed or emptied, and his soul in resonance was lifted into the higher spheres from its profane torpor.[26] He was then initiated into the higher states of knowledge hidden in the meaning of the poetry. Ficino's vision was expressed in the poet Pontus de Tyard's *Solitaire second* (Lyon, 1555).[27] Solitaire's adoration of Pasithee, the mythical union of music and poetry, unfolds in a tale that functions both as an intellectual journey from scholastic reason to the experience of transcendental intuition and a return journey for the soul back to the divine clarity of the place whence it had originally fallen in the time of Adam, and out of the camouflage, discord, and chaos of profane matter.

This is also Polyphilus's task, as he journeys from monument to monument built in memory of his unfortunate lovers. Were these lost loves traces of the perfect unity of prelapsarian experience? Were the monuments' hieroglyphs alchemical clues to recovery of experience through the work? It was precisely the desire to engineer his soul's return from the chaos of personal history that animated Palissy's walk and invited the muses to induce a dreamlike state of forgetfulness of history after the Fall. "I forgot my first thoughts," he wrote, "and stopped to listen to the psalm; setting aside the pleasure of their voices, I began to contemplate the meaning."

Palissy's "response" to the measured verse was a programmatic example of the doctrine of effects, instantly recalling similar moments in the *Hypnerotomachia, Le Roman de la rose,* and *Solitaire second.* But again, unlike the harmonic song of Polyphilus, Palissy's muse encourages him to grasp meaning linked to a specific historical moment by his *personal* understanding of the word through a soulish inspiration by God. As the perfect harmony of the song signified the timelessness of divine authority, it allowed King David's text to enter contingent experience simultaneously, filling him with the sense of hearing. But pure sensations of "pleasure," where Palissy located the main effect, could only be obtained when the soulish heart was animated to form a conjunction between macrocosm and microcosm, becoming a bridge for the astral body. The *plaisir* of Palissy's animated heart granted his spirit a moment of divine insight into the negation of history—history here revealed in negative relation to pleasure—by the gift of forgetfulness. Still, this was a gift that could never completely negate the truth: in the same moment his being was still riveted *bodily* to a real place by the river in war-torn Saintes.

Only insofar as there existed the *external* disorder of man's existential history could Palissy unveil his intoxicating experience of timeless *internal* order. This specific reciprocal relation both framed and animated his Neoplatonic epiphany. Like the conceptual barriers separating macrocosm from microcosm, this relationship was now experienced as "awe" (*tout confus,* literally, "all disordered"), as the two cosmic spheres came together in his animated heart, which was invaded, breached, and interpenetrated by the anarchic violence of "the strife of love." Emerging from this "disorder," there was a sense, not of chaos, but of profound equilibrium: metamorphosis, a moment of historical transformation when the disruption of old categories left in its wake an aperture sufficient to release the energy of new creation. This energy inspired Palissy's quest for the metaphysical union of matter and spirit in his artisanry. In his colossal *Platonic Theology,* Ficino systematized the movement of the soul in matter through his paradigmatic formulation of the five ontological hypostases (or substances), namely, the One, Mind, Soul, Quality, and Body. This formulation enabled him to define, through the mediation of the soul, the ultimately universal relationship of the absolute to the apparently fragmented and pluralistic universe of fallen matter.

The hypostases divided reality into a hierarchy of ontological states, so, as a system, "the higher subsumes the lower and the lower emanates from the higher and ultimately from the absolutely prime hypostasis, the transcendent One."[28] The equilibrium of Palissy's epiphany may be graphed onto Ficino's continuum, with the Soul occupying the nexus integrating spirit and matter. As Ficino wrote in an often-quoted phrase, the soul served as "the universal countenance, the bond and knot of the world."[29]

This provides a framework for interaction between macrocosm and microcosm inspired by the divine song of the muses, the sound by which the activation of the soul overcame the death of the body through an animated heart and effected a new, discrete harmonic order.

❧ "The Sound" ❧

In the seventeenth century, Böhme, following Palissy, merged this Ficinian musical model with the Protestant emphasis on the Word and Paracelsian alchemical principles in ways that clarified the redemptive qualities of reborn matter in the hands of physicians as well as rustic artisans. For Böhme, the harmonized voices of the glade were abstracted into the "Sound" of Nature, emerging from the soulish bowels of the earth. "The Heat, Light, Love, and the Sound or Tone, is hidden," Böhme wrote:

> and maketh the outward *moveable,* so that the outward gathereth it self together, and generateth a Body . . . the Word is the Sound or Tone, which riseth up in the Light . . . [but] the *Sound* of Gods Word must rise up through the astringent bitter Death, and generate a Body in the half-dead water, thereupon that Body is Good and also Evill, dead and living; . . . as the Earth its Mother doth . . . the Life lyeth *hid* under and in the Death of the Earth, as also in the children of the Earth. . . . Behold! Man becometh weak faint and sick, and if *no remedy* is used, then he soon falls into Death. . . . Now if a Learned Physician inquireth from the sick Person from what his disease is *proceeded,* and taketh that which is the *cause* of the Disease . . . the Astral birth remaineth in its *Seat* . . . mingleth with this water or powder . . . it can *take away* the Disease from a Man: for the Astral Life

riseth up through Death . . . the power or *vertue* of the Word and eternal life in the Earth and its *children* lyeth hidden in the center in Death, and springeth up through Death . . . it hath Life in its Seat, and that *cannot* be taken from it . . . the Spirit speaketh to *thee*, and not to the dead spirit of the flesh.[30]

From his many attacks on writing and eloquent speech, Palissy implied a failure of language to come to grips with the disruption of old categories and the accompanying ephemeral flash of essence. In the end it was his artifacts, transformed from dead matter into quality, that documented Palissy's moment of conjunction and unity with the whole, because craft infused with soul's truth carried by the astral spirit was the material of Palissy's spiritual experience. From the realm of disorder—local history, war, and violent language—arose a visionary order, the dulcet garden modeled after Psalm 104. This psalm attained critical importance in the Huguenot Psalter during the war period and beyond into the refuge during the seventeenth century precisely because it was the Genesis psalm (its temporal and narrative structure derive from Genesis 1), a hymn in praise of creation. The semantic importance of this celebration of the presence of God in Nature was as clear for Palissy as an artisan and natural philosopher as it was for Böhme.[31]

Moving past the effect of the sound on bodies and, by extension, Paracelsian chemical medicine, Böhme's Neoplatonic analysis linked these earth spirits (or, "children") to God's artisanal work in the creation, in Genesis, of "curious . . . Ideas forms or Images": shadows of macrocosmic perfection out of the bowels of the earth: "Now the purpose of God was, to make a curious excellent Angelical Hoast or Army out of the *Earth*, and all manner of Ideas forms or Images. For, in and upon that all should Spring, and generate themselves *anew*, as we see in mineral Oares, Stones, Trees, Herbs and Grasse, and all manner of Beasts; after a *heavenly* Image or Form."[32] In this context, Palissy's unlearned rustic artisans were the children of God and Mother Earth, and hearing her song, they, too, were moved, with the astral spirit's assistance, to help make an "Angelical Hoast or Army out of the Earth." Thus, his rustic "figulines" became disguised figures of Christian soldiers, intended to endure and rise up at the end of time. This was also one purpose of Palissy's garden and amphitheater of refuge made in the rustic style, which was decided upon when Palissy thought that "paintings do not endure." Ceramics had endured buried underground since beyond memory and kept their form, "and though those Imagings were *transitory*, being they were not pure before God," a chiliastic Böhme pointed to the apocalyptic future: "yet God would at the End of this time, *extract* and draw forth the Heart and the kernel, out of the new Birth or Geniture, and *separate* it from Death and Wrath, and the new Birth should Eternally spring up in God, without, *distinct* from this place, and bear Heavenly fruits *again*."[33]

First, Palissy's Huguenots *qua* overlooked creatures were reborn an army of rustic images; last, with patience and endurance, they would hear the sound, be extracted from death, and experience the "new Birth . . . Eternally." This was the crucial task of Paracelsian artisanry. Palissy's desire was to construct an exact parallel of God's creation of Nature in a microcosm made of the earth itself, harnessing artisanal *sûreté* to patience. He confronted the pious artisan's problem of building endurance, if not permanence, in history. The garden, with an amphitheater of refuge next to it, was built to the specifications of God's word carried by harmonic sound. Raised out of the half-dead matter of the aging earth, it was still granted the endurance of sacred authority, because Palissy's hands followed his animated heart and "created this garden in my spirit."

❧ Psalm 104 ❧

David's poem began by praising God ("Bless the Lord, O my Soul!") only—in a move standard in the Hebrew poetic tradition—to circle back to its beginning again in the end (35:2) ("Bless thou the Lord, O my soul!") as the ultimate artisan taking pleasure in the construction of his masterpiece. "Clothed with light as with a garment" (*Amictus lumine*), his kingly (1:4) "glory and majesty" was embodied in the very act and form of creation as the light of creation. Just as God possessed the power to will creation, so too providence provided, at his discretion, sustenance, and renewal (the spirit here was the breath of life):

> 29. Hidest thou thy face, they are terrified:
> Withdrawest thou their breath, they expire,
> And return to their dust:
> 30. Thou sendest forth thy spirit, they are created,
> And thou renewest the face of the earth.[34]

Palissy emerged from his epiphany in "awe," praising the skill of God the artisan ("the works of your hands"). Simultaneously, he possessed the will to materialize as artisanry the insight provided by his moment of astral conjunction. But the delectable garden of Psalm 104, though full of edenic imagery, was no Eden. It was at most a rustic landscape located in time *after* the Fall, where man feared real threats and had to labor for his subsistence:

> 20. Thou makest darkness, and it is night:
> Wherein all the beasts of the forest do creep forth.
> 21. The young lions roar after their prey,
> And seek their meat from God.

294 ✤ THE ART OF THE EARTH

> 22. The sun ariseth, they gather themselves together,
> And lay them down in their dens.
> 23. Man goeth forth unto his work
> And to his labour until the evening.

Thus the garden, like Palissy himself, occupied a space in history between the Creation and the return. Although no longer protected by God—indeed, He could take away the breath of life at any moment and return its creatures "to dust"—the garden remained an open space for creation. There is safety for man in labor, for only after toil ends in the evening do the lions come out of their dens and "seek their meat from God." This was space for waiting; a trope for the refugee artisan's escape into the private refuge for the self and others. Like Palissy's dreamy walk, the garden, anchored by its (*limace*-shaped?) amphitheater of refuge, became a fixed arena; a hidden fortress, natural-philosophical laboratory, and alchemical matrix that processed natural matter into artisanry and the artisans themselves. The separation and solitude of the refuge was cultivated and displaced into work toward Paracelsus's material-holiness synthesis: "which would be a holy pleasure, and an honest occupation of body and spirit." But, despite Palissy's expectation that his garden, wrought in the image of Psalm 104, would endure longer and more usefully than paint on panel or glass, his creation was a temporarily ordered personal space. It merely offered refuge from violent sequence. Yet even if it was not the final stopping point and the permanent, universal resolution of dualities (which was not the domain of human artisanry), here was a place where bits of the earth were redeemed and converted alchemically; evidence that the aging earth was moving toward final things.

Misunderstanding the amphitheater of refuge for "exiled Christians" to be yet another "city of refuge," Question dismisses the concept as no longer useful and naïvely turns to historical event—the "present peace"—as proof that refuge is unnecessary. Citing Matthew, he argues that Huguenots can now resume their evangelical role as preachers of the gospel in France and beyond. But Question is not a philosopher. He uses Scripture to support historical discourse but is unable to escape its limitations. Unlike Answer, who penetrates the meaning of Psalm 104 because it enters him on an "astral chariot" of harmonic sound, he cannot link macrocosm and microcosm through communion with God. Hence Question has little hope of penetrating the hidden truth of the divine message, which he "badly misread." But Answer, the philosopher, is able to assert with conviction that "the children and chosen of God" will have no peace in history. Everyone will *see* God's truth, but few will perceive it. The many will try to destroy what they cannot possess. The few will endure persecution "until the end," exiled until the return; an existence of mythological torment within a history that is not theirs, even while they labor in refuge and wait.

In the end, these Neoplatonic components of Bernard Palissy's Paracelsian discourse provided an available language to address the Saintongeais Huguenot artisan's materio-spiritual preoccupations, if such difficult language was set in "narrative" terms he understood. Hence Palissy asked his patron Catherine de Médicis to overlook his rustic discourse, at the same time that he asked: "I implore you to instruct those laborers who are illiterate that they should study natural philosophy industriously, following my counsel."[35] Despite Palissy's obvious identification with certain written traditions, a suspicion of language remains in his writing, a tension between the oral culture of an enthusiastic artisan with intimate connections to God and a natural philosopher and martyrologist who knew that print culture was necessary for his "counsel" to "endure" and be useful to other refugee artisans after his death.

When Palissy took his walk by the Charente River, he expressed his motivations emotionally in a language of the senses, a language that proceeded like a "dialogue" from hearing to feeling to seeing to prelapsarian remembering (through forgetfulness) and, finally, to artisanry.[36] Palissy's "simple" artisanal "language," although it survived in both pottery and writing, was crafted cautiously out of a Faustian bargain between converging oral and literary traditions. As such, it contained an intractable irony intended to meet the challenge of writing and thus maintain the primacy of the culture of sound in the very domain in which it would be destroyed.

❧ Nebuchadnezzar's Dream and the Materiality of Time ❧

The sound resonated from the outer rim of the macrocosm down into the microcosm, all the way to the bowels of the earth, before it emerged cleansed as virginal harmonies to Palissy's ears. So it seems appropriate here to join Question and Answer in the midst of a heated dialogue about geology. By the time the dialogue finally turns the *Recepte* to the subject of "stones," Answer has already alluded to a central problem in sixteenth-century natural science—what geologists subsequently came to call "subaerial denudation"[37]—the erosion of the surface of Planet Earth. In early modern times, this was referred to eschatologically as the "decay" of the sublunar world. Answer is thus rejoined pro forma by Question, who extends his role as defender of the inviolable authority of the written text to include biblical wisdom on geomorphology:

QUESTION: The opinion that you have told me now is the biggest lie that I have ever heard: for you say that the stone that has recently been made is subject to decomposition, because of the damage of time, but I know that from the beginning God made heaven and earth, and he also made all the stones and hasn't made any since. And even the Psalm [104] on which you want to build your garden gives testimony that all was made in the beginning of the Creation of the world.[38]

Palissy thus began to search the bowels of the earth to unravel the scientific and scriptural problems that attended the excavation of "proofs" of a historical body undergoing the aging process. This task forced him to account for a logical discrepancy—or even, as Question's accusation implies, willful misreading—when compared with the authorities already cited: Genesis and Psalm 104.

Both state, as Question attests, that heaven and earth were created in their totality in the beginning ("all was made in the beginning of the Creation of the world"). Therefore, according to a literal reading of Scripture, all geological structures ("all the stones") were also brought into being by fiat "in the beginning of the Creation." But if stones were subject "to breaking up" because of "the injuries of time," then Genesis was suspect as history, because other rocks had to replace those lost or else earth would dissolve into nothingness. The heretical implications of this observation were clearly not lost on Question. And so his argument follows, according to the logic of the biblical scientific tradition, that the earth's geology retains precisely the same structures now as then.[39]

Question's bibliolatry is understandable if taken in the context of Renaissance science and its veneration of the Genesis as "containing God's own impeccable account of the Earth's creation and early history."[40] A Genesis cult emerged, on one level, because it was commonly assumed that Genesis and the other books of the Pentateuch had been transcribed directly from words dictated by God, heard and presumably written down verbatim by Moses. The five books of the Pentateuch were believed to be the most ancient of all artifacts containing the Word and, as such, were regarded as chronologically closest to God's presence. Its divine provenance guaranteed the infallibility of Genesis as scientific discourse. As late as 1709, a British polemical tract hailed "the Mosaick System of the Creation; [with Moses,] the greatest Natural Philosopher that ever lived upon this earth."[41]

From the early Christian era until at least the Enlightenment and beyond, Genesis functioned as the West's universal textbook of geomorphology. In Palissy's time, discrepancies between text and Nature were assumed by authority to be the result of human error in any number of interpretive categories. Included among these were exegetical misreading; sensual misperception resulting from the devil's mischief; or, as Question charges against Answer with respect to the dogma that "all was made in the beginning of the Creation of the world," outright lies.[42] But we have seen how Question personifies a half-blind "literal" reading of Scripture, especially when confronted with the natural philosopher Answer's access to the primacy of experiential authority, validated by communion with God in conjunction with the light of Nature. Question's literalness and catechistic reliance on the written word make the *potentially* living text—and, by extension his unimaginative discourse—a dead letter.

Palissy thus began to address the eschatological component of Paracelsist artisanry during his walk by the river, when he decided to base his garden on Psalm 104, the Genesis psalm. In Palissy's Paracelsian geomorphology, the eschatological antitype of Genesis is typically Revelation's "a new heaven and a new earth" (Rev. 21:1). Northrup Frye argues in his typological reading of the Bible that with Revelation "we reach the antitype of all antitypes, the real beginning of light and sound of which the first word of the Bible is the type."[43] The Bible was interpreted in its original form as one huge codex in which each book existed in reciprocal relation to each of the others. This sort of textual reciprocity was probably very similar to the way in which enthusiastic Huguenot theologians encouraged disciples to read the books, with constant reference back from the New Testament to the Old for "authority" as type. Indeed, *désert* Huguenots such as Palissy quoted as much from the Old Testament as from the New.

Answer replies to Question's rigidity from the perspective, not only of the enthusiastic interaction of Genesis and Revelation, but also of his geological understanding of the Paracelsian chemical millennium. This encouraged the simultaneous reading of material signifiers of first and final causes in geological specimens taken from the "bowels" of the earth:

> ANSWER: I have never seen a man as dense as you are: I know very well that it is written in the Book of Genesis that God created all things in six days, and that He rested on the seventh day: but nevertheless, God did not create these things to leave them idle, thus each does its own duty, according to the commandment that it was given by God. The stars and planets are not idle, the ocean shifts from one coast to another and labors to produce beneficial things; similarly, the earth is *never* idle: that which is naturally worn out, she reforms immediately, if not in one way then in another. [And that is why you ought to manure the earth so that it immediately takes up the sustenance that it has been given.] Therefore, it is necessary to note here, that just as the outside of the earth labors to give birth to something: so too the inside and matrix of the earth also labors to produce [*produire* suggests a triple meaning here, including "to create" and "to give birth"].

Just as there was perpetual motion toward the industrious production of "beneficial things" in the macrocosm ("the stars and planets are not idle"), so too in the microcosm ("similarly, the earth is *never* idle"). As it was for Böhme, for Palissy, the earth was feminine—a mother who "labors to give birth to something"—and an alchemical "matrix" for the "refinement" of matter gestated over the fullness of time. Knowledge of the means by which perpetual industrious labor to separate purity from impurity in the bowels of the earth takes place would be especially useful to farmers. "That is why you ought to manure the earth," Palissy admonished. He believed that manure, like the farmer's philosopher's stone, replicated the earth's hidden treasures, leading to agricultural fecundity. So too artisans would benefit. If the earth's matrix took raw matter and returned "benefical things" from her labor, and if the artisan could some-how replicate the action of that matrix in his shop, then, conceptually speaking, he could replicate the process of production. Purification of self was also implied; the question then became, how did the artisan attain to the labor of the matrix? How could he return to the "mother" for rebirth without destroying himself in the process?

The intermingling of Genesis and Revelation was also apparent in Palissy's under-standing of the Paracelsian concept of the *quinta essentia,* the "potential" or "seed," that, over time, moved slowly, *observably* (like living organisms), toward ripeness or perfec-tion. Perfection, "inasmuch as he is perfect," could only be achieved in full at the end of time:

> Although the land and sea daily produce new creatures and various plants, metals and
> minerals, nevertheless, as early as the Creation of the world, God put into the earth all
> the seeds that are in it and ever will be: inasmuch as he is perfect, He has left nothing im-
> perfect . . . [and] . . . even as God has commanded the surface of the earth to busy itself
> producing and germinating things that are necessary to man and beast, it is certain that
> the interior of the earth does likewise, producing many kinds of rocks, metals and other
> necessary minerals.[44]

"The seeds" put into everything on earth were at the core of the chemical millen-nium; they contained both the beginning and end, impurities and purification simul-taneously. It followed there was a reciprocal relation of growth toward purification be-tween the history of the microcosm (the "bowels of the earth," its geological history) and the macrocosm (whence the seeds came). Paracelsians believed each element in Nature (including geological formations) was connected to the macrocosm by the as-tral spirit, which also gave it identity and form: "as the astral spirit penetrated matter it became specified and gave form and function to the objects which it generated," Hannaway observes. "The spirit is thus best comprehended, not as a continuous, ho-mogeneous spirituous entity, but as the vehicle which contained and transmitted the totality of discrete specifying individual powers of nature."[45]

For Palissy, the astral spirit was vitally materialized in form. He conceived of it as part of an ordering "fifth element": "although all philosophers have concluded that there are only four elements, there is a fifth, without which nothing could say I am . . . there is in human things a beginning of form held up by the fifth element, and other-wise all natural things would remain jumbled up together without any form."[46] Böhme called it the "*fifth* fountain-spirit; . . . the *hidden* source fountain or Quality, which, the corporeal being *cannot* comprehend or apprehend." "This fountain-spirit," while hid-den, did take on elemental properties, for it "taketh its original at *first* out of the *sweet* Quality of the water."[47] But this was water unlike any other.

Likewise the potter was also convinced from experiments that the astral spirit—

and hence the "fifth element"—must materialize as *water* mixed with seminal salt from the earth, because salt seemed always to be what remained behind after raw materials were reduced by burning or boiling during alchemical distillation:

> I have proven to you that in all species of trees, herbs, and plants there was salt. . . . and where do you think that the trees, herbs, and plants get their salt if it isn't from the earth . . . there is also salt in all kinds of stones . . . and not only in all kinds of stones but I tell you also, in all kinds of metals: for if it had none, nothing could be; and therefore would be suddenly reduced to ashes.[48]

If salt in the fifth element was fundamental to gathering earthly matter together and to giving it form, then it followed that it was fundamental to the birth, aging, dissolution, and death of the earth as well. Animated by the astral spirit and combined with the sweet water of the fifth element, salt was the principal congealing agent in the microcosm. As such, it helped give each specific thing on earth its own form, identity, life, and death, which all came from God but nevertheless had a basis in these materials as well.

Hence, all natural things in the microcosm were born of seeds and had encoded in them through discrete materials and elements a specific identity and fate. All were subject to the exigencies of historical and eschatological time, which was also encoded in them by the macrocosm. Every substance, whether visible or invisible, above or below the earth's surface, had to reveal to the Paracelsian artisan material evidence of its age, history, and life course in the macrocosm and the microcosm that would enable him to judge the appropriate alchemical process by which the material's impure life would be ended in fire (or on the turner's lathe) and reformed in its purified state. Because each thing on (and in) the earth was animated by individual astral spirits—hence it could "say I am"—there were no guarantees that purifying one species of the earth would cause all other "earths" to follow simultaneously. Still, Paracelsians believed that although the aging process was slow and staggered, in the end, the entire earth would die together. Although every stone had its own identity and life cycle in history, like fallen man, they were simultaneously linked by the universal experience of final things. According to Böhme and most Neoplatonists, at that moment, half-dead Nature, hitherto merely a shadow of prelapsarian perfection, would be fully perfect again.

This Paracelsian revival of the medieval notion of the aging earth gave rise to Palissy's conceptual framework. Paracelsus had been influenced by Joachim of Flora, and Palissy may well have acquired his understanding of the aging earth not only by reading Paracelsus but by coming into contact with another branch of the same large tradition of which Joachim was a part, one that was perhaps more appealing to potters.

The medievalist James Dean suggests that the discourse of aging earth entered the Renaissance via a circuitous route. Plato had refuted the notion that the world could age like worldly creatures. Aristotle and Plato both thought that the world was eternal. Many sixteenth-century Neoplatonists, however, inherited the discourse of aging earth from Augustine and the medieval scholastics, who themselves ultimately derived it from the Jewish apocalyptic: "The conception of an aged, decaying world was formulated . . . in late Jewish apocalyptic—in Isaiah and 2 Esdras. From Iranian (Magian-Chaldean) sources, the author of the Book of Daniel inherited the degeneration of world empires from gold to silver to brass to iron to iron mixed with clay."[49]

Historical and geological decline, devolving from gold to iron mixed with clay, was a pattern of degeneration conceptualized by the scholastics in terms of six world ages of Christianity. The first, or golden age, declined into the sixth age, or present time, which signified the world's old age. Geological materials thus possessed relative optical and other intrinsic values as indicators of purity or loss thereof. Gold signified man's origins in innocence and righteousness, while clay conveyed weakness, chaos, the confusion of history. Iron, the hard ore of labor and war, suggested the brutality of the present time.[50]

Conceptualizing eras as a sequence of metals declining in value from first to last is at least as old as Hesiod. But the crucial shift of this classic temporal metaphor in subsequent historiography occurred with the Old Testament Daniel (2:1–49) and the great dream-vision of Nebuchadnezzar.[51]

The story of Nebuchadnezzar's dream told in Daniel 2 is well known. It ranks second in importance among apocalyptic biblical dream-prophesies only to the New Testament Revelation of St. John, to which it is related as a type. "During the second year of his reign, Nebuchadnezzar had dreams, and his mind was so troubled that he could not sleep" (Dan. 2:1–2). Calling together his wise men at court, the king "gave orders, to . . . the magicians, exorcists, sorcerers, and Chaldeans to tell him what he had dreamt" (Dan. 2:2). Unable to get a response from his metaphysicians except for their sensible request to hear the dream in order to interpret it, Nebuchadnezzar falls into a murderous rage and orders "the death of all the wise men of Babylon" (Dan. 2:12, 13). One of these, the Jew Daniel, prays to discover the king's secret, and God reveals it to him. Daniel recounts Nebuchadnezzar's dream and its significance to the king, leading to his recognition as the favored instrument of "he that revealeth secrets" (Dan. 2:29):

> [T]here is a God in heaven that revealeth secrets, and maketh known to the king Nebuchadnezzar what shall be in the latter days. . . . Thou, O king, sawest, and, behold, a great image. This great image, whose brightness was excellent, stood before thee; and the form thereof was terrible. This image's head was of fine gold, his breast and his arms of silver, his belly and his thighs of brass, his legs of iron, his feet part of iron and part of clay. Thou sawest till that a stone was cut out [of a mountain] without hands, which smote the image

upon his feet that were of iron and clay, and brake them to pieces. Then was the iron, the
clay, the brass, the silver, and the gold, broken to pieces together, and became like the chaff
of the summer threshingfloors; and the wind carried them away . . . and the stone that
smote the image became a great mountain, and filled the whole earth. (Dan. 2:28, 31–36)

Daniel interprets the dream as predicting the rise and fall of a succession of king-
doms. The feet and toes of the statue are most vulnerable to the shattering stone, yet
also the fissured seedbed of the mountain:

And the fourth kingdom shall be strong as iron; forasmuch as iron breaketh in pieces and
subdueth all things, . . . shall it break in pieces and bruise. And whereas thou sawest the
feet and toes *part of potter's clay* and part of iron, the kingdom shall be divided; . . . partly
strong, and partly broken. And whereas thou sawest iron mixed with miry clay, they shall
mingle themselves with the seed of men [by intermarriage]; but they shall not cleave one
to another [such alliances will not be stable], even as iron is not mixed with clay. (Dan.
2:40–44)

As he read this passage, Palissy must have remembered ways that potters routinely
glazed common clay with iron (iron-based mineral glazes), and indeed how brittle this
mixture was on the finished product. Moreover, Christian historiographers quickly accommodated the fall of the Roman empire to Daniel's metaphoric scheme. St. Jerome
suggested diplomatically that Babylon could be "compared" to gold. He envisioned
Medes and the Persians as silver and Greece as brass. The Romans were iron, which,
like the empire, "breaketh in pieces and subdueth all things." So it followed that the
feet of iron mixed with potter's clay signified the decline and fall of Rome's empire by
internal strife, war, impiety, and barbarian contamination.[52]

The second-century author of Daniel, who suffered under the persecution of the
Jews by Antiochus IV Epiphanes, sought comfort in a prophecy that guaranteed that
earthly tyranny would ultimately succumb to the transience of history. Other parallels
between this author and Palissy's Saintongeais Huguenots run deep. In the fourth
chapter of Daniel, the tyrannical Nebuchadnezzar himself experiences exile after "a
voice from heaven" tells him: "The kingdom has departed from thee," transforming
him into an archetype of medieval and early modern wild men.[53] Nebuchadnezzar is
"driven from men, and did eat grass as oxen, and his body was wet with the dew of
heaven, till his hairs were grown like eagles' feathers, and his nails like birds' claws."
In the end, however, "I Nebuchadnezzar lifted up mine eyes unto heaven, and mine
understanding returned unto me; and I blessed the Most High. . . . the glory of my
kingdom, mine honour and brightness returned unto me . . . and I was established in
my kingdom, and excellent majesty was added unto me. . . . those that walk in pride
he is able to abase" (Dan. 4:31–37).

The author of Daniel represented the temporal tension between history and prophecy in material form for the first time. James Dean writes:

> The Daniel author . . . intends to offer consolation . . . through understanding; the Providential historical perspective—whereby the flux of events is seen as subordinate to the divine will and finally beyond the control of the imperialist persecutors—is in itself a consolation. The Daniel author here puts forward an important interpretation of temporality. So far as I know, he is the first historian to give time a definite *shape*. History is comprehended, as it were, in the limbs of the dream-statue, which takes the form of a man. By visualizing the statue, we can in effect visualize time itself—at least as much of it as the Daniel author chooses to show us. By portraying time *sub specie hominis*, the Daniel author inaugurates a tradition, the history of the world (the macrocosm) with the life of each man (the microcosm). Daniel does not use the terms "microcosm" and "macrocosm." These come up only later. The world, like a man, enjoys its best periods at the beginning of its history; afterward, there is only a decline and ultimately death.[54]

The path of Nebuchadnezzar's powerful dream imagery can be traced through the popular apocalyptic genre and Christian historiography that it evoked until Philippe de Harvengt (d. 1183), abbot of the Premonstratensian Abbey of Bonne-Esperance, Cambrai, Belgium, a contemporary of Joachim of Flora's whose work was of seminal influence. Philippe's great importance lay in the resonance his work created when read with other medieval and subsequent eschatological historiography. Philippe chose to concentrate on the Hebraic tradition encompassed by the six ages of the world (as opposed to Jerome's three) and the dream sequence in Daniel.

Philippe's *De somnis regis Nabochodonosor* made plain the statue's status as a figure of the materiality of time. Because Philippe's was Christian historiography, his discourse focused on Daniel 2:34–35 and the *lapis* "cut out of a mountain without hands" as a figure of Christ immaculately conceived. The stone, according to the author of Daniel, would finally break the statue and "become a great mountain [that] filled the whole earth." Philippe rejected the series of empires traditionally associated with Nebuchadnezzar's dream—Babylonians, Medes, Greeks, Romans, and even the Frankish, or Holy Roman, empire—and substituted his own interpretation of the statue based on materials and anatomical features. His material analysis broke its body down into six world ages:

1. Gold (Adam-Noah): head
2. Silver (Noah-Abraham): breast
3. Brass (Abraham-Moses): arms
4. Iron (Moses-David): belly

5. Iron and Clay (David-Christ): thighs
6. Stone: *lapis* (time of Christ): legs

Ages one through four generally repeated the theme of decline from pure to impure materials, though in an often unclear or contradictory manner in Philippe's schema.[55]

By the fifth age, Philippe's stake in the new interpretation becomes clearer. Just as iron and clay cannot combine successfully, so too Jews and Gentiles. In a variant that would not have been lost on sixteenth-century readers of *De somnis*, Philippe interpreted Nebuchadnezzar's statue with feet of iron mixed with clay as a time "that is future." Jews were not mentioned. The prophesy read only that "the man of this last age will not be able to be contained in the one bosom of holy Church." By the sixth age of stone, Philippe's apocalyptic vision is focused:

> Christ, the stone cut from the mountain without hands . . . smashes the whole statue, which Philippe now glosses as "the glory of this world that is base and contemptible." Christ destroys the statue by replacing the world's glory with spiritual poverty. "For when He told His disciples: 'Blessed are the poor in spirit: for theirs is the kingdom of Heaven'" (Matt 5:3), He placed spiritual poverty before gold, silver, brass, iron, and all the wealth of this world."

The age of stone, or Christ, thus replaced all the preceding eras of more sensuous and splendid materials devoid of spirit. Philippe would only regret the passing of the golden age, an age of natural law when man could still know God through the light of Nature: "For as gold has no color except its natural hue, so the men of the first age had no law by which they might know God except the natural law."[56]

There is no direct evidence that Palissy knew *De somnis*, but the potter would have been most sympathetic to the leveling of the statue with the stone of Christ and "replacing the world's glory with spiritual poverty." There can be no doubt, however, that Palissy knew the dream of Nebuchadnezzar and reformulated it to fit the purifying eschatological program of Paracelsian artisanry:

> All earths can become clays. . . . All clays are the beginning of rock. . . . If rocks did not exist, there would be no mountains. . . . The material of all rocks, both the common and the rare and precious ones, is crystalline and diaphanous. . . . If the main material of all rocks were not a pure and transparent water, diamond, crystal, emeralds, rubies and garnet could never exist, nor could any diaphanous rocks. . . . There are very few things in this world which cannot be made transparent by art.[57]

Palissy thus assumed the chiliastic role of "Elias Artista" and worked to wrest an artisan's millennium from the decline of the aging earth, *incrementally* separating pure from impure matter "by art." The move here was from "earth" and "clay" to the highest form of matter with "crystalline . . . diaphanous . . . transparent" attributes, suggesting the artisanal conjunction of the macrocosm (glaze) and microcosm (clay) formed as a ceramic pot. It followed that such a process could be realized prematurely in history, both by potters in their kilns and through alchemic distillation. According to Paracelsus:

> Nothing has been created as *ultima materia*—in its final state. Everything is at first created in its *prima materia,* its original stuff; whereupon Vulcan comes, and by the art of alchemy develops it to its final substance. . . . For alchemy means: *to carry to its end something that has not yet been completed* [emphasis added]. To obtain the lead from the ore and to transform it into what it is made for. . . . Accordingly, you should understand that *alchemy is nothing but the art which makes the impure into the pure through fire.* It can separate the useful from the useless, transmute it into its final substance and its ultimate essence.[58]

Palissy cautioned, regarding the purification of matter by fire, that "all those who seek to generate metals by fire, wish to build with the destroyer."[59] Yet he knew also that the history of Saintonge was a trial by fire ordained by Providence, which to purify ultimately required the violence and "esmotions" from which he separated himself and hid in terror. Just as Palissy's concept of artisanal *sûreté* allowed him to survive by inhabiting the disguise of the last humble creature of the earth moving imperceptibly among the blasted limestone ruins of his culture, so too the purification of humble "rocks" and "potter's clay"—the last, quintessentially *Christic* remnants of the "aging earth"—would also require that he "build with the destroyer."

❧ Disinterment ❧

> And there he told the whole history; but especially how the water-spirits had brought back those stones that I had cast into the lake, in the midst of the thunderstorm, and had lain them where they came from, but in exchange had taken me down with them. So some believed him but most accounted it a fable. —H. J. C. VON GRIMMELSHAUSEN, *The Adventurous Simplicissimus,* "How Simplicissimus Journeyed with the Sylphs to the Center of the Earth"

How did Paracelsians practice a geology in which the pursuit and disinterment of diaphanous stones, and understanding of their growth in Saintonge, was a precondition for Huguenot millennial artisanry?[60] Like the Charente River, which had its own local "diction," Palissy argued, geology was completely site-specific. The geology of Saintonge, therefore, was specific only to what was hidden beneath the ground in Saintonge and its peculiar earth history: "in some places she [the earth] produces Coal which is very useful, in other places it conceives and gives birth to iron, silver, lead, pewter, gold, marble, jasper, and all kinds of minerals, and kinds of clays, and in many places it will engender and produce bitumen, which is a kind of oleaginous gum that burns like resin." While each particular region produced varied "species" of stones, the embryonic growing process was universal "within the matrix of the earth," where all were "built up by heat from the fire."[61]

Palissy carefully documents this fecund process of insemination, change, and growth in Mother Earth to repudiate the Mosaic philosophers for whom she had remained unchanged (Palissy uses the word "ossified") since the Creation. His most compelling argument against this ossification concerned his close observation of fossilized shells:

> Many times I have found stones, which can be broken anywhere; similarly there are shells that are hard as rocks. . . .
>
> . . . For a few days I admired and contemplated them, but my spirit was tormented and debated the process and cause of this. And on a day that I was on the island of Xaintonge, on my way from Marennes to La Rochelle, I caught sight of a freshly cut pit from which had been dug over 100 carts of stones, which, anywhere you broke them, were full of shells, so near to each other that you could not have put the edge of a knife between them without touching them: . . .
>
> . . . from then on I lowered my head as I walked down the road so that I could not see anything that would have prevented me from imagining what could be the cause of this: and while my mind was working on this, I thought, and I still believe it now, and I'm sure that it's true, that near the pit, there once were houses, and that those who lived there, after having eaten the fish that were in the shells, threw the shells away in this valley where the pit was located, and as time went by, these shells dissolved into the earth, and also the earth of this quagmire was modified, the dirt rotted and reduced into fine earth like a clay: that is how these shells were dissolved and liquefied and the substance and virtue of their salt was attracted by the earth around it and reduced it into a stone with itself and in itself, every time, because these shells contained more salt in themselves than they give up to the earth, this [new] stone jelled even harder than the earth: but one and the other became a stone without these shells losing their form. This is the cause that since then has led me to imagine and nourish my spirit with many secrets of Nature.[62]

Palissy's discourse on fossilized shells discovered on a walk between Marennes and La Rochelle exemplifies his ability to combine (in fieldwork and natural observation) the Neoplatonic structures revealed at the river with Paracelsian eschatological structures of gradual organic growth toward separation and purification. Palissy often found stones that were a "bit broken" (*peu rompre*), with little shells "reduced . . . into a stone with itself and in itself" inside them. How had this transmutation come about? As at

FIGURE 7.2. *Conjunctio sive coitus*, in *Rosarium philosophorum* (Frankfurt: Ex officina Cyriaci Iacobi, 1550). Courtesy Harry Ransom Humanities Research Center, The University of Texas at Austin. The conjunction of astral opposites (sun and moon) as the sexual union of monarchs.

the river, he says, "my spirit was tormented and debated the process and cause of this." Then, on the way to La Rochelle, in the "freshly cut pit," he discovered a kind of incision into the matrix of the earth in the process of growing embryonic stones, analogous to a telluric cesarean section. Peering down into the hole, he found that digging had disinterred numerous stones that also contained shells. This discovery sent him off on another walk, lowering his head and turning inside himself to look into his soul, "so that I could not see anything that would have prevented me from imagining what could be the cause of this."

By purification in the earth's matrix, he reasoned, impurities were separated out and returned to the earth, which absorbed them as potter's clay, a process analogous to the alchemical operation called putrefaction. Matter had to be putrefied (made "rotten") before it could be purified. Earth's matrix functioned as a pottery kiln to harden the clay into a more perfect (or millennially advanced) material (stone), just as a potter fired glazed ceramics.

At this point in the process, "these shells were dissolved and liquefied and the substance and virtue of their salt was attracted by the earth around it." Thus the salt's astral properties served to congeal new earth to the now distilled shell in a liquid state "and reduced it into a stone." "This new stone jelled even harder than the earth: but one and the other became a stone without these shells losing their form." The "new stones" had congealed from the interaction of distilled liquid and surrounding earth in the matrix because they "contained more salt in themselves, than they give up" in their marriage (*conjunctio*) to the earth and thus retained more of the astral spirit's "secrets" of form production. The more salt earth matter contained, the harder (and purer) its properties.

By his discovery that these artisanal processes in the matrix worked by spiritual and alchemic means, Palissy established that God had intended the earth to change (and grow old) since Genesis, because the shells must have fossilized and been embedded in the stones in the pit *after* creation. Questions of how Palissy's purified shells may be related conceptually to shells of *sûreté* are inevitable, as is the relation of the tiny shelled creatures who were consumed and discarded "near this valley," only to be remade while hidden in the Saintonge earth as permanent versions of their former selves. This posture of hiding in the rocks was also revealed as waiting without "losing their form."

Conjunctio meant that the earth possessed masculine qualities in combination with its maternal ones. In effect, it could, in this way assume both feminine (moon) and masculine (sun) attributes simultaneously. The androgynous qualities of the hermaphrodite were ubiquitous in the alchemic literature on *conjunctio* (see, e.g., fig. 7.2), and both masculine and feminine readings are fundamental to the verb *travailler*.[63] If Palissy met resistance to his observation that the birth given by the earth to "these stones was natural," not artificial, it came from men "of letters." A "lawyer by the name of Babaud, . . . a famous man," was "really astonished," and maintained "that these stones were carved by the hand of some Artisan." Yet in response to such scholastic skepticism, Palissy simply replied that he had "found" not only shells but also "the bones of men sealed in the stones. . . . Isn't that fine proof that the stones grew in the earth?"[64] The earth "sealed" and "grew" new "bodies" around the bones of dead men.

Palissy's geology of diaphanous stones began with his notion that water as well as salt was a principal element of separation in the alchemical chart of materials, and that this combination was also a principal element in the generation of stones: "all of the water that passes through earths converts into stone, but only in part." As in the case of fossilized shells, salt acted as the main agent of congelation between water and earth, such that the resulting stones contained "no water inside." "The water that was joined with the salt of the earth," Palissy argued, and by using a phrase associated with God's chosen people, he gave new meaning to his conclusion that this "was evaporated by the violence of the fire, and the other parts were permanently dried up."[65]

As a result of this process, some stones became harder than others and separated out, while the rest were congealed into dense, amorphous, and soft lime, or limestone. The most important variable affecting these differences in hardness was duration of time in the fire and compression of the matrix: "in stones that were made for a very long time, the water and the other parts are so well united that it is impossible to make lime out of them, because their state of congelation is more perfect . . . but stones that are good for lime, they have not congealed and firmed up for very long."[66]

Other determining factors were the quality of the water, earths, and salts used in the formation of stones, if their shape allowed water to pool in them, and the depth at which raw materials entered the earth's matrix. Palissy's analysis of water and rocks occurring in and around natural springs and fountains made this point, while suggesting the relation between rock vessels and rustic pottery:

> Rocks were used as vessels and receptacles for those waters: for otherwise, the waters would descend to the abyss or the center of the earth . . . from the rocks and mountainous places many beautiful fountains give forth: and the most beautiful ones come from the furthest places, as they go in and out of good earth, these waters will be made healthy and purified and of good taste. At the beginning, the waters that come from these rocks are more salty and taste better than the others, because each day they attract a bit of the salt of these rocks.[67]

Having established the principles behind the growth of common rocks in the bowels of the earth, Palissy then turned to the cause of diaphanous stones, applying evidence from the observation of craft processes to his observations of the cause of diaphanous materials grown in the natural matrix. He drew upon his experience as a painter in glasshouses. The artificial matrix was the glassmaker's furnace and the crucial agent of congelation was again salt. However, here, stones already grown in the earth were processed further and transformed; in effect, grown again by human hands through the process of liquefaction and congelation: "Have you ever seen glass being made in which there is no salt? Have you ever seen anybody who knows how to melt or liquify stones without salt?" Palissy then proceeded to reveal the process by which salt was used to make glass:

> It is necessary in order to liquefy stones that one put some kind of salt [in with them]: the best one for this is salicor [*salicorne (christe-marine)*] and the next best is salt of tartar [cream of tartar (potassium tartrate)] . . . when it is put in a very hot furnace, like the furnaces in which you make lime of glass or any other such furnaces, in which the fire is extremely violent, these stones become vitrified by themselves, without any mixing, which proves notably that the stones carry in themselves a great quantity of salt, which causes them to vitrify, seeing that the salt that is inside them holds tight together the other matters . . . which in stones are fixed and inseparable . . . the moisture of the lime will evaporate in the fire, but when there is salt in that stone, I wouldn't say it evaporates, but that it dissolves . . . that is why the most beautiful glass is made of salt and stones: Now then it is fixed as much as the matter of this world, as I told you: however, it is transparent, which is an evident sign and appearance that there is little earth [in it] . . . we can say that there is not much else than water and salt and very little earth: for the earth is not diaphanous by itself, and if there was a quantity of it, the glass could not be transparent.[68]

Exactly replicating Palissy's vision of the growth taking place in the earth underfoot, the glassmaker transformed and purified matter for use in homes and churches. For Palissy, the production of glass in an "extremely violent" furnace was thus a prime example of Paracelsian artisanry.[69] The practical function of glass could not be separated from its spiritual material, even in domestic settings.

Protestant artisans and alchemists possessed the "industriousness" to speed the growth of stones, in the violence of a fiery furnace, to a much later stage in their eschatological and material progression toward ultimate purification. Palissy's example, the glassmaker, liquefied stones and combined them with salt in a furnace. Though all stones possessed salts, or else their watery generating element would not congeal with elements in nearby earths, these would also be "exhaled" during the firing process. So it became necessary for the artisan to extract and then provide "salicor" or "sel de tartar" to serve as the active agent of congelation. The principal function of the artisan then, was to intervene as God's intermediary with the earth to effect congelation between materials.

"The most beautiful glass," resulted from a sort of martyrdom of earth matter in the most violent separating and purifying action of the furnace. When finally congealed, the purest liquids were crystallized and "made transparent, which," for Palissy, "is sign and clear appearance that there remains not a bit of earth . . . *of this world.*" This notion of the diaphanous was shared by Böhme, who imagined that transparency was manifested in the microcosm by a material akin to ceramic glaze: "the sweet quality is a thin or transparent lovely *pleasant* sweet fountain or spring-water." The water survived the furnace, as "it allayeth the heat, and *quencheth* the fire, . . . so there remaineth, only the *joyful* light." This glaze of water and light originated in God before the Fall, before there were earth and stones: "Before the Times of the Creation He sate [sat] in the *Salitter* of the Earth, when it was yet Thin or Transparent, and stood in a heavenly holy Birth or Geniture, and was in the *whole* Kingdom of this world, therein it was neither Earth nor Stones, but a heavenly *Seed,* which was generated out of the . . . fountain spirits of Nature."[70]

The glassmaker's craft, as well as the production of ceramic glaze—because these artisanal materials were the least "of this world"—were understood to be most advanced in the direction of a chemical millennium. Macrocosm and microcosm were here conjoined such that transparency preponderated and there was "little else but water and salt, and very little earth. "For earth," Palissy wrote, was full of fallen matter, so "is not diaphanous in itself, and if there is any quantity in it, glass cannot be transparent." Transparency and diaphanousness, then, were prelapsarian unity materialized by work.

The earth also labored to separate diaphanous material in its matrix, and Palissy searched both above and below the Saintongeais landscape to find geological evidence of evolution of the microcosm toward separation and purification. Palissy's research into the formation and generation of geodes became, for him, a crucial type of historical research and an indirect commentary on the historical relationship between outer and inner bodies: "In this country of Xaintonge, we have a great quantity of marshland, in which one can find a number of stones, which are newly formed every year in the earth, and they are well-horned and knotty, and unsightly on the outside, but inside they are white and crystalline, very pleasant, and right for making glass and artificial stones."[71] One can extend this clear analogy between these geodes and Palissy's language, which though inelegant (*mal orné*) conveyed truths, to the southwestern Huguenot artisan's history of disguise as *sûreté* and Palissy's social and scientific program. In all facets of southwestern Huguenot artisanal culture, a naturalistic exterior that reflected the violent assaults of war masked the growth of internal purification, which augmented daily, almost in dialectical relation to scarring on the surface. Only "extreme violence" produced diaphanousness.

The growth of these crystalline structures inside the matrix of the geode was explained sexually as well, beginning with Palissy's understanding of the earth's insemination by a solution of salt and rain water: "there will be a certain kind of rain that will take away the salt of the earth and of the herbs that had rotted in the fields: and so the water will run along the furrows of the field, [where] it will find the hole of a mole or mouse, or [some] other animal, and the water will enter in that hole." A seminal liquid penetrated the earth's corpuscular surface through an animal hole; that part of the landscape was impregnated, and an embryonic "rock" was conceived and grown: "The salt that it will have brought will take what it needs from the earth and from the water, and according to the size of the hole and of the matter, it will congeal into a stone, or pebble as I have told you . . . which will be knobbly and knotty, and unsightly, according to the form of the place where it was congealed."[72]

Once again, Palissy was "tormented and debated the process and cause of this." He discovered that if he dissolved a quantity of saltpeter—potassium nitrate (KNO_3), which occurred naturally and was commonly used in gunpowder and fireworks—in water and boiled the water away in a huge caldron, "cubes of saltpeter. . . formed into a most pleasing [pattern of] grids and points" once the caldron had cooled down. Distilled saltpeter was well known to alchemists, and Böhme, among many other Paracelsians, later speculated that saltpeter was the principal material manifestation of the astral spirit in the microcosm.[73] Palissy was a proponent of this alchemical thesis, as he made clear in his conclusions about the cause of the crystals "like little diamond points" that appeared in the interiors of rocks found near the salt marshes:

> What did I consider in my spirit then, I saw that the pebbles of which I spoke to you were also congealed: but those that were massive were a sign and evident proof that there was enough matter to fill up the pit, and that those that were hollow showed that there was a superfluity of water, which had dried out while the congelation happened in the other parts: and when the central humidity dried out, the matter proper to the pebble stayed firm and congealed from the inside like little diamond points.[74]

Palissy's description of the geode remains the quintessential geological representation of the Paracelsian Huguenot artisan's understanding of the chemical millennium. In slow, incremental progress toward the culmination of the natural history of Saintonge, as the light of Palissy's soul augmented inside his persecuted and corruptible body, the light of nature sparkled clandestinely, emitting "little diamond points," which lay waiting sealed in the stones of Saintonge. Palissy's millennium could not be quantified, prophesied to arrive in an exact number of days. His was a *subterranean* millennium in every sense of the term, wherein Protestant artisans could understand the passage of time materially. For "signs and proofs" of material history, Huguenot artisans would be forced to turn inward, away from exposed surfaces and the artificiality of calendrical time and toward the inner sight of millennial experience. Only after intense introspection could an artisan hope to construct what he had seen.

Palissy's signs and proofs were given a very specific optical language. That language was encapsulated in his description of a "crystal ball" once in his laboratory:

Once I had a crystal ball, which was neat, round and well-polished: when I held it up to the light, I perceived certain sparks, within this crystal, afterward, I would take a vial full of clear water, and would also see little sparks similar to that of the crystal. I also took a piece of ice, and held it up to the light, and similarly, I perceived little and big sparks.[75]

It was now possible to add "little flashes and sparks" to the "grid and points" and "diamond points" to complete Palissy's small but precise vocabulary of descriptions for the spirit's appearance in the rustic artisan's soul as the light of Nature. This language communicated that the material-mind and material-holiness synthesis hidden in these stones was also grounded in refugee history: "this gave me occasion to understand and know that all transparent stones are for the most part airy, and the more airy they are, the more valiantly they resist the fire."[76]

That was another reason why the twelve oldest, hardest, and most diaphanous stones grown in the earth's matrix—above all, "Jasper . . . Topaz . . . Emerald . . . Turquoise . . . Saphire . . . [and] Diamond"—were "figures" for the twelve "foundations" of the "everlasting" city of New Jerusalem in Revelation (15–22); a city so enormous that once it emerged, it would fill the whole world.

QUESTION asked: Since you have been looking for a way to understand stones and pebbles, and the effect of their essence, could you give me some reason, for the twelve rare stones, which Saint John in his Apocalypse uses as a figure of the twelve foundations of the Holy City of Jerusalem? For one must understand that the twelve stones are hard and insoluble since Saint John takes them to represent an everlasting building.[77]

In response, Palissy repeated his understanding of the cause of such diaphanous stones. They were derived from the congelation of purified ancient earths, salts, and waters and subjected to heat of "extreme violence" for long periods of time. To account for the colors, Palissy, in effect, offered his recipes for ceramic glazes:

Topaz is a water, which also has passed through an iron mine, in which it took its yellow color, and from this comes the metallic substance that gives it more hardness . . . the Emerald is a very neat water, which has passed through brass mines or *coupe-rose* from which brass is made, and that is where it took its color of glass, and the salt that caused its congelation: for the said *coupe-rose* is nothing else than salt. . . . The diamond is as much a water as a crystal; but it is congealed by some rare kind of salt, pure and clean. . . . Thus jewelers say: "There is a diamond that has a beautiful water."[78]

Hence, the transparent stones in the foundation of the colossal "everlasting building" of New Jerusalem were merged with Palissy's glazes as he set his millennial vision of the tiny, hidden, and overlooked to work.

Subterranean matter dug up from the Saintonge *désert* fought "valiantly" against the violent flames to find its reward in pure transparency and was not far removed from Palissy's personal history and from his history of the Church of Saintes. Just as each rock recorded its own history in gradations of light and color, so, too, Palissy's progression toward the artisan's millennium was materialized as pottery glazes disinterred from the Saintongeais earth: "Sometimes I searched for pebbles to make enamel glazes and artificial stones: now then, after having assembled a great number of pebbles and wanting to pound them up, I would find many that were hollow inside; there were certain points like those of a diamond, glistening, transparent, and very beautiful."[79]

Palissy's millennial glazes showed a profound continuity between the histories of subterranean Saintonge and its "rotting" outer shell beset by demonic forces. His task as a potter became to shatter the barriers between these exterior and interior bodies, disinter Nature's light from below, and set it perpetually into his work.

What better way to subvert and overcome written history than from below, with an *artisanal* history of the earth where, as the millennium approached, oral traditions and natural sounds could not be "choked" by absolutism; natural language retained primacy and endured as an "everlasting building"; and historical truth became ever more visible over time as it crystallized to surround artifacts of the history of the millennium in progress, left behind by long-dead artisans as evidence of their faith and hope. Thus we can return to Palissy's rustic basins with new understanding.

Viewed in cross section, as in figure 8.8, the most frequently used shape of these basins suggests a geode split in two. A slice of the living earth beneath Palissy's feet has been excavated. All the elements of Palissy's artisanal consciousness are present: earth (clay); salts (in the tiny creatures, stones, and plants); and the standing and running water—the principal element of separation and regeneration. His colors followed the spectrum of the stones of New Jerusalem, and they often proceed from astral white (shellfish and water) in the middle toward the outer edge, where green generally predominates. Fire was implicit, hidden in the firing of the dish and the Saintongeais ground. The uneven surface of the interior, split with rocks and eddies for water, sparkled and glittered in the light. Here is the natural spring whence pure waters sink back into the matrix of the earth to congeal with salt and generate diaphanous stones.

What of the tiny "industrious" creatures crawling or swimming among the flora: snails, snakes, lizards, tortoises, crabs, insects, crayfish, amphibians? All were capable of metamorphosis, like the *désert* Huguenots or, indeed, like earths in the ceramic process. All were by nature small, secretive, ambiguous, dualistic creatures, and most were at home in more than one element. Although exposed, they were capable of quickly returning to the safety of their alternate element, be it water, air, a hole in the earth, or, in the case of the salamander, fire. There they could hide in safety from larger creatures and each tend to their inner lives.

But these tiny creatures perpetually at work on (and in) the marshes also once lived in reality. Palissy pioneered the use of direct casting techniques in France. Like the ideas of Luther and Paracelsus, this knowledge was diffused to rural France from similar sixteenth-century German bronze-casting traditions.[80] The direct cast substituted the body of a plant or animal to be cast in a mold for the traditional wax, which was then "burned out" and replaced by molten metal, an exact positive image of the disintegrated body left after cooling. Adapting this process for ceramics, Palissy pulled his molds from the dead bodies of his tiny creatures, making them permanent. Their former bodies endured in clay, their spirits worn inside out on their backs. The little creatures were perpetually glazed with "little flashes and sparks" as they appeared to push their way up from the matrix of the earth to emerge on its surface inseparable from— or intermediary *between* the elements of—its matrix-surface continuum.

Turning the basin so that its sparkling "inside" is down to follow the topographical "horns" and "knots" of its underside (the "unattractive" surface), it is clear from the negative space articulated between them that this was precisely what Palissy had in mind. Palissy's ceramic earths thus communicated the credo of the Saintongeais Huguenot artisan after the first war of religion had decimated the region. There were permanent possibilities lying latent in each tiny, vulnerable, transitory life on earth. These secret possibilities were the ultimate *sûreté*.

Yet within the scope of Palissy's materiality of time, the universal synthesis of the millennium would be a long time coming. At that moment of ultimate distillation, the difference between macrocosm and microcosm would dissolve, the artisan's shells of *sûreté* would disappear, and the "sparks" of Palissy's glazes would be transformed into an intense, uninterrupted light. Until that moment, however, the southwestern Huguenot artisan had to labor inwardly and "industriously" to separate and perfect himself and his world, leaving traces of his inner salvation in his work. He needed to cultivate the habit of waiting. For each artisan, however, the Paracelsian chemical (or artisanal) millennium personalized and made intimate his own eschatology of waiting.

Hillel Schwartz observes that the southeastern Huguenot community of Cévenol prophets exiled in London did not become disillusioned with their theatrical millennial tradition until as late as 1730, when they were guided in the Continental roots of the southwestern tradition by Hannah Wharton and Ann Lee:

> In the 1730s [the French Prophets] had given up this desire for a public sign of victory and sought instead to renew the group internally. . . . In the 1730s, influenced by quietist and pietist ideas, they knew that waiting was the root metaphor for all religious experience. Continental religious forces had guided the French prophets to a new understanding of the millennial timetable. Accustomed to a ritual waiting in worship, to a slow internship through the stages of illumination, to images of growth rather than cataclysm, they coordinate the millennium with internal rather than external events.[81]

These same "Continental religious forces" had taught southwestern Huguenot artisans the eschatology of waiting as early as the 1540s. The southeastern prophetic tradition disintegrated in London in the 1730s, the victim of its program of frontal assault against forces that were too powerful to subdue with arms or the bombastic language of imminent apocalypse. By that time, however, southwestern Huguenot artisans, in places as far from Saintes and La Rochelle as New York Colony, were employing strategies of waiting that had been implemented successfully against dominant cultures in their home region for almost two centuries.

CHAPTER EIGHT

The Art of the Earth

"And you," she said to her youngest son, "what have you brought me?"

The prince then took the nut from his pocket. This caused the entire assembly to break out in laughter. But the queen had already cracked open the shell and found a silk gown of indescribable fineness and color hidden inside.

"To you my kingdom," said she, "but on one condition, you must tell me who made this gift."

—"The Prince and the Frog," or "The Tower of Broue,"
a traditional Saintongeais folktale

The near absence of an authentic, continuous oral tradition, which logic dictates should survive in some form from the sixteenth century, is a remarkable feature of southwestern France's artisanal history. This curiosity was compounded when, in 1971, a government-sponsored archaeological team headed by Jean Chapelot of the École pratique des hautes études arrived in the region to begin an intensive investigation of medieval and early modern Saintongeais kiln sites, potters, and pottery.[1] Until 1971, these humble artisans and their production had only been superficially investigated by early twentieth-century British antiquarians, interested primarily in certain narrow aspects of pottery diffusion along La Rochelle's Atlantic trade network with England, starting around the thirteenth century.[2] Chapelot, however, was concerned with diffusion to the North American market, where Saintongeais pottery has consistently been found in significant quantities at early modern archeological sites.[3]

Saintongeais pottery was produced at more than twenty-nine kiln sites between the twelfth and eighteenth centuries, which Chapelot's team unearthed at nine towns in an arc around Saintes: La Chapelle-des-Pots (with the earliest, most renowned sites);

Ecoyeux, Brizambourg; Venerand; Saint-Cézaire; Fontcouvert, Le Douhet; Saint-Bris-des-Bois; and Chaniers.[4]

Polychrome shards discovered at these sites suggest that the kilns were in continuous operation from the twelfth century—with a decline during the war years of the late sixteenth and early seventeenth centuries—until the last traditional *atelier* (built ca. 1857), which belonging to the potter Philippe Machefer, ceased operations at the tiny hamlet called Chez Lorin (Venerand) in 1925.[5] Ten medieval and eighteen eighteenth-century kiln sites were found, but only three can be verified for the anarchic sixteenth and early seventeenth centuries, all three at La Chapelle-des-Pots, where Palissy claimed he was picking up potter's clay in March 1563 when the Catholic church in Saintes was being vandalized by heretics.

Chapelot's modern Saintongeais informants, hindered by a dim understanding of the intense violence of their region's religious and artisanal history, exhibited almost *no* authentic local memory going very far back:

> It is difficult to hope to get, from local informants, oral data going back further than the second generation of their ancestors. It is very awkward for an archaeologist in this particular region to deal with a memory that is still alive, though distorted most of the time, of regional ceramic activity, despite the fact that it has ceased to exist for at least two generations. The answers lead systematically toward the most recent vestiges or are narrowly conditioned by a local mythology of a "savant" origin founded on "memories" and the "tradition" of Bernard Palissy. Because of these two aspects, recent memories of the *artisanat* [and] Palissian "mythology," it is very difficult, even more difficult than elsewhere, to obtain commonplace information such as, for example, that inevitably given by a plowman or a winegrower [as to] whether any archeological vestiges exist in their fields.[6]

It is fascinating that Chapelot's quest for oral testimony about commonplace details should have proven so unproductive, especially because the majority of his informants were small landowners working an agrarian landscape, where contours have changed little since medieval times. One might suppose that in such a milieu, the "average" farmer or winegrower would have formed a quite specific (almost genealogical) mental map of the history of his domains and probably those of his near neighbors as well. However, Chapelot's team could obtain information about only two generations, remarkable in comparison with the long memory of informants elsewhere in France under apparently similar conditions. Huguenot informants from southeastern France, in the oral tradition of ten generations of ancestors, have long been actively engaged in the revision of official historiography to correspond more closely with the Camisard saga of the civil wars.

To be sure, commonplace details are the foundation of Chapelot's discipline, yet he is perhaps too dismissive of "local mythology" as a mnemonic "distortion." One task of archeology is to define boundaries between history and myth with precise empirical markers. Unfortunately, such boundaries are blurred as they emerge from Saintongeais popular memory. For Chapelot, the "narrowness" of "Palissian 'mythology'" has reduced Saintongeais oral testimony to mere rhetoric and childlike repetition—"'savant'. . . 'memories'. . . 'tradition'"—of no practical value to archeologists. Chapelot thus fell into the trap of mystification. He conflated cause with effect.

It was not just mythology or a failure of long-term memory but rather war, demography, geography, and migration that caused the responses that misled him. The vast majority of Saintongeais Huguenot artisans (potters included) had emigrated from the southwest by 1730, and precious few Protestant families remained in the region to remember the early years of ceramic production in the Charente River Valley.

Although isolated on land, southwestern Huguenot culture was molded by its proximity to the Atlantic trade routes. Whether they were wealthy Rochelais merchant-shipowners or common potters producing ceramics for export, all Huguenots were tied together by this overarching oceangoing mercantile commerce. When, by 1685, the Revocation of the Edict of Nantes made life for Huguenots unsupportable, the structures of escape for the Saintongeais were already firmly established. The region's Huguenot artisans took their oral history with them when they left, diffusing centrifugally from France. By the time of the French Revolution, the most coherent vestiges of southwestern Huguenot culture could be located in the centers of refuge in northern Europe, Dutch South Africa, and British North America.

Not so for the southeastern Huguenots. The Camisards' was a centripetal *mountain* culture with limited access for dispersion en masse to the larger Protestant world. While a number of "prophets" and others from that region made it to London and elsewhere, the majority of southeastern Huguenots could not escape France in the way common Saintongeais artisans were able to do. Perhaps because they could escape by sea to join a network of family members already in place in new host countries, southwestern Huguenots were more susceptible to an eschatology of waiting. They could afford to be patient. In the absence of such a safety valve, southeastern Huguenots, isolated in a pressure cooker of war from which they saw no real escape except martyrdom, might naturally have adopted the millennial tradition of imminent apocalypse. Unlike the southwestern Huguenots, then, the southeastern "tribes" stayed in their region in great numbers, where they cultivated a sophisticated oral tradition beginning in the war years of the sixteenth century.

That is why the great weakness of Chapelot's otherwise valuable study lies in his inability to document the confessional allegiance of Saintongeais artisans. In most cases, however, the documents that survive in the region are unyielding on this subject. Predictably, the best information Chapelot has yet been able to uncover about the religion of one of his potters, Jean Aumier, was found in Québec, where the name of

Aumier (or Houlmier or Osmier) appears in archives beginning in May 1676, when he entered into partnership with a brick maker named Jean Vivien. In another document dated November 30, 1676, Aumier is referred to as a "maître-potier" and the son of Jean Houlmier of Escoyeux, also a "maître-potier de terre." This sent Chapelot back to the archives of Ecoyeux, where, in a document dated 1653, he discovered Jean Hommier (probably the father), a Calvinist who abjured his religion for Catholicism.[7] The specific context of Hommier's abjuration is unknown. That he did so was possibly linked to his decision to emigrate to New France. Had he gone to Britain or colonial America, he would certainly have remained an overt Protestant. But the larger point is made. Following what we know from Palissy's history, this brief biography of Aumier and others indicates that a great many, perhaps the majority, of these Saintongeais potters began their lives as Protestants. When they left the southwest in the sixteenth and seventeenth centuries, however, there remained only a dwindling number of examples of their pottery (many examples of which are also to be found in museums in the host countries of the diaspora) and, whether Chapelot accepts it or not, what Palissy tells us in his books.

That is why the catechistic oral style Chapelot recorded is perhaps more indicative of a commonly shared grammar or parochial school rhetoric. This rhetoric is based upon mnemonic repetition of certain appropriate themes and key phrases common to the education of a French *écolier* rather than local oral history surviving in living memory. This is particularly true of the so-called Palissian myth. What Chapelot heard was likely the result of a regional revival of interest in Palissy's writings beginning with the reprinting of his *Oeuvres complètes* in 1844 and 1880, two centuries after the dispersion. Following the final eighteenth-century edition of his works in 1777, the potter was forgotten locally for almost one hundred years. The 1880 Charavay edition, with an introduction by Anatole France, inspired a popular one-act play in French verse by Eugène Brieux (1880), which has been taught to southwestern schoolchildren ever since.[8] Palissy's ascension as a local cultural hero was a nineteenth- and early twentieth-century phenomenon.

Local memory of regional material culture in general and of Saintongeais pottery specifically runs a roughly parallel course. On Christmas 1924, the popular journal of regional French folklore and material culture *La Vie à la Campagne* produced a special issue on the houses and furniture of southwestern France, in which even passing mention of Saintongeais pottery was conspicuously absent.[9] This particular issue was also the first publication of any kind to include a systematic discussion of Saintongeais regional house types and furniture. Local memory of indigenous pottery and craftsmen in general was reconstructed as late as the 1930s, partly as a result of the rise of fascism and regional interest in folkloric subjects in France as well as Germany, but primarily because of British interest. In 1933, the influential British antiquarian journal *Archaeologia* published an article by G. C. Dunning in which he reported the discovery of curious green-glazed and polychrome pottery dug from sites scattered about medieval London, as well as from contemporary rubbish trenches in the foundations of a gatehouse at Kidwelly Castle, Carmathenshire, South Wales.[10] Dunning concluded that London was only a transshipment point for this pottery. In a call for future research, he wrote.

> This is as far as we can carry the problem at present. . . . The manufacture of these somewhere in southern France seems probable; it will be observed, moreover, that their distribution in Britain favors Bordeaux or some adjacent port as the place of shipment. Research in the museums of southern France and, it may be added, those towns in Ireland reached by the Medieval wine trade, is clearly indicated as likely to produce definite results.[11]

Following up quickly on Dunning's pathbreaking research, British colleagues and archaeologists from all of La Rochelle's early modern trading partners soon discovered that the "local" pottery in their museums had originated in the towns around Saintes, and they began to map its diffusion to the north and west, out into the Atlantic world. As with so much of the history of southwestern France, its material culture was not defined by itself but by others. Neither mythology nor distorted memory was the cause of the "narrow" oral history of Saintonge; rather, Chapelot's peasant informants were indirectly communicating that the vestiges he sought were remnants of an alien culture, discontinuous with their own. That was why they did not remember.

❧ The "earthen cup" ❧

Of all the many "Palissian myths" that burdened Chapelot's research, the one he undoubtedly endured most often involved the story still taught to schoolchildren from La Rochelle to Bordeaux: how Bernard Palissy used his furniture and floorboards to feed his kiln while searching for the secret of the elusive white glaze.[12] This particularly dramatic scene was taken from Palissy's most important contribution to the literature of Paracelsian artisanry, his essay "On the Art of the Earth, its Usefulness, On Enamels and Fire," first published in his *Discours admirables* in 1580.

This essay has been commented upon by decorative arts scholars concerned with the potter's shop practices, methodology, and the geographic origin of the faience cup that obsessed him. Palissy biographers have extracted one or another vivid scene to humanize their accounts of the potter's apparently unhappy personal life. And, of course, modern schoolteachers in the Charente River Valley use the essay didactically, to educate their young students about the importance of personal sacrifice to achieve a greater goal. But none of the Palissy literature analyzes the essay as a revelation of his apprenticeship as a Paracelsian artisan, an adaptation and extension of traditional accounts of alchemic initiation rites, or as a commentary from the rustic periphery on the skilled craftsman's concept of spiritual honor.

The essay is structured as a dialogue between Theory and Practice, a form Palissy employs throughout both his books. In the *Recepte véritable*, Question is the unenlightened novice and Answer the natural philosopher possessed of great wisdom and many valuable craft secrets. In "On the Art of the Earth," Theory plays the role of an ambitious artisan's apprentice to Practice's experienced master:

> THEORY: You promised to teach me the art of the earth: and . . . I was very happy, thinking that you wished to teach me the whole of this art; but I was quite surprised when instead of continuing, you told me to come back later in order to make me forget my affection for this art.
>
> PRACTICE: Do you think a man of sound judgment would want to give away the secrets of an art that cost him who invented it dearly? As for me, I am not willing to do so unless I know a reason for it.
>
> THEORY: There is indeed no charity in you. If you wish thus to keep your secret hidden, you will carry it to the grave and no one will benefit from it, and thus your death will be accursed: for it is written that every man, according to the gifts he has received from God, should give to others: from this I can conclude that if you do not teach me what you know of this art, you are misusing the gifts of God.[13]

Practice's task in the remainder of the text is to prove the power and "benefit" to others of his hidden understanding. For the Paracelsian artisan, experience was crucial, and the real significance of "On the Art of the Earth" lay precisely in the "extremely violent" quality of artisanal experience that Practice passes on to his would-be apprentice. In these and other ways, this essay served as a natural culmination of all the inferences—both metaphysical and material—about Paracelsian artisanry that came before it.

Palissy's experience also taught him to reserve the secrets of the trade to himself for economic reasons. He remembered the hard lessons he had learned as a painter of stained glass, during which time (much as in the case of the Boston leather chair), manufacturing the product had become "too mechanized," causing overproduction, devaluation, and a glut on the market:

> PRACTICE: My art and its secrets are not like others. I am sure that a good remedy against a plague or some other pernicious disease ought not to be kept secret. The secrets of agriculture ought not to be kept secret. The hazards and dangers of navigation ought not to be kept secret. The word of God ought not to be kept

secret. But in the case of my art of the earth and many other arts, that is not so. Many charming inventions are contaminated and despised because they are too common. Also, many things are highly prized in the houses of princes and noblemen that would be less prized than old kettles if they were common. I pray you consider a little the glasses that are so low in price because they are too common, so that those who make them live more poorly than the porters of Paris. The profession is noble and the men who work at it are noble: but many who are gentlemen because they practice this art would like to be commoners and have money enough to pay the income of princes. Isn't that the trouble of the glassmakers of Périgord, Limousin, Xaintonge, Angoulmois, Gascogne, Béarn, and Bigorre? Where glassmaking is so mechanized that they are sold and auctioned off in the villages by the same men who peddle old clothes and iron, so much so that those who make them and sell them have a hard time making a living.[14]

To glassmakers, Palissy added makers of enamel buttons and Limoges enamels (including makers of "badges of office . . . but also . . . ewers, salt-cellars and all kinds of other vessels and other things"); "painters and clever draftsmen" (who had been undercut by "coarsely printed" images); and sculptors (whose original work was cheaply copied and resold by cast makers). Indeed, as in New York, refugee Huguenot artisans became well known themselves for underselling originals with copies. And Palissy, of course, substituted clay for metal in medallions and perhaps badges as well. Still, he listed many other kinds of tradespeople who had been put out of business by "mechanization," which he traced to the free dissemination of tradecraft:

> PRACTICE: You can easily understand by these examples and a thousand others like them, that it is better for one man or a small number of men to make a profit from some art while living honorably, than for a great many, who will harm each other so much that they will be unable to make a living save by profaning the arts, leaving things half done, as is commonly seen in all arts whose number is too great: however, if I thought you would keep the secret of my art as jealously as it deserves, I would not hesitate to teach it to you.[15]

Theory calls Practice's bluff and cajoles "If you will please teach it to me, I promise to keep it as secret as any man to whom you could teach it."[16] But Practice's response seems to suggest that the economic benefit of secrecy, though probably pertinent, is at the same time an obfuscation secondary to a larger purpose. A subtle shift in the dialogue occurs at the moment when Practice says: "I should like to do much for you, and to advance you as willingly as I would my own child: *but I fear that if I teach you the art of the earth, it would retard rather than advance you*" [emphasis added].[17] Practice thinks of Theory's progress "as I would my own child." Hence the secrets of the art of the earth were not forthcoming easily, but through the hard travail of creative birth. Theory presses on nonetheless. He freely acknowledges all that Practice has endured but now requests that the specifics of Practice's tradecraft passed on to him *in writing:*

> THEORY: I know that you have borne much poverty and trouble in learning it: but that won't happen to me: because the reason of your trouble was that you had a wife and children. [Moreover] you had no knowledge of it before and had to guess . . . you could not leave your family to go and learn this art . . . [and] you had no money to pay servants who could help you. . . . But that won't happen to me: because, according to your promise, you will give me in writing all the means of guarding against the losses and hazards of fire: also the materials from which you make enamels and their proportions, measures and composition . . . why should I not make fine things without running the danger of losing anything?[18]

To which Practice predictably replies:

> Even if I used a thousand reams of paper to write down all the accidents that have happened to me in learning this art, you may be assured that, however good a brain you have, you will still make a thousand mistakes, which cannot be learned from writings, and even if you had them in writing, you wouldn't believe them until practice has given you a thousand afflictions. . . . you will see that nothing will be attempted or completed, to render it in beauty and perfection, without great and extreme labor, which never comes singly but is always accompanied by a thousand anxieties.[19]

"On the Art of the Earth" thus becomes Palissy's ultimate definition of "great and extreme" labor itself. In such a definition, "proportions, measures and composition," like writing, are superfluous. One must begin at the beginning: "I will give you here *in order* all the secrets that I have found about the art of the earth,"[20] Practice says, and with this he tells Theory:

> [M]ore than twenty-five years ago, I was shown an earthen cup, turned and enameled with such beauty that I was immediately perplexed. . . . and immediately, without thinking that I had no knowledge of clayey earths, I started to look for enamels, the way a man gropes in the dark. Without having heard of what materials these enamels were made, I cracked, in those days, all sorts of things that I though could be used, and after having pounded and crushed them, I would buy a number of earthen pots, and after breaking them to pieces, I would put the things I had crushed on them, and after making them, I would write down the compounds [*drogues*] I had put on each one, as a reminder, then after I had built a kiln to my liking, I put these pieces to bake to see if my compounds

could produce some white color: for I was looking for no other enamel than white: because I had heard that white was the basis of all other enamels.[21]

"Perplexed" is a word Palissy uses interchangeably with "awe" to signify his experience of a natural-philosophical epiphany at the nexus of the macrocosm and the microcosm. He experienced the same feeling during his walk along the Charente River. This time, however, the effect of the Neoplatonic harmonics of song and the Paracelsian separation, perfection, and regeneration of water and salt was signified by a man-made object: the turned earthenware cup with a beautiful enamel glaze.

The hypothesis has been made that the cup Palissy was shown was an example of either Italian majolica or Saint-Porchaire ware from the Poitou.[22] Both are reasonable suppositions. However, no matter what type of cup the potter actually saw twenty-five years before publication of the *Discours* in 1580, his quest may well have been influenced by his awareness of another cup, famously associated with Jean Calvin. In Théodore de Bèze's widely read martyrology *Histoire de la vie et mort de feu Mr. Jean Calvin*, Calvin's will was published to refute claims that he had profited from his ministry in Geneva. "He was a man clearly void of all greedinesse of the goodes of thys worlde," de Bèze wrote:

> Was there any house considering the estate of the man . . . more slenderlye furnished with moveables? And if men will not believe me and ten thousand witnesses with mee, at least let them believe the slender wealth of his brother and onely heire, and also the inventory of all his goods, and it shall be found that all that ever he lefte behinde him (accompting also hys bookes which were dearely solde because of his precious memorie, to all men that were learned) doth not exceed the value of two hundred crownes.

Indeed, Calvin bequeathed only one "moveable" in his will:

> Concerning the final portion of goods, which God hathe given me here to dispose, I doe ordaine and appoynt for my only heir, my welbeloved brother, Antonie Calvin, only for credites sake, giving him for all his part, the cuppe that I had of Monsieur de Varennes, praying him therwith to content himself (as I am assured he wil) seing that he knoweth wel that I do it for no cause els, but to the end that that litle which I leave, may remain to his children.[23]

This cup held great talismanic qualities as a container of Calvin's memory, augmented by the ancient association of the sacrificial cup with the Lord's Supper. Though Palissy had problems with Calvin's writings, through which, following de Bèze, it "pleased God to make him to speake [and] . . . be heard of the posteritie to the ende of the world," his search for an artisanal voice may have been influenced by Calvin's one surviving household possession.[24]

Palissy's obsession was to make the perfect glaze, in much the same way as he was moved to construct a delectable garden by hearing the words of Psalm 104. For Palissy, the white glaze signified the flash of astral spirit materialized and then merged with the macrocosm in enamel: "I had heard that white was the basis of all other enamels," he says. From Palissy's understanding of the generation of stones, the white enamel was for him a pure fusion of salts and water, so that all color—and hence the earth's impurities—was removed, refined, and made transparent by fire in the furnace. The white glaze existed in the *absence* of earth. It was the potter's diamond from the foundation of the New Jerusalem: "nothing else but a water, . . . but it was jelled by some rare species of salt, pure and mordant, . . . its excellent beauty came in part from its hardness."[25]

As an artisan who had "taught myself alchemy,"[26] Palissy could appreciate the possibilities for a material-holiness synthesis in the ceramic process, a synthesis that had been achieved before by artisans only with painted glass. The insight that the "flash" or "sparkle" of the astral spirit could appear in a simple, everyday hand-wrought vessel was also revealed to Jakob Böhme in the second and most famous of his three visions of divine light, which took place in 1600 and which survives in the relation of his friend, the German theologian Abraham von Frankenberg:

> At the beginning of the seventeenth century, notably in 1600, when he was about twenty-five years of age, [Böhme] was, for the second time, seized by the divine light, and the sidereal spirit of his soul was introduced by the sudden appearance of a pewter vase . . . in its bottom or center the most intimate aspect of its nature was hidden, and thereupon, a bit suspicious, he went into the countryside to hunt for this spirit of his imagination . . . and for all that, to experience more and more clearly this gift of sight that he had come to receive, in such a manner that, by the medium of ["brilliant and jovial"] signatures,[27] or figures, traces, and colors, he was able to penetrate with one look into the heart itself and into the most intimate nature of creatures . . . after that, pierced with a great joy, he praised God and returned to his place of business [a cobbler's workshop] and spoke very little or not at all about his experience.[28]

Alexandre Koyré's characteristically metaphysical analysis of Böhme's "vision" is pertinent to our understanding of Palissy's "perplexed" experience with the earthenware cup:

> Boehme does not speak, it is true, of the exterior manifestation of his vision—of the light playing on the surface of a pewter vase—but we have no reason to doubt its reality . . . Frankenberg—who obviously did not understand this meaning—could not have invented this luminous symbol of one of the aspects of Boehme's doctrine; he did not see, as Boehme saw, the light that, invisible in itself, would reveal itself in its splendor and its

brilliancy as it set itself, and as it hit a polished and opaque pewter surface, the true symbol of God, of the divine light, which to reveal and manifest itself needed an "other," a resistance, an opposition; which, to sum it up, needed the world in which to reflect, express, oppose, and separate itself.[29]

Both pewter and ceramic—two of the most common and inexpensive materials to be fabricated in a furnace—shared opacity as a principal optical quality. There is little doubt that Palissy's encounter with the enamel cup can be understood in much the same way as we now understand Böhme's perception of "the sidereal perception of his soul," "playing . . . at its bottom or center" over the surface of a pewter vase. This enabled him "to penetrate with one look into the heart itself," like Paracelsus, "by the medium of signatures, or figures, traces, and colors"; what Koyré calls "the true symbol of God, of the divine light." Such optical qualities encompassed Palissy's observations about light refracting in stones, which included "diamond points," "sparks," and "flashes," the same optical effects he tried to replicate in the rustic figurines. And both Böhme and Palissy would agree that divine light could *only* become visible in *opposition* to the pain, corruption, and materiality of the microcosm. Recall that Palissy's astral light borrowed substance from salts in adjacent earths and, as Koyré points out, Böhme's light "needs the earth to reflect in, to express itself, to oppose and to separate." The essence of a glazed ceramic for Palissy was that it could make *permanent* the optical effects perceived in his luminous but evanescent moment of opposition of "love and wrath" between spirit and matter.

Böhme's response to his vision was to turn inward and begin to write a multitude of volumes in the most energetically oppositional language imaginable for his time. So much so, in fact, that Hegel championed Böhme's work as the origin of the German dialectic.[30] Palissy also turned inward, but he was initially seized with a Paracelsian artisan's mimetic desire to crystallize his vision out of the earth's natural materials. More than Böhme could probably have imagined, Palissy's obsession with his found artifact grew out of his personal history as a Saintongeais Huguenot artisan whose consciousness was formed during the civil wars of religion, and consequently also out of the structural complexities of his social and historical experience. Who could now argue that Palissy did not at some level also perceive the totality of his community's history of liminality, disguise, ambiguity, mimetic oppositional violence, and reversal contained in the charismatic little cup that, unlike the pewter vase in Böhme's vision, the potter could feel with his own artisan's hands and copy?

At the moment that Practice begins to draw Theory deeper into his consciousness as a rustic artisan, he simultaneously suggests the ambiguity of such a journey by drawing himself physically deeper into the earth's matrix. "On the Art of the Earth" broke down the conceptual and physical barriers between man and Nature and joined the maternal qualities of subterranean earth with the potential for generation of purity hidden beneath the corrupted shell of his own body. Just as Palissy had to excavate, reduce, and dissolve stones in order to disinter the earth's astral light through the process of distillation, so too the potter had to submit himself physically to an analogous, intensely intimate and personal form of excavation and disinterment. This was his ultimate act of mediation between macrocosm and microcosm. When Practice describes his ordeal in seeking to invent the white glaze for Theory, he wants him to understand that this journey into the private recesses of the self had also been an excruciating physical experience of bodily decay and transformation.

❧ Tables and Floorboards: Artisanal Rituals of Sacrifice and Exchange ❧

Palissy's artisan's pilgrimage in search of the white glaze became a journey of mythological torment. He could not control the violence of the kiln fire so that the white glaze would hold:

> Now, since I had never seen earth fired, and did not know at what heat this enamel would melt, I could do nothing in this way, even if my compounds had been good, for at one time my work had been heated too much, at others too little, and when these materials were too little baked or burned, I could not find out why I was making nothing good, but put the blame on the materials, although sometimes the work might have been good, or at least I could have got some hint toward achieving my goal if I could have controlled the fire according to the requirements of the materials.[31]

After years of failure, Palissy decided to try a kiln belonging to another potter (probably in La Chapelle-des-Pots) only to discover that common pottery furnaces fired too low to melt his "compounds":

> When I had thus blundered about unwisely for several years, with sadness and sighing, because I could achieve no part of my goal, and remembering my waste of money, I thought of sending the compounds I wanted to try out to some potter's kiln, to avoid such great expense; and having made up my mind about this, I immediately bought several earthen vessels, and after breaking them into pieces, as usual, I covered three or four hundred pieces of them with enamel and sent them to a pottery a league and a half away from my home requesting the potter to fire these experimental pieces inside some of their vessels; which they did willingly; but when they had fired their kilnful and drawn out my pieces, I had only shame and loss from them, for they included nothing good, because the potter's fire was not hot enough, also because my experimental pieces were not fired as they should be nor according to what I knew; and because I knew not why my experiments had not turned out well, I put the blame . . . on the materials: I would immediately make

numerous new combinations and send them to the same potters, to be treated as before: Thus did I lose time, suffer confusion and sadness many times, always at great cost.[32]

Yet he was virtually unstoppable. If one experiment failed, he would try another. Only when Palissy manipulated the far hotter temperatures attainable in the glass furnace did he begin to see that success in achieving the white glaze was possible:

> seeing that I had been unable to do any thing in my kilns or in those of the potters, I broke about three dozen brand new pots, and having crushed a great quantity of various materials, I covered all the shards of these pots with drugs brushed on: but you must understand that of two or three hundred pieces there were only three of each mixture: having done this, I took all these pieces to a glass house, to see if my material and mixtures might not turn out well in the kilns of the glass works. Now, because their kilns are hotter than those of the potters, after putting all my experiments into the kilns, the next day when I had them taken out, I saw that part of my mixtures had begun to melt, which caused me to be further encouraged to seek for white enamel, for which I had worked so hard. As for other colors, I did not worry about them at all; this little showing which I had found them, made me work for two more years looking for white, during which two years I did nothing but come and go to the nearest glass works, trying to achieve my goal.[33]

In the next set of passages, however, Palissy revealed for the first time what had been implicit all along; that is, how closely linked his quest to craft a white glaze on ceramic had become with his personal quest for self-mastery, purification, and salvation:

> God willed that just as I began to lose hope, and for the last time had gone to a glass works with a man carrying more than three hundred kinds of experiments, it happened that one of them melted within four hours of being put into the kiln *which was so white and polished as to cause me such joy that I thought I had become a new man* [emphasis added]: and I thought immediately that I had complete mastery of white enamel: but I was far from my goal.[34]

"I had become a new man," was of course, another way of saying that Palissy felt "born again" when he perceived the white glaze as the externalization, through labor, of his own newly purified soul. By analogy, "complete mastery of the white enamel" should have signified that Palissy's internal process of separation and purification had been "mastered" as well, and his pilgrimage of revelation ended. But Palissy's use of such language in this context has to be considered both ironic and didactic. Mastery implied an artisan's successful journey from apprenticeship to master status. However, in the soulish discourse used by enthusiasts and natural philosophers, it also connotes a negative characteristic of personal willfulness, a surfeit of profane carnality, akin to a surfeit of unpurified earths in the alchemical process. For the astral light to enter freely, such willfulness had to be negated, violently if necessary, to achieve sufficient bodily transparency. Only the deity determined the appropriate moment, which was unknowable. The Paracelsian artisan's journey was time-consuming. His spirit would not emerge quickly. As Practice painfully moves from the first to the third stage of his experiments (kiln 1: his own construction; kiln 2: a potter's kiln; kiln 3: a glass furnace), he drew closer to the hottest source of creation in the microcosm—the generative power of the earth's matrix. In exchange, he had to sacrifice that much more of his corporeal self to the kiln for the power to "control" the "violence" of the fire and finally achieve the pure white glaze.

This could not be done by "thought" alone. When Practice says, "I *thought immediately* that I had complete mastery of the white enamel," it is only a mirage. For the Paracelsian artisan, experience *preceded* theory (or "thought"). As Böhme argued, information was transmitted by feeling (or touching) in the body first, and only after the *heart* was animated did understanding reach the brain. "On the Art of the Earth" thus proceeds with Practice demonstrating to Theory that only through immense internal and external suffering could authentic performance be transformed into the beginning of a millennial event: "I was so stupid in those days, that as soon as I made this white which was singularly fine, I started to make earthen vessels, although I knew nothing of clay, and having taken seven or eight months to make these vessels, I started to put up a kiln like that of the glassmakers, which I built with incredible labor."[35]

Why did Palissy report it had "taken seven or eight months to make these vessels," and after that "I started to put up a kiln like that of the glassmakers, which I built with incredible labor" to finish production and grow the enamel? Counting the time he took to build the kiln and fire the pots, the potter describes a nine-month birthing process. With these passages, Practice begins an account of his metamorphosis from a man with artisanal powers limited merely to external and artificial labor to the inner, androgynous craftsman capable of natural labor. Indeed, he was transformed, experientially, into a hermaphrodite.

Here was a figure par excellence of the liminal body and a standard alchemical trope for astral conjunction. The astral seed with which Palissy was inseminated could now be brought forth in the form of a white glaze by "incredible labor." "Labor" took on its obstetric meaning necessary for the issue of the union of love and wrath in the macrocosm and microcosm to emerge. Like the sexually ambiguous creatures on Palissy's rustic pottery, he used his ambiguous sexual status to generate new life out of himself *autogenously*, its seed inseminated by an invisible light from God. After Practice "made this white" and "had become a new man," he "started to make earthen vessels" like Mother Earth, which took "seven or eight months" and after gestation began the labor of birth in the ninth month.

This labor was "incredible" in terms of both maternal pain and artisanal work, for the delivery of the white glaze occurred through a vaginal matrix like that in the earth that generated transparent stones and the glassmaker's furnace that generated crafted material with precious little of "this world" in it:

> for I had to do the stone work alone, mix my mortar, draw the water for mixing it, and fetch the brick on my own back because I had no money to pay a man to help me with this business. I baked my vessels for the first firing: but when it came to the second firing, *I had sorrows and labors such as no man would believe* [emphasis added]. For instead of resting from my previous labors, I had to work for more than a month, night and day, to crush the material from which I had made that beautiful white in the glassmaker's kiln; and when I had crushed these materials I covered the vessels I had made with them: this done, I lighted my fire at both openings, as I had seen the glassmakers do; I also put my vessels in the kiln, to melt, I thought, the enamels I had put on them: but that was an unfortunate thing for me: for although I spent six days and six nights in front of the kiln without ceasing to burn at both openings, it was not possible to melt the enamel, and I was like a desperate man: and although I was quite groggy from the work, I went and thought that my enamel contained too little of the stuff that was supposed to melt the other materials, and so, I started to proceed and crush this stuff, without, however, allowing my kiln to cool, so I had to do double work, pound, crush, and fire up the kiln.[36]

Ambiguous mixing, cosmic dualism and androgyny intensified. Practice began to merge with the earth, becoming male and female, a process signified by the sentence, "I had sorrows and labors such as no *man* would believe." This process of firing the kiln and crushing materials for the enamel took "more than a month, night and day" to add up to the requisite nine months gestation before birth. He lit his fire "at both openings" in the kiln, which he tended for "six days and six nights"—the duration of creation in Genesis—"without ceasing to burn at both openings," to do which would threaten the success of the synthesis of macrocosm and microcosm. But Practice thought his "enamel contained too little of the stuff that was supposed to melt the other materials" (astral salts), so he was forced to "pound and crush this stuff, without, however, allowing my kiln to cool, so I had to do *double work*." Practice's "double work" refers to the Paracelsian cosmos as well as the heat and compression functions of the matrix. These were now inseparable from the functions of his own creative body in the throws of birthing spiritual matter.

Practice then had to do the one thing that caused Palissy's memory to remain alive for the schoolchildren of southwestern France:

> When I had thus made up my enamel, I was forced to go out and buy more pots, to try out the enamel: since I had lost all the vessels I had made: and having covered the pieces with

the enamel, I put them into the kiln, keeping the fire high: but then another unfortunate thing happened which made me very angry, which is that when the wood was used up . . . I was forced to burn the tables and the floor of my house, in order to melt the second mixture. I was in such anguish as I could not describe: for I was quite dried out because of the work and the heat of the kiln; for more than a month my shirt had not dried on me.[37]

Practice here, in effect, takes inventory of his bodily dissolution and distillation. When he sacrificed his tables and floorboards to the kiln, Practice took three steps toward the end of the process. First, he began to feed the kiln's flame with domestic extensions of himself, extensions that protected his laboring body from the natural elements crucial to alchemical distillation. Second, the tables and floorboards signified two levels of horizontal barriers, fixed below the body, which separated Practice physically from the compressive and heating properties hidden deep in the bowels of the earth, with which he began to merge without protection beneath his feet. Third, the process began to take its toll on Practice's body; it became desiccated because of "the work" and "the heat of the kiln." At the same time, "for more than a month my shirt had not dried on me," while distilled fluids from his body condensed as in an alchemic experiment. Just as geodes grew diaphanous interior crystals so too Practice's astral body began to separate and distill as his bodily salts congealed with bodily fluids, emerging even as his body became "quite dried out."

The brutal process of sacrifice of physical and material gifts of the self to the kiln continued when Practice hired a potter to make "some vessels according to my ideas" and was forced "to give some of my clothes as salary."[38] And the gradual decomposition of his independent household worsened when "I suffered another affliction related to the above, which is that the heat, cold, winds, rain and leaks in the roof spoiled most of my work before it was fired; so much so that I had to borrow lumber, lath, tile, and nails to establish myself."[39] When Practice lost the roof to his workshop air and water mingled with the earth and fire, thus creating a storm of biblical proportions, which left him vulnerable to all of the elements, except the fifth growing inside of him, the one that allowed everything to say "I am":

I was every night at the mercy of rains and winds, with no succor, aid or consolation [fig. 8.1], except for the owls hooting on one side and the dogs howling on the other; sometimes winds and storms sprang up which blew so hard over and under my kiln that I was forced to leave everything, losing my labor; and it happened often that having left everything, without a dry rag on me, because of the rains that had fallen, I went to bed at midnight or at dawn, dressed like a man who had been dragged through all the mud holes of the city.[40]

The result of the process of his own putrefaction and decomposition, in which he had sunk deep into the earth and "all the mud holes," was "that I did nothing but build

FIGURE 8.1. "The old man transformed in a dismal rock pit," from Johann Daniel Mylius, *Philosophia reformata* (Frankfurt, 1622). Courtesy Glasgow University Library, Department of Special Collections. Paracelsus believed that the magi—or the elect—through wisdom mobilized by inner powers, possessed free will to resist the outer influences of the stars, or we "shall not know from one moment to the next whence a gust will come and where we shall be blown." An old philosopher retreats to a subterranean refuge where he is brought to the edge of bodily death by buffeting, demonic winds representing the higher elements of air and fire (see also figs. 10.7, 8), while a scavenging raven hopes for a meal. Yet instability and bodily destruction also begins a process of inner soulish expansion, as the earthy cavity serves as a sort of crucible for this adept who simultaneously resists the stars aligned above his head. He is connected to benign sources of animation in the macrocosm by the two angelic messengers. Internal conjunction of macrocosm and microcosm is signified by tightly crossed arms (see fig. 7.2)—indicating a man withholding powerful secrets—and the shape of his beard, a Trinitarian triangle clipped to point upward. This completes a soulish conduit from the heavens to the earth that is repeated in a similar context in figure 8.5. The younger Winthrop—his Calvinist predestinarian tradition notwithstanding—assumed the magis' position of patience and exerted powerful influence over the stars from his physician's chair (fig. 6.2).

and tear down." This artisan was "building with the destroyer." Practice gave up to the kiln everything he needed to maintain his outer body, for he "was forced to use the things that were necessary for my sustenance to build the commodities necessary to my art."[41] Yet by this sacrifice Palissy knew he stood to gain far greater wealth and power. By exchanging sustenance for art, Practice was committing metaphoric suicide, offering his decaying body to the kiln in exchange for mastery to build his second, astral body in white ceramic glaze. Like his tiny, live-cast creatures, his body would remain *permanently* transparent, durable, and pure. Far from "accursed," the "death" of Practice during this process was sanctified.

Practice's bodily decay during this process of separation and quest for alchemical purification, was mirrored by the stages of his separation from the community. He was accused of bizarre, asocial behavior. His denial of sustenance and loss of personal protection were only the beginning. Practice also rejected commercial aspects of his trade and therefore his status as prideful artisan and paterfamilias. This resulted in his marginalization, loss of honor, and ultimately complete social ostracism. Practice became the wild man of Saintes:

> to console me I was jeered at, and even those who should have helped me, went about the town shouting that I was burning up the floor: and thus I was made to lose my credit, and I was thought to be crazy. Others said that I was trying to make counterfeit money [a common charge against alchemists], which was an evil thing that made me dry up on my feet; and I went about the streets hanging my head, like a man ashamed: I had debts in several places, and usually two children being nursed and could not pay for it; no one helped me: but on the contrary they jeered at me, saying: he richly deserves to starve to death, for he neglects his trade. All this news reached my ears as I passed in the street . . . [and later] as I drew out my work I was given nothing but shame and confusion. For all my pieces were dotted with little pieces of pebbles that were so well stuck to them and bound into the enamel, that when the hand was passed on them, the pebbles cut it like a razor; and although the work was spoiled by this, still some people wanted to buy some at a low price: but because that would have been a mockery and a loss of honor for me, I completely broke up the whole kilnful and went to bed from melancholy, not without reason, for I no longer had the means to support my family; . . . my neighbors, who heard about this, said that I was nothing but a fool and that I should have had more than eight francs for the work I had broken up, and all these things added to my sorrow.[42]

But the bodily transformation that the dishonored Practice was forced to endure brought the most singularly painful episode of "sorrow" and "shame" to his own house. It is important to remember that in early modern France, sorrow also described the legacy of Eve, and shame connoted the feelings of pregnant women who had conceived out of wedlock or were forced to expose their "private parts" during childbirth.[43]

As Caroline Walker Bynum and Thomas Laquer have shown, just as Jesus was conceived as both male and female, so too were the reproductive bodies of men and
women. The female body was more material, and the male more formative and spiritual. "On the Art of the Earth" shows Practice's body continue to take on qualities of
both sexes. "Woman's reproductive system was just man's turned inside out," Bynum
writes. "In the sixteenth century, Ambroise Paré even suggested that woman could
turn into man if, owing to an accident, their internal organs were suddenly pushed outward."[44] The opposite could also happen in a context of "extreme violence." Not surprisingly, then, the marriage bed was the focal point of Practice's "anxieties" and the
battlefield upon which the results of his sexual metamorphosis were contested:

> in my house I got nothing but recriminations; instead of being comforted I was cursed.
> . . . And what is worse, the motive of these jeers and persecutions came from those of my
> household, who were so unreasonable as to wish me to work without tools, which is more
> than foolish . . . the more this was unreasonable, the more the affliction was great for me
> . . . [until finally], and in retiring thus, I stumbled about without light, and falling on one
> side or the other, like a drunkard, filled with great sadness: because after having worked a
> long time I saw my labor lost. Now, *in retiring thus dirty and wet, I would find in my bed-*
> *room a second persecution worse than the first, which makes me wonder now that I did not die of*
> *sadness* [emphasis added].[45]

The scene of consummation had shifted from the bedroom, where "I saw my labor
lost," to the kiln. More female now than male, Practice sacrificed his male sexuality by
castration ("to work without tools"). Physical symbols of male honor, fertility, willfulness, extension, and penetration *outside* of self were reversed, so that Practice could
open up and passively receive the astral spirit in his body through the space of absence
left behind by his neutered penis, as a woman would receive semen from a lover. At
the moment of *conjunctio,* Practice experienced the "similitude" of love with God
through Nature.

Like Palissy and Paracelsus, Böhme seems to have had unsatisfactory sexual relationships: "But this *Earthly* love is only cold Water, and is not true Fire: A man cannot find any *full* similitude of it in this *half-dead* world; Only the Resurrection of the
Dead at the Last Day, is a *perfect* Similitude in all *divine* things, which receive *the true*
Love-fire."[46] But Palissy's transparent stones were taken from Revelation, and although
for Böhme, true consummation between spirit and matter must await the apocalypse,
he was still able to write:

> And this is wholly hidden as to my Body, but not as to my animated or soulish spirit, for
> so long as it qualifieth or worketh with and in God, it comprehendeth the same, but when
> it falls with sin, then the Door is shut against it, and the Devil holdeth it up fast, and it

must be set open again with great labour and industry of the spirit . . . [for] I cannot resist him, though my earthly Body should go to wrack for it, yet my God will *glorifie me* in my knowledge.[47]

Where then, was the "door" on the body of Practice? Further, after insemination with the astral seed, Practice's "earthly Body" was crushed, dissolving even as the glazing material was pulverized and the desiring spirit grew inside him:

I had to do work that I thought would *kill* me. For after many days during which I tried myself pounding and calcinating my material, I had to crush them without help, with a hand mill, which *it usually took two strong men to turn:* the *desire* [emphasis added] I had to attain my goal made me do things that I would have thought impossible. . . . The next day, when I took out my work, after putting out the fire, my sorrow and pain were so heightened that I lost all countenance [thus Practice literally loses "all appearance," becoming invisible].[48]

The crucial moment of transformation comes when Practice's body finally succumbs utterly to the wracking presence of the spiritual seed growing inside:

For having made a certain number of rustic ewers and fired them, some of my enamels turned out fine and well melted, others were poorly melted, others were burned, because they were made of various materials that were fusible to various degrees; the green of the lizards was burned before the color of the serpents had melted, also the color of the serpents, crayfish, turtles and crabs had melted before the white had attained any beauty. All these mistakes have caused me such labor and mental anguish that before I had made my enamels fusible at the same degree of fire, I thought I would be at death's door: also as I worked at such things for more than ten years my body was so wasted away that my arms and legs had no form or trace of muscles, but on the contrary my legs were like sticks: so that the laces with which I tied up my stockings fell down to my heels with the rest of my stockings as soon as I walked. I often went for a walk in the meadow of Xaintes thinking over my misery and troubles. And above all that in my home itself *I could obtain no patience* [emphasis added], nor do anything that was considered good. I was despised and jeered at by everyone.[49]

Now in the final stages of putrefaction, Practice's "was at death's door." His body resembled the *transi* state Richelieu and others described in their accounts of the physical condition of the last survivors of the siege of La Rochelle in 1628. Like the stone that liquefied in the bowels of the earth, Practice's "body was so wasted away that my arms and legs had no form." Recall Palissy's "fifth," form-giving element, without which "nothing could say I am." And yet, Practice still avoids giving Theory any specific information. He reveals nothing that even vaguely resembled the operatic

336 • T H E   A R T   O F   T H E   E A R T H

emergence of the white glaze as an end in itself. Indeed, Practice hints at this, and early on, long before the final pages of his discourse, when he says to himself, "[W]hat are you sorry about, since you have found what you were looking for?"[50] In a sense, the *vision* of the earthen cup, and the lifelong quest for understanding "the work" it animated, are sufficient. Still, Theory complains: "Why are you giving me such a lament? Is it rather to turn me away from my invention than to make me get closer to it; you have really made a fine speech about the mistakes that are made in the art of the earth, but that only serves to scare me: for you haven't said a thing about enamels."[51]

Practice, however, has *already* said everything he intends to say—a fortiori, everything a Paracelsian artisan needed to know—about enamels. And what he has said returns us forcefully to this southwestern Huguenot's artisanal formulation of the Paracelsian millennial quest and above all, to his artful conceptualization of the materiality of time. Practice describes a scene of *premature* or mistaken birth, rather than rebirth. His tiny creatures suffered violence in the fire only to emerge from the kiln grotesquely deformed in precisely the same way as fetal "monsters and marvels" that Palissy's friend Ambroise Paré documented.[52] Many of the mothers of such monstrous offspring, Paré thought, had suffered "the wrath of God," because "the ordinary course of Nature seemed to be twisted."[53] The time was not yet right for the birth of Palissy's rustic figurines as a complete millennial event. The astral seed for the enamel had not received a gestation period sufficient to allow the various colors and materials to fuse together "at the same degree of fire" at the end of the process ("at death's door"). That was why some of the millennial glazes finished "fine and well melted, others . . . poorly melted . . . others were burned. Indeed, "the green of the lizards was burned before the color of the serpents had melted." But, most important, the white glaze, the material of desire as the "basis" of all the other colors, set insufficiently to form the astral foundation of the work: "the color of serpents, crayfish, turtles and crabs had melted *before* the white had attained any beauty." A pious artisan could not construct the surface without its framework of support.

The ultimate reason for this failure to achieve unity in the glazes was, then, essentially one of timing. Practice "could obtain no patience" at home for his sexual metamorphosis and the resulting pregnancy and labor of generating transparent material. Thus he did not add the most important ingredient of the recipe. Böhme would later say of this predicament that it was shared by all men of the spirit: "thus I stand yet as an anxious woman in travell."[54] The initiation of Theory by Practice ends with a clear message: the southwestern Huguenot artisan was actively engaged in constructing artifacts of an eschatology of waiting that were the embodiment of millennial historical processes. More than mere "virtue," the operative component in this combination of internal and external labor was above all patience. Premature interference by uninitiated and hence inexperienced artisans with the orderly unfolding of natural obstetric processes would be catastrophic and could engender the birth of monsters. Consequently, telling Theory outright, without his personally experiencing the pain of the laboring spirit, would also be premature, even dangerous. If Theory wished to know how to perform "the work," he must put aside a false sense of the superiority of scholastic reason and patiently endure the same long experience of "incredible labor" as Practice in order to achieve practical knowledge, or *praxis:*

> The mistakes I made while I found out the dose for my enamels taught me more than the things that were easy to learn: therefore I judge that you should work to find this dose, just as I have done: otherwise you would esteem the knowledge too lightly, and perhaps that would cause you to despise it: for I am certain that no one in the world takes lightly the secrets and the arts save those who got them cheaply: but those who have learned them at great cost and labor do not give them away so lightly.[55]

❧ Palissy and Cellini: Toward a Common Language of Things? ❧

Historians of the Italian Renaissance will doubtless recognize certain structural similarities between Palissy's "On the Art of the Earth" and the Roman Catholic sculptor Benvenuto Cellini's well-known *Autobiography* (dictated to his studio boy, 1558–66; first published edition, Rome, 1728). This is particularly true in Cellini's extensive account of his heroic personal travails in the casting of a bronze statue of Perseus:

> I fought these threatening disasters for several hours, exerting myself beyond my strength until I could stand it no longer. A sudden fever, of the utmost intensity, overcame me, and I had to go and fling myself on my bed. I dragged myself away from the spot, after entrusting the rest of the job to my assistants, ten or more in all what with master founders, handworkers, country fellows and my own special journeymen.
>
> "Observe all the rules I have taught you," I said to my apprentice. "Do your best with all speed, for the metal will soon be melted. You cannot go wrong. These men will have the channels ready. You will be able easily to open the two plugs and my mold will fill like a miracle. I feel sicker than ever before in my whole life and I believe that this fever will kill me before many hours are past."
>
> With despair in my heart, I left them and betook myself to bed, where I spent two hours battling with the fever, calling out all the time that I felt I was dying. While I was writhing in agony, the twisted figure of a man came into my room and, in a mournful, doleful voice, like one announcing their last hour to men condemned to die on the scaffold, he moaned to me, "Oh, Benvenuto, your statue is spoiled and there is no hope of saving it."
>
> I no sooner heard the wretched shriek than I let out a howl that could have been heard from hell, jumped out of bed, and throwing on my clothes, strode out to my workshop de-

termined to make trouble. . . . I filled the grate under the furnace. The logs caught fire, and oh! how the caked metal began to stir under the fearsome heat, to glow and sparkle in the flames! The new, roaring fire intensified the conflagration on the roof, so I sent men up to beat the flames out. I ordered boards, carpets and other hangings to be set up to protect us from the violence of the rain in the garden.

 The cake stirred and was on the point of melting. . . . The dead had come back to life against the firm opinion of all those ignoramuses. Such strength surged through my vein that all the pains of my fever vanished.

 . . . But I noticed that the liquid metal did not flow as rapidly as usual. . . . So I sent for all my pewter plates, my porringers and dishes, numbering in all about two hundred pieces, and cast part of them, one by one, into the ducts and into the furnace proper. The expedient worked miraculously. My bronze was in the most perfect liquid state and in a moment my mold was filled. Seeing my work finished, I fell on my knees and with all my heart gave thanks to God . . . then turned to a plate of salad lying on a bench there, and with a splendid appetite ate and drank, and all my gang of men along with me.[56]

The similarities between the essays by Palissy and Cellini are quite marked. These would include among other things: the labor-pregnancy metaphor; the interrelationship between birth and death; the disasters; the stupid, directionless apprentices and laborers; the sparkling optical effects; the disintegration of the workshop roof; the sacrifice of personal domestic items including boards in exchange for cosmic protection or for the cooperation of the kiln; and the mold with two channels which "will fill like a miracle." It is difficult to draw confident generalizations from the similarities between these two artisans' discourses other than that they were obviously drawn from a shared alchemical discourse of artisanal self-fashioning or mythologizing, including a sense that under certain conditions, artisans could actively enter the cosmic process through their work.

Although Paracelsus was widely read in Italy, no common literary source for these particular passages can be located, and the survival rate of such artisans' texts from the sixteenth century is rare. Yet there is the intriguing possibility that Palissy and Cellini may have influenced one another. We know that Cellini was in Paris in the employ of François I between 1540 and 1545, after which he returned to Florence under contract to Cosimo I, where he cast the Perseus. Palissy took up residence in Saintes during this period, where he stayed until 1565. So the chances of personal contact seem remote. There remains the possibility that some of Cellini's thoughts may have been written down while he was in the employ of François I—although the Perseus was cast for Cosimo—and they might then have fallen into the hands of Palissy when he entered royal service in the 1560s. Palissy may also have obtained a manuscript copy of Cellini's *Autobiography* before publishing his *Discourses* in Paris in 1580. In that case, a likely source would have been publisher and translator Jacques Gohory or a contact in Gohory's publishing network.

As intriguing as the similarities between the casting of the Perseus and "On the Art of the Earth" are the differences. These differences may be explained by religion. Cellini was a Roman Catholic who had fought bravely against Protestants in the sack of Rome in 1527. Although timing is crucial in both essays, Cellini encouraged his apprentice to "do your best with all speed," whereas Practice counsels "patience." Moreover, while Cellini had his share of enemies, he did not suffer social ostracism in making the Perseus, nor did he work completely alone. Practice did not have the benefit of a work crew, and he refuses to tell Theory anything about the glazing process beyond the incredible labor it necessitated. Conversely, although he was finally forced to take matters into his own hands, before collapsing on his bed, Cellini took care to remind his apprentice, "Observe all the rules I have taught you." There is, in short, a sense of companionship and camaraderie—of male bonding and society—in the *Autobiography* that is painfully absent in the *Discourses*. This may be partially explained by Palissy's commitment to the Paracelsian idea that the road to knowledge was a lonely, interior one. But I am convinced that Palissy's inability to articulate the sense of a community of practice was a metaphor for Huguenot life, labor, and martyrdom in the *désert*. When Practice finally discovered the most heinous sort of "persecutions . . . in my home itself . . . [where] I was despised and jeered at by everyone," it was as much a lament on history and the loss of community as on a sexual failure and the disintegration of an artisan's household.

That was also one reason why the endings stand in such stark contrast to one another. As Theory is the first to complain, Practice shows him virtually nothing of the actual process of fashioning the white enamel. Theory is pointedly denied access to the final product as well, and with it, the sense of an ending. Cellini, on the other hand, provides a detailed account of how he made the Perseus, complete with an operatic conclusion when the cast "came out admirably" and he "fell on my knees and . . . gave thanks to God." Conversely, Cellini, "and all my gang of men along with me," almost immediately turned from the spiritual component of their work "and with a splendid appetite ate and drank" to replenish those parts of their physical selves sacrificed but not lost to the kiln. While these two episodes of generation and production ended differently for the artisans involved, both articulated experience through a metaphysical language of things.

🌱 Anthropomorphic Vessels from La Chapelle-des-Pots 🌱

For Palissy, there could be no replenishment of loss in the *désert*, no quick sense of closure. Hence, the final lines of "On the Art of the Earth" refer to the Jews of the dias-

pora in their function as brickmakers. Practice speaks only of endurance and the sacrifice of the artisan's body to the perpetuation of spirituality in workmanship. But there
was also hope for the wrought millennial artifact made from such bodily sacrifice,
because Practice could now finally argue that clay vessels had greater potential for
longevity in history than stone:

> How highly do you think our ancestors prized the usefulness of the art of the earth? It is
> well known that the Egyptians and other peoples have built many splendid buildings
> through the art of the earth, many emperors and kings have built great pyramids of clay,
> to perpetuate their memory, and some of them did this fearing that their pyramids would
> be ruined by fire if they were made of stone. But knowing that fire has no power against
> buildings of baked clay, they had them built of brick, as witness the children of Israel, who
> were terribly oppressed while making the bricks for these buildings. If I had to write down
> all the uses of the art of the earth, I should never have done: therefore I leave it to you to
> think about its other uses. As for its esteem, it is now despised, but it has not always been
> so. The historians assure us that when the art of the earth was invented, vessels of marble,
> alabaster, chalcedony and jasper fell into disrepute: and many earthen vessels have even
> been consecrated to the service of temples.[57]

There is artifactual evidence to indicate that at least some of the ideas that Palissy
committed to paper in "On the Art of the Earth" were "perpetuated" into the seventeenth century by potters working at La Chapelle-des-Pots. Practice may also make
veiled reference to this place-name when he says, "and many earthen vessels have even
been consecrated to the service of temples." Several remarkable anthropomorphic ceramic vessels have survived, glazed in variegated polychrome patterns and measuring
between 15 and 35 centimeters in height (fig. 8.2). These vessels are known to have been
fired in the kilns of La Chapelle-des-Pots, ca. 1625–1650.[58]

Chapelot's cursory commentary on these artifacts is restricted to his description of
them as "bottles in the form of a woman" and his speculation that they had functioned
"to contain a liquid, perhaps alcohol." But he questions their practicality, for "the openings to fill them up, above all for the smallest vessels in the group, are very narrow and
of little practical value."[59] This fascinating group of artifacts deserves a more complex
archeology. Chapelot is only partially correct when he describes the form of the containers as feminine. He neglects to mention the proportionally outsized, erect, and un-
circumcised "phallus" (the male prepuce is represented by the deeply scored graduated
rings modeled on its shaft) that projects out and sharply up from the "feminine" gen-
ital area hidden underneath the folds of the figure's apparently noble dress, except in
terms of its most obvious use as a passage for distilled liquid.

Again, Chapelot is only partially correct about the opening. His assertion that it is
there so that the bottle can be filled up is true, because no other opening is available.

FIGURE 8.2. Anthropomorphic lead-glazed earthenware vessel, La Chapelle-des-Pots, France, early seventeenth century. H: 35 cm. Does this ceramic refer to the royal wedding depicted in figure 8.3? Louvre. © Réunion des Musées Nationaux / Art Resource, New York.

But this information once again raises the problems of utilization and context. Wine or spirits, water, oil, animal blood, and milk were five liquids for which specific ceramic containers were made in seventeenth-century Saintonge, and indeed, the liquid in this case would probably have been an alcohol. La Chapelle-des-Pots would undoubtedly have supplied all the ceramic needs of the Cognac area. One can assume, then, that the anthropomorphic vessels were originally modeled to contain eau-de-vie, for which Cognac was famous by early modern times.

"Eau-de-vie," of course, translates literally as "water of life." We have already seen how crucial water was in Palissian science, where it was perceived as a principal life-generating element. But "eau-de-vie" was also an idiomatic expression related to the "breath of life" alluded to in Psalm 104 (and commonly) as a well-known figure for the Holy Spirit. Here was the ceramic embodiment of what had become, by the seventeenth century, a regional ceramic type for the cosmic hermaphrodite that was first introduced to the southwest within Palissy's artisanal community. The degree of "circularity" in this instance can never be measured precisely. One can say that Palissy's most important contribution to southwestern Huguenot artisanal culture (and to historians who seek to understand it) was that he possessed the peculiar ability to systematize and act as intermediary. He bridged the gap between local folkways and the larger scientific, economic, and political world. He was able to articulate those folk conceptions in both writing and artisanry, using charismatic Paracelsian language that he had absorbed and taught from his earliest arrival in the region. That language mediated his experience and launched an enduring regional Huguenot artisanal tradition, which was dispersed with its artisans but "reseeded" itself in places throughout the Atlantic Huguenot community.

From the perspective of Palissy's discourse, the hermaphroditic vessels left behind in Saintonge were complete symbol systems. The liquid "breath of life" was poured through the phallic spout and into the empty outer body made of clay, just as the androgynous Practice was inseminated by the animate seed of his astral body. As the "water" replenished the container, the feminine form was also filled up and impregnated by the motion of the liquid until it expanded to press the limit of the vessel's "womb" and threatened to spill out through the spout. With the inner body of the container full, synthesis occurred, and the sparkling glazes attained their potential for transparency on the vessel's outer body. When the spirit bottle was held up and poured down in a stream from above, the drinker drew the eau-de-vie through his mouth, like the word, and, instructed by the language of the vessel, experienced his own body transformed into a vessel that contained the regional signifier par excellence of the conjunction of macrocosm and microcosm.

Might this courtly figure imagined in rustic pottery represent some historical or mythological personage? Perhaps it was the contemporary Princess Elizabeth of England (fig. 8.3), whose widely disseminated image in a similar costume resembles the vessels. Her marriage to the Elector Palatine of Bohemia in 1613 reminded Huguenot artisans of Protestantism's roots in the Germanic Reformation. Elizabeth's marriage also symbolized a portentous moment of astral conjunction for Rosicrucian inheritors of the Paracelsian tradition, who prophesied apocalyptic end times during the Thirty Years' War, and it was commonly called "the marriage of the alchemical king and queen."[60] Some of these vessels from La Chapelle-des-Pots show the figure with a small animal, too crude to identify precisely. Engravings of the royal couple are often accompanied by the Palatine lion, and occasionally a dog. Both are possibilities. Other female candidates are figures that appear in courtly dress in addition to Elizabeth, including nature, the moon, and planets. There were many women in local Saintongeais folklore as well, and it may be that like the frontispiece in Simplicissimus, the vessels were a composite image.

Yet a far more direct comparison may be made to another group of contemporary vessels, also with a Germanic lineage, with further links to Calvinist material culture in the British Isles. Starting in the last quarter of the sixteenth century, drinking vessels made of silver, called "wager cups," "marriage cups," and "maiden cups" (*Jungfrauenbecher*), were produced by goldsmiths in Nuremberg and Augsburg (fig. 8.4). Like the pottery, parts of these metal vessels appear to have been fired with enamel surfaces. The German maidens wear courtly dresses similar to those on Saintongeais vessels. The distinctive costumes were copied from designs by the Italian Cesare Ve-

FIGURE 8.3. The Chemical Wedding of Princess Elizabeth of England and the Elector Palatine Frederick of Bohemia, king and queen of Bohemia, in February 1613. Unknown artist. Courtesy the National Portrait Gallery, London. The marriage of Frederick and Elizabeth ushers in a period of natural rebirth and sacred violence. Three figures from Reformation history, including Luther and Calvin, gather around the Bible, with rustic plowmen and sowers in the background. The Word, combining evangelical ministry with simple labor in the earth, routs the all powerful forces of the Antichrist. Meanwhile, the union of Frederick and Elizabeth is also an act of alchemical conjunction, as the Holy Spirit descends through Elizabeth's scepter and Fredericks orb. Below, four crowned lions of the chemical millennium—perhaps a reference to the Swedish lion—gather at the couple's feet; one holds a single heart, the bodily site of their union and insemination in the Holy Spirit, the motion of which is revealed by its double tail, crossed over itself, with floral tips. Is the spout in figure 8.2 analogous to Elizabeth's scepter? Images of Elizabeth holding her scepter were diffused throughout the hotbeds of international Protestantism, including Saintonge.

cellio and the refugee Theodore de Bry, Robert Fludd's main image maker, who published most of his designs in Frankfurt, suggesting common sources for both the German and French vessels and perhaps for images of Elizabeth's costume as well.[61] Did Elizabeth's marriage inspire some German examples?

Unlike the Saintongeais vessels, where the spout extends from below the waist, the maiden cups were built in two parts; each was a receptacle for spirits. The maidens'

FIGURE 8.4. Hieronymus Imhof, wager or marriage cup, Augsburg, ca. 1610–15. H: 8″, W: 4″, D: 4″. Silver gilt and enamel. Courtesy Metropolitan Museum of Art, Gift of J. Pierpont Morgan, 1917.

skirts form the larger cup, while another, smaller cup was placed on a pivot between upraised hands. The wager referred to a game at table where a host awarded his guests the cup if they succeeded in draining both the small and the large receptacles simultaneously without spilling the contents. The association with marriage comes from the custom of offering the groom the larger cup and his bride the smaller. Like the survivals from Saintonge, the market for such vessels had faded in Germany by the mid seventeenth century, but not before it had extended briefly to Holland and especially England. In England, while both the form and function remained generally the same, the maidens' costumes were decidedly more bourgeois, more befitting the wife of a tradesman or a lawyer than a courtier. Hence, English variants have been linked with Puritan influence during the commonwealth period. Be that as it may, the last surviving English wager cups were made for use in guild rituals by the Worshipful Company of Vintners in London. In these ribald instances, however, Puritan asceticism may have been the butt of a joke.

Despite differences, certain similarities between the Germanic and Saintongeais anthropomorphic vessels seem suggestive. Applying what we know of the French vessels to their German counterparts, there is cosmological resonance. The Augsburg and Nuremberg goldsmiths were much closer to the source and language of Paracelsianism than were Palissy and his followers. Is it unreasonable to say that alchemic discourse was built into the maiden cups? Is it only a coincidence that the ritual interplay between the larger and smaller cups, which must operate together simultaneously to function properly, seems also to imply the larger and smaller world of the macrocosm and the microcosm? Synthesis and risk in the alchemic operation is also implicit in the marriage game, as are the dangers of court life. To drink from the cup of courtly patronage was a two-edged sword for artisans such as Palissy.

What then, are the consequences of the fact that hermaphrodite vessels were made at La Chapelle-des-Pots just when La Rochelle was facing its final siege?

❧ "A Delectable Garden" as Fortress of Patience ❧

> Behold the discourse of the four cabinets! . . .
>
> . . . And in order that ingratitude shall not be expressed even by the things which are insensitive and vegetative, here will be inscribed on the frieze a quotation taken from the book of wisdom, where it is written: *When fools will perish, then they shall call upon wisdom, and she will mock when their fear cometh, because they would have none of her counsel when she uttered her voice in the streets, when she cried in the chief places of concourse and in the openings of the gates, and uttered her words in the city.* This will be written in the said frieze, so that the men who reject wisdom, discipline, and doctrine shall even be condemned by the evidence of vegetable and insensible objects. . . .
>
> . . . I . . . would like to make certain statues, which shall hold a vase in one hand and in the other a tablet of writing, and thus when someone shall come to read the writing there will be an engine which shall cause the statue to pour the vase of water on the head of the one who would read the said epitaph.　　—BERNARD PALISSY, *A Delectable Garden*

In *A Delectable Garden*,[62] Palissy expanded his invention of a refuge for self-transformation to include a community of others in a pluralistic subterranean matrix that was also a rustic fortress of deception and waiting: "in which to retire and recreate my spirit in times of domestic quarrels, pests, epidemics, and other tribulations which confound us mightily in these days."[63] With the successful completion of his small-scale "experiments," Palissy achieved the competency required to undertake the realization of his total Neoplatonic vision (a garden and amphitheater modeled on Psalm 104), "dreamt" as a consequence of the musical doctrine of effects while walking along the Charente River as it bisected war-torn Saintes. These material-holiness harmonies signified a material-temporal synthesis in which figures for history (the clay earths) and the chemical millennium (diaphanous glazes) coexisted in simultaneous relation to one another. All existed in a state of both being and becoming at once, in historical time and artifactual material, just as they did in the most secret, intimate refuges of both the heart and body of the philosophical artisan himself.

The location had to be mountainous for many reasons. In a play on words that refers obliquely to final things, Answer informs Question "that *for the last days* I have been busy going from one place to another seeking a mountainous location proper and appropriate for constructing a garden."[64] This passage recalls the apocalyptic mountain of Nebuchadnezzar's Dream, refugee strongholds in the mountainous Cévennes and, of course, the fact that mountains had long been associated with the literature of final things.[65] Yet Answer seeks a mountainous location, Question points out, because it is specific to his historical concerns: "you say you require a mountainous place in which to build a delectable garden . . . because you say that you wish also to build a sanctuary for the exiled Christians."[66]

Above all, however, a mountainous location was the best place to apply the principles of rustic natural philosophy to Palissy's historical problem of building a "sanctuary" that also functioned "over the succession of time" as an appropriate place "to retire and *recreate* my spirit." Height for movement of water was key:

> ANSWER: To find a proper place suitable for a garden there must be some fountain or rivulet which runs through the garden, and for that reason I shall choose a level place at the foot of a mountain or rising ground in order to take a spring of water from the said height and cause it to flow according to my pleasure to every part of my garden.
>
> QUESTION: And where do you think to find a height where there will be a spring and a plain at the base of a mountain, as you require?
>
> ANSWER: There are in France more than four thousand noble domains where such situations are easily to be found and especially nigh unto rivers. . . . This is not unattainable. I will soon find a suitable place on the banks of a river which fulfilleth my requirements.[67]

Hence, the Neoplatonic river of separation, purification, and reunification was to issue "through" the garden "plain" located "at the foot of a mountain or rising ground."

The spring water or generating element would be taken "from the said height" and caused "to flow according to my pleasure to every part of my garden." In Palissian geology, mountainous regions represented a topography of particularly fertile—that is to say, pregnant—locations on earth. Palissy tells us that natural springs that emanate from mountains draw waters from the deepest reaches of the earth's matrix. Answer would "take" this seminal fluid from the "height" of his phallic "mountain or rising ground" and cause it to flow . . . to every part of my garden." The artisan thereby ordered the earth's reproductive powers for his own "pleasure" so that the generating element seeped back into the earth's matrix through animal holes and other cracks and crevices, in which the astral seed was planted and the generation of diaphanous materials could begin. Mountainous locations were also the most logical places for Huguenots to go underground in grottoes—defined as "an excavation or structure made to imitate a rocky cave"[68]—to await and work toward the chemical millennium.

The formal structure of Palissy's garden was initially laid out (in a manner familiar to all his artisanry) with compass and rule:

> In the first place I would mark the quadrature of my garden of such a length and breadth as I would deem necessary, and would make the quadrature in a plain, environed with mountains hills or rocks, facing the north and west winds, in order that the said mountains, hills, or rocks could serve a purpose. . . . But above all I would devise my garden in a place where there is a meadow below it, so that one could pass sometimes out of the said garden into the meadow. . . . And thus having laid out the site of the garden, I would then divide it into four equal parts, and to separate the four said parts there would be a pleached alley, formed like a cross, in the garden, and at the four ends of this cross there would be at each end, a cabinet, and at the center of the garden and cross, there would be an amphitheatre. . . . At each of the four corners of the said garden there shall be a cabinet, which shall make in all eight cabinets and an amphitheatre, which will be built in the garden; but thou must understand that all eight cabinets will be diversely carried out of such contrivance as has yet never been seen or heard tell of. That is why I wish to build my garden from the one hundred and fourth psalm. . . . I also wish to build this admirable garden in order to give men occasion to become lovers of the culture of the earth, and to relinquish all other occupations or vicious pleasures and evil traffic.[69]

Palissy's garden, from the very inception of its design, took on the tripartite functions of fortress (amphitheater surrounded by rocks), matrix (androgyny, generating waters), and utopian space (the Psalm 104 archetype: "give men occasion to become lovers of the culture of the earth, and to relinquish all other occupations").

Answer's task after laying out the general plans of the garden is to provide details specifying the construction and function of the first four cabinets. In sixteenth-century French, a *cabinet* was an article of furniture, but also "a little chamber . . . wherein one keeps his best, or most esteemed, substance; also an arbor in a garden."[70] In Palissy's garden, cabinets can connote all three meanings, but may be imagined as the equivalent of separate rooms "or bower[s]" enclosed by "nature":

> *Of the First Cabinet:* The first cabinet or bower . . . at the base of and joining the foot of the mountain or rock, I will build of baked bricks; but these will be fashioned in such a wise that the cabinet shall have the semblance of a rock, which might have been quarried on the very spot. Within the walls there will be several concave seats, and in the space between the seats there will be a column, and under this a pedestal, and above the capitals of the columns there will be an architrave, frieze and cornice . . . on the side of the north and the side of the west the cabinet will be cemented against the hills or rocks, in such a fashion that in descending from the higher level one could walk atop of the cabinet without knowing that any building was below it. . . . I shall have planted on the roof of it several shrubs, bearing fruits to delight the birds and certain herbs they feed upon in order to accustom the said birds to come to the bushes to rest and sing their little songs, which shall please those who shall be within the cabinet or garden.
>
> And the outside of the cabinet will be built of large stones from the rocky hills without being polished or carved, so that the outside of the cabinet shall not bear any resemblance to a building. . . . I will lead the water in a pipe, which I will build between the rockwork and the wall, and it will issue again in jets, which shall flow out of the cabinet in such a fashion that, the cabinet resembling a rock, the people will think the jets flowed from the cabinet without artifice. . . . But I wish . . . to discourse thee of the beautiful shining surface of the inside of the cabinet.
>
> When the cabinet shall have been thus constructed, I will cover it with several colours of glaze from the height of the vault to the ground and pavement of the aforesaid; this done, I will make a great fire inside the cabinet until the said glazes shall be melted or liquified on the masonry. In melting, the glazes will flow, and in flowing will intermingle, and in intermingling will form highly pleasing figures and patterns. The fire being extinguished in the cabinet, it will be found that the glazes will have covered the joints of the bricks of which the arbour shall be built, and in such a way that the arbour will seem all of one piece upon the inside, there being no sign of jointures. And the cabinet will shine so brightly that the lizards and crayfish which enter in will see themselves as in a mirror and will admire the images; if someone come upon them by surprise they will not be able to mount the wall of the cabinet because of its polished surface. And in this fashion the cabinet will last forever, and will not need any tapestry, for its decoration will be of such beauty as it were of jasper, porphyry, or chalcedony, well polished.[71]

The "discourse" of the cabinets was, in effect, a synthesis of all we have learned from Palissy's personal history, thoughts about artisanal *sûreté*, and notions about the geology of clay and glazes. The entire edifice was to be built with materials taken from local geological formations or naturalistic materials made in the manner of Palissy's "On the Art of the Earth." Question is encouraged to perceive the first cabinet as encapsulating the earthly element moving in the Paracelsian continuum between its "raw" state as unpurified earth and its ultimate millennial "cooked" state as purified diaphanous glazes. Like Palissy's little earthen cup, the first cabinet was also an allegory of temporality materialized.

Palissy's rustic figurines meant for domestic spaces and his outdoor garden cabinets were inextricably intertwined. The garden was conceptualized and intended to be constructed in the manner of the basins, scaled to gigantic proportions. Imagine one such basin reversed so that its innocuous clay underside is turned-up to face the surface as a disguise to inhibit unwanted visitors. As a result, the molded and glazed interior is turned down to form the subterranean ceilings, walls, and furniture of the grotto-bower. That was why the edifice was built of "baked bricks . . . fashioned in such a wise that the cabinet shall have the semblance of a rock, which might have been quarried on the very spot." It was also why "the cabinet will be cemented against the hills or rocks, in such a fashion that in descending from the higher level one could walk atop of the cabinet without knowing that any building was below it . . . and the outside . . . will be built of large stones from the rocky hills without being polished or carved, so that the outside of the cabinet shall not bear any resemblance to a building." After having "planted on the roof of it several shrubs, bearing fruits," Palissy will have completed the surface prospect of his fortress of deception. Here was the perfect counterpoint to the fortress and enceinte of La Rochelle, standing visible to the state as the very definition *of noblesse d'épée sûreté* and defiance. The enceinte of Palissy's fortress however, was to be understood as a *literal* womb hidden in a subterranean shell of earth and rocks, so its interior matrix remained imperceptible from the rest of mountainous nature outside. Resonances from Palissy's written texts are multiple, but the "knotty" exterior of his geode comes to mind immediately.

The geodelike matrix manifested precisely the opposite effect, with its "beautiful shining surface of the inside." When Palissy built "a great fire inside the cabinet until the said glazes shall be melted or liquefied on the masonry," the interior of the cabinet itself became a kiln to expand its capacity for internal growth. At this point, while the flow of liquefied glaze settled into its final pattern, Palissy allowed a rare insight into this Paracelsian artisan's thoughts about surface decoration. They are in no way iconographic in the traditional sense of the symbolic lexicon from which historians of the fine arts draw most of their understanding of the term. Here, it is clear that the significance of the glaze was communicated first by its rather haphazard optical effects, next, in the movement of the material itself as it mapped the interior process of its "growth," and finally in its permanent disposition on the cooled ceramic surface.

In the formal sense, especially, the *movement* of the liquefied diaphanous glazes as they flowed down in the subterranean matrix was a perfect ordering and figuration of Paracelsian Neoplatonism. Recall the moment of internal intermingling of the macrocosm and the microcosm experienced by Palissy as his dream-vision of Psalm 104. This signified as the "shining surface of the inside of the cabinet," when "in melting, the glazes will flow, and in flowing will intermingle, and in intermingling will form highly pleasing figures and patterns," probably much like the surface patterns on the hermaphrodite vessels. Astral conjunction in the fusion of the glazes was nowhere better represented than when "it will be found that the glazes *will have covered the joints* of the bricks . . . there being *no sign of jointures*," such that all perception of difference is eliminated. This was the essence of natural artisanry: that no artifice was revealed in the construction of the potter's perfectly invisible joints. Hence the "lizards and crayfish" (Palissy's tiny industrious creatures) "will see themselves as in a *mirror* and will admire the images." The mirror reflected parallel worlds in which they faced each other, even as the tiny creatures faced and "admire the images" of their "permanent," astral selves.

Palissy's figures for Huguenot refugees safely awaited the millennium in a desiring, pregnant condition, because the "brightly shining surface" of the interior was so well "polished" from the hermetic conjunction of its "jointures" that "someone" (perhaps the snail's enemies?) would be unable "to mount the wall" to devour them. The bower of the just was protected by a hidden internal light. Diverse internal events were completely obscured to those outside the community by deceptions, and yet were still perceived to be completely natural and hence totally "without artifice."

Within this setting, furniture for the eschatology of waiting was introduced for the first time: "Within the walls there would be several concave seats . . . which shall run around the said cabinet." The furniture of the millennium will be "natural" chairs (ones made "without artifice"), and so the bodily position of waiting became sitting. "Seats" in the first cabinet were set back into the rocky wall of the matrix facing out into public view. The front of the sitter, as well as the chair itself, would therefore also have to function as a part of the deception. The southwestern Huguenot's history of disguise would serve him well in such a position and it must also be remembered that, conceptually speaking, as in Winthrop's chair, the sitter's hidden back would be molded by the heat, sparking light, and transformative powers of the internal matrix. In the light of Practice's revelations about his androgynous sexual metamorphosis and astral impregnation, it is reasonable to assume that the cabinets in *A Delectable Garden* would also reveal elements of Palissy's sense of his own internal bodily matrix in the process of producing diaphanous matter.

The second through fourth cabinets contained extrapolations or variations on themes introduced in the first.[72] The second cabinet:

will be built entirely of bricks . . . and there will be several terminals inside . . . which shall serve as columns . . . placed upon a continuous base, which shall serve as a seat for those who would be seated in the cabinet. . . . The glazes . . . would be melted in the spot itself . . . the joints of the masonry shall not be perceived and the whole shall shine like crystal.

The third cabinet would "be entirely rustic, as if the cavern had been hewn out of the rock with great blows of the hammer . . . in the cabinet there will be certain cavities hollowed out of the wall which shall serve as seats." The sitters would take their places in the "cavities" of this cabinet like seeds absorbed into the uterine wall of the earth mother. Unlike the seating arrangement in cabinet one, the furniture in cabinet three was entirely inside, facing the matrix (fig. 8.5). Therefore, the chairs would "be covered with a white glaze, which shall have divers colours mottled, speckled, and marbled upon it in such a way that the glaze and divers colours will cover the joints of the bricks and masonry." This would give the chair *backs* (and by implication the absent sitter's upper body) the optical effect of Palissy's "sparks and flashes" and Böhme's "figures, traces, and colors." The fourth cabinet would "be lined with bricks" as the others "and present no appearance whatever of sculpture or labour of the hand of man." Finally,

the outside of the cabinet shall resemble a natural rock. And since the cabinet will be erected against the foot of the mountain . . . having the top covered with earth and hav- ing several trees planted in this earth, will have very little semblance of a building, because descending from the height above, one will be able to walk on the roof of the cabinet with- out perceiving that there is any manner of building there.

The remaining cabinets outlined in the beginning of *A Delectable Garden* generally followed the same framework as the first four except that in addition to earths and clays, Palissy introduced wood as his second basic material. His interest here was again to subvert (indeed, to reverse) the classical (and hence, artificial) order with the "rus- tic" order. Palissy's polemic revolved around his reading of "Vitruvius and Sebastian who wrote books on architecture." These architectural treatises demonstrated that the "rules [proportional relationships] they have adopted in fashioning their columns" were derived not only from the human body but, of far more import to Palissy, the gar- dener, from trees grown in Nature as well. In the divine order of things, then, trees made by the deity superseded columns made by man in imitation of them:

If you had read the books of architecture which you quote, you'd have found that the an- cient creators of excellent edifices took the examples and models for their columns from the trees and from human forms. . . . And also the columns made of trees will always be found rarer and more excellent than those of stone; but if you wish so to honour those of stone as to prefer them to those made of the trunks of trees, . . . it is against all order of

Quæ funt in fuperis, hæc inferioribus infunt :
Quod monſtrat cœlum, id terra frequenter habet.
Ignis, Aqua et fluitans duo funt contraria : felix,
Talia fi jungis : ſit tibi ſcire ſatis !

D.M.àC.B.P.L.C.

FIGURE 8.5. Seven earth spirits sitting in a subterranean refuge and matrix, from *Musaeum hermeticum* (Frankfurt, 1625). Courtesy Harry Ransom Humanities Research Center, The University of Texas at Austin. Compare figure 8.1. Triangles point simultaneously up to the macrocosm (fire and air) and down to the microcosm (earth and water), their conjunction manifested by the six-pointed star at center, known as the mystical seal of Solomon's wisdom. Hidden wisdom at the center of the earth is made accessible by the well, a motif that is central to figure 8.6, and one famously associated with Jesus in John 4:14, when he says that "the water that I give him will become in him a spring of water welling up to eternal life," and so a source for conversion and baptism. One of the earth spirits plays a lyre. Could these be the "virgins" Palissy heard harmonizing on his walk along the Charente River?

divine and human right, for the works of the First Builder should be held in greater honour than those of human builders.

Item, you know that where a portrait has been copied from another portrait the copy will never be as much esteemed as the original from which one took the portrait. It follows that columns of stone cannot glorify themselves against those of wood, nor say, "We are more perfect," and this especially since those of wood have engendered or at least taught us how to make those of stone.[73]

Palissy admitted, however, that columns made of diaphanous stone would always take precedence, even over those "grown" by God from wood: "and since the Sovereign Geometrician and First Builder set His hand to it, we must esteem them [wooden columns] more than those of stone, rare as the stone may be, *save that they be of jasper or other semi-precious stones.*"[74] Palissy made this single qualification because transparent stones were further along toward the chemical millennium than wood, and also because he perceived that *wood and stone, both of which grew out of the earth's matrix, existed in precisely the same alchemical material-growth continuum.* Hence, trees and other wood and vegetative elements became crucial signifiers of subterranean activity *on the surface.* If we return to Palissy's geological discourses, it becomes absolutely clear that in the hands of the Paracelsian woodworker as well as the potter, turning and joinery would contain within its primary material the seed and potential for hardness, diaphanousness, and astral animation just like earths and shells. In the proper context, wood could and would become stone and, without losing its original form, be purified by the earth over the succession of time:

> There is some wood that is reduced to stone . . . and I know why it happens. . . . It may be hard for you to believe it: but for me I know it is the truth . . . there was a certain forest of Fayan, which was in part a bog. From this I conclude in my spirit that the wood of Fayan contained more salt than any other kind of wood: because of that, we must believe that when this wood is rotten, and when its salt is moistened, [this] reduces the wood which is already rotten to a kind of manure or earth, and from then on, the salt that is dissolved from this wood hardens the rotten humor of the wood and transforms it into stone, which is, as I told you, what happens to shells; it is for that reason that when [the wood] softened and reduced into a stone, it didn't lose its shape: in the same way, the wood being reduced to stone still keeps its shape of wood, just as the shells did. And this is how [one state of] Nature is never destroyed without being reborn immediately into another state, which is what I have always told you, that the earth and other elements are never idle.[75]

That was why Palissy imagined that an additional "four green cabinets" would be fashioned, in part, from "the trunks of the elms [which] shall serve as columns and the branches form an architrave, frieze, and cornice, tympanum, and pediment"; or would contain wooden "coils fashioned in the manner of spiral lines . . . twisting"; or "on the right and on the left of the [third green] cabinet there will be several seats between the columns, which shall be made of certain sprouts, rising from roots of the young elms which form the columns, for it is the nature of elms to produce off-shoots from their roots; or finally, in the last green cabinet, "between the columns, which shall be the trunks of the poplars, there will be certain soft vines, which shall be woven, interlaced, and arranged in such a way that they will serve as partitions, seats, and backs between the columns; and above the seats and backs a portion will be woven flat to form a platform, upon which will be set several dishes and cups."[76] The potter imagined that "over the succession of time," when subject to the action of the astral waters, salts, and matrices that animated his *Delectable Garden*, the wooden components which he helped to fashion themselves would, if worthy, grow not only externally but internally as well. In this, the final Palissian reversal modeled on the Genesis psalm, the artisanry of man was silently upended by the subterranean artisanry of nature, both operating to restore the natural historical order and to assure the millennial continuity of animate matter.

❧ La Chapelle-des-Pots: Seventeenth-Century Extensions ❧

> It is to be stressed that the sixteenth century, with the research of Bernard Palissy in the area around Saintes, has a particular importance in this region and that its value as a yardstick in the evolution of local ceramics is without any doubt primordial. —SERGE RENIMEL

Serge Renimel, an archeologist who accompanied Chapelot's team to Saintonge in 1971, discovered a mysterious anomaly in his data.[77] The kiln sites in and around the immediate vicinity of La Chapelle-des-Pots showed evidence of intensive production during the Middle Ages (ca. 1250–1320) and again in the later seventeenth and eighteenth centuries (ca. 1650–1750). However the kiln sites also revealed perceptible gaps in production during the fifteenth century (perhaps a result of the Hundred Years' War?) and, above all, from the mid-sixteenth through the mid-seventeenth centuries (ca. 1550–1650). Although Chapelot's team refused to consider the problem of religious conflict in its report, this time frame also roughly encompassed the period of intense evangelism from Germany. This was followed by enthusiastic conversions in the local artisan community that led ultimately to uninterrupted civil war in the region until 1628.

But war provides only part of the answer. Also central (yet this too is an effect of war) is Renimel's observation that this period saw relative economic decline. As a result, Saintongeais artisans departed the region or relocated to the nearest urban area in search of work. For Saintonge, that could only mean Saintes, where, during this time Palissy had his workshop. Reminel has observed Palissy's "primordial" influence on the local seventeenth-century style, but fortuitous location was not the sole reason. Palissy *himself*, in "On the Art of the Earth," lamented that pottery was "now despised." Palissy's material-holiness synthesis would surely have had a profound and convincing effect in such a fluid, oppositional milieu, where artisanal morale, honor, and self-esteem were in decline. Recall that Palissy's *own* conversion experience occurred at a similar point in his personal history.

In addition, one can speculate that Saintongeais potters may have become too ingrown. Over the course of centuries, ceramic production among isolated, town-centered networks of intermarried families may have left local potters ill equipped to meet the challenge of the international Renaissance and early modern molded, naturalistic styles originating in Italy and Germany. Because he had traveled and read extensively in the Paracelsian tradition, and had therefore experienced many places far beyond his place of birth, Palissy served as the needed agent of change to help local artisans comprehend a marketplace driven by the thirst for innovation and novelty. And indeed, in this context, change amounted to a paradigm shift. But Palissy's program was, as we have argued, profoundly spiritual in nature. It would be naïve to attribute its local success solely to the marketplace. While Practice expressed his regret that pottery was "now despised," he ended with a hopeful reminder that in the past, when the art of the earth predominated, pottery had "even been consecrated to the service of temples."

Jean Chapelot expands in more specific artifactual terms upon Renimel's initial observations. These violent years between 1550 and 1650 also bracketed the time Palissy first arrived in Saintes, his removal to Paris and eventual death in the Bastille, and the beginning of the first massive dispersions from both Aunis and Saintonge to northern Europe and America following the collapse of La Rochelle. Chapelot's scrupulous research in the kiln sites, in conjunction with similar findings in places in northern Europe to which the pottery of Saintonge was exported, allows him to offer the following important information about *precisely* what sort of ceramics were being produced by Palissy's artisan followers during this period:

> It is, moreover, in this last category that a new kind of ceramic production belongs. It appeared at a date in the sixteenth century that is hard to pin down today and seems to have continued to exist into the middle of the seventeenth century without any modification. It went on to influence future regional production to a greater or lesser degree until the nineteenth century.
>
> This new sort of ceramic is characterized by a taste for applied decoration in relief, [and] the use of polychrome glazing, often in pursuit of colors that will produce a marbleized or jasper decoration. This kind of production, which uses a white slip [liquid clay

undercoat below the glaze], limits itself to ceremonial forms: warming plates, platters, bottles in the shape of a woman . . . and they must certainly have been made in conjunction with ceramics for everyday use. . . .

This manufacture poses historical problems: first of all, its relationship to Bernard Palissy's work is now little known. . . . One knows that Bernard Palissy worked in Saintes. The technical relationship between his products and those of the regional workshops are assured, as well as the decorative and iconographical relationships. But it is difficult to know in which direction the influences traveled. . . .

What is significant in relation to this [type of] ceramic is its relative rarity in the ceramic material of Port-Berteau. . . . It is possible that from the fifteenth to the mid seventeenth century, there was either a reduction of production in Saintonge or a relative stoppage of exportation by the [Charente] river.[78]

This new ceramic type had never appeared in regional material culture before Palissy's arrival and is attributable to Palissy's artisanal paradigm. Like Palissy's "rustic figurines," the earliest of these new molded forms had polychrome glazes, often in marbled or jasper (mottled) patterns. But just as often they appeared in the overall vivid copper oxide green that has also been discovered in excavations of Palissy's workshop in Paris and that became the dominant Saintongeais pottery glaze beginning with the early seventeenth century. Most ceramics installed in the "green cabinets" of the delectable garden would have been glazed in this color.

Most important from the perspective of social history, however, hard archaeological evidence clearly attests that this heavily molded and relieved pottery was not the work of a few highly skilled and specialized elite artisans, but was, rather, within the competence of *every "common potter"* (to borrow Palissy's term) who had an established working kiln near Saintes during this period. The diffusion of the Palissian paradigm throughout the region of La Chapelle-des-Pots is proven by the survival of an abundance of molded shards lying side by side with everyday, unadorned common pottery in most of the kilns. While one might argue that this evidence suggests an abundance of molds available for all, it also means that "common" and not "art" potters were producing both everyday and molded wares *simultaneously.* Moreover, this archaeological information is supplemented by the crudity of these seventeenth-century molded wares compared with shards found in excavations of the Louvre and Tuileries that are attributable to Palissy himself. Clearly, this local pottery is not of "elite" workmanship. Even Chapelot, who earlier in his report attacked the "Palissian myth," here allows that Palissy's influence may have been the cause of the paradigm shift, albeit with the caveat that "it is difficult to know in which direction the influences traveled."

Although again he is not sure why it should be so, Chapelot shows that molded Saintongeais pottery was evidently *not* made for export, inasmuch as very little was found left at Port-Berteau, an important loading site on the Charente. And, although a few examples of such molded ware has been discovered at British sites, Chapelot (like Renimel) concludes only that there was a marked diminution of production ca. 1550–1650, probably owing to market conditions. Perhaps the most simple answer to the complex problems posed by this significant but anomalous (in that it was not exported) ceramic type is that Saintongeais Huguenot potters made molded ware primarily for *themselves,* local courtly patrons, and their immediate communities, in hundreds of individual, private Paracelsist "experiments."

But this fails to address the question of production during the siege years (1620–28 specifically), when export of most materials from the Saintongeais hinterlands ceased through the port of La Rochelle. Archeologists are relatively certain that most surviving *green*-glazed molded pottery was produced in the first third of the seventeenth century, some undoubtedly during the siege years, when there was little hope of export. Like Palissy before them, perhaps some Saintongeais Huguenot potters engaged in an Paracelsian artifactual dialogue with war and even with the siege of 1628, perceived from La Rochelle's periphery, through the production of things. Based on these undated artifacts alone, however, such speculation must remain just that for the moment.

Consider two examples of the green molded pottery from this period. Each is a monument of the style, and in that sense communicates more fully than the numerous other survivals, but they are far from unique forms, and an understanding of their symbolic language can therefore serve to illuminate most, if not all, the other survivals of this type.

Chapelot calls the first example a "large circular platter." Here it will be addressed (in lieu of its unknown period name) as a circular ceramic cosmology (fig. 8.6).[79] Measuring 35 centimeters in diameter (5 centimeters in depth), it is currently in the collections of the Musée national céramique de Sèvres in Paris.[80] The second example (fig. 8.7) is called descriptively a "decorative vase in green glaze; closed form, with two holes under the foot," but here it will be addressed as a hermetic vessel.[81] This measures approximately 35 centimeters in height and has been in the collections of the Louvre Museum since 1897.[82] Not much is known about the provenance of the two artifacts, except that the vessel was donated to the Louvre by a certain Bardac, who also presented the museum with other distinguished examples of molded green-glazed pottery from La Chapelle-des-Pots. Even a glancing comparison between the circular cosmology and any standard basin by Palissy reveals a strong family resemblance. The Palissian heritage of this seventeenth-century follower is especially marked when one considers that molded and applied decoration in relief has no history in the region before Palissy's arrival. The question of color is basic to Palissian ceramics, especially in distinguishing between sixteenth- and seventeenth-century types.

The predominant colors in both cases are the legendary white and green. We have

FIGURE 8.6. Cosmology. Early seventeenth-century lead-glazed earthenware, La Chapelle-des-Pots, France. Diameter: 35 cm. Musée national céramique de Sèvres, Paris. © Réunion des Musées Nationaux / Art Resource, New York. Here the well serves explicitly as the vehicle of rebirth and eternal life cited in John 4:14. The youthful figure emerges from the well carrying a bouquet of flowers intertwined with the sweet smell of sanctity, cosmological unity, and resurrection.

already witnessed the associations that the color green had in the history of the violent beginnings of the "primitive" Church in Saintes and the symbolic significance of the green man, as well as the green cabinets in Palissy's garden. From Paracelsus to Palissy and beyond, to Francis Bacon and his circle, the color green was always intimately associated with both the natural philosophy and the metaphysics of water as a generating element in vegetative matter.[83] In his *Garden of Cyrus* (London, 1658), Sir Thomas Browne (1605–82), a follower of Bacon devoted to writing a full explanation of Bacon's notions about the water principle, made the scientific association between

FIGURE 8.7. Hermetic vessel. Early seventeenth-century lead-glazed earthenware, La Chapelle-des-Pots, France. H: 35 cm. Louvre. © Réunion des Musées Nationaux / Art Resource, New York. The bottom knot simulates *conjunctio* (see fig. 7.2).

seminal water and vegetative greenness plain: "And this is also agreeable unto water it self, the alimental vehicle of plants, which first altereth into this colour [green]; And containing many vegetable seminalities, revealeth their Seeds by greennesse."[84]

The white and green of the glazes on a basin from Palissy's workshop move outward from the cluster of four white shells at its epicenter (fig. 2.2), which appear to

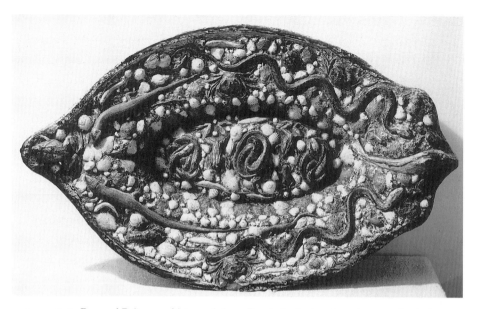

FIGURE 8.8. Bernard Palissy and his workshop. Rustic lead-glazed earthenware basin in a womblike form analogous to a geode, uterus, or alchemical matrix split open to reveal the hidden, inner life of elemental earth as productive mother of infinite conjunctions. H: 45.5 cm. W: 75.5 cm. Courtesy Musée des Beaux-Arts de Lyon. Photo, © Studio Basset.

emerge at least partially from below the surface. The next concentric level up and out on the earth's surface is green, and is occupied by vegetable matter, spiral-shelled creatures, and frogs. The green frogs are touching the next concentric band of white water, because they are amphibious creatures at home in both elements. We are reminded immediately of the relationship of the frog to the snake in figure 2.4. The snake descends from above (sun) to join the frog (moon)—perhaps to gently consume it to complete the conjunction—as the frog emerges from the earth's subterranean regions. Indeed, basins attributed to Palissy survive where the frog and snake appear together in an analogous relation (fig. 8.8). Within the water itself there are minnows swimming centripetally, in opposite directions. The smaller ones are all white, while the larger ones are green and white, having grown somewhat from the watery seed. The next green level (following the spiral growth suggested by the spiral shellfish) includes more frogs, taller plants, flying insects (elemental air), spiraling snakes or worms slithering toward conjunction on the margins, and a chameleon, which of course encompassed multiple levels, because it can exist in either green or white.

Palissy's ceramic cosmos suggested that life bubbles up from inside the watery matrix, moves upward with the seminal fluid (astral white) and out by anastomosis through vegetable and animal matter (green) to the rivers of the earth (white), and so on to every classification of life on earth. White, "the basis of all other colors," was clearly the foundation and animating color. That man was also derived from this process of combination of water and salts ejaculated from the matrix was of course implied and may in fact be represented in the form of the tiny "industrious creatures" that populate the Palissian cosmos and functioned as metaphors for Huguenot artisans during the war years. Paracelsus said of the outward circular movement of waters from deep inside the earth's matrix: "For, as the element of water lies in the middle of the globe, so, the branches run out from the root in its circuit on all sides towards the plains and towards the light. From this root many branches are born. One branch is the Rhine, another the Danube, another the Nile, etc."[85]

For Palissy, the Saintongeais "branch" was doubtless the Charente, always represented as the white watery element circulating among Palissy's "rustic figurines." In addition, he insisted that there had to be a "meadow" below the delectable garden, upon which the waters might eventually flow. Palissy's seventeenth-century follower conceptualized the relationship between white and green in precisely the same way, although he crafted it somewhat differently. Here the white is hardly in the glaze at all; rather, as the basis for all other colors, it is almost hidden underneath the green in the clay material itself, which, during this period, fires almost completely white. As if to make the subtle point that the astral white can emerge in spots like flashes or sparks, the potter allows certain tiny points to glaze white so that they appear to emerge through the green.

This connection between the white clay and green surface glaze would not have been readily apparent but for the fact that the potters of La Chapelle-des-Pots had extracted all the clay that fired white in their region before 1650 and were thereafter forced to use clay that fired a fleshy red color. Hence, the famous "vert et rouge" pottery shipped from La Chapelle-des-Pots through La Rochelle to the entire Atlantic market in the century between 1650 and 1750. Potters compensated for the red with a white slip, which they applied just beneath the green glaze, evident on the pitcher and saucer, ca. 1680, depicted in figure 8.9. These artifacts were excavated from the subaquatic site at Port-Berteau, where they were discovered by divers lying side by side when the sand was vacuumed away.[86] If the astral spirit was the thin agent of conjunction between macrocosm and microcosm, then what better material embodiment for it than a white slip that conjoined the fleshy pink ceramic body to the diaphanous millennial green glaze? The seminal quality of the slip was made all the more obvious by the drippy veil with which it was inevitably applied.

It is interesting to consider that by the late eighteenth century, at a time when the last of the Huguenots of the *désert* and even the *nouveau convertis* had either died out or departed the region, the white slip also disappeared from La Chapelle-des-Pots. Though nineteenth-century potters still used the red clay, most did not bother to apply the slip, and with their production, a vital material link to Palissy and the Huguenot

FIGURE 8.9. Pitcher and plate, La Chapelle-des-Pots, France, ca. 1680. Private collection, 1983. Photo, Neil Kamil. These examples of common "vert et rouge" export ware, of a sort found in archeological sites throughout the Americas, were excavated by divers from the Charente River. They probably fell from a pirogue that had just shoved off from Port-Berteau with its delivery of local wares intended for a coastal skiff heading up to La Rochelle (and transshipment north), or even a large merchant ship anchored near the mouth of the river in the Bay of Biscay.

artisans of the *désert* was lost. The loss, however, was of little consequence. Faience produced in La Rochelle and decorated with fashionable scenes from the Orient had begun to supplant traditional Saintongeais green earthenware as early as 1750. By 1800, the traditional ware was no longer important in the local economy.[87]

But in the early seventeenth century, when the ceramic cosmology in figure 8.6 was fired at La Chapelle-des-Pots, green earthenware and the mental and material context with which it was inextricably intertwined were still intensely vital elements in the artisanal landscape of Saintonge. The clay for the cosmos would have been gathered, not by the potters themselves, but by the highly marginal members of local society whose job it was to dig clay for them. In this way, these marginals performed a valuable service and were able to make enough money or barter to survive. After the clay was sifted for impurities and the air pockets removed by beating and kneading, in a process not dissimilar to preparing dough for bread, it was portioned into workable quantities and dried (or moistened) to a malleable consistency. Then a measure was gathered, kneaded still further, and rolled out on the potter's bench like a piecrust.

Taking his compass in hand, the potter placed its point at the epicenter of the mass of rolled clay and drew an arc to the desired diameter of the cosmos. In this particular example, the potter, after cutting away the excess clay around the circumference, simply turned one more arc in the center to mark the boundary of the central molded elements. At this point, while the circle was still flat, the mold and star punches were applied with pressure or a gentle hammer strike. It is also possible that the entire molded surface was applied by a plate mold. If that were the case, the flattened clay would be cut out, left blank, and lifted into the mold to achieve its final form before firing. The wet clay was allowed to rest in this position until completely dry, then it was partially fired, the glaze applied, and the whole fired to completion.

Let us take inventory of the molded elements as they appear in this artisan's cosmology. Remember that "the earth and stars are never idle," so these molded elements are also in perpetual motion. At the center is a circular image containing three figures; two figures are dressed, with the third naked and emerging from what appears to be a central portal by climbing a ladder. All three figures are animated by expansive gestures, their arms signaling up and out. The central figure also appears to be holding up two flowers in his right hand, while the witness to this event on his left is touching a tall plant. There is a roundel of floral images surrounding the event. Behind the second witness on the right of the climbing figure is a chimneyed, one-bay structure, with steps leading up into another large arched door. The body of the platter is earth, from which all the elements except air emanate. The second tier outside the central roundel contains a fish (water). It also has a bird (air) as well as a salamander consuming its own tail (the alchemical fire). A crenellated fortress structure also occupies the second tier, along with another man with a similar upraised arm gesture. Finally, the capital letters "F" and "H," both crowned and touching at their bottoms float by and vie for space with opposed connecting linear volutes.

The third, outermost, and final level shows the man with upraised arm twice more in revolution, an image that may have found its inspiration in the device Barthélemy Berton used for the title page of Palissy's *Recepte veritable* (see fig. 14.34). Both images are conjoined with winged effigies (one rides a bird, the other's hands have wings). This suggests elemental air and the movement of angelic or astral bodies in the outer rings toward heaven. This is reinforced by the reappearance of the bird. There are three grotesque masks, two of which are identical and sprout phallic horns from their heads. Two other images are up in the airy realm, one an armorial shield with three fleurs-de-lis, and the other is now almost lost, although it appears to have represented a repetition of the bird. In this context, the bird may recall the dove that was sent to find the earth after the Flood. Finally, though star punch decoration saturates the elements of water and air, there is none in the innermost central element. This implies that these

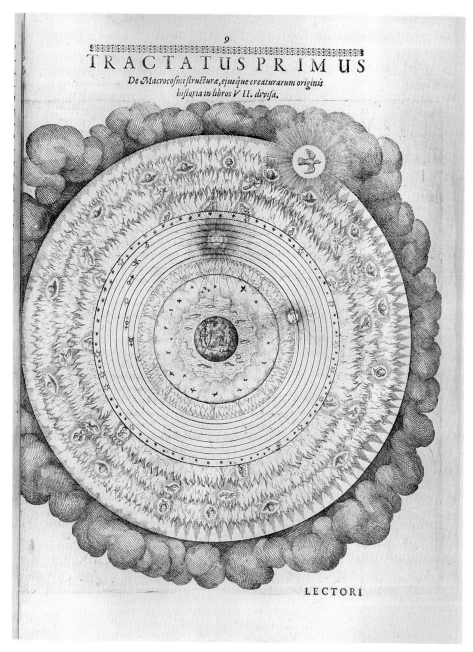

FIGURE 8.10. Johann Theodore de Bry, *De macrocosmi structurae*, from Robert Fludd, *Utriusque cosmi majoris scilicet et minoris metaphysica, physica atque technica historia in duo volumina secundum cosmi differentiam divisa . . . tomus primus De macrocosmi historia* (Oppenheim, 1617; 2d ed., Frankfurt, 1624). Courtesy Harry Ransom Humanities Research Center, The University of Texas at Austin. A Ptolemaic macrocosm showing how the disunification of the cosmos and its ultimate duality proceeded outward from the original sin of Adam and Eve at center, creating the sublunary world.

effects appear in time *after* the primordial creative event has already occurred, because floral elements fill the voids between figures and edifices instead.

What are we to make of the entities inhabiting this artisan's molded cosmos of clay and enamel? Chapelot claims that the central element "evokes the legend of Saint-Eutrope saving a child who fell into a well."[88] It is easy to understand how Chapelot could read the crucial central image in this way. Saint-Eutrope is the patron saint of Saintes, and the legend of the child and the well is a principal one in Saintongeais folklore. Though I will argue here for a somewhat different reading, Chapelot has led us in the right direction. He perceives the naked, climbing figure as a child.

Had Chapelot not denounced Palissy and his "mythologies" as superfluous impediments to his archaeology, he would have been able to give this artifact the sociocultural context it needs in order to communicate in its own historical language. Like the language of the hermaphroditic vessel to which this cosmology was intimately related, that language is inseparable from Paracelsian discourse, as it was refracted, in southwestern France, through the lens of the Palissian artisanal paradigm. After Palissy's removal to Paris and death, rustic naturalism emerged in combination with far more overt seventeenth-century Rosicrucian discourses developed by a new generation of Paracelsians. This was a new political language used in response to the horrors of the Thirty Years' War in general, and, in southwestern France, the siege of La Rochelle in particular.[89] In many ways, this cosmology provides a supreme example of the intimate relationship the Saintongeais had developed between print culture and artisanal culture by the early seventeenth century. One might read this molded surface as the ceramic equivalent to a printmaker's woodblock print. Both were effected with carved wooden "molds," and both emerged from Germanic artisanal origins. Moreover, there is every indication that the iconography of this artifact was derived almost entirely from contemporary (and mostly German) prints, adapted for local use. The sense of a "printed" cosmology begins with the winged effigy that appears in the outer two rings, but it is also a visual analogue (with its outstretched wings) for the central figure with outstretched arms. As a result, flying or rising is both implicit and explicit on all three levels.

The winged effigy synthesizes the "flying eagle" (fig. 2.4) and the "dove of the Holy Ghost," the image of which was widely disseminated throughout the Continent, Britain, and America. The bird appeared in originals and reproductions of an engraving (fig. 8.10) of "The Creation of the World" (after original sin) first printed in Robert Fludd's influential and widely copied book of Paracelsian cosmological images, *Utriusque cosmi majoris scilicet et minoris metaphysica* (Oppenheim, 1617; 2d ed., Frankfurt, 1624). The creation of the world, according to Rosicrucian Trinitarianism and Paracelsians such as Jakob Böhme and Robert Fludd, proceeded from a cloud representing the perpetually hidden Father, to "FIAT," the Word or the Son, whence it flew on the wings of the Holy Ghost in a gigantic circle, which formed the circumference of the Rosicrucian ceramic cosmology. When the dove was sent again after the Flood, it was, in effect, re-creating this moment of the birth of nature. Fludd's "universe wholly created" showed the conjunction of the Ptolemaic and Copernican cosmos resulting from Trinitarian creative impulses (fig. 2.3). Earth occupied the central sphere and proceeded outward to the elemental water (fish), air (birds), and fire. The sphere of fire appears in the Saintongeais cosmology as the alchemical mercury devouring its tail, implicit in the "fired" ceramic itself. The dove continued on its circular flight until the end of history, and so all the other spheres had also to be imagined in a vital "spinning" motion—to use a Boehmian word—in perpetuity.

Let us leave the sphere of the bird for a moment and return to the enigmatic central image. This return should call to mind not simply the image of a well but instead the wealth of subterranean cave and matrix images that animate the "discourse of the four cabinets" in Palissy's *Delectable Garden*. And indeed, those subterranean images were again merged with thresholds when related to Heinrich Khunrath's *Porta amphitheatri sapientiae aeternae* (The Gate of the Amphitheater of Eternal Wisdom) (Magdeburg, 1609), in which the philosopher ascends the stone steps of the Platonic cave of shadows toward a gate (or portal) that opens onto the light of Nature infused with the light of grace (fig. 8.11). Note the trees and other foliage that grew atop the cave, thus, in Palissy's conception, obscuring it like a fortress of patience. Frances Yates argues convincingly that the source of many of Khunrath's ideas was Palissy's English contemporary John Dee, who also published his important *Mones hieroglyphica* in 1564 and who therefore may have influenced the *Recepte véritable*.[90]

Yates also argued that Dee's ideas were behind the "rise of Christian Rosencreutz," the central mythological figure of Rosicrucianism, whose legend of rebirth was expounded in the so-called "Rosicrucian manifestos" (ca. 1612–15), the context of which, Yates is quick to point out, was allegorical and not intended to be taken literally by their authors.[91] I would argue, then, that far from being a representation of the legend of Saint-Eutrope saving a child from a well, the central image of the Saintongeais artisan's cosmology, while indeed representing a "child," was instead indicative of the chemical *rebirth* of an adult, much as Palissy was reborn in "Art of the Earth." The central roundel thus represents the seminal event of Rosicrucian mythology, which occurred in 1604, when, according to the manifestos, Christian Rosencreutz's "mystical sepulcher" was said to have been opened and his reborn aged "child's" body disinterred by adepts of the third circle, after 120 years of entombment (fig. 8.12).[92]

Yates argues that "the opening of the door of the vault symbolizes the opening of a door in Europe," for the great chemical instauration.[93] Unfortunately, the original image from 1604 is now lost. The engraving shown in fig. 8.12, published as the frontispiece to Denis Zacaire's *Die Naturliche Philosophia* (Dresden, 1724), an early eighteenth-

FIGURE 8.11. *Porta amphitheatri sapientiae aeternae*, from Heinrich Khunrath, *Amphitheatrum sapientia aeternae solius verae Christiano-kabalisticvm, divino-magicum, nec non, physico-chymicvm, tertriunum, catholicon* (Magdeburg: Levinum Braunss Bibliopolam, 1609). Reproduced by permission of The Huntington Library, San Marino, California. RB 601408.

century attempt by adherents of Rosicrucianism to retrieve its sixteenth- and seventeenth-century iconography, is probably a close copy of the original. Until the original image of Rosencruetz' mythological disinterment surfaces, the molded version on the Saintongeais artisan's cosmology remains an important copy from the period.

There remains the possibility as well that the mold is instead an adaptation from numerous written accounts of the event. Within this context, the "child" with arms outstretched became a figure for "Rosencruetz," the "well" (like the one in fig. 8.5) his subterranean tomb—which was really a matrix when it is understood that the chimneyed one-bay structure is also a kiln—and the two witnesses adepts of the third circle. The two roses the child holds in his hand signify the growing together of macrocosm and microcosm and hence personal hermetic transformation.[94] The ladder is Jacob's ladder of the six stages of transformation, from the world of the senses to the inner

world of the imagination and hence knowledge. The "child" stands well above the sixth and final rung, not unlike the children in Johann Theodore de Bry's *De macrocosmi structurae* (fig. 8.10).[95]

The juxtaposition of the two images of disinterment clarifies the relationship between them, just as it does that of Palissy's sixteenth-century subterranean fortress-garden and the seventeenth-century Rosicrucian fantasy of hermetic rebirth to a new world of chemical unity. While Palissy's subterranean fortress considered patience in awaiting the chemical millennium, and planting seeds in the wall of a matrix of light that is animated but yet hidden from the world of violence, this cosmology wrought by a seventeenth-century inheritor of his program manifested the artisan's unrealized dream of rebirth in perfection from the womb of the chemical millennium in the midst of a new dawn for mankind. But, of course, this was merely the extension to its logical end of the material-holiness synthesis through the rebirth of materials that Palissy planted in the region in the sixteenth century with his experiments in search of the white glaze. The Paracelsian artisan, exploiting his special transformational relationship with materials, could in this sense experience a spiritual rebirth every time he performed artisanry to externalize his internal millennial event. In this way every Paracelsian artisan became "Christian Rosencreutz" by separating purified matter—and his soulish self—from the earth's impurities. The extension of Rosicrucianism into Saintonge during the Thirty Years' War then, was a local reiteration of Palissian natural language, which used an expanded, more overtly occult symbolic language.

After having emerged from the subterranean garden-matrix, the language of the second and third tiers of this cosmological amphitheater became even more overtly

FACING PAGE:

FIGURE 8.12. *Mons philosophorum* (The Philosophical Mountain), frontispiece to Denis Zacaire, *Die Naturliche Philosophia* (Dresden, 1724). Courtesy Science Special Collections, University of Michigan Library. This is the earliest known copy extant of the lost 1604 image of Christian Rosencreutz emerging from his subterranean sepulcher. Unlike later copies, it does not have the date 1604 engraved on the plate. Here again, as with *In patientia sauvitas* (fig. 9.1), the mountain is also a fortress of concealment that reveals its alchemical secrets after a long period of maturation in earth's underground crucible. The hermetic vocabulary that dominates the molded surface of the pottery from La Chapelle-des-Pots seen in figs. 8.6 and 8.7 is repeated here. A furnace billows smoke to the right of the lion (cf. fig. 8.3) that guards the visible door to the fortress, while Christian emerges below. A nesting hen waits patiently for her eggs to hatch; and scampering rabbits, their ears forming the downward angle, scoot, like Christian, from holes hidden in the earth. Christian's white beard forms the upward angle like that of the adept in figure 8.1, to complete the circuit (with the rabbit) between macrocosm and microcosm. Disciples fall to their knees and raise their arms, amazed at their vision, in history, of the Second Coming.

PHILOSOPHORVM.

CONCEPTIO SEV PVTRE
factio

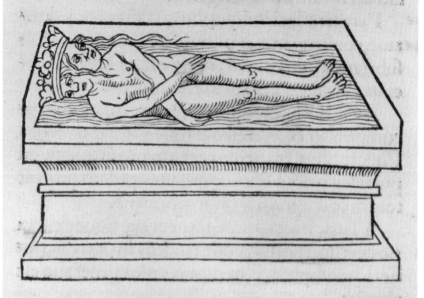

Hye ligen könig vnd köningin dot/
Die sele scheydt sich mit grosser not.

ARISTOTELES REX ET
Philosophus.

Nunquam vidi aliquod animatum crescere sine putrefactione, nisi autem fiat putris dum inuanum erit opus alchimicum.

FIGURE 8.13. *Conceptio seu putrefactio*, from *Rosarium philosophorum* (Frankfurt, 1550). Courtesy Harry Ransom Humanities Research Center, The University of Texas at Austin. Putrefaction in the alchemical process represented as postcoital synthesis. Male and female figures unite under a single crown, forming a kind of chemical hermaphrodite.

Palissian. This is particularly true in the images of the hermaphrodite floating in the liquid element. Palissy's friend Ambroise Paré provided a valuable clue that suggests what the crowned initials "F" and "H" may have stood for in "On Hermaphrodite or Androgynes, That Is to Say, Which Have Two Sets of Sex Organs in One Body," in *On Monsters and Marvels,* where he wrote: "Hermaphrodites or androgynes are children who are born with double genitalia, one masculine and the other feminine, *and as a result are called in our French language hommes et femmes. (Androgyne in Greek means man and woman, woman and man)* [emphasis added]."[96]

The crowns were again derived from prints of the *conjunction* of macrocosm and microcosm when represented as the crowned sun and moon engaged in inseparable coitus—and hence they are effectively one androgynous entity—as in figure 8.13, taken from the *Rosarium philosophorum* (1550). The bottoms—figuratively speaking, the "genitalia"—of the letters, were in contact as they moved in opposite directions, connoting the conjunction of opposites. As if to confirm this analysis, the reborn child now floats also, though barely perceptible, in the liquid near the crown of "H," where it seems to display swollen feminine breasts and masculine genitals. Inasmuch as the hermaphrodite is flowing in the liquid element, its image resonates with that of the virgin lactating distilled liquid into the sea of renewal, in Daniel Stolcius de Stolcenberg's *Viridarium chymicum* (1624) (fig. 8.14). The swollen breasts and male genitals are again made quite pronounced in both molds depicting the reborn child "riding" his spirit around the cosmos through the elemental air. Like Practice before him, this child is engaged in the spiritual regeneration of himself out of his own body, through the astral conjunction of macrocosm and microcosm—or in artisanal terms, a material-holiness synthesis—in the earth's matrix. In this, one of the most significant of the anonymous southwestern Huguenot artifacts of desire for soulish conjunction, the artisan built his astral body emerging into the light of a new world, cleansed and purified. Even if his corresponding corporeal body had to remain behind in historical time, a shell of disguise contained his animated spirit until the millennium.

The desire for alchemical conjunction is most famously depicted in Heinrich Khunrath's engraving of Paullus van der Doort's *The Cabalist–Alchemist* (fig. 8.15), also from Khunrath's *Amphitheatrum sapientia aeternae.* Here, the alchemist is depicted kneeling in prayer before the light emanating from a book opened to cosmologies of the macrocosm and the microcosm on succeeding pages, positioned next to another book representing either the Scriptures or the Book of Nature. His arms are spread in a gesture of both passive embrace and astonishment as he tries to accommodate the conjunction of both the big world and the little world to the celestial center in his own body. Following mannerist perspective back into deep space, the engraving ultimately resolves in a central vanishing point that is also a "prospect door" framed, once again, by columns of the Doric order. The door opens inward and yet out into the light,

FIGURE 8.14. Virgin lactating into the sea of renewal, from Daniel Stolcius de Stolcenberg, *Viridarium chymicum* (1624). Courtesy Yale University, Harvey Cushing / John Hay Whitney Medical Library. Dualities are purified by alchemical synthesis and find unity in "the sea of renewal."

in much the same way as the alchemist's physician's armchair, situated just before the door in the beholder's line of perspective, seems to repeat the door's open framing of the light in its back.

While the open door may have carried much the same meaning for Khunrath as it did for the writers of the Rosicrucian manifestos, it simultaneously calls to mind Böhme's analogy of the body's opening up to the spirit as similar to a kind of open door that must also be barred against entry by the devil. In this context, the open door in the far distance adumbrates the alchemists' goal, to be achieved only at the end of much labor and time, to experience the astral conjunction he can only desire in his imagination in the foreground. The advantage to utilizing the artisan's glazed ceramic cosmology as an artifact of desire for conjunction is that, conceptually speaking, the glazed ceramic had *already* undergone conjunction in the kiln and hence represented the *material* unification of the two cosmologies, which must be depicted separately in Khunrath's printed representation. But in the cosmology from

FIGURE 8.15. Paullus van der Doort, *The Cabalist-Alchemist*, in Heinrich Khunrath, *Amphitheatrum sapientia aeternae solius verae Christiano-kabalisticvm, divino-magicum, nec non, physico-chymicvm, tertriunum, catholicon* (Magdeburg: Levinum Braunss Bibliopolam, 1609). Reproduced by permission of The Huntington Library, San Marino, California. RB 601408. The room is bracketed by a shrine to metaphysical contemplation on one side, where the worshipful alchemist opens his arms to contain and unify occult images of the macrocosm and the microcosm illustrated in the open cosmology on the altar; and, on the other, the crucible and forge, a shrine to "Experientia" and the manual arts. On the table are musical instruments and a scale to signify harmony and balance between these dual forces of spirit and matter. The physician's chair, its diamond-carved back connecting the sitter's heart with God's secrets, revealed only to adepts (such as John Winthrop Jr.), directs his spirit through the narrow door of inner illumination at the room's vanishing point.

FIGURE 8.16. Detail of figure 8.6. Reproduced by permission of The Musée national ceramique de Sèvres. © Réunion des Musées Nationaux / Art Resource, New York.

La Chapelle-des-Pots, macrocosm and microcosm were literally superimposed on (and
in) one another.

Other images of balance and conjunction of opposites occur in the second and third
levels and in the intertwined volutes (fig. 8.16), which are nonetheless in motion in opposite directions, as well as in the multitude of "star" punches. The volutes represent
an early attempt in the region to express the physics of the movement between the
macrocosm and the microcosm in an abstract, linear way. This innovation would have
profound implications for Huguenot artisans working in other mediums but especially
in woodworking, where the tastemaker Daniel Marot adapted them for his influential design book. And the "stars" were later abstractions of Palissy's "sparks" and
"flashes," a mixture of air and fire so common in printed cosmologies. When perceived
in flickering candlelight, the star punches would produce the desired sparkling effect
by increasing opportunities for refraction in the glaze of the already raised and irreg-
ular surfaces of the cosmology. In corpuscular theory, no space is a vacuum; the air is
filled with imperceptible atoms. Finally, the two grotesque bearded masks in the elemental air suggest standard figures for the winds. With phallic horns expending in
opposite directions—inferring sexual conjunction—this also connoted a representation of Moses, the most pervasive Old Testament type with which *désert* Huguenots
identified in the seventeenth century, and perhaps the wild man as well?

If the conjoined crested volutes signifying the conciliation of opposites in the artisan's cosmology are suggestive of the seventeenth-century shift towards linear abstraction where impulse diagrams demonstrated the physics of the Paracelsian chemical millennium, then the hermetic vessel in figure 8.7 is a fully articulated and self-contained artifactual equation of the metaphysical movement of astral conjunction in matter. Unlike the cosmology, the vessel is ambitiously constructed in several parts, which are either turned, built with coils of clay, applied or molded, and then connected just before firing.

The vessel is sealed hermetically with the exception of two openings hidden up underneath the foot, which serve as the only access to the inner hollow body of the oval. These two holes served both practical and metaphysical functions. The practical function was simply to prevent the main body of the pot from exploding in the kiln, the victim of expanding interior gases with no opening for escape. The metaphysical function is far more arcane and implicitly Neoplatonic. James Nohrnberg performs an intriguing reading of the hilarious moment in Ariosto's *Orlando Furioso* when Astolfo flies to the moon to recover Orlando's lost wits. There he discovers that everything lost on earth goes to the moon where it is kept in jars. Of course, there are more jars of lost brains than anything else.[97]

Nohrnberg chooses, however, to read these passages from *Orlando Furioso* as a serious joke. He suggests that Ariosto was interested in exploring the "loss and recovery of self," wherein the jars "function as repositories for potential being."[98] That Orlando's wits were kept in a jar on the moon recalls Plato's well-known pun linking the shifting movement of the desiring soul with a jar, because it can be swayed and easily persuaded. But Porphyry, whose treatise *On the Cave of the Nymphs* from the Odyssey was widely read in the Renaissance, chose to explain Plato's pun in solemn Neoplatonic terms:

> Plato also says that there are two openings, one of which affords a passage to souls ascending to the heavens, but the other to souls descending to the earth. And according to the theologist, the Sun and Moon are the gates of souls, which ascend through the Sun and descend through the Moon. With Homer, likewise, there are two tubs,
>
>> From which the lots of every one he fills, / Blessings to these, to those distributes ills.
>> (*Iliad* 24.528 f.)
>
> But Plato, in the *Gorgias*, by tubs intends to signify souls, some of which are malefic, but others beneficent, and some of which are rational, but others irrational. Souls, however, are tubs, because they contain in themselves energies and habits, as in a vessel.[99]

Yet it was the *Timaeus*, Plato's natural-philosophical treatise on the operation of the soul in the creation of the universe, that, directly or indirectly, was the most influential of Plato's texts for Neoplatonic artisans as regards the forms taken by the soul's containers. Sections 16–18 of the *Timaeus* speak specifically to concerns displayed by the Saintongeais potters who made both the circular cosmology and hermetic vessel. The sections are titled: "The receptacle of becoming"; "The names fire, air, water, earth really indicate differences of quality not of substance"; and, most germane, "The receptacle compared to a mass of plastic material upon which differing impressions are stamped. As such it has no definite character of its own."[100]

In section 16, Plato says the universe "is the receptacle and, as it were, the nurse of all becoming and change." In section 17, we are told, as by Palissy, that elemental change is permanent in the universe. Everything is merely a container for something else in process, therefore all things must be mutable by definition, both more and less than they appear:

> There is in fact a process of cyclical transformation. Since . . . none of them [the elements] ever appears constantly in the same form, it would be embarrassing to maintain that any of them is certainly one rather than the other. . . . Whenever we see anything in process of change, for example fire, we should speak of it not as *being a thing* but as *having a quality* . . . the things we suppose we can indicate by pointing and using the expressions "this thing" or "that thing". . . have no stability and elude . . . permanence. . . . We should only use the expressions "this thing" or "that thing" when speaking of that in which this process takes place and in which these qualities appear for a time and then vanish.[101]

And in section 18, Plato explains that molds are impressions of these inner processes taking place in the receptacles. From an artisan's point of view, this also represented a craftsman's projection onto elemental matter that went into making the receptacle. Hence, clay was a perfect "plastic material upon which differing impressions are stamped" by the souls of natural artisans, as well as their patrons or spectators. Like the pious body, this material too must be void to receive the soul's impressions:

> The same argument applies to the natural receptacle of all bodies. . . . it continues to receive all things, and never itself takes a permanent impress of any of the things that enter it; it is a kind of neutral plastic material on which changing impressions are stamped by the things which enter it, making it appear different at different times. And the things which pass in and out of it are copies of the eternal realities. . . . We may use the metaphor of birth and compare the receptacle to the mother, the model to the father, and what they produce between them to their offspring; and we may notice that, if an imprint is to present a very complex appearance, the material on which it is to be stamped will not have been properly prepared unless it is devoid of all the characters which it is to receive. For if it were like any of the things that enter it, it would badly distort any impression of a contrary or entirely different nature when it received it, as its own features would shine

FIGURE 8.17. *Accipe ovum et igneo percute gladio,* from Michael Maier, *Atalanta fugiens* (Oppenheim, 1618). Courtesy Beinecke Rare Book and Manuscript Library, Yale University. Great wisdom in the manipulation of fire is needed to wield the alchemical sword of separation.

through . . . those who set about making impressions in some soft substance make its surface as smooth as possible and allow no impression at all to remain visible in it.[102]

In the hands of the Saintongeais artisan, the "energies and habits" desiring souls "contain[ed] in themselves" assumed specific patterns of movement, and that movement "in which this process takes place," occurred in a hermetic "tub," "vessel," or "receptacle" of very specific form. The oval shape set on a single turned foot had a long tradition in alchemical work and discourse. Its most basic, organic referent was the philosophical egg illustrated as emblem 8 (fig. 8.17) in Michael Maier's book of Rosicrucian emblemata, *Atalanta fugiens* (Oppenheim, 1618). Here the alchemist uses the ubiquitous sword of separation in an allegory of alchemic purification, death, and rebirth, which includes references to fire and the metaphysics of deep spatial perspective in yet another door open to the light.[103]

But perhaps the most explicit images of alchemic separation, distillation, and rebirth that use eggs or wombs as substitutes for the alchemist's matrix are to be found

FIGURE 8.18. Plate 9 of the *Mutus liber* (La Rochelle, 1677). Courtesy Beinecke Rare Book and Manuscript Library, Yale University. Embryonic mercury created inside an egg in the alchemist's fortress/crucible. Compare with figure 2.6.

in the *Mutus liber,* an edition of which was published in La Rochelle in 1677. Plate 9 of the La Rochelle edition depicts the process that occurs in the alchemist's fortresslike matrix (fig. 8.18). The upper level portrays an image of Mercury distilled in the philosopher's droplike egg (or vial), standing on the "gates" of sun and moon—represented on the central round of the present hermetic vessel—which signifies both his dual nature and the astral conjunction. The egg is held aloft next to the scorching rays of the sun (which sweats, ripens, and fills the distilling Mercury with the astral spirit), by two cherubs on the wings of doves whose function it is to occupy the transitional space as a moving bridge up and down between macrocosm and microcosm. The lower level of the image (male quality versus female quality) is another referent to the duality of matter, which has the potential for androgynous unity in the matrix signified here by the distillation of the egg as it drips, like seminal fluid, into an open funnel.

This form of the Neoplatonic concept of duality and conciliation of opposites is repeated in both the construction and molded and glazed surface decoration of the Saintongeais hermetic vessel in figure 8.7, beginning with the Janus-faced masks on the handles, surmounted by voluted returns to the center of the crest. While the inside of the vessel is absolutely hollow and hidden, the central roundel functions as a sort of eye, a window opening into the inner workings of the soul in its synthesis with its material vessel in the alchemists quest for the philosopher's stone. In short, the vessel becomes a trope for the animated astral spirit at work hidden inside the empty vessel of the desiring Paracelsist artisan. But while the inside signifies dark, empty, and hidden internal space, the outside glows and sparkles with the green glaze of generation, as the light, represented moving inside out, is manipulated by surface hatching and fluting to emit the effect of "sparks and flashes."

The centripetal flow diagram of soulish impulses in matter as the processes of separation, purification, and reunification occur circulates around a Trinitarian shield consisting of a pyramid form dominated by an ascending triangle signifying fire and air (which is also a compass in perfect position to draw arcs to form the body of the vessel), encompassing an astral heart, which is itself half-enclosed by the arc of the half-moon—recall Porphyry on Plato—of the microcosm. The placement of the heart *inside* the arc of the moon is a figure for the astral animation of the half-dead (half-dark) matter of the microcosm that also works in the generation of the ceramic vessel itself. The two heliotropic flowers bend toward the light along the upright planes of the equilateral triangle recall the bouquet brought up from the center of the earth by the androgynous child-figure in the artisan's cosmology.

An engraving (fig. 8.19) from Samuel Norton's *Alchymiae complementum* (Frankfurt, 1630)—which proceeds upward from the mouth of a Palissian frog—reveals that the roundel from the vessel signifies the stages of hermetic transformation of the Mercurius *homo philossophicus.* The elemental tree with anastomosing roots supplies the

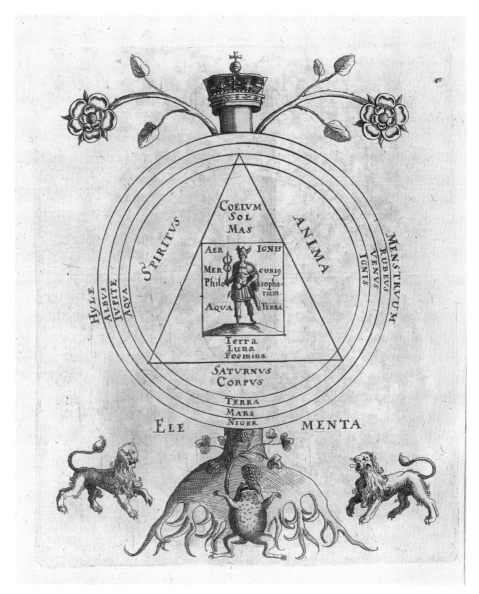

FIGURE 8.19. *Elementa*, from Samuel Norton, *Alchymiae complementum, et perfectio, seu, Modus et Processus argumentandi: sive multiplicandi omnes lapides, & elixera in virtute . . .* (Frankfurt: Typis Caspari Rotelii, Impensis Guiliemi Fitzeri, 1630). Courtesy Beinecke Rare Book and Manuscript Library, Yale University. A Palissian frog consumes the fruit of the vine while rooted in the earth and its subterranean regions at the base of an elemental tree. Philosophical mercury connects all the elements. The frog is flanked by two alchemical lions reminiscent of those in figs. 8.3 and 8.20.

animate heart of the philosopher at center (in a gnostic square inside a triangle inside the third of three cosmic revolutions, as on Winthrop's chair) with seminal water from the microcosm earth (recalling J. B. van Helmont's famous and influential Paracelsian willow tree experiment of 1648, which concluded that "all Vegetables do materially arise wholly out of the Element of water") even as the sun complements this action and feeds the waters of the earth in return with astral rays from the macrocosm. Indeed, all the elements converge at the heart of the philosophical man.[104]

In the image from Norton's *Alchymiae* (as in the Saintongeais vessel) the flowers representing "corpus" and "anima" are the five-petaled rose or blue and white "golden flower" of alchemical conjunction. This conjunction begins with the root of the flower in the seminal waters of the microcosm, and travels up the stem to the open flowers, which receive astral rays from the sun, thus completing a bridge or connection between the two. Closer to the context in which the hermetic vessel was made, however, is emblem 2 of Basil Valentine's *Azoth*, published in French translation in 1660 (fig. 8.20). Yet this emblem had appeared in France much earlier in the century, when it was incorporated into the frontispiece of Salomon Trismosin's *La Toison d'or* (The Golden Fleece), published in Paris in 1612.[105] Here, the figure of the philosophical mercury is represented by Jon Dee's monas sign for the philosopher's stone, taken from Dee's *Monas hieroglyphica* of 1564; a symbol that also served as John Winthrop Jr.'s ex libris. Valentine's occult motto, which can be roughly translated to read "Go VISIT THE IN-TERIOR OF THE EARTH AND YOU WILL PERFECT YOUR ART AND DISCOVER THE PHILOSOPHER'S STONE," might have been written by Palissy himself. To be sure, this command encapsulated perfectly the elemental ideology of Palissy's seventeenth-century artisan followers, as well as of the master himself.

The hermetic vessel thus functioned as a conduit between macrocosm and microcosm through the material-holiness synthesis of Paracelsian artisanry. In this context, the Neoplatonic function of the vessel's two openings becomes even more specific. This vessel is connected to the microcosm in the earth's matrix through the two openings in its foot, where the seminal "water"—the source of its brilliant sparkling "greenesse"—passes up into the inside. Simultaneously, astral rays from the macrocosm are absorbed into the vessel through the alchemic rose (or is it a sunflower) at its crest, and enter the vessel as well, where they "intermingle" with the seminal waters. The animated internal motion of intermingling is represented in the eye or window of the pot. As the two flowers grow together toward the light at the triangle's uppermost point of intersection inside, they are unified outside at the vessel's "crown" by a single flower, which opens back down, returning the light to the inside. Hence, there is reciprocity between the macrocosm and microcosm—the "ascending" and "descending" souls—through the material elements inside and outside the vessel.

Most important, however, the *movement* of the process of material-holiness syn-

FIGURE 8.20. *Visita interiora terra rectificando invenies occultum lapidem,* emblem 2 from
Basilius Valentinus, *Les Douze Clefs de philosophie de . . . Basile Valentin . . . traictant de la vraye
medecine metalique. Plus L'Azoth; ou, Le Moyen de faire l'or caché des philosophes* (Paris: Pierre
Moët, 1660). Courtesy Beinecke Rare Book and Manuscript Library, Yale University. A monas
sign representing philosophical mercury and the philosopher's stone appears to grow out of a
Grail-like vessel with gates for souls opened by the sun and moon found at the center-top of
this emblem of the chemical wedding of elemental earth and its subterranean regions. Ultimately from Paracelsus's *Das Buch azoth,* it was published in Paris as early as 1612, when it was
incorporated into the frontispiece of Salomon Trismosin's *La Toison d'or* (The Golden Fleece).

thesis— what Porphyry calls the "energies and habits" of the Platonic soul—was conceptualized as linear movement around and below the perimeter of the crests of Mercurius.

   Listen again to Jacob Böhme describe the generation of light in the Trinity between
macrocosm and microcosm. At the same time, continue to follow the impulses of soulish movement "inside" the vessel:

the Sonne is allways generated *continually* from eternity unto eternity, and restoreth always continually from eternity, unto the powers of the Father again, whereby the powers of the Father are always from Eternity to Eternity *continually* impregnated with the Sonne, and generated him continually. . . . Out of which, the Holy Ghost *continually* Existeth from eternity to eternity, and so continually from eternity to eternity goeth forth from the Father and the Sonne, and both neither Beginning nor End.[106]

Hence, the Saintongeais hermetic vessel was the materialization, not only of a seventeenth-century artisanal conception of Paracelsist optics, but of millennial history as well. But the movement of the soul inside the vessel was also evidence as well of the primacy of its *own* artisanal role:

For the Soul comprehendeth the *highest* sense, it beholdeth what God its Father acteth or maketh, also it Co-operateth in the heavenly Imagining or framing: And therefore it maketh a description draught platform, or modell, for the Nature-spirit, shewing how a thing should be Imaged or framed. . . . And according to this delineation or prefiguration of the Soul, all things in this world are made; for the corrupted soul worketh or endeavoreth continually, to bring forth or frame heavenly Ideas shapes or figures . . . [and that is why] when a Carpenter will build a curious house or Artificial piece of Architecture, or any other *Artist* goeth about the making of some artificial work, the *Hands* which signifie *Nature,* cannot be the first that begin the work; but the seven [Nature] spirits [fig. 8.5] are the first Workmasters about it, and the animated or soulish spirit sheweth the form figure or shape of it to the seven spirits. . . . And then the seven spirits Image or frame it, and make it comprehensible, and then the hands *first* begin to fall to work.[107]

Plate 15 of the *Mutus liber* (fig. 8.21) reinforces the central window as a soulish inner "eye" with its title: *Oculatis abis* ("Second Sight"). It represents the completion of the process of linear movement in the material of a rope knotted together with the arms of angels and man in the motion of joint double infinity—the conjunction of macrocosm and microcosm—which nonetheless continues to pulsate in animate matter throughout eternity. On the ceramic vessel, the "rope" is knotted at the bottom, "inside" the earth, to signify that the material of conjunction (green-glazed pottery) is of the earth. But while the material with which the pulsating animation of matter is described may be ceramic or rope, these are still essentially tropes for the elemental tree, the material of which is wood.

This was made plain by *Dialogue Between Nature and the Alchemist* (fig. 8.22), a miniature painted by Jean Perréal (ca. 1455–1530) in 1516 to illustrate his alchemical poem *La Complainte de nature à l'alchimiste errant.*[108] Here, androgynous Nature uses a signifier of astral conjunction, in this case a wooden tree, as a *chair* surmounted by an inverted flower to turn the light inside (like the one in fig. 8.7), from which the "homme

FIGURE 8.21. Plate 15 of the *Mutus liber* (La Rochelle, 1677). Courtesy Beinecke Rare Book and Manuscript Library, Yale University. The adept at bottom has captured the Golden Fleece, which he wears, inspiring "second sight." This eye of the imagination, signaled by both the text and the adept's hand (touching his mind behind the eye), allows mystical perception (see fig. 14.17) to pierce the deception of the senses and unify the macrocosm and microcosm.

FIGURE 8.22. *Dialogue Between the Alchemist and Nature,* 1516 (vellum), by Jean Perréal (ca. 1455–1530). H: 18.1 cm × W: 13.4 cm. Courtesy Musée Marmottan, Paris, France / Bridgeman Art Library.

et femme" debates with the alchemist, who has one foot in Nature's domain and the other at the door to his matrix. Thus, while the chair of Nature is a conduit between macrocosm and microcosm, the alchemist draws impulses from its conjunction to his matrix, which, as we have seen in the Saintongeais vessel, was analogous.

When read together with Saintongeais Huguenot pottery, this little painting has great implications for a new understanding of seating furniture constructed by south-western Huguenot artisans dispersed to colonial America in the seventeenth century. Perhaps we might now better understand the genesis of the London caned and New York leather chairs with the elaborately carved crest rail? Though they are by no means identical, it can be suggested that these chairs emerged from the same conceptual framework of Paracelsian artisanry that produced the Saintongeais hermetic vessel. The carved crests (figs. 15.26 and 15.40) follow similar ideas of the perpetual motion of binary separation, intermingling, and return seen, albeit in a different form and context, at the upper corners of the shields of the pot.

By the time the New York chair was turned and joined, the Palissian paradigm of the interiority of animate matter had emerged from the camouflage of tiny industrious creatures to the explicit—but short-lived—symbolism of the Rosicrucians. Ultimately, it took final form in the refugee Huguenot artisans' linear mapping of the centripetal journey of astral bodies, now mostly located in chairs. What was explicit in the early seventeenth century was internalized by the time of the Revocation and therefore became implicit in the hands and commodities of New York Huguenot artisans. These concepts were later expressed in the chairs themselves. As meaning was finally absorbed into the material itself, creating a new materialism, so too the subterranean culture came home in artifacts and was diffused within the colonial system. Chairs became the perfect furniture to uphold and maintain the patient body.

All this was predicted already in *A Delectable Garden*, which forms our earliest understanding of the historical and material connection between the Saintongeais "art of the earth" and wooden seats. Wherever the feet of the New York chair touched the earth, and depending upon who was sitting there, an astral conjunction between the macrocosm and microcosm was made, as if completing an electrical circuit.

Palissy concluded, therefore, that no matter what form it took, iconography stood in an a posteriori relationship to the discourse of materials and optics. Following Ficino, Palissy's artisanal practice presumed that the power to transform existed not in the magic of imagery but inside the materials themselves, which at most may be compressed or warmed into greater animation by molds and other tools.[109] In the final analysis, the discourse of molded pottery may only have amplified what had already been communicated about process and history by the plain, green-glazed pottery with which it was produced simultaneously. The difference remains that the plain pottery was produced for export, while the molded pottery remained "experimental" and, as such, at home. Perhaps, after all, some southwestern Huguenot artisans exported a hidden "second body" to the New World before their first was ready to go.

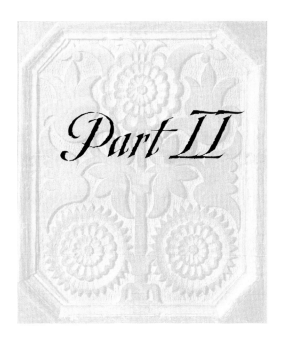

Part II

The Fragmentation of the Body

CHAPTER NINE

"In Patientia Sauvitas," or, The Invisible Fortress Departs

Thus I stand yet as an anxious woman in travel, and seek *perfect* refreshing, but find only the scent or smell or savour in its rising up, wherein, the Spirit examineth, what power *sticketh* in the true Cordial; and in the mean while refresheth it self in its sicknesse with that *perfect smell* or savour, till the true *Samaratan* doth come, who would dresse and bind up its wounds and heal it, and bring it to the eternal *Inne* or Lodging, then it shall enjoy the *perfect Taste.*   —JAKOB BÖHME, *Aurora*

When Palissy's Saintongeais followers were firing their hermetic receptacles, the discourse of Rosicrucianism and the subterranean language of artisanal security also converged in a representation of the siege of La Rochelle. The iconography of the Society of the Rosy Cross harnesses the martyrdom of La Rochelle's material body to the rebirth of its invisible soul in the fertile waters of the Atlantic world in a print entitled *In patientia sauvitas* (Sweetness in Patience) (fig. 9.1).[1] After this moment of convergence, in which iconography allowed visualization of the hidden soul of southwestern Huguenot culture during its migration from violence and corruption to the west, this public, if obscure, symbolic language became disengaged from the refugees' multitude of private concerns. Explicitness was no longer necessary. The invisible fortress had departed in the artisans of its region to create new material forms in new worlds.

La Rochelle's earliest heretics understood "subterranean" in the literal sense. The fortress became the dominant symbol of open Huguenot defiance in Catholic France, and the decades before its great Protestant revolution in 1568 saw many episodes of the violent persecution of heresy. Following publication of Luther's theses in 1517, more

IN PATIENTIA SVAVITAS.

Rochelle.

Qui mala fert male, fert tempus grave, bisq; dolore Fit miser: ast mala qui fert bene, victor abit.

Der Vnglück trägt mit vngduld sehr,
Dem wirt es zweymahl noch so schwer.

Der es aber trägt mit Geduld
Vhr wind entlich bkompt Gottes huld.

FIGURE 9.1. *In patientia sauvitas.* Print. Germany, ca. 1627–28. Courtesy Archives départe-mentales de la Charente-Maritime. Photo, Neil Kamil. A whipsaw of the type shown ripping through "the rock" called for two sawyers laboring "against" each other at opposite ends, one pushing and the other pulling.

than a generation of Rochelais Protestants experienced oppression under the state re-ligion before the tables were turned on the Catholics, and there is much archeological evidence of clandestine activity in La Rochelle, although it was very short-lived.[2]

Inconspicuous doorways, hidden in shadows cast by the city's covered arcades and porches, still open to houses with stone staircases that descend under the rues Saint-Sauveur, des Gentilshommes, and Bletterie. These former merchant houses, mostly tall and narrow, spiral around the church of Saint-Sauveur, a towering medieval cathe-dral that gives the quarter its name. Just below the second oldest church in La Rochelle, then, lies an underground network of limestone cellars, tunnels, and crawl spaces where Protestant conventicles assembled by night and heretical books were hidden. Depending on political circumstances, this secret labyrinth of forbidden scriptoria and printing presses, walled-in libraries, and closeted reading rooms was maintained and expanded or left to fall into disrepair from lack of use. After 1568, subterranean La Rochelle was forgotten by the victorious Huguenots. The underground was revived by the city's secret Protestants after 1628, but by then there were too few for it to matter.

The chamber of commerce and city hall of this prosperous community seem con-tent with the town's spruced-up archeological survivals. The façade of the old port has been remarkably well maintained for the benefit of the tourists who spend summers windsurfing off the Île de Ré and Les Minimes. But disliking the dark, dirty Renaissance revival façade of the late-nineteenth-century building that used to house the region's archives, situated across the place Foch from the prefect's office (an appropriately Palladian *hôtel*), La Rochelle's city fathers decided in the 1980 to replace it with a new building north of town.

Formerly, however, after negotiating the shadows of the old archives building's ill-lit hall and damp stairwell, visitors were surprised to enter the dry, bright intimacy of its reading room, a cabinet of curiosities collected for display by earlier archivists, whose portraits line the walls. The tiny engraving *In patientia sauvitas* (fig. 9.1) was once discreetly hung in one corner of this room. It had no provenance—no history outside the reading room—and had occupied the same spot for longer than anyone could remember. Most of the learned habitués doubtless found its Latin and German epigrams and hermetic references obscure—the work of irrational minds—and so thought the engraving unworthy of being taken down for serious inspection. Notwithstanding this, and although it was printed nearly forty years after Bernard Palissy's death, *In patientia sauvitas* remains a compelling epitaph for the passing of the Palissian moment from southwestern France to colonial America.

❧ Translation and Inventory ❧

The *In patientia sauvitas* print was clearly pulled from a German Protestant press. It is captioned "The Rock" in French below the title, and below the image we read, in Latin: "Those who endure adversity with impatience find the time interminable and the anguish twice as painful, but those who hold fast will carry off the victory." And below that, in German: "He who carries misfortune with great impatience / For him it will become twice as heavy. / He however who carries it with patience / Overcomes in the end and receives the Grace of God."

This grim yet playful representation of patience by a mournful Protestant artist contemplating the death throws of La Rochelle from the perspective of Germany articulates the same double meanings as Palissy does in "On the Art of the Earth." The relation between patience and adversity for Huguenots under siege in the fortress was clearly analogous to the misfortunes and finally the experience of pregnancy and soulish rebirth that Palissy endured in his quest for the white enamel. The triple repetition of the verb "carry" connotes the pain and risk of carrying a child to term in the fullness of time. Thus, if personal "misfortune," which was at the core of the Germanic sectarian conception of receiving grace, was carried with "great impatience," then the weight of the child, "for him," would "become twice as heavy." Patience allowed the desiring soul to "overcome the end and receive the grace of God." "The end" and "the time" was the loaded language of final things associated with both Revelation and the chemical millennium. As Palissy admonished, "the end" would only arrive "over the succession of time."

Let us take an inventory of the image itself. The eastern perspective from behind the walls and through the towers implies that the eyes of Europe, and especially Germany, were focused on the great events as they transpired. Also from the direction of Germany, an intense light shines on and apparently right through the apocalyptic mountain. In John Winthrop the Elder's diary of inner religious "Experiencia" of 1616–18, written while he still lived in England, the future governor of Massachusetts reveals a bodily assault similar to La Rochelle's trials. His resolve—and that of international Protestantism—was to remain steadfast like "the rock" of Mount Zion, laboring to mortify the flesh to create spiritual purity. And, like the narrow aperture opened up by the space between the towers of La Rochelle, such pious labor was "the narrowe waye that leads to heaven" (and, for Winthrop, to the New World as well):

> But God being mercifull to me, forced me (even against my will) to lay more load upon it [the flesh], and to sett it a greater taske, for he lett in such discomforts, of anguish, feare, unquietnesse, etc, upon my soule, as made me forgett the grones of the fleshe and take care to helpe my pore soule, and so was the flesh forced to be more strong and lively, when it was putt to greater labour. . . . Through Christ Jesus the world is crucified into me, and I to the world; I owe nothing to it, nor to the fleshe, but have hidden defiance to them with my whole heart . . . I am in the right course, even the narrowe waye that leads to heaven . . . all experience tells me, that in this way there is least companie, and that those which doe walke openly in this way shall be despised . . . yet all this is nothing to that which many of thine excellent servants have been tried with. . . . Teach me, O Lord to putt my trust in thee, then I shall be like mount Sion that cannot be removed.[3]

On the right of this mountain, the light strikes the image of La Rochelle's Huguenot Temple, casting the church of Saint-Sauveur into shadow. On the left of the mountain, diametrically opposed to the temple, stands what is probably the image of the church of Notre Dame de Cougnes, obscured except for its roof and steeple, where Richelieu himself chose to celebrate the victory mass after La Rochelle finally capitulated. Hence, the fortress was divided into a binary structure of confessional opposition and strife.

The situation of the mountain, with La Rochelle spread out at its base and the waters of the Bay of Biscay seeming to percolate gently outward, giving life to the stagnant flats beyond, calls to mind the design of Palissy's *A Delectable Garden*. The mountain itself is a remarkable image, taken along with the title *In patientia suavitas*, from Jacobus Typotius's *Symbola diuina & humana* (Prague, 1601–3; Frankfurt, 1652) (fig.

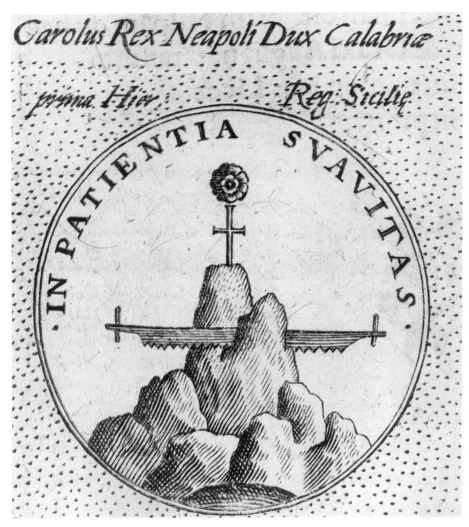

FIGURE 9.2. *In patientia sauvitas* from Jacobus Typotius, *Symbola diuina & humana pontificum, imperatorum, regum* (Frankfurt: G. Schönwetter, 1652). Courtesy The Winterthur Library: Printed Book Collection, Henry Francis du Pont Winterthur Museum, Winterthur, Delaware.

9.2). The whipsaw of a woodworker cuts a deep gash across the peak of the mountain, exposing the interior, out of which has emerged a rosy cross that projects up and through the famous towers of Saint-Nicolas and the Chain to inseminate the transparent elements of the Atlantic ocean and the air to the west. As such, the rosy cross, growing out of the earth scorched by fire (cannon are deployed everywhere), and into the remaining elements of water and air, is a sort of elemental tree. The whipsaw (or pit saw), unlike most other saws, is a tool that must be manipulated by two artisans laboring together. One pushes, the other pulls. It is not by coincidence, that the saw handles are placed in the vicinity of the two opposing churches whose strife engendered the violence of the siege.

The geometric planes encompassed by the saw, and the saw and rosy cross together, are meaningful. The superficial equilibrium suggested by the saw stretched between Catholics and Protestants refers to "the scale" of good and evil, a convention in Huguenot apocalyptic iconography. Here, all the wealth and possessions of the pope and Roman Catholicism are outweighed by the Word, even when the weight of the devil is added to the balance in favor of the Catholics. But when the triangle formed by the planes of saw and cross is taken into consideration, a Trinitarian and elemental pyramid is formed, like the one seen on the hermetic vessel from La Chapelle-des-Pots. References to Rosicrucianism also extend to the five petals of the alchemic rose, which are repeated in the five main battlements of the fort's enceinte, which suggests Robert Fludd's (and Palissy's) preoccupation with "perfect" fortifications that joined the macrocosm and microcosm together.[4]

Palissy, as we know, understood the growth of mountains to be a logical extension upward of the obstetric and alchemic processes by which stones were "given birth" deep inside the matrix of the earth:

> Just as the exterior of the earth labors to give birth to something, so too the interior and matrix of the earth labors to bring forth. . . . [In certain places] fire nourishes itself, and is kept going under the earth: and [it] happens often that over a long period of time, some mountains will become valleys because of an earthquake, or a violent movement created by the fire, or that the metallic stones and other minerals that held up the mountaintop burned, and as they were consumed by fire, this mountain would possibly decline and be brought low little by little: also other mountains could erupt and grow, through the joining together of the rocks and minerals that grow in them; or else it would happen that a region will be swallowed up or lowered by an earthquake, and then what is left will be mountainous: and so the earth will always find something with which to labor [*travailler*], internally or externally.[5]

For Palissy, as for Winthrop the Elder, mountains grew slowly "over a long period of time" inside the earth's matrix and womb. They also declined over time. Sometimes mountains were devoured quickly by fire or in an earthquake, or were reduced by a hidden inner history of death and rebirth. At other times, they were flattened out by the equally incremental process of telluric putrefaction. But as Palissy's discourse on geodes clearly demonstrated, the process of exterior putrefaction was also one of crystallization of the astral light hidden inside the rotting exterior shell of growing stones. Just as the transparent "sparks and flashes" of the interior of geodes could be revealed by cracking them open with a sharp instrument, it followed that the interior light hidden beneath the gnarled surface of a mountain of growing stones was revealed in the same way. This was the logical extension of the Paracelsian mineralogy of the concil-iation of opposites in the "extreme violence" of the kiln to induce separation and ulti-mately purified animate matter.

Separation was effected by the whipsaw's ripping action on the peak of the grow-ing mountain of light. Here again, the tool itself is the focal point. The cutting sword in figure 8.17 was the ubiquitous signifier of alchemical separation. But the sword was wielded by one person (the solitary philosopher) alone. It had only one hilt. The whip-saw, however, required two participants, one on either side. Therefore, the two op-posing Churches became the artisans of their own millennium, Huguenot purifica-tion, and the astral insemination of souls migrating to new worlds.

Like all Paracelsian cosmologies, this one too must be imagined in constant mo-tion, above *and* below the surface. Above the ground, the whipsaw ripped steadily back and forth across the rock, tearing down into the surface of earthen materials. The phys-ical effect was of an intense heat. Heat was generated in the metal of the saw as well as the cutting area in the earth. Thus the subterranean heat generated in the earth's matrix, which labored to grow transparent stones, was paralleled and abetted by the action of an artisan's tool, laboring to cut through the surface. The "extreme violence" of the heat of the subterranean matrix was thereby paralleled by, and made inter-changeable with, the heat and "extreme violence" "nourished" by warring factions in-side the matrix contained by the fortress walls (or enceinte).

Böhme's elucidation of this oppositional sawing action and the generating heat it effected formed his core of insights about the birth of the divine spirit within the earth at that *precise* point where it was touched or stirred.[6] Oppositional violence, and the emotional and physical "heat" it created, was another way of describing separation and the deeply sexualized, Neoplatonic attraction and marriage of opposites; that is, *the conjunction* of macrocosm and microcosm in the alchemical matrix of nature:

> And the hot quality also loveth *all* the other qualities, and the love is so *great* therein toward, and in the other, that it cannot be likened to any thing, for it is generated from and out of the other. . . .
>
> . . . First there is the astringent quality, *then* the sweet, *next,* the bitter: the Sweet is in the *midst* between the astringent and Bitter. Now the Astringent causeth things to be hard, cold, and dark, and the bitter *teareth, driveth, rageth,* and *divideth* or *distinguisheth.* These two Qualities *rub* and drive one another so hard, and move so eagerly, *that* they generate the Heat, which now in these two Qualities is *dark,* even as Heat in a *Stone* is: . . .
>
> . . . And when a man taketh a stone, or any hard thing, and *rubbeth* it against wood, these *two* things are heated. . . .
>
> . . . *Now further into the Depth* . . .
>
> . . . When the astringent and bitter quality *rub* themselves so hard one upon the other,

that they generate Heat, and so now the sweet quality, the sweet fountain-water, is therein in the midst or center *between* the astringent and bitter quality, and the *heat* becometh generated between the astringent and bitter quality, in the sweet fountain-water, *through* the astringent and bitter Quality. . . .

. . . And there the Light kindleth . . . *the beginning of Life:* for the astringent and Bitter Qualities, are the beginning and cause of the heat and of the Light, and thus the sweet fountain water becometh a *shining* light, like the Blew or Azure Light of heaven . . . and shineth into, and *through* all the Angelical Gates. . . .

. . . Now these . . . Qualities would be Dark and Dead, if the *Heat* were not therein: but as soon as the *Spring* time cometh, that the Sun with its *Beams* (supplieth) and warmeth the earth, the spirit becometh living by the Heat in the Tree, and the spirits of the Tree begin to grow green, *flourish* and Blossom . . . for that Quality of spirit . . . riseth up in the Body as a *flower* springeth up out of the Earth.[7]

In patientia sauvitas, in the Boehmian sense, portrayed a distant father's consoling perspective on the labor and deep suffering that attended the birth of his child. The father was the sixteenth-century Germanic sectarian enthusiasm that had inseminated Saintonge through the disguised "mouths" of three heretical monks and their artisan followers, including Palissy. The inseminating light emanated from Germany and was absorbed into and through the androgynous mountain—both pregnant and phallic simultaneously—as "sweet water," until it emerged on the other side to illuminate and impregnate the Huguenot Temple. The "tearing" motion of the saw held between the "bitter" and "astringent" qualities of the two implacable enemies performed a cesarean section *and* a circumcision on the rock to release its inseminating "sweet waters" and light into the matrix "at the base." Circumcision is, of course, the ritual of separation and purification of male Jews, a mark of the chosen people sent into exile. This imagery was made available by northern artists such as Lucas Cranach the Younger (1515–86), who began to associate circumcision with the experience of Christian martyrs in the sixteenth century; as in the German Cranach's engraving of St. Simon, who suffered a gruesome martyrdom when his body was ripped in two from groin to head with a whipsaw (fig. 9.3).

The rosy cross, here in the guise of the elemental tree, grew upward with the sweet waters of the subterranean matrix ascending inside of the mountain into the matrix of La Rochelle and through the narrow door formed by the famous towers. This second androgynous insemination, so reminiscent of the hermaphrodite vessels of La-Chapelle-des-Pots, thus occurred through the port's vaginal opening (which modern Rochelais sailors still call La Rochelle's "mother") and out into the seminal sea of separation and renewal surmounting a "blew" astral sky, which was absorbed back into the tree again through the rose. A conduit between the macrocosm and microcosm was

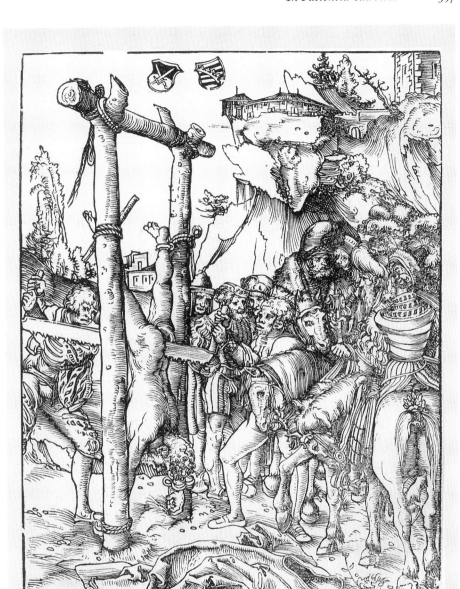

FIGURE 9.3. Lucas Cranach the Elder, *The Martyrdom of St. Simon.* Woodcut, 1512. H: 16.2 cm × W: 12.5 cm. Courtesy Metropolitan Museum of Art, Rogers Fund, 1917.

completed and stood in direct formal and historical relation to the Saintongeais molded pottery and Huguenot chairs made by artisans dispersed to New York. In this, La Rochelle's final moment of autonomous heretical life, the walls were leveled to invisibility and the subterranean artisan's clandestine fortress of patience emerged from beneath the great regional *place de sûreté* onto the surface at precisely the same time that it disappeared again in a flash of light. The Huguenots were launched into the Atlantic world as tiny seeds of light dispersed from the elemental tree.

In his essay "On Trees" from the *Recepte*, Palissy elucidated a science in which apparently unfeeling things having "vegetative and insensible natures," nevertheless, under the surface, "suffer to produce," experiencing the pain and labor of alchemical self-sacrifice to diffuse "seeds and fruits prematurely" in response to "accidents" in nature, or attack or catastrophe. In this way, their young would survive and perhaps flower elsewhere on earth. Just such a tree emerged from inside "The Rock" that "endure[d] adversity" with patience to become the transatlantic mountain of *In patientia suavitas:*

> Nothing in Nature produces fruit without extreme labor [*travail*], indeed pain [*douleur*]. This is the case with vegetative natures as well as the ones with sensibility. If the hen becomes faint to push out her chicks, and the bitch suffers to give birth to her young, consequently all species and genus, even the snake, which dies to produce its own kind, then I can assure you that [things] with vegetative and insensible natures suffer to produce the fruits of the earth. . . . Many times I have contemplated trees and plants, which in draught, or other accident . . . before they die, they hasten to flower in order to produce seeds and fruits prematurely.[8]

On this sea of Atlantic renewal sailed the ship of "grand peregrination" to carry the children of the light on their pilgrimage in search of unity (fig. 9.4). The ship symbolized migration to new worlds; but alchemists knew that ships also meant international commerce, as well as the relationship between distant travel and experience, craftsmen carrying skills in their memories and on their backs to faraway places, and the exchange of words and things.[9] Yet as in Practice's heroic quest for the white glaze, this journey too was incomplete, and so it would remain until end times. No final rebirth had taken place in the Huguenot diaspora, only another opportunity for insemination. As Böhme lamented, the *suavitas* of his rose of *patientia* offered "only the scent or smell or savour in its rising up . . . and in the mean while refresheth . . . in its sicknesse with that *perfect smell* or savour, till the true *Samaratan* doth come."[10] Until the true transparency of perfect unity finally arrived, southwestern Huguenot artisans reinvented themselves in different guises wherever the ship dropped anchor, making security out of the "sparks and flashes" of salvation and profit. This covert process created powerful hybrid forms such as the New York leather chair, overcoming "strife" by combining silently with dominant structures made to symbolize their hosts.

The iconographic relation between unhewn rock and chiliastic patience had been established in the siege of La Rochelle. This relation began with Dirck Coornhert's definitive engraving of Maarten van Heemskerck's *Patientia triumphus* (ca. 1555)

FIGURE 9.4. Johann Theodore de Bry, *The Grand Peregrination,* from Michaelis Maieri, *Viatorium* (Oppenheim, 1618). Courtesy Beinecke Rare Book and Manuscript Library, Yale University. An armored explorer (Magellan or Drake) in an oceangoing man-of-war consults a globe, conceptualizing a world connected, not divided, by the western oceans. The eagles fly off in opposite directions to circumnavigate the globe in search of a new geographical as well as alchemical unity, represented by Jason wearing the Golden Fleece, and, implicitly, the modern explorer's violent quest for a northwest passage to the east. The elements of air and water are thus signifiers of a new age of exploration.

(fig. 9.5). Van Heemskerck had depicted a figure of Patience *seated,* waiting on a rock, holding an animated heart.[11] This was adapted in 1565 for La Rochelle's civic gift to Charles IX and revived in the seventeenth century in Jeremias Drexel's *Heliotropium seu conformatio* (1634). Drexel depicts the patience of Moses during Exodus, using as in figure 9.6 alchemical images, including growing rocks, a heliotropic sunflower for which an angel pours water, which it absorbs while growing up toward the sun's astral rays, and finally another angelic figure holding the conjoined astral heart containing both macrocosm and microcosm.

Moses' position of waiting is kneeling, a bodily attitude quite close to sitting (with knees up), and his arms are supported by the twin rocks of Patience and Constancy.

FIGURE 9.5. Dirck Volkhertsz Coornhert (1519–90), *Patientia triumphus*, etching and engraving, after Martin van Heemskerck (1498–1574). H: 20.7 cm × W: 25.7 cm. Plate 1 of a set. Courtesy Metropolitan Museum of Art, Elisha Whittelsey Collection, Elisha Whittelsey Fund, 1949. Triumphant Patience sits upon the rock. In one hand, a heart inflamed by the Holy Spirit is made all the more powerful in its faith by the hammer of war that beats it on an iron anvil. In the other, a banner depicts a rose similar to the one that emerges between the towers of La Rochelle in figure 9.1; this time it grows between a door formed by two branches of thorn: the narrow way of Christ. The Lamb rides next to Patience on her chariot (foreshadowing the militant Lamb of Revelation, when Christian patience will be revenged). The chariot is pulled by Hope and Grief, while blind Fortuna is dragged behind, bringing up the rear, as she labors in vain to repair her wheel broken on the rock. In the background is a shipwreck, a catastrophic event of human history that must be borne with patience to triumph in the end.

The implication here is that Moses is carrying the growing astral spirit inside his illuminated body, like a maturing child. Just as the sunflower grew to complete its conduit between macrocosm and microcosm, so too Moses patiently awaited the growth and conjunction of the astral spirit inside his own suffering body. Just decades later, a New York Huguenot joiner and carver crafted an armchair fit for an American Moses (see fig. 15.40).

FIGURE 9.6. *Adiumenta*, from Jeremias Drexel, *Heliotropium, seu, Conformatio humanæ voluntatis cum diuina* (1628, 1634). Courtesy Department of Special Collections, Sheridan Libraries, Johns Hopkins University. Just as the faith of Moses was both supported and augmented by the weathered rocks of patience and constancy, so too purified "holy" water (distilled like a kind of eau-de-vie?), is poured by an angel, helping the heliotropic sunflower fulfill its natural potential and rise toward the sacred light of the sun. The representation of heliotropism was a constant in the iconography of Huguenot refugee artisans.

❧ Elias Neau in the Dungeon ❧

The eschatology and bodily attitude of waiting depicted in *In patientia suavitas* suffuses the image of *Elias Neau in the Dungeon* (fig. 9.7), a scene taken from the Huguenot Neau's account of his imprisonment as a galley slave in Marseille. Neau's immense importance for understanding the intense period of piety and revival among Huguenots in New York's French Church in the 1690s and the great significance of his work to influence the spiritual and material condition of the city's African slaves in the violent context of rebellion and reprisal in the early eighteenth century are well known.[12]

Born in Saintonge in 1662, Neau was trained as a mariner, as were many coastal Protestants. "Because the Gospel commanded me," Neau wrote, "when I was persecuted in one Kingdom, to fly into another Country," he fled to Saint-Domingue in 1679.[13] Neau left the Caribbean and married Susanne Paré in Boston, in 1686. He finally settled in New York City permanently by 1691, where he became a merchant. While sailing to London on business in 1692, he was captured by a French privateer. As an escaped Protestant who refused to abjure the Reformed faith for the state religion, Neau was sentenced to life as a slave on Louis XIV's galleys in the Mediterranean. The experience of galley slavery influenced his subsequent decision to open a school for enslaved Africans when he returned to New York. After he converted a fellow prisoner to Protestantism, Neau was imprisoned on the islet of If, near Marseille, where he endured a period of isolation, physical torture, and quietist contemplation that recalled sixteenth-century Saintongeais experiences.[14]

The image of Neau in the dungeon depicted his cell on If, whence he wrote a remarkable series of letters back to his wife in New York, as well as to several other correspondents in New York and on the Continent. In 1696, Neau's prison letters were published by New York's Quaker printer William Bradford, in the original French, titled: *A Treasury of consolations, divine and human, or a treatise in which the Christian can learn how to vanquish and surmount the afflictions and miseries of this life.* In 1698, Cotton Mather reached for a broader Protestant audience and published, in Boston, a single lengthy letter to Neau's wife, which he translated into English and called *A Present from a Farr Country.* The framework of this particular letter served as the basis for the publication, the following year in London, of the influential first-person *Account of the Sufferings of the French Protestants, Slaves on board the French Kings Galleys. By Elias Neau, one of their fellow sufferers.* Subsequent editions of the *Account* followed in Rotterdam (1701), and in London (1749). This final version contained the engraving of Neau in the dungeon and appears to support the revamped millennial program of the so-called French Prophets (tongues-speaking Camisard refugees in England to whom

Elias Neau *in the Dungeon,*
as described in Page 46.

FIGURE 9.7. *Elias Neau in the Dungeon,* from J. Morin & J. C. Jacobi, *A Short Account of the Life and Sufferings of Elias Neau* (London, 1749). Courtesy Special Collections & Rare Books, University of Minnesota Libraries. The refugee Saintongeais New Yorker, captured by former countrymen during a transatlantic trading voyage from New York and sent to a Marseille dungeon, sits prayerfully on the rock of patience wearing the garments of a heretical prisoner.

some Quakers trace their origin), which had been converted to the quietistic eschatology of waiting in the decade of the 1740s.

The effect of Neau's prison writings from France on the New York Huguenot population was galvanizing, precisely because they had reactivated the old tradition and
discourse of southwestern Huguenot artisanal piety begun by the martyred monks and
Palissy in the primitive Church of the 1540s. Though such discourse was submerged
in artifacts of commerce, Neau's local voice brought it back to the surface again
through vivid descriptions of religious persecution and imprisonment in France, where
absolutism still reigned under Louis XIV. The context of Neau's imprisonment played
a pivotal role in the visibility of Palissian language in New York in two important ways.
First, the Glorious Revolution of 1688 hardened the position of New York's refugee
population against Louis XIV and encouraged the political authority of Protestant
factions in the city. More than any time since the fall of La Rochelle, New York
Huguenots dreamed of a victorious return to France under English protection. Second, in 1689, rumors of Louis's plans to invade New York City from New France were
being spread, which terrified most residents of Manhattan and Long Island, where the
thrust of the attack was to be directed. New York's refugee population was particularly
threatened, inasmuch as Louis instructed the comte de Frontenac to make prisoners
of all "fugitive Frenchmen whom he may find there, and particularly those of the *religion prétendue reformée.*"[15] In the late seventeenth century, it was not difficult for New
York's Huguenot refugees to imagine themselves galley slaves, or perhaps one of Elias
Neau's "fellow Sufferers" in a Marseille prison.

The engraving depicts Neau sitting on the rock of *patientia,* which has grown up
from the earth's underground matrix, in his masonry prison cell, which is simultaneously a fortress tower and a kiln. He is wearing a costume of humiliation, complete
with devil's cap (a sort of heretic's mitre imposed on the victims of autos-da-fé), and
his hair and beard have grown wild. The cell floor is littered with debris and excrement. But the trash at Neau's feet is also good evidence of alchemic putrefaction, and
the astral light pierces through a trinity of wooden slats on the door to his inner light
and falls on his open body, spiritually penetrating and inseminating it. Neau accepts
his insemination with arms held up in prayer, a Mosaic gesture of patience, constancy,
and stillness. "The Birth or Geniture of God is thus," Böhme had written (in language
particularly resonant with his many Quaker readers); the natural body "doth not *reach
back* into its Father, which generateth it." It may receive light when it "holdeth still and
is quiet as a Body, and letteth the Father's Will . . . to form and image in it, how *they*
please."[16]

Neau's *Account* illuminated the discourse of the image, inventorying his experiences
of external affliction paralleled by the inner growth of secret impregnation after "about
a year":

in the year 1694, orders came from Court to transfer me to the Prison of the Cittadel. . . . I was forced to lye upon the Stones, for I could not obtain for a year together any Bed, not even Straw to lye upon. There was a strict order to suffer no body to speak to me, nor me to write to anybody, and the Aid Major came every night to search my Pockets. . . . I remain'd there about a year without seeing anybody; but about that time the Director of Conscience came to see me . . . he cry'd out, Lord, in what condition are you, Sir! I re-ply'd, *Sir, don't pity me, for could you but see the secret pleasures my heart experiences, you would think me too happy.* . . . The priest . . . sent me a Straw-bed to lie upon. . . . I continued 22 months in that Prison, without changing any Cloaths, my Beard being as long as the hair of my head, and my face as pale as Plaster.[17]

At the end of this period of time, Neau was caught having a forbidden conversa-tion with another prisoner, "just under me, . . . so much tormented, that they had turned his brains." Because of this transgression, Neau was banished to a "*subterrane-ous* Hole,*"* where he underwent further bodily decay for over a year. Finally, he was re-moved to the fortress on the island of If, where we see him sitting in a dungeon reached through yet another underground hole:

I was immediately removed into another Prison. . . . I was put on the 20th of May 1696 in a *subterraneous* Hole, wherein I remained till the first of July next following, [then] I was sent . . . to the Castle of If. . . . I and the poor Gentleman I have spoken of, were put in a Hole. . . . The place was so disposed, that we were obliged to go down a Ladder into a dry Ditch, and then go up by the same Ladder into an old Tower through a Canon hole. The Vault or Arch wherein we were put was as dark, as if there had been no manner of light in Heaven, stinking, and so miserable dirty, that I verily believe there is no more dismal place in the world . . . all our senses were attacked at once; sight by darkness, taste by hunger, smell by the stench of the place, feeling by Lice and other vermin, and hearing by the hor-rid blasphemies and cursing.

After being removed to two other such "pits," Neau went "for some time, without see-ing any light at all." Before Neau was finally "reclaimed" from this crucible by the earl of Portland, like Practice in Palissy's *On the Art of the Earth,"* whose shirt was perpet-ually wet from putrefaction and distillation, Neau reported "the place being very damp, our Cloaths were rotten by this time."[18]

It was in the letter to his wife published by Mather as *A Present from a farr country,* where Neau revealed the passionate textures of his prison experience, saying that God had given him "the Grace, to suffer, the Breaking of my Bones, the Roasting of my Flesh at the Fire, and my Marrow on the Live-Coals, and to be cast into a Burning Furnace." Deprived of the physical closeness he desires with his wife, Neau tells her his strategies to augment soulish intercourse in the face of a kind of rape (or blockage) of the pious body in the pit:

> the Devil and men are so animated against me, that they employ all their power and industry to hinder me from receiving any External Consolations; and to speak the truth, experience shows me that herein they succeed; and if they could oblige God to deprive me of Internal Consolation they would do it with pleasure . . . [yet] as he sees me deprived of all humane relief, he gives in unto me of Divine . . . in vain they try to destroy the work of the Holy Ghost. The Almighty Power of God is too much interested therein to suffer them to attain the end which they propose; they labor more and more to surmount my patience . . . the hope of Love, despises generously the assault which they make upon it. Nay, My Dear Wife, they at present attack me more ardently than ever.[19]

❧ The Miracle of Protection ❧

Neau's growing internal power in conjunction with the Holy Ghost is revealed in the only miracle recounted in "the Story of my Persecution," how all of his forbidden writing implements were saved, hidden in plain sight from his enemies. During one of Neau's many moves, "The commander ordered them to fetch my poor Straw Bed," where his things were cached:

> They did it, but without success, for the [Eternal] hid all that was therein, namely an English Bible, a Quire of Large paper, whereof this is some, a Bag, wherein was my Pocket Book, an Inkborn, and now, my Dear Wife, will you not praise the King of our Souls, who does such strange things?

Neau's problems were not over, however. The bed was too small to put into the hole leading to his next prison cell; it would have to be taken apart and then shoved through in pieces. His secret stash was certain to be revealed:

> Now comes a Second Alarm for me: my Straw Bed could not come in at the hole; the Straw was fain to be taken out by little and little . . . I address'd my self to the Officer who Led me; I declared to him all that was in my Straw Bed; I Pray'd him to save all that was there; promising to recompense him; he accepted the offer: he himself empty'd the bed . . . and caused it to be carried up to me by little and little; but he kept a little of the Straw, with all my concerns, in my Straw Bed, and brought them to me himself. Admire the Protection of the King of Kings![20]

Signs "that cannot be comprehended unless experienced," were becoming more "frequent and sensible." Neau would finally have a second birth in the last "Burning Furnace" of a dungeon. Indeed, Neau narrated his entrance through the crucible's narrow opening as if it were a physical reversal of his life course, an alchemical return to concealment and rebirth in the earth's womb. In every sense of the word, the Huguenot refugee had returned through the towers of La Rochelle to experience its "tragedy" again: "the spectators of this Tragedy, told me that I must go in, my feet foremost; so that I was fain to crawl in at the hole, the Wall being about eight foot thick. I entered into that . . . habitation; I found my self envelop'd with profound Darkness; but the Eternal created that, as well as the Light." Once inside, "without Light, in a place full of stinking ordure," Neau was forced to "undergo a double Martyrdom" in this fortress of patience.[21]

Neau experienced his rebirth as a chance to communicate in a deeper, more intimate way with his wife in New York. Uncertain that his letters had gotten through to her, and receiving none in return, he admitted that "the Distance and Difficulties are so great, that we can have no mutual Communications by Writing."[22] So he experimented with other forms of transatlantic communication, though the motions of the universal soul. In the hope that this letter would find her, and although he expected no response, Neau asked after their children:

> I pray you to let me know the State of my dear Children, if they be yet alive, and what Dispositions to vertue are found in them . . . neglect not this; labour to be their mother a second time, by endeavoring with all your might that they may be Born again by grace: All the world talk of Regeneration, but there are only a few that know it by experience. Men know how to say that Nicodemus was gross in his conception of it . . . but it often happens that those who thus speak, feel the efficacy thereof no better than he. Know then, that it is not the corporal or animal life which is renewed, but that of the Soul; the affections, desires & thoughts are sanctified. When a person is Regenerate . . . the sentiments of the heart are conformed to the light of the Spirit, that is to say, the love of *our* heart conformed to the Law of God in Spite of all the reminders of our Corruption, which abide in the inferior part of our soul, which the Scripture calls the Flesh: Endeavor then to obtain this *New-Birth* for your self, and your Children, without which you can never *see God.*[23]

After having described the "secret pleasures" that accompanied the horrors of his own "labour," Neau counseled patience and wrote his wife that she too must labor to become a mother "a second time." Neau's soul was freed by fire from his dungeon and "conformed with the light of the spirit" at precisely the same moment that it was released from the prison of "the Flesh." He was inspired by his desire and the power of his new birth to project his astral spirit west, flying free from his imprisoned body, and was thus rejoined with his wife, despite "the distance and difficulties," by "the love of our heart conformed to the Law of God." In New York, Neau's wife and children were inseminated again, "that they may be Born again by grace." Neau also disseminated

his metamorphic moment of labor and astral conjunction to other refugee New Yorkers when he wrote to express gratitude for his torment. He asked God to "Endow me
with a soul, that I may be thy Spouse, and worthy of that name, and that has its true
voice and language." The elders of the New York Huguenot community empathized
deeply: "How can we be insensible of your affliction," they replied, "since you are a
member of our body?"[24]

Neau's experience of slavery and imprisonment taught him that the "true voice and
language" of the soul was silent and hidden. The "exquisite pain" of life meant that
Huguenots must not judge Nicodemus harshly, but must follow the soul's own invisible path to make it "frequent and sensible" in New York. By the time Neau returned
to the city at the end of the seventeenth century, its Huguenot artisans were experiencing the full effects of anglicization. Neau's response to English cultural absolutism
was to become a member of the Church of England under false pretenses of adherence to its principles to acquire legitimacy and funding for his school for African slaves.
His deception was revealed to the English authorities in 1712, when he was charged
with being the alleged secret moving force behind New York's violent slave rebellion,
when some of his students were executed.

Inspired by the revival of primitive Palissian discourse and the eschatology of waiting, New York Huguenot craftsmen responded just as their artisanal culture had done
habitually for over two centuries when confronted with the demands of absolute power.
This time the structure of patience would emerge in the form of a chair. After all, is
not *siège* but another word for seat?

CHAPTER TEN

Being "at the Île of Rue"

Science, Secrecy, and Security at the Siege of La Rochelle, 1627–1635

You have bin at the Île of Rue,
and at Rochell, a poore people that lye nowe in the dust.
—EDWARD HOWES TO JOHN WINTHROP JR., March 26, 1633

Postscript—Salomons wisdome, 7 chap. 21 vers: And all such things as are
either secret, or manifest: them I knowe. . . .
   . . . The fyre cannot destroye whats written in the Harte.
—EDWARD HOWES TO JOHN WINTHROP JR., January 22, 1627

My sonne give me thy heart.
                    —John Winthrop's "Experiencia" (1616–18)

❧ Being There: "alchemy in its widest sense" ❧

Edward Howes's 1633 letter from London recalled events that had occurred only six years before. John Winthrop Jr. (1606–76), who received the letter in Boston, had been "at the Île of Rue, and at Rochell," and the letter was a pointed reminder that Winthrop's scientific friends throughout the Atlantic world would never forget this. Winthrop had *experienced* the most theatrical and resonant spectacle of absolute power, violent containment, and confessional genocide to occur in Europe during their lifetimes. Winthrop had emerged from this apocalyptic experience sanctified and alive, chosen by God to salvage fragments of the Reformation that still remained pure and hence viable. His task: to reanimate and make them whole again in the New World, something that weighed heavily on the young man's mind as he sailed away from 20,000 Huguenot co-religionists who, as Howes lamented, lay "nowe in the dust."

Like many of his fellow alchemists, Howes was anxious to obfuscate his contributions to "the work" (to prevent interception by the vulgar), and he was clever at allegory and linguistic games. But his wordplay here was neither original nor new. After the fall of La Rochelle in 1628, virtually every Protestant in the rapidly expanding Atlantic world would hear or read the basic narrative of this event and understand the sad irony of "Île of Rue." This painful new place-name entered popular discourse as both pun and lament for England's failure under Charles I's favorite, the duke of Buckingham, to gain a secure foothold on the Île de Ré, a strategic outer island guarding the entrance to the fortress of La Rochelle. The familiar narrative of this event cannot recapture the emotional nightmare that the fall of La Rochelle to the Counter-Reformation was for international Protestantism.[1]

Nearly two decades of correspondence shrouded by metaphor and secret codes had passed between Howes and Winthrop. Transatlantic religious and military history was harnessed to news of the latest experiments from European and American laboratories, urgent orders for current scientific books and apparatus were made, and the quest for the philosopher's stone was undertaken. A latitudinarian and moderate Calvinist, Howes reminded his "lovinge frind" and equally moderate colleague that even before Winthrop embarked to join his father's exclusive social experiment in Boston, his place in *both* eschatological history *and* the *universal,* inclusive networks of international science had already been privileged by experience. Winthrop had seen far worse violence than was perpetrated by his father against heterodoxy in New England. For John Winthrop's generation of natural philosophers, the fall of La Rochelle was one of those crucial events in history that adumbrated the end of the world. It was a kind of natural laboratory for adepts, where the chosen could see the future of man. Here was a prophetic instance that revealed the interior gestation of a long mental and material process of the history of final things that would culminate with a "great instauration" of primordial knowledge lost in the Fall.[2]

Much has been written about the life and career of Winthrop "the Younger," most of it curious reflection on the life of his authoritarian father. Despite this venerable historiography, which reaches back to the extraordinary hagiographies published after his death in 1676, and while it is well known that Winthrop served one of Buckingham's admirals as clerk aboard the *Due Repulse* (a command ship in Buckingham's ill-fated armada that laid siege to the Île de Ré from July 17 until October 29, 1627), historians have not analyzed this episode closely. Natural-philosophical concerns, coinciding with fears for the security of international Protestantism generally—and the protection of the forthcoming New World experiment in particular—were behind the younger Winthrop's strenuous personal efforts to persuade his fearful and protective father to use valuable family contacts to find a place for his son as an observer with the expeditionary force. The famously secretive Winthrop's decision to gain experience at the simultaneous sieges of the Île de Ré and La Rochelle was not prompted merely by a youthful thirst for adventure and travel, a character defect, most of his biographers allege, rooted in "indecisiveness" and lack of a firm sense of purpose and duty. Rather, the explanation for his peripatetic nature lies in private concerns and ambitions having to do with his international career as a Paracelsian physician, alchemist, natural philosopher, and would-be inventor of novel weapons to rearm a Protestant world in retreat. Winthrop linked these personal and scientific concerns—and his transatlantic experiences   less with the local problems that obsessed his absolutist father, who feared innovation, than with similarly innovative and clandestine strategies shared by heterodox Huguenot refugees from southwest France and their Protestant allies. Ultimately, these interests harnessed John Winthrop Jr. to the internationalist, permeable, free-floating, and geographically nonspecific culture of the Long Island Sound region.

The story of the younger Winthrop's journey to the Île de Ré in 1627 began after he left home in 1622 to attend Trinity College, Dublin, his first extended sojourn away from the family estate at Groton in East Anglia. On the face of it, the choice of Trinity was an unorthodox break with family tradition. Every other Winthrop male who attended university both before (and after) John Jr. did so at Trinity College, Cambridge. Yet there were good reasons for him to have decided for Ireland. By 1622, some Cambridge colleges required scholars to swear an oath to the Thirty-nine Articles of the Church of England, which many nonconforming Calvinists refused to do. Oaths were not a requirement at Trinity, Dublin, and hence it was considered a sort of refuge from growing ecclesiastical interference in England. At the same time, Dublin's curriculum followed the Cambridge model (with theology as the central discipline), and it was cheaper. But above all, in 1622, Ireland was the first place of refuge envisaged by the group that would by 1629 become the senior Winthrop's New England Company of Massachusetts Bay Colony. John Winthrop's sister and brother-in-law, Lucy Winthrop Downing and her husband, the loyal family attorney Emmanuel Downing, had already moved to Ireland. Depression in the East Anglian woolen trade to the Netherlands forced the sale of family lands, and fears for the progress of the Reformation in England and on the Continent gave this project greater urgency. It made sense, therefore, that when John Winthrop Jr. prepared to leave home, he became part of this family advance team—an extension of his father's eyes and ears—a role he filled later at the sieges of the Île de Ré and La Rochelle. By April 1623, the elder Winthrop was prepared to move, writing his son in an often quoted remark: "I wish oft God would open a waye to settle me in Ireland, if it might be for his glory."[3]

The elder Winthrop's God neglected to "open a waye to settle" him in Ireland, how-ever, and by late 1623, the Downings had returned permanently to London. The younger Winthrop then left Trinity College (against his father's wishes) and followed them there. According to convention, this was a portent of "declension" for the father; "the first hint of trouble" in the young man's personality, which slowed his future de-velopment as a public figure based on the old patriarch's famously decisive example. John Winthrop Jr.'s problem, it would seem, "was a simple lack of staying power."

> His studies required persistence, but the young man lacked the capacity (or willingness) to persist. So pronounced was this form of immaturity that it was already in the way of becoming a character defect. Indeed, it would linger for years, until the generally re-markable career of John Winthrop, Jr., became uncomfortably littered with unfinished tasks and abandoned designs. It too often was the distant grass that grew greenest. . . . To be sure, he was quite devoid of ideas for his own future . . . young Winthrop remained, insofar as a career was concerned, quite without impulse.[4]

Even as a mature adult and leader of the Connecticut Colony, Winthrop "literally found it difficult to keep a single iron in the fire."[5]

In fact, the opposite was true. Winthrop's "character defect" was not a sign of "im-maturity" that led to a lifetime of constant travel, "littered with unfinished tasks and abandoned designs." Rather, it was indicative of movement and experiment that de-fined the well-considered career of a focused Paracelsian searching for signs of meta-physical unity in apparently unrelated places and practices. The choice of Trinity Col-lege, Dublin, was appropriate beyond the conventional reading. Trinity's provost since 1609 was William Temple, a celebrated anti-scholastic and a proponent of the criti-cal pedagogy of Palissy's Huguenot colleague Pierre de la Ramée, or Petrus Ramus, which deeply influenced seventeenth-century Calvinist analytical theory. Temple's natural-philosophical treatises made him one of Dublin's Anglo-Irish elite. Temple later joined the circle of the universalist Invisible College, which centered around Trin-ity College, and included Benjamin Worsley and Robert Boyle. The clandestine In-visible College may be defined as a Neoplatonic and internationalist alchemical col-lege with "invisible" members, all sharing a profound interest in Paracelsism and the practice of alchemy as instruments of social reform. In the context of the British-American response to the wars of religion and absolutism, this clearly meant "an en-thusiasm for Baconian natural history [that is to say, experimentalism], and anti-authoritarianism, both in natural philosophy and medicine."[6] That the younger Winthrop found himself at William Temple's Trinity College, Dublin should not be considered a mere coincidence. This circumstance was thus the subject of a query from Charles Webster:

Within the Anglo-Irish group, the Invisible College would have found many patrons . . . in a position to provide encouragement and information. "Invisibility" would have been forced on the group by virtue of their unsettled fortunes and obligations outside London. While London provided a focus, it was necessary to maintain communications with Stalbridge, Ireland, Paris and various other locations on the continent and perhaps even New England. . . . John Winthrop, Jr., . . . so close in outlook to Worsley and Boyle, . . . would have made [an] invaluable member of the Invisible College. It is interesting in this context that Winthrop was educated at Trinity College, Dublin, and that his father had been concerned with Irish plantations. . . . Although small in membership . . . the Invisible College was by no means unproductive. Through this agency Robert Boyle was launched into his scientific career. . . . He believed that Histories of Trade and Nature of the kind undertaken by his friends were as much a fertile basis for scientific inquiry as a means to promote economic innovation. . . . Support from politically active patrons of the Invisible College was probably important in securing Worsley's appointment to civil service positions from which he could further his utopian schemes. . . . The investigations into chemistry, metallurgy, agriculture and surveying were to a large degree a reflection of the aspirations of a social group whose primary ambition was to re-establish profitable Irish plantations.[7]

This implies that the choice of Trinity College, Dublin, rather than Trinity College, Cambridge, was the younger Winthrop's as much as his father's. Both men may have had specific plans in mind for the younger Winthrop's role in the colonization movement. Winthrop may have intended from the start to matriculate at Dublin to further his natural-philosophical training. Therefore, it is a mistake to assume that he began his alchemical studies in London with Howes upon his return from Dublin. It is just as likely that Winthrop began to read Paracelsus and his followers, as well as the currently popular Robert Fludd (whose earliest publications on the microcosm and macrocosm began in 1616), in Trinity's library. This was the first important library Winthrop explored in a systematic way, and it undoubtedly influenced the beginning of his career as a bibliophile with a love of natural-philosophical texts. The younger Winthrop began to ask his father to send ever-larger sums of money for the first time during this period in Dublin, presumably in order to purchase alchemical books. Financial difficulties at home in Suffolk did not staunch the flow of funds; the elder Winthrop wrote his son in 1622, "I will shorten my selfe to enlarge you."[8]

There was every reason for the younger Winthrop to be happy in Dublin, and the indications are that he was content and productive. His father acknowledged the promising conditions of an Irish education and hinted at hoped-for practical results to be directed toward the colonization project. In a letter dated August 6, 1622, the elder Winthrop wrote, "I am very gladd to heare that you like [it] so well in Ireland, if your profitinge in learning may be answerable it will muche increase my comforte."[9]

Yet after a year, without explanation, John returned home to England. Neither his father nor grandfather had completed their studies at Cambridge either, but his "abrupt" return home in 1623 may have been prompted by very real intellectual concerns. More than the failure of the Ireland project and a young man's loneliness for the departed Downings (his surrogate family in Dublin) influenced his decision.

The Paracelsian dictum that university life and scholasticism were the dead letters of knowledge was in play here. In order to find wisdom, young men were instructed to leave the university and travel widely in Nature and exotic places, to learn from the lowly folk practitioner and simple artisans. Through manual philosophers, young alchemists gained practical experience. Winthrop the Younger's exit from Trinity College had precedent in Paracelsus himself. It was harnessed to Winthrop's conversion experience in Paracelsian natural philosophy. His mobility represented the first step along this young alchemist's path to the Île de Ré and La Rochelle four years later.

Moreover, the years 1622 and 1623 were formative ones in France and Britain for scientists who aspired to join the universal community of "invisibles." The formal inception of the Invisible College may have been the 1640s, but the first real mention of "the invisibles" occurred in 1623, when Gabriel Naudé published his *Instruction à la France sur la vérité de l'histoire des Frères de la Roze-Croix* (Instruction to France About the Truth of the Story of the Rose-Cross Brothers), the apocalyptic context of which was the military triumph of the Counter-Reformation in Germany. Claims about the existence of the secret society of Rosicrucians had caused a sensation, which diffused to England in Naudé's books, but also through the hugely influential work of Robert Fludd. Edward Howes and Winthrop were both passionately interested in Rosicrucianism and Robert Fludd, as indicated by their correspondence, and the wave of interest in the Rosicrucians extended to student laboratories in Dublin. An essential attribute of the "invisible ones," Frances Yates explains, was their mobility, complemented by a chameleonlike aptitude for disguise. Naudé revealed that Rosicrucians sold their souls to the devil and "abjured Christianity," not unlike Huguenots (and witches) as banefully represented:

> In return they were promised the power to transport themselves wherever they wished, to have purses always full of money, to dwell in any country, attired in the dress of that country so that they were taken for native inhabitants, to have the gift of eloquence so they could draw all men to them, to be admired by the learned and sought out by the curious and recognized as wiser than the ancient prophets.[10]

With this in mind, the pattern of the younger Winthrop's life when he returned to London in 1623 takes on a more specific logic and set of meanings, contradicting the notion he was "intellectually adrift and oppressed with ennui."[11] He was expected to take up the law, like his father and grandfather before him, and upon his arrival,

Emmanuel Downing, then attorney of the Court of Wards and Liveries, secured him a coveted place in the Inner Temple. Once again, however, he renounced an established institution of formal education: refusing to take up residence in the Inner Temple, he instead moved in either with the Downings or with Thomas and Priscilla Winthrop Fones, his uncle and aunt.

Aspects of the two households were particularly attractive to Winthrop at this early stage of his alchemic career. Edward Howes was Downing's clerk. Howes was then also a young scholar at the Inner Temple and, like Winthrop, an aspiring natural philosopher with an aptitude in mathematics and a collection of alchemic books and laboratory equipment. This marked the beginning of the lifelong scientific friendship between the two. True to the Paracelsian credo of searching for knowledge among artisans and tradesmen, Winthrop devoted most of his time during this period to working with his uncle Thomas Fones, an apothecary. Whereas "ancient" physicians trivialized apothecaries and other "skillful" folk as mere technicians, Paracelsian physicians sought them out as unlearned possessors of natural secrets hidden to university professors, but available to adepts. Fones's shop had a complete pharmacopoeia of chemical and herbal ingredients essential to the new homeopathic and chemical therapies, and his apothecary's apparatus and expertise with fire, crucibles, and distillation were also basic to alchemical laboratory practice.[12] By 1625, then, Winthrop's natural-philosophical career was right on track.

On April 18, 1626, Winthrop's younger brother Forth, the family member most readily conversant with John Winthrop Jr.'s scientific and bibliophilic interests, was sent to university—not to Trinity College, Dublin, but to Emmanuel College, Cambridge.[13] Unfortunately, Forth died in 1630, when he was just twenty-one. However, surviving letters from Forth to John bracket the latter's participation in the expedition to the Île de Ré. Although usually dense with alchemical metaphor and other obscure language, they are very revealing of John's natural-philosophical tradition, training, and motivations during this period. Apparently, John had become so deeply involved with his laboratory practice at both the Downing (with Howes) and Fones households that he isolated himself and neglected to communicate with his brother. At the end of December 1626, Forth wrote a mild yet telling letter of rebuke from Cambridge, which acknowledged that he had no idea where his older brother was but hinted that he knew the secretive nature of John's mysterious isolation, observing:

> [Y]ou are occupied about serious affaires, and perhapps that is the reson I have not heard
> from you of soe longe time . . . I should have trobled you with my letters many times, but
> I knew not at which door to knock, one while hearinge you weare at London, in which
> you weare as hard to be found of me as in a Labyrinth, for I doe nether know where my
> uncle Downing kepeth, whom I would have wrot toe, nether did I remember the Sine of

my uncles Foneses house . . . my letters to you goinge came backe with a non est inventus [nowhere to be found].[14]

The learned Forth's careful use of the key word "Labyrinth," in conjunction with his intimations that John was "occupied about serious affairs" at the houses of their uncles Downing and Fones was perhaps a cryptic reference to book 3 of *Paragranum* and book 5 of *Labyrinthus medicorum errantium,* where Paracelsus "set out the full dimensions of this alchemical activity."[15] Owen Hannaway sheds light on the significance of these seminal texts for physicians in training such as John Winthrop Jr., whose passage through the labyrinth indoctrinated in the Paracelsian "theology of the priesthood of the laborer," transforming natural materials to serve man and God (as would an apothecary):

> The principal theme of these loci was that God had given to every product of nature a natural end which, in conformity with the anthropocentrism inherent in the macrocosm-microcosm doctrine, was defined in terms of man's needs. In addition, God had assigned to man the task of transforming, by means of alchemy, the raw products of nature into a state appropriate for man's utilization. Thus God had endowed man with crops, animals, minerals, and medicaments in all three realms of nature, but not necessarily in a condition to be immediately assimilated or utilized by man. Man had to garner them, segregate them, separate the pure from the impure, and bring them to perfection, usually employing fire at some stage. This was *alchemy in its widest sense* [emphasis added]; and it made an alchemist not only of the physician but also of the farmer, the miller, the baker, the stoker, the smelter, the smith—in short, of every craftsman who employed his skills in the preparation of nature's products for man's ends. This alchemy might involve more than one stage and more than one alchemist. To illustrate with Paracelsus's own favorite example, the alchemical preparations of bread involved the alchemist-farmer, who cultivated the wheat; the alchemist-miller, who separated the grain from the chaff; the alchemist-baker, who produced the loaf of bread in his alchemical oven.[16]

Hence, this labyrinth was both mental and physical; the process of alchemic purification involved an internal and external pilgrimage of discovery to locate and connect this hidden labyrinth of skilled artisans, in order that they might be "elevated to the status of an alchemist, [and] allotted a positive role in a great cosmic drama which was nothing less than the redemption of the world."[17]

The subject of the younger Winthrop's desire to travel to exotic places was at the forefront of family discourse and action. On April 24, 1627, Joshua Downing (d. 1629), brother of Emmanuel and well situated as one of the commissioners of the Navy (and hence one of Buckingham's protégé's), wrote John Winthrop Sr.:

Concerning Mr. John Wenthrops inclinacion to the Sea, I will use my best endeavors for hym; but I have no part in shipping that goes for Turkie, and the marchantes that are owners, doe comonly place their owne servauntes for pursers; but if he pleaseth, to goe alonge in those shipps as a passinger to see the countries; the chardges of his dyett shall not be great, and I will comitt hym to the care of them, that wilbe tender over hym, so shall he have more libertie for hymselfe, and have all occasions to make the best observacions, for his owne good. But what if you send him, nowe out with this fleet with the Duke; the lord Harvey is Rear admyrall, and I thinck a well disposed gentleman; The Captain under hym is Captain Best; in whom I have some interest. If you shall please to thinck well of it, advize me speedily, and I will deale with Captain Best accordingly.[18]

When the younger Winthrop considered a sea voyage, his first choice thus seems to have been to follow the route of many an aspiring alchemist in search of the philosopher's stone and head for Constantinople. Seventeenth-century alchemical travel narratives tales conventionally depict young Europeans gaining sage advice from alchemists "from the east." Arabic texts carried west in the wake of the Crusades were known to be the sources of much alchemical knowledge, as was Kabbala, a mystical Jewish doctrine that was thought to embody knowledge of hidden numerical codes that were the key to biblical secrets.

Winthrop would indeed travel to the Mediterranean soon after his return from the Île de Ré, but the expedition to relieve the great fortress of La Rochelle was given priority, because the military experience it provided would be of use in his family's projected colony in the New World. The elder John Winthrop had questions about the viability of a stone fortress on the American coast in the face of an attack by Counter-Reformation forces. John Winthrop Jr., on the other hand, would be able to pursue two aspects of his natural-philosophical craft in Buckingham's service: fortress construction and the manufacture of new sorts of missiles and torpedoes to deliver gunpowder over great distances at sea. Bearing in mind that he subsequently became master of fortifications for the Massachusetts Bay Colony (his first official function), and considering his father's statement of 1622 that "if your profitinge in learning may be answerable it will muche increase my comforte," it is logical to assume that the two men opted for La Rochelle for two basic reasons: first, to prepare the novice physician-alchemist for the task of supervising the design and construction of the new colony's fortifications and arsenal as it prepared for the inevitable attack by the armies of the Antichrist; and second, to serve as the elder Winthrop's eyewitness to international Protestantism's penultimate line of defense in its "declining days." God's wrath, the elder Winthrop felt sure, would turn toward England if La Rochelle succumbed.

In the event, this was precisely what happened. On June 27, 1627, John Winthrop Jr. shipped out from Portsmouth for the Bay of Biscay as purser on Rear Admiral

William Hervey's flagship, the *Due Repulse,* an aging 40-gun warship built in 1596, which was deployed in the armada's second division, under Captain Thomas Best, the friend and loyal client whom Joshua Downing had recommended.[19] The young purser carried a letter from his father concerning the wisdom of minding one's tongue and behavior with strangers and in any military action, mailed from London on June 6:

> My Good Sonne, I received your letter from Gravesend, and doe blesse God for your safe arrival there, but I heard not from you since, which I impute to the suddaine departure of your Captaine out of the Downes upon the Dukes cominge thither; but I hope to heare from you soone, for I longe to understande how you fare, and what entertainment you find with your Captaine, that accordingly I may be stirred up to prayer for you and to blesse God for his mercyes towards you. I know not what further advise to give you, than you have already received, and as your owne observation, upon occasion, shall direct you: onely be carefull to seeke the Lorde in the first place, and with all earnestnesse, as he who is onely able to keepe you in all perills and to give you favour in the sight of those, who may be instrumentes of your wellfare: and account it a great pointe of wisdom to keep diligent watch over your selfe that you may neither be infected by the evill conversation of any that you may be forced to converse with, neither that your owne speeche or behavior be any just occasion to hurte or ensnare you. Be not rashe upon ostentation of valor, to ad-venture your selfe to unnecessarye dangers, but if you be lawfully called, lett it appeare that you houlde your life for him, who gave it you, and will preserve it unto the furthest period of his owne holye decree, for you may be resolved, that while you keepe in your waye, all the cannons or enemyes in the worlde shall not be able to shorten your dayes one minute: for my parte, as a father who desires your wellfare as much as mine owne, I cease not dayle to commende you to God, beseechinge him, to preserve prosper and blesse you, that I may receive you againe in peace, and have assurance of enjoying you in a better life, when your course heer shalbe finished.[20]

Given the younger Winthrop's penchant for dissimulation and secrecy in public life—including with his father—these Machiavellian words of advice from colonial America's master of the frontal assault seem to adumbrate a future career of hidden behavior and silence under pressure. Was the elder Winthrop merely acknowledging aspects of his son's behavior that would prove useful for survival during the siege (as well as in the harsh political and religious warfare in the New World)?

Evidence of Winthrop's personal habits and comportment toward strangers aboard the *Due Repulse* is unavailable, except to say that his duties as purser were not taxing and that he had plenty of time for what correspondents called his "observations." He attended faithfully to his duties as military observer and security advisor for his father's transatlantic Calvinist community. Significantly, during the five months Winthrop spent at sea off the Île de Ré, he was closely associated with Abraham Kuffeler, a Paracelsian physician-alchemist from Holland who joined the expedition as an explosives expert.[21] Kuffeler's task was to develop a "torpedo" to disrupt the French fleet and burst through Richelieu's blockade at the mouth of the old port.

The Kuffeler family was famous for technological innovation in northern Europe's artisanal community long before the potential of Abraham's torpedo drew Buckingham's attention. The alchemist and inventor Johann Sibertus Kuffeler, Abraham's brother, was, of the two, most responsible for building the torpedo used at La Rochelle, although Abraham went on the expedition alone. J. S. Kuffeler was initially known for innovations in dyeing techniques pioneered by his father-in-law, the natural philosopher Cornelius Drebbel (d. 1607).[22] Following Paracelsus's credo, Drebbel engaged in dialogue with local tradesmen and devoted his life to returning the favor by coming up with artisanal innovations. The idea for the La Rochelle torpedo probably originated with Drebbel, who had experimented extensively with submarines and torpedoes and other "fireworks" and "pyrotechnics." The Kuffeler torpedo was partially successful in 1628. The aim was true, but observers saw the timing mechanism ignite the explosives before the torpedo rammed into its target.

The Kuffeler brothers resettled in England in 1628, where they continued to perfect the weapon, apparently with some success. In 1653, J. S. Kuffeler claimed to have "perfected a dreadfull Engine for the speedie and effectuall destroying of Shipping in a Moment." He presented plans for deployment to the Council of State. Samuel Hartlib warned of dire consequences if the new weapon fell into the hands of enemies of religion, however. Pressing Cromwell to secure English control, Hartlib projected "the dreadfull effect of this invention to be such as would enable any one nation that would be first master of it, to give the law to other nations."[23] Cromwell witnessed the spectacle of a full trial of the torpedo at Deptford in August 1658. It performed "exceedingly beyond expectation and did a far greater execution than what the petitioner had promised." Cromwell offered the Kuffelers his patronage, but he died shortly thereafter, and interest in torpedoes faded with the Restoration. Meanwhile, J. S. Kuffeler had his hand blown off while installing a torpedo, underscoring the dangers of using them. Samuel Pepys felt Kuffeler's torpedoes were too unsafe, and naval gunners dreaded igniting the unstable time fuse before the torpedo was launched.[24]

In 1628, however, the threat of impending apocalypse overrode such considerations, and Winthrop hoped that the La Rochelle expedition would provide opportunities for testing torpedoes capable of reversing the fortunes of international Protestantism. He not only remained committed to experimentation on the Kuffeler brothers' project long after the siege but corresponded with the Kuffeler family all his life and visited them in Holland.

However, Winthrop's best natural-philosophical opportunities at the Île de Ré, where he had a clear view of maneuvers at La Rochelle just to the east, were in observations of fortress construction and defense against mass assault. A letter survives from the *Due Repulse* reporting the younger Winthrop's military analysis of the dual sieges of the Île de Ré and La Rochelle. Written to his father and dated September 1627 (a month before the English defeat at the Île de Ré and before the tide turned against La Rochelle), the letter remains an acute, prescient account that expertly balanced the strengths against the weaknesses—and prospects for survival—of both fortresses:

> Sir . . . I wrote unto you the last opportunity which I found by two severall messengers, whether they came to your handes I know not: but yet I doubt not but that you have had so full Intelligence of our proceedings till that tyme that it should be needlesse to write anything thereof. As touching our affairs how you shall understand now thereof, Our army lieth still the most part at St. martins some few Garrisons in other partes of the Iland. The Cittadell [at Saint-Martin-de-Ré] is now Intrenched Round, our trenches come in some places within a stones quoite of the Enemies the centinels on both sides continually playing with their small shotte watching as narrowly as the fouler after a bird how they may come at a shotte the great Ordinance on both sides shoot not so often as they did at first: every day there come some running out of the Castle who bring diverse and uncertaine reportes what they thinke of the tyme it can holde out, but it is thought they had yeilded it up by this tyme had it not been for 3 or 4 boates which in a darke and foule night stole over undiscovered of the shipes but tis thought they could not furnish them with much victuales, and if that be spent there is such order taken that they shall very hardly get any more, for besides the ships which lie there close together, and our boats scoutinge out all night they have made a boome with mastes chained together which lieth crosse that place where they shold go in so that they must needes be foule eyther of the shipes or that. Those boates which gott over were guided by two Dutchmen who Ridinge among our shipes had taken notice of the order of our fleet and the likeliest place they might come by them without discovery. They are now taken and to be executed. We tooke the other night two boates which were goeing to the Castle with victualls some other there were which escaped backe againe. We have now arrived 2400 soldiers out of Ireland, and doe expect a supply of shipes and men out of England when they be come I hope we shall not stay here long after I thinke soone after Michaelmos we shall be at home. The King of France [Louis XIII] hath had an army about Rochell ever since our comminge they are reported to be 12000 men but the town and they were on good termes till the 30 of August and then they began to fall out with some store of great shott on both sides but they feare not the kinges forces so long as our fleet keepe the sea open to them When I had well viewed the towne I marveiled not that it holds out so long siege, for I thinke it almost Impossible to take it by force if they be not shut up at sea as well as by land.[25]

Winthrop's narrative tells the tale of two sieges. After recounting the story of the resupply of Marshal Jean de Toiras's starving garrison at Saint-Martin, which succeeded despite a giant floating boom of masts chained together to form a blockade, Winthrop observed that La Rochelle would be "impossible to take by force if they be not shut up at sea as well as by land." This could not occur, "so long as our fleet keepe the sea open to them," ensuring a lifeline to the Atlantic. In the end, of course, the English fleet was unable to keep the sea lanes open at Île de Ré, and the royal architect Clément Metezeau's celebrated dike was built across the open mouth of La Rochelle's harbor. Unlike Buckingham's giant boom, this marvel of military engineering was successful, and the fortress was sealed off from the rest of the Protestant world.

After returning from the Île de Ré in early November of 1627, John Winthrop Jr. pursued his interests in natural philosophy and military innovations with vigor, especially as regards fortress design and torpedoes. Yet ultimately, the failure of the most powerful fortress in the world to withstand the siege of a determined and innovative enemy would cause him to reconsider old strategies of stationary fortress defense and turn to stealth and craftsmanship in ways that closely approximated artisanal *sûreté*. He also planned future alchemical journeys to discover the powerful secrets of the philosopher's stone and achieve the status of adept.

La Rochelle's fall was now expected. Thus, the discovery of the philosopher's stone was essential to the economic and military plans of international Protestantism. Hence, Winthrop renewed his scientific correspondence with Edward Howes as soon as he had settled in again at Groton. Howes's first letter to Groton was typically obscure. Reference to an alchemical recipe was cloaked in a secret code, one of several the two scientists employed in letters. Here, Paracelsian metaphor was used artfully, with the overall effect to convey joy at Winthrop's safe return in alchemical terms:

> Serenissimo mio Amigo, Yours came to me in serena die the supposed cloudes with soe gentill a gale of wind being driven from the horizon of our Auncient yet not old growing Amity. Your Newes was as welcome, as my thankes is readie to express my gratefullnes for givinge cause unto me of new borne, or at least renewed Meditations.
>
> I perceive he whoe trustes most in god and least in man, him will god undoubtedly assist in all his enterprises he that trusts in anything but God, that thinge shall faile him, if not shame him, he that is proud of his knowledge, the simple shall put him to silence . . . let me intreat you to send me an Rx to molify Agyarso [meaning "gas," in an alternate letter code].[26]

For Howes, Winthrop's letter announcing his return signaled a bright new Boehmian dawn. The clouds of war having been blown away by "soe gentill a gale of wind"— the breath of the spirit?—the two alchemists were united again, and Howes felt the quickening "of renewed [internal and soulish] Meditations," on earth's decline, now hastened by events at the Île de Ré and the crucible of La Rochelle. To "trust most in

God and least in man" was all that was necessary. "Him will God undoubtedly assist in all his enterprises," Howes assured Winthrop, just as "he that trusts in anything but God [Buckingham?], that thinge shall faile him, if not shame him." The philosopher's stone might now at last be found by "the simple" who will "put" the "proud . . . to silence." The secrets of the prolongation of life—the proverbial fountain of youth— might perhaps soon be revealed.[27]

These themes were reiterated and ramified one month later, when Winthrop received a similarly cryptic letter from his "very lovinge Frinde." This time, Howes played the client's role of the humble supplicant to a powerful alchemical patron, alternately reflecting and then "daylie seeinge my selfe . . . fall a loathinge," in the constant purity of his master's God-given inner light. This friend was content to accept the "deformed"—and hence, imperfect—material status of a dependent moon, at once "loving" but incapable of generating its own light from within. As in a Copernican solar system, Howes was "veiled" and sublimated with the "daily" rise of his exalted sun and patron. Howes's supplication was raised to the level of privileged natural-philosophical discourse, as he chose to "vaile" his words again in the shadow of alchemical metaphor:

> Deare Sir, The skillfullest painters some tymes bestowe theire best colours upon deformed Pictures And wisely some Orators to blazon the vices of some Catliffe speaketh of the contrarie vertues; Soe you (according to your gentle nature) have provided a vaile to cover my deformitie; that I daylie seeinge my selfe through it, may thereby appeare the more deformed and soe seeinge, fall a loathinge, and then (by divine assistance) leaving my deformitie, become conformed to what you would have me, Even to a conformitie of mynd and manners which as yet I am farre shorte of, though my study be for such perfection. It hath pleased you to conceive better of me than ever I could of myself Yea doe for me more than ever I would have done for my selfe which maketh my love (which you call frindshipe) a duty ever vowed to you. I love to write playnely for I knowe it pleaseth you, and to displease you, if it weare possible I might I could not. As for the universitie . . . of what neede you be a scholler there, where of you are president, I being but a sophisticall studient studie as I am bound to give accompte of my tyme come when you will, I shall be fitted with a plus ultra or something meane while I meane to make hollyday nowe and then when I can but find a holy hower to praye for our prosperous proceedings which God graunt to his glorye and our comforte Amen.

And in a postscript, Howes added; "And all such things as are either secret, or manifest: them I knowe" (Wisd. of Sol. 7:21).[28]

Ambiguity was used by natural philosophers to control the diffusion of sacred knowledge, and Howes was a masterful inventor of anagrams and other tools of linguistic mystification. Yet he acknowledges in his letter how this practice "displeases" his correspondent. Most of these metaphors conform to ideas and practices widely understood by early modern "chymists" such as Winthrop, whom Howes first compares to "the skillfullest paynter," arguably a figure for the Genesis God. When the author "speaketh of contrarie vertues," it is reasonable to assume that he was representing the conjunction of microcosm and macrocosm (and, by Neoplatonic analogy "downward," of spirit and matter); so too with "leaving my deformitie, become conformed to what you would have me" (the alchemist's purification of "deformed" or fallen matter, which thereby achieves a perfect state of being and light); the "conformitie of mynd and manners" (the adept's synthesis of theory and practice); and "a plus ultra or somethinge meane . . . pray for our prosperous proceedings which God graunt to his glorye" (implicit acknowledgement of linkage between Winthrop [*qua* sun] and Howes [*qua* moon]). This relation infers a symbiotic cosmic quest to discover the philosopher's stone, the holy grail of alchemists; a universal elixir of purification and infinite reproduction that could transmute all things into its own substance. As such, the stone *was* Christ: a gift from God of the spiritual made material to "simple" men who, like the incarnate Son (also "sun") himself, was simultaneously exalted (spiritual: "plus ultra") and banal (material: "somethinge meane").[29]

Howes was an elusive figure who moved through the lower levels of London's natural-philosophical circles with relative anonymity. He was known in the city's libraries and laboratories because of his association with the Downing family, or as a supplier of new scientific books and laboratory instruments, not for his own accomplishments. Scholarship concerning Howes's minor contribution to the history of science is as invisible as he represented himself to be in the letter to Winthrop. Still, he has received passing attention from historians of seventeenth-century New England. Howes is remembered as Emmanuel Downing's law clerk and usually trivialized as a singular individual with bizarre intellectual tastes. Thus he is portrayed as a mystical interloper among the sober, rational, and orthodox Winthrops. In effect, he has been depicted as a slightly disrespectable playmate until the governor's son overcame his personality defect and matured enough to leave childish things behind.

Howes's letters nonetheless chronicle decades of scientific friendship with the younger Winthrop. He was Howes's most influential patron in the New World, and Howes remained Winthrop's lifeline to the main publishing centers and booksellers in London and Frankfurt. This epistolary link was important to Howes for many reasons, but the key connection between the two men would be the search for the philosopher's stone in the Long Island Sound region and New Netherlands. Howes did not emigrate in the end. This decision was influenced by the changed context in England during the interregnum (when Winthrop himself nearly returned to London) and because Howes was finally able to support himself by teaching. Howes also expressed reservations and anxieties about reports of social repression and religious intolerance in Massachusetts. These fears, combined with his patron's failure to secure a firm economic foothold in America and to find the philosopher's stone, despite his formidable hermetic skills, undoubtedly played a large role in Howes's thinking.

By 1644, Howes had left the Downing household to become master at the Ratcliffe Free School in London. He adapted the school's classical and scholastic pedagogy to the new Paracelsian medical and alchemic tradition. Charles Webster has shown that this program was conducive to the English Calvinist program, when its practitioners domesticated its mystical and occult origins by suppressing them in public. If his letters to Winthrop are indicative, the practice of secrecy was a consuming aspect of Howes's everyday life. Not much more about the younger Winthrop's secretive protégé is known, except for one nineteenth-century reference to Howes having entered "holy orders." Howes's mystical and Neoplatonic reputation suggests membership in the Rosicrucian brotherhood, and there is plenty of evidence to support the claim that both Winthrop and Howes were at the very least engaged by the promise of this occult society.

An obscure letter of August 1635 showed the intensity of this mutual interest, which was not so arcane among scientists. Howes wrote Winthrop at Ipswich that "I have bin 2 or 3 times since with the Dr. and can get but small satisfaccon about your queries." The "Dr." remained unnamed, presumably for reasons of security. Howes continued in a furtive tone, to suggest that his metaphorical informant was associated with the Rosicrucians ("the *fratres scientiae*"):

> I doubt he hath some prejudicate conceipt of one of us, or both; yet I must confesse he
> seemed verie free to me, only in the maine he was misticall. This he said[:] that when the
> will of God is you shall knowe what you desire, it will come with such a light, that it will
> make a harmonie among all your authors, causing them sweetly to agree, and putt you for
> ever out of doubt and question. To discerne the *fratres scientiae* I cannot as yet learn of
> him.[30]

Perhaps Winthrop sought to discern members of the brotherhood as a means of achieving insight into the "harmonie" (or metaphysical unity of knowledge), to link the fragmented knowledge contained in all the natural-philosophical texts in his library ("amonge all your authors"), but the doctor's main insight was obscure and "misticall." Harmony would "come" when the "light" of God's "will" unified macrocosm and microcosm. Howes encountered Rosicrucianism early in his career and, like the younger Winthrop, took it very seriously, as many early modern natural philosophers did, although his occult interests did not prevent him from serving as Calvinist rector of Goldanger in Essex in 1659.[31] Although theoretical mathematics—mostly universalist and Neoplatonic in nature—played an important role in Howes's correspondence with Winthrop, Howes's only known book, *A Short Arithmetick*, was a primer that elicited no comment in mathematical circles.[32]

❧ Wisdom on the Margins ❧

Like Palissy's, Howes's Paracelsian Neoplatonism was harnessed to religious violence. This was certainly the context of the letter of January 22, 1627, coming as it did only two months after Winthrop's return from the Île de Ré, now that the final, catastrophic outcome was in view. To give formal shape to apocalyptic themes of personal security under assault, Howes provided Winthrop with a parting fragment of marginalia (fig. 10.1)—in effect, a pictorial commentary on the letter's written text—that purported to contain an illuminist's insight into the cosmological meaning of Winthrop's recent experience at La Rochelle, with a postscript: "And all such things as are either secret, or manifest: them I knowe." This is Howes's translation of Wisdom of Solomon 7:21, an apocryphal text written ca. 30 B.C. by the exiled Hellenistic Jew Philo of Alexandria. Chapter 7 of the Wisdom of Solomon is devoted to the relationship between divine

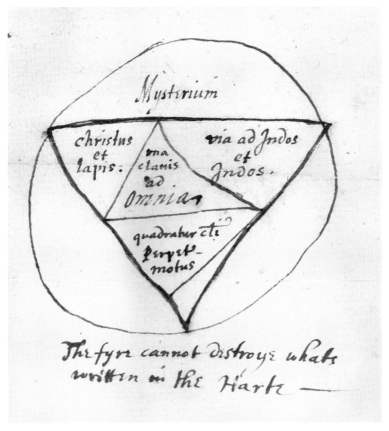

FIGURE 10.1. Edward Howes, marginalia in a letter to John Winthrop Jr., London, January 22, 1627. Winthrop Family Papers. Courtesy Massachusetts Historical Society.

wisdom and the human—or microcosmic—sciences and crafts. This was another key text in formulating the early modern natural-philosophical analogy of macrocosm and microcosm. It is also thought by some philologists to show the earliest use of the word "craftsmanship" (*ergateia*), in Greek (although it should be said that *ergateia* more generally means labor, work, or handicraft). Wisdom—like the earth, a feminine "artificer of all"—is God's beautiful handmaiden and the divine messenger between microcosm and macrocosm. She is the carrier of Adamic knowledge of the prelapsarian natural world, master of the skills of artisanal replication of Nature's hidden forms and processes. *Wisdom* is thus a fundamental text for the fusion of Neoplatonic and Paracelsian alchemy, with the universal soul as intermediary between God and man as the artisan and the physician-alchemist. Solomon (like Palissy) was taught by God through Wisdom to master the microcosmic crafts: the full range of secret skills belonging to the natural philosopher. These included, above all else, the alchemist's prophetic knowledge and visual perception of "the structure of the universe and the operation of the elements; / the beginning, and end, and middle of times":

> God grant that I speak in accord with his wish,
> and conceive thoughts worthy of his gifts,
> for he himself is both the guide of Wisdom
> and corrector of the wise.
> Both we and our words are in his hands,
> as well as all understanding and craftsmanship.
> For it was he who gave me unerring knowledge of existent
> being,
> to know the structure of the universe and the operation of
> the elements;
> the beginning, and end, and middle of times,
> the changes of the solstices and the vicissitudes of the
> seasons;
> the cycles of years and the positions of the stars;
> the natures of living creatures and the tempers of beasts;
> the violent force of spirits and the reasonings of men;
> the species of plants, and the virtues of roots.
> *I learned both what is hidden and what is manifest,*
> for Wisdom, the artificer of all, taught me.[33]

Apropos of Philo's ambiguous status as an exile from both the land of Israel and Judaism (because of his immersion in Hellenistic natural philosophy), David Winston has constructed a narrative of Philo's context and personal experience that has much in common with Winthrop's and Palissy's narratives of the war years. As "an unabashed Platonist," Winston writes, Philo was concerned with "the hidden meaning which appeals to the few who study soul characteristics, rather than boldly forms."[34] At the end of his letter to Winthrop, after the postscript, Howes for his part represented a soulish presence who alone comprehended the hidden meaning of the seemingly incomprehensible sacrifice of the sacred fortress with a Stoic aphorism, which may have been a crude adaptation from Deuteronomy (11:26) or a Ciceronian source: "Dic—Quid lex est illi qui sibi lex est, / Lex mihi Onus et Honus"; "It is said—The law is a thing unto itself, / But for myself the law is both a burden and an honor."[35] Appeal to the primacy of the hidden world was not merely a decontextualized intellectual project; rather, knowledge and ambiguous elucidation of "what is hidden and what is manifest" were inextricably linked to Philo's liminal religious, social, and political status within and outside of his own cultural community and its hosts:

> His mode of exposition is characterized by a deliberate ambiguity, which allowed him to cover his tracks when the philosophical views he adopted would have struck the wider Jewish audience he was addressing as essentially alien to their native ways of thinking. I find nothing dishonest nor any lack of integrity in this studied use of ambiguity, but only Philo's assured conviction that simple faith is for the simple and philosophical faith is for the philosophical.[36]

At the moment of millennial reversal, however, the need for ambiguity would disappear, as would separate nations; a new universal society of the soul would destroy nationalism, war, and the obscuring boundaries between faiths, and a "patrician lineage" of adepts, often hidden invisibly in quotidian occupations and waiting since primitive times, would arise and lead the skillful weak to victory with God's help:

> In response to the divine chastisements visited upon them, the people will repent and make a full confession of their sins. Their conversion in a body to virtue will strike their masters with amazement, who, ashamed to rule over their superiors, will set them free from their captivity. With one impulse they will hasten from their areas of dispersion to one assigned place, guided by a vision divine and superhuman, though invisible to others. Their ruined cities will be rebuilt, the barren land will be rendered fruitful, and they will have wealth so copious it will make that of their progenitors seem negligible by comparison. There will be a sudden reversal of all things. God will turn curses against the enemies who had exulted over their failures, not realizing they were but pawns in the hands of God who had employed them for the admonition of his people. When they begin to receive the wages of their cruelty, they will find that they had wronged not the obscure and inconsequential but men of patrician lineage who had retained the sparks of their noble birth. [Hence,] Philo's denationalizing and psychologizing tendency . . . refer[s] to the rule of the wise generally, and universal peace . . . [and] appears only as a consequence of

a more important good, man's inner peace of soul . . . God is designated by Philo not as the God of Israel, but of all people . . . Philo's messianic vision . . . reveal[s] the inner tensions in his thought between nationalism and universalism, the mystical and the this-worldly . . . when Philo is justly described as "a man between two worlds," the metaphor needs to be understood in a double sense, for not only does he join Athens with Jerusalem, but also the supernal, celestial Jerusalem with its lower, terrestrial image.[37]

Surely, this utopian society brought into being by the sacred conjunction of violence and wisdom, and elucidated by an exiled Jew caught "between two worlds" in the metaphorical "double sense" was also an elucidation of Winthrop's experience at the Île de Ré as he pondered the situation of two opposing fortresses, and of Palissy's at Saintes, La Rochelle, and later Paris.

In the margin of his letter to Winthrop, Howes drew a hermetic hieroglyph captioned "Mysterium" (fig. 10.1), beneath which he wrote: "The fyre cannot destroye whats written in the Harte," a motto that both echoed these resonances with Philo and paid homage to Francis Bacon's great utopian fragment *The New Atlantis* (1626), published after Bacon's death but just a year before Howes's letter to Winthrop. This essay exerted a profound influence on Calvinist leaders as they pondered colonization and looked through the books of Elizabethan projectors. *The New Atlantis* described the operation of a universal scientific laboratory on Philo's pansophic model, a connection made clear by Bacon's choice of "Solomon's House" as its name. We read that Solomon's House served the "harmonious and devout society" of Bensalem, island refuge of "a Christian people, full of piety and humanity." Charles Webster says of *The New Atlantis*:

This island was situated off the coast of America and Bacon's vision of a perfect society was undoubtedly influenced by the imaginative and optimistic accounts of America and the Islands of the West Indies published by Hakluyt, Ralegh and Harriot, or even by the stream of propaganda on the wonders of the New World issued by the promoters of the Virginia Company between 1606 and 1624. Bacon himself devoted one of his *Essays* to the subject "Of Plantations" and took an active interest in schemes for the plantation of Ireland, Virginia and Newfoundland.[38]

Howe's hieroglyph is a crude freehand ink drawing of a circle encompassing a square within an equilateral triangle with angles pointing east, west, and south. Inside are fragments of deliberately obscure, abbreviated text, that defy anything more certain than a provisional translation. Fortunately, however, all possible interpretations seem close enough in meaning to proceed on fairly secure ground. The arched space between the "bottom" of the upside-down triangle—at the uppermost ("north") section of the circle—(meant to signify the white space all around the triangle) contains the "Mysterium," or "Religious Rites," connoting rites of initiation or secrets of the adepts that cannot be divulged. Inside this shaky triangle Howes sketched what he clearly intended to be an aggregate of four more equilateral triangles. Two of these intersect at points on the circumference of the circle—"christus et lapis" (west), and "via ad Indes et Indes" (east)—but taken together their inner and outer angles are all roughly directed toward the four main compass points. As a result, the centrifugal triangles are congruent, and though aimed in opposing directions, form the basis for a hermetic puzzle centered around the phrase "una clamis ad OMNIA" ("one cloak for all things"). This linked Howes with Winthrop in a grand hermetic project in which they worked together secretly toward a single Neoplatonic solution for all God's answers hidden in Nature. This interpretation is supported by the form of Howes's hieroglyph, which may be seen in the depiction of "Mercuri Philosophorum" from Samuel Norton's *Alchymiae complementum* of 1630 (fig. 8.19) that itself may have derived from a plate depicting "Alchemy and Geometry" in *Atalanta fugiens,* Michael Maier's Rosicrucian manifesto of 1618, which was available to Howes when he wrote the letter.[39]

The mystical mathematician in Howes had composed an axiometric pictograph intended to be deciphered from a God's-eye view. This perception, of course, was privately joined with that of his privileged reader (Winthrop)—already deified by analogy with the "skillfullest painter" in the text of the letter—as he gazed down at the image on the page from above. Meditating upon this image, Winthrop saw that if the triangles were folded together as a three dimensional unity, (like origami), the image would then be transformed, on the outside, into a blank paper pyramid—with a square on the inside composed of two more triangles—pointing up from a vanishing point at the center of the sacred circle. Thus, simultaneously, it also pointed up, at Winthrop, now secretly singled out by Howes and identified as an adept whose authentic place was with God in the tiny, nearly imperceptible middle of the sacred circle. The role of the adept was therefore to reach down and open up this Trinitarian enigma like a flower (a Rosicrucian rose?)—here, the "Mysterium" of Nature (mysterium also connotes a puzzle)—to search its hidden interior for the key to unifying dispersed humanity under "one cloak." This was accomplished by reading the "light" in the ancient texts of Nature that only he was privileged to see inscribed beneath the surface. One is reminded instantly of "In patientia sauvitas," where "the fire" of the siege of La Rochelle is perceived as freeing the purity hidden beneath the ravaged surface, while a rosy cross grows out of the top of the Huguenot Mt. Zion.

Howes optimistically represented this task to Winthrop as a fait accompli (fig. 10.2); after all, his loving friend had already "gently" opened the petals of this sacred flower to reveal a Paracelsian seed at the base of its deepest receptacle—the pyramid's foundation—to read "una clamis ad OMNIA" ("one cloak for all things"). In this instance, the secret combination unified the three other spiritually seeking triangular depend-

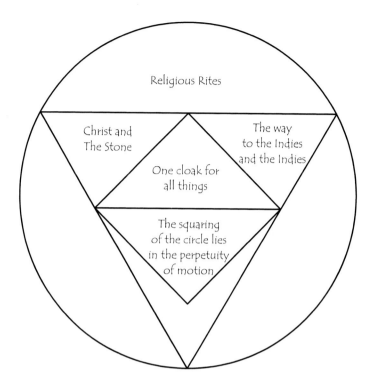

FIGURE 10.2. Reconstruction and translation of drawing in figure 10.1. The abbreviation "cli" has been translated as the genitive *circuli;* "perpet-" has been completed as the nominative *per-pet[uatio]*.

encies surrounding it in the "Mysterium." Howes represented the upper left (west) tri-angle as the philosopher's stone ("Christ and the Stone"). This was linked inextrica-bly to the upper right (east) triangle ("The Way to the Indies and the Indies") by the secret combination to unite all things, such that the East and West Indies—and the insurmountable distance between Eastern and Western hemispheres—are finally uni-fied by the replicating power of the spirit in the stone. The south triangle, "quadratur cli Perpet-[uatio] motus" ("The squaring of the circle lies in the perpetuity of mo-tion"), having a downward motion, is also made to point north simultaneously, har-nessed to the upwardly pointing unity of macrocosm and microcosm with Winthrop as the chosen intermediary. This makes sense for three reasons. In the simplest mathe-matical terms, the quadrature refers to the act of squaring; in this instance something akin to the Vitruvian squaring of the circle, inasmuch as the two central triangles form a square. In sacred and hermetic terms, the quadrature was generally analogous to God's heavenly geometry; His empyreal vault in the sky, as opposed to fallen man's orbicular world. As such, alchemists referred to the existence of a gnostic square and the monistic unification of the macrocosm and the microcosm might then be represented geometrically as the circle squared. In astronomical terms, it can also mean the conjunction of two heavenly bodies within the quadrature (when they are ninety degrees apart), as in horoscopes of the period.[40] Howes may thus refer to the "perpetual" conjunction of the sun (Winthrop) and moon (Howes) in God's sacred cosmology. This fortuitous arrangement is also inferred by Wisdom of Solomon 7:18–19, in which "the positions of the stars" are underscored.[41] Linking the north and south triangles then, is an alchemic figure for the conjunction of the macrocosm and microcosm, which come together in the spiritual and material experience of the adept—in this instance, Winthrop himself.

The image guaranteed Winthrop the faithful service of his dependent moon (Howes), no matter where he traveled on the geographical plane; that is to say, after he went west to the colonies. Just as they moved in conjunction under "one cloak for all things," so too the quadrature of Christ (also the cloak of heaven) would square the circle "in the perpetuity of motion" after the sun departed, wherever Winthrop traveled, collapsing the historical fiction of time and space between them. After all, the Copernican sun—as in Winthrop's chair—was always at the heart of the animate and spinning cosmos. To square the circle perpetually in history meant that Winthrop himself was the American capable of creating a permanent, active synthesis of macrocosm and microcosm on earth through his own connection to the celestial body and the discovery of Christ's philosopher's stone.

The three keys, then, to understanding this pictograph for Howes and Winthrop and their agenda for security in the wake of La Rochelle lay in the alchemic quest for the philosopher's stone, which Howes implies was harnessed to the to the discovery of the Northwest Passage in America; the affinity of this quest to the influential physician-alchemist Robert Fludd's theories of the "Fortress of Health" and its "enemies"; and the relation of all this to the inscription underneath, which reads "The Fyre Cannot Destroye Whats Written in the Harte."[42] Therein lies the final piece of the puzzle. Other forms of Howes's pictograph, such as Norton's and Maier's, invariably depict the upturned macrocosmic triangle representing elemental fire and air. Howes inverts this convention and replaces it with the microcosmic water and earth, suggesting that the destructive fire has been mastered and sublimated by Winthrop's heart and that the story written inside this bodily container of his soul will be revealed where earth and water meet.

❧ The Passage and the Stone ❧

Howes' puzzle tells us that to unify "Christ and the Stone" the alchemic voyager must travel "The Way to the Indies and the Indies." This meant to acquire the stone, John Winthrop Jr. was poised to find the legendary Northwest Passage and with it the East Indies itself. It is unclear which comes first—the passage or the stone—but the implication is one of simultaneity and clearly one cannot be discovered without the other. Thus, Winthrop was himself set in perpetual motion, having been presented with three choices in 1627–28 after returning from Île de Ré: go back to the university to find the key to the stone there in his books and the laboratory; go immediately to America to gain experience and begin his exploration for the Northwest Passage; or, set off for the Mediterranean (the east), as he had initially intended to do before the Île de Ré expedition intervened. Howes, in his letter of January 22, prescribed the stance of the Paracelsian, when he writes: "As for the university . . . of what neede you be a scholler there, where of you are president." Winthrop had apparently floated the idea to Howes, who advised rejection of Trinity College, Dublin, or Cambridge, in favor of the school of experience.

Winthrop's final decision to opt for the latter is indicated by another revealing letter from his clever brother Forth, written from Cambridge sometime in late 1627 or 1628. Forth's letter is a sort of personal allegory contrasting scholasticism and Paracelsism, as if "brothers educated by different mothers." To emphasize his role as family scholastic, Forth wrote in Latin:

> We are brothers (beloved brother); and yet, what may seem strange, brought up and educated by different mothers and in different soils, it happens that from our different discipline we have derived different habits, and pursue a different kind of life. I, indeed, an alumnus of Cambridge, my alma mater—if I may deserve that title—cling to her beloved halls and chapels, to her sacred precepts of the Muses, and to her illustrious fountains of learning, with so much ardor and affection, and admire them all so greatly, that, there amid the divine abodes of philosophers, I have decided to search out and unravel the secrets which Nature still holds in her silent bosom, to penetrate the labyrinths of philosophy and the obscure sources of sacred letters, even as an astrologer observes the motions of the stars, as the husbandman the plants of the earth, as Oedipus his knotty enigmas, or as an infant clings to the mother's breast. . . . When, however, I enter on a longer journey than you have undertaken, it is only among my books; where in a little space of time I can sail to Constantinople, and even reach the Indies with a dry foot. . . . Here I am fixed, and such is the fortune of my life. But you, nourished on a foreign soil, your country left behind, are laboring with the desire of seeing unknown lands, and of beholding strange cus-

toms; and so go on with a fortunate foot, and may God be your guide among the rocks of the ocean. To him fly as to an asylum and the sacred anchor of your safety . . . who is he Way, the Life, and the Truth to all who make him their refuge. Farewell.[43]

Both John and Forth were sons of Mary Forth, first wife of the elder John Winthrop. But Mary died when Forth was only two years of age, after which their father remarried, and hence they had been "brought up and educated by different mothers." But this was also a metaphor for different paths taken. Forth recognized the significance of John's leaving England for Trinity College, Dublin, while he himself matriculated at Emmanuel College, Cambridge. For Forth, his brother had followed a wanderer's career from the start. With Paracelsus as his model, John had been educated "on different soils." This referred not only to Trinity but also the expedition to the Île de Ré and La Rochelle, to which Forth gestured, "may God be your guide among the rocks of the ocean." John was thus freed from the ancient constraints of scholasticism: "you, nourished on a foreign soil, your country left behind, are laboring with the desire of seeing unknown lands, and of beholding strange customs; and so go on with a fortunate foot." Forth would stay among "the Muses" at Cambridge, following his older brother's calling without leaving the library. Forth may have felt physically weakened when this letter was written—too weak to join his brother on an alchemical journey except in the mind—he was to die just two years later. "Here I am fixed," said this mind traveler, "and such is the fortune of my life."

Having decided on the philosophical school of experience in the natural world—of "the fortunate foot"—John Winthrop Jr. thought first about America, but plans for the New England Company were hardly in the formative stages, and his father was uncertain about the timing. "For your Journey entended," the elder Winthrop wrote in April 1628, "seeinge you have a resolution to goe to sea I know not where you should goe with such a religious company and under such hope of blessinge, onely I am loth you should thinke of settling there, as yet, but to be goinge and cominge awhile and afterward to doe as god shall offer occasion."[44]

As the time was not yet right for "settling" in the west, the younger Winthrop voyaged first to the east, where he resumed searching for the stone in the Mediterranean. By June 1628, with Downing's help, he signed on with the merchant ship *London* (again as purser), and headed for the Levant. The *London*'s first port of call was Leghorn (Livorno), in Tuscany. Winthrop visited Pisa and Florence, where he did not wish to spend time viewing art and architecture but in exploring botanical gardens; these marvels—the Italian grottoes of Palissy's artisanal passion—were also famous outdoor natural-philosophical laboratories of man's dominion over the elements of nature. From there, the *London* continued east to Constantinople, where Winthrop considered voyaging on to Jerusalem. Money problems and interesting travel companions encouraged him to remain on board the *London,* however, as the vessel doubled back, then sailed up the Adriatic for Venice, the most pluralistic and heterodox city in the Catholic Mediterranean. Finally, Winthrop set sail for London in July 1629, but unfavorable winds in the English Channel forced a quick detour to Amsterdam, and he was unable to return home until August.[45]

As one might expect from a seeker in quest of the arcane and secret knowledge of eastern alchemy, Winthrop wanted to meet other like-minded friends. One of those Winthrop met on his travels was the Dutch linguist and natural philosopher Jacobus Golius (1596–1667), who gave him access to a formidable collection of Arabic and Persian manuscripts that he had collected on journeys through the Ottoman Empire.[46] Winthrop met Golius in Constantinople, and they traveled together to Venice on the *London,* after which they remained correspondents.

The other preoccupation on the Mediterranean voyage was Richelieu and the army of Louis XIII, whose progress Winthrop seems to have followed. After the fall of La Rochelle, Richelieu and the king led this powerful army of 35,000 foot soldiers and 3,000 cavalry into Italy. They entered the War of the Mantuan Succession against the Hapsburgs in support of the Bourbon candidate for the duchy of Mantua (Charles de Nevers), a settlement to which was reached between France and Savoy on March 11, 1629.[47] Winthrop sent two letters from Venice on March 9 and 28 with his observations, again as a military authority.[48] Hence, Winthrop was present to report on Richelieu's two greatest military thrusts of the 1620s, in which he moved huge armies great distances to engage in foreign actions. This was precisely the sort of offensive program that the leaders of international Protestantism expected from absolutism and the Counter-Reformation, and Winthrop continued to formulate his post–La Rochelle defensive strategies in advance of American colonization.

Meanwhile, the elder Winthrop's plans for colonization finally crystallized with the emergence of the New England Company in 1629. And on August 21, 1629, having just returned from the Mediterranean, his oldest son announced an end to his traveling in a famous letter that has been quoted so often that it has become almost invisible:

> For the business of N[ew] E[ngland] I can say no other thing but that I beleeve confidently that the whole disposition thereof is of the lord who disposeth all alterations by his blessed will to his owne glory and the good of his, and therefore doe assure my selfe that all thinges shall worke together for the best therein, and for myself I have seene so much of the vanity of the world that I esteeme noe more of the diversities of Countries then as so many Innes, whereof the travailer, that hath lodged in the best, or in the worst, findeth no difference when he commeth to his Journies end, and I shall call that my countrie where I may most glorify God and enjoy the presence of my dearest friends, therefore herein I submit myself to Godes wil, and yours, and with your leave doe dedicate my selfe

(laying by all desire of other imploymentes whatsoever) to the service of God, and the Company, with the whole endeavors both of body and mind.[49]

On one level, if read conventionally, John Winthrop Jr. is offering a variation on the time-honored theme of telling the old man what he wants to hear—that the wandering (if not prodigal) son has finally returned and is willing to come to heel.

But given what we know about the natural-philosophical context of this letter, it may be read as an alchemical narrative as well. While the younger Winthrop frames his letter as the kind of conventional pilgrimage his father might expect in this context, I think this begs the question: what does the oblique Winthrop mean by the seemingly innocuous statement that "I shall call that my Countrie where I may most glorify God and enjoy the presence of my dearest friends, therefore herein I submit myselfe to Godes wil, and yours"? The answer lies in Winthrop's very specific perception of what it meant to "submit myselfe" to the will of God. Following his correspondence with Howes—and indeed the focus and experience of his life to that point—this meant Winthrop's aspiration to the status of adept through the spiritual practice of the Paracelsian physician-alchemist, whose ultimate quest was the philosopher's stone. Howes meant precisely this in his letter of January 22, 1627, writing that he must "finde a holy hower to praye for our prosperous proceedings which God graunt to his glorye and our comforte." This was no mere catechistic closing, as Palissy has shown, but an essential opening up of the alchemist to the Holy Spirit. Yet the younger Winthrop also desired to submit to his father's will ("and yours"), hence the appeal for God's favor would have been understood from the father's authoritarian perspective, quite different from the son's. Having to submit to both God and his father meant the use of a discourse of double meanings for common religious and social language.

If different perceptions between father and son of the meaning of God's will may be called into question, what was the identity of "my dearest friends"? The assumption has always been the Calvinist community that joined together to form the New England Company and the Winthrop family and friendship network in America. It is logical to assume that this was the way the elder Winthrop would have been expected to read the word "friendship" by his son; that is to say, through his own narrow vision. But we have already seen how the younger Winthrop was building an international network of correspondence and patronage with natural-philosophical friends. When Howes wrote Winthrop about "our friends," this was what he meant.

What, then, does one make of the correspondence where Howes associates instruments in his alchemic laboratory, and even scientific books, with the word "friendship"?[50] Consider, that for all Winthrop's talk about his desire to "enjoy the *presence* of my dearest friends," he spent as little time as possible in the presence of anyone he knew in New England. Almost from the moment he arrived in Boston, the younger

Winthrop followed the same pattern of personal geographical and physical isolation as he had in Europe. In the Old World, he traveled north from England to Dublin, then south to the siege of La Rochelle, then briefly to England again, then south to the Mediterranean, and then went to America. In New England, he spent little time as commissioner of fortifications in Boston before moving north to Essex County, where he set up the Saugus ironworks and tried to harvest salt in pans like the ones Palissy described being used in the marshes of Saintonge. Then, after several exploratory searches to the Connecticut Valley—during which time he went back and forth between Ipswich, Boston, and Connecticut—and the decisive moment of the death of his father in 1649 (which allowed him to move far from Boston), John Winthrop Jr. settled permanently on the Connecticut side of Long Island Sound, *his* Mediterranean, on the border of the pluralistic New Netherlands.

Even before this, Winthrop had again become very hard for correspondents to find. Many were forced to address their letters to "somewhere in New England." In 1650, having moved south to the Long Island Sound basin, Winthrop received a letter from Dr. Robert Child, a natural philosopher exiled from Massachusetts, detailing Child's opinions of available books by four prominent Paracelsians (von Helmont, Glauber, Rulingius, and Harvey). Child, following Winthrop's early experience, planned to settle in Ireland. He did not expect to return to New England, where the oligarchy alienated him "by their discourtesye," but "if they would returne me my fine, I would adventure it with you." Still, "at Kilkenny a new Academy is to be Erected," he reported hopefully, or failing that, "I shall retreat to a more solitary life, as I can Commaund myselfe, with 6 or 7 gentlemen and scollars, who have resolved to live retyredly and follow their studyes and Experiences, if these troublesome times molest not."[51] Child knew that Winthrop had, from the start, begun his retreat to a more solitary life in which he too resolved to live in seclusion and follow his studies and experiences. Now the long waits between his letters made Child "suppose you are to your Plantacion, *out of the way*" of the infamous religious and cultural intolerance that so disturbed the younger Winthrop and his moderate friends, the latitudinarian scientists Howes and Child. In such a solitary life, Winthrop included among his "friends" the books in his alchemical library and his laboratory apparatus, as well as all the correspondents from his inclusive transatlantic scientific network. "Commaund me Sr. if I Can serve you," Child signed, "for truly I am Your loving frind."[52]

Alchemical friendship was quietistic, bound by a loving soul, ramified by common natural-philosophical languages found in the Bible, experience in Nature and with natural materials in the laboratory, and knowledge available in the infinitely portable book. When John Winthrop Jr. wrote carefully to his father on the eve of colonization that "all thinges shall worke together for the best therein, and for my selfe I have seene so much of the vanity of the world that I esteeme no more of the diversities of

Countries then as so many Innes . . . the travailer, that hath lodged in the best, or in the worst, findeth noe difference," that is precisely what he meant. In his Paracelsian pilgrimage, he thought he had discovered clues to knowledge of the philosopher's stone, which would enable him to burn off the corruption of "the diversities of Countries" and unveil from beneath the dross the universal spiritual force that would unify mankind. That is why the "travailer" (a fusion of "laborer" and "traveler") who had "lodged in the best" (pure spirit) "or in the worst" (corrupted matter) "findeth no difference when he commeth to his Journies end." At that final millennial moment, refined prematurely in the alchemist's fire, all social as well as material difference would dissolve under "one cloak for all things" through action by the universal elixir, which—like the soul itself—transmuted all things to its own substance in time. As the father built barriers that led to the forceful exclusion of "innovation" and "difference" from the body of Christ in New England, his peripatetic son moved south and settled on the borderlands of the middle colonies, "out of the way," to a place of hybrid openings where he could exploit his knowledge.

Thus, with Winthrop's emigration to America, we return at last to unresolved problems in Howes's pictograph: the link between the philosopher's stone and the Northwest Passage in the colonies; the influence of Robert Fludd on the puzzle's formal arrangement and Edward Howes's coded messages to Winthrop; and, by extension, the part Winthrop's experience at the Île de Ré and La Rochelle played in the correspondents' view of their natural-philosophical "proceedings." How did the "Île of Rue" figure in Howes's prophetic epigram: "The fyre cannot destroye whats written in the Harte?"

❧ The Fortieth Parallel and the American Mediterranean ❧

On March 26, 1632, Howes wrote implicitly of their continuing mutual interest in the Northwest Passage, hoping the letter carrier would find "his worthy frind Mr. John Winthrop the yonger at Boston in Mattachusetts Bay or else where these deliver in N: England."[53] Clearly, Winthrop was searching, and on the move again:

> I thought good to entreate you to acquaint me with some particulars of your Countrie; vizt. howe farre into the Countrie your planters have discovered, 2 what rivers, Lakes, or saltwaters westward, 3 howe farre you are from Hudsons River and from Canada by land, 4 what are the most useful commodities to send over to traffick with Th[e]Indians, or among your selves; 5 what kind of English graine thrives with you and what not; and what other thinge you please; daringe not to trespasse any farther on your gentle disposition, only be pleased to send a map or some discription of your land discoveries. *For you know well the cause of my desire to know New England and all the new world, and alsoe to be knowne there, yet not I but Christ, in whom I live and move and have my beinge* [my emphasis].[54]

In a letter dated November 23, 1632, their tacit understanding was made fully explicit by Howes, through his gift of a book:

> You would wonder what discoragements the divell putts in most mens mouths against your plantations, some that you are all comminge home, others that you are all gone or going for Virginia. For my parte I shall and will by gods leave endeavuour towards you and the work;..here inclosed you shall find a booke of the probabilities of the N: West passage, not in the 60 or 70 degree of N: latitude, but rather about the 40th. I sore suspect the Hollanders will have the glory and benefitt of the passage about Hudsons R[iver] yet God the Author and Finisher of all good works will (I believe) that all shalbe for the good of his Saints. I heare the french have this summer transported a company of priests and Jesuits and such vermine to Canada; but how longe they will staye there, it is a question. I conceive the land too cold for theire hott natures.[55]

The book to which Howes referred was Sir Dudley Digges's *Of the Circumference of the Earth, or, A Treatise of the Northeast Passage* (London, 1612). The title is known because it survives in the collection of the Massachusetts Historical Society with some other books of Winthrop's. According to Digges, the passage would not be found at a forbidding 60 or 70 degrees north, which would put it at the northern reaches of Hudson's Bay. Rather, Winthrop should explore the fortieth parallel, which ran directly through New Amsterdam and the Hudson River to the west. The context of Howes's letter—the rumors that the Massachusetts Bay settlers were moving to Virginia or soon would return home to England; the proximity of the Dutch ("I sore suspect the Hollanders will have the glory and benifitt of the passage"); the Counter-Reformation threat to the security of the passage from the influx of Jesuits and other "such vermine" in New France—seems to suggest that in order to protect the interests of "God . . . and his Saints," Winthrop should remove to the region of New Netherlands, find the passage, and thereby immediately discover both the Indies and the secret of the stone.

Howes's inscription in the copy of Digges's *Of the Circumference of the Earth* he sent Winthrop made this new map of America's mystical geography clear. To begin with, Howes altered the title page itself, changing "Northeast" to "Northweast." Then, to underscore the urgency of this project, Howes changed the date in the imprint from "1612," to the current year, "1632." But it was Howes's inscription to Winthrop on the verso of the gift's title page that told the whole story:

> Happie thrice happie should I be if this little treatise should add any thinge to your knowledge, Invention, or Industrie, to the atcheivinge of that Herculean worke of the Straits of N: England, which I am as verilie perswaded of; that there is either a Strait, as our narrow seas, *or a mediterranean Sea* [my emphasis], west from you. The dutch O the

dutch I doubt will prevent your discoverie, for they are the nearest, of any that have not as yet discovered it. But doubtlesse there is a man (or shalbe) sett aparte for the discoverie thereof, thereby to communicate more freely more knowingly, and with less charge, the riches of the east with the pleasures of the west, and that the east and west, meetinge with mutual embracements they shall soe love each other, that they shalbe willing to be disolved into each other; and soe God being manifested in Christ through all the world, and light shininge in thickest darknesse, and that palpable darknesse being expelled, how great and glorious shall that light appear. With God of his mercy hasten to accomplish. To the right noble and worthy Religious and vertuous gent[leman] john Winthrop the yonger all health and felicitie.

yours E. Hows.[56]

With the discovery of the Northwest Passage, the puzzle will be solved. "Christ and the Stone" will be unified through "the Way to the [East] Indies and the [West] Indies." This comes to pass because Christ set the sacred "quadrature" in perpetual motion, squaring the circle permanently and allowing the sun (Winthrop), moon (Howes), and earth (Nature) to correspond (both literally—by letter—and figuratively) as a body in unison (with Winthrop at the heart) to complete "the work" through shared wisdom of a universal Neoplatonic soul, utterly unfettered by encumbrance or physical separation. However, for this prophesy to materialize, it was first necessity for Winthrop to find the American Mediterranean Sea—a "midland" (or "intermediate" sea)—located "west from you," on (or "about") the fortieth parallel. Once the Northwest Passage had been found, a circuit between east and west would be completed, alchemically "hastened" before the natural course of its preordained millennial completion by God's decision to intervene with a specially chosen adept: "a man . . . sett apart for his discovery thereof." This convergence was analogous to other sexualized conjunctions of opposites: the coitus of macrocosm and microcosm; spirit and matter (see figs. 7.2, 8.13). At that passionate moment of universal alchemic convergence, "the east and west, meetinge with mutual embracements they shall soe love each other, that they shalbe willing to be disolved into each other," as the ultimate weapon in reforming both Old and New worlds.

Here was the perfect conjunction of clay and glaze of the Huguenot potter's imagination. The effect of a union at America's fortieth parallel would be perceived as a continuous "light shining in the thickest darknesse, and that palpable darknesse being expelled, how great and glorious shall that light appear." This was the pure, unfragmented light that Palissy and Böhme perceived only through dead elemental earth, as a tiny, seductive "flash" or "estincelle," sparkling through the dark matter of an earthenware pot or pewter pitcher. Winthrop was, of course, that "man . . . sett apart." Like Howes, he took Long Island Sound to be the eastern extension of the American

FIGURE 10.3. Rustic tin-glazed earthenware "Palissy dish." Possibly by Richard Newnham, an English follower of Bernard Palissy. Southwark, London, 1630–65. H: 3¼", L: 17½", W: 14⅛". Courtesy Longridge Collection.

Mediterranean; a fortiori, part of the Mediterranean proper. To control the Sound—and ultimately all of New Netherlands and the Hudson River opening up into the western inland sea—would also be to take the narrow path to the fortieth parallel, the Northwest Passage, the philosopher's stone.

The timing of this correspondence between Howes and Winthrop on the Wisdom of Solomon, the puzzle of the "Mysterium," and the Northwest Passage in America overlaps significantly with the extension and enormous ramification of Palissy's alchemical ceramic project into London's potteries almost immediately after the fall of La Rochelle in 1628. I am thinking here, not only of the few rare survivals of London-made rustic dishes (fig. 10.3), but more particularly of the series of "fecundity" scenes made in free imitation of the Palissy-type molds in rustic relief, of which over twenty examples survive. I say "Palissy-type" because while clearly made by close French and English followers, no exact prototype by Palissy's hand is known. They were made from different molds, some imported directly from France, and hence at different London factories. Indeed, at least eight different groups have been identified. Most dated examples range between 1633 and 1697. These provocative and sexualized forms were formed as basins and sometimes made to commemorate a marriage. They were called "Palissy dishes" in England, presumably beginning in the early modern period. The name is an interesting phenomenon in itself, although direct artisanal links beyond obvious linguistic, formal, and technological ones have yet to be established.[57]

The earliest dated Palissy dish to survive (1633) marked the marriage of Stephen and Elizabeth Fortune (fig. 10.4). This tin-glazed earthenware basin displays one of the eight standard London "fecundity" scenes in a classical courtyard with prominent tiles. The original source for the "fecundity" dishes is arguably a fresco of Danaë painted circa 1533–40 by Giovanni Battista de Jacopo Rosso (1495–1540) on the south wall of François I's Grande Galerie at Fontainebleau; although individual potters took great liberties with Rosso's design, particularly by using other print sources with which they were more familiar. At the center of a mythological court scene is a seductive maiden, naked except for her necklace, carrying what appears to be a St. George's or

FIGURE 10.4. Tin-glazed earthenware "Palissy fecundity dish," inscribed "1633 Stephen: Fortune: &: Elizabeth." Probably made in Southwark, London, by a follower of Bernard Palissy. H: 2⅛", L: 19⅜", W: 16⅛". Courtesy Longridge Collection.

Maltese cross. Such a pious symbol is unexpected, since the maiden reclines in a suggestive position, legs almost open. She is surrounded by a group of cavorting cherubs, one of whom has his arms around her while he reaches for the cross. Perhaps the playful putto wants to remove the seductive maiden's last vestige of piety. Yet on another level, this was a trope for the Neoplatonic quest for the highest spiritual love, that of the imagination. Here, the wrestling putti in the background of the dish suggest "contending desires" within the fecund imaginations of Stephen and Elizabeth Fortune. Ultimately, these contenders are banished, with only one true spiritual love—the little spirit reaching for the maiden's necklace—emerging triumphant and ennobled (like the redeemed materials in the earthenware dish itself, ennobled by alchemical fire).[58]

Scholarship on this celebrated group of artifacts is quite extensive. The broad current consensus is that "English delftware potters apparently chose such motifs for their decorative merit alone rather than for any interest in their meaning."[59] This may prove to be a premature conclusion for many of the potters, given the strong possibility that a version of Palissy's Paracelsian natural philosophy had gained currency among artisans—especially potters—by the seventeenth century, and because it may be argued that the fecundity scenes were derived from the same natural-philosophical tradition that inspired Howes and Winthrop's alchemical agenda. The motives of the seventeenth-century potters who made fecundity dishes, and of their patrons, can scarcely be known, but arguably some, if not all, of them were motivated by more than "decorative merit alone." Both the iconography of the fecundity basins and knowledge that they have been linked to Palissy by refugee migration, artisanal and collecting traditions, and common language suggests that at least some potters in seventeenth-century London shared Palissy's agenda. This logic is supported by the probability that both Howes and Winthrop understood the source and meaning of the available natural-philosophical language of these artifacts; that is to say, it was neither strange to their code-obsessed eyes nor would they have necessarily thought the motifs were merely decorative.

Read from the alchemical perspective of Howes's postscript from the Wisdom of Solomon and understood as part of the passionate and deeply sensual rhetoric of Paracelsian Neoplatonism that informed his dedication of Digges's *Of the Circumference of the Earth* in 1632, a sense of meaning emerges, and becomes available for the "Palissy-style" fecundity basins in the transatlantic context. The seductive and playful woman in an attitude of sexual arousal performs a central role in the Wisdom of Solomon: that of Sophia, goddess of wisdom, God's "lover," and his first creation to serve as master artisan in the construction of the earth. David Winston elaborates on Philo's personification of Sophia as God's consort, a receptacle and mother figure of "indefinite potentiality":

The personified Wisdom already makes her appearance in Proverbs and Job in the guise of a charming female figure playing always before Yahweh, having been created by him at the beginning of his work.[60] It is above all in the Wisdom of Solomon, however, that the figure comes into her own . . . Sophia is described in this work as an effluence or effulgence of God's glory and his agent in creation, and it is implied that she contains the paradigmatic pattern of all things . . . the author refers to her as his bride and boasts of living with her and enjoying kinship with her. Sophia anticipates those who desire her and those who seek her will not weary . . . [thus] Philo describes Wisdom . . . as "the mother and nurse of all". . . words used by Plato in the *Timaeus* to describe the Receptacle, and Philo himself elsewhere similarly adopts them as a description of matter . . . Philo sometimes employs an alternate pattern in which God is said to have intercourse with his Knowledge or Wisdom and thus produces his only beloved son, the sense-perceptible World . . . in the same terms that were applied to matter . . . [Philo] would employ the figure of Sophia . . . which is characterized by indefinite potentiality.[61]

The figure of Sophia immediately reminds us of the plaque of Flora the *feuillue* (fig. 5.2) and of the female colossus in Johann Theodore de Bry's *Integrae naturae (fig. 2.3)*, but also of Palissy's reconstruction of himself as feminine: an aroused, open receptacle for God's fiery sexual passion through intercourse with the soul in order to achieve the "fecundity" to construct his New World artisanry out of matter that had already passed through the fire of sacred violence in Saintonge. As it happens, of course, the forms Palissy chose to make were also Platonic receptacles—mostly basins survive— as are the London "Palissy dishes." Where there were camouflaged, metamorphic lizards, amphibians, and insects that moved furtively through the subterranean flora of Palissy's natural grottoes, now there were tiny human figures reborn as creatures of the light.

This relationship is also ramified by the source of the cherubic figures playing all around Sophia. Consider the thirty-first figure in Paracelsus's *Propheceien und Weissagungen* (1549), "Four Dancing Children" (fig. 10.5), and the "elucidation" of its meaning in *Prognosticatio eximii doctoris Theophrasti Paracelsi* (The Prophesies of Paracelsus [Strasbourg, 1566]).[62] Here playful "children" (some with strikingly adult faces) nearly identical to those on the fecundity dish of 1633 dance and cavort in what is arguably a print source of the tiled courtyard, with a forested garden in the distance. The pair of boys on the right are convincing as a direct source for their counterparts in the right background of the basin, under the fluted column. "There shall be such a total renewal and change," Paracelsus explained, in his prophesy that accompanied the woodcut:

that they will be as children that know nothing of the cunning and intrigues of the old. This shall be when they count LX [When LUX, Lux, Light, comes]. . . . Therefore it is

FIGURE 10.5. "Four dancing children" from Paracelsus's *Propheceien und Weissagungen* (1549). Courtesy National Library of Medicine, Bethesda, Maryland. Compare the putto in figure 10.4. Two of the "children" appear to be reborn Roman Catholic monks, as indicated by their characteristic tonsure. The monkish putto figure on the right displays rather dissonant aged features as well. Unlike the boy on the dish in figure 10.4, the child on the right does not support a small spaniel on his shoulder, perhaps a veiled reference to Charles I? Some of the London Palissy-style dishes contain tiny portraits concealed in the borders of Charles I and his queen, though more appear to depict a furtive Cromwell. "Alchemy must be revealed only to children of philosophy," wrote Palissy. "They are children of knowledge and . . . God."

> well that we should remember that the time appeareth to be a long time according to a
> man's lifetime, but as a short time should we observe and consider it. For to cause so much
> to fall and to be overthrown, with such a raging and roaring lion that has so long grown,
> this cannot be done in a moment. But how well it shall be with him that shall be as a little
> child, for human knowledge causeth but unrest and grief.[63]

In a very real sense then, these *spiritelli*, or childlike "sprites," were also precursors of Böhme's "sparks," as well as of Palissy's *étincelles*, which play with bodily perception across the surface of pottery from La Chapelle-des-Pots.[64]

The rustic Paracelsian artisan, returning to first principles, was reborn a man-child through conjunction with Sophia—figure of God's wisdom in the light of Nature—who "know[s] nothing of the cunnings and intrigues of old . . . for human knowledge causeth but unrest and grief." The horrors of war and religious violence that began this process of rebirth are sublimated into material life because human knowledge is forgotten. This rebirth of prelapsarian Adamic knowledge will usher in a new world that will unify the separation of spirit and matter. "They shall be willing to be dissolved into each other like transluscent glaze and occluded clay, and cause light to shine throughout the microcosm, unimpeded by dark matter." A material-holiness synthesis represented in God's master artisan Sophia was thus "characterized by indefinite potentiality." At the exact moment that "Palissy's" follower's child reached for nourishment at the breast of the mother/nurse Wisdom and found hope in the symbol of the English refuge and new beginnings after 1628, Howes and Winthrop were preparing to dissolve differences and barriers by unifying east and west in the American Mediterranean. They would meet "with mutual embracements" through a door hidden in the far western reaches of Long Island Sound. The door opened onto the Northwest Passage and the secret of the philosopher's stone as well. "Then will the New World begin," Paracelsus prophesied, "and the White and the Black shall disappear . . . and the plumes of the bird of the East shall be burnt by the Sun of the South."[65] This mystical imagery of childlike regeneration continued on the Palissy dishes until at least 1697 and also appeared on articles of domestic use in other media associated with the Huguenot diaspora in England and America: for example, a "Huguenot chair" of post-1685 London (fig. 15.35) exhibits "boyes and crown" carving adapted from a church on the Île de Ré.

❧ The Fortress of Health ❧

Of the part played by the influential English alchemist Robert Fludd in this transatlantic story of the fortieth parallel much more will be said later. For now suffice it to say, that the design of Howes's pictograph—a complex of interconnected triangles within a circle—was instantly recognizable by natural philosophers of the late 1620s and 1630s as derived from Fludd's famous "science of pyramids" (*Pyramidum scientia*) (fig. 10.6), his alchemic representation of the descent into the microcosm and reascent into the macrocosm of the soul. Howes would certainly have known that this science was one of the sacred arts explained in Fludd's *Philosophia sacra*, published just a year before his letter to the younger Winthrop of January 22, 1627.[66] Winthrop knew Fludd's work through his interest in what was known widely as the weapon salve. As we shall see, Winthrop's well-known correspondent Sir Kenelm Digby marketed this recipe—original to Paracelsus—to his personal advantage. But in 1632, Howes wrote Winthrop to advise the purchase of virtually every Fludd title whenever they became available, having:

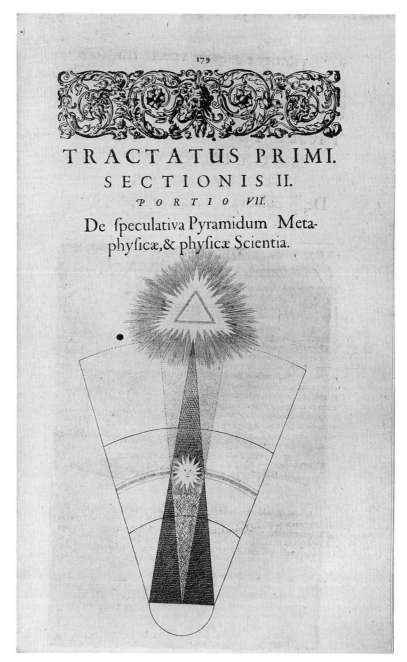

FIGURE 10.6. Johann Theodore de Bry, *Metaphysical and Physical Science of the Pyramids*, from Robert Fludd, *Utruisque cosmi majoris* (1624). Courtesy Harry Ransom Humanities Research Center, The University of Texas at Austin. Foundational to his profoundly Neoplatonic project, Fludd understood the linkages between the purity of God's realm in heaven (*metaphysicae*) and the corruption of the earth (*physicae*) as a series of hierarchical scales interpenetrated by light and dark Trinitarian triangles. He also depicted these scales as a fret board on a stringed musical instrument.

sent you a taste of the famous and farre renouned English man of our Tymes Fr. Fludd, whoe as you may remember published a booke in defence of the weapon salve before you went over, but that is nothing in comparison to these here menconed, which are all folio bookes, and full of brasse peices [engravings], the like I never saw, for engines, fortificacions, and a touch of all opperative workes, as you may conceive by the titles; yet let me tell you this, that the titles, nor my penn, is not able to express, what is in those bookes, as they are, no more than you in a map or sheete of paper, can exactly describe the rivers, creeks, hills, dales, fruite, beasts, fishes and all other things of your contrie; for I think it is impossible for man to add unto his macrocosme and microcosme, except it be illustration or comment, and that hardly too; his bookes are so bought up beyond sea, we can gett none brought over . . . here you see the titles which I could with all my heart wish the bookes themselves were in your hands as certaine as any thing you have.[67]

Among the fourteen titles on Howes's wish list was *Medicina catholica* (1629), which included a plate called *Homo sanus* ("The Sound Man"), also known as *The Fortress of Health* (fig. 10.7). The companion piece to this engraving, *Hostilis munimenti salutis invadendi typus* ("Enemies Invading the Fortress of Health") (fig. 10.8), did not appear until 1631, when it was finally published in Fludd's *Integrum morborum mysterium*. *Integrum* was not on Howes list in 1632—which included titles up to 1629—but copies of both of Fludd's medical treatises survive from Winthrop's original alchemical library.[68] Given the subject of these extraordinary engravings, and knowing Fludd's commitment to a long and productive relationship with the de Bry family of refugee Huguenot publishers from Frankfurt and Oppenheim in prior years, a strong case can be made that both of these images of the fortress of health under attack were at least partially a response to the siege of La Rochelle. *Homo sanus* was published in 1629, so it was created during the siege year. Did *Hostilis* simply extend an original idea to its logical conclusion, or was it a recognition of the historical context—a completion of the siege of "sound man" in which the walls surrounding his body finally crumbled under assault from demons—represented in medical and cosmological terms?

Homo sanus is secure in the "fortress of health" because he prays to God: "Show thy servant the light of thy countenance, and save me for thy mercy's sake; to which God replies "No plague shall come nigh thy dwelling; for I will give my angels charge of thee, to keep thee in all thy ways."[69] The four archangels Gabriel, Michael, Azazel, and Raphael guard successfully against evil angels of the four winds who unleash plagues of winged diseases against the walls of the fortress. These are certainly "the violent force of spirits and the reasonings of men" of Wisdom of Solomon 7:20, which were always taken to mean "the mighty winds . . . before they became angels [of holiness] . . . are spirits that are created for vengeance. . . . Fire and hail, and famine, and death."[70] They were arguably the same winds that Palissy claimed assailed his

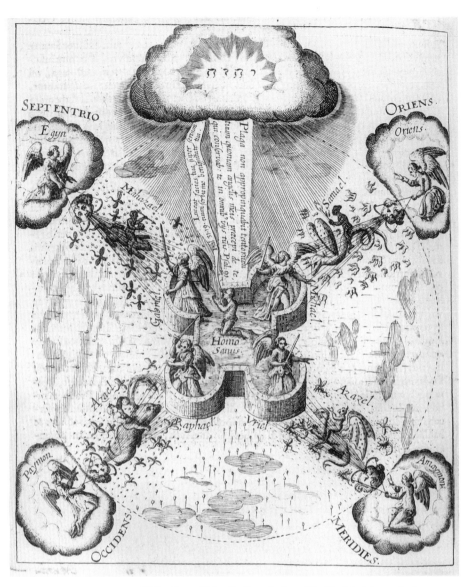

FIGURE 10.7. *Homo sanus* ("The Sound Man"), from Robert Fludd, *Medicina catholica*
(Frankfurt, 1629). Courtesy Yale University, Harvey Cushing / John Hay Whitney Medical
Library. To construct a fortress of health, the Sound Man prays God to "show thy servant the
light of thy countenance, and save me for thy mercy sake" (Ps. 31.16); to which God replies
from out of the light that "no plague shall come nigh thy dwelling; for I will give my angels
charge over thee, to keep thee in all thy ways" (Ps. 91:10–11). Hence, as in figure 8.1, the Sound
Man patiently resists corruption with divine wisdom. He is protected in a fortress of the soul
from evil angels who assail him with plagues carried by the four winds. The four archangels of
God guard the fortress, divided into four chambers, like the anatomy of the heart, the location
of the soul in the body. Fludd was a disciple of the physician William Harvey. Translations
from Joscelyn Godwin, *Robert Fludd: Hermetic Philosopher and Surveyor of Two Worlds* (Boulder, Colo.: Shambhala, 1979), 56, fig. 62.

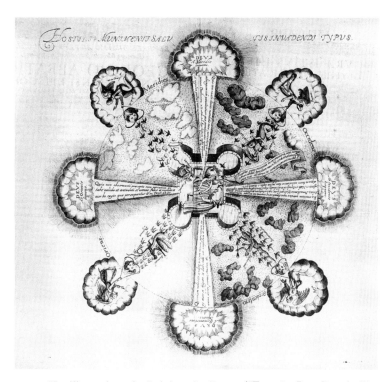

FIGURE 10.8. *Hostilis munimenti salutis invadendi typus* ("Enemies Invading the Fortress of Health"), from Robert Fludd, *Integrum morborum mysterium: Sive medicinae catholicae* (Frankfurt, 1631). Courtesy Yale University, Harvey Cushing / John Hay Whitney Medical Library. Mortal illness assails this man through the shattered south wall of his fallen fortress of health, which is not guarded by archangels and so is easily breached by the evil angel Azazel. His physician, who examines a urine sample, attends at his bedside. Aware that "The arrows of the Almighty are within me, the poison whereof drinketh up my spirit: the terrors of God do set themselves in array against me" (Job 6.4), the sick man has little hope. The word of God assails him from all four directions: "Because thou hast not hearkened unto my voice, I will afflict thee with . . . cold and will give thee a fearful heart and a sadness of soul until thou perish" (Deut. 28); "Because thou hast not kept my commandments, I will afflict thee in the summer with corrupt air, and give thee the pestilence to pursue thee until thou perish (Deut. 28) . . . I will send serpents among you, which will not be charmed" (Jer. 8:17); "Because thou hast not observed my precepts I will afflict thee with hot and seething . . . and fever"; "I will afflict thee with dropsy" (Luke 14); "I will make thee a lunatic, and afflict with a heavy spirit" (Matt. 17); and "I will dissolve thee with palsy, so that thy enterprises are hindered and thy mouth stopped, that thou canst not speak" (1 Macc. 9:55). Translations from Joscelyn Godwin, *Robert Fludd: Hermetic Philosopher and Surveyor of Two Worlds* (Boulder, Colo.: Shambhala, 1979), 59, fig. 66.

"dwelling" in Saintes from all sides, where he found security and overcame death by laboring to bring forth the translucent white glaze from the fire. Thus, Palissy wrote, he would "build with the destroyer," which was also the primary instrument of alchemy. Here, Fludd had represented a credo of Paracelsian medicine: that bodily health and illness were essentially spiritual not physical conditions. "They are not under Divine Justice," Fludd wrote of the four winds, "but come from Injustice, which is a figment of the Divine Darkness. Health is from God alone, given by his angels whose ruler is Jesus Christ . . . God's will is carried out by both good and evil Angels, but we, as creatures of the Light, can only be saved and remain healthy by prayer to God."[71] Were Richelieu's and Louis XIII's forces of the Counter-Reformation that besieged La Rochelle thought to "come from Injustice, which is a figment of the Divine Darkness"? This would be a significant reversal, since Richelieu argued that the siege was the way to excise demons from inside the fortress and hence from the body of absolutism.

Using Paracelsian medical-alchemic language and imagery, Fludd's *Homo sanus* graphically restated passages from Paul's Letter to the Ephesians that influenced Huguenots in Aunis-Saintonge during the region's most fragmented years of confessional violence. Paul, a "prisoner for the Lord" (Eph. 4:1), writes that God has "a plan for the fullness of time, to unite all things in him, things in heaven and things on earth" (Eph. 1:10). Fellow "prisoner[s] for the Lord" must therefore await the fruition of this plan "with all lowliness and meekness, with patience [and] forbearing" (Eph. 4:2), as in the engraving of *In patientia suavitas.* "Finally," Paul's eschatology of waiting required oppressed members of the Lord's "body" to fashion strategies of security to protect against supernatural forces too powerful for fortresses of mortar and stone to withstand:

> Put on the whole armor of God, that you may be able to stand against the wiles of the devil. For we are not contending against flesh and blood, but against the principalities, against the powers, against the world rulers of this present darkness, against the spiritual hosts of wickedness in the heavenly places . . . above all taking the shield of faith, with which you can quench all the flaming darts of the evil one. And take the helmet of salvation, and the sword of the Spirit, which is the word of God. (Eph. 6:10–20)

Unlike La Rochelle before 1628, the fortress Paul describes is an *invisible* one— a fortress of the soul—that emanates from the hidden relationship between God's universal spirit and the human heart. This was the meaning of the epigram Howes sent Winthrop on his return from the Île de Ré: "The fyre cannot destroye whats written in the Harte." The fire could destroy things of the earth detached from the spirit, but by destroying the carnal body, violence could also release the sacred into the material world. Winthrop's prophetic destiny was as "a man sett aparte for the discoverie" of the Northwest Passage "at or about" the fortieth parallel, at the gateway to New

Netherlands and the middle colonies: Long Island Sound. As a survivor of the disaster at La Rochelle, where the fallen were sacrificed by God to purify the body of Christ, Winthrop acquired the status of an adept whose spirit had emerged prematurely. This was also the essence of the secretive and domestic forms of artisanal security practiced by Palissy and his followers, who did not possess a great fortress in Saintonge. Thus, Palissy predicted the fall of La Rochelle long before anyone inside the fortress could have imagined and suggested the practice of artisanal security for the New World experience that would follow. In Fludd's *Hostilis munimenti salutis invadendi typus* (fig. 10.8), Winthrop and Howes perceived La Rochelle's failure to "put on the whole armor of God," not as a failure of the outer walls of the fortress of health, but as a collapse of the inner spirit of the heart. Fludd had, in fact, dissected human hearts with his friend William Harvey and knew from personal experience that the heart had four lobes—north, south, east, and west—just as the fortresses in *Homo sanus* and *Hostilis* each have four watchtowers (figs. 10.7, 10.8).

In *Hostilis*, the patient is afflicted with the diseases of the south wind carried through the crumbling south wall of the fortress by Azazel, because, as the dying man proclaims with Job: "The arrows of the Almighty are within me, the poison whereof drinketh up my spirit: the terrors of God do set themselves in array against me."[72] This resonated perfectly with the elder Winthrop's famous letter to his wife Margaret on May 15, 1629—on the eve of colonization—in which he compared the fall of La Rochelle to God's poisoning his corrupt children: now "he is turning the cuppe towards us also, and because we are the last, our portion must be, to drink the very dreggs which remaine."[73] Despite widespread sympathy in the Atlantic world for the people of La Rochelle, most Calvinists suspected that the Rochelais had been corrupt, and hence responsible for their own illness and destruction by God's dark forces. There is no evidence that Howes or Winthrop felt anything but sympathy for their Huguenot co-religionists as "poore people that lye nowe in the dust." Yet their authority seemed more useful when reconstructed in memory. Howes alluded to the sacrifice of the Rochelais, and to Winthrop's endurance and triumph, in a prophesy that emerged from their pain, in his motto: "But for myself the law [that is, God's law] is both a burden and an honor." It would also be hard to miss the significance of the messages of vengeance that Fludd had his *Deus* send from all points of the compass into the dying man's fortress: "Because thou hast not hearkened unto my voice; . . . kept my commandments; . . . observed my precepts; . . . I will afflict thee," with every variation of biblical plague, all leading to "a fearful heart and a sadness of soul until thou perish." In a sense, then, the victims' personal lack of faith and self-mastery caused the "Île of Rue," which afflicted their hearts (and that of international Protestantism).

For Winthrop the physician-alchemist and master of fortifications for Massachusetts Bay, the question was thus how to rebuild the *pure* underlying spirit of the

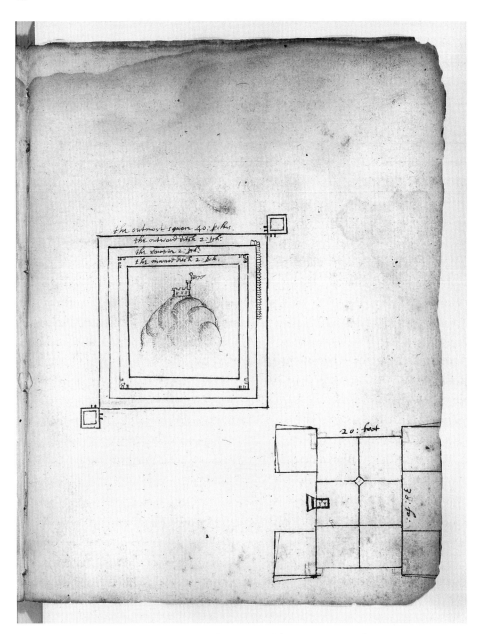

FIGURE 10.9. John Winthrop Jr., plans for a colonial fortress, ca. 1630, Boston or southern coastal Connecticut. Courtesy Massachusetts Historical Society. Both these and the drawings in figure 10.10 were found among miscellaneous notes at the end of the first volume of the elder John Winthrop's journal.

shattered fortress to secure the remnant of international Protestantism that had survived and escaped to America? Winthrop spent time studying fortress design in England soon after returning from the Île de Ré, but before his emigration to America, as is evidenced by a series of letters from December 1629 concerning the design of a particular English fortress, which is described in exquisite detail, down to "the dimensions of the fort and all things about it, as likewise of what severall materialls what Kinde of Earths or wood the severall parts are framed off." It was deemed "likely [that John Winthrop Jr.] may inquire of some thereabouts, labourers—artificers or artists that helped to make it." Winthrop now needed practical experience with the design, as it had been decided that this would be the prototype for the first fortress at Boston.[74] His early designs for three such fortresses survive, probably drawn for use in coastal Connecticut in consultation with Lion Gardiner, a student of the principles of fortification in Holland under the prince of Orange, and a future grandee of Long Island (fig. 10.9).

But after these plans for the construction of stationary late medieval fortresses in the New World, Winthrop became less interested in corporate fortresses designed on the *noblesse d'épée* pattern. Nor was he absorbed with the invention of novel weapons as he was in 1627, when he observed the use of the Kuffeler torpedo against the French fleet. Having seen the failure of this ancient mode of security in 1628, Winthrop turned inward, to the mobile, protean, and naturalistic method Palissy proposed as a "recipe" for refugee life, which did not depend for survival on others.

Palissy's method was private, mobile, and invisible—a moveable defense system that traveled with the refugee the way a snail's shell did with the snail. Survival was not based on violent frontal defense of authoritarian religious precepts, but rather on quiet, stealthy, and skillful use of domestic space for the cultivation of "Knowledge, Invention or Industrie," in Howes's words; for Palissy, it was the place to "multiply the talent you have received from God." Domestication and commercialization of the spirit negated the curse of "poverty that is the obstacle to happiness and safety."[75] Domestic practice was above all private and latitudinarian, and it observed the flexible presence of the universal spirit "written" in the heart of every individual artisan, farmer, or laborer as they moved through, and improved, the natural world. This was a way of self-mastery *and* cultural mediation fit for the Mediterranean of the New World, where it was necessary "to communicate more freely more knowingly and with less charge," across the cultural, material, and spiritual boundaries of pluralistic society.

❧ The Refuge Project on Long Island Sound ❧

In 1635, John Winthrop Jr. returned to Britain. He visited Ireland and Scotland, as well as England. His overriding concern during this first return was to clarify his role in the so-called Warwick Patent, signed in London by a like-minded group of Calvin-

ists on July 7, 1635. The terms of this patent charged the younger Winthrop with gaining control of "the River Connecticut in New England [and] . . . the harbors and places
ajoining." At the same time, Winthrop was to supervise the construction of fortifications and dwellings "at the River" that were suitable for the many "men of quality" who
were signatories to the patent, and who planned to use them as places of refuge should
religious war spread from the Continent to England, as seemed likely. This group of
"Lords and Gentlemen"—which included Lord Saye and Sele, Sir Arthur Hesilrige,
Lord Robert Greville Brooke, Henry Lawrence, Sir Richard Saltonstall, John Pym,
George Fenwick, and Henry Darley—instructed Winthrop to undertake this project
"with all convenient speede."[76]

The signers of Warwick Patent were not only united by their courtly status and a
shared interest in land and refuge in the New World; they converged in other ways as
well. For one thing, they were dismayed by the authoritarian religious regime in Boston
on both spiritual and material grounds, and they perceived similar doubts in the
younger Winthrop. As a result, while the search for refuge was a priority, settlement
near Massachusetts Bay was out of the question. Hence, these same figures also became involved in the West Indies, with the Providence Island Company.[77] Although
the litany of transatlantic schisms that beset Calvinism was only fully articulated
in public discourse by many of these men during the Antinomian Crisis of 1635–37,
Howes revealed the rumblings of discontent in London years earlier. "I have heard diverse complaints against the severity of your Governement," Howes warned Winthrop
In April 1632. "I would and doe desire all things might goe well with you all. But cer-
tainely if you endeavor in all mildnesse to doe gods worke, he will preserve you from
all the enemies of his truth; though there are a thousand eyes watchinge over you to
pick a hole in your coats."[78] By November of that year, in response to more "mut-
teringe," Howes adumbrated the position both he and friends in England and America would take in the Antinomian Crisis. "Allas, alas," he wrote Winthrop of the hidden soulish principles and belief in cultural pluralism and perhaps sympathy for the
Nicodemite he knew they shared, "it is not any outward . . . worship that god requires,
but god being a spirit ought to be worshipped in spirit and truth. There are many guifts
by one and the same spirit yet not all given to one man."[79] Winthrop's careful resistance to joining his father's attacks on heterodoxy and his decision to stay in Connecticut to keep his distance during Anne Hutchinson's trial, suggest tacit agreement.

There is no doubt that Howes himself was known to the Warwick group (through
Winthrop and Emmanuel Downing) or that they shared the same spiritual and
natural-philosophical concerns. Still in 1632, Howes thanked Winthrop for an introduction to Saltonstall: "by your meanes and good words of me to him, I have obtained
a most singular sweet frind of him . . . I had inward familiarity with him; he per-
swadinge me it was your desire that I should imparte my selfe unto him, on your be-

halfe, and for the good of N: E."[80] There is good reason to believe that the entire group was deeply concerned with Winthrop's natural-philosophical and alchemical projects for the fortieth parallel, and that all were not only latitudinarian but also Paracelsians with strong backgrounds in Neoplatonic universalism. Pym and Brooke in particular were patrons of the great Paracelsian reformers Samuel Hartlib, John Dury, and Jan Comenius and supported the idea of a universal laboratory that began to gain favor by the 1640s and would attract Winthrop's close attention in 1649. Brooke's ideas were explicitly conducive to the reformers' universalism. In his book *The Nature of Truth* (London, 1640), Brooke explained that while truth was atomized by experience into "particular rivulets," it was "that learned, that mighty man Comenius [who] doth happily and rationally endeavor to reduce all into one." Multiplicity and unity thus coexisted harmoniously in both nature and human society. With this theory in mind, Winthrop the Younger tried unsuccessfully to persuade Comenius to settle in America and accept the presidency of Harvard College.[81]

Having returned from London in late 1635, Winthrop proceeded "with all deliberate speede" to conform with the wishes of his new patrons, while still laboring to gain a foothold on the fortieth parallel. The result is shown in Winthrop's detailed design for a courtyarded dwelling in Saybrook, Connecticut, well south of the forty-first parallel, on the north shore of Long Island Sound (fig. 10.10). There, he could borrow Robert Child's description of his desired life in Ireland, and "I command myself, with 6 or 7 gentlemen and scollers, who have resolved to live retyredly and follow their studyes and Experiences, if these troublesome times molest not." Did Dr. Child use Winthrop's Saybrook project of 1635, "out of the way" of Boston, as a prototype for his refuge on the Celtic fringe in 1652?

Winthrop's design for his courtyarded dwelling is significant for the dwelling itself, which is located in the upper right corner of the page, as well as the diagram of the rural farm complex into which it is set. That plan is located diagonally across and down from the dwelling and may be found in the lower left corner of the same page. Winthrop clearly reserved space for the open courtyard, a sort of amphitheater surrounded by four galleries of chambers and workspaces in the lower right corner of the large enclosed complex of interior buildings, yards, and finally one acre of meadow. In the rooms surrounding the courtyard amphitheater, there are a dairy, larder, hall, kitchen, "parteyre" (parterre), and a 30-foot-long "servants Chambre," containing thirteen "cabbins," undoubtedly intended for African slaves. At Winthrop's death in 1676, his primary laboratory assistant was a slave; early modern European alchemical laboratories required large numbers of workers to turn a profit searching for the great elixir.[82] There are two or three spaces with no specific function designated by Winthrop, which may have been reserved as alchemical laboratories for the gentlemen refugees, with space for their servant assistants and workmen.

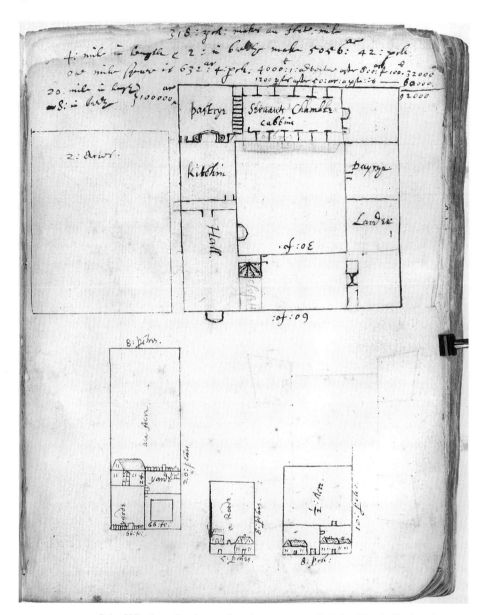

FIGURE 10.10. John Winthrop Jr., design for a large courtyarded dwelling in Saybrook, Connecticut. Courtesy Massachusetts Historical Society. Numerous spaces were set aside for "Servants Chambre cabbins." Winthrop's plan included not only domestic and field servants but laboratory operators and manual laborers as well. The latter extracted and handled ore and performed other physically demanding tasks in Winthrop's alchemical "factory" on Long Island Sound. Winthrop owned at least one enslaved African-American, who probably served as a laboratory operator.

Pamela Smith has demonstrated that the business of alchemy at the Hapsburg court involved factory-scale production, with a series of different rooms devoted to specific, interconnected alchemical functions. This enabled alchemists in the Holy Roman Empire to synthesize breaking down, grinding, boiling, and distilling materials. Indeed, the design of the Saybrook courtyard, hidden from outside view, yet simultaneously open on the inside to form a central stage for interior dialogue, recalls seventeenth-century natural-philosophical academies and certain European private laboratories. A stage was needed where the adept—in the European context, the alchemist-prince—taught or directed proceedings in the surrounding laboratories.[83] We shall see how the walls of such surrounding galleries and architectural spaces also suggest a good setting for a "Theater of Memory" based on Fludd's engraving "Theater of the World." Winthrop's use of the term "parterre" may also have been specific to the Saybrook court as a stage. A parterre was associated in early modern parlance with a space located on the ground floor beneath the galleries or behind the auditorium of a theater.[84]

Kitchens especially, as places containing fire and caldrons, but halls as well (as spaces with multiple uses), were also commonly used in laboratory settings.[85] This was not only practical, but also part of the natural-philosophical ideology of alchemy as part of everyday life. For his Saybrook laboratory on the edge of the Northwest Passage, Winthrop designed an independent, self-contained, secure, rural complex of farm and domestic buildings. Here were medicinal gardens for pharmacopoeia and pleasure gardens with grottoes for contemplation of the elements, laboratories, libraries (he kept many of his alchemical books in Saybrook), and servants' quarters for labor to facilitate large-scale experiments, exploration of the Long Island Sound region, and the production of commercial goods.

Winthrop's laboratory-refuge in Saybrook thus provided security and sustenance while he and his courtly colleagues pursued their agenda in the New World. Winthrop's interest in the promotion of heavy industry and manufacture, as well as the production of salt and mining, shows that his Saybrook agenda encompassed not only the quest for the Northwest Passage and the philosopher's stone but also the profit motive of the artisan philosopher who wished to use his manual skills, labor, and talent for innovation, to manufacture and market profitable things. For Winthrop, as for Palissy, these projects went hand in hand. They were alchemists (and in Winthrop's case, a physician as well) concerned with the mobile natural laboratory as both a Paracelsian microcosm of human salvation and reform and "a model of civic *negotia* and manufacture."[86] In Winthrop's cosmos—as for the Huguenots of the refuge—the hidden paths to security, commerce, and salvation needed to be inextricably linked. Howes remained very interested in all these aspects of Winthrop's firm "resolution to plant in Conectecut." It seems that the further his friend removed from Boston toward the southwestern frontier and the pluralistic Long Island Sound region, the more curious

Howes became, and the more seriously he considered joining him there. "I shall not need to request of you some knowledge of your plantation," Howes wrote about Saybrook in 1636:

> and howe farre you have discovered the [Connecticut] River, and howe you like it, and what newes of the Lake, and howe far you are from the Dutch, and from Boston, I am perswaded you will acquaint me with that which you thinke is fittest for me, and reserve for me the rest untill a seasonable tyme. Only I would gladly see a Mapp of the longe Iland and the coast from Cap Cod to River Hudson when you have one to spare.[87]

Robert Blair St. George, a folklorist, demonstrates that the design for Winthrop's courtyarded structure came from an unexpected source. He finds that the evidence for this "is so strong that it almost qualifies as a fifth architectural report in our New World landscape."[88] Although Winthrop lived and studied in Ireland, the design source for the Saybrook refuge was not specific to an Irish bawn—with clear, traditional, and overt military fortifications and intentions (and a long history of use in the colonies). Rather, the design source arose from the influential work of a Frenchman of Palissy's generation, Charles Estienne (1504–ca. 1564), a translation of whose book on naturalistic rural fortification to protect and multiply production, *Maison Rustique, or, The Covntrie Farme* (London, 1600), was in Boston in 1629 and in Winthrop's library by 1630. "Making it," St. George claims, "the first book containing precise architectural advice known to have been in the British colonies."[89] *Maison Rustique* was the centerpiece of a campaign of architectural reform among English rural farmers in the late sixteenth and early seventeenth centuries—such as Adam Winthrop, John's grandfather, who also built a courtyarded dwelling at Groton in the 1590s—that used Estienne's intensive compounds, courtyards, and scientific fertilizing techniques to maximize efficiency in labor, production, and security. *Maison Rustique* was a Paracelsian text, based on practical experience, which "stimulated among . . . freeholders a new commitment to the reclamation of the land, to experimentation with new plow types, and ultimately, to increasing England's annual crop yields."[90]

But if *Maison Rustique* was a Paracelsian text it was also, above all else, a Palissian text. In the sixteenth century, when Estienne was gathering material for his book in France, the very word "rustique" was immediately associated by natural philosophers with Bernard Palissy, the famous maker of "rustique figulines." His name was harnessed to "rustique" throughout the early modern period in France and England as well. Witness the fashion for "rustic" Palissy plates in London at precisely the same time that *Maison Rustique* promoted reform of rural English architecture. This was one reason the authors chose to use this key word in their title, to associate themselves with the venerable reformed artisanal tradition of Bernard Palissy. Palissy was by then famous in England for his promotion of *marne* (gypsum) to fertilize crops and to increase productivity. If, as Robert Blair St. George correctly argues, the fashion for courtyarded residences in the French style came to England's urban centers with Huguenot textile merchants during the 1560s, the natural philosophy and reform of the Huguenot *rural* farmstead and above all *refuge*—the core of Winthrop's charge from the signatories of the Warwick Patent—was adapted for *Maison Rustique* ("The Natural House") from the same sources that informed Palissy's famous amphitheater of refuge for Huguenots who survived the civil wars of religion in Saintonge. As Winthrop knew from his copy of Palissy's *Discours admirables,* and from his experience at the Île de Ré within sight of La Rochelle's impenetrable walls in 1627, artisanal security was a reliable foundation for a natural fortress of refuge. "I would have you feare nothing more then securitie," Howes reminded his patron, remembering the Île of Rue.[91]

✦ Reading Outside the Walls ✦

Winthrop's copy of Palissy's *Discours admirables* (see fig. 6.1) is still in the plain vellum cover in which it was originally bound. We cannot be sure in what year he acquired it for his alchemical library. "Discours Admirable[s]" is written in ink on its spine, but "Eues et Fontaines:–" also appears on the book's underside, which suggests that Winthrop shelved it on its sturdy spine with this rubric facing outward for identification. Produced in a small octavo format (6¾″ by 4⅔″ by 1″), this was also an easily portable book. It would fit comfortably in a small scholar's cabinet, a sea chest, or even a reader's pocket.[92]

During the five months he spent at anchor off the Île de Ré watching England's hopes for the liberation of La Rochelle go awry, Winthrop pondered the hidden reality behind La Rochelle's looming walls. Perhaps he had his little edition of Palissy's *Discours* with him. No other book in his library provided a record from deep inside the culture of southwestern Huguenot science and material life at the beginning of the wars of religion. Palissy had already foretold the ultimate failure of the quest for refuge behind La Rochelle's limestone walls. Absent God's direct intervention at the end of the world, hope for the security of the faithful in the *désert* was to be sought rather in ambiguity and in invisible "natural" fortresses of one's own making.

Palissy and his followers were the precursors and earliest practitioners of the universalist artisanal security projected in Saybrook by Winthrop. In the Huguenots' apocalyptic new world, every individual was compelled to fashion and "put on" a fortress of the soul, the "recipe" for which was "written in the heart" and built "by the destroyer." That is why during the civil wars of the 1550s, Huguenot artisans and natural philosophers began to ponder the questions Winthrop considered between 1628 and 1635: what quotidian material and commercial forms would the "*whole* armor of God" take when the walls of ancient strongholds gave way to a "shield of faith," experiential knowledge, and manual skill? How would innovation and commercial profit make the pious refugee safe? And when the potter's dark prophesy was realized in 1628, refugees from Saintonge clung to a warning from Proverbs: "Do not remove an ancient landmark or enter the fields of the fatherless; / For Their Redeemer is strong; he will plead their cause against you" (Prov. 23:10–11).

CHAPTER ELEVEN

The Geography of "Your Native Country"

Relocation of Spatial Identity to the New World, 1628–1787

❧ Flowering Plasters ❧

The fall of La Rochelle reformed perceptions of human geography. Change paralleled the unprecedented diffusion of natural-philosophical books throughout a rapidly expanding Atlantic world. Following the events of 1628, the extent to which Winthrop adopted the rustic persona as part of his New World Paracelsian project may be measured by books he owned and used as laboratory and clinical texts. Paracelsus's most influential books on alchemic medicine and natural philosophy have survived from Winthrop's library: *Archidoxorum* (Basel, 1582); *Baderbuchlin* (Mulhouse, 1562); *Das Buch meteorum* (Cologne, 1566); *De secretis creationis* (Strasbourg, 1575); *Philosophiae magnae* (Basel, 1569); and *Volumen medicinae paramirum* (Strasbourg, 1575).[1] These volumes not only formed the core of Winthrop's alchemical library; some of them were inscribed copies, which carried enormous talismanic significance.

In 1640, Winthrop acquired at least two of the Paracelsus titles from the library of John Dee (1527–1608), the pioneering author of the famous *Monas hieroglyphica* (Antwerp, 1564). Dee, an alchemist and mathematician, explored the mystical relation between geometry and Nature, and was the most revered first-generation English Paracelsian. Dee's fame spread quickly throughout the learned culture of the Atlantic world, and after the master himself, he became the most celebrated hermetic figure of the sixteenth century. These volumes of Paracelsus, along with seven other alchemical books and assorted manuscripts originally owned by John Dee, may have been given as presentation copies to Winthrop by Dee's alchemist son Arthur, as was Arthur's own *Fasciculus chemicus* (Paris, 1629). Such gifts were indicative of the exalted status Winthrop eventually attained among European colleagues as a New World natural philosopher and patron.

Winthrop's copies of the *Baderbuchlin* and *Das Buch meteorum* are each heavily annotated with drawings of laboratory apparatus and alchemical notes in John Dee's delicate hand, as Winthrop himself noted with unprecedented pride on the flyleaf of both volumes:

> [*Baderbuchlin*]
> This above written and the name on the top of the frontisspice of tis booke & yt writing
> in the middle of the frotispice and the severall notes in the margent through the whole
> booke, was written by that famous philosopher and Chimist John Dee. wth his owne
> hand. this J: Dee was he yt wrote the philophicall treatise called Monas Hieroglifica. also
> Propaidenmata Aphoristica also the learned preface before Euclides elements in English
> in folio. he was warden of Manchester. I have divers bookes yt were his wherein he hath
> written his name and many notes &c: for wch they are worthyly the more esteemed. John
> Winthrop. [Jr.] Jul: 25. 1640.

> [*Das Buch meteorum*]
> The writing on ye next leafe & ye next leafe & ye name on the top of the ffrontispice &
> ye marginall notes in ye booke were writen by that famous and learned philosopher John
> Dee, warden of Manchester, wth his owne hand writing, this booke was his while he lived
> I have divers other bookes both printed & some manuscript yt came out of his study, in
> them he hath likewise written both his name & notes: for wch they are farre the more pre
> cious . . . Jul: 25: 1640.[2]

The mystical Dee was to become so important to Winthrop's identity as a Paracelsian and book collector that he transcribed the hermetic "monas" (see fig. 11.3) signifying philosophical mercury from the frontispiece of his copy of Dee's *Monas hieroglyphica* as his ex libris. When Howes sent Winthrop an important shipment of alchemical books, including Robert Fludd's *Opera* (Frankfurt, 1619–1629), in 1632, he marked the outside of the box with the monas symbol.[3]

Winthrop collected mystical books by Oswald Croll, Peter Severinus (Peder Sørensen), and Michael Sendivogius (Michal Sedziwój) to complement those of Paracelsus, which (especially if annotated by Dee "wth his owne hand writing") were the talismanic core of his alchemical library, around which other texts rotated like planets around the sun. These followers clarified Paracelsus's theoretical language and thera peutic recipes for both practical and political purposes. Winthrop's editions of Croll's *Basilica chymica* (Frankfurt, 1609); Severinus's *Idea medicinae philosophicae* (Basel, 1571); three volumes of Sendivogius, who thought deeply about the relationship between manual experience and the philosopher's stone, including *A New Light of Alchymie* (London, 1650), an important new English translation by John French of *Novum lumen chymicum* (the 1628 Geneva Latin edition of which Winthrop already had); and, finally, *Von dem Rechten wahren Philosophischen Steine* (Strasbourg, 1613) meant that his library contained the four basic primers on seventeenth-century Paracelsian medicine.[4]

The didactic and lexicological nature of these primers and the publishers' intention to respond to a demand in the early-to-mid-seventeenth-century book market for readable introductions to Paracelsus is made absolutely clear on the title page of French's London translation of Sendivogius:

> A New Light of Alchymie: Taken out of the fountaine of Nature, and Manuall Experience. To which is added a Treatise of Sulphur . . . Also Nine Books Of the Nature of Things, Written by Paracelsus, viz. Of the Generations Growthes Conservations Life: Death Renewing Transmutation Separation Signatures of Naturall things. Also a Chymicall Dictionary explaining hard places and words met withall in the writings of Paracelsus, and other obscure Authors.[5]

These primers elucidated Paracelsus's perception that matter was interconnected by the same spirit that animated man. "Man could not separate himself in time and space from natural events," Owen Hannaway explains. "Nature was within him as well as without him, and all was encompassed within God. As such, man was inextricably caught up in the pulse of cosmic events stretching from the Divinity to the lowest of the elements." Thus, Hannaway concludes, "such knowledge was a unique gift of God granted to each individual according to his own lights." Croll's *Basilica chymica,* his only published book, argued for new standards of evidence for chemical and mineral therapy, so, "in this study, no man is further to be believed, than as everyone findeth by his own proper experience."[6] Paracelsians believed that physicians could learn more from humble artisans, chirurgeons, midwives, and others taught by direct experience of natural materials than from the theories of schoolmen who trivialized manual labor as merely instrumental.

An exemplary instance of such a Paracelsian appropriation of folkloric cures occurs in an exchange of letters between April 11 and 18, 1628, in which John Winthrop Sr. and his physician son discuss alternative therapies for an illness afflicting the father. This exchange took place six months after John Winthrop Jr. had returned from the Île de Ré. The last letter was delivered to London just days before the younger Winthrop embarked on the Mediterranean journey that preceded his final decision to join his father in the colonies. Paracelsus used systemic constitutional and chemical therapies, but he was not averse to topical treatment. In this instance, the experience of a skillful woman synthesized the Galenic approach and iatrochemistry. When Winthrop counseled his father to let the medicine "grow well," he alerted him to follow the Paracelsian practice of "flowering"—which *In patientia suavitas* shows in a political and historical context—where pathology and therapy interacted sympathetically to achieve a cure.

The elder Winthrop was in residence as lord of Groton Manor in Suffolk, when he experienced a debilitating affliction of his right hand. Fearing gangrene, a local physician counseled surgery for the removal of "mortified fleshe." This was a painful and risky alternative in the seventeenth century; the surgeon's knife killed with greater efficiency than most diseases. When this treatment was proposed to the younger Winthrop in London, he became alarmed and wrote his father to recommend the use of a poultice instead of surgery. He called these applications "plaisters," a noninvasive therapy learned during a recent visit to a "scilfull" woman living in London's artisans' quarter:

> I am very sory to heare that your hand continueth so ill, but I hope, by godes providence, you shall finde helpe by those thinges I have sent you, which I receyved from a woman that is very scilfull, and much sought unto for these thinges, she is sister to Mr. Waterhouse the linnen draper in Cheape side, by whose meanes, I was brought to her, she told me if you were at London she made noe doubt but to cure it quicly, but because you cannot come up she therefore gave me these plaisters to send to you, and said that if it were not Gangreend she would warrant them by godes helpe to do you present good, the use of them is as followeth Take the Yellow plaister, as much as will cover your sore finger all over to the next Joynt below the sore, and on the rest of your finger whereon this plaister does not ly, lay as much of the blake plaister as will cover it all over, this must be done twice a day in the morning, and evening till it beginneth to grow well, and then once a day. The other blacke plaister you must lay all over your hand, and that you must shift once in 2 or 3 dayes. You must not wash it nor lay any other thing to it. this will draw out the thorne if any be in and heale it both. she will take nothing for it, and therfore I doe the rather credit hir, for she doth it only for freindes etc. I pray therfore use it, *and leave of any other course of surgery.* I wish you were here at london where she might dresse it her selfe.[7]

Unfortunately, the hand had already "gangreend," and by the time the younger Winthrop's letter arrived in Groton with the package of "plaisters," the surgeon had done his work. Winthrop's father was forced to use his left hand to write his son four days later with news of the apparently successful operation, but he still labored to note tactfully that he applied the "scilfull" woman's therapy as well:

> My Good Sonne, As I have allwayes observed your lovinge and dutyfull respectes towardes me, so must I needes allso now, in that sence which you have of my affliction,

and that care and paynes you have taken to procure my ease; . . . I prayse God, my finger is well amended, my Surgeon did his parte well, and stayyde the gangreene and tooke out the mortified fleshe, but because your love and paines should not be loste, I have betaken my selfe wholly to your plaister, which the Surgeon likes well enough of . . . My yellow plaister wilbe spent this week, but of the blacke I have more than I shall use. My naile is allmost shotte of, I feare. The short bone under my nayle is putrified, but my finger will not be the shorter for the losse of that bone.[8]

The elder Winthrop, like his son, was utterly dependent on his writing "hand" to extend an epistolary reach from the country into the "outside world" of London, through the careful maintenance of family, mercantile, religious, and courtly patronage networks. That is why he added a postscript to explain that he would soon visit London personally, because "this trouble of my hand hath so hindered me in the disposinge of my affaires as I must be forced to come downe."[9] The younger Winthrop was pleased at the news of improvement and the impending visit, but he replied warily, cautioning his father to take his advice seriously by using the "plaisters" exclusively without recourse to further surgery:

I receyved your letters, my self and all our freindes heere much rejoycing to heare from you so good newes of your hand, whereof your former letters put us in noe small feare. I have sent you some more plaisters. I told the Gentlewoman of the bone which you feared was putrified, she saith that her plaister will draw it out, if it be, and heale it both without any other thing. I hope you wilbe at London before you shall need any more.[10]

❧ A Frontier Library ❧

We hear of the importance that colonial observers attached to John Winthrop Jr.'s alchemical library on December 15, 1640, when he was just thirty-four years of age and already a magistrate of his father's Massachusetts Bay Colony. The library was then in its formative stages—Winthrop had only just acquired Dee's volumes of Paracelsus—but given the context, such an enormous assemblage of books was perceived as a sort of spectacle by colonial observers. According to a journal entry recorded on that date by Winthrop's father (always fearful that his son's scholarship might lead to apostasy), he "[had] many books in a chamber . . . there were above a thousand." As historians of science have long noted, Winthrop's library was already "the most significant and extensive . . . in colonial America."[11] Winthrop's was also among the most complete natural-philosophical libraries in private hands anywhere in the seventeenth-century Atlantic world.[12] When, in 1648, the Bermudan George Starkey—who would eventually forge a controversial career in both Boston and London as a self-proclaimed "Philosopher made by the fire, and a professor of that Medicine which is real and not

Histrionical"—needed to consult "chemical bookes" in one of Winthrop's frequent absences, he wrote: "If your W[orshi]p would be pleased to remember the keyes of the cabinets wherein your bookes are, I should count it an extreame facility once to have the view of the chemical bookes wch I have not read a long time."[13] Ten years later, two "chemical bookes" written by Starkey himself—*Natures Explication and Helmont's Vindication* (London, 1657); and *Pyrotechny Asserted and Illustrated* (London, 1658)—found a place in Winthrop's cabinets.[14]

Winthrop also lent chemical books and gave advice and instruction to Jonathan Brewster, a trader in New England's backcountry and the son of Plymouth Colony's William Brewster Sr. Winthrop's clear intention was to patronize the peripatetic Brewster's research, while making him a sort of advance scout for potentially productive mineral sites in uncharted territories. Jonathan Brewster's correspondence is important because it shows that his interest in backcountry commerce was intertwined with a career as an enthusiastic alchemist in fierce pursuit of the philosopher's stone ("the red Elixer") on the Connecticut frontier. Brewster's deferential letters were appropriate to his status as a governor's protégé. But Brewster was also writing to an acknowledged adept who held keys to a great scientific library that was indispensable to his work. Books from Winthrop's library helped Brewster to achieve a sophistication in alchemical knowledge and laboratory practice that would have been judged competent even by London standards. The fictitious Nicolas Flamel's *Hieroglyphical Figures* (London, 1624)—the first English translation of a French treatise published in Paris in 1612 by a native of Poitou named Arnaud de la Chevalerie (who borrowed the pseudonym "Flamel" from a fourteenth-century bookseller)—was particularly helpful.[15] In returning Winthrop's book, Brewster tells us much about the significance of reading words simultaneously with allegorical images in seventeenth-century colonial material life. Brewster reported that his interpretation of Flamel's first hieroglyphical figure provided the key to understanding the "first ingredient." He meant the *prima materia*, basic to the discovery of the philosopher's stone. "I have sent your worshipp, by John Elderkin [the chair maker], the booke you sent," Brewster wrote in 1656. Laboring to decode the hieroglyph, he continued, "I will write as clear as a light, as farr as I dare to, in fyding the first ingredience . . . the first figure in Fflamonell doth plainly resemblle the first ingredience: what it is, & from whence it comes, & how gotten."[16] Surely, Elderkin, to whom figures 6.2 and 6.3 are attributed, was similarly influenced by the alchemical imagery in his master's books.

Meanwhile, there is no mistaking the violent, "wilderness" context of Brewster's enterprise. Indeed, his preoccupation with death in the midst of his experiments and the foundation of pure white materials in the process is remarkably similar to Palissy's. In another letter to Winthrop in 1656, he wrote that the "red elixir" would achieve perfection only after the "white." Yet time—essential to the formula—was not on his side. Would he have the time to be patient?

> it is 5 yeares, wanting two monthes, befor the red Elixer be perfected, and 4 years before the white, soe that my worke will be yet till December next, befor the coullers bee, & 5 monthes after before the white appeare; and after the white stands a working till perfected by the hott fyerey imbibitiones, one whole year after till September. I ffeare I shall not live to see it finished, in regard partly of the Indianes, who I feare will raise warres; as also I have a conceit that God sees me as not worthy of such a blessing, by reason of my manifold miscariadges.[17]

Fear of violent death or "miscariadge" before "the work" could "grow" and achieve "perfection" was as fundamental to the existential reality of New World alchemists practicing on the frontier as it was central to the narrative structure of transatlantic alchemic texts such as Palissy's. By 1658, Winthrop had resigned himself to the possibility of such a truncated outcome in his lifetime. After the failure of his experiments with Dr. Robert Child to produce viable amounts of "black lead" (or graphite) in the "Tantiusque" hills, sixty miles west of Boston—one of a series of commercial disappointments—Winthrop intimated to colleagues that he might not live to see the fruits of his labor. "It may be," he wrote with stoical resignation, that "God reserves such of his bounties to future generations."[18]

Early modern European alchemists often worried that processes that had not yet been written down might be forgotten and "the work" lost. Aside from the dangers of disease, such as the Great Plague in London in 1665, which killed George Starkey and 70,000 other citizens, many scientists experienced wars of religion so violent, enduring, and widespread as to make the bloody Indian wars of seventeenth-century America seem almost trivial by comparison. It is thus perhaps not surprising that in their sagas of heroic suffering, endurance, or even death in pursuit of the philosopher's stone, in addition to evidence of Ovid's *Metamorphoses*, we encounter Stoic ideas suggestive of Seneca, Plutarch, and Tacitus, who were read closely, sometimes in English translation, by Calvinists in the seventeenth century.

The Catholic world shared these interests. In 1555, André Thevet, a Franciscan friar who eventually served both Catherine de Médicis as chaplain and Charles IX as royal cosmographer, traveled to the new French colony in Brazil, where he stayed nearly three months. Thevet left shortly before the arrival of the famous Huguenot historian and natural philosopher Jean de Léry, whom he blamed (along with Léry's coreligionists), for the colony's religious schism and ultimate failure. Shortly after his return to France in 1556, Thevet published *Les Singularitez de la France antarctique, autrement nommée Amerique* (Paris, 1558), an ethnography of Brazilian Indians that made his reputation as a world traveler in the epic tradition—a sort of French Ulysses come home to tell the tale. A year after Charles IX died, Thevet produced an influential *Cosmographie universelle* (Paris, 1575), which celebrated the metamorphoses and transformative powers of a panoply of heroic figures, many of whom were doubtless later adapted to the dramatic logic of alchemic narratives.[19]

It would in any case be a mistake to regard Brewster's alchemical experimentation on the dangerous colonial frontier as the work of an eccentric loner "in hot and sanguine pursuit of the grand elixer in his cabin on the Connecticut frontier with the Indians howling at his kitchen door."[20] Far from being rare, such rustic natural-philosophical activities may have been "nearly routine for early [colonizing] ventures."[21]

An intact locally fired ceramic "alembick" found buried near several well-preserved pieces of late medieval English armor—including a close helmet and visor—in a refuse pit on the Carter's Grove tract at Martin's Hundred, Virginia (fig. 11.1) suggests that Brewster's frontier experience was far from unique to the borderlands of New England. A seventeenth-century fortified "bawn" called Wolstenholme Towne once stood on this exposed site overlooking the James River. This tiny edifice was little more than a flimsy English toehold in the Chesapeake. It was cobbled together within a generation of the defeat of the Armada. The settlers used log and posthole construction, which, until as late as 1740, was ubiquitous in the region's domestic and military architecture.[22] Ironically, given Wolstenholme Towne's fate at the hands of indigenous people, its cannon were trained toward the sea and potential Spanish adversaries. Yet the town's history was so short that the Spaniards had insufficient time even to notice its existence.

One of an alembic's functions was to serve as a condensation funnel or "head" of a tripartite alchemical still. The still and furnace were perhaps the most basic apparatus found in seventeenth-century laboratories.[23] It may be that Tidewater versions of Brewster's "red elixer" and medicinal substances such as "potable gold" were condensed in this artifact at Martin's Hundred in addition to alcohol. After all, were it not for the rare survival of his letters to Winthrop, Brewster would have labored in complete obscurity and we would know nothing of his experiments. Given what we have learned about the vast intellectual and commercial importance assigned to natural philosophy in virtually every early modern European imperial court that had interests in the Americas, future research may reveal that colonial expeditions to frontier outposts commonly included individuals like Brewster. Aided by an alchemical still and available Paracelsian books, they performed the dual functions of physician and alchemist.[24] Winthrop's natural-philosophical interests are well documented, as are those of, among many others, the Quaker diarist James Logan—who purchased a pewter "Limbeck" from the London-trained Philadelphia pewterer, brazier, and merchant Simon Edgell

FIGURE 11.1. Lead-glazed ceramic alembic, Martin's Hundred, Virginia, ca. 1620. H: 13⅛",
spout bore: 5⁄16". Courtesy Colonial Williamsburg Foundation. The rim is turned up inside the
alembic, forming a channel to carry the distilled liquid down to the narrow spout, now broken,
whence it finally dripped out into the alchemist's distilling flask, or cucurbit. Archaeological
excavation of the ca. 1607 site at Jamestown has unearthed just such a cucurbit, made of unglazed earthenware, imported from London. Illustrated in Beverly Straube, "European Ceramics in the New World: The Jamestown Example," in *Ceramics in America, 2001*, ed. Robert
Hunter (Hanover, N.H.: University Press of New England, 2001), 49, fig. 4.

(1677–1742) in 1724—and the Pennsylvania German pietists Johannes Kelpius, who led
a spiritual brotherhood called The Woman in the Wilderness, and Johann Conrad
Beissel, who founded the Ephrata Cloister. These individuals, unlike Brewster, set up
alchemical laboratories in the relative security of established settlements founded during the late seventeenth or early eighteenth centuries.[25] Though unclear to what ex-

tent, this archaeological evidence links the Saybrook and Martin's Hundred settlements.

Moreover, Sir John Wolstenholme (d. 1639), principal financial backer of Martin's Hundred, was also a backer of earlier voyages by Henry Hudson (1610) and William Baffin (1615), both of whom sailed to the New World in search of the Northwest Passage. This was an enterprise laden with alchemical associations from the start of Atlantic exploration, drawing Winthrop to the fortieth parallel and New Netherlands. Like Brewster, other, as yet unknown first-generation American alchemists must have felt threatened with violent death and feared the destruction (or appropriation) of their alchemical enterprises at the hands of Spanish or French competitors, or local Amerindians.

The date assigned the archaeological strata in which it was found suggests that the user of the Martin's Hundred alembic must have experienced the attack by Indians from the Powhatan Confederacy in March 1622 that destroyed Wolstenholme Towne except for two houses and "a peece of a church." He may have lost his life along with seventy-seven other colonists, or he may have been among the sixty-two survivors who retreated to the fort built at Jamestown in 1607. By 1622, James Fort had barely survived its own calamitous beginnings, and the refugees were lucky anyone at Jamestown was alive to receive them. After years of searching, archaeologists have discovered postholes and decomposed traces of rough hewn logs that are the remnants of James Fort's original palisades and bastions. Further clues to the alchemical context of the Martin's Hundred alembic, a fragment of one of colonial America's earliest laboratories, may yet be unearthed there.[26]

From the correspondence of Brewster and other rustic colonial natural philosophers, we can understand something of how Winthrop's vast network of scientific patronage influenced the circulation of books into and out of his library. Title-page dedications were an important aspect of this practice. The circulation of books to facilitate patronage was a strategy Winthrop shared with many seventeenth-century European collectors. These included Winthrop's Catholic correspondent Sir Kenelm Digby (1602–65), his would-be patron during the 1650s, whose famous libraries in London and Paris functioned as design studios and staging areas for gifts. The use of books in this fashion was therefore entwined with portability; books were among the most "mobile," widely diffused artifacts of the early modern era. It was Winthrop's habit as New England's most influential and "princely" natural philosopher to lend or make presents of alchemical books that were considered indispensable to the replication of certain seventeenth-century laboratory practices, thus extending his network to the periphery of New England and solidifying his connections with alchemical clients exploring the frontier. The borderlands of southern New England drew his attention after 1635, when the Saybrook project with its laboratory and manufacturing complex got under way. Simultaneously, European clients and patrons in the metropole, including Howes and Digby, attempted to do the same with Winthrop. In the process, Winthrop played the role of "adept," extending his identity through Dee's "monas" bookmark, to distant places—backcountry laboratories he would never have found time to visit (or perhaps have dared risk going to) in person. When books were returned with appropriate letters of gratitude after the completion of experiments in which they were used, he might also expect—as in Brewster's case—a report on a promising client's progress. Patronage provides a functional explanation for such an ambitious alchemical library in colonial America, yet this tells only part of the story. Above all, Winthrop used his library personally in his extensive laboratory experiments and astronomical observations and in preparing medicinal therapies.

Winthrop's informed reading in natural philosophy may be found everywhere in the letters, but particularly in the constant stream of correspondence with Howes— his primary supplier of books before 1650—about the relative merits of new titles currently available in London or at the Frankfurt book market. If friends, agents, or clients passed by way of Frankfurt, they offered to courier books for their esteemed patron. In 1629, for example, while Winthrop was visiting Venice during his lengthy tour of the Mediterranean, he received a letter from Judah Throckmorton informing him that "the stay wee have at Franckfourt (be it more, or lesse) I will employ to finde your booke."[27] The value of a book's contents—and hence its suitability for accession to the library—was hotly (and jealously) contested. In 1650, Dr. Child wrote Winthrop to dismiss as a mere gloss a book by the influential Belgian medical writer J. B. van Helmont. Writing that "though they conteyne many good things, yet they fall very short of the expectation which the world had of him, and truly he hath extracted most out of Paracelsus He bein[g] as easy to be understood as this man," Child assumed a familiarity with the complete works of Paracelsus and debates in London about plainness. His poor assessment of van Helmont's *Obscula medica* (Cologne, 1644) failed to dissuade Winthrop from adding this important seventeenth-century defense of Paracelsus to his library, however.[28]

❧ "Gov. Winthrops Ring" ❧

Winthrop's role as patron, librarian, and intermediary for seventeenth-century colonial alchemists and natural philosophers in his network of correspondence was also operative for adepts of "future generations." Above all the Reverend Dr. Ezra Stiles, who showed that he too "hath extracted most out of Paracelsus." During his thirty-year tenure as Yale's president and primary professor of American ecclesiastical history, Dr. Stiles (1727–95) also taught courses in a variety of related subjects, ranging from the practice of medicine and natural philosophy to law. It was in his double role

as ecclesiastical historian and natural philosopher that Stiles recorded his scientific encounter with minerals extracted from the legendary "Gov. Winthrops Ring." In his
Literary Diary, buried inside a routine inventory of pedagogy and laboratory experiment for May 31, 1787, Stiles recalled:

> I gave my Lect[ure] on Ecc[lesiastical] Hist[or]y, viz. [the] beginning [of] the American
> Churches . . . & also Mr. Erkelens . . . shewed me the Process for reducing Cobalt to
> Smalt, so that one Ton of Cobalt, with pulverized Flints & Potash will produce Eighteen
> Tons of Smalt, worth 2/ ster[ling] p[er] pound. The Mountain, called Gov. Winthrops
> Ring, abounds with it, & Mr. Erkelens owns it, about 1800 acres. He is going to carry
> Twenty Tons [of smalt] to China . . . with w[hich] is made the beautiful Blue on china
> Ware.[29]

Since first mined for ore in the seventeenth century, "Gov. Winthrops Ring," in
East Haddam, Connecticut, had been associated with folk legends of the younger
Winthrop's mystical practices. In the summer of 1787, Stiles invited Erkelens, a merchant, mariner, and "projector," to his laboratory in New Haven. Erkelens's visit
prompted reflection in Stiles's diary entry the next day on the seventeenth-century der-
ivation of the place-name "Gov. Winthrops Ring."[30] The cobalt experiments at Yale
triggered Stiles's memory of a conversation with Governor Jonathan Trumbull, his fellow local historian of colonial Connecticut, in which oral and written history merged
with hermetic legend, local folklore, and mythology. Thus, an otherwise unremembered "Mountain in the N.W. corner of East Haddam," on the Connecticut River just
north of Long Island Sound, was associated with Winthrop, whom Stiles called "an
Adept." Stiles understood adepts to be a worthy seekers selected by God to possess the
alchemical philosopher's stone for the transmutation of metals. The Yale cobalt experiments allowed Stiles to harness himself to Winthrop's rustic natural philosophy,
and hence to an elite international community of alchemists, with whom the former
colonial governor remained "intimately" connected over the course of his lifetime:[31]

> Gov. Trumbull has often told me that this was the place to which Gov. Winthrop of
> N[ew] Lond[on] used to resort with his servant; and after spend[ing] three Weeks in the
> Woods of this Mountain in roast[ing] Ores & assaying Metals & casting gold Rings, he
> used to return home to N[ew] Lond[on] with plenty of Gold. Hence this is called the
> Gov. Winthrop's Ring to this day. Gov. Winthrop was an Adept, in intimate Corre-
> spond[ence] with Sir Knelm Digby and [the] first chemical & philosophical Characters
> of the last Century.[32]

As late as 1787, it was thus common knowledge that Winthrop had by the time of
his death achieved the lofty status of adept and possessor of the stone. This status was
famously poeticized in an elegy by the Harvard-educated schoolmaster, physician, and

alchemist Benjamin Tompson entitled: "A FUNERAL TRIBUTE To the Honourable Dust of that most Charitable Christian, Unbiased politician and Unimitable Pyrotechnist John Winthrope, ESQ: A Member of the Royal Society, & Governor of Conecticut Colony in New England Who expired in his Countreys Service, April 6th, 1676."[33] Tompson's elegy read, in part:

> / . . . Great Winthrops Name Shall never be forgotten / . . . Projections various by fire he made / Where Nature had her common Treasure laid. / Some thought the tincture Philosophick lay / Hatcht by the Mineral Sun in Winthrops way, / And clear it shines to me he had a Stone / Grav'd with his Name which he could read alone / . . . His common Acts with brightest lustre shown, / . . . But in Apollo's Art he was alone. / . . . Sometimes his wary steps, but wandring too, / Would carry him the Chrystal Mountains to, / Where Nature locks her Gems, each costly spark / Mocking the Stars, spher'd in their Cloisters dark.

Tompson thus provided an early textual source for the legend of "Gov. Winthrops Ring," but why does the famous Catholic Kenelm Digby warrant favorable mention by the faithful "old Puritan" Dr. Stiles? To elucidate the transatlantic political, cultural, and scientific context that inspired "intimate correspondence" between Digby and Winthrop, one must revisit Stiles's intense reenactment of the seventeenth-century governor's alchemical experience at "Gov. Winthrops Ring." How can Stiles's retrospective absorption into a moment of personal experience of seventeenth-century metallurgical experimentation—indeed his identification with this rustic moment and its "wandring" protagonist—be better understood in the context of his gloss on colonial America's place in the Atlantic world and his own late-eighteenth-century natural-philosophical pilgrimage?

Consider that for Stiles, the significance of the experimental cobalt lay not merely in the specific natural phenomena manifested by the thing itself but its shared material history with the adept. During the 1640s, Winthrop experimented with cobalt extracted from his property in East Haddam to exploit its potential as a mineral dye to compete with indigo, just as Erkelens and Stiles would do 150 years later. To reveal again in Stiles's laboratory the hidden potential of this "lowly element," unearthed from inside Winthrop's hermetic "mountain," which "abounds with it," was also to stand with a heroic ancestor among sacred stones in the philosophical "ring." It was no coincidence that Stiles's interest in Winthrop grew after 1758. In a philosophical quarrel reminiscent of the great English debates of the 1640s and 1650s, Stiles rejected his early association with the "enlightenment" principles of deism, mechanistic thought, and "rational" religion and reached back beyond the revivalism of New England's Great Awakening to embrace the seventeenth-century millennial cosmology of the "old" English Calvinists.[34] "I am in principle," he wrote in 1770, "with the good old Puritans." The totality of Stiles's intellectual reversal and embrace of filial pietism caused him to identify so closely with seventeenth-century predecessors that by the late 1760s, he had virtually reinvented himself as an "old Puritan."[35]

Stiles felt he transcended the early eighteenth-century New Light revivalism of Jonathan Edwards (though Edwards's natural philosophy was not far removed from his own) and the later New Divinity of Samuel Hopkins and stood behind "those evangelical Doctrines for which their learned and pious Ancestors were eminent." Those ancestors included Edwards's grandfather Solomon Stoddard, Thomas Hooker, and such "old" English Puritans as William Perkins, the Elizabethan minister and Cambridge University theologian who mentored many of New England's first-generation divines.[36] In 1775, Stiles wrote Edward Wigglesworth, Harvard's professor of divinity, that modern evangelical models were insufficient to retrieve seventeenth-century doctrines of grace, which had been corrupted by Arminianism:

> I fear also a loss of the Evangelical Doctrines and the Doctrines of Grace as held by the good Old Puritans and by our Ancestors. They have evanished from the Church of England since Archbishop Laud, they are evanishing apace from the churches of Scotland and even Holland, and from the Dissenters in England . . . be instrumental, in your Day, of making such a Sett of Ministers as those made by the Tuition of that eminent Man of God Mr. Perkins of Cambridge.[37]

"The Writings of that excellent Divine are worthy [of] the Attention of every Student in Divinity, not for any Systematic order in them," Stiles argued, "but for the Perspicuity and Justness of his theological Principles."[38] Stiles also knew that Perkins "theological principles" elucidated doctrines of grace and justification that extended well beyond the pulpit into "physick" and the scientific study of the natural world and material life of "our ancestors." It was in the natural world that the key would be found to unlocking the secrets of a lost past. The writings of Perkins, along with those of a few other early seventeenth-century English Calvinists, such as John Preston and William Ames, played a crucial role in the mediation of abstract theological theory and Protestant scientific practice in everyday life on both sides of the Atlantic.[39] David D. Hall has demonstrated how deeply Perkins's "Old Puritan" views on divine will, providential experience, and the free working of the Holy Spirit influenced popular cultural practice in New England during the 1640s. This was especially true of theological debates on the reform of almanacs. Perkins wished to expunge representations of agency at the expense of spirituality and rituals asserting ways of dying deemed inappropriate for the godly. It is not until the late 1670s, or the second generation of settlement, that Hall sees signs of Perkins's influence on the wane.[40] Stiles thus yoked his program to Perkins when he inveighed against the Arminianism that had infected the Church of England "since Archbishop Laud." Human reason could never achieve philosophical unity; "God's works or his word . . . must be poured down upon the human intellect, as an emanation into the soul directly from God himself."[41]

Long before the Yale cobalt experiments, Stiles already provided an alternative for alienated colleagues who "lamented" the degree to which his scholarship embraced the religious enthusiasm "of our ancestors," at the expense of modern reason. When his mystical *Discourse on Saving Knowledge* was published in 1770, Stiles acknowledged in print that man was utterly helpless to understand "God's works" in the natural world without divine agency in the process. God alone could "raise divine Illuminations, and spiritual influences, to a degree of irresistibility" in human experience. Stiles's enthusiasm followed closely in the footsteps of Ficino, Paracelsus, Palissy, Croll, and especially van Helmont.[42]

Among the most influential "Helmontians" was George Starkey, Winthrop's close friend and colleague in both Europe and America. William N. Newman has proven that Starkey secretly constructed an elaborate fictional narrative and false identity around his "close friend," alter ego, and pseudonym, the charismatic, world-renowned adept and *philosophus Americanus* ("American philosopher"), "Eirenaeus Philalethes" ("Peaceful Lover of Truth").[43] Winthrop's reputation as an adept, his friendship with Starkey, and his location in New England caused many to identify Winthrop himself as Philalethes. This was a logical hypothesis in the 1650s. There can be no doubt from surviving correspondence that Winthrop and Starkey influenced each other directly, perhaps to the point where their laboratory practices in pursuit of the philosopher's stone ran in parallel courses. But, as Newman has also shown, it was Starkey in particular—often writing in the fictional guise of Philalethes—who profoundly affected the curriculum in chemistry at Harvard in the seventeenth century. And it was Starkey who, in the 1650s, translated van Helmont in ways that resonate powerfully with the spiritualist epistemology of Stiles's discourse from 1770:

> But I beleeve that the Almighty alone, is the only way, truth, life, & light, both of things living and al things else, not Reason. And therefore it behoves our mind to be intellectual, not rational, if it hold forth the immediate Image of God. This Paradox wil be very necessary to be unfolded, before wee enter upon the search of al things knowable, *but most Especially of such things which are Adepta.*[44]

In this sense, Stiles reasserts that worship was the primary function of old Christian adepts such as Winthrop. "The study of nature led to God," Hillel Schwartz writes; "by means of curiosity, diligence, logic and faith, the fortunate virtuoso ascended the spheres of religious illumination."[45] Stiles's soulish reading of the seventeenth-century past in terms of the Paracelsian light of Nature supports revisionist scholarship on

pietism in early New England. Despite the dramatic stance against religious enthusiasm taken by its Calvinist leadership, many orthodoxies contested for spiritual space
in seventeenth-century Massachusetts.[46]

For revisionists, New England—especially in places distant from Boston, on the
Massachusetts "near frontier"—experienced diverse patterns of religiosity similar to
parts of England and most of the post-Reformation Atlantic world. Thus it would
tend, in places, to look like the middle colonies.[47] The cultivation of a fluid, nonspecific
experimental cultural setting was as crucial to Winthrop's personal experience as settling on the coast of Long Island Sound and the fortieth parallel was to his natural-
philosophical and economic agenda.[48] Stiles's preoccupation with local history in and
around New Haven suggests that he knew that his personal embrace of "seventeenth-
century" religious enthusiasm at Yale in the 1760s was a necessary precondition to forging links between his natural philosophy and the beginnings of the Paracelsian tradition in the southern New England borderlands.

But Stiles's archaeological interest in Winthrop had already extended beyond the
heady experience of mystical communion with the first American adept through reen-
actments of legendary seventeenth-century experiments. Stiles wanted the words of
his ancestor heard at the same time that he touched, handled, and founded ores that
had been disinterred from Winthrop's ring and "roasted and assayed" in Winthrop's
laboratory. Like a sixteenth-century humanist questing for power from knowledge recovered in ancient texts, Stiles sought to recover and transcribe vast sections of early
Winthrop papers and manuscripts. These primordial texts from New England's "ancients" began with a cache of "old" English documents from the year 1498. Mainly,
however, they contained seventeenth-century archives that had passed through the
hands of Adam Winthrop (1548–1623) of Groton, England, his son, John Winthrop
of Groton and Boston, and his grandson, John Winthrop Jr. The Winthrop archives
remained mostly intact and were passed down through the family until 1767, when
Stiles borrowed the volumes directly from John Still Winthrop, Winthrop the
Younger's great grandson. After they had been in his possession for four years, Stiles
began his laborious transcription of the archives in January 1771. Stiles's will indicates
that when this task was completed, he had filled one manuscript volume in quarto with
"Extracts fr[om] Mss of Gov. Winthrop and others" and a second quarto volume
bound with "Extracts from John Winthrop's MS History of New England."[49] When
Stiles finally returned the borrowed documents to John Still Winthrop, they were lent
to Governor Jonathan Trumbull. Often the *Literary Diary* notes that Trumbull shared
Stiles's fascination with the younger Winthrop, the predecessor Trumbull revered most
as the first governor of the newly chartered Connecticut Colony.[50]

The alchemical foundation of Stiles's medical practice was inspired by passionate
spiritual engagement with the natural philosophy of his ancestors. Thus, Stiles's copi-

ous extracts from the Winthrop archives were also an archaeology of what for him represented "prelapsarian" sacred texts. For Stiles, the Winthrop archives documented Puritan seventeenth-century hermetic experience with "original" New World materials in their purest form, free from subsequent historical corruption. The same conceptual framework must also have been operative when Stiles undertook to master Hebrew, which Winthrop also mastered. Such linguistic skills had been common among seventeenth-century ancestors, who had read the Old Testament in Hebrew, and they were needed to facilitate an intensive analysis of the "antient . . . pure Knowledge" of the Kabbala in what was perceived to be its original language.

Among alchemists, the Kabbala was the traditional first step in decoding mystical and prophetic meanings in the Old and New Testaments, and through inspired biblical exegesis that transcended the corruption of time, in nature as well. By the mid seventeenth century, "the Kabbala . . . had burrowed deep into English religious thought."[51] In Stiles's day, thanks to the Kabbalistic inquiries of numerous transatlantic millennial sects including the French Prophets, Philadelphians, and Behmenists (followers of Jakob Böhme), the book of Revelation was perceived as a vast Kabbalistic code. It was thought that Jewish mystical code "ran through the entire New Testament," and French *millenarians* living in eighteenth-century London contended that over "1500 passages [were] incapable of being understood without knowledge of the Kabbala."[52] In a letter of 1773 to a Jewish talmudic and Old Testament scholar from Rhode Island who assisted with his Hebraic studies, Stiles claimed in "obscure" metaphorical prose to have distilled mystical knowledge from this ur-hermetic text. Several standard alchemic tropes were used to connote purification as a process of separation from historical dross:

> Much of this antient Knowledge is gone to ruin, being swallowed up and polluted in other streams that have issued forth from corrupt fountains. But as Gold mixt with reprobate Silver, or the Iron in the Image of Nebuchadnezzar which mixeth indeed but will not unite and cleave to the Clay; so a great deal of this pure Knowledge may be preserved among the Traditions and in the Caballa of the Nations.[53]

Mystical readings of the Old and New Testaments—and, as we have seen, the story of Nebuchadnezzar's Dream (Dan. 4:4–27) in particular—were fundamental to the artisanal Paracelsian material-holiness synthesis as it was put into practice by Palissy, Winthrop, and others. The importance to Huguenot artisans of the narrative of Nebuchadnezzar's Dream is clear from the ways in which Bernard Palissy interpreted this story, using both written texts and material artifacts, to elucidate the material history of an aging earth. It is noteworthy that Stiles, in the role of Neoplatonic alchemist, reactivated this story in a Kabbalistic context. Together with such "antient" hermetic texts, Winthrop's seventeenth-century laboratory notes and alchemical archives were transcribed by Stiles as unimpeachable ancestral authorities. By harnessing his experience to the replication of these aspects of Winthrop's laboratory practice taken from oral history or archives in the adept's own hand—and by working to complete certain unfinished Winthrop projects—Stiles thought himself able to cobble together an "antient," or uncorrupted, natural-philosophical identity. Then he would attract "emanation[s] into the soul directly from God himself," which, in hermeneutic fashion, would have circled back to authenticate his personal exegesis of Winthrop's writings.

Stiles's concern with America's ancient texts and minerals was a conduit to a deep well of universal soulish experience, capable of putting him in mystical contact with Winthrop himself. In so doing, we return to his "intimate" interest in Sir Kenelm Digby's natural-philosophical relationship with the old Connecticut adept during the seventeenth century.

Stiles's mystical thought experiments at Yale were the most idiosyncratic of his many personal initiatives in cosmology. Stiles amplified the occult astronomy of John Dee and Robert Fludd, because this was key to Winthrop's identity as a physician-alchemist and bibliophile. Fludd diagrammed elegant proportional relationships between microcosm and macrocosm, a well-known project in Neoplatonic cosmology, in which he developed the harmonic theory of the heavens in aesthetic as well as mathematical directions.[54] But following Dee, Stiles calculated the rate at which the universe expanded, something he understood to occur each time a new soul was created. Stiles's astronomical thesis was a proportionally elegant synthesis of animate materialism. Stiles perceived the perpetually expanding material boundaries of the universe as symbiotic in the spiritual sense, and so cosmological expansion was paralleled in precise order by a proportionally exact soulish expansion. Reading Paracelsian Neoplatonism, combined with the "face-to-face" archaeology of his Winthrop archival research, fieldwork, and laboratory practice, Stiles theorized that even as souls never die, they retain their names and historical identities. Familiar souls are eternally knowable in the Platonic consciousness of the dead, and also by living adepts with access to what Digby called the "Universal Spirit." "When we have left these Regions of incarnate spirits," Stiles claimed with anticipation, "and [have] entered into the intellectual World or Abodes of unbodied Minds—not only [will we] renew our Acquaintance with departed Friends, but personally converse with Moses, Isaiah, Paul, Plato, Cicero, Newton, Locke, and . . . with exalted Minds assembled from all parts of the moral Dominions of Jehovah."[55]

Nowhere is this fusion of unbodied minds in the Neoplatonic universal spirit better represented than in the portrait of Ezra Stiles painted in 1771 by Samuel King (1749–1818) (fig. 11.2).[56] Stiles is portrayed in clerical garb, as both a scholar of ecclesiastical history and Paracelsian physician-alchemist—in his own words, an "Effig[y] in a Green Elbow Chair." Behind him, on the shelves of his library, volumes from diverse

FIGURE 11.2. Samuel King (1749–1819), *Portrait of Ezra Stiles,* Newport, Rhode Island, 1771. H: 34″, W: 28″. Oil on canvas. Courtesy Yale University Art Gallery, bequest of Dr. Charles Jenkins Foote, B.A. 1883, M.D. 1890. This portrait was painted while Stiles was minister of the Second Congregational Church in Newport, Rhode Island, where he remained until joining Yale in 1778. Books visible on the top shelf of Stiles's library include Newton's *Principia* next to Plato, the Cambridge Platonist Ralph Cudworth's *Intellectual System,* and works by the "old" Puritan divines Isaac Watts and Cotton Mather. Aristotle is conspicuous by his absence. The second shelf groups together the Roman historian Livy (presumably his *Historia romanae*) and the *Historia ecclesiae* of Eusebius of Caesarea. Jean-Baptiste du Haldes *History of China* confirms Stiles's recent interest in the material science of such China trade commodities as cobalt blue on Chinese export porcelain, as well as the older quest for a Northwest Passage, while the Hebrew text from the Talmud—with the names of the early Jewish philosophers Abraham ibn Ezra, Solomon ben Isaac, and Maimonides inscribed on its spine in Hebrew and Aramaic—illustrated commitment to the languages of the Old Testament. The second shelf shows that the old Jewish, pagan, Christian, and Asian authors were now "Happy in God," commingling in a universal soul—and in the Neoplatonic Stiles's mind—despite their differences, as represented by the orb of light with *Yahweh* written in Hebrew at center, for Stiles, an "Emblem of the Universe or intellectual world" (David L. Barquist, *Myer Myers: Jewish Silversmith in Colonial New York* [New Haven: Yale University Press, 2001], 232–33). The diagram on the column shows the elliptical course of a comet intersecting with earth's orbit, a reminder—like Plato's pride of place next to Newton—that God's intervention in human affairs belies vulgar misunderstandings of mechanistic philosophy.

minds, religions, and disciplines converge. Newton's *Principia* and Plato's *Works* sit together on the top shelf, at the upper left, conjoining the revealed and the hidden in Nature. Also pictured are the works of Livy, the *Ecclesiastical History* of Eusebius of Caesarea, books by Cotton Mather and Isaac Watts, and the Jesuit J.-B. du Halde's *History of China.* Volumes in Hebrew (including "one inscribed Talmud B., Aben Ezra, Rabbi Selomoh Jarchi in Hebrew letters, and a little below R. Moses Ben Maimon Moreh Nevochem") and Arabic, as well as great histories of East and West, are shelved together. "By these I denote my Taste for History," Stiles wrote in his diary entry for August 1, 1771. "Especially of the Roman Empire, & of the Ch[urc]h in the 3 first Centuries & at the Reformation—the State of China as contain[in]g a systematical View of an antient p[eo]ple for 4000 years, being one Third or more of the human Race." He combined natural philosophy and primitive theology "on the other shelf [in] Newton's principia, Plato, Watts, Doddridge, [and] Cudworth's Intellectual System; & also the New Engl[an]d primaeval Divines Hooker, Chauncy, Mather, Cotton."[57]

Stiles's mastery of mystical powers—represented by the orb of atomized light particles that floats above his head to the right, and the linked circles on the column that diagram the conjunction of macrocosm and microcosm—show that death was not necessary to unite Stiles with the authors in his library. With one hand over his heart (where the sacred mysteries are hidden in the conduit of the soul), "in a Teaching Attitude," and the other "holding a preaching Bible" (from which he wishes to decode a hidden unity of knowledge), Stiles communes with his authors and his students through the transit of astral energy in the form of atoms that descend and then reascend from the orb of the universal spirit, as instructed in the Fludd cosmologies. The orb of light reveals the name "Yahwah" in large Hebrew text at the center; and barely visible in English is the unifying phrase, "all Happy in God," emanating out with the astral light of the soul toward the circle's periphery, called down into Stiles's heart from the macrocosm into the microcosm. Did Stiles or King intend that every atom of light emanating from God embody one of the "departed friends" or "exalted minds"? "At my Right hand stands a Pillar," Stiles wrote, in an extensive elucidation of "these Emblems" painted by King to his specifications, as they "are more descriptive of my Mind, than the Effigies of my Face":

> On the Shaft is one Circle and one Trajectory around a solar point, as an emblem of the Newtonian or Pythagorean System of the Sun & Planets & Comets. It is pythag, so far as respects the Sun & revolv^g Planets: it is newtonian so far as it respects the Comets moving in parabolic Trajectories, or long Ellipses whose Vertexes are nigh a parab. Curve. At the Top of the visible part of the Pillar & on the side of the Wall, is an Emblem of the Universe or intellectual World. It is as it were one sheet of Omniscience. In a central Glory is the name [Jehovah] surrounded with white Spots on a Field of azure, from each Spot ascend three hair Lines denoting the Tendencies of Minds to Diety & Communion with the Trinity in the divine Light: these Spots denote [*Innocency,*] a Spirit, a World, Clusters or Systems of Worlds, & their Tendencies to the eternal central yet universal omnipresent Light. This world is represented by a Cluster of Minds whose central Tendencies are turned off from Gd to Earth, self & created good—and also in a state of Redemption. Intervening is the Crucifixion of Christ between two Thieves—both Tendencies going off, but one turned back to the Light. Denotes also a converted & an unconverted Man. . . .
>
> . . . At a little Distance on the Left hand is a black Spot—the Receptacle of fallen An-

gels & the finally wicked. And as we know only of two Worlds (out of infinite Myriads) that have revolted; so this is big eno' to contain all these if none were saved. And the collection of moral Evil & Misery, in comparison with the moral Perfection & Happiness of the immense Universe, is but a small Spot & as nothing in proportion to the [whole]. So that under this small minutesimal Exception of the Misery of all the fallen Angels & even most of the Posterity of Adam, when we consider what is held forth in the Description of Coloss, i. 16. of Principalities, Dominions &c innumerable grand assemblages of Intelligences, we may say ALL HAPPY IN GOD.[58]

As Edward Howes wrote Winthrop after consulting with a "misticall" doctor in London, the unification of human knowledge would "come with such a light, that it will make a harmonie among all your authors, causing them sweetly to agree, and put you forever out of doubt and question."[59] Like Connecticut's original adept, Stiles practiced rustic philosophy in an invisible college thousands of miles from the center of science at the Royal Society in London, in the presence of Winthrop's words and things and the other exalted minds in his library.

🐦 A New Model Catholic and the Prodigal's Return to La Rochelle 🐦

Thus, it was partly because he associated himself with Kenelm Digby's well-known belief in the ability of the "Universal Spirit" to reconcile differences and obliterate the natural boundaries of time and space that Ezra Stiles privileged the Catholic Digby's "intimate correspondence" with Winthrop above other "friends" and placed him among the "first chemical & philosophical Characters of the last Century." The other impetus was Stiles's knowledge of a pivotal letter from Digby to Winthrop, written in 1655.

Winthrop's transatlantic community of "friends" was dominated by Protestants—albeit many were independents and sectarians—and most were Reform-minded scientists whose libraries and laboratory methods were similar to his own. Most followed Francis Bacon's interpretation of Paracelsus, which found voice in Bacon's skepticism and his firm belief in the primacy of evidence obtained by experiment alone. Webster argued that Bacon's experimentalist ideology was a natural outgrowth of the uncertainty of Calvinist predestinate theology and science, which appropriated Paracelsian thought in an effort to overturn the scholastic canon in natural philosophy during the Civil War and the interregnum. While Webster is revised to broaden his analysis beyond "Puritan" science to include all early modern Protestant natural philosophy, Stiles's anointment of Sir Kenelm Digby as one of seventeenth-century Europe's "first chemical & philosophical Characters" begs for further inquiry.

Stiles, a Calvinist minister with strong psychological and cultural ties to the Reformation, declared openly that Rome's intellectual and religious legacy was corrupt. However, it is possible to argue, with Webster, that Digby's status should be raised from "proselytizing Catholic" to "rehabilitated Catholic." The very ambiguity of Stiles's assertion of Digby's role as "intimate correspondent" suggests an entry into Winthrop's conception of his own religious and scientific identity. This opening arranges itself in the few traces that remain of Winthrop's complex transatlantic relationship with Digby and the risky context within which Sir Kenelm was forced to operate during the 1650s.[60]

Despite Stiles's enthusiasm about Digby's "chemical & philosophical" career, it would be a gross exaggeration to claim that the latter made significant contributions to seventeenth-century science. It *is* fair to say, however, that Digby was a successful courtier under the early Stuarts and the Protectorate, and that at least some of his success may be attributed to his transatlantic connections and the practice of natural philosophy. Sir Kenelm attended Charles I as "gentleman of the bedchamber" and was a member of the king's council. Like his father, James I, and indeed most seventeenth-century European monarchs, Charles demonstrated a passionate interest in alchemy. According to the diarist John Evelyn, natural philosophy helped Digby gain credibility and status at court, especially after "he had fixed [mercury]" for the young king.[61] And, unlikely as it may seem, Sir Kenelm also advanced for a time under Oliver Cromwell (when he was known as the Lord Protector's "Catholic favorite"). In seventeenth-century England, it would appear that noble bloodlines, court politics, and favorable patronage could forge a notable figure in transatlantic natural-philosophical circles even out of a relatively minor, though famously theatrical, Catholic philosopher.

Digby is known to specialists in seventeenth-century English literature as Ben Jonson's literary executor and the author of commentaries on Sir Thomas Browne's *Religio Medici* (1642) and Spenser's *The Faerie Queene* (1609), and much can be learned about the trajectory of his courtly career from his two greatest personal triumphs. Both were brief, dramatic, and early.[62] First, Sir Kenelm wooed the famously beautiful Venetia Stanley from a very public array of aristocratic suitors. In 1625, the two were married; and in 1628, Digby led a bloody but politically adept and, to be sure, highly profitable privateering mission to the Venetian-held port of Scandaroon (Iskenderun, formerly Alexandretta, in southern Turkey). Whatever else might be said about this mostly derivative natural-philosophical writer, Digby's maritime diary is among the most keenly observed reports on British privateering in the Mediterranean written in the seventeenth century.

Indeed, following the humiliating rout of the British navy under Buckingham at the Île de Ré in 1627, it is notable that the first appearance of Digby's "relation" of his "brave and resolute sea fight . . . (on the Bay of Scanderone)" was published together with the earliest English translation of the punitive articles of capitulation dictated by

Louis XIII in 1628. To borrow a set of adjectives from a contemporary polemical pamphlet titled *An Unhappy View of the Whole Behavior of my Lord Duke of Buckingham, at the French Island, called Isle of RHEE. Discovered by . . . an unfortunate commander in that untoward service* (1648), Sir Kenelm's was an example of "an undaunted heart" in the "true" English aristocratic tradition of courage and steadfastness in the face of an ancient enemy.[63] The ideological purpose of Digby's story of a knight's faithful service to king and nation with his sword was made clear by juxtaposition with the most palpable reminder yet published of England's dishonoring by the despised Lord Admiral Buckingham and his purportedly "effeminate," "desperate," and "perfidious" comportment on the field of battle just the year before.[64]

In 1629, in recognition of the didactic and political force of this juxtaposition, Digby was named naval commissioner. In 1630, doubtless for the sake of a rising career at court, Sir Kenelm converted and joined the Church of England. Anti-Calvinist Arminianism was in the ascendancy at court, and William Laud, who acted as Digby's patron while gaining the confidence of Charles I, was to become archbishop of Canterbury just three years later. Since the assassination of Buckingham in the aftermath of the Île de Ré, Charles had not selected a new favorite. Partially to fill the vacuum, Laud gained greater access to the king's inner circle of advisors. This, of course, was a well-known contributing factor in the great Calvinist migration to New England during the 1630s. What better time for an aristocratic Catholic to convert to this new and, from the Calvinist perspective, "papist" version of the Church of England?

Unfortunately, Digby's once promising career at court was interrupted on May 1, 1633, when Venetia succumbed to an untimely death. By all accounts, Sir Kenelm was devastated emotionally by his personal tragedy. He retreated into monkish seclusion in the alchemical laboratories at Gresham College and devoted himself to the study of natural philosophy, at first with particular emphasis on psychological and spiritual healing by analogy with material processes of death and rebirth. When Digby finally emerged from Gresham in 1635, the situation at court had changed sufficiently that he chose to abandon London for Catholic Paris. Before doing so, he prudently abjured the Church of England and reconverted to his natal faith.[65]

Sir Kenelm spent the next six years pursuing scientific interests in France and Holland while crisscrossing the Channel to appeal to English Catholics for funds on Charles's behalf.[66] One might presume a reversal of Digby's career at court during the Puritan Revolution and interregnum. However, despite close associations with Archbishop Laud and Charles I, and even despite his recent reconversion, this royalist chameleon made the best of the fall of his Stuart masters. Sir Kenelm continued his natural-philosophical research while casting about for new patrons to serve. The Long Parliament finally removed him from Charles's Council in March 1641, and while Charles I was on the run in November 1642, Parliament confined Digby under house arrest at Winchester House, a former episcopal palace in London. Far from languishing in his elegant prison, Digby revisited a Paracelsian project that was probably initiated when he attended Gresham College from 1633 to 1635. Because aristocratic prisoners were given extraordinary privileges, Sir Kenelm managed to hire a glassmaker named John Colnett, and with this local artisan as his skilled operator, he established a laboratory to experiment with the production of glassware for domestic and scientific use. By 1662, Digby was successful enough in this to apply surreptitiously for a patent, in Colnett's name, for a new process to manufacture glass bottles.[67]

After Digby petitioned for release, Parliament exiled him to France. There he joined forces with Henrietta Maria's expatriate court at the Louvre as chancellor to the Vatican. Charles I's French queen—who secretly practiced Roman Catholicism throughout her marriage and for Puritans remained the papist sister of Louis XIII—was sent across the Channel in 1642 by her husband, then a fugitive. Charles returned Henrietta Maria to her homeland to secure her safety. But she was also asked to locate royalist allies on the Continent and acquire munitions to mount a defense of the Stuart monarchy. Chancellor Digby was thus in attendance at the Vatican from May 1645 until January 1648 to negotiate in Henrietta Maria's name for 500,000 scudi in financial support. This was for arms to support Charles I in the Civil War, but also to bribe Calvinist members of Parliament to inspire conformity to the Arminian Church of England.

In return, Pope Innocent X negotiated to dismantle the Reformation in England. He demanded toleration for English Catholics under Rome's stewardship and stipulated that should the royalists triumph, he expected that the conversion of Charles I would follow shortly thereafter. Both of these demands were of course impracticable, and, in the end, moot. On June 24, 1646, after a series of defeats during the "first" Civil War that led to the capitulation of the royalist capital at Oxford to revolutionary troops, Charles chose to surrender himself to Scottish forces at Newark, where he was promptly ransomed to the Long Parliament for £400,000. Charles escaped captivity in November 1647, an often-told story that needs no particular development here. This event initiated a second round of warfare and decided the king's fate. Cromwell moved quickly to ensure that Charles's freedom was temporary. After a decisive battle in the north of England, the king was recaptured, and his trial and beheading outside Whitehall Banqueting Hall on January 30, 1649, followed.[68]

As late as 1647, Henrietta Maria hoped that Digby would be able to gain papal support for Charles's dwindling forces in the field. However, the military situation exacerbated a growing polarization between the principals, who had learned to loathe one another. The negotiations ended disastrously in July 1647, after another frustrating papal audience. In November of that year, Digby wrote a bitter statement of grievances to the pope. Innocent responded through the Venetian ambassador that Sir Kenelm was "full of crazy whims and phantasms." Digby's rhetoric, in turn, sounded more like that of a Puritan M.P. than a staunch defender of the Roman faith. He wrote Henrietta Maria at the Louvre to complain that "this prodigal Pope," had reduced their Church to a "sordid and impious" court.

Despite this exchange and Innocent's subsequent alienation, there was still support for Sir Kenelm and the royalist cause in the Congregation of Cardinals. At the last minute, the cardinals voted in favor of supplying the English royalists with financial support. No one in Rome except perhaps Sir Kenelm was surprised when Innocent intervened to overturn the cardinals' vote. The volatile Digby finally lost his temper and berated the pope in public, before leaving Rome in January 1648 for an extended tour of the Mediterranean, as if to obscure this failure by reminding observers of past triumphs for king and country. His heated speech amounted to political suicide for Digby and the royalist cause in the Vatican. But for Protestants at home, Sir Kenelm's behavior in the face of papal authority was surprisingly heroic, even if both his cause and religion were suspect. To dejected royalists who felt they had lost their main chance, however, the seventeenth-century antiquary John Aubrey's summary of Digby's catastrophic Roman sojourn seems particularly apposite. Sir Kenelm "grew high, and Hectored with His Holinesse, and gave him the Lye," Aubrey wrote. "The Pope said he was mad."[69]

The failure to form an alliance with Rome transformed Digby into a bitter anti-papist. Sir Kenelm now pinned his hopes on a risky plan to construct an anglocentric hybrid out of the fragments of the Roman Church that remained after the English Revolution; in effect, Digby posited a "new model" English Catholicism. After returning to join Henrietta Maria in Paris in February 1648—where the Gallican movement pursued similar goals for an independent French Church—Digby conspired with other Catholic nationalists to form a secularized English Catholic episcopate with stronger ties to the English state than to Rome. This conspiracy became known as Blacklo's Cabal. Blacklo was the pseudonym used by Digby's friend and co-religionist Thomas White, the leader of the ultra-secret cabal. White was an ordained priest, president of the English College of Lisbon, and a respected philosopher. He was also accused of heresy by Rome for publishing a series of attacks on the doctrine of the infallibility of the Church, which earned him a place on the Vatican's Index.[70]

When exiled in Paris in 1652, Digby published his *Discourse, Concerning Infallibility in Religion* in English, for an audience across the Channel, which he hoped would include all Christians.[71] Digby's religious, political, and natural-philosophical career was thus tied to a quest to unify Christianity and negate confessional difference. This was arguably a goal he shared with the silent Neoplatonist and latitudinarian Winthrop.

Once the initial impetus for the Digby-Winthrop relationship is understood, it is understandable that Blacklo's shrewd reformist program voiced concerns about tramontane institutional corruption that seemed to parallel aspects of the elder John

Winthrop's anti-Arminian experiment in New England and Parliament's revolt against Archbishop Laud in London. Since Rome had fallen into a state of intractable decadence, the task would fall to White *qua* Blacklo and his "Blackloist" co-conspirators—including Digby, John Belson, Hugh Cressy, Peter Fitton, Mark Harrington, Henry Holden, John Sergeant, Dr. George Leyburn, Abbot Walter Montagu, Dr. Humphrey Waring, and Bishop Richard Russell—to reconstruct Catholicism on English soil with "Papists of the new Modell." Although the conspirators were drawn initially from the royalist ranks, Blacklo's cabal accommodated the new power structures of the interregnum at the expense of both the Stuarts and orthodox English Roman Catholicism. Denying the Roman Church's infallibility was the theological and political basis of the Blackloists' goal of achieving toleration for Catholic worship in England. The Blackloist program also questioned the existence of purgatory, which obviated the vexing question of indulgences. Above all, it advocated transfer of power of appointment of English Catholic bishops from Rome to Westminster. Once a bishop and canonical chapter had been established in England, the plan called for a French prelate to consecrate the new English bishop. The bishop would then take an oath that circumvented the pope, whose commands were meaningless anyway without Parliament's approval.[72]

The plot began to unravel as early as 1650. Animosity toward the program of religious and political accommodation increased from both orthodox Catholics and deposed royalists. The Blackloists were prepared to trade theology for pragmatism, but their English co-religionists, in particular the Jesuits, were firmly opposed to "the most formidable faction, which has ever yet endangered our small national church."[73] In 1655, despite professions of loyalty to the deposed Stuart monarchy, White urged English Catholics to accommodate the Lord Protector's new religious and political order. In this White was clearly counting on Cromwell's growing sense of moderation and the assertion of his belief in "liberty of conscience." Such latitudinarianism coming from the mouth of the Atlantic world's most notorious Calvinist predestinarian caused astonishment and tortured soul-searching among Puritans in both old and New England. And indeed, Cromwell's tendency to recognize the practical benefits of international Protestantism and sectarian inclusivity in both foreign and domestic affairs did provide an opening for the enemies of those whom he derisively called "the preaching people."[74] Since the Blackloists openly disavowed the pope, White and his followers espoused a new model English Catholicism that would follow the letter of the Protectorate's written constitution of 1654, which guaranteed liberty of Christian worship, "provided that this liberty be not extended to Popery and Prelacy."

This was precisely the strategy Digby pursued aggressively on his own account, and he reminded English Protestants of his legendary denunciation of Innocent X. Working to ingratiate himself at Cromwell's "court," Digby also traded on his potential to

the Lord Protector as a diplomatic intermediary between the revolutionary government and expatriate Stuart royalists and their new royal masters dispersed throughout
the European monarchies. Above all, Cromwell was interested in Digby's strong
French connections. The Lord Protector made clear his intention to rally international
Protestantism behind England in support of the revivification of La Rochelle and the
greater Huguenot cause. Cromwell asserted, as had the Parliamentarians before him,
that the cause of the Reformation in France had been lost by Buckingham and the
Stuarts in 1628.[75] Cromwell's interest in La Rochelle and the memory in England of
the younger Winthrop's role as scientist and observer for his father's Puritan faction
in 1627 thus piqued Digby's interest in Winthrop's return.

In 1660, Blacklo's risky enterprise was finally undone by the Restoration of the Stuart monarchy. The cabal's association with the Long Parliament and ultimately with
Cromwell's Protectorate itself branded the group as Catholic anti-royalists. Ideologically, the Blackloists were neither anti-Stuart—as Digby's association with Henrietta
Maria attested—nor, to be sure, were they anti-royalist. Rather, the Blacklo conspirators were ambitious opportunists who chose to support the establishment of an illegitimate monarch, who had effectively disinherited the Stuart dynasty, in order to lead
elite Catholics such as Sir Kenelm away from the margins and toward the center of
power in English civic life.

Meanwhile, the vast majority of the Blackloists' Catholic co-religionists continued
to repudiate the cabal's political and theological unorthodoxy as self-destructive heresy.
Digby was deeply wounded by this outcome, though not yet finished politically. This
was in large part because Thomas White became the universal scapegoat for the conspiracy and for the fears it engendered among various constituencies of England's
established political and religious orders. White was forced to flee for his life to the
Netherlands. With the exile of Blacklo, the cabal disintegrated in a flood of recrimi-
nations. Its vindictive members attacked one another over perceived lapses in security,
which were ultimately blamed for the plot's failure. Digby's indiscretions were denounced by his co-conspirator Henry Holden: "You may do well not to open your
mouth . . . (for your freedom of speech ruins all your affairs)."[76] But Digby's political
and religious interest in the reconciliation of opposites—England's old Church with
the new—was also seen in alchemical terms as part of a project to unify fragmented
geographies, polities, and confessions by transmuting all things to one substance.

❧ The Universal Courtier ❧

Although Holden advised Digby "not to open your mouth," evidence abounds that the
latter's linguistic virtuosity was legendary under both the Stuarts and the Protectorate.
Indeed, Digby's ability to survive during the interregnum owed much to the dramatic

practice of courtly natural philosophy. Digby's verbal performance at court balanced the dual handicap of religion and a derivative intellect. Sir Kenelm's theatricality was motivated by the courtier's traditional desire to please the powerful and accumulate prestige through service, which was later amplified under Cromwell by adding the fluid eclecticism of Blackloism. Thus, beginning with the accession of Charles I, Digby worked to overcome marginalization by developing a framework within which to domesticate Paracelsus and hold the middle ground at court. This stance allowed him to pursue novelty with the enthusiasm of a gentlemanly virtuoso—as he did when he demonstrated for Charles I the use of a new powder with which to fix mercury—while never appearing openly to embrace either occult obscurantism or sectarian Calvinist millennialism. To recontextualize language from Hillel Schwartz's brilliant study of Huguenot millenarian scientists and prophets who sought refuge in London during the seventeenth and eighteenth centuries, Digby's "theatrical ambivalence" allowed him to play both sides of the street, depending on his audience.[77] His mutability would prove especially useful given Cromwell's close association with the Cambridge Neoplatonists in the 1650s, during which time he openly distanced himself from orthodoxy, supporting something approaching freedom of conscience and Protestant universalism.[78]

Digby moved boldly to trade on the courtly and economic value of a variety of Paracelsian scientific initiatives pioneered by others. His aristocratic pedigree and the verbal facility of his storytelling at court (in which he played the metamorphic role of Ovidian hero) enabled him constantly to reinvent himself as a courtier, while directing and starring in a personal theater of scientific innovation, burnishing his reputation as a natural philosopher. An intriguing if suitably ambiguous body of research and writing resulted. This oeuvre might be interpreted to reflect Digby's lukewarm adaptation of traditional Aristotelian theory to the "new" philosophies. While this position is not indefensible—Digby often invoked Aristotle to frame arguments—it has the potential to overstate the "rear-guard" significance of Sir Kenelm's "Catholic" Aristotelianism.

An argument can be made that even Digby's public discourses intended for courtly and scholastic consumption (where he tended to cite Aristotle most often) were distanced from "purely" Aristotelian natural philosophy. Sir Kenelm grappled bravely with the pivotal relation between Paracelsus's emphasis on experience and Bacon's expansion of this philosophical attitude into skepticism, which Bacon refracted through the lens of the Reformation into the principal of uncertainty of outcome inherent in experimentalism.[79] This was a period when innovation in natural philosophy remained under the powerfully anti-Aristotelian Neoplatonic influence of Paracelsus, with his fundamental emphasis on hidden interior experience, ineffable occultism, and the monistic unity of animate spirit and matter. However, Digby also came into contact with Descartes. But if Digby felt it politically prudent to assert public explications of the natural world based on appearances and traditional scholastic systems, he was also too well aware of Paracelsus's axioms about contingency and the centrality of personal experience to accept the formal, binary logic of a Descartes. "Digby cannot properly be called a Baconian in method at all, even though he was devoted to experience, and, or, experiment," the historian of science Betty Jo Dobbs observes.

> [H]e did not, like Bacon, want to discard all systems completely and begin anew in a systematic way to build from experience. Digby preferred to use experience to modify Aristotle. . . . Nor can Digby be called a Cartesian in any real sense, though he knew Descartes from 1640 and admired him greatly. Digby was only too conscious of the complex actuality of the world to allow him to follow Descartes all the way . . . Digby's criticism . . . was essentially that Descartes . . . did not accord with experience.[80]

If Digby attacked the obscurantism of Paracelsus rhetorically while publicly he adopted only parts of Bacon's experimentalism, then it is still fair to say that his critique of Descartes on the basis of experience was fundamentally a Paracelsian critique. This would tend to support Webster's interpretation:

> It is possible to argue at one extreme that the English Catholics (e.g. . . . Sir Kenelm Digby), or at the other, that religious radicals . . . were [both] highly receptive to the new philosophy or experimental science . . . the entire Puritan movement was conspicuous in its cultivation of the sciences . . . developing a scientific outlook consistent with its doctrinal position . . . [this outlook] was so productive that the influence of their work and outlook extended to many figures (e.g. Evelyn, Cowley, Digby, Aubrey) with whom they had otherwise little in common.[81]

It may be much too strong to position Digby in dialectical opposition to the "religious radicals," or indeed to *anyone* with power in mid-seventeenth-century England. It was his business to find things in common with those in a position to provide patronage and to accommodate his philosophical discourse to religious and political change. In this sense, he shares the younger Winthrop's courtier's reputation for "indecisiveness." While some historians may find it tempting to view Digby as a "transitional figure" who occupied a position between two oppositional poles represented by Aristotle on the one hand and Webster's "modern" reformers—including Paracelsus, Galileo, Bacon, Newton, and, by extension, Winthrop—on the other, it is probably more accurate (if also less elegant) to conceptualize his work initially in its specific courtly context and then as part of an eclectic, inclusive, multifaceted synthesis of traditions that had been active in Europe since the late Middle Ages. Digby's status as a philosophical hybridizer working to expand the scientific margins of an oppressed religious subculture would seem to fit the notion that such ill-defined categories as "ancient" and "modern" were conflated in the actual practice of seventeenth-century natural philosophy.[82] Digby's interest in inclusiveness was also fundamental to the Neoplatonic search for unity and order in all things. While Webster credits the "productive" nature of the new philosophy with having brought alienated and marginalized Catholic scientists into the same fold with Calvinists, it should not be forgotten that scholarly elites from both camps shared enduring institutional and political structures outside the laboratory: these would include the court, the religious wars, and the shifting quest for power. The historian of philosophy Beverley G. Southgate has pursued the argument that even after 1660, Digby's philosophical program was intertwined with the changing religious and social context that produced Blackloism. For Southgate, Sir Kenelm's science sought, in part, to counteract the skeptical effects of Calvinist predestinarianism:

> despite the demise of any practical political aspirations, the philosophical and theological positions associated with Blackloism long persisted. Expounded by White and Digby in the 1640s and '50s, these were essentially concerned with countering the challenge of [extreme] scepticism. In face of what seemed a growing threat to the possibility of any certain knowledge, the Blackloists sought to present a coherent intellectual package which would guarantee that certainty on which they believed human salvation ultimately depended. So they formulated a remarkable intellectual synthesis, combining elements of new thought with old, and . . . of science with religion.[83]

If, like Howes, Winthrop and Stiles, Digby wished to be "put forever out of doubt and question," his revolt against skepticism can also be overdrawn, in part because his "courtly" philosophy during the interregnum—like so much of the Blackloists "secret" discourse against Roman infallibility—was constructed for public consumption. Synthesis of science and religion during the seventeenth century was, first and foremost, a quintessentially Paracelsian project. However, while Paracelsus was perceived by critics to have willfully couched his synthesis in the occult, White and Digby extended their public discourse of the symbiosis of comprehensible phenomena and "new model" Catholicism to natural philosophy. In this way, the Blackloist compromise paralleled a shift in seventeenth-century science toward appropriation of the occult to clarify the inexplicable through experiment. Thus, elements of "mechanical" philosophy began to absorb the occult as its proper subject because scientists such as Boyle and Descartes perceived the unknown to be only temporarily unintelligible.[84] This aspect of the Blackloist program—to make sense of the inexplicable—sent Sir Kenelm on a Christian humanist's quest for both old and new texts in natural philosophy to provide occult observations of natural phenomena suitable for reinterpretation. The new books were primarily alchemical texts, again making the Paracelsians the core of Digby's library and his main frame of reference.

❦ Digby's Library ❧

Sir Kenelm's resources and courtly ambitions—and the enormous prestige that his important alchemical library conveyed through the gift, loan, or dedication of books—makes it understandable that he spent a large percentage of his income on his library.[85] Digby's first library was among the most celebrated collections of books and manuscripts in England. With the exception of gifted books that survive today in public collections, most of Digby's English library was either confiscated or burned during the Civil War or, after the Blacklo debacle, the Restoration. Sir Kenelm also built a second important library of more than 3,500 volumes during his exile in France. This was not an outstanding library in quantitative terms, especially by the high standards of the French court (Mazarin's contained 40,000 volumes); but it was famous for the quality, expense, and style of its dazzling, full red morocco bindings. The most theatrically self-referential example of Digby's devotion of capital to the embellishment of the finest bindings occurred in 1634, when he spent over £1,000 on the production of just one volume: an imposing Digby family history that is now lost. Almost 600 vellum pages long, Sir Kenelm's homage to his family name was enormous not only in length but also in sheer physical scale. Digby designed the book himself to function as a bibliopegistic spectacle—a sort of memory theater of filial pietism—which encompassed in microcosm his family's outsized history for visitors to the library. Observers marveled that the appearance of the Digby genealogy's intricate medieval calligraphy and painting, mounted with the finest enamelwork in the "antique" Byzantine style, exceeded that of any Bible in England.

Sir Kenelm's lavish expenditure on the binding of books in his collection accentuated their status as luxury objects, in part because of their frequent use as gifts. The style of his morocco bindings was so well known among seventeenth-century English bibliophiles that most could probably identify Digby's gifts of patronage at a glance, long before taking a book down off the shelf to read the inscription or find the ex libris. Some sense of the protean Sir Kenelm's strategy as a courtly book collector can be gleaned from the legendary quality of his gift in 1634 to Oxford's Bodleian Library—England's first noteworthy "public" library—where 238 manuscripts in medieval literature and sixteenth- and seventeenth-century natural philosophy marked "Digby MSS" remain deposited. Perhaps most significant was the enormous personal honor, prestige, and capital at court Digby must have expected to accumulate as a result of the Bodleian gift.

The gift was sponsored at Oxford by Archbishop Laud, a fellow bibliophile whom Digby was anxious to serve. A new west wing was constructed at the Bodleian to house the Digby gift, and the ceremony of acceptance performed by Laud and the heads,

492 ✦ THE FRAGMENTATION OF THE BODY

proctors, and other principals of Oxford was said to be "similar to that made for foreign rulers or dignitaries of the Church." Laud also solicited Digby to join him in a
combined gift of Arabic, Hebrew, and Asian manuscripts to St. John's College, Oxford, at the start of the Civil War.[86] Dobbs summarizes Digby's life as that of "a private gentleman, sometimes *virtuoso*, sometimes servant of the crown," by concluding
that Sir Kenelm "fits the ideal of the post-Elizabethan period very well; he held a book
in one hand and a sword in the other . . . he was *persona grata* at courts and watering
places, in salons and laboratories and the meetings of learned societies on both sides
of the Channel . . . he was the man who knew everyone and took an interest in every
advance."[87] It was in his role as opportunistic courtier that Digby would take "an interest" in John Winthrop the Younger and enter Stiles's field of vision.[88]

✦ The Weapon Salve: Artifactual Memory in the Powder of Sympathy ✦

Winthrop associated the name of Sir Kenelm Digby with the famous weapon salve
long before the two natural philosophers first corresponded. Winthrop maintained an
interest in this mystical therapy since the early 1630s, when Howes reminded him that
Fludd had first come to his attention with a book about the weapon salve.[89] Digby
published two widely read discourses in natural philosophy that appeared almost simultaneously in France and England: *Two Treatises. In the one of which, the nature of
bodies; in the other, the Nature of mans soule; is looked into: in way of the discovery, of the
immortality of reasonable soules* (Paris, 1644); and *Discours fait en une celebre assemblée,
par le Chevalier Digby, Chancelier de la Reine de la Grande Bretagne &c. touchant la guerison des playes par la poudre de sympathie* (Paris, 1657). Whether Winthrop possessed
these volumes is unclear; neither survives with the small remnant of his alchemical library. The discourse on the "poudre de sympathie" appeared in its first English translation, as *A Late Discourse Made in a Solemne Assembly of Nobles and Learned Men at
Montpellier in France . . . Touching the Cure of Wounds by the Powder of Sympathy* (London, 1658). Both texts were ultimately published together in an omnibus English edition of Digby's essays under the title *Of Bodies, and of Mans Soul. To Discover the Immortality of Reasonable Souls. With two Discourses: Of the Powder of Sympathy, and of the
Vegetation of Plants* (London, 1669).[90] *Two Treatises* ran through an impressive eight
editions by the eighteenth century. Despite the success of *Two Treatises*, Digby made
his name outside court and academic circles with *Of the Powder of Sympathy*, a brief,
wildly popular essay derived from Paracelsian occult medicine, which was to remain
in print continually until 1704, when the last of an astonishing forty different editions
appeared.[91] Thus, Digby's essay on the sympathetic powder, otherwise known as the
weapon salve, was reprinted for a new audience of readers about once a year on average for nearly a half century.

Though he denied it publicly, Digby's idea for the sympathetic powder clearly originated with Paracelsus. First appearing in the 1582 edition of *Archidoxorum* as the
"weapon-salve," Paracelsus's original recipe called for a gelatinous mixture of human
skull-moss, mummy, human fat, human blood, linseed oil, oil of roses, and a claylike
substance known as "Bole Armoniack."[92] Digby sanitized Paracelsus's macabre recipe
for polite consumers by reducing its grisly ingredients to a pure white anhydrous powder. The sympathetic powder did possess a mild styptic property, but in the end Digby's
version of the famous mixture was derived from nothing more corporeal than common green crystals of English vitriol baked white in the sun. Although he mixed different ingredients in the master's pharmacopoeia, it would appear that Digby's source for
the powder was again Paracelsus, who used vitriol as a homeopathic mineral therapy
for patients "when you see Erysipelas," an ulcerous inflammation of the skin.[93]

Erysipelas bacillus commonly presents symptoms of ulcerous lesions on the hand,
resembling the malady that caused the elder Winthrop to write for medical advice in
1628. The skillful woman in that case prescribed black and yellow "plaisters" (green and
white were usual in vitriol compounds), but it is not inconceivable that her remedy was
derived from similar minerals to those used by Paracelsus in his well-known homeopathic therapy for skin diseases.[94] As early as 1617, the English Paracelsian physician
John Woodall wrote in *The surgions Mate,* a treatise for "the benefit of young Sea-
Surgions, imployed in the East-India Companies," that common vitriol, or a mixture
of vitriol and alum both "burn'd" [black?] and used as a precipitate, "keepeth the flesh
moyst and from putritude, consumeth, contracteth and purgeth ulcers," when applied
for "outward ordinary uses." Woodall openly credited Paracelsus for prescribing vitriol
in the recipe.[95] Winthrop's skillful woman would have known the value of vitriol and
alum from common usage, while Digby, the well-read mariner, learned about earlier
versions of his sympathetic powder from Woodall's ubiquitous "Sea-Surgions" manual, if he had not already acquired it from other texts.

Clearly, Digby's sympathetic powder was far from unique in the seventeenth century, which occasioned a virtual growth industry in weapon salves. Demand was great
in the wake of continual religious warfare experienced everywhere. And dangerous occupations such as seamanship in the service of conquest and colonization, as well as
the growth of oceangoing commerce to Asia, Africa, and the Americas, placed a premium on topical cures.

What *is* surprising is that Digby's remedy should have cornered the extensive market in the literature of weapon salves and that his name was linked in perpetuity with
the sympathetic powder. The source of Digby's personal association with the sympathetic powder and his ability to market the therapy as unique, despite fierce competition from numerous similar therapies, was a function of blatant dissimulation, self-
promotion, and the dramatic persona of a seasoned courtier. Digby understood from

watching the success of such royal favorites as the duke of Buckingham that the true origin and content of a Stuart courtier's message was negotiable if hidden artfully under the subterfuge of physical beauty and represented with the appropriate rhetorical conventions.[96]

The handsome and charismatic Digby—acclaimed by noble audiences as a brilliant storyteller at court—inserted himself personally into a seductive alchemical legend he fabricated about the origin of the sympathetic powder. This was not the first time Sir Kenelm had made himself the heroic protagonist of legend; in fact, Digby's "autobiographical" *Private Memoirs*, which was purported to recount the events of his life until his return from the Mediterranean in 1628, was written very much in this style.[97] Sir Kenelm related the story of the sympathetic powder in the form of an early modern romance. The first audience was apparently the "Assembly of Nobles and Learned Men at [the medical college at] Montpellier," and thereupon, in 1657 and 1658, it was promptly published in both French and English. As the story goes, Digby did a great favor for a Carmelite monk who had returned to the West after having traveled widely in India, Persia, and China. In his debt for the favor, the monk, though reluctant to part with his secret, relinquished the recipe for the sympathetic powder. But Digby's romance takes on truly heroic proportions at the court of James I, when he used the sympathetic powder with astonishing success to cure the injured hand of a fellow courtier, James Howell. This feat was accomplished in the presence of the king, the royal physician, Theodore de Mayerne, and Lord Chancellor Francis Bacon. Digby then gave the well-known secret "freely" as a gift to James I, from whom the royal physician and Bacon obtained it, after which the episode was common knowledge among physicians. Though the now royally verified narrative legitimized Digby's story, Bacon certainly knew that the origin of the therapy was Paracelsus, not the wandering Carmelite monk.[98] Focusing on aristocratic political exploitation of the rhetorical conventions of fictional romance during the Restoration, the literary scholar Elizabeth Hedrick has explored Digby's use of the sympathetic powder to advance his ambitions at court during the late 1650s:

> Not only did his story purify the weapon-salve of its nefarious Paracelsian origins . . . Digby's dating of his story about Howell and the Carmelite monk to the early 1620s served the specific purpose of allowing him to include James I in his account, and to portray himself to Charles II—after his attempts to establish an English Catholic church and to curry favor with Cromwell had helped factionalize the royalists—as a personal favorite of Charles II's grandfather. Indeed, Digby's tale of sharing the secret of the powder with King James is . . . clearly calculated to show, without Digby saying so, that he and the Stuarts had always shared a mutual regard . . . in sniffing the political wind of the late 1650s, Digby detected an opportunity to recuperate his political fortunes and his natural philo-

sophical reputation in one stroke by writing his account of the sympathetic powder . . . a story like the one Digby uses to obscure his reliance on Paracelsus . . . was at once more noticeable and more fully necessary to producing natural philosophical innovation than it would be now; and it exists at the extreme end of a hermeneutic continuum in which the mere act of glossing a text can constitute an alteration of it—for all the interpreter's claims to pious originality.[99]

If Digby used the tale of the Carmelite monk to distance himself from Paracelsus at both Montpellier and the court of Charles II, it nevertheless remained hard to explain how the weapon salve worked. For, as Paracelsus had prescribed in the original weapon-salve therapy of 1582, to heal James Howell's injured hand, Digby applied the sympathetic powder, not directly onto the wound, but indirectly, to an old bandage in which Howell's bloody hand had been wrapped. Paracelsian weapon-salves were believed to heal through the air, even at a great distance, by activating the "material memory" of things that had come into contact with the wound during or just after the injury: the bandage was one of two appropriate place to apply the powder; the other, better one was the weapon that had actually caused the injury. As for the wound itself, the therapy basically ignored it, or prescribed simply that it be washed thoroughly and kept clean, or covered with a bandage soaked in the patient's urine, a natural disinfectant.

This in fact explains the relative effectiveness (and popularity) of the weapon salve compared to other early modern therapies. Unlike most treatments, weapon-salve therapy saved patients from contact with overzealous but incompetent physicians and, more important, prescribed sanitary treatment of the wound.[100]

Paracelsus and his followers attributed the success of the weapon salve to divine intervention. For Paracelsus, the healing virtues of the weapon salve traveled on an astral bridge from microcosm to macrocosm and back again. A soulish sympathy existed between the blood left on the weapon (or the old bandage) and the blood still inside the wounded patient's body. Indeed, there was an irresistible cosmological attraction between them. Distance was completely irrelevant to the operation of the salve, since for adepts the microcosm and macrocosm always existed in perfect proportion and mathematical symmetry to each other. Thus, the sympathetic agent in the patient's blood remaining on the weapon was activated by astral influences, which carried the salve's healing virtues with them through the air, where they were made more potent by further spiritual purification, after which the cure finally returned to the wound.[101]

In the *Late Discourse,* Digby explained sympathetic powder in an elaborate "Geometrical Demonstration," that reconfigured the occult motions of the Paracelsian weapon salve into an eclectic mix of corpuscularianism and mechanistic philosophy. Here, the inner workings of occult natural philosophy were purportedly laid bare. "The

Air is full throughout of small Bodies or Atomes," wrote Digby. "When fire or some hot body attracts the Air and that which is within the Air. . . . The source of those spirits or little bodies, which attract them to it self, draws likewise after them that which accompanies, and whatever sticks, and is united to them." Within this conceptual framework, where "spirits" were "divisible" "little Bodies," it would follow logically that under certain conditions such spirits could be perceived to move with almost mechanistic predictability:

> [T]he Sun and Light will attract, a great extent and distance off, the spirits of the blood. . . . [T]he Spirit of Vitriol, being incorporated with the blood cannot choose but make the same voyage together with the atoms of blood. [The wound] expires and exhales, in the meantime, [an] abundance of hot fiery Spirits, which stream as a river out of the inflamed hurt: nor can this be, but the wound must, consequently, draw to it the air which is next [to] it . . . so there will be a kind of current of air drawn round about the wound [which] will come to incorporate at last the atoms and Spirits of the Blood and the Vitriol. . . . [T]he atoms of the blood, finding the proper source and original root whence they issued will stay there, re-entering into their natural beds and primitive receptacles . . . [T]he Spirits of the Vitriol [being inseparable from the blood], both the one and the other will joyntly be imbibed together within all the corners, fibres, and orifices of the Veins which lye open about the wound; whence of necessity be refresht, and in fine imperceptibly cured.[102]

As a Catholic survivor stigmatized in the England's Protestant courts and laboratories, Digby was, like Palissy, a masterful manipulator of the ambiguity of perception for career advancement and personal security. Digby's clear intention was to make a name for himself by providing an explanation for why the weapon salve worked in the first place. While this explanation gestured boldly in print toward Paracelsus's competitors, the powder remains "sympathetic," and if Digby's "little bodies" are no longer overtly astral, they are still implicitly so. Like Stiles's disembodied minds pictured in King's portrait (fig. 11.2), they remain moveable "spirits" directed by an ineffable God. Digby never considered placing his version of Paracelsus's salve directly on the wounded patient. Not only was this mundane procedure less theatrical, but it was common knowledge that such cures must travel through the air bonded to spirits. Digby understood that "imperceptible" spirits, though material, transcended barriers of distance and difference of confession, because "little bodies" were part of a unified whole he knew as the "Universal Spirit."

The Neoplatonic source for Digby's conception of cosmological unity was neither Aristotle nor Descartes but again the theoretical convergence of Marsilio Ficino and Paracelsus. These authors were deeply influential in forging the synthesis of metaphysical and epistemological questions that concerned Benjamin Whichcote, Ralph

Cudworth, John Worthington, John Smith, and Henry More, the most important of the English Platonists centered at Emmanuel College, Cambridge, Forth Winthrop's beloved school.[103] Perhaps Forth's letter to his brother John on the eve of the latter's Mediterranean voyage may also be read as a Neoplatonic allegory on an advancing illness, necessitating scholarly travel via the universal spirit among the books at Emmanuel, rather than following John's "fortunate foot" of experience?

Digby knew Cromwell had taken strong personal interest in the latitudinarianism of the Cambridge group. Most were Calvinists who shared his belief in "liberty of conscience" and the doctrine of "liberty in non-essentials." The Lord Protector consulted Cudworth on policy and made Worthington vice-chancellor of Cambridge. In 1656, Cromwell's sister Robina married John Wilkins, a member of the group.[104] Given the political necessity for Digby's frequent sojourns across the channel however, and the congruence of Huguenot alchemy in Catholic France to his own situation in England, French alchemic Neoplatonism became more specific to Sir Kenelm's personal history and laboratory practice than did the Cambridge school.

❧ Digby's Book of Secrets ❧

Unlike the books he published during his lifetime, Digby's book of *Rare Chymical Secrets and Experiments in Philosophy*—compiled in the crucial 1650s and 1660s and published posthumously by his friend and laboratory operator George Hartman in 1682—is unambiguous on mystical and occult influences. *Secrets* shows that while he described the hybrid sympathetic powder in Aristotelian or mechanical language for courtly display or polite viewing, bound in morocco, for visitors to his library, Digby's secret laboratory journals contained voluminous evidence of Sir Kenelm's private passion for the experiments of Paracelsus, Croll, and Bacon. The work of Aristotle is insignificant in *Secrets*. Scholasticism is supplanted by private experimental discourse; Digby credits seven occult writers with influencing his work. "Crollius" is included as the master who best "teacheth the preparation and use of Chimike medicines." But Digby reserved the highest praise for Paracelsus himself, whose universal approach "aymes at all learning." Sir Kenelm admitted that Paracelsus's prose might have been "writt . . . when he was drunk; yet," he refused to quibble, "his workes generally a[re] worthy ones."[105]

During his exile in France, Digby demonstrated his complete understanding of why Paracelsus "ayme[d] at all learning." He did so by further exploring the implications in Nature presented by the profound linkages that Paracelsus perceived between the material practice of alchemy and the universal soulishness that connected all things at the level of "simplicity," as elucidated by the Neoplatonism of Ficino and Plotinus.[106] By the time Digby returned to England in 1654, he had harnessed his secret alchemical experiments to closely related French Neoplatonic theories of the "Universal

Spirit," as elucidated by the seventeenth-century natural philosophers Nicasius le Febure (Nicolas Le Fèvre [1615–69]) and especially Jean d'Espagnet (1564–1637).[107]

Like Winthrop and the generation of British-American natural philosophers that came of age after the fall of La Rochelle and matured during the Protectorate, when he returned to England, Digby assimilated the influence of the pansophic social reformers of the Hartlib circle. Samuel Hartlib's political principles and his attention to nuances of patronage and parliamentary support were especially attractive to Digby. They reflected his courtly experience and resonated with the Blackloist program of nationalistic inclusion across confessions. Theoretically, Hartlib's utopian universalism had the radical potential to absorb stigmatized religious minorities into civic culture, including English Catholic adepts. Religious inclusion was the primary goal of Hartlib's Scottish associate John Dury, an ecumenical Presbyterian, whose program called for reunion of the British Church. Cromwell encouraged alchemical Neoplatonism, the Blackloist philosophy of pragmatic accommodation, and Hartlib's pansophic ideas about the communitarian role of adepts in civic institutions that functioned openly for the public good. Sir Kenelm focused what remained of his personal wealth, and his hope for the convergence of the "Universal Spirit," on the philosophical language, theoretical premises, and material armature of "a general chemical council" whose goal was to erect a "Universal Laboratory" in London.[108]

This was an enterprise of such enormous ambition and scope—of such utopian potential for making transatlantic common cause through a general material-holiness synthesis of the metropolitan center with its colonial peripheries—that Digby thought the laboratory would enable him to seduce John Winthrop Jr. away from the New World and back to "your native country" in 1655. Though the inclusive ideology of its principal planners was pluralistic in nature, in different hands, the universal laboratory might have become a state-sponsored enterprise, adumbrating the aggressively imperialistic cultural stance that England took toward the colonies after the Restoration, when Whitehall attempted to bridge the growing social, cultural, and economic gap between America and the mother country by flooding the colonies with British functionaries and consumer goods.

But his courtier's history suggests that Sir Kenelm did not look deeply into the future. He had more immediate problems. Whatever else might become of Digby's elaborate stratagems of 1654–55, his most pressing ambition was to survive and avoid another exile. To accomplish this goal, he planned to return John Winthrop Jr. to Cromwell as a gift to help validate the Puritan Protectorate. Unlike the contents of the Bodleian gift, the learned expatriate from New England's founding family was to be presented at the Protector's newly established "court" as a sort of speaking text, the prodigal returned. Winthrop's return would serve as a conduit of pansophism, solidify shaky linkages between Old and New World Reform movements, and facilitate transatlantic commerce and industry. Finally, a new expedition to reverse the catastrophe of 1628 and liberate La Rochelle was in the offing, this time under the more inclusive flag of international Protestantism. Winthrop himself was to lead its alchemists and pyrotechnicians. Sir Kenelm Digby thus gambled that he could persuade Winthrop to join his Universal Laboratory and lead the expedition back to La Rochelle; in return, the grateful Lord Protector would solidify his tenuous toehold as "Catholic favorite" at court, and religious tolerance would return to England.

❧ Your Native Country: 1628 and 1655 ❧

In 1655, two exchanges took place between John Winthrop Jr. and Digby. Prompted by Winthrop, Sir Kenelm sent a handsome gift of some 40 natural-philosophical and theological books to Harvard College to help build a library begun in 1638, which stood at a meager 350 volumes in 1655. Given Digby's practice of using gifts of books for political purposes—and Winthrop's habit of accepting (and lending) scientific books to expand his patronage network—this gift commanded reciprocity.[109] The impulse behind the gift became clear in a remarkable letter from Digby to Winthrop written on January 31 the same year:

> I hope it will not be long before this Iland, yr native country, do enjoy yr much desired presence. I pray for it hartily, and I am confident that yr great judgemt, and noble desire of doing the most good to mankinde that you may, will prompt you to make as much hast hither as you can. Where you are, is too scanty a stage for you to remaine too long upon. It was a well chosen one when there were inconveniences for yr fixing upon this. But now that all is here as you could wish, all that do know you do expect of you that you should exercise your vertues where they may be of most advantage to the world, and where you may do most good to most men.[110]

Digby's letter is a source for Stiles's representation of the Catholic courtier as an "intimate Correspond[ent]" of Winthrop's, and one of the "first Chemical & philosophical Characters of the last Century." It is unclear whether Stiles was interested in Digby's career before finding the letter, or if its discovery prompted him to do further research. Knowing his compulsively "inclusive" nature and understanding the occult and universalist directions his work took in the 1750s, it is probable that Stiles read everything Digby wrote. As a physician, Stiles might reasonably have learned about Digby and the weapon salve in the natural course of his medical training with vitriol compounds. Indeed, when combined with the mystical universal spirit of Digby's *Secrets* and the younger Winthrop's alchemical archives, the occult theory of the Paracelsian weapon salve was very close to Stiles's own emerging Neoplatonic program. After the letter revealed Digby's personal association with Winthrop and his admiration for the adept, the decision to absorb Digby's "new model" Catholicism into one or another of these larger categories would not have been difficult.

Cited by Winthrop biographers as evidence of his growing international reputation, which was not enticing enough to tempt him from moral and familial responsibilities in colonial America, Digby's letter deserves closer scrutiny from the transatlantic perspective. It contained an artful combination of historical references to New England's eschatological "errand" and courtly puffery. This potent mix of seduction and status anxiety was calculated by Digby to make Winthrop's head spin.

In "John Winthrop, Jr., Industrial Pioneer," written in 1930 for *Builders of the Bay Colony,* Samuel Eliot Morison presented the canonical analysis of this pivotal quotation from Digby's letter. Morison rightly situated Digby's "warm invitation to London" in the context of fierce local and international competition for the relocation of Winthrop's skills as an "industrial" projector.

After the death of his father in 1649, it was now possible for Winthrop to remove himself completely from Boston's authoritarian sphere of influence, something he had done in fits and starts in the past. So during the 1650s, with a permanent move in the offing, Morison observes, "everyone wanted the younger Winthrop . . . he was the most sought-after person in New England."[111] Official invitations ensued from settlements with attractive inducements of land. He could reside south of Boston, including Connecticut Colony (where he was already a magistrate and assured of the governorship); New Haven Colony (where he was offered a plantation house complete with maidservant in exchange for the development of a local ironworks); Providence Plantation (Roger Williams suggested this was a logical spiritual home for Winthrop, as "You have been noted for tendernes toward mens soules, especially for conscience sake to God"); and most intriguing, New Netherlands (where Peter Stuyvesant sought to co-opt his cosmopolitan, land-hungry correspondent of many years by offering "accomodation" in land and slave-rich Brooklyn, "soe large and ample as hee hath power to give").[112] Stuyvesant's offer was the most complex, and Winthrop had long planned to appropriate the director-general's chair for himself.

Without mention of the fortieth parallel, the American Mediterranean, or its proximity to the Saybrook project, Morison concludes that Winthrop ultimately chose New London—on Long Island Sound, adjacent to Fishers Island at the mouth of the Sound, where Winthrop raised livestock—because the Pequot territory of southern Connecticut offered the richest mining and metallurgical prospects. These inducements were very real, but probably less significant to the younger Winthrop than the territory he hoped would become available south and west of the Sound. Once he became governor of Connecticut, Winthrop worked ceaselessly toward the ultimate goal of absorbing New Netherlands. As a final inducement to settle there, in May 1651, the general assembly of Connecticut Colony granted Winthrop a monopoly in perpetu-

ity over any rocks and minerals he discovered and improved to form the "staple commodity" that, as the architect of the Massachusetts General Assembly's Edict of 1646,
which encouraged the development of local trade and manufacturing in the *absence* of
a staple, Winthrop had failed to find in the Massachusetts Bay Colony:

> Whereas in this rocky country, among the mountains and rocky hills, there are probabil-
> ities of mines and metals, the discovery of which may be of great advantage to the coun-
> try in raising a staple commodity; and whereas John Winthrop . . . doth intend to be at
> charges and adventure for the search and discovery of such mines and minerals:—for the
> encouragement thereof, and of any that shall adventure with the said John Winthrop . . .
> in the said business, it is therefore ordered by the Court that if the said John Winthrop
> . . . shall discover, set upon and maintain such mines of lead, copper or tin, or any miner-
> als, as antimony, vitriol, black lead, allum, stone salt, salt springs, or any other the like,
> within this jurisdiction, and shall set up any work for the digging, washing and melting,
> or any other operation about the said mines and minerals, as the nature thereof requieth—
> that then the said John Winthrop . . . his heirs, associates, partners or assigns, shall enjoy
> forever said mines, with the lands, wood, timber and water within two or three miles of
> said mines, for the necessary carrying on of the works and maintaining of the workmen.[113]

Like Palissy, Winthrop had directed his gaze downward, looking for a synthesis of
salvation, security, and profit in the "bowels of the Earth." Stiles's understanding of
the folkloric connotations of "Gov. Winthrops Ring," had historical origins in a competitive land grant. By law and custom, Winthrop's name was associated with ore excavated from his East Haddam "mountain," including Erkelen's cobalt. As for Digby's
invitation, Morison argues that a triumphant return to continue his laboratory research
among peers in London would have proven "irresistible" had it been not for Winthrop's hopes that this promising new situation in Connecticut would allow him "to
retrieve the family fortunes, sadly wasted by the old Governor's lavish hospitality and
too great devotion to the public weal."[114]

Although he does not cite it fully, Morison refers to a letter Digby sent Winthrop
from Paris, on January 26, 1656, after Winthrop refused his invitation in a letter sent
four months earlier:

> Yr most welcome letter . . . was sent me . . . the same day I went out of London to come
> to this towne: wch made me lament the lesse the necessity of those affaires that call me
> hither for a little while; since I learne by it that you are not as yet minded to make our
> country happy wth yr presence. I pray God you may so alter yr resolutions that by the
> return of the shippes I may meete you att London. For I can not subscribe to your rea-
> sons—the maine of wch is, *res augusta domi* to a numerous family. For wheresoever you
> are, I am sure you can not want.[115]

Digby usually made for France when the political situation in England was dangerous. All the more reason to use Winthrop as leverage to improve his unstable place at
Cromwell's court.

Digby was quite right in implying that Winthrop was being disingenuous in using
family problems as an excuse. Winthrop's extensive correspondence with Dr. Samuel
Hartlib, whom he called "the great intelligence of Europe," about books, medical practice and above all the competitive, worldwide quest for the philosopher's stone, contain many reports concerning Sir Kenelm (whom they called "the Knight"). These
indicate that Digby knew Winthrop well enough to understand when he was obfuscating. Winthrop himself had certainly continued to keep a jealous eye on Digby's
travels, political intrigues and quest for the stone, long after their exchange of letters
in 1655. In a letter from London dated March 16, 1660, for example, in response to
Winthrop's query regarding Digby's whereabouts, Hartlib writes:

> Sir Kenelme Digby hath been up and down in Germany for the liquor Alkahest the great
> elixer. He hath now returned to Paris where he is for the present. My correspondent from
> Paris writtes unto me as followeth; we were with the generous knight (meaning Sir Kenel.
> D. but found him just stepping in his coach for to visit a person of quality . . .) . . . so I can
> give you no account at all of his voyage into Germany and the experience he hath had of
> that countrey onely I heare . . . that there is an Italian gentleman . . . at Strasburg neces-
> sitated to retire thither from Rome for having spoken too freely of the Popes aequality
> with other bishops; which person the Knight extolleth highly for his profound knowledge
> in Chymestry, and rare happiness in curing all manner of desperat diseases; About which
> I intend God willing to learn Sir K. D. ['s] own relation at our first meeting.

Digby was arguably just as familiar with his American correspondent and competitor's personal history; at least enough to know that in the past, Winthrop had not
hesitated to sacrifice family for the sake of ambition or travel. It would be a simple
matter to paint a picture of cruel indifference to the basic emotional and material needs
of both his wives and his children. Winthrop's first wife, Martha, died unlamented in
childbirth in 1634; Elizabeth, his second wife, spent much of her married life alone;
she was left behind while her husband traveled and "prayed often and tearfully for his
return."[116] Like those of Bernard Palissy, Jakob Böhme, and virtually all of the intensely
self-contained, sexually sublimated Paracelsian natural philosophers in this story,
Winthrop's emotional relationships with the women and children in his life were cold,
physically ambivalent, or absent.

Let us suggest other, more probable and complex reasons for Winthrop's rejection
of Digby's proposal that he take his rightful place among adepts of the universal laboratory in his native country. In 1655, Winthrop continued to believe that the greater
potential universal showcase for his skills as the New World's one authentic natural-

philosophical prince would be located at the fortieth parallel, where the Northwest Passage bisected Manhattan Island and where the philosopher's stone would unite east and west, macrocosm and microcosm. Evidence of a grand obsession with the conquest of New Netherlands is abundant in the plan he formulated to absorb the Dutch West India Company's colony into Connecticut. Winthrop was already deeply involved in a well-documented plot to extend his domain to Long Island, Manhattan, and the Hudson Valley, where he planned to use the region's abundant resources to maximize the manufacturing, mining, and alchemical projects started in Ipswich, Saybrook, and New London. When he received Digby's invitation, he had already made bold moves to grab land in the lower Hudson Valley and on Long Island from Stuyvesant. This was preliminary to his actions of 1664, when Winthrop was on the verge of the "peaceful" conquest of New Amsterdam just as the duke of York's fleet arrived to stake the latter's prior claim.

Winthrop knew Digby's ulterior motives regarding Cromwell's plans to return to La Rochelle with the legendary New World Puritan adept accompanying him, this time to play a leading and successful role in retrieving the fortress. If the Lord Protector, an accomplished general, with Winthrop at his side, could reverse the apocalyptic defeat of Buckingham and Charles I in 1627–28, he would gain a foothold against absolutism, trump the Stuarts again, and provide an elegant sense of closure. After all, the elder Winthrop had cited the fall of La Rochelle as a portent of final things that had sealed the fate of the Reformation in Europe and sent the New England Company into hiding across the Atlantic. After his father's death and the recovery of international Protestantism's great lost fortress, the younger Winthrop could lead the American exiles back to the mother country to rejuvenate English Protestantism through moderation and internationalist belief in the universal spirit. This was also the Cromwellian subtext in Digby's claim that a rustic New World refuge "was a well chosen one when there were inconveniences for your fixing upon this."

Cromwell's and Digby's interest in Winthrop's return for a second La Rochelle expedition was not limited to its symbolic value. Winthrop knew the territory well, having spent five months on the scene. His expertise in pyrotechnics and fortress design would also prove valuable to his friends, the Küffelers, in redeploying their torpedo and a new generation of underwater "engines." By the mid 1650s, Cromwell had become the torpedo's main patron in Europe, with an eye toward its use in a second siege of La Rochelle. "Dr. [Johann Sibert] Kuffler . . . presents his service to you," Hartlib wrote Winthrop on March 16, 1660, "hearing that you had written to me, by the letter here inclosed":

> He hath many excellent and usefull inventions which I cannot yett obtain that the publick should take notice of them. Only I sped in one towards the late Lord Pro[tecto]r

[Oliver Cromwell] which was to destroy ships in a moment which the Dr. made good near Deptford, to the great astonishment of all beholders; His highness was wonderfully affected with it, and would have done some great matters for him, but he soon died after. I shall send you God permitting the propositions and uses of all his undertakings by the next occasion.[117]

After the Lord Protector's death in 1658, however, first Richard Cromwell and then Charles II cut the Küffelers off. Not coincidentally, all talk of a return to La Rochelle was ended by Charles II, who had become the younger Winthrop's new and valued royal patron for the Connecticut Charter, which granted him New Netherland. Stuart interest in the New World was on the rise. Above all else, however, much had changed in Winthrop's approach to security since 1627. By 1655, his conceptions of international security and the declining value of fortresses conformed more closely to Palissy's than ever before. In a letter dated August 25, 1660, in response to Hartlib's offer of more details on J. S. Küffeler's latest experiments, Winthrop revealed just how far he had come: "I wish you could prevaile with Dr. Keffler to bury that fireworke (which you mention he would have made knowne) in oblivion and not by any meanes divulge it. There are means ynough already knowne to the world of ruin and destruction to mankind by sea and land."[118] Having "bin at the Ile of Rue," Winthrop did not wish to return.

What, finally, did Winthrop make of Digby's double-edged play on his colonial status anxiety—both flattering and condescending—that asked for a return to "your native country," because "where you are, is too scanty a stage for you to remain too long upon"? One might begin, with Forth Winthrop, by inquiring whether John Winthrop Jr. had ever really had a "native country." In his famous letter to his father of 1629, Winthrop wrote that every place seemed the same to him now, and that he would call home that place where he could be near his "dearest friends."

But even that seemingly innocuous phrase is problematic when wielded by a master dissimulator. For who *were* Winthrop's dearest friends: his family, the other "Puritans" from Suffolk in the New England Company, his transatlantic network of scientific correspondents spread all over the world, his laboratory apparatus, or perhaps, even most likely, his library of natural-philosophical books, which traveled with him wherever he went? This latter group of friends had no geographical limits, no "native land." As Forth was the first to recognize in his brother, Winthrop's "native land" was an interior, rustic, and natural place; that is, anywhere capable of camouflage, where his portable skills and experience could be carried in head, hand, and heart.

His rustic stage on the pluralistic borderlands of Long Island Sound, with access to abundant land, natural resources, and perhaps the Northwest Passage was simultaneously unified with the universal spirit, circulating everywhere in the Atlantic world at once, just as it did in Stiles's portrait. From the perspective of colonial America, Digby's personal belief in a universal spirit that allowed the efficacy of the weapon salve—a belief that Winthrop, Howes, and Stiles shared—belied the need for a universal natural laboratory located specifically in London. The soulish energy that supported any universal project was available everywhere, it need only be channeled to the fortieth parallel to find "Christ and the Stone" and (in the words of the rustic potter) "multiply your treasures." At that latitude, Winthrop's heart was centered like Fludd's cosmological figure at the center of the microcosm, encompassing the universe within his reach. Just as Saintongeais Huguenots developed the skills to survive the apocalyptic loss of the regional fortress in 1628 and their subsequent dispersion into the Atlantic world, so too Winthrop's rustic New World periphery negated the primacy of "this Iland['s]" metropolitan core.

One of Sir Kenelm Digby's philosophical heroes, the French magistrate and Neoplatonist Jean d'Espagnet, elucidated the hermetic relationship of the universal spirit to the secret of the philosopher's stone in his book *Enchiridion physicae restitutae* (Paris, 1642). "Before the creation of the Universe [God] was a book rowld up in himself giving light only to himself," d'Espagnet explained:

> but, as it were, travailing with the birth of the world, he unfolded himself, and that work which lay hid in the womb of his own mind, was manifested by extending it to view, and so brought forth the Ideal-world, as it were in the transcript of that divine Original, into an actual and material world . . . so that the extreames of the whole worke [are connected] by a secret bond [and] have a fast coherence between themselves through insensible mediums, and all Things do freely combine in obedience to their Supream Ruler.

Winthrop the Younger possessed a copy of d'Espagnet's book in his alchemical library.[119] Written on the inside cover of Winthrop's tiny volume is an unusual spelling of his name "Johanes Winthrop" in what may be his own hand (or perhaps that of the friend who gave him the book as a gift), with John Dee's monas sign placed above it, bracketing the "th"—and hence joining the "east" and "west"—of "Win-th-rop," making Winthrop emblematic of a passage of unity (that is, the Northwest Passage) bisecting the center of his own name (fig. 11.3). Below "Johanes Winthrop," formed like a Latin declension, is a phrase identified as an "Anagr[am]," which reads: "I Hope Wins a Throne." Because an anagram is defined as a transposition of the letters of a word or name, whereby a new word, name, or phrase is formed, this breaking of the code was above all a performance of linguistic alchemy. The hidden truth had been distilled out from behind the dissimulation that overlaid the façade of "John Winthrop." Names were significant when transmuted into anagrams by alchemists, as they were thought to possess enormous prophetic power associated with the discovery of the philosopher's stone and the "naming" of an adept. Anagrams were thus frequently

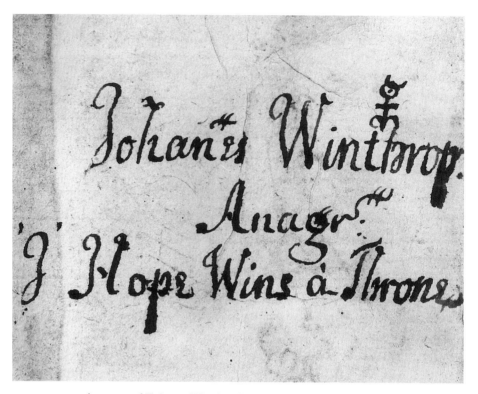

FIGURE 11.3. Anagram of "Johanes Winthrop" with the "th" surmounted by Dee's monas sign, possibly by John Winthrop Jr., from his copy of *Enchiridion physicae restitutae* (Paris, 1642), a pivotal French Neoplatonic text on the mystical relationship between natural philosophy and hermeticism. Courtesy New York Academy of Medicine Library. Fludd interpreted the four unified elements of the sign to mean, bottom to top: *ignis* (fire); *elementa* (the elements); *sol* (the sun); and *luna* (the moon).

associated with geological excavation, and in the seventeenth century, they were often harnessed to Palissian figures of subterranean, prelapsarian life emerging from underneath the ruins of history. "Heaven descends into the Bowels of the Earth," one commentator claimed in 1677, "and, to make up the Anagramm, the Graves open and the Dust ariseth." "His body," another wrote the next year, was like Fludd's gargantuan microcosm, "that stupendous frame, Of all the world the anagram."[120]

The Johanas Winthrop anagram and our knowledge of its decoder's ambitions suggest that the "throne" Winthrop hoped for was an adept's, whose status as secret royalty among virtuosi would be acknowledged with the discovery of the Northwest Passage on the fortieth parallel. At the same time, he knew, the philosopher's stone would be his and the gnostic circle squared in perpetuity. Thus, let us return for a final look at Winthrop's physician's chair, made in the Long Island Sound region shortly before Winthrop was elected the first colonial American member of the Royal Society (1661).

We do not know at what date Winthrop's copy of *Enchiridion* entered his library. It was published in 1642, so if he acquired the book within a few years of its publication, then he had already spent a decade on or about the fortieth parallel. That would suggest his hopes of finding the Northwest Passage were undiminished, and that he felt close to his goal. Certainly, it is also possible that he entered the anagram in *Enchiridion* much later, on the eve of becoming a member of the Royal Society.

Is it unreasonable to speculate that Winthrop chose precisely this volume in which to reveal himself because Jean d'Espagnet's (and by extension Kenelm Digby's) understanding of the universal spirit was analogous to that which Winthrop himself desired be made material in his "physician's chair?" Did not Stiles have representations of the motion of the universal spirit in mind when he sat for his portrait by King in 1771, hand over heart? Surely he knew where to aim his heart when he sat in Winthrop's chair, as he must have done at some point in his life, as an ultimate act of communion with the disembodied spirit of the dead alchemist.

Having begun with the "invisible" Edward Howes's memories of Winthrop "at the Île of Rue, and at Rochell," scattered among "the dust" of its dead, conjured across the Atlantic, it seems fitting for Howes to have the final word on the geography of the universal spirit:

> But to our sympathetical business whereby we communicate our minds to one another though the diameter of the earth interpose . . . I would have you so good a geometrician as to know your own centre. Did you ever yet measure your everlasting self, the length of your life, the breadth of your love, the depth of your wisdom & the height of your light? Let Truth be your centre & you may do it, otherwise not. I could wish you could now begin to leave off being altogether an outward man . . . the Ruler can draw you straight lines from your centre to the confines of an infinite circumference, by which you may pass from any part of the circumference to another without obstacle of earth or section of lines, if you observe & keep but one & the true & only centre, to pass by it, from it, & to it.[121]

Winthrop's chair now stands empty in its museum, extending its original function to the present. When the American adept took his seat, he too became invisible.

CHAPTER TWELVE

La Rochelle's Transatlantic Body

The Commons Debates of 1628

❧ Adam's "scattered bones" ❧

Military security and preservation of the remnants of their scattered flock in retreat were of primary concern to the surviving leaders of international Protestantism. The Counter-Reformation's forces had experienced a powerful resurgence in France and the Palatinate during the second and third decades of the seventeenth century. The reduction of La Rochelle and nearly complete erasure of its population was a reversal of cosmic consequence that led to victories for the Antichrist in Germany. In 1629, Ferdinand II and Wallenstein asserted their mastery, and an imperial edict restored to Rome the ecclesiastical estates lost in the peace of Passau in 1552. On May 22, 1629, Christian IV of Denmark, the last hope of the Protestant forces on the Continent, accepted the peace of Lübeck. He then withdrew his army from the Thirty Years' War, abandoning all his allies in northern Europe to extermination or submission to Catholic governance.

The Winthrop family watched from England with increasing apprehension as the apocalyptic endgame was played out at La Rochelle. Sometime in February 1628—the first month in which Rochelais physicians began to record the experience of mass starvation during the siege (see fig. 4.2)—Margaret Tyndal Winthrop, John Jr.'s stepmother and his father's third wife,[1] sent an undated letter to her husband, who was in London on business. Conveying concern about serious illness in the family, Margaret's letter soon expanded its scope outward from domestic anxieties in Groton to encompass Calvinist hopes for God's constancy and her metaphysical understanding that La Rochelle's deliverance from its near-mortal "condition" hinged ambiguously on God's favor and the potential for purification in suffering:

> I hope the lorde will heare our prayers and be pleased to stay his hand in this visitasion which if he please to doe we shall have great cause of thankfulness. but I desire in this and all other things to submit unto his holy will, it is the lord let him doe what semeth good in his owne eyes. he will doe nothinge but that shall be for our good if we had harts to t[r]ust in him, and all shall be for the best what soever it shall please him to exersise us with all. he wounds and he can heale. he hath never fayled to doe us good, and now he will not shake us of[f] but continue the same god still that he hath bin heare to fore the lorde santify unto us what soever it shall please him to send unto us that we may be the better for it and furthered in our corce to heaven. I am sorye for the hard condishtion of Rochell. the lord helpe them and fite for them and then none shall prevayle against them or overcome them. in vaine thay fite that fite against the lorde who is a myty god and will destroye all his enimyes.[2]

But by late spring 1628, God appeared to have forsaken La Rochelle and the Continental Reformed Churches. In a decisive letter to Margaret of May 15, the elder Winthrop gave vent to despondent thoughts of final things and fears for their safety, acknowledging that millennial signs had appeared everywhere "before our eyes." The time had come to abandon England before the European catastrophes—in which the Puritans themselves were made so obviously complicitous by their own corrupt behavior—crossed the channel to consume them "at last."[3] Thus Winthrop prepared his wife, family, and "our Companye" for the reality of their forthcoming emigration to New England:

> My good wife, I prayse the Lorde for the wished newes of thy wellfare and of the rest of our Companye, and for the continuance of ours heer: it is a great favour, that we may enjoye so much comfort and peace in these so evill and declininge tymes and when the increasinge of our sinnes gives us so great cause to looke for some heave Scquorge and Judgment to be cominge upon us: the Lorde hath admonished, threatened, corrected, and astonished us, yet we growe worse and worse, so as his spirit will not allwayes strive with us, he must needs give waye to his furye at last: he hath smitten all the other Churches before our eyes, and hath made them to drinke of the bitter cuppe of tribulation, even unto death; we sawe this, and humbled not ourselves, to turne from our evill wayes, but have provoked him more then all the nations rounde about us: therefore he is turninge the cuppe towards us also, and because we are the last, our portion must be, to drinke the very dreggs which remaine. . . . I am veryly perswaded, God will bringe some heavye Affliction upon this lande, and that speedylye: but be of good Comfort, the hardest that can come

shall be a meanes to mortifie this bodye of Corruption, which is a thousand tymes more dangerous to us than any outward tribulation, and to bringe us into neerer communion with our Lo: Je: Christ, and more Assurance of his kingdome. If the Lord seeth it wilbe good for us, he will provide a shelter and a hidinge place for us . . . we shalbe safe.[4]

The New England group was not unique among English Calvinists in its wrenching emotional response to the fall of La Rochelle, and in the sense of an ending inspired by painful evidence of "evill and declininge tymes." What did set them apart, of course, was the decision to abandon England for the New World, where these new Israelites could wait out the inevitable "general destruction" and "staye" in safety "till it come."[5] Here, as Winthrop clearly tells us, the apocalyptic events of 1628, and the resulting quest for refuge and safety, played a central role. But evidence is also widespread that all English Calvinists, at every level of society—including those Puritans who chose to stay behind because they failed to perceive that God's "Affliction upon this lande" would come "that speedyly"—shared many of Winthrop's sentiments, though not necessarily his sense of timing, and grieved deeply at the "troubles and sorrows of the Rochellers."[6] A broad cross section of England's Protestant population either participated in—or knew someone at—the siege of La Rochelle. Many Protestant soldiers joined Buckingham's huge expeditionary force of 1627, sent by Charles I to overrun the tiny French garrison that occupied the small but strategic fortress at Saint-Martin-de-Ré. The younger Winthrop, like so many others, wrote home on a fairly consistent basis over the course of five months of naval service off the coast of La Rochelle. Certainly, the Winthrop letters survive because the bulk of the family archives were preserved as sacred relics by descendants. However, one John Bradshaw, about whom nothing would be known were it not for another, less predictable, accident of survival, also wrote relatives to convey his experience at the "death" of La Rochelle.

Bradshaw was a nephew of the London Puritan artisan Nehemiah Wallington (1598–1658), about whom we know many things. Wallington was a deeply pious wood turner, whose introspective, thousand-plus page manuscript diary of melancholy and despair has also survived intact. This provides a window into the everyday life of an ambivalent, barely competent, and yet deeply religious seventeenth-century tradesman. Wallington could not have maintained himself as one "of the middling sort," without the guild connections and constant emotional and financial support of his family. Bradshaw sent an account of his observations on the suffering of La Rochelle to his grandfather, John Wallington Sr. Nehemiah borrowed this from John, and made two copies to include in his diary.[7]

Similarly, Nehemiah preserved four letters on La Rochelle's afflictions from the minister Livewell Rampaigne, his brother-in-law. Rampaigne's letters suggested sev-

eral ways in which the suffering of their French co-religionists might be used for didactic purposes to serve the faithful at home. Unlike the elder Winthrop, however, the
moderate Rampaigne—like many Puritans who did not join the New England experiment—was less than certain that England's apocalyptic future was at hand. On
the contrary, while Calvinists had now learned in their own time "that God's dearest
servants . . . are not privileged from bloody and fiery trials," England had clearly escaped the finality of La Rochelle's fate because of God's special favor. To be sure, this
logic was not wholly dissimilar from Margaret Winthrop's when she reassured her husband in 1627 that the Rochelais would prevail *if* "the lord help them and fite for them."
But Rampaigne's complacency in assuring Wallington that God's favor "is duly to be
observed and with praise forever to be acknowledged" would have infuriated Winthrop. Instead of conceding the chiliastic immediacy of the warning of God's terrible
judgment on La Rochelle for England, Rampaigne aloofly informed Wallington that
"the English should learn a grateful patience with their own troubles."[8] Rampaigne's
letters to Wallington, while expressing sympathy for La Rochelle, nevertheless assert
a palpable detachment from the apocalyptic events on the Continent. To be English,
in Rampaigne's eyes, was security enough.

Winthrop's letter to Margaret and "our Companye" in Suffolk on the eve of emigration, however, indicates a love, compassion, and spiritual unity with the suffering
of the martyred dead that allows of no historical separation. This dialectic of insepa-
rability—or, unity in separation—was ultimately carried to the point of identity with
La Rochelle, even as the New World colonists prepared to distance themselves physically from the Bay of Biscay. After all, Winthrop prophesied that "we are the last" to
drink the "very dreggs" from the *identical* cup of "bitter" tribulation that the Rochelais
had been forced by God to swallow first. And in "A Modell of Christian Charitie,"
Winthrop's seminal lay shipboard sermon of 1630, he moved to extend and codify this
discourse of unity in the face of violent separation. Historians seldom linger on these
sections of the long and often quoted "Model," which is usually cited in reference to
Winthrop's notions of social reciprocity, or, most famous of all, his "Citty upon a Hill"
metaphor, taken from Matthew 5:14.

Reactivating the venerable Augustine in this ur-text from the Puritan "middle passage," "Written On Boarde the Arrabella, On the Attlantick Ocean . . . In His passage . . . from the Island of Great Brittaine, to New-England," Winthrop likened the
Church to a single human body. Here, Winthrop knew, was a trope with a long oral
and written history; first encompassing the ascetic eucharistic piety of the later Middle
Ages, then, as early seventeenth-century Calvinist exegetics would have done, reaching back to Paul's letter to the Corinthians, in which he appeals for Christian unity so
"that there be no dissensions among you."[9] ("Now ye are the body of Christ," Paul states
rhetorically in 1 Cor. 12, "and members in particular.") Such a metaphor suggested

specific meanings when reactivated to serve the dual "wilderness" themes of exile and separation explored in "Christian Charitie." Here, Winthrop comprehended an anatomy of contraries that entered (or exited) the body through the mouth, inasmuch as "pleasure and content that the exercise of love carries with it"—as well as the fatal swallow of tribulation from God's poisonous cup—"wee may see in the naturall body the mouth is at all the paines to receive."[10]

In 1630, as fragmented parts of the main body of Christ lay dismembered or mortally wounded on the Continent, the potential for revivification and, ultimately, reunification through dispersion of living parts to places of safety, lay with the emergence of soulish love from the physical mortification of the Thirty Years' War. That is to say, because the soul was capable of moving freely "by secret passages" through matter at God's behest, while "giving any motion . . . to the body and the power it hath to sett all the faculties on worke."[11] Although the soul's pathways were God's secret, its anatomical seat in the loving heart was well known. Yet perhaps more than most sectarians—who believed in the heart as the soul's central passageway into the body but also that it was free and so sometimes took wayward and unexpected motions—Winthrop underscored the heart's ability to "frame" and hence order soulish motion. This is a very subtle distinction, but control of this motion was essential to Winthrop's project: first, to prevent the social and religious chaos of disordered motion, but perhaps above all to fulfill the direct, enduring linkage to God contrived by the theology of the covenant. The soul labors "upon all occasions to produce the same effect, but by framing these affeccions of love in the hearte which will as natively bring forthe the other, as any cause doth produce the effect."[12] Thus, citing Colossians 3:14—and directly paralleling contemporary Neoplatonic theory espoused by his son and most English alchemists (who followed Plato's dictum that the soul was bond and knot of the world)—Winthrop elaborated on a conjunctive metaphor of soulish love as a "perfect" connecting "ligament" for a fragmented Church:

> Love is the bond of perfection . . . or ligament . . . it makes the work perfect. There is noe body but consistes of partes and that which knitts these partes together gives the body its perfeccion, because it makes eache parte soe contiguous to the other as thereby they doe mutually participate with eache other, bothe in strengthe and infirmity in pleasure and paine, to instance in the most perfect of all bodies, Christ and his church make one body . . . when christ comes and by his spirit and love knitts all these partes to himselfe and each to other, it is become the most perfect and best proportioned body in the world.[13]

Winthrop had in mind the part of Christ's mystical body that had perished two years earlier with "many thousands of the Saintes" at La Rochelle, when he wrote of the common experience of pain that would naturally reverberate throughout the unity when any single part suffered. Christ—as the primordial heart of the mystical body—

sacrificed himself while contained in mortal, crucified flesh. Thus, Christ experienced mortification and ultimately the promise of ecstasy for mankind. Both of these conditions would maintain a historical dialectic that circulated throughout the mystical body as physical memory of sin and sacrifice until the millennium finally purified the chosen and redeemed them from pain and suffering:

> All the partes of this body being thus united are made so contiguous in a speciall relacion as they must needes partake of each others strength and infirmity, joy, and sorrow, weale and woe. . . . If one member suffers all suffer with it. . . . For patterns we have that first of our Saviour . . . becomeing a parte of this body, and being knitt with it in the bond of love, found such a native sensiblenes[s] of our infirmities and sorrowes as hee willingly yeilded himselfe to deathe to ease the infirmities of the rest of his body and soe heale theire sorrowes: from the like Sympathy of partes did the Apostles and many thousands of the Saintes lay downe theire lives for Christ againe.[14]

Knowing his profound hatred of religious enthusiasm in New England, it is noteworthy that during the passion and anxiety of the escape on the *Arabella*, Winthrop perceived that under certain conditions, it was possible that man could experience "continuall" intimations from Christ of redemption in historical time. The elder Winthrop perceived, with Calvin, that bodily decay, dispersion, and fragmentation began with original sin, when "Adam Rent in himselfe from his Creator, rent all his posterity allsoe one from another . . . till Christ comes and takes possession of the soule . . . and infuseth . . . love." The animate soul was thus the medium by which a *historical* return to prelapsarian grace—and hence the rebirth and reunification of martyred bones—became conceivable, their embodiment manifested in what Winthrop called famously "the new Creature":

> And this latter having continuall supply from Christ . . . little by little expels the former . . . soe that this love is the fruite of the new birthe, and none can have it but the new Creature . . . thus formed in the soules of men it workes like the Spirit upon the drie bones. [In Ezekial 37:7] bone came to bone, it gathers together the scattered bones [of] perfect old man Adam and knitts them into one body againe in Christ whereby a man is become againe a living soule.[15]

"Knitt[ing]" "old man Adam['s]" "scattered bones" "into one body againe in Christ," reclaiming "perfect" Edenic symmetry by supplanting man's fall with his resurrection, Winthrop's "new Creature" also perfected mystical communication between all the disparate parts of his cosmological "body"—through a shared, mediating heart—no matter at what distance in time or space the individual fragments might exist in relation to one another: "professing our selves fellow members of Christ . . . though wee were absent from eache other many miles, and had our imploymentes as farre distant, yet wee ought to account our selves knitt together by this bond of love, and live in the exercise of it."[16]

The primacy that the fall of La Rochelle played in joining a historical event with Calvinist theology in the formation of his millennial thought allowed Winthrop to conclude the segment of his text that addressed the mystical nature of international Protestantism by finding the ultimate "pattern" for tacit, soulish communication among Christians in "the Waldenses," or Waldensians. This group was the most significant pre-Reformation heretical movement in early modern France, usually perceived as the primitive precursors of the Huguenots. The elder Winthrop noted that soulish networks of communication were "notorious in the practice of the Christians in former times, as is testified of the Waldenses from the mouth of one of the adversaries: 'they use to love any of theire owne religion even before they were acquainted with them.'"[17]

In theory, then, the elder Winthrop's lay sermon preached a shipboard gospel of fluid, integrating, soulish love to redeem the body Christian fragmented by violence and dispersion. It was well known throughout the Protestant world as early as the mid 1630s, however, that the governor's dangerous intolerance of heterodoxy, and of transplanted Germanic pietism in particular, had hardened in everyday practice in Massachusetts. Once settled in America, he adhered closely to the standards of Old Testament wrathfulness toward heterodoxy. Because the elder Winthrop perceived his own heart at the center of the Christian body—one that framed the soul in an almost intractable fashion (as a king might have done)—his notion of the body's unity in the midst of fragmentation was unilinear. Hence, the direction of the soul was clear and, if not completely visible, comprehensible. Pietists and sectarians, however, perceived soulishness as multiple, interior, and hidden. The movement of the soul was thus impossible to guarantee; it had to be felt emotionally and with immediacy. While there was only one God, witness of the spirit took infinite forms; fragmentation and unity were therefore personal, and the spirit had the subversive potential for "framing" in infinitely different ways (and, in infinitely different, independent hearts).

Moreover, while many English Puritans took a more moderate view than Winthrop on how fast the millennial clock was ticking in 1628 and 1629, it is not surprising that for some, moderation on the question of temporality also extended to that of religious toleration. This caused many convinced predestinarians to reconsider initial millennial impulses to join the Puritan experiment in New England. For example, unlike the elder Winthrop and most of Wallington's Massachusetts correspondents—including Edward Brown, a fellow turner who emigrated to Ipswich (Wallington wrote Brown in 1645 to denounce religious discord in New England)—Wallington himself shunned doctrinal schism and seemed tolerant of Calvinist heterodoxy.[18] This issue of intolerance in Massachusetts Bay also generated a great degree of controversy among the younger Winthrop's scientific correspondents in London. Edward Howes, for one, hesitated to join his old friend and colleague in America for just this reason. Despite relative moderation, and geographical, social, and doctrinal distancing, most English Calvinists shared the elder Winthrop's intense anxiety and remained watchful of the international scene both during and after the siege of La Rochelle. This was predicated on spiritual communication through the doctrine of Christian unity of the fragmented body. The historian Paul Seaver, Wallington's most attentive reader, has placed the "world" of his subject firmly within the unified geographical field of international Protestantism dispersed by the religious wars. In this, the humble artisan possessed a much more inclusive spiritual cosmos than did his ministerial brother-in-law:

> Almost all Wallington's connections . . . created a network of concern that stretched to
> Massachusetts and Connecticut on the one side and to France and Germany on the other
> . . . he saw himself primarily not as a citizen turner, a Londoner or Englishman, but as a
> member of a more select or temporally limited group—the children of God. On occasion
> he referred to them as "the people of the Lord" or simply as "His People". . . among the
> children of God were also coreligionists abroad . . . [Wallington] lamented the harsh fate
> that had recently befallen the French Protestants at La Rochelle, "the general report" of
> which "filled me with much . . . sorrow of heart that the people of God should endure
> such great miseries scarce heard of in our age". . . [thus] Wallington had learned to see
> politics in terms of a . . . struggle between the forces of Christ and Antichrist, a battle
> whose fate was determined as much by the fall of La Rochelle or by the appearance of the
> Swedish Lion on the plains of Pomerania as by events in London or Westminster.[19]

❦ Bodily Disorders ❦

The source of Wallington's and Winthrop's shared awareness of themselves as actors in international apocalyptic politics, like many of their co-religionists, extended beyond personal and familial experience to Calvinist ideological identification with Parliament. This sense of identity was both personal and professional for Winthrop. As lord of Groton Manor, it was an economic necessity for Winthrop to study the law (or else spend scarce resources to hire a lawyer) in order to competently discharge his traditional duties as the judge of the manorial court and justice of the county court. He was thus intimately familiar with the theory and practice of English common law. Although he failed to complete his studies at Cambridge, in time he was to become a respected parliamentary antiquarian and scribe. Indeed, his knowledge of parliamentary language and precedent expanded Winthrop's world beyond Groton Manor to the metropolis. When Suffolk's woolen industry suffered a deep depression beginning in the 1620s, in addition to selling off parcels of land, the cash-poor Winthrop diversified further. He spent part of the year with family in London, where he supplemented his income by serving as counsel on drafting legislation for parliamentary committees. By 1627, Winthrop had risen to the more lucrative position of common solicitor in the Court of Wards and Liveries.[20]

Also beginning in 1620, with the onset of Louis XIII's bloody annual military campaigns against Huguenot strongholds in the south and west of France (which lasted until 1629, when cleanup operations following the siege of La Rochelle ended), parliamentary advocates of an international Protestant program to counteract the devastating effects of the Thirty Years' War started to speak of "the Huguenot cause as part of the general Protestant cause."[21] But with the "mortification" of La Rochelle and its linkage to the rise of the Counter-Reformation warrior-cleric Cardinal Richelieu, who simultaneously reached the height of his political and economic power in France and on the world stage in 1628, the stakes had also risen dramatically. This initial perception had grown to represent the Huguenots as the first piece in a domino theory of apocalypse. In this scenario, it was sometimes difficult for Protestants to distinguish between narratives of earthly and supernatural tyranny. Princely sinners like Charles I and his French Catholic wife, besotted by the treachery of a beautiful court favorite, and the blood-drunk Louis XIII, maddened by the quest for glory and absolute power, worked in tandem with the Antichrist to desecrate the cosmos and consume the world with evil.

J. G. A. Pocock and others have shown how the political language of the Puritan saint had come into common usage in England during the late sixteenth century,[22] but it found fullest parliamentary expression beginning on June 14, 1628. The widespread publication of the Commons' Remonstrance to Charles I summarized eight days of heated speech in the Calvinist-dominated lower house.[23] The Commons debate linked the devastating geopolitical consequences of the incomprehensible defeat of a Royal Navy armada of over 30,000 soldiers, sailors, and marines by the tiny French garrison at Saint-Martin-de-Ré—with a reported loss of some 7,000 men[24]—to the internal subversion of the once-proud nobility's primitive English virtue and religious piety by insidious individuals who had gained "nearness" to Charles I. The primordial ties linking Church and state were now in mortal peril. The duke of Buckingham, in particular, who had been excoriated by Calvinists since the early 1620s, was commonly portrayed as a secret Arminian or, worse, an agent of the pope. Now, in the wake of his repulse at Saint-Martin, Buckingham was represented by critics as an "effeminate," "counterfeit," crypto-Catholic enemy of the state—one who used dissimulation, disguise, and the illicit "pleasures" of a malicious heart to gain access to the most intimate part of the royal household.

Much of the available language that articulated the public's notion of Buckingham's ambiguous sexual tastes and appearance was delivered to Parliament in the form of eyewitness accounts of the duke's strange behavior at the unsuccessful siege of Saint-Martin. These bitter polemical pamphlets were published under the names of disgruntled officers on their return from France, although it is unclear how much of a hand they had in the writing. None was more scathing than *An Unhappy View of the Whole Behavior of my Lord Duke of Buckingham, at the French Island, called Isle of Rhee,* by Colonel William Fleetwood, "an unfortunate commander in that untoward service."[25] "Upon the point of our first setting to sea," Fleetwood reported, the duke's cowardice had revealed itself "out of a distrust of some miserable death that might befall him in the voyage . . . being for a time estranged from his effeminate pleasures here at home, from which no warlike service could ever withdraw him."[26] The duke's intention, therefore, was not to defend England's honor as befitted a brave and experienced knight sent to a foreign battlefield in the name of the king, but rather "to redeem all his lost honour at home . . . in a desperate manner." Fleetwood goes on to accuse his Lord Admiral of assassinating a field officer with whom Buckingham had disagreed. "The malice of a vindictive heart," he wrote of the bodily container of Buckingham's corrupt spirit, "is never appeased, but remains still inexorable and devilish." Sir John Burrows, although "cleare out of all danger of the Fort, was in an instant stricken dead in the place with a musket, shot by an unknown hand." The angry Fleetwood detailed similarly suspicious actions at every turning point in the battle, and each time Buckingham's "whole behavior" had favored the outnumbered and outgunned French defenders.[27]

Most egregious of all, on the day before the final battle, retreat, and slaughter of thousands of English soldiers that led to the chaotic flight of the armada from the Île de Ré, Buckingham called his officer corps together and "told us, that he had secret intelligence out of the Fort, that most of Their best Souldiers had conveied Themselves away by night." Thus, Fleetwood claimed, the duke misrepresented the still heavily defended fortress to initiate an open assault he knew secretly was destined to fail. To underscore this soldier's narrative of "our counterfeit Generall's" effeminate dissimulation and weakness, leading to his poisonous treachery—and perhaps to recall Calvinist contempt for his famous androgynous roles as the lead dancer in Inigo Jones's masques at the Stuart court—Buckingham dressed for battle in womanly disguise, hiding inside the clothing of a "faint and impotent soldier":

> The very next morning after this consultation, which fell out to be the day of doom to most of us, the Duke being sensible of his perfideous dealings, & that this was the day that the Defendants would encounter us to death . . . attired one of his own followers, every way much resembling himself, in his warlike habit & colours, with instructions suitable to the deceipt, and then disguised as a faint and impotent soldier, got himself a ship-board, and not only left us ignorant of the bloody intent towards us, but also made us incapable to prevent it, when we should . . . truely should the revenge of the Parliament

seize upon him . . . [for] the utter confusion of the poore Protestantes in France, now daily massacred without all pity, through their needlesse defense of their Religion. Yet it is the Kings pleasure still to afford him his wonted grace and connivance for all this; And treason it is apparent to denounce him faulty in any thing; But let his Magesty look at it, for his longer sheltring of this rich Traytor, and false-hearted man, both to God and his Country, which will be to [the] ruine both of himself and his kingdom at last, yet I have hope (out of the integrity of his heart, now whilest it is called today, and before the evill day come) he will give him over to the Parliament, whilst it is of strength to punish him. And that they for their parts will send him to H[ell] without any more ado.[28]

Nicolas Tyacke has argued persuasively that the religious controversies between English predestinarians and Arminians peaked when the Parliament of 1628 assembled. So Buckingham's place at the center of the tumult invited orthodox Calvinists to demonize him as the embodiment of national decline. Not only was the Commons faced with Buckingham's failings as Lord Admiral at the Île de Ré, but it was impossible for M.P.'s to separate the context of the Huguenots in France from their intense anxiety over two specific domestic issues of enormous theological and political importance in the late 1620s: first, the suppression of public debate on the "truthfulness" of the Thirty-nine Articles had caused orthodox clergy and laity to lose confidence in the state; and, second, the scandalous appointment of leading Arminians to bishoprics over the objections of Parliament had led to widespread fear of "counter-revolution" in the Church of England. Thus, a Catholic minority with strong courtly patronage under Buckingham's control could dominate English religious life, with the inevitable result that orthodox Calvinists would be pushed to the margins and stigmatized as "Puritans."[29]

Calvinist M.P.'s militated against "subversion of our true religion" in violent, unexpurgated debate. On June 5, 1628, the great historian of the common law Sir Edward Coke (1552–1634; Coke condemned Sir Kenelm Digby's father to a singularly horrible death) led the way and then allowed Edward Kirton, Christopher Sherland, Richard Knightley, and John Hampden to elaborate on his themes. All used the dangerous political language of heresy and slavery to attack Buckingham. Kirton, who was later censored for his provocative speech, called outright for the duke's assassination:

> COKE: I think verily that God has laid this punishment upon us because we have hoodwinked ourselves. . . . There is nothing grown to abuse but this house ought to reform. Because men have been named, I will name a man, the Duke of Buckingham. He is the grievance of grievances. Let us tell the King so, and though we have patents[30] which we complain of, yet that we ought to complain [about Buckingham] before any other.
>
> KIRTON: The great Duke . . . has gotten the strength of the kingdom into his

hands; he endeavors to make us slaves; he connives at our enemies; and in my conscience has some dangerous plot upon us. I pray let us make him known to the King. The Duke is an enemy to the kingdom, and so to the King; and I hope every good subject will before long draw his sword against the enemies of the King and kingdom.

SHERLAND: All that we have in the world is going to ruin, and the courses of late time have only tended to the subversion of our true religion and to raise the faction of the papists throughout Christendom. Are not papists in great favor at court? Are they not sent to be commanders, even in the last voyages which seemed to be made for the help of the Protestants? All our voyages have been turned contrary.

KNIGHTLY: All our miseries come from the undervaluing of the true religion, and no kingdom can flourish where the true religion does not. In many parts of this kingdom popery flourishes as much and is of equal power with the true Protestant religion.

HAMPDEN: For innovation of religion, it is like to come by this great man for, though he be not a papist, yet he is allied to papists, supports papists, and puts papists in places of trust.[31]

On June 6, Sir Nathaniel Rich and Lawrence Whitaker completed the long list of Calvinist grievances against Buckingham, Laud, and the Arminians. Rich and Whitaker showed how the duke's support for recusants and his failure to suppress heresy had caused papism and Counter-Reformation to "spread itself everywhere," especially in London:

RICH: Religion is the first, and heresies reign too much. Arminianism spreads itself everywhere. I have heard of clerks, at the induction of ministers, should ask them that were to be inducted whether they were Calvinists or Arminians. Books of orthodoxal doctrine are stopped, and others have free passage.

WHITAKER: There is an infinite flocking of these people around this town [London]. I once knew of a place about this town that for the diligence and devoutness they showed in religion were called "the Little Geneva." I can show you now a little Rome or a little Douai. There is amongst them nobility, gentry, clergy, lawyers; there is 3 papists to one Protestant. In Drury Lane more go to mass than to the church. There is a general want of preaching, which causes idleness, drunkenness, and all manner of debauchedness.[32]

This list was edited and formalized by Sir John Eliot (1592–1632) to become the first grievance in the Remonstrance of 1628 to Charles I, which explicitly named certain Jesuits in disguise as the mortal enemies of the "orthodox church":

our fear concerning change or subversion of religion is grounded upon the daily increase of papists . . . so are the hearts of your good subjects no less perplexed when with sorrow they behold a daily growth and spreading of the factions of the Arminians, that being (as your Majesty well knows) but a cunning way to bring in popery, and the professors of thse opinions . . . being Protestants in show but Jesuits in opinion . . . are much favored and advanced, not withstanding friends even of the clergy near to your Majesty, namely Dr. Neile, Bishop of Winchester, and Dr. Laud, Bishop of Bath and Wells, who are justly suspected to be unsound in their opinions that way. And it being now generally held to be the way to preferment and promotion in the church, many scholars do bend the course of their studies to maintain those errors. Their books and opinions are suffered to be printed and published, and on the other side the impressions of such as are written against them and in defense of the orthodox church are hindered and prohibited.[33]

Tyacke reminds historians of the baneful meaning seventeenth-century Calvinists assigned to the term "Puritan," since it was commonly used by "anti-Calvinists" in polemical contexts to identify intractable predestinarians. In his second spiritual "Experiencia" of 1616–18 (written after his second wife, Thomasine Clopton, died in childbirth), the elder Winthrop refused to accept such an identity assigned by others and adumbrated use of the word "Puritan" as an epithet of political marginalization in the Church of England. In this instance, however, he angrily turned the pejorative—among many others—into a defiant mark of spiritual steadfastness and courage in the face of adverse, "heated" speech:

[Christe Jesus] assurest my heart that I am in a right course, even the narrow waye that leads to heaven. Thou tellest me, and all experience tells me, that in this way there is least companie, and that those which doe walke openly in this way shallbe reviled, despised, pointed at, hated of the world, made a byworde, . . . slandered, rebuked, made a gazing stocke, *called puritans,* nice fooles, hypocrites, hair-brained fellowes, rashe, indiscreet, vain-glorious, and all that naught is; yet all this is nothing to that which many of thine excellent servents have been tried with, neither shall they lessen the glorie thou hast prepared for us.[34]

These multiple areas of religious contention in the Church of England engulfed its titular head, the king, and the royal favorite (a "false counsellor" who secretly pursued papist interests in the king's name), and contributed mightily to the atmosphere of hatred and paranoia that gripped Parliament in 1628. This, in turn, spread rapidly among the thousands of highly literate Calvinists who followed published accounts of the debates closely from both pulpit and pew. Indeed, as a direct result of violent ad hominem attacks and threats of assassination in the Commons over his abuse of power, which it said led to the duke's personal failure in the fall of La Rochelle, Buckingham was assassinated on August 22, 1628, by John Felton, a Suffolk seaman under his command. Felton was a devout predestinarian who had served as a lieutenant on the expedition to the Île de Ré. He was already dismayed by that result and deeply disturbed by long delays experienced in obtaining promotion and back pay. In fact, Buckingham had already been threatened with murder by roving bands of sick and impoverished sailors from the Île de Ré expedition. On May 19, 1628, he blamed Parliament and complained defiantly in a pamphlet, *My Lord Duke's Protestation against the Mariners:* "The King has no means to pay you till the parliament give it. . . . As for your threatenings to pull down my walls of my house around my ears: when I shall see you come with any such intention, I will let you know that I can and will correct you as sharply for your insolences and disorders as I have been forward to procure you satisfaction and have been sensible of your sufferings."[35]

While awaiting execution, Felton was anxious to set the record straight and deny pecuniary motives. He told inquisitors that by "reading the remonstrance of the House of Parliament . . . it came into his mind [that] by . . . killing the Duke he should do his country great service."[36] Thomas Scott's vengeful attitude toward the duke was not dissimilar. Scott, a Calvinist yeoman from Kent, was embittered and ultimately politicized by Buckingham's decision to billet troops returned from the Île de Ré throughout the southern coastal counties. This was a broadly unpopular action, particularly among devout Calvinists, for whom the disorders of billeting interrupted and finally defiled the religious life of the family. In light of the Calvinist emphasis on private family piety and the patriarchal role of reading the word aloud in domestic settings, Scott's pious perspective on the dangers and inconveniences of housing soldiers is understandable. He further complained that those billeted were Irish Catholic mercenaries used in the battle for Saint-Martin. In the end, Scott employed a scribe to assist in writing two lengthy narratives to present his grievances to Parliament. These gave the Commons an account of his arrest and appearance before the Privy Council for refusing to billet soldiers from Buckingham's command in his home.

Like the Wallington diaries, the Scott manuscripts exemplify the intersection of political and millennial experience in an unlearned English Calvinist household in the wake of Buckingham's defeat. But Scott had even greater personal involvement with the aftermath of the expedition than did Wallington, because on October 5, 1628, Scott's long account of day-to-day events in his besieged household was transformed into a prophetic meditation on the millennial power of two dates: July 17, 1628 (billeting ends), and August 23, 1628 (Buckingham's death following Felton's attack):

> How many are the days of thy servant? When wilt thou do judgement on my persecutors? As when on the 17 of July last the days of my affliction did end, but especially when on the 23 of August following judgement was done on my persecutors. The Lord laughs at him

(on the 17 of July) for he sees that his day doth come (on the 23 of August). They that come after this shall be astonished at his day (23 August) as they that went before were affrighted.[37]

This inspired Scott's last recorded prophesy, that Felton's sacrifice of Buckingham would finally cleanse the kingdom with blood. This expunged "the evil which for His sake I have suffered from these tyrannous lords." By "tyrannous lords," Scott meant both Buckingham and his uninvited Irish guests. Simultaneously, Scott had a miraculous vision, "brought into me," that La Rochelle itself had been delivered from death at the hands of absolutism:

> On this day and yesterday, which was the Lord's day, the news of Rochelle's deliverance is brought into me, for a certain truth (I pray God it prove so) of which before I heard many uncertain rumors. On this day also I brought into my barn all my corn after a long and late harvest, but ever since the Duke's death fair and seasonable beyond expectation of any experience within the memory of man.[38]

Scott's prophesy of La Rochelle's deliverance did not prove so, and Louis XIII's punitive "Articles of Agreement . . . upon the Rendition of the Town" were issued just three weeks later.[39] The Commons debates that culminated in the Remonstrance of 1628 reveal the extent to which the Calvinist majority, already anxious over failures in its domestic program, perceived that the arsenal of international Protestantism on the Continent had been compromised. The Commons also discerned that in this fluid context, it could assert the existence and primacy of a "true orthodoxy" in the Church of England and thus turn the chaotic situation in France to the advantage of its political and social program. The fall of La Rochelle was, therefore, inextricably linked to the decimation of the external frontier of spiritual, military, and economic security that England had nurtured and enjoyed since the defeat of the Spanish Armada during the golden age of Elizabeth. The elder Winthrop and melancholy Wallington, heroic Felton, and messianic Scott spoke for a large constituency of now anonymous Calvinist correspondents and diarists. Members of Parliament responded with anxiety over the apocalyptic instability of history, ambitions for God's favor, and a thirst for revenge, wondering aloud what they must now do to prepare themselves and their institution for the imminent arrival in England of the armies of the Antichrist.

One such M.P. was Sir John Eliot, vice-admiral of Devon, who served in the House of Commons until he was imprisoned by Charles I in the Tower of London in 1629. The spokesman for a large, complex faction of members disaffected on many levels with perceived corruption in early Stuart rule, Eliot took the greatest personal risk in the debates of 1628 and was made an example as a consequence. The king held him personally responsible not only for his prominent performance on the Commons' floor leading up to the Remonstrance of 1628—which Eliot's subcommittee wrote—but for the far greater offense of conspiring to incite the assassination of the royal favorite. Indeed, Eliot's naval experience gave him the professional authority to lead the withering parliamentary attack on Buckingham's failure as Lord Admiral of the navy. Initially, this took the form of a critique of Buckingham's part in turning a potentially successful expedition against the Spaniards at Cadiz in 1626 into a costly failure. But ultimately, the Commons turned to his "shameful" command of the fleet at the Île de Ré. Eliot also led Parliament's search for precedents to fashion the apocalyptic political language necessary to give cosmological meaning to the Commons' discourse on the fall of La Rochelle.[40]

The Remonstrance itself represented the culmination of a series of aggressive strategies against Buckingham that were deployed openly for the first time in March 1626, intended first to separate the favorite from his royal protector and then to have him impeached. These moves were orchestrated by Eliot and his group, which cobbled together a faction of disaffected peers, Calvinist predestinarians, and antiquarians in the lower house, all of whom shared an interest in the claim that Buckingham's role at court privatized "ancient" parliamentary privilege to counsel the king in the name of his people. "We sit here as the great council of the king," Eliot began on June 3, "and in that capacity it is our duty to take into consideration the state and affairs of the kingdom and . . . to give them in a true representation by way of counsel and advice . . . and to see that all things that are out of order be represented to him."[41] The appropriation by any private individual of the time-honored duty of the Commons to represent "our . . . true . . . order" was above all an illegal structural "innovation." Innovation threatened the mythical balance of continuous English institutions of liberty thought to have originated prior to the Norman Conquest of 1066 with the Germanic Anglo-Saxon tribes of the fifth century A.D., and later elaborated by humanist inquiry into Greco-Roman and feudal law. Sir Edward Coke—who, according to Pocock, "discovered law and parliament among the pre-Conquest English" and whose "essential belief" was, moreover, that "the common law had been proved good because it lasted from time immemorial"—argued that Buckingham's most egregious sin was the radical innovation of "what had been proved good" by time, a crime that Coke discovered carried with it ample legal precedent for impeachment of the royal favorite.[42]

Although historians label him a religious radical whose actions anticipated the Civil War, Eliot claimed to be a reformer whose goal was the overthrow of institutional and religious innovation and the retrieval of orthodoxy as defined by his (and Coke's) reading of England's first historical principles. Eliot took advantage of chaos and political instability that accompanied the loss of La Rochelle to merge his antiquarian scholarship of 1626 with the charismatic popular millennialism of 1628. However, from the

beginning, Eliot built his arguments for restoring stability on an "orthodox" foundation of the *maintenance* of institutional balance, precedent, and privilege *within* a well-
functioning monarchy, a strategy that would seem to be opposed to the radical parlia-
mentarianism of the 1640s. On the contrary, however, Eliot argued that the "cause of
causes" of England's decline was the "offense unnatural" of placing too much "honor"
in the hands of a single individual who was *not* the king but acted in his name. The
unnaturally ennobled favorite threatened the balance of power by destabilizing the old
equilibrium between king, privy council, and Parliament. Eliot insisted that by subtracting the ultimate "cause" of destabilization and disorder—and so its bodily and
spiritual corruption—the kingdom would return to its natural symmetry once again.
So Eliot's impulse achieved institutional reform through a process of subtraction of
corrupt elements to return to the primitive purity of first principles. These were still
available, known from time immemorial to the "true English heart." The question became, then, how to define the true heart? This question resonated powerfully with both
Reformation ideology about the primacy of the primitive Church and humanist programs of classical legal scholarship.[43]

As such, the Commons debates of 1628 represented the most forceful assertion of
the legal and political language of the "ancient constitution" yet heard in a seventeenth-
century Parliament.[44] This linkage seemed natural given the shared sense of an Anglo-
French crisis that the Counter-Reformation on the Continent conveyed to English
Calvinists during the late 1620s. The state of Protestantism in France, and La Rochelle
in particular, was likewise of special concern, because of long historical associations
with England. As the consequences of Charles IX's journey to La Rochelle in 1565
made clear, these cross-channel associations also had firm twelfth-century origins in
the southwestern French historical consciousness as well. The fortress's allegiance to
Paris was ambiguous at best, reactivating the quarrel over identity and communal privilege between La Rochelle and the French monarchy fully articulated by Louis XIII
in the Articles of Agreement in 1628.

English historians argued that the ancient individual liberties of the Rochelais—
which they conflated with the communal liberties of La Rochelle's municipal privileges—had been brutally suppressed by an absolutist Catholic tyrant. Thus, in direct
"bodily" relation to England's own battle with the Stuarts' tyrannical favorite, this political discourse meshed neatly with the elder Winthrop's trope of orthodox exclusivity in the model Body Christian. With "primitive" roots in the early Church, such
expressions of late medieval eucharistic piety and covenantal theology channeled
communication with its physical (and geographic) extremities through the nexus of a
soulish heart.[45] Parliament's researchers showed that La Rochelle's liberties circulated
from a common Germanic bloodstream shared by Anglo-Saxon progenitors and primitive Christian martyrs. Blood was now spilled together in one confluent stream of vir-

tuous resistance to violent oppression that animated the souls of English and French co-religionists.

Connected as they were in one world body that was under attack from within and without, Calvinists alleged that France's Counter-Reformation was now moving from the Continental extremities of the body Christian toward Charles I and the heart of international Protestantism. A papist vein carried infected blood to supply England's mortal disease with sustenance. After all, the francophile Buckingham (and the countess of Buckingham, his Catholic mother), Buckingham's Arminian "creature" Dr. Laud (who by 1628, had made sufficient progress at court to write most of the king's reply to the Remonstrance), and Charles's French queen, Henrietta-Maria (daughter of Henri IV and Catherine de Médicis and sister of Louis XIII) were joined together in their "nearness" to the king. There was a sinister conspiracy to infect England with the poison of Catholic absolutism, a cannibalistic disease whereby the monarch, an unknowing disciple of the Antichrist, would ultimately devour first the law and then his subjects. The Remonstrance thus posited an apocalyptic battle for dominance between two competing orthodoxies: Calvinism and absolutism. In the middle, by reason of his nearness to the king, stood the royal favorite, Buckingham, leading an advance guard of Arminian agents provocateurs and Jesuitical imposters.

Eliot was explicit in blaming internal weakness, the major symptom of this disease, for disabling England's historically symbiotic relationship with southwestern France. This, he argued bitterly, would effectively force the kingdom to radically redefine its worldview. England now faced new and immediate threats to its identity as the world's touchstone of stability and historical consciousness of having inherited its security from the immemorial past. Eliot saw the origin of this historical linkage in the "wisdoms of our ancestors," which had been put into practice and achieved a golden age in his own lifetime in the rule of "that never to be forgotten excellent Queen Elizabeth." Indeed, with Buckingham's "disorder" of James I and then his son Charles, Eliot argued that the duke's religious and sexual ambiguities had an innovative effect on early Stuart rule. Buckingham's corruption as a succubus on the body politic reestablished a context for cataclysmic historical reversals like the one at the Île de Ré. The favorite had substituted a perverse form of government for a balanced one, which instilled pathological weakness, enabling the emergence of a new anti-Elizabethan cosmology at court.

Elizabeth had "advanced" England powerfully, while suppressing dangers in a world she created with the help of her French alliance against Spain. Yet Buckingham had proceeded "directly contrary and opposite, *ex diametro,* to those ends":

> the cause of those dangers were our disorders, and our disorders are yet our greatest dangers, and not so much the potency of our enemies as the weakness of ourselves do threaten

us. . . . And if in these there be not reformation, we need no foes abroad: time itself will ruin us. . . . For if we view ourselves at home are we in strength, are we in reputation equal to our ancestors? If we view ourselves abroad, are our friends as many as our enemies? . . . What counsel to the loss of the Palatinate[?]. . . . What counsel gave direction to that late action whose wounds are yet ableeding? I mean the expedition to Ré, of which there is yet so sad a memory in all men.[46]

"What counsel" had dismantled France's internal unity, dangerously interrupting the natural continuities of national security between "our ancestors" and Elizabeth?

You know the wisdoms of our ancestors, the practice of their times; how they preserved their safeties. . . . Against this greatness and ambition we likewise know the proceeding of . . . Queen Elizabeth. . . . You know how she advanced herself, how she advanced this kingdom . . . how she enjoyed a full security . . . she built on . . . unity in France . . . the division in France between the Protestants and their King . . . has made an absolute breech between that state and us.[47]

❧ Huguenot Historians Write English history ❧

Refugee French Huguenot historians forged ancestral links with England's consciousness of its primordial past. Despairing for a homeland lost to absolutism, Hugh Trevor-Roper argues, Huguenot historians were central to the development of English historical Pyrrhonism—a skeptical "distrust of all great schemes of history" that, Trevor-Roper contends, "was the chief contribution of the Huguenots to the study of history in the half-century after the Revocation."[48] As Pocock and others noted long ago, however, Pyrrhonism became widespread earlier than the Revocation of the Edict of Nantes, easily as early as the sixteenth century, and not just among English Huguenots.[49] For Pocock, the techniques of historical criticism were common during the Italian Renaissance. Diffused via the Venetian book trade into northern Europe by the later sixteenth century, the new criticism circulated first among French and then among English and Netherlandish humanists.

New histories formed a wide spectrum from Pyrrhonist despair about the future of literary narrative ("as to whether," Pocock writes, "the story of the past could be told at all") to highly original and complex "critical methods." These methods determined "the reliability of facts" about the past, as developed by French scholars such as Jean Mabillon and adapted to the English context by legal historians including Coke.[50] Still, Trevor-Roper's thesis is useful, particularly if his chronology is adjusted backward to include pivotal events that occurred more than a century before the Revocation. Huguenot historiography, including historical Pyrrhonism, found its formative impulse in the genocidal violence of the 1560s, in the midst of the first civil wars of religion. It was elaborated following the loss of the Palatinate and La Rochelle. By 1685, depending on regional context and individual experience, the critical tradition in Huguenot historiography was already in place inside France, from which it had long since traveled to the refugee historians' Atlantic hosts.

Trevor-Roper appears to muddy his argument against the limitations of skepticism with surprisingly nativistic aspersions against foreign historians "[in]capable of original thought." At the same time, however, he shows intense engagement with the mythic past by the refugee historians and their English Calvinist allies. The essence of that process of reading English history through the Huguenots' tumultuous *désert* experience was not its derivativeness but its ambiguity. Having first reduced the problem to unproductive binary oppositions between retrograde French criticism and progressive British creativity, Trevor-Roper then tries to break out of his predicament by reassuring readers that "Huguenot historians were not entirely destructive" after all.

We may extrapolate from Trevor-Roper's critique of Pyrrhonic despair that Huguenot historians were again engaged in a kind of *bricolage.* This signified the fluidity of their identity with the lived experience of dispersion; of being, *simultaneously,* destroyers and artisans of reconstituted historical and scriptural texts that tied past and present together. This constructed a textual continuity with the past in "real time," suggesting an experiential foundation from which Huguenot historians may themselves have asked Trevor-Roper's essential question: once "inadmissible" historical systems were deconstructed to fit the present context, "how was the historian to begin again?"

The answer was found in the libraries of both Calvinist and humanist scholars. For most sixteenth-century Huguenot historians and early seventeenth-century English parliamentary historians, these identities were combined: "He must go back to first principles, re-examine the sources," Trevor-Roper writes, "and so provide a new basis on which . . . a more accurate system could afterwards be built." The urgency of the French civil wars of religion propelled this program of historical reconstruction and reinterpretation forward until common sources of cross-channel confluence in the mythic Germanic root of Anglo-Saxon law and ancient liberty were found. This project joined the great sixteenth-century Huguenot jurist and publicist François Hotman—whose enormously influential *Francogallia* was written in 1573, partially in response to the terror of the St. Bartholomew's Day Massacre—with Coke and Eliot writing the Remonstrance of 1628.[51]

Narrowing his focus to the late date of 1685, Trevor-Roper claims this program found its first and last great practitioner in the Huguenot historian Paul de Rapin-Thoyras (1661–1725), exiled to Holland and then England following the Revocation. Rapin emerged from the wreckage of the Revocation and historical Pyrrhonism to find refuge in his paradigmatic "Old Whig" *History of England: As Well Ecclesiastical as Civil*

(1726–47), which extols the unifying virtue and stable continuity of primordial English institutions of individual liberty.[52] The Glorious Revolution seemed to signal a second Reformation, and Rapin was bitterly disappointed that the Huguenots did not return en masse from exile to France behind the armies of William of Orange. In 1688, it finally seemed possible to reverse the catastrophe of 1685 by overthrowing absolutism and in its place reactivating the tradition of Anglo-Saxon liberty and religious tolerance in France, as it had been in England.[53]

Trevor-Roper argues that Rapin's *History* stood alone as England's master narrative of its past until the Scottish natural philosopher and historian David Hume (1711–76) refuted Rapin's model. Hume is Trevor-Roper's heroic Enlightenment figure— a "far greater man" than the reactionary Rapin and one fully "capable of original thought"—who framed his modern narrative of *The History of England* in terms of its "material progress." Trevor-Roper thus implicitly attacks both Whig history and French intellectuals simultaneously. He praises Hume's language of change, elucidated in terms of late eighteenth-century scientific empiricism, because it destabilized the synchronic logic of the "Old Whig" synthesis of the early eighteenth century.[54]

Trevor-Roper is only half-right. Rapin's work may have signaled one ending for this tradition in Anglo-French Calvinist culture, but since its historiographical origins are also found in the war years of the 1560s, this process was more complex than he imagines. Religious violence provided the immediate context for Hotman's and Coke's work in the history of the law, as well as Jean de Léry's natural history of Brazil and, most important for our purposes here, Bernard Palissy's artisanal, religious and natural philosophical history of La Rochelle and its Saintongeais hinterland. Trevor-Roper's derision of the parasitic impulse in Huguenot writers of English history reflects a one-dimensional view of refugee craftsmanship. At once creative and "unoriginal," Huguenots built history into available materials provided by their Atlantic hosts. The same pattern appears in Palissy's work and in the commercial triumph of the New York leather chair.

The "cause of causes": England as "sudden prey"

Eliot's aim was also to "go back to first principles, to re-examine the sources." His task carried specific historical languages and meanings that auditors had long since associated with France in general and La Rochelle in particular. It was this language of first principles against heterodoxy and innovation that provided the charismatic religious and political framework for the Remonstrance. This was also the language of last resort for Eliot's faction, just as the Remonstrance was clearly the last parliamentary instrument available to bring Buckingham down after the first attempt in the Commons to impeach him failed in 1626. The earlier failure was largely due to the king's intercession to protect his royal prerogative on behalf of his favorite, and the role of the House of Lords, which could be relied upon to defend the king's interests.

In 1626, Eliot's inquiry provided the framework for a subcommittee called "Causes of Causes," which undertook a broad review of the grievances against Buckingham. These grievances were pursued under the dubious legal (but telling social) category of "common fame" (or that which was accepted as common knowledge). It included "multiplicity of offices in one man's hand"; "not right ordering of the king's revenues"; "anticipating of revenues"; "exhausting of honour and buying them"; and the "growth of popery." In 1626, however, the Commons had only limited authority to pursue specific charges against the duke, because it possessed no judicial powers of condemnation and punishment. Traditionally, such powers resided in the Upper House, where the Lords, acting on the king's behalf, sat in judgment on Buckingham. But the king himself was the greatest obstacle. In the Parliament of 1626, Eliot claimed that Buckingham had acted illegally *and* in "common fame" so far as "the people" were concerned, yet paradoxically *without* the king's knowledge. In other words, the duke had acted alone but in the king's name, an impeachable offense according to parliamentary precedent. Charles I easily countered this tenuous maneuver, which he considered a threat to his sovereignty, by personally accepting responsibility for Buckingham's actions, affirming that they had been directed from the throne. With that, the threat of impeachment ended, and Buckingham continued on his path toward the Île de Ré.[55]

However, in 1628, when Eliot and the Commons regrouped and attacked the excessive power of the duke once again, they cohered behind the negative public opinion that animated the Calvinist majority in the aftermath of the calamity in the Bay of Biscay, and they also showed how much had been learned from experience about the subtleties of parliamentary procedure. A remonstrance gave the Commons far greater latitude in systematically making its case to both the king and his literate subjects than was possible within the strict legal limitations of an impeachment trial. Better yet, Eliot understood that unlike impeachment proceedings, remonstrances did not require the judicial cooperation of the previously recalcitrant Lords. Finally, a remonstrance allowed Eliot to exploit the legal possibilities of the role of the Commons as the king's "Great Council":

> Acting as the "Great Council" of the king, the Commons could complain of matters which could not form the basis of criminal charges. Their function was "truly to present to the king what he doth not know alreadie about his ministers and officers." At the same time he showed that he thought the Remonstrance was a more moderate way of proceeding than impeachment.[56]

As a document that represented the collective voice of the king's "Great Council," the Remonstrance of 1628 effectively harnessed Eliot, an advocate of constitutional privilege and balance of power, to the growing millennialist faction in the Commons. Together, they composed a lengthy list of "Causes" that finally reached back beyond the failure at the Île de Ré to Buckingham himself—the "cause of causes"—whose religious and political transgressions led inevitably to lamentations that the insidious power of hidden corruption at court had infected and sickened the state, both at home and abroad. The intractable effect of that primary cause was a kind of death on the historical margins of the British archipelago; that is to say, the death of La Rochelle, and with it, an apocalyptic sense of England's profound material and spiritual insecurity in the rapidly diminishing world of international Protestantism.[57]

Metaphors of medical pathology saturate the Remonstrance, which often approaches the eulogistic tone of a deathwatch over England's weakened "body." The Commons finally diagnosed the cause of this potentially fatal disease to be both internal and unnatural. If death was to be the ultimate outcome, it was also willful and premature—the act of a murderer. But first forensic evidence of the progress of pathology must be sifted, classified, and presented to the king. This search for a systemic "cause of causes" was an extension into Calvinist political culture of the new universal Paracelsian medicine of the sort practiced by the younger Winthrop and his scientific community. It was not sufficiently therapeutic to treat the symptoms or humoral conditions; the central cause of the corruption was at the core of the disease, and it must be revealed, located, and treated. Ernst Kantorowitz has called attention to the central role played in the mythology of the divine right of kings by the notion that the monarch had two bodies, one human and secular, the other sacred and mystical, which, as in the mortal incarnation of Christ were inextricably, if sometimes ambiguously, intertwined.[58] That is why in the Remonstrance of 1628, the Commons appealed to Charles I to consider that he alone possessed the mystical power to reverse the course of the mortal disease that afflicted his kingdom, because it also afflicted his own physical body. To eliminate the cause, the Commons remonstrated with the monarch to turn inward and purify his own heart—which had now become the cancerous Buckingham's host—by expelling the illness from his presence.

Buckingham's "nearness" to Charles's body was thus harnessed to the fear of contagion. In the final clause added by Eliot's subcommittee on causes (which generated the written text), the Commons reminded the king of his duty to himself as well as the nation to protect the safety of the monarch's two bodies (his "royal person") from the effects of proximity to corruption:

> And our humble desire is that your Majesty would be pleased to take into your princely consideration whether, in respect the said Duke has so abused his power, it be safe for your majesty and the kingdom that he continue still in his . . . place of nearness to your Majesty's royal person.[59]

The Commons was saddened to report abundant evidence that the king had failed to protect himself from this plague of "nearness." "The great and urgent affairs of this church and commonwealth . . . at this time in apparent danger of ruin and destruction" had opened the doors even wider to deadly infection by England's adversaries, for "the multitude and potency of your enemies are abroad, what be their malicious and ambitious ends[?]" The king need look no further for answers than "the dangers threatened thereby to your sacred person and your kingdom and the calamities which have already fallen and do daily increase upon your friends and allies."[60] "Calamities" had befallen friends and allies in La Rochelle, showing how "near" the symptoms of England's "strange" internal malady had come to finally claiming Charles's kingdom (and so the king himself) as its final and most passionately desired victim. "Vigilant and constantly industrious" enemies brought "weakness" to the court that threatened the symbolic and physical heart of England's health and security. Equal measures of "orthodox" Calvinist vigilance and industriousness on the part of the monarch were required to reverse the course of the disease, before England, like La Rochelle, became mere "prey," hunted down and devoured by Richelieu or other bloodthirsty predators sent by the Antichrist:

> To which end we most humbly entreat your Majesty to cast your eyes upon the miserable condition of this your kingdom of late so strangely weakened, impoverished, dishonored, and dejected, that unless, through your Majesty's most gracious wisdom, goodness, and justice, it be speedily raised to a better condition, it is in no little danger to become a sudden prey of the enemies thereof, and of the most happy and flourishing to be the most miserable and contemptible nation in the world.[61]

❧ Secret Working and Combination ❧

The Remonstrance of 1628, "in the name of all the commons of your realm (whom we represent)," begged Charles "to cast your eyes upon . . . your kingdom." This rhetoric allowed the Commons to focus the king's vision and assumed primary importance in the presentation of claims against Buckingham. Eliot's faction began to construct a powerful argument about concealment, insisting that Arminian and other papist heresies had been secreted in a conspiratorial cabal at court, in plain sight to the Commons but strangely obscure to royal perception. Perception was thus dissembled under the guise of "specious pretenses":

> And we do verily believe that all or most of the things which we shall now present unto your Majesty are either unknown to you, or else by some of your Majesty's ministers offered under such specious pretenses as may hide their own bad intentions and ill consequences . . . take notice . . . there is a general fear conceived in your people of secret work-

ing and combination to introduce into this kingdom innovation and change of our holy religion, more precious unto us than our lives and whatever this world can afford . . . at which your Majesty out of the quick sense of your own religious heart cannot but be in the highest measure displeased.[62]

The Remonstrance proceeded in its tragic narrative of the "innovation," decline, and death of "orthodox" Calvinist religious culture to expose a multitude "of the things . . . unknown" to Charles, including knowledge that Catholics "do find extraordinary favors in court from persons of great power and quality there." Buckingham, though a leading member of the Church of England, was directly implicated through his mother, "the Countess of Buckingham, who, herself openly professing that religion, is a known favorer of them that do the same."[63]

After the king, the duke was the primary patron at court. This was a position of unsurpassed power and wealth in England—and most early modern monarchies— where systems of governance, prestige, and economic opportunity were based on courtly patronage. The favorite therefore commonly attracted intense hostility from would-be clients who felt marginalized or had fallen to the status of outgroup and were thereby denied lucrative access to power. While sincere religious sentiment was present, it was not the only motivation behind aspiring Calvinists whose courtly status and acquisition of places in the government bureaucracy had diminished in the middle to late 1620s. They and Eliot wrote in the Remonstrance that the procurement of "honor, offices, and places of command" by allegedly Catholic courtiers was "a toleration odious to God, full of dishonor and extreme disprofit to your Majesty, of great scandal and grief to your good people, and of apparent danger to the present state of your Majesty and of this kingdom."[64] More scandalous yet, just as the countess of Buckingham cast doubt on her son's religious reputation by familial association, so too Charles's French queen, Henrietta Maria, tainted her husband by holding "publicly frequent mass at Denmark House [the queen's residence]," thus "combining their counsels and strength together, to the hazard of your Majesty's safety and the state . . . especially in these doubtful and calamatous times."[65] In such an atmosphere of tolerance at the highest levels of the state, was it any wonder that the Arminian Bishop Neile and especially Laud—"being Protestants in show but Jesuits in opinion"— should also infiltrate the court "to further increase our fears concerning innovation of religion"? At this point in his text, Eliot began to merge the language of "unnatural" "innovation" in the balance of power from the impeachment proceedings of 1626 with that of orthodox Calvinism's "innovation of religion," so that by 1628,the rhetoric of international politics and religion converged in the Commons. The relation between the elder Winthrop's governance of Massachusetts and his former patrons in the Commons is particularly resonant here.

Internal spiritual threats to a formerly pure and balanced body and soul, together with external military threats to the kingdom's security, were thus to emerge as fearful symmetries at the core of the Remonstrance's cosmology. It seemed inevitable to its authors that the effects of such baneful connections would be defenses that were disabled by heresy and the newly "replenished" Counter-Reformation, which functioned inside a diseased organism. The protective boundaries—both metaphorical and material—between home and abroad were negated. While a "strangely weakened" England played a tragic role in the fall of international Protestantism's venerable "allies and friends" on the northwestern fringe of the British isles, another violent tragedy was brewing to test the kingdom's dwindling strength: the Irish were "kept in ignorance and are apt to be easily seduced to error and superstition." Here, the Roman Catholic Church grew unchecked under "popish jurisdiction" because the monarch failed to have Ireland "seasonably repressed" (later to become Cromwell's brutal task):

> It does not a little to increase our dangers and fears in this way, to understand the miserable condition of your kingdom of Ireland, where without control the popish religion is openly professed and practiced in every part thereof, popish jurisdiction being there generally exercised and allowed—monasteries, nunneries, and other superstitious houses newly erected, re-edified, and replenished with men and women of several orders, and in a plentiful manner maintained at Dublin and most of the great towns and diverse other places of the kingdom.[66]

Thus, with the fearful specter of Irish barbarians on England's borders, the Remonstrance presented ominous new evidence that England itself was finally experiencing secret intimations of the same "open force and violence prosecuted in other countries." In addition to the Irish troops billeted in Thomas Scott's Kent, other "strangers," including "the scum of Germany," were "placed in the inland of the country" by an unwitting king under the influence of corrupt advisors. Relying on the authority of "an author in fashion," Sir John Maynard cited "this design out of Machiavelli," (chapter 12 of *The Prince*), "that it is absolutely the destruction of a country to entertain mercenaries either they are valiant or coward; if valiant and the prince conquer, he is prisoner to them; if a coward, all is lost."[67] Maynard went on to remind the Commons that the Germans were especially dangerous as cavalry, because "one horseman is worse than 10 footmen." Eliot, who used humanist rhetoric to good effect throughout the debates, recalled classical precedents to predict that Germans were enlisted covertly by "our intestine foes" to form a modern day "praetorian cohort," a fortiori, a "trojan horse"; "making it too apparent that there is a great probability of . . . some ill design upon his Majesty's person."[68] This news was especially alarming in light of "the standing commission granted to the Duke of Buckingham to be general of an army within the land in the time of peace":

> The report of the strange and dangerous purpose of bringing in German horse and riders
> . . . gave us just cause of fear. . . . There wanted not those that . . . might secretly . . . con-
> trive to change the frame both of religion and government . . . the bringing in of strangers
> for aid has been . . . to England fatal . . . we are bold to declare to your Majesty and the
> whole world that we hold it far beneath the heart of any free Englishman to think that
> this victorious nation should now stand in need of German soldiers to defend their own
> King and kingdom.[69]

As Scott's anguished petitions to Parliament show on a deeply personal level, throughout southern coastal England—which local custom and resistance placed almost beyond the reach of London's legal and military authority in the early seventeenth century[70]—the billeting of soldiers increased the pressure on the kingdom's mounting military and religious insecurity. Indeed, "the conditions of their persons (many of them not being natives of this kingdom, nor of the same, but opposite, religion), the placing them upon the seacoast where making head amongst themselves they may unite with the popish party at home if the occasion serve, or join with an invading enemy to do extreme mischief."[71] The threat of a Spanish conspiracy played a prominent role here again. On June 6, Sir Nathaniel Rich argued that to arm the Irish Catholics now billeted in Kent for the Île de Ré expedition was subversive: "For the Irish soldiers, some know the state of Ireland. And it has been against the practice of our state that that the Irish should wear or use weapons at all. And in Spain they instruct them what they can in war. Now, when religion is in peril, it is dangerous to instruct the Irish in arms. It is such a counsel as brings danger into England."[72]

On April 10, 1628, Thomas Scott summarized Calvinist feelings of fear and despair from hard personal experience, after a mercenary from the Île de Ré expedition named "Ferrier, the serjeant, is commanded to bring two lusty Irish popish soldiers unto my house and to leave them there. They enter my house and will not out except my wife will allow them 6s. apiece by the week." In a letter to Herbert Palmer, a Calvinist lecturer and friend in the parish of St. Alphege, Scott remained defiant:

> I would billet none nor pay any money. It is against the liberty of a free Englishman and
> gentleman and of a parliament man, and intended by the Duke to do us a mischief. For
> to what other use can Irish popish soldiers . . . serve? They, together with the . . . popish
> and Arminian . . . faction . . . must help set up popery and the excise and, as some of them
> do already give out, cut the Puritans' throats.[73]

This "strange and dangerous" conjunction of England's inner and outer demons in 1628—of Catholicism's secret power growing steadily at home (while "weakening" the "body" of the kingdom almost beyond recovery), and the Counter-Reformation's outward military strength abroad (demonstrated at La Rochelle)—was no mere accident

of history. It was the Old Testament God's cosmic warning to England of an apocalyptic future of sacred purification and "dispersion" by violence. In the language of the
Remonstrance, the kingdom would be scourged if it failed to root out the "cause" and
effect a cure. Just as the elder Winthrop wrote Margaret to reveal his grim prophesy
of the turning cup that signified the approach of final things following the fall of La
Rochelle, so too the Commons perceived the same awesome hand of divine retribution falling on England for "some secret and strange cooperating here . . . for . . . neglect of his holy religion":

> And now, if to all of these your Majesty will be pleased to add the consideration of the
> time, wherein these courses, tending to the destruction of true religion within these your
> kingdoms, have been taken here, even when the same is with open force and violence
> prosecuted in other countries, and all the reformed churches in Christendom either dis-
> persed or miserably distressed, we do humbly appeal . . . that there is some secret and
> strange cooperating here with the enemies of our religion abroad for the utter extirpation
> thereof . . . remember the displeasure of almighty God always bent against the neglect of
> his holy religion, the strokes of whose divine justice we have already felt and still do feel
> with smart and sorrow in great measure.[74]

Finally, "out of the depth of sorrow, [we the Commons] lift up our cries to heaven
for help and, next under God, . . . appeal ourselves unto your sacred Majesty," to understand how, "in consideration of the time," England's weakness was now so palpable,
its decline so precipitous, its vulnerability so complete, that even with the king's
"speedy help and reformation," England was no longer a "victorious nation." On the
contrary, the hard lessons learned at La Rochelle about England's humiliating new
military and spiritual insecurity were abundantly clear; the cost to the kingdom's shattered defenses in men and ships had been overwhelming:

> We do humbly pray [your Majesty] to consider whether the miserable disasters and ill
> success that has accompanied all your late designs and actions, particularly [at] . . . the Isle
> de Ré and the last expedition to Rochelle, have not extremely wasted the stock of honor
> that was left unto this kingdom, sometimes terrible to all other nations and now declin-
> ing to contempt beneath the meanest. Together with our honor we there lost those . . .
> who, had they lived, we might have some better hope of recovering it again: our valiant
> and expert colonels, captains, and commanders, and many thousand common soldiers
> and mariners, though we have some cause to think that your Majesty is not yet rightly in-
> formed thereof, and that of six or seven thousand of your subjects lost at the Isle of Ré,
> your Majesty received information but of a few hundreds. And this dishonor and loss was
> purchased with loss of above a million of treasure.[75]

Having thus witnessed the utter decimation of the royal navy, and with it, the vanguard of England's most experienced and ideologically dependable Calvinist officer corps by Richelieu's forces at the Île de Ré, the Commons' turned to England's land defenses in the search of security. But the island's last hope to repel the invasion now expected daily from the Continent—the line of aging late medieval fortresses along England's coast—"are exceeding weak and decayed, and want both men and munition."[76] The Commons asked by what "strange improvidence" the vast stores of gunpowder kept in the Tower of London for defense of the kingdom had fallen to levels of unprecedented scarcity in England's time of greatest need. The answer to this and every rhetorical question was that in each case, the "cause of causes" was the same secret cabal of crypto-Catholics led by the seemingly omnipotent Buckingham. This cabal was responsible for all the other "miserable disasters" that had befallen England, including above all else the fall of La Rochelle and the decimation of the other "allies and friends" of international Protestantism.[77] The Commons concluded "the principal cause of which evils and dangers we conceive to be the excessive power of the Duke of Buckingham, and the abuse of that power." Therefore, "we humbly submit unto your Majesty's excellent wisdom," whether "so great power as rests in him by sea and land should be in the hands of any one subject whatsoever . . . in respect the said Duke has so abused his power, [can] it be safe for your Majesty and your kingdom to continue him either in his great offices of trust or in his place of nearness and counsel about your sacred person."[78]

❧ The Anatomy of Princely Love ❧

The appropriate answer should have been as transparent to the king's "sacred person" as it was to the "faithful hearts" of the Commons. Charles had to remember that Parliament, not the favorite, was by right of precedent the king's authentic "Great Council," and that, "in discharge of the duty we owe," the devastating claims of the Remonstrance were "a true representation of our present dangers and pressing calamities." The deferential politeness of the Remonstrance tempered the tough message contained in its concluding paragraphs. Thus when the House finally "beseech[ed] your Majesty graciously to accept [our council] and take the same to heart," this was also by way saying that the king's heart could not be given freely to any individual favorite, something only private persons could do. Beyond the limits delineated by natural philosophy and historical precedent, the monarch's heart was not, in the opinion of the Commons, within Charles's princely power to give. Despite its multiple nature, the king had to learn to master the mysteries of his heart; to constrain its natural passion to operate in an orderly manner; to "frame" his mutable heart within a strict metaphysical hierarchy. This structure was ordained by God and assured each dynasty's claims to the awesome power of divine right because it contained the essential mystical nexus that balanced the soulish love of England's "royal person" between heaven and earth. Thus, the Commons insisted that the royal heart was to be shared simultaneously with the sacred realm (also claimed by the "orthodox" Commons), where it extended upward to embrace "the honor of almighty God and the maintenance of his true religion"; the dual-bodied (or middle) realm, where it functioned as both spirit and matter to provide "the safety and happiness of your most excellent Majesty"; and finally, by extension downward, the secular realm of the commonwealth, where it secured "the safety and prosperity of your people your greatest happiness, and their love the richest treasure."[79]

The irony of Eliot's diagnosis of the anatomy of princely love was not lost on Charles I. More famously than any English monarch before (or since), Charles had been personally associated with the natural philosophy of the heart. By autumn 1628, it was "common fame" throughout European learned culture, that William Harvey (1578–1657), Charles's brilliant court physician, had dedicated his *De motu cordis* (*On the Motion of the Heart and Blood in Animals*) (Frankfurt, 1628) to his royal patron. The dedication came as the culmination of three years of intensive personal interaction with the Stuarts as an aspiring courtier, royal physician, natural philosopher, and loyal protégé.

Harvey's status climbed rapidly at court after he impressed Charles with his political discretion as attending physician during the mortal illness of James I, who died, possibly of kidney failure, on March 27, 1625. Harvey's value to Charles I and Buckingham was proven after a much publicized episode when the duke was accused of poisoning the dying king on his sickbed. Unknown to his "sworn physicians," suspicious witnesses saw secret "plasters and potions" applied to James in his bedchamber, "the Lord Duke's folk having brought it in." Suspicions became accusations when James took an immediate turn for the worse and died.[80] Harvey, the only physician on record attending at that hour, had apparently approved the treatment without consulting his colleagues, and he was subsequently implicated with Buckingham as a regicide by Dr. George Elsingham, James I's displaced personal physician. Elsingham's charges were published in *The Fore-Runner of Revenge*, a sensational pamphlet that first appeared in anticipation of Buckingham's impeachment trial in 1626, and then again in 1642, the second time as a Civil War polemical tract.

The conspiracy theory was aired in 1626, along with a spate of other charges against the duke. Like the trial itself, these accusations came to nothing. Popular suspicions of Buckingham as a poisoner of kings did not disappear. Fear of a repeat performance to finally kill the troubled Stuart dynasty altogether had migrated quickly to Charles as next in succession. Uncertainty about the king disquieted readers of the Remonstrance and informed the meaning of the duke's "dangerous nearness" to the presumably increasingly vulnerable Charles. As if to reinforce this reading, Coke—while careful to elide reference to Buckingham's complicity in James's death (since the duke was officially exonerated in his 1626 impeachment trial)—cleverly reactivated this subtext by presenting terrifying evidence from the sainted Elizabeth's reign. This showed a historical correlation between invasion, regicide, poison, and, above all, religious toleration, which "patronized" papist "weapons." Like Elizabeth (and unlike James), would the weakened and declining Charles emerge, with his kingdom, a survivor?

> We shall never know the commonwealth flourish but when the church flourishes. They live and die together. . . . If you have laws and they be not executed, it will patronize wicked doers. When Queen Elizabeth, in '88, had repelled the Spaniards, there was a conspiracy to poison our Queen, and no three years but some attempt was threatened . . . If there be so many recusants now we are not safe. They intend to make Spain a monarchy [over England]. If we proceed against these weapons, I fear no invasions. Let the laws be executed against papists. I saw a commission for a toleration. I dare say Queen Elizabeth would never have consented to the like.[81]

Although Harvey's role as a whole in the alleged conspiracy in 1625 was unclear, he had definitely been in attendance at James's bedside when the disputed medications were administered, and he had later testified that they were relatively harmless and ineffectual. It seemed suspicious that within a few weeks of the end of Buckingham's trial, Charles (with Buckingham's approval) quietly rewarded Harvey for his tact (or perhaps his silence) with a "free gift" of £100 "for his pains and attendance about the person of his Majesty's late dear father." Such suspicions were not allayed when, on February 10, 1626, the king granted Harvey an extraordinary "general pardon" for his part in the affair, though an explanation of the actions that warranted pardon are absent from the document.[82]

In December 1627, his loyalty and discretion beyond dispute, Harvey was ordered by Buckingham and the Privy Council to come to the duke's aid once again, this time by assuming the politically sensitive task of overseeing the court's medical efforts on behalf of thousands of sick and wounded soldiers and marines from the Île de Ré expedition, who had returned to Portsmouth and Plymouth early in November. The astonishing mortality rate of the returnees indicates that Harvey (and four fellows from the Royal College of Physicians) could do little to help the men.[83] But as the Commons also claimed in the Remonstrance, the final, devastating figures were intentionally hidden from the king and Parliament. This was a convenient fiction that served the purposes of the Commons, but may also have served Harvey equally well, as it would his interested patrons, especially Charles and Laud.

It is thought that *De motu cordis* first appeared at booksellers in Frankfurt a few months *after* the Remonstrance was written. By June 1628, however, the publication of

Harvey's work had long been anticipated in London's learned culture. Harvey was no-toriously slow to publish and had completed the manuscript years before finally send-ing it to press. The manuscript's contents and association with Charles I's patronage were already well known in court and philosophical circles, the result of a celebrated series of public lectures and anatomical demonstrations Harvey gave in 1627 at the Royal College of Physicians, using notes taken directly from the original text. In ad-dition, as was the custom among most favored natural philosophers, Harvey gave fre-quent demonstrations for visitors at his laboratory. He did the same at court, where Charles was an enthusiastic amateur natural philosopher with a special interest in medical subjects.[84]

Therefore, it is probable that the patronage and thesis of *De motu cordis* were com-mon knowledge in early Stuart London, as well as among scientific patrons in Euro-pean courts, university medical faculty, and private laboratories, at least one year before the book actually appeared in print. Since by 1627 the manuscript was at the workshop of his German publisher, Willem Fitzer (and out of Harvey's hands), the now famous dedication was probably sent to press after Buckingham's expedition be-gan to go badly, but before the start of the debates:

> To the most illustrious and indomitable Prince, Charles, King of Great Britain, France, and Ireland, defender of the faith.
>
> Most illustrious Prince!
>
> The heart of animals is the foundation of their life, the sovereign of everything within them, the sun of their microcosm, that upon which all growth depends, from which all power proceeds. The King, in like manner, is the foundation of his kingdom, the sun of the world around him, the heart of the republic, the fountain whence all power, all grace doth flow. What I have here written of the motions of the heart I am the more embold-ened to present to your Majesty . . . because almost all things human are done after human examples, and many things in a King are after the pattern of the heart. The knowledge of his heart, therefore, will not be useless to a Prince, as embracing a kind of Divine example of his functions,—and it has ever been usual with men to compare small things with great. Here, at all events, best of Princes, placed as you are on the pinnacle of human affairs, you may at once contemplate the prime mover in the body of man, and the emblem of your own sovereign power.[85]

"The knowledge of his heart" that Harvey's Paracelsian experiments on circulation throughout the body famously revealed to his king and patron textualized precisely the same portion of his corporeal and metaphorical anatomy that Charles I was asked by the Commons "to . . . contemplate" in the Remonstrance of 1628. As we have seen, however, Eliot and his faction emerged from its polemical dissection with quite the

opposite result. Unlike Harvey's benign, coordinated, and, above all, stable representation of the homeostatic system in *De motu cordis,* when Charles was forced to contemplate Eliot's diagnosis of the weakened "microcosm" of his interior world, he failed
to find a healthy "sovereign of everything within . . . the heart of the republic, the fountain whence all power, all grace doth flow." Instead of a Copernican "sun of the world,"
the flawless, infinite function of which naturally balanced the "flow" of power between
microcosm and macrocosm, Charles was asked to "contemplate" the wreckage of a
royal heart ebbing at the center of a cosmos in mortal peril; one that was diseased, "disordered," and, from the perspective of a House of Commons trivialized by its king,
dangerously out of balance. The Remonstrance thus claimed inextricable cosmological linkage with La Rochelle. First in France and then in England, an angry God had
been forced to intervene with millennial force, to instill terror, and, a fortiori, the sense
of an ending. Far from beating forever with "sovereign" precision (as Harvey would
have it), time had run out on Charles's anarchic royal heart. Without immediate healing (nothing less than the cleansing of his soul to cast out contagion), apocalypse would
overcome his "ruined" dynastic house and kingdom: "A rueful and lamentable spectacle we confess it must needs be to behold those ruins in so fair an house, so many
diseases, and almost every one of them mortal, in so strong and well tempered a body
as this kingdom lately was."[86]

The intractable reality asserted by this rhetoric ensured that Charles would never
take advice from the Remonstrance "to heart," for its diagnosis aggressively presumed
to reveal morbidity in the very "fountain" of his mystical power. Predictably, within
days of receiving the document, the king dissolved Parliament. The story of Charles's
subsequent struggle with the Calvinist opposition until his execution by Cromwell in
1649 is very well known and does not require further elaboration here. In the short
term, however, after the monarchy's constant search for "supply" to pay down debt and
revive its crippled foreign policy necessitated a final stormy session in 1629, Charles
dispensed with Parliament altogether for eleven years, and extracted funds from the
wealthy mercantile sector "by right," using the much despised "forced loan" or the lucrative "Tonnage and Poundage" duty as his preferred instruments of taxation.

The Arminian ascendancy quickened under Dr. Laud, whose career at court flourished while the unrepentant Eliot sat in prison. Nevertheless, Eliot contributed in a
minor fashion to a distinguished body of prison literature that marked the early Stuart era. The books that emerged from Eliot's confinement celebrated without irony
"the never dying glory" of the monarchy, the "ancient" mystical principles of which—
including the "mysteries of state" and *arcana imperii*—he still intended to reform from
"innovation."[87] This Calvinist vice-admiral of Devon was neither a radical nor a precursor of regicide. However, despite his personal losses, the Remonstrance achieved
Eliot's main purpose. After all, the assassin Felton proved a most attentive reader. J. N.

Ball argues to the contrary that Eliot's ultimate "failure" was his "persistent refusal to face . . . genuine structural tensions instead of . . . personalities," when he adhered anachronistically to political theory which "saw . . . political discords . . . in terms of ill-disposed individuals but for whose manoeuvrings and ambitions the political scene would have realized the state of ideal 'Elizabethan' harmony." Still, if Eliot's analysis of the "cause of causes" of discord, fragmentation, and insecurity was anachronistic, it was also informed by the most current theoretical principles available in seventeenth-century natural philosophy.[88]

On June 17, 1628, the day he received the Remonstrance, Charles could not disagree with Eliot (or the elder Winthrop) when it was observed that of the "many . . . mortal" diseases that beset the kingdom's "body," the annihilation of the Huguenots at La Rochelle by Richelieu and Louis XIII was the most debilitating. On the same day, in Dr. Laud's proposed reply to the Remonstrance, the bishop could not advise Charles to deny the enormity of the loss, only to defend Buckingham on the grounds that "Rochelle is acknowledged a very difficult work, and what may be done about it wise men doubt." "And as for the Isle of Ré," Laud gamely deflected the blame away from the dishonored duke: "we know too well it was our fault at home in not sending timely supplies, not his, who in the view of Christendom did service full of honor there."[89] While Eliot's articulation of the parliamentary consensus that portrayed Buckingham as the "cause of causes" may be challenged if analyzed retrospectively in terms of "structural tensions," if *experienced* from the floor of the Commons of 1628, such rhetoric would not have seemed exorbitant to listeners. The favorite's very real power of patronage (and so access to the king), affected the worldview of everyone in Parliament. That power was compounded by heightened feelings of fear and insecurity posed by the threat from "secret combinations" that gripped the Protestant world after the duke's failure at the Île de Ré. The Commons' elaborate construction of Buckingham's physical "nearness" as the ultimate cause of bodily contagion thus provides a useful beginning toward understanding the very large problem of "orthodox" Calvinist cosmology as the fragments of the body of international Protestantism entered the darkest days of defeat and "dispersion." Buckingham became the repository of all sickness and evil in an apocalyptic religious culture beset by attacks of fear and anxiety, yet by tradition unprepared to affix blame directly on the king himself. "In this way and method," Sir Robert Phelips argued on June 6, "if anything fall out unhappily, it is not King Charles that advised himself, but King Charles misadvised by others and misled by misordered counsel."[90]

Thus, between 1625 and 1628, the Commons' construction of the persona of the favorite framed and contextualized millennial fears about the internal presence of evil in the body. The duke alone possessed the secret powers of intimacy and dissimulation to carry poison from king to king along the same dynastic line, first, as the sexually

ambiguous lover and stealthy murderer of James I, then as source of unnatural nearness and spiritual ambiguity that caused the heart of Charles I to succumb to its mortal illness. Attacking the heart of the body of the kingdom, Buckingham simultaneously attacked the body's appendages throughout the world. And in the instance of
the most important of those appendages—the last great Huguenot *place de sûreté* at La
Rochelle, the orthodox "heart" of seventeenth-century French Protestantism with "ancient" ties to the English monarchy—Buckingham's nearness to the fortress at the Île
de Ré effectively "caused" its death as well. As "the cause of causes" of England's mortal illness was violently excised from its politico-religious body by the assassin Fenton
after the duke's catastrophic failure at the Île de Ré, Buckingham served to define the
linkage of internal and external disequilibrium of a chaotic, international world of
strangers that afflicted orthodoxy with an anxious sense of the infinite expansion of
geographic and spiritual insecurity at its heart.

A "weak" Calvinist monarch, engaged in a "strange" and "innovative" relationship
with a favorite of an ambiguous sexual and spiritual nature was "dangerous" in part because he privatized counsel to the exclusion of ancient institutional norms. To make
"effeminate" was to engage in transgressive acts of suppression and dissimulation: to
hide the transparent and make it secret. Orthodoxy stigmatized the effeminate—and
the effeminate courtier in particular—precisely because it feared the subversive power
of the hidden. It was the outward manifestation to Calvinists who feared "innovation"
of what they knew was the secret and insecure ambiguity of the heart. Thus an effeminate heart "never hathe spirite to any hie or noble dedes."[91] For if the heart was a "fountain" of primitive spiritual "power" for the children of God, when out of control and
disordered, it was open to seduction by weakness and disease that would poison and
ultimately kill the body of Christ. This body was unified in its *exclusive* construction
by the Holy Spirit only when channeled through a single "pure English heart." In his
"Experiencia" of 1606, the elder Winthrop wrote, "it must be only God that must
worke in the hearte." Or else the heart would find the space to become inflamed, "with
a seacrit desire after pleasures and itchinge after libertie and unlawfull delightes . . .
whence came much troble and danger." "All the imaginations of the thoughts of [such
a] heart," Winthrop concluded, "are onely evill continually."[92] With this in mind, Sir
Edward Coke lamented that secret and "personal matters are the grievance of grievances," the cause "of all our miseries."[93]

To British-American Calvinist orthodoxy, the personal and private "nearness" of
the corrupt equivalent of strangers like Buckingham to the secret heart of the kingdom was the ultimate source of mortal disease of the body Christian. But what did
more latitudinarian English moderates such as John Winthrop Jr. or the soulish pietists
and enthusiastic sectarians think of personal nearness to the heart of cultural and religious difference? Was it possible that soulish hearts in close communication with

strangers could achieve Christian unity—in the words of Jean d'Espagnet, so "all things do freely combine"—without deadly infection of the entire body? Indeed, could nearness effect the opposite, and cure heresy by transmuting corruption into purity?

The now-decimated Consistory of La Rochelle had from the outset of its Reformation shared the Commons' exclusive view of the body of international Protestantism; it had aspired to become notoriously repressive, like its model in Calvin's and Théodore de Bèze's Geneva—or, for that matter, the elder Winthrop's Boston. The great fortress had tried to keep Protestant heterodoxy at a distance, just as it did the Counter-Reformation and nascent absolutism. But the famous walls were leveled soon after the Commons was dismissed by Charles I, ending the tumultuous session of 1628. Though the fragmented body of Christ converged elsewhere in the Atlantic world, it was never reconstructed in quite the same way again.

CHAPTER THIRTEEN

"Fraudulent father-Frenchmen"

The Huguenot Counterfeit and the Threat to England's Internal Security

❧ Universal Artisans ❧

Fear of outsiders bringing innovation "near" spread to the refugees themselves. Hence, life in the shadows did not end for Huguenot artisans upon their arrival in London, that great transatlantic entrepôt for refugee labor on the way to the New World. In many cases, despite talk of unity among Protestants, the refugees' subterranean culture was extended to new contexts in the refuge. Highly skilled Huguenot and Walloon weavers, drapers, furniture makers, and metalsmiths used new "French" styles, family networking, and cheap labor to undercut London's native craftsmen. As a result, they faced ostracism in the guilds and xenophobic violence from local competitors.[1] Merchants with vested interests in the old English-made woolens fought back, supported by native artisans threatened by outsiders with superior skills, new markets, and productive technology. "The French make fortunes in London," Cosimo III de' Medici observed on a visit to England in 1668; "for being more attentive to their business, they sell their manufactures at a lower price than the English."[2]

The sudden appearance of Huguenots and Walloons in the 1550s was particularly ominous to Francophobes in coastal England. Large refugee artisan communities settled in London, Southampton, and the Cinque Ports. Within a generation, refugee artisans had dispersed further to form significant concentrations in the textile towns of Norwich, Colchester, Canterbury, and Maidstone. With their arrival in force in the mid sixteenth century, England's artisanal sectors were thus ambivalent hosts to a sizable, widely dispersed ethnic minority population for the first time in historical memory.[3]

Riots against Huguenot craftsmen broke out in London first in 1517 and again in 1593. Norwich experienced similar crowd action during the rebellion of 1570, when plotters seeking the duke of Norfolk's release from the Tower of London harnessed their plan for the government's overthrow to a popular call for the violent expulsion of Norwich's 4,700 Huguenot artisans and their families. Complaints that resulted in litigation by town magistrates during the 1570s usually accused Huguenots of hoarding wealth at the expense of native English artisans, claimed that strangers were drunk and disorderly (which resulted in an eight o'clock curfew in Norwich), expressed anxiety that the French were monopolizing the finest wool for their workshops, or decried the ways in which foreigners broke local ordinances governing craft practice.[4]

Although the large influx of Walloon woolen workers threatened traditional labor practices that had supported native craftsmen in southeastern England since the early fourteenth century, refugee artisans were nevertheless championed by some of London's international merchant houses and master craftsmen in the more cosmopolitan shops. Potentially great benefits in the shape of innovations were projected for native English weavers and merchants, who were expected to acquire foreign skills. The new weaving techniques mastered by Huguenots to produce profitable textiles called "new draperies" were especially sought after.[5] "[W]e ought to favor the strangers from whom we learned so great benefits," the author of a 1577 treatise on relations between the English and Huguenot artisanal cultures concluded pragmatically, "because we are not so good devisors as followers of others." While "the native weavers seemed always ready to complain about aliens taking advantage of their hospitality," writes Joseph P. Ward, capturing the ambiguity of this process of acculturation for London, "this concern came with the corollary that if the strangers would play by the economic rules laid down for them, then the Londoners would treat them kindly." Unfortunately, the rules were seldom clear, and when they were, the refugees proved masters of clandestine means of getting around them.[6]

Other economic treatises added scholarly weight to an already substantial record of mercantile correspondence by leading international merchants. Everyone adumbrated the economic historian Warren Scoville's primary assertion of the baneful effect of religious persecution on French economic development. Migration of reformed French textile workers who carried industrial secrets with them to the British archipelago (as well as to the Netherlands, Switzerland, and the Protestant Germanic principalities) eroded France's ability to compete internationally. In the instance of the new draperies, this was effected by absorption into the most highly capitalized segment of the British economy of France's most innovative and integrated artisanal and mercantile sector.[7]

Most new draperies produced and sold by this sector were lightweight "bays" (baize) and "says" (serge).[8] Unlike the traditional heavy domestic English broadcloth, these finely woven fabrics had already captured the lucrative Mediterranean market, where lightweight clothing was in great demand. Merchants also saw potential for Iberian transshipment to expanding markets in Latin America and, by the 1620s, to southern British America and the West Indies as well.

The economic benefit refugee artisans and the new draperies provided to England's textile-producing regions in Essex and East Anglia is well known. One example from Norwich should suffice here to illustrate their combined potential to stimulate local economies.[9] In the year 1566–67, records for the Norwich Cloth Halls indicate that woolen workers had officially produced a total of 1,200 "cloths." However, by the time the new draperies were fully integrated into Norwich's textile industry, between 1583 and 1588, the Hall count indicated that production averaged over 36,000 cloths per year, and Norwich ranked second in urban wealth behind London.[10] Not surprisingly, as Norwich's wealth grew and spread economic competency to tradesmen during the 1580s, Anglo-French artisanal relations also began to improve. By law, native weavers were apprenticed exclusively to foreign artisans, and English boys anglicized their Huguenot masters while learning the art and mystery of weaving the new draperies in French shops.

Still, it is misleading to say that periodic economic recessions in the international woolen markets did not make scapegoats of Huguenots. The London riots of 1593 triggered a Commons debate on immigrants' rights, which reiterated earlier claims that Huguenots were enriching themselves through illegal retail trade practices, which victimized "thousands" of true Englishmen, whose only recourse was to beg alms in the street.[11] When an act of Parliament to outlaw such practices was not forthcoming, frustrated London artisans posted broadsheets in Huguenot neighborhoods that revealed the cultural depth of English tradesmen's fears that French secrecy and duplicity were fragmenting the Reformation and subverting the once-unified religious body of the state:

> You fraudulent father-Frenchmen, by your cowardly flight from your own natural countries, have abandoned the same into the hands of your proud cowardly enemies; and have, by a feigned hypocrisy and counterfeit show of religion, placed yourselves here in a most fertile soil, under a most gracious and merciful prince, who hath been contented to the great prejudice of her natural subjects, to suffer you to live here, in better ease and more freedom than her own people.[12]

This sense of the French material and spiritual "counterfeit"—that even French Protestantism was fraudulent and that stranger artisans remained crypto-Catholic during the sixteenth century—pervaded English discourse on authenticity in commerce and the question of "secret" Huguenot materials and "unnatural" artisanal practices. Within the new categories of woolens, for example, Walloon weavers and dyers from the Hainaut region specialized in the production of mockadoes (a variant of the Italian *mocajardo*, derived from the Arabic *mukayyar*, for mohair), as well as carrels and grograms. All were colorful, technically complex dry-woven luxury goods, more prestigious and expensive overall when first introduced as novelties than the standard bays and says. Exotic woolens were sometimes made of mixed materials; they combined uncertain proportions of wool with mohair, silk, or linen. In part because the mockadoes' true material nature was concealed, the word itself received wide comment in both English consumer and political discourse as a synecdoche for Huguenot artisanal culture.

The *Oxford English Dictionary* traces the linguistic transformation of these products from sought-after novelties to targets in attacks on effeminate French politesse as early as 1562, when London's materialistic aristocracy was accused of having lost its manly English virtue under a labyrinth of deceptive new draperies.[13] Mockadoes were often used as curtains for new-style "French beds" or as fringes on expensive chairs made stylish in London court circles by Huguenot upholsterers. By the late sixteenth century, however, in addition to talk of usefulness, these words commonly appeared as pejoratives. They were often ridiculed in sarcastic wordplay or accompanied by suspicious modifiers such as "trumpery," "mockery," "mak-a-dooes," "tufted," "padding," "ridiculous," and "mockado Eloquence." Thus, they connoted baneful dissimulation, surface polish without ballast of core substance, superfluity, and sham "French" artifice. The noun "mockado" was also an adjective synonymous with French refugee artisans, reflecting their allegedly fraudulent substitutes for authentic, natural materials of intrinsic and enduring value to English consumers. Ersatz material explained how Huguenot artisans produced and sold goods cheaply, undercutting native artisans. "Sham" silk was one such artfully adulterated material, because silk remained relatively scarce in England until, again, Huguenot artisans and merchants upgraded the "new draperies" and came to dominate the London silk industry a century later.[14] Having reinvigorated the English woolen industry with new draperies to end decades of recession for many native artisans and merchants in the textile towns, French weavers and upholsterers nevertheless remained suspected of hidden impurities.

London's guilds were at the forefront of English assaults on Huguenot artisanal secrets. Their most important weapon was the Ordinance of 1483, written into the *Statutes of the Realm*. This ordinance stated that foreign-born artisans were required to take native-born Englishmen as apprentices, and English weavers in textile centers such as Norwich tried with considerable economic success to appropriate the new technology from French refugees.[15] Still, the London guilds claimed that through secrecy and dissimulation, hidden Huguenot craft networks managed to manipulate the rules to the strangers' advantage. In the early seventeenth century, similar complaints were heard from other than the weavers' company, albeit some of these trades—the joiners and carvers in particular—were often closely related in the luxury market. By quantifying the yearly Returns of London's aliens, combined with an analysis of apprenticeship records of its Worshipful Company of Joiners, the furniture historian Benno Forman documented remarkably high numbers of Huguenot woodworkers in residence, indicating their conspicuousness among foreign craftsmen who migrated to London before 1626. So high, in fact, was the percentage of Huguenot furniture makers that it is reasonable to assume that the vast majority of seventeenth-century Huguenot artisans who fled to London—and probably Amsterdam, Leiden, and Frankfurt as well—practiced either the textile or elite woodworking trades. Indeed, Forman concludes, "with the exception of the Weavers' Company, the total of joiners and carvers exceeds the stranger craftsmen listed by all the other companies of the city combined."[16]

That these two crafts followed parallel trajectories was no coincidence. It underscored the intensive interaction then taking place between refugee Huguenot drapers and woodworkers, which was set in motion by the growing demand among elite consumers for the cosmopolitan tastemaking and technical skills represented by the Huguenot upholsterer's craft. By the early seventeenth century, Huguenot upholsterers laid personal claim to the dissemination of an anglicized (or Batavian or Germanic or Scandinavian) Bourbon court style, which was then in the process of relocation with the migrating diaspora to the urban style centers of Protestant northern Europe. Before the influx of refugee artisans, English "upholders" (later "upholsters," then "upholsterers") were relatively uninvolved in the design and manufacture of the woodwork used in their products. At best, they were concerned primarily with the supply and manufacture of a range of products made out of fabric. Although a guild ordinance of 1474 recognized the upholders' "right of search" over feather beds, pillows, mattresses, cushions, and curtains, the clear reference to scavenging remnants indicates that their historical status in the English trades could be very low indeed. The first edition of John Stow's *Survey of London* (1598) also noted that in the reign of Henry VI (1422–61), many upholsterers had dealt in secondhand goods and could be found on "Birchover's Lane [in Cornehill Ward], on that side street down to the stocks," where "Fripperers or Upholders . . . sold old apparel and household stuff."[17]

But near the end of Elizabeth's reign, refugee upholsterers redefined and revolutionized the trade in England. Upholstery was harnessed to elite fascination with the accessories of French courtly manners and the development of expanding markets for the new draperies. Upholsterers redefined their own artisanal identity and status as well. Thus, for the first time in the history of the English trades, upholsterers became directly involved in the design and production of the wooden frames that would house their fabrics. Indeed, the Huguenot style derived its aesthetic identity entirely through the prescribed deployment of fashionable textiles; that is, the new draperies were "upholded" ("held up" and nailed onto wooden frames) in uniform sets of expensive upholstered "French beds" and conforming upholstered seating furniture. Taken together, all this required an enormous quantity of costly new fabrics, which Huguenot weavers (or their English apprentices) provided.[18] A most complete description of the upholsterer's new "universal" artisanry was made by Robert Campbell in 1747 in *The London Tradesman:*

> I have just finished my House, and must now think of furnishing it with fashionable Furniture. The Upholder is the chief Agent in this Case: He is the Man upon whose Judgement I rely in the Choice of Goods; and I suppose he has not only Judgement in Materials, but Taste in the Fashions, and Skill in the Workmanship. This Tradesman's Genius must be *universal* [emphasis added] in every Branch of Furniture; though his proper Craft is to fit up Beds, Window-Curtains, Hangings, and to cover Chairs that have stuffed Bottoms: He was originally a species of the Taylor; but, by degrees, he crept over his Head, and set up as a Connoisseur in every article that belongs to a House. He employs Journeymen in his proper Calling, Cabinet-makers, Glass-Grinders, Looking-Glass Frame-Carvers, Carvers for Chairs, Testers and Posts of Bed, the Woolen Draper, several species of Smiths, and a vast many Tradesmen of the other mechanic Branches.[19]

French refugee upholsterers and weavers thus worked together in the new courtly style to add value to the single most marketable immigrant product. This, in turn, increased capital and presented skilled Huguenot artisans with expanding opportunities to acquire prestige and patronage through the medium of London's luxury trades. Upholsterers positioned themselves as middlemen serving both elite consumers and artisanal producers simultaneously. So the multilingual Huguenot upholsterer synthesized the tastemaker, textile merchant, and elite woodworker.

❧ Buckingham's Universal Tastemaker ❧

Access to noble households that commanded mastery of such a formidable synthesis of international skills could also arouse suspicion. The Huguenot Balthazar Gerbier began his career as a courtier in 1617, becoming England's most notorious tastemaker when Buckingham granted him unlimited state funds to design for his expanding household. Although Gerbier admittedly had a remarkable patron, his own background and combination of skills were not unique. Huguenot tastemakers with Gerbier's skills were in demand, and skilled refugees were numerous enough to compete for patronage at every level throughout Protestant Europe. Gerbier's post required constant travel and the ability to undertake extended multilingual negotiations with both international art dealers and London's refugee craft communities. He was fluent in French, Dutch and Spanish, and possessed a natural philosopher's ability to unify a multitude of skills. As he promoted himself in his book *To All Men Who Love Truth* (London, 1646), Gerbier marketed a "good hand in writing, skill in sciences such as mathematics, architecture, drawing, painting, contriving of scenes, masques, shows and entertainments for great princes." He was experienced as an itinerant, knocking about Europe in search of courtly patronage. So he was experienced in the coded languages that belonged to the submissive creature of influence. He quickly developed a confident relationship as his master's mentor. Buckingham took Gerbier's lessons in connoisseurship as essential instruments for his self-realization as a great man. Their relationship was the subject of intense public scrutiny.[20]

By 1621, the duke had become a collector of international renown. Buckingham also felt sufficiently secure both in his position at court and of Gerbier's abilities to commission the refugee to travel the Continent and "choose for him rarities, books, medals, marble statues, and pictures [in] great store." Gerbier would accomplish this task in a remarkably short period of time, in part because of his natural acquisitive zeal, but primarily because he had immense quantities of cash at his disposal. Much was gifted to the favorite in lands, rents, and jewels by his lover James I, and during the reign of Charles I, he benefited from the high price of patronage and access to the king. But most was borrowed from Buckingham's growing list of creditors, at an interest rate calculated at between 30 and 40 percent yearly. In the seven years that remained until the duke's assassination on August 22, 1628, he accumulated one of England's greatest collections of paintings, sculpture, and furniture. With it, he acquired England's foremost collection of creditors as well. More important for our purposes however, Gerbier was much more than Buckingham's agent in major transactions involving art. He also had a strong hand in the day-to-day details of the duke's housekeeping designs.

In 1624, Gerbier glorified his patron with the news that Inigo Jones (1573–1652), the favored designer of mechanical marvels and courtly spectacles produced under the Stuarts, had come in person to see the favorite's new Titian, *Portrait of a Secretary*.[21] Gerbier had recently acquired the painting and put it on display in the duke's rooms in York House, which were then undergoing a major remodeling. In the process of playing his all-important role as interpreter reconstructing the subtleties of this unveiling for his master, Gerbier provided insights into the function of their relationship and the guile of the Huguenot upholsterer's craft. Consider the effect of Gerbier's manipulation of interior space using the new draperies and, with it, the intentionality of dominant artifacts and the phenomenology of levels of perception. Gerbier thus represented his mastery over space and materials to Jones, his rival and the designer of Buckingham's apartments at the royal palace of Whitehall in 1619.[22] He claimed to read Jones's practiced eye as it surreptitiously withdrew from its intended viewing of Titian's masterpiece—which occupied the room's privileged position—to the French textiles that were the talk of London's artisanal and mercantile communities, which competed for the beholder's attention on the painting's perceptual margins. This subversion of artifactual hierarchies was simultaneously cultural and economic. In effect, Gerbier's reading subtly asserted his interest in establishing a symmetry of desire between his mastery of the new Anglo-French taste and a masterpiece of the historically dominant Italianate style.

Buckingham was aware that Jones's experiments with Italian Renaissance design, following his Roman travels, constituted the earliest adaptation in England of the work of Andrea Palladio (1508–80). As a result, Jones was also considered a leading local authority on Italian painting. The Palladian style came under fire as papist design by some Calvinist ideologues during the Long Parliament, but Jones had already begun a prestigious career at court as designer of theatrical masques for James I (featuring Buckingham's famous dancing).[23] Jones's fusion of classical Roman architecture and modern Roman ornament drew the attention of the anti-Calvinist William Laud, the duke's powerful ally at court, who favored the high baroque Italianate style for his Arminian program, then ascendant in the Church of England. With an alchemist's skill at designing mechanical marvels, including automata and other self-animated novelties, and having the support of such lofty patronage, Jones was rewarded with the title of Surveyor of the King's Works in 1615, a post he held until Civil War began in 1642. While Gerbier effused that Jones "almost threw himself on his knees" in front of the Titian, he also conveyed the news that after having been drawn initially to the painting's riveting beauty, the connoisseur was compelled to turn away toward something unexpected. Jones was instantaneously "surprised and abashed," distracted by the novelty with which the painting was framed and contextualized by the new velvet hangings that Gerbier—now playing the role of French upholsterer—had used to redecorate the rooms.[24] Buckingham was impressed with Gerbier's gloss on the power of textiles, deployed in the Huguenot style, to destabilize the perception of London's most sophisticated beholder. Gerbier's career was assured when the duke passed his protégé on to Charles I in 1625.[25] Others in government were less than pleased with the results of Gerbier's work, however. In the two impeachment proceedings against Buckingham, and additionally during the Commons debates of 1628, the vast cost of Gerbier's designs was blamed for the favorite's unprecedented household expenses. This was a fair assessment, because Buckingham's spending on interior decoration, combined with his lavish clothing requirements, meant that the price of his art collection may have been exceeded by capital outlay on fabric alone.[26] The duke's implacable enemies in the Commons could only speculate as to what transpired in rooms presumably designed by Gerbier. Had the simultaneously counterfeit and absolutist French style secretly influenced his "effeminate" crypto-Catholic master to undermine

the state and corrupt the king's manly English virtue? After all, by 1625, Gerbier constituted yet another hidden link between the corrosive Buckingham and the household of Charles I. Notwithstanding the risk of being caught up in the eclipse of Buckingham's star, Gerbier hung on; the measure of risk versus benefit was a way of life for
refugee Huguenot artisans in search of patronage at court (as Palissy demonstrated by
his dangerous alliance with Catherine de Médicis in 1565).[27] Huguenot upholsterers
understood that Gerbier's access to Buckingham meant money, prestige, and protection, and with the possible exception of Amsterdam, nowhere outside France was Gerbier's synthesis of skills more in demand than in metropolitan London.

The second edition of John Stow's *Survey of London* (1603) is important in the history of British-American material culture, because it included an early, polemical
"Apologie against the opinion of some [country] men, concerning that citie, the greatnesse thereof." In updating his 1598 *Survey,* Stowe asserted that London had been made
a metropolis by commerce, specifically the expanding market for luxuries, catering to
the "greater" numbers of Stuart courtiers now drawn for the first time to live permanently in the capital and "vain" young members of the urban elite.

Moreover, both groups of voracious consumers were more "gallant" in both public
and private life than before. In this context, the definition of the word "gallant," is best
understood to conform with new and ferociously contested rules of beauty, desire, and
comportment—and, by extension, consumption—devised by the duke of Buckingham under Gerbier's direction to help gain and maintain the post of royal favorite. The
new rules that Stow called "gallant" in 1603 were simultaneously absorbed into the
specifically French—hence deeply problematic—political and cultural category of *politesse,* with which, for both good and evil, Buckingham's courtly behavior was associated.[28] In short, by the 1620s, new courtiers and members of the urban elite were willing to incur unprecedented debts in pursuit of prestige and to accommodate their
household furnishings and public presentation of self to the French courtly style epitomized by the success of Buckingham and others:

> To aunswere the accusation of those men, which charge London with the losse and decay
> of many of the auncient Cities, Corporate Towns and markets within this Realm by draw-
> ing from them to her selfe alone, . . . all trade of traffique by sea, and the retayling of
> Wares, and the exercise of Manuall Arts also, . . . it is no maruaile if [Handicraftes men]
> . . . resort to London: for not onely the Court, which is now a dayes much greater & more
> gallant then in former times, and which was wonte to bee contented to remaine with a
> small companie [in the country], . . . is now for the most part either abiding at London,
> or else so neare unto it, that the provision of thinges most fit for it, may easily be had from
> thence: but alos by occasion thereof, the Gentlemen of the shires do flie and flock to this
> Citty, the yonger sort of them to see and shew vanity, and the elder to save the cost and

charge of Hospitality, and house keeping. . . . Artificers . . . do leave the Countrie townes, where there is no vent, and do flie to London, where they be sure to finde ready and quicke market.[29]

❧ "Like Israel in Egypt": The Demographics of Politeness ❧

Glossing Neil McKendrick and Joyce Appleby (with links to T. H. Breen's "empire of goods" in British America), Lawrence Klein reiterates the current consensus (and the thrust of Stow's *Survey* of 1603). To wit, although economic historians trace the origins of England's market economy to the fourteenth century, "only in the early modern period did commercialization in the economic and social organization of English society proceed at a rate sufficient to force people to reflect and write about the phenomenon . . . England was rapidly becoming a consumer society."[30] The commercialization of "vanity," "hospitality," and the culture of politeness may have supported demand for fashionable products that benefited elite Huguenot upholsterers and other suppliers of the materials of "disguise and dissimulation," but this did not mean that the middling and low-level Huguenot joiners and carvers who provided the underlying armatures for such materials enjoyed a warmer reception from native woodworkers threatened with displacement than did their counterparts in the textile trades.

London's woodworking guilds were already under intense pressure as a result of an influx of skilled English craftsmen from the countryside, according to Stow, when the pressure effectively doubled because of a new influx of French-speaking refugees after Philip II of Spain (r. 1556–98) sent 10,000 troops under the duke of Alba in 1567 to crush Calvinist resistance to faltering Roman Catholic authority in the Walloon region of the southern Netherlands (later Belgium).[31]

With Henri II's death in 1559, confessional violence increased in France, and with it, the number of refugees. But the first civil war of religion did not erupt until March 1562, after a massacre of Huguenots at Vassy planned by the ultra-Catholic Guise family under the personal direction of François de Guise. The fighting ended briefly in 1563, with the Edict of Amboise, and in France, as elsewhere in war-torn northern Europe, the lull provided opportunities for uprooted refugees to move. Regional populations dispersed in waves, following the pattern of religious warfare, and there was an upsurge in emigration.

This was followed in France by the brutal second war of religion, which began with a massacre of Catholics by Protestants at Nîmes in 1568, and the pattern continued with a third, which ended in 1570. But this was just the beginning of a decade of massacres, cresting in the infamous St. Bartholomew's Day Massacre in 1572, an event that caused many Huguenots north of the Loire to flee the country or seek refuge in La Rochelle, which was besieged in 1573, as was Jean de Léry's refuge of Sancerre. There

were eight civil wars of religion in France in the years between 1562 and 1598, not counting the innumerable undeclared local wars, village massacres, settlings of personal
grudges, and episodes of gang violence that complete the picture of sixteenth-century
French confessional violence. France experienced a lull in the violence when the Edict
of Nantes was signed in April 1598, however, and the crisis shifted temporarily from
the battlefield to polemics.[32]

Demographic evidence is available from the seventeenth-century records of London's Threadneedle Street Eglise française, but quantifying French refugees in sixteenth-century England is tricky. In the absence of corroborating evidence—above all,
genealogical evidence—judging ethnicity based on surnames is unreliable at best.[33] To
make things worse, reports on immigrants were politicized, with disgruntled guild
wardens and M.P.'s exaggerating their numbers. Moreover, depending on the political
climate when counts were taken, immigrants tended to report numbers that were probably much too low.

By 1628, when Laud (1573–1645) was named bishop of London (five years in advance
of becoming archbishop of Canterbury) and was blamed by ideologically "orthodox"
Calvinists for conniving with his patron Buckingham in ways that led to the devastating defeat at La Rochelle, he responded by turning Parliament's praetorian guard
argument on its head. As Charles I's chief minister during the Eleven Years' Tyranny
(1629–40) of rule without Parliament, Laud portrayed England's Huguenots as being
"like Israel in Egypt"; the refugees, with their own ecclesiastical institutions and sectarian tendencies, which were particularly troublesome in the face of Laud's Act of
Uniformity of 1634, were thus subversive of the kingdom's moral, economic, and military security. The Huguenot leadership responded by reporting defensively after the
siege of La Rochelle that only 5,213 French Calvinists lived in the entire realm, with
2,240 at most in London.[34] However, 4,700 immigrants were reported in Norfolk alone
in 1579 (even after the great plague), 1,300 in Colchester in 1586, and London and its
environs averaged about 4,000 during the second half of the sixteenth century. If we
are to believe the earlier figures, then the census of 1635 tells us that London's immigrant population had fallen approximately 13 percent to 3,546. This decline may be explained, in part, by the "urban graveyard effect": early modern urbanites experienced
lower birthrates and higher mortality rates overall than did their rural counterparts,
and Huguenots were primarily town dwellers. Recent transatlantic regional studies,
including studies of New York City, offer preliminary support for this hypothesis.[35]
The number of French immigrants remained steady or declined slightly until an upsurge of 1,182 new members was recorded in the Threadneedle Street French church
in 1681, the year the dragonnades began in southwestern France.[36]

The relatively low figures also reflect London's status as a way station. Most refugees passed through temporarily, staying if there was opportunity and moving on if

there was none. If the population of London grew to about 200,000 by the time of Elizabeth's death (and publication of the second edition of Stow's *Survey*) in 1603, then immigrants accounted for no more than 4 percent of the city's total population in the sixteenth century. But this was clearly perceived by artisans, merchants, and many consumers as an important 4 percent. Gross quantification cannot possibly account for the complex variations that obtained in the neighborhood-centered experience of early modern urban life. The vast majority of Huguenots lived in notorious artisan "guettos" in Westminster, Southwark, Bishopsgate, and Spitalfields, where their *occupational* visibility was much higher there than elsewhere in London. More important, the rise in commercial discourse in the early seventeenth century made it common knowledge among producers and consumers that Huguenot artisans dominated the production of novelties in the textile and woodworking trades. Together with new technologies for the reproduction and diffusion of quantities of consumer products in the "French taste"—that is to say, things in daily conversation identified *specifically* as signifiers of one cultural group—it is easy to see how anxious natives amplified the number of Huguenot craftsmen into hidden armies of aliens hard at work in London's subterranean niches. Moreover, Huguenot dominance in trades such as upholstery tended naturally to heighten these anxieties. Amplification was also a response to the glut in the supply of skilled Huguenot labor during the war years. Refugee churchwardens monitored supply and demand in the local labor force before directing newcomers to leave or stay. Yet newly arriving craftsmen were almost always available to work.

❧ The Appropriation of Novelty ❧

The fluidity of Huguenots' artisanal life was harnessed to their production and hence to native perceptions that Huguenots "dwelled" in every artifact associated with their artisanry. Therefore, in the metaphorical as well as the physical sense, Huguenots were present *virtually* everywhere in the expansion of English material life by the late 1620s—and, if the diffusion of new draperies is taken fully into account—throughout the Mediterranean and Atlantic worlds as well. Because of the transformative power associated with Huguenot craftsmanship, and the fact that it represented cheap, available labor, the English were ambivalent about the French refugee artisans' ability to channel innovation through work to create novelty in unprecedented abundance. Indeed, much of the rage of native craftsmen during the weavers' riots of 1675 was directed at the refugees mechanized new "engine-weaving-looms," which were dragged out into the streets of London's craftsmen's ghetto and burned. New things were thereby conflated and made almost interchangeable with the new people who produced them, as well as the new words that were used to communicate their novelty.

In the Ordinance of 1474, English "upholders" were little more than ragpickers—

mere "fripperers" (from the French *friperie* meaning "cast-offs")—granted "right of search" in the streets of London, to recover vile remnants from the corpses of homeless vagrants or the houses of the dead.[37] By the end of the sixteenth century, English Huguenot artisans seemed to embody the alchemists' dream exactly as written in the ancient texts. After all, they had somehow acquired the mechanical knowledge to discover the philosopher's stone, which had given them the means to transmute, purify, replicate, and, in Palissy's words, "multiply their treasures," in the form of valuable substances for the market from base materials and thus transform worthlessness into cash and power. And if Huguenot artisans had not discovered the stone, they were nonetheless masterful counterfeiters. Moreover, if "the stone" lay in the streets and was available to even the poorest artisan by "right of search," adepts would argue that this was final proof of authenticity. How many refugee Huguenot artisans there may have been thus seems less important than why this "declining minority" were constructed by their hosts as mankind's most powerful and mysterious manipulators of the material world.[38]

Countermeasures were taken by the authorities, but these affected only public performance of craft. On March 11, 1563, in response to the refugee crisis in the trades occasioned by the first war of religion in France, the Joiners' Company of London appointed four masters to an alderman's court to consider the "workmanship and conning" of twelve immigrants proposed for membership by the guild wardens. Six were admitted after they agreed to pay a £5 "redemption," which many other refugees found prohibitive. Just as illuminating, there remained ninety-nine foreign joiners in London available to fill the six places.[39] On July 12, 1571, the Joiners' Company adopted an elaborate set of restrictive ordinances for foreign woodworkers, although only a tiny minority qualified for membership and enjoyed guild benefits. First, it was stipulated that immigrant joiners residing in London not practice their craft without paying the same fees assessed company members. Moreover, after having paid membership fees from which they received no benefit, immigrants were limited to two apprentices, for whom they were expected to record contracts of indenture at Guildhall at the member's fee. Guild members were also denied the right to employ foreigners except as apprentices and could not instruct foreigners except apprentices. In addition, no immigrant could "take in hand any work" from anyone but a member; immigrants had to make a proof piece that passed company inspection; foreign-made wares were to be brought to Guildhall and marked as such; and finally, immigrants were denied the right to hawk their wares in the street.[40] The ordinance against retail commerce was a particularly onerous one and was debated in the Commons. The London riots of 1593 followed, when there were incidents of heated speech and action in the streets against alien craftsmen.

In practice, although repressive, most guild ordinances were unenforceable in the large, complex city that London had become by 1603. What was enforced was precisely what nativists feared: the incorporation of refugee Huguenot artisans into an underground, low-cost craft economy, something they were already familiar with from long experience in France, where similar restrictions were imposed on Protestant tradesmen by Catholic guilds and royal edicts in regions where Catholics were dominant. The opposite held true, of course, in Huguenot-dominated strongholds such as La Rochelle, where Protestant artisans maintained control of the city's guild system by victimizing Catholic members, a state of affairs reversed with a vengeance by the Catholics in 1628.

❧ Huguenot *maleficium* ❧

In addition to encouraging the dissimulation and development of hidden craft and retail practices they were ostensibly meant to negate, the ordinances forced many Huguenots to circumvent guild wardens by falling back on discreet organization and natural forms of personal and artisanal security available in family craft networks whose members were accustomed to an underground economy. To preface a list of immigrant craftsmen requested by the lord mayor of London in April 1583, the Joiners' Company virtually conceded the success of these tactics by French competitors in the increasingly open marketplace:

> The Master and Wardens of the Companye of Joyners never licensed nor admitted any of the persons hereunder expressed to use their said trade, yett they, dwelling some in [the Huguenot "ghettos"] Westminster, somme in Sainct Katherins, and somme in Sowthworke, do use the sayd occupation, and have joyned themselves togeather . . . to worck in London as fullye as a Freeman may doe, to the utter undoing of a great number of Freemen Joyners, mere Englishe men, who are allsowayes ready for any service for her Majestie, this Realme, and Citie of London.[41]

These themes were reiterated and amplified in a report to James I in 1616. This report consisted of a collection of petitions from London guild wardens who attested to the secret and malevolent activities practiced by Huguenot artisans who had managed to infiltrate no less than 121 separate occupations.[42] The timing of the report also reflected a long period of depression in the production of the old heavy woolens, which fell on southeastern England's core textile regions. By the 1620s, the depression in the Suffolk woolen industry was so profound that John Winthrop the Elder and his neighbors began to slaughter their flocks and sell choice meadowland. Winthrop also chose to spend more time in London to increase his income. With the help of Emmanuel Downing, Winthrop diversified into mercantile activities, pursued attorney's fees at Parliament, and pondered resettlement in Ireland.[43]

This situation sent anxious Stuart officials scrambling for political cover, and they found it in Huguenot artisanal *maleficium*. The 1616 report to King James documented the penetration of a veritable encyclopedia of trades by insidious Huguenots, and there were renewed calls from native artisans for the expulsion of the aliens. The metaphor of Huguenot *maleficium* endured into the Protectorate. Although Cromwell was a friend to the Huguenot cause in religious and international affairs, he did not prevent London artisans from circulating a petition in 1654 that claimed that refugees "take large houses, divide them, take inmates, and so breed infection."[44]

Second only to workers in the textile and upholstery trades, members of the London goldsmiths' guild were challenged to change their practices in response to a paradigm shift brought about by innovative Huguenot technology and design of naturalistic cast mounts. Methods akin to Palissy's live casting were used by French goldsmiths in the early seventeenth century. Consequently, many English goldsmiths lost capital and commissions and blamed it on the influx of this famously talented group of provincial Huguenot goldsmiths.[45] The Goldsmiths' Petition of 1616 provides insight into the sense of powerlessness and conspiratorial presence felt by certain members of the majority of London's guilds. They inveighed against the octopuslike qualities of this clandestine network of "aliens and strangers," who usurped English enterprise with alarming ease: "the said aliens and strangers in their habitations are dispersed in many lanes and remote places of this city and suburbs, working in chambers, garrets and other secret places where the wardens of this company may not have convenient access and recourse to search."[46] And in 1622, the Goldsmith's Company pursued this inquest into the subterranean world of artisanry to its logical conclusion, accusing 183 Huguenot goldsmiths of using alchemy to counterfeit jewels.[47]

In guild petitions to Elizabeth and James in 1583 and 1616, London's guild wardens represented their dismay at Huguenot middlemen's access to elite English households and political patronage. Long accustomed to maintaining surveillance over native craftsmen clustered openly along the streets of the city's traditional artisan neighborhoods, London guild wardens failed even to *locate* (or perceive) the covert, "dispersed" sources of their "secret" competition. A dread of counterfeiting and radical expansion of the license accorded professional informers to spy on their neighbors resulted.

Opportunity directed the attention of this expanding group of spies to the artisanal activities of immigrants, and their income grew accordingly. Informers ostensibly pursued information that concerned Huguenot violation of many craft ordinances restricting specific sorts of manufacturing by immigrants. By law, in the event of conviction, informers were awarded one-half the stranger's fine as a reward. However, there was considerable slippage in the system. The obvious potential for blackmail and extortion from the refugees was commonly exploited. Clearly, informers were interested in any information that might find a buyer.[48] This tended to be political or religious in nature, and at times there were even allegations of conspiracies between the

French monarchy and "fraudulent" Huguenots who immigrated to England to form a praetorian guard. The role of urban informer was certainly not restricted to Tudor-Stuart England. A similar pattern developed in colonial New York at the height of the Huguenot response to the Boston leather chair. In 1707–8, a Dutch informer charged the Rochelais upholsterer Benjamin Faneuil with conspiring to subvert the colony's defenses by providing secret information on its fortresses and militia to invading "French compatriots."

Questions of being and appearance pervasive in the British-American perception of refugee Huguenot artisanal culture makes Lawrence Klein's work on the third earl of Shaftesbury, and in particular his reading of the anglicization of *politesse* through the material culture of commercialization and the consumer society in seventeenth-century England, of great interest to historians of the early modern transatlantic world. Shaftesbury adapted for England the functional essence of the French absolutist notion that politeness was not merely a political instrument, but rather "a total cultural condition . . . [that] amounted to civilization."[49] Shaftesbury's anglicization project was holistic: to reconcile French courtly theatricality (*politesse*) with what he took to be native English "sincerity." To understand, master, and encourage the links between the domains of form ("of style and fashion, of 'air' and manner") and of morals ("the substance of things: nature, reason, virtue").[50] "What are all those Forms & Manners wch come under the notion of good-breeding?" Shaftesbury asked rhetorically, "the affected smiles, the fashionable Bows, the Tone of Voice, & all those supple carressing & ingratiating ways? what is this but Embroidery, Guilding, Colouring, Daubing? . . . [its Huguenot purveyors] talk of nothing but Ease, Freedome, Liberty, Unconcerndness."[51]

Still, natural philosophy was the knot that integrated this superficial world of form with substance. "Shaftesbury embraced the word 'politeness' and the concern with sociability that it raised," Klein explains, "but he sought to avoid its moral turbidity by anchoring it in philosophy. . . . Where polite learning was 'ornamental', 'philosophy' was 'solid' or 'useful.'" Such knowledge was extended to consumers, who were expected to perform an active critique of materials in the marketplace; and of artisans as well, who were judged by their competence in negotiating the proper balance of ornament with utility. As a "total cultural condition," this process had powerful resonance among English and anglicizing French artisans in creating a world of interactive things appropriate to elite comportment in social contexts where civic discourse took center stage. Mirroring larger social and cultural processes, metropolitan British artisans and elite patrons worked together with exiled Huguenot artisans, designers, and patrons to domesticate the material culture of *politesse*. Making it "polite" meant facilitating the integration of things into the total culture of polite performance.

At the core of the performance of politeness, from the inner workings of the polite mind to, by analogy, literary, artistic, and artisanal expression, and ultimately to polite physical comportment that facilitated commerce and conversation in the economic and social world, lay freedom of motion throughout the urban landscape, balanced by simplicity of expression. These skills were perceived as a counterweight to the growing consumption of artifacts of cultural elaboration and a way to help negotiate the ever-smaller and more complex spaces in the interstices between them. The enemies of politeness then, were privacy, ambiguity of intention, and life in the shadows. The comportment of politeness, unlike that of *politesse*, had to be functionally transparent. Shaftesbury's phenomenology of politeness proscribed disjunctions between being and appearance. Mere simulation or mimesis without grounding in a philosophy, potentially rampant in a consumer society, was attacked as subversive. Unethical behavior was a danger inasmuch as politeness was "*more sensibly to be perceived* [emphasis added], than described."[52]

❧ Shadow Worlds ❧

It was precisely in the shadowy interstices between being and appearance that English Calvinist critiques of both Buckingham and Huguenot artisanal culture intersected and were harnessed together by polemicists in the decade before the favorite's assassination in 1628. The producer and consumer of exiled French courtly culture were both stigmatized and made to represent the counterfeit—or the uncertainty, fluidity, and social instability (and hence the potential tyranny) of undomesticated politesse. The subversive dangers of the wild man were thus inverted and applied to artifice and social polish; the pendulum swung too far in the opposite direction from rusticity. This was to become Benjamin Franklin's field of play in the late eighteenth century.

That Buckingham was counted the most "natural" performer in the Stuart masques was, of course, indicative of the threat to virtue by false transparency. Just as lines of demarcation over Buckingham and his status as favorite were drawn in the Commons, so too tensions remained in English political, artistic, and natural-philosophical culture in response to innovations in theatricality. Buckingham's Calvinist critics (who thought masques corrupt) and courtly friends (for whom masques were pleasurable and sometimes instruments of revenge) would both have confirmed—for different reasons—the validity of Arnold Hauser's reading of the masque's relevance to courtly cultures formed in the apocalyptic years of the late sixteenth and early seventeenth centuries:

> The frequency with which characters in drama masquerade as others and question their own identity, are [sic] only ways of expressing the fact that, while the objective world had grown unintelligible, the identity of the self had been shattered, had grown vague and

fluid. Nothing was what it seemed, and everything was different from what it purported to be. Life was disguise and dissimulation, and art itself helped to disguise life as well as to penetrate its masks.[53]

Powerful English courtiers such as Buckingham were accused of being counterfeit—of only *seeming* to be what they apparently were—by conspiring to obscure transparent truth through theatrical dissimulation of their impure, un-English hearts. At the same time, beginning in the early 1560s, and peaking during the years 1628 and 1685, refugee artisans, as producers of the material culture of politeness and theatricality, were accused of artisanal *maleficium*. Huguenot artisans had thus made things that inverted the moral force of their clients' polite behavior. Interiority, stealth, cryptic modes of communication, secretly altered materials, alchemical counterfeiting, and hiding in the shadows to avoid detection were their insidious modus operandi. Exposure of this dangerously unstable dialogue between structures of being and appearance in the clandestine artisanal culture of the Huguenots was fundamental to critiques of the expansion of commercialism and consumerism in British-American material life through the end of the eighteenth century and beyond.

CHAPTER FOURTEEN

"The destruction that wasteth at noonday"

Hogarth's Hog Lane and the Huguenot Fortress of Memory

Turning over the Bible which lay before me . . . I cried out, "Well, I know not what to do; Lord, direct me!". . . ; and at that juncture I happened to stop turning over the book at the 91st Psalm, and . . . I read . . . as follows: "I will say of the Lord, He is my refuge and my fortress: my God, in Him will I trust. Surely He shall deliver thee from the snare of the fowler, and from the noisome pestilence. He shall cover thee with His feathers, and under His wings shalt thou trust: His truth shall be thy shield and buckler. Thou shalt not be afraid for the terror by night; nor for the arrow that flieth by day; nor for the pestilence that walketh in darkness; nor for the destruction that wasteth at noonday . . . Only with thine eyes shalt thou behold and see the reward of the wicked. Because thou hast made the Lord . . . thy habitation; there shall no evil befall thee, neither shall any plague come nigh thy dwelling."

I scarce need tell the reader that from that moment I resolved that I would stay in the town, and casting myself entirely upon the goodness and protection of the Almighty, would not seek any other shelter whatever; and that . . . my times were in His hands.

—DANIEL DEFOE, *A Journal of the Plague Year* (1722)

How might historians enter the shadows where refugee artisans "dwelled"? Once inside, can we pose the question: How did dwelling therein enable the construction of an identity at once both hidden and representational? Let us begin with what we know:

the matrix of refugee work and worship in London was inextricably intertwined with the human geography of the immigrant ghetto in Soho. The Eglise des Grecs, the Huguenot church, received its unexpected name from the Greek Orthodox congregation that had worshipped there before the Huguenots replaced it. After the peak years of the sixteenth century, the steady influx of French refugees to London did not increase greatly again until the 1660s and ultimately the turbulent 1680s. By that time, the immigrant population finally exceed the seating capacity of existing immigrant churches. The Eglise des Grecs accommodated the rapid overflow of worshippers and became the "daughter" church of the Savoy Chapel, one of the largest and best-connected French churches in early eighteenth-century London.

William Hogarth (1697–1764) learned his trade as a painter-engraver after years of life study with Huguenot instructors, at the Parisian Louis Cheron's Academy, which by 1718 was located in St. Martin's Lane, directly behind the Eglise des Grecs.[1] Hogarth's name was closely associated with Cheron's Academy beginning in the 1730s, and he kept a studio nearby.[2] Once reaching a position in his profession whereby he could hire engravers to make prints after his original designs, he hired French refugees almost exclusively. Of the twelve engravers known to be associated with Hogarth's shop during the eighteenth century, seven were French, four English, and one Dutch. To put this into perspective, most of Hogarth's non-French engravers were also trained by Huguenot masters, some at the St. Martin's Lane Academy. Indeed, so close was William Hogarth's personal and professional "friendship" with the French refugees of Soho that he was reputed to know all of their "secrets."[3]

Hogarth put his intimate knowledge of the variety of Soho's refugee terrain—and so of Huguenot history, piety, and artisanal secrets—to use in his painting *Noon, L'Eglise des Grecs, Hog Lane, Soho* (fig. 14.1).[4] He worked from experience. Painted in 1736 as the second in a cycle of four paintings depicting *The Four Times of the Day*, *Noon* was once thought to have been commissioned by Jonathan Tyers for display at the popular public pavilion at Vauxhall Gardens, which was known for eclectic architectural styles as well as licentious behavior, both of which appear in the painting. The Tyers-Vauxhall association is apocryphal, however, in fact, Hogarth sold the entire series at public auction on March 1, 1745. *Noon* and *Evening* sold to the duke of Ancaster.[5] Any attempt to reconstruct a viewership at Vauxhall is therefore futile. Even if something more might be said about the painting's viewership in situ, the real life of the image in *Noon* is as a prototype for reproduction and international diffusion throughout the Atlantic world as an engraving, beginning with its publication by Hogarth in 1728.

Still, other opportunities present themselves in *Noon*. The construction of subterranean refugee culture by both the Huguenots and their detractors is seldom plumbed below the surface rhetoric. Were its hidden foundations represented in interaction between the shadow world of private artisanal memory, piety, and technology and the

FIGURE 14.1. William Hogarth, *Noon, L'Eglise des Grecs, Hog Lane, Soho.* Oil on canvas. London, 1736. Courtesy Trustees of the Grimsthorpe and Drummond Castle Trust. Photograph: Photographic Survey, Courtauld Institute of Art.

public performance of consumers; that is, aspiring natives with enough cash to buy the external trappings of polite identity built into products of Huguenot craftsmanship? Because *Noon* addresses these questions, it is Hogarth at his most ambitious. He attempts nothing less than to unify perceptions of the hidden links between consumption and production that animated Huguenot material life in the early eighteenth century. More than that, however, because he was privy to the "secrets" of the Huguenots, plus a few of his own, *Noon* stands alone as a personal manifesto on natural-philosophical and alchemic secrets that Hogarth shared in the form of a transatlantic artisanal cosmology with refugee colleagues, friends, and neighbors. Hogarth's painting, then, is both historical and scientific: first, it specifically contextualizes the new London congregation formed from the cohort of French Calvinist refugees of the 1680s, a group sanctified by the violence of Louis XIV's *dragonnades;* and second, it unearths the refugees' natural-philosophical cosmology and reintegrates it into a reading of the Huguenots' function as the invisible artisans of modern life. This act of reintegration demonstrates intimate knowledge on the part of both Hogarth and his audience of basic continuities between the metaphysical concerns of Bernard Palissy's generation of civil war Huguenot artisans and the material culture of politeness carried throughout the Atlantic world by refugees by the late seventeenth century.

Excavation of the shadow world begins as spectators peer with difficulty into the murky background in Hogarth's painting of the Huguenot ghetto to search for the church. They can barely discern an ethereal congregation of sober French Calvinists as they move through an amorphous veil of dark paint. Some of the worshippers have already gone. They emerged silently from the noon prayer at L'Eglise des Grecs, evading notice altogether. Others seem to pass quickly from the scene, disappearing into the shadows. Covertness is the natural condition of the pious refugees in *Noon.* Hogarth's Huguenots search out the shadows. This is their territory if they venture into the public spheres of the microcosm, which must be carefully negotiated after prayer to reclaim the private worlds of their workshops.

✲ Terrestrial Time ✲

Hogarth invites his audience to negotiate their labyrinth of historical, scientific, and spiritual trails through his art. Such paths constitute metaphorical passages into the secret life of Hog Lane, analogous to journeys into the self taken by earlier Huguenot artisans, moved by religious violence, to embark on soulish quests for mechanical knowledge of earthly materials. Hogarth begins by punning on the title, *Noon,* an indispensable clue to his symbolic program. The time of the day is exploited as a verbal and visual palindrome of dazzling flexibility. The mirror structure of these palindromes ramify, deployed like a mathematical puzzle; a kind of fractal based on contingencies of Huguenot history, artisanry, and natural philosophy.

Noon implicitly invites spectators to reflect upon themselves and others, as if in a mirror; to move beyond the stance of casual spectator and discover what lies beneath what we see that animates the world. Spectators are given options to consider the invisible depth of experience that accompanies production. Ephemeral moments of exchange were infinite in London, an expanding commercial city. Yet even superficial commercial transactions in Soho are products of hidden artisanal languages and subcultural memories. Production required access to astonishing historical, scientific, and aesthetic knowledge overlooked by the consumer. Such knowledge was available to some. For most others, the shadowy paths of access were ignored, obscured, invisible, or blocked.

Shaftesbury argued that the material culture of politeness must be transparent to avoid the stigma of disjunction between being and appearance and function smoothly as a medium of commercial exchange in English civil society. But Hogarth *shows* how the self-conscious affect of transparency through public display of polite artifacts obscured an oblique and deeply coded natural-philosophical dialogue about the dangers of ignoring elemental material processes behind the polished surfaces of words and things. Paracelsian discourse on the spirituality of material life, although widely known in the host culture since the sixteenth century, was practiced in the cash economy by Palissy and Huguenot refugees from southwestern France. Like these artisans, the congregants of the Eglise des Grecs labored to relocate secret knowledge of the synthesis of spirit and matter to the British-American world. Following the lead established by such successful predecessors as Bernard Palissy in Medician Paris and Balthazar Gerbier in Stuart London, they strategized to gain access to powerful patrons in the core culture.

Hogarth thus faced a considerable pictorial problem: how to represent the instant when hidden transactional events occur? How, he asked himself, does one represent an absence? How do artists reveal as their subject that imperceptible moment in time when it is in the process of changing, without reducing the complexity of lived experience hidden in the moment? Hogarth pursues the problem analytically, testing the limits of perception and the hypothesis that multiple levels of experience exist simultaneously in a single moment. The painting plots the results on a mystical terrestrial clock integrated with human, artificial, and natural components.

When clocks struck twelve in 1736, the longer minute hand passed directly over the short hour hand at the apex of the clock face. In so doing, the minute hand obscures the hour hand, which it supersedes in the beholder's field of vision. Noon is thus one of the times of the day when two hands—or perhaps the big world and the little world—merge seamlessly into one. The hour hand is then thrown into shadow for precisely one minute, before the minute hand separates from the hour and continues on its way around the dial.

This clockwork action mimics the foreground placement of the polite strollers in "Noon," at the moment they cast an obscuring shadow over the worshippers emerging from a midday service in the background. Significant contradictions remain, however, as life bends to conform to the outward demands of Hogarth's plays on the clockwork mechanism and its analogy to Newton's cosmos. Although in shadow, the pious

Huguenots remain barely visible behind the self-absorbed strollers. Moreover, if this event actually occurred at the precise second the church clock tolled twelve, then both the theatrical strollers and covert Huguenots would merge to form a kind of horological total eclipse, thereby obscuring the Huguenots completely from view. But Hogarth indicates by the clock on the church steeple that the time of the scene as we see it in his art is actually 12:10, not noon, as the title suggests. Therefore, the strollers and the Huguenots stand on their respective parts of Hogarth's terrestrial clock at 12:10. New curiosities appear and questions arise: Does the lowest point of the strange sign hanging high above the strollers signify an advertisement of some sort, or (given the painting's temporal theme) a sundial's gnomon, a pendulum, or a clock hand, or perhaps an amalgam of all three? Whatever else it signifies, it directs notice down to a specific quadrilateral space pointed out by the man's right hand and contained by the left feet of all three strollers, as well a piece of unidentifiable debris at which the boy gestures with his walking stick. Are these the four main compass points commonly engraved on a sundial, an astrological analogy for *The Four Times of the Day*?

Consider that Hogarth has constructed a terrestrial clock with human "movements." This clock is animated by light and obscured by darkness, like all sundials. A converging mass of humanity inverts and conflates the mechanistic certainty of the great clock high on the steeple of Savoy Chapel, which is literally cast into the uncertainty of shadow *on the ground*. These differences suggest that *Noon*-time is lived on at least two different, yet interlocking, levels of experience, and that the action on the ground may be influenced by the invisible, mythological, inner demons of noonday.[6] Action on the Savoy clock face parallels the dancelike positions of the strollers' left toes. These form points of an equilateral triangle, bisected with precision by the lady's stylish shoe at 12 o'clock. The toes of the man and boy point to 11 and one o'clock respectively. When read from directly in front of the polite group, at the point where the acute angle in the left foreground lines up with the high sign and the church clock, then the walking sticks form the "hands" of the terrestrial clock. They trace the movement of their shadows cast on the cobblestones of Hog Lane toward ten past the hour, even as the strollers walk along.

The well-dressed boy's tiny "hour-hand" walking stick, which he points from a slight distance to the left (with his left hand) at a morsel of food (or dirt), lines up with his mother's toe at 12 o'clock. His father complements this action by gesturing with his open right hand to "twelve," while his left thumb and forefinger rise above the top of his long "minute-hand" walking stick. These actions are mirrored by the boy's right hand and arm. There is precedent for this representation in the eighteenth century. It is in fact, much like the stiff action of the automaton (fig. 14.2), an automatic machine that by Hogarth's time was a commonly used metaphor in political discourse for the tension between Continental authoritarianism (the automaton) and British "natural"

FIGURE 14.2. Automaton in the form of a nef, with a side removed to reveal its hidden clockwork mechanism, attributed to Hans Schlottheim. Augsbourg, ca. 1580. © Copyright The British Museum. The eight courtiers marching on deck have been restored after the example of two similar nefs, also by Schlottheim. The royal and ecclesiastical figures on the upper deck (to the left) are original. Schlottheim is also known to have automated tiny marsh creatures similar to the ones found on Palissy's rustic dishes.

anti-mechanistic, self-regulated liberty. Hogarth writes frequently about "clock-work machines" in *The Analysis of Beauty* (1753). He was fascinated by one "brought from France some years ago . . . with a duck's head and legs fixed to it, . . . : which was so contrived as to have some resemblance of that animal standing on one foot, and stretching back its leg, turning its head, opening and shutting its bill, moving its wings and shaking its tail; all of them the plainest and easiest directions in living movements." Yet Hogarth ultimately disparages "this silly, but much extolled machine [which] being uncover'd, appeared a most complicated, confused and disagreeable object." Much like the unnaturally polite threesome in *Noon*, the clockwork machine instructs human beings (and the artist who paints them) that "the more variety we pretend to give our trifling movements, the more confused and unornamental the forms become; nay chance but seldom helps them.—How much the reverse are nature's! the greater the variety her movements have, the more beautiful are the parts that cause them."[7] An automaton was a sophisticated toylike machine, wound up with a key and operated by a clockwork mechanism. The figures were programmed for amusing, stereotyped gestures; imitating life, yet inspiring the pejorative use of the word "automaton" if applied to people interacting with others. With that in mind, the father's walking stick is slightly elevated and in automatic motion around the "dial" to his left, toward 2 o'clock (and 12:10). Thus his gold-tipped "minute hand" lines up like a surveyor's arrow with gold-tipped spire of Savoy Chapel clock tower.

Meanwhile, back in the shadows, a tiny walking stick belonging to a diminutive Huguenot child, who gestures minimally with his body and occupies ground space so close to the street that he is nearly indistinguishable from the earth, crosses this path to form an X. He is, in effect, congruent to the polite boy's mirror image. Like his polished counterpart, the homespun Huguenot lad holds his stick to the ground at about twelve o'clock, yet has none of the disdain for the flotsam down below manifested by the other. It is hard to be certain where time stands now for him, since this pious child is the inversion of his polite counterpart, and he is obscured by his opposite's shadow as he walks away with his back to the spectator. However, if the spectator continues to follow sundial logic as the basis for Hogarth's terrestrial clock, then the gutter bisecting Hog Lane is a surrogate for the shadow cast by the invisible gnomon at 12:10. This is confirmed as the shadow passes under the stylish man's minute-hand walking stick, with the murky debris to the left of the gentleman's left foot marking the direction of the shadow's course as time progressed.

From the inverted perspective, the departing Huguenots stand on the shadow line (the brown ocher gutter) marking 12:10, while the polite threesome stand, facing south, gesturing in the vicinity of the sun and the origin of noon's shadow. Ironically, what seems at first to be the shallow, house-of-mirrors depth of the everyday temporal process depicted here transforms a ribald street scene into discourse on the interaction of cosmology, history, and time. Mirrors may be shallow, but they also connect everything reflected in them. Thus, Hog Lane's fashionable "sun" figures move forward toward the spectator observing present time as, simultaneously, most of the refugees move back, into the past. Or are they moving in the opposite direction, into the future? This depends on the viewer's perspective on the status of light and shadow. Meanwhile, the sun reaches its peak at noon and begins its descent in the midday sky, while the architectural arch above the foreground actors' heads is thrown into half-shadow to mark the moment.

Hogarth presents more clues in the foreground light, perhaps to entice the spectator to look closer for the meaning of what is happening there. Large orbs of sun-bright orange makeup circle the polite lady's cheeks, with five orange buttons crowning her bonnet. These mischievous references to the transitory nature of style and appearance by analogy to the five standard sundial stages (south/southwest/west/northwest/north), that mark the sun's transit from sunrise until noon in conjunction with the earth's rotation. Just so, the coquettish tilt of her head shows the sun rising on the southwestern side of her face to the foreground (about 6 A.M. on the dial), making its daily transit across her bonnet, and beginning its descent into background shadow to the northeast on the sunset side of her face.

As Huguenot "earth" figures in the background begin to rotate north, receding away from the sunlight into shadow, they turn back into their future, toward darkness at the end of day and the rising of the moon. The rotation is prefigured by the transition from the architectural arch on the Eglise des Grecs (already in half-shadow) to the dark oval window (cloaked fully in shadow) placed directly over the church door as the earth figures exit. Hence, there are at least "four times of the day" occurring simultaneously in *Noon:* past, present, future, and cosmological time. The interaction of microcosm and macrocosm is linked in the motions of the human body, which are influenced, as in Winthrop's chair and Howes's pictograph, by the motion of the earth and moon. All rotate—or "dial"—around the Copernican sun. These temporal dimensions are linked oppositionally and interact like mirror images. Like the Hebrews living in millennial time in Jeremiah 7:24, most of the action in *Noon* goes "backward and not forward."

Like the automaton, such temporal motions were often predetermined by popular misreadings of Newtonian physics as revealing a clockwork universe, although, in fact, Newton and his followers vigorously denied any such belief. Newton never used the clock metaphor, and his dynamic cosmology based on God's continuous maintenance of the universe seems much closer to Paracelsus than Descartes.[8] At first glance, the motions in *Noon* appear to be locked into structures already defined by mechanistic philosophy, rather than the sort of inner-directed spiritualist animate materialism we have associated with the Paracelsians. However, the actions and intentions of the figures presented in *Noon* are far too fluid or obscure to define. They shift ambiguously over time. Depending on position bodies may be hidden or distorted by a surfeit of light or shadow. A cryptic Hogarth plays off the relationships between the variety of visual perception and monolithic readings of Newtonian natural-philosophical concepts in a time-travel game. This starts with the painting's title, which is *Noon,* after all, not 12:10. Hogarth's time game thus revolves around perceptions of history, since the central action has already happened in the past.

Witness the outcome of a catastrophic transaction on the other side of Hog Lane, resulting in a broken earthenware pie dish and a hurt and crying child. In both the foreground and background, the polite threesome and the worshipful Huguenots are in the process of leaving the central pictorial space. Since the passage of time is linked to the movements of the actors, whatever happened on Hog Lane ten minutes earlier is no longer fully visible in *Noon.* Yet time's internal logic in the unmechanized shadow world of Hogarth's art allows as much for unforeseen accident as clockwork fate.

In other words, rewinding the hands of the steeple clock—or running an automaton in reverse—will not suffice to reverse human experience, and hence the full history of events that led to the broken plate. The pieces of pottery in Hogarth's painting cannot be put back together again retrospectively; neither can spectators reconstitute the hidden history of *Noon* as in a time machine. No mechanism can rewind the past in form and substance. The whole story cannot be retold without knowledge of what occurred in the shadows. This is complicated further by the culture of Hog Lane itself. What is hidden is out of style and so beyond consumption. But the seduction of the labyrinth keeps Hogarth's audience in the game. Spectators become historians complicitous in the production of a complex pictorial text in urban pluralism, which guarantees the pleasure of many possible readings and outcomes, and exits from the labyrinth. Indeed, the introductory paragraphs of chapter 5 ("Of Intricacy") of *The Analysis of Beauty* leave no doubt whatever of the intentional complexity of Hogarth's project:

> The active mind is ever bent to be employed. Pursuing is the business of our lives; and even abstracted from any other view, gives pleasure. Every arising difficulty, that for a while attends and interrupts the pursuit, gives a sort of spring to the mind, enhances the pleasure, and makes what would else be toil and labour, become sport and recreation.
>
> . . . . It is a pleasing labour of the mind to solve the most difficult problems; allegories and riddles, trifling as they are, afford the mind amusement: and with what delight does it follow the well-connected thread of a play, or novel, which ever increases as the plot thickens, and ends most pleas'd, when that is most distinctly unravell'd?
>
> The eye hath this sort of enjoyment in winding walks, and serpentine rivers, and all sorts of objects . . . composed principally of what I call the *waving* and *serpentine* lines.
>
> Intricacy in form, therefore, I shall define to be that peculiarity in the lines, which compose it, that *leads the eye on a wanton kind of chase*, and form the pleasure that gives the mind, intitles it to the name of beautiful."[9]

Given the clockwork pace at which the motion occurs, one may presume that as the clock struck twelve, the Huguenots were just emerging from the church door to descend into the shadows. At the same time, the fashionable threesome—the sun figures—approach the church door from the direction of Savoy Chapel, coming face to face with the exiting congregants. At that moment, the Huguenots eclipse the threesome and are briefly exposed to sunlight just as their counterparts are cloaked in shadow. Having been conjoined at noon, the solar threesome walk through into the foreground to their appointed position just exiting center stage, and the earthly Huguenots, returning to their natural habitat, continue to descend "in winding walks" into the shadows in the background at right. For a brief instant, the congregants of the Eglise des Grecs are revealed converging with polite culture, as the artisans of politeness. To perceive such an easily overlooked incident suggests that to understand the relation between production, consumption, and time on Hog Lane, the spectator must look in detail at the whole surface of reality in flux at the margins of peripheral vision. To *"teach us to see with our own eyes,"* as Hogarth commands (his emphasis),[10] it is necessary to take inventory of the interaction of public and private bodies moving in a continuum from atomized detachment to brief moments of convergence.

❧ Inventory of the Peripheral ❧

To make sense of Hogarth's narrative, we have to begin again in "real time," where nothing is as innocent as may appear at first glance and periphery is center. Pious congregants descend in procession from a church door, rotate their faces away from spectators in the light, and converge silently into the darkness like ghosts behind the façade of Hog Lane. Blurring in and out of focus, they retreat surreptitiously back into the streets of Soho, a French stronghold after the Revocation of the Edict of Nantes. Underneath the half-seen arch, two elderly Calvinist women—one of whom clutches a sacred text (perhaps a book of psalms) under her right arm—separate from the majority of their co-religionists, and embrace in a covenant of spiritual friendship. Their embrace signifies the presence of a mobile community of the faithful joined together by the Word animated by the Holy Spirit.

But even this scene shields secrets and will not yield to the comfort of a transparent piety. Is there a face hidden ominously beneath the black tricorn hat with gold frills that floats directly behind and just slightly above the ancient women, leaving virtually zero degree of separation? This spectral figure reveals not a face but the presence of something absent. Who is this mysterious third party? Does the memory of Huguenot dead stand guard over the heart of the community's oldest survivors, the knot of violence and the sacred that bound kinship ties together with the history of refugee culture? Is this an allegory of the mystical cope of heaven that conjoins macrocosm and microcosm through the living Word, and that was also materialized in the canopy of portable pulpits Huguenots used for their clandestine assemblies of the *désert?* Multiple readings are available for this apparition, so sometimes a hat is not just a hat. In this sacred context, this hovering presence reveals the existence of the invisible Holy Spirit in everyday life, or simply the ineffable, mystical quality of the sacred mysteries, which cannot be controlled by any mechanism: Trinitarianism, as it were, in a three-cornered hat. The hat seems almost to fit the "head" of the two embracing women at once. To pursue Hogarth's cosmic themes of doubling and inversion, are the two heads are joined permanently at the mouth, connecting the breath of spirit with the bodily organ of the Word contained in the book?

Unlike the elderly women, most of the congregation shun pious display. Reversing direction, it turns away from the polished sun figures. Like a monolithic sun, oblivious to the human drama that transpires all around it, Hogarth's fashionable threesome proceed just past the church door and stroll blithely past the two pious women as well. This group comprises a discrete social unit. The adult couple affects polite conversation. They present themselves and their possessions narcissistically, with their public gestures of exorbitant and self-conscious theatricality. But where is their audience beyond themselves? Surely not their preoccupied offspring, who uses his walking stick to delicately prod a scrap discarded in the street. Neither are the subaltern characters on the other side of Hog Lane interested in the conspicuous display of fashion; they are absorbed with their own carnal desires for sex and gluttony. The only actors fully concerned with this bit of theater are the couple themselves, Hogarth's audience of consumers, and that lone figure who stares back at his audience knowingly from the narrow space still available between the polite couple.

The painter stops time to expose the civic benefits of Lord Shaftesbury's philosophy of virtuous interaction. The idealized social and material discourse of politeness is embodied here by this solipsistic couple and young child—a family that labors not to produce but to consume sufficient goods and knowledge to abide by the rules of the distinctive social system advertised by their clothing and gestures. Hogarth and those who viewed his work knew very well that the costumes, cosmetic masks, and other ostentatious courtly French bodily adornments fashionable in England were designed and produced by ascetic Huguenot artisans who retreated behind a cloak of invisibility when their clients theatrically displayed themselves. Thus private and public life are inseparable realities, even if only the public domain at center is perceived by most spectators.

This dialectical framework also directs our attention to the soiled condition of the polite man's left coat sleeve (which hovers directly over the gutter), and hence another hidden reality: no matter how lightly they may seem to tread—or how self-consciously they distance themselves from the "low culture" of production—the all-consuming sun figures cannot rise completely above the flotsam of dirt and refuse that spatters up from the street. This, after all, is a story of production as well as consumption. We perceive the remnants of an obscure transaction between the Huguenots and their clients, which took place when their paths crossed ten minutes earlier. Here is raw evidence that like the human body, polished goods derive from gross earthy matter. "Our necessities have taught us to mould matter into various shapes," Hogarth reminds us, "and to give them fit proportions for particular uses." Thus, the fashionable hands of time must pass through the muck of the terrestrial world.

Playing off his story of mass production, social quotation, and the superficiality of style, another peculiar sign hovers over the hidden boutique fronting the narrow background space that opens in the direction of the departing refugees. The headless sign reminds spectators of the faceless hat in the foreground. They can draw a connecting line between the hat and the sign. Here is a Hogarthian pun on seduction by self-deception: the refined sun group defines its social self-identity through imported clothing and gestures. This is reproduced and multiplied in the sign: the polite woman's mirror image in the "French style." So, like the tyrannical court style of the sun king's absolutism, style functions here to negate individual "faces" and difference within the group, while setting up boundaries of social distance and "distinction" outside.[11] Thus, the boutique advertises the dress of a headless female. This image is an inversion of the spirituality of the Huguenots' headless hat. It is animated during its brief existence as fashion solely by the transitory nature of style itself; by its life as a transaction and a conduit of a theatrical gesture at the moment of consumption and display. After these ephemeral moments in the sun vanish, fashion disappears from the scene as human waste, indistinguishable from a joint of rotten meat, the carnal body dumped from the window above the dispirited boutique sign down into the gutter below. At the same time, one cannot overlook the probability that this shop sign directs consumers to a boutique that belongs to a congregant. Did the stylish threesome purchase their clothing at the boutique? The discarded meat draws attention from the stylish foreground back across the gutter that bisects Hog Lane. The gutter is an open sewer streaming waste, marking the "fluid" boundary between being and appearance. Here again Hogarth inverts the fashionable threesome into the figures of the racially mixed couple and child. On a sign above their heads for Hog Lane's public house that reads "Good Eating" (a grotesque pun for the platter of meat), we find advertised a disembodied head on a platter. This was standard iconography for the beheaded St. John the Baptist. It shows him after he lost his "head" to Salome's sexual frustration, a stoic who refused to be seduced by carnal desire. Here his emblem is a bawdy double entendre to the action taking place directly below at street level. "Good Eating" thus completes a triangle of floating bodily signifiers and unifies three fragmented figures. The disembodied hat of the invisible spirit, which transcends all the categories of sublunar temporality on display here (including being and appearance, night and day, sun and moon, darkness and shadow, high and low), reconnects the disembodied head of the spirit that resisted porcine consumption (St. John) with the headless body of soulless fashion (the headless woman).

Under the sign of the beheaded saint, the stylish threesome emerges as distinctively unpolished, in formal opposition to their polite counterparts across the gutter. Here the process of "Good Eating" is revealed as a crapulous riot of sexual transgression and rampant (re-)production in the service of premature, displaced or wasted consumption. This is harnessed to an orgy of carnal desire that conflates such disorders of bodily discipline as gluttony and unrestrained sexual appetite. The flushed and aroused shop girl presents consumers with her anatomically suggestive meat pie, which she casually offers for sale. The pie drips condensed streams of hot juicy liquid from a tufted hole at center, as if an ornament on a bizarre sexual fountain. She has been caught by surprise in a salacious, behind-the-back embrace by an opportunistic "African." The construction of this figure's furtive yet aggressive persona on the painting's margins plays on local stereotypes inspired by the common sight of black craftsmen or seamen passing through London's artisans' ghettos during the eighteenth century.

Large numbers of both freed and enslaved "black jacks" could possess a relatively high degree of personal autonomy (compared with plantation slaves) while serving on transatlantic ships that carried raw materials such as sugar, tobacco, and wheat from the American colonies to the metropolis.[12] Superficially, Hogarth presents most casual observers with a lewd image of the libidinous African. This was a variant of the ubiquitous and corrosive eighteenth-century racial trope of impure desire. It is also an archetype of the shadowy Anglo-American fetish for the seductions of darkness, famously elaborated by Thomas Jefferson in *Notes on the State of Virginia*. This text summarizes Jefferson's natural philosophy, drawn from Aristotelian sources and clearly refracted through the lens of the Chesapeake slaveholding elite. Included is a "scientific" essay on early Virginia's race relations. Jefferson reasoned against racial mixing and that enslaved Africans, contrary to the natural symmetry of the white race, were burdened with an unequal balance of rational and emotional impulses. Africans' surfeit of undisciplined emotion and raw sexual energy necessitated restraint and domestication through the rational assertion of white mastery (that is, slavery). For Jefferson, the natural racial equilibrium was achieved in Virginia, thus linking both races.[13]

✦ The Unforeseen Consequences of Desire ✦

It was natural for a depiction of miscegenation to show the African in charge in the one arena in which he was accorded dominance in British-American culture, that of transgressive desire. He gropes roughly around the servant's back (under her left arm and over her right shoulder), to encircle her body and possess her orblike breasts. Meanwhile the girl turns her head lustfully, to receive his kiss. The tip of her right breast is squeezed between his black thumb and forefinger and her nipple is exposed. Given its proximity, this suggests the servant's breast was a natural font for her meat pie's milky stream of waste. However, the African's disordered and profane movements to possess the shop girl are the cause of a chaotic chain reaction with unforeseen consequences.

In addition to spilling the fountain of liquid, the surprised servant knocks her dripping pie onto the head of her frizzy-haired child (the hair perhaps a sign of African paternity) hard enough to cause the boy to cry, grab *his* head, and drop an identical earthenware pie plate he is carrying down below at street level. This "lesser" plate appears linked on a parallel plane to the one above. The plate below smashes in two, causing its unrecognizable contents to go crashing down to the cobblestones. This has oc-curred ten minutes earlier—prematurely, at noon—because the boy has by now re-trieved the plate's broken half from the street. Even wasted material finds its proper consumer at the lowest level of existence. Close to the open sewer, a spectral street urchin sneaks in and scavenges hungrily for soiled scraps in the rubble, like a pig on Hog Lane.

To complete the first level of Hogarth's metaphysical dialogue between the alchemy of politeness and its dark, chaotic underside, the *prima materia* of base materialism: the transgressive desire that triggers the impulse of wasteful consumption is refined and redirected from the physical absorption of "Good Eating." Here it appears first as bodily waste in the gutter; then, transmuted into highly valued commodities, it takes the commercial form of polished materials displayed by the polite group across the street. Still, every material contains remnants of its history and the potential (as on the coat's unclean sleeve) to degrade and revert to human waste. On the other side of the street, the African's openly crude gesture of encompassing sexual consumption is mir-rored and distilled in his polite counterpart to a delicate touch of thumb to forefinger.

Finally, out of the corner of his eye, the beholder returns to the pious Huguenot women joined in holy embrace. The pious embrace of heaven and earth gives birth to a sacred book that meditates on the meaning of spiritual life, and it is still within reach. But the Word speaks the Huguenot's shadow language of interiority; thus it is out of fashion (the book receives in passing the back of the lady's gloved right hand). This lady of fashion's hyperaesthetic politeness is elaborately rhetorical. Her comportment resists the "plain style" fundamental to the Reformation's moral passion, fervently pos-sessed by the Continental reformers who elucidated the personal experience of inner grace by both verbal and material subtraction, another refining process. At the same time, using his right hand, the stylish male in white powder completes the polite anal-ogy to the subversive sexuality of his black alter ego, with a delicate, openhanded ges-ture toward the result of this amorous "touch": a fully formed, miniature reproduction of himself (and his self-love). The child of this shallow union is a kind of homuncu-lus; that is, a play on Paracelsus's artificial, self-contained "little man." A composite male and female, made in his father's image to scavenge at his feet. Idiosyncratic ges-tures reinvent in alchemic terms the conventional iconography of misalliance and bas-tardy, signaled by the smashed vessel, still partly possessed by the despondent child crying loudly over his misfortune on the other side of Hog Lane. Thus, three diminu-tive figures form the basis of another triangle composed of mirror images, at street level, with the Huguenot child leading the way to form the hidden apex/head. This deepens the viewers perspective into the shadows of the workshops of Soho. It rotates back into memory, simultaneously moving forward into the millennial future, along the path taken by the Huguenots in retreat from the disorder of consumption they quietly created on Hog Lane.

❧ Robert Fludd and the Metaphysics of Hog Lane ❧

The presence of alchemical signs extends Hogarth's invitation to further natural-philosophical inquiry beyond the mechanistic reading of time. Perceptive spectators may now move to deeper levels of meaning hidden in a metaphysical reading of materialism on Hog Lane. This is further reinforced by oblique references to the mystical quest for universal knowledge, diffused by a number of well-known alchemical texts published in response to the religious violence suffered by Huguenots in La Rochelle, as well as by other refugee groups in the Netherlands and the German Palatinate during the last stages of the Thirty Years' War.

Hogarth harnessed alchemical themes to specific images from a series of engraved books by the influential second-generation English Paracelsian and hero to Howes and Winthrop: the Oxford physician, natural philosopher, and cosmographer, Robert Fludd. These huge folio editions were engraved by the foremost refugee printer, Johann Theodore de Bry, and published ca. 1617–29, in Frankfurt and Oppenheim. Fludd and the first-generation Paracelsian John Dee (1527–1608) were the two widely read English mystics of the early modern period. Winthrop's alchemical library has shown that both bibliophiles and print collectors pursued the magnificent volumes resulting from the Fludd–de Bry collaboration. Prized for the quality of de Bry's cosmological engravings after Fludd's drawings, these images were elucidated in the occult text. Fludd–de Bry collaborations were thus considered the crowning glory of all English natural-philosophical libraries throughout the early modern Atlantic world. John Winthrop Jr.'s library still contains eleven titles by Fludd alone. Hog Lane layers Hogarth's perception of profound linkages between memories of the Soho Huguenots' hidden modes of production, the gaudy spectacle of theatrical consumption, and the natural-philosophical imagery and texts of Robert Fludd.[14]

Hogarth's cryptic pictorial references to the Fludd volumes found a knowledgeable audience of learned English book and print collectors in 1736. Old print culture was yet another category of consumable with an expanding market from commercialization and the consumer revolution. Consumers with the finances and libraries to acquire the Fluddian texts may be represented by individuals from both groups of characters on the left side of Hog Lane. There was a keen interest in the occultism of philosophers such as Dee and Fludd. Their cosmologies were both fashionable and intellectually respectable in Hogarth's time, in large part because of the growth of Freemasonry and the fascination of London's large community of scientists and literati with the millennial performances staged during the early eighteenth century by the French Prophets. Unlike the stoical Calvinists on Hog Lane, these Huguenots expressed their religious enthusiasm in theatrical ways (at least until the 1740s), and were attracted to open performances of their interpretation of Paracelsian apocalyptics to wrest meaning out of violent experience in southeastern France. These Camisard "Seekers, Citizens, [and] Scientists" were deeply engaged in alchemic experimentation toward a universal theory of animate materialism based on laws of motion in matter. The personal and prophetic theory of motion developed by these scientists differed sharply from mechanical philosophy. Clearly building on the work of both Paracelsus and Palissy, the French Prophets experimented with salt (*Sal volatile oleosum*). It was, they argued by the 1740s, the hidden, germinative element in nature and man, linking the motions of microcosm and macrocosm.[15]

Hogarth's audience of *erudits* and collectors had at hand the research materials necessary to identify the source of *Noon*'s alchemic code, which represented earth's status as one of the four primordial elements, providing a key to deciphering the painting's semiotics of Huguenot artisanal experience. I would argue that Hogarth in fact intended *Earth* as a hermetic title and a sort of subtextual surrogate for *Noon*. While it is not my task here to analyze all *The Four Times of the Day* to assess how the logic of this assertion might extend to the others as well, one might speculate that the set may have functioned as an alchemical allegory of the four elements. By harnessing the cycle of time as it completes its passage from beginning to end, together with the four elements of nature essential to mankind's material life (and in particular to geochronology), Hogarth links the natural philosophy of "Noon" to the millennial discourse of an aging earth. Many artisans also encountered this influential millennial worldview at the same time that it was reactivated by Europe's reformed sectarian groups—in particular, the Anabaptists—during the era of religious warfare.[16] Palissy showed the discourse of the aging earth was resonant with the early modern natural philosophers and was fundamental to Paracelsian medical practice and alchemy. By extension, Joachim's chiliastic framework for knowledge of the past, present, and future ages of earthy materials, powerfully informed the materio-holiness synthesis forged by the potter and his Huguenot artisanal community in Aunis-Saintonge during the civil war years. Remnants of this community ultimately relocated to the Eglise des Grecs and New York City in the 1680s.

Fludd's mystical presence in *Noon* dwells in a third, "high sign," the unusually shaped escutcheon that appears in the upper left foreground hovering near the cornice of the Eglise des Grecs. With its back to the audience, yet fronting the Huguenot ghetto, it floats at the painting's highest margin. A backward sign occupies virtually the same supermundane plane of material existence as the church steeple in the deep background, and so it emits an aura of spiritual lightness and transparency that would be singular on Hog Lane were it not for its resonance with the hat that also levitates below without visible means of support. The floating signifier, at once Hogarth's most enigmatic artifact of Fluddian philosophy and his most mysterious, is distinguished by sheer physical ambiguity: what manner of sign is this? Since only an armature in the back is barely visible, making none of the usual product advertisements or even a simple place-name available, what message was it meant to convey to Hogarth's audience? Is it really untethered, floating up in the air like a sort of kite; alternatively, does it hang down by a rope, like the one carried by the ascending Christlike figure, upheld by angels, illustrating "second sight" in figure 8.21, from some unseen place on the cornice gutter; yet more linguistic doubling, this time of the gutter that collects raw sewage down on Hog Lane? That gutter is now elevated to its mirror image, its function to collect and redirect transparent rainwater as it flowed down off the roof of the Eglise des Grecs, just before it descended into its impure state, mixing with dirt and waste down in the filthy street.

Unlike the two conventional signs of conventional construction across the lane, there are no wooden brackets visible or other means of attachment beyond the enigmatic floating rope or chain with tasseled end. Where then, and how, is this strange object physically mounted to the building? How is it connected to the tripartite dynamics of the scenes below? What does it mean that nearly transparent materials are used in its craftsmanship? Are they meant to convey—like the Huguenot congregation—a sense of ethereal refinement and attenuation, one that keeps its distance from the lower world of Hog Lane, at the same time the sign seems attached to the terrestrial sphere? The tension between material translucency and earthy mixing punctuates the sign's high status in the continuum of man-made earthy materials, from unformed dross in one gutter to refined luminosity in the other. The sign floats like a plumb line above the church, pointing down at the enclave of false transparency. Here, at least, we locate a standard reference to Shaftesbury's admonition against the disjunction of being and appearance; the synchronic depth of near transparency illuminates the transience of mere polish.

Since the audience sees only the back of the sign, the front—presumably containing the message that would end speculation—is hidden to those who occupy Hog Lane's foreground, and to Hogarth's spectators above all. Should we assume that secret knowledge of the special materials used in its manufacture is available to the pious Huguenot artisans alone? They have the sign side in plain sight. Situated in a natural place for a church sign, it may also serve as a sign of the palindrome (another sign of reversals). Or it could signify the Huguenot artisans' social simultaneity; their shifty, protean quality of both being in back (as hidden producers) and appearing in front (as finished products displayed by clients). As such, the sign may have many names—backward sign, high sign, church sign, Huguenot sign—in the shifting context of Hog Lane. The sign's elegant formal structure, its linear trajectories that send two opposing cyma-recta curves in parallel motion to connect at the bottom, has a finely wrought seam at the intersection that also bisects the uppermost acute angle. This construction joins the apex of a slightly concave compass, dividing the whole in two halves. Its formal structure thus reinforces the light sensation of simultaneity in perpetual motion. This was the line of beauty.

❧ "The line of beauty" ❧

Contextualizing the aesthetics of natural philosophy and the formal logic of perpetual motion was precisely what Hogarth had in mind when he called the cyma-recta or S-curve the "line of beauty." On the title page of *The Analysis of Beauty,* the subtitle of which is *Written with a View of Fixing the Fluctuating Ideas of Taste* (1753), Hogarth's critique of the "fluctuation" of modern tastes in fashion, are variations of his serpentine line. He chose to focus on and illustrate a form widely understood among connoisseurs of French taste as an object of Huguenot artisanal manufacture: a curved chair leg (fig. 14.3, boxes 49, 50).[17] Hogarth was aware that knowledge of the curved leg in London was traceable at least to 1702, when the Huguenot architect and designer Daniel Marot (1661–1752) published his first collection of designs, containing 236 leaves of engraved plates.[18]

Marot entered William III's service in London as a refugee of 1685. Yet the *Oxford English Dictionary* shows that the word *cabriole* was first used in English as early as the sixteenth century, although not specifically in reference to an article of furniture. Rather, it signified the spirited caper of a leaping goat or horse. Thomas Fitch, a Boston upholsterer of leather chairs, called such a leg a "horse bone" or "Crookt Foot" in his account book, a lexical pattern that soon became common in appraisals of chairs with these legs. Such legs were identified as ubiquitous on artifacts of politeness in probate inventories taken in affluent colonial households.[19] Why serpentine chair components were idealized in British-American transatlantic culture, and hence considered analogous to a part of natural bodies essential to the "caper" of politeness, is also essential to the natural philosophy of *Noon.*[20]

Hogarth was unambiguous on this point. If a "grand secret of the ancients, or great key of knowledge" existed, he had found it in the serpentine line which connected "an infinite variety of parts." Like Palissy, Hogarth looked to Nature for the source of this foundational line, and, like Palissy, he found it in the inner and outer bodies of the shell, where his eye went, "in the pursuit of these serpentine-lines, as in their twistings their concavities and convexities are alternately offer'd to its view":

> [L]et every object . . . be imagined . . . to have nothing of it left but a thin shell, exactly corresponding both in its inner and outer surface, to the shape of the object itself . . . whether the eye is supposed to observe them from without, or within; . . . we shall find

FIGURE 14.3. William Hogarth, *The Analysis of Beauty* (London, 1753), pl. 1. Courtesy Harry Ransom Humanities Research Center, The University of Texas at Austin. Compare sections 49 and 50 to see the "line of beauty" materialized as a chair leg. Sections 38 and 39 refer to patterns for turned legs on other sorts of furniture, such as the high chest of drawers in figure 16.17. Numbers 17 and 18 recall earlier images of crying and posing children on Hog Lane.

the ideas of the two surfaces of this shell will naturally coincide. The very word, shell, makes us seem to see both surfaces alike.

. . . the [more often] we think of objects in this shell-like manner, we shall facilitate . . . a more perfect knowledge of the whole . . . because the imagination will naturally enter into this vacant space within this shell . . . and make us masters of the meaning of every view of the object.[21]

With the important exception of the outsized earthenware pitcher cloaked in shadow on a pedestal in the deep background, no other "moveable" figure down on street level in "Noon" shows the line of beauty seen on the Huguenot sign. Indeed, Hogarth's polite threesome can only manage to convey a sort of angular—even geo-metrical—stiffness. Rather than repeating the requisite series of mobile serpentine lines like the ones floating effortlessly above their heads, at first glance the sun figures present instead an image of arrested action. Here, light and spirit are forced through a maze of straight lines that bend into triangles and converge at the head, arms, legs,

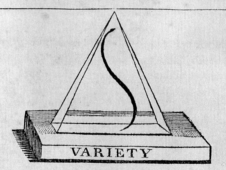

THE
ANALYSIS
OF
BEAUTY.

Written with a view of fixing the fluctuating IDEAS of
TASTE.

BY *WILLIAM HOGARTH.*

So vary'd he, and of his tortuous train
Curl'd many a wanton wreath, in ſight of Eve,
To lure her eye.-------- Milton.

VARIETY

LONDON:

Printed by *J. REEVES* for the *AUTHOR,*
And Sold by him at his Houſe in LEICESTER-FIELDS.

MDCCLIII.

FIGURE 14.4. William Hogarth, *The Analysis of Beauty,* title page. Courtesy Harry Ransom
Humanities Research Center, University of Texas at Austin. In both the subtitle and his epigram from Milton, as well as in the famous image of VARIETY, Hogarth plays with "views" of
fixing ever-changing relations between form, perception, and meaning in material life.

and feet. Here, too, Hogarth's agenda is inferred from *The Analysis of Beauty*. Elucidating the aesthetic relation between philosophical language and animate form, Hogarth reinvented seventeenth-century artisanal and scientific images, "with a view of
fixing the fluctuating ideas of taste."

In a second engraving of the line of beauty published on the title page (fig. 14.4),
Hogarth contains the fluctuating line of taste in solid geometric form. This thought
experiment in the aesthetics of matter in motion (or put another way, motion hidden
inside of matter) focuses the line vertically and in two directions at once. Here an animate spirit undulates between macrocosm and microcosm in perpetuity inside a transparent crystal pyramid; that is, inside of four transparent triangles connected with a
common point at the apex, which Hogarth explains suggests the alchemical symbols
connoting fire and air. Just as Hogarth appropriated the line of beauty for the chairs
in figure 14.3 (boxes 49, 50) from Marot's designs for William III's chairs, so, too, he
gathered the conceptual framework for this system of triangles from a cryptogram on
the title page of Fludd's *De technica microcosmi historia,* or History of the Microcosmic
Arts (Oppenheim, 1619), an elaboration on Renaissance drawing in deep perspective.
Fludd identified this formal representation as his most influential natural-philosophical
conception, the "science of pyramids" (*pyramidum scientia*) (fig. 10.6). Hogarth used it
as a fragmentary source for the backward sign. When Fludd's multiple volumes of
cosmology were engraved and published by the refugee de Bry in Oppenheim and
Frankfurt between 1617 and 1631, they were contextualized as major contributions to
the Huguenot corpus that, as Frances Yates and Frank Lestringant show, emerged
specifically from apocalyptic conditions created by the Thirty Years' War. The Fluddian images from *Microcosmi historia* explored the metaphysics of movement in the
context of flight from religious warfare. Both were necessary for the construction of
the crystal pyramid in *The Analysis of Beauty,* and the system of materialism configured
in the form of the backward sign of the Huguenot church in *Noon.*

As we have learned from the introduction to his chapter "Of Intricacy" in *The Analysis of Beauty,* Hogarth also followed an older tradition of representation in showing
the linear movement of numerous bodies through geographical space. Serpentine lines
had been used cross-culturally to document passage over distances by important court
or religious processions ever since the Middle Ages, when the courtly progress was a
common event. But it became a conventional artistic schema of dispersion in early
modern times, when it underwent a process of elaboration. In 1661, a similar serpentine composition was elaborated in a Dutch engraving of La Rochelle that reimagines
the largest outmigration of refugees from the city after 1628 as a frantic flight by diasporic Huguenots carrying the tools of their trades and material belongings with them
(fig. 14.5).

FIGURE 14.5. Jan Luyken (1649–1712), *Vervolging in Rochell* ("Persecution in La Rochelle"), engraving, Amsterdam, ca. 1661. Courtesy Collections du Musée d'Orbigny-Bernon de La Rochelle. Photo, Neil Kamil. The legend reads: "Three hundred Reformed Huguenots flee from [*trekken voor*] the persecution in La Rochelle in the month of November 1661." By the 1640s, Protestant demographics had begun a brief recovery from 1628, especially among artisans, who, demonstrating greater industry than their Catholic counterparts, began to reclaim trades after guilds were suspended by the articles of capitulation and trades became free (*métiers libres*). This occasioned a rise in Catholic anti-Protestant workers' organizations and ultimately a massive purge of Protestants from La Rochelle in 1661 by the police courts, directed by the Catholic corporations, which said they were only targeting illegal residents. (On the 1661 purge, see Katherine Louise Milton Faust, "A Beleaguered Society: Protestant Families in La Rochelle, 1628–1685" [Ph.D. diss., Northwestern University, 1980], 101–15.) In fact, Huguenots were banished—literally thrown out into the street, as Luyken dramatized—for minor offenses. Among the homeless is the orphan pointed out in the foreground, certain to be rebaptized a Catholic. Luyken's composition follows the conventional serpentine pattern. A large number of these families made their way to New Amsterdam, where they were recorded in town records a few years before the English takeover.

The serpentine line was thus also a trope for migration of refugees during wartime. Hogarth's education as a printmaker probably owed more specific debts to representations of the siege of La Rochelle. Hogarth's fascination with the Jacques Callot's seventeenth-century engravings of the "horrors of war" is well documented. One of his earliest commissions—John Beaver's *The Roman Military Punishments* (London, 1725)—was modeled on Callot's *Misères de la guerre.*[22] Hogarth thus knew the many reproductions available in England of Callot's enormous composite engraving of *The Siege of La Rochelle* (1628), a watershed in seventeenth-century French engraving. These overlapping contexts formed the natural-philosophical and aesthetic foundations for Hogarth's "analytical" discourse on the serpentine line. The hidden, albeit "fluctuating," history of Soho's refugee Huguenot artisans was particularly well suited on many levels to function as *Noon*'s primary historical text.

Specific linear forms assume greater historical meaning here. Just as the cyma-recta merges into the angle atop the pyramid in *The Analysis of Beauty,* so the opposing S-curves at the top of the Huguenot sign merge together to form a compass. If one imagines a line that connects its bottom two points above the curves, it forms the top of a triangle as well. A small segment of the audience was prepared by knowledge of natural-philosophical principles to follow the motion of the opposing serpentine lines down through the arrowlike point at the bottom of the sign. If spectators knew it was plausible for that descending motion to continue downward through the physical and material mass of the enclave of politeness into the ground in exactly the same way— like an invisible effluvium that passes through purified earthy matter like a Palissian snake just as it passes through the lightness of air—then they also understood that motion must follow this path through a gauntlet of congruent triangles.

The first triangle points up. It is composed of the heads—or, rather, the vacant and triangular noses of three individual actors. The fashionable couple facing each other make up the base of an equilateral triangle. At its apex—in the place taken by the enigmatic hat to his right—is a shadowy male figure (who mingles among the congregants but does not appear to be one of them, for he is not dressed in black). The stranger has long black hair, the most prominent nose of all, and stands almost invisibly behind the couple. Is this the maker of the automaton's mechanism or a puppeteer hidden behind his marionettes? Or, like the carved crest of an upholstered chair, is he the upholsterer between the customary pair of turned finials. Is this a cryptic representation of Hogarth himself as the earthly conduit for the animating spirit, standing behind the theatrical, two-dimensional world of pictorial creation?

The figure does not, however, resemble the known Hogarth self-portraits. Still, allusions to the spirit-animated hidden theater of behind-the-scenes manipulation fit Hogarth's (and the artist's) traditional role as animator of pigments, materials, or otherwise dumb characters. They would also seem to fit the role Hogarth and English craft culture had assigned the shadowy Huguenot artisans in their traditional behind-the-scenes relation to elite clients. The stranger stands *among* the Huguenots in the shadows, so he may also share their identity as a marginalized outsider with hidden transformative powers, who stands *behind* as operator of a theater of powerful public actors. In another variation on the automaton, while Huguenot artisans supply the taste in fashionable goods that ornament the homes and bodies of elite consumers, the stranger helps set the scene, and seems to direct narrative and gesture to enable otherwise wooden figures to be set in motion. Secretive Huguenot artisans and designers were industrious in private life, but were they also virtuous? Where did the shadowy operators of Hog Lane acquire their authority?

To answer these questions about *Noon*, we must reconstruct the geometry of the polite family and the stranger to see how Hogarth, like Ezra Stiles, tracked metaphysical impulses as they circulated from macrocosm to microcosm. This would establish a specific nexus for time and motion in the formation of animate matter. While the illusion of volume gives depth to the outline of the equilateral triangle of heads and noses, this abbreviated form is merely the "head" atop a large pyramid composed of the lower bodies of the threesome. As these triangular human containers interact with one another in polite discourse, they simultaneously appear to labor to envelope the line of beauty just as Hogarth would later demonstrate in his schematic diagram on the title page of *The Analysis of Beauty*. If the outer edges of their fashionable attire mark the sides of the polite triangle in two dimensions, then the seams that form its inner edges, as well as the placement of feet and arms, push the triangle forward, forming the illusion of the outside front and back of a pyramid. Closed, and yet politely transparent, this interactive space, encompassed in the midst of the triumvirate of fashion, signifies the sanctum sanctorum of the crystal pyramid. Now, in *Noon*, it is prepared to receive the spiraling line of beauty from the sign above. Hogarth shows us that the line moves through space in the much same pattern as the necklace around the lady's neck moves over her heart. Its movement is directed by the gentleman's right hand, which functions like a pendulum, and is open to the precise center point of the pyramid, and that of the two wooden walking sticks, which are held upright, (again) like hidden boundaries, to contain the double helix on its path of descent to the ground, as well as on its return journey upward again through the pyramid with its system of triangles.

Hogarth's voyeuristic stranger stares back, inscrutably, at his audience, over the shoulders of the two awkward marionettes, who are, of course, oblivious to his presence as he animates their bodies. As if by chance, the polite lady points her closed fan, which is also the side of a triangle, directly at the lurking interloper's nose. Thus, Hogarth playfully directs the motion of the dual effluvial lines to pass like breath, or *spiritus* (or less "subtly," like a sneeze?), through the stranger's two nostrils, which point the way down, bisecting the "base" of the uppermost triangle. The base of this triangle of nasal passages is congruent to the base of an isosceles triangle directly beneath it. However, the central angle of this one is aimed downward, toward the ground. The serpentine lines must now pass "lightly" through the fingertips of the gentleman's strangely shaped right hand, with bizarre fingers curved like the claw of a crab. The two central fingers are seamed together like the sign above to form one appendage. This echoes the earthbound movement of the lines, as the hand closely follows the shape of the rococo cartouche (see fig. 14.3, boxes 1–7) accompanying Hogarth's chair legs in *The Analysis of Beauty*. That grotesquely curved double fingertip—in careful opposition to the perfect anatomy of the gentleman's elegant left hand—forms the apex of another isosceles triangle pointing up, its base composed of the tip of the boy's cane touching the cobblestones and the tip of his father's daintily deployed left foot.

Finally, the Huguenot sign's two cyma-recta lines pass down into the earth of Hog Lane, but not before bisecting the common base of two congruent equilateral triangles that lay flat on the ground. The bases of the two earthly triangles are formed by the two left feet of father and son, while their apexes are formed by the morsel of debris prodded by the boy, and the point of the lady's left foot. The foreground triangle points in the direction of the audience, while the background triangle creates a sense of closure, by pointing back over the voyeur's shoulder at the pious Huguenot congregation as it emerges from the Eglise des Grecs. The line of beauty mingles with the Huguenots as they snake their way back into Soho, directed by the hand of the couturier's sign. That pathway leads to a congruent system of vertical triangles already linked with the Huguenot sign. These connect the pyramidal steeple of the church in the background with the Huguenots on the ground, in precisely the same way that the Huguenot sign is joined to the group of polite strollers displaying themselves on Hog Lane. The sacred aspect of the line of beauty, its traversing spiritual course, travels backward and forward on its serpentine path between the gold cross at the top of the church and the two conjoined women who are embracing in the foreground; an act of cosmic reciprocity. The line's movement is delineated by the valley amid the peaks and cornice ridges of the triangular gabled roofs. It flows directly into the steeple and back again, down the corner of the building. Then it merges into the shadow of the Huguenot effluvium.

We are thus confronted with the two most significant elements in *Noon*'s structure of palindromes: the "hidden" spirit (or being) that animates the painting's Huguenot artisanal community in relation to that of the audience. Depending on the spectator's place in the continuum of production and consumption between being and appearance, do spectators form a community with the polite threesome in the foreground. Where does the beholder stand? As the stranger stares out from behind his marionettes at his audience, does he see inversion or duplication, wasted effort or opportunity? We have already seen how in *Noon*'s terrestrial clock, the lady's foot marks twelve, and, by analogy, the morsel of waste pointing back at the audience is on precisely the same timeline. Does this mean that the beholder, on whom the stranger alone casts a judgmental eye, lives in the very same moment?

If the terrestrial clock of the aging "earth" conforms to the palindrome logic of *Noon*, the foreground triangle mirrors and inverts its opposite. Hogarth's audience of consumers may thus have been witness to the prophesy of an unhappy millennial ending. From where the spectators stood on the imaginary chapter ring (at the point of the gnomon's angle), their backs to the light shining on the painting, with faces cast in shadow as they beheld mirror images on the sundial, the aging earth's reading of geological time was midnight and not midday. Even as the Huguenots disappear behind them into the background, the consumers must stand still, under the floating sign. Like a gnomon, the beholders are riveted by the transiting sun to the one position on the dial that provided both a reflection of solar light and a pyramidal shell in order to direct "fluctuating ideas of taste." Politeness may be polished in the light, but it is a fragile vessel, one that merely contains and stiffens, gesturing conformity to angles that can only reflect and encompass light and motion. Politeness is thus represented as an a posteriori effect of the light, rather than its embodiment.

The Huguenots are superficially dark and recessive, but their amorphous spirituality is the embodiment of motion itself. Their movements forward and backward with serpentine fluidity inside of dark matter cause its transformation by *imparting* the essence of light and motion. Unlike their polite counterparts, the Huguenots are animate in the shadows, without exterior light (it is already hidden inside). They move physically beyond the brightness of *Noon*, away from Hog Lane and back into Soho, where for them the time is now 12:10. For some mechanistic philosophers, this meant matter would remain inanimate without the "vivid ray" of external light to provide the impetus for industriousness. Was Hogarth playing with the triangular, refractive structures of mechanistic optics (the mechanistic hypothesis of primary and secondary fields of vision) in his design of the polite family's angular lines as they ascend to (and descend from) the source of astral light in the Huguenot sign? Hogarth's subterranean Huguenots function on interior time during the metaphoric night. They operate without regulative power or optical illumination provided by the external light of the sun. Like the Germanic pietists who inspired their reinterpretation of rural Calvinism during the early years of the civil wars of religion, southwestern French Huguenots carried the light with them into the shadows.[23]

On Hog Lane, even symbols easily visible in the light of day masked false reciprocity and incomplete exchange. For example, at first glance the Huguenot sign could read as the bottom half of an hourglass split in two at middle by the top of the picture plane. It is directly in line of sight to the church steeple, where the clock reads 12:10.

This is a reminder that noon is midday in the light (in the dark, its metaphorical inverse: millennial midnight). Yet the shape does not conform to the round glass baluster at the bottom of a figure eight; it devolves to a directive point instead, with its escutcheon shape. There is no funnel to a receptacle at top, and it is difficult to explain the significance of the cord in the context of an hourglass.

Yet cords are central to the image of a pair of scales titled *The Weighing of the Worlds* in Fludd's *De praeternaturali* (Frankfurt, 1621).[24] While the serpentine form and pointed bottom is absent here as well, it is an explicit emblem of the interaction of microcosm and macrocosm, and a narrative of elemental earth in particular. *The Weighing of the Worlds* pictures the hand of Iod (God) holding a pair of scales with the sun as balancing point (or fulcrum) at the center of the cosmos. The rising scale of the "empyrean heaven" consists of "light fire"; the descending scale (congruent to the Huguenot sign) signifies the "elemental realm" of "heavy earth." The "wings" on the sign's bottom half suggest the back of an earthbound dove descending in flight (its "beak" at the lowest point). This spirit figure of the soul's downward motion through the air into the heart was commonly linked by a jeweler's chain to the bottom of a Maltese cross (fig. 14.6), perhaps similar to the one worn around the maiden's neck in figure 10.4, and in this instance, clearly a symbol of the Huguenots of the *désert*. This symbol of cultural continuity was worn outwardly as a sacred medal in the presence of coreligionists, or secreted under clothing, near the heart. Sometimes incorporated into public monuments, more often craftsmen blended it discreetly into objects such as furniture or other utilitarian things. This signaled the identity of an artifact of the diaspora in everyday life. This is closer to what we would expect to see high above the Eglise des Grecs, almost—but not quite—out of sight. Like the legend of the philosopher's stone, it was obscured by the seductive theater of the street. Many messages were intended to make sense in passing; interchangeable at a general level of busy urban life, simulacra for a host of possible signs.

Consider again that the palindrome was the central metaphor of Hogarth's system of signs. Itself a backward sign, it automatically conveys inside knowledge of an alternative perspective on refugee artisanal culture working "behind" the scenes. If the Huguenot sign in *Noon* is also a palindrome that reads the same backward and forward, then its duality is deeply problematic: the back we see is simultaneously the front we thought we did not. This fundamental misreading of front and back does not mean at all that the sign is functionally transparent. Like a mirror, it is reflective rather than transparent. Casual viewers are unaware the sign has no back—or two backs and two fronts—or that the private message available only to the Huguenots of Soho was apparently immediately available to everyone all along.

Thus Hogarth conjoins hidden and revealed aspects of refugee artisanal society at the margins of perception. The intentions of the Huguenots of Hog Lane remain un-

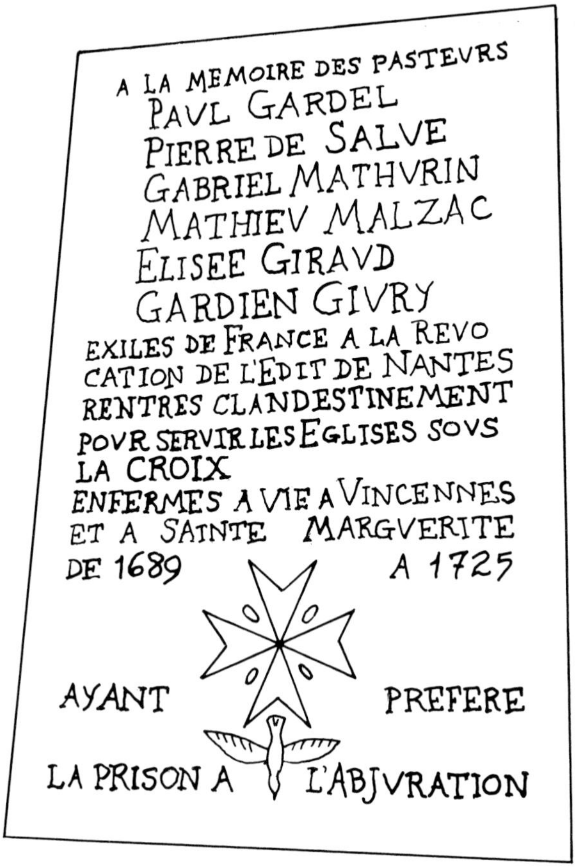

A LA MEMOIRE DES PASTEVRS
PAVL GARDEL
PIERRE DE SALVE
GABRIEL MATHVRIN
MATHIEV MALZAC
ELISEE GIRAVD
GARDIEN GIVRY
EXILES DE FRANCE A LA REVO
CATION DE L'EDIT DE NANTES
RENTRES CLANDESTINEMENT
POVR SERVIR LES EGLISES SOVS
LA CROIX
ENFERMES A VIE A VINCENNES
ET A SAINTE MARGVERITE
DE 1689   A 1725

AYANT   PREFERE

LA PRISON A   L'ABJVRATION

FIGURE 14.6. Maltese cross with descending dove (the "Huguenot cross"). Monument to six Huguenot martyrs, Fort Réal, Île de Sainte-Marguerite, Bay of Cannes. Drawing by John Cotter. The monument reads, "In memory of the pastors . . . Exiled from France at the Revocation of the Edict of Nantes who returned clandestinely to serve churches under the cross. Imprisoned for life at Vincennes and at Sainte Marguerite from 1689 to 1725, having chosen prison over abjuration."

clear. They seem to blend the sacred and material worlds, hovering ambiguously on the periphery of their clients', spectators', and host culture's vision. Hosts inadvertently support unclear and potentially subversive intentions by politely ignoring the inner realities of the shadowy strangers in their midst, limited as they are by a hierarchy of vision that is focused on distinctive objects and materials that shine in the light and satisfy their own private concerns. Hogarth not only asks viewers of his picture to expand their peripheral vision to accommodate its margins but expands his inquiry into the uncertainty of face-to-face interactions between immigrant and host cultures. He reframes the question in terms of the extent to which ethical ambiguities influence the relation between the production and consumption of earth materials.

Hogarth thus posits the moral complicity of artisans in the social process of politeness that supports (and is supported by) commerce. He links the narrow visual field of consuming English elites possessed by novelty, theatricality, and self-advertising narcissism and their gluttonous subaltern counterparts on Hog Lane, who consume carnal materials in a disordered porcine manner under a sign that infers cannibalism. Such grotesque carnality is instructive precisely because it functions without the mediation of politeness. Ultimately, Hogarth confronts the paradoxes of Soho's southwestern Huguenot artisans themselves: "hidden" at high "noon"; and yet represented by strangely blatant, in-your-face displays of spiritual practice performed with secrecy, denial, self-effacement, self-discipline, accommodation, and security. Appearing to consume nothing at noon, with the exception of the Word, these Huguenots seem to receive nourishment subtly, as it were, through the air. We have seen how these cultural traits were transformed by refugee artisans into habits of survival during the religious wars that drove them out of southwestern France and into the Atlantic world. In this context, Hogarth shows how they serve equally well in the quest for profit. But it is not enough to say that *Noon* is merely a visual rehearsal for the advent of classical Weberian pieties. By emphasizing the role played by the inner workings of soulishness, natural philosophy, alchemy, the transmutation of earth materials, and, above all, refugee Huguenot artisans, and adding to the mix the complicity of secrecy, politeness, and commerce in the immigrant communities of eighteenth-century London, Hogarth constructs a total artisanal history from the fragmentary elements of a subterranean culture with origins in sixteenth-century Aunis-Saintonge.

❧ Terrestrial Astrology on Hog Lane: The Huguenot Sign ❧

To review the thread of my argument thus far: Hogarth locates a natural-philosophical dialogue between macrocosm and microcosm and being and appearance at the intersection of at least three apparently different realities of human experience, all of which converge in front of the Huguenot Church on Hog Lane in *Noon*. While superficially unlike one another, these three different yet simultaneous experiences in the nexus of parallel universes are interconnected by a very specific time and place, inside a hierarchical semiotic system, at the apex of which "floats" an idiosyncratic backward sign. I have also called this the "Huguenot sign."

The sign is a metaphysical message, which delivers us to the next level of Hogarth's natural-philosophical labyrinth. It also serves to reinforce intuitive claims that the fulcrum of *Noon* is not the sun per se, but rather the hidden light of refugee Huguenot artisanal culture, which absorbs energy from deep inside earth's subterranean places. Insurmountable cultural, social, historical, and even perceptual boundaries fragment and separate pluralistic Hog Lane, but these differences are simultaneously collapsed and linked by a mysterious materio-holiness synthesis of parallels, palindromes, and inversions. The nature of these linkages resists reductive, mechanistic explanations of distribution of energy in matter. They were capable of supporting multiple and relativistic responses to the same cosmological impulses, since animate spirits of light and motion did not enter all matter in the same way at the same time. *Noon* transcends superficial perception. Rather, it is a complete *cosmology* for elemental "earth." Here Huguenot artisans are represented as intermediaries at the limen of Soho's spiritual and material life. Like noon itself, Huguenots are in the middle, balancing cosmic forces of time, space, spirit, matter, and history.

Despite its appearance on the remotest perceptual margins of *Noon,* the backward "Huguenot" sign, assumes an optimum position as Hogarth's core metaphor for the Huguenot artisan and his production. In fact, the sign is positioned to mediate between all three groups. Its peripheral position in the pictorial space also begs reconsideration of Hogarth's notion of the status of communication in commercial society, and possible ethical problems in conveying perceptions of "pure" innocence. Knowledge is suddenly available in the Huguenot sign's underlying material foundation (or, by analogy to natural philosophy, metaphysical foundation), which once seemed innocent of symbolic intention. Does this new information compel eighteenth-century beholders to reevaluate perceptions of innocence projected by the pious Huguenot refugees of the Eglise des Grecs? Their sign is apparently composed of mute materials. It is devoid of conventional languages of iconography, yet represented at the top of a hierarchy of all signs. There are private languages here, assigned to the "art and mystery" of artisanal materials. What do raw earthen materials communicate? Are spectators asked to reevaluate the cultural and ethical status of the production and consumption of materials?

Following the linguistic structure of the palindrome that Hogarth used to give its form meaning, the sign's construction is binary on its surface; it has two identical "wings" in the subtle shape of vertical cyma recta curves, bisected in the middle by a joined seam held together by three horizontal cleats that run parallel to the ground.[25] Having already inventoried similar formal and philosophical analogies between the parallel worlds of *Noon,* it is reasonable to assume that Hogarth intended this dark seam down the middle as yet a third gutteral analogy. A vertical axis this time, it provides a conduit for the ethereal "flow" between the gutter bisecting the middle of Hog Lane (the receptacle of effluent waste occluded in the microcosm) and the one attached to the cornice of the Eglise des Grecs (the receptacle of transparent waters distilled in the macrocosm, descending as astral raindrops). The sign is connected to (but also far above) Hog Lane's heterogeneous urban landscape. It contains binding agents missing (or displaced) from the other signs. While the signs for couturier fashion and "Good Eating" on the other side of Hog Lane advertise the personal and social fragmentation of blind consumption, this entity lacks conventional commercial language to provide direction. Yet it is clearly unified by a trinity of binders that joins symmetrical halves into a self-contained whole. This infers that the binding power of the soul—what Ficino called the "knot" of the world—remained inside the Huguenot sign. On the other hand, the floating tricorn hat (of the trinity bound by the Holy Spirit) reconnects (and hence unifies and reanimates) the separated head and torso of the other two street signs from a distance. The signs for "Good Eating" and the couturier's boutique give the appearance of clear, unambiguous public discourse advertising specific products. In contrast to the transparency and depth of the Huguenot sign, however, commonplace iconographic languages suddenly seem insufficient.

The armature of the Huguenot sign reads three-dimensionally as a construction of segmented parts, seamed together and joined by three cleats nailed parallel across the joint. But our hypothesis about the sign's material-based symbol system indicates that it might be possible to adapt portions of the methodology developed by Michael Fried in his phenomenological reading of eighteenth-century French painting, to follow a related path of inquiry for a semiotics of *Noon*. Consider that Hogarth may also have represented the sign as a two-dimensional text to convey knowledge of materials as such; that is, as an array of marks and lines, dots and dashes, that infer primordial themes concerning the relation of earthen bodies to the creation of form. If we follow Fried in focusing on surface gesture as much as illusion of depth, Hogarth may be supposed to have represented this series of lines to form a geometric language on the surface of the escutcheon. We have read artisanal construction as discourse generated from a cosmological dialogue about the materiality of an aging "earth," with a grammar and lexicon intended to communicate the natural-philosophical and temporal program of *Noon*. Thus the surface of the sign, which shows its construction, may be read as an outline of Robert Fludd's abstract emblem for the occult art of geomancy (*Geomantia*), or "terrestrial astrology."

✦ Geomancy as Art of the Earth ✦

Fludd's emblem for geomancy appears prominently on two different occasions in his oeuvre: first, on a cosmological wheel engraved by de Bry on the title page of his 1618 *De naturae simia seu technia macrocosmi historia* (Nature's Ape, or History of the Macrocosmic Arts), the second treatise of eleven of his *De macrocosmi historia* (History of the Macrocosm); and second, on the title-page of the second volume of his seven-volume series on the microcosm, *De technica microcosmi historia* (The *History of the Microcosmic*

FIGURE 14.7. Johann Theodore de Bry, title page of Robert Fludd's *De naturae simia seu technia macrocosmi historia* (Nature's Ape, or History of the Macrocosmic Arts) (Oppenheim: Johann Theodore de Bry, 1618; 2d ed., Frankfurt, 1624), the second volume of Fludd's *De macrocosmi historia* (History of the Macrocosm). Courtesy Harry Ransom Humanities Research Center, The University of Texas at Austin. Geomancy is located over the ape's left shoulder.

Arts), where it is included in a cosmological wheel. On the title page of *De naturae simia*, the eleven macrocosmic arts—mathematics (the ape points to an arithmetic primer with his stick); geometry (a surveyor plots a triangle); perspective; painting; fortifications; engineering; timekeeping; cosmography; astrology; geomancy; and music—are depicted in clockwise rotation (fig. 14.7). On that of *De technica microcosmi historia*, the seven microcosmic arts—prophesy (*prophetia*); geomancy (*geomantia*); memory (*ars memoria*); natal astrology (*genethlialogia*); physiognomy (*physiognomia*); and palmistry (*chiromantia*)—similarly reveal hidden aspects of the macrocosm (fig. 14.8).

Fludd's cosmologies are quintessentially Paracelsian in that they chart the interaction of microcosm and macrocosm through the medium of inspired artisanry and search for evidence of metaphysical process in the banality of everyday life, and Hogarth used Fludd's influential innovations in the "science of pyramids" (*pyramidum scientia*) to show the connection of man in the microcosm by soulish analogy to spiritual motion in the universal macrocosm.

The construction of prophetic texts out of random dots of tossed dirt, sand, or cracks found on the earth's surface defines geomancy in a general way. The same effect was sometimes achieved with a sort of "unconscious" or automatic writing. Both were read for answers to questions about the future, prophesies divined from earth's elemental secrets. But there were many variations on this practice of what was essentially a form of terrestrial astrology. By the sixteenth century, natural philosophers in the West knew of an ancient Middle Eastern form of geomancy based on marks impressed into sand, called *khatt al-raml* ("sand writing") in Arabic.[26] During the Crusades, the practice was adapted by the Western alchemic tradition, and the word "geomancies" appears in Chaucer and the medieval romances. With numerous definitions used by secretive operators or mystical commentators to mislead the vulgar who were unworthy to receive such knowledge, geomancy had a long if undefinitive history of practice by the eighteenth century. Certain technical rules were, however, believed to be fundamental to all forms of geomancy. "A question is 'proposed' by the geomancer himself or by a person consulting him," the Fludd scholar C. H. Josten notes; the geomancer then projects a pattern based on the number four (as in times of the day?):

> Then the geomancer jots down ("projects") four times four rows of a random number of dots. The geomancer must not count the dots while making them. According as their total in a row is an odd or an even number, one or two dots are considered to be the result of that row. The results of each row thus obtained become the constituent parts of four original "figures" called *matres*, each of which is derived from one of the four sets of four rows. . . . Any one of sixteen different figures, each consisting of four lines of one or two dots, may . . . result from each *mater*. Each of them has a Latin name, its special significance, and its zodiacal, planetary, and elementary correspondences.[27]

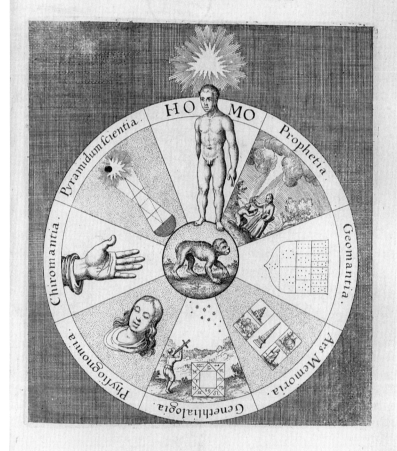

FIGURE 14.8. Johann Theodore de Bry, title page of Robert Fludd's *De technica microcosmi historia* (History of the Microcosmic Arts) (Oppenheim: Johann Theodore de Bry, 1619).

The *matres* are then ramified into the figures of four *filiae* (fig. 14.9), and together this first group of eight figures are connected contiguously into a line of "houses." Eight houses from the upper row of *matres* and *filiae* are subsequently paired to form four new houses called *nepotes;* these twelve houses are analogous to the twelve astrological houses. Following the genealogical method used in the upper rows, two *nepotes* are paired with two *testes* below, which in turn devolve finally to a single *judex* figure at the bottom point of the escutcheon.[28]

Translation of these Latin categories underscores both the hermaphroditic and dynastic nature of geomancy, for the practice was presented in a kind of genealogical structure. Four primordial houses of earth "mothers"—*matres* are a similitude in this context for (the singular) *mater,* or matter, the stuff of which everything is composed—produce four "daughters," and together they are the parents of four houses of grandsons. These Adamic male descendant figures give birth to the "genitalia" formed at the bottom of the geomantic scheme: *testis* means "witnesses," but the word also makes sense here as "testicles" (*testes*), "earthen vessels" (*testae*), or the Palissian metaphor of security and artisanal recreation, "shells" (also *testae*). A witness ("one who gives evidence"), is an appropriate source of information for the oracular *judex,* or phallus figure, which translates as "judge." The binary geomantic scheme conjoins two opposing sexual worlds like a hermaphrodite. As such, its hermetic means of production recalls the fully formed alchemical homunculus, with progenitor earth figures ascendant in the female upper houses, declining to the prelapsarian Adamic male reproductive "organ" (a representation of adept aspirations).

Hogarth's innovation was to transform the early seventeenth-century Fludd–de Bry interpretation of the centuries-old geomantic chevron—a heraldic escutcheon with straight dexter and sinister sides—by adapting its form and function to the serpentine line's movement. Whoever stands in watchful pose toward his audience underneath the Huguenot sign—whether a surrogate for the artist himself, or perhaps a figure for the tastemaking Huguenot couturier emerging from midday prayer, or some composite figure—appropriates the *judex* role for himself. Comical nose size and shape is strong supporting evidence for this identity, as Hogarth's judges on *The Bench* (1764)—one of his last engravings—attests (fig. 14.10). Here, Hogarth identifies his signifier of a British judge's face as the radically long, downward pointing, boldly triangular nose. If the *judex* figure in *Noon* does not wear a powdered periwig, his long curly hair seems appropriately juridical. Perhaps the inspiration for this particular subject was Hogarth's contemplation of his own impending mortality and judgment, since the title is followed by a humorous apology: "This Plate would have been better explain'd had the Author lived a Week longer." Hogarth did live long enough to explain "the different meaning of the Words Character, Caracatura and Outre in Painting and Drawing," all of which are demonstrated in *The Bench.* "As to the French word Outre," the

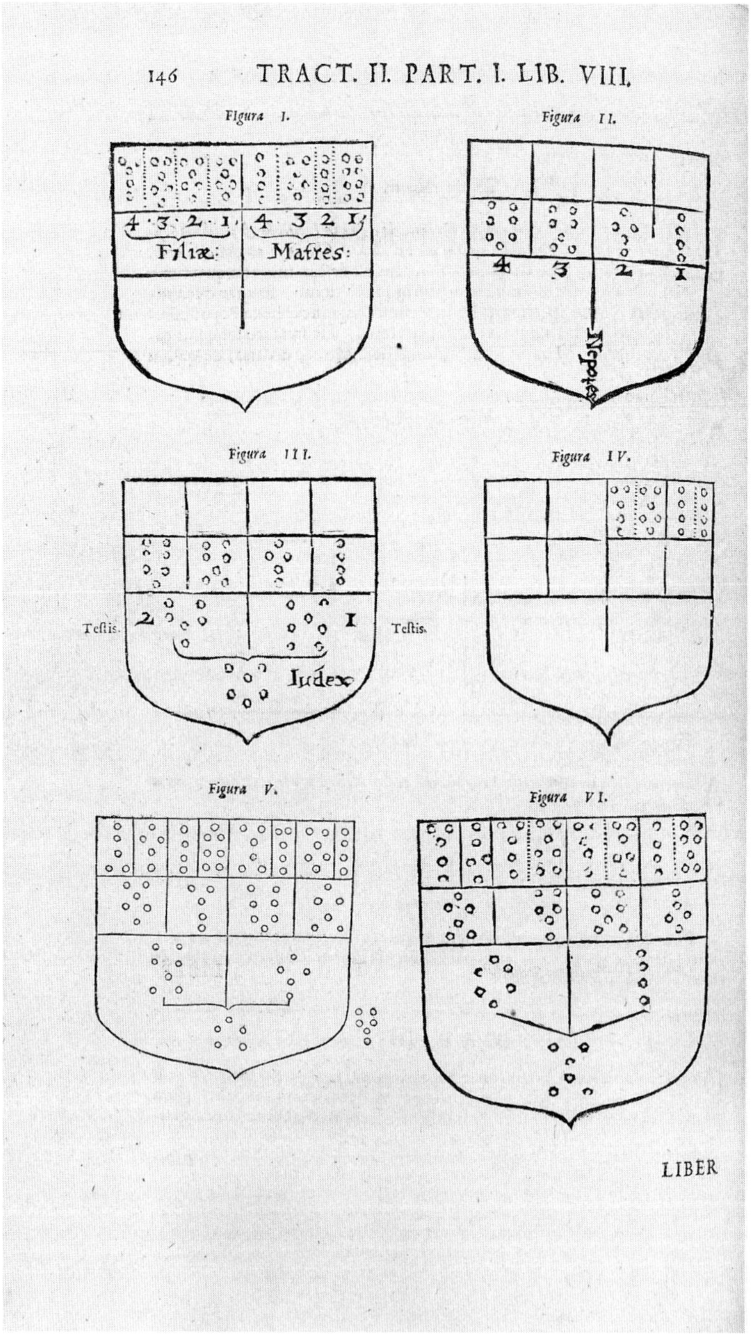

FIGURE 14.9. Johann Theodore de Bry, geomantic escutcheons from Robert Fludd's *Utriusque cosmi majoris scilicet et minoris metaphysica, physica atque technica historia in duo volumina secundum cosmi differentiam divisa . . . tomus primus De macrocosmi historia* (Oppenheim, 1617; 2d ed., Frankfurt, 1624). Courtesy Harry Ransom Humanities Research Center, The University of Texas at Austin. The *filiae, matres, nepotes,* testis, and *judex* are located on these escutcheons, which are represented like a genealogy of heraldic devices descended from noble houses.

FIGURE 14.10. William Hogarth, *The Bench:* "Of the different meaning of the Words *Character, Caracatura* and *Outré* in Painting and Drawing," engraving, London, September 4, 1758. H: 12⅜″, W: 6¼″. Courtesy Yale Center for British Art, Paul Mellon Collection. *Outré,* used in the caricature of judges, with the outsized nose serving as a judicial signifier, is explained in the caption as "in the French word . . . the exaggerated outlines of a figure . . . so any part as a Nose, or a Leg, made bigger or less than it ought to be."

accompanying text reads: "it . . . signifies nothing more than the exaggerated outlines of a Figure all parts of which may be in other respects a perfect and true Picture of Nature. A Giant or a Dwarf may be call'd a common Man Outre. So any part as a Nose, or a Leg made bigger or less than it ought to be, is that part Outre."

Geomancy had a long history of adherents in England after its introduction in the fourteenth century. Despite their rhetoric of ambivalence (at least in public) about the ethical and scientific value of occultism, the evidence suggests geomancy was considered practical science by many later English natural philosophers. The *Oxford English Dictionary* notes a citation from 1569 of an English translation of a Latin text published in 1531 (by the alchemist Cornelius Agrippa of Nettesheim), which defined "Geomancie," as that "which doth divine by certaine conjectures taken of similitudes of the crackinge of the Earthe."[29] By 1591, the English status of geomancy had risen from mere conjecture to "a Science and Art which consisteth of points, prickes, and lines, made in steade of the foure Elements." Geomancy was devalued as science in Hogarth's time—having been assigned the ambiguous rhetorical status of "occult philosophy"—but this did not necessarily mean its venerable magic was dismissed as trivial by empiricists. Just as Ezra Stiles rediscovered Paracelsus and Fludd through his antiquarian experience with the "ancient" alchemical legends, library, and archives of John Winthrop Jr., late Enlightenment natural philosophers still honored (and consulted) "old" books by Fludd as science. Indeed, "all the renowned authors" (1774), from "certain colleges in old times, where . . . magical sciences were taught (1820)."

As a matter of available disciplinary knowledge, eighteenth-century scientists knew the fundamental element of geomantic divination was a millennial link between the puzzle's beginning and its end. Thus, the *alpha* house of the first *mater* was unified with the *omega* of the *judex* figure. Even as Genesis adumbrated Revelation, posing problems for which answers would ultimately be revealed in the experience of final things, so, too, questions posed to the geomancer would be answered by pairing these two metaphorical "projections" of Earth's original creation as *mater* of nature and the final judgment of the *judex*. This formula was perceived by natural-philosophical practitioners of geomancy to channel random variation in the same way experiments were conducted in the laboratory. In the end, only one set of the original sixteen geomantic figures remained and were available for interpretation.

Despite Neoplatonic strategies of reduction of the many to the one, and the "mechanistic" rigidity that superficially controlled the external form of the geomantic scheme, an infinite variety of internal arrangements, refinements, and subtleties were available for interpretation of this single figure. Shades of meaning were divined from the position and interaction of the figures *inside* their individual houses and, above all, the context in which the question itself was asked.[30]

❧ "Mixed composition," Pluralism, and the Philosophy of History ❧

Fludd received his M.A. degree from Oxford in 1598 (at age twenty-four). Like the younger Winthrop and other Paracelsians in search of worldly experience beyond the academy, he importuned his father to supply funds and embarked on a six-year journey to the centers of alchemic research in France, Spain, Italy, and Germany. In southeastern France—the center of Camisard resistance—Fludd supplemented his father's stipend by working as a tutor for the children of the ultra-Catholic nobility. The Protestant Fludd found himself the tutor of (among others) Charles de Lorraine, fourth duc de Guise, and his brother François. Here, Fludd repeated a classic pattern seen in Palissy's quest for patronage among both the local Huguenot and "foreign" Parisian Catholic aristocracy. This provides a level of insight into Fludd's use of the lingua franca of the Paracelsian program to further his career, but also his latitudinarian belief in the transcendence of religious difference through an animate spirit that ignored confessional distinctions and was both universal and personal at once.[31]

Most interconfessional encounters in France were not benign, however. While attempting to cross the Alps into Italy during the winter of 1601–2, Fludd was delayed in Avignon, which harbored a Jesuit community hostile to magic and Protestant scientific ideas. His dangerous experience of the ensuing debates with undisguised religious adversaries in Avignon was in a sense destabilizing, but it also compelled him to synthesize fragments of ancient geomantic practice. Fludd naïvely sought spiritual and material unity with these most zealous defenders of papism in France, but he found confessional competition and intellectual animosity instead. Thus, the model he chose to reinvent the experience as natural philosophy was Palissian. Fludd conceptualized geomancy as his Neoplatonic metaphor par excellence for the animate soul's hidden unity behind the appearance of all duality and difference in matter—including bodily matter—derived from elemental earth. He used his geomantic program to reconfigure infinite varieties of contingency available for action, perception, and contemplation in the microcosm. Fludd published two essays on the subject under de Bry's refugee imprint in Oppenheim. Read together, these texts constituted the most comprehensive theory of geomancy available to Western readers in the seventeenth century.

The first essay, concentrating on the macrocosm, appeared in 1617–18; the second, on the microcosm, completed the argument in 1619. Fludd's theory of geomancy is also one of the earliest methodologies available for the study of urban human geography in the chaotic and protean urban context that tumbles out onto Hogarth's atomized London cityscape in *Noon*. Flood adumbrated this for the composition of Hogarth's pictorial narrative, because his theory of geomancy laid the cosmic groundwork in the spiritual direction, elemental composition, and relative spatial disposition of the human body on earth:

> The rows of geomantic dots comprise and express the idea of the whole world no less than does the human body. The human body is seen only outwardly, whilst we contemplate . . . inwardly, with our spiritual eyes. As in the body we discern the elements, *invisible in their mixed composition*. . . . Likewise, in every one of the four sets of four rows of geomantic dots, one of the four elements lies concealed: the element of fire in the first set, that of air in the second, the element of water in the third, and that of earth in the fourth set. In the figures produced from these four sets, the seven planets and the twelve signs of the zodiac are present, though they may only be perceived with the eyes of *spiritus*.[32]

Internal mixing of the elements is explicitly illustrated both in de Bry's engraving of Fludd's science of the pyramids (see fig. 10.6) and in descent from the Huguenot sign to Hog Lane. But where is the element of fire? The only one of the four elements not represented openly in the narrative of the painting is fire. Does this element exist implicitly in the light of the empyrean sphere, the sun figures on the polite lady's cheeks or the furnacelike bowels of the earth? Does the fire in the earth also figure in the servant's bubbling meat pie—a bawdy sign of her "fiery" sexual passion? Thus, by analogy, questions of elemental mixing informed the practical and formal logic of natural-philosophical theory, elucidating the structure and function of mixed societies in the new, commercialized, and densely populated early modern city.

Knowledge of these influential essays was widespread among natural philosophers during the eighteenth century, not only from the original de Bry editions, but also from the diffusion of lengthy extracts reprinted under Fludd's name in *Fasciculus geomanticus*, a Veronese compendium of geomantic treatises that found sufficient readers for two editions (1687 and 1704). The essay of 1617–18 appeared in its entirety in both editions of *Fasciculus geomanticus* as "Roberti Flud tractatus de geomantia," printed immediately following a modified version of chapters 1 through 6 of Fludd's 1619 *De technica microcosmi historia*. Fludd's chapters were ranked above his competitors; the Englishman's preeminent place in the modern history of geomancy was clear.[33]

Fludd begins with a definition of the language of geomancy and the metaphysical forces behind it. All terminology had a specific task in animating the geomancer's insight into essential questions of being and appearance:

> Geomancy is an act of the *anima intellectualis*. *Mens* rules over *intellectus* and *ratio* as a king over his subjects, or a master over his servants. *Intellectus* and *ratio* in turn convey the impulses of *mens* to the region of *imaginatio*. In their service *imaginatio* operates as a vehicle. It is drawn by the senses as a chariot is drawn by horses. Thus it is the action of the horses that ultimately delivers the remote impulses of *mens*, the king and master, to the visible

world. The servant, in carrying out the master's command, does not know what the intentions and secret motives of the master are. *Ratio, imaginatio,* and *sensus* will be ignorant thereof as the servant, the chariot, and the horses. Yet *ratio* is far better equipped to
make conjectures, than *imaginatio* or the senses. Like a servant, *ratio* may indeed sometimes, as it were, presume or guess the idea prevailing in the master's mind, though never
with absolute certainty.[34]

Following Ficino, Palissy, and mystical contemporaries such as Jakob Böhme,
Fludd defined *anima intellectualis*—and hence geomancy—as "an act" of "soulish perception." As animated perception, it greatly exceeded the common senses. Moving
between macrocosm and microcosm, it enabled the hidden world of the spirit to communicate impulses from the macrocosm directly into the part of the human soul
governing the geomancer's ability to make sense of what he perceived in the world of
the elements ("*intellectus* [sensual perception] and *ratio* [calculation])." Thus, geomancers had the skill to discern hidden unities behind the "visible" chaos of the postlapsarian world. *Mens,* that is to say, "understanding"—also, "to remember" (as in
moments of lucidity when lost memories of Adam's primordial unity with God are
retrieved and understood retrospectively)—is superior in relation to man's superficial
thoughts and perceptions. *Mens* is literally the noetic "master": *intellectus* and *ratio*
serve their "king" by transporting his "remote impulses" to the imagination, which carries them as would a chariot. From thence, "it is drawn by the senses as . . . by horses
. . . to the visible world." *Mens*'s "impulses" are "remote" to his noetic servants, inasmuch as they are hidden to the "inferior . . . region" of sensate perception and inanimate thought. "The servant," Fludd writes, "in carrying out his master's command,
does not know what the intentions and secret motives of the master are."[35]

Hence, invisible or "secret" "intentions" and "motives" are privileged over "the visible world" in geomancy, just as they are by Hogarth in *Noon,* where they inhabit the
ethereal geomantic sign and the shadowy domain of the Huguenot "masters." Like the
Saintongeais artisans who communicate (or "operate") mysteriously through Nature's
fallen media (or matter), "in geomancy *mens,* operating through the media of *intellectus* or *ratio, imaginatio,* and *sensus,* is made to exert its divine virtue, in the same way
as *mens* operates more openly and potently in the act of prophecy." It is even possible
to discern a more subtle distinction here between the inward experimental pietism of
southwestern Huguenot culture and the outward, radical enthusiasm of the southeastern Camisard speakers in tongues. Indeed, Fludd claimed it was possible for *mens
humana* to infuse servant media with a sort of internal prophetic power. This could be
accomplished without direct infusion of sacred impulses (or *radii superiores*), hence
without the operatic drama that ensued openly after the conjunction of macrocosm
and microcosm. Yet this too may have been witnessed by the senses: "Whereas in

prophecy *mens [humana]* is united to *mens divina*, whereby a multitude of *radii supe-riores* is introduced into the process, *mens humana* may by itself and without the aid of any divine *radii* infuse the geomantic process with a prophetical power whose effect can be apprehended by the senses."[36]

This assertion would seem illogical or physically impossible, except that "the science of geomancy is very occult and inward; it is difficult to account for it in a rational way." Fludd continued as if in response to those mechanists who perceived pluralism as mere chaos, while ignoring the power of man's inner world to order and reverse "vulgar" outward direction: "geomancy transcends vulgar understanding to which it must ap-pear foolish, inane, absurd, and ridiculous."[37] Neoplatonic logic in "De geomantia" ex-tolled the primacy of hidden realities behind perception. It also recalled a creative ten-sion in Palissy's "The Art of the Earth," which itself explored the chasm that existed for Huguenot potters who sought to craft a synthesis of macrocosm and microcosm in their translucent earthenware glazes. This early modern problematic had derived from the imperfect, postlapsarian knowledge of the hidden intentionality of God:

> We know nothing of the [macrocosmic] *ratio* [that is, the mind of God] lying behind the acts of *mens*. Human reasoning on this subject relies entirely on *effectus* [behavior] and leads only to conjectures. As we may not know God but *a posteriori*, so also we may know [a thing] only by its effects. Likewise, we know indeed nothing with any certainty of the source, the vehicle, or the reason of the life we receive in a wondrous way from above, though we reason about them from performance and by way of conjecture.[38]

Following Palissy and Böhme, Fludd inveighed against the "obstacle" of sexual desire and the bodily need for consumption as an extension of the chasm between macrocosm and microcosm. Whereas Palissy and Böhme represented themselves as sublimating sexual desire to adopt chastity and heighten their experience as natural philosophers, Fludd claimed to have remained an "unstained virgin" all his life. This certainly trumped Palissy, who was chased from the bedroom by his irate wife. Not only did Fludd identify with his image of Christ as the unstained Word incarnate, but he also tended to read Adam's sexual desire as the absolute cause of expulsion from Eden and so the source of separation and difference between the natural world and God.[39]

Thus, in the uppermost band of Fludd's geomantic schema, the progenitor of the family tree is at first entirely female, and so the earth "mother" or "matter" was in-seminated with the invisible "seed" from the macrocosm. This is conjoined by the middle band into the liminal figure of the hermaphrodite. By the lowest two bands (closest to the microcosm), the most overt representation of sexuality is sublimated into the *judex* figure. This phallic figure is a surrogate for the Adamic geomancer. He is fallen yet still an extension—if the lowest and potentially most corruptible—of the macrocosmic world. Sublimation of the "obstacle" of sexual desire was therefore necessary to avoid dissembling commotion within the atomized dot pattern. It was also in the arena of the deceptions of untrammeled desire that Hogarth reactivated Fludd's ideas and images most explicitly. Their critical narratives on consumption on (and of) elemental earth had intersected on Hog Lane. "We are prevented by the obstacle of the flesh," Fludd continued, "and the darkness [surrounding us] from having a proper knowledge of the marvelous effects in man by *mens divina*. We are content to recognize a monk by his habit, and a thing by its effects."[40]

The adept's God-given skill to stand in the golden circle and transcend the retrospective necessity of historical "effects," to "penetrate" with spiritual eyes the essential unity of space and time hidden behind the chaos represented by bodily dots of fallen matter, defined the task of the Stoic, Protestant geomancer:

> By the effects, however, the practitioners of the *artistae* [the "art," also "occupation" or "knowledge"] have found geomancy to be a true science through which things future, present, and past may be revealed, provided the geomancer's judgement is not obscured by the obnoxious influences of the body or the deceitful action of the senses. . . . Geomancy is not accessible to all. Fools would never be able to penetrate to that center of the action, that unity and very point of the *mens*. For that point lies beyond the degree of *ratio* and *intellectus*, and only those may reach it who manage to leave the habitation of their bodies.[41]

With the same now familiar "out-of-body" logic that harnessed the geomantic process to the global distances covered by similar particulates of "aerial niter" sent by the weapon salve through the "ether," geomancy forged soulish connections and "convey[ed] the [prophetic] message" over space and time and between bodies, by using misunderstood gestures and following established Neoplatonic theories of motion for animate matter:[42]

> The sixteen lines of dots which the geomancer produces at the beginning of the operation are not caused merely by an advantageous movement of the hand, as the ignorant would say; but in the number and proportion of the dots of those sixteen lines a prophetic message of the soul lies concealed. Inasmuch as the dots establish correspondences with the twelve signs of the zodiac, the seven planets, and the four elements, they convey the message of the soul by the macrocosmical vehicles of ether and the four elements. Without the aid of those macrocosmic vehicles, neither *mens* nor *intellectus* could have descended into man; and nothing *real* [emphasis added] or essential can issue from *mens* unless it passes through those media.[43]

Fludd's occult science of triangles conceptualized reciprocal movement between worlds using "macrocosmic vehicles," and Hogarth's line of beauty imagined the form in which "the message of the soul" was "conveyed" through them. *Noon*'s silent pictorial narrative forges astral and elemental links throughout the mirror worlds of atomized and dissonant humanity on Hog Lane, "as the dots establish correspondences."

Like Palissy's Neoplatonic glazes, which settled into preordained patterns on the clay body naturalistically with only minimal direction from the potter's hand, Fludd claimed the hand's movement in tossing (or drawing) the geomantic dots on the ground—if pure and "unhindered" by the "accidents of the flesh," the obstacle of desire—was not accidental:

> The movement of the hand producing the geomantic dots is not accidental in so far as it proceeds from the human soul, man[']s very essence. That movement acts, therefore, in an essentially significant way if it be unhindered by the accidents of the flesh and the senses.[44]

It followed, therefore, that accidents of the flesh were analogous to the accidents of the "inexperienced" (code for non-Paracelsian nonadepts) during the alchemic process, both of which set similar obstacles in the path of the growth and purification of matter:

> Similarly we say that the mineral natures of lead and iron tend in their essence towards the nature of gold; but by accident, namely by [the presence of] impure sulphur, they are arrested in their natural growth, so that they may not attain the aim of nature. The inexperienced will object that the like impediments will always occur to the human body, because of the impurity of the flesh and the darkness of error into which our existence is plunged.[45]

❧ The Broken Pie Plate ❧

Prominent mention of such key alchemic words as "accident," "impure sulphur," and "inexperience" returns us once again to the servant girl and her African lover in *Noon*. This sequence, which begins with a moment of transgressive sexual desire, surprise, and arousal, and ends in a chaotic chain reaction that results in the injured child, broken earthenware platter, and contents spilled into the street, is arguably a Hogarthian figure of Fludd's "accident" of impurity. This intertextual reading is supported by our belated ability to identify the "impure sulphur" from Fludd's text (its characteristic yellowish hue contaminated with white dross) as the probable contents of the boy's broken platter, ultimately consumed by a hungry street urchin. Thus, while the sulphur actually signifies the "contents" of the platter, it is never carried "in" the thing, in the functional sense, like the servant's pie. Rather, it is literally inside of the pottery in the material sense; seeming to be in the process of decomposing (or leaching out) from *within* elemental *matter*, from which the earthenware vessel was built and fired by the potter. Even as this crude *misalliance* of ill-matched opposites progresses, the soulish, Neoplatonic "bond and knot" of alchemic mercury that holds the "atoms" of the boy's earthly possession together as a material unity has deserted its microcosmic hosts. Before the spectator's very eyes, the detritus of impurity descends into chaos, falling under the weight of gravity to a kind of material death.

Contrast the comportment of Hogarth's servant and African lover with figures 14.7 and 14.8, as well as with figure 2.3, the de Bry engraving in Fludd's *Utruisque cosmi majoris* (1617).[46] Both contain the geomantic escutcheon in cosmological wheels of the arts in the microcosm and their sources in the macrocosm. In fig. 2.3, *Integrae naturae speculum artisque imago* (The Mirror of the Whole of Nature and the Image of Art)—Fludd's most famous and fully integrated cosmology—we confront the sources for Hogarth's amorous couple. The servant is a similitude for the naked virgin ("not a goddess") who stands as intermediary (or gatekeeper): "her right foot stands on earth," Fludd wrote, "her left foot on water, signifying the conjunction of sulphur and mercury without which nothing can be created." Thus she is chained in her liminal reality between God (as manifested by the light of the Word) and the microcosmic simian in figures 14.7 and 14.8. Nature's ape is a dark and ambivalent creature who sits upon the sublunar world (measuring the globe as if a navigator with his compass). His head was arguably a model for Hogarth's animalistic African sailor (another sort of navigator). This is particularly persuasive if the use of the African as signifier of the "universal tincture" (fig. 14.11) is any indication. In this seventeenth-century image, the African holds the sun and moon in either hand—the sun and moon also cover the virgin's breasts and vagina in figure 2.3—inferring the potential of the arts of elemental earth to conjoin macrocosm and microcosm.

We have come across the "Mater" Nature figure before, of course; in the London "Palissy dish" and in Edward Howes's cryptic reference to Sophia in the postscripted marginalia of his letter to the younger Winthrop in 1630, about the fall of La Rochelle—the figure's prototype as God's consort and helper—in the Wisdom of Solomon. *In Fludd's Utruisque cosmi majoris,* we read:

> She is not a goddess, but the proximate minister of God, at whose bequest she governs the subcelestial worlds. In the picture she is joined to God by a chain. She is the Soul of the World (*anima mundi*), or the Invisible Fire. . . . It is she who turns the sphere of the stars and disposes the planetary influences to the elemental realm, nourishing all creatures from her bosom. On her breast is the True Sun; on her belly the Moon. Her heart gives light to the stars and planets, whose influence, infused in her womb by the mercurial spirit (called by the philosophers the Spirit of the Moon), is sent down to the very center of the Earth. Her right foot stands on earth, her left in water, signifying the conjunction of sulphur and mercury without which nothing can be created.[47]

FIGURE 14.11. *The Universal Tincture as an African King.* Seventeenth century. From *Handbuch zu welchen ordentlich.* Courtesy Glasgow University Library, Department of Special Collections.

Having plainly seen earth, air, and water, three of the four elements, in *Noon,* we are finally shown the container of the last, "Invisible Fire." Unfortunately, however, the servant—like Nature (and the one other female figure, located in the realm of "Animalia") in *Integrae naturae* (fig. 2.3)—is opposed to the sun figures of politeness, and so is lit darkly by an inverted quarter moon, situated on the source of carnality on her lower anatomy (note the shape and position of the servant's apron). The inner invisible fire (and "light" of the heart) are, in this instance, thrown out of balance with the sun's outer illumination by "accident"; the "accidents of the flesh" deform them too: "the more the rays of the *mens* are impeded in their movement by the filth of the body, the more the effect the action of the *mens* is weakened. *Imaginatio* may indeed be so affected by the world of matter that it will lie like a thick cloud over the senses, not allowing them to receive the sun-like rays of the *mens.*"[48]

But part of the function of Hogarth's chaotic *Integrae naturae* on Hog Lane is to insist that accident and destruction, too, are inescapable (and even perhaps redeemable) parts of this essentially artisanal process. The ostensible cause of the carnal accident that interrupted the equilibrium of the material economy of production and consumption on Hog Lane is the violent physical impetuosity (or "inexperience") of Hogarth's African sailor; that is, Flood's simian figure, the craftsman, qua ape of Nature. In figures 14.7 and 14.8, this image refers to both the darkness of earthy matter, unpurified by conjunction with the spirit, and man's efforts—usually incomplete or in folly—to imitate God's work and in so doing to unite with him through metaphorical coitus with his seductive "proximate minister." Like Palissy's *Recepte Veritable* and *Discours Admirables,* Fludd's discourse on Nature's ape (fig. 14.7) concerns itself with art and artisanry as modes of contemplation of the soul and of personal and material transformation and metamorphosis. Fludd also sought to represent the ape's potential to become a benign metaphysical figure into which he could collapse Hermes, Mercurius, and perhaps above all (in the instance of geomancy) the simian Thoth, inventor of writing and other communicative arts.[49]

Hogarth's African fails to exploit his artisanal potential to change the darkness of his own materiality through work, into the translucency of the Huguenot sign, and thus complete the material-holiness synthesis. Overwhelmed by desire for Nature's superficial bounty, he opts for "the obnoxious influence of the flesh and of crapulence,"[50] and impedes the free movement of spirit in matter necessary to effect change. The process of transformation through conjunction of opposites is prematurely interrupted, and Fludd's accident ensues with Hogarth's burlesque depiction of *coitus interruptus* as wasted spillage.

Even in a highly charged and transgressive sexual context, this gesture seems to infer that the subaltern virgin of Hog Lane may have retained her chastity after all; the African's dark hand does not dissolve matter into purity. Instead, it functions to obscure and sully the transparency of Nature's absolute whiteness and the dissemination of her light as "Soul of the World." That is why, as he encircles his unprepared lover from behind with his arms (with a bowed gesture analogous to that of the earthbound simian in fig. 14.8), the African deflects Nature's "true" (inner) sunlight as he squeezes her right breast, and spills—rather than narrowly pours—her "milk" down in a crooked (not serpentine) stream. Without the narrow spiritual direction and discipline in the elemental realm, Nature cannot moderate the flow of terrestrial time, or "turn the sphere of the stars and dispose the planetary influences to the elemental realms, nourishing all creatures from her bosom." The conjunction of microcosm and macrocosm ends in failure, and in this sense at least, natural time and—in a Hogarthian aside to smug mechanists—progress stops in the material world.

Indeed, the millennial discourse of an aging earth suffused Hogarth's reinvention of Fludd's two cosmological wheels (figs. 14.7 and 14.8) encompassing man's mastery of the arts and crafts, both of which are divided into distinct sections—eleven and eight respectively—surrounding the craftsman figure of the ape at the hub. That these cosmological wheels are segmented is important, since Geomancy then forms only one segment of a large pie shape that closely resembles the meat pie held by Nature qua female servant in *Noon*. In a larger sense then, all the arts are represented in *Noon,* and it is especially noteworthy that the duality of timekeeping, represented by *both* the twelve-hour sundial and the twenty-four hour mechanical clock, is pictured on the title page of *De naturae simia*. But Hogarth carries the cosmological metaphor further. The servant's sexually charged pie also mirrors the circular window over the church door across the street. Though darkened, it is still visibly segmented into quarters, interspersed with a profusion of minute panes of glass, around a central opening at the hub. It is as if Nature had taken her sacred macrocosm from the wall of the Huguenot church.

This makes it possible to identify the orange bosses of the "sun" that transit the cap of the polite lady as analogous to the course of brickwork that forms a rotational pattern around the window. Here is the stellar halo light that surrounds Nature's head in *Integrae naturae*—and flows above Saturn into the uppermost orbit of the *caelum stellatum* ("heavenly stars")—but has now been separated from the moonlit persona of the servant. Nature's diadem, in turn, recalls the crimped edge of the servant's meat pie. It also resonates with the numerous globular pendant drops, called "hanging flagons" (tavern signs) by Hogarth's biographer Ronald Paulson. Perhaps there are also heavenly lights that fall from the overhang of buildings in the deep background and continue on the "Good Eating" side of Hog Lane. Like the tiny degrees of time that circulate around a sundial's chapter ring, the drops and crimped crust circulate completely "around" the painting from light to shadow to light again.

This inversion of Copernican perspective is engraved in the "transit" function of sundials, which is to say that they track the "movement" of the sun. Even as the earth revolves around the sun in astronomical terms, in the archaic language of sundials, it is the sun that transits and circulates light. Visualize the entire geomantic street scene as a shaky system of hidden and revealed rotating parts animated by fragmented and competing elements that consume parts of the "Soul of the World": the sun (the polite and fashionable trio); the moon (the weakness of the flesh); and the hidden inner spirit (the Huguenots of the Eglise des Grecs). Having closed a cosmological circuit between the two sides of Hog Lane, the dark metaphysical light of the church window across the street is projected down through the girl's pie, into both halves of the boy's broken earthenware pie plate, and then into the street, where the waste adds to the confusion of superfluous geomantic dots. Here, finally, is Hogarth's figure par excellence of the dilemma of the Paracelsian artisan seeking to purify and transform himself by conjunction with the light of Nature. While Nature holds her macrocosm above and parallel to the earth—just as she does in Fludd's *Integrae naturae*—the crying boy holds his half-decayed orb (the microcosm) below in its appointed place, his sorrow attesting to the inability of art and Nature to achieve unity in modern times.

The identity of the impure and decaying microcosm in the boy's grasp is again confirmed by the legendary "pillar" upholding what is left of the little world in the shadow underneath. The process of the distillation of "nourishing" liquid dripping from Nature's breast in the macrocosm down to the elements in the microcosm is, by simple analogy, precisely the same process that occurred in the alchemic crucible.

And as Palissy and Böhme believed, and Fludd reiterated in "De geomantia," the danger for "inexperienced" operators of the alchemic crucible is of spreading the "accident" of impurity throughout mankind—instead of reversing the impurity of the Fall—which results inevitably from the catastrophic failure to know the spiritual essence of their materials. Such an elemental failure in the circuit of mankind's ever-increasing commercial engagement with urban production and consumption could have the unintended consequence of increasing the speed with which the earth decayed and aged. This gave new currency to Böhme's admonition that postlapsarian man must exploit every moment of transient lucidity to pierce the veil of the half-blind, and reduce his bodily self in order to absorb the spiritual light of Nature. That is why the fragments of man's aspirations for unity in the transparency of his artisanal materials are in perpetual decline from the perfect circle of the uppermost cosmos, which remains intact, to the shards on the bottom. This process of descending from the mountaintop of purity and perfection to the infinite variety of error and disorder that suffused the everyday life of the street mirrors the tripartite arrangement of binders on the backward sign. It is an inversion of the fictional unity of the world of polite consumption and the reality of incompleteness and fragmentation it alternately masks and reveals.

Here precisely, Hogarth begins to read the natural philosophy of "De geomantia" through the lens of the subterranean earth of Hog Lane's pious Huguenot artisans. Fludd inquires how the body prepares to receive the transparent perception of geomantic prophecy; to see all the way through the "multitudinous" impulses that accidentally impact the senses "to the simplicity of nature"? "The body must," Fludd writes:

> be prepared for the operation by some kind of abstinence that will temper and subtiliate it, that will humble the arrogance of the flesh, and will make the dissipated central rays of

the soul contract towards their center. The whole man must outwardly and inwardly be reduced to the simplicity of nature. He must neglect and hate all that is composite and multitudinous. Thus, by the virtue of *mens humana* herself, will he be best prepared for the production of works not accidental, but essential. His intellectual functions will not be impaired by the flesh, and [he] . . . will become as alert, docile, pure and unperturbed as will render him a fit receiver of the prophetic message conveyed by the luminous rays of *mens*. In a mystical way *it will show the objects of truth as in a looking-glass* [emphasis added], and it will make the sense and movement function precisely as *mens* directs. The geomancer should be in good health, his mind unperterbed, his stomach not overburdened with food and wine; he should not be oppressed by poverty, nor under the influence of lust or wrath. Quiet religious contemplation is conducive to the proper state of mind; so is a moderate and temperate way of life, in accordance with nature. The geomancer should abstain from carnal intercourse, but rejoice in spiritual copulation [that is, the union of *anima* and *mens*]; instead of wine, the illuminating fluid of *mens* should inebriate him; he should prosper not in worldly riches, but in the affluence of *intellectus divinus* ["divine perception"]; he should be replete with spiritual food, not with crapulence.[51]

Hogarth's title tells us the Huguenot congregation of the Eglise des Grecs prays at "noon," consuming only the Word at midday. In a remarkably Palissian gesture, having turned their backs on "Good Eating" and open participation in the world of polite culture, they would seem on the surface to refuse to partake of London's culture of raw or fashionable consumption. The Huguenots choose another path, which sublimates carnal and material desire into the refugee artisan's passion for synthesizing religiosity and work into both innovation and production.

As for prophets resisting the sins of the flesh, the Huguenots of Hog Lane—with few exceptions—are already reduced physically by Hogarth's rendering of their advanced age, their state of physical decrepitude and projection of otherworldly desire. In a very real sense then, these are the last living refugees of 1685, painted a half-century after the Revocation. For them, "noon" is literally the final age of man. "Subtiliate"— taken from St. Augustine's description of the "invisible, active" bodies of the angels in *City of God* was a key word for both Fludd and Hogarth. It directed the manner in which Hogarth painted Soho's Huguenots, how he interpreted their history in London after having survived the crucible of sacred violence. This made them the logical choice for the natural-philosophical artisans of *Noon*.

The *Oxford English Dictionary* tells us that the word "subtiliate"—defined generally as "To make thin or tenuous; esp[ecially] to rarefy (a fluid); to sublime; to refine; purify"—entered common usage for the first time during the fifteenth century. From the beginning, it was an alchemical term. The process of subtiliation produced "quicksilver," or philosophical mercury (the key element in the philosopher's stone) in 1408. By

1579, this mystical process of spiritual refinement was widely known among English natural philosophers, and it was "supposeth [that] the body of Christe might be subtiliated, by his Divine power, to passe through the doores."

In Sir Hugh Platt's popular book of secrets, *The Jewell House of Art and Nature* (1594), this English gentleman and natural philosopher, who translated and glossed Bernard Palissy and was the subject of a Howes-Winthrop dialogue in the 1630s, was skeptical of a certain alchemist who claimed to have produced "Sol so subtiliated by often reiteration of *Aqua Regis* upon it, as that it became almost an impalpable powder [that is, Palissy's philosophical salt, the potter's 'fifth element']."[52] When combined with a secret packet of "medicine" and left in "the crucible in the fire . . . within one halfe hour," Platt reported, it was said that "the Mercurie were sufficientlie tincted into Sol" that the deceptive alchemist "willed to be taken out of the fire and conveyed into an ingot . . . twoe ounces of perfect Sol [gold]."[53] Still, it was only by dint of this fluid and clandestine process of bodily subtilation that Hogarth's Huguenot refugees could have moved between, inside, and around the parallel worlds of macrocosm and microcosm, which they now occupied simultaneously, and so were able "in a mystical way . . . [to] show the objects of truth as in a looking-glass."

But it also stands to reason that Hog Lane's Huguenots were just as capable of synthesizing memories of southwestern French history and culture, combining their lived experience of Soho at the same time as their old and new worlds. Internalizing Palissy's artisanal reinvention of the social, religious, and material processes of Calvinist self-mastery, the refugees alone were shown "outwardly and inwardly . . . reduced to the simplicity of nature." Neoplatonic "simplicity" or an attitude of plainness could take the social form of refugee hiding and mobility, because simplicity was seemingly imperceptible amid the self-conscious theatricality of Hog Lane. Here, the binary universe mediated by Nature was not made whole (*integrae*) but rather confused and conflated. "Simple" Palissian artisans had become agents and invisible intermediaries between "all that is composite and multitudinous" in the commercial city. Thus, filtered through the chaos of Hog Lane, Fludd's prophetic "De geomantia" offers an implicit critique of counting heads (or dots) from the interactive perspective of two early modern philosophers of English natural history. Fludd and then Hogarth devalued the "*a posteriori*" / "*ab effectu*" analysis of behavior in everyday life—and of the usefulness of superficial mathematical quantification per se (as opposed to mystical geometry)—to infer social meaning. Here, then, was a philosophical basis for Huguenot stigmatization by native tradesmen, although demographic counts suggest that such fears went beyond mere numbers. Above all, it was necessary to avoid the obfuscations and sensual confusions that would follow, if one began what was essentially an experiential process, with a mechanical, a posteriori count. This Paracelsian critique formed the core of Fludd's advice to inexperienced operators, who also had to endure the rigorous personal preparation of internal moral cleansing before the geomantic process could properly begin:

> Before you proceed to the projection of the dots, I want you to know that the dots, while being made, must not be counted. If you count them, the result of the operation will be useless; for this science has its foundations in the soul and therefore, the number of dots must depend on the will of the soul, and not in any way on the appetite of your senses. He who approaches this work should not begin with anything unless his heart be well disposed, his conscience clear and sound, his *spiritus* or *anima* not vexed by any troubles; so much so that he do not wish anything worse to any other man than to himself. When so prepared, let him trust God, the master of the sciences, and pray to Him that by the virtue of this science He may open the truth to him. Immediately after sedulously performing these acts he may proceed to the projection and disposition of the dots.[54]

In 1562, mortified by the chaos and extreme "esmotions" of mimetic violence in war-torn Saintonge, Palissy was compelled to walk along the serpentine Charente River, where he contemplated the soulish relation between macrocosm and microcosm through his perception and excavation of the hidden elements of subterranean earth. Suddenly, as Fludd prescribed two generations later, the potter experienced harmonic epiphany. He acquired Neoplatonic insight to "approach" his experiments in the kiln with "his heart . . . well disposed, his conscience clear . . . his *spiritus* not vexed by any troubles; . . . not wish[ing] anything worse to any other man than to himself." Thus, like Palissy's potter, who transformed matter from the ruins of a Saintongeais Huguenot culture that was fragmented and "dispersed" by war into translucent glaze, Fludd's geomancer marries the "Soul of the World" to unify "all that is composite and multitudinous" and achieve the aesthetic of divine perception. Palissy and Fludd staked their political and natural-philosophical programs on their understanding of Neoplatonic materialism. Here a migrating, vital soul makes quantity meaningless by focusing perception on all man-made things as mere fragments of a larger whole dismembered at the onset of postlapsarian time.

Because it was in the nature of this mystical whole to be infinitely greater than the sum of its parts, a few individuals chosen by God to have access to its unifying power could secretly control the motion and production of things in the microcosm. When Palissy made rustic figures and fashioned subterranean grottoes crawling with snails and lizards, he indicated that the sacred power could—perhaps must—be contained in vulnerable bodies like those of their Huguenot makers. Strength was embodied in tiny or nearly invisible things in everyday life. When such things were made by nature in the bowels of the earth and were discovered as marvels or curiosities, they showed workmanship of breathtaking intricacy and almost supernatural beauty hidden inside.

Fascination with the inner workings of fragmented Nature and its replication in art and artisanry endured well into the age of mechanical philosophy. This was why Platt was so popular and one reason for his contemporary English translation and gloss of Palissy's work. For Platt, Palissy was an honored founder of the books-of-secrets tradition. There was a direct relation between the perception of smallness and truth in these texts. Paracelsian natural philosophers acknowledged that their metaphysical project (like Hogarth's moral tales) was voyeuristic, but (in a strategy of distancing itself from the wars) nonviolent and benign. Narratives of natural exploration and experimentation, the historian of science William Eamon explains, used language that was a byproduct of the Neoplatonic sexualization of nature:

> Natural objects were often described as curious by virtue of their smallness, exquisiteness of workmanship being exhibited more strikingly in miniature. [The natural philosopher and microscopist Robert] Hooke [1635–1703] noted that when examined under a microscope, the most "curious" works of art appear crude, "whereas in *natural* forms there are some so small, and so curious, and their design'd business so far remov'd beyond the reach of our sight, that the more we magnify the object, the more excellencies and mysteries do appear; And the more we discover the imperfections of our senses, and the Omnipotency and Infinite perfections of the great Creator." If exquisite workmanship made objects of art worthy of inquiry (and of acquisition), the subtle and intricate secrets of nature were the most curious of all possible objects of interest . . . Hooke openly acknowledged the voyeurism of the new philosophy. Far from condemning it, he extolled it. Hooke contrasted the microscope's ability to peek at nature without being noticed to the more violent methods of dissection. Instead of "pry[ing] into her secrets by breaking open the doors upon her," with a microscope the observer can "quietly peep in at the windows, without frightening her out of her usual byas." To the almost exclusively male company of virtuosi, nature's secrets were as wonderful and mysterious as those of women. As nature was feminine, natural philosophy was "a Male Virtu" whose "curious sight" followed nature "into the privatest recess of her imperceptible littleness."[55]

The famously vaginal imagery of Hogarth's tiny (1¼-inch diameter) print of his "cottage" (fig. 14.12) had a long history in the natural-philosophical books-of-secrets tradition, and its ultimate intellectual source in the shadows of Plato's cave. Indeed, consider the image itself as a supplicant's prospect of the virginal Nature and Soul of the World (in Fludd's *Integrae naturae*), as viewed from below across still waters and through a narrow gate by the Nature's ape. There, rising above Nature's right breast, "is the true Sun . . . infused in her womb by the mercurial spirit." "Hogarth's Cottage"—with its triangular gable end pointing upward to the macrocosm (and to God above Nature's head)—would thus be located on the dark side of the vaginal moon. As if to punctuate Hogarth's habitation in the "privatest recess" of Nature, the triangular well handle and chain remind us of the seven nature spirits hidden in figure 8.5

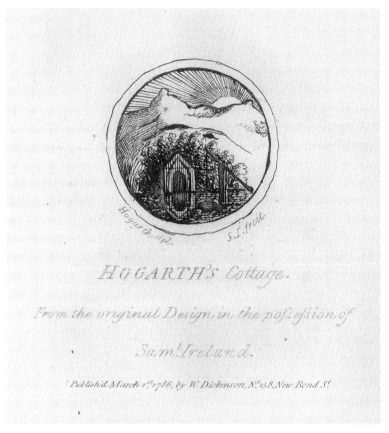

FIGURE 14.12. William Hogarth, *Hogarth's Cottage*, March 1, 1786. Posthumously published engraving. 1¼″ diameter. Courtesy Lewis Walpole Library, Yale University.

and form another sort of gnomon to cast the cottage itself into the shadows. Hogarth would seem to identify with two ostensibly oppositional characters created for *Noon:* the sanctified Huguenot artisans of the Eglise des Grecs, who silently replicated the secrets of nature in their clandestine workshops, and, in an unexpected way, the artless African lover, whose simian assault on Nature's virtue is, in this instance, carnal and premature. The achievement of *Hogarth's Cottage* in the countryside is that its author (in Fludd's words) could "rejoice in spiritual copulation."

For Fludd, it followed that "geomancy must be performed in a kind of rapture or ecstasy."[56] But this prophetic conjunction and moment of sublime soulish excitement is unseen by others and by definition remains internalized and hidden. Geomantic prophesy thus cannot exist in a world governed by mechanical philosophy, because it derives from "immediate" interaction with an *engaged* God. Fludd's deity communicated with the geomancer at the very moment of ecstasy: "In prophecy, this rapture or ecstasy is caused by an abstraction, alienation, and illumination of *mens humana*, proceeding *immediately* [emphasis added] from God; in geomancy a similar effect is produced by the gathering together of the of the rays of *mens* into, as it were, a narrow place, namely the human body, so that the soul may by their light see the simple truth more brightly."[57]

Gathering *mens* for projection into "a narrow place, namely the human body," materialized in Hogarth's containment and redirection of the animated line of beauty. By virtue of this gathering, Fludd establishes the occult principles of terrestrial astrology, thereby enabling Hogarth to adapt them to his pictorial narrative. Outward sight reflected by sunlight on the elemental earth of Hog Lane is inverted into its mirror image, contracting its "formerly diffuse" force to the "center" of the Huguenot congregation's now inwardly illuminated body. Hogarth thus privileged the inner metaphysical light of nature, over the multitudinousness of sensual perception:

> The rays of *mens* must, therefore, be made to contract by diverting them from the objects of the external world . . . so in this . . . rapture of geomancy those rays of the human soul which are normally sent forth in an outward direction and are dispersed hither and thither are called back towards their center and reflected into *mens*. Thus an inward illumination may be produced that is comparable to the concentration of formerly diffuse light into the center of the Sun, which took place on the fourth day of Creation. When the rays of the soul are collected in this way, the nature of inward man is reduced to simplicity. He thinks about himself within himself; he is there only by himself and has forgotten matters alien to his real self. In such a rapture or ecstasy, he may to others appear to be without himself, whereas really he is more than ever with himself. There will be little distance between him and the divine.[58]

Hogarth's reading of Fludd provided a philosophical language for the pictorial performance of the Huguenots on Hog Lane. After consuming the Word at noon, the refugees "contract"—or absorb—the spirit into themselves, focus their eyes on "inward illumination," and turn their backs on "the objects of the external world." They occupy a world of shadow, hidden from the sun's external governance, which is "diffused" on the complex, chaotic, and "crapulent" modes of consumption depicted in the foreground. In reality, the power of the sun has moved inside of the refugees own pious bodies, where it instills divine "simplicity" (hence clarity) unnoticed by the outside world. This "is the nature of inward man," to "think about himself within himself." But such contemplation of the conjunction of macrocosm and microcosm merely reflects off of the self-absorbed narcissism of the polite threesome as in a mirror. Carnality and crapulence centered around the African have the same limited effect. Contemplation is the "experience" of self-knowledge, of "truthful" self-mastery. To love oneself in this way, is to love God. In the moment of ecstatic gratification, "there will be little distance between him [the geomancer] and the divine." Given what I am ar-

guing is his enormous debt to Fludd, it is unsurprising that this assessment of the geomancer's bodily metamorphosis parallels the bodily discourse supplied the sitter by
John Winthrop Jr.'s physician's chair. Like Palissy's withdrawal into his natural laboratory hidden from chaos to build his ceramic material-holiness synthesis in the presence of the holy spirit, it was necessary to have "withdrawn from the multitude."[59] The
smaller the "distance" from the divine presence, "the more he may appear to others to
be without himself." Being "without" self describes Hogarth's darkly ethereal Huguenot artisans, who were "really . . . more than ever with" themselves after experience
with the living word in the Eglise des Grecs. In the spectacle of diverse humanity on
crowded Hog Lane, the Huguenots alone embody "such simplicity and unity . . .
which ignores the multitudinous objects of the external world of the senses . . . and
linger[s] in . . . ecstasy to behold, as in a polished mirror, things mundane as well as
divine."[60]

For some, this begs the question of whether the Huguenots on Hog Lane embody
the geomancer or chosen geomantic dots—the observer or the observed? The answer—like everything else in this cosmos of sundials, mirrors, and palindromes—remains ambiguous and fluid, with significant seepage on both sides. Hogarth provides
clues, holds his cards close to his vest, and relies on some members of the audience to
deconstruct the visual text. Meaning in Hogarth's universe of "multitudes" is thus revealed slowly, parsed from the confusion and simultaneity of street life, where the
"without" and "with[in]" logic of artisanal experience (and Hogarth's "conceit" of the
shell) required that the Huguenot occupy both territories.

Actually, such duality of perspective is also permissible in Fludd, since the *anima*
directing the divine eye of the geomancer would be drawn interactively—like the
Paracelsian homeopathic process—to the analogous truth represented by the pairs of
dots resonating mystically with his soul. Additionally, two broad themes emerge from
fragments of meaning deciphered so far: first, inasmuch as the vast majority of Soho's
Huguenots were artisans of luxury goods, then the pious congregation of the Eglise
des Grecs were the producers on Hog Lane; and second, while *The Four Times of the
Day* seems anomalous in the times-of-the-day tradition (instead of the morning/af-
ternoon/evening pattern), it *is* analogous to the conventional parable of the four ages
of man, which, by extension, blends seamlessly with the four elements of nature.
Within this context, "Noon," functioned as a modern history painting. Thus it "documented" the interaction of natural-philosophical and artisanal history at a precise
moment of elemental *and* millennial time, as it passed for the aging and decaying
Earth. This was, of course, *the* essential Palissian project. Reenacted by the most widely
observed artist-philosopher in the transatlantic world two centuries after the *Recepte
veritable* appeared in La Rochelle, this link was confirmed by Hogarth when he
adopted the public persona of "tradesman."

❧ The Philosophical "tradesman" in the "*Theatrum orbi*" ❧

Depicting the materiality of the aging earth from perspectives of decayed humanity to which the elements were inextricably linked through the microcosmic body was a millennial project of personal importance to Hogarth. Witness his publication on March 3, 1764, of *Tail Piece, or The Bathos,* with its caustic farewell to London's adversarial dealers in "authentic," "old master" history paintings, competitors of Hogarth's new, "modern" histories. The old-style pictures were obscured by aging varnish; as Hogarth chided in his sarcastic dedication, "or Manner of Sinking in Sublime Paintings, inscribed to the Dealers in Dark Pictures." Hogarth could afford to be nasty. He was dying; *Tail Piece* was the last print marked "design'd and engrav'd" by the artist in his lifetime (fig. 14.13).[61] As Paulson has remarked, "for here Time's darkening means also that the scene is darkening, the sun and moon are failing."[62] Paulson deciphers the "profusion" of Hogarth's puns on the project he called "the End of all Things":

> some are paralleled, the great with the small, a cracked bell and a broken bottle, the sun going down and a candle guttering out, the world on the tavern sign and the world in *The Times* print being consumed by fire. A gallows, an unstrung bow, and a broken crown indicate the "end" of a robber, a poet and a king. These examples become increasingly verbal, as Hogarth puns on a scale unprecedented even in his work; Time himself, dying with his scythe and hourglass broken and his pipe snapped, comes to his end uttering "FINIS." Near him is "The World's End" tavern, and around him lie the last pages of a play ("Exeunt Omnes"), a rope's end and a candle end, the butt end of a musket, the worn stump of a broom, and a shoemaker's "waxed end" twisted around his wooden "last."[63]

Hogarth's punning synthesis of word and image is superimposed as rhetorical ornament on the conclusion of the Paracelsian natural-philosophical dialogue that informed both *Noon* and *Tail Piece.* Thus, Hogarth returned at the end of his life to retrieve and open up for further public scrutiny a subject he had introduced as a hidden subtext in the process of gestation twenty-eight years earlier, in *Noon.* This decision was made doubly complex because the earlier work contained obscure intertextual dialogues with the seventeenth-century Paracelsian Fludd, harnessed to the clandestine history of London's diasporic Huguenot artisans, in the generation following the Revocation of the Edict of Nantes, which had to be accounted for in *Tail Piece.* That is why the natural-philosophical program that undergirded Hogarth's final print cannot be fully comprehended without *Noon.*

Hogarth's infirmity undoubtedly played a decisive role in his choice of subject, but the historical context of *Tail Piece* was his witnessing of a natural phenomenon with cosmic and millennial overtones. On April 1, 1764, a total eclipse of the sun, the first

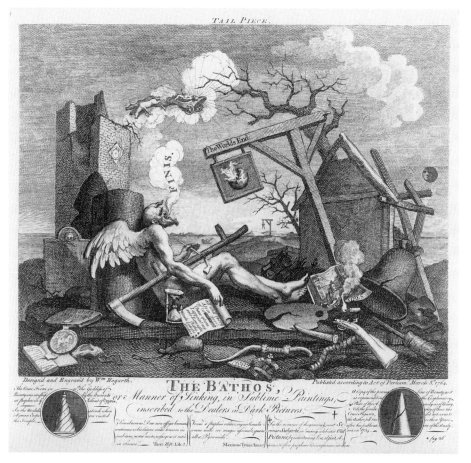

FIGURE 14.13. William Hogarth, *Tail Piece*, or *The Bathos*, engraving, London, March 3, 1764. H: 10¼″, W: 12¹³⁄₁₆″. Courtesy Lewis Walpole Library, Yale University. Hogarth's "dark picture" of "The World's End," painted the year he died, showing "Nature bankrupt" as Time's astral chariot draws near.

to occur in forty-nine years, darkened the sky over London. Two weeks later, *Tail Piece* was advertised in the *St. James' Chronicle.*[64] Hogarth's apocalyptic sun did not end its life in *Tail Piece* like a clock mechanism winding down. It expired organically, as a body in the midst of its daily *transit gloria*. An androgynous creature that has lost animating light, the sun is now prone in agony with legs spread. This was a carnal end for Fludd's figure of "Mater" Nature as well. Deprived of the spirit of fertility, she dies in fruitless labor. The sun begins its catastrophic descent into the microcosm. Without light, it is now falling into stasis. Here it stalled in a chariot riding on Flood's broken cosmological wheels, drawn behind a powerless team of dead horses. Harnessed together like the inseparable trinity, this threesome have relinquished the spiritual power necessary to pull the sun across the heavens. The darkened sun disables the sundial over Time's head (extending the subterranean darkness in the Huguenot half of *Noon* throughout the picture), turning midday into permanent midnight. The mechanical dial can neither illuminate the industrious nor cast a clandestine shadow. Even the inner light of piety seems absent. Indeed, the gnomon—like all the artifacts of human history—has fallen away from its interior moorings on the chapter ring.

The Paracelsian synthesis is in the process of decomposition; spirit separates from matter, which disconnects into aimless atoms, form devolves into formlessness. *Noon* located structures of Neoplatonic unity behind the multiplicity and fragmentation of everyday life, but here the very matter of elemental earth loses coherence. Like the misconceived crying boy's earthenware platter disintegrating into sulphuric waste, the world reverts to a state of chaos and entropy without benefit of time for artisanal repair and maintenance. In *Tail Piece*, as in *Noon*, momentous events have already occurred or are about to happen. Time has crossed "the Earth" off his last will and testament at the moment of his death. God is receiving Time's immortal soul, which ascended in his last breath. Instead of returning his body to the vanishing earth, whence it came, Time bequeaths "all and every Atom thereof to Chaos whom I appoint my sole Executor." In death, Time's atomistic legacy is literally unraveled into dots of chaos. Just as the Lamb breaks the seven seals of the Apocalypse to reveal the scroll in Revelation 5–8, opening the scroll unravels the harmonic balance maintained by the line of beauty, which connected the macrocosm and microcosm. This appears three-dimensionally in the subtext as "The Conic Form in w[hi]ch the Goddess of Beauty was worshipped by the Ancients."

Revelation and the discourse of production and consumption on Hog Lane are converged in Hogarth's image of "A Nature Bankrupt," a final judgment on Nature's remaining assets, written matter-of-factly on the side of a probate portfolio tossed in a corner, its notarial seal conspicuously broken. The image on this seal seems to have released the fourth and final horseman of Revelation 6:7–8: "a pale horse, and its rider's name was Death." Yet the first three horsemen have already been released to complete their grim task, witness the broken weapons of war in the center foreground. These belonged to the first rider (Rev. 6:1–2), who "had a bow; and a crown was given to him, and he went out conquering and to conquer."

Hogarth's simultaneity reveals fundamental millennial linkages between the history of heaven and earth, as he did in *Noon*. Here, however, as the things of everyday life collapse into an undifferentiated mass of matter in a state of fragmentation from the unity of spirit and matter, dying artifacts of production and consumption fulfill the potential for complete chaos implied by the shop signs on which fragmented bodies advertised goods and services on Hog Lane. If *Noon* shows that a precarious balance

FIGURE 14.14. William Hogarth, *The Times*, pl. 1, engraving, London, September 7, 1762. H: 8⁹⁄₁₆″, W: 11⅝″. Courtesy Lewis Walpole Library, Yale University. This apocalyptic scene harkens back to the Great Fire of London of 1666 and also contains references to Britain's transatlantic imperial wars, in particular, the costly Seven Years' War in North America, then about to draw to a close. Perhaps the dove, surveying the chaos below in the London streets, heralds peace in America while pondering the catastrophic economic and political damage caused in the metropolis by the war?

between the worlds of production and consumption has been achieved at great cost to the resources of Nature, *Tail Piece* shows that the bill has finally come due. Just when Time expires (FINIS), gives up the ghost, and "sinks" into the "dark" alchemical "sublime," "The Worlds End" is announced on another shop sign, which topples to the ground. The earth is destroyed by the hidden internal fire of corruption and decline, and like Time, animate forces exit the "body" at the end. To reiterate this point, a hanged man's dead body is suspended from a gibbet in the deep background. The conflagration itself had been prefigured in 1762, by plate 1 of *The Times*. In *Tail Piece*, a copy of this print is set on fire by a fallen candle, reanimating its subject and making its prophesy "real." The print prophesied a second great fire of London as a harbinger of final things (fig. 14.14), and showed penitence wasted as time has run out. A burning globe similar to the sign in *Tail Piece* appears as a pediment over a door in *The*

Times, upheld by a pair of serpentine brackets. *The Times* thus forms a narrative bridge between *The Four Times of the Day* and *Tail Piece;* roomlike compositional elements in the enclosed urban landscape are repeated in all three images.

Noon and *Tail Piece* exploit Fludd's science of pyramids and triangles. If the scene at "The Worlds End" were put right again—that is, if the clock were turned back to the final moment before the collapse of Time and the aging earth—then the signpost would still stand upright. In this vertical position, its brackets formed a downward triangle that aligned perfectly with the upward triangle of the gable end on the collapsed building. At the moment of FINIS, a shop sign announcing "The World's End," also announces the dissipation of the "Soul of the World," and with it the structural security that has held the formal and aesthetic elements of Nature's material life together since the beginning. All this is exhaled into nothingness as millennial Time—the internal time of God and the soul of men and materials—expires, an event that coincides with the collapse of the Fluddian conduit through Nature between microcosm and macrocosm. Does Hogarth represent himself here, by harnessing Fludd's geomantic powers, as the last of the old adepts? Will life and art revert to chaos after his death? Was no artist left of "experience" to search for the stone?

The "bathos" of *Tail Piece* thereby linked postlapsarian man's ultimate descent into chaos with the catastrophic failure to perceive the monistic relation between his own body and soul and the plain animating essence of the natural world hidden below the fragmented surface of modern material life. Like the philosopher's stone that lay ignored in the street, hidden from the vulgarity of inexperience under a translucent cloak of naturalness, Hogarth also offers his knowledge—albeit covertly—to his many publics. Having completed a semiotic pilgrimage that traversed a labyrinth of clues, it was finally possible for the newly "experienced" to perceive that their silent "withdrawal from the multitude," had returned the Huguenots of Hog Lane to a memory theater of primitive origins. The conclusion of Fludd's geomantic text again served as Hogarth's street map to the refugees' secret spiritual and material world:

> Deeper still, towards the center [of geomantic interpretation], the *spiritus* of empyreal heaven lies hidden, which is the revealer of things future and present, namely [in] the rational or intellectual collection of these figures [the formerly hidden sequence of dots] and of *the things mundane that are therein contained* [emphasis added]. It becomes thus even more apparent how carefully *spiritus intellectualis* should be protected against the obnoxious influence of the flesh and of crapulence, for the first impulse in the production of the geomantic dots issues therefrom and carries away with it, in an occult manner, the natures of the celestial signs, of the planets, and of the elements, concealing them all under the number and proportion of the dots, as a treasure is concealed in a chest. If we wish to open that chest, so that we may penetrate first to the elements, then to the planets and celestial

signs, and finally to the limit whence this motion originally ensued, we shall *find under the figures* [emphasis added], as it were, hidden in that chest, the will of *mens* in its sanctuary, in the ointment-store. . . .

Thus it becomes evident that, as the prophesy of those touched by [a divine] afflatus [or communication of knowledge] is caused by a union of *mens divina* and *mens humana* (whence originates the fullest and greatest vaticination), so also prophecy may sometimes occur in persons not so touched, when, *withdrawn from the multitude* [emphasis added], *anima* with her rays is united to her vertex, i.e. to *mens humana*, which, without any doubt, in conjunction with *anima* may perform very great actions and may direct them towards a felicitous climax and issue.[65]

To confirm Hogarth's performance of Fludd's conclusions on the power of geomancy to prophesize the aging earth's historical secrets, it is necessary to revisit *Noon* for a final look at the Huguenot retreat from Hog Lane. Picturing the refugees' departure from the Eglise des Grecs is at once his most culturally specific and cosmologically resonant act of mirroring. I would suggest this moment of retreat is, moreover, a metaphorical reenactment of the process of artisanal "dispersion" from Huguenot strongholds such as Saintonge, to which the Eglise des Grecs was harnessed after 1685.[66] Their departure from Hog Lane is part of a pictorial dialogue between the natural unity of "primitive" artisanal memory rooted in the Huguenots' civil war past and the veil of fragmentation from the distortions of fashionable consumption in London's historical present. Again, a serpentine line of "progress" unites forward and backward motion in space and time and requires congregants to exit the church through the one clearly visible doorway in the painting, only to turn back and enter immediately into another, metaphorical one—a sort of double door—presumably visible only to themselves.

To achieve this effect, Hogarth revived and syncretized two closely related early modern engravings with impeccable credentials as icons of the refugee corpus: Johann Theodore de Bry's 1620 rendering of Robert Fludd's *Theatrum orbi* ("Theater of the World") (fig. 14.15), and the title page of Clément Marot and Théodore de Bèze's key translation of the Psalms into French poetic vernacular in 1562 (fig. 14.16). Both images (like Hogarth's profane "cottage" in fig. 14.12) famously focus on liminality and feature mysterious doorways; thresholds to the hidden secrets, pains, and rewards of private, metaphysical space.[67]

French Protestant families commonly possessed at least one copy of the ubiquitous Marot–de Bèze Psalter, and the iconic image on the title page was the most familiar one in Huguenot culture. As with all Reformation emblemata, text and image were read together. Having opened the book to "Sing to the Lord who lives in Zion, & proclaim his deeds among nations," the choir scanned down to a two-inch engraving of a

Loci iterum *temporales* funt *duplices*, cùm *alius* fit orientalis, qui fcilicet in eo-
dem figno orientalem mundi plagam refpicit, atque hunc locum theatro albo
impleri imaginabimur: *Alius* verò *occidentalis*, five occidentalis figni portio, in
qua ponetur theatrum quoddam nigrum, de quo pofteà dicemus.

CAP. X.

De theatri orientalis & occidentalis defcriptione.

THeatrum appello illud, in quo omnes vocabulorum, fententiarum, particu-
larum orationis feu fubjectorum actiones tanquam in theatro publico, ubi
comœdiæ & tragœdiæ aguntur, demonftrantur. Hujufmodi theatrorum *fpe-
ciem unam* in puncto orientis fitam effe imaginabimur; quæ realis feu corporea,
fed quafi vapore æthereo confideranda erit: Sitque illa theatri umbra fimilitu-
dinibus fpirituum agentium repleta. *Primum* ergo theatrum habebit colo-
rem album, lucidum & fplendidum, præ fe ferens diem, diurnasque actiones.
Quare in oriente collocabitur, quia Sol ab Oriente fe attollens diem incipit,
claritatemque mundo pollicetur: *Secundum* verò fingetur imbutum colore ni-
gro, fufco & obfcuro: illudque in Occidente pofitum imaginaberis, quia Sol in
Occidente exiftens noctem & obfcuritatem brevi venturam dénunciat. Quod-
libet autem horum theatrorum habebit *quinque portas* ab invicem diftinctas, &
ferè æquidiftantes, quarum ufus pofteà demonftrabimus.

CAP.

FIGURE 14.15. Johann Theodore de Bry, *Theatrum orbi* (Theater of the World), from Robert
Fludd, *Utriusque cosmi majoris scilicet et minoris metaphysica, physica atque technica historia in duo
volumina secundum cosmi differentiam divisa . . . tomus primus De macrocosmi historia* (Oppenheim, 1617; 2d ed., Frankfurt, 1624). Courtesy Harry Ransom Humanities Research Center,
The University of Texas at Austin. The exemplar for refugee memory theaters in the seventeenth-century transatlantic world. The five geometric forms in the foreground represent
spaces reserved for columns. Memory is transmuted into material form—architecture and furniture (or interstitial shadow inside them), or ubiquitous consumer goods—in personal "memory places," located anywhere and available throughout the world, to be recalled by a traveler
passing through or a settler.

FIGURE 14.16. François Perrin (for Antoine Vincent), title page from Clément Marot and Théodore de Bèze, *Les Pseaumes mis en rime Françoise* (Paris, 1562). Courtesy Societé de l'histoire du protestantisme français, Paris. This title page device from the crucial Marot Psalter, which was small enough to hide in one's sleeve and was arguably possessed (in one of its multiple editions) by every French Protestant family, illustrates the admonition from Matthew 7 juxtaposing the choice of the wide or narrow gate to perdition or salvation. Compare the bottom border of the same device with the carving on the New York chairs illustrated in figs. 15.26 and 15.40.

walled garden, a mannerist trope for the pilgrim's entrance to the soul's fortress and an image of the struggle between good and evil in the seeker's own corrupt heart.[68]

Inside the walls and situated on what may be the top of the world, two abutted arches stand juxtaposed, one narrow, one wide, boxed in by a second boundary: a wall of words. Here the text distills a scriptural admonition about the purifying effect of endurance and suffering taken from Matthew 7:13–14: "Enter by the narrow gate [*porte*],[69] because it is the wide gate and spacious path that leads to perdition." The narrow gate or, in this instance, arch, is of plain construction, with no discernable ornament or historical style (except the simple brickwork and naturalistic, rough-hewn stone columns). However, to pass through to the other side would be an ordeal. The narrow arch is obscured and guarded by a thorn bush, which reaches out to impale those approaching the threshold. With its roots hidden in the shadows behind a column, the bush grows all the way through the passageway, from back to front, where its branches block the entrance. A metaphor for the steady growth of faith through sacrifice, painful barbs slowly inch their way up the narrow arch. The rustic "capitals" form a sort of crucifix as they traverse the opening (a metaphysical keyhole). This test of love of God provides the raw materials for the construction of Christ's heroic crown of thorns. The narrow way, in other words, is a painful yet ecstatic memory, recalled by the psalms, of the path taken by Jesus himself.

The wide arch is, by contrast, lavishly ornamented in popish italianate style. It has fluted neoclassical columns framing thornless, sweet-smelling flowers set in the middle of the path behind the cavernous opening. Thus, the devil seduces the unwary into his deathtrap in the hellfire (above the wide arch). The application of this allegory to the enticements of untrammeled, narcissistic desire available on Hog Lane is self-evident, but it is also worth remembering that the original context for this was a message of self-mastery. The psalms promoted stoic endurance and harmonic transcendence to the faithful to overcome the physical and spiritual trials and fragmentation of wartime. Ultimately, they sang of the sanctity of violent martyrdom, while offering the hope of eternal salvation and the transcendence of fallen bodily matter through physical pain and ascetic self-denial. Was this not one source for the narrow, cruciform path taken through its towers by La Rochelle's martyrs in 1628, as seen through the Germanic lens of the anonymous engravers of *In patientia suavitas* (fig. 9.1)?

But if this were only a story of pious suffering, what are we to make of Palissy's transcendence during the first war, from the "pleasure" of the psalms? Again, there are affinities here with Hogarth's aesthetics of knowledge, and revelation of philosophical truth through close analysis of tiny things of beauty. To quote Matthew in full, recalling Palissy's application of Neoplatonic principles to the social logic of Saintongeais civil war artisanal discourse: "Enter by the narrow gate; for the gate is wide and the way is easy that leads to destruction, and those who enter by it are many. For the gate is narrow and the way is hard, that leads to life, and those who find it are few." Not coincidentally, the epiphany Palissy experienced as an individual, isolated from the community of the "many," occurred during a walk by the banks of the Charente River in 1563, just one year after the Marot–de Bèze Psalter appeared. At that moment, harmonic voices overwhelmed the isolation and carnality of his body and sublimated his senses while calling the vital power of the macrocosm down through the light of nature and into his animated soul.

Fludd also believed the "experienced" could call down the powers of harmonic convergence through the conduit of music, as well as with the science of pyramids. Fludd elaborated this claim in "The Temple of Music." The temple combined a magico-religious edifice with a kind of music machine. This marvel was illustrated by de Bry in *De naturae simia* (1618).[70] Is the little book clutched under the right arm of Hogarth's elderly Huguenot woman who embraces her friend outside the Eglise des Grecs, a copy of the Marot–de Bèze Psalter? (The 1562 edition was similarly small and portable; the title page measured 6 by 3½ inches.) The "narrow" front end points "the way" through her companion's heart in the wake of the departing congregation, toward the "double door." This cosmological gesture is noteworthy. Hog Lane is packed with such obscure directional signals.

If Hogarth linked the Marot–de Bèze Psalter with the Huguenot congregation in *Noon,* he grafted Fludd's fortresslike *Theatrum orbi* even more firmly onto its pictorial, natural-philosophical and historical armature. By extension, *Theatrum orbi* was meant to be read together with its companion image in *Ars memoriae* (The Art of Memory), the second volume of Fludd's *Utriusque cosmi* (fig. 14.17). It is not my task here to elucidate Fludd's immensely complex and historically learned inquiry into the origins of occult knowledge hidden in the shadowy recesses of human memory. Frances Yates has accomplished this in conjunction with her pathbreaking study of the adaptation of classical memory systems in Renaissance culture. In the process, Yates has also posited a provocative and convincing argument relating the form and function of Shakespeare's Globe Theater and de Bry's engraving of Fludd's two-tier *Theatrum orbi.* A famously visible, material construction was plausibly linked to the process of seventeenth-century memory formation. A stage thus found a central place in the invisible and transatlantic worlds of private religious experience and noetic imagination.[71]

Taking the universalist, cosmopolitan geography of the *Theatrum orbi* at its word, I am concerned with Hogarth's specific use of Fludd's memory theater as a template for ways of perceiving the unity of the past hidden behind the pluralistic babel of Soho's internationalism. I shall show that Hogarth elucidated this framework to mediate the clandestine nature of Huguenot artisanal experience and the chaotic

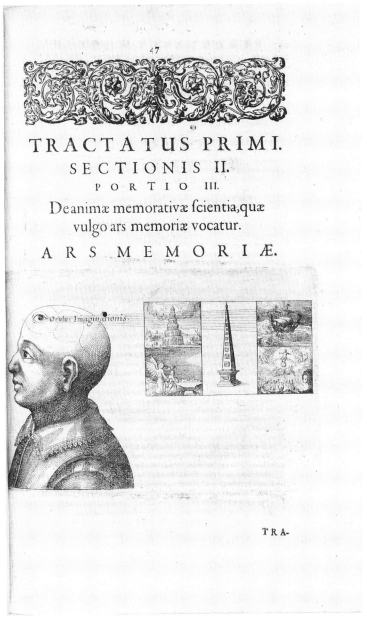

TRACTATUS PRIMI.
SECTIONIS II.
PORTIO III.
De animæ memorativæ fcientia, quæ
vulgo ars memoriæ vocatur.

ARS MEMORIÆ.

TRA-

FIGURE 14.17. Johann Theodore de Bry, title page of *Ars memoriae* (The Art of Memory) in Robert Fludd's *Utriusque cosmi majoris scilicet et minoris metaphysica, physica atque technica historia in duo volumina secundum cosmi differentiam divisa . . . tomus primus De macrocosmi historia* (Oppenheim, 1617; 2d ed., Frankfurt, 1624). Courtesy Harry Ransom Humanities Research Center, The University of Texas at Austin. Fludd's understanding of the eye of the imagination, or third eye, which looks backward in time from the first of three ventricles in man's brain that structure memory. Memory places collected by man's bodily eyes are brought forward from shadowy obscurity in the third ventricle at the back of the head up to the eye of the imagination. Divine light from the third eye is refracted backward through universal memory experiences contained in scenes from the Tower of Babel, Tobias and the Angel, a storm-tossed ship at sea, and Revelation, all of which are connected by the mediating pyramidal figure of an Egyptian obelisk.

consumption of Hog Lane. Read in an interactive way—as a sort of historical dialogue between past and present—Hogarth's theatrical and densely populated painting fills the empty space made available in Fludd's vacant, heavily defended, and yet
strangely open and passive, *Theatrum orbi*.

Walls or buildings are removed in the foreground. Space is thus allotted for spectators to look through three-sided boxes, which display abrupt perpendicular back-
drops that form shallow theatrical stages. These open boxes are pierced with additional
mysterious openings, all darkened by shadow. One depicts an urban setting, the other
a sort of fortress, including battlements. One has opposed urban rooflines, the other
fortified walls. Both are cropped abruptly at about 45 degrees, compressed beneath the
top of the picture plane. These shallow settings seem to offer refuge to occupants (of
Noon) and potential occupants (of the *Theatrum orbi*), as well as the option of entering either a catacomb of secret warrens (backstage / deep shadow) or shallow, utterly
exposed public space (center stage / bright sunlight).

Figures might fill openings in the walls away from center stage, but they are secured—as by the obscuring outer layer of Fludd's geomantic dots—by the boundaries
of the spectators' visual perception. Perimeter walls have already been breached in both
instances: "real" Huguenot fortress walls by siege in the early seventeenth-century
image; figurative nativist walls that protected "fortress" England from unwanted (but
needed) aliens in the early eighteenth-century image. Still, security inside remains
available to both sets of furtive refugee artisans who manipulate shadows in the international theater of perception. Even as both experienced and inexperienced spectators
engage in the practice of observation, the logic of these images enables shadow actors
hidden "offstage" to mirror spectatorship and survey transactions taking place in the
light. The spectating public is itself caught in the act; the public observer is observed
clandestinely. Neoplatonic and occult dialogues between the hidden and revealed of
the macrocosm and microcosm animate Fludd's "De geomantia," tacitly implying
powerful invisible presences and experiences despite the absence of figures appearing
openly on stage in "the world." Oblique themes of hiding for refuge and security—a
sort of natural-philosophical weapon to retrieve memory or obtain other useful knowledge—are ramified by the aggressive display of rough-hewn stones used to build the
walls of the *Theatrum orbi*.

Common in fortress construction since ancient times, such blocks are nevertheless
remarkably similar in size and shape to those used to fashion the famous limestone
walls of La Rochelle, which had already endured more than one unsuccessful siege by
1620. The visually opaque, impenetrable nature of these stone blocks may be quoted
in *Noon*'s background in the generic shape of Soho's densely packed windows, which
indicate that Hogarth may have read refugee homes as "blocked" in shadow. As a
Paracelsian physician in search of experience, John Winthrop Jr. may well have imag-

ined witnessing the invasion and fall of La Rochelle and the creation of international Protestantism through its destruction, as a variant of Fludd's *Enemies Invading the Fortress of Health* (1629–31) (fig. 10.8). Did the refugee de Bry's seemingly abandoned *Theatrum orbi* infer that once the walls were breached, the dispersion of refugees into the Atlantic world would ultimately revive the dead and fragmented fortress, transforming it into an international memory theater? If so, the fortress was carried in memory; following Palissy's "simple artisan," and ultimately Hogarth's "tradesman," this was especially true in the art and mystery of craft memory.

The appearance of the Fludd–de Bry *Theatrum orbi* in Oppenheim in 1620, and its reappearance on London's Hog Lane in 1736, suggests that both Flood and Hogarth actively reconsidered Palissy's pivotal questions about the fate of the Saintongeais reformation without La Rochelle in particular, and of fortress culture in general. How would communal security, lost after Louis XIII's reduction of the stone walls of the Huguenot fortress, be reconstituted in the refugee artisans' atomized New World? By what "art and mystery," practiced in the shadows for display on stage, can the hidden artisan amplify his diminished status in the light?

Begin with Hogarth's use of the mysterious and idiosyncratic Fludd–de Bry masonry arch. Consider the pair of plain arches floating behind the *Theatrum orbi's* crenellated balcony on either side of the overhanging turret. Unlike the walls below the battlements, which are laid in stone, the arches are set into walls above the battlements laid in a Flemish bond similar to the walls of Hogarth's Huguenot church. These arches are both blocked at bottom by a single battlement and so are only partially visible. Yet they, too, are clearly framed by a brick course laid in alternating Flemish bond, while the two stone arches at stage level are not. Hogarth's extensive quotation of Fludd's "De geomantia," makes it logical that Hogarth should also include the floating, half-visible arch on the Eglise des Grecs, which, like the walls, is laid in Flemish bond. The sturdy narrow arch built of plain brick on the Marot–de Bèze title-page emblem, which identifies individual Huguenot martyrs with the universal memory of Christ's martyrdom and patient suffering on the cross, merges with the similarly plain brick arches engraved on the fortress of memory. Jesus' absence and millennial return is fundamentally present in Fludd's magico-religious *Theater*, hidden inside the half-seen shadow images in eschatological waiting for the opportune moment to reappear on center stage.

Alternative readings also present themselves. Fludd's strong association with the early mythology of Rosicrucianism in England was well known to Hogarth. His use of Fludd in *Noon* harnessed the seventeenth-century natural philosopher to Hogarth's position in debates over forms of public discourse used by British Freemasonry, a problem that has been discussed thoroughly elsewhere.[72] Popular historical narratives contended that there was a formative relationship between the two secret societies, which shared artisanal symbol systems based on tools and were both connected to ideals of universal learning. Yates, Margaret C. Jacob, and Hillel Schwartz, have, of course, shown the close relationship of individuals and narratives at the center of the Freemason movement with French refugee communities in urban England, Holland, Germany and colonial America.[73]

Exorbitant displays of the foundational components of the art of masonry—which stand out in the otherwise plain construction of the Fludd–de Bry and Hogarth arches—suggest metaphysical meanings beyond the built architecture of "operative" masonry. Displays of stone and ceramic building blocks of operative masonry here merged seamlessly with the "speculative" architecture of Rosicrucianism, including Fludd's reading of the art of memory and, by extension, Hogarth's vision of a street language for Freemasonry. We are also reminded of the subterranean "vault" of Rosicrucianism constructed with walls, a ceiling and floor, and perhaps Elias Neau's prison "furnace" as well; all of which, we have seen, was adapted to the Saintongeais folkloric tradition.

The mythological narrative of the Rosicrucian arch was also syncretized with the dominant Masonic symbolism of eighteenth-century "Royal Arch" masonry. For Yates, these outsized "royal" arches, each encompassing a secret yet rigidly prescribed language of columns, geometrical figures, and emblems, merged long-standing Christian and occult traditions—as well as the tradition of occult memory—to comprise a synthetic mythology of the mystical arch. The mythology of the arch, shared in common by these two secret societies, bridged the narrative "gap" between the submergence of Rosicrucianism as an active discourse with the end of the civil wars of religion, and Freemasonry's lodge records and written histories, which first began to appear in the early eighteenth century.[74]

Hogarth quotes other passages from Fludd's memory theater in tandem with his reading of "De geomantia." Both Fludd (charting "terrestrial astrology" with geomantic dots) and Hogarth (mapping a "masonry" ground built with rough-hewn cobblestones resembling the theater's walls) require scrutiny of obscure street languages located virtually on the ground, where the rules of social grammar are represented in geometrical form. Fludd's *Theatrum orbi* complicates the composition of the ground by picturing base marks or sites for the construction of architectural columns of differing profiles. Yet, if taken literally, these, too, are subject to multiple readings as floating two-dimensional forms and could also signify openings to subterranean worlds— or perhaps Fludd's stage marks. Did Hogarth position his polite threesome underneath the Huguenot sign as a sort of human column between microcosm and macrocosm, deployed around the pattern set by geometric templates? (Indeed, the diamond, stage right—also fronting an arch, as on Hog Lane—seems plausible for this strategy.) Geometric forms mapping the floor include circles, diamonds, and a central hexagon (the latter two reducible to the science of triangles)—all of which also give form to Fludd's cosmologies. Circles and diamonds are repeated on the balcony; circles alone on the battlements that obscure the arches.

Recall the outsized circular window that hovers above the door of the Eglise des Grecs. The church door itself is squared about a third of the way down from the lintel by a "line" bisected by the head of Minister Herve at center, and bracketed behind each of his shoulders by the heads of two anonymous Huguenot congregants. Taken together, the circular window, in deep shadow, relates less to the door than specifically to its half-seen companion, the equally shadowy Fluddian floating arch. The front façade of the Huguenot church exhibits the three quintessential forms of Fludd's memory theater: the arch, the circle, and the square, all cloaked in Giordano Bruno's shadow of memory.

And if the arch had a venerable history as a symbol of refuge ranging from the title page of a civil war Huguenot Psalter to a central place in the elaborate symbolic vocabulary of early modern Rosicrucianism and Freemasonry, then the context from which *Noon* was constructed also attached very specific Fluddian meanings to the Renaissance conjunction of the Vitruvian circle and square, already seen at work in Edward Howes's pictograph naming John Winthrop Jr. the adept of the New World (fig. 10.1). Given Hogarth's high status among London's freemasons, and taking evidence that he performed a close reading and pictorial reimaging of Fludd's *Theater of the World* into consideration, these were meanings that Hogarth would have known and manipulated for public consumption and private Masonic ritual.

For example, in volume 2 of *Utriusque cosmi . . . historia*,[75] Fludd uses the circle and square to propose a binary structure for "the science of spiritual memorising which is vulgarly called *Ars Memoriae*." He defines two distinctive forms of this spiritual art, which he calls the "round art" (*ars rotunda*) and the "square art" (*ars quadrata*). These are the only forms in which the art of memory can be practiced. The "round art," produced by inspired imagination, is simultaneously magic and "fantasy." Somewhat like the geomantic *mens*, round art operates "through ideas, which are forms separated from corporeal things." However, like *mens*, these ideas can nevertheless interact with corporeal things. In effect, the round art of memory functions outside the limits of common perception, through the intercession of hidden "things, such as":

> spirits, shadows (*umbrae*), souls and so on, also angels . . . we . . . use this word "ideas" . . . for anything that is not composed of the four elements, that is to say for things spiritual and simple conceived in the imagination; for example angels, demons, the effigies of stars, the images of gods and goddesses to whom celestial powers are attributed and which partake more of a spiritual than of a corporeal nature; similarly virtues and vices conceived in the imagination and made into shadows, which were also to be held as demons.[76]

While the shadow discourse originated with Bruno's writings, Fludd's "spiritual" and intellectual task was to reintegrate them into reformed Christian natural philosophy by sanitizing the Italian's memory systems for consumption by international Protestantism.[77] Ultimately, the task of reintegration proved more manageable for Fludd than for the Roman authorities. When Rome decided that Bruno's pre-Christian and ancient Egyptian occult philosophies, and above all his high-profile publications and volubility, were no longer possible to ignore, he was lured back to Italy and executed by the Inquisition.

Of particular concern for our purposes, however, is Bruno's influential sojourn in Elizabethan England (1583–85). During this period, Bruno produced a gigantic book on magical emblemata, which he called the "seals" of memory.[78] Yet the loquacious Bruno found ample time to alienate politically connected English Ramists and scandalize important Calvinist churchmen. Both groups thought his discourses on memory were the centerpiece of a dangerously foreign (read Roman) medieval revival, thought by some alarmed Puritans to infect English natural philosophers like a virus. Bruno's fiercely polemical university lectures on figuration of magical memory, which privileged the vitalism of nature and the creative force of the personal imagination above abstract logic and written texts (two elements that alienated English listeners), may have received a warmer reception by Saintongeais refugees.[79]

Stuart rehabilitation of original Christian and Trinitarian forms of the Paracelsian natural-philosophical tradition was nevertheless inspired by Fludd's universalist response to the wars of religion on the Continent. While Fludd and de Bry readily adapted Bruno's theory of the shadows into their memory system for displaced survivors of the apocalyptic French wars of religion and the Thirty Years' War, Fludd's reading of the Italian's dangerous "medieval" paganism was domesticated by the work of John Dee. Neoplatonic and Paracelsian explanations of ancient hermetic mysteries informed Dee's *Monas hieroglyphica* (Winthrop's ex libris sign), and the *Monas*—as well as Fludd's own reading of Ficino and Paracelsus—influenced his Christian revision of Bruno's art of memory.[80] Hence, Fludd's discourse of "angels" and "demons," his belief in the occult power of the Holy Spirit, and the Trinity's role in the "spiritual" art of memory. Fludd's Christian revision of Bruno's hermetic philosophy was continued by Hogarth as well. Signs of Huguenot Protestant worship and specters of Trinitarianism placed on Hog Lane are agents of coherence and geomantic unity behind the appearance of fragmentation and chaos.

Therefore, if the "round art" consisted of magical "ideas" that operated exclusively in the "shadows," then the "square art" was practiced with "images" of things seen whole. The "square art" was thus concerned with memory images embodied in aspects of the corporeal world. The corporeal included people and animals, but also inanimate objects of all kinds. Fludd intended the "square art" primarily for common folk interested in the ordinary practice of memory. Of the two types of memory, the square was inferior, fit for practitioners with relatively "inexperienced" imaginations. "Square art" was deemed inferior because it used artificial memory places and images that stood out in the man-made environment. The "round art" was superior because it was "natural," and—like Palissy's "rustique fugulines"—blended invisibly into the chaos of the microcosm. Infinitely more difficult than ordinary memory, the construction of memory theaters from the "round art" could only be practiced by the "experienced."

Fludd's distinctions between artificial and natural memory were clearly drawn from the same Paracelsian framework as was Palissy's discourse on artificial and natural artisanry. Palissy was living in Paris and probably encountered Bruno in natural-philosophical or court circles after the Italian arrived for a two-year stay beginning in 1581, but the timing of Bruno's arrival postdates the potter's last known publication in 1580, so evidence of influence is unavailable. For more direct links to the potter's knowledge of memory theaters, we must look again to Jacques Gohorry, founder of Paris's influential medico-magical academy and its near neighbor, Baif's Academy of Poetry and Music.

Gohorry's academy disbanded in 1576, five years before Bruno arrived in Paris. However, in *De usu & mysteriis notarium liber* (Paris, 1550), Gohorry described the great "wooden amphitheater" of memory Guilio Camillo built for François I. Camillo's influential amphitheater was paradigmatic for Bruno and Fludd, as well as for most early modern practitioners of the art.[81] Prints and descriptions of Camillo's memory theater were widely diffused throughout France and England, and Gohorry's description of this marvel almost certainly influenced Palissy's own discourse on the rustic amphitheater of refuge and contemplation for Saintongeais Huguenots. The circular form of Palissy's amphitheater had both cosmological and elemental overtones (as did the "art of the earth"), but the memory function of the amphitheater may also have been a corollary to the potter's elaborate ceramic plateaux, which served as naturalistic habitats; "invisible" places where tiny "rustique figulines" could hide and safely endure the ordeal of their alchemical, Christian and Ovidian metamorphoses. Were Palissy's basins and the cosmic forms made by followers used by patrons who practiced the "square art"?

So far as the "round art" was concerned, Fludd followed Bruno closely in his claim that shadow images were naturally recessive. But corporeal images of people and animals must be overt, lively, and active to transcend inanimate status; obviously. Eye-catching images were remembered best in the "square art." Thus, Bruno and his international cadre of followers thought the human figure could be useful in a memory system, but only if arrayed hyperbolically in astonishingly beautiful or (its mirror image) utterly ridiculous poses.[82] It followed that Hogarth saw the potential to create an inverse dialogue between these two arts of memory in *Noon*.

Hogarth, as England's master of the *outré*, clearly relished creating the two groups of strikingly theatrical consumers, mirrored in the light of Hog Lane's foreground, to fill Fludd's corporeal roles. By joining circle and square to form another sort of Huguenot arch out of the doorway of the Eglise des Grecs, Hogarth announces covertly to the experienced spectator that a synthesis of both *ars rotunda* and *ars quadrata* was quietly at work in the memories of its congregants.

Etymological questions present themselves here: how did early seventeenth-century readers name the memory theater's conspicuous and pronounced architectural features? What would audiences call the mysterious cantilevered projection hovering ambiguously at the upper center of the back wall, jutting above the battlements; its pendant drop coming to rest like the nib of a scribe's pen, above the joint of the double door? Trapezoidal in form when viewed frontally, extending on top into a similarly trapezoidal hipped roof, and supported by a circular gadrooned foundation, this curved and faceted projection—like the window over the door on the Eglise des Grecs—is basically circular and squared simultaneously.[83]

Arched openings again appear in deep shadow. To punctuate related themes, Fludd puns on geometry in his title, THEATRUM ORBI, written on a placard (another hanging sign), attached to the front. "Theater of the World" (*orbis*) reads as architecture and astrology; that is to say, as "Theater of the Circle" (or of the "rotation" of the world). Yates suggests a plural reading here as well; hence, a "Theater of the World(s)." This translation implies a space of magical lucidity where microcosm and macrocosm interact in "round" memory. The word *theatrum* translates literally as "theater," but also generically any place where action transpires and is observed (standard reference is usually made to the Roman forum). Therefore it is logical to infer Fludd's cosmological sense of "Action of the Circle" on man in the microcosm, as for Edward Howes, and that "the squaring of the circle lies in the perpetuity of motion" (fig. 10.1).

In Fluddian contexts, circles and squares synthesized opposed geometric and, by extension, philosophical forms. Some trapezoidal architectural forms were therefore meaningful. Trapezoidal meanings were thus dualistic, ambiguous, and contingent on experience and practice. In Fludd's cosmologies of the microcosmic arts and crafts of man, trapezoids tend to function as geometric signifiers of the potential for a universal monism; that is, for Neoplatonic sexual *conjunctio* of the dyadic cosmos through Paracelsian natural-philosophical or artisanal practice. This included construction and use of memory theaters.

Medieval builders standardized such trapezoidal projections, adapting them to fit multiple contexts. Is this a theatrical prop seen anchoring Fludd's *Theatrum orbi*, part

FIGURE 14.18. Léonard de la Reau, architect, Hôtel de Ville, La Rochelle, ca. 1544. The left pavilion of this courtyarded public building, fortified like its city, has the requirements of an ideal memory theater. The stair to the left of the bell tower is part of a nineteenth-century addition.

of a forgotten or lost fortification, or a species of pulpit (called a minister's "desk" and scriptorium in the period)? Clues may again be found in Neoplatonic protections medieval church builders sought in use of the hexagon; for what is the overhang if the hidden part in back is considered only a six-sided form?[84] This particular overhang is clearly part of a theater. Fludd tells us so on the placard. On one level then, it functioned in a theatrical mise en scène. But the theater was also a self-contained fortress of memory, part of an internalized arsenal—carried in the form of a book or already memorized as a "system"—newly available in the late sixteenth century for transport along with the mobile New World cultures of international Protestantism. In a fortress, Fludd's overhang most closely resembled watchtowers or lookouts built into the walls. The French word was *échauguette,* literally "troop guard," also a kind of fire watch (for the sentry's use of a torch to signal other *échauguettes* down the line), and they were essential to protect vulnerable individual soldiers who operated as warning scouts.

The man in the *échauguette* occupied the most liminal and exposed spot in a fixed fortress culture. This was defined by the limits of the walls (were "lookouts" standing

FIGURE 14.19. Seal of La Rochelle attached to a document dated 1437. The counterseal represents a knight on horseback wielding his weapon. Document conservé au Centre historique des Archives nationales, Atelier de photographie, sceau D/5459/B. La Rochelle was simultaneously the *noblesse d'épée* fortress par excellence and a great naval and mercantile power.

inside or outside, or within the fabric of the walls?). As such, these were thresholds related to closed doors. Even a simple comparison shows that an *échauguette* (fig. 14.20) served as de Bry's model for the memory theater's fortified central architectural element, where the theater's universal sign was placed.

When Louis XIII commanded that La Rochelle's walls be razed in 1628, hundreds of *échauguettes* went down with them. Only the three enormous watch and bell towers still stand guard over the inner harbor. The sixteenth-century interior court of the Hôtel de Ville, with its fortress of memorylike theatrical space (fig. 14.18), still stands guard over what remains inside the old city itself. The Hôtel was indeed an ideal site for a memory theater, and it was undoubtedly used as such by readers of Gohorry, Bruno, and Fludd. We know Bruno and Fludd traveled the cities of Europe to "collect" in their memory the images contained in such idiosyncratically packed urban places. They direct novices to acquire similar experiences in their books. Imagine refu-

FIGURE 14.20. Sixteenth-century *échauguette* at Brouage. Photo, Nicolas Faucherre.

gees traveling from city to city to practice their urban trades, absorbing famous memory sites along the way.

La Rochelle's Hôtel de Ville's enclosed and arcaded courtyard is densely crowded with discreetly framed niches. Most niches were built to contain statues and plaques related to the fortress's long and contested history. Taken as a whole, the courtyard's discourse confirmed and continually asserted La Rochelle's ancient privileges according to the town's master narrative of its history. While the niches claim fealty to the crown, at the same time, as Charles IX witnessed contemptuously in 1565 and Louis XIII finally reversed in 1628, these same images reiterated La Rochelle's sense of autonomy. The ship carved into the arch at the Hôtel's entrance, as well as the city's *jetons* (fig. 14.19), and not the crown, was the real source of La Rochelle's communal memory and identity in commerce with the Atlantic world.

Unlike La Rochelle, its bitter rival to the north before 1628, the relatively modest ramparts of Brouage are still extant. The little fortress guards the Bay of Biscay from what was a dominant port for seventeenth-century Saintonge's most valuable, productive, and historically contested stretch of coastal *marais*. Brouage's fortifications survive because they were reinforced in 1630, with funds provided by Richelieu himself, after he had made certain La Rochelle's were razed two years earlier. This renovation campaign reflected Richelieu's vast financial interests in the region's salt production. He envisioned Brouage as a transatlantic entrepôt for the state in a oncemighty Huguenot region. Richelieu's investment in Brouage left twenty-two stone *échauguettes* (fig. 14.20) to guard its walls. Some predate 1630; most still resemble the "lookout" on Fludd's *Theatrum orbi.*[85]

Surviving *échauguettes* are small fortified spaces. Like a knight's oversized, armored close helmet, they have with enough room available for a single soldier to stand, take cover inside, and scan the flat marshlands with his weapon in hand. Unlike the Fludd-

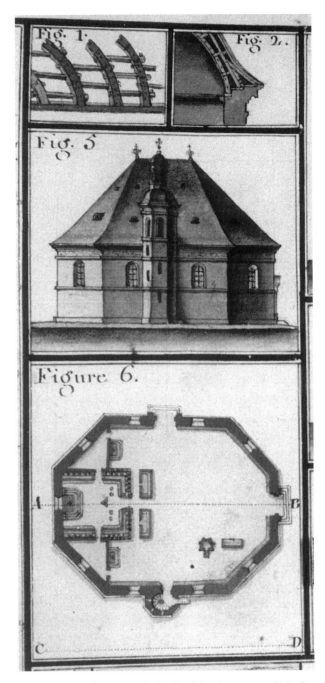

FIGURE 14.21. Claude Masse (1650?–1737), detail of the *Coupe et profil du Grand Temple de La Rochelle*, La Rochelle, ca. 1717. Courtesy Bibliothèque municipale de La Rochelle, and by permission of the Archives historiques de la marine, Vincennes. Photo, Neil Kamil. This engraving from Masse's original drawing shows the famous hexagonal plan of the Protestant Grand Temple and its tower. The temple was built through the war years of the late sixteenth century. It was founded in 1600, converted to a Catholic church by Richelieu himself in 1628, burned in 1687, and finally demolished in 1689.

de Bry *échauguette* with its large ocular openings, most have extremely small openings—usually gothic arches or mere slits in the stone—from which to survey surreptitiously and fire a weapon. The function of the *échauguette,* then, was twofold: first to provide cover for surveillance over a specific stretch of fortress wall and also a point of triangulation between a neighboring *échauguette* and the enemy in the distance; second, to provide an elevated fortified platform from which to shoot in the event of a siege. These were primarily stealthy and defensive functions, but *échauguettes* were also meant to warn outsiders that the fortress was not blind and that intruders were always being watched at a safe distance from "inside" the walls. It was well known that sentinels were capable of sending withering crossfire down into the ranks of enemies who approached their defensive positions.

Variations on trapezoidal themes are evident in Reformation ecclesiastical architecture and interiors. The Grand Temple de La Rochelle (fig. 14.21) was begun in 1569, reconsecrated as a Catholic church in 1628, and destroyed by an arson fire in 1687. The temple was built "in the round." It was actually hexagonal (two opposing trapezoids), with a freestanding hexagonal tower attached to the façade opposite the front door with a design similar to the Fludd *échauguette.* Commenced just four years after Charles IX's visit during the most contentious period of the civil wars, the Grand Temple represented La Rochelle's Calvinist consistory at the height of its militancy. With its heavy limestone foundation climbing nearly halfway up the façade and an overall appearance of armored resistance, the temple was perceived by Huguenots and Catholics alike as a virtual fortress of the Reformed Word. In fact, many reformed meeting houses were heavily fortified against attack, in both Europe and America.[86]

Most Calvinist temples posed a visual dialogue between the architecture and the interior. This was particularly true of the minister's pulpit. The Grand Temple's pulpit does not survive, but a sense of its form can be gleaned from the hexagonal tower, paintings of the interior of the other Protestant temples, and from surviving seventeenth-century Calvinist pulpits. A Netherlandish pulpit (or *predickstoel*), with a high arcaded façade found on early Dutch woodwork, survives from New York's colonial period (fig. 14.22), and is still used at the First Church of Albany. To compare this form to the memory theater's *échauguette* is plausible. Especially striking is Fludd's use of the open door directly underneath the edifice itself. An open door is made clearly visible at the base of the Grand Temple tower as well. The bounded sacred space of a seventeenth-century Protestant pulpit was commonly entered by the minister from below, usually through a door placed somewhere in the lower section. He then ascended the pulpit to confront the sacred text on the scriptorium, at the "desk." Unlike the Albany pulpit (which has been altered), but like the memory theater, many pulpits were covered. Additionally, the surviving portable pulpits used by fugitive predicants of the assemblies of the *désert* exhibit both of these important features (fig. 14.23). Did the

FIGURE 14.22. Pulpit of the First Church in Albany, New York. Amsterdam, 1656–57. Oak. Courtesy First Church in Albany. Photo, Robert S. Alexander. The sounding board originally suspended above the Dutch Reformed minister's head and the spiral staircase by which he entered the pulpit have been removed. The pedestal was made by Tiffany Studios in the 1920s, when the chancel was remodeled, to replace the much higher original. The pulpit was received as gift from supporters in Amsterdam and arrived in Albany in August 1657.

FIGURE 14.23. *Désert* pulpit, possibly from the Poitou region, ca. 1690–1720. Various woods, iron rods, nuts and bolts. Courtesy Musée protestant de La Rochelle. This pulpit was built for portability, a basic requirement of life for heretics in the *désert,* especially after 1685. Although over six feet high, it can be broken down quickly into a box the size of a suitcase for transport. The minister could exit from a secret door in the back.

theater's double door "double" the form of an open book, to underscore Fludd's re-formed program of re-Christianization of the art of memory?

Just as doorways in the *Theatrum orbi* defined the metaphorical boundaries of coming and going, Fludd's practice of "spiritual" memory in the seventeenth-century Protestant world began and ended with experience of the living Word, now, along with artisanal skill, the refugee's only real security against the enemies of faith, both internal (soul) and external (body). A painter's adaptation of graphic sources to his own work is seldom as exact as historians might wish. Nevertheless, imagine Hogarth's elderly Huguenot lady (in possession of the Marot–de Bèze Psalter) magically transported from Hog Lane to the *Theatrum orbi.* Once there, were she to take a congruent position under the arch on the left (in the corner where the back of stage right and the wall join at right angles), she could look up at the back wall toward the *échauguette.* From there she could perceive a portion of the arch in the *Theatrum orbi* to her left in about the same position as the church's arch. At the angle where she stood and her closeness to the wall, her line of vision at its highest point would allow her to see merely the pendant drop hanging down from the turret. Here—with minor changes in drawing to adapt de Bry's mannerist pendant to Fludd's geomantic escutcheon and Hogarth's line of beauty—is yet another apparition of the Huguenot backward sign.

These congruities are not merely formal. Taken together with Fludd's essay on geomancy, Hogarth grafted *Noon* onto the structure of Fludd's memory theater to associate Soho's Huguenot artisanal experience with the Fludd–de Bry natural-philosophical tradition. Because of Hogarth's initiation into the art and mystery of his trade by French artisans from that neighborhood—an initiation amplified by his activities as a Freemason—he claimed a filial association. Thus, Hogarth revealed indirectly how fragments of Palissian artisanal memory were still maintained and operated by the "future and present" craftsmen of Huguenot London.

Transatlantic Memory Furniture: Palissy and Hugh Platt

According to Fludd's thesis, fragments of memory were stored by inventing an orderly inventory of "memory places." Images of memorable things are then systematically stored in these places, until ultimately recalled by the eye of imagination (see fig. 14.17) to the first of the brain's three ventricles of consciousness and revisited. The *Theatrum orbi,* with its hidden arches, doors, windows, columns, segmented floor and interstitial spaces, was the ideal warehouse of memory places. Palissy's artisanry also showed how a specific thing made by a pious craftsman functioned as a sort of Huguenot memory theater. And while Palissy's written work on memory was indirect and unsystematic (if compared with Bruno's and Fludd's), his discourses on personal experience in the amphitheater of refuge and the function of his naturalistic grottos are strongly suggestive of this tradition. *Jewell-house of Art and Nature* (1594), Hugh Platt's immensely popular book of secrets—and, as the author readily admitted, a more or less direct translation of Palissy's *Discours admirables*—shows Palissy's influence on this subject in England as well. Platt's *Jewell-house* of instructions on building with natural materials was so popular among seventeenth-century rustic natural philosophers that in the 1630s, Howes and Winthrop corresponded more frequently about it than any other specific title.[87] The potter's English translator and interlocutor followed the philosophical lead of his Huguenot artisan—addressed as "Master Bernard" in his text— to bridge the brief chronological gap between Palissy and Fludd. The *Jewell-house* predated Fludd's earliest publication (1617) by only a few years, but emerged from the same occult tradition. Platt may well have influenced Fludd, learning the "Art of memorie which master Dickson the Scot did teach of Late yeres in England, and whereof he hath written a figurative and obscure treatise, set downe briefly and in plaine termes according to his owne demonstration, with especiall uses thereof."[88]

Here Platt refers to Alexander Dicson, a Scottish apologist and popularizer of Giordano Bruno, whose *De umbris idearum* (The Shadow of the Idea; 1582) formed the theoretical basis of Fludd's *Theatrum orbi*. Just as Platt imitated Palissy, Dicson did Bruno. Possessing the invaluable ability to communicate "briefly and in plaine termes" Bruno's "figurative and obscure" ideas about shadowed memories, Dicson fit well into Platt's commercial project in the book-of-secrets tradition. With only minor modifications and self-promoting commentary, Platt passed Dicson's "plain" translation of Bruno's secrets along to practical-minded readers. Included among these were the adept John Winthrop Jr. and Edward Howes. Howes, much to Winthrop's repeatedly expressed displeasure, was never able to please his friend and "write plain," because of his innate fear of revealing secrets to the public.

Unlike Howes who operated in utter obscurity, both Dicson and Platt created natural-philosophical careers by virtue of ability to perform in public. Platt's first encounter with Dicson's work was the result of a closely watched debate that occurred some ten years before publication of *Jewell-house*. The Scot burst onto London's scientific scene in 1584 during a high-stakes religious controversy over the theological status of Bruno's memory system. In its wake, Dicson made his name by publishing a vigorous defense of Bruno's occultism against the Cambridge Ramist William Perkins (idol of Ezra Stiles).[89] Like Palissy and other Paracelsians who chose—for economic and philosophical reasons—to perform experiments in public, Dicson had "his owne demonstration" to prove the merits of Bruno's system in practice.

Platt also offered similar demonstrations, though (turning shamelessly on his intellectual benefactor) he claimed that these were given "freely," while Dicson's were performed for substantial sums of cash in what was a competitive market in memory systems. Platt marketed his method as a facilitator in table talk. This was a skill known to increase prospects for Stuart courtiers like Platt who, "would discharge . . . the *re-membrance* of all such pleasant tales and histories as shall passe in table talke, from con-ceipted wits." Platt moralized however, that this powerful "invention" was wasted by certain baneful practitioners for "meere craft and cousenage." Cleverly targeting the competition, the resourceful Platt planted the seed of illicit profit: "Maister Dick-son['s] . . . schollers . . . have proved such cunning Card-players heereby, that they coulde tell the whole course of the Cardes, and what every gamester had in his hand."[90]

Platt's largesse in foregoing his demonstration fee may also have been conditional. His generosity seems to have been limited to secrets "disclosed alreadie . . . by any publique impression," to imply that further instruction was available to patrons who had a copy of his book in their possession. If a "scholler" arrived at Platt's laboratory empty-handed, a book would be provided at the usual price. Platt, then, never hesi-tated to advertise firsthand experience (and promote the sale of his book) at Dicson's expense. *Jewell-house* "censored" Dicson's laboratory demonstrations (using French terms, following Palissy's dialogue structure) as too "Theorique," and insufficiently "practique." Neither were they "plaine" or "manuel" enough for "my Country men." They were also costly, Platt claimed, since students paid mostly for an intentionally mystifying performance of "that great and swelling Arte":

> Behold heere that great and swelling Arte, for which Maister Dickson did usually take of every Scholler twentie shillings, making one whole Moneths discourse of the Theorique part thereof, but in the practique hee coulde scarcely tell which way to bestowe a full houre in demonstration . . . I have often exercised this Art for the better part of mine owne memorie, and the same hath never failed mee. . . . And if there be any that doe either make doubt of this art, or shall think I have dealt too compendiouslie in so large a Sub-ject, I will according to my ancient promise, be at al times readie, and that freely, as well in this as in any other secret which I have disclosed already, or shal hereafter by any publique impression disclose unto my Countrey men, be readie to manifest the same by plaine tearmes, or manuel demonstration, to their best contentment.[91]

Yates dismisses Platt's insistence on a "plaine" reading of Dicson's reading of the metaphorical and occult Bruno as naïve, inasmuch as he "seems to have been taught a simple form of the straight mnemotechnic which he did not know was a classical art but thought was 'Maister Dickson's art'. He was evidently not initiated into Hermetic mysteries."[92] Given Palissy's influence however, it would be a great mistake to conclude that Platt misunderstood the classical foundations of "that great and swelling Arte." Platt privileged experiential, "manuel" metaphysics practiced by the Huguenot potter he called "Master," so, like Palissy, he consistently reinterpreted the dubious wisdom of "the ancients." Thus, he reduced "great and swelling" classical and hermetic mysteries to fit into a "simple artisan['s]" quotidian sphere, one filled with *mobilier:* small, moveable containers of information about the past.

We have seen Palissy's natural philosophy privilege "simple form[s]" which, after much labor and voyaging were discovered in familiar places close to home. Diminutive forms were known to conceal Nature's greatest mysteries and fecund processes of continuous reproduction. Palissy's simple artisans of the earth and Fludd's primitive ape of nature also labored to reproduce them through the Neoplatonic transmutation and recombination of spirit and matter. Following Palissy's artisanal philosophy of the small and using the discourse of the worshipful apprentice, Platt's book further domesticated the "Art of memorie," providing readers with detailed instructions on mapping secret memory places in intimate spaces made available by practical household goods and artifacts. "Familiar," concrete things taken from the everyday life world of the household, were "animate[d]" deep in shadow, and transformed into personal containers for "subjects" (as Platt called them) of historical contemplation and discourse:

> You must make choice of . . . Chambers or Galleries . . . so familiar unto you, as that everie part of each of them may present it selfe readily unto the eyes of your minde when you call for them. In everie of these roomes you must place . . . severall subjectes at a reasonable distaunce one from the other, least the neerenesse of their placing should happen to confound your Memorie. . . . These subjectes would be such as are most apt either to bee agents or patients [active or passive subjects], uppon whatsoever you shall have cause to place in them. And therefore a fire, a Dunghill, a Carte, a paire of Bellowes, a Tubbe of water, an Ape, a Shippe, a night-gowne, a Milstone, and such like, are apt to make your subjects of, wherein you may place all such things as you woulde remember, and as Maister Dickson tearmed it, to animate the *umbras* [shadows]. . . . But heerin everie man may best please his owne witte and memorie . . . your Bed-steed . . . at the head whereof, you maie by a strong imagination place an extreeme burning fire, and at the feete thereof a smoaking Dunghill. In your Chimney . . . you maie imagine a Tubbe full of water. . . . Then upon your court Cubbarde, you may place an Ape with her clogge.[93] . . . Upon your Chaire you may imagine a night-gowne furred with Foxe skinne, having wide sleeves, and great pockets belonging to the same. Then uppon your Table standing in the middest of the roome, you may place a Milstone, or a Drumme, and in the top of the seeling [ceiling] over your Table, a Target, a sword, or a Lute hanging downwarde.[94]

By powerfully emphasizing the familiar and the real as three-dimensional grounds for containment of "a strong imagination" in the shadows, Platt's Palissian book of secrets served (along with John Dee's work on Paracelsus) as an important English precursor to Fludd's British-American domestication of Bruno's memory system. Fludd found balance and practicality in the "square art," even as Bruno's system was based primarily on the internal creation of a "speculative" architecture of the imagination. For Bruno, memory was nothing less than man's window onto "the *fabrica mundi,* the divine architecture of the world," and as such, "an object of religious veneration and a source of religious experience."[95] "He creates inwardly the vast forms of his cosmic imagination," Yates writes, in part responding to his historical context: "in the later sixteenth century, the more troubled age in which Bruno passed his life, the pressures of the times, both political and religious, may have been driving the 'secret' more and more underground."[96] Unlike the artisan Palissy and his followers, who, as we have seen responded to similar pressures by the material "externalization" of Huguenot secrets in the "art of the earth," Bruno:

> externalises these forms in literary creation. . . . Had he externalised in art the statues which he moulds in memory . . . a great artist would have appeared. But it was Bruno's mission to paint and mould within, to teach that the artist, the poet, and the philosopher are all one, for the Mother of the Muses is Memory. Nothing can come out but what has first formed within, and it is therefore within that the significant work is done. . . . With untiring industry he adds wheels to wheels, piles memory rooms on memory rooms. With endless toil he forms the innumerable images which are to stock the systems.[97]

Contrary to Bruno's internal method of adding "wheels to wheels" (but following Platt's popular book-of-secrets approach), Fludd argued firmly for practice of the square art, if for no other reason than the vast majority of potential practitioners were sure to be too inexperienced (and hence without sufficient imagination) to apply the more difficult round art. Yates found particular significance in what she called Fludd's "polemic against":

> the use of "fictitious places" in the square art. . . . "Real" places are real buildings of any kind used for forming places in the normal way in the mnemotechnic. "Fictitious" places are imaginary buildings or imaginary buildings of any kind which . . . might be invented if not enough real places were available . . . Fludd is very much against the use of "fictitious" buildings in the square art. These confuse memory and add to its task. One must always use real places in real buildings. "Some who are versed in this art wish to place their square art in palaces fabricated or erected by invention of the imagination; . . . this opinion is inconvenient. . . ." The buildings which Fludd will use in his memory system will be "real" buildings.[98]

In "real" buildings, Platt inventoried "familiar," overlooked articles of household furniture for use in his memory system—a bedstead, chair, and center table—and perhaps the most intriguing, a "court cupboard." This elaborate and still mysterious artifact was found on both sides of the Atlantic. In the colonies, the vast majority were made in New England, with two known survivals from the Chesapeake region. Because it was an elite form with unusually high survival rates for seventeenth-century domestic furniture, court cupboards have been studied extensively by furniture historians. They are customarily associated with the social, cultural and technological history of early New England family life, in part because of the unchallenged antiquarian status that such artifacts have acquired in the nineteenth century as signifiers par excellence of Calvinist filial piety. As such, court cupboards are usually associated with names of "founding" families that settled towns in both north and southeastern New England.

Genealogical priorities have fossilized these artifacts by obscuring contexts that might seem improbably exotic to modern sensibilities but help explain the puzzling ambiguity of the court cupboard's basic functions. Much scholarship has been devoted to court cupboards, but little of it has suggested why enormous amounts of scarce labor, capital, and interior space were expended by elites on outsized cupboards, most of which present a peculiarly arranged, inadequate, and indeed awkward storage capacity. Consider the well-known court cupboard carved with "P 1680 W," probably for Peter Woodbury (1640–1704) of Beverly, Massachusetts (fig. 14.24). The family history of this artifact is well documented; its anonymous makers are believed to have worked in either Ipswich or Newbury, in northern Essex County, Massachusetts.[99] If the Woodbury cupboard was made in Ipswich or Newbury in 1680, it was a form familiar to inhabitants of the same Massachusetts county where the younger Winthrop first settled in the colonies after he set out from Boston (it is dated just four years after his death). Indeed, some products of this shop have been associated with Winthrop through marriage. The furniture historian Robert Trent, a specialist in Essex County material culture, notes the identifying features of the surviving cupboards associated with this anonymous shop:

> The . . . cupboards . . . are among the most heavily constructed and ornamented cupboards to survive from seventeenth-century New England. Almost all have turned pillars in both top and bottom cases. Seven have trapezoidal storage areas in the upper cases, two have open shelves in the lower cases, eight have straight-fronted enclosed bottom cases with either drawers or storage areas with doors, and four have framed jetties or overhangs or overhangs resembling the framed jetties on houses. These complex compositions with many recessed stages and drawers make necessary heavy internal flooring to enclose the various areas, with the result that these cases are far heavier than most cupboards and must have been very expensive.[100]

Recent research has found precedent for these unusually constructed forms in sixteenth-century French court furniture and argues that this craft knowledge was also

FIGURE 14.24. Court cupboard, northern Essex County, Massachusetts, 1680. H: 57¾″,
W: 50″, D: 21⅝″. Red oak, maple, sycamore, and yellow poplar. Courtesy the Henry Francis du
Pont Winterthur Museum, Winterthur, Delaware. Carved with "P 1680 W," probably for
Peter Woodbury (1640–1704) of Beverly, Massachusetts. Robert Fludd's Theater of the World,
illustrated in figure 14.15, was available to the patron of this two-story structure with dramatic,
aggressively architectonic, overhanging jetties, and potential for hundreds of shadowy, com-
partmentalized places. This was precisely the sort of theatrical furniture that functioned as a
memory theater for colonial elites.

carried to England by Huguenot refugees. Still, if a retrospective taxonomy of form and construction based on high survival rates is achievable, Trent's insights into the court cupboard's original functions remain superficial and unsatisfying:

> While the ostensible function of cupboards was the storage of table linens and table gar-
> nitures like glasses, galley pots, and relish dishes, their actual purpose was ornamental.
> The shelves and top often served for the display of ceramics and silver, which were sel-
> dom used, and many cupboards have charred areas over the shelves, indicating that can-
> dlesticks were placed on them . . . the Woodbury inventory indicates . . . cupboards most
> often stood in rooms used for dining (generally speaking, the parlor), but they do appear
> listed in halls and in the best chambers of houses as well.[101]

Informed discussions of court cupboards derived from Trent's work do not extend beyond "ornamental" function. The exception is Laurel Ulrich's analysis of an early eighteenth-century cupboard, a late example of the form, thought to have been made in the area of Hadley, Massachusetts. Ulrich was drawn to write about this artifact by the painted inscription of "Hannah Barnard," a unique instance of a woman's name being displayed prominently on the cupboard's upper section (fig. 14.25).

While Ulrich's chief concern was the cupboard's function to identify, secure, and contain Hannah's marriage portion—mostly valuable textiles—and its discourse de-claring her ultimate right to control its legacy, in a larger sense, Ulrich also examines its place in personal and family memory. Ulrich does not attempt to treat this article of household furniture as a domestic container for the art of memory in the Fluddian sense of the "square art, wherein, perhaps, each block letter or part of a floral pattern might serve this function perfectly." Yet it may be argued that what she elucidated in-tuitively was, in fact, a superb example of an elaborate memory system formulated for a female consumer in the rustic Connecticut River Valley.[102] That the Hannah Barnard court cupboard contained a memory system that was directed toward family succes-sion in one of the few regions of colonial America where family economy was para-mount from the first generation on (and where court cupboards survive in quantity) is highly significant.

I say this because a comparison of the Woodbury cupboard with Fludd's "theater of the world" reveals striking similarities in form, and, I would argue, function. Trent's perfunctory description of function does reveal the cupboard's basic theatricality. At the same time, his very useful analysis of the outer form and interior technology of all the surviving artifacts from this group reveals the enormous effort expended on "heavy internal flooring" and exorbitantly complex "jetties or overhangs resembling the framed jetties on houses." Indeed, I would argue that the elevated, projecting, trape-zoidal "jetty or overhang" (or *échauguette*) on the fortresslike Woodbury cupboard, read in the context of its elaborate discourse of arches, doors, pillars, "many recessed stages

FIGURE 14.25. Court cupboard inscribed "Hannah Barnard," area of Hadley, Massachusetts, ca. 1715. H: 61⅛", W: 50", D: 21¼". Oak and yellow pine. From the collections of the Henry Ford Museum & Greenfield Village, Dearborn, Michigan. The block letters of Hannah's name dominate the memory places available on the upper section of the cupboard.

and drawers," resembling the *theatrum orbi*'s stone walls, and above all its idiosyncratic drop pendants, find their ultimate source in the back wall and side arcades of Fludd's "*theater of the world.*" Inasmuch as Platt revealed the secret of the court cupboard as an exemplary staging area for memory subjects as early as 1594, thus elevating its status as an elite household possession among colonial readers such as John Winthrop Jr., who was obsessively concerned with natural-philosophical memory far from the metropole, then it is logical that after the appearance of Fludd's immensely influential *Ars memoriae* in 1620, court cupboards were actively constructed in its image to serve as a domestic "theater of the world" in microcosm.

This also explains the enormous investment in this form by New England's landed families—the oligarchical "fathers of the towns"—who tried to maintain an iron grip on their families' control and possession of seventeenth-century transatlantic historical memory to maintain political and economic authority. Ulrich's analysis of Hannah Barnard's cupboard is thus all the more significant. While the association of women's names with chests and cupboards having "dowry" functions is fairly common south of New England—especially among Germanic pietists of the middle colonies and south—women's names appearing alone (without the husband's name or initials intertwined) are relatively uncommon on artifacts produced north of Long Island Sound.[103]

Much work remains to be done on memory furniture, but is it unreasonable to say Peter Woodbury's court cupboard satisfied the specific demands of both Platt's and the Fludd–de Bry version of Bruno's memory system? Consider also, that despite its impressive size and weight, the whole unit, as an article of furniture (not real property), was easily disassembled for transport from place to place. A portable fortress of memory made for mobile consumers, this artifact was useful in an international system that claimed universality, yet asserted a methodology that privileged the physical presence of "some large edifice or building."[104] Public structures fitting this grand description were to be found in central London, Amsterdam, and Frankfurt in 1680, but were unavailable in Woodbury's hometown of Beverly, or even Boston (with the exception of the defunct Triangular Warehouse). As in Platt's system (in resonance with the old Calvinist system of adapting domestic furniture for ecclesiastical use), the use of available furniture—a "center table" or "chair"—to animate the extensive system of shadows was arguably as common as there were readers of *Jewell-house.*

A luxury market for domestic memory places made especially to serve as altars for private contemplation and use seems to have accompanied Fludd's books to the New World by the 1630s as well. The small ceramic, metal, glass, and wood objects that were imported from the metropolis and made available for display on its tiers and inside its niches amplified the material discourse of the court cupboard's memory system. Indeed the de Bry family was among the influential publishers of images of densely packed grotesques, marvels, curiosities, and other exaggerated—outré, eye-catching, and memorable—designs used by artisans who made small household goods in the mannerist style (fig. 14.26, a, b).

This is not to make the claim that "mannerist" design originated in the universal call for memory images like the ones Bruno "created" out of his visual imagination. I

FIGURE 14.26. Details: (a), (b). Salt-glazed stoneware mug with applied decoration, possibly from Siegburg, Germany, inscribed "Jan Allers 1594." H: 4⅜", Diameter: 3". Private collection. Photo, Brian Cullity. Jan Allers—the surname suggests a French refugee background—worked in both Nijmegen and Culemburg in the Netherlands, where, in 1580, he began to trade in second-quality Rhenish stoneware. This name, therefore, represented a wholesale shipper, not a maker's mark. The distinctive frieze applied to the central panel was adapted from an engraving signed by Theodore de Bry (1528–98). The choice of the de Bry was specific to this German maker and Dutch wholesaler, since many different *Modellbücher* (pattern books) were more popular among Rhenish potters and just as easily available. (a) In a potter's joke, this naked forest figure, both exposed and vulnerable, carries a chamber pot rather than the open book plainly illustrated in the original pattern by de Bry. (b) She is threatened by a devil figure that emerges from a shell with fiery hair and a ferocious expression. This molded creature looks remarkably like images of the pope as Antichrist (without the emblematic spired hat) that poured out of Lutheran kilns up and down the Rhine. Meanwhile, a Palissian snail from de Bry's pattern edges along a volute of foliage to the lower right, as in figure I.1, undetected by his enemy. Quantities of similar Rhenish stonewares are commonly excavated from American archaeological sites. On Jan Allers, see David Gaimster, *German Stoneware, 1200–1900: Archaeology and Cultural History* (London: British Museum Press, 1997), 52, 149 (for ceramic images of the pope as Antichrist), 208–9, and 66; for an illustration of the pattern by Theodore de Bry, see Brian Cullity, *A Cubberd, Four Joyne Stools & Other Smalle Thinges* (Sandwich, Mass.: Heritage Plantation of Sandwich, 1994), 7, fig. 1; for further discussion of the Allers mug, see 69, fig. 58.

(a)

(b)

merely wish to propose a visual dialogue peculiar to the violent milieu of early modern life; the same naturalistic milieu that informed Ambroise Paré's book on monsters and marvels, *Des monstres et prodiges,* and the cabinets of curiosity associated with early modern explorers, colonizers, and natural philosophers. Here are Bruno's brief descriptions in *De umbris idearum* of a few "star images":

> First image of Saturn: A man with a stag's head on a dragon, with an owl which is eating a snake in his right hand.
>
> First image of Mercury: A beautiful young man with a sceptre, on which two serpents opposed to one another are entwined with their heads facing one another.
>
> First image of Luna: A horned woman riding on a dolphin; in her right hand a chameleon, in her left a lily.[105]

Seekers of memory images acquired objects in every material with similar motifs for display on court cupboards at home, following Fludd's recipe for the square art of memory. Fludd encouraged domestic consumption of an array of memory images for use in and around personal memory theaters by inventing an alphabetic and mathematical language based on common household forms ("Ordo alphabeticus rerum inanimatarum"; "Figurae rerum inanimatarum pro hac arte") or rustic carved and molded imagery ("Ordo characterum arithmeticorum in hac arte") (fig. 14.27). In this context, a high-backed upholstered armchair, much like the one illustrated in figure 15.9, might be used to recall the letter H, while a Palissian snake or snail stood in for the number

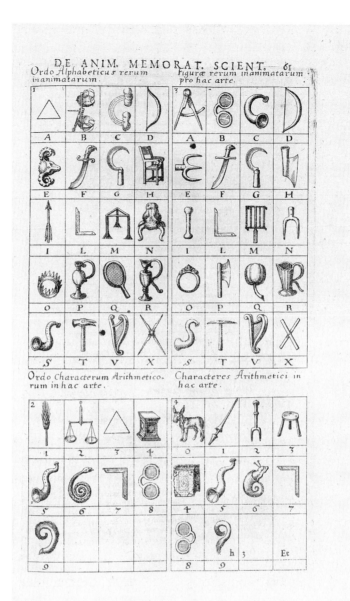

FIGURE 14.27. Johann Theodore de Bry. "De anim. Memorat. Scient," from Robert Fludd, *Utriusque cosmi majoris scilicet et minoris metaphysica, physica atque technica historia in duo volumina secundum cosmi differentiam divisa . . . tomus primus De macrocosmi historia* (Oppenheim, 1617; 2d ed., Frankfurt, 1624). Courtesy Harry Ransom Humanities Research Center, The University of Texas at Austin. "Inanimate" consumer goods, including upholstered armchairs (compare the figure for the letter H with the armchair in fig. 15.9), ceramic pitchers, weapons, or artisan's hand tools served as memory places, in this instance, for letters of the alphabet. Similarly, Palissian rustic creatures, such as a coiled snake or a snail, were memory places for the number 6. These were only obvious suggestions, however, as Fludd encouraged readers to invest domestic objects with personal meanings.

6. Palissy's Anglo-French artisan followers—the makers of "fecundity" plates—may also have adapted his work for the post-1628 English market because, in part, it was appropriate for such a purpose.

Thus, the universalism of the *theatrum orbi* emphasizes transatlantic intertextual relations that linked the production of books with the consumption of things. This is visible in the ways in which specific spaces are prepared both outside and inside the cupboard and in de Bry's engraving as well; to receive, frame, or conceal the personal memory subjects that are now absent in both. The Woodbury cupboard thus follows Fludd closely in presenting shadowy voids waiting to frame real or imagined subjects, to complete the cupboard's memory discourse and set it in motion. Therefore, the material culture that supported Fluddian memory systems was usually intended to be flexible, interactive, and custom-made for personal use. A single large public edifice such as La Rochelle's Hôtel de Ville could contain thousands of individual memories. So too, in the intimate, private space available in the shadows, niches, and cabinets of British-American court cupboards. Space was made for new subjects when old ones were lost, removed, or replaced by a succession of subsequent owners, usually in the same family. But memory systems on court cupboards were private, so certain patrons had artisans develop strategies that diverged from Fludd's universal *theatrum orbi*.

Packed surface decoration on Hannah Barnard's cupboard allows less flexibility for placement of new memory images and hence manipulation of its original memory system than does the openly staged and framed layout on Peter Woodbury's cupboard. Everywhere this artifact asserts Hannah's unwillingness to concede her place to an uncertain future. Covered over with printed text, surrounded by naturalistic imagery of death and rebirth so that available "white space" (and with it potential displacement) was banished like the final report on a Calvinist tombstone, colorful messages codified the memory of Hannah's personal experience, her intentionality, and ultimately her legacy. If new memory images were placed in front of her name by posterity, remnants of "Hannah Barnard" (almost a double palindrome) would bleed through like palimpsest on medieval incunabula.

The Huguenot Peter Blin (1640–1725), a joiner and carver who lived and worked in Wethersfield, Connecticut, and his apprentices—including a son named Peter Blin Jr., of Guilford and Branford, Connecticut (1670?–alive in 1741)—is also thought to have decorated the surfaces of court cupboards overall. Peter Blin the Elder, in particular, was known by inhabitants of the Long Island Sound region to carve and mold (fig. 14.28) his products with schematic floral motifs surmounted by complex geometric shapes. (Peter Blin the Younger is associated with a group of similarly painted chests.) These botanical carvings—most commonly tulips, sunflowers, and marigolds—are generic decorative motifs that appear across cultures in seventeenth-century Europe and America. The expression of naturalistic iconography of sunflowers and marigolds

FIGURE 14.28. Court cupboard traditionally attributed to Peter Blin (d. 1725) and his circle, coastal Connecticut, 1690–1710. H: 56¼″, W: 49½″, D: 21½″. White oak, yellow pine, yellow poplar, and possibly eastern red cedar. Courtesy Yale University Art Gallery, bequest of Charles Wyllys Betts, B.A., 1867. Peter Blin was a Huguenot woodworker. Too many artifacts showing the "sunflower" and with this style of idiosyncratic carving have been attributed to his hand. Construction differences among the many survivals suggest the work of several shops. However, Blin and his circle in Wethersfield, along with family shops of English woodworkers in nearby Windsor, Connecticut, created the paradigm for this regional style. Rising sunflowers or related heliotropic symbols such as marigolds or tulips on the bottom panels and the upward triangle facing the one who opens the bottom door, resonate powerfully with Jeremias Drexel's representation of the heliotropic sunflower in figure 9.6. This flower has traditionally been associated with the Huguenot search for refuge, because it will find the sun (the spirit) wherever it is planted. Four double hearts link macrocosm and microcosm, and the flowers on the bottom to the sunburst panels on the top of the cupboard. These panels (on the top left and right) also resemble the Maltese cross, commonly incorporated in similar contexts into woodwork and ceramics produced by Protestant artisans in Aunis-Saintonge.

was idiosyncratic, however. This may have possessed spiritual meanings in the context of seventeenth-century refugee material culture, particularly in regard to the heliotropic nature of such flowers (see fig. 9.6). The type of flower, though the subject of some debate, seems much less significant historically than what the iconography may tell us about an artisanal culture known for mobility and its association with the portability of inner light to new worlds.

This hypothesis is supported indirectly by the probable source of similarly idiosyncratic sgrafitto (shallow carved) decoration, common to ceramic ware (figs. 14.29, 14.30) made both in southwestern France and the southwest of England (in Barnstable and Bideford in North Devon and at Donyatt in Somerset). During the mid sixteenth century, when sgraffito wares were produced in the region for the first time, the southwest of England was susceptible to seaborne influence from southwestern France and other areas of the Continent, including Germany and the Netherlands. Ready access to foreign ideas and trade was available through the port towns of Barnstable and Bideford. Barnstable in particular attracted refugee artisans because of its function as a regional market town. Evidence indicates French and Germanic sources for this form of sgraffito decoration came into England directly through trade or migration from northern or southwestern France. Also indirectly, via Holland or the Rhineland by refugees resettling in the southwestern coastal pottery region, which must have reminded some Huguenots of Saintonge. The complex history of Devon pottery may thus illuminate the near simultaneous appearance of the heliotropic carving and painted styles in the neighboring Connecticut River Valley towns of Windsor (where recent research argues prototypes for the style originated) and Wethersfield (where it appeared soon thereafter). At least some members of the shops in Windsor had strong religious, craft, and genealogical connections with Devon and so may have carried the style west with their regional material culture, while Blin the Elder, a French refugee, had direct knowledge from European sources. Once in close proximity in the Connecticut Valley, the carving (if not the construction) of the Windsor and Wethersfield shops converged further. Frankly, however, the question of convergence in this instance is probably after the fact. Interaction of refugee Protestant groups leads inevitably back to Europe and the existence of a cross-Channel heliotropic style. Contemporaneous carved forms with rosettes and vines that are virtually identical to those found in Windsor and Wethersfield were common in Germany and the Netherlands in the period after the Revocation of the Edict of Nantes in 1685.[106]

Little is known about Peter Blin the Elder's personal history or Anglo-French regional origins. A substantial artifactual record remains, but Blin's story in the colonies is otherwise restricted to documentary evidence of service as an attorney and translator for two Huguenot merchants. An intriguing fragment of oral history does survive. A youthful descendant claimed to have seen an old carved chest in 1919, which was

FIGURE 14.29. Detail of pierced openwork lead-glazed earthenware vase, La Chapelle-des-Pots, France, ca. 1590–1625. Courtesy Musée d'Orbigny-Bernon, La Rochelle. Photo, Neil Kamil. This green vase was extremely difficult to construct and fire successfully. The openwork suggests the possibility of ritualistic functions, as a flame could light the pierced openings, a practice that was common using ceramic pots in regional funerary rites in the early Christian and medieval periods. The sunflower in this detail is an obvious choice for such treatment which makes it appear that the light of the spirit emerges from within. Sunflower motifs dot the surface, as do pierced Maltese crosses and scrollwork similar to that found on the cupboard in figure 14.28, the title page to the Marot Psalter (fig. 14.16), and carving on the New York leather chairs in figs. 15.26 and 15.40.

FIGURE 14.30. Joseph Hollamore (at Samuel Hollamore's Pottery), lead-glazed earthenware harvest jug, Barnstaple, North Devon, England, signed and dated 1764. Courtesy Colonial Williamsburg Foundation. Recent research argues that Devon potters may have been influenced by imported French ceramics and immigrant potters, suggesting a similar pattern to Peter Blin and his followers and members of the Windsor group (some with Devon connections) in Connecticut. Once again, the sun and sunflowers do their heliotropic dance, here with a decidedly material and agricultural theme. The sun says: "I[,] like bright Phebeous Do apear When my B[el]leys full with good Strong Beer."

FIGURE 14.31. Detail of the lower cupboard door in figure 14.28. Courtesy Yale University Art Gallery, bequest of Charles Wyllys Betts, B.A. 1867. Like the Paracelsian spiritualized seed, a star punch in the form of a Maltese cross is barely perceptible at the center of each of the trinity of sunflowers, which may be imagined spinning like cosmological wheels in perpetual motion. The star punch is not unique to this carved panel in the French refugee artisanal tradition; it was available to other craftsmen. However, its specific, consistent use in this context is particular and resonant.

remarkable because it was full of books in French. When he asked his mother about this oddity, she identified the chest and books as having originally belonged to their refugee ancestor.[107] There is also a miniscule private message that may have been left behind for the "experienced" on the artifact's surface—indeed on almost all surviving woodwork thought to have been carved in the Blin shops—although it is almost impossible to see as more than a dot at the very center of the flowers in bloom (fig. 14.31). The endurance of a specific cultural heritage, as well as universal Neoplatonic fecundity, may be concealed in an image of the universal seed planted in the "soul" of the refugee woodworker's material. In effect, Blin may have "signed" his work covertly with an impression (made with a punch) of the Huguenot Maltese cross in the middle of a flower, marking the nature of his material with a symbol of Paracelsian inner growth. The heliotropic style was, after all, part of the transatlantic discourse of the Paracelsian artisan. Sunflowers reveal another Huguenot signature: the face of this flower grows spirally, like a snail shell.

We know something about Blin, and his fellow carvers of heliotropic flowers in Windsor, but very little physical or documentary evidence remains to recall the original operators' use of domestic colonial memory theaters. Enough scorch marks exist, both inside and out, on Peter Woodbury's court cupboard (as on other surviving examples) to be noteworthy. Yet surely it is unremarkable that candles would be used to illuminate objects placed along edges and pockets of the overhang, or locked behind the front door. Still, given Fludd's instructions, would it have been common practice to animate memory subjects and illuminate hidden shadow images by candlelight? Did tenebristic effects at the atomized edges of a fat lamp's sputtering flame help an operator define the optical boundaries of sacred space in early seventeenth-century domestic settings?

The nocturnal scenes of the Jansenist painter Georges de La Tour of Lorraine (1593–1652) are suggestive. I am thinking in particular here of his St. Joseph rehabilitated as an artisan in *Christ with Saint Joseph in the Carpenter's Shop,* painted between 1635 and 1640 (fig. 14.32). La Tour was Catholic, though Jansenism and Calvinism shared comparable ascetic styles. Yet so were Bruno and Paracelsus, who received the last rites on his deathbed. As in Palissy's obsession with growing translucency in the dark matter of earthy materials, La Tour's work with the metaphysics of light and dark asserts his position as a Neoplatonist whose own rustic production was powerfully influenced by a charismatic international style.[108] La Tour's early years also produced work intended as a religious response to political and geographic displacements of the 1620s. Like Palissy's Saintonge, La Tour's Lorraine, situated on France's strategic northeastern borderlands, suffered invasion by expansionist monarchs and was fragmented into a state of regional entropy during the Thirty Years' War.[109]

FIGURE 14.32. Georges de la Tour (1593–1652), *Saint Joseph the Carpenter,* Vic-sur-Seille, Lorraine, France, ca. 1640. Oil on canvas. Courtesy Musée des Beaux-Arts, Besançon, France. © Giraudon / Art Resource, New York. Vic-sur-Seille, a prosperous, fortified provincial town, was a center of Jansenist reform of Catholicism in Lorraine. La Tour's painting shows the full extent to which Joseph had been rehabilitated and spiritualized as a hard-working artisan and paterfamilias of the sacred family of Jesus after his former status as a cuckold was overcome in the later Middle Ages.

❧ Experience and Perception in Shadow ❧

What shadow secrets interested Fludd and ultimately Hogarth, who privileged darkness as pious and creative space occupied by veiled Huguenot artisans at the intersection of Newtonian and terrestrial time in his ambivalent picture of the social history of Hog Lane? Art historians rightly stress the sacred iconography of La Tour's spectral night scenes, where isolated biblical figures are posed in painful or contemplative gestures. These scenes take place either before or after the pivotal action in their stories has already happened. Candlelight opens up a space of security or spiritual creativity in the shadows. La Tour's individual places of refuge picture the embattled self at rest—the body static, hidden, and, above all, anchored in place—inside a shell obscured by the hovering darkness.

Following Bruno, however, Fludd's memory system transforms stasis into a metaphor of fluidity. He expands and redirects the protecting shadows that covered La Tour's finite group of primitive Christian martyrs into the construction of a universal fortress. Thus, protection was made available for the tiny, everyday martyrs of international Protestantism, each carrying their own inner light sanctified by religious violence and materialized by skill. Fludd's "De geomantia" instructs geomancers—and hence, by extension, operators of the fortress—to engage in prophetic practice in the light of perceptual *experience*. Through these practices, refugee operators labored to order chaos that overlay the deep historical, cultural, and material past while settling in—or moving through—new worlds.

Hogarth's inversions from beneath the Enlightenment master narrative implied shadow languages operated in everyday life and were available as privileged linguistic and material discourse. This was particularly true in pluralistic urban societies such as London (and, in the colonial context, New York), where diasporic groups displaced by confessional violence converged, drawn by the centripetal pull of commercialization. Hogarth's reinvention of Fludd's theory of terrestrial astrology, understood in the context of the debate in Freemasonry over the new constitution with its overt codification of symbolic languages and narrated in terms of the hidden artisanal history of the Huguenots, is closely related to the essence of Bruno's shadows of ideas, and makes sense when applied to this universalist historical and cosmological framework. If carried in the Neoplatonic imagination (and hence mobilized), La Tour's candle could have provided access anywhere through the half-open door into the interior of the *theatrum orbi* (as actual candles must have done for operators of Peter Woodbury's cupboard), and so into protected sacred space in the darkness.

Carried forward to 1736, this transpired in furtive moments between noon and 12:10, when Hogarth's Huguenots turned away from the doorway of the Eglise des Grecs and circled back into the privacy of London's artisan ghetto. The civil wars of the 1560s and 1620s provided Palissy and Fludd with the "recipe" of physical violence, natural-philosophical motion, and historical entropy to produce new forms of identity with the prelapsarian past through the alchemical process of material destruction, renewal, and artisanal replication. Yet Hogarth harnessed the entropy and premature disruption of the cycles of nature and craftsmanship he saw in commercialization to alchemy itself. Hogarth's analogy to the chaos, waste, fragmentation, and displacement of religious warfare in Fludd's "theater of the world," and his installation of Huguenot masters and neighbors in the shadows behind the scenes on Hog Lane, suggest Paracelsian hopes of Neoplatonic unity in the serpentine line of beauty. The corrupt fragmentation of material life evident in *Noon* can be reversed through material purification and convergence. The perception of hidden purity in the alchemic renewal of man and Nature will emerge at the end of the four times of Hogarth's long millennial day.

Natural-philosophical texts varied in interpretation of what was hidden in the shadows, but after Platt and above all Fludd domesticated Bruno by reformulating his medieval shadows of ideas in more familiar and accessible materialistic, commercial Protestant Christian language, most English memory theaters tended to follow the same program well into the late eighteenth century. At that point, this discourse was adapted by speculative Freemasonry. The force of later adaptation was elucidated clearly by William Preston (1742–1818) in his widely diffused and influential *Illustrations of Masonry* (London, 1772), where he codified the use of "allegorical" memory "emblems" from the Bruno-Fludd "method" to facilitate "immediate" perception of "serious and solemn truths": "Everything that strikes the eye more immediately engages the attention, and imprints on the memory serious and solemn truths. Hence Masons have universally adopted the method of inculcating the tenets of their order by typical figures of allegorical emblems to prevent their mysteries from descending within the familiar reach of inattentive and unprepared novices."[110]

Platt suggested as early as the 1580s that emblems built in the imagination be attached in the figurative sense to real articles of household furniture, but it was for purposes of Masonic ritual that such emblems were crafted in the form of tools and used to elevate domestic items. The use of applied emblematic impressions, sometimes appearing as molded encrustations linked by analogy to congruent parts of the sitter's body, is most evident on the many lodge master's chairs that survive from eighteenth-century America (Fig. 14.33).[111] Differences between overt "public" imagery built into Masonic artifacts and the "private," "shadow" imagery of memory theaters such as the Woodbury court cupboard were probably contextual. After all, Masonic chairs were displayed in lodges where they were seen only by members of a secret society "admit-

FIGURE 14.33. Masonic master's chair attributed to Anthony Hay, Williamsburg, Virginia, ca. 1765–70. H: 52½″, W: 29½″, D: 26¼″. Mahogany. Courtesy Williamsburg Masonic Lodge No. 6, A.F. & A.M. Photo, Colonial Williamsburg Foundation, where the chair is on long-term loan. This master's chair has remained in possession of Williamsburg's Lodge No. 6 since at least 1770. By tradition, it was commissioned for use in the lodge by Lord Botetourt, the royal governor of Virginia (1768–70). Although a late-eighteenth-century example of the genre and stylized by a provincial hand, the effect of this dense attempt at naturalistic carving recalls molded Neoplatonic detailing in sixteenth-century rustic designs, filtered through early-seventeenth-century Rosicrucian iconography. It may not be coincidental, therefore, that the carving bears more than a passing relationship to that on the Windsor-Wetherfield woodwork (see figs. 14.28 and 14.31). The chairs back follows ascent to master's status: intermingled between the columns of Solomon's temple, signifying the Masonic trinity of wisdom, strength, and beauty, are vines and roses (related to early carving in Île de Ré [fig. 15.38]) in syncretic motion, similar to the branches at the back of Nature in figure 8.22. On either side of the central column, this natural foliage rises up and is transformed by the skilled hand tools of the aspiring manual philosopher, among them, the senior warden's level and the junior warden's plumb. To achieve mastery, however, one must unify the microcosm and macrocosm, signified by both the heart and pentagonal star above the tools and at the point where—as in Winthrop's chair—the back aligns with the sitter's heart. Unity is achieved through spiritual knowledge of the Bible, on one side of the column, and, on the other, the meaning of proposition 47 of book 1 of Euclid's *Geometry*—the Pythagorean Theorum—which was considered essential in the mastery of mathematics and hence philosophy. These books opened "the door" to the highest level: at "the head" are the arms of the London Company of Masons, with helmet and four alchemic castles. Political unity and the growing together of spirit and matter, skill and knowledge, are conjoined in the serpentine conjunction of the rose and thistle on either side of the master's head.

ted into the mysteries." Court cupboards were meant for the display of memory images and subjects in private space, and contained personal (or family) rather than corporate memory. Guests were impressed by the wealth of these images, but they were not necessarily expected to understand their meaning as "typical" of anything beyond the exalted social position of the owner. Masonic artifacts were, to the "admitted" (a variant of "experienced"), unambiguous extensions of the "universally adopted" material culture informing Palissy's rustic figures molded "from life," as well as the molded ceramic wares of his Saintongeais followers during the Thirty Years' War, who substituted Rosicrucian iconography for the ostensible silence of naturalistic forms.

These allegorical emblems further "inculcated" the long-standing hypothesis that all shadow discourse was essentially astrological and followed the principles of alchemical materialism in its psychic applications. The stars are images of imperceptible astral intermediaries that carried the light of pure "ideas" down from the macrocosm to the microcosm. Star images, because they occupy an upper, liminal space between sacred and fallen terrestrial terrain, are also a cycle closer on Fludd's cosmological rings to knowledge of the supercelestial world. Given the position occupied by the translucent backward or Huguenot sign on the Eglise des Grecs, it is not unreasonable to infer its place on just such a higher plane of reality. The task of the "experienced" artisan (or the adept) was to find ways to manipulate and multiply star images from below, because such images were always closer to Neoplatonic reality than their *mirror* objects in the microcosm, which were made of earth materials and depended on astral impulses to give them form.

The task of primordial memory was to reveal the perfect form of images hidden behind macrocosmic veils since postlapsarian time. Memory systems worked on star images by arranging them in logical patterns, then manipulating them into particular places where they could be located, framed, and ultimately held in the imagination for the future. Bruno's star images "*are* the 'shadows of ideas', shadows of reality which are nearer to reality than the physical shadows in the lower world." Thus, star images were imprinted on the memory, such that lower things in the natural and artificial world may be understood as part of a symbiotic dialogue with their ideal and superior "agents" above. Paré's "monsters" and de Bry's shape-shifting anthropomorphic creatures, caught in the violent international imagery of Huguenot material culture, imaged "ideas" of anguished "refugees" caught in-between elemental realms. "The forms of deformed animals are beautiful in heaven," wrote Bruno. "Non-luminous metals shine in their planets. Neither man, nor animals, nor metals are here as they are there . . . illuminating, vivifying, uniting, conforming yourself to the superior agents, you will advance in the conception and retention of the species."[112]

Every deformed image contained memory of its primordial ideal form. Laboring to "conform yourself" to this active "agent," the new Adamic adept reached back into the shadows and perceived things in prelapsarian time. Palissy wrote of his reconstruction of hidden natural languages in artisanry, in part because of his ambivalence about writing, and also to limit perception of politically powerful enemies in control of written culture. The potter's perception of silent interaction between written and material texts has much in common with Bruno's mystical Neoplatonism. Much as

Bruno understood shadows of ideas to function as a sort of "inner writing," Palissy's naturalistic ceramic marvels were perceived by their author to supplement—and at times move far beyond—the artifice of writing. Yates argues that Bruno was a visual artist forced to externalize cosmic insights as written text rather than material form. Palissy reached his full potential by constructing memory systems in ceramic form, which he then *supplemented* with written text.

Bruno imagined private Neoplatonic ideas to inhabit universal mental machines revolving in the form of interior cosmological wheels. Set in motion, these shadow worlds within worlds ramified their images to form infinite image structures. Essentially pictograph permutations of sacred and ordinary memory, these were conceptualized in much the same way that adepts perceived the philosopher's stone multiplied alchemic materials.[113] Coding this process as mankind's "multiplication of . . . treasures," Palissy demonstrated that he understood the form of his concentric production from the *désert* experience—everything from the geodal basins to the self-contained grottoes—in terms of refined material brought out from inside subterranean Huguenot shadow worlds.

Bruno cast the "eye" of his imagination upward to conform to "shadows of ideas," but Fludd's "De geomantia"—which was, after all, "*terrestrial* astrology"—also invited practitioners to look down; to perceive empyreal secrets in earthy terrain, hidden "in the lower world," concealed by "physical shadows." Much important action on Hog Lane is located here. We are reminded of Barthélemy Berton's emblem for *Recepte veritable* (fig. 14.34): the rustic caught between his rising spirit on the one hand, and a rock tethered to the other; the dead weight of unrefined earthy matter *and* poverty. That is one reason why Fludd's Paracelsian concept of geomancy—based on a Protestant archeology of sacred secrets refined from dots of dust scratched from elemental earth—has such a strong familial relation to Palissy's "Art of the Earth." Indeed, Berton's emblem for the Recepte reappears as an imprinted "image" on the Saintongeais ceramic cosmology illustrated in figure 8.6, which was made around the same time that Fludd's "De geomantia" was published. However, it was Bruno who called his willful conformation to superior agents "astral memory," arguably the direct astrological source for Fludd's geomantic scheme to perceive order behind chaos. "There is," Fludd wrote, "in your primordial nature":

> a chaos of elements and numbers, yet not without order and series. . . . There are, as you may see, certain distinct intervals. . . . On one the figure of Aries is imprinted; on another, Taurus, and so on. . . . This is to form the inform chaos. . . . It is necessary for the control of memory that the numbers and elements should be disposed in order . . . I tell you that if you contemplate this attentively you will be able to reach such a figurative art that it will help not only the memory *but also all the powers of the soul in a wonderful manner.*[114]

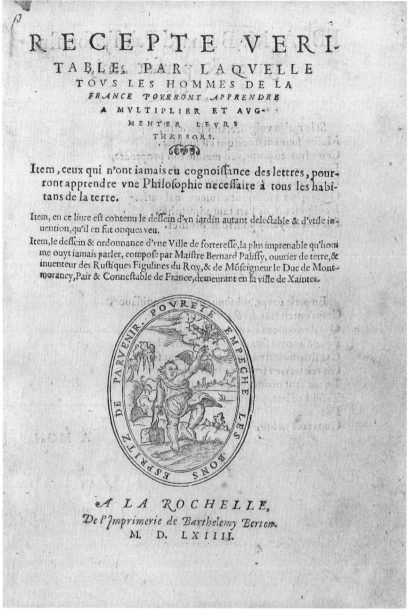

FIGURE 14.34. Barthélemy Berton, title page of Bernard Palissy's *Recepte veritable* (La Rochelle, 1563, 1564). By permission of the Houghton Library, Harvard University. Berton's device from this rare (perhaps unique) copy of a 1564 edition shows a young rustic whose soul aspires to the heavens while his material body is weighted down to earth by a rock (a play on La Rochelle?). The legend translates: "Poverty limits the reach of good spirits." Compare the in-between condition of Berton's impoverished rustic with a similar image molded onto the surface of a Saintongeais ceramic cosmology in figure 8.6 and the lighter-than-air joyfulness of Paracelsus's four dancing "children" of the millennium in figure 10.5.

Here again, a Fluddian adaptation: where Bruno's "primordial nature" functions in tandem with the inward *anima* and *mens* as it pulsates subtly between the upper and lower states of being, the ability to "contemplate . . . attentively" is transformed into a mental act of seeing elemental essences hidden in the microcosmic world. Thus, as the "mixed composition" of man's body remains partially attached to its divine origins by the "powers of the soul":

> The rows of geomantic dots comprise and express the idea of the whole world no less than does the human body. The human body is seen only outwardly, whilst we contemplate its *anima* and *mens* inwardly, with our spiritual eyes. As in the body we discern the elements, invisible in their mixed composition, so also we discern . . . in the figures produced from these four sets [where the elements are concealed], the seven planets and twelve signs of the zodiac are present, though they may be perceived only with the eyes of *spiritus*. . . . The geomantic figures express the natures of the twelve signs in the following way: *Acquisitio* corresponds in an abstruse manner to Aries, *Laetitia* and *Fortuna Minor* to Taurus, [and so on, "down" to Pisces].[115]

Astral correspondences between the twelve astrological houses and the human body, so central to Fludd's geomantic scheme, had also been a fundamental part of folk medical knowledge in the West since classical times. Astrology can be documented in England beginning with medieval medicinal texts. The Paracelsian "Man of Signs"— Aries corresponds to his head and Pisces with his feet—depicted in seventeenth-century almanacs showed the controlling analogy between the health of the inner body (of the little world) and the great outer world of the macrocosm, which, Paracelsus believed, was itself subject to control by adepts, such as John Winthrop Jr. Thus the elemental body, internally mixed and invisible to the inexperienced eye in the microcosm, may be signified by separation into its component anatomical parts. In this context, especially, Hogarth's street signs showing fragmented body parts (the headless woman's torso and the disembodied head of John the Baptist) add layers of meaning to symbols of ill-health on Hog Lane.

For example, Johann Martin Bernigeroth's raising of the French master Mason in 1745 (fig. 14.35), shows eleven illuminated standing figures "raising" the murdered body of a twelfth (perhaps the rebirth of the Huguenot in refuge), "connected" to the upper circle through the points (or dots?) of a triangle of drawn swords. This ritual reunified the twelve astrological houses, separated and made incomplete by violence, through the alchemic rebirth of the fallen member. His fragmented (headless) body, about to be reborn a new man and "master," lies on a platform dotted with what are traditionally called "teardrops." These dots also double as distilled drops of alembic condensation, or alternatively, flames that surround a body rising purified from the fire of a crucible.

The folkloric use of the "Man of Signs" survived the presumed "death" of magic in

FIGURE 14.35. Johann Martin Bernigeroth, *Assembly of French Masons for the Reception of Masters*, from *Les Coutumes des francs-maçons dans leur assemblées* (ca. 1745). Copyright, and reproduced by permission, of the United Grand Lodge of England. This performance of the so-called French "teardrop" ritual or third-degree raising of the master Mason was analogous to the distillation process and was probably unique, at least at first, to French refugees. The caption reads: "The recipient lies down on the sepulchre appointed by the lodge, his face covered by a linen shroud tinged with blood. And all those in attendance draw their swords, presenting their points to the body." The grand master supervises from the apex of the sacred triangle (or pyramid), and two "surveillants" stand watch at the angles at the base.

Enlightenment medicine to endure as an icon of the astrological body in popular American print culture. Boston's John Foster is credited with the first surviving colonial version in a woodcut for *An Almanack of Coelestial Motions for the Year of the Christian Epocha 1678*. However, the most widely diffused version was *The Anatomy of Man's Body as Govern'd by the Twelve Constellations*, a woodcut that appeared in Benjamin Franklin's *Poor Richard Improved* for the year 1749 (fig. 14.36). The "Man of Signs" was originally drawn in a seated position, but in *Poor Richard*'s "improvement," he stood (as in Foster's *Almanack*), awkward but upright. Franklin succeeded in marketing his almanac to practical-minded barber-chirugeons, midwives, and other skillful therapists. The standing pose was actually adapted from a cheap German medical manual with anatomical charts drawn *vom Aderlassen und Schropfen* ("for Bloodletting and Cupping"). The "Man of Signs" in *Poor Richard Improved*, was thus transformed into "Vein Man," an old image of Paracelsian medicine harnessed to a specific therapeutic function.[116]

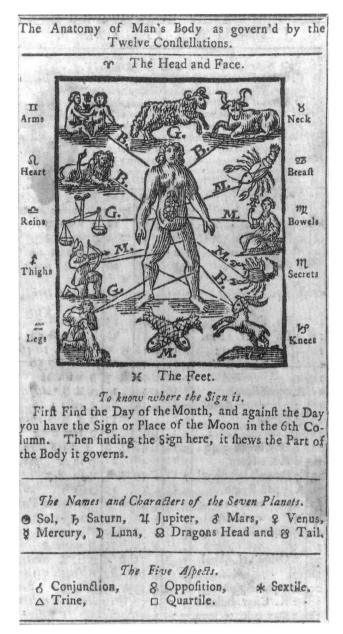

FIGURE 14.36. Benjamin Franklin, *The Anatomy of Man's Body as Govern'd by the Twelve Constellations,* or "Sign Man," from *Poor Richard Improved* (Philadelphia, 1764). Courtesy The Winterthur Library: Printed Book and Periodical Collection, Henry Francis du Pont Winterthur Museum, Winterthur, Delaware. This was the public face of Paracelsian medicine in late colonial America, widely diffused by Franklin's and many other almanacs.

❧ Urban Blindness and Mastery of Insight ❧

Hogarth's pictorial history for London of Fludd's theories of geomancy and memory maps and inventories similar strategies of "invisible mixing," alchemic "withdrawal from the multitude," and astral rebirth. In effect, it represents the "modern" artisan and natural philosopher's ethnography of pluralism and street life in London's most cosmopolitan urban ghetto. We have seen Hogarth's Huguenots enter the chaos of Hog Lane by exiting the Eglise des Grecs—the church of the Greeks, hence scholasticism—through a barely "visible" door, already in shadow, and rotate at noon like celestial bodies by turning away from sunlight's "regulative power" into the protective darkness that veiled deep perspective. Ultimately, the congregants return to the "art and mystery" of their workshops and Masonic lodges through the "double door" of Fludd's fortress of memory. The pious Huguenot craftsmen and women truly become *de naturae simia,* "This Ape of Nature we call Art." Celestial revolution is thus simultaneously an act of artisanal pilgrimage to the center of Fludd's cosmology of the microcosmic arts (see fig. 14.8).

This is in juxtaposition to the un-self-mastered African's "inexperienced" and "crapulent" figure, caught in his premature embrace of a surprised, spiritually unprepared and hence fragmented Nature, all arrayed under the sign of St. John the Baptist's decapitated head in the right foreground. A misalliance of nature and craft such as this could never achieve "felicitous climax and issue." The authentic *simia* is dark, because his existence in shadow is a metaphysical extension of the primordial memory of terrestrial matter. *Simia,* therefore, is the embodiment of Bruno's memory system, since he aspires to light from shadow. He crawls or squats close to earth, an animate primitive (or, following Palissy, a learned rustic), caught in the darkness of aspiring matter. Here is a dialectical "consort" to the light of Nature, as the elevated light of Nature is consort to God. Fludd's naked and hence Adamic HOMO stretches from earth toward God through his arts and sciences in the guise of *simia naturae*—the foundation on which man stands—inasmuch as "in his sciences he follows the nature which God has created."[117] Man and Nature are thus sacred links in the proverbial seventeenth-century chain of being, where artisanal man labors to continue Nature's work on earth through the reinvention, in the memory of experience, of primordial mimetic processes. When Hogarth grafted Fludd's microcosm of man's arts and sciences onto the everyday life of Hog Lane, he also reinvented Fludd's "useful" guides to the prelapsarian Adamic return through self-knowledge. These valuable guides are coded against impure consumption by a labyrinth of mirrors and palindromes. Encrypted writing and layers of images appear everywhere to guide the pilgrim along this "narrow path," as do emblemata of natural-philosophical and Masonic allegories on mathematics; geometry;

perspective; painting; fortification; timekeeping; cosmography; astrology; and above all *pyramidum scientia, prophetia, geomantia,* and *ars memoriae.*

That is why the celibate Fludd admonished aspiring adepts to remember that astral conjunction in the lower world "should be *protected* against the obnoxious influence of the flesh and of crapulence," which sought to besiege the "fortress of health," guardian of the *spiritus intellectualis.* Sexual intercourse, the repetition of bodily interpenetration that was a primary effect of original sin, left the *spiritus* to languish in an unprotected and insecure state by the body, just as the Fall left mankind outside Eden, walled in since the advent of postlapsarian time. Above all else, the spiritual eye was occluded, blinded to the protective secrets of the shadows, like the headless sign over the Hog Lane couturier's shop.

Philo scholars will recognize here an allusion to Sodom itself, which for Philo meant "blindness" and "barrenness" of the soul. Thus, by the early Christian period, "the city of Sodom stands for the animal nature . . . the soul barren of good and blind of reason."[118] Blindness in the unprotected spiritual eye, its shield of faith overcome by the chaos and miscegenous "mixing" of bodily invasion, is precisely the outcome of the carnal interaction between Hogarth's African sailor and the servant girl hawking meat pies. Hogarth's graphic source for the couple's plainly in-"felicitous . . . issue," the inconsolable crying boy, decodes the pictorial riddle of this fragment of London street theater. The source may be found in *Oculus imaginationis* (Eye of the Imagination), Johann Theodore de Bry's iconic frontispiece for Fludd's *Ars memoriae,* published in Oppenheim in 1619 (see Fig. 14.17), during the early years of Louis XIII's violent campaigns against Huguenot fortresses south of the Loire Valley. Unexplained by Fludd, its meaning is nevertheless clear enough in the light of the text of *Ars memoriae,* and Hogarth adapted its central figure and memory images for *Noon.* The mysterious iconography displayed in *Oculus imaginationis* was actually fairly standard in natural-philosophical discourse by the seventeenth-century. First Bruno, then Fludd, and finally English translations of Böhme's *Aurora* found an audience for similarly occult theories of perception in Britain.

The place to begin is the oculus itself—a version of which appeared in La Rochelle as late as 1677 (see fig. 8.21)—which functions here as the proverbial third eye, or rather an eye aimed at primordial memories of the distant past, situated behind the back of the head. Acting alone, man's frontal or bodily eye, perceives life as flat, superficial form, hidden behind a veil of dense façades. The supplement of the inner eye is necessary to pierce these shadows of historical memory. In Hogarthian terms, man's bodily eye perceives the superficial sunlit images fronting social life on Hog Lane; his *oculus imaginationis,* its shadow images hidden behind. Margaret Jacob has noted that the concept of "second sight" was perhaps the earliest structural link between Rosicrucian mythology emerging out of the Thirty Years' War and the rise of British speculative

Masonry. Witness a boastful mid-seventeenth-century Scottish poem: "For we brethren of the rosie cross; / We have the mason-word and second sight, / Things for to come we can foretell alright."[119] Fludd's "experienced" man has the power of "second sight." He sees backward (into memory) and forward, like a prophet (to "foretell"), at once. "Second sight" even had a specific anatomy, facilitated by the tripartite ventricular structure of the experienced man's brain. The three ventricles were the physiological means by which things to be memorized were initially retrieved from primordial "rooms," where they were held in storage somewhere in the obscurity of the rear ventricle, and then gradually brought forward to the front, where they were exposed to the eye of the imagination and classified for use.[120]

In the instance of the crying boy—the mixed, impure "issue" of unprotected flesh—Hogarth signified the catastrophe of total blindness. The boy reaches back to hold the part of his head that contains the brain's rear ventricle, a corrupt inversion of the prophetic moment represented by the adept in figure 8.21. The pathways to his eye of the imagination have been painfully blocked, interrupted by the transitory pleasure of crapulence. He cannot access second sight to see behind him into the shadows of prelapsarian Adamic memory now occupied by the retreating Huguenots. The boy bursts into tears, perhaps suggesting distillation; but here more an act of remorse forcing his bodily eyes to shut tight, signifying man's descent into blindness without benefit of memory and experience. The artisan's earthenware pie plate microcosm, now devoid of the light of nature, dissolves and begins its soulless descent back down to the street as a result of the sailor's premature connection to the macrocosm, held up as an object of aspiration by fallen Nature. This death of animate matter creates the chaos of superfluous geomantic dots that obscure the perception of monistic unity before sightless eyes. While the crying boy holds his head and is blinded by a failure of the imagination, his polite counterpart across the gutter covers his heart as if to signify the narcissistic blindness of self-love. As Paracelsians from Harvey to the younger Winthrop and his friend Howes to Ezra Stiles knew, an impure heart impeded circulation of wisdom between the worlds and was itself the cause of blindness. Such blindness was costly: is that the philosopher's stone the stylish boy prods ambivalently in the street?

The five memory places penetrated, not by physical coitus, but by the rays of Fludd's *oculus imaginationis* suggest images the crying boy would have seen through the shadows behind him were he not blinded by "obnoxious influence[s]." The large central image at the nexus of the other four is an obelisk; it stands as a symbol of unity in the Fluddian memory chamber. The obelisk is bracketed on the left by smaller images of the Tower of Babel and Tobias and the Angel; and on the top right, by the storm-tossed ship carrying Jason and the Argonauts in their legendary quest for the Golden Fleece worn by the adept in figure 8.21 (an alchemical trope for the philosopher's stone). Finally, at bottom, is the descent of the damned into the mouth of hell—a scene from the last judgment.[121]

The story of Tobias and the Angel speaks directly to the triumph of blindness over insight suffered by Hogarth's crying boy. Like the Wisdom of Solomon, which helped form the younger Winthrop's alchemic identity, this popular narrative from the Book of Tobit was from the widely read Old Testament Apocryphal tradition. Written by refugees who experienced the early periods of Jewish military defeat and dispersion, Tobit was hugely popular among the Christian laity during the period of the wars of religion, in part because the story was about exile and redemption told in a folkloric style. Indeed, Tobit was canonized by the Council of Trent (1546), even while it was found acceptable by many reformed theologians. It was published in conjunction with English Bibles until at least 1629. Wisdom and Tobit represent the apocryphal Jew as God's chosen, but these stories also record Jewish experience as scorned wanderers and universal strangers. Both tell didactic tales that recount a pious protagonist's secret struggles to maintain the purity of biblical practice among hostile, unclean hosts. As an allegory of sight and perception, the Book of Tobit became an emblematic narrative for visual artists. Among seventeenth-century reformed artists, Rembrandt (1609–69) was particularly concerned with this text and its relation to tenebrism.[122] Its privileged position in the literature of exile and sanctification of physical movement as pilgrimage toward the ultimate restoration of Israel, and with it, second sight, appealed to displaced, mobile Huguenot artisans and refugees such as de Bry.[123]

✿ The Story of Tobias ✸

Tobias was the son of Tobit, a pious Jew exiled in Nineveh with his kinsmen from the Naphtali tribe after they survived the devastating invasion of Israel by Assyria. Unlike most of the rest of his exiled kinsmen (who assimilated forbidden Assyrian food ways), Tobit maintained strict Jewish dietary laws. Although well-known for charity and good works in the exile community, Tobit personally undertook the illicit burial of dead kinsmen executed for crimes against the state and left unburied. The risk and danger that accompanied this task came from the authorities, but also from constant contact with the dead. The secret burial of one such corpse caused Tobit's ritual defilement. Made unclean by the ceremony, Tobit could not return to his household on the night of the burial. Forced to separate from others of his tribe for a period of time prescribed by Jewish law, Tobit slept outdoors under a courtyard wall. But Tobit, in a sign of spiritual blindness, slept with his eyes wide open.

Sparrows landed on the wall above him, and after settling on top of and breaching this insecure boundary, the birds blinded Tobit by dropping dung into the unprotected openings. Eyelids may thus be compared to walls in the fortress of health, breached for good or evil by airborne emissaries. The excretions of waste left a veil of obscuring white film (a cataract) over Tobit's eyes. Here was a decisive early metaphor for the "mixed composition" of occlusion and transparency. Indeed, the pluralism of strangers encountered during exile and migration is signaled by the bodily presence of "crapulence" that for Fludd, thwarted the sight of the Neoplatonic geomancer or prophet, an act that obscured perception from the *oculus imaginationis.*

As a gravedigger, Tobit intuited that he had experienced a sort of spiritual death through veiled sight. "I cannot see the light of heaven," Tobit lamented. "But," comparing himself to a living corpse (or to the unburied and hence displaced dead), "I lie in darkness like the dead who do not see the light anymore. Living, I am among the dead!" An exile taken from the core of his culture and left straining for reunification, "I hear the voice of men, yet I cannot see them."[124] The pious Tobit can only pray for divine assistance to retrieve his sight and return to the land of the living; to a place where "the light of heaven" may be seen even from the distance of exile. This light led the pilgrim back to Israel (the millennial New Jerusalem) and out of the metaphorical wilderness.

At the same time that Tobit was blinded by excrement after crossing the boundaries that separate the living from the dead, a woman in Ecbatana prayed to drive away an evil demon that had killed each of her seven husbands before the marriages could be consummated. The youthful Tobias enters the narrative at this point. Impoverished by age and blindness, Tobit desperately recalls a sum of money owed him in a distant city. As he is no longer able to go himself to claim this outstanding debt, Tobit chooses instead to send Tobias, his naïve and inexperienced son. Because of the danger posed to inexperienced travelers, Tobit hires a traveling companion to guide young Tobias on his journey. He does not know that the guide is in fact the disguised angel Raphael. The author of Tobit thus employs another aery spirit to transcend the obscurity of both waste and crapulence dropped by the sparrows to obscure perception of the "narrow path." The title page of Fludd's *De technica microcosmi historia implies that* Tobias actually embarked on an adept's alchemical journey from innocence to experience, guided by God's angelic intermediary between macrocosm and microcosm. In Tobit, as in Fludd's essay on geomancy, this journey marks the transition from physical blindness to metaphysical insight. The angel Raphael shares his experience of the narrow path with his novice in secret, by effectively forming a working synthesis with the innocent, natural eye of Tobias. God's spiritual eye is thus embodied to direct Tobias to contemplate the outward chaos of the material world inwardly, and then, via the *media* of *anima* and *mens,* to map the territory of his journey to "invisible" knowledge by seeing through and behind a labyrinth of "mixed composition."

In the hands of the Fludd–de Bry partnership, although this story functions on one level as an alchemical tale, it also has a natural place in the much broader tradition of artisanal piety. Given its significance for visual artists such as Rembrandt, it is surely reasonable that the father's initiation of a working relationship between Raphael and Tobias was understood by seventeenth-century readers (or auditors) as analogous to an aging and unskilled parent giving his child in apprenticeship to a pious master to guide him through the next passage of life toward self-mastery by teaching the art and mystery of craft skills. To be sure, eighteenth-century Freemasons such as Hogarth would have found affinities between the apocrypha and the mythology of their secret societies. This reading would suggest that Raphael performed the role of master and second father. Tobias's mobile "artisan" guide would thereby have conducted the pious transition to craft competency and ultimately the life of an independent householder or freeman. Noteworthy in this respect is that Tobias finds both his wife and a "dowry" (his inheritance of Tobit's recovered debt) at his journey's end.

In this sense especially, the story of Tobias shares powerful affinities with the late medieval rehabilitation of Joseph the Carpenter. The context of rehabilitation from cuckold to saint is pious labor and Joseph's warm domestic relationship with the young Jesus, who is sometimes represented in the mundane role of shop apprentice. Joseph is not, of course, the Christ's biological father, and "God the Father['s]" decision to apprentice his son to a carpenter was understood as affirmative. It drew on a deep well of regional folkloric traditions, making available new and pious (rather than ribald) interpretations of the quotidian meaning of the Christ-Joseph relationship.

This impulse informed La Tour's Jansenist reading of *Christ with Saint Joseph in the Carpenter's Shop* (fig. 14.32), completed in war-torn Lorraine sometime between 1635 and 1640. The theological and psychological relationships between Protestant Calvinism and Catholic Jansenism—named after the Dutch theologian Cornelius Jansenius (1585–1638)—are well known. Note, for example, these striking similarities in Roland Mousnier's Old Testament–like assessment of "Jansenism, so strong in France," during the seventeenth and eighteenth centuries:

> Conceiving the most lofty idea of the greatness and omnipotence of God and impressed by the weaknesses and miseries of mankind, the Jansenists formed the notion of a terrible God whose designs are unfathomable and whose decrees are beyond our understanding. Without this God, man can do nothing. Man goes wherever his pleasure and gratification lead him, and, since the Fall, they have led him only into evil. His intelligence works in a void that can attain to no reality; his reason, contradictory and various, is a joke; his will, mere impotence. Man is a plaything. Crushing external forces, the fortuitous play of circumstances, habit and custom, these are what guide him, making him turn about like a weathercock with every wind that blows. Egotism, self-regard, individual appetite, these are his driving forces. Man can do nothing about it. But God, the All-Powerful, by

his grace causes man to find gratification in the observance of his commandments. God gives his grace to men whom he has chosen for all eternity, whom he has predestined. Christ died for them alone, redeemed only them. They cannot avoid God's grace, it is imposed upon them. Man is not free, he is God's slave. This kind of psychology and theology went badly with the idea of the king as hero, the divine king, the king as God. . . . The Jansenist doctrine was not easy to reconcile with the foundations of the idea of absolute monarchy.[125]

In *Christ with Saint Joseph in the Carpenter's Shop*, Christ, performing the role of dutiful apprentice, provides spectral illumination in the dark for his weary master, who refines raw material into finished product. Yet, even as Joseph bends low to pierce a block of wood, his hands twisting the transverse handle of a suggestively cruciform auger, the master artisan chooses not to look down at his work. Rather, his demeanor infers the psychic toll of true artisanal knowledge and experience; he looks up sorrowfully from his labor and directly into the candlelight reflected by—and through the back of—Christ's translucent hand. Its fleshy matter flattened, suffused, and permeated with the metaphorical *spiritus* of the light—as is the newly pierced wood that adumbrates the cross—the floating, ethereal, almost dualistic quality of Christ's illuminated hand cannot help but remind us of the strange translucent materiality of Hogarth's "backward," or Huguenot, sign.

In *Christ with Saint Joseph in the Carpenter's Shop*, metaphysical light, characteristically rendered by La Tour as ordinary candlelight, merges with the two figures' complicity in their premonition of sacred violence. The perception of Joseph's bodily eye, ultimately connected to the work of his hand, is directed by the appearance, hidden in the shadows, of an inner light refracted down from the macrocosm through Jesus, the chosen vessel of pain and redemption. Following Fludd's *Oculus* and Bruno's study of the role of primordial imagination in parsing mystical memory from the shadows, is it not reasonable to infer, given what we know about the mystical foundations of La Tour's Jansenism, that Joseph's inner eye could see through time hidden "behind" as well as ahead of him, as Hogarth's crying boy is unable to do?

Bruno's discourse was available to La Tour when he painted Joseph. Perhaps he peered into the shadows of primordial memory as he worked? The shadows that surround Joseph seem oppressive, as if to weigh the pious craftsman down. They signify a third, "invisible" protagonist in La Tour's ecstatic memory painting foreshadowing Christ's future crucifixion. Here in the shadows is the image of a historical event that has already transpired but has been stored away in the obscurity of mankind's collective memory, from which it is now drawn forth into the light of artistic experience. La Tour's rendering of Joseph's perception in the darkness and the form his work will inevitably take as a result is also a prophesy of the apprentice's suffering and the chosen fragment of mankind's redemption from sin. In the secret world of alchemy, personal and collective histories of violence and the sacred were artfully synthesized.

Memory of this moment of supreme sacrifice also signifies Christ's acquisition of unified knowledge and the experience of macrocosm and microcosm. This is an experience he could only have achieved by inhabiting a frail body suffused with a powerful, universal spirit. As such, his experience of conjunction and synthesis remains the one against which all others are measured through time. The enormous intellectual and emotional effort that Palissy expended in "Art of the Earth" explains his experiments in the annealment of translucent glazes to coarse rustic figures in the kilns of La Chapelle-des-Pots. Such a bond transpired precisely *because* it was crafted by artisans who made a practice of reconstructing the pain of primordial Christian experience and sacrifice in their materials. Palissy's task as a Huguenot artisan was to document, as artifactual history, the symbiotic martyrology of his personal journey and that of his co-religionists, together with the materials of the dying earth in the process of rebirth. We have seen how that passionate process of alchemic death and rebirth informed the methodology of Palissy's natural philosophy of the Saintongeais earth. Saintonge endured a regional passion in the local wars of religion, resulting in the potter's redemptive material-holiness synthesis and the "invention" of Huguenot "natural" craft. From across a permeable and eclectic confessional "divide," religious violence animated the translucent spirit in Palissy's pottery kiln, while La Tour envisioned Christ holding his light so that memory work could proceed in the shadows of a carpenter's shop.

Just as Palissy's Paracelsian natural philosophy sought a pilgrim's peripatetic solutions to the geomorphology of elemental earth in the subterranean stones and hidden aqueous creatures he disinterred from its "bowels" on walks along the Charente River Valley near Saintes, so, too, Tobias finds medicinal properties in the belly of a giant fish the travelers encounter on the first evening of their journey. Indeed, de Bry's image shows the young traveler carrying this strange creature under his arm; a reference to the moment in the story when a fish rises up from the deep to break through the filmy and opaque surface of the Tigris River, only to be captured by the startled Tobias and disemboweled under the direction of the angel Raphael:

> So they both journeyed along. When night overtook them, they lodged by the Tigris River. And there leaped a great fish out of the water and sought to snap at the feet of the young man and he screamed! "Seize and hold fast to the fish!" cried the angel to the young man. So the young man seized the fish and hauled it upon the land. "Cut open the fish," the angel thereupon instructed him, "and take out its gall and its heart and its liver; keep them with you, but throw away the entrails. The gall and the heart and the liver of it serve as a beneficial remedy." When the young man had dissected the fish, he put together the

gall and the heart and the liver; then he roasted part of the fish, and ate, and left over some of it to be salted. Then they went on together until they drew near Media.

Whereupon the youth inquired of the angel, saying to him, "Brother Azariah [literally, "God helps"], what is the medicinal property in the heart, in the liver of the fish, and in the gall?" "With regard to the heart and liver of the fish," he answered him, "make a smoke in front of a man or woman whom a demon or evil spirit has attacked; then every ailment will flee from him, and they will never lodge with him any more. And as for the gall, anoint a man's eyes over which white films have crept, blowing upon them, over the white films, and they will become well."[126]

Thus, the story is resolved when Tobias makes a fire of the heart and liver of the fish to raise smoke and stupefy the evil demon haunting Sarah (the unfortunate virgin of Ecbatana) whom he discovers (again from the angel), is, like himself, a lost member of the exiled Naphtali tribe. Sarah and Tobias are thus ultimately able to marry. The angel continues to guide Tobias to the holder of the debt. He retrieves the money, which becomes Tobias's competence. Finally, the now experienced Tobias returns with Sarah and the angel Raphael to Nineveh, where he applies the gall removed from the fish's belly by "dissection" and clears the cataract of white film that obscures Tobit's eyes. At journey's end, reconciliation of the experience of old age (father), pious innocence (son), and a member of the lost tribe (Sarah) has overcome fragmentation and separation under angelic direction. The father's sight magically returns—literally, he acquires "second sight"—while his son achieves the pure insight of an adept who possesses the pharmacopoeia and skill to "blow upon" a filmy surface and perceive profound secrets in its hidden depths.

The symbolic resolution of this apocryphal tale conforms with certain aspects of Palissy's natural philosophy of Saintonge, while resonating with the work of Fludd and Hogarth in interesting ways. The fish is not an uncommon motif in Christian iconography or pottery made by Palissy or inspired by him. Fish may be found swimming in his basins, and one may imagine that fish were a mainstay of the grottoes, but *only* in their proper element: in proximity to snails, lizards, frogs, and other aqueous creatures. Protean in their ability to negotiate the permeable and productive territory where elemental earth and water interact, these tiny amphibians are mobile hybrids, at home on land and under water. It is instructive to note, however, that unlike Palissy's tiny rustic creatures who follow the subterranean practice of Saintongeais Huguenot artisans and hide their secrets in plain sight, Tobias's fish—presumably at God's direction—does the inverse, by presenting itself openly, leaping out of the obscure depths to snap aggressively at the young traveler's feet.

The fish is ultimately "dissected" (cut open like Palissy's geode), and secrets are ripped out of its belly and carried away to provide economic profit and spiritual rebirth for the slaughterer's family and tribe. Pure "philosophical" parts (the heart, liver, and gall), are extracted and saved for future use as elixirs. The unrefined interior waste left behind in the process (the entrails) is "thrown away." Then the flesh is partitioned for consumption. Tobit teaches that though the exterior flesh is corrupt—an article of commerce in other contexts—it may be purified and consumed by the innocent Tobias if dietary precautions are taken to preserve purity. Tobias eats part of the fish straight away, after the fire has purified it, and salts the remainder for future consumption.

When Tobit was written, salt was understood to have certain preservative qualities when applied to meat or fish, but it was also considered a powerful spiritual preservative. This was especially true in Semitic folk traditions. Salt used in cooking and preservation of food was thought a prophylactic against the evil and corruption of dead flesh.[127] We know that Paracelsians ascribed seminal powers to salts in the alchemic process. Palissy, as we have seen, took this a step further, describing certain salts as the mysterious fifth element. This soulish material lingered in the microcosm after the Fall to act as a means of convergence when combined with other elements. All this was possible because Tobias follows an angelic guide. The angel directs him to see beyond the exterior chaos of mixed composition and corrupted flesh to the depths of second sight, where adept's tools to effect material and philosophical purity lie hidden.

If the image of Tobias and the Angel signifies the mobility of the spirit in Fludd's *Oculus*, its use in the context of his art of memory reveals real social concerns. These were at the heart of Fludd's—and by extension, Hogarth's—natural-philosophical and memory programs. They informed an ongoing process of convergence and hybridization in urban contexts made pluralistic by the influx of refugees from the Continent to commercial centers beginning in the sixteenth century. Therefore, if the Fludd–de Bry Tobias of 1620 stands in for the spiritual movement of refugees searching the shadows for the angelic light of guidance out of exile, then the obelisk provides a conduit for the inner perception of convergence and reconciliation that unified the Huguenots' primitive past, chaotic present, and millennial future.

The Egyptian obelisk is Fludd's gesture toward Bruno's memory system, with its foundations in pantheistic readings of Egyptian hermetic practice. Thus, the eye of the imagination projects its visual impulses through the confusions of the mixed composition of matter, represented here by the polyglot chaos of the Tower of Babel and Hogarth's painting of Hog Lane. The conduit for these impulses of visual memory is the *upper* triangle of the obelisk, which guides perception in the direction of the desired goal—the Golden Fleece (or philosopher's stone) sought by Jason and the Argonauts—just as the angel Raphael guides Tobias safely on his journey in search of second sight. In the ca. 1745 Bernigeroth engraving (fig. 14.35), the headless body lies dead at the base of an obelisk formed by a canopy of curtains. Presumably, the master Mason is "raised," reborn through the top. Since de Bry's Raphael guides Tobias toward the obelisk, this implies that if the *Oculus* fails to find its proper level of transcendence, the pilgrim will fall victim to a permanent blindness, shipwrecked by the violent storms of history. Descent into the mouth of hell follows. There, the chaos is intractable.

Again, Hogarth follows Fludd's iconographic and philosophical leads precisely. The top of the giant church steeple and clock tower looms over the center of Soho in *Noon,* derived in form and function from the Egyptian obelisk that anchors Fludd's *Oculus.* Because of its formal position in this hybridized image of the Bruno-Fludd memory systems, and its function as a bridge for the four memory chambers, Yates has wisely argued that the obelisk also signifies Bruno's faith in the pivotal power of the "'inner writing' of the art [of memory]." Memory negotiates the macrocosm and microcosm, imposing order on chaos, in much the same way that Ficino conceptualized the soul as "bond and knot of the world."[128]

Through the intermediary of inner writing, the five memory images collapse together in *Oculus* and *Noon.* Hogarth's modern history painting thus becomes an eclectic synthesis of Bruno's "medieval" Egyptianism; the Fludd–de Bry reinterpretation of Bruno as Paracelsian natural philosophy hidden in the borderless experience of Huguenot refugees; the resulting ethnic and cultural heterodoxy of modern urban artisanal life, further amplified by the centripetal pull of commercialization; and, finally, the emergence of eighteenth-century British Freemasonry out of the remnants of sixteenth-century Rosicrucianism. This provides a meaningful context for one of the pivotal moments in *Noon,* when the Huguenot congregation rotates away from the Eglise des Grecs (and the false eloquence of ancient and scholastic philosophical traditions). Turning back to the future hidden inside the shadows of memory, they find direction by heading toward the steeple (the obelisk of convergence in Fludd's *Oculus* and Bruno's privileging of the Egyptian hermetic tradition in *De umbris idearum*). Why else did Hogarth represent himself as a fierce champion of what was, for want of a better term, pictorial "inner writing," but to show common cause with Bruno and Fludd?

❧ "Find the grammar of the art" ❧

In the tradition of early eighteenth-century Paracelsian discourse, Hogarth's autobiographical *Anecdotes. . . Written by Himself* (1781) betrays the same persecuted craftsman's anti-scholastic disdain for the dangers of "ancient" eloquence that attended Palissy's efforts to privilege the authenticity of the production of rustic artisanal language over writing. In this brief but closely written autobiography, Hogarth takes up the discourse of the oppressed "natural" artist and craftsman, proving such rhetoric could survive the absence of religious violence, finding inspiration in the very real (if less operatic) pressures and anxieties of an urban commercial context. Language of artisanal oppression may have been cobbled together from bits of Palissy, whose written and craft production had been known in Soho since the early seventeenth century. Or from shop talk with the Huguenot goldsmiths and engravers with whom Hogarth apprenticed as a young printer and later worked alongside as a master. It may also have blended with the private "craft" discourse of Hogarth's Masonic lodge. Clearly, it was derived self-consciously from materials with a strong history in the Huguenot corpus.

Hogarth's *Anecdotes* reads like a narrative of a Paracelsian craftsman's coming of age as a disciple of Robert Fludd in early eighteenth-century London.[129] At the very beginning of *Anecdotes,* Hogarth locates "the natural turn I had for drawing rather than learning languages" in the ambivalent relation that his father Richard—a classical scholar and writer of a Latin dictionary—had with the corrupt publishing industry. Constructing an allegory out of his personal history, Hogarth recounts how he intentionally charted his professional course away from the "cruel" and insecure "labour" of writing. This was exemplified by the failed latinate scholasticism of his father, Richard Hogarth. Thus the youthful Hogarth moved toward security in his apprenticeship in the unwritten, manual, and natural language as a tradesman in visual art and artisanry:

> Beside the natural turn I had for drawing rather than learning languages, I had before my eyes the precarious situation of men of classical education. I saw the difficulties under which my father laboured, and the many inconveniences he endured, from his dependence being chiefly on his pen, and the cruel treatment he met from booksellers and printers, particularly in the affair of a Latin Dictionary, the compiling of which had been the work of some years. It was deposited, in confidence, in the hands of a certain printer, and, during the time it was left, letters of approbation were received from the greatest scholars in England, Scotland, and Ireland. But these testimonies . . . produced no profit to the author. It was therefore very conformable to my own wishes that I was taken from school, and served a long apprenticeship to a silver-plate engraver. I soon found this business in every respect too limited. . . . paintings . . . ran in my head; and I determined that silver-plate engraving should be followed no longer than necessity obliged me to do it. Engraving on copper was, at twenty years of age, my utmost ambition.[130]

Learning his trade as an engraver, Hogarth confronted the same superficial and catechistic repetition that limited inquiry in the old scholastic method. Hogarth sought a "method" to "draw objects something like nature" in painting and printmaking, a task that required a deep philosophical knowledge of the anatomy and material structure of the natural world: "I had learned, by practice, to copy with tolerable exactness in the usual way; but it occurred to me that there were many disadvantages attending this method of study . . . even when the pictures or prints to be imitated were by the best masters, it was little more than pouring water out of one vessel into another."[131] Simply to draw matter "after the life" did not guarantee sufficient mastery to animate the artist's subject: overcoming the ontological disconnection between the artist "in the academy" and the memory of engaged experience in the natural world: "Drawing in an academy, though it should be after the life, will not make the student an artist; for as the eye is often taken from the original, to draw a bit at a time, it is possible he may know no more of what he has been copying, when his work is finished, than he did before it was begun."[132] The analogy is again with scholasticism. Here the problem lies with fragmentation and disunity, the "dull transcriber['s]" inability to "embrace the whole":

> There may be, and I believe are, some who, like the engrosser of deeds, copy every line without remembering a word; and if the deed should be in law Latin, or old French, probably without understanding a word of their original. Happy is it for them; for to retain would be indeed dreadful.
>
> A dull transcriber, who in copying Milton's "Paradise Lost" hath not omitted a line, has almost as much right to be compared to Milton, as an exact copier of a fine picture by Rubens hath to be compared to Rubens. *In both cases the hand is employed about minute parts, but the mind scarcely ever embraces the whole* [emphasis added] . . . Yet the performer will be much more likely to retain a recollection of his own imperfect work than of the original from which he took it.[133]

Hogarth also carried the linguistic analogy one step further to its logical conclusion. Loathe to play the role of superficial copyist, "employed about minute parts" of form devoid of meaning of "the whole," from which "to retain a recollection" when removed by the eye from the original context and set down in another, Hogarth reasoned that a solution to the problem lay in the communicative function of art. Building on Fludd and anticipating the extension of Ferdinand de Saussure's structural linguistics into an analogy with the "language" of modern culture and art developed by Roland Barthes, Meyer Schapiro, Norberg-Schultz, and others, Hogarth asserted his ability to deconstruct the retrospective logic of any painting's linguistic structures and then commit them to memory to reconstruct them in practice. Thus, nearly a half-century after Hogarth completed *The Four Times of the Day*, he reveals his great intellectual and artistic debt to the Fludd–de Bry partnership in writing as well as painting.

This information was not revealed openly. As in *Noon*, knowledge was made available covertly to the initiated, who had the experience to decode the Fluddian references embedded in the text. These linguistic structures "fix[ed]," in the figurative sense, as "forms and characters in my mind." Following Bruno's "axiomatic" contribution to the English art of memory, these structures were "perfect *ideas* of the subject [Hogarth] meant to draw":

More reasons, not necessary to enumerate, struck me as strong objections to this practice [of the copyist], and led me to wish that I could find the shorter path,—fix forms and characters in my mind, and, instead of *copying* the lines, try to read the language, and if possible find the grammar of the art, by bringing into one focus the various observations I had made, and then trying by my power on the canvas, how far my plan enabled me to combine and apply them to practice.

For this purpose, I considered what various ways, and to what different purposes, the memory might be applied; and fell upon one which I found most suitable to my situation and idle disposition.

Laying it down first as an axiom, that he who could by any means acquire and retain in his memory, *perfect ideas of the subject he meant to draw* [emphasis added], would have as clear a knowledge of the figure, as a man who can write freely hath of the twenty-four letters of the alphabet, and their infinite combinations (each of these being composed of lines), and would consequently be an accurate designer.[134]

Hogarth's ambitions in exploiting the art of memory were complex. Here, it was to realize the full potential for profit that eluded the meticulous scholarship of his father Richard, who suffered loss of his labor when publishers appropriated his Latin definitions without compensation. The skillful but inexperienced Richard made these readily available because he did not hold the copyright. As a result, William sought far more mastery than to acquire great skill as an "accurate designer." He sought complete control over his own labor through sale of products unique to his imagination. This is the context for Hogarth's famous application for copyright protection to Parliament in 1735, just three years before *Noon* was published as a print.

❧ Commerce and the Oppressed Tradesman ❧

More interesting for our purposes, is the Palissian language of the corrupt oppression of "innovation" and "the ingenuity of the industrious," Hogarth appropriates for his summary of the incident in *Anecdotes*. "It will also be proper to recollect," he wrote:

> that after having had my plates pirated in almost all sizes, I in 1735 applied to Parliament for redress; and obtained it in so liberal a manner, as hath not only answered my own purpose, but made prints a considerable article in the commerce of this country; there being now more business of this kind done here, than in Paris, or any where else, and as well.
>
> The dealers in pictures and prints found their craft in danger, by what they called a new fangled innovation. Their trade of living and getting fortunes by the ingenuity of the industrious, has, I know, suffered much by my interference; and if the detection of this band of public cheats, and oppressors of the rising artists, be a crime, I confess myself most guilty.[135]

Hogarth's intense fear of oppression by dominant forces was not limited to commerce. It was also available in the traditional language of ambivalence adopted by the earlier artisan-heretics, who negotiated the risks and consequences of self-representation and public exposure to pain, humiliation, and loss through the insecure production of a written text.[136] Listen as Hogarth decodes the "principles" of visual language in writing. Note the use of artisanal analogies—in particular, textile and upholstery—as well as the tension between the security of innovation kept private and the risk of ridicule when made public. Now familiar references to "malicious attacks" on self and family appear as well:

> Though the pen was to me a new instrument, yet, as the mechanic at his loom may possibly give as satisfactory an account of the materials and composition of the rich brocade he weaves, as the smooth-tongued mercer, surrounded with all his parade of showy silks, I trusted that I might make myself tolerably understood, by those who would take the trouble of examining my book [*The Analysis of Beauty*] and prints together; for, as one who makes use of signs and gestures to convey his meaning in a language of which he has little knowledge, I have occasionally had recourse to my pencil. For this I have been assailed by every profligate scribbler in town, and told that, though words are man's province, they are not my province; . . . accused of vanity, ignorance, and envy; called a mean and contemptible dauber; represented in the strangest employments, and pictured in the strangest shapes; sometimes under the hierographical semblance of a satyr, and at others under the still more ingenious one of an ass.
>
> Not satisfied with this . . . they endeavored to wound the peace of my family. This was a cruelty hardly to be forgiven: to say that such malicious attacks and caricatures did not discompose me would be untrue, for to be held up to public ridicule would discompose any man . . . I knew that those who would venture to oppose received notions, must in return have public abuse.[137]

"My only chance for eminence," Hogarth wrote, was to transcend and devalue technical skill with the burin—a skill in which many others exceeded him—and to use, in this instance, the square (or "technical") art of memory, to recombine old images he had stored, and reinvent them "in my own mind" like bricolage. Memory emerged from this process as novelty and was exchanged for cash:

> This I thought my only chance for eminence, as I found that the beauty and delicacy of the stroke in engraving was not to be learnt without much practice, and demanded a larger portion of patience than I felt myself disposed to exercise. Added to this, I saw little probability of acquiring full command of the graver, in a sufficient way to distinguish myself in that walk; nor was I, at twenty years of age, much disposed to enter on so barren and unprofitable a study as that of merely making fine lines. I thought it still more unlikely,

that by pursuing the common method, and copying *old* drawings, I could ever attain the power of making *new* designs, which was my first and greatest ambition. I therefore endeavored to habituate myself to the exercize of *a sort of* [emphasis added] technical memory; and by repeating in my own mind, the parts of which objects were composed, I could by degrees combine and put them down with my pencil. Thus, with all the drawbacks which resulted from the circumstances I have mentioned, I had one material advantage over my competitors, *viz.,* the early habit I thus acquired if retaining them *in my mind's eye* [emphasis added], without coldly copying on the spot, whatever I intended to imitate. Sometimes, but too seldom, I took the life, for correcting the parts I had not perfectly enough remembered, and then I transferred them to my compositions.[138]

In the end, despite the fact most of his prints were executed by Huguenot shop printers, contemporary critics noted that Hogarth developed an idiosyncratic style with the "graver." Given his natural philosophy, his quickness, his aim to achieve a "grammar" of natural language rather than the "polish"—even if he relied on memory and rarely "took the life"—prints attributed to Hogarth's hand and not his shop were usually described positively as "struck off at once," "rough," "warm from the imagination," and full "of the force and spirit of his expression."[139] Even the Reverend William Gilpin, a contemporary of Hogarth's and a critic of the artist's "low" subject matter, his technical inadequacies in "composition," his "distribution of light," and his "drawing," conceded:

> He etches with great spirit, and never gives one unnecessary stroke. For myself, I greatly more value the works of his own needle, than those high-finished prints, on which he employed other engravers. For, as the production of an effect is not his talent, and this is the chief excellence of high finishing, his own rough manner is certainly preferable, in which we have most of the force and spirit of his expression.[140]

In the sixteenth century, the words "rough" and "rustic" would be synonymous.

Hogarth's elision of "more reasons, not necessary to enumerate," which "struck me as strong objections to this practice" of copyist, may be linked to reading Fludd on the art of memory, Palissy in the original (or in Platt's English book-of-secrets edition), as well as other "secret" Paracelsian materials. His reticence may also be linked his admission into the mysteries of Freemasonry. Be that as it may, overwhelming evidence of Fludd's prevailing influence pervades discussions of methodology in *Anecdotes,* including a plain reference to the use of "striking" memory images "from nature," thus leading to animated compositions which succeeded in communicating the painter-printmaker's unified messages to society, "although similar subjects had often failed in writing and preaching":

My pleasures and my studies thus going hand in hand, the most striking objects that presented themselves, either comic or tragic, made the strongest impression on my mind; but
had I not sedulously practiced what I thus acquired, I should very soon have lost the power
of performing it.

Instead of burthening the memory with musty rules, or tiring the eyes with copying
dry and damaged pictures, I have ever found studying from nature the shortest and safest
way of attaining knowledge in my art. By adopting this method, I found a redundancy of
matter continually occuring . . . choice of composition . . . naturally led me to the use of
such materials as I had previously collected; and to this I was further induced by thinking,
that if properly combined, *they might be made the most useful to society in painting, although
similar subjects had often failed in writing and preaching* [emphasis added].[141]

"Studying from nature" was also key to competitive success for the dominant
Huguenot textile workers, couturiers, and artisans in the other luxury trades, who filled
London's refugee ghettos, and Soho in particular. The Huguenot St. Martin's Academy, where Hogarth mastered his skill, was renowned specifically for this practice.
Hogarth apprenticed with (and hired) many such artisans with connections to southwestern France. Thus, it is noteworthy that at the conclusion of a sarcastic discourse
on prospects for academic drawing classes for native apprentices under the auspices of
an English "Society for the Encouragement of Arts, Manufactures, and Commerce"—
a domestic strategy for narrowing the huge French advantage in the luxury trades—
Hogarth wrote tellingly about a variant of the Palissian method (of "casting" from life),
used by his own Huguenot master engravers:

How absurd it would be to see perriwig-makers' and shoemakers' boys learning the art of
drawing, that they might give grace to a peruke or slipper. If the study of Claude's landscapes would benefit the carver of a picture fame, or the contemplation of a finely painted
saucepan by Teniers, or Basson, would be an improvement to a tinman, it would be highly
proper for this Society to encourage them in the practice of the arts. But as this is not the
case, giving lads of all ranks a little knowledge of everything, is almost as absurd as it
would be to instruct shopkeepers in oratory, that that they may be thus enables to talk
people into buying their goods, because oratory is necessary in the bar and in the pulpit.
*As to giving premiums to those that design flowers, &c, for silks and linens, let it be recollected
that these artisans copy the objects they introduce from nature* [emphasis added]; a much surer
guide then all the [then fashionable] childish and ridiculous absurdities of temples, drag-
ons, pagodas, and other fantastic fripperies, which have been imported from China.[142]

"Studying from nature" to gain knowledge of its variety, and *experience* with the
"sportiveness" of Nature's complex patterns of fluidity and contingency, became Hogarth's credo and the basis for his reactivation of a sixteenth-century Paracelsian cri-

tique of the neoscholastic natural philosophy of modern painting. Painting without seeing by the inexperienced was based on theory acquired mainly from books. For Hogarth, this meant "giving rules for the operative part of the art," not privileging practical experience with the "physiological . . . nature of the objects."[143] "The first attempts that were made to fix" and reify as absolute the reversal of nature's authentic hierarchy of visual knowledge "were by natural philosophers." Unlike Paracelsus, the scholastic school failed to ground useful Neoplatonic ideals in experience, and:

> who, in their amplified contemplations on the universal beauty displayed in the harmony and order of nature, very soon lost themselves; an event that, from the way in which they set out, was inevitable; for . . . it necessarily led them into the *wide road of order and regularity* [rather than the narrow path of faith and discipline?], which they unexpectantly found crossed and intersected by many other paths, that led into the *labyrinths of variety;* where, not having passed through the *province of painting,* they became confused, and could never find their way. To explaining the order and usefulness of nature they might be equal; *but of her sportiveness and fancy, they were totally ignorant* [emphasis added].[144]

Like Palissy, Hogarth found the intersection of order and variety (or synchronic and diachronic time) in the "province" of naturalistic painting (and rustic ceramics) formed out of the primordial art of memory. Also like Palissy, Hogarth disdained, rhetorically, all but "simple" knowledge learned directly from the book of Nature:

> Nature is simple, plain, and true, in all her works, and those who strictly adhere to her laws, and closely attend to her appearances in their infinite varieties, are guarded against any prejudiced bias from truth; while those who have seen many things that they cannot well understand, and read many books which they do not fully comprehend, notwithstanding all their pompous parade of knowledge, are apt to wander about and about it, perpetually perplexing themselves and their readers with the various opinions of other men.[145]

Put in the natural-philosophical language of *Noon:* without insight into the hidden metaphysical nature of composite material bodies and things Raphael provided Tobias to give him experience, the scholarly traveler, lacking *oculus imaginationis* and although he had "seen many things," might finally stumble across the narrow path to truth only "to wander about it and about it." As did the proverbial professor of theology, he might also wander past the philosopher's stone unnoticed—hidden in plain sight—like refuse in the street. Fludd's geomancer would also agree that those who "closely attend" and *experience* Nature's "appearances in their infinite varieties" without "prejudiced bias" find inner perception to see behind pluralities and composite existence. As would those reading through the appearance of chaos in the refugee "Babel" of Hog Lane, or who discern hidden order within the surface of the fluid glazes that Palissy dripped and dotted in unencumbered patterns down the body of his art of the earth. These chosen few who had overcome the temptation of their own fallen bodies were put on earth to perceive in Nature what is "simple, plain, and true, in all her works."

Hogarth's *Anecdotes* thus amplifies Fludd's art of memory and its influence on the painter's natural-philosophical agenda in *Noon*. In effect, an autobiographical text served as discursive supplement to the composite pictorial narrative in this oblique history painting of Huguenot artisanal experience in the shadows. In *Anecdotes*, Hogarth reconstructed his personal experience as a modern tradesman to merge almost seamlessly into the alchemic narrative of the Paracelsian artisan. He found particular affinity with the wartime discourse of the "oppression" of the "industrious" and "innovative" Protestant craftsman, made available beginning with the French civil wars of religion in "New World" texts exemplified by the writings of Jean de Léry and Bernard Palissy and reaching full development in England in the Fludd–de Bry universalist response to the ravages of the Thirty Years' War. In the midst of it all, the fall of the fortress at La Rochelle remained the central icon of lost security and millennial anxiety for reformers. I have argued that Palissy's innovations emerged out of his war experience as a Saintongeais Huguenot craftsman, necessitating the invention of covert artisanal languages to compete with the fixity and exposure of writing. We have seen, in a parallel way, how Hogarth also pursued innovation in the analysis, memorization, and naturalistic recomposition of what he called the "grammar" of painting, as a fluid alternative language of self-expression, self-mastery, and self-protection in the face of perceived corrupt trade practices and belligerent patrons and critics who "discomposed" Hogarth and his household with "cruel" attacks.

But above all, it was the unbounded, synchronic universalism of Fludd's memory project that attracted the innovator in Hogarth, whose response was the line of beauty that animated the art of Nature. He opposed the catechistic copy as self-limiting and unnatural, but the "drudgery" of modern mechanical reproduction was stigmatized as unprofitable. Art harnessed to mere repetition for its own sake was the inverse of novelty. "I could not bring myself to act like some of my brethren," Hogarth wrote with disdain, "and make it a sort of manufactory, to be carried on by the help of back-ground and drapery painters, it was not sufficiently profitable to pay the expenses my family required."[146] Fear of slavery to technique as a mere "operator" exploited by employers as well as the quest for a novelty to "pay the expenses," caused Hogarth to conceive "modern morals" as his subject.

"To prove his powers and vindicate his fame," Hogarth harnessed morality and materialism together using seventeenth-century Neoplatonic and alchemic language, to recreate a new sort of modern history painting. Hog Lane transcended national, disciplinary and temporal boundaries and unified cultures fragmented by the violent dislocations of history. Having been admitted into the mysteries of seventeenth-century Huguenot natural philosophy through cosmopolitan apprenticeship and Freemasonry, Hogarth "turned my thoughts to a still more novel mode, *viz.* painting and engraving modern moral subjects, *a field not broken up in any country or in any age* [emphasis added]."[147]

Hogarth's moral subjects, based on social interaction in "those scenes where the human species are actors," replaced overt religiosity "rejected . . . in England."[148] Like "intermediate" souls in serpentine patterns, these subjects were bridges to connect apparently disconnected disciplinary fragments across space and time. The task of this new sort of painting, then, was nothing less than to synthesize what he defined as a modern dialectic "between the sublime and grotesque." The sublime and grotesque may be taken as Hogarthian stand-ins for macrocosm and microcosm. The modern painter's role in the natural-philosophical exploration of intermediate territory where, like Palissy, Hogarth found "totally overlooked . . . *species* of subjects" hidden in the shadows was analogous to the adept's conjunction of opposites at the nexus of the monism. This was something no mere alchemic "operator"—or artful "copyist"—was capable of performing: "The reasons which induced me to adopt this mode of designing were, that I thought both writers and painters had, in the historical style, *totally overlooked that intermediate species of subjects,* [emphasis added] which may be placed between the sublime and grotesque."[149]

Hogarth's final homage to the art of memory virtually glossed Fludd's *Oculus,* merging his text and de Bry's images in *Theatrum orbi* with the novelty of moral subjects. Hogarth reconfirmed that his unified art was performed in a memory theater that was technically "difficult" because of the universality of its proportions. On stage was ground where "intermediate species . . . may be placed," while exposed to the light to perform roles in public. Here they risked interstitial transition between the theater's many levels. Or else they had to wait, hidden in the shadows of the infinite niches and memory chambers, for other, more opportune moments to appear:

> I therefore wished to compose pictures on canvas, similar to representations on the stage; and further hope that they will be tried by the same test, and criticised by the same criterion. . . . In these compositions, those subjects that will both entertain and improve the mind, bid fair to be of the greatest public utility, and must therefore be entitled to rank in the highest class. If the execution is difficult (though that is but a secondary merit), the author has claim to a higher degree of praise. . . . Ocular demonstrations will carry more conviction to the mind of a sensible man, than all he would find in a thousand volumes; and this has been attempted in the prints I have composed. Let the decision be left to every unprejudiced eye, let the figures in either pictures or prints be considered as players dressed . . . for high or low life. I have endeavored to treat my subjects as a dramatic writer:

my picture is my stage, and men and women my players, who by means of certain actions and gestures, are to exhibit *a dumb show*.[150]

In this "dumb show" "of actions and gestures" and performance without words, the tradesman Hogarth "made all possible use of the technical memory which I have before described": "by observing and endeavoring to retain in my mind lineally, such objects as best suited my purpose; so that be where I would, while my eyes were open, I was at my studies, and acquiring something useful to my profession."[151]

Use of the art of memory to recreate natural life, allowed Hogarth to project a certain equivalence onto all the memory images in his pictures; an overall effect that could not be achieved with the camera obscura. In this sense, all images were equally important for the spectator to see clearly, since images on the periphery of a canvas (or in the shadows) were connected with those at the core and informed their meaning. Hogarth implies reading hierarchies may be "difficult," requiring the reader to acknowledge that every memory figure is inextricably linked and must be considered as part of an interactive cosmology of painting. The moral, then, "of the greatest public utility" in "moral subjects" is that *no* subject may be safely "overlooked" in modern public life:

> By this means, whatever I saw, whether a remarkable incident, or a trifling subject, became more truly a picture than one that was drawn by a *camera obscura*. And thus the most striking objects, whether of beauty or deformity, were by habit the most easily impressed and retained in my imagination. A redundancy of matter being by this means acquired, it is natural to suppose I introduced it into my works on every occasion that I could.[152]

❧ Tiny, Industrious, Overlooked ❧

Sixteenth-century Saintonge thus comes full circle, emerging again in Hogarth's London. We hear the humble artisan of Palissy's rhetorical voice at the end of a "modern" Paracelsian craftsman's narrative of experience. We witness the theatrical reemergence of the Huguenot potter's miniscule, hidden, metamorphic, "rustique figulines" in Hogarth's exposure of the "trifling subject" as public actor on a global stage.

To look down into the marshy rocks and grottoes of civil war Saintonge's "intermediate" earth was to recognize that "the most striking objects, whether of beauty or deformity," were also the smallest, most vulnerable, and yet also most skilled survivors; natural creatures who—like Palissy and his fellow heretics—crafted themselves and their surroundings to blend transparently with the elements of the earth. "Overlooked" by predatory enemies, "industrious" creatures manipulated the condition of invisibility to effect a reversal of power, which Hogarth plays out on Hog Lane. "Four things which are little upon the earth, but they are exceedingly wise," Proverbs 30:24–28 says.

After the ants, conies (or rabbits, "a feeble folk, yet make their houses in the rocks"), and locusts, which " have no king, yet they go forth all of them by bands"), have been listed with their attributes, the fourth is the spider, which, like Palissy himself, "taketh hold with her hands, and is in kings' palaces." And like the Protestant autodidact Palissy—as well as Paracelsus, Bruno, and Fludd—the similarly anti-scholastic and self-promoting Hogarth "grew . . . to admire nature":

> beyond the first productions of art, and acknowledged I saw, or fancied, delicacies in the life, so far surpassing the utmost efforts of imitation, that when I drew the comparison in mind, I could not help uttering blasphemous expressions against the divinity even of Raphael, Urbino, Corregio, and Michael Angelo. For this, though my brethren have unmercifully abused me, I hope to be forgiven. I confess to have frequently said . . . the style . . . I had adopted . . . might . . . be made more entertaining and useful than the eternal blazonry, and tedious repetition of hackneyed, beaten subjects, either from the Scriptures, or the old ridiculous stories of heathen gods; *as neither the religion of one or the other requires promoting among Protestants, as it formerly did in Greece, and at a later period in Rome* [emphasis added].[153]

To validate the authenticity of "innovative" and "industrious" "labor" in the reformation of modern painting, Hogarth appropriated the last measure of autobiographical identity from the experience of his artisan predecessors in the shadows of Hog Lane. His was a geomancer's labor, using experience to remove the veil of the "white film" of iconography from the eyes of the public. What was revealed behind the chaotic fictions of catechistic "repetition" of history were remnants of primordial meaning hidden in the "dumb" natural history of quotidian materials. Yet the hidden was simultaneously exposed by the "actions and gestures" of the "trifling, overlooked, intermediate species" of elemental earth. By extending the secretive strategies of the sixteenth- and seventeenth-century artisanal reformation of Greek and Roman "divinity" into the commercial "theater of the world" of *"modern"* Protestantism, Hogarth created novelty out of the refugee quest for security, and hence profit out of moral subjects derived from the "heretical opinions" of Huguenot craftsmen.[154]

Soho's aging and experienced master artisans circle back in time and then forward in *Noon.* By circling into the sundial's shadow and out of the light of authority, they enter simultaneously into the shadow of memory and the realm of prophetic time. On this centripetal route to the heart of refugee spiritual and economic culture, the congregation follows the round art of memory on its slippery cosmological path. There, the pious artisan locates the source of nature's Neoplatonic soul in the animate material world of Fludd's "microcosmic arts." "Deeper still," wrote Fludd in "De geomantia," "towards the center the *spiritus* of empyreal heaven lies hidden"; what is *spiritus* but "the revealer of things future and present." Turning inward to contemplate this material-holiness connection with the unity, the congregation has prepared itself by its experience with sacred violence and the forced pilgrimage of exile to participate bodily in the recreation of earth's elemental obstetric processes.

The pious refugees reject temptations of the street that lead others to the chaos of impious mixing and to "hoggish" crapulence and sustain their sacred bodies with the Word alone. Still, they do not reject the marketplace, where they "multiply" their "treasures." Instead, they reject style for personal consumption and with it the superficial "repetition" of the history of material life. They separate from the "high life" symbolized by the theatrical trio of narcissists dressed in French fashions promoted and purchased in Huguenot shops. Self-contained and implicitly celibate (most are long past child-bearing age), this ancient community is immune to the distractions of sexuality. The refugees are not involved with the fleshy concerns that consume their neighbors across the gutter and that troubled Palissy, Fludd, and Böhme in their quest for order in the pure fecundity of alchemic rebirth.

The Huguenots return, therefore, to locate the soul's hiding place in the shadow world of the fortress of memory (fig. 14.15). In so doing, the group *almost* disappears amid the distracting hurly-burly of the street. Like Palissy's chameleons, which can assume the color of earth, they are present and absent at once. This power also allows them to appear "in kings' palaces." Yet for all these representations of an identity of ascetic purity, one may also legitimately open the painting up to alternative readings according to spectators' various perspectives (or position in the market). Here the shadow figures may appear to be either benign or ominous. Multiple readings are supported by the claim that Huguenots could disperse like the "subtle effluvium" of the soul described by the French Prophets then preaching in the streets of London.[155]

Hogarth's moral subjects naturally beg moral questions. Are the Huguenots, Hog Lane's producers, exempt from doubt about the purity of their intentions in the marketplace, even if they are represented as the prophets of materialism, pure in body and soul? How have their artisanal activities contributed to the creation of the chaos this group apparently deplores? As "counterfeits" and producers of materials that sink to the level of frippery when acquired by inexperienced consumers, do self-interested Huguenot artisans conflate the crucial difference between being and appearance for the sake of novelty and profit? Does anything go in the name of security and self-preservation in the modern urban world? Hogarth cannot fail to ask of his subjects and himself: Who benefits most from consumption of dissimulation and camouflage, literally built into artifacts of politeness? Hogarth's metaphor of the glutton begs the question further: if the race and spiritual inexperience of the African sailor *qua* ape of nature eliminates him as a possibility, who alone in this picture possesses the artisanal skills and mastery necessary to transform "raw" materials into "cooked," polished products for the delectation of the spiritually weak and morally undisciplined? The chaotic simultaneity and the reflected ambiguity of *Noon* make such questions about personal complicity in these "moral subjects" a matter of personal perception.

These are also natural subjects, however; various specimens of humanity who perform discreetly as well as overtly on Hog Lane. Information is revealed quickly for the adept, but knowledge comes more slowly and uncertainly for most, through the contingency and accident of face-to-face interaction. Unfortunately, Hog Lane's babel of chaotic interaction effectively denies all but the most experienced spectators the unities of moral, visual, or even temporal clarity. The canonical tropes and empirical authority of Enlightenment science cannot but fail to reach into every corner of Hog Lane. Here, in the shadows, authority has been reversed, devolving *naturally* to reside among intermediate species of overlooked subjects in life and memory, who spend their time scuttling in and out of the light of publicity. In these camouflaged places, social and cultural rules are seldom uniform. They are private and unclear, improvised for safety or maximum benefit in negotiation. Among refugees, rules were cobbled together from individual, family, and community memories with origins in religious persecution or the everyday danger of relative powerlessness and the consequent necessity for secrecy. At midday (or, following the series' title, the "intermediate" time of day), in the transactional, largely oral culture of artisanry and street commerce, Soho's Huguenots are intermediate actors par excellence.

Recall our preliminary discussion of Hogarth's debt to de Bry in his placement of the double door on Hog Lane. Look closely, for the last time, at the two central elements in Fludd's *"theater of the world."* As Herve and the elderly congregation of the Eglise des Grecs descend from beneath the pulpitlike *échauguette* and "look out" from the shadows, they project the calm power of Stoic self-mastery. At the same time, they also conduct surveillance on the scene of impious mixing, consumption, and anxiety. Like a soldier standing lookout in his individual *échauguette,* who was also capable of firing out anonymously from behind the tiny gun sight, a double sense of personal security is revealed. Congregants display the potential to mount a complex and hidden defense of one's interests through a dialogue of surveillance and aggressive response to information surreptitiously gathered. The aggressive "defense" of self-interest might include invention and production of fashionable items of material culture sold on Hog Lane, a source of capital, prestige, and security. Detached and strategic surveillance of consumer desire was the historical role of innovative Huguenot tastemakers and designers.

Over a century after the fall of La Rochelle, refugee artisans had the skills to preserve the lost walls of the enceinte of the great *place de sûreté* as a private fortress of constructed memory, reinvented by Palissy, Fludd, and de Bry as a mobile, universal fortress to be carried with every individual into the Huguenots' New World, like the snail's shell. Diffused in the Atlantic world during the critical decade in which La Rochelle succumbed to the catastrophic fragmentation that Palissy first predicted in 1563, and elucidated from the natural-philosophical perspective of contingency, adaptation, and spiritual universality, the mutable fortress of memory, hidden "under the figures" of the theater of the world, manifested Palissy's rustic plan for an interior and hence unassailable program of artisanal security. Everyman now constructed and disassembled his own fortress, according to his skills and assets, wherever needed.

When the Huguenot refugees leave the Eglise des Grecs and turn back "deeper still" in a serpentine line to extend the "rays" of the *spiritus* of pious experience into the world of their workshops, they disappear under the sign of the headless woman (jutting halfway over the narrow path between the two buildings that open back into Soho). Simultaneously, they enter on the narrow path occupied by the half-open door under the *échauguette* in de Bry's "theater of the world." Inside, only the sign of a ceramic pitcher on a pedestal remains to be seen; is this a memory image or a Huguenot relic in the shadows? Perhaps this most obscure of all the signs on Hog Lane advertises the premises of an invisible shop where wine may be purchased. We know Hogarth has played this game many times before. By now, only naïve spectators perceive merely a transparent signifier of production and consumption on Hog Lane. The experienced spectator remembers to expect that every sign on this street carries multiple meanings, and that experience carries with it the supplement of the *oculus imaginationis*.

That this particular sign is an earthenware pot is suggestive on at least two levels of interpretation: first, because Hogarth was widely employed by the English ceramics industry to provide designs from his popular paintings and prints for use on pottery, he was the most knowledgeable painter in London about the early history, materials, and technology of this subject. This included the crucial role of naturalistic Huguenot potters such as Palissy and his followers in England during the early seventeenth century, particularly in the production of the so-called "fecundity dishes" that appeared in London just after the fall of La Rochelle.[156] Hogarth apprenticed and worked among Huguenots. He knew their "secrets." Hogarth's interest in Palissy would be spurred by intimate knowledge of local oral tradition and his desire to learn the universal "grammar" of the ceramic art. Palissy's historical and natural-philosophical discourses were available in alchemical libraries in the original editions, and interest in his writings revived during the eighteenth century; witness the edition of his works dedicated to Franklin. It is very probable, then, that Hogarth read Palissy, as did many self-invented Protestant artists and natural philosophers. Certainly, he examined examples of rustic pottery made by Palissy and English followers of his. Moreover, Hogarth esteemed Franklin as a kindred spirit and correspondent (he purportedly lay in bed reading a laudatory letter from Poor Richard himself at the moment of his death); he would have been attentive to the dedication. And second, we now understand that *Noon* was intended to be read as both an allegory of Fludd's treatise on geomancy and a formal exposition of its visual "language" and "grammar." This is broadly defined as "terrestrial astrology": the alchemical art of divining forms of natural order out of historical chaos by "producing" and deploying associated dots of elemental earth. With this in mind, it is worth noticing that a similarly formed pitcher is deployed as a sign of distillation in Hogarth's *Gin Lane* (1751).[157]

This definition also serves as a reasonable definition of Palissy's "humble art of the earth." "Without any doubt," Fludd's geomancer wrote, if *mens divina* and *humana* unify, "in conjunction with *anima*, [they] may perform very great actions and may direct them towards a felicitous climax and issue." Here was a later variation on the alchemic art of Palissian self-mastery. The Neoplatonic natural philosopher was liberated from the obscuring veil by disciplining sublimated sexuality. He experienced pious pleasure and material fecundity, as represented in the seventeenth-century "Palissy Plates" of London manufacture, made and traded by Fludd's and Winthrop's contemporaries. Dispersed dots of elemental earth—"persons" (like the dispersed refugees)—were also made into enduring structures by Hogarth's artist's "grammar," and tested for alchemic purity by the primordial experience of refugee lives: the fire of sacred violence.

Thereupon, the chosen survivors were "withdrawn from the multitude." "Under the figures" of geomantic perception, they were found again, after having been distilled from chaos to simplicity by the art of memory. Thus, they were available as discrete images for perception of the *oculus imaginationis.* New forms of prophetic earths were "issued" and reborn, resulting from the conjunction (or metaphorical coitus) of the universal soul with Nature descended into the microcosm. Given form by artisanal memory of Adam before the Fall, stirred by the craftsman's animate soul, a process was begun that unified those disparate earthly parts of Christ's body, fragmented by war and dispersion. The fragments of Christ's body that were dispersed like relics into the refuge from apocalyptic events in La Rochelle in 1627–28, rematerialized through this process as artifacts linked to the millennial status of those humble artisans who constructed interconnected "constellations" of tiny things that comprised the "natural" matter of everyday life. In *Noon,* Hogarth confirmed the presence of a constellation of things by the "transit" of the sun on the polite lady's face and cap, a motion we have traced into the shadows, where sunlight was submerged and reconfigured as a row of earth-colored architectural lights or pendant drops. Deep in the background, the earthenware pitcher, analogous in form to these inner lights, merges into the transit of the star as it recedes in shadow on the sundial.

❧ A Rustic Pot in the City: Seeing in the Metropolis ❧

Like Palissy and the potter of final things in Jeremiah, when Soho's aging Huguenot "artisans of the [aging] earth," enter the half-open double door of the *theatrum orbi* at the appointed "time of the day," and so the protective shadows of the fortress of memory, their spiritual bodies transmute into an amorphous state like earth brown clay or gray slip. They are distilled, and then molded into the secret source and material creation of "felicitous" reproductive power. Here, the philosophical tradesman's power of infinite reproduction is contained in an earthenware pitcher, once overlooked as the mere marginalia or ephemera of Hogarth's text; a naïve, rustic, and styleless container distinguished only by its banality.

Like Palissy's geode, his snail, Fludd's geomantic dots, or Hogarth's moral investigations of the art of memory, the external appearance of this dull, timeless object is an ontological inversion; in effect, an artifactual palindrome. Unlike the mechanistic sun, pietistic beauty had a charismatic light. It shone recessively, in the private constellation of things. Hidden in plain sight in humble containers, this aesthetic was viable in the dark, while others slept, like tiny nocturnal creatures on Palissy's pottery. "The natures of the celestial signs, as a treasure is concealed," as Fludd said, "in a chest." "If we . . . penetrate to the limit whence this motion originally ensued," he concluded, "we shall find . . . hidden in that chest, the will of the *mens* in its sanctuary, in the ointment store." Was this willful ointment for passive bodies taken from the same "store" that Tobias, under angelic direction, found hidden in the belly of the fish, that provided the cure for the refugee Tobit's spiritual blindness?

When perceived "under the figures" by an experienced reader, a last triangle points to the pitcher at its apex. This apex is defined not by sun but by shadow. The two remaining points on the triangle are composed of the crying boy's broken earthenware pie plate (or microcosm) as it dissolves in chaos back down into the street, and the airy, translucent "Huguenot," "backward," or (according to Fludd's geomancer) "celestial" sign, an aspiring construction of ineffable lightness that floats, animated by the fluctuating wind, above the dark door of the Eglise des Grecs. Hence, this is a figure of the contingent status of the refugees themselves. This is also a hybrid sign—a fugitive kite caught on an invisible platform—an escutcheon shifting tentatively on its tether, poised Janus-faced to negotiate space between the two worlds.

The nature of the hybrid points to a synthesis of the opposing elements of earth and air. Again, the kernel of the Huguenot idea of aspiring synthesis was represented by Berton in the influential emblem used by his printshop at La Rochelle (fig. 14.34). This tiny, awkward image appeared in a oval at the bottom of the title page of Palissy's

Recepte veritable, as well as the printing house's other sixteenth-century Protestant tracts. As an intellectual and pictorial precursor for the metaphysical ideas that informed Hogarth's celestial sign of the Huguenots, this was a graphic image of an impoverished Huguenot rustic stretched between two worlds. He is dragged down by one hand tethered to the heavy rock of intractable matter, and hence "poverty," at the same time that the other hand, connected to a winged "spirit" reaches impossibly for the distant figure of God as it beckons down from the clouds.[158] In his publisher's emblematic representation of Palissy's and, I would argue, Hogarth's later incarnation of the same cosmology, the mastery of manual skills, manifested by soulish interaction of pious experience, artisanal industriousness, and alchemical innovation, remove man's tether from the dead weight of the repetitious cycle of poverty.[159] This frees the flight of man's spirit to reach God. Having followed the narrow path of virtue to unearth the philosopher's stone, the experienced artisan can reconcile spiritual and material wealth through the "issue" of the mechanical arts imitating Nature. For Palissy, this meant the artisan-adepts' "multiplication" of Nature's hidden "treasures"; the commercial tradesman's equivalent of the philosopher's stone.

The historian of science Pamela H. Smith has demonstrated intimate spiritual and economic relationships that associated alchemy and commerce and has shown how its clear and systematic elucidation occurred in the mid seventeenth century in the work and pedagogy of Erhard Weigel (1625–99) and his students. Weigel was a "practical" mathematician at the University of Jena. He may be linked to Hogarth through Gottfried Wilhelm Leibniz (1646–1716) and Samuel Pufendorf (1632–94), two students influential in eighteenth-century British natural-philosophical and Masonic circles. However, Weigel's work also had undeniable affinities with Fludd's *De technica microcosmi historia.* The pragmatic Weigel simply redefined these practices as "mechanical arts" and retained most of Fludd's arts, including fortification (not painting and timekeeping; and he stigmatized the occult rhetoric in geomancy, chiromancy, and cosmography as "unnecessary"). While Weigel's intellectual genealogy leads directly back to Paracelsus, by the 1650s, Weigel was no enemy of the academy. Instead, he insisted that the mechanical arts be privileged over scholastic pedagogy, and they were shifted to the core of his university curriculum. Weigel conceived "the practice of the mechanical arts capable of yielding a new kind of knowledge that would reform" natural philosophy *and* commerce.[160] Above all else, this was the sort of experiential knowledge that began—in the historical and practical sense—with movement of the human body per se. Knowledge was thus a contingent, material thing in motion, reformed by productive experience, rather than an instrument of absolute authority "that would stand in contrast to the past of war and confusion." As Palissy revealed to his Huguenot followers in Saintonge during the civil wars, alternative artisanal languages had become a necessity for both cultural and economic survival, as the violent insecurity "of the past . . . was grounded in disputation and words." "In a treatise on the mechanical arts," Smith concludes, "Weigel explained how *ars* came into being:

> Before the Fall, humans had known the secrets of God and nature, but afterward *these things were obscured from sight* [emphasis added], and humankind had to rely on its own power of creation to supply its daily needs. This power of creation lay in art; a uniquely human trial-and-error *imitation* of the nature left behind in Paradise. The goal of the liberal arts, which arose naturally out *of the movement of the body,* such as speech and discourse, was understanding. While understanding was mainly a tool for individual perfection in the knowledge of God, it also used the power of the body and the body's movement in order to create and produced the necessities that eased human life. *Thus, the mechanical arts originated from an understanding of the creative capacity of the body* . . . Weigel believed every university student should complete a propaedeutic course in the mechanical arts. . . . The faculty of the mechanical arts would pursue a new kind of knowledge, which he called "*Real-Weisheit*" (knowledge of things or *realia*). This knowledge was grounded in material things rather than words, and involved inactive doing and creating rather than talking and writing. The result of such knowledge would be material increase and economic prosperity . . . to usher in a reign of peace and prosperity that would stand in contrast to the past of war and confusion, which had resulted in an education *grounded in disputation and words.* Commerce, as a component of the mechanical arts, formed part of this knowledge of material things. . . . The knowledge that brought about this material reform depended on *ars,* artisanal practice, and the harnessing of the productive knowledge of artisans.[161]

Hogarth leaves no doubt that the crying boy's decomposing pie plate is the mirror image of the pitcher in the shadows. Both are innocuous articles of unglazed earthenware set on nearly identical rustic stumps for pedestals, which do not appear anywhere else in the painting. Moreover, pitchers and basins—similar in form to the pie plate—were commonly used together and sold as a set (in this instance, the pitcher was used to stand in its basin to catch spillage and retain overflow). Here, of course, the fragmented plate has lost all its original contents and is furthermore unable to hold the overflow of juice (or seminal liquid) that continues to drip out and down from the serving wench (that is, Nature's) pie. Inexperience, illicit sexuality, crapulence, free and undisciplined "emotions" (as Palissy would have it), and rampant physicality have resulted in the incomplete conjunction of macrocosm and microcosm. The "issue" of this miscegenous coupling is thus both "mixed" and premature. While the premature forcing of matter to its fully mature state is, as I have argued, a primary goal of Paracelsian artisanry, this can only be accomplished by adepts. Suffering blindness (both the cause and a result of this failure) in the *oculus imaginationis,* the boy is unable to see behind him into the Huguenots world of humanity's primordial past mediated by memory objects in the shadows.

In the shadow world of the Huguenot artisan, the public and theatrical failure of this racially mixed issue to achieve unity and hence inner perception is transmuted by art into its mirror. Then we perceive secret unity and success in the microcosmic arts of the experienced artisan of natural things. Shadows, absent the bright mechanical light of the false authority of man's historical past, provided the obscure territory necessary to succeed in the hidden work of Soho's pious refugee artisans. They alone found and deciphered memory images in the dark through pious experience and insight. Coming face to face with the inverted image of the boy's platter, the congregation perceives what he cannot. At the same time, the Huguenots merge seamlessly with *their* issue—an unbroken, self-contained pitcher—born not of mixed composition but of the soul-purifying pain of sacred violence and exile in the body of Christ.

These Huguenots have found and crafted a Fluddian "sanctuary" in London. This was the metaphysical source of their shadowy power: a tiny, artisanal fortress hidden in a universal fortress of memory; a safe, overlooked place to hold the tincture of the soul. Here was Fludd's "treasure." Celestial "rays" were transmuted into an animate liquid or "salt" capable of binding and purifying the fragmented particles of elemental earth when used by experienced artisans to give matter the inner life necessary for production. This primitive skill was lost to the muddled memory of the boy. He grieves over his loss as the pie container "dies" in his hands after evidence of the premature ejaculate dribbles from the pie hole before completing insemination. The plate spills the wasted seed before blind eyes, an event clearly reminiscent of the fate of the millennial artifacts in Hogarth's "Bathos" (fig. 14.13), their material essence dying in "chaos" under the sign of the apocalypse at "The World's End." If the word contained in the old refugee's book is overlooked, misread, or unheard, so, too, the pitcher, the terrestrial container in *Noon,* "whence this motion originally ensued," was also the "hidden" sanctuary for the squandered source of creation that traveled to the microcosm. There it was spilled out onto the cobblestones of mixed production and wasted consumption on Hog Lane.

This rustic pitcher of distillation, then, contains the seminal liquid of the microcosmic arts concealed in its dark body. It is also a hidden relay point between artisanal memory and craft production, and the on-stage world of commercial consumption where the liquid was wasted before it could effect synthesis. But the seminal liquid itself was originally animated and purified by transparent celestial rays that descended from the macrocosm and through the Huguenots' celestial sign, the highest relay point between the two worlds. Thence the rays were refracted through atoms of air and into the pitcher, where they were synthesized with natural matter from the microcosm, alchemically transmuted and contained for everyday use in the art of the earth. Now it

might be used in a medicinal "ointment," for example, by Fludd's geomancer to remove the veil from the eye of the imagination, or by Kenelm Digby to cure a wound
with his cosmic weapon salve; or, to give form and translucency to handcrafted materials, as in Palissy's art of the earth. This tincture, like the philosopher's stone, was infinitely mutable.

The downward path of motion from the celestial sign into the fortress of memory
and the Palissian pitcher is now possible to discern. A sign of the Huguenot temple,
the celestial rays in motion follow the serpentine path of the retreating congregation.
It is there with them as they walk through the half-open double door of the theater
after worship, and disappear into the shadows of the fortress. The sign of the headless woman is at the midway point on a line between the pitcher and the celestial sign.
All three line up in precise order from highest (celestial sign) to lowest (earthenware
pitcher). The linear pattern is underscored by the mimetic grammar of the three articles of material culture: all three are formed on the template of Hogarth's serpentine
line of beauty, and so all are variations on the same core structure. Having the same
structure, the three are subject to moral studies on the relationship between perception of inner and outer beauty. In much the same way, Hogarth might compare the
grammar and rhetoric of words and things, or Palissy, the suppression of "rustic" artisanal languages by the artificial and "beautiful."

Hogarth requires that spectators understand and follow the perspective of the de
Bry's engraving of the *Theatrum orbi* precisely here, to decode the material relationship between the three artifacts. Inexperienced spectators, taken in by Fludd's Babel
of false appearances issued by mixed composition, stand and face center stage, located
slightly to the right of where the gutter-gnomon intersects with the bottom of the picture plane in the foreground (the territory of carnality and crapulence). From here they
look straight at the presumed center of the painting: the sign of the headless woman.
From the ambiguous perspective of the *Theatrum orbi,* however, the vision of stage
center spectators was veiled. They were unable to see *inside* the heart of the fortress of
memory through the back of the half-open door. This was the "white veil" of headless (and hence mindless, eyeless) adherence to the seductive rhetoric of fashion. Like
Babel, such accretions were built up like dross in circular layers of earth or clay matter on the surface of the ground, rather than beneath its secretive and productive subterranean spaces.

Style thus obscured the elemental nature of things crucial to material reform and
fecund increase in production and consumption that "we shall find under the figures."
There, *underneath,* Palissy searched for the primitive material language of the artisan.
A surfeit of artificial discourse was both morally and politically dangerous, even as latinate eloquence disfigured natural art. This was Palissy's Babel: a posteriori iconography overlaid on top of the knowledge of things. "The Art of the Earth" explained the

nature of *raw materials* and then the clay earths brought up from the "bowels of the earth," before turning to a more circumspect discussion of refinement in the potter's kiln.

It was impossible to separate the essential relation between raw materials brought up from the bowels of the earth from the polished artifacts made from the skillful transformation of the same materials. This ecology of things posited the perception of the surface disfigured the basic materials and grammar of nature. Hogarth's written and pictorial texts thus presented a dialectic of memory and forgetting. Only the Huguenots remembered the natural material relations of the artifacts in *Noon.* Rustic nature did exist in modern urban babels like London and New York, uncovered and reactivated by artisans of the art of memory.

However, in Hogarth's "modern" life, the simplicity principle hidden in natural relations in the human species must be perceived through the mixed mediation of complex commodities of commerce, all of which tended by design or accident to obscure their origins in the raw materials of elemental earth. Great moral and ethical danger accompanied the disconnect between spirit and matter that led to artifactual chaos among consumers on Hog Lane, who "forgot" the natural material order of the things that supplied the body.

At the same time, and for many of the same reasons, human atomization threatened prosperity with chaos in the new commercial cities of the pluralistic Atlantic world. Without memory of the unity of spiritual and material knowledge understood by refugee natural philosophers of the sixteenth and seventeenth centuries, there was no real hope of human convergence, or of economic reform leading to the integration of production and consumption.

This veil also overlaid the path of celestial rays in motion down toward the earthenware pitcher. The eye of the inexperienced spectator would be drawn to the fashionable sign, only to overlook the essential hidden messages of the plain pitcher of shaped earth. Since these were "French fashions" on the sign, manufactured by the Huguenots themselves, we are again left with the impression that Hogarth perceived these eye-seducing (and so manipulative and directive) artifacts as a fortress of perceptual security for secret production and trade.

Here, perhaps, was an obscure source for English fears of the French counterfeit: the historical sense that what was visible and available for consumption was not really the "true" material. In fact, what was exhibited for purchase mystified and obscured the real thing. If alchemists made false gold by claiming possession of the philosopher's stone, could they not also make things of false value in their artisans' workshops? In an unexpected way, following the Paracelsians, Hogarth infers that enormous economic and social power comes with universal knowledge of the elemental materiality of everyday things and in the mysterious refining processes of artisanal products, in which matter is transformed into artifacts of commerce and domestic life. This was the dream of John Winthrop Jr., as well as Hartlib, Comenius, and Weigel.

Could such potent knowledge dissolve the barriers between hidden production and the "waste" of mindless consumption without self-regulation, and dismantle the bitter rhetoric of the polite counterfeit? Even this inference is problematic. We have seen how alchemists from Edward Howes to George Starkey developed complex ideologies of personal secrecy at the same time they displayed a rhetoric of openness. And no one in the history of art fought more vigorously to establish proprietary rights over the commerce of secrets and "innovations" than Hogarth. Hogarth insists only that vulgar and mindless consumers have the *potential* to transcend spectatorship through the innate perception of simultaneity in the microcosmic arts represented by the visual language of *Noon*. Only after having negotiated this perceptual labyrinth to gain experience and enter the fortress of memory can theoretical knowledge become available as practice.

Seeing beyond the door, through the narrow opening to the left—an act that allowed personal access through the eye of the imagination to the soulish *immanence* of the fortress—required spectators of life on Hog Lane to resist visual chaos and so, too, the superficial voyeurism of spectatorship. Detached observers who lay visual siege to the outside of the fortress walls can never enter the narrow door to knowledge and, in the end, take the wide path to perdition. To follow the narrow path traveled by Hogarth's seventeenth-century refugee predecessors, spectators must *engage* with street life as an integral part of nature's material landscape. Painful experience initiates the metamorphosis from subjects of corrupt authority and scholastic repetition into refugees and innovators. Only Hogarth's refugees perceive images in the shadows and so carry with them the artisanal memory to craft material things in imitation of nature. To follow the narrow path mapped in both *Theatrum orbi* and Hogarth's *Noon* was therefore to see into the half-open door and plot an unimpeded line between the celestial sign and the pitcher. Thus, it was necessary to hew close to the margins. In *Theatrum orbi*, that means the rear wall of the stage, under the *échauguette;* in *Noon,* the space along the front wall of the Eglise des Grecs, occupied exclusively by Huguenot congregants. This marginal territory also appears to be the only sacred space left on Hog Lane.

But smallness was advantageous in the transatlantic world. On the narrow path taken by the refugees, a doorway is open for astral rays emanating from the translucent celestial sign to converge with the plain terrestrial container in the shadows. Experienced intermediaries trading along the narrow path where the trajectories of shadow and light intersect, Huguenots found protection in the artfully conflated space between spiritual refinement and material elaboration.

As primitive witnesses to a moment of convergence when spirit and matter merged ambiguously into the art of the earth, who can say with certainty whether the material of Tobit's white veil of blindness was transmuted by the memories of Hogarth's refugees into a talisman of Palissy's transparent white glaze? By appropriating the rustic potter's clandestine discourse of artisanal security as the hidden reality behind the impurity and confusion of life on Hog Lane, Hogarth's art of the human species transmuted the art of the earth into the essence of modern experience.

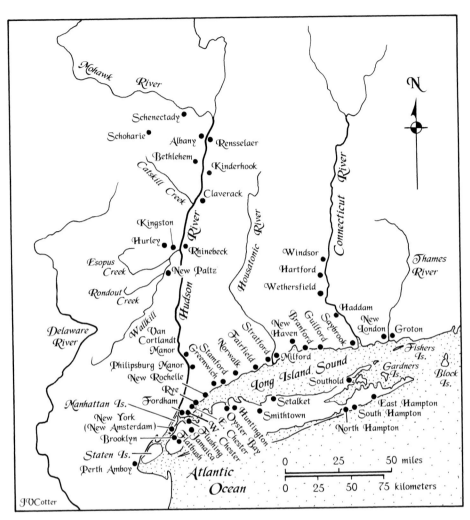

MAP 2. Eastern New York Colony and the Long Island Sound Region. Drawn by John Cotter.

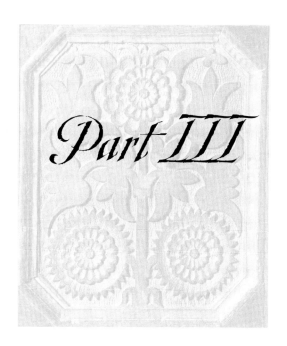

Part III

The Secrets of the Craft

CHAPTER FIFTEEN

Hidden in Plain Sight

Disappearance and Material Life in Colonial New York

> October 29, 1716. Monday. New York . . .
> I walked round this town. There is here three churches, the English
> church, the French and the Dutch church. . . . The French have all the
> privileges that can be in this place and are the most in number here. They
> are of the council, of the parliament, and in all other employments here.
>
> —JOHN FONTAINE, Huguenot traveler

❧ "Ingate" and "Outgate": Dialogues about Words and Things ❧

The current state of New England regional studies indicates that traditional notions of dominance and cultural homogeneity are finally undergoing revision.[1] Recent scholarship suggests that the region, once thought to have been "monolithically" Puritan, was in fact settled intermittently by diverse groups of migrants, not only from a variety of East Anglian settlements, but from all over England and America. Given our awareness of the limitations of this traditional assumption, it is ironic that historians of colonial America who venture into the middle Atlantic region must again confront similarly reductive, one-dimensional ethnic models.

The most enduring scheme of ethnic reductiveness in middle Atlantic regional studies is the one that posits successive Dutch and then English cultural hegemony in colonial New Amsterdam / New York, with 1664—the date of English conquest of the colony—representing the chronological break between the two periods. Transatlantic historians might well ask how one even begins to define the pluralistic, shifting

Netherlands in such monolithic "Dutch" terms. One must also consider persuasive quantitative evidence that, although New Netherlands came into being as a colony of the Dutch West India Company, it never had an effective ethnic Dutch majority. Indeed, many of the earliest colonists were French-speaking Huguenots and Walloons who came in search of refuge and economic opportunity. Immigrants from all over Protestant Europe, African slaves, and local native groups contributed to creating some of the most pluralistic societies in colonial America in New York City and its dauntingly large hinterland. This social and geographic context has enormous implications for understanding the fluid history and culture of New York Colony.[2]

The stereotype of "pure Dutchness" owes much to the nostalgic ethnic myths and fairy tales popularized by the nineteenth-century New York essayist and historian Washington Irving (1783–1859), particularly in his *Dietrich Knickerbocker's A History of New York* (1809).[3] This perception powerfully shaped the historiography of New York and limited the analysis of the colony's many other important and linguistically distinct subgroups, which were engaged in constant cultural conflict and accommodation on many levels of interaction. New York's material culture was not Dutch or English per se; rather, it was ethnically and culturally diverse, with both the Dutch and the English playing appropriate parts.

The French words for "furniture," *mobilier* and *meubles*, literally mean "moveables," and one way to begin understanding such ambiguous issues as regional identity in diverse colonial settings, ethnic stereotypes, and cross-cultural conflict and accommodation is by considering the journey (or diffusion) of an instantly recognizable colonial artifact—the Boston plain leather chair (fig. 15.1). Thanks largely to the work of the furniture historian Benno M. Forman, we now know that because of intercoastal trade the Boston leather chair—a shoddily made provincial adaptation of the fashionable London caned chair—was the single most influential moveable produced in colonial America between the Restoration and the end of the French and Indian War. Forman's main concern was what he and other art historians of his generation called connoisseurship, an intensely "presentist" word directed toward highly subjective questions of universal quality and difficult to define or contextualize historically; nevertheless, because of his project, we can separate similar leather chairs made in Boston, New York, Philadelphia, and other coastal style centers and focus on new sets of questions and concerns.[4]

What, after all, was the leather chair's significance as it was carried as merchant cargo from place to place in the colonies, inspiring local copies nearly everywhere it was sold? Why were "style" and "fashion" such key words for the artisans, merchants, and buyers of leather chairs in the port towns of early eighteenth-century America?

Historically, the Boston leather chair's significance centers on its role as an important English symbol for colonial elites. Made primarily for export to the middle At-

FIGURE 15.1. Boston leather side chair, ca. 1700. H: 34¼", W: 17¾", D: 14¾". Maple and oak; original leather upholstery. Courtesy Wadsworth Atheneum, Hartford. Wallace Nutting Collection Gift of J. Pierpont Morgan. 1926.440. In New York, Boston "plain" leather chairs of this type outnumbered carved examples approximately six to one.

lantic region and the south by a network of Boston chair makers and upholsterers, the chair remained at the nucleus of New England's coastal furniture trade for more than a century. New York City and western Long Island were among the most important markets; however, only the elite owned leather chairs. A survey of 560 inventories probated between 1700, when the new, high-backed leather chair first made its appearance, and 1760, when appraisers consistently described a later version of that form as "old," "very old," or "old-fashioned" indicates that only thirty-one households (5.5 percent) possessed leather chairs.

These were important households, however; the average valuation of estates that list leather chairs was £982.8.[5] The chairs were clearly luxury items, and they ranged in value from 10s. to £3 or more apiece, depending on model and condition. Most significantly, households valued near the average were seldom without at least one leather chair, indicating that they were a necessary symbol of status for New York's elite. Their owners were generally "merchants" or "gentlemen" who lived in the city, where 77.4 percent of all leather chairs were inventoried. The remainder were evenly distributed in Flushing, Jamaica, and Hempstead, the largest towns on western Long Island. These towns were also the traditional strongholds of New York's prosperous Quaker community. So widespread was the trade in leather chairs that some colonial officials protested to the British Board of Trade that New England artisans and merchants were undermining the spirit of the Navigation Acts by infringing on England's natural prerogative to provide her colonies with manufactured goods. In a contentious report presented to Parliament on January 22, 1733, Lieutenant Governor William Gooch of Virginia complained that "scrutoires, chairs and other wooden manufactures . . . are now being exported from thence to the other plantations, which, if not prevented, may be of ill consequence to the trade and manufactures of this kingdom."[6] Gooch's report clearly reflects the fact that his constituents in the Chesapeake Bay Region produced tobacco and other agricultural products for export, not chairs.

To compensate for the lack of an overarching staple, New England merchants and artisans produced and exported chairs and other manufactured goods so aggressively that transatlantic economic historians now conclude that New England's conscious mercantile strategy was to assume the role of English metropolis in the New World. It has been said that, "New England resembled nothing so much as old England itself. And that, of course, was the problem . . . it was in the expansion of domestic processing and manufacturing, of a far-reaching export business . . . that New Englanders . . . mounted a growing challenge to the hegemony of the metropolis."[7]

By 1700, the middle Atlantic, southern, and Caribbean plantation economies, which exploited slave labor to extract and refine staple commodities, had far outdistanced New England in terms of direct credits with metropolitan England and the empire's Atlantic market. The Massachusetts General Court had become conscious of this imbalance as early as the empirewide depression of the 1630s and 1640s. In New England, the depression intensified as immigration (the colony's main source of liquid capital) dropped off following the great Puritan migration of the 1630s. Having observed that "our ingate [imports]" were to exceed our outgate [exports]," such that "the ballance needs be made up," the court passed an edict in 1646 that allowed for the active development of local manufactures, in explicit competition with the metropolis, to address the crippling structural problem in the colony's balance of trade.[8] The export of such new manufactures as clothing, shoes, boots, ironware, and chairs was one of the few means for New England merchants and artisans to boost exports back into balance.

Shortly after the edict, upholstered chairs were among the most common items of New England manufacture carried south on sloops from Boston. Indeed, by the 1670s, references to the earliest form of the low-backed, leather-upholstered "New England" chair or "back stool" (fig. 15.2) appear in Maryland inventories. By 1700, inventory appraisers in every colony were specifically referring to leather chairs as either "Boston," "New England," or "Boston made." The artifactual language of the Boston leather chair thus proved distinctive enough to warrant the acceptance of new terminology into colonial discourse. In the small world of North American commerce, the chair became a medium for intercolonial communication.[9]

FIGURE 15.2. Side chair, Boston, 1650–1700. H: 35″, W: 18″, D: 15″. Birch, maple, and ash. Courtesy Henry Francis du Pont Winterthur Museum, Winterthur, Delaware.

But what could chairs communicate? What were the cultural associations that the word "Boston" carried along with the chair on its travels south into the regions of staple production? What, beyond its point of origin, were the signifiers of its Bostonness? Such implicit cultural associations attending the chair trade were imperative to Boston's mercantile strategy. From 1646 until at least the 1730s, Boston acted as the mother country's cultural broker, albeit without British approval. As far as fashionable furniture was concerned, the other colonies looked chiefly to Boston. "In the city of New-York, through our intercourse with the Europeans, we follow the London fashions; though by the time we adopt them, they become disused in England," William Smith Jr. observed in his *History of the Province of New-York from the First Discovery to the Year 1732* (1757). "Our affluence . . . introduced a degree of luxury in tables, dress, and furniture, with which we were before unacquainted. But we are *still* [emphasis mine] not so gay a people, as our neighbors in Boston."[10]

Nowhere was Boston's stake in controlling the discourse of novelty and style more evident, than in the frequent correspondence between the Boston merchant and upholsterer Thomas Fitch (1669–1736) and Benjamin Faneuil (b. La Rochelle 1658–d. New York 1719). Faneuil, the eldest child of the merchant Pierre Faneuil and Marie Depont Faneuil of La Rochelle, was Fitch's principal agent in New York and a French Huguenot merchant exiled to London in 1685, before first arriving in Boston in 1688. Benjamin, his immensely wealthy son Pierre (b. New York 1700–d. Boston 1742), and his brothers André (b. La Rochelle 1657–d. Boston 1737) and Jean (b. La Rochelle 165?–

in Boston 1688–d. La Rochelle 1737) established one of the most important refugee trading firms in early eighteenth-century America. The Faneuil family's importance resulted not only from the emergence of a strong Boston–New York coastal axis, but also its long-standing transatlantic financial connections with other relatives and members of its patronage network still living in La Rochelle, as well as in Rotterdam, Louisbourg, and Québec.[11]

Fitch's letters concern multiple shipments of leather chairs from Boston to New York, and they demonstrate how important the coastal furniture trade was to Boston's merchant elites and their clientage networks in the early eighteenth century. They also inform and complicate the arbitrary geographical boundaries usually assigned to the "middle colonies," which suggest that the area actually consisted of two distinct "human regions":

> New York, parts of western Connecticut, eastern New Jersey, and the northeast corner of Pennsylvania comprised one region. Most of Pennsylvania, part of Maryland, and all of western New Jersey and Delaware formed another. Each region had peculiar characteristics, and the inhabitants of each interacted mostly with themselves. What inter-regional contacts they did have tended to be with the South, for the Philadelphia-centered region, and with New England, for the New York-centered region. Each region was different from the South and from New England in important respects, to be sure, but for different reasons and in different ways.[12]

Although this chapter underscores the strong interregional socioeconomic and cultural connection between New England and New York during the late seventeenth and early eighteenth centuries, it also considers transatlantic extensions of New York's human region. Transatlantic concerns clearly influenced Fitch's performance as cultural broker and the acceptance of that performance in New York. Fitch maintained social distance and cultural dominance over Faneuil precisely because of his self-proclaimed knowledge about what was stylish in London and Boston. Fitch's letter of April 22, 1707, in which he chastised Faneuil for ordering something out of fashion in both London and Boston, is the best example of the asymmetry of the patronage relationship between this fully Anglicized Boston merchant and his French refugee client: "Sir . . . leather couches are as much out of wear *here* [emphasis added] as steeple crowned hats. Cane couches or others we make like them . . . are cheaper, more fashionable, easy and useful."[13]

Faneuil and some of his fellow New Yorkers did not, however, sit idle while Fitch and others flooded the affluent New York market with Boston leather chairs. Fitch was so overwhelmed with orders from New York by 1706 that he wrote Faneuil, "I would have sent yo some chairs but could scarcely comply with those I had promised to go by these sloops"; yet three years later, there was a glut of leather chairs on the

FIGURE 15.3. Side chair, New York City, 1705–1710. H: 46¾", W: 18", D: 18¾". Maple and oak. Courtesy Henry Francis du Pont Winterthur Museum, Winterthur, Delaware

market for the first time. On September 9, 1709, Fitch began a series of anxious letters that despaired of Faneuil's inability to sell his consignment: "I wonder the chairs did not sell; I have sold pretty many of that sort to Yorkers, . . . and tho some are carved yet I make it six plain to one carved; and can't make the plain so fast as they are bespoke. *So you can assure them that are customers that they are not out of fashion here* [emphasis added]. . . I desire that you would force the sale of the chairs . . . I also submit the price of them to your patience. It's better to sell them than to let them lie." Fitch added, "It might be better to have them rubbed over that they may look fresher," even though the expense of polishing would come out of his rapidly diminishing profit margin.[14]

Boston plain leather chairs had enjoyed uninterrupted popularity in New York for more than a decade (or for more than forty years, if one includes earlier related seating forms) so Fitch's exasperation was understandable. Even his old trump card to sway the presumably unanglicized elites in New York—his protests about the chairs' stylishness in Boston—failed to bolster sales. What had changed? To start with, New York chair makers began producing a modified version of the Boston leather chair by the end of the seventeenth century (fig. 15.3). Subsequently, several New York shops produced a number of variants, all incorporating recognizable features of the Boston chair. By 1709, they supplied enough competition to cut into Fitch's formerly secure market. Thus, on a very local level and in just one sort of export manufacture, we begin to see early evidence of the unraveling of Massachusetts's strategy outlined in the edict of 1646.

Even those regions engaged primarily in the exploitation of staple agriculture diversified by developing an artisanal component to compete with New England's export market in manufactured goods. Relative population growth is a good general indicator of the potential for regional development of the artisanal sector. In 1660, New England's total population (including slaves) exceeded 33,000, while the middle colonies' was less than 6,000 (a ratio of over 5:1). But by 1710, while New England's population had grown to 115,000, the middle colonies' increased to nearly 70,000 (a ratio of less than 2:1). Beginning in 1705, a flurry of correspondence crisscrossed the Atlantic, indicating for the first time that the Board of Trade in London saw *New York's* growing manufacturing sector as a potential threat to British mercantilism.[15] New York had begun to replicate elements of Boston's mercantile strategy of 1646 successfully enough to gain notice both in Boston *and* in the metropolis.

Still, why would New York prove to be among the first to support an artisanal sector powerful enough to respond so rapidly to a formidable mercantile engine largely in place in New England since the 1640s? Given Fitch's condescending attitude toward Faneuil, it seems ironic that many of the artisans and merchants who usurped Fitch's enterprise were from southwestern France, particularly Aunis and Saintonge, La Rochelle's hinterland. La Rochelle was the birthplace of Benjamin Faneuil (his family was one of the ruthlessly resourceful survivors of 1628), and his craft network consisted mostly of Aunisian and Saintongeais refugee immigrants, many of whom shared Old World trade or family associations.[16] Indeed, Faneuil was a central figure among a powerful religious, linguistic, and occupational cohort that converged on colonial New York by the early eighteenth century. Arguably, just 11 percent of the city's total population were Huguenot refugees (still a considerable improvement over the approximately 4 percent in London), but an astounding 31 percent of its merchants were French, exceeding the percentage of English merchants, who came in a clear second.[17] Faneuil and his compatriots had put their hard-won experience dealing with the dominant order into practice in the middle colonies, just as they had in La Rochelle and London.

❦ The Year 1685 and New York's "Old" Culture ❧

Although 1685 was the starting point for the largest migration of Huguenot artisans from Saintonge to New York, the foundation for the city's leather chair-making in-

FIGURE 15.4. Side chair, Boston, 1690–1705. H: 41¾″, W: 20″, D: 18″. Maple and Oak. Courtesy New York State Education Department, Albany.

dustry was laid earlier, since its heterogeneous artisanal sector developed along with its population. Until the late 1680s, the vanguard of international Protestantism in New Amsterdam / New York had consisted of family networks of merchants and artisans from Dutch, German, and Scandinavian regional cultures, Walloon refugees from the Spanish Netherlands (who spoke a French dialect), and "old" diaspora Huguenots who founded churches in exile among sympathetic hosts throughout the North Atlantic Protestant community by the 1550s.[18] The Huguenots of the dispersion were the final and primary catalyst that enabled New York's artisans to compete successfully with Boston imports and challenge that city's role as disseminator of metropolitan style and fashion.

On April 16, 1705, Fitch wrote Faneuil, "Please to inform me in yor next whether Turkey worke chairs would see with yo, If yo think they will shall send yo some from 15 to 20s a pss here."[19] Presumably, these chairs were Boston-made high-backed stools similar to the one illustrated in figure 15.4. Although no response to Fitch's letter survives, Faneuil probably replied negatively, since this type of chair was outdated in London and Boston.[20] Fitch often remarked that New York was behind the times, and he probably assumed that heavy woolen Turkey-work chairs might still be stylish there.

Fitch evidently underestimated and misunderstood the development and sophisti-

FIGURE 15.5. Side chair, New York City, 1660–1700. H: 36¾",W: 18¾", D: 15½". Maple and Oak; original sealskin upholstery. Courtesy Old Saybrook Historical Society. Photo, Gavin Ashworth. The ball-and-cove and vase turnings on this chair differ from those on seventeenth-century Boston examples such as figs. 15.2 and 15.4. Sealskin was used when leather was unavailable.

FIGURE 15.6. Side chair, New York City, 1660–1700. H: 34",W: 18¼", D: 15½". Oak and black ash; original leather upholstery. Courtesy John Hall Wheelock Collection, East Hampton Historical Society. Photo, Joseph Adams. This chair descended in the Wheelock family of East Hampton, Long Island.

cation of both New York tradesmen and consumers. Inventories indicate that high-backed stools were out of fashion by 1701 at the latest. Huguenot Captain Nicholas Dumaresq[ue]'s inventory, taken on June 12, 1701, listed "four old high Leather Chairs" and "one old Low chair." Given the proximity and similar language of these listings, the "old Low chair" probably resembled the ones illustrated in figures 15.2 and 15.5–8. Appraisers often used the term "old" interchangeably with "old-fashioned," and in this case, "old" probably referred to style rather than condition.[21]

By 1701, two predecessors of the new plain leather chairs were anachronistic in both Boston and New York. What is most significant, however, is that a great variety of low-backed leather, Turkey-work, and other woolen upholstered chairs were apparently manufactured in New York during the late seventeenth century (figs. 15.5–8), but not enough to effectively challenge the Boston trade. Nevertheless, several shops from various cultural traditions were clearly established to lay the basis for New York's powerful cultural response—spearheaded by the Huguenot immigration from Aunis-Saintonge after 1685—to the introduction of Boston leather chairs like those exported by Fitch (fig. 15.1).

If the "old high Leather chairs" in Dumaresque's inventory were made in one of New York's earliest shops, rather than in Boston, they may have resembled the grand chair frame illustrated in figure 15.9. Evidence suggests that this late seventeenth-century "high [upholstered] chair" may be a rare colonial interpretation of the Parisian

FIGURE 15.7. Side chair, New York City, 1660–85. H: 37″, W: 18″, D: 15⅛″. Red oak. Courtesy Pocumtuck Valley Memorial Association, Memorial Hall Museum, Deerfield, Massachusetts. Photo, Helga Studio. The inverted case-and-barrel turnings on this and another related example at the Wadsworth Atheneum followed Amsterdam prototypes in an era when Netherlandish design was on the wane in New York City.

FIGURE 15.8. Side chair, New York City, 1685–1700. Maple and oak. H: 35½″, W: 18½″, D: 18½″. Private collection. Photo by Gavin Ashworth. The turnings on this chair are closely related to those on late-seventeenth-century London caned chairs and early-eighteenth-century New York leather chairs, such as the one illustrated in figure 15.3.

FIGURE 15.9. Grand chair, New York City, 1680–95. H: 44¼″, W: 22½″, D: 22¼″. Maple stained red. Private collection. Photo by Christopher Zaleski.

FIGURE 15.10. Escritoire, New York City or northern Kings County, 1685–95. H: 35¾″, W: 33¾″, D: 24″. Red gum, mahogany, and yellow poplar. Courtesy Metropolitan Museum of Art, Rogers Fund, 1944. The turnings on the side stretchers are closely related to those on the front stretcher of the grand chair illustrated in figure 15.9.

"grand" chair, a form that appeared mainly in France and on the Continent around 1670 (the grand chair seems, anomalously, not to have proven fashionable in London). More important, it is a New York–made predecessor to the high-backed leather chair form introduced to New York from Boston during the early eighteenth century (fig. 15.1).[22]

In formal terms, the design of the armchair's turned front stretcher relates directly to the side stretchers of a New York escritoire (fig. 15.10) with a Dutch inscription detailing a business transaction and the date 1695 under its lid. The escritoire and the grand chair, however, could date from as early as the mid 1680s, when the word "escritoire" first begins to appear in New York inventories. The escritoire has long been considered a keystone for understanding late seventeenth-century urban New York cabinetmaking. Collected from a house on [Jacques] Cortelyou Road in the Flatbush section of Kings County early in this century, it may have been made in Brooklyn, or brought there from New York City.[23]

Certainly the escritoire, like the grand chair, may have originated in either place, because competent artisans capable of working in "urban" idioms existed on both sides of the East River, which connected rather than separated these areas. The close proximity of lower Manhattan to the northern tip of Brooklyn—a brief ride on the Long Island ferry across the lower East River, and so easily accessible to the docks, or the business end of New York City—is confirmed by the diary of John Fontaine, an Anglo-Irish Huguenot of southwestern French parentage who wrote on October 26, 1716: "About eleven we came to the ferry which goes over to New York. There is a fine village [Brooklyn] upon this island opposite to New York. The ferry is about a quarter of a mile over, and water runs very rapidly here, and there is good convenient landings on both sides. About 12 we landed at New York." Fontaine's appraisal of Manhattan's roads was far less encouraging: "[They] are very bad and stony, and no possibility for coaches to go only in the winter when the snow fills all up and makes all smooth, then they can make use of their wheel carriages. There is but two coaches belonging to this province though many rich people, because of the badness of the roads."[24]

By the late seventeenth century, Kings County surveyors had established a passable network of roads, which connected all the major western towns to the Long Island ferry. The stylistic relation of New York City to Kings County furniture is thus a difficult problem to unravel with utter assurance. Consider the problems that accompany the neat separation of kasten—upright, freestanding Dutch-style closets (see, e.g., fig. 16.18)—with New York City and Kings County histories. These artifacts share many of the same details. Intraregional interaction is also suggested by the distinctive finial of the New York grand chair (fig. 15.11), which has much in common with drawer pulls found on a number of early New York City or King's County kasten (fig. 15.12) and with the standard finial on its successor, the New York plain leather chair (figs. 15.3). Moreover, between the English takeover and the Revocation of the Edict of Nantes, cross-generational, transatlantic cultural continuities, solidified by strategic marriages that connected families, shops, regions, and neighborhoods, clearly played a significant role in the linkage and maintenance of New York's most enduring continental craft networks. Some seventeenth-century Kings County artisans from New York's "old," pre-1685 Huguenot culture, including members of the Lott family of southwestern France, Amsterdam, and Kings County—plausible makers of both the escritoire and the grand chair—worked for elite patrons in New York City while simultaneously developing cheap land and maintaining numerous slaves in the more homogeneously Continental towns across the river in Brooklyn. As we shall see, Quaker merchants and artisans had followed a similar bifurcated yet symbiotic pattern on western Long Island since the time of Peter Stuyvesant's restrictions on Quaker "conventicles," which led to the publication of the Flushing Remonstrance on December 27, 1657.[25]

FIGURE 15.11. Detail of the finial of the grand chair illustrated in figure 15.9. Private collection. Photo, Christopher Zaleski.

FIGURE 15.12. Detail of a drawer pull on a kas, New York City or northern Kings County, ca. 1740. Courtesy Milwaukee Art Museum, Layton Art Collection, L1994.3.

The material evidence strongly suggests that the maker of the grand chair was of Continental European descent. The unusual carved arms with concave elbow rests relate less to turned and upholstered metropolitan prototypes than to joined great chairs made in the British Midlands and West Country. However, a more closely analogous arm occurs on an early eighteenth-century turned armchair of vernacular French or Germanic origin.[26] There is also the distinct possibility that the New York armchair represents the collaborative work of a turner and a joiner—perhaps individuals from different cultural backgrounds. If so, this would further complicate the quest for ethnic origins in what is most likely a "creolized" chair of hybrid form.

Two of the most intriguing components of the chair are its trapezoidal seat and recessed back, which frames three squared, partially unfinished spindles (the surfaces have deep horizontal saw marks). The chair maker constructed the trapezoidal seat by chamfering the front and rear ends of the seat lists and side stretchers at opposite, though parallel, angles to accommodate the wider front (fig. 15.13). Another method, commonly used on British and Boston examples, was to leave the ends of the side elements cut flush, an economical technique that allowed for thinner stock, while chamfering the inside back of the two front posts beneath the seat to receive them, thus angling the posts instead of the stretchers (figs. 15.14, 15.15). It would be simplistic, how-ever, to conclude that one solution was "Continental" and the other "British," since these conceptually opposite construction techniques commonly appear in chairs at-tributable to *both* Boston and New York.

Peter Thornton has demonstrated how seventeenth-century French and Low Country chairs had "bucket" seats or backs designed to contain removable, mattresslike "carreaux" (or "squabs"). The three rough hewn spindles on the New York armchair were not meant to be visible, but rather to serve as tying posts for the carreau's fasteners, probably made of woven ribbon or "tape." Both transatlantic and cross-generational structural continuities are suggested by the height available for the car-reau on the grand chair's back, which measures 15½ inches, as does the height of its seat. Reciprocal, one-to-one vertical symmetry remains constant on New York's high-back leather chairs as well (see figs. 15.3, 15.41d), although not on Boston plain chairs. Boston chairs accentuate verticality, such that the height of the back typically exceeds that of the seat. The back structure of an unusual southern armchair at Colonial Williamsburg suggests that it also had a carreau; however, the framing members of the back are larger, and they are smooth-planed and molded. The latter example possibly represents the work of a Huguenot tradesman from one of the large French settle-ments in the South Carolina low country.[27]

Although the upholstery materials used on the seat of the New York grand chair are unknown, nail holes indicate that it had a sacking bottom (rather than girt web-bing), that was probably covered tightly by leather or a woolen. Print sources suggest that a high cushion may have surmounted the seat, rising to fill the gaping hole be-

FIGURE 15.13. Detail of the understructure of the trapezoidal seat of the grand chair il-lustrated in figure 15.9. Private collection. Photo, Christopher Zaleski.

FIGURE 15.14. Side chair, Boston or New York City, ca. 1700. H: 47″, W: 20″, D: 21″. Maple and oak. Private collection. Photo, Christopher Zaleski. This chair, branded "PVP," for Philip Verplank of Fishkill, New York, is related to three carved leather chairs at Washington's Headquarters, Newburgh, New York, which are also branded "PVP."

FIGURE 15.15. Detail of the understructure of the side chair illustrated in figure 15.14. Private collection. Photo, Christopher Zaleski.

tween the top of the frame's seat lists and the bottom of its lofty stay rail. Presumably, the carreau and seat cushion had matching textile covers. In his discussion of continental seating styles, Thornton also cites "a French chaire hollow in ye back." To accommodate the shape of the sitter's shoulders and ribs, such chairs had concave backs formed by subtly curving the crest and stay rails backward. This shell-like feature principally occurs in British America only on early eighteenth-century New York leather chairs (figs. 15.16, 15.17) and may represent a Huguenot innovation, but it originates with sixteenth-century French caqueteuse and Italian sgabello armchairs. The sgabello was a rustic chair associated with the grotto; the backs of these chairs were carved to represent concave shells that enveloped the sitter.[28]

The "grand" armchair suggests by its very singularity that only a few were made. The advent of the "new fashioned," high-backed London cane and Boston leather chairs (fig. 15.18), combined with the Parisian grand chair's apparent rejection in London, assured that this form quickly passed out of fashion in New York. Fitch's 1701 letter to Faneuil stressing the availability of presumably cheap, high-backed Turkey-work chairs currently out of fashion in the metropolis indicates that he was intent on capturing what remained of the dwindling New York market for these luxury items. Evidently, the *new*, high-backed "Boston" plain leather chair was just coming into fashion in New York around the turn of the century.

FIGURE 15.16. Side chair, New York City, 1700–25. H: 45⅝", W: 18⅛", D: 15¼". Maple and oak. Courtesy Milwaukee Art Museum, Purchase, Layton Art Collection, L1982.116. Photo, Richard Eells. This chair reportedly descended in the family of Pieter Vanderlyn of Kingston, New York, who immigrated to New York City from the Netherlands in 1718. In light of the date of his arrival, he may have acquired the chair from an earlier owner.

FIGURE 15.17. Detail of the "French hollow" back of the side chair illustrated in figure 15.16. Courtesy Milwaukee Art Museum, Purchase, Layton Art Collection, L1982.116. Photo, Gavin Ashworth. The curvature is similar to that of the London carved leather chair illustrated in figure 15.35.

FIGURE 15.18. Caned chair, London, ca. 1700. Dimensions not recorded. Beech and cane. Private collection. Photo, Neil Kamil.

Two high-back leather chairs made in New York about 1700 (figs. 15.19, 15.20), have the same seventeenth-century turning sequences as the grand chair (fig. 15.9). These are the only known high-back chairs of the later variety with these early turnings. Anomalous survivals such as these were undoubtedly considered anachronistic by the early eighteenth century, particularly when compared with new turning patterns drawn from fashionable London cane chairs. Fashion did not erase all memory of the grand chair however. For example, arm supports with bilaterally symmetrical balusters—a classical form that was updated and called a *double poire* (double pear) by the French architect Charles-Augustin d'Aviler in his *Cours d'architecture* (1710)—appear on several, early eighteenth-century high-back New York leather armchairs (see fig. 15.27).[29] The earliest New York example with this turned element is a joined great chair (fig. 15.21). Made a decade or two earlier than the grand chair, it attests to the longevity of this turning pattern; however, the *double poire* and urn finial with its proud boss turned in the round (figs. 15.9, 15.11), were the only parts of the short-lived New York grand chair consistently repeated on later upholstered furniture.

❧ Human Geography and Material Life ❧

By 1701 Fitch had enlisted Faneuil to act as a middleman and to persuade New Yorkers of every ethnic stripe that the leather chair was no less popular in English Boston than in heterogeneous New York. In that capacity, Faneuil was able to maximize his personal power, as had generations of other multilingual Rochelais merchants in northern Europe and the British Isles. Evidence suggests that Faneuil may have endured Fitch's arrogant scorn to his eventual profit while serving as the upholsterer's submissive apprentice in the subtleties of Anglo-Boston material culture. The profit, of course, came precisely when Faneuil and his network of Huguenot artisans understood the social and cultural connotations of the Boston leather chair and quietly made it their own through adaptation and innovation.

The most compelling artifact asserting the role artisans from Aunis-Saintonge played in the New York leather chair industry after 1701 is a carved armchair made for Stephanus Van Cortlandt (1643–1700) or his son, Philip (1683–1748) (fig. 15.22).[30] Found

FIGURE 15.19. Side chair, New York City, ca. 1700. H: 44⅜″, W: 17¾″, D: 14½″. Maple. Private collection. Photo, Gavin Ashworth. The front stretcher is related to that of the chair shown in figure 15.9.

FIGURE 15.20. Side chair, New York City, ca. 1700. H: 44¼″, W: 17⅝″, D: 14½″. Maple. Private collection. Photo, Gavin Ashworth. This chair is closely related to the one illustrated in figure 15.19.

FIGURE 15.21. Joined great chair, New York, 1650–1700. H: 43″,W: 23¾″, D: 21″. Oak. Courtesy Wadsworth Atheneum, Hartford. Wallace Nutting Collection Gift of J. Pierpont Morgan. 1926.393. Photo, Joseph Szaszfai. The left arm and seat have been replaced, and the feet are missing.

FIGURE 15.22. Armchair with carving attributed to Jean Le Chevalier, New York City, 1705–10. H: 47½″,W: 25½″, D: 27″. Maple with oak and hickory. Courtesy Historic Hudson Valley, Tarrytown, New York. Photo, Gavin Ashworth. The finials are incorrect nineteenth-century restorations; the feet are more recent.

among the family collections of Van Cortlandt Manor in Croton, southern Westchester County, the armchair appears in a late nineteenth-century photograph of the second-story hall.

Among the most distinctive features of the armchair are its carved crest rail and stretcher, both of which have angular scrolls with stylized flowers at the interstices and acanthus leaves shaded with a parting tool (a V-shaped carving tool). The crest rail and stretcher are virtually identical to those of a contemporary armchair that descended in the Chester-Backus families of Albany (fig. 15.23), the armchair illustrated in figure 15.24, and the side chair fragment illustrated in figure 15.25 (see also fig. 15.26).[31] The acanthus leaves on all of these examples are also similar to those on the arms of a more conventional New York leather armchair (fig. 15.27), but the technical relationships are insufficient to attribute them conclusively to the same hand. Nevertheless, the turnings on the latter example and the Chester-Backus armchair are directly related to those on the standard New York version of the Boston leather chair (fig. 15.3).

Several different turners and chair makers were involved in the production of these leather chairs, although at least four are tied together by a single carver. All have trapezoidal seats that are constructed differently. The Chester-Backus chair maker joined

FIGURE 15.23. Armchair with carving attributed to Jean Le Chevalier, New York City, ca. 1700–10. H: 53¾″, W: 22⅞″, D: 16⅜″. Maple and oak. © 2003 Museum of Fine Arts, Boston, Gift of Mrs. Charles L. Bybee, 180.379. Photo, Edward A. Bourdon, Houston, Texas. This chair was damaged by fire while in the Bybee collection.

FIGURE 15.24. Armchair with carving attributed to Jean Le Chevalier, New York City, 1705–10. H: 52″, W: 24¾″, D: 17½″. Maple and oak. Courtesy Chipstone Foundation, Fox Point, Wisconsin. Photo, Gavin Ashworth. The low placement of the carved front stretcher is reminiscent of late-seventeenth-century French fauteuils, as well as of some varieties of London caned chairs, which took French court furniture as a stylistic paradigm under the influence of refugee Huguenot artisans, especially after 1685. The left scroll volute of the crest is a replacement.

FIGURE 15.25. Side chair with carving attributed to Jean Le Chevalier, New York City, 1705–10. Dimensions not recorded. Maple and oak. Private collection. Photo, Gavin Ashworth.

the side stretchers and front posts in a manner once thought exclusive to Boston leather chair makers (fig. 15.23; see also fig. 15.15); the chair maker of figure 15.25 utilized the same techniques as the maker of the New York grand chair (see fig. 15.13); and the Van Cortlandt chair maker awkwardly combined both methods—perhaps indicating an idiosyncratic, "creolized" solution or mere confusion over the application of a difficult new construction technique (fig. 15.22).[32] There is strong circumstantial evidence that the carver of these chairs was Jean Le Chevalier, a Saintongeais Huguenot who provided carving for the royal customhouse barge in 1700. Le Chevalier was born around 1670, probably in the region of Mortagne, in Saintonge. The Chevalier family was deeply involved in the Reform movement in the small coastal seafaring villages of Moise, Soubise, Saint-Seurin, and Mortagne from the sixteenth century until the family's emigration to London and New York in the late seventeenth century. Although he did not arrive in the colonies until around 1688, the stage for his entrance into New York's artisan community may have been set twenty years earlier by another Jean Chevalier, probably his grandfather.[33]

The elder Jean Chevalier and a relative named Thomas (possibly his brother) were in Martinique in January 1661. The following month a "John Cavlier" married "Eleanor La Chare" (*sic*) in New York City. She was probably the daughter of Salomon La

FIGURE 15.26. Composite detail showing (from top to bottom) the crest rails of the chairs illustrated in figs. 15.23, 15.24, and 15.25 and the stretcher of the chair illustrated in figure 15.22. Compare carving with the scrollwork at the top and base of the device in figure 14.16.

FIGURE 15.27. Armchair, New York City, ca. 1700–10. H: 47¼″, W: 23½″, D: 22⅜″. Maple and oak; original leather upholstery. © 2003, Museum of Fine Arts, Boston, Arthur Tracy Cabot Fund, 1971.624. Acanthus-carved arms such as these were common on late-seventeenth- and early-eighteenth-century French upholstered seating furniture.

Chaire, who served as Notary of New Amsterdam from 1661 until 1662 and was a powerful member of the city's bureaucracy. Like so many of the earliest colonists in New Netherlands, Salomon was a Walloon, born on the Lindengracht in Amsterdam. His father was Pierre La Chaire, a weaver from La Haye, Normandy, who became connected with the Normandy branch of the Le Chevalier family when he married Marguerite "Cavulier" in Amsterdam. The elder Jean Le Chevalier's social and political connections undoubtedly helped him secure important public contracts, like framing and repairing the royal coat of arms on the front of City Hall. Such commissions also increased his exposure to the city's Church of England elites.[34]

This complex transatlantic web of patronage ramified by marriage and familial interconnections provides fragmentary evidence of a migrating colonial craft network. Salomon La Chaire's brother Jan was a carpenter who emigrated from Valenciennes, a town in northeastern France bordering Flanders, and who arrived in New Amsterdam on September 2, 1662. Jean Chevalier (Cavlier), thus married a cousin who was related to another family of refugee woodworking artisans, setting the stage for his grandson's entrée into a preexisting New York craft network, which probably originated generations earlier in heretical outposts of northern and southwestern France, before extending its web to Amsterdam, London, and finally to colonial America.[35]

On June 27, 1692, Jean Le Chevalier Jr. married Marie de La Plaine in the Dutch

Reformed church in New York. However, when their two daughters were born in 1693 and 1695, they were baptized in the new French church. Le Chevalier's name appears often in the records of the French church after 1688 (the date of his arrival), a strong indication of the multiple public and private allegiances that many New York City Huguenots maintained with dominant local cultures. Marie de La Plaine was the daughter of Nicolas de La Plaine, a Huguenot from the Seigneurie de La Grand Plaine, near Bressuire, just north of La Rochelle in Poitou. Nicolas was living in New Amsterdam by April 1657, when he took the oath of allegiance to the Dutch government. By marrying into a French Protestant family established during the period of Dutch ascendancy, Le Chevalier forged additional ties with New York's "old" French culture. Joshua Delaplaine, Marie's brother, was one of New York's most successful joiners, thus Jean may have also benefited from the commercial associations established by his brother-in-law.[36]

An alien under British colonial law, Le Chevalier received letters of denization in New York on September 28, 1695, and was made a freeman the following October. On June 11, 1700, "John Chevalier joiner" sued "gentleman" Duie [*sic*] Hungerford, for "non-payment for making [a] Screwtore [escritoire], table and other joiners work." Evidently, Le Chevalier was an extremely versatile tradesman, capable of producing a variety of joined forms, carving, and turning. Something may be learned about his training as a turner from a note attached to the inventory of Magdalena Bouhier (also "Bouyer," from Marennes in Saintonge) taken on July 15, 1698, and designated "To John Le Chavallir by tornors tools of s[ai]d heredity 12s." Magdalena's husband Jean Bouyer was a cloth maker, so a close male relative or a previous husband may have taught Le Chevalier the "art and mystery" of turning. The turner's tools "of s[ai]d heredity" could refer to the set of tools often given an apprentice at the end of his term. It is uncertain whether Le Chevalier served his apprenticeship in France, London, or New York.[37]

Le Chevalier's personal history suggests that he learned his trade both within the nuclear family and without, in shops belonging to closely related southwestern Huguenot craft networks. We know, for example, that he was apprenticed to a member of Magdalena Bouhier's family and so was trained as a turner in the Saintongeais tradition, that he probably learned to carve from either his grandfather or father (assuming his grandfather "Jan" trained his father), and that he was connected to at least two Huguenot craft and patronage networks through marriage. He was also well known to the entire New York Huguenot community through his active participation in the French church. In addition to close social and occupational ties with his native community, Le Chevalier was connected with older New York continental cultures through his long association with the Dutch Calvinist church. Nevertheless, evidence suggests that many of his patrons were New York elites of British descent and other craftsmen.

From the fall of 1700 until the summer of 1701, the British customhouse and fort in New York underwent extensive renovation. On October 15, 1700, "Jno Chivaleer Carpenter" received £6 "for work done in the Custom house" and he earned £86.11 for Joiner's work done ye Fort" the following June. At least five other carpenters and joiners worked on the customhouse and its interior, but Le Chevalier received the highest payment.[38] Le Chevalier gained access to New York's anglicized elites through public projects and by supplying piecework for English joiners such as John Ellison Sr., one of the most successful and well respected Anglican woodworkers in the city. Among the debtors and creditors listed in Ellison's ledger and inventory are several prominent local artisans including Le Chevalier, who may have sold him turned or carved components or entire chair frames.[39] Le Chevalier's public commissions and his close association with Ellison suggest that he was one of the busiest early New York carvers. Indeed, no other carver is documented in New York at the turn of the century. Given the relatively low demand for carving in early eighteenth-century New York (Fitch's correspondence suggests that he sold six plain leather chairs for every carved one), it is plausible that Le Chevalier and his shop could easily provide most of the carving needed by New York chair makers and joiners. New York merchants and chair makers did not develop an extensive export trade, so it is unlikely that the city could support more than a few professional carvers.

Although it can only be inferred that Le Chevalier made leather chair frames, there is direct evidence that at least two other Huguenots with connections to southwestern France made leather chairs—Richard Lott and Jean Suire (John Swear). The earliest references to Lott are in Thomas Fitch's letter books. On September 9, 1706, Fitch sent "Richard Lott NYC" a "bill Lading and Invo[ice] of one bale of upholstery being what yo bought amounting to forty two pound 7/9d shipd as yo odder'd . . . hpe will get safe to [New] York." Apparently, Lott, who was referred to as an "upholsterer" and "chairmaker" by 1707, imported most of his upholstery materials from Boston. The following month Fitch wrote: "I had not one brass nail nor tack by all these ships Tho a supply of other goods. That I shall be forced to buy Some here if can get them and if I can meet with any shall send yo some."[40]

On April 22, 1707, Fitch wrote Faneuil, to whom Fitch had transferred Lott's debt, "I hope Lott has paid all: as to his chairs being somewhat lower priced, ye reason is they were not Russia, but New Eng. leather, he had done here." Fitch apparently understood that Lott and his fellow New York chair makers were a source of competition, but he continued to sell him the upholstery materials. Fitch's patronage of both Faneuil and Lott may have exemplified an "unintended performance," since the combination of chairs imported from Boston and those produced locally saturated the New York market with leather chairs by 1709.[41]

Fitch may have been partially mistaken, or perhaps intentionally misleading, in his analysis of why Lott's chairs were "somewhat lower priced." Although Lott imported upholstery materials from Boston, several factors gave him a competitive advantage over Fitch: Lott did not have custom duties and other carrying costs to factor into his price; he did not make chairs for venture cargo, therefore he assumed far less risk than Fitch who, by 1709, had a number of unsold chairs on consignment in New York; and Lott was intimately connected with and answerable to the local market, which may have required him to produce chairs that were better made and more ornate than conventional Boston examples—ones closer to the Huguenot-inspired, prototypical London caned chair (fig. 15.18).[42]

Little is known about Lott other than what is found in the Fitch letter books and court records. The progenitor of his family in New York was probably Peter Lott, who emigrated from the Lott River Valley in south-central France, not far from Saintonge, in 1652 and settled in Flatbush, Kings County. Since Richard Lott became a freeman in 1707, he must have been born around 1686, probably in Flatbush. Assuming that Peter Lott was his grandfather, Richard would have been a second-generation New Yorker from the "old" French culture, a relative rarity among early eighteenth-century Huguenot artisans, most of whom emigrated in the 1680s. Peter may have left France in response to one of Richelieu's periodic military forays against Protestant strongholds south of the Loire Valley. The southwestern experience certainly supports the hypothesis that the persistent wars of religion caused thousands of Huguenots to leave in distinct waves long before the Revocation of the Edict of Nantes. Peter may also have been a woodworker. Several of the Kings County Lotts were woodworkers, some until well into the eighteenth century.[43]

The New York chair maker and joiner Jean Suire emigrated from Saint-Seurin de Mortagne, a tiny coastal village just north of the Gironde River in Saintonge. A Jean Suire appears often in Mortagne's consistorial records as an active participant in local church activities from Saint-Seurin. The Suire name remains common in coastal Saintonge and Aunis and is distinctly regional. It may be counted repeatedly in the archives of merchant and artisan heresy in southwestern France, where the Suires were usually recorded as woodworking or textile-producing tradesmen and occasionally as small shopkeepers. Members of the family were prone to conflict with both religious and secular authorities, to whom they were very well known. As early as 1661 (the year of the great "persecution" illustrated in the engraving in fig. 14.5), La Rochelle's police undertook the "Expulsion of the Reformed: Suire, of Marans [a fishing village just north of La Rochelle]." In 1748, police in La Rochelle fined "Suire and his wife, publicans [*cabaretiers*]"—suspected as secret, "newly converted" Huguenots who remained in France after the Revocation—"for having served drinks to apprentice shoemakers and operated [for this purpose] during prohibited times and by night." Were the Suires serving heresy along with their wine? It is not difficult to imagine that Jean Suire may have been forced to leave Saintonge because of similar heretical activities.[44]

Nothing is known about Jean's route from Saint-Seurin, how long he may have resided in England or Holland, or the specific circumstances that caused him to immigrate to America. He was naturalized in New York in 1701, where he lived and worked in the West Ward until his premature death in March 1715. Suire's name appears seldom in the public records, although on December 6, 1715, he signed the Oath of Abjuration to George I. Virtually everything known about Jean's working life in the New World is contained in his inventory, a rich record that documents the shop of an industrious New York joiner, chair maker, upholsterer, shoemaker, and sleigh maker. Evidently he died in his prime, for he left many things "done in part" or "not finish'd."[45] Suire was certainly not alone in practicing multiple trades. The theory that specialization was an urban phenomenon and that real diversity only existed in rural areas is refuted by the inventories of several New York woodworkers. Personal, familial, economic, and cultural factors, as well as geography, all influenced artisans' decisions about diversification.

Suire's estate was inventoried on March 12, 1715, by two English appraisers, who knew him as "John Swear late of this City Joyner." The correct spelling of Suire's name and his ethnicity might have been lost had not his wife, "Marjan Suirre," signed the document and made several notations in French. The latter consist of computations from her husband's account books taken shortly before she and her son Cezar left the city and moved north to the Huguenot settlement at New Rochelle.

Suire's possessions suggest that he was relatively successful. The Anglo-French word "Due" mixed with Marjan's creolized French, denotes outstanding debts totaling over £75.

> 1 ps Oxenbrix 93 Ells Brown . . . 5.8.6.
> 1 crokas & wooden Screen 8 Leaves . . . 1.18.0
> a parcel fo Iron worke 16 box Locks 30 small
> Locks & 8 pair of Chest hinges 9 dozen of .0.0
> Brass Drops & 3 dos. Scutchins a parcel of Nails & brads
> 11 short thread Laces . . . 0.4.0
> a parcel of Joyners Tools viz sws chizels gouges plaines &c . . . 10.0.0
> 2 pair scales and weights . . . 1.0-.0
> 8 Indian drest Deerskins . . . 1.3.0
> 2 skins of Neat Leather & 1 pair Shoes . . . 1.0.0
> a parcel of Lumber . . . 1.0.0
> 1/2 barrel Lamp black 1 bird cage and one small box of paint 0.18.0

part of a New Bedstead . . . 0.6.0

3 Small Cupboards not finish'd . . . 1.7.0

1 Jug with about 1 gallon Varnish . . . 0.9.6

1 old grindstone . . . 0.4.6

28 square ps Timber

50 boards whitewood & Gum & some black wallnutt 3.10.0

1 Sleigh without Irons . . . 1.4.0

1 Negro about 8 yeares. . . . 12.0.0

1 chest Drawers not finish'd . . . 0.18.0

2 old cross cutsaws 2 old guns & a parcell of rushes for chairs .8.0

80 yds bristole stuff . . . 3.0.0

Pour argen recu 15//14//3
Pour Due Sur Le Livre 16//4//9
Pour Due Sur le Livre 59—.0 8.

Marjan Suirre

Suire's inventory, including household goods, totaled £126.9.1, and his joiner's and turner's tools were among the most expensive inventoried during the late seventeenth and early eighteenth centuries, indicating that he probably had the means to produce elaborate furniture forms. Lumber on hand included whitewood (yellow poplar), gumwood (or "bilsted"), and black walnut, along with "28 square ps Timber," probably intended for turning. The "parcell of rushes for chairs" and other upholstery materials such as leather, "oxenbrix," "crokas," and "bristole stuff" indicate that Suire was both a joiner and a chair maker. Most intriguing are the "8 Indian drest Deerskins" and "2 Skins of Neat Leather." The Indian deerskins may have been used for upholstery, but it is also possible that Suire stocked them for making shoes.[46] The "neat leather" was probably for chair upholstery, since Fitch and other upholsterers commonly used that term to denote furniture-grade material. The locks, hinges, brass drops, and "Scutchins" were expensive articles of hardware, largely imported from England, and the "Lamp black," "small box of paint," and "1 gallon Varnish" were finish components.

An artisan with a cultural background similar to Suire's may have constructed the Van Cortlandt armchair (fig. 15.22). Of all the New York armchairs known, it is the least indebted to Anglo-Boston prototypes and the closest to Saintongeais antecedents. With its undulating arms that sweep downward from a block high on the sharply raked rear posts and its low massing of details (an unusual combination of features for an Anglo-American leather armchair) the basic form of the Van Cortlandt armchair is generically related to seventeenth- and eighteenth-century French provincial fauteuils and to fauteuils made by French craftsmen in the upper St. Lawrence and

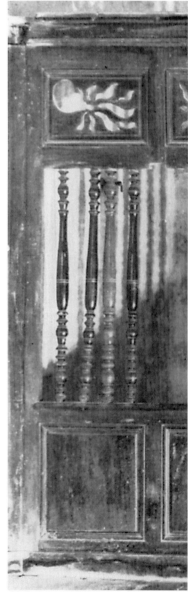

FIGURE 15.28. Details of oak baptismal screen in the church of Saint-Étienne, Ars-en-Ré, Île de Ré, 1625–27. From *Inventaire général des monuments et des richesses artistiques de la France, Commission régionale de Poitou-Charentes, Charente-Maritime, Cantons Île de Ré* (Paris: Ministère de la culture, Direction du patrimoine, 1979). Photo, Christopher Zaleski.

lower Mississippi River valleys. The turned elements on the Van Cortlandt armchair are virtually identical to those on the posts of the baptismal screen (*clôture des fonts baptismaux*) (fig. 15.28), in the medieval parish church of Saint-Étienne, in the canton of Ars-en-Ré on the Île de Ré. The woodwork in the church dates between 1625 and 1627, just before the siege of La Rochelle. After the siege, the most openly practicing Huguenots were systematically purged from the regional guilds.[47]

The interior woodwork of Saint-Étienne is essential for understanding the turning patterns favored by southwestern French Huguenots during the seventeenth century. Very little seventeenth-century interior woodworking from the war-torn region of Aunis-Saintonge (where churches were favored targets for iconoclasts) remains in situ. Moreover, the Île de Ré lies just off the coast of La Rochelle, in Aunis, and is perfectly situated along the traditional trade routes used by Protestant merchants and mariners as they traveled north through the Bay of Biscay to Britain, the Netherlands, and ultimately the New World. This woodwork reflects the interaction of artisanal ideas from La Rochelle and other Reformed metropolises in Northern Europe and vernacular traditions from Saintonge carried up the coast by journeymen woodworkers who regularly made the short journey to the island by sea in search of seasonal work. Despite the fact that Saint-Étienne was Roman Catholic, Huguenots were in the majority in the port towns, where they dominated most of the Île de Ré's artisanal guilds by 1625. During the renovation of Saint-Étienne, Huguenot culture was probably more pervasive on the Île de Ré and in La Rochelle, its powerful patron and protector, than ever before.

The unusual turning sequences shared by the chair posts and screen balusters are distinguished by an attenuated ovoid element bracketed by delicate filets and spools that rise into sharply ridged and molded bands. The maker of the Van Cortlandt chair rejected the attenuated balusters common on Saintongeais prototypes in favor of the radically cut-down, tapered, and stacked column common to leather chairs and London caned chairs influenced by Huguenot designers and turners in England. His turnings therefore blend Saintongeais forms with Huguenot-inspired London ones.[48]

The positive and negative space created by the balusters of the baptismal screen are similar to those formed by the spindles of a side chair that descended in the Schuyler and Dey families of New York and New Jersey (fig. 15.29) and the spindles of an armchair with a history of ownership in Tarrytown in Westchester County, New York (fig. 15.30). Both probably represent the work of Huguenot chair makers trained in southwestern coastal traditions. Commonly referred to as "black" or "colored" chairs, such forms were almost invariably painted, and fitted with simple rush seats. Suire, for example, had all the materials necessary for the production of black chairs, including lumber prepared for turning, "1/2 barrel Lamp black . . . and one small box of paint,"

FIGURE 15.29. Black chair, Long Island Sound region, perhaps southeastern Westchester County, 1705–30. H: 48″, W: 18⅜″, D: 13½″. Maple and ash. Courtesy Passaic County's Dey Mansion, Wayne, New Jersey. Photo, Neil Kamil.

FIGURE 15.30. Black great chair, probably Tarrytown, Westchester County, 1705–1730. H: 44½″, W: 23″, D: 26¼″. Wood unidentified. Courtesy Historic Hudson Valley, Tarrytown, New York.

and "a parcell of rushes for chairs." New York inventories indicate that black chairs were commonly used in combination with caned chairs (though rarely with leather chairs), so they represented a relatively inexpensive turner's alternative to upholstered furniture.[49] Evidently, Suire and his Huguenot contemporaries made chairs for consumers of all income levels.

Turnings similar to those of the "black chairs" (figs. 15.29, 15.30) are typically associated with chair making in coastal Connecticut, but evidence suggests that similar work was produced along the entire coastline of the culturally permeable Long Island Sound and in Connecticut River Valley towns that traded with communities commercially linked to the Sound. The couch illustrated in figure 15.31 reflects the shifting transatlantic human geography of Long Island Sound. Probably made in either Rhode Island or New York, it belonged to Ezekiel Carré, a Huguenot minister, a native of the Île de Ré who emigrated in 1686 with twenty-five other French refugee families to the short-lived settlement of Frenchtown in East Greenwich, Rhode Island.[50]

Perhaps the best material evidence documenting the extensive migration of refugee turners and chair makers from southwestern France to the Long Island Sound region is the cross-generational shop production of the Durand Family of Saint-Froul (a town of 400 in seventeenth-century coastal Saintonge) and Milford, Connecticut, and of the Coutant Family of the Île de Ré and New Rochelle in southern Westchester County, New York. Benno Forman, Robert Trent, and Kathleen Eagen Johnson have documented the production of these shops, including their turned alternatives to metropolitan leather chairs. More important, they have also demonstrated an overlap between the end of the so-called "heart-and-crown" phase of coastal Connecticut chair making at mid-century and the beginning of the "York" (New York) phase of chair making in the Hudson, Connecticut, and Delaware River Valleys and the Long Island Sound region.[51]

FIGURE 15.31. Couch, New York City or coastal Rhode Island, 1700–1715. H: 42⅛″, W: 74⅜″, D: 25⅛″. Maple. Courtesy Henry Francis du Pont Winterthur Museum, Winterthur, Delaware.

FIGURE 15.32. Detail of early-eighteenth-century oak confessional in the church of Sainte-Catherine, Loix, Ars-en-Ré, Île de Ré. From *Inventaire général des monuments et des richesses artistiques de la France, Commission régionale de Poitou-Charentes, Charente-Maritime, Cantons Île de Ré* (Paris: Ministère de la culture, Direction du patrimoine, 1979). Photo, Christopher Zaleski.

Given what we know about the refugee origins of these shops, it is plausible that many of the relationships between these diverse artifacts reflect common familial, craft, and patronage ties that originated in southwestern France. However, this is *not* to say that only Huguenot artisans produced turner's chairs—or, for that matter, New York leather chairs. Instead the evidence suggests that, at the very least, a process of Anglo-French creolization was active in the cultural and material life of New York City and the Long Island Sound region. The decorative arts historian Peter Thornton has documented a similar process among French refugee artisans living in London after 1685.[52] In both instances, creolization occurred as a result of face-to-face interaction in French-speaking artisan networks of refugees from the same regional diaspora and through common artisanal discourse. In New York the latter included the ubiquitous use (in several different combinations) of architectonic superimposed balusters.

Huguenot turners such as the Coutants, for example, were undoubtedly familiar with early eighteenth-century baluster shapes such as those decorating a confessional (fig. 15.32) in the parish church of Sainte-Catherine, also in the canton of Ars-en-Ré on the Île de Ré. This French regional turning style, introduced to England and the New World by refugee woodworkers from the Continent, is manifest in a prototypical "first-generation heart-and-crown chair" made in Milford by Andrew Durand (1702–91) or his master, possibly Pierre Durand (fig. 15.33). The latter may have emigrated to America as early as 1702.[53] Similarly, refugee woodworkers active in this artisanal network were aware of the carving pattern that survives on a pew door in the Église d'Esnandes, a tiny twelfth-century fortified church (fig. 15.34). This pattern was

FIGURE 15.33. Side chair attributed to Pierre or Andrew Durand, Milford, Connecticut, 1710–1740. H: 45¼", W: 19½", D: 14¾". Maple and ash. Anonymous collection. Photo, New Haven Colony Historical Society.

FIGURE 15.34. Enclosed pine pew with carved door, Église d' Esnandes, Aunis, France, ca. 1740–50. The church of Esnandes was constructed between the twelfth and fifteenth centuries, when it was fortified with turrets and crenellated walls. This pew, with its heart and crown crest rail on the door, was installed in the second quarter of the eighteenth century, when the vestiges of medieval interior woodwork were replaced. Photo, Neil Kamil.

common to several varieties of heart-and-crown chairs. Located on the Atlantic coast just north of La Rochelle near the mussel-farming town of Marans, the pew was built as part of a campaign to replace the church's interior woodwork during the early eighteenth century. The Durands and Coutants were thus connected over the course of more than a century by two bodies of water—the Bay of Biscay and Long Island Sound—as well as by common languages and artisanal traditions carried west in the Huguenot diaspora from Aunis-Saintonge.

Just as New York City Huguenot chair makers began to wrest a share of the local market for metropolitan upholstered furniture from Boston English merchants and artisans, rural Huguenot shops began to dominate the regional market for inexpensive stylish alternatives to urban leather-upholstered seating. Both drew patterns from similar Old World sources but adapted them to different economic and social milieu. Although southwestern French patterns were often cloaked under the guise of the dominant Boston English fashion for leather chairs, many details endured and were adapted to inexpensive vernacular forms. In some rural settings, French turning styles persisted long after the "mannerist" superimposed baluster style became anachronistic in the metropolis. The baptismal screen in the church of Saint-Étienne (fig. 15.28) also yields important information about the human geography of southwestern French Huguenots in New York and the Long Island Sound region. Architectural carving installed during the same period as the screen (see figs. 15.38, 15.39) foreshadows, at the very least, the emergence of plain leather New York chairs, heart-and-crown chairs, and perhaps most of all, their anglicized antecedents. Indeed, the heart-and-crown chair may have been the most enduring adaptation of a southwestern Huguenot artifactual language that began for many refugee artisans on the coast of the Bay of Biscay around the middle of the sixteenth century, and ended on the coast of Long Island Sound in the middle of the eighteenth. The New York leather chair was just as profoundly indebted to that artifactual language as its rural counterparts, only its debt was much more dissonant and ambiguous.

Benno Forman was the first to recognize ambiguities in how the historical and for-

FIGURE 15.35. Side chair, London, 1685–1700. Wood and dimensions not recorded. Photo, Symonds Collection. Courtesy The Winterthur Library: Decorative Arts Photographic Collection, Henry Francis du Pont Winterthur Museum, Winterthur, Delaware.

mal structures of New York leather chairs interacted. Forman understood that any inquiry into the nature of New York's material life must focus on the complex, contingent *relation* between history and form—the *life* of form. Yet he was unable fully to apply this methodology to the pluralistic New World societies of the middle Atlantic region and the South. His struggle with the conceptual problems pluralism posed focused ultimately on his thwarted formal analysis of the one "European" leather chair (fig. 15.35) that he considered absolutely central to the "origins of the New York style."[54]

This "European" chair had many of the standard features of the New York leather chair that differed fundamentally from standard Boston models: superimposed baluster posts wherein the turner's scansion is sharply punctuated by compressed caps, filets, reels, and ellipsoids (see fig. 15.3); compressed, urnlike finials surmounted by distinctively rotund bosses (see fig. 15.11); leather upholstery pulled through a slit in the crest rail and nailed in the back—a device that appears on many standard New York leather chairs with carved crests and rectangular back panels (see figs 15.23–26); thick, double side stretchers that connect with a rear stretcher tenoned with a single peg at the same level as the bottom side stretcher—a feature that appears on most, but not all, New York plain leather chairs (see fig. 15.3); symmetrical balusters on the posts below the seat and often, in lieu of a cylinder, on the turned juncture of the rear posts between the bottom of the back and the top of the seat (see fig. 15.16); and a concave or "French hollow" back (see fig. 15.17). "If this European chair is English," Forman wrote, "then the style of the New York chairs is English, and the New York high-back leather chairs took their inspiration from a part of the English tradition unknown or less influential in Boston. If, on the other hand, this European chair is continental, then the New York chairs are northern European in inspiration." But, when Forman looked to Holland, a logical northern European source for immigrant New York craftsmen, the stylistic origins of the chair became more ambiguous. Chairs with verifiable Netherlandish provenances shared remarkably similar features with the European leather prototype, its London caned derivatives, and New York leather chairs.[55]

Forman also reached an intellectual cul-de-sac when he attempted to ascertain the origins of a finial turning shared by a Dutch highchair, the New York-made Chester-Backus armchair, *and* some Boston chairs: "The Dutch highchair also has a finial almost identical to that on the . . . [Chester-Backus chair]. Were these attributes brought to New York by an emigrant craftsman from Holland? The picture is further complicated by a version of the finial of the Dutch highchair and the [Chester-Backus] chair that is also common on Boston-made chairs in this period. How did that come about? Did this particular form of the finial make its way from Holland to England and thence to Boston and New York?"[56] Regrettably, the human context had disappeared over three hundred years before these chairs caught Forman's eye.

Part of the problem lies in the quest to locate static territorial origins for the New

York leather chair, indeed for New York history per se. Both were products of converging *human* geographies; of unstable, shifting, and above all infinitely mutable Atlantic communities, atomized and dispersed across Britain and Protestant northern Europe by vicious religious wars that beset Europe and colonial America from the sixteenth to the eighteenth centuries. Historical context, contingency, and above all human interaction dictated that *all* and *none* of the place-names cited in Forman's analysis were the provenance of the New York leather chair. Thus the New York leather chair, like the "European" leather chair and the London caned chairs that preceded it, was not purely French, English, Dutch, Bostonian, or American. Instead the New York leather chair is a material manifestation of the interactive and competitive discourse of cultural convergence, quotation, and creolization whereby different regional cultures communicated their perception of difference to themselves and others.

Forman's intuitions about the "European" chair and the physical evidence embodied in it ultimately help portray Huguenot artisans as cultural creoles who used available artifactual languages in an innovative process of negotiation and conservative adaptation that could accommodate changing contexts and power relations throughout the early modern Atlantic world. Forman speculated, on the basis of its Russia-leather upholstery (commonly imported to London), that the "European" chair was

FIGURE 15.36. Side chair, London, ca. 1690–1700. H: 48¾″, W: 21⅞″, D: 17⅝″. Beech. © 2003, Museum of Fine Arts, Boston, Gift of Mrs. Winthrop Sargent, in memory of her husband Jun. 17.1629.

FIGURE 15.37. Side chair, New York City, 1685–1700. H: 48″, W: 20¼″, D: 22″. Maple. Courtesy Chipstone Foundation, Fox Point, Wisconsin. Photo, Gavin Ashworth. The sunflower is combined with spiral—also called "twist" or "French"—turnings.

"probably" made in urban England. This attribution is validated by its close relation to London high-back caned and Turkey-work chairs (compare figs. 15.18, 15.36). The carved and turned elements on the caned chair in particular share much with New York leather chairs, as do details on many other types of high-style London caned chairs. The post turnings—vases surmounted by a sharply articulated reel and baluster—on the European chair are related to all but one New York leather chair illustrated here (fig. 15.22), as well as the Durand side chair (fig. 15.33), and a distinctive group of contemporary New York City tables (e.g., figs. 16.3 and 16.5). The Turkey-work chair (fig. 15.36) also has a slit crest rail and carved elements associated with the "European" leather chair (fig. 15.35) and its London caned and New York leather contemporaries, and its frame is strikingly similar to that of a carved New York side chair with "barley twist" posts and stretchers (fig. 15.37). The fleur-de-lis and the sunflower motif on the latter chairs (fig. 15.37) spread from France in courtly and religious iconography that preceded the Huguenot dispersion and became part of the decorative vocabulary in England and Scotland during the sixteenth century. However, as we have seen, on these early chairs, the fleur-de-lis and the heliotropic sunflower (of whatever variety) may relate specifically to Huguenot artisanal culture and patronage.[57]

Assuming that the "European" leather chair (fig. 15.35) was made in London, then the *earliest* date assignable to its "boyes and crown" crest rail and stretcher is extremely significant. The term "boyes and crown," which probably derives from the same craft and etymological tradition as "hearts and crown," first appears in the accounts of the English Royal Household *after* 1685, in reference to carving on new caned chairs made for James II and William and Mary. This date coincides with the Revocation of the Edict of Nantes, after which Huguenot refugee artisans flooded into London. The publisher, architect, and interior designer Daniel Marot (1661–1752), was one of many highly skilled Huguenot artisans who received royal patronage during the mid 1680s. Although he and his father Jean certainly helped introduce the court style to England and Holland, many French baroque designs, such as the "boyes and crown," are too generic to attribute specifically to them. Even the Marots did not invent many of the designs they published; rather, their work represents an ingenious and marketable compilation of Huguenot design dialects carried north from the courts of Paris and Versailles as well as from small towns and regional centers such as Aunis-Saintonge.[58]

The appearance of the "boyes and crown" in London in 1685, and its stylistic relationship to the earlier architectural carving in the church of Saint-Étienne (figs. 15.38, 15.39) strongly suggest that this motif, like most of the decorative vocabulary on the wooden *frames* of the "European" leather chair and its New World counterparts, was developed in both metropolitan and colonial contexts through direct interaction with southwestern Huguenot craftsmen and their merchant patrons such as Jean Suire, Jean Le Chevalier, Richard Lott, the Durands, and Benjamin Faneuil. After 1685, most refugee craftsmen resided in Huguenot artisanal communities in metropolitan England (as did the family of Jean Le Chevalier) or, before 1664, Holland (as did the family of Richard Lott). The duration of their stay generally depended on economic prospects and the existence of familial or craft networks in other areas of Europe or America.

The carved elements of the choir screen in the church of Saint-Étienne (fig. 15.38) are also important in understanding the movement of artisans and ideas.[59] The façade contains sixteen square, rectangular, or demilune panels depicting scenes of Christ the Evangelist and His Apostles (fig. 15.38a). The biblical representations are punctuated by acanthus foliage (fig. 15.38b) or woodlands grotesques (figs. 15.38c, 15.39). The latter are carved naturalistically in deep three-dimensional relief and framed by sharp, complex applied moldings.

Half of the carved panels are friezes representing opposing winged cherubs with flowing curly hair, goatlike hooved legs (similar to those of Pan, god of the forest), and

FIGURE 15.38. Details of three carved panels in the choir screen in the church of Saint-Étienne, Ars-en-Ré, Île de Ré, components ca. 1629: (a) Jesus gathering his flock; (b) acanthus-leaf foliage; (c) winged cherubs holding an urn. Oak and walnut. From *Inventaire général des monuments et des richesses artistiques de la France, Commission régionale de Poitou–Charentes, Charente-Maritime, Cantons Île de Ré* (Paris: Ministère de la culture, Direction du patrimoine, 1979). Photo, Christopher Zaleski.

FIGURE 15.39. Details of one of the earliest panels in the choir screen (fig. 15.38) in the church of Saint-Étienne, Ars-en-Ré, Île de Ré, ca. 1580. Photo, Christopher Zaleski.

FIGURE 15.40. Joined great chair, probably New York City, ca. 1675. H: 42½″, W: 25″, D: 22½″. Oak. Courtesy Henry Francis du Pont Winterthur Museum, Winterthur, Delaware. Jean Le Chevalier's grandfather, called "Jan Cavelier," was a prominent carver in New York during the era when this chair was made. Compare the crest rail with the scrollwork at the base of the device in figure 14.16.

aquatic serpents' tails. Most (see fig. 15.38c) hold between them an urn containing tiny flowers that are remarkably similar to those *unique* to some New York carved leather chairs. The latter typically conjoin the opposing halves of S-scrolls (fig. 15.26, bottom). The lower half of the urn has a mature flower flanked by opposing foliate volutes joined by a clearly delineated band, perhaps forming a rosy cross. The articulation of this motif, often represented in both Rosicrucian and Huguenot iconography of the seventeenth century, recalls the carved fleur-de-lis on the London high-back Turkey-work chair (fig. 15.36), Windsor-Wethersfield work (fig. 14.28), and the leafy carved crest rail of a seventeenth-century joined oak great chair (fig. 15.40) found in Southampton, Long Island, in 1875.[60] Here was a rustic chair fit for an American grotto.

Fourteen of the carved screen panels date from the late 1620s, about two generations before the "boyes and crown" appeared in London. The two remaining panels, which date from the sixteenth century, also depict winged cherubs with goat feet and serpents' tails (fig. 15.39), a pattern of hybridization similar to the bizarre, morphed creation of the Thirty Years' War that served as the frontispiece (fig. 5.3) for Grim-melshausen's *Simplicius Simplicissimus* (1668). Since they probably served as the proto-type for the later panels, this Italianate and/or Germanic imagery may have appeared in the Aunis-Saintonge area as early as the 1560s. Although the "boyes and crown" on the "European" leather chair is not by the same hand as the later church carving, it is clearly the work of a Huguenot refugee—or a Huguenot-trained "native"—who emerged from the same southwestern French regional craft traditions.

Forced out into the Atlantic world, Huguenot craftsmen sought to form new so-cial and economic identities through artisanal interaction. Long experience in craft-ing heresy at the French court, the core of French absolutism, had revealed that skill in manipulating the material languages of concealment and display was absolutely nec-essary to maintain a semblance of cultural equilibrium amid the asymmetries of the New World. For the Huguenots, asymmetry and the quest for equilibrium had be-come a permanent condition of life in the *désert*, which was, after all, a place to await the millennium at the end of time—the Huguenots' only real "home" in history. The apocalyptic moment of perfect social and spiritual harmony would accompany Christ's return and, with it, the annihilation of all difference. Concealment, the armature of a displaced, shifting identity, would then simply dissolve into transparency.

❧ Hidden in Plain Sight ❧

New York's successful response to the importation of Boston leather chairs began with the massive influx of French Huguenot merchants and craftsmen into New York City from the Aunis-Saintonge region of southwestern France following the Revocation of the Edict of Nantes in 1685. Within a decade, New York had a mature community of Huguenot artisans, many of whom arrived in kinship networks that migrated virtu-ally intact in the same craft diaspora that transformed notions of courtly style in En-gland and Holland. In this context, the Huguenot diaspora of the 1680s compares closely with the migration of Puritan craft networks to Boston and other parts of southeastern New England during the 1630s. By the end of the seventeenth century, New York also had a well-developed community of "native" artisans, including "old," pre-1685 French or Walloon refugees who migrated west during earlier periods of con-fessional violence. These craftsmen linked the newcomers with French-speaking groups that were already established in New Amsterdam prior to the English takeover in 1664. Comprised of individuals from both artisanal sectors, New York's leather chair makers from Saintonge and their merchant patrons from La Rochelle were perfectly positioned to compete effectively in the heterogeneous market for luxury goods that Boston's merchants and artisans had dominated since the mid seventeenth century.

As Fitch and Faneuil's correspondence about the rigorous demands of metropolitan style and fashion indicates, commercial success in New York was contingent upon interaction and convergence with the dominant anglicized culture. Fragmented and asymmetrical, the process of convergence manifested itself in discrete yet perceptible cultural boundaries arranged specifically within the internal spatial dynamics of the chairs themselves. The chairs, therefore, encoded a sort of narrative; a "fictional consensus" between competing merchant-elites and artisan communities that represented competing cultures on the colonial core and periphery—a material discourse interacting with multiple histories whereby both specific and generic perceptions of metropolitan style encompassed fundamental questions of identity, social distance, and boundaries in a pluralistic New World society. This problem was a transatlantic one, however, wherein marginalized cultures acted to subvert and redefine core cultures in relation to themselves, particularly in arenas of social and economic action that remained viable after political and military battles were lost. By the early eighteenth century, the negotiation of shifting identities between "natives" and "foreigners" had a long history in absolutist France owing to the enduring presence of Huguenots and Jews. Both "foreigners" and "natives" pinned their hopes on shifting, circular dialogues: "foreigners" hoped for manipulation toward change from below, "natives," for maintenance (or extension) of the status quo from above. "A 'native resident,'" wrote the French chancellor Henri d'Aguesseau in 1742, "is the opposite of a 'foreigner'; and as opposites ought to define one another, in defining the term 'foreigner' we will know the full limits of the 'native resident.'"[61] Although they could not remain pure "opposites" in a Protestant America that granted them refuge, New World Huguenots found meaning in the negotiation of an identity in which their historical status as perpetual "foreigners" was reactivated as a defining element. Following Böhme's animate materialist epiphany, they were most comfortable when playing off the dull surface of pewter like little sparks of light.

In Saintongeais Huguenot society, artisans had a powerful formative influence on virtually every facet of economic life in the countryside and in lay spiritual life as well. Tradesmen pursued strategies that linked local religious discourse and materialism at the most basic levels of experience. Yet, the one-dimensional linear framework employed by many historians of the American Huguenot experience virtually "predetermines" the rapid decline, "assimilation," and "disappearance" of Huguenot culture in New York. Although this monolithic approach documents simple superficial evidence of their absorption into the dominant English culture, it is too shallow to confront change as process. Because it overlooks or misinterprets the Huguenot experience in southwestern France, it provides no foundation for understanding the complex, dynamic processes of transatlantic convergence and creolization in the middle colonies.

FIGURE 15.41. Composite diagram of the New York side chair illustrated in figure 15.3. Drawing, Neil Kamil; art work, Wynne Patterson.

(a) Trapezoid representing the ground plan of the central axes of the four posts considered from an axiometric perspective.

(b) Dimensions of the trapezoid providing basic units of measurement.

(c) Trapezoid extended vertically to form framework in three dimensions.

(d) Chair's overall dimensions indicating a one-to-one symmetrical relationship between the seat height and the height of the leather back panel (compare to fig. 15.9).

(e) Backward rake of the rear posts viewed from the side.

(f) Proportional system of horizontal elements viewed from the side: overall symmetry and balance, as opposed to the verticality of the Boston prototype, is achieved by equidistant tripartite repetition traversing areas both above and below the seat (bc/gh/lmn); balancing and then reducing the three spaces beneath the seat using the largest measurements available in the system to accentuate a "bottom heavy" effect (jk/kl/lmn); and the static repetition of the turners pattern above the seat (ji/gf/ed/; hg/cb; fe/dc/ba).

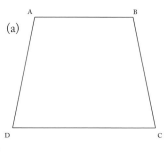

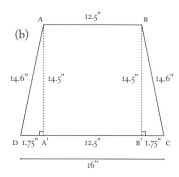

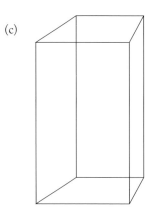

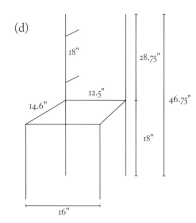

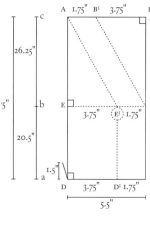

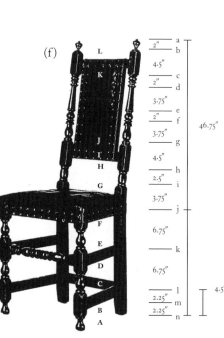

The most fundamental stumbling block for the assimilationists, however, is their perception of Huguenot culture as transparent; they take traditional Huguenot masking behavior—or "disappearance"—at face value. As early as 1611, a bemused Catholic observer at the great Huguenot assembly at Saumur cautioned against the danger of such generalizations: "When the Protestant beseeches the king *tres humblement* [he does so with] hand held high, sword drawn from its scabbard."[62]

Nearly three centuries of continuous religious war and violent reversals of power in the region caused southwestern Huguenots to become anything but transparent. To survive they had to develop strategies of interaction with others that were devious, obfuscating, and subterranean; they had to remain invisible while close to the heart of power. This strategy is reflected in the Bourbons' use of disease metaphors such as "virus" or "cancer" to describe "poisonous," insidious "attacks" by heretics hidden within the "body" of the state, which was precisely the same language as was used by Parliament to denounce Buckingham—and to justify brutal, cleansing excisions. By the mid sixteenth century, southwestern Huguenots had developed a mobile, mutable, largely artisanal culture that expressed its values, attitudes, and beliefs obliquely, usually in material form, by converging invisibly, yet within plain sight, with the most powerful symbols of the dominant host culture. A marginalized people, they chose to display their personal symbols on the margins of their work.

When New York Huguenots such as Jean Le Chevalier, Richard Lott, Jean Suire, and Benjamin Faneuil appropriated the Boston leather chair, they radically transformed only the surface treatment of the frame (the cheapest and most inconspicuous or *marginal* component) leaving the generic structure and leather panels of the Boston prototype undisturbed (fig. 15.41); however, the compositional logic of the New York leather chair conveys a dissembling, almost subversive quality. By subdividing the smooth, classical scansion of the Boston chair frame and substituting symmetry where there was asymmetry, the producers of the standard New York plain leather chair inverted the primary aesthetic intended by the producers of the Boston prototype—the abrupt, centrifugal verticality that represented the very essence of New England's mercantile reinterpretation of the most novel features of imported Anglo-French metropolitan caned chairs. Because the language of the chair was defined by its upholstery, and because he was not restrained by the economics of production for export, the New York chair maker could make significant changes in the disposition of ornament on the frame without making a different chair. New York chair makers creolized the Boston chair's artifactual language. They borrowed all of its basic lexicon, yet worked to change the generative grammar—fluid substructures that interact with the surface of the lexicon to generate meaning—to suit contingencies associated with their (or their patron's) own sociocultural requirements for the same price (or less) as the Boston leather chair.[63]

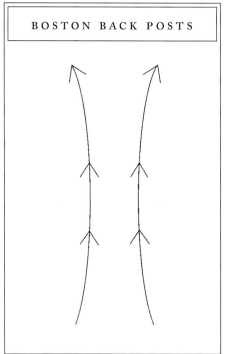

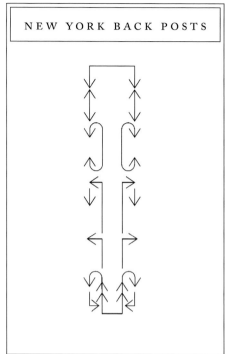

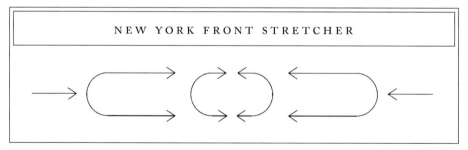

FIGURE 15.42. Flow diagram representing the formal reversal and redirection of turning patterns on the Boston and New York plain leather chairs exemplified by figs. 15.1 and 15.3 respectively. Drawing, Neil Kamil; art work, Wynne Patterson.

The exact percentage of the Boston prototype transformed by the New York artisan can be calculated by taking the surface area of the New York chair viewed frontally and subtracting significant "grammatical" change from the Boston prototype. The composite is nearly four parts prototype to one part alteration. Although the New York Huguenot artisan altered only one-fifth of the space of the Boston form, he did so by reactivating "old" cultural turning patterns derived from Anglo-French London cane and leather chairs, earlier New Amsterdam / New York Franco-Walloon chairs, or specific southwestern French regional woodworking paradigms, patterns that would have meaning for artisans and patrons from Aunis-Saintonge. In doing so, he constructed a new socio-material identity that brought together multiple, symbiotic, yet partially discrete "human regions" in a single dominant artifact.

Jack P. Greene has argued that colonial British America was an "uncertain, unequal, exploitative, restless, and, in many respects, chaotic world," in which "the psychology of exploitation" was so "normative" that there existed a "symbiotic relationship between independence and dependence." Pluralistic cultures in British America were constantly engaged in a struggle to "establish their mastery over their . . . several distinctive cultural spaces." As an artifact of cultural convergence with perceptible internal boundaries, the New York leather chair was a medium through which the struggle over mastery could be negotiated in a relatively benign manner—as "commerce"—and ultimately redefined in terms of economic "improvement" useful in elaborate, mutually acceptable (if not mutually inclusive) rituals of "politeness" and "civility." These contexts provided the appropriate discursive conditions for acceptance by upwardly mobile colonial elites.[64]

The elements of the New York chair that evidence the most radical centripetal motion are the very ones that move centrifugally on the Boston prototype: the columns on the back posts and the balusters on the front stretcher. Indeed, the attenuated "classical" columns and smooth surfaces were precisely the spaces chosen for a kind of serpentine reversal by patrons, artisans, and designers using southwestern Huguenot forms (fig. 15.42). On the back posts of the Boston chair, the animate motion of the line follows its narrow path upward with no opposition, and on the front stretcher the impulse is away from center. By contrast, the molding sequences on the back posts of the New York chair interrupt the upward momentum: impulse ascends, rebounds, twists, and returns to its starting point. The front stretcher, the only component common to almost all New York plain leather chairs, turns movement inward towards center to such a degree that it is the virtual opposite of its Boston counterpart. The same is true of Boston and New York leather chairs with carved crests. While the scrollwork of the Boston model flows away from center, the New York crest begins its outward movement, but stops, pivots on an acute angle, and returns just as abruptly. These

differences represent a dialogue between Anglo-Boston artisans expressing a centrifugal artifactual language and New York artisans from Aunis and Saintonge responding
centripetally.[65]

The analysis of leather chairs and other artifacts can be likened to the analysis of
text, a hermeneutic process. As such, the historian must strive to contextualize and reconstitute an artifact's entire scope, including "what they were intended to mean and
how this meaning was intended to be taken."[66] Yet, as with the New York chair's physical attributes (or symbolic language), intentionality may be turned in upon itself. If
read one-dimensionally, as Fitch intended his leather chair be read by New York's merchants and consumers, that perception could be manipulated from "below," as part of
an oblique dialogue about the contingency of culture, commerce, and ultimately power.
The New York plain leather chair was consequently constructed to contain alternative
"intentions" responsive to many levels of experience.

One school of perceptual theory maintains that man's fundamental impulse to gen-
eralize and order his experience causes him to "abstract single properties and regard
them as if they were the whole object." In a pluralistic setting, however, monolithic
perceptions are not necessarily generated by the artifacts themselves but are conditioned and potentially refracted and multiplied through social interaction with multiple personal and cultural histories. This "floating chain" of signifiers accommodates
areas of instability where contradictory intentions converge and are internalized. Multiple social realities can then be ordered hierarchically as "finite provinces of meaning."
New Yorkers were thus socialized to understand that certain phenomena mediated certain artifacts and institutions (or, like the Boston leather chair and the craft community that produced and marketed it, artifactual institutions), and this attitude tended
to govern their perceptions. This begs the essential historical question: How were seventeenth-century theories of visual perception practiced in pluralistic social settings?

Clearly, a seductive set of social expectations, associations, memories, and perceptions accompanied the "news" about style, fashion and status that the Boston leather
chair and its local variants carried into virtually every elite New York consumer's household under the thrall of anglicization. The control of knowledge was, therefore, also
at stake.[67] The Boston leather chair can thus be interpreted as a strictly coded symbol
system with its signifiers, *Boston* and *leather,* plainly defined in the early eighteenth-
century lexicon, making it an artifact accompanied by a verbal and written text to facilitate understanding. The primary signifier of the chair—its rectangular leather back
panel—was intended to be perceived first as the center of focus. It possessed the chair's
general social, cultural, and economic attribute—its sign of Bostonness, and was the
one aspect of the chair that was necessary for all viewers to experience. The back panel
conveys the sign in a clearly defined geometric form: a rectangle, preferably made of
patterned Russia leather, always framed with one or two rows of shiny brass nails and

bracketed by doric columns. Refractory textiles with crystalline optical qualities, such as Russia leather, were highly prized components of the court style. Jean-François Nicéron's 1638 *La Perspective curieuse,* for example, diagrammed "the optics" of domestic objects, such as upholstered chairs, "by direct sight." Niceron was particularly interested in the "refraction of crystals" and the "reflection of flat, cylindrical and conical mirrors" as optical paradigms that would be "very useful to painters, architects, engravers, [and] sculptors." On leather chairs, the rake of the back panel, upward, in "sight" of the beholder, determined the interplay of pattern and light that reinforced the textile's communicative power.[68]

New York Huguenot artisans capitalized on the production of "polite" artifacts—things that had both private and public functions—and so had the potential to generate multiple layers of meaning, perceptible to some and obscure to others. By retaining the generic leather back panel, a powerful symbol of British metropolitan style and culture, French chair makers were able to subvert the secondary codes embodied in the frame of the Boston chair with patterns borrowed from their "old" culture, creating a creolized form that would "pass" in the dominant anglicized culture while it remained in opposition on a more subliminal level. For most New Yorkers of British descent, the New York leather chair *was* a locally made Boston chair and a requisite status symbol linking them with other anglicized elites. Huguenots from Aunis-Saintonge however, undoubtedly perceived vestiges of their own refugee culture attached discreetly to the cognitive edges, the space that Buckingham's tastemaker Garbier manipulated to draw the eye of Inigo Jones. While historians can never fully know the variety of cultural associations that colonial New Yorkers may have carried with them when they took their seats during the early eighteenth century, there is reason to believe that beyond their obvious practical use, some chairs were made to function interactively, to help mold and direct those associations, and so, in a sense, the sitters themselves. Perhaps that is why after having "walked round" "English," "French," and "Dutch" New York in 1716, the Huguenot voyager John Fontaine finally beheld, to his amazement, a "French" town.[69] Everyone could construct their own convergence narrative.

Huguenot artisans and their merchant patrons quietly revealed in New York what they had learned under absolutism. Even the most powerful, seemingly inflexible symbols of dominance afforded valuable opportunities as vehicles for access, manipulation, and, in the end, appropriation through the "hidden" mediation of craft. For Faneuil, Lott, Le Chevalier, and Suire, the Boston leather chair, made ubiquitous by the volume, duration, and scope of that city's mercantile activity—indeed, made a "natural" part of colonial America's aesthetic reality—provided an open door to the homes of their hosts. Early New York was a place where, in practice, notions of mastery and totality were notoriously unstable. There, the powerful impulse of anglicization was transformed into an armature of commerce and transformation upon which French refugee merchants and chair makers harnessed their own concerns about mastery and its limitations.[70]

The struggle for mastery in New York had its price for the refugees, however; on February 10, 1708, eight leaders of the Huguenot merchant and artisanal community including Faneuil, Elias Neau, Stephen de Lancey, and François Vincent published a broadside demanding: "A Full & just Discovery of the weak & slender foundation of a most pernicious SLANDER Raised against the French Protestant Refugees Inhabiting the province of New-York generally, but more particularly affecting Capt. Benjamin Faneuil, A Person of considerable note amongst them."[71]

In 1706, an informer named Morris Newinhuysen accused Faneuil of a "very infamous, pernicious, and detestable report . . . *clandestinely* and *industriously* [emphasis added] spread abroad amongst the inhabitants of this City and Province." Newinhuysen, a New York Dutch mariner, claimed to have been aboard a ship where he saw letters in Faneuil's handwriting, "directed to *Rochell*," and "writ in *French*," that read, "to this effect, that if the *French* Squadron that took *Nevis* [in the British West Indies], had come hither, they would have met with less Resistance."[72]

This French threat to New York's security gave rise to another "false Rumour," claiming Faneuil and other Huguenots had "held and maintained a Correspondence with some of the Inhabitants of the kingdom of France, discovering the weakness of the strength and Fortifications of this Province, and how easily it might be made a conquest to the *French*, her Majesty's declared Enemies." A broadside claiming innocence in response to these new charges of dissimulation and conspiracy was posted on March 9, 1708, signed by ten French New Yorkers, most from La Rochelle. After learning that Newinhuysen was actually unable to read French, the case fell apart, and Lord Cornbury and the Mayor's Council cleared Faneuil and the other Huguenots. Yet the underlying insecurity and fear of hidden "conquest" from which the attacks emerged lingered on for many years to come.[73]

What, beyond his native country, enviable success in trade, and a few letters written in French had drawn such baneful attention from New York's English authorities, leading to allegations of clandestine activity in combination with popish enemies in France? The story of the chairs seems to have been only a part of a larger picture of Faneuil's perceived duplicity and *maleficium*. In fact, the francophobe accusations of 1706 may have originated with Faneuil's disappearance from New York between March 1701 and April 1705. His activities in those years tell us much about the shadowy nature of experience in the Huguenots' New World.

The whereabouts of Benjamin Faneuil during the lapse in the New York archival record between 1701 and 1705 might be accounted for by any number of explanations (including the notorious incompleteness of New York's colonial archives). The French government archives, however, contain an enigmatic document that may reveal something about the transatlantic behavior of the Faneuil family in general and (possibly) in particular, Captain Benjamin Faneuil's own risky role as a Huguenot *negociant-armateur* (merchant-shipowner) in early eighteenth-century colonial culture.

In 1698, the comte de Pontchartrain, who was to become Louis XIV's chancellor of state just one year later, began an extensive correspondence over the course of the next seven years with Michel Begon concerning royal strategies to suppress continuing heretical activity in southwestern France. Begon, who came from a venerable noble family of the robe, was among the king's most trusted and experienced administrators, which was why, soon after the Revocation, he was named intendant for the still unstable and politically sensitive Generality of La Rochelle (a relatively new bureaucratic unit, created after the siege in 1628). In a series of letters written between January 10 and June 6, 1703, Ponchartrain instructed Begon to "arrest Faneuil who came to La Rochelle, from Boston, where two of his brothers are established, with his belongings and who is a religionist [Protestant]: it may well be that he was sent to observe the preparations that are being made for the colonies neighboring New England." Faneuil was set free after having abjured Protestantism and was converted to Roman Catholicism, but despite this overt (though extorted and, as his later reconversion reveals, duplicitous) demonstration of Faneuil's loyalty to the state religion, Pontchartrain wisely remained suspicious. Begon was ordered to continue covert observations of the returned refugee, with an account of Faneuil's conduct to be delivered into the hands of the king himself.[74]

Faneuil was arrested in his native La Rochelle in 1703, under suspicion of having been "sent" to spy on behalf of New England's neighbors, presumably New York. Like New Yorkers who would be equally suspicious of Faneuil in 1706 (if from the opposite perspective), Louis XIV was particularly concerned that his ongoing plans to invade British America from New France might be intercepted by his enemies.

This was not an unreasonable assumption, since, as Pontchartrain indicated, New England and New York both maintained a constant state of readiness for war with the Catholic colonists of New France and their native allies on the northern frontier. Pontchartrain was concerned that France's ongoing preparations for supplying the Anglo-French imperial wars in North America from the port of La Rochelle—long a central staging area for expeditions to New France (as well as Louisiana and the French Antilles)—might be compromised. Was this also the source of Newinhuysen's fear of Faneuil's letters "directed to *Rochell*," and "writ in *French*"?

It is impossible to say with certainty if this was Benjamin Faneuil of New York, or one of his brothers, André and Jean. That he was identified as "from Boston" might suggest the latter. But inasmuch as Benjamin disappears from the New York archives during this period, it is possible that he set sail from Boston (or was understood by the French to represent the Boston firm of Faneuil and Company) on a commercial and/or espionage mission in partnership with his brothers and their political patrons in the colonies. It is noteworthy however, that Pontchartrain informed Begon of the existence of "two brothers" in Boston. If Pontchartrain meant to convey knowledge of three brothers, including the one Begon was about to arrest in La Rochelle, then Benjamin had to be directly involved as a protagonist in either Boston or La Rochelle.

But there are other clues. Charles W. Baird, whose nineteenth-century antiquarian history of the Huguenot migration to America remains the standard for transatlantic archival research, discovered a letter written in French on May 22, 1690, from Benjamin Faneuil, then living in Boston, to his brother-in-law, the Rochelais merchant Thomas Bureau. The Bureau family, like the Faneuils and numerous other refugees from Aunis-Saintonge, was also a major investor (and loser) in the disastrous Huguenot settlement project on the Massachusetts frontier at New Oxford. After New Oxford was destroyed twice by Indian attacks in 1696 and 1699, it was ultimately abandoned, and the Bureau family along with Benjamin Faneuil and many other refugee investors moved to New York. Baird correctly assumed that the letter had been intercepted by the French government somewhere between Boston and London, since the original is now in the French archives. The subject of the letter was Massachusetts's recent capture of Port Royal, Nova Scotia, and it conveyed in no uncertain terms Benjamin Faneuil's passionate hope that Québec would soon fall as well:

> Our fleet which we sent out from here to take Port Royal, has sent back a ketch, which has arrived this day, with news of the taking of that place, on capitulation they have seized six ketches, or brigantines, loaded with wine, brandy, and salt, together with the governor and seventy soldiers, and have demolished the fort. They have also taken twenty-four very fine pieces of cannon, and thirty barrels of powder. We expect them hourly. Our fleet which was composed of six vessels, one of which carried forty guns, will be reinforced with a number of strong ships, and will be sent with twelve hundred men and some Indians, to take Canada. I hope it will succeed.[75]

Soon thereafter, a combination of harsh weather and Frontenac's skillful defense of Québec overwhelmed the colonists' demoralized forces. But Benjamin Faneuil's intentions to begin to reverse the Huguenot defeat in the French Civil Wars of Religion by achieving a victory over French Catholicism in the New World would have been easily perceived by Pontchartrain or Begon had they intercepted his letter.

We know that André left Boston for Holland during the 1690s, where he attended to the family's business interests overseas until 1699, when Benjamin was forced by the business reversals at New Oxford to leave Boston for New York. Presumably because of that vacancy, André reappears in Boston.[76] One wonders whether Benjamin's absence from New York in 1701 was necessitated by European commitments that André was no longer able to fulfill because he had to take Benjamin's place in Boston? But given passionate political and military convictions, espionage against his former—and, from the perspective of refugees still secretly pursuing the revival of the Reformation in La Rochelle, present—oppressors, could have been a viable course of action for Benjamin Faneuil and his family's firm. Whatever the reason for the return to La Rochelle, and whoever the Faneuil was, Pontchartrain and Begon had reason to take defensive action and apparently were well advised to maintain surveillance. If we assume that Benjamin Faneuil was the subject of Begon's surveillance, then having disavowed his false conversion to Catholicism upon leaving La Rochelle for a second time, he was back again in New York City by April 1705 to inspire similar suspicions of conspiracy among his New World hosts.

But on June 24, 1705, Pontchartrain made yet another cryptic reference to "Faneuil"; this time an *armateur* who put into La Rochelle from Noordingh in Holland. This Faneuil was the owner, together with a certain "Daniau," of a suspicious vessel the chancellor ordered seized and searched for a hidden cargo of Rochelais *nouveaux convertis* seeking escape routes north and west to the New World.[77] The traffic in refugees to Britain, Holland, and ultimately America was active and lucrative throughout the early modern period and, as earlier events that transpired during the siege of La Rochelle have shown, Rochelais merchants were not above exploiting the plight of desperate coreligionists for profit. There was money to be made at both ends of such transactions: the price of this risky passage out of French territory was high for those who could afford to pay, and for those who could not, merchants negotiated indentures in labor hungry New World environments such as New York or the French Antilles. Might this last mention of a Faneuil have referred to Jean, who was to die in La Rochelle in June 1737, presumably also under suspicion as a *nouveau converti*?[78] When Benjamin finally made his way back to New York in 1705, and with André needed in Boston, was it Jean's turn to take his place in this transatlantic family's subterranean rotation?

The Faneuil spy cases that transpired sequentially in La Rochelle and New York City in the early eighteenth century emerged from the same strategic worldview that produced the New York leather chair that captured the local market from Boston a year after Lord Cornbury dismissed all charges against the upholsterer and his fellow refugees from Aunis-Saintonge. Depending on the local power relations of the moment, or as *nouveaux convertis,* southwestern Huguenots were notorious for their reliance on fictional performances—textual and material—masking personal convictions, motivations and behavior, in combination with other forms of duplicity, to achieve their religious, commercial, and political goals.

Ultimately, the "clandestine" and "industrious" Huguenots who migrated from southwestern France to colonial America were part of a dispersed Atlantic culture of almost pure contingency, of infinite adaptation to niches made available by their skills. Never in their history had they lived outside the shadow of a more powerful "enemy." When considered from the refugee chair maker's subterranean perspective of a violent and troubled past, the presumed "disappearance" of southwestern Huguenot culture in early New York becomes the best historical evidence of its continued vitality. What is regionalism, after all, but another word for human geography?

CHAPTER SIXTEEN

Fragments of Huguenot-Quaker Convergence in New York

Little Histories (Avignon, France, 1601–1602; Flushing, Long Island, 1657–1726)

❧ Table Talk: Theories of Visual Perception in Avignon (1601) ❧

> In the penultimate year of the life and reign of the glorious Queen
> Elizabeth of England [1558–1603] (whose fame will never die), I was
> compelled to spend the whole winter in the city of Avignon, because the
> winter was very severe, with so much snow covering the mountains of [St.]
> Bernard that the passage into Italy was entirely blocked.
>
> —ROBERT FLUDD, *De naturae simia*

So begins Robert Fludd's hugely entertaining alchemic romance and travel narrative, written ostensibly from memory, which takes the form of a personal history of youthful geomantic experiences in France.[1] After taking his M.A. at Oxford in 1598, Fludd's task, like that of many other young disciples of Paracelsus before and after him, was to wander the world to learn directly from the novelties of Nature, illiterate "folk," and the practical school of experience. Playing the well-rehearsed role of a Paracelsian seeker and traveler en route through France to northern Italy—the same path of experience taken by John Winthrop Jr. after he had witnessed the sieges of Saint-Martin-de-Ré and La Rochelle in 1627—Fludd was "compelled" by Nature to spend the winter of 1601–2 in Avignon, when snow blocked the Saint Bernard Pass, France's "passage" and natural "doorway" to Italy. Thus Fludd preceded Winthrop the Younger to Italy, where both journeyed on a natural philosopher's pilgrimage in search of alchemical secrets. After finally departing Avignon in 1602, Fludd met the great Paracelsian physician and rising courtier William Harvey, his fellow countryman, in Padua. This occurred soon after another encounter in Rome with one "Grutherus," a conveniently obscure (and perhaps fictitious) Swiss adept. Fludd claimed that it was Grutherus who had taught him the lucrative secret of the weapon salve.[2] Reading Fludd's "De geomantia" together with de Bry's pictograph of the *oculus,* we are immediately aware that his language of obstruction and passage was borrowed from Tobit, and was common to Fludd's geomantic allegory.

As the voice of the wandering narrator trapped in contested territory where acts of confessional violence against Protestants were a common occurrence, Fludd was suddenly forced to identify with a Protestant refugee. Like Hogarth, he assumes the liminal identity of the Huguenot artisan and natural philosopher. This represented the persona of an outsider who relies on memory of artisanal skills and "the art" to survive contact with the politically dangerous, philosophically inexperienced Jesuits and "other young men," all of whom were "former pupils of the Jesuits."

Fludd called his deceptively simple narrative *Of the Internal Principle of Terrestrial Astrology or Geomancy.* The striking simplicity of its language seems, moreover, to be grounded mostly in disarming storytelling. Where "De geomantia" parses *mens, intellectus, ratio, imaginatio,* and *sensus, Internal Principle,* like Palissy's *Recepte* and *Discours,* collapses these technical terms together and unifies them in the soul as the universal divine messenger. When de Bry harnessed Fludd's practical history as a preface to the highly theoretical "De geomantia" in the second volume of *Fludd's De macrocosmi historia* in 1618, his strategy was to supply the author with appropriate bona fides of Paracelsian experience to buttress the secretive and obscure rhetoric to follow.

So, at age twenty-seven, Fludd found himself stranded in Avignon "with many other young men of gentle birth and of sound education."[3] While the education of these companions was "sound," Fludd found that it was also suspect, for the young gentlemen were "pupils of the Jesuits." As a result, they had been indoctrinated in the repetitive pedagogy of militant Catholic scholasticism at the Jesuit school and noviciate at Avignon.[4]

Fludd confides that geomancy first came up in Avignon as conversation in table talk. Cleverness in polite philosophical debate was crucial for alchemists seeking patronage. To be sure, Fludd performed *Internal Principle* as an entertainment for noble auditors at court long before committing it to print. In the high-stakes battle for patronage, aspiring alchemist-courtiers such as Kenelm Digby, Fludd, and Harvey had to demonstrate mastery over this strategic form of charismatic "talk," which, it seemed, was always constructed around copious amounts of alcohol. Fludd's narrative thus cen-

ters around a debate at table over the "validity" of geomancy as an art. This was to become the main subject of an evening's entertainment "at the house of a certain captain," where "I received board and lodging":

> One evening, while we were drinking at table, I discussed philosophical subjects with the
> others and noticed their various opinions on geomantic astrology. Some of them denied
> its virtue altogether; others, with whom I sided, defended stoutly the validity of that art.
> I adduced many arguments whereby I proved myself fairly well versed in geomancy. The
> meal being over, I had no sooner repaired to my chamber, when one of my companions
> followed me there and asked me for our love's sake to try my art (which, he said, he had
> seen was considerable) in the resolution of a problem of some importance which, he said,
> filled his mind with much anxiety. Having made many excuses, I was at last prevailed
> upon by his entreaties. So, instantly I projected a geomantic scheme for the question he
> proposed.[5]

Fludd convinces us that his position won the evening, as it was the most charismatic demonstration of table talk. As a result, Fludd's companion "entreats" the geomancer to go beyond theory, and he comes to Fludd's chamber with a "problem which
. . . filled his mind with much anxiety." The "question he proposed," for which Fludd
"projected a geomantic scheme," drives the story and distills the complex theory of "De
geomantia" into the narrator's testimony on a single "historical" moment and its context. Titillating, given Fludd's vow of chastity (which, nevertheless, allowed the geomancer to see the "scheme" clearly): "This question was: whether a girl with whom he
had vehemently fallen in love returned his love with equal fervor, and her entire mind
and body, and whether she loved him more than anyone else."[6]

Fludd's lengthy response turns on his perception in the geomantic scheme of an obscure deformity: a sort of dot "or blot" on the girl's left eyelid: "Having drawn my geomantic scheme, I assured him that I could rather well describe the nature and bodily
disposition of his beloved and, having duly described to him the nature and shape of
the girl's body, I indicated also a particular and rather noticeable mark or blot thereon,
namely a certain kind of wart on her left eye-lid, which he confessed was there."[7] Once
he has perceived the impurity of Tobit's cataract in the "certain kind of wart" on the
left eyelid of his companion's lover, an answer to the question is already prophesied.
To establish his credibility, first Fludd gives certain other details about the girl that
only an intimate would know, then tells his companion that his beloved is indeed "in-
constant and by no means steady in her love of him, and that she loved somebody else
more than him. Whereupon he said that he had always very much suspected that this
was the case and that he was [now] seeing it, as it were, with open eyes."[8]

Through the mediation of the *oculus imaginationis,* Fludd's companion himself saw
"with open eyes" the meaning of the mark on his lover's eyelid, a symbol of her im-

purity and a reflection of his own blindness. He perceived, for the first time, a hidden reality beneath the surface of fleshy matter that he had always overlooked as nothing more than an ephemeral thing. In effect, he was unable to see his own reflection in his lover's deformity. Yet publicizing this skill at seeing made Fludd's situation even more dangerous. His life was jeopardized when the blot on the lover's eye remained invisible in plain sight to the gentlemen, educated in the local Jesuit school, who attended the dinner party earlier that evening:

> He left my room in haste and then related to his companions with some admiration the verity and virtue of my art. Yet some of them, who knew the girl rather well, denied altogether that she had any such mark on her eye-lid as I had described, until they talked to her the following day and thus became witnesses of the correctness of that detail which I had discovered to them by the art of geomancy and which even they had never previously noticed.[9]

Acting the role of the angel Raphael, Fludd leads his blind and inexperienced doubters and potential adversaries to perceive what was always there but had been invisible to them. An English Protestant "refugee" among hostile French Jesuits had *negotiated* their perception of the significance of a hidden form, as a contingency of social interaction in the "mixed composition" of a pluralistic urban context.

As in the work of refugee Huguenot artisans in colonial New York, however, noticing the overlooked could also be strategically reversed as a function of dissimulation, to protect the vulnerable, facilitate commerce, or simply to be secretive. If messages sent via an experienced refugee's perception of "a particular" form were revealed to one group of hostile or competitive "companions" in Avignon, the same perceptions might also be concealed from another in New York. The moral purity and alchemic skill necessary to see through the veil of "mixed composition" to essential signs meant that composite forms could also be deployed *from behind*, to form a perceptual shield against the perceptions of outsiders.

Revealing his esoteric skill to his importunate companion ("despite having made many excuses") puts Fludd—now exposed as a Protestant—in great danger from the Jesuits. "Thus," he wrote, "I became better known than I desired, so much so that rumours of this matter reached the ears of the Jesuits."[10] A conspiracy is hatched, and "two of them went secretly to the Palace and impelled by envy, reported to the [papal] Vice-Legate that there was a certain foreigner, an Englishman, who had made predictions of future events by the science of geomancy, which science had been reproved by the Catholic Church."[11]

Far from becoming the subject of an official papal inquest, "a few days later," the vice-legate "kindly invited me to a meal," where once again, Fludd engaged in table talk with his host:

When I had duly made my reverence in the customary manner, the Vice-Legate began to discourse with me as follows:

"I hear," he said, "that you are well versed in the art of geomancy. What then is your considered opinion of that art?"

I replied *experience* [emphasis added] had proved to me that it was a valid science, built on occult foundations.[12]

The vice-legate's reference to "that art" and Fludd's use of the Paracelsian code word "experience" identify them to each other as secret adepts.

It is now safe for Fludd to reveal further trade secrets to his inquiring host, as one experienced practitioner to another. "'How can there be any certainty', he said, 'in a method that operates by means of accidental dots?'" Fludd's response to this question, using plain language, unlike in "De geomantia," was that geomancy was never really accidental, since—as with Palissy's glazes—the human hand was directed to perform inward artisanry by a "peaceful" and "impartial" soul. Harmonic adjectives such as these adumbrate theoretical explications that were to follow in "De geomantia." More than that, they conform well to Palissy's abhorrence of the unbalancing effect of confessional violence and "esmotions" on the conjunction of macrocosm and microcosm, and by extension, the spiritual work of the soul on the material art of the earth.

Recall that Palissy's metaphor for this harmonic conjunction is the angelic chorus of the seven earth spirits singing psalms along the banks of the Charente. Recall, too, that *Homo sanus* is protected by the "fortress of health" (see fig. 10.7) and sings psalms that put him in harmony with God (the "temple of music," a giant cosmological music machine, was one of Fludd's greatest projects). Suffering man, on the other hand, with walls crumbling around his body and beset by "enemies invading the fortress of health" (see fig. 10.8), cannot connect harmonically with the divine voice. He hears only God's admonition that "because thou hast not harkened unto my voice, I will afflict thee [Deut. 28:15–22]; . . . I will dissolve thee . . . so that thy enterprises are hindered and thy mouth stopped, that thou canst not speak [1 Macc. 9:55]." Fludd, a heretic and refugee in Catholic France, desired "peaceful" and "impartial" judgment from the strangers and religious antagonists who were his hosts:

I said the principle and origin of those dots made by the human hand was inward and very essential, since the movement emanated from the very soul. I added that errors of geomancy were by no means caused by the soul, but by a base and incongruous mutation of the human body moving against the intention of the soul. For that reason it was a general rule in this art that the soul must be in a peaceful condition, and a condition in which the body is obedient to the soul; also that there must be no perterbation of body or soul, nor any partiality concerning the question; that the soul must be a just and impartial judge.[13]

And, in the context of Fludd's construction of his personal refugee history, his "plain" elucidation of the animate role of the *mens* and its astral function to perform secretly and fly unbounded and invisibly over great distances, takes on specific historical meanings. We are already familiar with these ideas in general from reading "De geomantia," our encounter with Digby's weapon's salve, and John Winthrop Jr.'s physician's chair:

> [It follows] that the human body is to the soul as a servant is to his master. "The master can send his servant hither and thither with letters, whilst the servant is not in any way aware of his master's plans. And an eminent painter may send to the king a fine picture through a servant wholly ignorant of the mixtures of the colours and of their symmetrical proportions. Likewise a king may impose taxes on his people through others, whilst the reason for his imposting them is known only to the king himself. In the same way, no doubt, can the body perform an action which the soul commands from its secret domain without the body's perceiving in any way the principles of that action if not merely by its effects."[14]

Having listened to this speech, the vice-legate, in earshot of "some bishops and deans," secretly called Fludd aside to "a table nearby where he took quill and ink, drew a geomantic figure, and disoursed about it in a most learned way, so that I saw clearly *he was far more learned and skilled than I in that science for which the Jesuits had denounced me to him* [emphasis added]. So, when the meal was over, I went away enjoying his favor."[15]

Fludd's dialogue with the vice-legate of Avignon represents the alchemical dream of the universal soul to reform the emotions of confessional difference and the baneful effect of both political and geographical displacement into a unified vision throughout the Atlantic world through convergence of spirit and matter. This utopian vision was to be directed by "impartial," "peaceful" adepts who were able to discern the divine motives in the relationship between material revelation and spiritual concealment. Fludd reflects on the humane political qualities and deep natural-philosophical skill of the vice-legate: "For I *noticed* he was a very ingenious prince, well versed in the sciences, friendly towards foreigners, and in no way given to tyranny."[16] By constructing an inversion of growing Bourbon absolutism—a monarchical system that depended on violence and the perpetuation of shape-shifting culture of appearances to maintain a superficial and unnatural monolithic order—Fludd creates a new prince of the natural world. The vice-legate of Avignon rules ingeniously over an harmonic order of friends and strangers alike, through the flexible "innovations" of practical experience gained by manual knowledge and insights into the "mixed composition" of mutable nature, rather than the tyranny of the received wisdom of kings written by inexperienced "artisans of glory," to uphold the corrupt power of hereditary repetition.[17]

Having found favor with the papal governor through shared practice of the geomantic arts, it remains for Fludd to reconcile with the despised Jesuits. Again, this transpires through his interaction with another natural philosopher. "When these events had become known among the Jesuits," Fludd recalled, "one of them, who was a praelector in philosophy, desired very much to confer with me . . . I called on the Jesuit and was gracefully received by him. After mention had been made of a number of philosophical subjects [that is to say, more code words were exchanged], he soon fell into [a discussion of] the geomantic science, believing perhaps that I might use facile arguments [read artificial rather than natural language] in my defence."[18]

Here, Fludd builds a metaphysical dialogue between ostensibly competing Christians, that unifies basic elements of the portable, uncontained, Neoplatonic discourse of the weapon salve, his friend William Harvey's dedication to Charles I in 1628, the physician's chair joined and carved for Governor Winthrop the Younger, and Dr. Ezra Stiles's late eighteenth-century transatlantic theory of the friendship of souls after death:

> "Well then," he said, "is it or is it not possible that somebody should be able to predict by the art of geomancy danger to a man, or death threatening him on a journey to Rome? Or is there a participation and communication between the soul of that man and your own, though either soul be contained within a human body?"

> I replied to him briefly thus:

> "Since the soul of every body is that especial light that has dominion over everything else in the body, even as the Sun is predominant among the other stars in the heavens, yea since the soul is the very Sun of the microcosm directing the whole body by her vivifying rays, there is no doubt that it throws forth its invisible rays invisibly through the pores of the body in the same manner as that celestial Sun transmits its rays, through the sieve of the elements to the inferior [world] . . . so also without any doubt are rays emitted between the soul of one man and that of another [both] which [souls] are invisible lights. In their emission the rays are so joined together that either the soul of the seeker or the seeker[19] himself be the one to whom danger is imminent, or else a friend of his; for the [soul] is very prophetical. Being immortal, it may know within itself things that are in the future and things present. Like a guardian foreseeing danger with which a body [in his charge] is threatened, it may explain the secret future of its body to another soul applying to it—a future which it had been unable to communicate to its body because of that body's grossness. And in this way may a quiet and peaceful soul, which is in a fit condition for judging, and to which the movements of its body are well subjected, prognosticate the future to that other soul . . . [such a soul could] leave its body so as to find a place whence it could enter into communication, and converse, with the souls of . . . friends. And, without any doubt, the rays of the soul extend imperceptibly outside the body and far beyond

the range of visible rays. They . . . may pass through elementary media without any hindrance, like an influence. This is so because their form is exalted and their origin sublime."

. . . We may conclude, therefore, that this art [of geomancy] is a way of knowing that depends immediately on the soul; that its root is the soul itself; and that, therefore, it is a science more subtle than any other science man may comprehend in this corruptible world.[20]

To comprehend "a way of knowing that depends immediately on the soul"—metaphysical logic that supports the only real attempt Fludd ever made to construct a lucid explanation of the practice of geomancy—is to consider seriously the proposition that historians (and in particular, students of the pluralistic American middle colonies) understand Fludd's occult treatises as a rational theory of early modern sociological practice. Was not Fludd's a useful framework for gaining access to the ways in which cultural mixing and convergence were perceived and manipulated by both hosts and refugees relocated to multicultural centers of commerce throughout the seventeenth-century world?

Hogarth demonstrated how perceptual boundaries between urban subcultures defined the subtle mastery of space as an artifact of the experience of cultural memory, economic competition, scientific process, and social distance. Hogarth acquired his mastery of both theatrical and private space by initially engaging in a series of famously public disputes with authority. To provide his carefully constructed image of the exalted outsider's philosophical legitimacy, Hogarth reactivated Fludd's Paracelsian texts on geomancy and the art of memory to identify his self-image, personal history, art, and commercial success with historically innovative outsiders and outcasts: the talented Huguenot artisans and refugees who made a virtue of being forced to live and work in the shadows by implacable enemies. The arc of Palissy's tumultuous early history of conflict with Catholic and Calvinist authority in Aunis-Saintonge, and his adaptation of Paracelsian cosmology and alchemic methods to his religious outlook and practical artisanry, intersects neatly with Hogarth's personal history and construction of an outsider's social self-identity. By the time Hogarth painted *Noon* in 1736, he shared with Palissy the eyes of the heretic and critical primitive. Hence, Hogarth mapped human dispersion, relocation, and convergence as part of a natural process of concealment and revelation of knowledge. The universal, hermaphroditic access of tiny things was shared, of course, with the snail, who generated armor inside-out to carry on his back snakes and lizards, or "the spider," from Proverbs 30:28. All moved invisibly in or out of cracks above the subterranean spaces in Palissy's ceramic grottoes. These were living things so utterly small, voiceless and apparently natural that they may enter surreptitiously and live "in kings' palaces."

Key to perceptual mastery and access to the overlooked, hidden in shadow behind the chaotic Babel of converging strangers, was the seeker's "participation and communication between the soul of that man and your own, though either soul be contained within a human body." I have argued that it is possible to understand such bodily participation and communication of hidden knowledge—coded in the available language of sanctified natural materials—as ways in which natural philosophers conceptualized potential for convergence as a process of tacit social interaction, often mediated primarily by material bodies and things rather than words in the pluralistic, commercialized, and largely artisanal contexts that emerged wherever Huguenot refugees settled in the early modern transatlantic world. The logic implicit in this social system was also central to the function of the alchemic tradition Fludd knew from his reading of Neoplatonism, Paracelsian medicine, and the scientific canon of the Huguenot corpus to which arguments on occult perception in "De geomantia" and *Internal Principles* were key contributions. This context supports constant dialogues based on analogies between metaphysical and material binary oppositions, including macrocosm and microcosm, spirit and matter, or even Catholic and Protestant. Such interaction was central to the pluralist, potentially chaotic language of the street: "participation and communication . . . himself be the one to whom danger is imminent, or else a friend of his . . . like a guardian forseeing danger with which a body is threatened." All this makes perfect sense when juxtaposed against the Neoplatonic ideal of "a quiet and peaceful soul" that could "leave its body . . . to find a place whence it could enter into communication, and converse, with the souls of . . . friends."

Fludd's theory of convergence detailed a complex synthesis of cultural, social, political, economic and material, as well as religious *practice*. Unlike the elder Winthrop's perception of the extension of Christ's monolithic body to New England in "Modell of Christian Charitie," Fludd's alchemist and geomancer perceives "participation" in the convergence of multiple social realities, where danger and dissonance, as well as love and unity are subjects of "communication." The differences between these Protestant positions as responses to the dual status of outsider and refugee as a result of reversals in La Rochelle and the Thirty Years' War also elucidate tensions in the development of the younger Winthrop as he silently distanced himself from his father's policies and grew to embrace his role as a New World Paracelsian physician.

This distance was manifested over time by the son's experiential peregrinations from Groton to Dublin to La Rochelle to the Levant to Massachusetts Bay to Essex County to Connecticut, and finally to the hinterlands in between New England and New York on the north shore of Long Island Sound, the Mediterranean of the New World. Land hunger and the quest to uncover the Northwest Passage and the philosopher's stone—or, failing that, mineral wealth in the form of exploitable resources—drove the industrious Winthrop south toward the fertile Hudson and Delaware valleys. That quest included the desire to live on the threshold of New York Colony. The quietly tolerant, multilingual Winthrop, an avid collector of Fludd's books, understood that alchemical mastery of the "mixed composition" of participation and communication was essential to mastery of space in the pluralistic middle colonies.

*   Practice: The Quaker Meetinghouse,   *
Flushing, Long Island (1693–94)

Fludd's *Internal Principles* reminds us of the relationship between the younger Winthrop's natural-philosophical and geographic orientations and his pursuit of the philosopher's stone through the Long Island Sound–Northwest Passage–middle colonial nexus. Yet this relation is powerfully reinforced by resonances that link geomantic theories of the body and animate matter with core Quaker beliefs and practices. Fludd's argument for the existence of an "especial light that has dominion over everything else in the body" was also, of course, the central metaphysical claim of seventeenth-century Quaker cosmology. What makes these linkages even more interesting however, is the widespread acceptance of some variation of the bodily light as a common language among a whole range of New World inheritors of the Germanic pietist tradition, including both the southwestern Huguenots and Quakers. Earlier we saw how the humiliating failure of the overt, bombastic style of south*eastern* Huguenot prophetic discourse forced many French Prophets in London to merge with quietism and some, ultimately, with Quakerism by the 1740s. I also showed how Palissy's introduction of strategies of natural security—including artisanal discourse—to southwestern Huguenots to function as covert communication and a supplement (or sometimes an alternative) to overt speech and writing, paralleled later Quaker patterns that were developed during the English Civil War.

It must be said that Palissy began to teach mastery of the covert natural style in Saintonge much earlier; indeed, as early as the first French civil wars of religion of the 1560s. Such cross cultural parallels are not coincidental. They lay in the common origin of both Quakerism and the Saintongeais heresy in religious civil warfare *and* the rustic tradition of Germanic pietism. The potter credited immigrant monastic craftsmen—presumably Lutheran or possibly even Anabaptist refugees from the Germanic regions of central Europe—with initial conversion of French settlements in the isolated *marais* region of coastal Saintonge during the early sixteenth century. He also showed how the Saintongeais Reformation remained predominantly in the hands of lay preachers from artisanal backgrounds because trained ministers were vulnerable and on the run. Moreover, the Paracelsian movement made rapid progress among dispersed artisans in Saintonge because it was a lay religious as well as a materialist Reformed movement, and because Paracelsus had personal, regional, and intellectual links to Germanic Reformed culture.

The historical significance of Quaker influence on Long Island lies in liminal strategies necessitated by the transatlantic sect's position among neighboring groups. These strategic patterns should be understood in geographical and theological as well as cultural terms. Quakers settled throughout western and west central Long Island, close enough to Manhattan Island for purposes of commerce, yet still maintaining the social distance required by both the wary Dutch colonial government and the Quakers' need to acquire arable land to ensure privacy, independence, and expansion. This heterodox territory was a geographical bridge in between the majority northern European "west end" (the western towns in Queens and Kings Counties) and the predominantly Calvinist East Anglian "east end," with ties to the New Haven Colony (from eastern Queens County through Suffolk County to Montauk Point). The east end was settled by New Englanders from coastal Connecticut, Lynn, Massachusetts, and Plymouth Colony, who migrated south across "permeable" Long Island Sound, beginning in the 1640s. In a very real sense, the Quakers of New Amsterdam and New York had a foot in each camp.

During the period of Dutch Calvinist religious and political authority that lasted until the capitulation of the fortress at New Amsterdam to English forces in 1664, Quaker farmers and craftsmen established new towns in Jericho, Jerusalem, Newtown, and Jamaica. They also attracted followers in the culturally mixed "Dutch" port town of Flushing. Flushing was called "Vlissengen" or "Vlishing" in the seventeenth century. Its Old World namesake had strong commercial and cultural ties to coastal England, Belgium, and France, as it was located on the Wester Schelde trade routes on the far southwestern coast of the Netherlands, directly across the Dover Strait from London and just north of Antwerp and Le Havre (and hence the Seine River Valley). In eastern Queens, Quakers families intermarried and influenced the diverse "English" towns of Oyster Bay and Hempstead. These prosperous towns straddled the fertile Hampstead Plains where they bisected the border with the more homogeneous "Puritan" settlers of Suffolk County.

The largest, wealthiest, most influential, and from Peter Stuyvesant's authoritarian perspective, most threatening Quaker enclave, was in the town of Flushing. This was also the home of several family dynasties of Quaker craftsmen, more than any other place in the middle colonies with the exception of Philadelphia and Chester County, Pennsylvania. Marriage records and letters of recommendation of good character for new members of the Flushing Meeting show that it was common for Philadelphia and Flushing Quaker artisan families to intermarry. This had the effect of sending craftsmen and their wives back and forth between New York and Pennsylvania throughout the year. The same may be said for land transactions. Quaker merchants from Flushing maintained valuable property holdings in Philadelphia and Chester County. In a late seventeenth-century notation written in his account book, John Bowne, the domi-

FIGURE 16.1. Friends meetinghouse, Flushing, Long Island, south elevation. Photo, Pasquali Cuomo. The meetinghouse was originally built in 1694, with many later additions. Among the major exterior alterations are the hipped roof and the porch. The eastern, or oldest, end is shadowed by the tree. The Quaker burial ground is no longer in use. Stone markers came into fashion after 1835. Permanent markers for Quaker graves do not appear to have been used in the seventeenth-century cemetery.

nant Flushing Quaker leader, recorded the sale of "my lott in ffiladelfa w[i]th all my lands [in] Chester County in penselvanie," to his brother Samuel for £50.[21]

In 1694, as a sign of the sect's growing population on Long Island and the place of Queens County at the center of its regional influence, the first Friends' meetinghouse in New York Colony was built in Flushing. Its latest incarnation still fronts Northern Boulevard (fig. 16.1). In 1696, the first Yearly Meeting in New York was held there. Conventicles gathered in John Bowne's house (ca. 1661, also still extant) before the meetinghouse was constructed. The use of private homes for secret meetings followed usual Quaker (and sectarian) practice from the English Civil War.

The original contract between the Flushing Yearly Meeting and the house carpenters John Feke and Samuel Andrews (both members of the meeting) is a rare document. It recorded the specific building practices for "strong and Sufficient" ecclesiastical architecture in the plain style acceptable to New York's Quakers under English rule during the late seventeenth century. It denoted nomenclature for framing and fenestration of the meetinghouse, as well as costs, including diverse modes of payment to the artisans:

> it is by ffriends agreed that Samm[uel] Andrews & John ffeakes shall make & sett a strong and Sufficient frame every waye [suitable] and Answerable for the End & use affore s[ai]d [and] they are to have the summe of fifteene p[ounds] which Summ is to bee p[ai]d: in wheate at 4s:6d, pease at 3s:6d, Indian [corn] at 2s:6d, porke at 4s [per pound.] [T]o all w[hi]ch: ye: d[ai]d John ffeakes & Sammuell [Andrews] are Contented with and promise they s[hall endeavor] to have it upp for the further fi[nishing by] ye: 30th daye of the first month: [16] 93: It is further agreed that for ye s[ai]d [sum Samuel] and John shall make: 8: windows [2 on] one side the house, & 2 on the other side &: 2: [in the] ends belowe all made fitte for glasse, together [with] window shutts [that is, "shutters"] & 2 windowes in the Gable ends [with] Shutts likewise they are to make 2 Doors One in one side of itt & the other in ye o[ther side]. Itt is to bee understood both these doors a[re pro]per duble doores with 2: dorment windowes & for makeing all these they [are] to have 5 [pounds]: mor[e which] makes ye: Sum 20 [pounds].[22]

The building was expanded when a new meetinghouse was built near the old one in 1716 to accommodate women excluded after services from the 1694 structure, because the men took over the space to conduct the business of the meeting. This would enable them to join the men in these discussions—something that was becoming more prevalent in these years—rather than retiring to the Bowne house, as had been the practice for the first twenty-three years of the building's existence.

Although the Flushing meetinghouse is among the few survivals close to the city of New York of regional architecture still visible above ground, it has been much altered both inside and out. So the contract provides an irreplaceable record of what the 1694 building looked like. The contract describes a fairly modest framed and clapboarded structure. The simple frame had gables at each end, but it was distinguished by the number (eight) and symmetry (two on each side) of its fenestration, which provided much light. It is tempting to link this plan of a plain, well-lit religious space to Quaker natural philosophy. There is however, no proof that extensive fenestration such as this was unique to Quakerism, or New York. Perhaps it indicated nothing more than affluence, as glass was imported and expensive. Still, this practice included the double doors on each side, which were to have frames for two dormer ("dorment") windows set into the top.

Alterations of the original structure began as early as 1704, when the building was shingled, plastered, and "further repaired." During most of the eighteenth century, John Farrington and various successors were paid £2 annually to maintain fires in a large medieval hearth in the center of the meeting room. In 1760, this opening was covered up and the meetinghouse heated by an efficient Franklin stove. In 1763, the building underwent its most dramatic (and disfiguring) renovation campaign. Unfortunately for historians of seventeenth-century artisanal practices, the original gallery overhead was removed and a new floor laid, making the building two stories. At the same time, the chamber was divided in two, and one of the rooms was devoted to a Quaker school. In 1776, the building was occupied by British soldiers, who found it useful as a prison, and then a barracks, field hospital, and storehouse. As a result, the New York Yearly Meeting was forced to move from Flushing to Westbury. The meetinghouse sustained enormous damage during the Revolution, when soldiers used every available piece of removable construction material as firewood. In 1783, the building underwent its final major renovation campaign before modern times, as it was rebuilt again after the war. By then little was left of the original Quaker joinery. In 1794, Flushing's dominance finally ebbed, and the Yearly Meeting was moved to New York City.[23]

❦ John Bowne's Network of Quaker Craftsmen: ❧
John Feke and Samuel Andrews

The builders of the original meetinghouse, Samuel Andrews and John Feke, were artisans with English backgrounds. And its framed exterior was designed as a modification of vernacular styles common to the late seventeenth-century British regional tradition. In the 1690s, New York City's and western Long Island's vernacular woodworking traditions were undergoing a period of intense change under the influence of anglicization as elite patrons began to support "Georgian" architecture and other building practices disseminated in international design books. The meetinghouse plan, with its plain, slightly old-fashioned "English" exterior, probably showed clear symmetry in the placement of windows and doors. This was a local colonial gesture toward the conservative adaptation of the new metropolitan style, a move that made sense in both religious and secular terms.

John Feke, a house carpenter, was the father or uncle of the accomplished portrait painter of aspiring colonial elites Robert Feke (1707?–52) of Oyster Bay, Long Island and later Newport, Rhode Island. In 1742, Robert married Eleanor Cozzens, thus tying two Quaker artisan families together across the Sound. John Feke was related by marriage to John Bowne, being a direct descendant of Elizabeth Feke Underhill, Bowne's influential sister-in-law.[24] The Feke (Feake, Feeke) family had its origins in Norfolk, but like many farm families from the English countryside, some members with artisanal skills migrated to London looking for work and then moved on to the colonies in the seventeenth century.[25]

John Feke's name first appears next to "Housecarpenter" in John Bowne's damaged and nearly illegible account book in 1666, when Bowne contracted his "brother" Feke to build a Norfolk-style thatched barn:

> on the 12 day of the month was agreed betwixt us John Bowne and John ffeake namely that I John ffeake doe undertake to beuld for my brother John Bowne a good strong suffishant barne of 40 fout long [and] 20 fout wide and 9 foot [high?] from the [ ] of the ground to the top of the [ ] all the maine postes to be [ ] full twelfe inches [square] with all the rest of the timber [answerable] a lentwo [lean to] to one side anserable to [torn] to be nine foute wide within and [torn] sides and ends and the lentwo [ ] [ ] the [ ] and tolath all the rest of the roufe fit for thatching and to make all the dores both aloft and [a loe/ that is, "below"] and fit them all to make fast and to lay a good [ ] flouer and all the worke that belongs to this building I am to doe finding my owne [timber?] onely my brother [that is, John Bowne] is to cart the timber and [gett] the clabord boult [bolts] and to cleve out [that is, to rive from the bolts] the planks for the flore and to provide help to rayse the house timber [rest torn away, except] . . . of the first mont 1665/6.[26]

Feke would not have done the thatching, a highly specialized task. The thatcher may have been John Shafton. Shafton was credited by Bowne in 1696, "for thathing the stable," at a cost of £1.12s.[27]

John Feke was also the house carpenter Bowne hired when he expanded his original 1661 house to half its present size (fig. 16.2); the addition was to be complete by November 1680. Since Feke was a house carpenter, he was responsible for framing the exterior timbers (or skeleton) of the building, and he was to be assisted by John Clay, a carpenter who added openings to Feke's frame for the doors, windows, and chimneys. Clay was also to prepare a lath foundation between the great timbers for subsequent carpenters and joiners to add the skin of sheathing, clapboards, and shingles necessary to finish the job and roof the building. Clay, like Feke, was a member of the Flushing Meeting. Bowne had to find a replacement when John Clay died of an unknown malady in February 1680, soon before work began on the addition. His replacement is also unknown. Bowne took charge of Clay's final days and kept "an account of charges for John Clay In his sicknes and at funerall," a not insubstantial total of £2.9.1½. This suggests he may have been considered part of Bowne's household, perhaps an indentured servant, speculation supported by the fact that Bowne bought Clay a pair of shoes in 1680. Clay was constantly at work around the Bowne house and farm until his death, almost always acting as an assistant on major construction jobs.[28] Unlike in the case of the barn Feke had built fifteen years earlier, the contract

FIGURE 16.2. The John Bowne House, Flushing, Long Island. Courtesy Historic American Buildings Survey, Library of Congress. Bowne's original house, built in 1661, is now encased in the east wing. The Georgian wing was added at the west end by his son Samuel (1667–1745), beginning in the early eighteenth century, and expanded by the family in the 1830s.

for the new addition to Bowne's house specified that Bowne was to be responsible for providing Feke with the framing timbers "[al]redy hughed." Such heavy materials were cumbersome to transport to the building site from the woods and required the labor of at least two men to dress down (or "hew") the fallen trees. Hence, the timber was made ready for Feke to finish, cut out, and saw the mortise and tenon joints for the frame. Suitable lumber—oak and hard pine (*Pinus taeda*) common in Long Island architecture—was available locally in Kings and Queens Counties, but it was shipped to New York City by boat from as far away as Staten Island and northern New Jersey. On September 9, 1732, for example, an Irish shipwright named John Blake, then living in the city's Dockward, was sued for trespass by Edward Stoughton, a sawyer who supplied Blake with wood. Stoughton sued for £13.8.3 "owed to Edward for carrying and transporting plank wood timber trees sticks and other merchandize from New Jersey to New York," as well as £19 in damages.[29] *Hewn* framing timber was thus a major expense, because it represented value added to the already substantial cost of rough sawn wood and transport:

> Agreement made with brother John ffeke ye 31th: of ye 11th: month 1680: at foloweth heeis
> to frame ye house I intend to build I providing ye: timber redy hughed [hewed] or sawne
> hee it to smooth frame and set by Joyning it Suffishantly to the house allredy built. John
> Clay to worke with him hee [Feke] in Structing J[ohn] C[lay] what hee cann in ye doing
> of it, [finishing] all framing both for doors windows and chimnis leveing it fit for clabor-

ding and Shingling and [Cobbing?] as it shall require for which I am to pay him six pounds t[h]ree in winter wheat and three in [different] good young sheepe at twelfe shillings a peece at the beginning of winter [that is, with a full coat of marketable wool].[30]

The last appearance Feke makes in Bowne's accounts before our final encounter with him when he framed the meetinghouse in 1693, took place in June 1684. At that time, Feke presented Bowne with a scrap of paper showing the "rest dew upon balance of acounts," for finishing the interior of the new addition. Feke did "six days worke towarde the laying of the hous flour," for which he was paid 18 shillings; and an additional "5 days worke about stayrs [that is, building the staircase] and other worke" (15 shillings). After finishing inside the house, Feke also charged Bowne 3 shillings for mending a spade and 5s. 6d. for "mending a Sadle a panill and making lath [bords]."[31] These entries reveal that in addition to framing houses, Feke was able to supplement his income through joinery (the staircase, mending a panel) as well as other interior finishing work (laying the floors). His record of repair work increased his value to farmers as a jack-of-all-trades specializing in maintenance. The Bowne accounts reveal that Feke commanded 3 shillings a day, a realistic benchmark for skilled artisans in both Flushing and New York City on the eve of the Revocation. When compared with the difficulty French refugees had in gaining a competency in highly competitive European labor markets flooded with refugee labor, including Amsterdam and London, the wages commanded by Feke must have provided a compelling reason for Huguenot woodworkers to come to New York in 1685.

The record is much less forthcoming about Samuel Andrews (Andrew, Andros) than about the house carpenter John Feke. Samuel Andrews was the grandson of an Englishman of uncertain regional origin named Edward Andrews. After a sojourn in Barbados, Edward migrated to Flushing in 1663, to join the Quaker meeting. Bowne knew Edward personally, and his background, through correspondence with Friends in Barbados or Long Island, where newcomers were usually well known by one or more families in the meeting. This was true in Edward's case. He came to settle in Flushing and join the meeting, to marry Mary Wright of Oyster Bay. He did so immediately, in a Quaker ceremony.

Although Oyster Bay was originally settled in the 1630s, the largest migration of New England sectarians joined the town in 1653. Oyster Bay's New England connections ran deep, which helps in part to explain its opposition to Stuyvesant's regime in New Amsterdam.[32] Connections included the intriguing presence, as witnesses at the ceremony, of Captain John Underhill and his wife Elizabeth Feke (John Bowne's sister-in-law), alongside many members of the Wright family.[33] Of the subversive Underhill and his activities as an agent provocateur on Long Island in the employ of his patron John Winthrop Jr., more will be said later. Suffice it to say here, that the Underhills' presence as witnesses establishes an early and close connection between the Andrews, Feke, and Bowne families. This suggests that in addition to his famously genocidal mercenary activities against local Amerindian settlements for New England's land-hungry magistrates and the equally grasping Dutch West India Company, Underhill was, at minimum, a Quaker sympathizer by marriage and ritual and arguably a member of the Society of Friends.

In any case, even if he was not one himself, Underhill took great risks for the Friends. At the height of the prohibition of Quaker conventicles on Long Island, Underhill held secret meetings in his house at Oyster Bay.[34] Indeed, by 1663, Underhill had broken with Stuyvesant—a military and political patron—and was now associated with Winthrop (his oldest ally from New England), as well as with John Bowne and his Flushing Quakers. All were the director general's mortal political and religious enemies. From the start, Roger Williams's letter to Winthrop of 1660 praising "your prudent and moderate hand in the late Quaker trials amongst us" reflected equal parts Winthrop's soulishness and his growing interests on western Long Island.[35]

Soon after Edward's marriage, a son named Samuel Andrews was born in Flushing. The exact date of birth of *his* son, who became the meetinghouse carpenter in 1693–94, is not certain. In 1683, the footloose Samuel Andrews Sr. moved his family to New Jersey and then to Charlestown, Massachusetts, where he died a year later. His son, Samuel Andrews Jr., may have stayed behind in Flushing when his father began his travels in 1683. It is possible that he returned home after his father's death, or he may have remained apprenticed. John Feke was once his master, so perhaps he was then a journeyman. In any event, Samuel Andrews Jr. was in Flushing by 1693, where he worked with John Feke—a member of a family of Quaker artisans with whom he was allied by marriage—to build the meetinghouse.[36]

❧ Huguenot and Quaker Artisanal Convergence: Germanicus Andrews ❧ of Flushing and the French Upholsterers of New York City

Germanicus Andrews—presumably named after the Roman general Germanicus Caesar—was the son either of Samuel Andrews Jr. or another Long Island Andrews of that generation. When he was made a freeman of New York City, on October 12, 1713–14, Germanicus was listed as an "upholsterer,"[37] an identification perhaps even more unusual than his classical name. Upholstery was a highly specialized craft, at the apex of the furniture trade—a long way up from house carpentry. Such upward artisanal mobility, assuming that Germanicus was indeed of Samuel Andrews Jr.'s son, would suggest that much more was going on behind the scenes in Flushing and New York than is easily coaxed from the archives.

We have already seen how upholsterers—Huguenot refugees, in particular—operated as quintessential urban artisans in Britain and colonial America. The year 1707 was most likely the first of the young Quaker's apprenticeship. To find an upholsterer's shop and a master, and then test the limited market for his skills in 1714, Germanicus had to abandon Long Island for Boston or New York. Germanicus moved to the city with the intention of upholstering leather chairs made locally by Saintongeais Huguenots in lucrative competition with Boston chair makers. His intention is very easy to know, because from 1707 to 1714, precisely, the leather-chair industry was thriving. It was the only upholstery work available, or known to be sufficiently productive, to draw these specialized artisans to the New York market. Germanicus Andrews thus belonged to a very select group of colonial producers of luxury goods. In the best of times, a relatively limited demand existed, and there was only enough work in town throughout the year to maintain an average of about two such specialists. Between 1701 (when Anthony Chiswell appeared in town) and 1738 (when John Schultz was named a freeman), only seven artisans (including Andrews) were called upholsterers in New York, eight if we include Jean Suire, who was called a joiner but also did upholstery work. Unfortunately, only this terse record of his occupation survives to show any sign of Germanicus Andrews's progress toward achieving his ambitious goal. The young man died prematurely in 1718, four years after becoming a freeman.[38]

Sudden death and disappearance plagued this highly skilled group in New York. Of the seven upholsterers who followed the trade in New York during the early eighteenth century, only two Huguenots, Benjamin Faneuil and Richard Lott, managed to survive and maintain themselves. Both families originated in southwestern France. Survival came through a skillful and secretive process of adaptation and innovation, and above all, the war-tested strength of a successful, migrating, regional refugee craft network. The fact of their survival in New York's limited market likely assured the disappearance (Wenman, Schultz) or diversification out of the trade (Wileman), of those competitors who did not die prematurely (Chiswell, Suire, Andrews).[39]

Still, given his known family and religious contacts, it is useful to speculate as to who Germanicus Andrews's master in upholstery was, and what sort of reception he received in 1714 from New York's existing luxury craft networks. Relationships between Flushing's artisans and the refugee craftsmen belonging to the southwestern Huguenot community in Manhattan were key. Consider the question of Andrews's apprenticeship. As a Quaker, he would not have been welcome in Boston to train with the Congregationalist upholsterer Thomas Fitch, owing to the long history of religious violence between the two confessions.

French Calvinists were acceptable in Boston on religious grounds, given the right circumstances. In May 1730, the mother of James Renaudet, a refugee from Saintonge who had settled in New York, wrote Fitch in Boston to inquire if he would take her son on as an apprentice. Fitch replied quickly:

relating to my taking your Son an Apprentice, I'm much oblig'd to you for your good & charitable opinion therein expressed [and] . . . your . . . desires would be a considerable inducement if it were consistent with my present circumstances. But . . . having my Son with me and an apprentice that has several years to Serve It will neither consist with my convenience nor the Service or advantage of a youth for me now to take another . . . I must defer to taking another to some considerable time hence.[40]

Of the master upholsterers available to train Andrews in New York in 1707, only Wileman, Faneuil, and Lott are known to be possibilities. But if Wileman intended to maintain his upwardly mobile status at Trinity, it seems doubtful that he would have risked incurring the disapproval of the anti-sectarian Church of England by taking on a Quaker apprentice with family connections in Flushing, with its long history of turbulent relations with the established churches in Manhattan. That leaves only the two Huguenots as possible masters for Germanicus Andrews.

It would have made economic sense, too, for either Faneuil or Lott to have taken on a new apprentice in 1707 to help manufacture leather chairs, production of which was expanding rapidly in New York by 1708–9. As we have seen, these Huguenot upholstery shops, and the chair makers in their craft network who built frames in imitation of the Boston style, captured the market from Thomas Fitch and other experienced competitors in New England. When consumer demand was high, production time was short. If Faneuil or Lott failed to supply an order, Fitch would fill the need. Thus, in New York City in 1707, leather-chair making became a competitive and very time-conscious enterprise, and an extra pair of hands would have been welcomed. Yet market forces alone cannot explain why Andrews himself was selected by one of these Huguenot upholsterers. Nor can the market tell us what sort of artisan's world Germanicus prepared to enter in 1714, when he finally went out on his own after the traditional seven-year training period. Consider that the negotiation of the young Quaker apprentice's selection by Faneuil or Lott transpired as part of a process of occupational and religious diffusion and convergence of economically, spiritually, familially, and ethnically related craft networks, made up primarily of Quaker and Huguenot artisans, and that Andrews's entrance into this world was already well prepared before he gained his majority as a freeman.[41]

Clues to this process of French-Quaker artisanal convergence originate in 1663, with the marriage of Edward Andrews and Mary Wright, which reflected many religious, economic, and craft alliances. Such alliances were not simply between the two principals. In practice, they also spun webs that involved the Feke, Bowne, and Underhill families, as well as corollary relations and, if need be, patrons (such as Winthrop) and clients. Dutch-period Quaker alliances, although over a generation old by then, were still very much in place in 1693, when John Bowne selected Samuel Andrews and John Feke to build the Flushing meetinghouse together. And they were also there in 1707, when the decision was taken to apprentice Germanicus Andrews to one of the two available Huguenot upholsterers. Andrews's seventeenth-century network of Oyster Bay and Flushing Quaker craftsmen and related families thus expanded into the lucrative urban market for polite luxury goods in the early eighteenth century. The strategic logic of this expansion to Manhattan, which had restricted open Quaker practice to Long Island since Stuyvesant's time, was to join allied Huguenot-Quaker families in an effort to maintain control of limited skilled labor for production in the trade. Because only two upholstery shops could operate profitably at the same time in New York in the early eighteenth century, control of labor effectively controlled domestic design and production in the local market.

❧ Commerce and Conversion: The Delaplaine French-Quaker ❧ Artisan Network in New York City

How was the way made for these Quaker families to carry their artisanal skills to New York City from the Manhattan side of the East River during the latter part of the Dutch period? The pattern was established in the personal history of another first-generation Huguenot refugee who sojourned briefly in Holland before settling in New Netherlands: Nicolas de La Plaine (1593–1697). Many skilled descendants of Huguenots became both Quakers and successful woodworkers in New York City, forming a cosmopolitan Huguenot / Long Island Quaker artisanal network, which centered primarily on the Delaplaine family.

Nicolas de La Plaine was born in the Seigneurie de la Grand Plaine, near Bressuire, just north of La Rochelle in Poitou. He migrated indirectly to the American colonies from "Bersweer in Vranckryck," a way station for war refugees in the Netherlands. On April 14, 1657, Nicolas was living in New Amsterdam, where he was granted the Small Burgher's Right, and identified as a "tobacco twister" by trade. On September 1, 1658, the sixty-five-year-old tradesman married Susanna Cresson in New Amsterdam's Dutch Reformed Church. Exactly like her husband, Cresson had followed a typical pattern for pre-1664 Huguenots; she fled initially to Ryswyk, in Holland, before emigration to New Amsterdam. Cresson's marriage to Nicolas merged substantial assets—clearly a major inducement for the much younger Cresson—inasmuch as Susanna brought a marriage portion of 200 guilders from her father Pierre. When the long-lived Nicolas died in 1697, he was worth an estimated £3,000.[42]

The origin of the Delaplaine family's conversion to Quakerism is unclear. "Nicolaes d'la Plyne" was declared a freeman of New Amsterdam on April 13, 1657, the year of the first major influx and persecution of Quakers in Manhattan Island and Long Island.[43] The Quaker "Remonstrance of the Inhabitants of the Town of Flushing to

Governor Stuyvesant," which was written to protest Stuyvesant's very public persecution of sectarian groups in New Netherlands, appeared later that year (on December 27). It is not known whether Nicolas's arrival in the colony was timed to coincide with that of the Quakers. We do know that he was married to Susanna Cresson in the Dutch Reformed Church of New Amsterdam in 1658, but this public display of loyalty to the only official confession in the colony may have been the price of doing business in Manhattan, rather than having to remove to the Quaker strongholds at Long Island's west end.

This hypothesis is supported by evidence that Nicolas was also present at the standard Quaker rituals that marked rites of passage for his children. In the "6th mo., 12, 1686," for example, when his daughter Elizabeth married Caspar Huet, a New York tailor, in a Quaker ceremony "at the house of Thomas Lloyd, New York," Nicolas and his wife attended as first witnesses.[44] Nicolas may, therefore, have been a Quaker from the start of his residence in the colony, or he may have converted later. That he married twice more during his long lifetime (to Mary "Delaplaine" and Rachel Cresson) may have influenced a later conversion. In any event, by at least 1686 (and probably as early as 1657), the French refugee Nicolas de la Plaine had strong family, religious, and occupational ties to the two important Quaker towns of Flushing and Oyster Bay on western Long Island. If he was converted by the late 1650s, as one suspects, Nicolas would surely have known John Bowne and Edward Andrews of Flushing. He may also have heard George Fox preach at Bowne's house in 1672—early Quakers were also known as Foxians—and have been fully converted then. If one is certain of de la Plaine's Quakerism after 1686, then he should have known the house carpenter Samuel Andrews, who built the Friends' meetinghouse along with John Feke.

The Cresson family that intermarried with the Delaplaines were Walloons, a family that migrated to New Netherlands "from Walslant," after finding refuge near Mannheim in the German Palatinate. The original name was shortened to two syllables from "Crucheron" (also Crocheron, Crosseron, or Cresseron) to facilitate pronunciation, or perhaps to sound like a typical southwestern French name. The Cresson family were among the first settlers of Staten Island, where the 1706 census shows that more than one-fifth (22 percent) of the 865 inhabitants were either French-speaking Waldenses from the Palatinate—a group with a long history of spiritual enthusiasm—or French Huguenot refugees from La Rochelle or Saintonge.[45] French refugees went to Staten Island because of the availability of large tracts of land for flax plantations near navigable waterways. They added value to the flax using their skill in textile manufacture to make linen, an enterprise that found many followers on Long Island as well. Virtually every Huguenot with property on Staten Island grew flax and possessed hatchels and spinning wheels. Many had slaves in their possession and as a result of slave labor, some had large textile operations.[46]

❧ French Quaker Artisans in Esopus and the Mohawk Valley ❧

In the 1650s, a group of Waldenses broke off from the Staten Island contingent and moved north into the Hudson Valley in search of land. Members of this secondary migration were granted lots in the Esopus Creek district in 1653. In 1662, Stuyvesant established an independent fortified town for them on Esopus Creek that he called Wiltwyck (renamed Kingston by the English in 1669).[47] Competition for the desirable land along the waterway brought the French refugees into direct conflict with the Esopus Indians, resulting in brutal warfare in 1659 and again in 1663. The settlement expanded first to New Village, later called Hurley,[48] and then, in 1677, to New Paltz ("le nouveau palatinat"), fifteen miles south of Kingston by boat on the Wallkill River, which was in due course granted a patent by the English. This was the most homogeneous Huguenot refugee community in New York outside of New Rochelle.

Most settlers at New Rochelle had strong family links with refugees from Aunis-Saintonge who worked in New York City; however, in addition to their close linguistic, religious, and occupational ties to Huguenot families in New York and Staten Island, the settlers of New Paltz also had noteworthy Germanic connections, many having originally fled from Saintonge to the Palatinate. Each town's New World name thus reveals something of the effect migration patterns had on transatlantic Huguenot cultural allegiance.[49]

❧ Artifactual Relationships ❧

More revealing, perhaps, is the stylistic relationship between a distinctive group of artifacts long attributed to New York City—specifically to the Delaplaine Huguenot-Quaker craft network—and furniture produced by French craftsmen in the region of human geography that centered on the three main Esopus Creek settlements adjacent to the Hudson River.[50] This relationship owes much to the rapid diffusion of the land-hungry craft network, brought to light by the marriage of Nicolas de La Plaine to Susanna Cresson in 1658.

A distinctive group of oval tables ca. 1685–1730 share a variant of the same theatrically turned baroque legs with stacked elements and falling leaves that are supported by heavy lopers (or "draw bars") drawn from under the table's frame (figs. 16.3, 16.4a, 16.4b). These tables all have strong histories of ownership in Kingston, Hurley, or New Paltz, where they were made. They also share clear stylistic affinities with another group of tables made in New York City (fig. 16.5). The falling leaves of the New York City group differ only in that they are supported by "gates" (legs that swing from underneath), the usual method commonly found in British woodwork, a concession to

FIGURE 16.3. Oval table with falling leaves, or "draw-bar table," area of Kingston, New York, ca. 1740. H: 28½″, W: 60⅜″, D: 50″. Red gum, pine and oak. Courtesy Huguenot Historical Society, New Paltz, New York. Photo, Gavin Ashworth.

the city's anglophile elites. But the theatrically stacked, vessel-shaped turnings, like those on the New York leather chairs, were unmistakably drawn from similar sources in the coastal region of southwestern France.

Look closely at similarities in the stacked structure and rotund articulation of the banister turnings on four related late seventeenth-century staircases that survive on Saint-Martin-de-Ré—also a source for New York leather chairs—and compare them with the turnings on tables from both the Esopus Creek region and New York City.[51] Of the four staircases, the one at the arsenal of the Citadel at Saint-Martin is the best documented and preserved (fig. 16.6). The arsenal was refurbished by Vauban between 1681 and 1685, so it was used in its unrefurbished state by Jean de Toiras when he defended the island against Buckingham in 1627. Still, the resemblance between the banister turnings and the New York tables from roughly the same period is striking. Consider, especially, the tripartite, vertical structure; the identical shape and breadth of the baluster with its compressed ball underneath; the use of the same large flat disc beneath the baluster and a double ring as primary elements of separation; and, though the position is reversed, the idiosyncratic truncated column at the bottom of the post. The distinctive use of lopers (or "draw bars") in Esopus, has convincing antecedents

FIGURE 16.4. (a) Detail of draw bar slide mechanism underneath the top of the table shown in figure 16.3; (b) loper, or "draw bar," from a similar table from the same or a related shop. Courtesy Chipstone Foundation, Fox Point, Wisconsin. Photo, Gavin Ashworth.

FIGURE 16.5. Van Cortlandt family table, New York City, ca. 1700. H: 30⅛″, W: 72¼″, D: 58″. Mahogany, cherry, and yellow poplar. Courtesy Historic Hudson Valley, Tarrytown, New York. Photo, Gavin Ashworth. Like the leather armchair shown in figure 15.22, this table probably belonged to Philip Van Cortlandt (1638–1748), and it was used in the family manor house in Tarrytown.

in the French Renaissance. A "table à rallonges coulissantes" ("table with sliding leaves") made in Paris in the late sixteenth century employed precisely the same peculiar loper system drawn from a stack of parallel tracks hidden underneath the frame (fig. 16.7), as do the Esopus tables, though on the latter they are drawn from the sides.[52]

Nicolas de La Plaine's son Joshua Delaplaine made tables exactly like the one in figure 16.5, since these were among the most stylish and expensive furniture forms made in New York City during the early eighteenth century. At that time, Joshua Delaplaine was among several Huguenots who crafted hybrid Anglo-French furniture using the finest workmanship then available in the colonies. Thus Delaplaine's approximated the best work done in London, where stylish furniture was made under the direction of refugee artisans. The high quality of workmanship and the fact that many of these tables were made of exotic imported materials, including mahogany from Latin America, meant they were purchased by the city's elite and used in complex rituals of politeness and table talk that centered around exorbitant displays of eating or drinking.

The most opulent survival of this form is a gigantic (h. 29½″; top 71″×78½″) mahogany table, so big that four gates were needed (two on each side) to support the oversized leaves. The need for a stagelike platform of such extraordinary size, at a time

FIGURE 16.6. Staircase in the Arsenal of the citadel at Saint-Martin de Ré, Île de Ré, 1681–85. From *Inventaire général des monuments et des richesses artistiques de la France, Commission régionale de Poitou-Charentes, Charente-Maritime, Cantons Île de Ré* (Paris: Ministère de la culture, Direction du patrimoine, 1979). A typical stacked baluster from the southwest coast of France made during the Revocation era, shows one of the many turning variations available to Huguenot refugee craftsmen that relate to early New York tables.

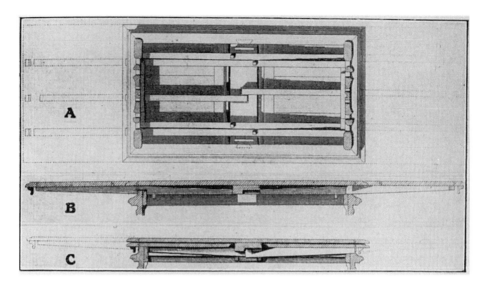

FIGURE 16.7. Engraving of the mechanism from a Parisian "table with sliding leaves," ca. 1580–1600. Compare with figs. 16.4 (a) and (b). From Guillaume Janneau, *Pour discerner les styles dans le mobilier—Les Arts decoratifs: Les Meubles de l'art antique au style Louis XIV* (Paris: Librairie d'Art R. Ducher, 1929), 31, figs. 29–31.

FIGURE 16.8. Unidentified New York cabinetmaker. Dining table. H: 29½″, W: 78½″, D: 71″. Mahogany, sweet gum, yellow poplar, and eastern white pine. Courtesy Albany Institute of History & Art. Gift of the heirs of Major-General John Tayler Cooper. Photo, Gavin Ashworth. This imposing table—a sea of exotic mahogany—is the largest of its form to survive from early New York.

when dining tables were usually small and light for portability, is explained by the fact that the table was owned by Sir William Johnson (1715–74), New York Colony's influential commissioner of Indian affairs (fig. 16.8), who presided over this territory , from the portico of a well-equipped Georgian country estate in the wilds of the Mohawk Valley during the long period of imperial warfare. Imagine the financial and political resources the ennobled Johnson required to stock such a grandiose stage with consumables. These included the appropriate accoutrements for dining, slaves (African and Indian) to serve or move things around (including the unusually heavy table), and a set of at least eighteen fashionable leather chairs to surround the table's vast circumference. Finally, Johnson required the power and prestige to command the presence of a sufficient number of clients worthy to fill them on a consistent basis.

✦ Germanicus Andrews and Joshua Delaplaine ✦

The British Quaker upholsterer Germanicus Andrews may not yet have been born when Nicolas de la Plaine finally died in 1697 at the age of 104. Nicolas was famously old in a city where Huguenot craftsmen mostly died young. Germanicus's connection to the city's French Quakers came through the large artisanal network associated with Nicolas's son Joshua Delaplaine (working 1707, d. ca. 1771), and Edward Burling, Delaplaine's master. Joshua was a productive joiner of luxury furniture in exotic woods, first recorded in New York in 1707, when he witnessed the will of another New York Quaker, a shopkeeper named William Bickley.[53] Bickley is mentioned in passing in the journal of Thomas Story (1662–1742), an itinerant Quaker preacher from Cumberland in England who found truth in 1689 and eventually traveled to meetings throughout the Atlantic world spreading the gospel. Much of Story's time was devoted to preaching in fertile territory in Flushing, as well as to the somewhat more resistant listeners in New York City. Yet he seems to have traveled the colonies ceaselessly on horseback between 1699 and 1705. Still, the Long Island Sound region became his main focal point north of Pennsylvania.

Story encountered William Bickley's son in 1702 on his way to a Meeting in Stratford, Connecticut. "William Bickley (William Bickley's son of New York)," Story recalled, "who (though gone from the Profession of Truth, in which he had been educated, yet retained a Respect for Friends and Professed no other Religion) came readily to us, and was very kind, and willingly let us have his house for a Meeting-place, and went himself, and also sent his servant about the Town, and invited the People."[54] William Bickley Jr. was typical of many of the people Story encountered in the Long Island Sound region who had never been—or were no longer—members of the society of Friends but remained in general sympathy with Quaker principles. Many, like Bickley, were former Quakers who still attended meetings from time to time. Others, as we shall see, were members of other sects that sought a religious or philosophical dialogue with Quakers; still others were nominally members of dominant religions, such as Calvinism.

Calvinists in this region engaged in diverse and wide-ranging varieties of Protestant practices. A number were internationalistic, heterodox, and often pietistic.[55] Many New York artisans were in this category, particularly those such as Andrews and Delaplaine, who were members of the Huguenot-Quaker craft network. Those who attended Quaker meetings in the Long Island Sound region should therefore be understood as having occupied a very broad spectrum of religious belief. If religiosity was deeply felt among the sects and heterodox Calvinists and Lutherans who attended meetings, along with the many Presbyterians who were almost always present, formal confessional connections seem to have been far less important than the quest for intensity and variety of spiritual experience.

❧ Master and Apprentice ❧

The year 1707 was the first of Germanicus Andrew's apprenticeship in the Faneuil or Lott shop. Joshua Delaplaine's apprenticeship records and his account book survive, so we know more about Delaplaine than most contemporary artisans in New York. We know, for example, that his own master and later the choice of his shop apprentices reflected almost precisely the hybrid, "mixed composition" of Delaplaine's New York French-Quaker worldview and craft network. Inasmuch as Nicolas was a tobacco twister, Joshua must have been apprenticed in the early eighteenth century to a joiner, although no indenture of apprenticeship survives. However, the earliest references in the Delaplaine accounts show him engaged in numerous shop transactions with Burling, a Quaker joiner with strong family ties to Long Island.

Two transactions in particular from the 1720s have an almost primordial quality. They suggest the ways in which Burling, as an extension of his former role as Delaplaine's master, traded goods for labor with the newly freed apprentice to ease the transition for himself and, in the process, also help set up a young artisan's shop. The first account, which runs from 1721 until 1727, shows Joshua Delaplaine in debt to Burling for a total of £65.5.7½ worth of the basic tools of the trade. The very first entry recorded "a tenant saw" worth 6 shillings. Burling subsequently provided Delaplaine with over fifty basic items, mostly tools and other equipment. These items included "a file and firmer . . . a hammer auger and pr of compass . . . 2 lb of nails . . . a file . . . some small nails . . . 8 chest lockes . . . 2 thous[an]d brads . . . 3 pr of chest hinges . . . 1 doz Screwers . . . 1 doz [cupboard?] locks . . . some Coffin handles . . . 6 Setts of bed screws . . . a cask of nails [worth £11.1.4] . . . 2 doz draps [imported brass "drop" handles for drawers] and [1] doz Scutches [imported brass "escutcheons": engraved cutout face-plates for lock holes or backing plates for handles].[56]

Year by year, Burling credited Delaplaine in full in exchange for joinery work on items of furniture as well as for work on three ships in port: the Samuel, Oxford, and Essex. These accounts seem almost interchangeable. For example, the credit lines read: "work and Stuf to the Ship Samuel . . . a table . . . a table . . . 1 ditto . . . work to ye Samuel . . . 3 chest drawer locks returned . . . Cash for ye 2 mehoginy boards . . . 34 candle boxes and other work . . . a table . . . acct to ye Oxford . . . 2 tables . . . [and] work to ye Essex."[57] Thus, Burling was able to maintain a measure of control over Delaplaine's valuable labor by extending his former apprentice credit, as Delaplaine went into debt to set up shop on his own account. This accommodation between the two artisans continued from 1728 until 1743, a total of eleven years. During this latter period, Delaplaine owed Burling £31.7.3 for more hardware and tools. Delaplaine made "6 oak Spars [for masts] . . . a box . . . a table for John Burling [Edward's second son, born on August 9, 1703] . . . a Chest of drawers [at an astonishing value of £11.10s., signifying both exotic woods and an enormous amount of labor] . . . [and] a tea table," in exchange for credit.[58] Clearly, Burling had a financial interest in the three ships. By 1736, he was no longer identified as a joiner, but rather as a merchant and freeholder of New York City. As early as 1728, Burling had already branched out considerably. He began to advertise real estate for sale in the *New York Gazette.* And due to his shipping interests, this ambitious Quaker quickly diversified into the trade in enslaved Africans, active among urban artisans in the busy East and Dock Wards. In 1731, Burling posted an advertisement in the *Gazette* offering for sale a "Negro man and two Negro Women and a Child."[59] Consignments of human cargo moved quickly in New York's heated market in enslaved Africans, with its strong connections to the West Indian trade.[60]

On June 11, 1737, in his upwardly mobile capacity, typical of successful artisans in colonial New York, Edward Burling joined a group of petitioners to the Common Council from the East Ward, a neighborhood where "men engaged in sea-oriented pursuits frequently dwelled." They succeeded in their petition to purchase water lots facing their properties on Van Cleeft's Slip. This was an effort by rising artisans and merchants to accommodate new shipping on their street and to facilitate the repair and refitting of boats. Hence, Burling Slip once faced his house.[61] Much more interesting to historians of New World artisans and material culture is the universal interchangeability of Delaplaine's joinery skills. He moved easily between high-style domestic furniture in the luxury trades and the heavy lifting of maritime woodworking. Indeed, if Delaplaine had not been credited with the fabrication of "6 oak Spars," one would assume he merely worked on the finish of a ship's interior. Such flexibility and adaptation was unheard of in the guilds of La Rochelle, from which, in any event, overt

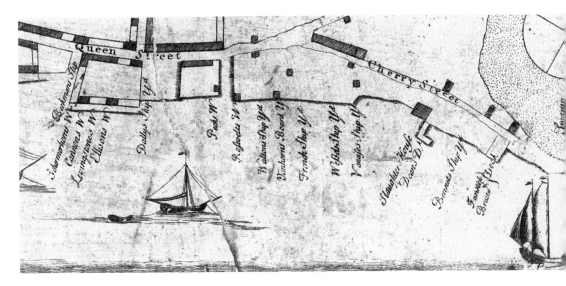

FIGURE 16.9. Detail of the "French
Ship Y[ar]d," engraved by Thomas
Johnson or Charles le Roux, from "A
Plan of the City of New York from an
actual survey, drawn by James Lyne,
printed by William Bradford, 1730."
Collection of The New-York Historical Society. New York French woodworkers were both shipwrights and
furniture makers.

Huguenots had been expelled in 1628. Still, overlapping woodworking skills were common enough in coastal Saintonge.

For Joshua Delaplaine, if such skills were commonly adapted to domestic woodworking, then the presence in New York by the late seventeenth century of the
Saintonge-dominated "French Ship Yard" (fig. 16.9) was a significant factor in both
the concentration and the success of Huguenots in the city's luxury trades. Being
skilled in two related trades, in which large amounts of capital were available, and able
to follow them more or less simultaneously, as Delaplaine did, provided the security of
constant work and the potential for supplementation when demand for labor in either
sector slacked. From the perspective of the survival of the constantly ramifying

Huguenot craft networks, "mixed" duty also allowed kinship groups living on both sides of the East River to overlap and expand. This practice helped Huguenot-Quaker networks to further consolidate control over demand for highly skilled woodworkers through intermarriage, thus greatly extending the influence of a core group of related refugee families in the city and on western Long Island.

❧ Hybrid Joinery Techniques ❧

Crossover phenomena among Saintongeais and related woodworkers in New York help explain the presence of hybrid local joinery techniques in some of the colony's refined early furniture. I am thinking here especially of the widespread use in furniture made along waterways of face-grain plugs to cover countersunk nail holes. This construction method is unique to the Long Island and upper New Jersey area. Perhaps it provided a smooth surface for finishes. Yet its use is not notable in the work of craftsmen from other regions, where exposed nails are commonly painted over. One might speculate that such plugs may have been adapted on Long Island from shipwright joints. Both nail holes and pins are known to have been concealed on wooden ships—northern European *bateaux* in particular—to keep hundreds of wood joints watertight and protect wrought-iron nails from corrosion.[62]

Hybridization was essential to development of shipbuilding in an era of expanding international trade, when a huge premium was placed on ship speed and adaptability to changing coastal contexts. Every busy early modern Atlantic port hosted ships made by all the major maritime powers, docked alongside colonial products. Local builders were thereby provided with a manual encyclopedia of international shipbuilding techniques. Ships' crews and carpenters were gathered from all available nationalities, and most competent shipwrights had an expansive and eclectic worldview. "The Dutch would have had no hesitancy in borrowing from the French," one historian of American colonial shipbuilding has observed, "or the French from the Dutch, or the British from both. Boat design is most certainly a mixing process of elements taken from many varied sources, both ancient and contemporary."[63] This cosmopolitan and improvisational theory of practice—long a hallmark of southwestern Huguenot artisanry—was fundamental to the crossover shop culture of the Burling-Delaplaine craft network.

❧ The Burling Family of Long Island and New York City ❧

Edward Burling was born into an English Quaker family on November 4, 1674 (d. New York City, May 1749). He and two young siblings (Grace, b. October 29, 1676, and

William, b. December 26, 1678) emigrated to Flushing with their parents, Grace and Edward Burling Sr., as a family. They joined the Meeting in 1680, establishing close networking bonds, especially with community leaders.[64] That same year, John Bowne's account book records that he "Reckened with Edward Burling ye 29th of ye first mont 1680: 81 and [rest] due to him six bushels Indian corn or else one barrill of Sie=der[,] which[ever] he [pleseth]."[65] The Edward Burlings were soon joined in Flushing by other members of their clan. The wheelwrights John Burling and Elias Burling were close relations (perhaps brothers) of Edward Burling Sr. Becoming members of the Flushing meeting, they were immediately established under John Bowne's patronage. Both newcomers were credited with wheelwright's work done for Bowne in 1681 in exchange for "Indian corn and cyder." By 1687, Elias Burling was also doing wheelwright's work for other Quakers on Bowne's account.[66]

Meanwhile, Edward Burling Sr. had left Flushing, and he was declared a freeman of New York City on October 1, 1683, without the usual reference to occupation. This is a curious omission, but since every male Burling was in the woodworking trades, it is likely that he was too. Despite this sojourn in New York—how long he stayed is unknown—the elder Burling returned to Flushing, where he took up his last residence. He died there in August 1697.[67] In the end, it was Edward Burling Jr. who found a way to reside permanently in the city. Transience was more or less commonplace for opportunistic Quaker craftsmen advantaged by strong artisanal networks and close proximity to waterways.

❧ John Bowne and the Burlings ❧

An intriguing notation was recorded as part of the transaction of 1681. Elias Burling paid John Bowne threepence for an unidentified "booke." Bowne sold the same book to a number of other artisans that year. Although the author is uncertain, imported books were consigned to Bowne by the colonial printer and publisher William Bradford, who commissioned Bowne as his agent to sell a stock of titles on Long Island.[68]

Bradford began his career as a Quaker but was passionately estranged from the sect in the early eighteenth century, when he published polemical pamphlets against sectarianism for the Church of England faction in New York City. In 1702, in his role as a polemicist, Bradford attacked the English Quaker preacher Samuel Bownas for heresy on Long Island.[69] As for the uncertain identity of Bradford's authors in 1681, George Fox (1624–91) preached at Bowne's house in 1672, so the Quaker theologian's books would have found a ready market in Flushing. A stronger possibility, however, is William Penn (1644–1718), Bowne's friend and business partner. Penn's *Brief Account of the Province of Pennsylvania* was published in London in 1681; his *Brief Account of the Province of East-Jersey* followed from the same publishing house the next year. Both books were of enormous interest to land-hungry Quakers in Flushing. They supplied valuable "information of all such persons who are or may be inclined to settle themselves, families and servants in that country."[70] John Bowne himself acquired considerable property in both Philadelphia and Chester County before 1690. Doubtless he profited handsomely from commissions on land sales in Pennsylvania to resettled Long Island Quakers.[71]

❧ Permeable Boundaries ❧

It is clear that by 1696, the year after John Bowne's death, Edward Burling Jr. had done substantial joinery work for him in Flushing. In April of that year, Samuel Bowne, John's son, settled accounts with Burling for £6. Cash was "taken out of ye stock and ped [paid] to friends [Quakers] as [I] find was dew by ye book from my father."[72] On June 11, 1700, Edward Burling was called a carpenter, when he married Phebe Ferris (fferris), in a Quaker ceremony. Phebe was the daughter of John Ferris (d. 1715) and Mary (West) Ferris (d. 1704). She was the granddaughter of Jeffrey Ferris (1610–66), an Englishman who immigrated to Boston from Leicestershire in 1635. Ferris was named a freeman at Watertown, Massachusetts. By 1636, he had gone in search of land to Wethersfield, Connecticut.

Land hunger is the common theme among New England Quakers who migrated to Oyster Bay (Underhill and Feke), Flushing (Bowne and Andrews), coastal Connecticut, and Westchester (Ferris). Sometime before July 1640, Jeffrey Ferris acquired land in Greenwich using Robert Feke (the artist brother of John Feke, the Flushing house carpenter) as his agent in the transaction. Given these rapid southerly migrations and this early connection to the Feke family, it is unsurprising that Ferris appeared next in New Netherlands, where in 1657, he signed an oath of submission to the Dutch in Stuyvesant's presence. The director-general was deeply suspicious of Ferris's regional background and ethnicity. With an inkling of his Quaker leanings, Stuyvesant also appended the proviso: "so long as we shall live in this jurisdiction"; both a threat and an invitation to leave. Perhaps Ferris found these terms too restrictive, as next year he sailed back across the Sound to Greenwich. After the death of his second wife in 1660, Jeffrey Ferris married Judith Feke and acquired more land in the Greenwich area near Westchester. This growing network of acquisitive Quaker artisans strengthened occupational, economic, and religious ties between the Ferris and Feke families of coastal Connecticut, Westchester, and Flushing.[73] Through the Fekes, the Ferris family was allied to the powerful Bownes and the dangerous, even more land-hungry Underhill.

John Ferris was a carpenter and originally a member of the Flushing meeting. Soon after 1664 (and the removal of the Dutch), Ferris took advantage of an Anglo-French land grab of former Dutch claims in the lower Hudson Valley. He migrated up the Sound just west of Thomas Pell's newly awarded patent. There, Ferris joined four other Quakers in settling Westchester Town, acquired in 1668, in a grant of former West India Company land from Governor Richard Nicolls. By 1670, Ferris and his fellow grantees expanded the town and set out new lots for a growing influx of settlers. Ferris also profited by building houses and furniture for them. Growth only increased the local Quaker oligarchy's appetite for further land acquisition.

Land expansion also meant expanded Quaker influence. Ferris stayed in constant contact with his former community, as New York Quakers traveled freely between Westchester Town and western Long Island. Intermarriage was common between these communities and Friends settlements in Rhode Island as well. A sense of this extreme mobility, with Flushing—and the Bowne family—situated at the nexus of travel, and the speed and efficiency with which Quakers could penetrate the entire permeable Sound region in small watercraft is clearly demonstrated by a packed itinerary noted in the journal of Thomas Story. In 1699, having just completed a Meeting in Oyster Bay, Story "went with Samuel Bowne and his wife to Flushing":

> where we had a glorious Meeting next day; and, the Day after, had a pretty large meeting in Jamaica, about four miles from Thence; and that Evening, we return'd to Flushing. . . . The next Day I went over the Sound, accompanied by several Friends, to West Chester; and the Day following, being the First of the Week, had a large Open meeting there, many Friends coming from Long-Island, and Abundance of People from all Quarters round. . . . The People were very still, and many affected with the Testimony of Truth. After the Meeting we returned over the Sound in a canoe.[74]

And, in 1702, after an unusually "comfortable" Meeting in hostile New York City, Story:

> then took [a] Boat back for Flushing, about 16 miles by water, and lodged with Samuel Bowne; and on the 26th, we had a meeting at West Chester, over the Sound, and returned to Samuel Bowne's in the Evening; on the 27th, were at their week-day meeting at Flushing . . . and then, accompanied with many Friends, we went over the Plains to Westbury, to a Quarterly Meeting, where we had good Service . . . the next [day] beiing the First of the Week, the Lord gave us a glorious Meeting in his Presence, in a new Meeting-house fitted up on that Occasion, and many Hundreds of Friends, and abundance of Other People were there, and generally satisfied, many things of Importance in Religion being clearly opened by the Wisdom and Power of Truth that Day.[75]

Note the careful, but still fluid, distinction that Story makes between Friends and "Other People" (or simply, "The People"). From Story's perspective, this marked the temporary boundary between Friends and the many others who almost always attended meetings in New York. Though there were important doctrinal differences among them, the nature of the give-and-take at these meetings indicated that for Story and his audience, the Quakers and heterodox "other people" communicated across diverse confessions using common pious languages derived from perceptions of the presence of the animated soul. That is one reason why so many other sectarians attended these extraordinarily heterodox meetings. All were seekers of common ground on the basis of their shared understanding of potential for "mixing" within a universal soul.[76]

To supply land to accommodate this population influx, Ferris engaged in nasty boundary disputes with neighbors in Eastchester and Fordham, as the men from Westchester Town tried to extend their original grant to encompass adjacent claims. During this period, Ferris continued to nurture old alliances on Long Island, which he exploited to broker advantageous settlements. To curry favor and gain political support for expansion, he also forged alliances in the city. A leading Huguenot Leislerian, Nicolas Bayard, was asked to arbitrate disputes, and Ferris used leverage to acquire Bayard's patronage. Edward Burling, a producer of elite goods in the city with strong ties to the pre-1685 Huguenot community through the Delaplaine craft network may have had direct influence with Bayard, whose public disgrace and trial did not occur until 1702. The Leislerians had strong economic and cultural interests in Westchester and would have been sympathetic to families with French connections. Jacob Leisler had powerful ties with New York's Huguenot community. His father was Jacob Victorian Leisler, a French Reformed minister in Frankfurt am Main, so Jacob the Younger spoke French and German interchangeably and shared a strong internationalist religious perspective with New York's French refugee community. Indeed, it was Jacob who organized the settlement at New Rochelle between 1687 and 1689, and made certain it was named after La Rochelle.[77] But Burling knew others in the Dock Ward whose patronage would prove very useful in Westchester, as it did in Flushing.

Burling married into a clan of aggressively expansive Quaker artisans, solidified by the establishment of networks of old family ties between Europe, southern coastal New England, Westchester, New Netherlands, and western Long Island. As in the case of the Ferris-Burling alliance, marriage was a good way to solidify holdings in Westchester, western Long Island, and New York City.[78] Successful establishment of this migrating network based on transatlantic ties, the universality of soulish religiosity and communication, acquisition of land, and dissemination of artisanal skill made Phebe Ferris an appropriate match for Edward Burling's ambitions. At the same time, Burling's family history, occupation, and geographic situation assured his ability to act as a broker between Westchester Town, Flushing, and New York. But the use of New York patronage for rural land acquisition was not the only reason for Burling to exploit his role as broker. The prospect of the expansion of an essentially rural artisanal network into the capital-rich city was equally attractive to Burling's in-laws. Jeffrey Ferris tried without success to gain a foothold in the city over a generation earlier (again, in 1657), under the suspicious eyes of the passionately antisectarian Stuyvesant. This path was ultimately laid out for Germanicus Andrews to take under English rule in the early eighteenth century.

❧ Quaker-Huguenot Apprenticeship Ties: ❧ Extensions of Artisanal Security to New York City

Delaplaine's indenture of apprenticeship to Edward Burling is not extant. If Delaplaine set up shop in 1718 (the date he took on his first apprentice), he started his apprenticeship anywhere from 1711 to 1714. There is a lacuna in the records for this period, but Burling's indentures are available for the years 1694 to 1707 and again from 1718 to 1727, so records of indenture for five other apprentices in Burling's service do survive and are instructive.

Very little is known about Thomas Sutton and Richard Berry. On June 1700 and February 1705, respectively, these two artisans with English backgrounds were the first apprentices Burling recorded in the presence of Robert Lurting, a city alderman. Sutton was eighteen years of age—old for an apprentice—and for that reason he was only expected to serve three years (rather than the usual six or seven), whereafter he was to receive "a good Sett of Carpenters Tools." Sutton also expected that his master "shall learn him to write Read & Cypher."[79] Other than his apprenticeship record, nothing more is available for Thomas Sutton. His religious affiliation is thus unclear, but he was probably connected with the Flushing Quaker network. Much the same may be said of Richard Berry, although we do know he was declared a "joyner" and a freeman of the city on September 7, 1725. It would be interesting to learn how (and where) Berry spent the fourteen-year-long interval, after his six-year apprenticeship expired.[80]

The Flushing connection was made perfectly clear on 8 February 1705, when the next apprenticeship recorded: the "indenture of Benjamin Burling, aged 16 years, with the consent of his mother to his brother, Edward Burling, joyner, for four years, from February 1st."[81] Sadly, like Germanicus Andrews, his close contemporary and coreligionist, Benjamin Burling died just four years later.[82] But even as the joiner Edward Burling rose in status to merchant and slave trader in New York City, while Edward's son James (b. 1701) added the rank of attorney as well,[83] Edward's grandson Thomas Burling (active 1769–97) remained an artisan and maintained the strong Flushing craft connections of his father, grandfather, and uncles before him. Again, the Bowne family is at the hub of the record. The cabinetmaker Thomas Burling was declared a freeman of New York City in 1769. Not long afterward, Thomas produced a small mahogany table, under the top of which he placed a label: "Made and sold by Thomas B[u]rling, in Chappel Street, [New York]." This meant that the table was probably made as venture cargo, or to be shipped out of town. Indeed, Burling sold the table to another Flushing Quaker, a descendant of John Bowne, and it remains in the collection at the Bowne House.[84]

The final two apprenticeships Edward Burling recorded are particularly interesting, given what we now know about his working relationship with Joshua Delaplaine. On October 8, 1707, Burling engaged his first Huguenot apprentice before Delaplaine's indenture in 1714, "John Vignoud Tillou, aged 15 years, with the consent of his mother," apprenticed, "to Edward Burling, Joyner, from November 6th, 1706, for five years." Young Tillou's indenture follows the conventional form, except that it lacks the usual reference to remedial education. Unlike the terms of Thomas Sutton's indenture, this apprentice was to be taught "to read write & Cypher *English* [emphasis added]." This is an intriguing alteration. Tillou could write. He signed his full name in its French form, Jean Vignau Tillou. The indenture implied, however, that Edward Burling (or someone in his household) understood French well enough to teach an already literate Huguenot apprentice to read and write in English.[85] Because of his mercantile interest in shipping and shipbuilding, it would not be unusual for Burling to converse in French, since many New York shipwrights, like Joshua Delaplaine, were Huguenot.

Indeed, the shipbuilding trades ran deep in the family of John Vigneau Tillou. He was the grandson of Pierre Tillou, who had fled from persecution in the old shipbuilding town of Saint-Nazaire, a short sloop trip of seventy-five miles up the Atlantic coast from La Rochelle, in 1681 and was naturalized in England on March 21, 1682. Pierre first appeared in New York in 1691, where he declared himself a French refugee and asked for protection and rights of citizenship. His son Vincent joined forces with another Huguenot family, of which little is known, when he married Elizabeth Vigneau. Before 1709, possibly about the same time that his son John was apprenticed to Burling, Vincent died, leaving another son, also Vincent, along with three daughters.[86]

Vincent was a favored Christian name for sons in the Tillou family. But it was also the surname of a prominent family of New York craftsmen, indicating strong connections between the Tillous and the Vincents. Two Huguenots witnessed the apprenticeship of John Tillou to Edward Burling: François Vincent and Benjamin d'Harriette. Both were artisans in the maritime trades with strong family ties to La Rochelle and Soubise in Saintonge. Vincent family members were seen working as block makers, sail makers, and coopers everywhere in New York's French shipyard. Moreover, they were allied during the eighteenth century with the upholsterer and merchant Benjamin Faneuil, their fellow émigré from La Rochelle and one of two masters available to Germanicus Andrews in 1707. Indeed, François Vincent signed the broadside in defense of Faneuil's loyalty to New York in 1708.

One of the few times a Vincent was recorded in a transaction outside the maritime trades was in making upholstery materials. John Vincent Jr. of New York City, was called a "leather dresser." Vincent *père* was a cooper.[87] In addition to shoe and saddle leather, John Vincent also dressed leather for upholstery. Faneuil and Lott were principal customers in this limited market. More typically in this family, when declared a freeman of New York on August 9, 1698, "Francis" Vincent was called a "saylemaker."[88] Vincent died in 1732, but his inventory was not probated until 1734, owing to the demands of his creditors. When the estate was settled, it was worth a substantial £1,700.[89] In order to settle the estate however, Vincent's three Huguenot executors—Ann Gilbert, John Dupuy, and the silver- and coppersmith Joseph Leddell (whose work we see in figs. 17.1 and 17.3)—posted an advertisement in the weekly *New York Gazette* for March 13 to March 20, 1732:

> All Persons that have any Demands on the Estate of Mr. Francis Vincent, late of the City of New-York, Sail-Maker, deceased, are to give notice of the same unto John Dupue or Joseph Leddell, Executors, or to Mrs. Ann Gilbert, Executrix to the said Estate, in order to receive Satisfaction. Also notice is hereby given that the Dwelling House of the said Francis Vincent, situate on the West Side of Broad-Street, near the Long-bridge, is to be SOLD, together with two young Negro Men, both good Sail-makers, and sundry Sorts of Household Goods. Those that incline to purchase the same, or any part thereof, may apply to the above mentioned Executors.[90]

The success of François (or Francis) Vincent in the sail maker's trade was manifested not only in the size of his estate and its extensive list of creditors, but also by evidence that he owned at least two African slaves trained in his craft. These two slaves were among the most valuable commodities at the vendue of Vincent's household possessions in 1732. This corresponds with abundant evidence of large numbers of slaves skilled in the maritime trades at work on the docks in eighteenth-century Philadelphia, Richmond, and Charleston. Not only did Vincent's slaves provide scarce skilled labor on those projects in which he had a personal stake, but they could be hired out to other New York artisans at high rates for day-to-day work on their projects during Vincent's down time, providing added income. The shorter the term, the higher the rate of return for slaves' labor. Most "other artisans" who hired from Vincent were usually linked to the Huguenot-Quaker network, whose members gained further competitive advantage by having available a familiar and reliable source of skilled slave labor. Certainly, Vincent could expect a similar arrangement in exchange from other members of the network if he needed to hire additional temporary help to complete a big project.[91] The artisans' business practice of hiring skilled slave labor at the docks was absolutely necessary for the success of the network. A group of Charleston master shipwrights, many of them French refugees, defended everyday use of skilled slave labor against fears expressed by less successful white artisans of black economic competition. The masters pointed out that "his Majesty's ships have been repaired and refitted only by the assistance of Our slaves, And . . . without these slaves the worst consequences might ensue."[92]

The Vincents undertook ambitious civic projects for the city down at Dock Ward. Because of the capital they commanded for such work, ownership of skilled slave artisans to labor in the maritime trades and add profit from the business of hiring out was the norm. It was folly to waste valuable time and energy of skilled slaves on the heavy, unskilled labor for which such civic projects involving maritime woodworking were known. This could be handled by younger family members, unskilled white laborers, and, ideally, large gangs of unskilled slaves gathered precisely for such tasks. Slave gangs were often shipped in from plantation populations in Brooklyn, the Hudson Valley, and Staten Island.[93]

It was commonplace for unskilled slave laborers to ship down the Hudson River to Manhattan, a practice followed constantly by the planter Frederick Philips, one of New York colony's most active slave traders. Philips's boatman Diamond, one of several slaves implicated in the conspiracy of 1712, made the trip south piloting his master's sloop at least once a week. He carried individuals back and forth from the community of forty-eight slaves at Philips's flour mill in Tarrytown, which specialized in making hard tack for New York shipping. Most slaves ferried by Diamond went to work at Philips's warehouse in New York. Philips profited from hiring out both skilled and unskilled slaves.[94]

In 1736, for example, it was necessary to gather large gangs of unskilled slave labor from a source such as Philips to do heavy work for Wynant "van Zandt," a batavianized "Vincent Vincent." A master turner and a maritime block maker, Wynant worked alongside several family members (represented by the city as "Mess:/rs Van Zandt"), when he was awarded an enormous city contract worth £4,137.11. Wynant, head of the Vincent–Van Zandt clan after the death of François, was paid in cash by the Common Council: "on account of the Expense of Improvements at the Battery . . . [the] Corporation Dock . . . [and the] Warren Street Bulkhead."[95] That year, the same prosperous Wynant Van Zandt joined forces with Edward Burling, his Quaker neighbor and another ambitious, upwardly mobile woodworking artisan, in a successful petition to the Common Council to acquire those valuable water lots facing Van Cleefts' Slip. Perhaps it was Edward Burling himself who sold Francis Vincent the two enslaved sail makers.[96]

This suggests that when John Vigneau Tillou signed an indenture of apprenticeship to the Edward Burling in 1706, he helped establish an alternating pattern of interchangeable and overlapping trades in shipbuilding and luxury woodworking that his fellow Huguenot Joshua Delaplaine followed when he joined the Quaker Burling's francophone shop. After Tillou's apprenticeship ended in 1711, he maintained this pattern with his former master. On January 9, 1718, Edward Burling registered his final and most unusual apprentice. In this instance, the witnesses were "John Tillou," and a Danish carpenter, block maker, and turner named Simon Breeste (Bresteade).[97]

This apprenticeship was unusual because it represents the only known female apprentice registered by a woodworking artisan in colonial New York City. The indenture was for Mary Mariot, another Huguenot, "aged about eleven years, with the consent of her Mother, to Edward Burling, Joyner, for seven years, from December 1st."[98] The language of the contract, also fairly unique, was extremely generous and included furniture often associated with dowries:

> the said Master dureing the Said Term Shall find and provide unto the Said Apprentice sufficient Meat, Drink, Apparell, Lodging and Washing fitting for an Apprentice, and at the Expiration of Said Term Shall give unto her a New Suit of Apparell both Woolen and Linen, besides her Common Wearing Apparell, and a New Cubboard worth three pounds and a Chest worth fifteen shillings and also three pounds in Money.[99]

Mary Mariot was promised no joiner's tools because, although her trade was not specified, she was not apprenticed as a woodworker. Women were not commonly associated with woodworking artisans in Europe unless they were involved with the cutting and application of textiles. Diderot shows women working alongside men in French upholstery shops, fitting covers to chair frames. Because Burling was not known to be an upholsterer but did build and repair boats, and since Mary Mariot was a French refugee accompanied by two witnesses who were shipwrights as well as furniture makers, it is logical to assume she apprenticed as a sail maker. By the time Delaplaine set up shop on his own in 1718, while continuing to work eleven years for Burling on credit, this pattern of Quaker-Huguenot artisanal communication and exchange was well established among craftsmen in the port and, based on the personnel in the Delaplaine shop, in Flushing as well.

While Burling may have indentured more than the six apprentices attributed to his shop, Joshua Delaplaine trained four known apprentices. Like Burling's six, however, these artisans were a mixture of English and French Quakers. When Delaplaine set up shop in early 1718, his first apprentice joiner was a Quaker with British antecedents named Francis Warne, whom he indentured for a period of eight years.[100] Not much is known about Warne's life in New York, except that he was made a freeman of the city on June 29, 1731.[101] The reason for his obscurity was Warne's decision to leave New York to test his skill in the West Indies. Unfortunately, like many colonists in Kingstown, Jamaica, he fell ill. Warne left his wife and sons behind, and they became the subject of a remarkable letter "to Joshua Delaplaine Joyner in New York," his former master whom he now addressed by the Quaker honorific, "Respected Friend." "I make bold . . . by this opportunity," Warne wrote on April 26, 1740, "to let thee hear that through the mercy of the Lord I am in a very likely way of getting of my health at ye last":

> I have had nothing but sorrow trouble and Sickness; as for hardship I have had my Share
> since I left New York but through the mercy of God I now begin to get a little health, tho
> I can safely say, I never enjoyed 2 weeks health since I left home. I Desire thee and thy
> wife will please to accept a pot of tammarins [tamarid][102] which I send by the bearer. it is
> but of a small value, stil I hope smal as it is I hope thee wil accept it. I wish I was able I
> would send more. I have got to work and hope I shall do wel at Last. if I can but get my
> health as I am in hopes I shal I should be very willing to come home but am very loth to
> come naked. it has cost me a great deal of money for to pay charges for sickness. I desire
> thee to advise my wife to put my sons to a good master and let her bind them out. I shall
> be very willing to it and hope to be at home next spring tho I shal be no ways wanting to
> do my best endeavor for my wife and children. I desire thee to advise her and tel her to
> make her self easy a little longer. I desire thee to be remembered to thy wife and Family
> and al Friends. I Rest thy Loveing Friend and old apprentice, Francis Warne.[103]

We do not know whether Warne survived his illness, or if he ever returned home to New York City. No evidence has been found that his sons were bound out to other joiners, or which of Warne's "Loveing Friends"—French or English—may have been their masters. Still, it is a measure of Warne's confidence in Delaplaine and the strength, reach, and memory of this Quaker-Huguenot network that in a time of personal danger, Warne turned to his old master to advise his wife to bind their sons out within the network. Warne's children would follow a strategy intended to reduce risk of failure and dependency and increase the chance of competence and security as skilled artisans. Warne's letter is poignant, both in the great regret he expresses over his decision to follow the path of artisanal transience—"to do wel," he left the relative security of New York and ran the very real risk of tropical disease in the West Indies—but also in its implication that in his absence, his sons had become vulnerable. These boys would not leave the shop floor and manual labor to rise to the status of merchant on the firm foundation of their father's work. Warne asked, in effect, that arrangements be made that his sons ensure his continuity (and theirs) by taking up his tools and resuming the artisan's interrupted life at "home" with "friends." Perhaps the next generation would achieve the lofty goals aimed at in his journey to Jamaica. Warne asked his "Loveing Friend" and Huguenot master to become surrogate father to his children. The powerful Quaker-Huguenot craft network was their best hope of an artisan's education, and hence employment and protection from the outside world.

Not all Delaplaine's apprentices felt as warmly about their master as Warne. The next Quaker apprentice to work at the bench Warne had formerly occupied in Delaplaine's shop was a contentious young man named William Jones, "the son of Margaret Jones, widow." On March 26, 1725, shortly before going out on his own, Warne had witnessed Jones's indenture to Delaplaine.[104] Jones, an ephemeral and transient figure, did not stay long in one place. A clue to his personality is his litigiousness; nothing about Jones's life is known outside of several appearances in court. By his surname and certain Quaker background, British ethnicity may be inferred. Yet Jones may also be Jansz. Guessing names is a risky business in New York. British or not, Jones is interesting for the meager record of his activities after he began his apprenticeship to Delaplaine in 1725.

His stay with Delaplaine was typically brief. Sometime before 1728, Jones entered into the service of yet another Huguenot master, Charles Jandine, who, like Delaplaine, had proven skills as a joiner and turner of elite goods. Jandine's work as a turner and designer was highly regarded by the city's anglicizing elites. This is made clear in the vestry minutes of Trinity Church for February 1, 1743, when the Huguenot's design for the new pews was accepted by the vestry: "Order'd that Each of the bloks and Squares of pews in the body of the Church as all the Owners of Each block Shall Agree to be turned Comfortable to the Draft made by Charles Jandine dated ye 7th day of December Last at the Charge of the Church."[105]

On October 1728, Charles Jandine took Jones to mayor's court, where the illustrious William Smith represented Jandine in a suit against Jones, who was cited for "leaving the employ of Jandine as a carpenter and joiner." By January 31, 1729, all the parties were back in court again. Jones was again identified as Jandine's apprentice and sued for breach of contract.[106] Charles Jandine's confessional allegiance is unclear. If Delaplaine took Jones on as his apprentice, with Warne as witness, then Jones was a probably at least a Quaker sympathizer. It may be that Jones had a falling out with the Quakers and opted for an Anglican master, or that Jandine had some Quaker associations as well, despite the fact that he designed and turned Trinity's pews and retained William Smith as his lawyer.

With the exception of Warne's signature as witness, the only contacts on record for Jones involved Huguenot masters. Most ended in litigation. Indeed, our final encounter with Jones involves yet another lawsuit. This time, Jones sued the Huguenot joiner Francis Bomier, who had hired him. Jones claimed that Bomier failed to pay him as agreed "for labor as a house carpenter and joiner at 5 s[hillings]" per day. If Jones was telling the truth about his wages, then skilled journeymen woodworkers in New York City could command between 20 and 40 percent more pay than their counterparts in Flushing, who normally expected to earn between three and four shillings per day. Jones managed to get Bomier thrown in jail in the end, despite William Smith's defense.[107] Lacking specific evidence, it is difficult to assign responsibility for these heated interactions between artisans. Was the problem transparently economic, or does Jones's litigiousness show animosity that runs deeper? Whatever the specifics, however, on complex levels of family, religious, and craft history that we can only begin to parse here, networks of New York Quaker and Huguenot artisans were *engaged* in intensive interaction on a number of levels. Between "friends," engagement was not always benign. There was tension as well as security in the shadows.

About a year after Warne signed on with Joshua Delaplaine in 1718, the Huguenot joiner and shipbuilder found enough work to add a second Quaker apprentice. On October 15, 1719, Benjamin Lawrence, the "son of Elizabeth Lawrence of Flushing on Nassau Island," was indentured to Delaplaine for a term of seven years.[108] The patron for this member of the Lawrence family was Edward Burling himself. Sometime in the 1730s, Edward Burling Jr.'s third son, also Edward (February 3, 1714–May 1749), married Mary Lawrence of Flushing (b. April 2, 1718). This marriage consolidated ties between the Burlings and the Lawrence family of artisans and merchants in both Flushing and New York City.

The Flushing–New York bilateral relationship made for similarities in the cross-river geography of occupational and religious lives. Mary Lawrence Burling was the daughter of Richard and Hannah Bowne Lawrence. Hannah was the daughter of John Bowne's son Samuel, thus further strengthening the already strong ties between the Burlings and Bownes. Soon after, the family web drew even tighter as Edward III's sister, Sarah Burling, married his brother-in-law Caleb Lawrence.[109] Elizabeth Lawrence "of Flushing on Nassau Island," the well-located mother of Delaplaine's new apprentice, was thus a member of this family—possibly the sister-in-law of Richard Lawrence. After registering his apprenticeship, however, Benjamin Lawrence disappears completely from the record.

Other woodworkers from the Lawrence family of Flushing and New York City remained active, however. All were intertwined with the rapidly expanding Quaker-Huguenot craft network in New York and on Long Island. A certain Thomas Lawrence was declared a freeman and joiner of the City of New York on May 4, 1725.[110] In 1725 and 1726, Thomas Lawrence signed a bond for £10 to John Bell, witnessed by a second Quaker joiner named Thomas Grigg. Bell, a carpenter of undocumented religious background, also aspired to merchant status. In addition to Bell's carpentry, when he could attract a profitable consignment from his London agent, he sold luxury goods to catch the eye of New Yorkers who aspired to replicate metropolitan style. Hogarth's trio of polite strollers on Hog Lane might be comfortable in some of these imports. Included was a combination of old-style native English ("Broad Cloths") and fashionable Huguenot textiles (baises, or "bases"). There was a stock of "Ready made Cloaths," and chinoiserie furniture; most were consumables then generally "in style," yet slightly behind the current London fashion, a fate that befitted rustic colonial consumers. When the shipment arrived in New York, Bell took out an advertisement in the *Gazette*. On December 9, 1734, a year before the appearance of Hogarth's painting in London, Bell's advertisement read:

> At the House of John Bell, Carpenter over against Capt. Garret Van Horne, there is to be Sold, Broad Cloths, Kersey's, Kersey [Plains], [Frize], Green Colloured, Dussills, Druggets, Shalloons, Miniken Blew Bases, Frize, and Plains, And some Ready made Cloaths, &c. By Wholesale or Retail at Reasonable Rates. Also, Looking Glasses, and Eight Day Clocks with Japan Cases.[111]

John Bell's confessional allegiance and ethnicity were undocumented. Yet in this they may resemble Thomas Lawrence's witness, Thomas Griggs, a Welsh Quaker joiner with early ties to western Long Island, as well as with New York's Huguenot maritime networks clustered around Dock Ward. Thomas descended from John, son of George Griggs, who immigrated to New England from Newport in Wales, a common port of entry for refugees from the civil wars of religion. John Griggs was living in New York in 1669, having left New England to join the English Quaker settlement founded at Gravesend in Brooklyn by Deborah Moody. Although his occupation is unknown, John Griggs acquired a substantial amount of land in and around Gravesend. He owned lots on Coney, Gishert's, and Ambrose Islands, as well as in "Gravesend Plantation," so he was probably a planter. The Kings County Census of 1698 showed John Griggs owned four African slaves. John had one child, also John (b. 1665), and the father of Thomas Griggs the New York joiner (b. ca. 1695). Thomas had property just across New York Bay from Gravesend on Staten Island, where he met and married the Huguenot Lena du Puy, whose family emigrated to New York from Artois in 1662 and settled, with so many French refugees, on Staten Island. Children from this couple married into the du Puy, Dey, and Bodin families, all Huguenot landowning families on Staten Island and in northern New Jersey.[112]

Like many Quaker woodworkers from Flushing, Griggs also followed his trade (if not the open practice of his religion) in the city. So, on April 24, 1716, Thomas "Grigg" was declared a freeman joiner of New York.[113] As on Long and Staten Islands, Griggs fostered close personal and working relationships with a number of pivotal New York Huguenot artisan families with ties to Quaker landowners in communities outside the city. For example, on April 29, 1719, "Thomas Griggs and Henry Gillam [Henri Guillaume, Guillam, Guillaim, or Guliamne], of New York City, Joiners," both posted bond for James McGrath, a Quaker carpenter from Flushing. McGrath died in 1726. His inventory was appraised by Adam Lawrence, a family member and close contemporary of Thomas Lawrence, the joiner and associate of Griggs.[114] Henry Gillam was declared a freeman joiner of New York on the same day in 1716 as his "friend" and cohort Thomas Griggs.[115] There is good circumstantial evidence of Gillam's Quaker sympathies, if not his formal membership in the society. Gillam's economic relation with Griggs and McGrath is suggestive. So was the location of Gillam's two houses, lots and fields in the Flushing and Oyster Bay extensions, Westchester Town, and Eastchester, where there was much French-Quaker interaction. When Gillam died in 1735, a notice was published in the *New York Gazette*:

> Notice is hereby given that . . . at the Court House in Westchester, there will be Exposed to Sale at Publick Vendue, the Dwelling-House and ground late of Henry Guillaim, in the Town of Westchester. Also, one lot of land in East-Chester, containing about three Quarters of an Acre, with a Dwelling-House thereon . . . and one other lot of land in East-Field of Bedford Township, containing about six acres; together with all other, the real Estate of Henry Guillaim.[116]

Ownership of these lands put Henry Gillam on the same side of the Long Island Sound as his father (or uncle), Charles Guillam (1671–1727) of Saybrook, in coastal Connecticut. Because of his ownership of French books and association with an idiosyncratic group of colonial American painted furniture made in the area of Saybrook, much research has gone into the location of Charles (and hence Henry) Guillam's Old World origin in Jersey, one of two Channel Islands in the Gulf of Saint-Malo off Normandy that remained French linguistic domains. Furniture forms and painting patterns traditionally attributed to Charles Guillam (as yet none can be traced definitively to Henry) also have distinctive Channel Islands antecedents (see fig. 5.8).[117]

Thomas Griggs's ties to New York's French refugee artisans were not limited to the northern Channel Islands. To be successful in New York, a city in which Saintongeais artisans dominated the maritime and luxury trades, they had to extend to southwestern France as well. It is noteworthy that on October 1, 1747, Griggs was chosen to build the coffin of the Huguenot Samuel Boyer (Bouyer, Bouhier), which was evidently not a simple five or ten shilling pine box, since he was paid a healthy £2.4.3, making it one of the most expensive on record. The progenitor of the Boyer family in New York was Jean Bouyer, a turner and weaver from Bordeaux (d. 1698), who was probably the master of Jean Le Chevalier from Saintonge, a major supplier of leather-chair frames to Lott and Faneuil for upholstery and resale. The Boyer family thus had associations with the New York leather chair and its artisanal network.

So Benjamin Lawrence, Joshua Delaplaine's second apprentice, entered his employ having come from a family of Flushing artisans with strong links to Delaplaine's New York Quaker-Huguenot craft network. The strength of these links cannot be underestimated, as the Lawrence family itself, like the South Carolina branch of the family, was arguably of Huguenot origin. John Lawrence, a merchant and the first of the family in New York, was a founder of Flushing in 1645. He was also one of three commissioners from New Amsterdam sent by Stuyvesant in 1663 to negotiate with John Winthrop Jr. over English claims to Dutch territory in New Netherlands. Following the English takeover, he was alderman, mayor, and supreme court justice of New York Colony until his death in 1699.

The name Lawrence is commonly thought to be ethnically English by New York historians.[118] It is true that John Lawrence immigrated from England, but so did almost all of his French ancestors, who, like Benjamin Faneuil and countless others, used London as a sort of relay point, just as the de La Plaines migrated via Holland. Despite the fact that the New York Lawrences must have left France a full generation before the South Carolina branch, John Lawrence and his Long Island Quaker family were known as the Laurent family of merchants in La Rochelle.[119] Hence, two old New Netherlands families, Delaplaine and Lawrence (Laurens, Laurent, Lorentz, or Laurence), planted American roots early for growing Quaker-Huguenot craft networks. These ramified as craftsmen, credit and sympathetic religious sensibilities were exchanged between numerous Quaker towns in the British Midlands, west of England, and western Long Island, and Huguenot strongholds in Aunis-Saintonge, Amsterdam, London, and New York City. The transatlantic convergence of Quaker and Huguenot networks in New Amsterdam and New York, provides further evidence that for these two refugee subgroups, a combination of artisanal skill, technical innovation, and advantageous geographical placement substituted for the security of numbers they lacked.

The last indenture of apprenticeship known to be recorded for the shop of Joshua Delaplaine, identifies "Nicholas Bellanger son of Ive Belanger late of little Egg Harbour [a town on the Delaware River near Philadelphia] in West Jersey, with the consent of his mother." He was apprenticed on May 2, 1720, "to Joshua Delaplaine, Joiner, for seven years." Benjamin Lawrence was on hand to witness the indenture, which the apparently literate Bellanger also signed in his own hand.[120]

Nicholas was the son of a weaver who arrived in Philadelphia in 1690, after coming to the colonies from Poitou. This followed the customary sojourn in England during the 1680s. Eves Bellangée (Ives Belanger, Belleng, Bellinger, de Bellinger, Ballinger, or Bellanger), the father of Nicholas, joined the maritime trades when he settled permanently in the Quaker-dominated area of Burlington County, New Jersey. There is fragmentary evidence that Nicholas had been preceded to a Quaker enclave by another family member with New York connections. On February 18, 1688, the Hempstead deed book recorded: "There was given to Michael Belleng, the Frenchman that lives on Mr. Spragg's land, twenty acres of woodland, lyng on the west side of Mr. Spragg's land, near the [Hempstead] plains."[121] Because he came directly to Philadelphia, it is possible that Eves Bellangée converted to Quakerism in London. Eves was surely a member of the Society by 1697, when he married Christain de La Plaine at the Friends Meeting in Philadelphia. Christain de La Plaine, the daughter of Nicolas de La Plaine of New York and his second wife Rachel Cresson, was Joshua

Delaplaine's sister. This meant that young Nicholas Bellanger, another Huguenot-Quaker joiner, was Joshua Delaplaine's nephew and the namesake of Joshua's father. When his father Eves died, the Delaplaine family welcomed Nicholas into the security of the New York French Quaker woodworking trades under his uncle's paternal eye.[122] Here was another link between New York City, Flushing, and Philadelphia, suggesting that parallels in patterns of woodworking resulted from the convergence of these family networks through intermarriage and migration. Indeed, large dining tables made simultaneously in the Philadelphia and New York shops of Burling, Delaplaine, Tillou, and their contemporaries are very similar in design, construction, and materials. Many display the same stacked baluster arrangement we know from the Île de Ré.[123] It may be that some furniture forms attributed to Pennsylvania were made in New York and vice versa.

Christain's marriage to Eves Bellangée in 1697 shows the utility of looking further into records of fragmentary artisanal alliances, through marriage, of the children of Nicolas de La Plaine and the Cresson sisters.[124] Indeed, such an inquiry does bear fruit for our reconstitution of the brief working life and unrealized potential of the unfortunate Flushing Quaker Germanicus Andrews. Maria Delaplaine, another daughter of Nicolas and the sister of Joshua, married the talented and well-connected Huguenot chair maker and carver Jean Le Chevalier on June 27, 1692. We know Jean and Maria Le Chevalier had their two daughters baptized in New York's French Church, a new place of worship for the refugees, its construction full of intense meaning and emotional solace after the destruction of the temples and exile in the *désert*.[125] Nevertheless, Jean Le Chevalier was thereby fully integrated into the Burling-Delaplaine craft network. That meant he had become a client "of the blood" of the most venerable of New York's Huguenot-Quaker artisanal dynasties. As the brother-in-law of Joshua Delaplaine, Le Chevalier assumed the pivotal brokerage role that brothers-in-law played in all Huguenot patronage networks. Le Chevalier was thus the perfect artisan to make the connection with his Huguenot patrons and broker Germanicus Andrews as an apprentice upholsterer to Faneuil or Lott. Had he survived, Andrews would have succeeded his Huguenot masters as one of two primary upholsterers of leather chairs in New York, thereby linking the Flushing Quaker artisanal and mercantile community to the most profitable medium of the international Huguenot style in urban America.

This is not to say that such linkages were absent on western Long Island or that they failed there to effect the "mixed composition" of hybridization and the creation of hybrid Anglo-French forms. The cultural, religious, artifactual, and documentary record points in just the opposite direction. Pluralistic interaction was pursued avidly on western Long Island by Quakers and other related regional sectarians and pietists. An improvisational cultural style circled back and forth between Manhattan and Long

Island as Flushing Quaker artisans converged with their Huguenot allies in the city. In addition to members of the Lawrence family, other Huguenot artisans lived and worked in Flushing. These included James Clement, a French joiner and a member of John Bowne's household, and his son Samuel Clement. The French-Quaker Clement shops were also essential to the process of cultural convergence and hybridization in Flushing.

❧ The Meetinghouse Bracket ❧

A successful French-Quaker craft network thus circulated between New Netherlands / New York and western Long Island. It is now possible, therefore, to pose new sets of questions. What material and spiritual evidence remains of this interactive artisan network? How can we identify the permeable and fluid process of circulation and "unities" among refugees who so industriously ramified their networks in the material culture of French-Quaker convergence to acquire land and labor through commerce and marriage? To repeat a basic question from Part I, how do artifacts from this craft network communicate the material-holiness synthesis fundamental to international artisanal pietism during the seventeenth century? Was there something in the religious *culture* of the network that bound these two very specific groups together in joint material and spiritual projects in New York? Why, in other words, did they come together in the ways they did?

When they signed the contract to build the Friends Meetinghouse in Flushing, Samuel Andrews and John Feke "promise[d]" their patron, John Bowne, that "they s[hall endeavor] to have it up for further f[inishing by] ye: 30th daye of the first month: [16] 93." That meant that the basic structure was to be standing for Bowne's glazier to finish the windows and for his carpenters and joiners in addition to Feke who specialized in interior woodwork to make the meetinghouse fit for use by the Society of Friends. Unfortunately, almost nothing of the original work from this initial building campaign survives to connect the makers with their production. What can be deduced from both the contract and surviving elements of the building suggests a variant of English "plain" architecture in the exterior form and plan. Sadly, little to signify the hand of Feke or Andrews—or subsequent artisans who finished the interiors—is available for analysis.

Only a few brackets (or corbels) that support a joint between a post and beam in the upper room of the meetinghouse are distinctive and indisputably part of the original structure (fig. 16.10a and b). Building elements in early modern house construction like this one, although obscured by banal utility and easily "overlooked," are not without interest. Interest is compounded by the realization that a similar distinctive bracket is found nearby, in the construction of John Bowne's house. Inasmuch as the

FIGURE 16.10. Friends meetinghouse, Flushing, New York, built for John Bowne by John Feke in 1694 and renovated in 1717 and 1763. Photo, Pasquali Cuomo. (a) One of the surviving brackets original to the 1694 structure. All the brackets are oak, with iron rivets and bars and oak and iron washers. The bracket was seated in the crook between a post and summer beam—itself secured by an iron strap nailed to the beam—and attached by nails and rivets toward the ends. At the stress points in the middle, bars secured by wooden and iron washers and staples pulled each corbel against its post. This bracket's close relationship to ship architecture suggests that Feke may have followed both trades. (b) Bracket, possibly from the 1763 renovation, when a second story was added and the roof raised.

Norfolk man John Feke is the only housewright known to have played a major role in building at both sites (Feke also contracted with Bowne to construct the addition to his house in 1680, along with John Clay), he seems likely to have fashioned this joint. It may be that Feke also built the original section of Bowne's house in 1661. Although the contract for this building does not survive, we know Feke built Bowne's thatched barn in 1666. This puts Feke in Bowne's employ as early as the 1660s, making him a likely candidate.

If Feke was indeed the maker, he probably did not learn to fashion such a corbel from Norfolk craftsmen, or from any English-trained artisan, for that matter, because they were not made in the vernacular English manner used in East Anglia. Abbott Lowell Cummings has shown that in early New England, all the surviving seventeenth-century New World English house brackets were joined to mortises in the post and beam with tenons. These thicker joints were then invariably fastened tight *solely* with long wooden pegs.[126] If John Feke was responsible for fashioning brackets for the meetinghouse and the Bowne House, then he must have learned how to do so through encounters with continental woodwork (or woodworkers) on Long Island. The staircase in the Arsenal of the citadel at Saint-Martin-de-Ré on the Île de Ré, for example, makes excellent use of similar brackets (see fig. 16.6). Such encounters would have been part of Feke's daily routine.

What, then, is distinctive, or even idiosyncratic about the meetinghouse bracket? To begin, this bracket is unusual in the colonies because unlike ones found in New England and the south, it is unusually attenuated in form—akin, perhaps, to beams that attached the crown post to the roof frame in early English construction—and not attached with standard English mortise and tenon joints fastened by pegs. Here, the support system was held together originally by a series of formidable iron rivets driven up through the arch of the bracket and into the post and beam. This method of construction is known in New York furniture from the period as well. The top of a late seventeenth-century draw-bar table in the Metropolitan Museum of Art is also attached with enormous iron rivets. In addition, rods were seated into the bracket with large iron washers, and then pinned by iron pins. This seventeenth-century blacksmith work is, in fact, so unusual, that it suggests an elaborate old repair. Perhaps the rods were inserted into holes vacated by rivets that had worked loose over time? Yet, the presence of an early iron strap hinge to support the post and beam above the bracket and evidence from a turned and joined table made around 1700 in New York City or western Long Island (fig. 16.11) advances the possibility that the weight-bearing ironwork may be part of the original bracket.

This portable table, with the deep vase on the baluster, has strong northern European antecedents, and it may have been made by Feke himself, or indeed by one of several Continental or Anglo–New York or Long Island woodworkers trained in the Dutch, German, or French tradition. Huguenots found refuge in all these places, and such ambiguous forms, like their makers, were infinitely adaptable, reflecting the influence of their travels. The table is, moreover, turned in the same shop tradition as a large group of turned chairs made in New York City or western Long Island ca. 1650–1720. One example (fig. 16.12) has descended, in situ, in the Bowne house. Dating from John Bowne's time, the chair's back balusters are turned similarly to one supporting the table.[127]

Nothing in the form or construction of this table corresponds with known English types. If the table is disassembled, two of the component parts reveal similar modes of regional artisanal practice used on the bracket. The maple baluster of the table has a rounded tenon turned at the bottom that fits through the two sets of legs, which overlap when assembled. All three elements were secured by an iron washer of the type on the bracket, which is slipped over the rounded tenon, flush against the inside top

FIGURE 16.11. Tea table, Flushing, Long Island, ca. 1690–1720. Possibly by John Feke. H: 26½″, diameter of top: 18¼″. Maple, oak, and black walnut. Private collection. Photos, Jeff Rowe. The top, with cup of tea, can be rotated toward a guest without lifting the table. Compare the turned shaft with spindles shown in figure 16.12 and the arm supports in figure 16.14. Chamfering on the top's bottom edge is reminiscent of similar treatment on the top of figure 16.3. (a) Detail below the base shows remarkable similarities to brackets illustrated in figure 16.10 (a) and (b), including the drawknife and chisel work and use of an iron washer and a pin (originally made of iron) to secure the shaft to the bottom and to facilitate movement of the shaft and top.

of the lapped legs. An iron pin (now missing) was pushed through the washered tenon, thus fastening all the pieces together. This is fundamentally the same system used in the meetinghouse. Just as this system was rare craft practice in colonial house construction, so too it is rare in American regional furniture outside New York.

The other idiosyncratic regional feature of the meetinghouse bracket are the deeply chamfered edges and ends cut with a drawknife. The chamfer was worked as a decisive ornamental element drawn along the inside edge of the bracket and termini. The

FIGURE 16.12. Great chair owned by John Bowne, western Long Island, probably Flushing, or New York City, 1660–90. H (reduced by wear): 36″, W: 23″, D: 17¼″. Ash and maple. Courtesy Bowne House Historical Society, Flushing, New York. Photo, Society for the Preservation of Long Island Antiquities. This chair has never been out of the Bowne House, where it was part of the seventeenth-century furnishings. The turnings, like those of a number of surviving chairs from related early shops on western Long Island and New York City, closely resemble the turned shaft on the tea table in figure 16.11.

attenuated edges thus formed an architectonic arch when paired with the opposing brackets and seen from below. Deeply channeled edgework is powerfully visible on both the top and bottom of the tea table's legs. When the table is apart, its lap joints form a similar bracket, articulated in the same forceful way.

Survival of the meetinghouse bracket in situ deepens our understanding of the historical processes that informed Long Island regional woodworking, just as it illuminates the fugitive hybridized culture of the local Quaker craft networks. Something as seemingly trivial to historians as this idiosyncratic form of chamfering may prove a signifier of cultural convergence, in particular when read together with related written and material documents of artisanal behavior and experience.

Consider the components of a joined great chair (fig. 16.13), from the middle Atlantic region, with no reliable history of ownership, but plausibly made in or around Huntington, Long Island, sometime between 1700 and 1740. The filial relation of this chair to one with an unimpeachable history of ownership in Huntington (fig. 16.14)—with turned elements under its arms formed like the blunted arrow terminus on the tea table—makes the intuitive attribution of figure 16.13 to an early Long Island maker seem reasonable. Resonance between the idiosyncratic crest in figure 16.13 and the arms in figure 16.14 is particularly convincing. Moreover, close comparison of specific elements on the chair with the meetinghouse bracket makes western Long Island its probable place of origin.[128]

FIGURE 16.13. Joined great chair, northwest shore, Long Island, possibly Huntington, 1720–40. H: 46½″, W: 23½″, D: 22¼″. Birch with a white pine back panel and seat. Private Collection. Photos, Jeff Rowe. (a) Detail of "hidden" edgework on back of scrolled crest and rear stile. The unusual carved volutes on the crest rail are perfect miniatures of the carved arms on the chair in figure 16.14.

FIGURE 16.14. Joined great chair, Huntington, Long Island, 1720–40. H: 54³⁄₁₆″,
W: 30⁹⁄₁₆″. White oak, maple, red cedar, and
hickory. Courtesy Henry Francis du Pont
Winterthur Museum, Winterthur, Delaware.
The initials "I C" inlaid on the crest stand for
Jacob Conklin (1677–1754) or his son Israel
(1719–77), both of Huntington, in whose
family the chair descended. The finials are
nineteenth-century additions.

This chair was the perfect artifact for a pluralistic social setting, precisely because
it could have come from anywhere on the Continent, perhaps one of the Quaker counties in the English West Country or Midlands. In short, any potential buyer might
have perceived something recognizable, competent, and comfortable in its artifactual
language. Following Hogarth, this chair had something for virtually every perceptual
grammar then known on Long Island. Above the seat, the dramatic scrolled crest and
inward-turning ears were available to regional artisans in the Palatinate, the Netherlands (particularly the province of Limburg), France, the Channel Islands, Wales, and
sometimes East Anglia; likewise the carved back and seat with perimeter moldings.
Carved backs and perimeter seat moldings also appear on some chairs from seventeenth-century Plymouth Colony, with its early history of settlement in Holland. Hidden below the seat, however, is a molded front stretcher backed by a medial H stretcher,
with no back stretcher. In the British Isles and British North America, this was uncommon (if not unheard of), and though much more common in the Netherlands and
the Palatinate, this arrangement below the seat absent a back stretcher is most common in France.

So, too, is deeply chamfered edgework by joiners. This was particularly true of chamfered legs, stretchers, and posts—although this may simply reflect a joiner without knowledge of turning, or one lacking the proper equipment (a lathe and chisels). All the regions that supplied artisans to New York also employed the deep chamfer to perform similar sorts of edgework. In Wales or the Palatinate, chamfered edges were also a significant part of the available artisanal language, though perhaps not used as often or as persistently as in Saintonge. As in certain particularly adaptable sounds in pidgin or creole dialects, the ubiquitous practice of chamfered edgework in Long Island may have helped to form the basis for a common visual grammar for artisanal discourse, innovation, and convergence; that is to say, the grammar of a hybrid regional style. The use of this idiosyncratic edgework certainly bound the language of the joined chair to the bracket, presumably made for John Bowne by the Norfolk-Flushing Quaker John Feke. Thus it was well known as a woodworking pattern by Quaker craftsmen attending the Meeting in Flushing.

Did Bowne specify this sort of work on the bracket, or was it simply considered natural in Flushing in 1693? Such specifications appear nowhere in the carefully worded contracts. Compare the deeply channeled edgework on the scrolls, legs, arms, and stretchers of the chair with the chamfered bracket (fig. 16.10a and 16.10b). The chair's maker paid exquisite, lapidarian attention to detail when he chamfered two tiny, essentially hidden elements: the ends of the scrolls tucked invisibly behind the ears at the crest; and the ends of a molding strip behind the seat, a "backstop" to be covered later with a stuffed pillow. The private performance of drawknife work, built in to be overlooked, was secreted in the chair's shadows as a kind of artisanal memory image. Was this simply to protect the sharp end grain from splitting, a consequence of disciplined self-mastery, or an act of convergence with diverse refugee artisans in the region who shared a common language with the maker of the meetinghouse bracket?

❧ The Meetinghouse Forms ❧

When John Bowne died in 1694, Samuel Bowne continued to use his father's account book, where he noted names of local artisans responsible "for further finishing" of the meetinghouse interior. John Everad (Everett?), presumably a sawyer or cartman, passed briefly through the book's pages in connection with construction between 1696 and 1701. Everad was paid, "for two load of bords fetching for formes [benches] for ye meetinghouse," "nails for ye meetinghouse," and "planks to use above ye meetinghouse."[129] The use of leveling, rustic forms for seating the meeting, rather than elaborate, hierarchical pews used by the Church of England in New York City, suggests that the main vehicle for English Quakers' unmediated rhetorical and aesthetic style was extended to Long Island's interior furnishings (fig. 16.15).

The Quaker vernacular style was thus analogous to a kind of anti-Babel: where the

FIGURE 16.15. Interior view of the gallery of Brigflatts Friends Meeting House, Cumbria, UK. © Library of the Religious Society of Friends, Friends House, London. In 1714, these gallery seats were low oak forms. They were raised in 1720, as seen here, by adding backs and arms. This pattern was repeated in Flushing. A number of the slab-ended pine benches visible in figure 16.10 (a) are old, perhaps added sometime around 1760, when the meetinghouse underwent another of its many renovations. The Brigflatts Meeting House in Wales displays interior woodwork with deep chamfering and turned elements in the same general column-and-urn pattern seen on artifacts from Flushing. Were these Welsh, international Quaker woodworking patterns or simply generic?

tower of Babel was ornate, striving, high, concentric, and atomizing; the Quaker form was natural, humble, low, straight, and unifying. Here was a place where simple artisans—like the builders themselves—could rise up to testify in Palissy's natural language (and in tongues) of the stark immediacy of their prophetic experiences and subtle encounters of the soul.

An account of one such experience was recorded by the itinerant Quaker preacher Thomas Story, who made Samuel Bowne's house in Flushing his center of operations for conversion in the crucial Long Island Sound region. In 1691, not long before he set out to evangelize in colonial America, Story wrote of the fluid convergence of spiritual experience he had experienced in northern England:

And, when we came to the Meeting, being a little late, it was full gathered; and I went among the Throng of the People on the Forms, and sat still among them in that inward Condition and mental Retirement. . . . For, not long after I had sat down among them, that heavenly and watery cloud overshadowing my Mind, brake into a sweet abounding shower of celestial Rain, and the greatest part of the Meeting was broken together, dissolved and comforted in the same divine and holy Presence and Influence of the true, holy and heavenly Lord; which was divers Times repeated before the Meeting ended . . . our Joy was mutual and full, tho' in the Efflux of many Tears, as in Cases of the deepest and most unfeigned Love.[130]

Thomas Story described his Neoplatonic convergence experience—chaste and sexual at once—in material, elemental, and spiritual language closely approximating natural-philosophical, alchemical, and artisanal discourse. Their bodies still, "the People" turned all physical motion inward toward the soulish examination of their one common heart and "Mind" in Christ. An inseminating shower of celestial rain, like the binding, replicating tincture of the philosopher's stone, thus caused their separated bodies, now met, to be "broken together, dissolved and comforted in the same divine and holy Presence." The truth of this experience of their plural bodies, reduced, atomized, and recombined nonviolently in a crucible of divine love, was proven because, "it was divers Times repeated before the Meeting ended." These temporary moments of repetition of bodily dissolution and soulish purification resulted in "mutual and full" convergence, while individuals were sitting side by side and back to front.

This action figuratively collapsed benches full of separate bodies together into a single spiritual seat. At the end of the process, the product of this purified solution was, in fact, *distilled*, "in the Efflux of many Tears." Such a subtle material effluvium from the body could only occur "in Cases of the deepest and most unfeigned Love." Every Paracelsian alchemist and natural philosopher, from Palissy to Fludd, understood that the primitive purity of deepest love was transitory. It was a shadow memory of Neoplatonic transparency, lost after prelapsarian times, recovered through the unity of the soul. The Quaker experiment was another sort of geomancy. It drew God's transparent light of truth down into their bodies—and, like Palissy's rustic figures, the material products of their artisanry as well—making security from the danger of corruption and personal assault a quotidian matter. Sir Kenelm Digby's thesis of soulish motion that gave the weapon salve its fabled potency comes to mind here. And in Fludd's *Internal Principle,* the inner movement of the light of the soul "communicated" from body to body, "like a guardian foreseeing danger":

In their emission the rays are so joined together that either the soul of the seeker or the seeker himself be the one to whom danger is imminent, or else a friend of his; for the [soul] is very prophetical. Being immortal, it may know within itself things that are in the future and things present. Like a guardian foreseeing danger with which a body is threatened, it may explain the secret future of its body to another soul applying to it—a future which it had been unable to communicate to its body because of that body's grossness. And in this way may a quiet and peaceful soul, which is in a fit condition for judging, and to which movements of its body are well subjected, prognosticate the future to that other soul . . . [such a soul could] leave its body so as to find a place whence it could enter into communication, and converse, with the souls of friends."[131]

Verbal communication—what Story calls "Tongue and Lip Religion"—was superfluous—a dangerous impediment to authentic communication between natural bodies. Hence, "the Meeting being ended" when Story stood up, and "the Peace of God, which passeth all the Understanding of natural Man, and is unexpressible by any Language but itself alone, remained, as a holy Canopy, over my Mind, in a Silence out of the Reach of all Words; and no Idea, but the Word himself, can be conceived."[132]

For Palissy and his transatlantic Huguenot followers—and their network of Quaker artisan patrons and clients both in and around New York—passionate, Neoplatonic quietism, experienced "out of the Reach of all Words," was the essential language of material things engendered in the subterranean "bowels" of Nature and imitated by calling on the "inward condition" of man, where the silent "peace of God" lay hidden in the soul. This condition created the "holy Canopy" of the Word, which hovered invisibly over the simple form. More important, this edifice could be constructed anywhere in the microcosm, as by Huguenots in the *désert*.

❧ James Clement of Flushing ❧

Many artisans performed work inside the shell of the Flushing meetinghouse. The Bowne accounts show that this was an ongoing process. In March 1696, one George Langly, a Quaker carpenter who may have been a member of Bowne's household, commanded a total of 16 shillings "for worke done about ye meeting hous." Two months later, Thomas Ford was paid 19 shillings, "for 6½ das worke at ye meetinghouse," and in March 1700, he earned £1.17.1½ for thirteen days of master carpentry. Not much more can be said with confidence about these and other unknown Quaker craftsmen. Blacksmiths did not usually warrant mention in the documentary record, but one Will Fowler was paid 12 shillings "for making hinges for ye meetinghouse."[133] Was he even a Flushing townsman? Blacksmiths were in short supply on Long Island and were often imported from elsewhere for specific jobs.[134] Did this quiet craftsman forge the ironwork for the meetinghouse brackets or the related wrought-iron washer and pin, hidden under the tea table's post for stability?

One craftsman from the Bowne accounts of the construction of the meetinghouse interior has enough history attached to his name to provide something more than a fragmentary biographical context. James Clement (ca. 1640–1725), was a Huguenot-Quaker joiner and, in an extraordinary synthesis, a scribe as well. Clement specialized in typical European notarial functions, including land transactions and similar economic documents for the Flushing Quaker community. He was also said to be "skilled in the law."

Clement's artisanal credentials are also readily apparent in the Bowne accounts. In December 1697, the same month that Clement received 2 shillings from Samuel Bowne for building "my Childs cofin," death struck another local artisan. Clement was paid 12 shillings to make "g [Langleys] cofin" as well. This was for the body of carpenter George Langley, credited one year earlier "for worke done about ye meetinghouse." Despite his lively trade in coffins—always a mainstay of any early modern carpenter's craft—Clement still found time that winter to undertake more "work done about ye meetinghouse." This remained a constant refrain in the accounts until September 1701, when the first campaign to finish the building's interior finally ended, seven years after it opened for use. At one point, Clement worked side by side with Thomas Ford. Both craftsmen were probably responsible for making the forms from two loads of boards fetched to the meetinghouse by John Everad in 1696.[135]

Clement did much of his notarial work for the Quakers. On May 3, 1696, he received 5s. 6d. shillings "for writing a bill of sale for ye me[e]ting house" in Flushing. This bill of sale may refer to construction of the meetinghouse itself, three acres of land purchased for the site for £40 in 1692, or the purchase of additional land. The bill was followed in the Bowne accounts by another credit for 5s. 3d., to "James Clement for a deed for [the New] York meetinghouse land." This property was acquired "from Jacob Were [Ware]." The month before, Samuel Bowne had paid 5 shillings "to James Clemant for recording the dead of Seal [deed of sale]" of the transaction.[136]

Who was James Clement of Flushing? How did he come to join the New York Quaker community in the dual capacities of craftsman and scribe? We do know that he was not the first of his line in the colonies. There were several individuals named Clement living in New Amsterdam / New York during the seventeenth century. All were clearly woodworkers, or in the building trades, and "close kin" to James and his family on Long Island.[137] This small cell of related craftsmen included "Charles Clement ye Cooper [a.k.a. Clement the Cooper]," who appeared in New York City records for the last time in 1677. Charles Clement can be traced along collateral lines south to settlers on the Raritan River in New Jersey and as far north as Schenectady, in the Mohawk Valley. More important for our purposes however, are Bastien Clement and Jan Clement, arguably brothers, whose first appearances in New Amsterdam / New York may be traced to 1659 and 1665 respectively.[138]

Bastien came originally from the northern French province of Tournay and, following the pattern of most of the first refugees in the "old" (or pre-1685) Huguenot colonization of New Amsterdam, he traveled the well trodden route from the northern French provinces (Picardy, Normandy, Maine, Brittany, and Tournay) to the New World Dutch colony, arriving by way of numerous temporary residences where work was available in the coastal Netherlands. Bastien, a wheelwright, made his way first to Doornick in 1657, and then to New Amsterdam in February of 1659.[139] The Clements split up to find work in various towns in Holland, which were burdened by a glut of skilled refugees. Then they migrated in a staggered pattern across the Atlantic. By 1665, a certain Jan Clement, a master mason by trade, had emigrated to Kings County, where he acquired land in New Utrecht and Flatlands and married Marie Bocquet (Bokee), another French refugee.[140]

There were other colonists named Clement with French refugee antecedents within reach of New York in the seventeenth century. All were skilled artisans. While asserting a direct relationship to James Clement of Long Island is uncertain, there are suggestive parallels. Abbott Lowell Cummings has found that Augustine Clement was the only decorative house painter recorded in Boston before 1650. Augustin is a common French name, and he pursued a quintessentially Huguenot trade. Indeed, the next acknowledged "painter-stainer" to advertise his services in Boston was another Huguenot, John Berger (fl. 1718–32). Augustine Clement embarked from Southampton in 1635. Described in Boston as a "sometime" (impermanent) resident of Reading, in Berkshire, Augustine enjoyed great longevity and also trained his son, Samuel Clement (1635–78), to master his rarified trade. James Clement trained his son, also named Samuel, but nothing more is known of either painter.[141]

In 1688, Richard Clement, another artisan with occupations related to James's, appeared in Casco Bay, Maine, a French refugee settlement established after the Revocation of the Edict of Nantes, whence many southwestern Huguenots dispersed to the Boston area and, after the failure of the Oxford, Massachusetts, resettlement project, to New York. In an intriguing document, written in French, Richard Clement was called a *[c]harpanteur* (roughly, "builder" or house carpenter)" and named "deputy surveyor" for the settlement. In his dual capacity, Richard Clement also assumed the role of scribe in charge of the documentation of land transactions.

That is how he was identified in a petition to Governor Andros by Pierre Baudouin, a refugee who emigrated from La Rochelle to Dublin, and thence to Casco Bay, where he acquired 100 acres of woodland. In a long "Supplication," Baudouin appealed "humbly" for tax relief to pay "the said Clement," who was hired "to do carpentry work, after which he had to make his report so that the patents or leases on the said property may be delivered." Baudouin claimed the exemption for hard times following religious persecution. He claimed further, that "because of hardships suffered by those of his religion, he had lost nearly all his assets," which he was forced to leave behind in La Rochelle. Inasmuch as the highly specialized rhetoric of this notarial document was written *about* Baudouin, essentially in the third person—then signed by the supplicant—one wonders if Richard Clement was the scribe. After all, Clement clearly stood to benefit if Baudouin's petition was successful.[142]

Our first encounter with James Clement of Flushing occurs in Amsterdam on May 30, 1663, when "James Clement of ye Buthrop-Bridge in Durham, in ye Kingdom of England" was bound as an indentured servant to "John Bowne, inhabitant in Flushing, in ye province of New Netherland, in America."[143] That James Clement came to Amsterdam from Durham, does not mean he was born there. Indeed, the date of Clement's indenture (1663) and the place (Amsterdam) tie his migration closely to that of Bastien and Jan Clement—perhaps James's brothers or cousins—whose arrival in New York and New Utrecht from Tournay via Holland may be dated to 1659 and 1665 respectively. Bastien was thought to have left Tournay around 1657. It is reasonable to assume James was made a refugee at about the same time, but instead of going directly to Holland, he first made his way to the Quaker region of Durham. He found work there and perfected his mastery of the scrivener's trade before using his contacts with Durham Friends to reach terms on a suitable colonial indenture with a Quaker master in Amsterdam. During the interim of six years in Buthrop-Bridge, he may have been apprenticed to a clerk. Befitting a servant with such useful skills, Bowne granted James Clement reasonable terms of indenture. He was to receive half the cost of his "freight or passage" to New Amsterdam, 250 pounds of tobacco, and, most unusual in standard artisans' contracts, cash "sufficient to Clothe him with two suits of Apparell, one fit to Labor, and the other fit to use on other occasions."[144] The other occasions were notarial in nature. James needed clothing that was appropriate to a public rank much higher than rough "Apparel . . . fit to [manual] Labor."

In 1663, John Bowne prepared his return to Flushing from Amsterdam, after successfully defending his town's right to follow enthusiastic beliefs to the directors of the West India Company. James Clement traveled to Flushing on his new master's triumphant voyage home. Clement's skills were of enormous value both to Bowne himself and to the Society of Friends, because his clients were then acquiring as much land as possible. Accurate, clear, and detailed documents were necessary to the success of this process, particularly since such acquisitions were often challenged in court. As a skilled house carpenter and joiner, Clement would also be invaluable in the numerous building campaigns to come, both on Bowne's expanding farm and other properties and as regards the new meetinghouse. Indeed, James Clement began to write deeds for land transactions in Flushing immediately upon his arrival in 1664. By 1669, he was identified as "clerk," "town clerk," or "clerk of the county court," as well as a carpenter or joiner from Flushing and John Bowne's servant. By September 1710, Clement had

risen in the local bureaucratic hierarchy to become one of the five supervisors of
Queens County.[145]

Clement may have been working privately on his own account as a freeman as early
as 1670. Yet, like Burling and Delaplaine, he was still routinely employed by Bowne
and continued to use the honorific "master," as in a final balance recorded in Clement's
hand in Bowne's account book:

> All reconkings [reckonings] made Ballanced betwixt one James Clement & my master
> Jon Bowne & their is dew to him two good cowes wth cave [calf] or & calfes by their side
> wch I doe ingadge to deliver to him ore his order in ye begining part of may next as also
> twenty shillings more in marchant pay, to be pd in at Robert S[hr]eyes at New Yorke as
> wittness my hand ye 20th October 1676.

The context of this transaction is lost, but by 1675, James possessed a small farm on
Little Neck Bay in Flushing (Bayside), where he raised cows. The agreement was significant enough to be witnessed by the politically influential Flushing merchant "Major" William Lawrence. A longtime patron of the Clement family, William was kin to
Benjamin Lawrence, who apprenticed to Joshua Delaplaine in 1719, and whose master was John Bowne's reliable client Edward Burling.[146] Moreover, William Lawrence
played host to the Quaker preacher Thomas Story if Samuel Bowne was unavailable,
and because Clement was associated with the household of John and Samuel Bowne,
he was known to Story as well.

By comparison with texts produced by the other two clerks we have encountered in
this book—the learned Edward Howes and the polished writer of the supplication for
Pierre Baudouin (perhaps Richard Clement)—James Clement's awkwardly written
account of his negotiation with John Bowne seems crude. Perhaps this shows that English was, after all, James Clement's second language, while the other scribes wrote
with facility in their native tongue. Still, the most significant aspect of this document
is Clement's failure to date it in the standard Quaker manner; that is to say, "20 d[ay]
8 m[onth] [17]19." Despite the crudeness of the text, this must be considered a conscious decision, not a trivial oversight. Clement was probably a member of the sect in
Amsterdam in 1663, or else it is doubtful Bowne would have accepted him into his
household. William Wade Hinshaw, the great Quaker encyclopedist, did not share
this opinion. Hinshaw believed that James Clement was an active member of the Society of Friends beginning in 1676.[147]

Evidence suggests that Clement was a member much earlier, however. Francis Coo-
ley and John Adams stood up in the Flushing Meeting in 1667 because they found "it
in their hearts to speak to James Clement about his absenting himself from meetings."[148] Did Clement's indenture to Bowne, a principal supporter of the meeting, end
in 1667? James Clement's name disappears from Meeting minutes after that date. Al-

though Clement absented himself from Meeting, he clearly remained a well-known adjunct of John Bowne's household—if no longer a bonded servant—and arguably also in sympathy with fundamental tenets of Quaker theology. All evidence suggests that if Clement was no longer formally Quaker, he remained all his life a primitivistic, quietist Calvinist, of the sort Bernard Palissy encountered routinely in the artisans' *désert* of Saintonge in the 1560s. In this posture, Clement was similar to many of the "other people" encountered by Thomas Story at meetings throughout the Long Island Sound region on his mission between 1699 and 1705. However, while Clement's name appears with a fair degree of frequency in the economic records of the society—as well as Bowne's accounts—in his capacity as craftsman and clerk for Quaker land transactions, the births of his children were not recorded there, and neither was his death. This was highly unusual among Friends in the New York Meeting. More anomalous still are the language and format of James Clement's will, which employs a secular rather than the familiar religious formula preferred by most active members of the society and again eschews the usual Quaker dating system. In such a ritualistic context, this was a statement by omission of Clement's religious independence and his desire for privacy.[149]

Yet some of James Clement's offspring became full members of the Society. Following Catherine Swindlehurst's research on refugee artisans in seventeenth-century Spitalfields and Hillel Schwartz's findings on the Huguenot Prophets in eighteenth-century London, the Huguenots of New York, given their background in the religious practice of Civil War Saintonge, were drawn to the pietistic quietism of Quakerism. This was amplified by the Friends' similar emergence from the fires of religious persecution. Still, some French refugee families did not join the confession until the next generation.[150] Gradualism was facilitated in New York because the meetings retained an inclusive style until well into the eighteenth century. Long Island meetings were subject to fluid spiritual and social give and take, as Story shows. This gave New York Huguenots the benefits of convergence signified by the meeting, without the necessity of relinquishing their old patterns of hidden religious practice in exchange for the permanent communal devotion of adherence to formal confession. In a very real, familial sense, tension between the "two reformations" of communal devotion and personal piety was played out in nebulous cultural territory that surrounded the Long Island Sound basin. Negotiable religious space available in this ill-defined territory—the inverse of Winthrop's Boston—was what drew the doomed Anne Hutchinson and her extended family to Long Island. Such unresolved spiritual tensions sometimes had crushing long-term consequences, however, perhaps more so for women.[151]

The name of James Clement's first wife, the mother of their nine children, is unknown. The identities of the children and of his second wife Sarah Hinchman (married on 2 July 1696) are to be found in the Flushing Census of 1698, taken by the Quaker

Jonathan Wright and James Clement, respectively the town's "Constable and Clerk," on "this Last of August 1698."[152] Clement's marriage to Sarah Hinchman solidified ties to the Quaker elite of Flushing, despite his stubborn resistance to open membership in the meeting.[153] Still, there is also evidence that Clement's religious practices caused "trouble or disturbance as much as in me lyes," as Sarah wrote in her will of June 15, 1725 (proved February 28, 1727). James Clement left all their daughters out of his will of May 5, 1724 (proved March 16, 1725), presumably because of their open religious affiliation with the Flushing Meeting against his wishes. This caused a tumult in the family, something Sarah sought to avoid (or perhaps compensate for) in her will by having three witnesses to reverse her husband's passion for secrecy and contrariness, all of them "being *known* Quakers [who] *did declare in due form* [emphasis added]."[154] For these and other reasons now lost with most of the early town records of Flushing, James Clement was judged an "unusual and peculiar man."[155]

The census was also taken idiosyncratically, which was the fashion of this "peculiar" Huguenot clerk. First, it listed the heads of some prominent families, where Samuel Bowne is not named, though James Clement was placed with the grandees. No reference to ethnicity is made in this list ("Col. Thomas Willetts, Justice Tho: Hukes, Major Wm Lawrence, Richard Cornell, John Esmond, Samll. Thorne and James Clement"). Yet in the lists of Dutch, French, and English inhabitants following the elite, ethnicity is noted. After these came unmarried landowners called "freemen-men."[156] The census thus contains the names of two Huguenot families—Clement and Lawrence—which James Clement felt transcended ethnic identity with social status.

One name appears unexpectedly in the category of unmarried "freemen-men," that of "John Clement," a servant "In the family of Coll: Thomas Willett." This could not possibly be Jan Clement the mason, who immigrated in 1665. Instead, John was almost certainly "Jan Clement 22 Jeare," when he took the oath of allegiance in New Utrecht, in Kings County, on September 3, 1687, two years after the Revocation.[157] This Jan (or John) would have been 33 years old in 1700. He was probably sent by Jan Clement the mason of New Utrecht to join their kinsman James Clement in Flushing, where he acquired some land and a place in the household of Thomas Willett, a town leader. In this way, John's situation paralleled James's modest beginnings in Flushing. Also like James Clement, John Clement was not—or did not dare stay—a member of his Quaker master's Meeting. Given James's harsh treatment of his daughters in the will, his distance from the Meeting may have been a condition negotiated in advance of John's arrival from New Utrecht.[158]

James Clement's local reputation for peculiarity also stems from a brief but ironically open theatrical performance during the Bownas controversy of 1702. I say ironic, in that James Clement's only recorded public utterance was a dramatic defense of the right to act quietly—in the shadows—in which he defended the absolute value and inviolability of both corporate and personal secrecy from intrusion by the state. In the absence of other evidence, it may be possible to extrapolate from this incident Clement's abhorrence of institutional intrusion on his material and spiritual privacy of *any kind*, including attendance at Meeting, where introspection can become a subject for analysis and judgment by the group.

❧ The Bownas Controversy ❧

The Bownas controversy was constructed in Quaker martyrology as a four-part passion play, set in three major western towns on Long Island, all of which contested for converts with the colony's authorized Church of England ministry and the flourishing (albeit officially illegitimate) sectarians. Samuel Bownas's year-long ordeal began in Hempstead, where he was charged with heresy by two New York judges; moved to the Flushing meetinghouse, where he was arrested; and culminated at Jamaica, where a grand jury refused to concur with the judges that a trial was warranted. Finally, he was imprisoned by Lord Cornbury despite the grand jury's findings. We also encounter James Clement in Jamaica, where he was a juror. But before turning to Clement's revealing moment on the grand jury, it remains to trace the momentum of prior events from accounts written by Bownas himself.

In November 1702, Samuel Bownas, an English Quaker preacher, traveled to Hempstead to preach at a Meeting held in a large barn, where he was to be the principal speaker. Bownas was trailed to Hempstead by two former Friends converted to fierce evangelical and political adversaries: George Keith ("once a Quaker," according to Bownas, "but now an Episcopal minister"), and William Bradford, John Bowne's main supplier of William Penn's books for resale in Flushing during the 1680s ("who had been a printer for Friends at Philadelphia, but deserting the Society, Friends took the business from him").[159] The barn was immediately divided into two halves by the rivals, and as Bownas preached to one group of seekers in one half, Keith (with William Bradford attending) preached to his group in the other. From Bownas's perspective, he easily carried the day in the open competition between orthodoxy and heterodoxy in early New York. "I being very young and strong," Bownas wrote, "my voice was plainly heard by the people who were with Keith, so that they all left his meeting and came to ours (for we had room enough for both meetings, it being a very large barn), except the Clerk and one William Bradford."[160]

Facing public humiliation and desertion, Keith and Bradford formulated a face-saving strategy. Both "agreed that the latter should come and try if no advantage might be taken of my doctrine: accordingly he [the printer William Bradford, acting the ancient role of inquisitor's scribe] came to my meeting and pulled out of his pocket a small blank-book, with pen and ink, and steadfastly stared in my face to put me out of countenance if he could. . . . He opened his book and writ about two lines in it, then shut it again, continuing his staring . . . but I was past his skill, for I felt both inward and outward strength, and divine power to fill my heart, and my face was like brass to all opposition." When Bradford failed to disconcert Bownas, he demanded a public dispute over doctrine. "I told him his questions being more for contention than edification," Bownas replied, "I did not think myself obliged to answer them. He turned from me, and in a very angry manner said I should hear of it another way."[161]

Bradford had in mind to produce a formal charge of heresy akin to Anabaptism (among other heresies) against Bownas in a deposition sworn before Edward Burroughs and Joseph Smith, justices of the court of New York, with a copy to Thomas Cardale, sheriff of Queens County:

> I, William Bradford, of New York, aged 40, depose that on the 21st of November, 1702, going into the Quaker's meeting, at Nathaniel Pearsall's, deceased, in Hempstead, I heard one Bownas, lately come out of England, preach; and the first words I heard him say, were: "The sign of the cross; and thus, friends, having gone through the Papist baptism, let us examine the Church of England. Well, what do they do? Why, the Bishop lays his hands upon those who have learnt the languages, and ordains them to be ministers. Well, what do *they* do? Why, they baptize the children, the young children, and sprinkle a little water in their faces, and by this they make the child a Christian as they say, and for so doing the parents must give the priest four pence or a groat: indeed, this is an easy way of making Christians for a groat! And how do they do this? Their own Catechism tells us, The priest says to the child: "What is thy name?" The child answers, Thomas, James, Mary, &c. Well, and "who gave thee this name?" *Ans.*—"My godfathers and godmothers in my baptism, whereby I was made a member of Christ." This is brave, to be a member of Christ. Who would not have a little water sprinkled in their faces? And "what did your godfathers and mothers then for you?" *Ans.*—"They did promise and vow three things in my name: 1. That I should renounce the Devil and all his works." &c. Ay! did they so? This is brave. Well, what did they promise more? "Secondly, that I should keep God's holy will and commandments," &c. And yet, in contradiction to this, they plead for sin term of life, and say they can't keep God's commandments in this life. Why, this is strange, that godfathers and mothers should promise what they believe and can't perform. Do they thus promise? Yes! they do. But this is strange, that their God should need a godfather and mother. But, friends, *our* God is the true and living God, and hath no need of godfathers and mothers. Well, and what do Presbyterians do? Why, they baptise their children also; but, as I take it, they do not make use of godfathers or mothers, nor the cross. They have thrown away that piece of popery. As to the Lord's supper I shall be brief. The bread and wine which they receive and call the Lord's supper, goes in at the mouth and into the

draught, and profits nothing. They call it a sign, yea, and an empty sign it is. But by these ways and forms the hirelings deceive the people. They will turn with every wind, and every turn that will answer their priests' ends, as we have seen largely fulfilled in our day.[162]

On November 24, 1702, Sheriff Cardale was empowered by the court to execute a warrant issued for Bownas's arrest. Less than one week later the scene shifted to Flushing, where Bownas traveled on November 29 to attend New York's "half-yearly meeting, which was very large, Keith being expected there,"

> when the meeting was fully set the Sheriff came with a very large company, all armed, some with guns, others with pitchforks; others, swords, halberds, clubs, &c.; as if they should meet with great opposition in taking a poor, harmless, silly sheep out of the flock. The Sheriff stepping up into the gallery, took me by the hand and told me I was his prisoner. We pro'd and con'd a little time, and. . . . The sheriff allowed me to stay with my friends until the 5th day. . . . The meeting increased, there being near 2,000 the last day; but Keith did not come.[163]

Cardale was patient; wisely allowing Bownas to come in his own good time, doubtless fearing the incitement of such a crowd by an abrupt or violent arrest.

Apparently, the crowd did not diminish by the time the careful sheriff arrived in Jamaica with his prisoner. Threat of mob action was perceived great by the authorities. "I appeared at Jamaica before four Justices," wrote Bownas. "A great crowd of people were deprived of an opportunity of hearing my examination, for want of a large hall, which they might have had," he continued in a sarcastic vein, "but by reason of the *cold* [that is, popular resentment in the streets] the Justices would not go there. They wrote a *mittimus* [arrest warrant], ordering the sheriff to safely keep in the common goal of Queens Co. Samuel Bownas, charged with speaking scandalous lies of and reflections against the Church of England."[164] Bownas remained a prisoner in Jamaica for three months, after which "a court was held. The judges came, attended with much company, in great pomp, with trumpets and other music before them. The grand jury were called over, a very uncommon charge given them, and on retiring a bill[165] was sent them. They had also before them sundry evidence [prepared by Bownas] to set Bradford's evidence aside."[166]

When the court met on February 29, 1703, James Clement was one of twenty-two members of a grand jury that included several Quakers and woodworking artisans. But Clement was by far the most vocal and memorable, so far as Bownas was concerned. "The Jury being asked what business they had to lay before the Court, presented the bill against me indorsed *Ignoramus:*

> The Judge was very angry. . . . On the Judge [Chief Justice Bridges] demanding their reasons for not finding a bill, James Clement, a bold man and skilled in law, answered: "We

are sworn to keep the Queen's secrets, our fellows' and our own." The Judge replied: "Now, Mr. *Wiseman* speaks. You are not so sworn, and I could find it in my heart to lay you by the heels, and a fine on your brethren." Clement retorted that neither Grand nor Petit Jurors are to be menaced with threats of stocks or fines, but they are to act freely to the best of their judgement on the evidence before them. Now, the Judge finding that he had not children to deal with, began to flatter, and requested the Jury to take back the bill and resume consideration on it. On this the Jury was in judgement divided, but at last all consented. Next morning the Judge asked the Forman [Richard Cornell]: "How find you the bill?" *Ans.*—"As yesterday." The Judge then charged the Jury with obstructing justice. "Why?" said Clement; "because we can't be of the same mind as the Court! We would have you know that we desire nothing but justice." The Clerk called over the Jury singly to show their reasons. Some refused to say more than: "That's our verdict." Others said: "How unreasonable for the Court to try to perjure the Jury by revealing their secrets in the face of the country!"[167]

In the heated and sarcastic dialogue between Chief Justice Bridges and Mr. *Wiseman*, it is difficult not to perceive in the habitually secretive Clement's overt and subversive role as Mr. *Wiseman*, the Long Island survival of Palissy's ironic "pauvre artisan sans lettres." It may be that Chief Justice Bridges's use of such figurative and rhetorical speech was merely an angry response to Clement's putative reputation as a local know-it-all. Be that as it may, we have no evidence that Bridges was even aware of Clement's existence before the County Clerk called the grand jury into session. To be sure however, it is absolutely certain that Clement's occupation as a carpenter and joiner was listed by the clerk, so Judge Bridges undoubtedly saw a "poor uneducated artisan," "boldly" standing before him in court to elucidate his reading of the common law—hence, Mr. *Wiseman*. Most un-Palissian, however, was the jury's open challenge in finding the charge *Ignoramous*, to block the extension of the state's authority to the hinterlands. With the one exception early in his career when Palissy openly expressed his Protestant beliefs to the local authorities in Saintes (the potter's openness nearly cost him his life), the "humble" Palissy tended to mask his contempt for the ignorance of authority in the indirect, flattering, and exorbitant language of patronage. This Clement found unnecessary in Jamaica.

The Palissian denunciation by Clement and his peers on the grand jury of the learned ignorance of arbitrary authority, was delivered from the ancient, experiential wisdom of the practical, natural artisan. Refugee tradesmen such as Clement kept essential secrets hidden, just as did the soul of nature. This competition between local and central authority in Jamaica, extended to the ultimate resolution of the Bownas controversy. The grand jury's defiance of the court's desire that jurors return a bill indicating just cause for prosecution, and the Huguenot joiner James Clement's vigorous defense (with other jurors) of the right to secrecy from the state, "angered the Judge so that he adjourned the Court for six weeks, and ordered the prisoner to be kept closer than before, on account of crimes and misdemeanors of the most dangerous consequence, as tending to subvert Church and State, and threatening to send me [Bownas] to London."[168]

In its desire to punish Bownas and warn his supporters, the court's anger led to the construction of an oppressively small, isolated rustic prison, reminiscent of the one occupied by Elias Neau in France (see fig. 9.7). This parallel would not have been lost on Huguenots, Quakers, and "other people" on Long Island whose families had been the victims of religious oppression; nor would Samuel Bownas's final refuge in artisanal production while a prisoner of the spirit have been lost on the many craftsmen living among these sectarian groups:

> I was now put up in a small room made of logs, which had been protested against as an unlawful prison, and my friends denied coming to me. I appealed to the Governor [Lord Cornbury], but all in vain. Not wanting to be chargeable to my friends I applied to a Scotch churchman, Charles Williams, to let me have tools and teach me to make shoes. By night I finished one shoe, and next day the other, and made such improvement as to earn 15 shillings a week, and thus diverted body and mind, and had plenty of money.[169]

Under painful pressure in which the body and spirit (or "body and mind") enter a sort of crucible, Palissy the Huguenot artisan reinvented himself as a preacher and Bownas the Quaker preacher mastered artisanry. The double roles become almost interchangeable in the literature of the history and martyrology of artisanal sectarianism, violent oppression of heterodoxy by the state, and ultimately secret refuge in the shadows. Just as Palissy imagined his spirit to be impregnated by the Neoplatonic soul of nature that planted the seeds of unity and recreation in the fragmentation of his besieged body, thus enabling the potter to communicate silently through the material language that emerged from his obstetric craft at the moment words failed or were choked off by absolutism, so, too, Samuel Bownas, silenced and isolated in a "small room" as an arbitrary prisoner of "Church and State," produced shoes in his enforced "confinement . . . and thus diverted body and mind." Was Bownas's curious pattern of making one shoe by night and the other by day a metaphor for conjunction of macrocosm and microcosm? Following material-holiness themes that animate spiritual artisanry in Palissy, Fludd, and Hogarth, had the now isolated Bownas "withdrawn from the multitude . . . [to] perform very great actions and . . . direct them toward a felicitous climax and issue"? Indeed, skill became his path to spiritual and material security; the besieged oppression of Bownas's body and soul was transmuted and hence reborn in the purification of materials. And, in the end, he "had plenty of money." Even (or, perhaps I should say especially) in prison, natural artisanal skill learned from God through Nature and the intermediary of the soul and crafted wisely in secrecy, privacy, and isolation, was transformed into redemption and cash.

In October 1703, after a year in prison, the judge offered Samuel Bownas his freedom if he paid the jailer's fees. He refused to acquiesce despite his cash reserves—a reward for patience, work, and steadfastness in adversity that he would not turn over to his persecutors—but he was released from his Long Island prison after Friends paid the charges. Upon Bownas's release, he returned to his Long Island ministry, and "he now visited every corner . . . and had very large open meetings."[170]

But tensions remained high between the Church of England and the Quakers and their sectarian collaborators. Almost as high as in the 1650s, when Stuyvesant persecuted sectarians in the name of the officially authorized Dutch Reformed Church. One can clearly see why New York City Huguenots remained vital to the Quakers' economic and religious prospects in the colony. The Huguenots were the Quakers' artisanal bridge to Manhattan's rich material culture. Inroads had been made since Stuyvesant's notorious prohibition of sects in New Netherlands. Quaker Meetings were now quietly held in private New York houses, while Lord Cornbury and his successors as governor usually looked the other way. But the controversy over Samuel Bownas poisoned the atmosphere between the Church of England and the Quakers and set up new boundaries against sectarianism in the city, which were not lifted completely until after the American Revolution.

In 1699, three years before the Bownas controversy, Thomas Story was amazed to hold a Meeting "at the House of one Thomas Roberts, a convinced man," because it took place "in the Heart of the City." After all, "the Testimony of Truth hath seldom any great Prevalence in that Place." And yet there was still space available for optimism and light: "the Room," at Thomas Roberts' house, "was large, and all about the Doors and Windows were full of People." By 1702, while Bownas was making shoes in prison, Story's hope for effecting a spiritual convergence between western Long Island and New York City lessened. His spiritual light was nearly extinguished "in that hard and dark Place." As Story wrote in 1704, "Samuel Bownas [was] still a Prisoner for the Testimony of the Truth, by the lawless arbitrary Imposition of that Government under the Administration of Edward Hyde, commonly called Lord Cornbury, an unreasonable and unjust Persecutor."[171] As a result, Story felt persecuted and threatened by Cornbury as well, and in advance of a Meeting that took place in New York later that year, he wrote in his journal:

> I went to New-York; and the Day after had a good and comfortable Meeting there; and though I had heard, two months before I went from home, that the Lord Cornbury had threatened, that if ever I should come into his Government he would confine me, for some Words falsely alleged to have been spoken by me in my Testimony, some time be-

fore in Maryland (with which he had no business at New-York) about the National Church of England, her Sacraments, Order, and Catechism; yet I did not go one step out of my way, nor at all Shun him about it, either in my going to New York, or now in my returning [to Long Island], though the common talk in these Parts was, that a Warrant was lodged in the Sheriff's Hand against me, at whose house I was several Times, yet the LORD preserved me free.[172]

✦ Samuel Clement of Flushing ✦

Of five sons remembered in James Clement's will, only Samuel Clement (born ca. 1686–died after June 1760), a carpenter and joiner who lived and worked all his long life in Flushing, is known to have carried on his father's trade.[173] Moreover, Samuel shared his father's ambiguous relationship with Friends. He was arguably a Quaker sympathizer—all his kin and network of association were Friends or related to known members of the Flushing Meeting—but no records for Samuel Clement are available other than the census of 1698, and his presence on a militia roll in 1715.[174] While Samuel Clement lived and worked in Flushing at least until sometime after 1760 (the year in which he appraised Samuel Lawrence's household inventory), the secular and religious record is virtually mute concerning his activities. We cannot even be sure of his wife's name.[175]

If Samuel Clement were formally a "convinced" Quaker, he would appear periodically in the Friends' records. Like James Clement, however, Samuel was not known to be an outward member of any other church or sect. Also, like his father, we cannot assume Samuel's resistance to oaths, or his formal absence from the Meeting's records (though probably not the Meeting itself)—and indeed his decision not to belong to another Church—connoted lack of religiosity. The inverse may have been true for both James and Samuel Clement. Ever since the sixteenth century, artisan refugees with Clement's Huguenot background had privileged private piety expressed in secret as material culture, and this may have held true in his spiritual and material life in Flushing. Is it possible that private individuals such as James and Samuel Clement depended on their wives to perform the public duties of communal devotion, including formal membership in the sect? Given this intermediary position, would Quaker women in a split household serve as go-betweens?

Appropriately, the only substantive historical knowledge of Samuel Clement's existence in the world is derived from material sources. By accident of survival—but above all because material culture sometimes reveals itself through an unexpected fragment of writing—Samuel Clement's name and town have been harnessed to two articles of early eighteenth-century joinery that provide an index to the vocabulary of

FIGURE 16.16. Samuel Clement, Flushing, Long Island, June 1726. Inscription secreted behind the lower central drawer in the base of the high chest of drawers in figure 16.17. Courtesy
Henry Francis du Pont Winterthur Museum, Winterthur, Delaware. The inlay on this drawer
resembles an open book, perhaps suggesting an appropriate "cover" for the author's hidden
signature?

woodworking and artisanal thought common to the French Quakers of western Long
Island.

If the utterly unique inscription in dark ink announcing (to whom?): "This was
made in ye Year 1726 / By me Samuel Clement of fflushing / June ye[]" (fig. 16.16) had
not been inscribed in an elegant, learned hand on the inside back board behind the
lower central drawer in an elaborate high chest of drawers (fig. 16.17), the name of this
otherwise obscure craftsman would not have surfaced. Part of an ambitious order of
fashionable and expensive furniture, the "Samuel Clement high chest" has come down
to us together with a dressing table made *en suite* for the Clement family's most reliable patrons, the French-Quaker Lawrence family of Flushing. Samuel Clement appraised these items himself when he inventoried Samuel Lawrence's household possessions in the summer of 1760. Included among Lawrence's polite personal effects
were "1 small chest Drawers & Dressing Table & Looking glass," a fashionable group-

ing valued at £4. Clement also inventoried "1 chest Drawers," together with a complete set of "1 Doz: Leather chairs," as well as a tablecloth and a few napkins, all appraised at a little more than £6.[176] Were these leather chairs made in New York City by Le Chevalier and upholstered by Faneuil?

The high chest (or "chest Drawers") (fig. 16.17), accompanying dressing table, and looking glass (now lost) represented the "mixed composition" that resulted from a Hogarthian dialogue between the innovation of novel international Anglo-French styles and prominent seventeenth-century Netherlandish forms that had been used traditionally to organize and contain valuable textiles. Such traditional forms remained popular and functional as signifiers of ethnic and family continuity in "Dutch" New York, at least until the influx of cosmopolitan Huguenot artisans from Aunis-Saintonge joined forces with their predecessors from the northern provinces of France. After that, these migrating Huguenot craft networks embarked on the transformation of material culture in New York and surrounding towns, just as they had done successfully in metropolitan London.

The chest of drawers became a likely focal point of change because it was considered an innovative, "English" furniture form, particularly in the pluralistic context of seventeenth-century New York, where such seemingly subtle distinctions of style and structure took on added significance. In Boston, the earliest chests of drawers were introduced to anglicizing elites by craftsmen from London—where the new form was already in fashion—sometime between the late 1630s and the early 1660s.[177] After the English takeover of New Amsterdam in 1664, the chest of drawers began to replace the Dutch kas among the rising Anglo-French elite, but for both symbolic and practical reasons, the kas (a type of large, freestanding upright cupboard with one or perhaps two exposed drawers at the bottom, found throughout Europe) (fig. 16.18), endured until the nineteenth century as an identifiable regional artifact among "Dutch" and other Continental inhabitants. However, as I argue elsewhere, virtually all the diverse European inhabitants of New Netherlands and New York owned kasten, and even inventories of British settlers list a kas or two in the household. This was invariably the case when English colonists married Netherlandish women, when the kas held the bride's trousseau of household linens and fabric. The kas identified this property as matrilineal, and it would remain with the woman throughout her lifetime. Despite their monolithic appearance, most kasten were easily disassembled, and hence mobile. Such massive, locked "cases" (presumably only women in the maternal line possessed a key) were intended for security and to keep special belongings separate from other property brought into the marriage through the wife's family, which might be claimed in common by the husband or male children. Women could use, transport, or bequeath the kas and its contents they pleased.[178]

This begs important questions about gendered material culture and its manifesta-

FIGURE 16.17. Samuel Clement, high chest of drawers, Flushing, Long Island, signed in the inscription and dated June 1726. H: 72″, W: 43⅜″, D: 24½″. Red gum, ash, elm, and catalpa. Courtesy Henry Francis du Pont Winterthur Museum, Winterthur, Delaware.

FIGURE 16.18. Oak kas, New York City or western Long Island, 1650–70. H: 67¼″, W: 66½″. © Art Institute of Chicago. This nearly square oak kas is the only surviving seventeenth-century New Amsterdam kas in the Netherlandish urban hardwood tradition. The design may have been derived from a pattern in Crespin de Passe the Younger (Dutch, 1593–1670), *Oficina arcularia* (Amsterdam, 1642).

tions in power relations, which cannot be answered here: were chests of drawers perceived by some subgroups of New York women as threatening novelties that unnaturally extended the boundaries of the traditional male domain? Did visible drawers demystify, reduce, reclassify, reorganize, or finally appropriate separate space formerly available to contain female possessions in the household?[179] Answers are not yet forthcoming, but because of competition from kasten, the metropolitan London chest of drawers, which performed the same practical function as the kas but relied on the innovation of a visible system of drawers that subdivided storage to organize fabrics and other accumulated items overtly appeared more frequently in the households of New York's Anglo-French (or Quaker-French) elite only in the 1680s. This may have reflected a lower percentage of English and Dutch intermarriage and higher aspirations to anglicization among non-British residents.

But if few early references are available for chests of drawers in New York, while many may be found for the "kas," "kast," or "Dutch cupboard," it is telling that the earliest record of a chest of drawers being *made* in the colony was noted in John Bowne's account book. In 1685, the year of the Revocation, Bowne hired the joiner William [Denears?; also Dener and Deneys] to build "one Chist of draw," arguably similar to the kaslike form from New York illustrated in figure 16.19. Bowne paid a hefty £1.13s., a substantial amount for furniture without textiles built into the cost.[180] This artisan was not from Flushing, as Bowne paid for shipping as well. Unfortunately, William's surname is barely legible through Bowne's unusually dense scrawl, but it is suggestive of the Huguenot de Nyse (or Denys) family of Flatbush. This family comprised a formidable clan of carpenters and joiners originating in La Rochelle, where "Denys" is one of the most common regional surnames. The first of the de Nyses emigrated via Utrecht to New Netherlands about 1638, an unusually early date for a southwestern origin. Many family members worked as carpenters or joiners in the western half of Long Island and Staten Island during the 1680s, though no William has yet come to light.[181]

It should come as no surprise, therefore, that the high chest of drawers and dressing table Clement made *en suite* in 1726 were hybrids of past and present patterns, forms peculiar to the region. The outlines of kasten thus remain visible as a palimpsest emerging from around the periphery of Samuel Clement's high chest. Memory of the older form is asserted in the large, overhanging cornice and wide, horizontal stance. A remnant of the gigantic kas was also framed visibly in construction of the tiny dressing table. Its "carcass" was joined to show the linked endgrain pins of Clement's distinctively sharp dovetails. Clement clearly used these joints decoratively: placing them as centripetal pendants on the object's two front corners. This idiosyncratic construction is common to kasten with western Long Island and northern New Jersey histories, where kasten continued to be made into the late eighteenth century. This method also survives on at least one other unsigned high chest attributed to Clement.[182]

Unmistakably of Flushing manufacture also are the heavily chamfered stretchers on the dressing table, which recall the meetinghouse bracket and the wainscot chair. Such chamfering is very unusual on dressing table stretchers. It has been identified only on artifacts attributed to the Clement family or with strong histories of ownership at the west end of Long Island. The robust turnings and flared edges of the legs on the high chest of drawers are also very characteristic of the New York French-Quaker style.

FIGURE 16.19. Chest of drawers, New York area, probably New York City, 1685–1715. H: 39½″, W: 41″, D: 23¼″. Black walnut, oak, yellow pine. Private collection. Photo, George Fistrovich. The subdivided English-style chest of drawers was slow to find space in New York households because of the cross-cultural endurance of the *kas*, which remained popular through the early nineteenth century. This rare early example of a chest of drawers from New York appropriated the standard English form but maintained both the square proportions and architectonic moldings of the *kas* in figure 16.18.

Here, the Clement artifacts harnessed the naturalistic three-dimensionality common to the Huguenot articulation of ornament on woodwork to the two-dimensional patterns of British ornamentation, which Palissy termed "artificial" and "unnatural." This emerged from the refugee affinity for the grotesque designs of sixteenth-century Italian grottoes and architecture. No wonder the slippery refugee Huguenot artisans were despised and emulated by London's native English craftsmen.

The cosmopolitan Samuel Lawrence must have found Clement's perfectly drawn

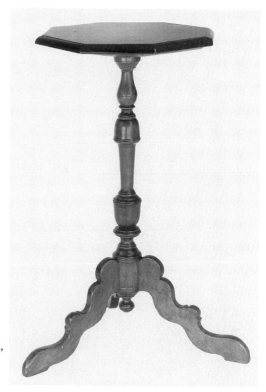

FIGURE 16.20. Stand attributed to Samuel Clement, Flushing, Long Island, 1720–30. H: 28⅝″, W: 18″, D: 18″. Red gum. Private collection.

baluster attenuated and its large molded disc and inverted flared vase "confortingly" (to borrow Story's word) reminiscent of baroque elements that his Laurent mercantile ancestors had seen everywhere on the Île de Ré and La Rochelle. The pattern was established when these same French sources were used for the stacked baluster tables made by the French-Quaker network in New York City. At the same time, however, there is no denying the resonance of this southwestern regional dialect with vernacular turned work seen in baroque northern French and Flemish furniture. After all, James Clement was likely from Tournay, not Saintonge. Yet by Samuel Clement's time, the new post-Revocation artisanal elite led by the likes of Faneuil and Lott had infiltrated and appropriated the old northern French and Flemish style—keeping some parts of it and jettisoning others—just as they had done to the old French–New Amsterdam craft networks.

The most effusive surviving example of this cosmopolitan style as it converged with Quaker life in the town of Flushing may be seen in a small stand with Samuel Clement's characteristic baluster: the signature Clement vase, inverted and doubled top and bottom in a mirror image, a tour de force of New-World French baroque turning (fig. 16.20). The conceptual framework of the mirror image—a classic Huguenot conceit, deployed by refugees in mediums from ceramics to silver and gold—was at the core of Palissy's cosmological use of live cast molds, virtual impressions of the natural world. So it is possible that Hogarth may have paid homage to this practice of doubling in palindromes and shadow worlds on and behind Hog Lane. Perhaps the extravagant scrolled and chamfered legs at the base, made in the fluid context of artisanal pluralism, were products of an alchemist's practical intuition (if not outright knowledge) of the plasticity of wood and other materials as they grew from seeds in the subterranean shadows of the natural world. Less speculative however, as we shall see, is the probability that Clement's expansive sense of the plasticity of his raw materials was linked to his exceptional skill as a calligrapher. In Clement's work, writing and artisanry communicated closely.

While it was possible to construct this partial inventory of Samuel Clement's very personal bricolage of diverse transatlantic and local material languages, how did his performance in making the high chest signify social and religious communication with people in Flushing? If the mirror image astonishes as a fragmentary conceit on the stand, then what results if the impulse was expanded like a genealogy, to build and contain the force of cosmological unity on the high chest? What distinguishes Samuel Clement's high chest from others outside the New York region is the binary subdivision of the drawers by use of light and dark inlay. This doubling effect was ramified by the superimposed pattern of hardware (shining like *étincelles*), a brass skeleton applied in the form of an exposed armature over the drawer fronts. The inlay gives the false appearance of separation. First, we confront the disguised double drawer, but appearances dissolve in hidden monistic unity after the drawers open to one receptacle inside. There, pulled from deep shadow, the effects of a life were contained and stored for future presentation.

According to the *Oxford English Dictionary,* the word "inlay" itself suggests the perfect material for refugee artisans in terms of both chronology and meaning. In 1598, inlay meant "concealment or preservation," as in, "to inlay or worke in among other things." Inlay also had strong linguistic or commemorative meanings in the seventeenth century, as in "Inscriptions and Epigraphs, cut, writ, inlaid, or engraven upon the Sepulchres." "[F]rom the worlds Common having sever'd thee, / Inlaid thee, neither to be seen, nor see," John Donne's "Elegie VII" (1631) reads. However, to infer the metaphysical operations laid bare in *In patientia suavitas* in 1628 (see fig. 9.1) from this remarkable etymology, taken together with the formal arrangement of inlay and ornament on a chest of drawers made in Flushing in 1726, will require more work. At the very least, if that "opening up" in 1628 resulted from violence of religious war, then by 1726, an analogous process occurred daily in the domestic solitude of Samuel Lawrence's French-Quaker home.

That is one reason why "skeleton" appropriately describes the unusual disposition of expensive brass hardware imported from London on Clement's high chest: a total of sixteen "drops" (handles) and backplates, and five "escutcheons" (lock plates), thirty-seven individual units of molded and stamped metal overall. In the same way that Leonardo's Vetruvian man mapped mathematical proportions onto the cosmological human body, and, more important for our purposes here, that the figure of man "microcosmus" centers all of Fludd's great universal cosmologies, the hardware skeleton on Samuel Clement's high chest of drawers maps the figure, spine, and head of the human torso, emerging as a microcosm from within the shadows of the double inlay.

But, following Fludd, this embodiment of form was not merely an exercise in the mathematics of proportion. The superimposed body emerges as an inextricable part of the material of the chest itself. Indeed, the shining brass armature stands in the nexus as the intermediary between matter and spirit, as a synthesis of both. To open the body of the high chest was to reveal the soulishness of its materials and construction; that is, of its artisan and perhaps its patron as well. As Fludd counseled, to look wisely at patterns of dots is to use experience to see beyond confusion on the surface to a place where beauty, truth, and unity are stored "in a chest" for use. This sense of body-spirit interaction inside and outside the material is also present in the dressing table, absent an all-important looking glass. This space of absence is decisive in its disfigurement of the early modern reality. For in 1726, to sit at a dressing table pondering one's image in the looking glass floating above its top was to see a vital reflection of one's upper torso "inlaid" (that is, set "in among") the material life of the furniture itself. The body in Clement's high chest was thus simultaneously light and dark, bifurcated and unified, spirit and matter, invisible and visible, as were Clement and Lawrence themselves.

❧ Spiritual Life in the Material World ❧

Material-holiness synthesis was a familiar part of everyday life for Huguenots and Quakers, as it was for many other sectarian groups with roots deep in Germanic pietism. Palissy spoke for Saintongeais Huguenot artisans in this vernacular. But the Quaker leader George Fox also thought deeply about this subject, writing that "the outward body is not the body of death and sin; the saints' bodies are the members of Christ and the temples of the living God."[183] Above all, of course, Fox stressed Quaker doctrines of bodily perfectibility in everyday life against the orthodox Calvinist emphasis on physical corruption and decline.[184]

Having found truth in the conversion experience, "children of the light" found perfect balance, calm, and vision. "Comfort" was achieved where no essential separation between spirit and matter in the natural world was perceptible. In this sense, every Quaker had the potential to possess the third eye of the geomancers. Historians of early modern science, especially Margaret C. Jacob, have shown how "inner light doctrines of the Quakers bore no small resemblance to the pantheism of the freethinkers," defined, ultimately, as a cosmology that *unified* matter and spirit:

> the pantheistic materialism of seventeenth-century radicals owed its origin to the magical and naturalistic view of the universe which Christian churchmen and theologians had labored for centuries to defeat. At the heart of this natural philosophy lay the notion that nature is a sufficient explanation or cause for the workings of man and his physical environment. In other words, the separation of God from creation, creature from creator, of matter from spirit, so basic to Christian orthodoxy and such a powerful justification for social hierarchy and even for absolute monarchy, crumbles in the face of animistic and naturalistic explanations. God does not create *ex nihilo;* nature simply is and all people (and their environment) are part of this greater All.[185]

Jacob's enterprise argues that sectarian passion for direct, emotional communication with the prelapsarian light of the Holy Spirit had the potential for universality. So, despite the desire for exclusivity on the part of scientists such as Howes and others, natural-philosophical practice as part of everyday religion was not exclusive and can be understood as an effective way in which Quakerism engaged and converged with other spiritualist and pietistic sects in colonial New York. Calling up the memory of the light, in order to see the world "with a *single Eye, in the unprejudiced Love of Truth,*" was the subject of dialogues with large numbers of "other people"—sectarians as well as heterodox Calvinists—who attended meetings in the Long Island Sound region to hear Story preach.[186] Examples are everywhere in the journal. At a Meeting in Taunton in 1704, one auditor challenged Thomas Story to reveal: "How do you know that it is not a Spirit of Delusion which you are guided by?" Story replied by analogy. "Then I asked him":

> "By what medium does thou discover the Sun in the Open Heavens? . . ." Then I continued and Said, "That as the Body of the Sun is not to be seen or known but by his own Light, and fully seen by that; neither is the Spirit of Truth, which is Divine, eternal, essential Light, known, or knowable but by himself; but is self-evident unto every Eye which he hath opened though the Children of Darkness of this world do not know Him: He who believeth hath the Witness in himself."[187]

How did the artisan Samuel Clement, an informal (or secret) Quaker, with his Huguenot family history, and his friend and patron Samuel Lawrence, who had a similar background but had long since acknowledged his membership in the Society of Friends, understand this complex process of cosmological synthesis and reunification of spirit and matter? How did they imagine that millennial experience was crafted into an article of material life for everyday use in the household? In other words, how do we elucidate the possibility that the dualistic pattern of inlay and brasses on the high chest, into which a figure of the human body as light in darkness may also have been inlaid, conformed perfectly with the available Bruno-Fludd paradigm for the art of memory in terms that Clement and Lawrence understood and might use themselves?

Thomas Story was a regular guest in the Bowne and Lawrence households between 1699 and 1705, so it is safe to assume that the Clement and Lawrence families both had an intimate knowledge of his teachings. Because both artisan and patron came of age by hearing him preach at local meetings, the very specific language of Thomas Story's conversion to the "truth" provides an opening onto how the cosmological framework of Flushing Quakerism was constructed by craftsmen in 1726. As Story made clear by making it prominent in his journal, and since his aim was conversion of "other people" to the truth, what could be more natural than to repeat the story of his own conversion experience at every Meeting on Long Island? Indeed, when the moment came in England in 1689 and he finally witnessed the truth unified and whole, Story drew an image with words of a pictograph that he might have seen in Fludd's great *Utriusque cosmi . . . historia;* or, for that matter, in a ceramic grotto crawling with "tiny" creatures constructed by Palissy:

> From henceforth I desired to know nothing but the Lord, and to feed on that Bread of Life which he himself alone can give, and did not fail to minister daily, and oftner than the Morning. And yet, of his own Free-Will and Goodness, he was pleased to open my Understanding, by Degrees, into all the needful Mysteries of his Kingdom, and the Truths of his Gospel; in the Process whereof he exercized my Mind in Dreams, in Visions, in Revelations, in Prophecies, in divine Openings and Demonstrations.
>
> Also, by his eternal and divine Light, Grace, Spirit, Power and Wisdom; by his word, he taught, instructed, and informed my Mind; and by Temptations also, and Provings, which he suffer'd Satan to minister; that I might see my own Weakness and Danger, and prove, to the utmost, the Force and Efficacy of that divine Love and Truth, by which the LORD, in his boundless Goodness and Mercy, has thus visited my Soul.
>
> By all Things I saw and heard in his wonderful Works of Creation; by my own Mind and Body, and the Connection and Duration of them as one for a Time; by their Separation, and the distinct Existence of each by itself in very different States and Modes, as if they had never been in Union, or composed one Man; by the differing States, Ranks, and Understandings of the Children of Men, their Superiority, Inferiority, Offenses and Aids, the Motive of every natural man to act regarding only himself.
>
> By the Animals, Reptiles, and Vegetables of the Earth and Sea, Their Ranks and Subserviences one to another, and all of them to the Children of Men.
>
> By the Sun, Moon, and Stars, the innumerable host of Heaven, and infinite Worlds, and that boundless Space that they move and roll in, without interfering, or in any way annoying one another, as all depending one upon another, as Meet Helps and Coadjutors;

all connected without a Chasm, and all govern'd by the steady Laws, which the Almighty Word and Fiat that gave them Being, and formed them, placed them under, and settled them in.

But, as the Diadim of all, and the only true and certain Way, when it pleased the Most High, by the Effusion of his own Goodness, to reveal in mye the Son of his Love, even his Wisdom and Power, by whom he design'd and effected all Things, then I was taught to fear him; then I was taught to love him; then, O! then, and not aright till then, was my Soul instructed and informed indeed.

But these secret Operations were confin'd to my own Breast, so that no one knew anything of them; only an alteration was observ'd in me, but the Cause of it was not seen . . . I declined the public Worship.[188]

Story's reinvention of the divine knowledge of Nature "by Degrees, into all the needful Mysteries," as a Quaker variation of Fludd's monistic universe created a viable context for pluralistic cultural interaction and the simultaneous maintenance of personal, material, and spatial boundaries. His ecstatic vision of a universe teeming with the fecundity of animated life on elemental earth, in the sea, and in the air, encircling one another—like the concentric orbs of Flood's cosmologies (see fig. 2.3), or Bruno's memory diagrams—reimagines the constellations of the "Sun, Moon, and Stars, the innumerable host of heaven, and infinite worlds, and that boundless Space that they move and roll in, without interfering, or any way annoying one another . . . all connected without a chasm." This seamless connection was the bond and knot of the soul, so it was internal, not to be found in "public worship." Thomas Story's international mission, therefore, was to *perceive* a universal community with others like himself, for whom "these secret Operations were confin'd to my own Breast, so that no one knew anything of them . . . the Cause of it was not seen." To see and hear from the perspective of tiny creatures below the tower (beneath the chaos of Babel) was reason enough for Quaker belief in the power of silence and the quiet, secure discourse of craft, like Bownas and Palissy before him. Story's was indeed a geomantic project, an alchemist's task: to dissolve surface confusions and see the profound and secret truths in order to become a "Coadjutor" (or magus); spiritual and material witness to "an Alteration . . . observ'd in me," in other people. To effect a convergence of everything alive in the spirit and remake the world with this shared "Wisdom and Power."

✧ Inner Writing ✧

The aim of Story's mission in the Long Island Sound region was to reconstruct in New York society "all the things I saw and heard in his wonderful Works of Creation; by my own Mind and Body, and the Connection and Duration of Them as one *for a*

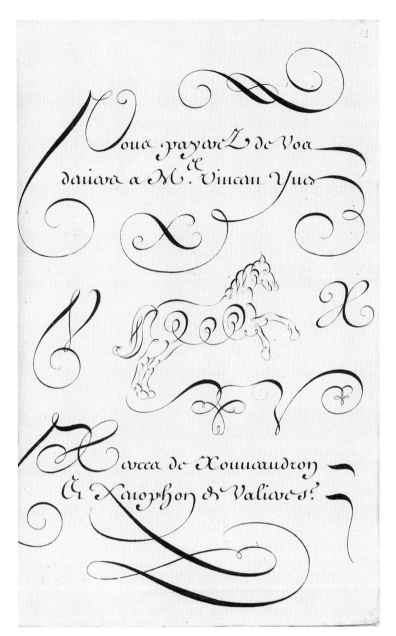

FIGURE 16.21. Page of exercises from Étienne de Blégny, *Les Elemens; ou, premieres instructions de la jeunesse* (Paris, 1702). Courtesy Harry Ransom Humanities Research Center, The University of Texas at Austin. This page for teaching young children penmanship is from the section entitled: "New examples of writing of singular beauty by Estienne de Blegny Master Writer in Paris." Compare the scroll behind the horse's rear with Samuel Clement's T in figure 16.16 and the scroll foot on the tea table in figure 16.22.

Time." This was not to demolish the all-important independence of each individual creature. Individuals moved like industrious atoms, each in its own orbit, "by their Separation, and the distinct Existence of each by itself, in very different States and Modes, as if they had never been in Union, or composed one Man." Thus, unlike the elder Winthrop's model of the body, these flexible parts could function separately *or* connected to the whole, as the universal spirit moved them, all according to God's plan. "Secret operations" of personal and communal experience converge in the form, function and material life of Samuel Clement's high chest. Here was a pluralistic body of diverse moveable parts. Clement tells us so himself, in the ornate language of the artifact's most secret "inlaid" element: its deftly hidden inscription. "This was made in ye Year 1726," he wrote in that baroque scrivener's hand, "By me Samuel Clement of fflushing" (fig. 16.16).

This fragmentary inscription carried the weight of layers of personal history and meaning for Samuel Clement, and he chose his words with care. I say personal, because the inscription was hidden. It is difficult to read a label of colonial advertising or a public warranty of workmanship here, since no patron was expected to know of its existence. Because his difficult and controlling father had died just the year before, and because this signature and inscription are unique in Clement's oeuvre, it is difficult not to read this as a sort of declaration of independence by a subjugated son and apprentice. This was made "By *me Samuel* Clement." Still, such loaded sentiments are never unambiguous; neither, to be sure, are language or motivation. The completion of this complex project was at the same time a mark of pride in his father's training, as if to say to himself, here is proof that I have mastered the family craft and am the next Clement in line, here in Flushing. Remember, Samuel was one of the favored sons gifted in James's will, so it is difficult to infer hard feelings on the face of things.

Much easier to see was Clement's obvious pride in mastery of elegant and learned penmanship, the other family trade. Here, too, was a hand tool skill, passed from master to apprentice (or father to son) with the help of penmanship manuals widely available in the Atlantic world since the sixteenth century. On the basis both of its intended audience and illustrated plates, one influential manual by Étienne de Blégny (active Paris, 1666–99), *Les Elemens; ou, Premieres instructions de la jeunesse* (Paris, 1691), seems particularly suggestive, given the relationship between James and Samuel (fig. 16.21). De Blégny dedicated his book to "fathers of the family," to help instruct their young sons in practical application of what he called the "principes des lettres." This immensely popular manual went through numerous editions between 1691 and 1751, making *Instructions de la jeunesse* widely available throughout the Atlantic world.[189] Did James, like so many other fathers, use this particular manual as Samuel's writing primer? If James Clement's single handwritten entry in the Bowne account books is indicative of his awkward skill as a scribe, then Samuel Clement far surpassed his father in this craft. In the shadows of his work, Samuel showed his own brand of "inner writing"; that is to say, his confidence and personal mastery of the hidden unity of material life, in private, by skillfully synthesizing the arts of the scribe and the joiner.

On first glance at the inscription, what appears to be an elaborate calligraphic $\mathcal{T}$ doubles as a powerfully drawn French baroque scroll. This flamboyant letter may have been copied directly from the exercise illustrated in figure 16.21, with particular attention to the scroll behind the hindquarters of the capering stallion; indeed, the scroll appears to echo the rearing horse's back leg and hoof. The deep chamfers "of fflushing" reappear here; stroked heavily along the upper pair of ascending and descending marks—Hogarth's lines of beauty—while the masterful volute at bottom, reminiscent of Palissy's snail, was performed without risk by using Clement's joiner's compass. Perceived as something other than a T, this collection of scrivener's marks also matches the "capering" foot of a tea table (fig. 16.22) made for the anglicized Dutchman Peter Schuyler in New York City or western Long Island in the same period as the high chest. Did Clement have a hand in its manufacture? Turned counterclockwise an imaginary ninety degrees (so that the bottom of the volute rests between the l in Samuel and the C in Clement), the T underwent another metamorphosis. Now it transformed into a scroll identical to those carved on the crest rail of the joined armchair (fig. 16.13), with drawknife work done in the tradition of the meetinghouse bracket. In the shadows of the work, writing and artisanry were "all connected without a Chasm." Samuel Clement's inscription, harnessed to a secret recess behind the "operation" of his high chest, was, like the soul of its maker, silent and eloquent at once.

Still, there is evidence that the specific language of Samuel Clement's inscription had a transatlantic history in public as well as private life. In both the artisanal and the political sense, the message was both a pluralistic and hybridized construction. For Clement to write: "made . . . By me," was an unusually formal method of framing a relatively common possessive sentence in English. The "me" seeming superfluous from this distance, though it might connote that "Samuel Clement" was his signature and not simply part of a declarative sentence about him. Here too, there are French antecedents. Furniture was rarely signed in eighteenth-century Aunis-Saintonge, or in the Poitou region, but if so, the artisan's signature commonly followed "faite par moi" (made by me).

Closer to home, Samuel Clement's inscription was the artisanal equivalent of the notarial inscription that ended the written text of the Flushing Remonstrance, the Quaker manifesto on Stuyvesant's absolutism. This inscription read: "Written this 27 day of December, in the year 1657, by mee Edward Hart, Clericus." James Clement would eventually succeed Edward Hart as town clerk of Flushing. So Samuel probably learned this idiosyncratic turn of phrase from his notarial father and adapted it to the inscription he hid inside his joinery: Samuel Clement's own manifesto. Nature's

FIGURE 16.22. Tea table, New York City, ca. 1700. H: 27½″, W: 30″, D: 19½″. Mahogany and cherry. Courtesy Henry Francis du Pont Winterthur Museum, Winterthur, Delaware. This table, incorporating mahogany, an exotic wood imported at great expense from Latin America, was first the property of Peter Schuyler of Albany. It conveyed lightness when moved into position to serve tea or other New World repasts using exotic staples, such as cocoa or rum. The scroll foot compares favorably with the scroll that emulates the hoof of the "capering horse" in figure 16.21, a related early-eighteenth-century artifact that also conveyed the hand's mastery of a light touch, and the scroll on the T in Samuel Clement's inscription in figure 16.16. The table's foot has pronounced edgework analogous to scrolls cresting the chair in figure 16.13.

ape had identified himself as an artisanal microcosm located at the celestial center "of fflushing," where "this was made in ye Year 1726 By me."

Samuel Clement had thus constructed for a Quaker patron a Fluddian cosmology of his bodily and spiritual world in the material culture of a specific place and its relation to the universe as revealed with precision in a single synchronic moment. Such lucid moments of unity were also the goal of Palissy's artisanry, mediated by his walks along the shore of the Charente River, where he heard the harmonies of Marot's psalms sung by the seven earth spirits. Here, then, was the theater of memory in which Story could imagine were contained "all Things I saw and heard in his wonderful Works of Creation; by my own Mind and Body, and the Connection and Duration of Them as one for a Time." Yet the Flushing Remonstrance codified as both social and political discourse the conceptual framework by which personal constructions of a pluralistic cosmos could take place and converge in colonial New York.

❧ The Flushing Remonstrance (1657) ❧

The Flushing Remonstrance is a crucial document of the multilayered history of the transatlantic struggles that pitted the interests of "orthodoxy" against vigorous response by sectarian dissent in the heterodox New Netherlands / New York colony. Official confessions—whether Dutch Reformed or Church of England—were on the defensive in the atmosphere of extensive religious privatization that prevailed throughout the Protestant world during the 1650s.[190]

Notions of the power of the Dutch Reformed Church to assert discipline in New Netherlands were mitigated by the social reality of life in a New World refugee culture filtered through the way stations of the Dutch Republic. Historians have estimated that while 37 percent of the population of the Dutch Republic belonged to the Calvinist Church in the 1640s, only 20 percent of New Netherlands's colonists *may* have been formally Calvinist.[191]

The usefulness of this statistic is complicated by the diversity of personal experience, linguistic, and ethnic difference and the variety of religious practices among refugee colonists who called themselves "Calvinist." Comparative scholarship on early modern Holland suggests that as early as the 1560s, in provincial Utrecht, 80 percent of the faithful actively and defiantly engaged in some form of heterodox lay piety, and often in Catholic backsliding.[192] The Utrecht Synod inventoried slight improvement in discipline by 1606, when "the state" of eight provincial churches was evaluated. In the town of Houten, "The minister reported the dismal state of his church; few attended because of a former priest . . . who keeps watch on the inhabitants . . . and threatens them with damnation if they go to church . . . also inducing some inhabitants to stand by the church and to jeer at those who enter. . . . [He] also showed certain sheep, etc., made of wax which the inhabitants even offered in church during service." In Abcoude, the minister "complained about some assembly of Anabaptists. Also . . . the inhabitants often . . . take part in papist exercises held in certain houses." And, in the town of Amerongen, the church "suffered from having been very badly ruined as a result of destruction inflicted by soldiers . . . the congregation also leaves the church when baptism is administered before the public prayer and general blessing; the superstitions associated with St. Cunerus's Day are very detrimental . . . [and] the schoolmaster teaches from books of all sorts, whatever comes to hand." The same problem of the availability of heterodox books and their use in pedagogy by universalist minded schoolmasters plagued Montfoort, where, "though the schoolmaster is of the Reformed religion, he uses books of all sorts."[193]

Intense competition over the formal and spiritual boundaries of religion extended to New Netherlands. The West India Company tried hard to exert a moderating influence on those orthodox Dutch Reformed churchmen who wanted the New World to be the place where full conformity, then unattainable in the Netherlands, might finally be achieved. When Flushing was granted a town patent by Director-General Willem Kieft on October 10, 1645, the pragmatic West India Company, shepherding New Netherlands through its early development from an isolated fur trading outpost to a fledgling colonial society, was more concerned with attracting settlers than suppressing sectarianism. After all, the Netherlands itself swelled with refugees from war and religious intolerance. This signaled a culture to support the general program of colonization. As a result, both the directors and investors in the West India Company were especially concerned with the need to protect their investments by keeping the English at bay, in part by peopling the fluid frontier zone between Manhattan Island and southern coastal New England.

In ideal terms, the West India Company preferred to plant a uniform religious culture in New Netherlands. However, the need for a huge influx of settlers, not potential for sedition or subversion of authority by religious dissenters, was the primary agenda in the 1640s and 1650s. The directors understood that they were engaged in an alarmingly fragile and fluid religious situation that required flexibility on the part of their director-general. Kieft followed orders closely in the latitudinarian terms he offered in the first Flushing patent, which clearly stated that townspeople (much like burghers in some areas of the Dutch Republic) could expect a high level of freedom from interference by magistrates in New Amsterdam in the conduct of personal religious affairs. Residents, "would have and Enjoy the Liberty of Conscience, according to the Custome and manner of Holland, without molestacon or disturbance, from any Magistrate or Magistrates, or any other Ecclesiasticall Minister, that may prtend Jurisdiccon over them."[194]

Nevertheless, "Liberty of Conscience" must not be misread as total. Officially, "free" public worship in New Netherlands meant Calvinist. The ambiguity was intentional; a strategy to privilege security of accommodation over risks of conflict. The unintended (but not necessarily unforeseen) consequence of this strategy was to encourage an increase in the defiant practice of religious interiority and privatization in New Netherlands, since "conscience" meant private "belief" extended to personal practice. By local custom and Company policy, director-generals were expected to "connive" (*conniventie*) or "wink at" (*oogluijckinge*) heterodoxy. In perceptual language that

Bernard Palissy, Robert Fludd, Samuel Bownas, Thomas Story, the Clements, and Hogarth all understood, authority agreed to see and overlook, simultaneously.[195] Put another way, the relation of perception to authority was negotiable in New Netherlands. Problems arose when one of the conniving parties decided something seen was non-negotiable. Usually, this occurred when tacit rules were thought to be broken.

The physical existence of Kieft's document, which came into the possession of John Bowne, would haunt Stuyvesant in the last two years of his term as director-general (1647–64). It allowed Bowne to describe himself and his Flushing "friends" as "oppressed" Christians to Company directors in Amsterdam in 1663, when he took James Clement as a bonded servant. Stuyvesant had seen the old rules that limited negotiable space, fostered by the intentional ambiguity of the Company's use of "liberty of conscience," expanded by sectarian practice to effectively neutralize his notion of what his masters meant by minimal orthodoxy and Church discipline. The established Church in parts of New Netherlands was facing the same degree of disintegration as was then occurring deplorably in parts of Utrecht. For Stuyvesant, the Flushing Patent assumed the status of a radical disestablishmentarian manifesto, which transformed western Long Island into virtually open religious territory—or, at least, even more heterodox territory than before.

Pluralism and heterodoxy had always been present. No single political document was the instrument of change when it may simply have reflected the reality already present on the ground. Still, codification of its language of ambiguity toward personal religiosity and heterodoxy should not be underestimated as a force in the cultural development of this region and in the social self-selection of its immigrants. More than ever before, western towns were targets of opportunity for settlement and expansion by land-hungry sectarians. Pietists, dissenters, and seekers of every persuasion flooded unabated into Long Island from England and Europe, as well as diverse varieties of nonconformists from Massachusetts, Rhode Island, coastal Connecticut, and Pennsylvania.

In August 1657, already chafing at the restraint applied by the patent's latitudinarian language, the famously choleric Stuyvesant, an orthodox Calvinist, was openly threatened by the arrival in New Amsterdam—"whither they had movings"—of five proselytizing English Quakers who had disembarked unexpectedly from an English ship called the *Woodhouse*, originally en route to Boston. The five English preachers were led off the boat on the East River shore by Robert Hodgson. He was followed by Richard Doudney, Sarah Gibbons, Mary Wetherhead, and Dorothy Waugh. Stuyvesant was strongly influenced by orthodox clergy in the Dutch Republic. His mentors back home had worked feverishly to fill the pews and suppress the sects and Catholicism throughout the seventeenth century, and he was already anxious over the relatively low numbers of Calvinists who attended the official Church of New Netherlands. Still, representatives of the group were received graciously by Stuyvesant, who appeared at first "moderate both in words and actions."[196] When two of the women attempted to preach in the streets of the city, however, they were arrested for disturbing the peace and imprisoned for eight days. Finally, they were paraded through the streets with their hands tied behind their backs and banished to Rhode Island. Stuyvesant responded to the challenge of heterodoxy in the city as the elder John Winthrop did in Boston. Heterodoxy and sectarianism was always dangerous to the colonial leadership. If it was tolerated by default on the near frontier, it must have been considered absolutely intolerable at the seat of government.

Thus, the remaining party of two men and one woman wisely crossed onto Long Island and traveled south and east to Gravesend, Jamaica, and Hempstead, where they knew there were "many sincere seekers after Heavenly riches, and were prepared to appreciate those Spiritual views of religion which these Gospel messengers had to declare."[197] Then two Friends continued east to the "Puritan" end of the island. From there they sailed north across the Sound to join the Quaker community in Rhode Island, leaving Robert Hodgson behind in Hempstead, where seekers "rejoiced in the spread of those living truths which were preached among them."

Hempstead was the site of a well-established Calvinist congregation in 1657, so there was local antagonism toward Hodgson's presence in town. Moreover, the justice of the peace, Henry Gildersleeve, owed his appointment to Stuyvesant. While awaiting a Friends Meeting that he had organized, Hodgson was arrested and imprisoned. Ultimately, a contingent of soldiers was sent out by Stuyvesant himself from New Amsterdam to take charge of the prisoner. Hodgson was tortured, dragged behind a cart from Hempstead to New Amsterdam, and imprisoned in the fort. After five weeks, he was freed to join his co-religionists banished to Rhode Island. This concluded the first period where violence was used to persecute Quakers in New York.[198]

Paralleling early Reformation history of Saintonge in the civil war years, when the cream of the Genevan ministry in the region was killed, retreated to the fortress at La Rochelle, or went in to hiding, Quakers, and other Long Island sects benefited from distance from the city and the absence of ministers from established congregations in New Amsterdam's hinterlands. Learned and lay sectarian preachers with ideas quite similar to Palissy's, and perhaps James Clement's, had the field to themselves. The case for conversion was undoubtedly made much stronger by calling attention to the despised practice in some of the western towns (including Hempstead) to tithe for upkeep of the established Church.[199]

Before his imprisonment and banishment, Robert Hodgson was thought to have been responsible for the conversion of John Bowne (1627–95), who migrated to New Netherlands from New England in the early 1650s, to become the most politically influential Quaker in New York during the seventeenth century. Bowne's house was favored for the first Flushing Quaker conventicles. The conventicles also occurred out-side in *désert* conditions or in other private houses until 1694, when the meetinghouse opened in Flushing. Stuyvesant challenged conventicles as subversive, secretive prac-tices, but he was largely unsuccessful in preventing them.

This is not to say that Stuyvesant's creatures on Long Island did not act vigorously in his name. Henry Gildersleeve always kept careful watch over Hempstead's inhabi-tants. In 1658, after Hodgson's tour of the region and capture, Gildersleeve presided over the trial of the wives of two prominent freemen of the town for heresy.

As with Ginzburg's and Martin's northern Italian heretics, there was circular ex-change between adversaries—in effect, an adversarial convergence of information—made more potent by the fact that all the participants in this dialogue were of the same social and intellectual order. Knowledge was communicated in trial testimony and by "woeful experience." Thus, dialogues between Quakers and inquisitors revealed that the Holy Spirit flourished in secret places outside the town, out in the "natural" world, and to "hold converse" in near proximity to these "seducing spirits" was to risk unity with them. Fear emerged from what Fludd's *Internal Principle* describes in both sci-entific and metaphysical terms as "a way of knowing that depends immediately on the soul," considering the soul's capacity to "leave its body so as to find a place whence it could enter into communication, and converse, with the souls of . . . friends":

> Forasmuch as Mary, wife of Joseph Schott, and the wife of Francis Weeks, have, contrary
> to the laws of God and this place, not only absented themselves from public worship but
> profaned the Lord's day by going to a conventicle in the woods where were two Quakers,
> and now justify their act by saying they know of no transgression they had done, for they
> went to meet the people of God, it is ordered that each party shall pay 20 guilders and
> costs. Whereas we find by woeful experience that of late a sect hath taken such ill effect
> amongst us as to seduce certain of our inhabitants who (giving heed to seducing spirits
> under the notion of their being inspired by the Holy Spirit of God) have profaned the
> Sabbath and neglected to join with us in the true worship of God as formerly they have
> done, now be it ordered that no person whatsoever shall give entertainment to or hold
> converse with the people called Quakers, or lodge them in their house but for one night
> only, and then they are to depart quietly and without debate next morning.[200]

This interdiction emanating to its hinterlands from New Amsterdam had little effect in places like Hempstead, and none in Flushing, where loss of Bowne's Quaker patronage was more feared by inhabitants than any government edict. To "hold con-verse with the people called Quakers" was to map the most significant family relations on the west end of Long Island in the seventeenth century. Bowne's sister-in-law was, moreover, the wife of the itinerant Boston mercenary and infamous Indian fighter

Captain John Underhill (1597–1672), the younger Winthrop's old friend, comrade-in-arms, and correspondent.

If Captain Underhill's formal religious allegiance is not absolutely certain, it is telling that his wife joined the Society of Friends a short time before, during a clandestine Meeting at the coastal town of Oyster Bay, on the north shore of Long Island.[201] Perhaps like the Clement men, Underhill was not necessarily a formal Quaker, but he was sympathetic and well connected by marriage to the elastic Quaker economic, political, and military networks dispersed around the Sound.

It is important to know that Underhill was associated closely with the antinomian controversy in Boston in 1637 and was in sympathy with John Wheelwright (1592–1679), who was banished to Exeter, New Hampshire, by the elder Winthrop for belief in personal dominion by the Holy Spirit. Underhill himself was accused of the heresy and was banished briefly as well. The Massachusetts general court recorded that after voyaging to Boston from England in 1638, Underhill:

> was questioned for some speeches uttered by him in the ship, viz: that they at Boston were zealous as the scribes and pharisees were and as Paul was before his conversion, which he denying, they were proved to his face by a sober woman whom he had seduced in the ship and drawn to his opinion; but she was afterwards better informed in the truth. Among other passages, he told her how he came by his assurance, saying that, having long lain under a spirit of bondage, and continued in a legal way [that is, as a follower of covenantal theology] near five years, he could get no assurance, till at length, as he was taking a pipe of the good creature tobacco, the spirit fell home upon his heart, an absolute promise of free grace, with such assurance and joy, as he never doubted since of his good estate, neither should he, whatsoever sin he should fall into. . . . The next day he was called again and banished. The Lord's day after, he made a speech to the assembly, showing that as the Lord was pleased to convert Paul as he was persecuting, &c, so he might manifest himself to him as he was making moderate use of the good creature called tobacco.[202]

Underhill's banishment was rescinded after he made an abject and tearful public apology for these heretical statements, especially that the spirit materialized in the smoke he inhaled from the "good creature tobacco," communicating to him "an absolute promise of free grace . . . whatsover sin he should fall into." An eccentric spiritual insight (or perhaps a joke) like this—while heretical in Boston—would not have seemed strange if voiced as testimony at most Quaker meetings attended by Thomas Story on Long Island.

Family relations seemed to facilitate John Bowne's conversion to Quakerism. New members were always "introduced" to the Flushing Meeting through family connections, testifying to the candidate's moral and economic fitness for membership. The younger Winthrop had already received a stellar letter of introduction from his old friend and comrade-in-arms John Underhill on Bowne's behalf, dated April 12, 1656, although this correspondence contained another sort of testimony. Underhill recommended Bowne to his powerful and expansionistic patron as a "verri jentiele young man, of gud abilliti, of a lovli fetture, and gud behafior."

This was not idle gossip. As a New World courtier, Winthrop wished to extend his already substantial scientific, economic, and military interests through patronage of aspiring elites of the Long Island Sound basin, including Bowne, always with a covetous eye on the ultimate prize of New Amsterdam.[203] Winthrop's ambitious political agenda included influence over the growing population of English and anglicized continental settlers in Flushing, already an affluent town of farmers, artisans, and traders. Flushing's strategic importance was evident: it stood on the water equidistant between Manhattan Island and Brooklyn. Soon after the death of his father in 1649 freed him from Massachusetts, Winthrop began to extend his patronage web through Long Island. His network of correspondence extended west to New Amsterdam, where Winthrop used his status and multilingual skills to maintain close contact with members of the city council. This included a constant dialogue with the director-general, who maintained cordial relations with this ambitious Englishman who wrote and spoke in Dutch, if only to keep an eye on him.[204] These actions on Long Island shed a somewhat different light on Roger Williams's praiseful letter of 1660, about Winthrop's moderation toward Quakers, and his "tendernes toward mens soules, especially for conscience sake to God." They also contextualize Winthrop's remarkable refusal to sign without qualification, the act of September 23, 1658, sponsored by the United Colonies of New England, to banish, maim, or put to death, any Quakers who entered its domain. Winthrop was the only U.C.N.E. commissioner to devalue the document by signing it "a query and not an act."[205]

Winthrop's relationship with Underhill was among the longest and most illuminating of all his network contacts on Long Island. Born in Warwickshire in 1597 (not far from John Bowne's home region of Northampton), Underhill trained as a soldier in the Netherlands. In 1630, he migrated west to follow his call to arms in the service of the insecure first generation of Massachusetts settlers. After the apocalyptic events of 1628, Underhill was employed to supervise militia training and instill military discipline in the colonists, whose leaders were fearful of French settlers to the north and the Pequot Indians in their midst.

Underhill's military training in the Netherlands and his approach to martial discipline and warfare was experiential and practical. This reformation of martial practices was shared by his Paracelsian patron. When serving as commander of Salem's militia, Underhill asserted a firm belief that experience and merit, not appointment as "placemen" based on patronage or social rank, was essential to the effectiveness and prestige of the Bay colony's officer corps:

> their own appointment made them a captain, lieutenant & enseign, & after such a man-
> ner as was never heard of in any school of war, nor in no kingdom under heaven. . . . For
> my part, if there should not be a reformation in this disordered practice, I should not ac-
> knowledge such officers. If officers should be of no better esteem than for constables to
> place them, & martial discipline to proceed disorderly, I would rather lay down my com-
> mand than to shame so noble a prince [of Orange] from whom we came.[206]

Having also served a military apprenticeship as part of his natural-philosophical training in Ireland and England—befitting the firm place of fortification in Fludd's *De naturae simia*—and then gaining practical experience at the siege of La Rochelle in 1627–28, Winthrop followed his father to Boston, where his first official title was master of fortifications. Underhill and Winthrop worked together on security matters in the colonies from the earliest date of settlement. Initially, this concerned matters of basic survival and defense, but increasingly over time security was redefined in terms of aggressive land acquisition and cultural expansion. Defense and aggression were inseparable.

The professional closeness between these two ambitious men was made clear in 1636 by their murderous cooperation in the bloody Pequot war. Governor John Winthrop Sr. authorized his son (then governor of Saybrook) to represent Massachusetts in negotiations with the weakened Pequot. The negotiations were a thinly veiled pretense for the younger Winthrop to issue a "provoking ultimatum" to the Pequot and their allies. From the New England perspective, a war to annihilate this group was both desirable and inevitable. Under Winthrop's strategic direction, and by John Endicott's and Underhill's military command, ninety heavily armed and armored volunteers set out on a punitive expedition. First, they sortied against the Indians on Block Island. Returning to the mainland, the volunteers were then to invade Pequot strongholds. Winthrop's strategy of land-clearing violence for profit was uncharacteristically unambiguous. He loathed the Pequot as savage and dangerous; an impediment to his plans. Once the volunteers reached Block Island, he made it known that "John Underhill, was commissioned to kill the men of the tribe, enslave the women and children as booty, and take possession of the island."[207] In the event, the Amerindians of Block Island avoided their frustrated adversaries by stealth.

After the ninety Massachusetts volunteers withdrew and went home to the Bay, a flabbergasted Lieutenant Lion Gardiner (1599–1663) and twenty men were left behind at Fort Saybrook to face the Pequot alone. Like Underhill, Lion Gardiner, was military client of John Winthrop Jr.'s. Gardiner had also trained in fortification under the prince of Orange and had acquired extensive landholdings on Long Island.[208] In 1640, Gardiner removed there from Connecticut. He bought a coastal island on Long Island's east end of some 3,300 acres, which the aspiring Gardiner called the Isle of Wight. In 1686, Lion's son David achieved his father's lordly ambitions and secured a manorial patent for the family's island.[209]

But before his removal to the Isle of Wight, Gardiner had to survive the nine-month siege of his contingent of defenders at Fort Saybrook, as the Pequot retaliated for the failed expedition from Massachusetts. Captain Underhill's next expedition against Pequot forces was more successful, as success was measured in bloodshed. Indeed, Underhill's role in the Connecticut-Mohegan attack in May 1637 against the Pequot fortified settlement on the Mystic River initiated one of the most appalling episodes in the entire history of English-Indian interaction.

This Pequot settlement controlled the strategic mouth of the Connecticut River, and its elimination had everything to do with John Winthrop Jr.'s designs on hegemony of Long Island. Both Winthrop and his New England allies were in competition with the equally aggressive Pequot to absorb the Montauk Indians of eastern Long Island, and with them, their unequalled capacity to produce and supply the wampum essential to the Indian fur trade. Were the Pequot to prevail, they would dominate the supply side of the fur trade. Moreover, a hostile force would gain control of the many Indian villages on the east end of Long Island, already a dangerous place for European settlers. The Pequot were therefore an enormous impediment for Winthrop and his imperialistic ambitions.[210]

Using an innovative combination of stealthiness and fire to contain their Pequot enemies, English soldiers under the command of Underhill and John Mason encircled Mystic Fort with an inner ring of English armed with snaphances (flintlock muskets) and a second, outer ring manned by their Narragansett allies (fig. 16.23). The English, headed by Mason's contingent from Connecticut, did not trust their Indian allies to attack, since the fort contained women and children, not warriors, as depicted in the famous print of the siege.

Mystic Fort was the Pequot's La Rochelle. As with the siege of the Huguenot fortress, the fall of Mystic Fort effectively ended the Pequot War. The destruction was total. To the surprise and disgust of the Narragansetts, Mason and Underhill ordered the fort burned and every survivor killed. Just five of the five hundred defenders and their families managed to escape.[211]

The mind of John Winthrop Jr. was behind the innovative, indirect, and ruthless strategy that allowed the English to surround the town undetected, leading to the fort's reduction. His hand is even more evident in the famous engraving by RH. Here, the attack on the fortress was raised to cosmological proportions in a Fluddian image largely inspired by the wars of religion, and above all by the siege of La Rochelle it-

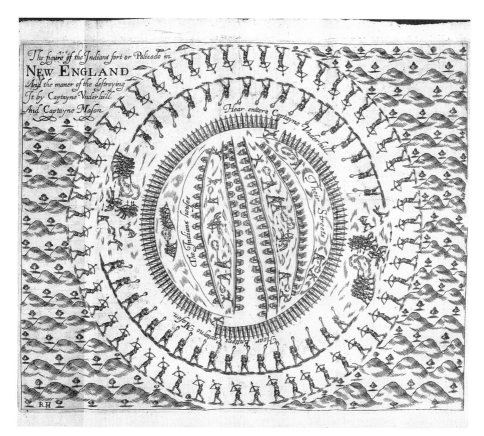

FIGURE 16.23. "The figure of the Indians fort or Palizado in NEW ENGLAND And the maner of the destroying It by Captayne Underhill and Captayne Mason." Engraving by "RH" from the text by Captain John Underhill (London: J. Dawson for P. Cole, 1638). Reproduced by permission of The Huntington Library, San Marino, California. RB 3391. Cosmological representation of the notorious reduction of the Pequot fortress at the mouth of the Connecticut River on Long Island Sound and subsequent slaughter of the inhabitants, under the command of John Underhill and John Mason, two clients of John Winthrop Jr.'s. This image contains striking similarities to Robert Fludd's "Enemies Invading the Fortress of Health," in figure 10.8, with God and his demonic winds attacking from every direction, proving the corruption of the victim's soul. The analogy may have an ironic historical source. The Narragansett warriors allied with the English (depicted on the outer circle) were so appalled by the loss of life by their enemy that they called the attack "evil." Winthrop collected most of Fludd's books for his alchemical library.

self. Violent "winds" of disease (see fig. 10.8) are reversed, and the winds of purification become destroyers of the Pequot. Like Palissy, Winthrop would "build with the destroyer."

Mason and Lion Gardiner also wrote accounts of the siege, but only Underhill's was published, along with a print depicting the attack (fig. 16.23), as part of a collection called the *Newes from America; or a new discoverie of New England* (London, 1638). It was an effective advertisement for other land-hungry patrons with designs on the colonies. After his widely publicized success of 1637–38, Underhill's military career flourished and merged with Winthrop's economic and natural-philosophical ambitions. With the mouth of the Connecticut River secure, these old allies turned their attention south across the Sound toward their goal of absorption of New Netherlands.

Now famous for his efficient removal of local impediments to European expansion, Underhill appeared in New Netherlands in 1643. Underhill's military training in the Netherlands, and his consequent knowledge of rudimentary Dutch, made him Director-General Kieft's logical choice for mercenary commander of an Anglo-Dutch militia in the ongoing Mohawk wars. Using the same stealthy strategy followed by encircling by the armored musketeers that had proved so successful at Mystic Fort, Underhill led a force of 130 men on a night attack against a large Tankiteke or Siwanoy village, which again resulted in the massacre of nearly five hundred Indians. The effectiveness and grim brutality of Underhill's involvement facilitated the signing of a friendship treaty between the Dutch, the Mohawk, and the Mahican at Fort Orange in July 1645.[212] Underhill was paid for his military service with land, including parcels in the city and on Long Island. He chose to remain in the region, where his military training in Holland, pidgin Dutch, impressive contacts among competitors in New England, ambiguous religiosity, and exploits in the Indian wars of the Hudson Valley facilitated his rapid rise in the Dutch colony's military bureaucracy. Ultimately, he joined the director-general's inner circle as a member of his advisory committee.

Using his new political influence, Underhill moved quickly to extend his landholdings on Long Island. In 1648, as part of this thrust into the hinterland of New Netherlands, he secured a sensitive appointment as sheriff of Flushing from Stuyvesant. Stuyvesant had tried in the past to extend political power onto the island through patronage and appointments of sheriffs and justices of the peace. In this instance, Stuyvesant felt that Underhill had been made *his* client at Winthrop's expense. This was a real mistake in light of Underhill's loyalty to Winthrop, his hidden Quaker sympathies, and network of association.

During Underhill's sojourn in Flushing, Underhill came into close contact with Bowne. Underhill then moved Southold, Setauket, and finally Oyster Bay, in 1662, where he set up a household with Bowne's sister-in-law, a Quaker. With that favorable marriage, Underhill further increased his value to Winthrop, having by then constructed alliances with western Long Island's three major ethnic and cultural groups: the Dutch, English, and Quakers. This allowed him to function as an intermediary among all three (as well as the numerous other sects that "conversed" with the Quakers). These groups were also internally diverse. Like his Amerindian adversaries,

Underhill played off one against the other, exploiting internal rivalries as he brokered military skill or covert information for leverage and strategic advantage.

Winthrop and Underhill converged over expanding interests in the region. After he left Stuyvesant's advisory committee in 1648 and began a near thirty-year residency on Long Island's north shore (just a short sail across the Sound to Winthrop's land-holdings on Connecticut's south shore), Underhill remained a thorn in Stuyvesant's side. Underhill stayed a highly visible and bellicose opponent of Dutch rule until the English takeover in 1664. He also performed the role of agent provocateur for Winthrop and his allies in the Long Island Sound region. Underhill was tireless in his noisy efforts to undermine the interests of the director-general and replace Dutch with English rule.[213]

Subversiveness was central to Underhill's personality. The younger Winthrop knew this well, and he understood that like most successful mercenaries who had cut their teeth in the wars of religion, Underhill was to be handled carefully, with financial rewards and blandishments to his personal prestige. Or else (as Stuyvesant discovered), an asset quickly turned into a liability. Underhill changed sides in the middle of battle if it suited his purpose, as mercenaries did as a matter of course during the religious wars in the old world. In 1638, following on the heals of the antinomian crisis, while training the Massachusetts militia, Underhill showed he was not above threat of violent rebellion against the regime of the elder Winthrop. "I profess, sir," wrote Underhill, complaining of unjust treatment of officers, "till I know the cause, I shall not be satisfied, but I hope God will subdue me to his will; yet this I say that such handling of officers in foreign parts hath so subverted them as to cause them to turn public rebels against their state and kingdom, which God forbid should ever be found once to appear in my breast."[214]

The regional goals that made Underhill useful as an agent on Long Island were harnessed to John Winthrop Jr.'s grand economic, political, and natural-philosophical program for the 40th parallel. In 1650, this led to a fragile diplomatic accommodation. Compared to his authoritarian father, the future governor of Connecticut was a natural-philosophical pluralist, but latitudinarianism did not temper his enduring desire for land, economic security, and political power. The Treaty of Hartford was negotiated between Stuyvesant's agents and the Commissioners of the United Colonies of New England and signed in 1650, temporarily defining a dangerous, contested boundary between New Netherlands and its land-hungry neighbors in the New Haven and Connecticut Colonies.[215]

After the Restoration of 1660, it was also Winthrop, as a Stuart courtier, who traveled to Whitehall to obtain Connecticut's 1662 charter from Charles II. The colonial astronomer (and new member of the Royal Society) compared the restored Stuart king to a "new and dazzling star," recalling Galileo's gesture of naming a star for his Medici patron.[216] The terms of the charter not only allowed Connecticut to absorb New Haven Colony but in effect delivered into Winthrop's hands the legal keys to all of western Long Island, if only he could wrest it from the Dutch. Under the charter, the Connecticut Colony now claimed possession not only of strategic Greenwich and Westchester Town on the mainland—with Westchester's growing population of Long Island Quakers—but the most prosperous settlements on western Long Island: Jamaica, Flushing, Gravesend, Hempstead, and Middelburg (or Newtown).

By then, Stuyvesant was politically and militarily weak, and he commanded a culturally diverse colony that had failed to consolidate behind his authority. Yet he responded in October 1663, when he appointed three commissioners from New Amsterdam: Cornelius van Ruyven; the Anglo-Huguenot John Lawrence, with his family ties to Flushing's friends; and Oloff Stevenz van Cortlandt. In a futile enterprise, the three agents went to Hartford to seek redress from Winthrop himself.

Plainly, the Connecticut governor was planning to quietly conquer his long-coveted "Mediterranean" colony at virtually the exact moment the forces of the duke of York actually invaded in 1664. New Netherlands's capitulation was arguably well within his grasp by negotiation and perhaps without violence, given the chaos of Stuyvesant's government. However, it is prudent to assume that the dangerous Underhill was also prepared to lend force to the negotiations with his presence. Underhill began preparations by providing Winthrop with intelligence toward these ends from the moment of his appointment to Stuyvesant's advisory committee in 1648. Winthrop—buoyed by the international triumph of the charter and his recent appointment to the Royal Society—was poised to begin the takeover in 1664 at Huntington on Long Island when Underhill brought the devastating news from Boston that the duke of York's forces were nearby, on their way to "settle government and reduce the Dutch." This message was written in Underhill's hybrid dialect, described condescendingly as an "untutored, half-Dutch scrawl."[217] On the verge of triumph over the Venice of the American Mediterranean, Winthrop was not defeated by the Dutch, but by another, better-connected courtier from England. Winthrop had circled his wounded prey like a shark since the death of his father in 1649, but the prize was seized at the last moment by a bigger predator from the same school. The pragmatic Winthrop had no alternative in the summer of 1664 but to join in the triumphal entrance into New Netherlands of the English force led by Richard Nicolls and help negotiate the final terms of Stuyvesant's surrender.[218]

This context of external strategic insecurity and internal religious and political instability helps explain why Stuyvesant often felt it was in his interest to risk sanction by his cautious masters in Amsterdam, who preferred connivance to confrontation in religious and cultural matters. The director-general finally reached the limit of his personal tolerance and moved to suppress all forms of heterodoxy in 1657—the year of the Quaker Hodgson's arrival and arrest—but he did so only after provocation by yet another outsider from the conspiratorial Winthrop's side of the Sound, who appeared suddenly in Flushing. William Wickenden, an itinerant "Baptist" preacher from Rhode Island, was arrested by Stuyvesant's men and sent back.

Despite his stubbornly imperious persona, Stuyvesant was never truly autonomous, and he took a substantial personal and political risk in acting forcefully against the sects. A director-general was more powerful than the other Dutch colonial officers, but he was also, in effect, a mere functionary. The West India Company Directors could (and did) overrule decisions he might take in conjunction with his council. Officially, the vote of his council could also overrule the director-general. Stuyvesant's vote carried the same weight—if not the same force—as that of his councilors, who, after all, were dependent on his patronage as well as that of the directors of the Company.[219] But as Stuyvesant prepared to intervene militarily and confront an ominous threat of unknown proportions originating from suspicious or hidden sources, who worked with local collaborators to usurp established authority, events simply underscored his inability to control dissent, with or without force.

Stuyvesant's defense of orthodoxy began in earnest when he issued a written "prohibition" against the influx of Quakers onto western Long Island and their participation in secret conventicles. This prohibition was mentioned in the trial later that year of the two Quaker women arrested for joining a conventicle in the Hempstead woods. Yet Stuyvesant clearly knew that the Quakers were only a part of a larger problem with sectarianism, which would certainly have included Huguenot spiritualists and sympathizers. Fearful of nonconformist subversion, which Calvinist magistrates associated with Anabaptism after what had happened at Münster in 1534, Stuyvesant "commanded," by his military authority as director-general, that "beside the [Dutch] Reformed worship and service, no conventicles or meetings shall be kept in this Province."

Stuyvesant listed a number of secret hiding places on coastal Long Island's millennial *désert* where heresy occurred in the shadows, out of sight of authority, "whether it be in houses, barnes, shops, barkes, nor in the woods, nor fields."[220] Here, the director-general's strategy to undercut Flushing's ambiguously worded patent of 1645 recalled the clear language of the colony's original principles articulated in the "articles and conditions" for government of New Netherlands of 1638, with its prohibition of "forbidden assemblies or conventicles":

> without . . . it being inferred . . . that any person shall be hereby in any wise constrained
> or aggrieved in his conscience, but every man shall be free to live up to his own in peace
> and decorum, provided he avoid frequenting any forbidden assemblies or conventicles,
> much less collect or get up any such; and further abstain from all public scandals and

FIGURE 16.24. *Portrait of Petrus Stuyvesant*, attributed to Henri Couturier, New Amsterdam, ca. 1661–62. Oil on panel. H: 22½″, W: 17½″. Collection of The New-York Historical Society. Director-General Stuyvesant is represented here as simultaneously warrior, pastor, and burgher.

offences, which the magistrate is charged to prevent by all fitting proofs and admonitions, and if necessary, to advise the Company, from time to time, of what may occur herein, so that confusions and misunderstandings may be timely obviated and prevented.[221]

This command also implied—incorrectly—that the director-general had either the police power or authority from the Company to ferret out subterranean groups then beginning to appear and to cause "public scandals and offences" everywhere in this growing colony of refugees.

But the theatrical Stuyvesant was the New World's master of bravado. His sense of owning a double identity as director-general is revealed in his only surviving portrait (1661–62), attributed to the Huguenot painter Henri Couturier (fig. 16.24). The vigilant director-general peers out from inside an oval enceinte and challenges the wary spectator to confront the evidence of his complete authority. What, exactly, is he wearing here? Is he posed in a costume that combined armor with a sort of clerical garb to symbolize the theatrical presence of a proud Reformation warrior-minister? Or is that a magistrate's robe he wears? The ambiguity is very effective. If the former, Stuyvesant's portrait embodied an absolutist vision of the synthesis of Church and state. The possible conflation by observers of ambiguous meanings of the clerical/magisterial robe in this context would also have served his purpose to project the presence of total authority. It would not be at all surprising if internal threats to his authority from dissenters during the late 1650s—in addition to the continuous threat of invasion by English forces under the command of the Stuyvesant's competitor John Winthrop Jr.—inspired the portrait's unified rhetoric of religious and military security.[222]

Stuyvesant must have been tempted to put on this armor on December 27, 1657, when the "inhabitants of Vlishing" (the signatories actually included a total of thirty-one freeholders from Flushing and Jamaica), chose to respond to his "prohibition" and "command" by issuing a defiant "Remonstrance" to the director-general, the language of which was simultaneously stinging, condescending, and pious. The use of the term "remonstrance" was itself an uncomfortable reminder to Stuyvesant of sedition. The most subversive recent usage of this word in the history of the Dutch Republic had been in 1610 to denote Dutch Arminian "remonstrants" who challenged orthodox notions of predestination. The Flushing Remonstrance that was served on Stuyvesant declared:

> You have been pleased to send up unto us a certain prohibition or command that we should not receive or entertain any of those people called Quakers because they are supposed to be, by some, seducers of the people. For our part we cannot condemn them in this case, neither can we stretch out our hands against them, to punish, banish or persecute them, for out of Christ God is a consuming fire, and it is a fearful thing to fall into the hands of the living God.
>
> We desire therefore in this case not to judge lest we be judged, neither to condemn lest we be condemned, but rather let every man stand and fall to its own Master. Wee are bounde by the Law to doe good unto all men, especially to those of the household of faith. And though for the present we seem to be unsensible of the law and the Law giver, yet when death and the Law assault us, if we have our advocate to seeke, who shall plead for us in this case of conscience betwixt God and our own souls; the powers of this world can neither attack us, neither excuse us, for if God justifye who can condemn and if God condemn there is none can justifye.
>
> And for those jealousies and su[s]picions which some have of them, that they are destructive unto Magistracy and Ministereye, that can not bee, for the magistrate hath the sword in his hand and the minister hath the sword in his hand, as witnesse those two great examples which all magistrates and ministers are to follow, Moses and Christ, whom God raised up maintained and defended against all enemies both of flesh and spirit; and therefore that which is of God will stand, and that which is of man will come to nothing. And as the Lord hath taught Moses or the civil power to give an outward liberty in the state by the law written in his heart designed for the good of all, and can truly judge who is good, who is civil, who is true and who is false, and can pass definitive sentence of life or death against that man which rises up against the fundamental law of the States General; soe he hath made his ministers a savor of life unto life, and a savor of death unto death.
>
> The law of love, peace and liberty in the states [of Holland] extending to Jews, Turks

and Egyptians, as they are considered the sonnes of Adam, which is the glory of the outward state of Holland, soe love, peace and liberty, extending to all in Christ Jesus, con-
demns hatred, war and bondage; And because our Saviour saith it is impossible but that
offenses will come, but woe unto him by whom they cometh, our desire is not to offend
one of his little ones, in whatsoever form, name or title, hee appears in, whether Presbyterian, Independent, Baptist or Quaker, but shall be glad to see anything of God in them,
desiring to doe unto all men as wee desire all men shall do unto us, which is the true law
both of Church and State; for our Saviour saith this is the law and the prophets.

Therefore if any of these said persons come in love unto us, we cannot in conscience
lay violent hands upon them, but give them free egresse and regresse unto our Town, and
houses, as God shall persuade our consciences. And in this we are true subjects both of
Church and State, for we are bounde by the law of God and man to doe good unto all men
and evil to noe man. And this is according to the patent and charter of our Towne, given
unto us in the name of the States General, which we are not willing to infringe, and vio-
late, but shall houlde to our patent and shall remaine, your humble subjects, the inhabitants of Vlishing. [223]

After the signature "Edward Hart, *Clericus*" followed the names of the other thirty signatories.

Stuyvesant's response—including the town's reminder of Kieft's charter of October 10, 1645 ("to have and Enjoy the Liberty of Consience, according to the Custome
and manner of Holland, without molestacon or disturbance, from any Magistrate or
Magistrates, or any other Ecclesiasticall Minister, that may prtend Jurisdiccon over
them")—was to instruct his agents on Long Island to increase surveillance over secret
activities of the sects. In 1662, after failing to staunch sectarianism in New Netherlands's hinterland, and fearful of continued inroads into the city itself, Stuyvesant
finally arrested John Bowne for disobeying his edict against harboring Quakers and
holding conventicles. And indeed, after the completion of Bowne's house in 1661,
many Quaker meetings were openly held there. Because Bowne was the "greatman"
and the leading patron of Flushing's Quakers, this was meant as a violent refutation
of the Remonstrance and its latitudinarian text. Stuyvesant put Bowne in prison. After
he refused to pay a fine that acknowledged wrongdoing and the director-general's
authority over religious practice in the colony, Bowne was banished from New Netherlands.

❧ John Bowne's Exile and Return ❧

Bowne took a copy of the Flushing town charter of 1645 with him into European exile in 1663. In the end, he used the document to win an appeal to Jacob Pergens, di-

rector of the Amsterdam Chamber of the West India Company, the bureau responsible for New Netherlands, for the reversal of Stuyvesant's edict and Bowne's banishment from the colony.

Bowne took copious, phonetically written notes in his tiny script that detailed his painful, ultimately triumphant experience of banishment to Europe. His account of exchanges with Jacob Pergens in Amsterdam demonstrate again the extent to which middle colonial sectarianism was a transatlantic phenomenon. Bowne spent a month in Amsterdam in his appeal to the company. He had eleven "sittings" with Pergens. In the meantime, he met with supporters, and arranged for his eventual return to Flushing with his newest servant, the joiner and scribe James Clement.

The crucial "sitting" with Pergens took place in Amsterdam on April 18, 1663, as the two men parsed confusions between company and colony over questions of liberty, privilege, governance, and law. Bowne wrote, "I was cald agen then hee [Pergens] said":

> the gentelmen here have considered of ye: things and desiers to know whether you intend
> to goe to feach your wife or to stay there I said nay I have no intent to feach my wife and
> Childern here but to laber to maintain ther as I use to do but wee thinke seaid hee you was
> best to stay heare and sen[d] for your wife and Childeren for wee doe not give liberty there
> I said liberty was promised to us in a patent given by vertue of a commision from the
> prince the stats generall and the westindea Companie; hee said who gave that patent governor Kifiet [Kieft] oh seaid hee that was before any or but few of your Jugement [that is,
> Quakers] was harde of I seaid wee are known to bee a peseable people hee seaid but if you
> bee pesable and will not bee subject to the Laws and plakados [placards] which are published wee cannot sufer you in oure Jurediction I seaid it is good first to consider whether
> that law or plackad that was published bee acording to Justis & righteousnesse or whether
> it be not quite contrarie to it and allso to that libertie promised to us in our patent and I
> desier ye Company would red it or here it red I have a copie of it by mee hee seaid if I
> would walke out a while the[y] would a pritie time after the[y] cald mee in a gen then hee
> [Pergens] standing up sett a bould face on a bad case and tould mee the[y] had read it and
> considerd of it and did find it verie good and like it well then[n] after some words a bout
> it . . . it was concluded that I should come the next sitting . . . to see there writing and to
> give my anser to it . . . the speker [Pergens?] called us in to another roume and gave us a
> bad paper in duch which I gott translated and left my anser in writing for them.[224]

The key document in this exchange was the copy made "by mee [John Bowne]," of Kieft's patent.[225] Bowne's answer (translated into Dutch) to the company's contentious "bad paper," shows the ways in which this international sectarian group—like its Huguenot collaborators in New Netherlands—exploited useful opportunities to reactivate the primitive Christian role of universal victim. Thus, Bowne begins by reciting the remonstrance's admonishment against asymmetrical power relationships as contrary to free motion of the spirit, by again invoking the golden rule and representing himself as one of those tiny creatures "oppressed" and "afflicted" by evil:

Friends, the paper drawn up for me to subscribe I have perused and weighed, and do find the same not according to that engagement to me through one of your members, viz.: That he or you would do therein by me as you would be done unto, and not otherwise. For which of you being taken by your wife and family, without just cause, would be bound from returning to them unless upon terms to act contrary to your conscience, and deny your faith and religion and this in effect do you require of me and not less. But, truly, I cannot think that you did in sober earnest ever think I would subscribe to any such thing, it being the very thing for which I rather chose freely to suffer want of the company of my dear wife and children, imprisonment of my person, the ruin of my estate in my absence here, and the loss of my goods here, than to yield or consent to such an unreasonable thing as you here by would enjoin me unto. For which I am persuaded that you will not only be judged in the sight of God, but by good and godly men, rather than to have mocked at the oppressions of the oppressed, and added afflictions to the afflicted than herein to have done to me as you in the like case would be done unto, which the royal cause of our God requires. I have with patience and moderation waited several weeks expecting justice from you, but behold an addition to my oppression in the measure I receive. Wherefore I have this now to request for you, that the Lord will not lay this to your charge, but to give eyes to see and hearts to do justice, that you may find mercy with the Lord in the day of judgement.[226]

The metaphoric opposition of seeing with closed eyes appeared vividly in the rhetoric of the Company's final instructions on the matter to Stuyvesant. While Bowne asked God to provide his "oppressors" with the equivalent of geomantic eyes to enable them to see truth, the Company ordered the stubborn director-general to shut his eyes to life in the shadows, *so long as it remained hidden and private.* In instructions dated April 16, 1663, the directors of the Amsterdam chamber sealed Bowne's victory in the visual language of pragmatic self-interest:

Your last letter informed us that you had banished from the Province and sent hither by ship a certain Quaker, John Bowne by name: although we heartily desire, that these and other sectarians remained away from there, yet as they do not, we doubt very much, whether we can proceed against them rigorously without diminishing the population and stopping immigration, which must be favored at a so tender stage of the country's existence. You may therefore shut your eyes, at least not force people's consciences, but allow every one to have his own belief, as long as he behaves quietly and legally, gives no offence to his neighbors and does not oppose the government. As the government of this city [Amsterdam] has always practiced this maxim of moderation and consequently has often had a considerable influx of people, we do not doubt, that your Province too would be benefitted by it.[227]

❧ Opposing World Views ❧

The practice of secrecy and the negotiation of perception were thus used successfully in the center of European heterodoxy and were absolutely essential to maintaining "a considerable influx" of refugees to the colony. Privatization of the besieged spirit was natural and hence God's will. Messages of heterodox solidarity and resistance, were encoded in the Remonstrance. Thirty farmer and artisan heads of family constructed this text as a cultural and ideological document of cosmological ideals representing the shadow world of international Protestantism. The furtive, tiny language of the soul, common to Paracelsian natural-philosophical discourse and Huguenot material culture, also suffused the alchemical library of John Winthrop Jr., as well as the libraries of his transatlantic scientific community. Had Winthrop accomplished his conquest of New Netherlands, would the laboratory practice this language entailed—the alchemical quest to unify diverse substances in the material world and, by extension, the fragmented refugee cultures of the seventeenth century—have achieved the political and social significance promised by the sponsors of the universal laboratory?

To be sure, Winthrop had demonstrated his inability to include Amerindians in the unity, except as human dross to be burned off. In contrast, the Remonstrance codified the worldview of Flushing and Jamaica, and indeed most of western Long Island. Its text reasserted the primacy of primitive Christian *inclusiveness* and defined the inhabitants' heterodox sense of local culture as both private *and* inclusive. This was seventeenth-century "multiculturalism," a perception of soulishness beyond the gross impurities of "mixed composition," extending even to the Jews and Islam. Flushing prospered *because* society was scrupulously private and hence secure, in stark contrast to the violent exclusivity of an expanding "state" religion from which many had originally fled, and that now again was a threat to peace and prosperity. The remonstrators thus reflected a somewhat safer New World context. They aligned openly with a subterranean transatlantic tradition, one that was still active in the memory of migrating Christian societies and New Netherlands's Huguenots in particular. Many New Netherlands families were uprooted by, or knew through oral history, the effects of the religious oppression and mimetic violence that was endemic to Reformation and Counter-Reformation warfare.[228]

The Remonstrance was a more fluid and open reading of the analogy of the bounded corporate body, adapted universally from St. Augustine's venerated texts. Orthodoxy usually reinterpreted these writings exclusively to provide oppositional armatures for both the "Modell of Christian Charitie" *and* French Catholic absolutism.

Both systems represented heterodoxy and cultural difference internal to the body as forms of attacking illness like a virus or cancerous growth. It was necessary to excise parasitic invaders with precise surgical violence. Recall the surgeon's removal of the dark growth that lingered on the elder Winthrop's hand, despite his physician son's Paracelsian chemical and folkloric argument against such aggressive external therapy.

By deploying a benign figure of peaceful domesticity instead, the Remonstrance gave form to an *open* "household of faith." This mystical core metaphor reminded readers of the availability of a shared "deep structure" in hopes of inspiring Protestant culture to reconstruct memory of what John Bossy calls the communitarian ethos of primitive Christianity, in response to historical violence and separation.[229] Reconstruction was taken literally—that is to say, materially—by artisans from all such groups that converged around basic spiritualist principles. Once again, the "going out and coming in," a sense of the near transparent domestic permeability of the unlocked door is both a spiritual and a material constant. (It was also, to be sure, a reasonable description of the human geography of the Sound region.) So this was a community of privatized individuals. Goals here were material and spiritual: to absorb the population absolutely necessary to the economic success and security of the sectarian towns, and to construct a place of messianic unity among independent sprititualists where "Christ at his coming again would find a home."[230] In a household of pluralistic man, exclusive discipline and bounded confessions were unnecessary. "Wee are *bounde*" solely, the Flushing signatories wrote, by both the gospels and the elegant simplicity of the golden rule: "the Law to doe good unto all men." As Story unveiled in his conversion experience, Flushing was intended to operate like a Fluddian theatre, with communal space available in the shadows for memories of all strangers in the world to mingle as friends. The permeability of the open household did not mean that the Calvinist purity of the narrow way was forgotten in Flushing—Quakers could be notoriously strict—only that spiritual *exclusivity* was harnessed to universal themes of individuality and soulishness and could never be defined by confessional difference alone.

The signers perceived that their personal risk of persecution for the sake of sharing the purity of the Holy Spirit was greater than before and invoked a malleable, quietistic reinterpretation of the relation between violence and the sacred. Although "death and the Law assault us," the remonstrators refused violence. There would be no "stretch[ing] out our hands" to block the door against strangers or to "punish, banish or persecute." Inner guidance on personal practice and comportment in refuge was defined only by spiritual laws. This information was communicated silently over the enormous distance "betwixt God and our own souls."

The total authority and ultimate protection for these acts also derived from God alone. The text continued confidently in a primitive assault, then millennia old, on Stuyvesant's assertion of a dual civil and ecclesiastical identity: "The powers of this world can neither attack us, neither excuse us, for if God justifye who can condemn and if God condemn there is none can justifye." Here was the authentic voice of the heretic. Soulish language confirmed the power of Christic weakness and sacrifice when enthusiasts had to confront laws "commanded" by magistrates given inquisitorial authority. Here was the primordial denial of the "righteousnesse" of the asymmetries of history that John Bowne articulated as well, as a warning to his "oppressors" in old Amsterdam and New. The weak were tiny and overlooked, and yet they were also "patient and moderate" by nature of their particular combination of spirit and matter. Bowne warned that it was dangerous to forget that patience carried the hidden and latent power of reversal. He appended this message implicitly to Director Pergens in saying that he hoped "that you may find mercy with the Lord in the day of judgement."

❧ Domestic Armor: The Lapidary Style ❧

Whether communicated silently through prayer or hidden in plain sight in memory contained and accessed daily in "household" goods in colonial America, the language of Remonstrance was firmly embedded in the transatlantic artisanal networks. Its epigrammatic rhetoric echoes small and quiet voices of Huguenot artisans carved into house masonry throughout Aunis-Saintonge. In the particular artisanal (and notarial) tradition of mediation through artifacts communicated by Samuel Clement's inscription, "made by mee," axioms of identity, or "inscriptions lapidaires" ("stone inscriptions"), were carved into Protestant doorways. Many survive in the region; another Huguenot shadow discourse made to blend in with the natural materials of the domestic setting. Doorways may be dated by the house's architecture. Inscriptions were also often dated. So taken together, we know that the lapidary style began to proliferate with the violence of the first civil wars of religion in the 1550s and 1560s. The last ones date from the late 1690s, most within a decade of the Revocation.[231] Catholic neighbors, local judges, and members of the constabulary read these messages from the discursive doorways in their midst; they were meant for friend and foe alike. Thus, as in New Netherlands, regional perception of invisibility was contingent on the maintenance of tacit agreements between heretics, and their enemies and competitors. These were akin to the darkened spaces, niches, and doorways in Fludd's memory theater and analogous structures behind the theatricality of Hogarth's Hog Lane. Hidden places such as these obscured processes and contained information against which Stuyvesant was ordered to shut his eyes by the directors of the West India Company.

As long as heresy was contained in silence, it was necessary to allow it limited space. Every region of the refuge in the transatlantic world had its own negotiable rules of perception of the extent and limits of what would "give no offence to . . . neighbors and does not oppose the government," in specific material contexts. Still, London's native artisans saw the refugees appropriate their local enterprise, and so they clearly considered the government's pragmatic acts of complicity a Faustian bargain. London's artisans wanted strangers rooted out of their secret place in the shadows and exposed as counterfeits, rather than allowing them more headway as successful competitors.

Exodus 12:3–11 is also applicable here, with its sign made with the blood of the sacrificed Paschal lamb to protect the chosen from the angel of death. The sacrifice of the lamb to display his blood as a code, hidden in plain sight on the front door of Jewish households as a lifesaving signifier of the covenant in Exodus 12:23, was the crucial archetype for Easter and the militant lamb who opened the seven seals of destruction in Revelation, but also for Palissy's alchemic "destroyer" as agent of sacred separation. To wit: "For the Lord will pass through to slay the Egyptians; and when he sees the blood on the lintel and on the two doorposts, the Lord will pass over the door, and will not allow the destroyer to enter your houses to slay you." Instead, Jews reconstructed their lives and diasporic community elsewhere, as an *effect* of horrific actions undertaken by "the destroyer" on their behalf.

If French Calvinists memorized Exodus as a fundamental text for the war years and periods of "dispersion," ministers and lay preachers alike commonly reminded auditors of Old Testament stories detailing an alchemist God who repeatedly destroyed the majority of his chosen people because of Adam's transgression and the many covenants broken subsequently. In this way, he continued to refine a purified minority over a long period of time. Huguenot craftsmen identified with Genesis 1 in particular; here, God's primordial work of natural creation was described as artisanal, as was Noah's in Genesis 6:11. After the Fall, but in advance of the Flood, God effectively passed the "tools" of his refiner's craft down. He provided Noah with a set of measurements and instructions on the practical application of appropriate materials and construction methods that are specific enough to recall ancient building contracts. Noah was commanded to use these methods and materials to "make yourself an ark of gopher wood."

Construction of the ark was essential for Noah's security and protection, as God had "determined to make an end to all flesh; for the earth is filled with violence through them; behold I will destroy them with the earth." Following Adam, Noah's master also instituted a profane syncretism between impurity of fallen earthly matter and violent fleshliness. Thus he was forced to destroy to recreate, leaving a small, yet purified human and earthly remnant, saved from the wreckage for reconstitution elsewhere. God told Noah "I will establish my covenant with you; and you shall come into the ark . . . your sons, your wife, and your sons' wives with you"; and two fertile survivors "of all flesh . . . of every sort" chosen from the natural world. The New Testament promise that "the last shall be first" made it especially meaningful to Palissy that God chose, in Genesis 6:20, to provide security for "every" tiny, nearly imperceptible, "creeping thing of the ground." The lowliest most vulnerable creatures were sanctified as the last included in a new, post-apocalyptic covenant.

Marot's title page (see fig. 14.16) for his psalms of harmonic convergence in response to the violence also influenced the lapidary style in ways that paralleled Palissy's Neo-platonic promenade by the Charente River, an act that inspired scientific and artisanal innovation, after Saintes descended into chaos under attack. The Passover and Exodus both seemed ever-present in southwestern Huguenot households at the height of the *dragonnades*. In 1683, "C BOVTIN" carved a defiant prayer into the lintel above the door of his windmill at Saint-Pompain, which pumped water in the lower Deux-Sevres *marais*. Boutin called down God's condemnation onto the heads of liars; and then, underneath, he added the talismanic words from the Passover story: "PASE MAL / FESANT [PASS BY EVIL / DOER]."[232]

We are reminded of the emblematic warning from Matthew about the narrow and wide paths quoted on the same famous title page of Clément Marot's ubiquitous Psalter (see fig. 14.16), familiar to those who carried it. Not surprisingly, quotations from Marot's verses appear over doors to Huguenot houses as early as the 1560s. Two inscriptions dating from 1566 that were found over the doorway of a certain François Perrin in Geneva suggest the sort of narrow confidence that was found on axioms carved over entrances to many "orthodox" Genevan households. Above, the uppermost inscription cites the Reformation's ur-text on doorways ("Enter by the narrow path . . ."); and just below was inscribed a closely related passage of the invitation from John 10: "I am the door; if anyone enters my way, he will be saved."[233]

The "lapidary" fashion in Protestant France may have originated in Geneva and then diffused west, but this is uncertain. Surviving examples of stark textual confidence are rare among the inscriptions recovered from southwestern France, however, and on those found over doors in other contested regions. Given the different security context, it makes sense that these tend to show widespread anxiety over confessional violence. Such Huguenot doorways reveal worried signs of hope for divine protection. As such, they were personal buttresses against the pain and vulnerability that beset heretical households on the losing side of the regional fighting. Flushing, a New World refugee community across the Atlantic, demanded an open household from a growing position of strength. In southwest France, however, the front door to the domestic world was the gateway to an inner fortress against the dangers of civil warfare raging outside in the streets. When a now-forgotten Protestant built his new house on Poitiers' rue de la Marche in 1557, he took care to have the words HOC. EST. REFVGIVM. MEVM ET IN DNO CONFIDO ("This is my place of refuge") inscribed above the windows on the second story.[234]

This same text formed the core of the Remonstrance's exegetic armature as well. It is not surprising that such language, forming the "armor of God," was common to material life throughout the embattled southwest, as random religious violence moved almost interchangeably from battlefield to street. Such a text was found in the Deux-Sevres region, just north of La Rochelle, when, in 1566, Romans 8:31, a text about God's authority over all civil authority, was carved in Latin over the doorway of the Robert house. The Roberts were Protestants who lived in the small coastal village of Breuil-Coiffault, located in Hanc parish.[235] In the nearby town of La Pommeraie de Clussais, in 1662, within just five years of the publication of the Remonstrance, the same venerable text from Romans was inscribed over the door to the Bonnel house: SI DIEU / EST / POUR / NOUS Q / UI SERA / CONTRA [NOUS] ("If God be for us, who can be against us?").[236] Variations on these words echoed in Flushing in 1657, just as they appeared over doorways of sixteenth- and seventeenth-century houses in the small coastal towns that surround La Rochelle in Aunis. Indeed, vigilant observers can still spot this inscription over some doorways inside the old fortress itself.[237] This text was identified with the Protestant cause, to be sure, but it was nonetheless difficult for many Catholics to openly reject such pious language. The debate turned, of course, over whose side God was "for." Several martyrologies, including Palissy's and Neau's, recount scenes of Protestant torture where prisoners were asked, "Where is your God now"?

The talismanic qualities inherent in this text were useful for protection in the early Christian era, when Romans was written in response to the experience of persecution. Revived as a primitive text, it flourished for much the same reason among Huguenots during the civil wars of religion. Inscribed over doors that could be defended in no other way, this and other memorable axioms were textual fortresses of the spirit for besieged believers. This was especially true during the *désert* experience and on Long Island in the 1650s and 1660s, when for want of ordained ministers, Huguenots and New Netherlanders turned to texts specified and disseminated by artisan lay preachers such as Palissy.

The implications of this text for community protection were publicized when carved into a cartouche placed on the "Tour de la Borde," a seventeenth-century tower on a ruined Huguenot fortress in Nere, a parish in Saintonge. Here, the inscription reads as both a humble prayer by the defenders for divine protection and a play on the fallibility of *noblesse d'épée sûreté*. The tower speaks in the first person: DIEV EST MA GARDE + / ET MA HAVLTE TOVR / EST LOBIET SVR LEQVEL / IE MASSEVRE ("God is my protection + / and my high tower / [He] is the sapwood from which / I draw strength").[238] Even such a powerful talisman provided limited protection for the static, frontal inflexibility of the tower, a flaw that Palissy showed was built into every Huguenot fortress. For Palissy and his artisan followers, a combination of corporate hubris and military theatricality doomed the stone fortress to the chaotic fate of Babel. Hope lay in domesticity, the obfuscations of artisanal security, and the refugees' mobile shadow culture.

❧ Fortress of Silence ❧

When the refugee Boston painter-stainer Jean Berger (working ca. 1718–32), whose family emigrated from La Rochelle in 1685, published his design book in 1718, readers opened to a frontispiece that depicted a large classical door surrounding the author's name. The door also showed the date the refugee relocated—as it were, through the door—to his new place of publication and refuge (fig. 16.25).[239] A pierced flaming heart appears in the pitched pediment between with his initials, "J. B." Here was an ardent sign of Berger's aspiring soul pierced by sin and sacred violence and yet inflamed by the heat of God's light. Berger thereby invited readers to enter the text as he did, at

FIGURE 16.25. Title page from Jean Berger's design book for Boston tradesmen (Boston, 1718). Watercolor on paper. Courtesy Historic Charleston Foundation. Photo, Gavin Ashworth. Berger's use of a door alludes to the narrow door illustrated in figure 14.16. Here, the way is paved by a Turkish rug inscribed *Dieu Est Mon Droy* (God Is My Right), a play on the concept of the divine right of kings. Many of Berger's designs are chinoiserie, and the Middle Eastern carpet revives the Renaissance trope of the New World as Cathay.

the end of a pilgrimage. Readers (other artisans in search of stylish designs), "walked" their eyes over the naturalistic garden of a eastern "Turkey-work" carpet, marking the "narrow way" through the door and simultaneously into Berger's new place of refuge, his craft and (literally above all), the secrets of his soulish heart. Here, the words DIEU EST MON DROY ("God is my right"), a play on an English monarchical motto, shows the right of way guided by the universal power of the Holy Spirit. This punning double entendre on the British royal coat of arms (representing Huguenot faith in English protection) merged with a Rochelais refugee artisan's personal faith that the light of his animate soul was directing him (and the perception of his readers) on the narrow path through the door and toward the innovation and skills revealed in this latter-day book of secrets. "The idea of the self," Orest Ranum has written, "was . . . centered in the heart;" [which was] "invariably . . . a sign of 'inwardness.'" Inwardness, but also hidden "passion," and, most challenging to orthodox sensibilities that shunned secrets and innovation, the threat of "ambiguity."[240] A symbol common in the *désert*, Berger's pierced heart may well have shared the same secret passion as both Palissy and the younger Winthrop.

Revelation prophesied that in the fullness of time, all the darkness Hogarth revealed under the cover of shadow in "Hog Lane" would be understood as temporary. Perhaps that is one reason why, in 1565, the Bergier family of La Jarrie, in Saintonge, ancestors of John Berger of La Rochelle and Boston, inscribed over their doors POST TENE-BRAS LUX ("After darkness, light"), a loose paraphrase of John 1:5.[241] About these Bergiers we know nothing more, yet their sense of safety and promise in the darkness was simultaneously both metaphorical *and* material.

Some families employed forms as well as words in inscriptions. The Mage family built the Château de Disconches, near Saintes. Unlike the Bergiers of La Jarrie, the Mages' place in Saintongeais reformation history is at least partially recorded. In February 1583, the château hosted a clandestine Huguenot assembly where records of the baptisms of Protestant children were made and saved. At the entrance to the château, as was the custom in noble families, the Mages displayed their coat of arms, which incorporated a play on words (Mage/Magi) that transformed the family name into the personification of alchemical metamorphosis. To the left of the escutcheon was carved: ASTRA / DVXERVNT / MAGEOS AD / CHRISTVM ("The stars guided the Magi toward Christ"), and at the right: CHRISTI / CRVX DVCET / MAGOS AD / ASTRA ("Christ's cross will guide the Magi toward the stars").[242] An alchemical *inscription lapidaire* such as this would surely have directed Palissy—the rustic magus of Saintes—and his artisan followers to the door of the "Magi." The heretical potters of La Chapelle-des-Pots labored close by to coax guiding lights from earth materials with translucent glazes dotted with *étincelles*. These flashes of sparkling light were the first "terrestrial astrology" of Huguenot artisans searching for the narrow path in heavenly light, by sharing in the darkness of Christ's pain. Fludd recognized these dots as artisanal geomancy. And what of the tiny Maltese crosses punched in a nearly invisible pattern into the seventeenth-century woodwork of southern coastal Connecticut? Were these astral signs intended to "guide the Magi" as well, in their perception of the material world and its basic patterns inside the chaos of nature? Located in Reformed matter (and history) between the visible and invisible, did these tiny marks represent the carvers' metaphysical signatures?

Palissy elucidated the ways that the silence and power of craft were keys to security for artisan refugees who were forced to live, work, and prosper in darkness . However, Palissy's Huguenots, like the Quakers, showed that a silent mouth did not always mean passivity. Palissy fled in search of noble protection and refuge from the authorities in Saintes after *he* had unwisely spoken in public of his heretical allegiances. Hence this final, exorbitant expression of the material life of silence, one very appropriate to Palissy's own context and experience.

Dated 1560, this door is from the Château d'Usson near the seminal Protestant bastion of Pons, to which Palissy fled around the time it was carved. No sensible historian would dare argue the typicality of this door. It displayed over a hundred carved inscriptions. Neither could one make the case for hidden discourse. Overtness was precisely the point. This door screamed silence in the faces of passersby. Here, the theatricality *of* absorption was materialized.

These *inscriptions lapidaires* were carved under the patronage of the powerful Rabaine d'Usson family—builders of the château between 1536 and 1548, the family did not convert to Protestantism until 1560—and all advertised the virtues of silence, presumably with talkative Huguenots in mind. Still, the Rabain d'Ussons were clearly powerful enough—and may have had plenty of reason—to launch these diatribes against the "slander" of gossipy local Catholics as well. Consider a few of the axioms available to visitors at the door: ANTE QVAM LOQVARIS DISCE ("Before speaking, listen") (Eccles. 18:3); PROVERBIVM 13 / QVI CVSTODIT O / S SVVM CVSTOD / IT ANIMAM SVAM ("He who guards his mouth guards his soul") (Prov. 13:3); LOQVACI NE CREDAS ("Put no faith in the words of a blabbermouth"); CITO NE CREDAS ("Don't rush to believe"); LINGVAM COHIBE ("Hold your tongue"): AVDI MVLTVM. LOQVARE PAVCA ("Listen much, speak little"; and NE MALE DICAS ("Never slander").[243] Intense inscriptions such as these should be read on many levels. Certainly, at least as an internal demand by this imperious noble family for co-religionists to listen silently upon passing through the imposing door to Château d'Usson, and to guard the secrets they learned once they left the household and reentered the dangerous world of the civil wars. Yet it would be impossible to come away from this door without feeling the power of silence in southwestern France during the civil wars and the awesome ability to discipline and redirect this power into work commanded by the internalization of speech.

The material culture of productive silence was adopted early among Protestant artisans. Yet continuity over time and across religions is suggested by the resonance between the natural-philosophical discourses of Palissy, first published in the 1560s, and the remarkable diary of the Paris glazier Jacques-Louis Ménétra, who began to write his *Journal de ma vie* in 1764, and who expressed much sympathy for both Protestants and Jews oppressed in France. Palissy, of course, was a painter of stained glass and applied this early knowledge of vitrification to ceramic kilns and glazes. Ménétra wrote a poetic coda for his journal in "Year XI, 25 Vendemiaire," that included the following lines:

> Remember my mind always stay calm
> You must see everything say nothing and no speeches / . . .
> And for your own peace and quiet you who pretend to be a fine mind
> renounce erase and cross out what you have written."[244]

While Ménétra finally abandoned the security of silence—and with it the "primitive" artisanal persona he inherited from his father and internalized daily with *compagnons* ("you must see everything say nothing and no speeches")—to take up the exposed language of the pen, he seemed (only half-playfully) to revert to old habits in the end to admonish "my mind," to "renounce erase and cross out what you have written."

Colonial administrators such as Stuyvesant learned that when silence of the spirit was *performed* to exploit the hidden social, political, and artisanal meanings of soulishness, it could also be manipulated strategically, sometimes with Rabain d'Usson–like aggressiveness. The Remonstrance strongly indicates that such strategies were performed by the Quakers of Flushing and their sectarian allies. This stance of aggressive silence supported by the invisible power of divine protection was also indicated by John Bowne's parting threat to Pergens. Following the text of the Remonstrance, if this was a personal "case of conscience betwixt God and our own souls," then by definition of the original "Articles and conditions" of 1638, it was a quiet operation, not a "public scandal and offence." Hence it "can not bee" a threat to Stuyvesant's power ("destructive unto Magistracy and Minstereye"); neither should it even enter his field of vision, as the directors' instructions of 1663 made plain.

The text argued that "all magistrates and ministers are to follow" the two "great "examples" of primitive communication between God and man's soul, namely "Moses and Christ," "whom," like the primitive Christians the sectarians perceived themselves to be, "God raised up maintained and defended against all enemies both of flesh and spirit." Because the flesh as well as the open households of such rustic primitives were given material form by their animate soul, magistrates and ministers were warned to temper their judgment, to sheath their "swords." Like the ceramic pie plate that dissolves in two so that only one-half remains material (and useless) while the other reverts to chaos before the blind eyes of Hogarth's crying boy, "that which is of God will stand, and that which is of man will come to nothing."

The authentic law of God and man must therefore privilege the expression of interiority over outward appearance. When the flesh is tempered then the spirit circulates freely—and universally—in nature, through the elements, from macrocosm to microcosm. That was the medium by which, "the Lord hath taught Moses or the civil power to give an outward liberty in the state *by the law written in his heart* designed for the good of all." This was what John Bowne meant by the "heart to do justice." If that law was secreted in Adam's heart by God in prelapsarian times, and then revived in the hearts of Moses and Christ in primitive times, who but God himself, and those sectarians in direct communication with God, "can truly judge who is good, who is civil, who is true and who is false, and who can pass definitive sentence of life or death."

Ambiguity over relationships between God's truth and the secrets of the heart was the underlying tension between orthodoxy and sectarianism in the Bownas controversy. It also informed James Clement's shocking challenge to the court's authority to know his mind. There is an undeniable relationship between Stuyvesant's struggle with the sects in the 1650s and 1660s and the continuity of that struggle with the Church of England from 1664 until the revolutionary period. Long Island was contested territory in 1657 and again in 1664 and 1702, in large part because of imperial fears that the disease of boundaryless soulishness would carry disorder and chaos from the shadow of the city's periphery to the brightness of its core. Put another way, acceptance of sectarianism on Long Island might allow the secret practice of New York City's sects to dispel the darkness, emerge from the shadows, and challenge the established political and religious authorities.

In this sense, the relation of Flushing to New York City in the seventeenth and eighteenth centuries was like that of Saintonge to La Rochelle a century earlier. The famously conservative Consistory of La Rochelle was anxious to keep Palissy and other heterodox elements outside its walls to prevent precisely what happened in New York City over the course of the eighteenth century.

The upheavals of New York's seventeenth-century history are well known. Following the Glorious Revolution, Leisler's Rebellion, and its bitterly divisive aftermath (including Leisler's execution and Nicolas Bayard's trial), there emerged a complicated political, cultural and theological schism between the anti-Leslerian ministry and an aroused pro-Leisler laity in the profoundly pluralistic New York Dutch Reformed Church. Thereby a very long period ensued when Calvinist sacerdotalism came under attack and lay participation in church ritual and other forms of lay enthusiasm, including private worship, increased dramatically. Thus decreasing church attendance may—in some instances at least—have represented an increase in religiosity.[245]

❧ Contesting Mastery ❧

After 1664, British colonial New York, as a royal colony, furthered Stuyvesant's efforts to support establishment churchmen in the struggle to coerce dissenters into orthodoxy. As in Europe, New York's new leaders continued to assert an authoritarian milieu within which dissent and heterodoxy traditionally flourished. This was certainly the case with New York's large and wealthy Anglican community, which was engaged in a vicious battle with dissenters throughout the 1750s, culminating temporarily in the churchmen's successful institution of King's College under the aegis of the Church of England. The president of King's College, Samuel Johnson, joined with local churchmen to call for an American Anglican bishop. This created the impression at least, so far as the Dutch Reformed and Anglican clergy were concerned, that New York's religious establishment was prepared to support a program of intolerance similar to that which had sent Old World heterodox groups underground to pursue their activities clandestinely. In this way as in many others, New York was perhaps the most "European" of the American colonies.[246]

The strength of heterodoxy in New York was still perceived as a real threat by the authorities. Speaking of growing sectarian piety in the city, one influential Lutheran cleric observed bitterly that by 1730, the sects thought it "a pious thing to honor disorder as an idol." Also in 1730, another minister lamented that sectarians had grown so successful in their quest to assure unmediated and unrestricted personal religious experience in the colony, that, in effect, "here [in New York] the church is like a vineyard without a hedge, like a city without walls, like a house without a door and lock."[247] The world of the fortress had been inverted. The sectarian domestic metaphor of the New World town as an open household for refugees of all confessions, posited as the social ideal by the Remonstrance on Long Island in 1657, was lamented as the infiltration of chaos from outsiders by New York City's churchmen in 1730.

Yet by 1730, the pietistic Lutheran Henry Melchior Muhlenberg explained how his concept of holy materiality linked the various sects—from Quakers to Ranters—despite differences between them. Thus, material life was harnessed to Muhlenberg's Palissy-like notion of the anti-rhetorical simplicity of holy speech. "High-flown words, artistic expressions, outward forms, and seemingly holy gestures," he wrote, following the Paracelsian tradition, "none of these effects anything whatsoever unless edification by the Word of God begins in the bottom of the heart."[248] Like the heart of the body, the armature of the world of forms was interior and hidden. Fludd's *Interior Principle* predicted the conflict to local readers, including the younger Winthrop.

Where New York's enthusiastic sectarians perceived unity through the third eye of the animated soul, inexperienced prophets of authority were blinded by the confusion and disorder of Babel. That is why the remonstrators reminded Stuyvesant that the colony of New Netherlands, like the Dutch Republic, was historically (and by nature), an open state, where refugees fled to escape the violence of religious "hatred, war and bondage." Anti-Semitism was in truth rampant in the Dutch Republic, but "the law of love, peace and liberty in the states," was extended even to the most affluent and productive of infidels, the "Jews, Turks, and Egyptians, as they are considered the sonnes of Adam," and hence postlapsarian sinners, like "all in Christ Jesus." Then in an apocalyptic threat reminiscent of the first paragraph of the text ("for out of Christ God is a consuming fire, and it is a fearful thing to fall into the hands of the living God"), the Remonstrance warned again that "our Saviour saith it is impossible but that offenses will come, but woe unto him *by whom* they cometh."

This merged exegetically with the millennial investment of the pietist artisan in animation of tiny, overlooked, invisible shadow-world bits of life. These were the mutable refugees who fled from Nature's predators, traceable from Palissy's metamorphic insects and amphibians cast alive into earthenware to Hogarth's painted "species" on the human perceptual periphery. Stuyvesant and other masters of "Newtonian" sunlight were warned to fear the hidden power of God's spiritual protection. These warnings were harnessed to "our desire . . . not to offend one of his little ones, *in whatsoever form, name or title hee appears in.*" Thus, "hee" was disguised to the unseeing inside the forms of the weak to balance the power of the strong. The mixed disguises, mobility, and infinite mutability of such "little" forms made it absolutely necessary that they be welcomed in love, and given "free egresse and regresse unto our Town, and houses, as God shall persuade our consciences." This "egresse and regresse" was to be "free" and natural, much like the movement of the universal soul as it permeated the "fit" body, or the light of nature called down by the Huguenot artisan to animate fallen matter.

❧ Personal Readings, Universal Affinities ❧

In its claim that the Quakers of Flushing "shall be glad to *see* anything of God *in* any of them," the Remonstrance provided the social, cultural, and theological precondition for the operation of Thomas Story's pluralistic ministry on Long Island. At virtually every meeting, Story engaged other sectarians—and other friends—whose autodidactic reading and experience had led to strange and idiosyncratic interpretations of natural philosophy and scriptural text. Dozens of examples line hundreds of pages of the preacher's dense journal. Two moments of interaction and convergence suffice. Story was only mildly surprised when a Quaker "who had professed the Truth about

20 years" testified at a Meeting in Hempstead in 1699 that he "had once believed, that if the Body of a Man were Burnt to Ashes, and those Ashes sifted through a Sieve over all the Earth, Sea, and Air, yet, at the Last Day, the same Dust should come together again, and the same Body should then arise; 'but,' said he, 'I now believe otherwise.'"[249]

Unfortunately, this unnamed Friend did not fully explain why he "now believe[d] otherwise." The scholarly Story considered this naturalistic and vaguely geomantic theory of bodily recomposition from the elements. He incorporated the man's millennial testimony into his carefully constructed, noncommittal response, which was intended to disagree dispassionately, and still not repulse the man from open the household of God. "Now," replied Story cautiously, "though we fully believe the Resurrection of the dead, both of the Just and Unjust, yet we take not upon us to determine the Mode of Existence in that State, or with what Bodies they shall Come; but leave it to the Almighty to give unto us Bodies as may best please him."[250] Story's permeable conception allowed for infinite bodily shapes at the Last Judgment; these were to appear "in whatsoever form" as well.

From the perspective of New York's consistories, outrageous and annoying spectacles of multiple interpretation were commonplace at meetings on Long Island. These were apparently absorbed by the Quakers as well, though undoubtedly with far less grace than Story showed in Hempstead. The Ranters, in particular, tested the open structure of the Remonstrance, because even a flexible cosmos was too formal for some sects:

> On the 28th [1699] we had a meeting at Tinnering [Long Island], on the occasion of a marriage, about nine miles from thence: To this Meeting came some of the *Ranters* of *Oyster Bay;* and, during the greatest part of the time, were pretty still, save only an old Man, who sometimes hooted like an Owl, and made a ridiculous Noise, as their Manner is: And the Marriage was solemnized, he stood up, and bare his Testimony, as he called it, against our set Forms; and cried for Liberty to the oppressed Seed, which, said he, is oppressed with your Forms, meaning the Manner of Celebration, of our Marriages; generally approved by Mankind as the most decent of all.[251]

The old man who "sometimes hooted like an Owl" witnessed against monogamous marriage and separate family life. For him, this was the main obstacle to victory over the corrupted flesh (Ranters represented themselves as God's unified flesh).[252] That the Ranters sought liberty from the oppressiveness of outward Quaker ritual (or "Forms"), is particularly significant in light of Story's response. Ranters were commonly mistaken for Quakers by "other people" (they sometimes claimed to be Quakers). Forms of outward convergence around the unity of belief in a universal soul caused such confusion at times that sectarian difference could only be determined from inside the sects themselves, so boundaries were virtually invisible to outsiders:

Now, that which these Ranters would be at, is a Liberty to all that profess Truth to do what they list, without being reproved, or accountable to any Person or People: For, they say, to be accountable to Man is Bondage; and for Man to judge is vain, since those actions he may censure may be done in the Motion of the Holy Seed and Spirit of Christ; under which Pretense they would cover many lewd and vile Practices, by reason whereof we had sometimes been upbraided in *Connecticut Colony;* where some of them, in Times past, had appeared, in their extravagant ravings, under the Name of Quakers.[253]

"Lewd and vile" they may have been, but the Ranters were protected by the Remonstrance's open code of judgment, accepting the notion that any action claimed to be made "in love," was potentially "the Motion of the Holy Seed."

❧ Menocchio(s) on Long Island ❧

Consider an extension of this logic of universalist affinity, such that John Winthrop Jr., Sir Kenelm Digby, or, for that matter, Comenius and Oldenburg might find coherent relationships between Fludd's geomantic theories of perception, the Remonstrance's text, and the words uttered at his trial by Carlo Ginzburg's Friulian miller Menocchio. We know Menocchio was a nominal Italian Catholic, and like Palissy, a literate artisan and autodidact. In 1601, around the time Palissy died a prisoner in the Bastille, he was burned at the stake by the Roman Inquisition. Menocchio's long trial and execution resulted in volumes of testimony. Like Palissy as well, these volumes reveal the extent to which the miller was a derivative cipher for the enormous body of literature and imagery of natural-philosophical and theological debate that was available to him and thousands of others throughout the early modern world during his lifetime. Included in these transcripts is a revealing exchange that blended Fludd's geomantic process of perception, with the miller's folkloric understanding of natural-philosophical texts he may have been reading (or, heard read). These may have included snippets of Bruno, Cellini, or even Palissy, as well as the Bible:

> INQUISITOR: What is this power of God?
> MENOCCHIO: To operate through skilled workers. . . .
> INQUISITOR: Is what you call God made and produced by someone else?
> MENOCCHIO: He is not produced by others but receives his movement within the shifting of the chaos, and proceeds from imperfect to perfect.[254]

Ginzburg infers that the philosophical Menocchio's execution was ordered in part because of certain affinities in his testimony with the profoundly heretical books of Giordano Bruno, who truly did terrify the Vatican. Outside this dangerous context, the quirky animate materialism of this talkative but insignificant miller might have been overlooked. This linkage would help explain why, ultimately, Pope Clement VIII personally targeted Menocchio, "who had become a rotten member of Christ's body, to demand his death."[255] Shortly before the miller's execution, an Inquisition scribe recorded on April 28, 1584, Menocchio's vigorous denunciation of "the pope, cardinals, and bishops [who] are so great and rich that everything belongs to the church and to the priests, and they oppress the poor." He then continued, full of the self-destructive passion of a terrified but inspired autodidact, to

> call for a church that would abandon its privileges and reduce itself to poverty alongside the poor . . . tied to a different religious concept, rooted in the Gospels, free of dogmatic requirements, and reduced to a core of practical precepts: "I would want us to believe in the majesty of God, to be good, and to do as Jesus Christ commanded when he replied to those Jews who questioned him about what law was to be kept: 'Love God and your neighbor.'" For Menocchio this simplified religion didn't call for confessional restrictions. His impassioned exaltation of the equality of all religions was based on the idea that illumination was granted to all men in equal measure—"the majesty of God has given the Holy Spirit to all, to Christians, to heretics, to Turks, and to Jews; and he considers them all dear, and they are all saved in the same manner."[256]

It would be a simple matter to locate numerous other examples of similar sorts of apostolic language taken from the Gospels (Matt. 26:24–25 was the common text). Such rhetoric was reactivated by almost all the sects, especially during times of tribulation, witness the events that led to the Flushing Quakers' response to Stuyvesant in the Remonstrance of 1657. This common language was taken from the period in which the bodily pain and affliction of Jesus and the apostles was a signifier of their devotion to the enthusiastic revival of what Palissy and all the sectarians called the primitive Church: the youthful age of the Church that brought Christianity closest to a prelapsarian, Adamic ideal. What was an open household but a figure of Eden before the Fall? Thereafter, the garden was "bounded" and "locked" from mankind. The Fall was the primordial separation of macrocosm from microcosm, mankind's punishment, half-blind perception. Hence, William Penn wrote in his famous preface to George Fox's *Journal:* "These things gave them [the Quakers] a rough and disagreeable appearance with the generality, who thought them turners of the world upside down, as indeed in some sense they were: but in no other than that wherein Paul was so charged, viz. to bring things back to their primitive and right order again."[257]

Palissy's rustic language, like Gerrard Winstanley's, had a powerful Leveler or Digger component, and his sarcastic (and, given his own quest for patronage, somewhat disingenuous) attack on the parvenu ministers of Saintonge who attended rich patrons (in their châteaux) at the expense of the poor (in huts), was a source of Palissy's troubles with the wealthy and authoritarian Consistory of La Rochelle during the period of

Calvinist consolidation. It is also useful to recall his encounter with the geode—a paradigm for his natural artisanry and for the internal condition of the earth's "bowels"—having "a rough and disagreeable appearance with the generality." When this world in microcosm was reversed, "to bring things back to their primitive and right order again," it became possible to see inside, at the "bottom," to witness the sparkling transparency of the soul of Nature distilled in crystalline rock.

Penn was able to achieve a rhetoric of religious tolerance in Pennsylvania rarely approached in colonial New York. Still, it is noteworthy that the idealized contours of his charge from Paul to effect this reversal and "bring things back to their primitive and right order again," were delineated in the Flushing Remonstrance. Thus, the town was particularly fertile territory for Fox's message, as well as Story's.

Interaction with lay interpretation of Pauline language is powerfully present when reading the Remonstrance, especially if juxtaposed with transcripts from Menocchio's trial: in the miller's devaluation of corrupt, learned culture, supplanted by a rustic lay dominion empowered by spirit made material in Nature; the equivalence of *all* religious piety as "dear," even alleged heresy, when illuminated by the light, thus ushering in a new age of universal, ecumenical piety. Pronounced in the Remonstrance as well, readers encountered the dialectical armature of refugee cultures. This emerged from the experience of subterranean worlds locked in mortal combat over the unified inclusivity of "love" and the utter fragmentation of religious "violence." A profound relation existed between "the law of love" and violence. For the remonstrators, "the law of love" was also the code of a marginalized social order animated as a conduit for the holy spirit, and experienced in "peace and liberty." That is to say, privately, inwardly, and hence in almost infinite outward variety. "In whatsoever form . . . [we] shall be glad to see anything of God in any of them," they wrote, inasmuch as to see God in them was to peer into the light of love's bodily receptacle and share the deepest recess of the soulish self: the "bottom of" the heart. In the words of Menocchio, God "receives his movement *within* the shifting of the chaos" of natural bodies, "and proceeds from imperfect to perfect."

On the other hand, "violence," as defined by Europe's civil wars of religion, was the suppression of difference in the name of absolutism, whereby independent piety, an expression of the secret self is turned inside out and made available to carnal blockage by the dominant order. This construct was central to the heterodox worldview—as in Aunis-Saintonge—and was entwined in its history. "They rather throve," John Bossy has written, "on persecution."[258] One reason the sects were so successful on Long Island and finally in New York City was that they were persecuted, but not officially "eliminated," as in Bourbon France.

Persecution created the context for material culture that asserted the appearance of a "plain" (or, "primitive"?) façade that, like Palissy's ceramic grottoes, Fludd's "theater of the world," and Hogarth's back streets of Hog Lane, simultaneously hid, protected, encoded, *and* displayed the existence of interiors that contained a multitude of secret passages, entries, recesses, and messages mastered by shadowy subgroups. Menocchio knew secrets were dangerous when exposed to the authoritarian gaze of inquisitors. Yet he was invested in the power of truth as he understood it to overcome the boundaries of difference and learning, and persisted in ridiculing the Inquisition's efforts to imagine the ineffable in overt or conventional ways.

Menocchio—who also claimed to see "with the eyes of the mind," because "without bodily eyes we cannot see everything"—gave primacy to inner experience for the same reason as Hogarth and Palissy, because it held out the utopian promise of novelty and innovation. "I have an artful mind," he told his amazed inquisitors in 1584, "and I have wanted to seek out higher things about which I did not know . . . my mind was lofty and wished for a new world and way of life." It was precisely this fear of innovation that alarmed the elder Winthrop, Stuyvesant, and Hogarth's and New York's Huguenot chair makers' competitors in the marketplace. The same year the Remonstrance was written, Stuyvesant complained in frustration to the West India Company about the chaos of innovation on western Long Island in his report on the "State of the Churches in New Netherland." Gravesend was already under the thrall of what he called "Mennonites," and Flushing's "Presbyterians [were] endowed with divers opinions" and had now "absented themselves from preaching." This was fertile ground for Huguenot and Quaker artisans, but in a larger sense, Menocchio, as well as Palissy and his followers, would have felt *comfortable* there searching for, and constructing, "a new world and way of life."[259]

❧ Huguenot-Quaker Affinities ❧

Like many Huguenots, Quakers migrated in family groups from borderland regions from which they often challenged authority with impunity. They were also highly artisanal. Most New York Quakers appear to have come from provincial northwest England bordering the anglophobe "Celtic fringe" of Wales and Scotland. After 1664, New York Huguenots emigrated mostly from provincial southwest France, bordering the Atlantic, and so had historical and economic ties to coastal regions of the English archipelago and the New World, while displaying tenuous, often violent relationships with landlocked and absolutist Paris. These two regional cultures also shared similar notions of anti-authoritarian personal enthusiasm and materialism, inspired by the interior presence of the luminous Holy Spirit, which emerged particularly in contexts of violence and oppression. Both groups were influenced by Continental (especially Germanic) pietism during the religious civil wars in France and England in the early modern period.[260]

Barry Levy's study of the "radicalism" of "frontier" (his terms) Quaker domesticity in northwest England and the Delaware Valley, and the extent to which Quaker universalism and ideas about the luminous body informed everyday life, also suggests modes of convergence between the Huguenot and Quaker artisans who extended their "spiritual tribalism" to New Amsterdam and New York. If "domesticity was an essential part of George Fox's and Margaret Fell's religious strategy," the core of domestic relations was their desire "to base worship on nonverbal spiritual intimacy." Levy concludes that British-American Quakers "wanted to make households totally spiritual and therefore morally self-sufficient," thus creating, "the most spiritualized household relations ever seen in England."[261]

This is a big statement given the variety of sectarianism throughout the British Isles, but it is not my plan to dispute Levy's conclusions for England. Yet this vision of domesticity may not have been restricted to seventeenth-century England. This Quaker sense of the domestic cosmos had strong affinities with Protestantism in southwestern France and, by extension, the refugees in England and New York Colony. These religious strategies were also firmly entrenched in Palissy's program for the survival of the Huguenots of Saintonge as early as the 1560s. Such strategies were part of a complex web of family resemblances whereby Huguenot and Quaker artisans found significant areas of overlap in which to converge in spiritual and material life, as groups from Long Island and the city merged networks and "tribes" and positioned themselves to dominate New York's lucrative woodworking and upholstery trades. Refugee craftsmen had occupied an enviable position as artisans in the city since the earliest days of New Amsterdam, but the stigmatized Quakers might not have obtained initial access to higher wages and the urban luxury trades without help from New World Huguenot networks.

What does it mean, in the context of seventeenth-century Flushing, to speak of a domestic cosmos that depended on "nonverbal spiritual intimacy" in Quaker households, which were "totally spiritual and therefore morally self-sufficient"? Perhaps that the material life of the household was integral to the totality of a great material-holiness synthesis for Quakers, just as for southwestern Huguenot culture. Was there not a close relationship between Palissy's notion of spiritualized domesticity as a keystone of artisanal *sûreté* for Huguenot refugees—hence the household as "natural" fortress of the soul—and Quaker domesticity? Huguenots and Quakers alike shared the fundamental understanding that silence and other modes of nonverbal communication allowed society's "tiny" creatures to see all with the "eye of truth" and remain invisible to those who controlled overt discourse. For all of his posturing and sexual braggadocio, Ménétra was arguably just a weak little man. It was from that small part of himself that occupied the very core of his being as an artisan that the glazier warned, "you must *see everything*," but, "*say nothing* and no speeches."

Levy does not concern himself with problems of material culture, and given his emphasis on social and family history, he pays little attention to close analysis of the theological texts that show how Quakers addressed the crucial relationship between quietist "spiritual intimacy" and domestic life. Yet this is the most logical place to begin to unravel what Braudel in another, not unrelated context, calls the pluralistic "structures within which the peoples . . . gradually found a place, collaborating . . . here and there curiously re-creating the patterns" of memory that were already shared or, "in play," between New York Huguenot and Quaker artisans.[262]

The folklorist Richard Bauman has elucidated Quaker construction of social and cultural identity, wherein the "symbolism of speaking and silence" was privileged. He combines analysis of seventeenth-century theological and natural-philosophical texts with methods pioneered by sociolinguists such as Dell Hymes. By a practice he calls an "ethnography of speaking," Bauman observes ways in which "silence as a communicative phenomenon," with "richly textured and multidimensional . . . kinds of meanings," was a product of the mystical synthesis of religion and science. (Also, one might add, of the unity of spirit and matter.)

Thus, the function of silence was specific to the same cosmological order that enmeshed Palissy, Winthrop, Flood, and de Bry in its web of relationships, and that Thomas Story revealed in the narrative of his conversion experience in England before coming to preach on Long Island. Following Weber, Bauman concludes that Quakers experienced the "routinization of charisma" over time in repetitive performances by ministers. Levy's location of spiritual charisma as being active in the routines of domesticity is more satisfying as social history. But the most logical space where the charisma of spiritual silence was routinized or communicated in everyday life was artisanry and the geomantic perception of material culture in the local workshop, alchemic laboratory, marketplace, and—as in Hugh Platt's domestic adaptation of Bruno's art of memory through the homey lens of his Huguenot mentor "Master Bernard"—in the British-American home.[263]

This is not the place to address the full force of Bauman's complex and subtle reading of seventeenth-century Quakers' verbal and textual performance. For our purposes here, suffice it to say that Bauman makes two crucial connections between Quaker spiritual practice and the dialectic of speaking and silence in the sectarian tradition of the English civil wars: first, Bauman underscores the centrality of the Tower of Babel mythology in Quaker discourse and the culture of silence; and second, he posits the significance of the natural-philosophical and alchemic writings of Jakob Böhme to the formulation of the Quaker program. Fox distinguished between what he came to call the "natural" language of postlapsarian times and prelapsarian Adamic, or "spiritual," language.

This is related to the Palissian paradigm of natural artisanry, since Palissy referred to earth materials he had already purified by alchemy as returned to a prelapsarian or Adamic state. Nature itself wasn't evil; only the corrupted part obscured by the dross of the Fall that concealed the fragment of pure spirit. This was what Böhme meant by "half-dead" nature. Palissy's *rustique figulines* were Nature reformed, inasmuch as the corrupt deadness was burned off and the primitive spirit of purified Nature was inseminated and reborn, made translucent by fire in the potter's kiln (as was the potter himself by the fire of sacred violence). "For the early Quakers," Bauman writes:

> speaking was basically a faculty of the natural man, of the flesh. Fox experienced early in his life the realization that 'the people of the world,' those who were joined to the flesh and servants of it, "have mouths full of deceit and changeable words.". . . It is not that languages or speaking were seen as inherently evil. . . . Rather, speaking in the service of the spirit had to derive in a special way from a proper spiritual source, and "carnal talk," talk that did not stem from that spiritual source, was inadequate to comprehend spiritual truth, the service of which was the most important business of man on earth. Fox . . . "*was afraid of all carnal talk and talkers, for I could see nothing but corruptions, and the life lay under the burden of corruptions* [emphasis added].". . . At the foundation of these principles was the powerfully resonant awareness that natural languages came into being at Babel and that only by regaining the "state to which Adam was before he fell" could one comprehend the eternal and "divine Word of wisdom." If carnal speaking, as the faculty of natural man, is inadequate for the attainment of the desired spiritual condition, which are the proper behavioral means by which this condition may be attained? For the Quakers, one of the most fundamental means was *silence*. Silence was very close to the center of seventeenth-century Quaker doctrine and practice.[264]

For Quakers, the object of faith became to suppress carnality, allowing the light of the spirit to enter the heart and suffuse the body like a beacon, and above all, to hear the voice of God through the conduit of one's inner spiritual voice (the verbal equivalent of Fludd's inner *oculus imaginationis*). The spirit of God within was thus God's voice ("God the *speaker*"), just as it extended God's eye to the experienced.[265] By the strictest comparison with the shifting, "changeable" nature of the Huguenot practice of *sûreté*, Fox's insistence on not hiding behind the "mixed composition" of "deceitful" words seems provocative. Silence was clearly safer, since such rhetoric conforms more readily with the anti-Nicodemite, martyrological ideal of Crespin, rather than Palissy's more usual practice of following the "medieval custom" of denying heresy "as far as possible to save one's skin, if one had not first succeeded in escaping capture."[266]

Still, in a typical contradiction, the potter hoped that Jehan Crespin would publish his account of Philibert Hamelin's life (see chapter 3). Here again, however, smallness was operative as a key metaphor of materiality, and spiritual silence, although in practice part of a dialogue of pilgrimage, was actually "a small still voice, moving in man

Godwards" toward completeness of the soulish circuit between microcosm and macro-cosm.[267] As with ambiguous symbolic plays on audience perception of the products of Huguenot artisanry, what was silence to those outside of "converse," but an opening to the small still voice to that experienced part of the craftsman's audience having both the memory and competence to achieve unification of perception?

Fludd's geomantic treatises posited similarly that the blindness of Babel emerged from carnality. Willfulness and other exertions of the flesh buried God's voice in chaos, destroying hope of prophesy: the tiny voice of the Holy Spirit "in converse" with man-kind by way of the open mind and silent mouth. Hence, Palissy's claim during the battle over Saintes that death did not frighten him. However, he did fear the chaos caused by carnal emotions that would interfere with passage of the tiny voice of the Holy Spirit at the last moment. At that moment, Palissy prayed for Stoic calm. Above all, the famous admonition "let your words be few" (Eccles. 5:2) originated with the Old Testament God. The constant refrain to the Israelites after virtually every trans-gression, was a reminder of their failure to *listen* to his word. Who could doubt that Fox quoted Ecclesiastes when he visited Flushing and preached at Bowne's house in 1672? Would it be redundant for Huguenot pastors to actually speak these words at the Château d'Usson, where newly converted Saintongeais Huguenots—including Palissy and his followers—held clandestine meetings and recorded baptisms in the mid 1560s? After all, the Rabain d'Ussons had already communicated their warnings silently in terse inscriptions carved "invisibly" in stone round their door. Was a conventicle in Pons as quiet as Quaker meetings in Flushing or in the Hempstead woods?

Bauman argues that the Quaker practice of Adamic silence punctuated by unex-pected bursts of mysterious, prophetic speech was appropriated and adapted from the "mystical tradition of the hermetic philosophers and Jacob Boehme." Tracing affini-ties to the "occult line of religioscientific thought," Fox's Quakerism is "informed by cabalistic, Rosicrucian doctrines," engaged by the Paracelsian tradition of "speculative cryptological, numerological, etymological, and allegorical attempts to reconstruct the language of Adam."[268] Bauman compares Böhme's transforming "experience of hav-ing 'the nature and virtues of things opened' to him in the year 1600" (allowing him to perceive the "flash" in the dull material of a pewter pitcher) to Fox's epiphanic "joy at attaining the Adamic insight of 'how all things had their names given them according to their virtue.'" For Bauman, Fox's joy was in decoding the Adamic language.[269] This conforms well with Böhme's idiosyncratic, very nearly incomprehensible figurative language in *Aurora,* an exorbitant use of metaphors that is arguably the inverse of Quaker silent performance.

Yet this metaphoric overlay was a move toward similar ends of recovering the Adamic purity of spiritual expression. Böhme's ecstatic visions and his ineffable emo-tions existed in the cosmic realm of mankind's common memory beyond the carnal containment of words. Hence, the highly charged, sexualized discourse of Böhme's *Aurora* was displaced and then reinvented as a Neoplatonic natural philosophy of intense material fecundity, "spoken," in the textual equivalent of "tongues." "This preoccupation with language," made for what was well known in seventeenth-century British America as "a distinctive, symbolically resonant Quaker communicative style." But, if the antecedents of "the Quaker communicative style" were Germanic (Böhme) and French (Palissy), as well as British (Fludd)—all part of the Paracelsian tradition—then Quakerism represented only the best-known of a profusion of sects, all privileging the reconstruction of the transparent language of Adam, leading to a "proliferation of sectarian speech styles . . . a prominent component of the Babelistic confusion of tongues that gave revolutionary England its characteristic din."[270]

Yet the silent reconstruction of certain Adamic languages in postlapsarian time was simultaneously an artisanal project, taken up in the visual, tactile, and especially spiritual language of earthy materials by such manual philosophers and alchemists as Palissy, Fludd, and Hogarth. Here, babelistic confusion was understood primarily as a perceptual problem of decoding pluralism and the conflated effects of "mixed composition" through alchemical vision. Thus, for sectarians, pietistic Huguenot artisans, as well as alchemists, the primordial "nature and virtue of things," and the metaphysical manner in which "all things had their names given them," were inextricably entwined by God in creating the original language of Adam. This was unified discourse, in which historical slippage between words and things was nonexistent, and the meaning of verbal and visual language was utterly transparent, inseparable. This was also the true aim of geomancy. Fludd's *Internal Principle* showed how the active agent of visual unification in "this art [of geomancy] is a way of knowing that depends *immediately* [emphasis added] on the soul; that its root is the soul itself; and that, therefore, it is a science more subtle than any other science man may comprehend in this corruptible world."

Through this alchemical operation of the soul, "structures of collaboration" join together in secrecy, combining for the sort of mutual protection and hidden security that the signatories of the Flushing Remonstrance—and Bernard Palissy, the younger Winthrop, Sir Kenelm Digby, and, over 100 years later, Dr. Ezra Stiles—would have comprehended. "Without any doubt are rays emitted between the soul of one man and that of another which are invisible lights," Fludd wrote. "In their emission," he continued, "the rays are so joined together that either the soul of the seeker or the seeker himself be the one to whom danger is imminent, or else a friend of his; for the [soul] is very prophetical:

> Like a guardian forseeing danger with which a body is threatened, it may explain the
> secret future of its body to another soul applying to it—a future which it had been unable
> to communicate to its body because of that body's grossness. And in this way may a quiet

and peaceful soul, which is in fit condition for judging, and to which the movements of its body are well subjugated, prognosticate the future to that other soul . . . [such a soul could] leave its body so as to find a place whence it could enter into communication, and converse, with the souls of . . . friends . . . the rays of the soul extend imperceptibly outside the body and far beyond the range of visible rays. They . . . pass through elementary media without any hindrance, like an influence.

The alchemical process works through the soul to find affinities with other purified bodies of "elementary media" through which it "may pass without hindrance, like an influence." These conversing souls seek to "find a place" to enter into silent, interior communication with "friends," as the many converge in unity and self-protection. But not only friends, enemies as well may enter into converse and be converted. The alchemical operation of the geomantic soul—like the philosopher's stone—allowed for the silent transmutation of another carnal "body's grossness" into transparent purity and friendship (what Stuyvesant and Cornbury called "seduction"). At the end of Fludd's romance, the peripatetic alchemist had only to convince one last Jesuit adversary before being allowed on his way. Verbal arguments alone did not transform the Jesuit from enemy to friend. Fludd gives this away subtly, as two former enemies come together physically and unify symbolically, passing the silent soul from one body to the other. The Jesuit "*embraced me humanely* and swore an oath that henceforth *he would look upon me as if I were his brother* [emphasis added]. He also asked me to visit him and his *confreres* as often as possible." The two men had entered into a sort of family relationship, revealed to them silently, through inner experience. Security was achieved by hidden "influence" rather than violence. The converted Jesuit now carried the invisible rays to his confreres, so that they might act on carnal enemies domestically, hidden in plain sight, even though the alchemist was long gone.

When last we encounter Fludd's character, he is moving on to even greater challenges. He is asked to accept the Jesuit's fraternal offer to stay in Avignon. "I was . . . prevented from doing so by my sudden departure from that city," Fludd wrote cryptically, "whence I went to stay with the Duc de Guise, then at Marseilles, he having sent for me that I might instruct him and his brother, a Knight of Malta, in the mathematical sciences."[271] Charles de Lorraine, the fourth duc de Guise, descended from the most powerful and despised of the noble Counter-Reformation families in France. The Guise family was well known to have been responsible for infamous massacres and other acts of violence committed against Huguenots during the civil wars of religion. The appearance of such a notorious name in this synthesis of alchemic myth and refugee history would have resonated powerfully with Fludd's partner the refugee printer de Bry, and every Huguenot of the many civil war generations. The story ends with Fludd's empathy with the oppressed Huguenots leading him to merge his character's identity with that of a refugee alchemist in France. Like Palissy in 1565, Fludd had become emblematic of a New World Huguenot who would enter the household of his greatest enemy to ply his trade and, in so doing, unify with his opposite through alchemical transmutation.

The provocative John Bossy—whose spiritual and intellectual heroes are the "authentic" early Christians, rather than their lesser Reformation emulators—has written dismissively of the seventeenth-century sectarians as "spiritual radicals" who, though "absorbing to contemplate," were "in the end only a footnote to the history of the transformations of Christendom."[272] This was because in the end,

> their millenarian background inhibited them from preaching the sort of mysticism of everyday life which would accommodate the conventional wisdom that good fences make good neighbors. It seems too strong to say that they were the end of an old song, not the beginning of a new one, for they were all scripturalists in their fashion and their feelings about oneness corresponded to something general in the Reformation; the Quakers are after all still with us. But on the whole they strike one as a bit old fashioned, inhabitants of a moral universe shaped by deadly sins. To the lack of staying-power characteristic of extraordinary motions of the Spirit they added the anachronism of having been born into a civilization of the word: in the long run, moreover, a civilization of the printed word. One answer to the Anabaptists was the baptismal register; another was the catechism. The spirituals could not compete in this field: imagine a Ranter catechism . . . the age of the Spirit was either gone, or not yet come."[273]

If "the spirituals could not compete in this field . . . of the printed word," they had learned to compete successfully in profitable fields that put a premium on the "silent" languages of the Hogarthian shadows: seeing, hearing, remembering, encoding, innovating, building, and rebuilding. Bossy's uncritical use of Walter Ong's notion of a pervasive "civilization of the printed word," has led him, following Hogarth, to overlook sectarian or heterodox artisans working in the Palissian tradition. Huguenots, Quakers, and more than a few Ranters had succeeded in constructing the "mysticism of everyday life," albeit more in things than in words. "Print situates words in space more relentlessly than writing ever did," Ong observes, such that "writing moves words from the sound world to the world of visual space, but print locks words into position in this space. Control of position is everything in print."[274]

Building on the work of Elizabeth Eisenstein, Marshall McLuhan, and George Steiner, Ong elucidates how conceptions of space and by extension the very materiality of meaning were transformed from primordial oral-aural patterns by early print culture, with its geometric reorganization of vision and obsessive emphasis on compartmentalization and closure. Which is precisely why Palissy and his artisan followers—and indeed most sectarians—maintained fluidity and openness in the oral tradition by turning away from "preaching" only printed text by supplementing the mute spiritual charisma of material culture. The Paracelsians, after all, put themselves in the uncomfortable position of writing books to attack the writing of books. Moreover, artisanal work was both sold and disseminated where artisans from places such as Flushing could not go "comfortably." Just as the remonstrators of 1657 likened their town to a household open to settlement by those with "anything" of God in them, the reverse was certainly possible: a sectarian thing was given the motion to silently "leave its body so as to find a place whence it could enter into communication, and converse," through commerce. After all, Kenelm Digby's weapon salve cured wounds by treating the offending weapon, half a world away, if needs be, from its victim. Therefore, while Bossy may find it impossible to "imagine a Ranter catechism," it is not so hard to imagine that Ranters—who called themselves Quakers throughout the Long Island Sound region—made the desk upon which the catechism was read, the house in which the desk was placed, or the paper it was printed on. Certainly, a sectarian may also have printed the catechism itself, if Benjamin Franklin's well-known encounter in Philadelphia with an odd fellow printer—a "French Prophet" who spoke in tongues, "and could act their enthusiastic Agitations"—is any indication. Franklin observed that "he did not profess any particular religion, but something of all on occasion."[275]

❦ Conclusion: Father Jogues Passes Through the Fortieth Parallel ❧

Had the American economic historian Benjamin Labaree followed the younger John Winthrop's European career in the aftermath of the siege of La Rochelle—when Winthrop traveled the Mediterranean in search of the philosopher's stone, and ultimately migrated south from Massachusetts Bay to the Sound region to continue his quest—he would not have apologized for his insight, that "Long Island Sound can be understood, tongue in cheek, as the Mediterranean of the New World." "It provided a magnificent waterway," Labaree goes on,

> for the European settlers of New Amsterdam and Connecticut, as well as for the native Americans on both sides of the Sound. The Sound stretches fifty miles from its lower end to the race at its opening into the Atlantic, and reaches 30 miles at its widest. Its waters are protected. . . . Most small craft . . . can handle its waters without much trouble. The Sound is ideal for shipping: its waters are wide enough to make a series of tacks in a good wind. Its strong winds can also help propel boats along. To further the Mediterranean analogy, Long Island Sound was also an area of conflict. The Sound's easily navigable waters promoted the mixing of cultures; however, peoples living in the Long Island basin experienced occasional friction, primarily because there were so many resources in the area worth fighting over.[276]

It was, of course, in the context of "mixing of cultures" in the pluralistic Mediterranean, that Fernand Braudel first used the term "structures of collaboration." It has been my task here to analyze the morphology—the pluralistic convergence of shared features, "bundles of relations," or "family resemblances"—that provided an underlying unity of structure "beneath" the "mixed composition" of New York's Huguenots and Quakers. Here were two primitivist, refugee artisanal cultures that, in effect, merged spiritual and material assets "primarily because there were so many resources in the area worth fighting over."

The historiography of this task to map convergence in the midst of apparent cultural chaos extends at least from Braudel's post-Nazi, Lévi-Straussian structuralism, in which the very word "collaboration" was heavily laden with meaning, to the approaches of Natalie Zemon Davis and Carlo Ginzburg—both of whom are also heavily influenced by cultural anthropology (and, in Ginzburg's work, folkloric studies as well). Davis demonstrates how effective the "metaphor of the network of human communication" among a heterodox polyglot population may be when it is applied comparatively by historians to the task of understanding how a set of complex yet subtle ties of urban piety, as well as other common early modern vernaculars, including artisanal skills, material life, and innovative entrepreneurship, bound together the most ethnically disparate members of Lyon's highly pluralistic Protestant minority in ways that resonate with the process in New York. Ginzburg unveils a dazzling collection of evidence of a folk cosmology that stretches the underlying unity of symbolic understanding across an array of histories and cultures, and hence "establishes affinities among a vast range of popular beliefs related, it is claimed, to the witches' sabbat."[277]

I make no such claims here. It is precisely the commonplace, quotidian aspect of the process that is most compelling about the convergence of Huguenot and Quaker artisans of New York City and Long Island. The affinities of these refugee groups lay in (1) shared histories of persecution and faith in the power of sacred violence and suffering to purify the spirit and matter of the religious body and produce innovate work, "reborn" out of chaos and entropy (Palissy's dictum: "build with the destroyer"); and hence, (2) fear of the power of absolutism to destroy local shadow worlds of private action; (3) a quest for spiritual and material security in the quotidian "open household" of "converse," convergence, and commerce rather than the elite martial paradigm of the great walled fortress of La Rochelle; (4) beliefs about the hidden motion of the soul to retrieve the unity of fragmented and dispersed Christendom as the "bond and knot of the world"; (5) the obstetric power of material production in interior silence in the shadows; (6) the metaphysical flight of the spirit over or through walls, and between material bodies (an affinity shared with most mythologies of the witches' sabbath); (7) the redemptive nature of primitive memory and the ability to overcome pluralistic difference through shared Adamic languages recovered through the movement of the spirit in the physical body and throughout the material world of Nature; (8) the charismatic spiritualism of domesticity in an "open household" of inspired laity that recovers memory through its containment in domestic furniture; (9) the power of biblical exegesis on the natural world if informed by the immediate workings of the spirit; (10) the Neoplatonic displacement of carnal sexuality into pure love of the spirit and artisanal work; and, by extension (11) security in one's personal mastery of craft skill as a portable commodity precious to migrating refugees in particular, as stated in Paracelsus's often quoted maxim on "experienced" travelers: "Qui omnia secum portat, non indiget alieno auxilio" ("He who carries all things with him needs not the aid of others");[278] (12) the manual philosophy of artisans as opposed to the learned rhetoric of scholars—a common language of artisanry and earth materials unified "simple" pious workmen "sans lettres" from many diverse cultures; and, finally, (13) the belief that the tiny and overlooked—including small metamorphic creatures and seemingly trivial, everyday handcrafted things—can carry the codes to unlock primordial secrets of the unity of matter and spirit, because, like the Holy Spirit's tiny voice, the overlooked were given the power of liminality. They alone were granted the ability to travel between the "little" and the "big" worlds of the microcosm and the macrocosm.

These "affinities" have many different sources in primitivist cosmology, but the most easily identifiable mode of convergence for Huguenots and Quakers in seventeenth-century New Amsterdam / New York was the Paracelsian tradition of natural-philosophical and alchemical discourse. This discourse merged seamlessly with that of the Protestant refuge. It was read and disseminated by figures in each group, both leading and anonymous, each through an intimate lens of private life. Paracelsism contains a "bundle of relations" in a comprehensive tradition, that ranges here from Paracelsus to Palissy, and beyond to Bruno, Platt, Böhme, Fludd, John Winthrop Jr., Thomas Story, the Clement family, and thousands of unnamed practitioners. In the end, Fludd constructed a theory of New World plural societies that fit the experience of each migrating Huguenot refugee artisan who carried "all things with him" in quest of a place in the Atlantic world to converge with other secret souls hidden in the shadows. This was the theory of the "internal principle," or geomancy, whereby the "experienced" traveler called on the *oculus imaginationis* of primordial memory to see beneath the chaos of Babel and perceive the unity of spirit that connected the material universe fragmented by the chaos of transgression and war and find friendship in converse with strangers and enemies.

In the spirit of Fludd's trip to Avignon, let me end, therefore, with the famous quotation from the narrative of Father Isaac Jogues, a Jesuit missionary to New France who was released from captivity by the Iroquois in 1643, only to be delivered by chance to the marginally less hostile territory of New Netherlands. Father Jogues's narrative of experiences on "Manate" (Manhattan) was told to another Jesuit, Father Buteux, who reported it to his superiors in 1645. As a result, the account usually refers to Jogues in the third person. The epigrammatic quotation reads: "The arrogance of Babel has done much harm to all men; the confusion of tongues has deprived them of great benefits." I have chosen to end with these words to posit a historiographical reversal. The quotation has become so familiar, of course, because it has been placed at the *beginning* of virtually every history of New York ever written. This move has all but obviated the necessity of further historical inquiry about perception of cultural confusion. Said by Buteux to have been taken verbatim from Jogues's appraisal of the historical failure of New Netherlands's mixture of cultures, this sentence has been repeated like a catechism. Indeed, it remains a mantra that reverberates throughout the historiography of New Amsterdam and New York as prima facie evidence of an *internal* "principle" of chronic cultural entropy in the colony.

Unfortunately, this famous sentence actually appears at the end of a longer, more complicated passage, one that must be quoted fully to consider the subtle personal contexts Jogues constructed through his interlocutor. This passage does not begin, therefore, in New Amsterdam, but in Rensselaerswyck, the large Hudson Valley manorial settlement surrounding Albany. Jogues was hidden there by a colonial Dutch "sutler" (or army camp provisioner) while waiting for an opportunity to ship out of Iroquois territory. Here, Buteux rehearsed Jogues's relation of the condition of his hiding place:

> In this garret where the Father [Jogues] was, there was a recess to which his guard continually led Hiriquois savages, in order to sell some produce which he had locked up there: this recess was made of planks so slightly joined that one might easily have passed his fingers into the openings. "I am astonished," says the Father, "that those barbarians did not hundreds of times discover me; I saw them without difficulty; and unless God had turned away their eyes, they would have perceived me a thousand times. I concealed myself behind casks, bending myself into a constrained posture which gave me gehenna and torture two, three, or four hours in succession, and that very often. To go down to the court of the dwelling, or to go to other places, was casting myself headlong; for every place was filled with those seeking my death."[279]

Having to choose between this life-or-death predicament and taking the next sloop down the Hudson to cast in his lot with hostile Protestants in Manhattan, Jogues sensibly chose the latter option. Once there, though treated by Kieft with the sort of kindness that Stuyvesant would never have offered a Catholic in later years, *his* own perception of chaos, an inability to see what lay beneath the surface of Babel, gave Jogues pause.

The Manhattanites tried to dress Jogues at least partially "in their own style," hoping he would become like one of them—which he was, as a refugee from persecution and violence—instead of just a stranger:

This good Father was received in Manate with great tokens of affection; the captain had a black coat made for him, sufficiently light, and gave him a good cloak and a hat in their own style. The inhabitants came to see him, showing, by their looks and their words, that they felt great sympathy for him. Some asked him what recompense the Gentlemen of New France[280] would give him, imagining that he had suffered those indignities on account of their trade. But he had given them to understand that worldly thoughts had not caused him to leave his own country; and that the publication of the Gospel was the sole good that he had in view when casting himself into the dangers into which he had fallen. A good lad, having met him in a retired place, fell at his feet, taking his hands to kiss him, and exclaiming, "Martyr, Martyr of Jesus Christ!" He questioned him, and ascertained that he was a Lutheran, whom he could not aid for want of acquaintance with his language; he was a Pole. Entering a house quite near the fort, he saw two images on the mantelpiece, one of the blessed Virgin, the other of our Blessed Louys de Gonzage.[281] When he betokened some satisfaction at this, the master of the house told him that his wife was a Catholic. She was a Portuguese, brought into that country by I know not what chance; she appeared very bashful. *The arrogance of Babel has done much harm to all men; the confusion of tongues has deprived them of great benefits* [emphasis added].[282]

The seventeenth-century language of spiritual perception is familiar. Father Jogues immediately identifies the Iroquois as "barbarians"—that is, the ultimate kind of stranger—devoid of spirit. Indians are carnal "savages," who appear in the European settlement for the sole purpose of acquiring material goods. As a result, Jogues remained invisible through his confident sense of purity, and he was "astonished" that though "I saw them without difficulty; . . . unless God had turned away their eyes, they would have perceived me a thousand times." Without the historical facility with which the Huguenots went underground (often to escape Jesuit persecution), Jogues "cast" himself awkwardly into the protection of the shadows, making the whole process of concealment strange, painful, and above all unnatural. The Jesuit refugee knew this had to be a temporary condition, because, though he had earned "my crosses,"[283] he could not bear to suffer the hellish pain of the subterranean life for too long: "I concealed myself behind casks," Buteux quoted him as saying, "bending myself into a constrained posture which gave me gehenna and torture." He found it impossible to move freely through this mercantile space, "for every place was filled with those seeking my death."

The situation was reversed once Jogues reached New Netherlands. The inhabitants received him with "great sympathy" as a refugee of religious violence. He was given local "tokens of affection" that allowed the Jesuit refugee to disguise his distinctive "black robe" and appear "in their own style." What was communicated by this symbolic gesture of stylistic inclusion? Maybe it was a simple attempt to absorb a stranger with the potential to access Church funds. Or perhaps the Manhattanites wanted to show they could help obscure the superficial perception of confessional differences and see Jogues, along with themselves, as a member of a community of Christ in the spirit? However, despite this good start, it was clear that Jogues and the friendly colonists had little in common from his perspective. The Jesuit informed his listeners that (presumably unlike them and the Iroquois barbarians) "worldly thoughts had not caused him to leave his own country." Thus he assumed the pose of moral superiority he supposed had saved him from being detected by the Iroquois in Rensselaerswyck.

Then the key moment arrives, offering Jogues the opportunity to achieve the potential of convergence. Jogues was invited to enter New Netherlands's spiritual community of the shadows. He had moved out of public view and encountered "a good lad [who] having met him in a retired place, fell at his feet . . . exclaiming 'Martyr, Martyr of Jesus Christ.'" This man was a Pole and a Lutheran, who called the Jesuit a martyr of Christ, a double reference to his religious house and his refugee status. In so doing, the colonist offered his presence to engage in open "converse" with the spirit. But Jogues could not communicate in this way. He perceived only linguistic and confessional difference, not potential for unity beneath the confusion of Babel. Father Jogues, therefore, "could not aid" the seeker, "for want of acquaintance with his language."

Jogues's experience of linguistic alienation was repeated at the house of another Protestant colonist and his Portuguese Catholic wife. Here, he perceived two Catholic "images on the mantelpiece." Yet Jogues was unable to move beyond narcissistic perception of commonality between himself and the "very bashful" woman, to extend his knowledge and absorb the deeper connections she might have made, not only with her Protestant husband, but with other Christians in New Amsterdam. Jogues perceived a familiar hierarchy of images but overlooked the possibilities of converging memories implied by the context in which they were embedded. In the end, the Jesuit could not speak her language either, so he concluded that, like himself, the Portuguese woman had been "brought into that country by I know not what chance."

Thus we arrive at last at the famous passage. Having failed to find comfort and communicate in the language of silence, Father Jogues succeeded in constructing a legacy of multicultural New York as Babylon. At the same time, however, Jogues's Protestant competitors found the "mixed composition" of New Netherlands / New York the perfect place to relocate a shape-shifting culture of being and appearance. In the Huguenots' New World, everything of consequence began life in the shadows.

CHAPTER SEVENTEEN

Reflections on a Three-Legged Chair

Sundials, "Family Pieces," and Political Culture
in Pre-Revolutionary New York

In 1736, William Hogarth explored shadows cast by the gnomon of a metaphorical sundial over the hidden world of his Huguenot neighbors in London. In 1751, a copper sundial (figs. 17.1, 17.1a, 17.1b), was engraved in New York by Joseph Leddell Sr. (also Leddel) that turned the tables on Hogarth by reflecting light on the sun's government of the fortieth parallel. A Huguenot engraver and pewterer with powerful anti-Catholic and anti-Jacobite political convictions, Leddell had connections to a French Calvinist artisanal network that may have originated in Saint-Malo. Leddell (1690?–1754) was actually born in England, to refugee parents in Hampshire, but he eventually resettled in New York, where he became a member of the city's French Church.[1] The philosophical maxim used by Leddell to title his sundial, "Emblematical Figures Better Conceive'd Than Express'd," is particularly well suited to Huguenot themes. New York City's coat of arms locates the New World's future in the unity of its polyglot crucible, where scriptural text, transatlantic history, and prophecy are combined by alchemic processes. Like Vulcan at his forge, the emblem of the alchemic crucible transmutes artifacts of war into articles of mercantile commerce, not plowshares fit for the countryside.

References to war served multiple purposes. Above all, they were a gloss on the brutal experience of New Yorkers on the frontier with New France, where fighting had been going on since the seventeenth century. Such figures also attempted to distance the city's Huguenots from local fears of conspiracy on the part of their French Catholic counterparts by calling attention to the long history of their own sanctification by violence beginning with the civil wars of religion and ending with the final separation of the diaspora from absolutist France in 1685.

To reiterate millennial themes of unity amid the potential for conflict inherent in middle colonial heterodoxy and pluralism, the dial face is engraved in English, while the gnomon, which casts the shadow, has additional maxims about passing time in several languages on both sides. These are written in classical Latin and Greek as well as the city's three commonly used languages: Dutch, French, and English. Plays on social unity connect the gnomon's linguistic messages, which make sense if read together as couplets. Leddell's choice for his French maxim is joined—as were most Huguenot New Yorkers—to an English one above it. The English and French lines form a couplet on the gnomon's east side referring to the metaphysics of security, that most venerable of Huguenot artisanal themes: "Mans life is nought without divine protection / Si nous y faisons une serieuse reflection [*sic*] [If we give it serious reflection]." There can be little doubt that Leddell used "we" to associate his work with New York's Huguenots. All the more reason for "serious reflection" to have a double meaning in French (as in English); the phrase puns on contemplation and reflection (or perhaps being and appearance). When new, this copper gnomon was as highly polished as gold, casting shadows in sunlight at the same time as the maxims reflected off the luminous dial. Like *Noon,* "Emblematical Figures" on the Leddell dial also exist in a looking-glass world of shadow and reflection.

Sundials reminded readers in implicit and explicit ways that the earth merely reflects (and is animated by) the sun's light. At the same time, however, earthly creatures can only be seen fully in the daylight. It is for this reason, of course, that sundial chapter rings count the hours of daylight only from five in the morning until seven in the evening. Mechanical clocks like the one on Hogarth's church tower were necessary for telling time at night. This liability was the common subject of jokes and humorous reproaches engraved on the dials themselves. Didactic aphorisms were a form of serious play: reminders that habits of industry, politeness, and internal self-mastery, on display during the day, should remain constant, or else the baneful effects of an unexamined or unrestrained life—impoliteness, conspiracy, chaos, and corruption—can reassert control at night or remain hidden in shadow during the day. Imperceptible behavior thus operates secretly outside the sun's (or the state's) "regulative power."

Supported on columns of Justice and Virtue, the two stanzas of verse engraved on Leddell's dial invoke a range of pieties that underscore social harmony and its connection with the daily rising of the sun. With the sunrise, mankind's industriousness can be timed to coincide exactly with the calm dispassion of a mechanistic cosmos. But the sundial cannot possibly reflect what transpires on earth between seven o'clock at night and five in the morning. In the absence of light, "this machine" loses both the

FIGURE 17.1. Joseph Leddell Sr. (1690?–1754), copper sundial, New York City, 1751. H: 4⅝″, W: 9¼″. Courtesy Henry Francis du Pont Winterthur Museum, Winterthur, Delaware. Visual and textual messages are engraved over the surface of the dial and its gnomon to promote political, temporal, linguistic, and religious pacifism in pluralistic New York City during an age of imperial warfare and factional competition. The main frieze depicts interaction and friendly commerce through trade and Roman soldiers turning swords into plowshares in the republican period. Leddell, a Huguenot refugee, engraved multiple texts about time, industry, and God's protection in a confluence of Latin, Dutch, Greek, French, and English to reflect his context but also to refute accusations by critics of its many non-English ethnicities that New York City was a modern Babel. (a) and (b): A dog chases a rabbit up and down the gnomon's serpentine bracket; a playful comment in the age of Hogarth on the perpetual interaction of time with the macrocosm and microcosm.

source of its power and its audience. "Like" the spectator, it is resigned to a "useless" half-life that invites disorder, lassitude, and (ribald) dysfunction:

Reader behold how this machine,　　　When Phaebus god of Light and day,
The fleeting hours display.　　　　　Moves o'er my plain his vivid ray.
Unurg'd by passion, or by spleen,　　If a slight look on me you'll cast.
Admits of no delay.　　　　　　　　I'll shew you when to break your fast
This emblem should our tempers give　By just degrees I tell the time.

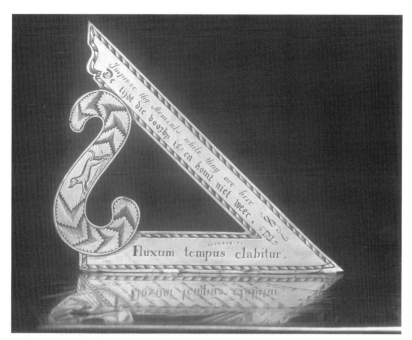

(a)

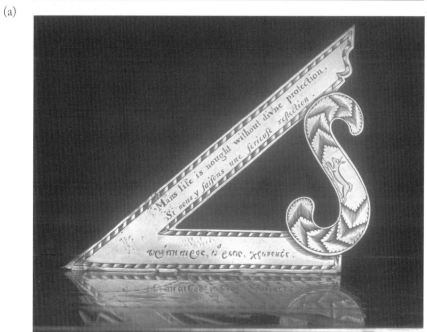

(b)

Its regulative power.
And virtuous action while we live
Distinguish ev'ry hour.
When thus inflexible we'r found,
Envy her yell gives o'er,
And endles raptures shall us
When time shall be no more.

And point you out the hour to dine.
By my assistance you may see,
When too regale with cake or tea.
And when the Sun to westward drops.
I'll shew you when to shut your shops.
But when he dos withdraw his crown, light,
Like you I am useless all the night.

Leddell's production of instruments of natural philosophy was not unique in the city. Another eighteenth-century New York dial maker who was conspicuous for having the widest range of technical and scientific skills (in addition to engraving) was an Irish manual philosopher named Christopher Colles (1739–1816). Colles settled in Manhattan in 1774, after three relatively anonymous years in Philadelphia. What little we know of Colles's sojourn in Philadelphia dates from August 26, 1771, when the newly arrived immigrant from Ireland advertised his intention in the *Pennsylvania Chronicle* to "instruct young Gentlemen . . . in the different Branches of . . . Mathematics and Natural Philosophy." There was much competition in Philadelphia among a well-established group of talented scientists and instrument makers—including Franklin and Benjamin Rittenhouse—so New York must have offered more plausible opportunities.

Because Colles's natural-philosophical interests focused primarily on experiments in hydraulic engineering, he sought patronage in New York for ambitious waterworks projects, while laboring to establish a day-to-day market for engraving and domestic scientific instruments made in direct competition with English imports. It is possible that the two enterprises were connected, since Colles may have produced sundials as gifts—to solicit subscriptions or other forms of patronage for his waterworks projects—as well as for sale. Nevertheless, only four Colles sundials are known to survive, in part because the vast majority of sundials used in early America were imported from England, and they were, in any event, simply discarded as out of fashion by the early nineteenth century. Mostly, however, the survival rate is low because Colles made his dials from the cheapest base metal available in the colony, locally mined paper-thin copper, with a wrought-iron gnomon loosely attached with a rivet at either end. When placed outside in the elements, the copper and iron tended to corrode, come apart, break free of rusted iron attachments to the dial post, and eventually disappear altogether into the refuse pit. While it is impossible to extrapolate Colles's output over the course of a forty-two-year-long career, the mere fact that four of these flimsy devices survived at all suggests that it was substantial. Moreover, he clearly had expectations of success, since the dials were engraved for reference of future patrons, as "fecit" (made by him), at "No 42 Pearl Str[eet] New York."[2]

FIGURE 17.2. Christopher Colles (Ireland, 1739–New York, 1816), copper and iron sundial, New York City, 1774–1816. Private collection. Photo, Christopher Zaleski. H: 5¼″, W: 8¾″, D: 8¾″. The dial is signed "Chris Colles fecit No 42 Pearl St. New York." Colles arrived in New York City from Philadelphia in 1774 and promoted himself as a hydraulic engineer, mathematician, and natural philosopher. He may have made sundials as gifts to promote patronage for his many waterworks projects, including a network of pipelines underneath the city's streets. This project showed promise but ended with the British occupation of New York during the Revolution. Whereas the poem on the front of Leddell's dial (fig. 17.1) ends with the line, "Like you I am useless all the night," engraved on the back of Colles's dial is the phrase "I fly while you sleep." Both sentiments were playful reminders that time's secret life goes on in the shadows.

When Colles took up Leddell's humorous lament about the perceptual limitations of sundials, he did so far more succinctly than his Huguenot counterpart. Atop the most complete surviving dial (fig. 17.2), Colles engraved daytime's motto in Latin, "Dum spectas fugio" ("Watch [me] fly while you can"). This suggested that a playful dialogue was under way with the unseen portion of the back of the dial. There he engraved nighttime's arch response in English, "I fly while you sleep."[3]

"A slight look . . . cast" at Leddell's sundial, perhaps situated on a dial post in the herb and medicinal garden just outside the door, must have had the daily effect of a subliminal précis of Benjamin Franklin's *Poor Richard Improved* (Philadelphia, 1763), or even his *Autobiography*. Both were elite texts adopting quotidian (often artisanal) poses. All attempted to lock in emblemata that "governed" social and astronomical harmony between microcosm and macrocosm, embodied by the relentless timing of industrious labor in support of the prevailing natural and ideological order.[4] The sundial displayed patrons' Enlightenment ideology conjoining time and natural law, but Leddell's personal and religious history was far too byzantine, and his pluralistic "readers" in New York City (as the sundial itself reminds us) were too much a part of a complex social milieu, for Leddell to be reduced to a mere cipher for the dominant order.

The best evidence that Leddell's work defined hierarchies of loyalty is drawn from an extraordinary group of his engravings on silver, which show that the mental world of a Huguenot living in mid eighteenth-century New York was still intensely historical and deeply rooted in seminal Reformation events of seventeenth-century Europe. Leddell's artifacts display fear of the continuing threat to overthrow the Protestant Hanoverian dynasty in England with, in effect, the reversal of the Glorious Revolution of 1688, plotted by Catholic supporters of Charles Stuart, the grandson of the deposed James II. With the obvious exception of books, overtly polemical artifacts that are known to have been made and used (here remade and reused) domestically, or even in ritual settings, by the same Huguenot artisan and his family rarely survive.

❧ A Language of Remembering ❧

However, a silver beaker with anti-Jacobite iconography (figs. 17.3a, b, and c) made about the same time as his sundial is one such artifact. Its provenance indicates Leddell had a deeply personal stake in its idiosyncratic design and manufacture as a relic of the Huguenot historical past, a guide to the present, and a prophesy of a bleak future that might cause a return to the dangers of the past once again. By the 1750s, Huguenot artisans such as Leddell felt less threatened by the inscription of an overt iconographic narrative on diasporic artifacts that were previously left silent, "plain," or natural." Earlier artisans who suffered a great deal in their refugee experience, such as Palissy, were constrained by sophisticated Nicodemite strategies that emerged out of fear of violent reprisal. Shunning openness, these artisans sought to communicate indirectly, through hidden artisanal languages they understood to be available in certain natural materials.

It is therefore a remarkable homage to changing contexts that the beaker has outsized images of the devil, the pope, and the pretender (Charles Stuart) engraved all around, rendered in the anachronistic caricatured style of the Germanic Reformation's mannerist woodcut. These woodcuts were cheap, widely diffused instruments of popular anti-papal propaganda, perhaps the most instantly recognizable prints in the history of early modern Europe. The beaker itself was neither of American manufacture nor engraved when first made. Rather, it was made "plain," in 1707 in Saint-Malo, France, by a provincial Huguenot silversmith named Huges Loissieux. Leddell inherited it from his parents—who, unlike him, had been persecuted in France—and carried it with him as a sacred family heirloom from the Old World to New York, where he himself added the engraving in 1750. Because the beaker remained in the possession of the Leddells in an unbroken line of descent to modern times, it served the personal use of the maker and his descendants, possibly for private communion at home, with family members and friends. Leddell attested in French to his work as "sculp"[ter] ("carver"), along with his name and the date, all of which are engraved on its bottom, next to the original Loissieux shop mark.

Perhaps Leddell left the French maker's mark behind as a vague reminder that its former history in France and England paralleled his own family's history and travels, showing also that his additions were not without foundation, but built on top of the sanctified experience of the beaker's original maker.[5] His mark superimposed on that of his predecessor, therefore, functioned as a palimpsest of refugee life. Hence, a formerly silent old cup from Saint-Malo was refashioned by a Huguenot artisan in mid eighteenth-century New York, where it now retold an old Reformation story in a languages that were universally recognizable, albeit on a private artifact of Huguenot family memory. Here, the devil drags a chain attached to the pope's nose, first through a doorway marked "Death," signified by the "Raw-Head and Bloody-Bones," and then down into the flaming mouth of hell. There, the Stuart pretender (in a Scottish tartan) follows prayerfully behind the pope Anti-Christ, with their necks yoked together in a noose drawn through a gibbet marked: "Danger." This evil procession allowed for space behind the pretender. Thus, if England and America were harnessed by the neck to Charles Stuart as their monarch, it would be the equivalent of marching in lockstep behind the damned into hell. Like most sixteenth-century Reformation prints, the beaker's engraved images from 1750 mingle easily with written text. Unlike prototypes published during the wars of religion, Leddell admonished friends and family—perhaps at the moment of the Lord's Supper—to "Remember" when they handled the relic. His engravings were living updates, not "dead-letter" anachronisms:

> Three mortal enemies *Remember*
> The Devil Pope and the Pretender
> Most wicked damnable and evil
> The Pope Pretender and the Devil
> I wish they were all hang'd in a rope
> The Pretender Devil and the Pope

(a)

(b)

FIGURE 17.3. (a) (b) (c) French Huguenot silver beaker depicting the devil leading the pope and the pretender into the mouth of hell, made in blank form by Hugues Lossieux, in Saint-Malo, France, around the time of the Revocation of the Edict of Nantes, and subsequently engraved by Joseph Leddell Sr. in New York City in 1750. Courtesy Museum of the City of New York. H: 3¹⁄₁₆″. Leddell reanimated this old family relic from the period of the *désert* by engraving it in the style of seventeenth-century Reformation propaganda to depict his perception of a continuous personal threat to religious and political liberty, from the Old World to the New.

French Calvinists had complex relationships with their kings, and Huguenot discourse on monarchy could vary greatly from moment to moment and by region in the transatlantic world. It ranged from a minority of so-called radical "monarchomachs" (or king-killers) on one end of the spectrum to unapologetic royalists on the other. Moderates, or "politiques," occupied shifting ground in the middle. Loyalties to monarchs divided families. After the Revocation, many Huguenots still attached strong emotional attachments and political hopes to the mystical body of their king, though the individual who inhabited his secular body may have been despised.

In New York City in the 1750s, Leddell harnessed his family's loyalty to the Hanoverian kings. He saw the return of a Catholic pretender to the throne as the greatest threat to British-American Huguenots, and the guarantee against this happening was a strong monarchy.[6] By extension, Leddell joined the royal governor's colonial clientage network. Huguenot artisans learned much from personal experience and family history in the dangerous internecine political battles of sixteenth-century France. They learned how loyalty to patrons tied to the established order of the moment could sometimes be seen as resistance, and loyalties to patrons were similarly flexible in mid eighteenth-century New York. That is why it is difficult to consider Leddell's loyalty to the Georgian kings separately from the specifics of his artisanal admonition: "remember" the past. As Leddell's near contemporary Paul Rapin de Thoyras demonstrated in his *History of England*, Huguenots throughout the Atlantic

(c)

world attached enormous providential significance to the Glorious Revolution. Rapin's *History* equates the momentous landing and subsequent installment of William and Mary on the throne with Julius Caesar's landing in ancient Britain. The year 1688 was thus Year One of a prophetic narrative that began with Louis XIV's impending defeat by William, followed by the reversal of the Revocation of the Edict of Nantes, and ending with the exiles' victorious return to France. When these events did not transpire as predicted, Rapin abandoned England for the Hague, and finally Wesel, where he subsisted on a pension from William III until his death in 1725. Despite their disappointment that the ultimate promise of the Glorious Revolution was not fulfilled by William of Orange, diasporic Huguenots of Leddell's generation remembered the significance of 1688 and nurtured millennial hopes of an eventual return to France behind a combined Anglo-French army led by a new English Calvinist warrior-king.

But any analysis of Leddell's worldview must also take into account his elevated status as an artisan who supplied the luxury trades, if only because he had access to coin and other forms of precious metal. Like most successful New York silversmiths, he was obliged by his business to maintain strong commercial and political ties with the city's English elites, while at the same time absorbing styles and fashions from the metropolis into his decorative vocabulary. Taken together, Leddell's motivations for crafting goods that idealized the submission of New York's factional groups to the natural order and "regulative power" of the cosmos are too complex to categorize neatly. That Calvinists were motivated by the sublimation of "passion . . . spleen . . . [and] tempers" (these are Leddell's words) into work must also find its proper place here. The negative experience of violent passions was recorded for posterity as a fundamental trope of Huguenot historiography, which was itself simultaneously a martyrology of victims. Huguenot historiography was a narrative of the baneful effects of centuries of "spleen [and] tempers"—Palissy's disordered "esmotions." Huguenots had learned to construct stories about tragic consequences that resulted from emotional disharmony, and to extend narratives of "memories" of victimization—so central to Huguenot identity as a diasporic culture—into Leddell's time.

Memory narratives of the dispersion were written in Europe and the Americas until well into the nineteenth century and provided the textual basis for founding Huguenot societies throughout the world.[7] Still, it seems problematic that "Emblematical Figures Better Conceive'd Than Express'd" was Leddell's axiom for manual philosophy in New York, if for no other reason than that its logic about the limited expression of metaphor underscored the limitations of the sundial's message in social practice. While Leddell's rhetoric traces the naturalness and hence the universality of "regulative power" as it flowed from God to God's allegorical figures—the sun and the king—the logic of his axiom automatically acknowledges its limitations.

As Leddell admits—and Hogarth demonstrates—the dial's "governing" paradigm for the regulation of time is complicated by the rules of practice, where everything is negotiable. Just as the normative rules "expressed" by sundials disappear during the night, so too metaphorical philosophies espoused by "this machine" can be as elusive in light of day as the shadows on Hog Lane. Indeed, one reason Leddell claimed a specific definition of this axiom was his realization that in practice the range of possible meanings ascribed to emblematic figures of the natural world were as multiple and fluid as they were tacit. All were "conceive'd" on the basis of invisible personal, cultural, and historical memories. Leddell also announces a strategy that social convergence around a natural-philosophical master narrative was accommodated under certain conditions in New York, but only if tacit agreement existed on a metaphorical level beyond language (and hence beyond debate).

❧ Natural Light and Imperial Politics ❧

However, reading the sundial's axiom as part of a larger discursive context, its maker and patron could not have been complacent about the universal acceptance of mechanistic natural philosophy and its political ramifications in New York City. The dial's mechanistic discourse blends seamlessly with language used by members of a mid eighteenth-century political faction that believed in the naturalness of royal prerogative in the colonial context. This faction was conscious of the problematic nature of achieving this worldview in practice, fearing disorder caused by rejection of the prerogative in New York. Leddell's engravings can thus be linked to a program to neutralize assembly power and domesticate monarchical notions of order and security by inserting Whitehall's ideas about the nature of prerogative, mediated by "Master" artisans but unsullied by the assembly, directly into the homes and private spaces of New Yorkers.

The metaphorical language of "emblematic figures" originated with Renaissance humanism and had important seventeenth-century antecedents in colonial New England. This language was firmly reactivated in New York politics during the early 1750s—just when the sundial was made—and written into polemical tracts that supported the immutability of royal prerogative (and the power of royal governors) in order to resist steady encroachment on it by the lower houses of colonial legislatures.[8]

With the British imperial administrator and mercantilist Archibald Kennedy's "From an Assembly We Have Everything to Fear" in his *Essay on the Government of the Colonies* (New York, 1752), a monarchist jeremiad was launched by this city customs collector of over twenty years' standing against privileges taken by the powerful and obstreperous New York assembly. "The design of the Settlement was the Extension of Commerce," Kennedy insisted, to clarify the assembly's willful misreading of its proper place in New York Colony's institutional history, "not the Foundation of a City, or a new Empire." Kennedy's criticism of the New York assembly's imperial ambitions in competition with the crown resonates with the growth of local artisanal production. Yet Leddell and other successful New York tradesmen also knew that Kennedy was sometimes an ally who had defended to his superiors in England the right of New York's artisans to expand their manufactures in the face of growing imperial policies demanding cutbacks or interdiction. This may have been cause for political alliances.[9] Still, at around the same time as his tract was published, or perhaps a decade or so earlier, an anonymous New York painter completed a rustic image of Romulus and Remus (fig. 17.4). Given the context of Kennedy's complaint, it is not far-fetched to suggest that the painting depicts precisely the sort of conception of the founding of an empire in New York that Kennedy warned against. In addition, the painter seems to use the Roman foundational myth as a call for political and cultural inclusiveness as the basis for empire building in the city. Here the orphan Romulus is received into the "open household" of the shepherd Faustulus, who presents him to his wife, Acca Larentia, gesturing an exorbitant welcome.

It follows, then, that what Kennedy called the "Fundamental Law" of colonies was meant to supersede indigenous authority and so was properly called the "Law of Europe."[10] For Kennedy, this meant law devolved directly from the monarch to colonial British America and that the multilayered imperial system was an instrument of royal prerogative. The king's laws were a benevolence extended as a gift to his English subjects in New York and were exercised directly through the offices of the royal governor—the king's chosen surrogate—and not the assembly, which diffused the purity of the original intention through pluralism and private interest. Unruly individuals wishing to advance personal agendas in pursuit of social and economic liberty did so at the expense of the whole, which, for Kennedy, stood to benefit most from the monarch's natural sense of order.

Liberties thus subverted the royal prerogative, accumulated unnaturally over time, and were finally institutionalized as inviolable assembly privileges. The exercise of royal

FIGURE 17.4. Unknown artist in the circle of Gerardus Duyckinck I (1695–1746), *Romulus and Remus Received into the Household of the Shepherd Faustulus and His Wife Acca Larentia.* H: 12″ × W: 18″. Oil on canvas with original stretcher of American white pine. Probably New York City, ca. 1700–30. Private collection. Photo, Christopher Zaleski. Another scene from early Roman history to which a New York artist drew parallels. Here the rustic theme infers that adopting refugees will, in time, make New York City a new Rome.

prerogative, which Kennedy thought natural, was perceived as negotiable by his political opponents. The constant state of hurly-burly that characterized negotiation over political power in New York was the cause of Kennedy's despair. Because disorder was, for Kennedy, an unnatural state, his rhetoric uses a variant of the microcosm/macrocosm analogy to satisfy his desperate desire to restrain social chaos and fluidity through a fictional consensus based on metaphors of "natural Prerogative":

> The Commission and Instructions directed to his Excellency the Governor, but intended for the Good of the Whole; which, by the Bye, I cannot help thinking, that if they were in every Body's Hands, as a Family-Piece or House Bible, and not scooped up like the *Sibylline Oracles,* to which Recourse was only had upon extraordinary Emergency, it might be of mighty Use; the People would become acquainted and in Love with their Constitution! they would there see through the Whole, the benevolent Intentions of our most gracious Sovereign the King, and our Mother-Country: Whereas, at present, they are

represented, by some of our Dealers in Politicks, as big with that Monster, *Prerogative,* a Thing which some of our weak Members are taught to dread as much as ever Children were that of *Raw-Head and Bloody-Bones.* Thus by wicked Instruments, for wicked Purposes, are weak Minds imposed upon; for whose Sake I shall endeavor to explain the Word, which, I doubt, is but ill understood.[11]

Using antiquarian strategies developed to argue opposing positions by the great seventeenth-century English parliamentarian and legal historian Sir Edward Coke ("The Oracle of Law," as he was called by New York's eighteenth-century historian and legal scholar William Smith),[12] Kennedy found ample historical precedent for royal prerogative in the Americas. He "explain[ed] the Word" philologically by tracing its origins beyond the earliest colonial governments chartered under Elizabeth, back through Henry VII and Sebastian Cabot, to speculation on Carthaginian sources. Predictably, after citing papers written in the powerfully symbolic year of 1664 by the famously autocratic Governor John Endicott (1588–1665) of Massachusetts Bay Colony, Kennedy settled on an authoritarian and paternalistic reading of Calvinist prerogative in relatively homogeneous seventeenth-century New England, while asserting the unifying value of a similar definition for pluralistic New York Colony. From this definition, he extrapolated the historical existence of a tacit colonial consensus—the unwritten foundation of an American ancient constitution—that confirmed tacit and customary rules of obedience to the king. This was "expressed" "emblematically" by the most basic Calvinist symbol for patriarchal authority available, the father's preeminent place as ruler in his household or shop. These tacit rules remained unfixed because their variety was as mysterious and infinite as there were numbers of households or shops, even as the contexts in which they usually applied were face-to-face and informal.

But if codification was "impossible," it was also unnecessary. The symbolic language of natural prerogative had stood the test of time. It had shown itself to be all-encompassing, flexible enough to accommodate the infinite variety of everyday life. It was, to gloss Leddell, as unnatural as delaying time to negotiate "The Father['s] or Master['s]" authority in the household; just as "His Majesty, as he is our political Father, his political Prerogative, from the like Circumstances and Reasons, is equally necessary." By both natural law and custom, this universal symbol of convergence was "perfectly understood" by every family. "And this political Authority has been allowed the supreme Director, in all States, in all Ages, and in all Places." Thus, Kennedy continued, "if I may be allowed to compare small Things with great,"[13] the natural prerogative to rule both "little" and "larger" governments was intertwined, because in either world, only one individual could effectively bestow justice on the plurality:

There is, in every Family, a Sort of Government without any fixed Rules; and indeed it is impossible, even in a little Family, to form Rules for every Circumstance; *and therefore it*

is better conceived than expressed [emphasis added]; but perfectly understood by every Individual belonging to the Family. The Study of the Father or Master, is for the Good of
the Whole; all Appeals are to him; he has a Power, from the Reason and Nature of Things,
to check the Insolent, or Indolent, and to encourage the Industrious: In short, the whole
affairs of the Family are immediately under the Care or Direction of the Father or Master; and this is a natural Prerogative, known and acknowledged by every Man living, who
has ever had a Family, in all Ages and in all Places. His Majesty, as he is our political
Father, his political Prerogative, from the like Circumstances and Reasons, is equally necessary. And this political Authority has been allowed the supreme Director, in all States,
in all Ages, and in all Places; and without it, there would be a Failure of Justice.[14]

When Kennedy added a third layer to form a tripartite analogy of king with father
and master, he cleverly extended the conceptual framework of "We Have Everything
to Fear." Now he included Leddell and diverse other New York master artisans—
whose craft and economic interests he supported in England—on yet another level of
ideology and patronage. Kennedy saw the economic and cultural common ground between elite patrons and the city's unusually heterogeneous group of masters as a useful bridge linking royal prerogative with the lower orders of urban artisanal labor. This
included journeymen, indentured servants, apprentices, and, after the slave rebellion
of 1741, New York's large, mobile, and threatening society of slave artisans as well.

Less conventionally "political," but more provocative from the viewpoint of both
the early modern transatlantic history of New York's refugee artisans and their artifactual record, on the one hand, and the synthesis of synchronic (universal) and diachronic (local) time contained in Leddell's sundial, on the other, is Kennedy's deceptively quotidian wish: "by the Bye, I cannot help thinking, that if [the governor's
instructions from Whitehall] were in every Body's Hands, as a Family-Piece or House
Bible, and not . . . only had upon extraordinary Emergency, it might be of mighty Use;
the People would become acquainted and in Love with their Constitution! *they would
there see through the Whole*" (emphasis added). Kennedy proposed the domestication of
contentious political discourse in the form of benign everyday artifacts, so common as
to appear almost invisible. Quietly discursive things would extend cosmological ideas
from the central authority into colonial households in ways that would invite casual
acquiescence by circumventing standard forms of political resistance. One wonders
how much Kennedy's published wish reflected processes that were already under way
in New York's material culture, or whether he intended a new challenge to the city's
artisans on the lookout for powerful patronage.

To be sure, the parallels between Kennedy's language of the benign transparency of
paternalistic intentions and the reflective and instrumental function claimed by Leddell's quotidian artifact, which merely synchronized the mechanical nature of man, are

striking in both chronology and rhetoric. Consider the functional precision with which man matched universal messages directed from "this machine" of God's macrocosm (the sun's rays) to every locality in the dial's adjustable microcosmic context. To decode the mystery of cosmic convergence, it was a simple matter to adjust the angle of the gnomon to the latitude of its geographical setting (as in Leddell's and Colles's gnomons, which are set permanently to Winthrop's mystical latitude of 40°, which bisects New York City). Consider, as well, that Leddell's playful pun on the French phrase *serieuse reflection,* may have been associated with the following passages from Kennedy: "If any impartial Thinker, or indeed that can think at all, would give himself the Trouble *seriously to reflect,* and *compare our present Situation and Constitution, with any other upon the Face of the Earth* [emphasis added], I am confident he would determine in our Favour."[15] Leddell crafted just such a situational instrument, to provide a context in which to consider and reflect upon these comparisons minute by minute.

In the end, however, Kennedy's rhetorical "confidence" in the transparent purity of the theory of royal prerogative was shaken by the instability of liberty in practice. "Family-Pieces" made by Leddell and his co-religionists were potentially useful political instruments, but Kennedy knew that without complicitous readers, artifacts were in themselves unpersuasive. Private messages could not be controlled. Objects were insufficient to fill "thoughtless, unwary Country-men" with knowledge of the tacit natural relationships revealed in the "whole" of "Emblematic Figures Better Conceive'd Than Express'd." Metaphorical relationships could not be contained whole within one confined symbolic system. Instruments reflecting the polish of royal prerogative in autonomous domestic settings had crude but successful competition in the assembly among "Perverters of it." While New York's heads of households might acquiesce to Kennedy's analogy of kingship to patriarchy, there was no guarantee that such a heterogeneous group would rule like Hanoverian monarchs, or even like one another. That is why the author's contempt for his colony's consumers "of our Dealers in Politics . . . [those] wicked Instruments, for wicked Purposes," was unvarnished. New Yorkers who perceived virtue in muddled and subversive assembly rhetoric and a multiplicity of laws and interests, rather than clarity in royal prerogative, were "weak Minds imposed upon." The cause of this weakness was "our Liberty . . . it must infallibly indanger our Constitution."[16] Thus "We Have Everything to Fear" from the loss of reciprocity and balance in the cosmological machine caused by contention and disorder. Instability in the microcosm threatened retribution from the king or an angry God, for Kennedy, the primary agents of government regulation between the two worlds. Kennedy reasoned that the danger to New York lay in its ever-present work-in-progress state of fluidity and becoming. Moreover, he represented the threat in a stunning paraphrase from Jeremiah, of the famous analogy God draws between himself and a potter at his wheel in the process of making and remaking a clay vessel: "We are but yet, as it were, in the Hands of the Potter; in a probationary State of Good-Behavior; if we totter upon three Legs, he can add or diminish, or turn us off in whatever Shape he pleases; and who dare say, *What doest thou?*"[17]

Did Kennedy perhaps borrow this asymmetrical image from Jonathan Swift, whose "A Beautiful Young Nymph Going to Bed (Written for the Honour of the Fair Sex, in 1731)" explores the disjunction between appearance and reality: "Corinna, pride of Drury Lane, / For whom no shepherd sighs in vain . . . seated on a three-legg'd Chair / Takes off her artificial Hair . . . / Untwists a Wire; and from her Gums / A Set of Teeth completely comes"?

Huguenot artisans and exegetics of the *désert* experience from Palissy to Leddell would recognize the source of Kennedy's analogy in the prophetic narrative of God's assessment of the punishments and possibilities for redemption awaiting unfaithful Israelites in Jeremiah:

> For in the day that I brought them out of the land of Egypt, I did not speak to your fathers. . . . But this command I gave them, Obey my voice, I will be your God, and you shall be my people; and walk in all the ways that I command you, that it may be well with you. But they did not obey or incline their ear, but walked in their own counsels and the stubbornness of their evil hearts, and went backward and not forward. (Jer. 7:22–24)

> [Then] word . . . came to Jeremiah from the Lord: Arise and go down to the potter's house, and there I will let you hear my words. So I went down to the potter's house, and there he was working at his wheel. And the vessel he was making of clay was spoiled in the potter's hand, and he reworked it into another vessel, as it seemed good to the potter to do so. The word of the Lord came to me: O house of Israel, can I not do with you as this potter has done? says the Lord. Behold, like the clay in the potter's hand, so are you in my hand, O house of Israel. If at any time I declare concerning a nation or a kingdom, that I will pluck up and break down and destroy it, and if that nation, concerning which I have spoken, turns from its evil, I will repent of the evil I intended to do it. (Jer. 18:1–8)

While Kennedy dared not ask God the potter, *What doest thou?* to stabilize the fearful three-legged disequilibrium of "an over Ballance of Power," Palissy, the philosophical potter, actively reconstructed the materials of divine knowledge in a quotidian, artisanal synthesis of macrocosm and microcosm. Combining words and things to document his self-conscious heroism in rebuilding the metaphysical monism by hand, something that seemed impossible after the Fall separated the cosmos, Palissy's artisanal history of Saintonge was also written from the perspective of the postlapsarian potter in Jeremiah. His too was a history of the dispersion of God's chosen people. Palissy labored to "pluck up and break down and destroy" his shape-shifting vessels in the furnace. Innovation had required these forms to be "spoiled . . . [and] reworked

. . . into another vessel," momentarily disappearing into tiny, overlooked fragments, but like the chosen people of the book, never allowed to vanish altogether. Still, if Kennedy's jeremiad inveighed against the vessel of New York City as an imperfect work in progress, he remained hopeful that if not destroyed prematurely by the chaos of everyday life, it might be perfected in time.

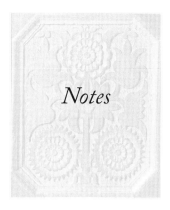

Notes

Introduction

1. George Wither, *A Collection of Emblemes, Ancient and Moderne (1635),* introduction by Rosemary Freeman; bibliographical notes by Charles S. Hensley (Columbia: Published for the Newberry Library by the University of South Carolina Press, 1975), 1: 19. I am grateful to Nancy Zey for bringing this reference to my attention.

ONE ✤ A Risky Gift

EPIGRAPH: Louis-Étienne Arcère, *Histoire de la ville de La Rochelle et du pays d'Aulnis,* 2 vols. (La Rochelle: René-Jacob Desbordes, 1756–57), 1: 345, 350. I am indebted to Marie-Aline Irvine for her help in reviewing my translations of certain passages in Arcère.

1. There are three excellent full length studies of the tour from political, social, and cultural perspectives, Pierre Champion, *Catherine de Médicis présente à Charles IX son royaume* (Paris: B. Grasset, 1937); Victor E. Graham and W. McAllister Johnson, *The Royal Tour of France by Charles IX and Catherine de' Medici: Festivals and Entries, 1564–6* (Toronto: University of Toronto Press, 1979); and esp. Jean Boutier, Alain Dewerpe, and Daniel Nordman, *Un Tour de France royal: Le Voyage de Charles IX (1564–1566)* (Paris: Aubier Montaigne, 1984), 61–63.

2. Still useful among the many general histories that are concerned with these well-known events placed within the overall political and social context of the sixteenth-century French wars of religion is J. H. M. Salmon, *Society in Crisis: France in the Sixteenth Century* (New York: St. Martin's Press, 1975), see esp. 146–95; see also R. G. Asch and A. M. Birke, eds., *Princes, Patronage, and Nobility: The Court at the Beginning of the Modern Age, circa 1540–1650* (Oxford: Oxford University Press, 1991). For the seventeenth-century context, see Ronald G. Asch, *The Thirty Years War: The Holy Roman Empire and Europe, 1618–48* (New York: St. Martin's Press, 1997); William Beik, *Absolutism and Society in Seventeenth-Century France: State Power and Provincial Aristocracy in Languedoc* (Cambridge: Cambridge University Press, 1985); Nicolas Henshall, *The Myth of Absolutism: Change and Continuity in Early Modern European Monarchy* (London: Longman, 1992); and John A. Lynn, *Giant of the Grand Siècle: The French Army, 1610–1715* (Cambridge: Cambridge University Press, 1997). On the synthesis of religious and political discourse and the dialogical nature of confessional conflict that informed such events during the French Reformation, see Donald R. Kelley, *The Beginning of Ideology: Consciousness and Society in the French Reformation* (Cambridge: Cambridge University Press, 1981); see also Euan Cam-

eron, *The European Reformation* (Oxford: Oxford University Press, 1991), and *International Calvinism, 1541–1715,* ed. Menna Prestwich (Oxford: Oxford University Press, 1985). On the formation of political thought and practice and Calvinist theories of resistance—particularly in England and France—from the late thirteenth through the late sixteenth century, see Quentin Skinner, *The Foundations of Modern Political Thought,* vol. 2: *The Age of Reformation* (Cambridge: Cambridge University Press, 1978), esp. 234–358; see also P. Collinson, *The Religion of the Protestants: The Church in English Society 1559–1625* (Oxford: Oxford University Press, 1982).

3. See esp. Skinner, *Foundations of Modern Political Thought,* 2: 243–44.

4. Ibid.

5. Ibid.

6. Judith Pugh Meyer, *Reformation in La Rochelle: Tradition and Change in Early Modern Europe, 1500–1568* (Geneva: E. Droz, 1996), 114.

7. "Either by charter or by custom, the most important section of . . . a town's inhabitants, those who bore the title of *bourgeois* of the place in question, formed a body that was endowed with a legal personality and was represented by a group of magistrates and municipal officers, *le corps de ville,* an organ that expressed its common will"; Roland Mousnier, *The Institutions of France Under the Absolute Monarchy, 1598–1789: Society and State,* trans. Brian Pearce (Chicago: University of Chicago Press, 1979), 564.

8. Meyer, *Reformation in La Rochelle,* 114; for the standard sixteenth-century local history of these events, see Amos Barbot, *Histoire de La Rochelle depuis l'an 1199 jusques en 1575,* ed. Denys d'Aussy, *Archives historiques de la Saintonge et de l'Aunis* 17 (1889): 200–203.

9. Barbot, *Histoire de La Rochelle,* 206–7, and Meyer, *Reformation in La Rochelle,* 114.

10. The monastery of Sainte-Marguérite was the Oratorians "house" (including living quarters) in La Rochelle after their return from banishment in 1628. The community expanded the monastery after 1652, when they built "a few secondary structures" on the same site. See Louis Pérouas, *Le Diocèse de La Rochelle de 1648 à 1724: Sociologie et pastorale* (Paris: S.E.V.P.E.N., 1964), 191 n. 1.

11. The Congregation of the Oratory, or Oratorians, a secular teaching order of priests that did not follow monastic orders, had its origins in sixteenth-century Rome and then diffused to Paris. There was a "house" in La Rochelle—an offshoot of the Paris oratory—by the early seventeenth century. The Oratorians proliferated throughout France, where fifty-eight Oratorian houses were recorded by the late eighteenth century. Their "Cartesian" teaching methods were influential in the universities beginning in the late seventeenth century. See Paul and Marie-Louise Biver, *Abbayes, monastères, et couvents de Paris, des origines à la fin du XVIIIe siècle* (Paris: Éditions d'histoire et d'art, 1970), 495–514 (I am indebted to Ann W. Ramsey for this reference and for her insights into the Oratorian movement); and Mousnier, *Institutions of France Under the Absolute Monarchy,* 343, 348–54, 714–15.

12. For an excellent study of the social effects of the catastrophic demographic reversal in La Rochelle after 1628, see Katherine Louise Milton Faust, "A Beleaguered Society: Protestant Families in La Rochelle, 1628–1685" (Ph.D. diss., Northwestern University, 1980); the most recent general study of Protestant demographic patterns in France in the seventeenth century is in Philip Benedict, *The Huguenot Population of France, 1600–1685: The Demographic Fate and Customs of a Religious Minority,* Transactions of the American Philosophical Society, 81, pt. 5 (Philadelphia: American Philosophical Society, 1991). The classical text for French international Protestantism in the North American context in general and La Rochelle / Aunis-Saintonge in

particular remains Charles W. Baird, *History of the Huguenot Emigration to America,* 2 vols. (New York: Dodd, Mead, 1885). This has been augmented recently from a number of different perspectives by a greatly expanded bibliography on the subject, including Philip Benedict, *Christ's Churches Purely Reformed: A Social History of Calvinism* (New Haven, Conn.: Yale University Press, 2002), 121–292; Jon Butler, *The Huguenots in America: A Refugee People in a New World Society* (Cambridge, Mass.: Harvard University Press, 1983); J. F. Bosher, *The Canada Merchants, 1713–1763* (New York: Oxford University Press, 1987); id., "Huguenot Merchants and the Protestant International in the Seventeenth Century," *William and Mary Quarterly,* 3d ser., 52 (January 1995): 77–102; David Ormrod, "The Atlantic Economy and the 'Protestant Capitalist International,' 1651–1775," *Historical Research* 66 (1993): 197–207; and Neil D. Kamil, "Hidden in Plain Sight: Disappearance and Material Life in Colonial New York," *American Furniture, 1995,* ed. Luke Beckerdite and William N. Hosley Jr. (Hanover, N.H.: University Press of New England, 1995): 191–249.

13. Arcère, *Histoire,* p. xix.

14. Ibid., 1: dedication (unpaginated), v–vi.

15. On the "artisanal culture" of *gloire* perpetuated by the Bourbon court historians of the early modern period, see Orest A. Ranum, *Artisans of Glory: Writers and Historical Thought in Seventeenth-Century France* (Chapel Hill: University of North Carolina Press, 1980).

16. Arcère, *Histoire,* 1: v.

17. Ibid., i.

18. Ibid., 1: xiv–xv. The "judicious and elegant author" was G.-H. Bougeant (1690–1743). *Arcère cites vol. 3, p. 316, in* Bougeant's *Histoire des guerres et des négociations qui précédèrent le Traité de Westphalie (1727).*

19. Mousnier, *Institutions of France Under the Absolute Monarchy,* 342–49, 353–55, 714–19. It is important to reiterate that the "Cartesian" movement within the French Oratorian order was a *late* seventeenth-century phenomenon and not always uniform. Under its founder Pierre de Berulle in 1602, the order was decidedly Christocentric and spiritually ardent, with particular communities displaying powerful mystical zeal at certain moments. Since the Oratorians were founded as small cells of secular priests, each cell might have a specific religious style or character and might respond idiosyncratically. In 1659, for example, Rochelais Oratorians such as Père de Launay were strongly associated with the Port-Royal movement; see Pérouas, *Diocèse de La Rochelle,* 261–62.

20. Mousnier, *Institutions of France Under the Absolute Monarchy,* 354.

21. Pérouas, *Diocèse de La Rochelle,* 128.

22. Ibid., p. 240.

23. Arcère, *Histoire,* 1: xi. For the publication history of Barbot's *Histoire de La Rochelle* see n. 28 below.

24. Arcère, *Histoire,* 1: vi.

25. Ibid., 1: xvi.

26. Ibid., 1: x.

27. Ibid., 1: xi.

28. A nineteenth-century edition of Barbot's original unpublished manuscript is to be found in Amos Barbot, *Histoire de La Rochelle: 1199–1575, publiée par M. Denys d'Aussy,* 3 vols. (Paris: A. Picard; Saintes: Mme. Z. Mortreuil, 1886–90); see also Publications de la Société des archives historiques de la Saintonge et de l'Aunis, vols. 14, 17–18. Arcère probably used the original man-

uscript (2 folio volumes, 771 pages), which is in Barbot's handwriting, although it also has a cover page dated 1732 that states that the manuscript was given to the Bibliothèque nationale that year (Fonds français no. 18,968), i.e., over twenty years before the publication of Arcère's *Histoire*. Père Jaillot had a copy of Barbot's manuscript transcribed—in 1732?—which may have served Arcère's purposes, perhaps prompting the donation of the original manuscript to the B.N. The title page of the original manuscript reads "Histoire de La Rochelle depuis l'an 1199 jusques en 1575, par Amos Barbot, escritte de sa main. Originale." Although the manuscript is undated, a tentative date of ca. 1613 is suggested in the introduction to the 1886 edition.

29. Arcère, *Histoire*, 1: xi. I assume "Caurian" refers to Philippe Cauriana, *Histoire du siege de la Rochelle 1573*, trans. Leopold-Gabriel Delayant (La Rochelle: A. Siret, 1856).

30. Abel Jouan, *Recueil et discours du voyage du roy Charles IX de ce nom a persent regnant, accompagnedes choses dignes de memoire faictes en chacun endroit faisant sondit voyage en ses paiset provinces de Champaigne, Bourgoigne, Daulphine, Provence, Languedoc, Gascoigne, Baionne, et plusieurs autres lieux, suivant son retour depuis son partement de Paris jusques a son retour audit lieu, es annees mil cinq sens soixante quatre et soixante cinq. Faict et recueilly par l'un des serviteurs de sa Majeste* (Paris: Jean Bonfons, 1566). The *Recueil* was also published at Lyon, Toulouse, and Angoulême in 1566, and at Lyon in 1567. These were all places the king visited during his tour. I have consulted the edition of Jouan included in Graham and Johnson, *Royal Tour of France*.

31. My translation from Boutier et al., *Tour de France royal*, 13–16.

32. Arcère, *Histoire*, 1: xvi.

33. Ibid., 1: xxii–xxiii.

34. Ibid., 1: 344.

35. Arcère, *Histoire*, 1: 344.

36. Ibid., 1: 345

37. Ibid.

38. Ibid. On the attempted coup d'état in 1563, see Meyer, *Reformation in La Rochelle*, 115.

39. Arcère, *Histoire*, 1: 346

40. I have consulted the annotated edition of Jouan's *Recueil* in Graham and McAllister, *Royal Tour of France*, 123.

41. Jouan, *Recueil*, 123. The most recent (and reliable) source for biographical data on Palissy's journey and stay in Paris is Leonard N. Amico, *Bernard Palissy: In Search of Earthly Paradise* (Paris: Flammarion, 1996); see esp. 32–40.

42. Jouan, *Recueil*, 124.

43. Ibid.

44. Ibid., 125.

45. For more on Montmorency's role, see N. M. Southerland, "Anthoine de Bourbon, King of Navarre and the French Crisis of Authority," in *French Government and Society 1500–1850: Essays in Memory of Alfred Cobban*, ed. J. F. Bosher (London: Athlone Press, 1973), 13. On the augmentation of military forces recruited when the tour reached heavily Protestant regions, see Boutier et al., *Tour de France royal*, 113–14.

46. Arcère, *Histoire*, 1: 348.

47. Ibid., 1: 346–47.

48. Quoted (my translation) in Boutier et al., *Tour de France royal*, 64; see also 65–69 for a provocative discussion of the allegory of Hercules and its emblematic function on the tour.

49. Arcère, *Histoire*, 1: 349.

50. On the presidial and the extension of royal courts during the Valois dynasty, see Salmon, *Society in Crisis,* 72–73.

51. Arcère, *Histoire,* 1: 349.

52. Michael P. Fitzsimmons, "Privilege and Polity in France, 1786–1791," *American Historical Review* 92, no. 2 (April 6, 1982): 270.

53. David Parker, *La Rochelle and the French Monarchy: Conflict and Order in Seventeenth-Century France* (London: Royal Historical Society, 1980), 34–35. See also Meyer, *Reformation in La Rochelle,* 19–30; and Bibliothèque nationale, Paris, MSS 7285–7286: "Privileges accordez aux habitans de . . . La Rochelle." On the towns called communes and the rapid removal of their privileges by the state beginning in the early seventeenth-century, see Mousnier, *Institutions of France Under the Absolute Monarchy,* 564–65.

54. Parker, *La Rochelle and the French Monarchy,* 7.

55. Arcère, *Histoire,* 1: xxiii–xxv.

56. Ibid.

57. On the politicization of La Rochelle's Calvinist elites in the 1560s, see Meyer, *Reformation in La Rochelle,* 113–52.

58. 1: Arcère, *Histoire,* 1: 347

59. Quoted in ibid., 1: 348.

60. Ibid., 1: 347–48

61. Graham and Johnson, *Royal Tour of France,* 8.

62. For an example of the fashionable form of an engraved silver and gold (parcel gilt) basin, almost certainly made by a Huguenot silversmith in London as an English royal gift celebrating dynastic history, see the extremely rare survival of an engraved commemorative basin (19^{11}/$_{16}$ inches in diameter) and ewer, ca. 1567–68, currently in the collections of the Museum of Fine Arts, Boston (accession numbers: 1979. 261–262), and illustrated and discussed brilliantly in Ellenor M. Alcorn, "'Some of the Kings of England Curiously Engraven': An Elizabethan Ewer and Basin in the Museum of Fine Arts, Boston," *Journal of the Museum of Fine Arts, Boston* 5 (1993): 66, fig. 1; see also 81, fig. 23, and 83, fig. 25. For Germanic examples that may have provided contemporary sources for French silversmiths in both London and La Rochelle, see ibid., 81, fig. 23, and the basin by the Nuremberg goldsmith Wenzel Jamnitzer, ca. 1550–60, now in the Louvre Museum, Paris, illustrated in Daniel Alcouffe et al., *Les Objets d'art: Moyen Age et Renaissance* (Paris: Réunion des Musées nationaux, 1993), 133.

63. Arcère, *Histoire,* 1: 350.

64. See esp. Graham and Johnson, *Royal Tour of France,* 12–66.

65. Arcère, *Histoire,* 1: 351.

66. Barbot, *Histoire de La Rochelle,* 17: 85–226; see also Meyer, *Reformation in La Rochelle,* 115.

67. Barbot, 17: 225–26; Meyer, 115.

68. Of his many works on the subject of the anthropology of gifts, see esp. Pierre Bourdieu, *Outline of a Theory of Practice* (Cambridge: Cambridge University Press, 1977), 190–93.

69. Meyer, *Reformation in La Rochelle,* 93–152.

70. Quoted in François de Vaux de Foletier, *Le Siège de La Rochelle* (1931; La Rochelle: Éditions Quartier Latin et Rupella, 1978), 148–51.

71. See Jean Petit, "Descartes et trois poètes au siège de La Rochelle," *Cahiers de l'Ouest,* 42 (January–February 1958): 48–49.

72. C.-F. Menestrier, *La Source glorieuse du sang de l'august maison de Bourbon* (Paris, 1687).

73. Jean Troncon, *L'Entrée triomphante de leurs majesties* (Paris, 1622), n.p.; quoted in Jean-Marie Apostolides, *Le Roi-Machine: Spectacle et politique au temps de Louis XIV* (Paris: Minuit, 1981), 15.

74. "Relation du siège de La Rochelle sous le tres chrestian et invincible Roy Louis XIII," in *Archives curieuses de l'histoire de France* (Paris, 1838), 37–137 (my translation).

75. For an excellent discussion of the *désert* experience, see Hillel Schwartz, *The French Prophets: The History of a Millenarian Group in Eighteenth-Century England* (Berkeley: University of California Press, 1980), 11–37.

76. Section epigraph from *The Admirable Discourses of Bernard Palissy,* trans. Aurele La Rocque (Urbana: University of Illinois Press, 1957), 243. *See chapter 10, n. 92, below for full citation of* Palissy's *Discours admirables.*

77. This story is well told and interpreted in Donald R. Kelley, *The Beginning of Ideology: Consciousness and Society in the French Reformation* (Cambridge: Cambridge University Press, 1981), 1–50 et passim; see also Carlos Eire, *War Against the Idols: The Reformation of Worship From Erasmus to Calvin* (Cambridge: Cambridge University Press, 1979), 189–93; and Benedict, *Christ's Churches,* 77–120.

78. See Schwartz, *French Prophets,* 11–37, 251–79.

79. For an inventory and detailed description of all the ceramic medallions discovered by archeologists in the latrines of Palissy's house next to his workshop under the cour du Carrousel, as well as the French and Italian bronze sources, see Jean-Robert Armogathe et al., *Bernard Palissy, mythe et réalité* (Saintes, Niort, and Agen, France: Coédition: Musées d'Agen, Niort, Saintes, 1990), 76–79, figs. 83–84. In addition to the ceramic medallion of Montmorency, others were recovered that depicted Isabelle of Portugal (wife of Charles V, 1526–39); three of Mary Stuart (queen of France in 1559, widow of François II in 1560); three of Henri II (king of France, 1547–59); two plaque fragments depicting Antoine de Bourbon (king of Navarre, 1555–63); Charles IX (king of France, 1560–74); Hippolyte de Gonzague (1535–63); Iosina de Matanca (?); two of Louis de Gonzague (son of Frederick II de Gonzague, duke of Mantua); and Philip II of Spain (r. 1556–98).

80. For a useful discussion of the ubiquity of the culture of patronage and its dominance of the politics and society of early modern France, see Sharon Kettering, *Patrons, Brokers, and Clients in Seventeenth-Century France* (New York: Oxford University Press, 1986).

81. On the extensive scientific culture that supported gifts and gift giving, see Mario Biagioli, *Galileo, Courtier: The Practice of Science in the Age of Absolutism* (Chicago: University of Chicago Press, 1993). Recent laboratory tests on Palissy's glazes found on survivals from the Tuileries have been the basis for the reattribution of several objects formerly thought to have been made by Palissy to anonymous contemporaries, showing how influential and widespread his new artisanal paradigm had become in France by the 1570s. No doubt many of the potters in his gift factory learned their trade secrets from the master. See Isabelle Perrin, *Les Techniques céramiques de Bernard Palissy,* 2 vols. (Villeneuve d'Ascq: Presses universitaires du Septentrion, 2001).

82. This theme runs through a large body of Palissy's work; it is encapsulated in James C. Scott, *Domination and the Arts of Resistance: Hidden Transcripts* (New Haven, Conn.: Yale University Press, 1990).

83. For more on display of ceramic medallions worn near the heart as emblems of loyalty during the Renaissance, including a group of terra-cotta medallions associated with the patronage of Cosimo de' Medici that were gilded to resemble precious medal, see Arne R. Flaten,

"Identity and the Display of *metaglie* in Renaissance and Baroque Europe," *Word and Image* 19, nos. 1 and 2 (January–June 2003): 61, fig. 1, and 65, n. 25.

TWO ✦ Palissy's Fortress

1. Except where otherwise indicated, the edition of Palissy's *Recepte véritable* (La Rochelle: Barthélemy Berton, 1563) from which I quote is that found in *Oeuvres complètes de Bernard Palissy,* ed. Paul-Antoine Cap (Paris: J.-J. Dubochet, 1844; reprint with an avant-propos by Jean Orcel, Paris: A. Blanchard, 1961). *Recepte,* or *recette,* can have multiple meanings in this context. I have settled loosely on "recipe," inasmuch as it corresponds to the *recettes de métier,* or "tricks of the trade," that were the artisanal contribution to the "Book of Secrets" tradition, popular during the early modern period. However, given Palissy's dual purpose of settling debts in print with both old enemies and old friends in the *Recepte véritable,* the receipt (as in the collection of a debt) may also be considered active.

2. Berton's press published several dramatic pamphlets by La Rochelle writers on the royal siege of 1572–73 under the command of the duc d'Anjou, the first of several the fortress withstood prior to succumbing in 1627–28. After Berton's death, his interest in the publishing house was inherited by his widow Françoise Pierres (probably the daughter of Jean Pierres, who was sieur de la Jarne in Saintonge and lieutenant general of La Rochelle). Françoise Pierres Berton formed a partnership with Jean Portau that lasted from 1573 to 1589. See E. Droz, *L'Imprimerie à La Rochelle,* vol. 1: *Barthélemy Berton, 1563–1573;* vol. 3: *La Veuve Berton et Jean Portau, 1573–1589,* Travaux d'humanisme et Renaissance, 34 (Geneva: E. Droz, 1960).

3. Evidence suggests that Palissy was known in Limoges and familiar to the town's artisans. See Leonard N. Amico, *Bernard Palissy: In Search of Earthly Paradise* (Paris: Flammarion, 1996), 16.

4. The specifics of Paul Berton's punishment remain unclear. Droz, *Barthélemy Berton,* 10–12. On Lyon's printers and heterodoxy, see the two seminal essays by Natalie Zemon Davis, "Printing and the People," and "The Sacred and the Body Social in Lyon," in her *Society and Culture in Early Modern France* (Stanford, Calif.: Stanford University Press, 1975).

5. Randle Cotgrave, *A Dictionarie of the French and English Tongues* [hereafter, Cotgrave's *Dictionarie*] (London, 1611; reprinted Amsterdam: Da Capo Press, 1971) defines Pons as: "Ponts. The name of a Towne in Saintonge, called so of the many Bridges about it."

6. Alexandre Crottet, *Histoire des églises réformées de Pons, Gemozac et Mortagne en Saintonge, précédée d'une notice étendue sur l'établissement de la réforme dans cette province, l'Aunis et l'Angoumois* (Bordeaux: A. Castillon, 1841), 101–11; on Louis XIII's southern campaign of 1620–21, see A. Lloyd Moote, *Louis XIII, the Just* (Berkeley: University of California Press, 1989), 112–36.

7. Bernard Palissy, *Les Oeuvres de Maistre Bernard Palissy,* ed. B. Fillon and Louis Audiat (Niort: L. Clouzot, 1888), 1: xvi.

8. Droz, *Barthélemy Berton,* 22.

9. See Emmanuel Rodocanchi, *Une Protectrice de la Reforme en Italie et en France: Renée de France, duchesse de Ferrare* (Paris, 1896; Geneva: Slatkine Reprints, 1970); and anon., *Some Memorials of Renée de France, Duchess of Ferrara* (London, 1859); for a discussion of the surviving architecture and interiors of the court, see Loredana Olivato, *Il palazzo di Renata di Francia* (Ferrara, Italy: Corbo, 1997).

10. John Martin, *Venice's Hidden Enemies: Italian Heretics in a Renaissance City* (Berkeley: University of California Press, 1993), 44–45.

11. Palissy, *Recepte véritable,* in *Oeuvres,* ed. Fillon and Audiat, 1: 18.

12. Crottet, *Histoire des églises réformées,* 82–86. Marie de Monchenu was unsympathetic to the Protestant cause, unlike her fervent predecessor, and her influence over Antoine prompted de Bèze to insult Marie, as "l'une des plus diffamées desmoiselles de France."

13. Bernard Palissy, *The Admirable Discourses,* trans. Aurele La Rocque (Urbana: University of Illinois Press, 1957), 24–5.

14. Théodore de Bèze, *Histoire ecclésiastique* (1559), 1: bk. 2; quoted in Palissy, *Oeuvres,* ed. Fillon and Audiat, 1: xvii.

15. Ibid., xx.

16. The short Latin title of 1536 was *Institutio christianae religionis;* for its publication history, see Jean Calvin, *On the Christian Faith: Selections from the Institutes, Commentaries, and Tracts,* ed. John T. McNeill (New York: Bobbs-Merrill, 1957), vii–viii.

17. Palissy, *Oeuvres,* ed. Fillon and Audiat, 1: xx–xxii.

18. Jean-Daniel Sauvin, *Philibert Hamelin, martyr huguenot (1557)* (Geneva: University of Geneva, 1957), 9–41; and Droz, *Barthélemy Berton,* 22.

19. The first book by Yves Rouspeau published by Berton was entitled *Traitte de la Preparation à la Saincte Cene de Nostre Seul Sauveur et Redempteur Jesus Christ, Propre pour tous ceux qui veulent dignement s'approcher a sa saincte Table du Seigneur, Plus un Dialogue contenant les poincts principaux, que ceux qui veulent recevour la Cene, doivent savoir & entendre* (La Rochelle: Barthélmy Berton, 1563).

20. *Architecture, et ordonnance de la grotte rustique de Monseigneur le duc de Montmorancy, pair, & connestable de France* (La Rochelle: Barthélmy Berton, 1563). See Droz, *Barthélemy Berton,* 14–15, 22–25.

21. The full text can be found in Amico, *Bernard Palissy,* 232, doc. XII.

22. See Droz, *Barthélemy Berton,* 24–25. The full text of the contract of September 3, 1563, is available in the original document at La Rochelle (ADCM, 3E 2148); it has also been reprinted in G. Musset, "La 'Recette veritable' de Bernard Palissy," *Recueil de la Commission des arts and monuments de la Charente-Inferieure* 17 (1906): 319–21, and in Amico, *Bernard Palissy,* 230–31.

23. An abridged copy of this inventory is in Amico, *Bernard Palissy,* 231, doc. VIII.

24. Ibid., 238, doc. XL.

25. See Martin Luther, *"Treatise on Christian Liberty" (The Freedom of a Christian),* in *Martin Luther: Selections from His Writings,* ed. John Dillenberger (Garden City, N.Y.: Anchor Books, 1961), 53, 58–63, 67–69. The classic formulation of the medieval tradition of man's "twofold nature" can be found in Ernst H. Kantorowicz, *The King's Two Bodies: A Study in Medieval Political Theology* (Princeton, N.J.: Princeton University Press, 1957).

26. *Oeuvres complètes de Théodore Agrippa d'Aubigné,* ed. Eugène Réaume, François de Caussade, , and A. Legouëz, 6 vols. (Paris: Alphonse Lemerre, 1873–92), 6: 248, and also 1: 56, 2: 526, 3: 432, 4: 201. For biographical information on Agrippa's multiple roles during the civil war era, see Jacques Bailbé, *Agrippa d'Aubigné, poète des "Tragiques"* (Caen: Association des publications de la Faculté des lettres et sciences humaines de l'Université de Caen, 1968), iii–102; Cotgrave's *Dictionarie.*

27. See Esther Cohen, "The Animated Pain of the Body," *American Historical Review* 105 (February 2000): 36–68.

28. For influential recent work on this subject, see Judith Perkins, *The Suffering Self: Pain and Narrative Representation in the Early Christian Era* (New York: Routledge, 1995), and Brent D. Shaw, "Body/Power/Identity: Passions of the Martyrs," *Journal of Early Christianity* 4 (1996): 269–312. For a classic overview of the subject, see Gerhard Oestreich, *Neostoicism and the Early Modern State* (Cambridge: Cambridge University Press, 1982); for studies of the intimate relationship between Neostoicism, art, and the representation of warfare and politics in England and on the Continent during the early modern era, see Andrew E. Shifflett, *Stoicism, Politics, and Literature in the Age of Milton: War and Peace Reconciled* (Cambridge: Cambridge University Press, 1998), and David G. Halsted, *Poetry and Politics in the Silesian Baroque: Neo-Stoicism in the Work of Christophorus Colerus and His Circle* (Wiesbaden, Germany: Harrassowitz, 1996).

29. Norbert Elias, *The Civilizing Process: Sociogenetic and Psychogenetic Investigations,* trans. Edmund Jephcott, 2 vols. (Oxford: B. Blackwell, 1978).

30. See esp. Philippe Ariès, *Western Attitudes Toward Death: From the Middle Ages to the Present,* trans. Patricia M. Ranum (Baltimore: Johns Hopkins University Press, 1974), 1–14.

31. Paul Seaver finds persuasive evidence of deep religious motivations behind the London wood turner Nehemiah Wallington's personal despair, leading to what appear to have been multiple suicide attempts. There is implicit evidence that the turner's family and guild may have had an informal social safety net in place for Wallington, suggesting that suicide was not unexpected in Puritan London. See Paul S. Seaver, *Wallington's World: A Puritan Artisan in Seventeenth-Century London* (Stanford, Calif.: Stanford University Press, 1985).

32. *Winthrop Papers, vol. 1: 1498–1628* (Boston: Massachusetts Historical Society, 1929), 161–64, 193.

33. Luther, *Treatise on Christian Liberty,* 66.

34. Ibid., 53. On Menocchio, see Carlo Ginzburg, *The Cheese and the Worms: The Cosmos of a Sixteenth-Century Miller,* trans. John and Anne Tedeschi (Baltimore: Johns Hopkins University Press, 1980).

35. Luther, *Treatise on Christian Liberty,* 70–71.

36. Caroline Walker Bynum, *Fragmentation and Redemption: Essays on Gender and the Human Body in Medieval Religion* (New York: Zone Books, 1992), 182.

37. Luther, *Treatise on Christian Liberty,* 67–8.

38. Ibid., 53, 67.

39. Ibid., 60, 58.

40. For a clear discussion of the function of astral bodies in Neoplatonic theology and their implications for Paracelsian science, see Owen Hannaway, *The Chemists and the Word: The Didactic Origins of Chemistry* (Baltimore: Johns Hopkins University Press, 1975), 27–29, and passim.

41. See Harold Bloom, *The Anxiety of Influence: A Theory of Poetry* (New York: Oxford University Press, 1973), *A Map of Misreading* (New York: Oxford University Press, 1975), and *Agon: Towards a Theory of Revisionism* (New York: Oxford University Press, 1982).

42. For a trenchant critique of modern historians' attempts to reconstruct authorial intentionality from the past, see Nancy S. Struever, *Theory as Practice: Ethical Inquiry in the Renaissance* (Chicago: University of Chicago Press, 1992), x–xii.

43. Frank Kermode, *The Sense of an Ending: Studies in the Theory of Fiction* (New York: Oxford University Press, 1967).

44. Ernest Dupuy, *Bernard Palissy: L'Homme, l'artiste, le savant, l'écrivain* (1894; rev. ed., 1902; reprint of rev. ed., Geneva: Slatkine, 1970), 17–18; Cotgrave's *Dictionarie* defines *pourtrait*

generally as "A pourtrait, image, picture, counterfeit, or draught of" virtually anything. The verb *pourtraire* meant "To pourtray, draw, delineate, paint, counterfeit."

45. Luther, *Treatise on Christian Liberty*, 84–85.

46. Palissy, *Recepte véritable*, 113–14. Translations of the *Recepte* are my own except where otherwise noted.

47. J. R. Hale, "To Fortify or Not to Fortify? Machiavelli's Contribution to a Renaissance Debate," in H. C. Davis et al., eds., *Essays in Honour of John Humphreys Whitfield: Presented to Him on His Retirement from the Serena Chair of Italian at the University of Birmingham* (London: St. George's Press, 1975), 99–100. On changes in the technology and tactics of siege warfare in response to the effective use of gunpowder against fortified walls, especially in late fifteenth-century France and Italy, see Ivy A. Corfis and Michael Wolfe, *The Medieval City Under Siege* (Woodbridge, UK: Boydell Press, 1995), 227–75.

48. Quoted in Hale, "To Fortify or Not to Fortify," 100–101.

49. Ibid., 101.

50. See chapter 12 below.

51. Quoted in Hale, "To Fortify or Not to Fortify," 103–4.

52. Here, a play on words, translated from *garnisons*, hence also garrisons.

53. Théodore Agrippa d'Aubigné, *Oeuvres,* ed. Henri Weber et al. (Paris: Gallimard, 1969), 36–37, lines 659–72.

54. *Oeuvres complètes de Théodore Agrippa d'Aubigné,* ed. Réaume et al., 2 (1877): 351. D'Aubigné's source and didactic intention in this dramatic bit of apocrypha—very much a part of a large, interesting, and relatively unexplored apocryphal tradition in Huguenot historiography of the civil wars—is clarified in his "Confession du sieur de Sancy" (in ibid., 3: 350), where the protagonist declares: "Voyez l'imprudence de ce belistre; vous diriez qu'il aurait lu as vers de Seneque, *Qui mori scit cogi necit,* on ne peut contraindre celui qui sait mourir." When d'Aubigné's dying Palissy paraphrases Seneca in *L'Histoire,* d'Aubigné is forging a didactic link between Stoic death and the Huguenot ideal of Christian martyrdom. A second, competing martyrological narrative exists of Palissy's last days in the Bastille. This one, an almost exact contemporary to that of d'Aubigny, was written by Pierre de L'Estoile, who signed the privilege to publish the *Discours admirables* in 1580. It is far more elaborate, containing lengthy interviews. For copies of two documents (ca. 1589–90), related to L'Estoile's narrative, see Amico, *Bernard Palissy,* 237–38, docs. XXXVIII and XL. The second document (1590) contains elements in common with d'Aubigny's narrative; the first plays on Palissy's mastery of fire. Threatened by an inquisitor with the stake, L'Estoile's Palissy responds, "Monsieur, do you presume that I am afraid of this fiery material? No, no, I am much more fearful of the Eternal fire, which was prepared by the Devil and his Angels."

55. John Calvin, *On the Christian Faith: Selections from the Institutes, Commentaries, and Tracts,* ed. John T. McNeill (New York: Bobbs-Merrill), 31.

56. Hale, "To Fortify or Not to Fortify?" 116.

57. Palissy, Palissy, *Recepte véritable,* in *Oeuvres,* ed. Fillon and Audiat, 1: 138–39.

58. The maintenance and constant expansion of La Rochelle's walls during the building boom of the late sixteenth century to meet the perceived military threat to religious and economic autonomy was an enormous financial strain on the city's economy. One example of this strain was the La Rochelle Consistory's inability to raise the funds to complete the Grand Temple in less than twenty-four years.

59. Palissy, *Recepte véritable,* 114. For images of du Cerceau's two plans, see Amico, *Bernard Palissy,* 184, figs. 167–8.

60. Cotgrave's *Dictionarie*

61. Palissy, *Recepte véritable,* 114.

62. For the classic period text on the life of the *compagnon,* albeit highly embellished by its autobiographer and protagonist and written exactly two centuries later (1764) than the *Recepte,* see Jacques-Louis Ménétra, *Journal of My Life,* ed. Daniel Roche, trans. Arthur Goldhammer (New York: Columbia University Press, 1986).

63. Luther's "hidden and revealed" dialectic may also be at work here. Note the relationships to the Neoplatonic theology of Palissy's near contemporary and co-religionist Moise Amyraut. Both Palissy and Amyraut were denounced by Huguenot scholastics for devaluing the covenant of laws. Both were committed to the covenant of grace that fueled their adherence to the Neoplatonic doctrine of the animate soul's triumph over corrupted flesh, and both paraphrase 2 Corinthians as an authority for the primacy of inner strength that identified with the humility of Christ's suffering. See Brian G. Armstrong, *Calvinism and the Amyraut Heresy: Protestant Scholasticism and Humanism in Seventeenth-Century France* (Madison: University of Wisconsin, 1969), 148–49.

64. Problems in the beleaguered "nature-culture opposition" as formulated by Noam Chomsky and Claude Lévi-Strauss have not generated much interest on the part of anthropologists or historians since the critique of structuralism in the late 1970s, esp. by Bourdieu in *Outline of a Theory of Practice* (Cambridge: Cambridge University Press, 1977), 27–32. Structuralist logic, supported by a hermetic reading of Chomsky's mentalist linguistics and leavened by E. P. Thompson on the English working class, has endured among some folklorists whose subject is American artisanry and material culture. Others have turned recently to the fluid strategies inspired by literary and cultural interpretation. For examples of both approaches in the work of one influential scholar, see Robert Blair St. George, "'Set Thine House in Order': The Domestication of the Yeomanry in Seventeenth-Century New England," in Jonathan L. Fairbanks and Robert F. Trent, eds., *New England Begins: The Seventeenth Century, vol. 2: Mentality and Environment* (Boston: Museum of Fine Arts, 1982), 159–88, and Robert Blair St. George, *Conversing by Signs: Poetics of Implication in Colonial New England Culture* (Chapel Hill: University of North Carolina Press, 1998).

65. Palissy, *Recepte véritable,* in *Oeuvres,* ed. Fillon and Audiat, 1: 132–33.

66. Geerat J. Vermeij, *A Natural History of Shells* (Princeton, N.J.: Princeton University Press, 1993), 13, 83. The specimen in Palissy's "De la ville de forteresse" was probably the common snail—a member of the largest molluscan class called the Gastropoda. This class possesses a univalve shell with a spiral posterior and has an anterior opening covered by a door (operculum) in times of danger.

67. Cotgrave's *Dictionarie,* s.vv. "Limace," "Limaçonner."

68. For illustrated examples, see Peter Kenny, "Flat Gates, Draw Bars, Twists and Urns: New York's Distinctive, Early Baroque Oval Tables with Falling Leaves," *American Furniture, 1994,* ed. Luke Beckerdite (Hanover, N.H.: University Press of New England, 1994): 113, figs. 11–13; for evidence of unmediated transmission to New World by French artisans, see Jean Palardy, *The Early Furniture of French Canada* (Toronto: Macmillan, 1963), 269, fig. 366.

69. Vermeij, *Natural History of Shells,* 11–13, 40–41; for a diagram of the gastropod shell, see 13, fig. 2.2; for images of shells glazed inside and out, see plates 1–21.

70. Ibid., 4, 32, 61. Vermeij reminds us that "ecology" is derived from the Greek *oikos*, meaning house.

71. Ibid., 95.

72. Ibid., 99.

73. Ibid., 83, 99–147.

74. Ambroise Paré, *On Monsters and Marvels,* trans. Janis L. Pallister (Chicago: University of Chicago Press, 1982), 91.

75. Amico, *Bernard Palissy,* 185.

76. In this context, if the snake in the basin referred to one particular iconographical meaning inferred by Palissy (which I am not suggesting), it may have been "wisdom" rather than the devil, the former a meaning from the Latin *anguis.* The root *ang* (or *angu*) commonly appears in Latin words referring to angles, corners, or narrow physical spaces, all specific to Palissy's *pourtrait* of the fortress town, as well as snakes. In astronomy, the snake appears in the constellation Draco.

77. Calvin, *On the Christian Faith,* 37–38.

78. Such as the one depicted by Lucas Cranach the Elder, in a wing panel of the Wittenberg Altar (1547), in the Stadtkirch, Wittenberg; panel reproduced in Oskar Thulin, *Die Lutherstadt Wittenberg und ihre reformatorischen Gedenkstatten* (Berlin: Evangelische Verlagsanstalt, 1968), fig. 30.

79. Carl C. Christensen, *Art and the Reformation in Germany* (Athens: Ohio University Press, 1979), 158–59.

80. A platter with a salamander turning back toward his own tail attributed to Palissy or his workshop is reproduced in Amico, *Bernard Palissy,* 114, fig. 98.

81. Augustine, *On Christian Doctrine,* 2.16, trans. D. W. Robertson Jr. (Indianapolis : Bobbs-Merrill, 1958), 50–51, as quoted in Lorraine Daston and Katharine Park, *Wonders and the Order of Nature, 1150–1750* (New York : Zone Books, 2001), 40–41.

82. Palissy, *Recepte véritable,* in *Oeuvres,* ed. Fillon and Audiat, 1: 133.

83. Palissy, *Recepte véritable,* 115, 120.

84. I am thinking here especially of Victor Turner, *Dramas, Fields and Metaphors: Symbolic Action in Human Society* (Ithaca, N.Y.: Cornell University Press, 1974), and id. and Edith Turner, *Image and Pilgrimage in Christian Culture: Anthropological Perspectives* (New York: Columbia University Press, 1978); *Process, Performance and Pilgrimage: A Study in Comparative Symbology* (New Delhi: Concept Publishing, 1979); and *The Drama of Affliction: A Study of Religious Processes among the Ndembu of Zambia* (Ithaca, N.Y.: Cornell University Press, 1981). The term "limen" was introduced by Arnold van Gennep in *The Rites of Passage (1908),* trans. Monika B. Vizedom and Gabrielle L. Caffe (London: Routledge & Kegan Paul, 1960); see also id., *Manuel du folklore français contemporain,* 7 vols. (Paris: Picard, 1938–58).

85. See esp. Caroline Walker Bynum, "Women's Stories, Women's Symbols: A Critique of Victor Turner's Theory of Liminality," in *Anthropology and the Study of Religion,* ed. Robert L. Moore and Frank E. Reynolds (Chicago: Center for the Scientific Study of Religion, 1984), 105–24.

86. Turner and Turner, *Image and Pilgrimage in Christian Culture,* 249–250.

87. Palissy, *Recepte véritable,* in *Oeuvres,* ed. Fillon and Audiat, 1: 133.

88. Ibid., 1: 135–36.

89. The mollusk *Purpurellus* was found off West Africa in the sixteenth century, though it

also has a Mediterranean fossil record; see Vermeij, *Natural History of Shells,* 171. Cotgrave's *Dictionarie* translates *pourpre* as "the Purple Shellfish."

90. *Industrie* is also defined in Cotgrave's *Dictionarie* as "diligence; vigilancie; active carefullnesse; indeavor; aptnesse unto, readinesse in, any thing."

91. Palissy, *Recepte véritable,* in *Oeuvres,* ed. Fillon and Audiat, 1: 136.

92. Ibid., 136–37.

93. Ibid. 137.

94. Ibid. This is suggestive of a level of access to Leonardo da Vinci's drawings after Vitruvius.

95. Ibid., 137–38.

96. Jean-Robert Armogathe et al., *Bernard Palissy, mythe et réalité* (Saintes, Niort, and Agen, France: Coédition: Musées d'Agen, Niort, Saintes, 1990), 38.

97. Amico, *Bernard Palissy,* 235, doc. XXIX (my translation unless otherwise noted).

98. Palissy, *Recepte véritable,* in *Oeuvres,* ed. Fillon and Audiat, 1: 138.

99. Ibid.

100. Ibid.

101. Ibid., 139.

102. Ibid., 140.

103. Ibid.

104. Ibid.

105. Ibid., 141.

106. Ibid.

THREE ❧ Personal History and "Spiritual Honor"

1. Jean Calvin, *Excuse de Jehan Calvin, à messieurs les Nicodemites, sur la complaincte qu'ilz font de sa trop grand' rigueur* (Zurich: Zentralbibliothek, 1544), in *Three French Treatises,* ed. Francis M. Higman (London: Athlone Press of the University of London, 1970), 131–53.

2. Ibid., 42–43.

3. No place of publication is given for any of the three editions of Crespin's *Actes* (subsequently *Histoire des Martyrs*). The actual title of John Foxe's *Book of Martyrs (1563),* first published in Latin at Basle in 1554 as *Rerum in ecclesia gestarum . . . commentarii,* is *Actes and Monuments of Matters Most Speciall and Memorable, Happening in the Church, with an Vniuersall History of the Same. Wherein Is Set Forth At Large the Whole Race and Course of the Church, from the Primitiue Age to These Latter Times of Ours, with the Bloudy Times, Horrible Troubles, and Great Persecutions, Against the True Martyrs of Christ, Sought and Wrought As Well by Heathen Emperours, As Now Lately Practised by Romish Prelates, Especially in This Realme of England and Scotland.* Tieleman Janszoon van Bracht, or Braght (1625–64), wrote *Martyrer Spiegel* (1660), translated by Joseph F. Sohm as *The Bloody Theater: Or, Martyr's Mirror of the Defenseless Christians Who Baptized Only Upon Confession of Faith, and Who Suffered and Died for the Testimony of Jesus, Their Saviour, from the Time of Christ to the Year . . 1660: Compiled from Various Authentic Chronicles, Memorials and Testimonies* (7th ed., Scottdale, Pa.: Mennonite Publishing House, 1964). On the relative ineffectiveness of martyrologies as tools for discipline in the countryside, see Euan Cameron, *The Reformation of the Heretics: The Waldenses of the Alps, 1480–1580* (Oxford: Clarendon Press, 1984), 224; see also Robert Kingdon, *Myths about the St. Bartholomew's Day Massacres, 1572–1576* (Cam-

bridge, Mass.: Harvard University Press, 1988), on martyrdom and witness; and Natalie Z. Davis, "The Rites of Violence," in *Society and Culture in Early Modern France* (Stanford, Calif.: Stanford University Press, 1975), 152–87.

4. Calvin, *Excuse de Jehan Calvin, à messieurs les Nicodemites,* 147–48.

5. Ibid., 135, 137.

6. John Calvin, *Institutes of the Christian Religion,* trans. Ford Lewis Battles, ed. John T. McNeill (Philadelphia: Westminster Press, 1960), 1: 56–58; Calvin constructs this argument in cha. 5 sec. 5, around a long excerpt from Vergil's *Aeneid* (6: 724–30).

7. Ibid., 54.

8. Ibid., 51.

9. Calvin, *Excuse de Jehan Calvin, à messieurs les Nicodemites,* 139.

10. Ibid., 150.

11. Martin Luther, *Treatise on Christian Liberty,* 45.

12. Calvin, *Excuse de Jehan Calvin, à messieurs les Nicodemites,* 132.; the 1558 edition lacks all the quotations.

13. Gerrard Winstanley, *Fire in the bush: The spirit burning, not consuming but purging mankinde, or, the great battell of God Almighty between Michaell, the seed of life, and the great red dragon, the curse fought within the spirit of man: with severall other declarations of the power of life* (London: Giles Calvert, 1650); see also John Rogers, *The Matter of Revolution: Science, Poetry and Politics in the Age of Milton* (Ithaca, N.Y.: Cornell University Press, 1996).

14. On Palissy and Agen, see H. Patry, "L'Origine de Bernard Palissy," 370–72; and Leonard N. Amico, *Bernard Palissy: In Search of Earthly Paradise* (Paris: Flammarion, 1996), 13–14; a number of *pirogue monoxyle* have been excavated from the Charente River bottom where they sank carrying pottery to Atlantic ships for export; see esp. Jean Chapelot, ed., *Potiers de Saintonge: Huit siècles d'artisanat rural: Musée national des arts et traditions populaires, 22 novembre 1975–1er mars 1976,* exhibition catalogue (Paris: Éditions des Musées nationaux, 1975), 110–13; and Jean Chapelot and Eric Rieth, *Navigation et milieu fluvial au XIe s.: L'Épave d'Orlac (Charente-Maritime),* Documents d'archéologie française, no 48 (Paris: Éditions de la Maison des sciences de l'homme, 1995).

15. Ernest Dupuy, *Bernard Palissy: L'Homme, l'artiste, le savant, l'écrivain* (1894; rev. ed., 1902; reprint of rev. ed., Geneva: Slatkine, 1970), 13; Amico, *Bernard Palissy,* 13–14.

16. Amico, *Bernard Palissy,* 13.

17. See Jan Craeybeckx, *Un Grand Commerce d'importation: Les Vins de France aux anciens Pays-Bas, XIIIe–XVIe siècle* (Paris: S.E.V.P.E.N., 1958).

18. Dupuy, *Bernard Palissy,* 17; on Menetra's travels in the glass trade with his *compagnons,* see his personal account in Jacques-Louis Ménétra, *Journal of My Life,* ed. Daniel Roche, trans. Arthur Goldhammer (New York: Columbia University Press, 1986); Palissy quote in Amico, *Bernard Palissy,* 16.

19. A reproduction of a typical *pourtrait* may be seen in *Inventaire général des monuments et des richesses artistiques de la France, Île de Ré: Inventaire topographique* (Paris: Ministère de la culture, Direction du patrimoine, 1979), 443, fig. 459; on the technology of glass painting, see Barbara Butts, Lee Hendrix, et al., *Painting on Light: Drawings and Stained Glass in the age of Dürer and Holbein* (Los Angeles: J. Paul Getty Museum; St. Louis, Mo.: St. Louis Art Museum, 2000), 57–65.

20. Quoted in Amico, *Bernard Palissy,* 16.

21. Dupuy, *Bernard Palissy,* 17–19. François I formally signed the edict establishing the *gabelle* in 1542; Palissy is thought to have been employed beginning sometime after May 1543.

22. Dupuy, *Bernard Palissy,* 18–19; Amico, *Bernard Palissy,* 18–19, speculates on various dates for the ceramic glaze experiments.

23. Cameron, *Reformation of the Heretics,* 224.

24. John Martin, *Venice's Hidden Enemies: Italian Heretics in a Renaissance City* (Berkeley: University of California Press, 1993), 125–46.

25. Bernard Palissy, *Recepte véritable,* in *Les Oeuvres de Maistre Bernard Palissy,* ed. B. Fillon and Louis Audiat (Niort: L. Clouzot, 1888), 1: 115–16.

26. Jean Calvin, *Institutes of the Christian Religion,* ed. John T. McNeill, trans. Ford Lewis Battles (Philadelphia: Westminster, 1960), 2 vols., 1: 72. Palissy knew the *Institutes* in Hamelin's edition, distributed in Saintonge by colporters.

27. For theoretical and methodological discussions of these problems, see Jon R. Snyder, *Writing the Scene of Speaking: Theories of Dialogue in the Late Italian Renaissance* (Stanford, Calif.: Stanford University Press, 1989); Michel de Certeau, "L'Ethnographie, l'oralité, ou l'espace de l'autre: Léry," in id., *L'Écriture de l'histoire* (Paris: Gallimard, 1975), 215–48; and Walter J. Ong, *Orality and Literacy: The Technologizing of the Word* (London: Methuen, 1982).

28. Frances A. Yates, *The Art of Memory* (Chicago: University of Chicago, 1966); Elizabeth L. Eisenstein, *The Printing Press as an Agent of Change: Communications and Cultural Transformations in Early Modern Europe* (New York: Cambridge University Press, 1980); and Natalie Z. Davis, "Printing and the People," in her *Society and Culture in Early Modern France* (Stanford, Calif.: Stanford University Press, 1975).

29. Jean-Daniel Sauvin, *Philibert Hamelin, martyr huguenot (1557)* (Geneva: University of Geneva, 1957), 11.

30. Palissy, *Recepte véritable,* in *Oeuvres,* ed. Fillon and Audiat, 1: 115–17. Palissy leaves the names anonymous in the *Recepte* and calls Robert "Robin," probably for reasons of security. The names of the monks and their orders have been identified by Henri Patry and Nathaniel Weis in "Frère Nicolle Maurel, apostat celestin, dit le predicant," *Bulletin de la Société de l'histoire du protestantisme français* 61 (1912): 193–203.

31. Sauvin, *Philibert Hamelin,* 13–15; Alexandre Crottet, *Histoire des églises réformées de Pons, Gemozac et Mortagne en Saintonge, précédée d'une notice étendue sur l'établissement de la réforme dans cette province, l'Aunis et l'Angoumois* (Bordeaux: A. Castillon, 1841), 16.

32. *LA BIBLE, Qui est toute la saincte Escriture, en laquelle sont contenuz. le vieil Testament, & le Nouveau, translatez en Francois, & reueuz: le vieil selon Hebrieu, & le nouveau selon le Grec* (Geneva: Philibert Hamelin, 1552). The 1552 edition of the Bible is in five volumes ("petit in-12°"), and the 1556 edition in two volumes ("petit in-quarto"). Most of the runs were intended for distribution in war-torn Saintonge, so surviving copies are rare. Copies of each edition are to be found in the Bibliothèque de Geneve (incomplete) and the library of the Société Protestante in Paris (complete).

33. Several copies of the *Oraisons* are available in libraries. Hamelin's edition of *L'Institution* is also located in the Société Protestante and was not attributed to his press until 1902. See also Sauvin, *Philibert Hamelin,* 35.

34. Sauvin, *Philibert Hamelin,* 17–24.

35. Palissy, *Recepte véritable*, in *Oeuvres,* ed. Fillon and Audiat, 1: 120.

36. Crottet, *Histoire des églises réformées,* 16–25.

37. Sauvin, *Philibert Hamelin*, 30–31.

38. Ibid., 38; Palissy, *Oeuvres*, ed. Fillon and Audiat, 120–21.

39. Palissy, *Recepte véritable*, in *Oeuvres*, ed. Fillon and Audiat, 1: 120–21; Sauvin, *Philibert Hamelin*, 38–41; order of the *parlement* of Bordeaux, April 12, 1557, in Archives départementales de la Gironde (Bordeaux). Hamelin was made to run the gauntlet, sealed in a pit for eight days with heavy leg irons dangling from his feet, and publicly tortured in unspecified ways on the day of his execution.

40. Palissy, *Recepte véritable*, in *Oeuvres*, ed. Fillon and Audiat, 1: 121; the provost marshal was the local informer, judge, and executioner combined in rural France, a hated and feared figure for Saintongeais Huguenots during the civil wars.

41. Ibid., 121–22.

42. Ibid., 114.

43. Ibid., 124

44. Ibid., 120–23; Sauvin, *Philibert Hamelin*, 38.

45. Palissy, *Recepte véritable*, in *Oeuvres*, ed. Fillon and Audiat, 1: 124.

46. Ibid., 126.

47. Dupuy, *Bernard Palissy*, 30–35.

48. Or "lords of particular jurisdictions."

49. Quoted in Dupuy, *Bernard Palissy*, 34–35.

50. The warrant of 1558 was dated September 25, Archives départementales de la Gironde (Bordeaux), 1B 195, fol. 177; see H. Patry, "Un Mandat d'arrêté du Parlement de Guyenne contre Bernard Palissy et les premiers fideles des eglises de Saintes et de Saint-Jean d'Angély (1558)," *Bulletin de la Société de l'histoire du protestantisme français* 51 (1902): 77–78, and Amico, *Bernard Palissy*, 229, doc. II.

51. Archives départementales de la Gironde (Bordeaux), 1B 256, fol. 146; see H. Patry, "La Captivite de Bernard Palissy pendant la premiere guerre de religion," *Bulletin de la Société de l'histoire du protestantisme français* 69 (1920): 21–25; and Amico, *Bernard Palissy*, 229–30, docs. IV–V.

52. Foremost among the royal officials whom Palissy claimed supported his release, along with Montmorency in 1563, was Guy de Jarnac, governor of La Rochelle, whose support for the monarchical faction was paramount during the visit of Charles IX two years hence. This may be a signal of Palissy's removal to Paris to work for Catherine de Médicis as early as 1563. For a discussion of Palissy's prison letter, see Amico, *Bernard Palissy*, 32.

53. Quoted in Dupuy, *Bernard Palissy*, 35; see also 62.

54. Palissy, *Recepte véritable*, in *Oeuvres*, ed. Fillon and Audiat, 1: 127.

55. Ibid., 127–28.

56. Ibid., 129.

57. Max Weber, *The Protestant Ethic and the Spirit of Capitalism*, trans. Talcott Parsons (New York: Scribner, 1950). My reading of Weber has been deepened by Alexandra Owen, *Magic and Modernity: Occultism and the Culture of Enchantment in Fin-de-Siècle Britain* (Chicago: University of Chicago Press, forthcoming), particularly chapter 7, "Magic and the Ambiguities of Modernity" (I am grateful to Professor Owen for the opportunity to read her book in manuscript); see also Guenther Roth and Wolfgang Schluchter, *Max Weber's Vision of History: Ethics and Methods* (Berkeley: University of California Press, 1979); Donald N. Levine, "Rationality and Freedom: Weber and Beyond," *Sociological Inquiry* 51, no. 1 (1981): 5–25; Rogers Brubaker, *The Limits of Rationality: An Essay on the Social and Moral Thought of Max Weber* (London: George

Allen & Unwin, 1984); and Scott Lash and Sam Whimsler, eds., *Max Weber, Rationality and Modernity* (London: Allen & Unwin, 1987).

58. Victor Turner and Edith Turner, *Image and Pilgrimage in Christian Culture: Anthropological Perspectives* (New York: Columbia University Press, 1978), 249–50.

59. Caroline Walker Bynum, "The Body of Christ in the Later Middle Ages: A Reply to Leo Steinberg," *Renaissance Quarterly* 39, no. 3 (Autumn 1986): 435; see also id., "Women's Stories, Women's Symbols: A Critique of Victor Turner's Theory of Liminality," in *Anthropology and the Study of Religion*, ed. Robert L. Moore and Frank E. Reynolds (Chicago: Center for the Scientific Study of Religion, 1984), 105–24.

60. Martin Luther, "Treatise on Christian Liberty" *(The Freedom of a Christian),* in *Martin Luther: Selections from His Writings,* ed. John Dillenberger (Garden City, N.Y.: Anchor Books, 1961), 56, 64.

61. *Salut* defies simple translation in this context. In the sixteenth century, according to Cotgrave's *Dictionarie, salut* meant not only "salutations" but also "health" and "safety" as well. Given my argument above, and that of the poem to follow, this greeting should be understood as having multiple meanings.

62. Palissy, *Recepte véritable,* in *Oeuvres,* ed. Fillon and Audiat, 1: 10.

63. *Secret de l'histoire naturelle contenant les merveilles et choses memorables du monde* [Secret of Natural History Containing the Marvels and Memorable Things of the World] (Paris: Jehan Kerver, n.d., but probably ca. 1580–1600); Bibliothèque nationale, Paris, MS Fr. 22791, fol. 60 verso; image also reproduced in Amico, *Bernard Palissy,* 182–83, fig. 165. However, Amico's interpretation of the image was limited to a few lines and his intention was to use it merely as an illustration of shells *qua* fortresses. My interest here is to interpret the image as part of a larger historical problem.

64. "Qui omnia secum portat, non indiget alieno auxilio," as translated in Pamela H. Smith, *The Business of Alchemy: Science and Culture in the Holy Roman Empire* (Princeton, N.J.: Princeton University Press, 1994), 52.

FOUR ❧ War and *Sûreté*

1. Étienne Trocmé, "L'Eglise reformée de La Rochelle jusqu'en 1628," *Bulletin de la Société de l'histoire du protestantisme français* 98 (July–September 1952), 133 (hereafter cited as ERLR). See also id., "De Gouverneur à l'intendant: L'Autonomie rochelaise de Charles IX à Louis XIII," in *Recueil de travaux offert à M. Clovis Brunel, membre de l'Institut, directeur honnoraire de l'École des chartes, par ses amis, collègues et élèves* (Paris: Société de l'École des chartes, 1955), 1: 616–32, and id., "Reflexions sur le separatisme rochelais," *Bulletin de la Société de l'histoire du protestantisme français* 122 (July–September 1976): 203–10; More recent work on pre-1628 La Rochelle is found in Judith Pugh Meyer, "La Rochelle and the Failure of the French Reformation," *Sixteenth Century Journal* 15, no. 2 (1984): 169–83; id., "The Success of the French Reformation: The Case of La Rochelle," *Archiv für Reformationsgeschichte* 84 (1993): 242–75; id., *Reformation in La Rochelle: Tradition and Change in Early Modern Europe, 1500–1568* (Geneva: E. Droz, 1996); David Parker, *La Rochelle and the French Monarchy: Conflict and Order in Seventeenth-Century France* (London: Royal Historical Society, 1980); and Kevin C. Robbins, *City on the Ocean Sea, La Rochelle, 1530–1650: Urban Society, Religion, and Politics on the French Atlantic Frontier* (Leiden: E. J. Brill, 1997).

2. ERLR, 133–34.

3. Resources at the Archives départementales de la Charente Maritime, Archives munici-pales, and Bibliothèque municipale, La Rochelle, and the Bibliothèque nationale and Archives nationales, Paris, currently available for La Rochelle for the period 1550–1628, are inventoried in Meyer, *Reformation in La Rochelle*, 165–67.

4. ERLR, 135–36. Meyer has mined La Rochelle's notarial registers to good effect; see her *Reformation in La Rochelle*, appendix D, 164–65. As Arcère discovered in 1756, Amos Barbot's history still remains a most useful resource for archival material.

5. ERLR, 137–38.

6. Meyer, *Reformation in La Rochelle*, 139; see also Mark Greenglass, *The French Reformation* (Oxford: Oxford University Press, 1987), 48–50.

7. Meyer, *Reformation in La Rochelle*, 141.

8. Ibid., 138–44.

9. Étienne Trocmé and Marcel Delafosse, *Le Commerce rochelais de la fin du XVe siècle au de-but du XVIIe* (Paris: A Colin, 1952); and Marcel Delafosse and Claude Laveau, *Le Commerce du sel de Brouage aux XVIIe et XVIIIe siècles* (Paris: A Colin, 1960).

10. Arcère, *Histoire*, 1: 310.

11. Étienne Guibert, "La Rochelle en 1628: État sanitaire des Rochelais et des assiegéants, mortalité, morbidité" (M.D. thesis, Université de Bordeaux II, June 26, 1979), 5.

12. ERLR, 137–38; see also Nathanaël Weiss, *La Chambre ardente: Étude sur la liberté de con-science en France sous François Ier et Henri II* (Paris: Fischbacher, 1889), 1–50; Paul Louis and Georges Musset, *Un Parlement au petit pied: Le Présidial de La Rochelle, étude historique* (La Rochelle, 1878).

13. ERLR, 137.

14. Philip Benedict, *Rouen During the Wars of Religion* (Cambridge: Cambridge University Press, 1981), 49.

15. In addition to the Aunis, the provinces of Champagne, Brie, Île de France, Picardie, Maine, Anjou, Touraine, Poitou, Angoumois, Beauce, Orléanais, Sologne, Berry, Nivernais, Lyonnais, Morvan, Forez, Auvergne, Bourbonnais, and Mâconnais were also included in the domain of Paris. Weiss, *Chambre ardente*, lxxii–lxxiii.

16. Ibid., lxviii. Blois in particular was targeted by the *parlement* of Paris as a center of Huguenot recruitment in the mid sixteenth century.

17. See chapter 1, pp. 39–40.

18. Weiss, *Chambre ardente*, lxxiii–lxxiv. Weiss includes transcripts of all surviving *procès* recorded in Paris of heretics transported there from the provinces, among them several from Au-nis-Saintonge; a general discussion of the structure of *parlements* may be found in Roland E. Mousnier, *The Institutions of France Under the Absolute Monarchy, 1598–1789: Society and State*, trans. Brian Pierce (Chicago: University of Chicago Press, 1979), 160–63, 278–79, 388, 431–42, and 609–27.

19. François Vaux de Foletier, *Le Siège de La Rochelle* (1931; La Rochelle: Éditions Quartier Latin et Rupella, 1978), 166.

20. Louis Pérouas, *Le Diocèse de La Rochelle de 1648 à 1724: Sociologie et pastorale* (Paris: S.E.V.P.E.N., 1964), 81.

21. Ibid., 96.

22. Ibid., 86.

23. Meyer, *Reformation in La Rochelle*, 141.

24. Kevin C. Robbins, *City on the Ocean Sea,* 107–427; on Toulouse, see Robert A. Schneider, *Public Life in Toulouse 1463–1789* (Ithaca, N.Y.: Cornell University Press, 1989).

25. ERLR, 187–93.

26. Ibid., 191.

27. Leonard N. Amico, *Bernard Palissy: In Search of Earthly Paradise* (Paris: Flammarion, 1996), 229, docs. II, IV, V; 236–37 docs. XXXV–XXXIX.

28. Ibid., 232–36, docs. XVI, XXIII–XXIV, XXVI, XXX–XXXII.

29. During his years in Sedan, Palissy's presence in La Rochelle can be documented only once, when he attended the baptism of Jehan, son of his daughter Margerite Palissy and Pierre Morysseau, in the Temple Sainte-Yon on April 17, 1575; ibid., 234, doc. XXI.

30. Epigraph to this section from Claude Lévi-Strauss, *Tristes tropiques,* trans. John and Doreen Weightman (New York: Pocket Books, 1977), 76, 34.

31. ERLR, 167; on Pierre Richier, see Olivier Reverdin, *Quatorze calvinistes chez les Topinambous: Histoire d'une mission genevoise au Brésil, 1556–1558* (Geneva: E. Droz, 1957), and Frank Lestringant, "Calvinistes et cannibales: Les Écrits Protestants sur le Brésil français 1555–1560," *Bulletin de la Société de l'histoire du protestantisme français,* 1–2 (1980): 9–26, 167–92; for the edition of Léry I use in the analysis to follow, see Jean de Léry, *History of a Voyage to the Land of Brazil, Otherwise Called America: Containing the Navigation and the Remarkable Things Seen on the Sea by the Author; the Behavior of Villegagnon in that Country; the Customs and Strange Ways of Life of the Various Savages; Together with the Description of Various Animals, Trees, Plants, and Other Singular Things Completely Unknown over Here,* trans. Janet Whatley (Berkeley: University of California Press, 1992).

32. Frank Lestringant, "The Philosopher's Breviary: Jean de Léry in the Enlightenment," in *New World Encounters,* ed. Stephen Greenblatt (Berkeley: University of California Press, 1993), 129.

33. Especially in *Tristes tropiques,* and *The Savage Mind.* In regard to Léry's influence on the anthropologist's earliest work on Brazil, it is noteworthy that Lévi-Strauss devoted much of the latter portion of his career to an anthropology of artisanal culture, specifically potters and pottery; see Claude Lévi-Strauss, *The Jealous Potter,* trans. Benedicte Chorier (Chicago: University of Chicago Press, 1988).

34. Paolo Rossi, *Philosophy, Technology and the Arts in the Early Modern Era* (New York: Harper & Row, 1970), 1–2, et passim; an overview of historians of science who investigate the circularity of learned and artisanal culture as fundamental to early modern epistemological inquiry would include Edgar Zilsel, "The Sociological Roots of Science," *American Journal of Sociology* 47 (1941–42): 544–62; Walter E. Houghton Jr., "The History of Trades: Its Relation to Seventeenth-Century Thought," in Philip P. Weiner and Aaron Noland, eds., *Roots of Scientific Thought: A Cultural Perspective* (New York: Basic Books, 1957), 354–81; J. A. Bennett, "The Mechanics' Philosophy and the Mechanical Philosophy," *History of Science* 14 (1986): 1–28; Alexander Keller, "Mathematics, Mechanics and the Origins of the Culture of Mathematical Invention," *Minerva,* 23 (1985): 348–61; Lisa Jardine, *Francis Bacon: Discovery and the Art of Discourse* (Cambridge: Cambridge University Press, 1974), 17–58; Pamela O. Long, "The Contribution of Architectural Writers to a 'scientific' Outlook in the Fifteenth and Sixteenth Centuries," *Journal of Medieval and Renaissance Studies* 15, no. 2 (1985): 265–98; R. Hooykaas, *Humanisme, science et reforme: Pierre de la Ramée (1515–1572)* (Leiden: E. J. Brill, 1958); William Eamon, "Technology as Magic in the Late Middle Ages and the Renaissance," *Janus* 70, nos. 3–4 (1983): 171–212;

and Owen Hannaway, *The Chemists and the Word: The Didactic Origins of Chemistry* (Baltimore: Johns Hopkins University Press, 1975).

35. Jean de Léry, *Histoire Memorable de la Ville de Sancerre contenant les Entreprises, Assaux et autres efforts des assiegans: les resistances, faits magnanimes, la famine extreme et delivrance notable des assiegez Le nombre des coups de Canons oar journees distngyuees. Le catalogues des morts et blesses a la guerre, sont a la fin du livre. Le tout fidelement recueilly sur le lieu, par JEAN DE LÉRY* (Rouen: Richard Petit, 1573); I have used the account given in Géralde Nakam, *Au lendemain de la Saint-Barthélemy: Guerre civile et famine* (Paris: Éditions Anthropos, 1975).

36. See Janet Whatley's strong archival evidence for Léry's status as a practicing shoemaker in Léry, *History of a Voyage*, 225, nn. 2, 4, and xvi.

37. Nakam, *Au lendemain de la Saint-Barthélemy*, 68.

38. For Theodore de Bry, see his fourteen-volume *Grands voyages* (Frankfurt, 1590–1634); for Urbain Chauveton, *Histoire nouvelle du Nouveau Monde: Contenant en somme ce que les Hespagnols ont fait jusqu'a present aux Indes Occidentales, et le rude traitement qu'ils font a ces povres peuples-la* (Geneva, 1579). Marcel Bataillon introduced the notion of a "Huguenot corpus on America," see his "L'Amiral et les 'nouveux horizons' français," in *Actes du colloque "L'Amiral de Coligny et son temps" (Paris, 24–28 octobre 1972) (Paris: Société de l'histoire du Protestantisme Français*, 1974), 41–52; on Calvin's role in Brazil, see Léry, *History of a Voyage*, 41–45, and David S. Lovejoy, *Religious Enthusiasm in the New World: Heresy to Revolution* (Cambridge, Mass.: Harvard University Press, 1985), 6–8.

39. See Frank Lestringant, *Le Huguenot et le sauvage: L'Amérique et la controverse coloniale en France, au temps des guerres de religion (1555–1589)* (Paris: Aux Amateurs de livres / Klincksieck, 1990); and id., "Philosopher's Breviary, 127–28.

40. Donald R. Kelley, *The Beginning of Ideology: Consciousness and Society in the French Reformation* (Cambridge: Cambridge University Press, 1981), 64; for alternative views of the origins of Protestant and Catholic Reformations of the sixteenth century, see John Bossy, *Christianity in the West, 1400–1700* (Oxford: Oxford University Press, 1985), 89–171.

41. Kelley, *Beginning of Ideology*, 64.

42. Léry, *History of a Voyage*, 53.

43. Ibid.; see also Charles W. Baird, *History of the Huguenot Emigration to America* (New York: Dodd, Mead, 1885), 1: 63–77 (hereafter cited as Baird); for a general discussion of the context of Coligny's colonization program, see Charles-André Julien, *Les voyages de découverte et les premiers établissements (Xve–XVIe siècles)* (Paris: Presses universitaires de France, 1948).

44. See the medal in Tessa Murdock et al., *The Quiet Conquest: The Huguenots, 1685–1985* (London: Museum of London, 1985), 30, fig. 13.

45. It is well known that the peopling of New France had a significant Calvinist component. For example, for an excellent discussion of the role played by the Rochelais Huguenot mercantile community in the society and economy of New France, see J. F. Bosher, *The Canada Merchants, 1713–1763* (Oxford, Clarendon Press, 1987); for insights into Calvinist culture among the largely Saintongeais "peasantry" in New France, see Leslie Choquette, *Frenchmen into Peasants: Modernity and Tradition in the Peopling of French Canada* (Cambridge, Mass.: Harvard University Press, 1997), 129–36.

46. Palissy, *Recepte véritable*, in *Oeuvres*, ed. Fillon and Audiat, 1: 29–35. Marl (*marne* in French) is a naturally occurring fertilizer composed of clay and calcium carbonate applied to

lime-deficient soils. Bernard Palissy, *The Admirable Discourses of Bernard Palissy,* trans. Aurele La Rocque (Urbana: University of Illinois Press, 1957), 204–32 (204 quoted).

47. Léry, *History of a Voyage,* 35.

48. Palissy, *Admirable Discourses,* 154–55.

49. Léry, *History of a Voyage,* 51–52.

50. Richard J. Tuttle, "Against Fortifications: The Defense of Renaissance Bologna," *Journal of the Society of Architectural Historians* 41, no.1 (March 1982): 189–201; see also Ivy A. Corfis and Michael Wolfe, *The Medieval City Under Siege* (Woodbridge, Suffolk, UK: Boydell Press, 1995).

51. Léry, *History of a Voyage,* 52.

52. Ibid.

53. Ibid.

54. Ibid., 50.

55. Ibid.

56. Ibid., 50, 53.

57. Ibid., 51.

58. Ibid., xx–xxi.

59. Ibid.

60. Ibid., xlvi.

61. Ibid., xlvii.

62. Ibid.

63. ERLR, 140; see also Guibert, "La Rochelle en 1628," 5.

64. E. Droz, *L'Imprimerie* à *La Rochelle,* vol. 1: *Barthélemy Berton, 1563–1573,* Travaux d'humanisme et Renaissance, 34 (Geneva: E. Droz, 1960), 22–24; Meyer, *Reformation in La Rochelle,* 96–98, 116, 141.

65. Yves Rouspeau, *Traitté de la préparation à la saincte Cène de Nostre seul Sauveur et Rédempteur Jésus Christ . . . plus un Dialogue contenant les poincts principaux que ceux qui veulent recevoir la Cène doivent savoir et entendre* (La Rochelle: Barthélemy Berton, [1563]), preface; and Droz, *Barthélemy Berton,* 24.

66. Meyer, *Reformation in La Rochelle,* 142; see Barbara B. Diefendorf, *Beneath the Cross: Catholics and Huguenots in Sixteenth-Century Paris* (New York: Oxford University Press, 1991), 30–35; and Virginia Reinburg, "Popular Prayers in Late Medieval and Reformation France" (Ph.D. diss., Princeton University, 1985).

67. ERLR, 138.

68. Meyer, "La Rochelle and the Failure of the French Reformation," 171–83.

69. Meyer, *Reformation in La Rochelle,* 142–43.

70. ERLR, 151.

71. Guibert, "La Rochelle en 1628," 5.

72. Catholic services were held at Sainte-Marguérite, next to the place du Château, in January 1571–September 1572, September 1576–December 1576, December 1577–1585, August 1599–May 1621, January 1624–Spring 1625, and Spring 1626–late September 1627.

73. ERLR, 139.

74. Benedict, *Rouen During the Wars of Religion,* 140–45; Robbins, *City on the Ocean Sea,* 287–92.

75. Heretics were still executed in La Rochelle as late as 1534.

76. ERLR, 144.

77. Ibid., 138.

78. Ibid., 142. Catholic numbers estimated from attendance at Sainte-Marguérite. For population figures, see Guibert, "La Rochelle en 1628," 152; for a more conservative tally of La Rochelle's population before and after 1628, see Philip Benedict, *The Huguenot Population of France, 1600–1685: The Demographic Fate and Customs of a Religious Minority,* Transactions of the American Philosophical Society, 81, pt. 5 (Philadelphia: American Philosophical Society, 1991), 51.

79. Guibert, "La Rochelle en 1628," 52–53. Between November and March 1627, 1,500 Catholics, "strangers," and "rich" evacuated the fortress. In addition, 250 sailors were accepted into the king's protection to serve in the royal navy, and 50 inhabitants escaped. For lower figures, see Benedict, *Huguenot Population of France, 1600–1685,* 51. Benedict counts La Rochelle's total population at 17,000 in 1610, and places the death toll in the siege at "close to 10,000 people." He does not cite the city census taken by Jean Godefroy in 1627 or Guibert's "La Rochelle en 1628," however.

80. Guibert, "La Rochelle en 1628," 45–55.

81. Ibid., 45; Trocmé and Delafosse, *Commerce Rochelais,* 116–25.

82. Guibert, "La Rochelle en 1628," 57.

83. Pierre Mervault, *Le Journal des Choses les plus memorables qui se sont passe au dernier siege de La Rochelle* (Rouen: J. Lucces, 1671), 312, 576, 577, 582; see also Arcère, *Histoire,* 1: 614, as quoted in Guibert, "La Rochelle en 1628," 58. Guibert argues that the Rochelais were suffering from "hypoprotidemie, hypoglycemia, hypolipemia et acedocetose et des modifications des compartiments corporels."

84. Vaux de Foletier, *Siège de La Rochelle,* 270.

85. Ariès, *Western Attitudes Towards Death,* 39–46. *Transi* may be understood as bodily purgatory, hence as the liminal state par excellence.

86. Armand-Jean du Plessis, duc de Richelieu, *The Political Testament of Cardinal Richelieu,* trans. Henry Bertram Hill (Madison: University of Wisconsin Press, 1961), 91.

87. For the most detailed description of cannibalism within the family in besieged Sancerre, see Léry's account of Simon and Eugènie Potard and their daughter in Nakam, *Au lendemain de la Saint-Barthélemy,* 290–96. That La Rochelle's was a seafaring culture is significant as well, since cannibalism was traditionally overlooked in cases of shipwreck.

88. As quoted in Guibert, "La Rochelle en 1628," 46.

89. See Nakam, *Au lendemain de la Saint-Barthélemy,* esp. 290–96.

90. Ibid., 295.

91. Léry, *History of a Voyage,* ch. 25: "How the Americans Treat their Prisoners of War and the Ceremonies They Observe Both in Killing and in Eating Them," 122–33.

92. Ibid., 131–33.

93. Nakam, *Au lendemain de la Saint-Barthélemy,* 136–38. See also Gérard Defaux, "Un Cannibale en haut de chausses: Montaigne, la différence et la logique de l'identité," *Modern Language Notes* 97, no. 4 (May 1982): 919–57.

94. Nakam, *Au lendemain de la Saint-Barthélemy,* 136–38.

95. On ordeal and purification, see Henry Charles Lea, *The Ordeal* (Philadelphia: University of Pennsylvania, 1973).

96. Lionel Rothkrug, "The 'odour of sanctity,' and the Hebrew Origin of Christian Relic Veneration," *Historical Reflections / Réflexions historiques* 8, no. 2 (Summer 1981): esp. 112–16.

97. Quoted in ibid., 113.

98. Ibid.

99. Ibid., 114–15.

100. On Sancerre, see Léry, *Memorable History,* ch. 10.

101. Léry, *History of a Voyage,* 132.

102. *Winthrop Papers, vol. 1: 1498–1628* (Boston: Massachusetts Historical Society, 1929), 359–60.

103. Guibert, "La Rochelle en 1628," 49.

104. Guibert is convincing in his assertion there was no evidence of plague in La Rochelle prior to 1628. After the capitulation, however, disease was carried into the fortress by the conquering army, which was afflicted, as was Louis XIII himself, from the very beginning of the siege. See "La Rochelle en 1628," 70.

105. Ibid., 16. This category of "gentleman-merchant" included *banquiers, changeurs, armateurs, titulaires, bourgeois, negociants, corsaires,* and *artisans parvenus* (artisans who rose to bourgeois status, escaping the stigma of manual labor).

106. Guibert, "La Rochelle en 1628," 75.

107. See Robbins, *City on the Ocean Sea;* also J. G. Clark, *La Rochelle and the Atlantic Economy,* esp. ch. 1 on the Rochelais economy and the relationship of intendants and merchants to municipal and central government; chs. 3–5 on dynastic merchant families and kinship; and p. 45, table 3.1, on the statistically predominant position of port families among important Rochelais families in the eighteenth century. For a case study of one such family, see Robert Forster, *Merchants, Landlords, Magistrates: The Depont Family in Eighteenth-Century France* (Baltimore: Johns Hopkins University Press, 1980). On the evolution of La Rochelle's Huguenot population after 1628, see Pérouas, *Diocèse de La Rochelle,* appendix, 475.

108. Katherine Louise Milton Faust, "A Beleaguered Society: Protestant Families in La Rochelle, 1628–1685" (Ph.D. diss., Northwestern University, 1980), 114–24.

109. Ibid., 10–20; Benedict, *Huguenot Population of France,* 51.

110. Faust, "Beleaguered Society," 13–14.

111. Joseph Bergin, *Cardinal Richelieu: Power and the Pursuit of Wealth* (New Haven, Conn.: Yale University Press, 1985), 46–61; see also id., *The Rise of Richelieu* (New Haven, Yale University Press, 1991), vii–115. Compare Bergin's analysis of Richelieu's financial interests with an early anecdotal treatment of the same in Aldous Huxley, *Grey Eminence* (New York: Harper & Row, 1941), 164–77.

112. Bergin, *Cardinal Richelieu,* 55, 58.

113. Ibid., 59–60.

114. Ibid., 64.

115. Ibid., 61–2, 66.

116. Faust, "Beleaguered Society," 143–363.

117. Elie Brakenhoffer quoted in ibid., 237, 244; Philippe Vincent, *Paraphrase sur les Lamentations du Prophète Jérémie* (La Rochelle: Jean Chuppin, 1646), 7.

118. Classically, the word "parasite," from the Greek *parasitos,* means "one who eats at the table of another, hence one who lives at another's expense by flattery or diversion" (*Oxford English Dictionary, s.v.*); biologically, it means "an organism living in or on another living organ-

ism, obtaining from it part or all of its organic nutriment, and commonly exhibiting some degree of adaptive structural modification" (*Webster's New World Dictionary, s.v.*). And in seventeenth-century French, according to Cotgrave's *Dictionarie, it meant:* "a trencher-friend, or bellie-friend, a smell-feast, and buffoone at feasts; a clawback, flatterer, soother, smoother for good chear sake."

119. ERLR, 147–49.

120. Ibid., 97. Synods were held at Jarnac (1560); La Rochelle (1562); Saint-Jean d'Angély (1563); Châteauneuf-s/Char (1570); Ligneres (1572); La Rochefoucauld (1581); Taillebourg (1591); La Rochelle (1592); Saint-Jean d'Angély (1593); Pons (1594); La Rochelle (1597); Saint-Jean d'Angély (1598); Pons (1599); Saujon (1600); Jarnac-Charente (1601); Taillebourg (1602); Saint-Jean d'Angély (1604 and 1605); and Pons (1606).

121. Ibid., 148.

122. Ibid., 146. Amos Barbot's *Histoire de La Rochelle* (Saintes, 1886), 1: 359, claims 76,000 persons—three times La Rochelle's population in 1627—flooded into the fortress after the Huguenot defeat at Moncontour in 1562.

123. Palissy, *Recepte véritable*, in *Oeuvres*, ed. Fillon and Audiat, 1: 122–23.

124. Archives départementales de la Gironde (Bordeaux), 1B 195, fol. 177, reprinted in Amico, *Bernard Palissy*, 229, doc. II. There was no record that Palissy was arrested in 1558 as were other members named in his group. Perhaps Montmorency or Pons also gave Palissy noble protection then, as well as in 1563?

125. See chapter 15, n. 44 . Guillemete's surname was probably Bodet, like her son's. "Patronne" undoubtedly referred to her status as owner of The Noble Vine.

126. Léry, *History of a Voyage*, 135.

127. Ibid., 134–35.

FIVE ❧ Scenes of Reading

EPIGRAPH: Hans Jakob Christoph von Grimmelshausen, *The Adventures of Simplicius Simplicissimus* (1668), trans. and ed. George Schulz-Behrend (Columbia, S.C.: Camden House, 1993), ch. 18, "Simplicius Takes His First Leap into the World, and Has Bad Luck," 28.

1. Hohenheim himself probably coined the name "Paracelsus" ("Beyond Celsus") by appending the Greek prefix *para* to the name of the patrician Roman physician Aulus Cornelius Celsus (ca. 1st century A.D.), whose reputation as one of the foremost medical writers in Latin was reestablished during the Renaissance when his *De medicina*—a medical treatise that contained chapters on agriculture, military strategy and fortifications, rhetoric, philosophy, and law—was published in 1478. This book was translated into vernacular editions for use as the standard medical textbook in the university lecture halls that Paracelsus would reject in print as inadequate. He thereby also claimed symbolically to be a superior teacher outside the lecture hall than his illustrious predecessor, by using his own books to supplement the great Book of Nature and confirm the centrality of experience over ancient and scholastic precedents.

2. For a lucid analysis of the significance of the Paracelsian movement in the early modern period, see H. R. Trevor-Roper, "The Paracelsian Movement," in id., *Renaissance Essays* (Chicago: University of Chicago Press, 1985), 149–99.

3. See Wayne Shumaker, *The Occult Science in the Renaissance: A Study in Intellectual Patterns* (Berkeley: University of California Press, 1979), 16, 53, 202–5; see also Walter Pagel, *Paracelsus:*

An Introduction to Philosophical Medicine in the Era of the Renaissance (Basel: Karger, 1982); Paul Oscar Kristeller, *The Philosophy of Marsilio Ficino,* trans. Virginia Conant (New York: Columbia University Press, 1943); Ardis B. Collins, *The Secular as Sacred: Platonism and Thomism in Marsilio Ficino's Platonic Philosophy* (The Hague: Nijhoff, 1974); André Chastel, *Marsile Ficin et l'art* (Geneve: E. Droz, 1954); on Ficino in sixteenth-century France, André-Jean Festugière, *La Philosophie de l'amour de Marsile Ficin et son influence sur la littérature française au XVIe siècle* (Paris: J. Vrin, 1941); and Jean Dagens, "Hérmetisme et Cabale en France de Lefèvre d'Etaples à Bossuet," in *Revue de Littérature comparée,* no. 1 (January–March 1961): 5–16.

4. Paul Oskar Kristeller, *The Philosophy of Marsilio Ficino* (New York: Columbia University Press, 1943), 203–40.

5. John Bossy, *Christianity in the West, 1400–1700* (New York: Oxford University Press, 1985), 108.

6. Nigel Hiscock, *The Wise Master Builder: Platonic Geometry in Plans of Medieval Abbeys and Cathedrals* (Aldershot, UK: Ashgate, 2000), 274.

7. Ibid., 97–101, 274–75.

8. Trevor-Roper, "Paracelsian Movement," 156. For the classic discussion of this doctrine as practiced by early modern alchemists, see Owen Hannaway, *The Chemists and The Word: The Didactic Origins of Chemistry* (Baltimore: Johns Hopkins University Press, 1975), 22–57.

9. Trevor-Roper, "Paracelsian Movement," 156.

10. Charles Webster, *From Paracelsus to Newton: Magic and the Making of Modern Science* (Cambridge: Cambridge University Press, 1982), 3–4.

11. Kurt Goldammer, *Paracelsus: Natur und Offenbarung* (Hanover: Theodor Oppermann, 1953), and "Paracelsische Eschatologie," *Nova Acta Paracelsica* 6 (1952): 68–102; see also Trevor-Roper, "Paracelsian Movement," 156–57.

12. Webster, *From Paracelsus to Newton,* 15–17, 21, 24–29.

13. On Joachim and the wide diffusion of his prophesies, see Marjorie Reeves, *The Influence of Prophesy in the Later Middle Ages: A Study in Joachimism* (Oxford: Clarendon Press, 1969), and Bossy, *Christianity in the West,* 107; on the influence of Joachimism on the adepts, see Frances A. Yates, *The Rosicrucian Enlightenment* (Boulder, Colo.: Shambhala, 1978), 35; and Trevor-Roper, "Paracelsian Movement," 157; on prophesy among the Paracelsians, see Webster, *From Paracelsus to Newton,* 15–47.

14. On the status of the operator and the relation between operators and philosophers, see William R. Newman, *Gehennical Fire: The Lives of George Starkey, an American Alchemist in the Scientific Revolution* (Cambridge, Mass.: Harvard University Press, 1994), xi–xiv; on smallness and purity, see 160–69.

15. Hannaway, *Chemists and the Word,* 6–7.

16. See D. P. Walker, *Spiritual and Demonic Magic from Ficino to Campanella* (London: Warburg Institute, 1958), "Paracelsus and Jacques Gohory," 96–106.

17. Ibid., 97.

18. Ibid., 96 and 105.

19. Palissy, *Admirable Discourses,* 100.

20. Alexandre de La Tourette, *Bref discours des admirable vertus de l'orpotable: auquel sont traictez les principaux fondemens de la medicine, l'origine & cause de toutes maladies, & quels sont les medicamens plus propres a leur guerison, & a la conservation de la santehumaine . . . Avec une apologie de la tres utile science d'Alchimie, tant contre ceux qui la blasment, qu'aussi contre les faulsaires, lar-*

rons & trompeurs qui en abusent . . . (Lyon, 1575); for further discussion, see Wallace Kirsop, "The Legend of Bernard Palissy," *Ambix* 9, no. 3 (October 1961): 148, an article that extends Walker's research on Gohory into a convincing analysis of Palissy's association with Gohory's scientific community.

21. Jacques Gohory, *Discours responsif a celuy d'Alexandre de la Tourete, sur les secrets de l'art Chymique & confection de l'Orpotable, faict en la defense de la Philosophie & Medecin antique, contra la nouvelle Paracelsique* (Paris, 1575). For the definition of "chymistry" as "the total of chemical/ alchemical terminology and theory as it existed in early modern Europe," see William R. New- man, *Gehennical Fire: The Lives of George Starkey, an American Alchemist in the Scientific Revolu- tion* (Cambridge, Mass.: Harvard University Press, 1994), xii–xiii.

22. Kirsop, "Legend of Bernard Palissy," 148; Kirsop argues that Palissy would have been aware of all the works by Paracelsus and his followers available in Paris in the mid to late six- teenth century, as well as the work of other medieval and modern alchemists, through his access to Gohory's community.

23. Palissy, *Admirable Discourses*, 23–24.

24. Ibid., 81.

25. Ibid.

26. Pagel, *Paracelsus*, 241–71.

27. Newman, *Gehennical Fire*, 93–94.

28. Ibid.

29. Ibid., 94–95

30. Ibid., 95–99.

31. See Frances Yates, "The Art of Ramon Lull: An Approach to It Through Lull's Theory of the Elements," *Journal of the Warburg and Courtauld Institutes* 17, no. 1–2 (1954): 115; and Mark D. Johnston, "The Reception of Lullian Art, 1450–1530," *Sixteenth Century Journal* 12, no. 1 (1981), 31–48.

32. Kirsop, "Legend of Bernard Palissy," 147.

33. Ibid.; Newman, *Gehennical Fire*, 103. The original work is Jean de (de Valenciennes) La Fontaine, Jean de Meung, Jean Clopinel, dit, *De la transformation métallique, trois anciens tractez en rithme françoise, asçavoir: la Fontaine des amoureux de science, autheur: J. de La Fontaine; les Remonstrances de Nature à l'alchymiste errant, avec la Response dudit alchy., par J. de Meung; ensem- ble un tracté de son Romant de la Rose concernant ledict art; le Sommaire philosophique de N. Flamel, avec la défense d'iceluy art et des honestes personages qui y vaquent* . . . (Paris: G. Guillard & A. Warancore, 1561).

34. Walker, *Spiritual and Demonic Magic*, 99–101; and Kirsop, "Legend of Bernard Palissy," 149.

35. Walker, *Spiritual and Demonic Magic*, 100.

36. Ambroise Paré, *On Monsters and Marvels* (1573), trans. Janis L. Pallister (Chicago: Uni- versity of Chicago Press, 1982), xv–xxxii.

37. Ambroise Paré, *Journies in Diverse Places*, trans. S. Paget, in *Scientific Papers: Physiology, Medicine, Surgery, Geology*, vol. 38 (New York: Collier, 1910).

38. Paré, *On Monsters and Marvels*, 3.

39. Ibid., 3–4.

40. For examples of monstrosity created out of lack of self-discipline and immorality, see esp. ibid., 74–84 (chs. 21–26).

41. Ibid., xxvi–xxvii; Jean Céard, *La Nature et les prodiges: L'Insolite au 16e siècle, en France* (Geneva: E. Droz, 1977), 290–320; see also Katharine Park and Lorraine F. Daston, "Unnatural Conceptions: The Study of Monsters in Sixteenth- and Seventeenth-Century France and England," *Past and Present,* no. 92 (August 1981): 21–54; and Lorraine F. Daston and Katharine Park, *Wonders and the Order of Nature, 1150–1750* (New York: Zone Books, 1998).

42. Palissy, *Admirable Discourses,* 154–155; *Oeuvres complètes de Bernard Palissy,* ed. Paul-Antoine Cap (Paris: J.-J. Dubochet, 1844; reprint with an avant-propos by Jean Orcel, Paris: A. Blanchard, 1961), 271; and Paré, *On Monsters and Marvels,* xxiii.

43. Thomas C. Allbut, "Palissy, Bacon, and the Revival of Natural Science," in *Proceedings of the British Academy* (London: Oxford University Press, 1913–1914), 224–47.

44. Bernard Palissy, *Recepte véritable,* in *Les Oeuvres de Maistre Bernard Palissy,* ed. B. Fillon and Louis Audiat, *Les Oeuvres de Maistre Bernard Palissy* (Niort: L. Clouzot, 1888), 1: 11–12, 13–14.

45. Ibid., 19.

46. On the relation between Washington and Cincinnatus, see Garry Wills, *Cincinnatus: George Washington and the Enlightenment* (Garden City, N.Y.: Doubleday, 1984); on Agricola and his influence, see William Emerton Heitland, *Agricola: A Study of Agriculture and Rustic Life in the Greco-Roman World from the Point of View of Labor* (Cambridge: Cambridge University Press, 1921); Cotton Mather, *Agricola. Or, the Religious Husbandman: The main intentions of religion, served in the business and language of husbandry; and commended therefore by a number of ministers to be entertained in the families of the countrey* (Boston: D. Henchman, 1727); Samuel Fisher, *Rusticus ad Academicos, or the Country correcting the Clergy* (London, 1660); John Robertson, *Rusticus ad Clericum, or, the Plow-Man rebuking the Priest* (Aberdeen?, 1694); and Bernard Bailyn, *The Ideological Origins of the American Revolution* (Cambridge, Mass.: Harvard University Press, 1967).

47. On the relation between Cato and Addison, see Julie K. Ellison, *Cato's Tears and the Making of Anglo-American Emotion* (Chicago: University of Chicago Press, 1999).

48. Bernard Palissy, *The Admirable Discourses of Bernard Palissy,* trans. Aurele La Rocque (Urbana: University of Illinois Press, 1957), 113–14; *Paracelsus: Selected Writings,* ed. Jolande Jacobi, trans. Norbert Guterman, Bollingen ser. 28 (New York: Pantheon Books, 1958). On Paracelsians and the primacy of experience, see Hannaway, *Chemists and the Word,* 4, 59–62. See also n. 1 above on the name "Paracelsus."

49. See n. 1 above.

50. John Calvin, *Institutes of the Christian Religion,* trans. Ford Lewis Battles, ed. John T. McNeill (Philadelphia: Westminster Press, 1960), 1: 52.

51. Palissy, *Admirable Discourses,* 10–13.

52. Ibid., 113–14.

53. On English skepticism, see Barbara J. Shapiro, *A Culture of Fact: England, 1550–1720* (Ithaca, N.Y.: Cornell University Press, 2000), 1–7. On the book trade in France in the sixteenth century, see E. Droz, *L'Imprimerie à La Rochelle,* vol. 1: *Barthélemy Berton, 1563–1573,* Travaux d'humanisme et Renaissance, 34 (Geneva: E. Droz, 1960); Lucien Febvre and H. J. Martin, *L'Apparition du livre* (Paris, 1958); Annie Parent, *Les Métiers du livre à Paris au XVIe siècle (1535–1560* (Geneve: E. Droz, 1974); David T. Pottinger, *The French Book Trade in the Ancien Regime, 1500–1791* (Cambridge, Mass.: Harvard University Press, 1958); Natalie Z. Davis, "Printing and the People," in *Society and Culture in Early Modern France* (Stanford, Calif.: Stanford University

Press, 1975), 189–206; and Robert Darnton, *The Literary Underground of the Old Regime* (Cambridge, Mass.: Harvard University Press, 1982).

54. *Désert* territory is well mapped and defined in similar terms for Protestant culture in southeastern France in two excellent and now classic studies: Philippe Joutard, *La Légende des Camisards: Une Sensibilité au passé* (Paris: Gallimard, 1977); and Hillel Schwartz, *The French Prophets: The History of a Millenarian Group in Eighteenth-Century England* (Berkeley: University of California, 1980). For the *désert* as metaphor, see esp. Schwartz, 11–36.

55. For a complete list of texts one can infer Palissy knew from hints in his writing, see Palissy, *Admirable Discourses,* 10–13.

56. Charles Webster, *The Great Instauration: Science, Medicine, and Reform, 1626–1660* (London: Gerald Duckworth, 1975); and, for a concise version of the Webster thesis, see id., *From Paracelsus to Newton.*

57. On publication of scientific secrets and their association with both commerce and personal power, see William Eamon, *Science and the Secrets of Nature: Books of Secrets in Medieval and Early Modern Culture* (Princeton, N.J.: Princeton University Press, 1994), 3–90, 168–233.

58. Carlo Ginzburg, *The Cheese and the Worms: The Cosmos of a Sixteenth-Century Miller,* trans. John and Anne Tedeschi (Baltimore: Johns Hopkins University Press, 1980), xii–xiii.

59. Ibid., xxiv.

60. Ibid., xxii–xxiii.

61. Ibid., xxiii; for the most sustained critique in English of this and other problems in Ginzburg's oeuvre, see John Martin, "Journies to the World of the Dead: The Work of Carlo Ginzburg," *Journal of Social History* 25, no. 3 (Spring 1992): 613–27.

62. Ginzburg, *Cheese and the Worms,* 127–28; on Bruno, see Frances A. Yates, *Giordano Bruno and the Hermetic Tradition* (Chicago: University of Chicago Press, 1964).

63. Jakob Böhme, *Aurora . . . that is, the root or mother of philosophie, astrologie, & theologie from the true ground,* trans. John Sparrow from the first German ed., Görlitz, 1612 (London: Giles Calvert, 1656), 48; for Böhme's intellectual biography, see Alexandre Koyré, *La Philosophie de Jacob Boehme* (Paris: J. Vrin, 1929); for Böhme's influence in England and America, see Schwartz, *French Prophets,* 8; Richard Bauman, *Let Your Words Be Few: Symbolism of Speaking and Silence Among Seventeenth-Century Quakers* (Prospect Heights, Ill.: Waveland Press, 1990), 3–5; Henry A. Pochmann, *German Culture in America: Philosophical and Literary Influences, 1600–1900* (Madison: University of Wisconsin: 1957), 31, 224, 226, 677 n. 2; A. G. Roeber, "'The Origin of Whatever Is Not English Among Us': The Dutch-speaking and the German-speaking Peoples of Colonial British America," in Bernard Bailyn and Philip D. Morgan, eds., *Strangers Within the Realm: Cultural Margins of the First British Empire* (Chapel Hill: University of North Carolina Press, 1991), 250; F. Ernest Stoeffler, "Mysticism in the German Devotional Literature of Colonial Pennsylvania," *Pennsylvania German Folklore Society* 14 (1949): 1–181; and Yates, *Rosicrucian Enlightenment,* 99, 186, 225–32.

64. Böhme, *Aurora,* 96–98, 196.

65. Ibid., 98.

66. Luther's open schism with the enthusiasts is usually dated to 1524; see Bossy, *Christianity in the West,* 107; and see also a useful overview of the violent quarrels following the rapid rise of Lutheran sectarianism during the sixteenth century in Quentin Skinner, *The Foundations of Modern Political Thought: The Age of Reformation* (Cambridge: Cambridge University Press, 1978), 2: 73–81.

67. Böhme, *Aurora,* 159, 162.

68. Ibid., 160–61.

69. Ibid., 146–47.

70. Ibid., 596–98

71. Ibid., 270, 403, 411, 472–73.

72. Peter James Klassen, *The Economics of Anabaptism, 1520–1560* (The Hague: Mouton, 1964), 14–16.

73. G. H. Williams, *The Radical Reformation* (Philadelphia: University of Pennsylvania Press, 1962); *Spiritual and Anabaptist Writers: Documents Illustrative of the Radical Reformation,* edited by George Huntston Williams, and Evangelical Catholicism as represented by Juan de Valdés, ed. Angel M. Mergal, Library of Christian Classics, vol. 25 (Philadelphia: Westminster Press, 1957); Steven E. Ozment *Mysticism and Dissent* (New Haven, Conn.: Yale University Press, 1973); and C. P. Clasen, *The Anabaptists: A Social History* (Ithaca, N.Y.: Cornell University Press, 1972).

74. "An Open Letter from Wolfgang Brandhuber to the Church in Rattenberg" (1529), trans. in Klassen, *Economics of Anabaptism,* appendix D, 128–33.

75. Böhme, *Aurora,* "Note," n.p.

76. Jean Seguy, "Religion and Agricultural Success: The Vocational Life of French Anabaptists from the Seventeenth to the Nineteenth Centuries," trans. Michael Schank, *Mennonite Quarterly Review* 47 (July 1973): 209–17.

77. Böhme, *Aurora,* 402–4.

78. Seguy, "Religion and Agricultural Success," 209–17.

79. Klassen, *Economics of Anabaptism,* appendix D, 128–33; on the term "Family of Love," see John Canne, *A Necessitie of separation from the Church of England, provided by the nonconformist Principles* (London, 1634), 132; and Ephraim Pagitt, *Heresiography: Or a Description of the Hereticks and Sectaries of these Latter Times* (London, 1645), 105.

80. Bossy, *Christianity in the West,* 106.

81. Ibid.

82. John Martin, *Venice's Hidden Enemies: Italian Heretics in a Renaissance City* (Berkeley: University of California Press, 1993), 121–2, 99–112.

83. Böhme, *Aurora,* "Note."

84. On the Essenes and the early Judeo-Christian sectarian tradition, competition, and confluence, see Gunther Sternberger, *Jewish Contemporaries of Jesus: Pharisees, Sadducees, Essenes,* trans. Allan W. Mahnke (Minneapolis: Fortress Press, 1995); Eric M. Meyers, ed., *Galilee Through the Centuries: A Confluence of Cultures,* Duke Judaic Series, vol. 1 (Winona Lake, Ind.: Eisenbrauns, 1999); and Eric M. Meyers and Michael L. White, "Jews and Christians in a Roman World," *Archaeology* 42, no. 2 (March–April 1989): 26–32.

85. Grimmelshausen, *Adventures of Simplicius Simplicissimus,* 250–52. This disciplined description is, in effect, a reversal of Palissy's dark vision of Saintes in chaos over the mouth of Hell after occupation by Counter-Reformation forces, with unmastered children, the violent heirs of their demonic heritage, divided by loathing into forces of mimetic opposition within the formerly unified community.

86. Ibid., 250, 252.

87. Bossy, *Christianity in the West,* 109–10.

88. Grimmelshausen, *Adventures of Simplicius Simplicissimus,* 113–18.

89. Bossy, *Christianity in the West,* 110–11.

90. For examples of what I call the southeastern prophetic "style," see Margaret C. Jacob, *The Radical Enlightenment: Pantheists, Freemasons and Republicans* (London: George Allen & Unwin, 1981); Joutard, *Légende des Camisards;* and Schwartz, *French Prophets;* on the theatricality of the southeastern prophets, see Schwartz, ibid., 251–78.

91. Bossy, *Christianity in the West,* 110.

92. Quoted in Frederick J. Powicke, *The Cambridge Platonists: A Study* (Hamden, Conn.: Archon Books, 1971), 99.

93. Bauman, *Let Your Words Be Few,* 1–32.

94. Roeber, "Origin of Whatever Is Not English," 250–51; Carter Lindberg, *The Third Reformation? Charismatic Movements and the Lutheran Tradition* (Macon, Ga.: University of Georgia Press, 1983), 55–178; Hannaway, *Chemists and the Word,* 9–11. Evidence of Grimmelshausen's sophisticated occult, astrological, and natural-philosophical interests is found throughout the text of *Simplicissimus;* see Helmut Rehder, "Planetenkinder: Some Problems of Character Portrayal in Literature," [University of Texas] *Graduate Journal* 3 (1968): 69–97; Günther Weydt, *Nachahmung und Schöpfung im Barock: Studien um Grimmelshausen* (Bern: Francke, 1968), pt. 4; and for a contrary perspective, Blake Lee Spahr, "Grimmelshausen's Simplicissimus: Astrological Structure?" *Argenis* 1 (1977): 7–29.

95. Canne, *Necessitie of Separation,* 132.

96. On the sociology of "front and back," see Erving Goffman, *Relations in Public: Microstudies of the Public Order* (New York: Harper Colophon, 1972).

97. Palissy, *Recepte véritable,* in *Oeuvres,* ed. Fillon and Audiat, 1: 115–17.

98. Ibid.

99. For one anonymous depiction of Peter's deliverance from prison, painted in eighteenth-century New York, see Ruth Piwonka, Roderic Blackburn, et al., *A Remnant in the Wilderness: New York Dutch Scripture History Paintings of the Early Eighteenth Century* (Albany, N.Y.: Bard College Center and Albany Institute of History and Art, 1980), 56, fig. 28 (note the eyes of the guard sitting on a bench in the right foreground).

100. Böhme, *Aurora,* 224–25.

101. Ibid., 438–39.

102. Ibid., 572.

103. Ibid., 411–12.

104. Ibid., 227–28.

105. Ibid., 441, 452.

106. Cotgrave's *Dictionarie.*

107. Jan Craeybeckx, *Un Grand Commerce d'importation: Les Vins de France aux anciens Pays-Bas, XIIIe–XVIe siècle* (Paris: S.E.V.P.E.N., 1958), 78–206; Sidney W. Mintz, *Sweetness and Power* (New York: Viking, 1985).

108. Jean Chapelot, ed., *Potiers de Saintonge: Huit siècles d'artisanat rural: Musée national des arts et traditions populaires, 22 novembre 1975–1ᵉʳ mars 1976,* exhibition catalogue (Paris: Éditions des Musées nationaux, 1975), esp. 108–13 and 119–21.

109. Schwartz, *French Prophets,* 11. The geographic origin of these artisans is obscure.

110. Ibid.; Joutard, *Légende des Camisards;* and Jacob, *Radical Enlightenment.*

111. Lynn White Jr., "The Iconography of *Temperantia* and the Virtuousness of Technology,"

in *Medieval Religion and Technology: Collected Essays* (Berkeley: University of California Press, 1978), 182–83.

112. Ibid.

113. Bossy, *Christianity in the West*, 11.

114. Ibid., 10–11.

115. Kathleen Basford, *The Green Man* (New York: D. S. Brewer, 1998)); Richard Bernheimer, *Wild Men in the Middle Ages: A Study in Art, Sentiment, and Demonology* (Cambridge, Mass.: Harvard University Press, 1952); William Anderson, *Green Man: The Archetype of Our Oneness with the Earth* (San Francisco: HarperCollins 1990); Hamish Henderson, "The Green Man of Knowledge," *Scottish Studies* 2, no. 1 (1958): 47–85; J. R. L. Highfield, "The Green Squire," *Medium Aevum* 22 (1953): 18–23; Lady Raglan, "The Green Man in Church Architecture," *Folklore* 50, no. 1 (1939): 45–57; R. O. M. Carter and H. M. Carter, "The Foliate Head in England," *Folklore* 78 (1967): 269–74; James Clarke Holt, *Robin Hood* (London: Thames & Hudson, 1982); and Christian Jacq, *Le Message des bâtisseurs de cathédrales* (Paris: Plon, 1980).

116. Anderson, *Green Man*, 20–30; Holt, *Robin Hood*.

117. Arnold van Gennep, *Manuel de folklore français contemporain* (Paris: A. Picard, 1943–66), 1: 1488–1502.

118. Anderson, *Green Man*, 26; Barbara Butts and Lee Hendrix, *Painting of Light: Drawings and Stained Glass in the Age of Dürer and Holbein* (Los Angeles: J. Paul Getty Museum, 2000), 312.

119. For photographs of these two ceramic pieces, see Amico, *Bernard Palissy*, 26, fig. 14; and Chapelot, ed., *Potiers de Saintonge*, 73, fig. 229. A full discussion of the plaque's attribution and source is found in Amico, 37, and Alan Gibbon and Pascal Faligot, *Céramiques de Bernard Palissy* (Paris: Librairie Seguier/Vagabondages, 1986), 42–45; on Palissy's Italian influences, see Gibbon and Faligot, 16–26.

120. Anderson, *Green Man*, 14, 33.

121. On Wisdom and Fortuna in Renaissance humanism, see Charles Dempsey, *Inventing the Renaissance Putto* (Chapel Hill: University of North Carolina Press, 2001), 184–85.

122. For close discussions of the *Simplicissimus* frontispiece, see Ellen Leyburn, *Satiric Allegory: Mirror of Men*, Yale Studies in English, 130 (New Haven, Conn.: Yale University Press, 1956), 7; and esp. Karl-Heinz Habersetzer, "'Ars Poetica Simpliciana': Zum Titelkupfer des *Simplicissimus Teutsch*," *Daphnis* 3 (1974): 60–82, and 4 (1975): 57–78.

123. For the relation between the carving of eyes wide open and eschatology in seventeenth-century New England Calvinist mortuary art, see David H. Watters, *With bodilie eyes: Eschatological Themes in Puritan Literature and Gravestone Art* (Ann Arbor, Mich.: UMI Research Press, 1981); on the widespread use of figures emanating vegetation in the frontispieces and title-page borders of British-American and Continental books in the early modern era, see R. B. McKevrow and F. S. Ferguson, *Title-Page Borders Used in England and Scotland, 1485–1640* (Oxford: Bibliographical Society, 1932); and Alfred F. Johnson, *German Renaissance Title-Borders* (Oxford: Bibliographical Society, 1929).

124. Böhme, *Aurora*, 114–15.

125. See Anderson, *Green Man*, 24, 80–88, 134; and esp. Basford, *Green Man*, 15–16. There is no mention of this program in Adolf Katzenellenbogen, *The Sculptural Program of Chartres Cathedral* (Baltimore: Johns Hopkins University Press, 1954).

126. See Eugène Canseliet, "Les Écoinçons des stalles de la cathédrale de Poitiers et leur in-

terprétation alchimique," *Atlantis,* 332 (1984): 291–308; C. J. P. Cave, *Roof Bosses in Medieval Churches* (Cambridge: Cambridge University Press, 1948), and *Medieval Carvings in Exeter Cathedral* (London: Penguin Books, 1953); Roland Sheridan and Anne Ross, *Grotesques and Gargoyles in the Medieval Church: Paganism in the Medieval Church* (Boston: New York Graphic Society, 1975); G. L. Remnant, *A Catalogue of Misericords in Great Britain* (Oxford: Clarendon Press, 1969); and James Jerman and Anthony Weir, *Images of Lust: Sexual Carvings on Medieval Churches* (London: B. T. Batsford, 1986).

127. *Oxford English Dictionary,* s.v. "misericord."

128. Anderson, *Green Man,* 135–36.

129. Bernheimer, *Wild Men in the Middle Ages,* 2.

130. The two chests of drawers are located in the collections of the Wadsworth Atheneum, Hartford, Connecticut, and Historic Deerfield, Deerfield, Massachusetts. See also Brian P. Levack, *The Formation of the British State: England, Scotland, and the Union, 1603–1707* (New York: Oxford University Press, 1987).

131. On the social history of witchcraft, see Carlo Ginzburg, *The Night Battles: Witchcraft and Agrarian Cults in the Sixteenth and Seventeenth Centuries,* trans. John and Anne Tedeschi (New York: Penguin Books, 1986), 1–98; id., *Ecstasies: Deciphering the Witches' Sabbath* (New York: Pantheon Books, 1991); Brian P. Levack, ed., *Articles on Witchcraft, Magic, and Demonology: A Twelve Volume Anthology of Scholarly Articles* (New York: Garland Publishing, 1992), esp. vols. 1–3, 12; id., *The Witch Hunt in Early Modern Europe* (London: Longman, 1995); Bernheimer, *Wild Men in the Middle Ages,* 4.

132. Bernheimer, *Wild Men in the Middle Ages,* 1–9.

133. Ibid., 7–12.

134. Ibid., 12–20.

135. Ibid.

136. Grimmelshausen, *Adventures of Simplicius Simplicissimus,* 30–31; these chapters show certain similarities to the medieval German epic *Der Busant,* which itself may have been derived from the French story *Peter of Provence.*

137. Ibid., 30.

138. Ibid., 34.

139. Ibid.

140. The ideal form of the society of orders—a rather static model—is exemplified by Roland Mousnier, *The Institutions of France Under the Absolute Monarchy, 1598–1789,* trans. Brian Pearce (Chicago: University of Chicago Press, 1979), and *Les Hiérarchies sociales de 1450 à nos jours* (Paris: Presses universitaires de France, 1969). Critiques have developed from Mousnier's Marxist contemporaries, Pierre Goubert, *Beauvais et le Beauvaisis de 1600 à 1730* (Paris: S.E.V.P.E.N., 1960), and id., *Louis XIV and Twenty Million Frenchmen,* trans. Anne Carter (New York: Pantheon Books, 1970); and A. D. Lublinskaya, *French Absolutism: The Crucial Phase, 1620–1629,* trans. Brian Pearce (Cambridge: Cambridge University Press, 1968); as well as gender studies, see Julie Hardwick, *The Practice of Patriarchy: Gender and the Politics of Household Authority in Early Modern France* (University Park, Pa.: Penn State University Press, 1998); Sarah Hanley, "Engendering the State: Family Formation and State Building in Early Modern France," *French Historical Studies* 16 (Spring 1989), and id., "The Monarchic State in Early Modern France: Martial Regime Government and Male Right," in *Politics, Ideology, and the Law in Early Modern Eu-*

rope: Essays in Honor of J. H. M. Salmon, ed. Arianna Bakos (Rochester, N.Y.: University of Rochester Press, 1994).

141. The word *verds* is read here as a variant of the verb *verdir,* "to turn green." I have chosen to translate *verds* as "verdure" or "greenery" because the use of vegetation seems to capture the sense of the passage most accurately.

142. Böhme, *Aurora,* 405–6.

143. Ibid., 406–7.

144. Ibid., 407.

145. Ibid., 409–10.

146. The historiography of torture in early modern France is dominated by Roland Mousnier, *The Assassination of Henri IV: The Tyrannicide Problem and the Consolidation of the French Absolute Monarchy in the Early Seventeenth Century,* trans. Joan Spencer (New York: Scribner, 1973); a transcript of Ravaillac's torture is found in Edmund Goldsmid, *The Trial of Francis Ravaillac for the Murder of King Henri the Great, Together with an Account of His Torture and Execution, Extracted and Translated from the Registers of the Parliament of Paris, 1610* (Edinburgh: Privately printed, 1885); see also John H. Langbean, *Torture and the Law of Proof: Europe and England in the Ancien Regime* (Chicago: University of Chicago, 1977); William T. Cavanaugh, *Torture and Eucharist: Theology, Politics, and the Body of Christ* (Oxford: Blackwell, 1998); and Darius M. Rejali, *Torture and Modernity: Self, Society, and State in Modern Iran* (Boulder, Colo.: Westview Press, 1994).

147. Jacob, *Radical Enlightenment,* 22.

148. Ibid., 47.

149. Quoted in François de Vaux de Foletier, *Le Siège de La Rochelle* (1931; La Rochelle: Éditions Quartier Latin et Rupella, 1978), 279.

SIX ❧ American Rustic Scenes

1. Ronald Sterne Wilkinson, "The Alchemical Library of John Winthrop, Jr. (1606–1676) and His Descendants in Colonial America, Part I," *Ambix* 11, no. 1 (February 1963): 33.

2. Ibid., 34.

3. Ibid.; and Ronald Sterne Wilkinson, "The Alchemical Library of John Winthrop, Jr. (1606–1676) and His Descendants in Colonial America, Part II," *Ambix* 13, no. 3 (October 1966): 139; see also John W. Streeter, "John Winthrop, Junior, and the Fifth Satellite of Jupiter," *Isis* 39 (August 1948): 159–63; Ronald Sterne Wilkinson, "John Winthrop, Jr., and America's First Telescopes," *New England Quarterly* 35 (December 1962): 520–23; Silvio A. Bedini, "The Transit in the Tower: English Astronomical Instruments in Colonial America," *Annals of Science* 54, no. 2 (March 1997): 161–96; and Robert C. Black III, *The Younger John Winthrop* (New York: Columbia University Press, 1966), 55, 169–71, 307–19.

4. Wilkinson, "Alchemical Library of John Winthrop, Jr., Part II," 174, cat. no. 196.

5. Estate Inventory, John Winthrop Jr., Boston, 1676: Connecticut State Library, Hartford District, file 6151; Jonathan L. Fairbanks and Robert F. Trent, eds., *New England Begins: The Seventeenth Century, vol. 2: Mentality and Environment* (Boston: Museum of Fine Arts, 1982), 217; and William N. Hosley Jr., ed., *The Great River: Art and Society in the Connecticut Valley, 1635–1820* (Hartford, Conn.: Wadsworth Antheneum, 1985), 192–93.

6. Fairbanks and Trent, eds., *New England Begins: The Seventeenth Century,* 2: 217–18.

7. Ibid., and Robert F. Trent, "The Spencer Chairs and Regional Chair Making in the Connecticut River Valley," in *Bulletin of the Connecticut Historical Society* 49, no. 4 (Fall 1984), 191.

8. Trent, "Spencer Chairs," 191–92; Hosley, ed., *Great River,* 192–93.

9. Peter M. Kenny, Frances Gruber Safford, and Gilbert T. Vincent, *American Kasten: The Dutch-Style Cupboards of New York and New Jersey* (New York: Metropolitan Museum of Art, 1991), 11–12, 36–39; Robert F. Trent, "New Insights on Early Rhode Island Furniture," *American Furniture, 1999,* ed. Luke Beckerdite (Hanover, N.H.: University Press of New England, 1999): 209–15; Robert A. Leath, "Dutch Trade and Its Influence on Seventeenth-Century Chesapeake Furniture," *American Furniture, 1997,* ed. Luke Beckerdite (Hanover, N.H.: University Press of New England, 1997): 21–39; and Black, *Younger John Winthrop,* 132–33.

10. Peter Follansbee, "A Seventeenth-Century Carpenter's Conceit: The Waldo Family Joined Great Chair," *American Furniture, 1998,* ed. Luke Beckerdite (Hanover, N.H.: University Press of New England): 209–10.

11. Quoted in ibid., 210.

12. Ibid., quoted on 211.

13. Elderkin's greetings are conveyed in Roger Williams to John Winthrop Jr., October 23, 1650, *Collections of the Massachusetts Historical Society,* 4th ser., 4 (Boston: Printed for the Society, 1863), 284. An early, popular widely disseminated illustration of "The Copernican System" was known to New Englanders from *An Almanack of Coelestial Motions for the Year of the Christian Epocha, 1675* (fig. 6.4), but this woodcut was only printed in Boston by John Foster (1648–81) some sixteen years after the chair was made. A second edition of the 1675 *Almanack* appeared in 1681. See Fairbanks and Trent, eds., *New England Begins: The Seventeenth Century,* 2: 147–48, 329–30.

14. Foster graduated from Harvard in 1667 and his press in Cambridge printed all New England's almanacs until 1676. Ibid., 147–48.

15. For a list of Robert Fludd titles in Winthrop's library, see Ronald Sterne Wilkinson, "The Alchemical Library of John Winthrop, Jr. (1607–1676) and His Descendants in Colonial America, Part IV: The Catalogue of Books," *Ambix* 13, no. 3 (October 1966): 155–56, nos. 86–95.

16. Ibid., 155, nos. 89 and 89a.

17. Robert Fludd, *Integrum morborum mysterium: Sive medicinae catholicae . . .* [and] *Katholikon* [Gr.] *medicorum katoptron* [Gr.] *. . .* [and] *Pulsus seu nova et arcana pulsuum historia, e sacro fonte radicaliter extracta, nec non medicorum ethnicorum dictis authoritate comprobata,* three works, forming the complete tractate 2 of vol. 1 of the *Medicina catholica* in one vol. (Frankfurt: Wolfgang Hofmann for Willem Fitzer, 1631), 343; Joscelyn Godwin, *Robert Fludd: Hermetic Philosopher and Surveyor of Two Worlds* (Boulder, Colo.: Shambhala, 1979), 65, fig. 77.

18. Robert Fludd, *Katholikon* [Gr.] *medicorum* katoptron [Gr.]: *In quo, Quasi Speculo Politissimo Morbi praesentes mor demonstrativo clarissime indicantur, & futuri ratione prognostica aperte cernuntur, atque prospiciuntur* (Frankfurt: [Willem Fitzer?], 1631), 255; Godwin, *Robert Fludd,* 64, fig. 76.

19. The seven-part color wheel is illustrated in Robert Fludd, *Medicina catholica* (Frankfurt: Willem Fitzer, 1629), 154.

20. See Roland Barthes, *Camera Lucida: Reflections on Photography,* trans. Richard Howard (New York: Hill & Wang, 1981), 26–27: "it is this element which rises from the scene, shoots out of it like an arrow, and pierces me. A Latin word exists to designate this wound, this prick, this mark made by a pointed instrument: the word suits me all the better in that it also refers to the

notion of punctuation, and because the photographs I am speaking of are in effect punctuated, sometimes even speckled with these sensitive points; . . . I shall therefore call [such a point a] *punctum.*"

21. On the metropolitan aspect of the significance of the Doric order on seventeenth-century American chairs, see esp. Benno M. Forman, *American Seating Furniture, 1630–1730: An Interpretative Catalogue* (New York: Norton, 1988), 182–83, 200–201, 276–77, and 304–5; see also Jonathan L. Fairbanks and Robert F. Trent, eds., *New England Begins: The Seventeenth Century, vol. 3: Style* (Boston: Museum of Fine Arts, 1982), 522–24.

22. Milo M. Naeve and Lynn Springer Roberts, *A Decade of Decorative Arts: The Antiquarian Society of the Art Institute of Chicago* (Chicago: Art Institute, 1986), 54–56; Ann Smart Martin, *Makers and Users: American Decorative Arts, 1630–1820, from the Chipstone Collection* (Madison, Wis.: Elvehjem Museum of Art, 1999), 16.

23. Jakob Böhme, *Aurora . . . that is, the root or mother of philosophie, astrologie, & theologie from the true ground,* trans. John Sparrow (from the first German ed., Görlitz, 1612 (London: Giles Calvert, 1656), 598.

24. Ibid., 599.

25. Ibid., 472.

26. Ibid., 157–58.

27. *Oxford English Dictionary*

28. Including *Architectura* (Antwerp, 1578), and *Perspective* (Amsterdam, 1628). See also Alexandre Koyré, *Metaphysics and Measurement* (Cambridge, Mass.: Harvard University Press, 1968).

29. Fairbanks and Trent, eds., *New England Begins: The Seventeenth Century,* 3: 514–15.

30. Benno M. Forman, "Continental Furniture Craftsmen in London: 1511–1625," *Furniture History* 7 (1971): 94–120.

31. This is to exclude, of course, beds and bedrooms where, cross-culturally and at various moments in history, visitors have been "publicly" received. This custom is especially noteworthy among noble families and the king in ancien régime France, but it can also be observed in England and America.

32. Fairbanks and Trent, eds., *New England Begins: The Seventeenth Century,* 2: 348–49.

33. Margaret C. Jacob, *The Radical Enlightenment: Pantheists, Freemasons, and Republicans* (London: Allen & Unwin, 1981), 38.

34. "Oswaldus Crollius [D.O.M.A. Osualdi Crollii Veterani Hassi Basilica Chymica Continans], 4 to, should be [16], 283, [25], Pp. but title and first leaf of preface is missing. Followed by 'Oswaldi Crolii Trectatus De Signaturis Internis Rerum, Seu De Vera Et Viva Anatomia Majoris et minoris mundi' and 'De Vera Antiqua Philosphica Medicina' (1608 or 1609)." Quoted from inventory provided by Wilkinson, "Alchemical Library of John Winthrop, Jr. (1606–1676), Part II," 150.

35. Owen Hannaway, *The Chemists and the Word: The Didactic Origins of Chemistry* (Baltimore: Johns Hopkins University Press, 1975), 28 and 31.

36. Böhme, *Aurora,* 130–31, 147–49.

37. Ibid., 148–49.

38. On the phenomena of "absorption" by artists into their work through the media of their tools, see Michael Fried, *Absorption and Theatricality: Painting and Beholder in the Age of Diderot* (Berkeley: University of California Press, 1980). I benefited greatly from participation in Fried's

"Eye and Mind" seminar as a graduate student at Johns Hopkins University. See also Robert S. Woodbury, *History of the Lathe to 1850: A Study in the Growth of a Technical Element of an Industrial Economy* (Cleveland: Society for the History of Technology, 1961); on lathes used by seventeenth-century American turners, see Joseph Moxon, *Mechanick Exercizes: Or the Doctrine of Handy-Works,* ed. Benno M. Forman (New York: Praeger, 1970 [London, 1677 edition]), pls. 12–18. For a discussion of Elderkin as a carrier of books, see chapter 11, p. 000

39. See Ellen Griffith, *The Pennsylvania Spice Box: Paneled Doors and Secret Drawers* (West Chester, Pa.: Chester County Historical Society, 1986). The "vine and berry" inlay that often decorates the doors, Griffith argues, was brought to England by French or Flemish artisans, whence it was diffused from the West Country to Chester County.

40. Martha H. Willoughby, "Patronage in Early Salem: The Symonds Shops and Their Customers," in *American Furniture, 2000,* ed. Luke Beckerdite (Hanover, N.H.: University Press of New England, 2000), 169–84.

41. Luther Samuel Livingston, *Franklin and His Press at Passy: An Account of the Books, Pamphlets, and Leaflets Printed There, Including the Long-Lost Bagatelles* (New York: Grolier Club, 1914).

42. *Oeuvres de Bernard Palissy, revues sur les exemplaires de la Bibliothèque du Roi,* ed. Barthélemy Faujas de Saint Fond and Nicolas Gobet (Paris: Ruault, 1777), vij–viij. This edition reprints the 1563 text but the editors also refer to a first edition published at Lyon in 1557, which remains unestablished. The consensus of Palissy's biographers and critics is that the first edition was the one printed at La Rochelle in 1563.

43. Robert Darnton, *Mesmerism and the End of the Enlightenment in France* (New York: Schocken Books, 1970), 10, 62, 64, 146, 152.

44. For a full-length study of Paracelsianism in relation to the republican tradition in early modern Europe, see Jacob, *Radical Enlightenment.*

45. The Saint-Aubin engraving is pictured in Charles Coleman Sellers, *Benjamin Franklin in Portraiture* (New Haven, Conn.: Yale University Press, 1962), appendix, p. 10.

46. Ibid., 96–108, appendix, p. 9.

47. Ibid., 105. "Several intact cases of these medallions, each pair packed back to back in paper, were discovered in a Bordeaux warehouse in 1885, 'as fresh as the day when they were first baked'" (*Franklin in France. From Original Documents, Most of Which Are Now Published for the First Time, by Edward E. Hale and Edward E. Hale, Jr.* (Boston: Roberts Brothers, 1887–88; reprint, New York: Burt Franklin, 1969), 1: xvi.

48. *The Writings of Benjamin Franklin,* ed. Albert Henry Smythe (New York: Macmillan, 1907), 7: 23–26.

49. Richard Bernheimer, *Wild Men in the Middle Ages: A Study in Art, Sentiment, and Demonology* (Cambridge, Mass.: Harvard University Press, 1952), 4–6.

50. Michel René Hilliard d'Auberteuil, quoted in Alfred Owen Aldridge, *Franklin and His French Contemporaries* (New York: New York University Press, 1957), 43.

51. Jacques-Louis Ménétra, *Journal of My Life,* ed. Daniel Roche, trans. Arthur Goldhammer (New York: Columbia University Press, 1986), 73; see also Lisa Jane Graham, "A Quest for Autonomy: Jacques Louis Ménétra, Glazier in Eighteenth-Century France" (Department of History European Seminar, Johns Hopkins University, April 21, 1988), 31, and René Moulinas, *Les Juifs du pape en France: Les Communautés d'Avignon et du Comtat Venaissin aux 17e et 18e siècles* (Paris: Privat, 1981).

SEVEN ❧ The River and Nebuchadnezzar's Dream

1. Frederick J. Powicke, *The Cambridge Platonists: A Study* (Hamden, Conn.: Archon Books, 1971), 99–100.

2. Ibid.

3. Owen Hannaway, *The Chemists and the Word: The Didactic Origins of Chemistry* (Baltimore: Johns Hopkins University Press, 1975), 44–45.

4. *Paracelsus: Selected Writings,* ed. Jolande Jacobi, trans. Norbert Guterman, Bollingen ser. 28 (New York: Pantheon Books, 1958), 4–6.

5. Carlo Ginzburg, *The Cheese and the Worms: The Cosmos of a Sixteenth-Century Miller,* trans. John and Anne Tedeschi (Baltimore: Johns Hopkins University Press, 1980), xxiii.

6. Bernard Palissy, *Recepte véritable, in Oeuvres complètes de Bernard Palissy,* ed. Paul-Antoine Cap (Paris: J.-J. Dubochet, *1844; reprint with an* avant-propos by Jean Orcel, Paris: A. Blanchard, 1961), 43.

7. Jean Chapelot and Éric Rieth, *Navigation et milieu fluvial au XIe siècle: L'Épave d'Orlac (Charente-Maritime),* Documents d'Archéologie française, no. 48 (Paris: Maison des sciences de l'homme, 1995), 9–93.

8. Bernard Palissy, *Recepte véritable,* in *Les Oeuvres de Maistre Bernard Palissy,* ed. B. Fillon and Louis Audiat (Niort: L. Clouzot, 1888), 1: 23–25.

9. Translated from original text reproduced in Mathieu Augé-Chiquet, *Les Amours de Jean-Antoine de Baïf* (Paris: Hachette, 1909), 149. For a description of Baïf's Ficinian academy, which was more universalist in nature than Gohory's, see D. P. Walker, *Spiritual and Demonic Magic from Ficino to Campanella* (London: Warburg Institute, 1958), 96–106.

10. W. H. Herendeen, "The Rhetoric of Rivers: The River and the Pursuit of Knowledge," *Studies in Philology* 68, no. 2 (Spring 1981), 107–8.

11. For a world history of this phenomenon, see Simon Schama, *Landscape and Memory* (New York: Knopf, 1995), "Water."

12. See Max F. Schultz, "The Circuit Walk of the Eighteenth-Century Landscape Garden and the Pilgrim's Circuitous Progress," *Eighteenth-Century Studies* 15, no. 1 (Fall 1981), esp. 1–5.

13. Leon Wencelius, "Musique et Chant Sacré," in *L'Esthétique de Calvin* (Paris: Les Belles Lettres, 1937), 285.

14. Quoted in Augé-Chiquet, *Amours de Jean-Antoine de Baïf,* 150, lines 70–87; and 154, lines 25–30.

15. Frances A. Yates, *The French Academies of the Sixteenth Century (London: Warburg Institute, University of London, 1947),* 84; id., "The Art of Raymond Lull: An Approach to It Through Lull's Theory of the Elements," *Journal of the Warburg and Courtauld Institutes* 17 no. 1–2 (1954): 136 n. 1; Ramon Llull, *Libre de meravelles, a cura de mn. Salvador Galmés,* 4 vols. (Barcelona: Editorial Barcino, 1931–34); and see also Josep Maria Ruiz Simon, *L'art de Ramon Llull i la teoria escolàstica de la ciència* (Barcelona: Quaderns Crema, 1999).

16. Palissy, *Recepte véritable,* 4.

17. For an account of the translation of the *Hypnerotomachia* into French, see Benjamin Fillon, "Le Songe de Poliphile," *Gazette des Beaux Arts,* 20 (July–December 1879): 60–64.

18. The most recent English translation is Francesco Colonna, *Hypnerotomachia Poliphili: The Strife of Love in a Dream,* trans. Joscelyn Godwin (London: Thames & Hudson, 1999); see also Anthony Blunt, "The Hypnerotomachia Poliphili in Seventeenth-Century France," *Jour-*

nal of the Warburg Institute 1 (1937–38): 117–37; Giovanni Pozzi in vol. 2 of *Francesco Colonna, biografia e opera,* ed. Maria Teresa Casella (Padua: Editrice Antenore, 1959); Emanuela Kretzulesco-Quaranta, *Les Jardins du songe: "Poliphile" et la mystique de la Renaissance* (Paris: Les Belles Lettres, 1986); and Alberto Perez Gomez, *Polyphilo, or, The Dark Forest Revisited: An Erotic Epiphany of Architecture* (Cambridge, Mass.: MIT Press, 1992).

19. Francesco Colonna, *Hypnerotomachia Poliphili,* trans. Robert Dallington as *Hypnerotomachia: The Strife of Love in a Dream* (London, 1592); reprint (New York: De Capo Press, 1969), 11.

20. Ibid., 11–14.

21. Ibid., 14.

22. Ibid., 15.

23. Ibid., 16; see also fig. 2, 13.

24. Yates, *French Academies,* 46; Wencelius, *Esthétique de Calvin,* 280–83.

25. Clément Marot, "L'Épître aux Dames de France" (August 1, 1543), quoted in Wencelius, *Esthétique de Calvin,* 282–83.

26. See D. P. Walker, "Orpheus and Theologian and the Renaissance Platonists," *Warburg Journal* 16 (1953); id., "The Prisca Theologia in France," ibid. 17 (1954); for a fine study of Ficino's Neoplatonic system in early modern music and song, and its effect on the body, see Gary Tomlinson, *Music in Renaissance Magic: Toward a Historiography of Others* (Chicago: University of Chicago Press, 1993), 67–228; see also id., *Metaphysical Song: An Essay in Opera* (Princeton, N.J.: Princeton University Press, 1999).

27. Pontus de Tyard, *Solitaire premier, ou Prose des muses e de la fureur poétique* (Lyon: Jean de Tournes, 1552); *Solitaire premiere, ou Discours des muses, e de la poétique* (Paris: Galiot du Pré, 1575); *Solitaire second, ou Discours de la musique* (Lyon: Jean de Tournes, 1552); *Solitaire second, ou Prose de la musique* (Lyon: Jean de Tournes, 1555).

28. M. J. B. Allen, "Ficino's Theory of the Five Substances and the Neoplatonists," in *Journal of Medieval and Renaissance Studies* 12, no. 1 (Spring 1982)., 19.

29. Quoted in ibid., 20.

30. Jakob Böhme, *Aurora . . . that is, the root or mother of philosophie, astrologie, & theologie from the true ground,* trans. John Sparrow (from the first German ed., Görlitz, 1612 (London: Giles Calvert, 1656), 504–6.

31. Psalm 104 was not only identifiable with the doxology of Protestantism. The Catholic apologist Guy Le Fèvre de La Boderie transposed the hymn nearly intact to serve as centerpiece for his *La Galliade* (1578), "Cercle IV." *La Galliade* is a celebration of the glory of Gaulle, for its composer the wellspring of music, and by extension, also of the harmonizing effects of the music of the spheres. Of course, from Palissy's point of view, one man's harmony was another's discord. See Simone Maser, *La Galliade* (Geneva: E. Droz, 1979), 11–12, 31–32.

32. Böhme, *Aurora,* 571.

33. Ibid.

34. For a discussion of this psalm, see Patrick Boylan, *The Psalms: A Study of the Vulgate Psalter in the Light of the Hebrew Text* (Dublin: M. H. Gill & Son, 1948), 2: 177–88.

35. Palissy, *Recepte véritable,* in *Oeuvres complètes,* ed. Cap, 9.

36. For a comparative discussion of tensions between the aural and the written text in early modern England, see D. R. Woolf, "Speech, Text, and Time: The Sense of Hearing and the Sense of the Past in Renaissance England," *Albion* 18, no. 2 (Summer 1986): 159–93.

37. Gordon L. Davies, *The Earth in Decay: A History of British Geomorphology, 1578–1878* (New York: American Elsevier, 1969), is a good general survey of the subject.

38. Palissy, *Recepte véritable*, in *Oeuvres*, ed. Fillon and Audiat, 1: 45.

39. Classical interpretation ran parallel to biblical in its rejection of an aging earth; see James Dean, "The Earth Grows Old: The Significance of a Medieval Idea" (Ph.D. diss., Johns Hopkins University, 1971), 5–10.

40. Davies, *Earth in Decay*, 9.

41. Thomas Robinson, *A Vindication of the Philosophical and Theological Exposition of the Mosaick System of the Creation* (London, 1709), 54.

42. See Davies, *Earth in Decay*, for numerous examples of persecution for questioning the dogma that "all was made in the beginning of the Creation of the world."

43. Northrup Frye, *The Great Code: The Bible and Literature* (New York: Harcourt Brace Jovanovich, 1982), 138.

44. Bernard Palissy, *Discours admirables de la nature des eaux et fontaines . . .* (Paris: Martin Le Jeune, 1580), 90, 103. For Paracelsus on the *quinta essentia*, see *Paracelsus: Selected Writings*, ed. Jacobi, 28–29.

45. Hannaway, *Chemists and the Word*, 28–29; also Walter Pagel, "Paracelsus and the Neoplatonic and Gnostic Traditions," *Ambix* 8 (1960): 127–32.

46. Bernard Palissy, *The Admirable Discourses of Bernard Palissy*, trans. Aurele La Rocque (Urbana: University of Illinois Press, 1957), 125–28.

47. Böhme, *Aurora*, 162–63.

48. Palissy, *Recepte véritable*, in *Oeuvres*, ed. Fillon and Audiat, 1: 42.

49. Dean, "World Grows Old," 12.

50. Ibid., 143.

51. Ibid., 142–43.

52. Ibid., 143–44.

53. See Richard Bernheimer, *Wild Men in the Middle Ages: A Study in Art, Sentiment, and Demonology* (Cambridge, Mass.: Harvard University Press, 1952), 12.

54. Dean, "World Grows Old," 143–44.

55. Ibid., 180–84.

56. Ibid., 185–88.

57. Palissy, *Admirable Discourses*, 254, 301, 47, 199, 228, 378.

58. *Paracelsus: Selected Writings*, ed. Jacobi, 141–43.

59. Palissy, *Admirable Discourses*, 93.

60. Epigraph to this section from H. J. C. von Grimmelshausen, *The Adventurous Simplicissimus: Being the Description of the Life of a Strange Vagabond Named Melchior Sternfels von Fuchshaim*, trans. A. T. S. Goodrick (Lincoln: University of Nebraska, 1962), 339.

61. Palissy, *Recepte véritable*, in *Oeuvres*, ed. Fillon and Audiat, 1: 46.

62. Ibid., 48.

63. On the hermaphrodite and *conjunctio*, see esp. *The Collected Works of C. G. Jung*, Bollingen ser. 20 (New York: Pantheon Books / Princeton, N.J.: Princeton University Press, 1953–83), vol. 12: *Psychology and Alchemy* (1953), 329; vol. 13: *Alchemical Studies* (1967), 123, 136, 139, both trans. R. F. C. Hull.

64. Palissy, *Recepte véritable*, in *Oeuvres complètes*, ed. Cap, 39.

65. Ibid., 41; for a more complete discussion of these issues comparatively, see Charles Web-

ster, "Water as the Ultimate Principle of Nature: The Background to Boyle's Skeptical *Chemist*," *Ambix* 13, no. 2 (June 1966): 96–107; and D. R. Oldroyd, "Some Neo-Platonic and Stoic Influences on Mineralogy in the Sixteenth and Seventeenth Centuries," *Ambix* 21, nos. 2 and 3 (July–November 1974): 128–56.

66. Palissy, *Recepte véritable*, in *Oeuvres complètes*, ed. Cap, 41–42.

67. Ibid., 53–54.

68. Palissy, *Recepte véritable*, in *Oeuvres*, ed. Fillon and Audiat, 1: 52–56.

69. Ibid., 50.

70. Böhme, *Aurora*, 153, 440.

71. Palissy, *Recepte véritable*, in *Oeuvres*, ed. Fillon and Audiat, 1: 56.

72. Ibid.

73. Alexandre Koyré, *La Philosophie de Jacob Boehme* (Paris: J. Vrin, 1929), 169–301.

74. Palissy, *Recepte véritable*, in *Oeuvres*, ed. Fillon and Audiat, 1: 57.

75. Ibid., 59.

76. Ibid., 59–60.

77. Ibid., 62–63.

78. Ibid, 63–64.

79. Ibid., 56–57.

80. See Ernst Kris, "Der Stil 'Rustique': Die Verwendung des Naturabgusses bei Wenzel Jamnitzer und Bernard Palissy," *Jahrbuch der Kunsthistorischen Sammlungen in Wien*, n.s. (Vienna: A. Scholl, 1926), 108–138; Klaus Pechstein, "Wenzel Jamnitzes Silberglocken mit Naturabgussen," *Anzeiger des Germanischen Naturalmuseums* (Nuremberg, 1967), 39ff.; and Erich Egg, *Veroffentlichungen des Museum Ferdinandeum* 40 (Innsbruck: Universitats-Verlag, 1960), for references to the direct bronze casting done by the Austrian sculptor Casper Gras (ca. 1584–1674).

81. Hillel Schwartz, *The French Prophets: The History of a Millenarian Group in Eighteenth-Century England* (Berkeley: University of California Press, 1980), 215. See also G.-H. Bougeant, *Les Quakres français, ou les nouveaux trembleurs . . .* (Utrecht, 1732). I am grateful to Peter Dreyer for calling this reference to my attention.

EIGHT ❧ The Art of the Earth

EPIGRAPH: Tale collected in Robert Colle, *Legendes et contes d'Aunis et Saintonge* (La Rochelle: Éditions Quartier Latin et Rupella, 1975), 127–31, my translation.

1. The report of Chapelot and his team is contained in Jean Chapelot, Claudine Cartier, Jean Cartier, Odette Chapelot, Serge Renimel, Eric Reith, et al., "L'Artisanat céramique en Saintonge (XIIIe–XIXe siècles): Essai d'archéologie extensive terrestre et sub-aquatique, rapport préliminaire (typescript, Musée national des arts et traditions populaires, École pratique des hautes études, 5th sec., 1972). See also Jean Chapelot et al., eds., *Potiers de Saintonge: Huit siècles d'artisanat rural: Musée national des arts et traditions populaires, 22 novembre 1975-1ᵉʳ mars 1976*, exhibition catalogue (Paris: Éditions des musées nationaux, 1975); and Jean Chapelot, "La Céramique exportée au Canada français: Trafic maritime et commerce de la céramique aux XVIIe et XVIIIe siècles," in *Dossiers de l'archéologie*, no. 27 (March–April 1978): 104–13; as well as Jean Chapelot, "Vaisselle de bord et de table à Saint-Mâlo–Saint-Servan du XIVe au XIXe siècles" (typescript, n.d., on deposit in the Archives départementales de la Charente-Maritime).

2. For the classic article on Saintongeais pottery from the earlier British perspective, see

G. C. Dunning, Cyril Fox, and C. A. Raleigh Rodford, "Kidwelly Castle, Carmarthenshire: Including Survey of the Polychrome Pottery Found There and Elsewhere in Britain. With an Inventory of the Polychrome Pottery Found in Britain," *Archaeologia* 83, 2d ser., no. 33 (1933): 93–138.

3. Chapelot, "L'Artisanat céramique en Saintonge," 2; id., "La Céramique exportée au Canada français," 104–13; and id., "Vaisselle de bord et de table," 156–63 (note esp. chart, "Les Principaux groupes céramiques à Saint Servan–Saint Malo: XIVᵉ–XIXᵉ siècles," located on 161, for evidence of diffusion of ceramics from southwestern France's principal trading partners).

4. For maps of the sites, see Chapelot et al., *Potiers de Saintonge,* 58, 68, 84, 89, 90–1; also id., "L'Artisanat céramique en Saintonge," 41, 48.

5. Ibid.; and Chapelot, *Potiere,* 44–48.

6. Chapelot et al., "L'Artisanat ceramique en Saintonge," 47.

7. Aumier was originally from Ecoyeux, a tiny village near La Chapelle-des-Pots; see Chapelot, "Céramique exportée au Canada français," 112.

8. Bernard Palissy, *The Admirable Discourses of Bernard Palissy,* trans. Aurele La Rocque (Urbana: University of Illinois Press, 1957), translator's introduction, 8–9.

9. "Numero extraordinaire: Maisons et meubles Poitevins, Vendéens, Saintongeais," *La Vie à la Campagne,* no. 5, Exceptionnels, xxx (Paris: Hachette, 1924; reprint, Paris: Librairie Guénégaud, 1976).

10. See n. 2 above.

11. Dunning et al., "Kidwelly Castle, Carmarthenshire," 118.

12. I learned this in a personal interview in 1981 with Bernard Demay, a native of La Rochelle and director of the Bibliothèque municipale de la Rochelle. I also sat in on a local *collège* (high school) class in La Rochelle, where I saw firsthand the impressive mnemonic skills required of local *écoliers,* especially in the ritualistic repetition of homework responses and the memorization of poetry and prose from French literature and history. It was clear from this experience that the Palissy stories would be remembered in substantially the same way by most members of the same cohort group.

13. Palissy, *Admirable Discourses,* 188. The La Rocque translation of this and the following passages from "On the Art of the Earth" has been somewhat modified.

14. Ibid., 188–89.

15. Ibid., 189–90.

16. Ibid., 190.

17. Ibid.

18. Ibid., 191.

19. Ibid., 192.

20. Ibid.

21. Ibid., 192–93.

22. See Jerah Johnson, "Bernard Palissy, Prophet of Modern Ceramics," *Sixteenth-Century Journal* 14, no. 4 (1983): 401.

23. *A discourse wrytten by M. Theodore de Beza, conteyning in briefe the historie of the life and death of Maister Iohn Caluin, with the testament and laste will of the saide Caluin, and the catalogue of his bookes that he hath made.* Turned out of Frenche into Englishe by I. S. (London, H. Denham for L. Harrison, 1564; facsimile, Amsterdam, Theatrum Orbis Terrarum; New York, Da Capo Press, 1972).

24. Ibid.; Elaine K. Bryson Siegel et al., *Eucharistic Vessels of the Middle Ages* (exhibition catalogue; Cambridge, Mass.: Busch-Reisinger Museum, 1975), 1–35.

25. Bernard Palissy, *Recepte véritable,* in *Les Oeuvres de Maistre Bernard Palissy,* ed. B. Fillon and Louis Audiat (Niort: L. Clouzot, 1888), 1: 52–53.

26. Bernard Palissy, *Recepte véritable, in Oeuvres complètes de Bernard Palissy,* ed. Paul-Antoine Cap (Paris: J.-J. Dubochet, *1844; reprint with an* avant-propos by Jean Orcel, Paris: A. Blanchard, 1961), 151.

27. This is probably a cryptic reference to "the jovial character," commonly used by alchemists in reference to the coordination of matter with Jupiter.

28. Quoted in Alexandre Koyré, *La Philosophie de Jacob Boehme* (Paris: J. Vrin, 1929), 19 (my translation), see also 19, no. 2.

29. Ibid., 20.

30. G. W. F. Hegel, *Vorlesungen über die Philosophie der Geschichte,* vol. 15 of *Werke* (Berlin, 1836), 301, et passim.

31. Palissy, *Admirable Discourses,* 193.

32. Ibid., 193–94.

33. Ibid., 194.

34. Ibid.

35. Ibid., 195.

36. Ibid.

37. Ibid.

38. Ibid., 196.

39. Ibid., 200.

40. Ibid., 200–201.

41. Ibid., 200.

42. Ibid., 195–96, 198.

43. Mireille Laget, "Childbirth in Seventeenth-and Eighteenth-Century France: Obstetrical Practices and Collective Attitudes," in Robert Forster and Orest Ranum, eds., *Medicine and Society in France: Selections from the* Annales: Economies, sociétés, civilisations, *volume 6,* trans. Elborg Forster and Patricia M. Ranum (Baltimore: Johns Hopkins University Press, 1980), 139–57.

44. Caroline Walker Bynum, *Fragmentation and Redemption: Essays on Gender and the Human Body in Medieval Religion* (New York: Zone Books, 1992), 220; Thomas Laquer, "Orgasm, Generation, and the Politics of Reproductive Biology," *Representations* 14 (Spring 1986): 1–41.

45. Palissy, *Admirable Discourses,* 198, 200–201.

46. Jakob Böhme, *Aurora . . . that is, the root or mother of philosophie, astrologie, & theologie from the true ground,* trans. John Sparrow (from the first German ed., Görlitz, 1612 (London: Giles Calvert, 1656), 168: 49.

47. Ibid., 363: 27 and 28.

48. Palissy, *Admirable Discourses,* 197. See also *Oxford English Dictionary,* s.v. "countenance."

49. Palissy, *Admirable Discourses,* 199–200.

50. Ibid., 196.

51. Ibid., 201.

52. Ambroise Paré, *On Monsters and Marvels,* trans. Janis L. Pallister (Chicago: University of Chicago Press, 1982).

53. Ibid., 6.

54. Böhme, *Aurora,* 185:46.

55. Palissy, *Admirable Discourses,* 201–2.

56. Benvenuto Cellini, *The Autobiography of Benvenuto Cellini,* abridged and adapted from the translation by John Addington Symonds by Alfred Tamarin (London: Macmillan, 1969), 133–37, and Robert Goldwater and Marco Treves, eds., *Artists on Art: From the XIV to the XX Century* (New York: Pantheon Books, 1972), 93.

57. Palissy, *Admirable Discourses,* 203.

58. Chapelot et al., *Potiers de Saintonge,* 79–82.

59. Ibid., 80.

60. See Frances A. Yates, *The Rosicrucian Enlightenment* (Boulder, Colo.: Shambhala, 1978), 49–56, and figs. 1, 8, 26a.

61. Yvonne Hackenbroch, "Wager Cups," *Metropolitan Museum of Art Bulletin* 26, no. 9 (May 1968): 381–87. On the goldsmith trade in Augsburg, see Reinhold Baumstark, Helmut Seling, et al., *Silber und Gold: Augsburger Goldschmiedekunst für die Höfe Europas* (Munich: Hirmer, 1994); Cesare Vecellio, *Vecellio's Renaissance Costume Book: All 500 Woodcut Illustrations from the Famous Sixteenth-Century Compendium of World Costume* (New York: Dover Publications, 1977), 29, 68–70, 73–74.

62. Bernard Palissy, *A Delectable Garden,* trans. and ed. Helen Mortenthau Fox (Falls Village, Conn.: Herb Grower Press, 1965), section epigraph quoted from 16, 26, and 50. This translation, which I modify, uses old English to approximate Palissy's sixteenth-century French.

63. Ibid., 1.

64. Ibid.

65. See Marjorie Hope Nicolson, *Mountain Gloom and Mountain Glory: The Development of the Aesthetics of the Infinite* (New York: Norton, 1963).

66. Palissy, *Delectable Garden,* 3–4.

67. Ibid., 4–5. For a series of engravings of such locations, where the town of Plurs in Switzerland is represented at the foot of an "apocalyptic" mountain, in response to a natural disaster in 1618 when half of the town was lost ("sa ruine terrible arrivée en 1618"), see Gunther Kahl, "Plurs: Zur Geschichte der Darstellungen des Fleckens vor und nach dem Bergsturz von 1618," in *Zeitschrift für Schweizerische Archäologie und Kunstgeschichte* 41, no. 4 (1984), cover illustration, 249–73, and figs. 28 and 29.

68. *Oxford English Dictionary,* s.v. "grotto."

69. Palissy, *Delectable Garden,* 6–7.

70. Cotgrave's *Dictionarie.*

71. Palissy, *Delectable Garden,* 8–11.

72. Ibid., 11–16.

73. Ibid., 20–21.

74. Ibid., 21.

75. Palissy, *Recepte véritable, in Oeuvres,* ed. Fillon and Audiat, 1: 60–61.

76. Palissy, *Delectable Garden,* 21. See George Edwards and Matthew Darley, *A New Book of Chinese Designs* (London, 1754), pl. 86, for an eighteenth-century design of such a rustic chair.

77. Section epigraph: Serge Renimel, "4.2.3.2. Les Sites XVéme–XVIéme siècles," in Jean Chapelot, Claudine Cartier, Jean Cartier, Odette Chapelot, Serge Renimel, Eric Reith, et al., *L'Artisanat céramique en Saintonge (XIIIe–XIXe siècles): Essai d'archéologie extensive terrestre et sub-aquatique*, rapport préliminaire (typescript, Musée national des arts et traditions populaires, École pratique des hautes études, 5th sec., 1972), 46.

78. Ibid., 78–80.

79. Chapelot, *Potiers de Saintonge*, 72.

80. Ibid., 74; Musée national céramique de Sèvres accession no. 53951.

81. Ibid., 76. See also a recently discovered vessel from La Chapelle-des-Pots of the same form with a molded image of the young Louis XIII on the side, now in the Musée régional Dupuy-Mestreau in Saintes. This establishes a probable date of ca. 1610 for this vessel and shows that courtly patronage for the green molded forms was available in the seventeenth century. For an illustration, see *Revue du Louvre: La Revue des musées de France* (Paris: Conseil des musées nationaux) 51, no. 5 (December 2001): 83, fig. 18.

82. Louvre accession no. OA 3989.

83. Charles Webster, "Water as the Ultimate Principle of Nature: The Background to Boyle's Skeptical Chemist," *Ambix* 13, no. 2 (June 1966): 96–97.

84. Quoted in ibid., 102.

85. Quoted in D. R. Oldroyd, "Some Neo-Platonic and Stoic Influences on Mineralogy in the Sixteenth and Seventeenth Centuries," *Ambix* 21, nos. 2 and 3 (July–November 1974): 135.

86. Chapelot et al., *L'Artisanat céramique en Saintonge*, 80.

87. Ibid., 80–81.

88. Chapelot, *Potiers de Saintonge*, 73–74.

89. The classic account of this relationship between war, Rosicrucianism, and political language is Frances A. Yates's *The Rosicrucian Enlightenment*, an ultimately enthusiastic but also pioneering and erudite book, the important and far-reaching implications of which have been extended though not necessarily superseded in a less subjective fashion by the historian of science Margaret C. Jacob, in *The Radical Enlightenment: Pantheists, Freemasons, and Republicans* (London: Allen & Unwin, 1981).

90. Heinrich Khunrath, *Amphitheatrum sapientia aeternae solius verae Christiano-kabalisticvm, divino-magicum, nec non, physico-chymicvm, tertriunum, catholicon* (Magdeburg: Levinum Braunss Bibliopolam, 1608); Yates, *Rosicrucian Enlightenment*, 38, 49–50.

91. Ibid., 38–39. Yates published a complete reprint of the manifestos in an appendix, 235–60.

92. Arthur E. Waite, *The Brotherhood of the Rosy Cross* (New Hyde Park, N.Y.: University Books, 1961), unpaginated eleventh image and caption. Although this text is definitely the work of a devout believer, it is accepted as a valuable and accurate source of basic information about Rosicrucian imagery and arcana.

93. Yates, *Rosicrucian Enlightenment*, 49.

94. *The Collected Works of C. G. Jung*, Bollingen ser. 20, vol. 12: *Psychology and Alchemy* (New York: Pantheon Books / Princeton, N.J.: Princeton University Press, 1953), trans. R. F. C. Hull, 393, fig. 214.

95. Joscelyn Godwin, *Robert Fludd: Hermetic Philosopher and Surveyor of Two Worlds* (Boulder, Colo.: Shambhala, 1979), 71.

96. Ambroise Paré, *On Monsters and Marvels*, trans. Janis L. Pallister (Chicago: University of Chicago Press, 1982), 26.

97. I am most grateful to Joe Marino for bringing this important reference to my attention.

98. James Nohrnberg, *The Analogy of the Faerie Queene* (Princeton, N.J.: Princeton University Press, 1976), 16.

99. Ibid., quoting *On the Cave of the Nymphs,* 13, trans. Thomas Taylor, in *Select Works of Porphyry* (London, 1823), 194f.; slightly modified here. Böhme calls man "either a vessel of honour or dishonour" in *Aurora,* 99: 4.

100. Plato, *Timaeus,* trans. H. D. P. Lee (Baltimore: Penguin Books, 1965), 66–69.

101. Ibid., 67–68.

102. Ibid., 68–69.

103. On the sword as symbol of alchemic separation, see H. J. Sheppard, "Gnosticism and Alchemy," *Ambix* 6, no. 2 (December 1957): 98–101.

104. Samuel Norton, *Alchymiae complementum, et perfectio, seu, Modus et Processus argumentandi: sive multiplicandi omnes lapides, & elixera in virtute . . .* (Frankfurt: Typis Caspari Rotelii, Impensis Guiliemi Fitzeri, 1630). For a fuller discussion of Van Helmont's "Willow Tree Experiment," see Charles Webster, "Water as the Ultimate Principle of Nature: The Background to Boyle's Skeptical Chemist," *Ambix* 13, no. 2 (June 1966): 96–99. Northrop Frye, *The Great Code: The Bible and Literature* (New York: Harcourt Brace Jovanovich, 1982), 135–38, contends the return of the tree and water of life "lost" after Genesis, in Revelation, signifies the typological relation between the two books.

105. See also Salomon Trismosin, *La Toison d'or: ou, La Fleur des trésors,* commentaires des illustrations par Bernard Husson; étude iconographique du manuscrit de Berlin par René Alleau (Paris: Retz, 1975).

106. Böhme, *Aurora,* 117: 55, 56.

107. Ibid., 347–48: 49–52.

108. Musée Marmattan (Wildenstein Collection); William Wells, "French Fifteenth-century Miniature Painting a New Hypothesis: Jean Perréal: From René to the Bourbon Master," *Apollo,* July 1986, 17.

109. On this aspect of Ficino's ideas, see Wayne Shumaker, *The Occult Sciences in the Renaissance: A Study in Intellectual Patterns* (Berkeley: University of California Press, 1979), 129–30.

NINE ✤ "In Patientia Sauvitas"

EPIGRAPH: Jakob Böhme, *Aurora . . . that is, the root or mother of philosophie, astrologie, & theologie from the true ground,* trans. John Sparrow, from the first German ed., Görlitz, 1612 (London: Giles Calvert, 1656), 185.

1. *Patientia* can also connote endurance or resignation in this context. I wish to acknowledge Donna Evergates for her help with translations from the Latin and Arnt Bohm for his help with the German.

2. Maurice Ricateau, *La Rochelle 200 ans huguenots: 1500–1700* (La Rochelle: Imprimerie de la Charente-Maritime, 1978), 6–8; Adrien Blanchet, *Les Souterrains-refuges de la France: Contribution a l'histoire de l'habitation humaine* (Paris: Picard, 1923), 253–82; J. R. Colle, "Les Souterrains-refuges en Saintonge," *Bulletin de la Société géographique de Rochefort,* 2d ser., 2 (1968): 87–91; Paul Cantaloube, "Souterrains-refuges," *Recherche de la Commission des arts et monuments de Charente-Inferieure* 14 (1897): 102–6; Pierre-Amedée Brouillet, "Inscriptions, tombeaux, statues, laternes des morts, souterrains-refuges de Haut Poitou" (Bibliothèque municipale, Poitiers, MS

865, nineteenth-century typescript); Jérôme Triolet and Laurent Triolet, *Les Souterrains: Le Monde des souterrains-refuges en France* (Paris: Érrance, 1995); and Nicolas Faucherre et al., *Les Fortifications du littoral: La Charente-Maritime* (Paris: Éditions Patrimoines et Médias, 1996), 67–81.

3. *Winthrop Papers*, vol. 1: *1498–1628* (Boston: Massachusetts Historical Society, 1929), 194–96.

4. Fludd, of course, was not alone in this preoccupation. See esp. Joscelyn Godwin, *Robert Fludd: Hermetic Philosopher and Surveyor of Two Worlds* (Boulder, Colo.: Shambhala, 1979), 82–83.

5. Bernard Palissy, *Recepte véritable, in Les Oeuvres de Maistre Bernard Palissy,* ed. B. Fillon and Louis Audiat (Niort: L. Clouzot, 1888), 1: 46.

6. Böhme, *Aurora,* 196–97; see esp. 196: 107.

7. Ibid., 168: 52; 169: 57; 163: 23, 24; 164: 28, 29; and 162–63: 21; 112: 25.

8. Palissy, *Recepte véritable,* in *Oeuvres,* ed. Fillon and Audiat, 1: 40–41.

9. See Pamela H. Smith, *The Business of Alchemy: Science and Culture in the Holy Roman Empire* (Princeton, N.J.: Princeton University Press, 1994), 152, fig. 7.

10. On digging up bones of martyred dead by pilgrims in search of the sweet smell of sanctity, see Lionel Rothkrug, "The 'odour of sanctity,' and the Hebrew Origin of Christian Relic Veneration," *Historical Reflections / Reflexions historiques* 8, no. 2 (Summer 1981).

11. For an informative essay on this cycle of engravings, see Priscilla L. Tate, "Patentiae Triumphus: The Iconography of a Set of Eight Engravings," in Gerald J. Scheffhorst, ed., *The Triumph of Patience: Medieval and Renaissance Studies* (Orlando: University Presses of Florida, 1978), 106–138.

12. Jon Butler, *The Huguenots in America: A Refugee People in New World Society* (Cambridge, Mass.: Harvard University Press, 1983), 161–65; id., "Les 'Hymnes ou cantiques sacrez' d'Elie Neau: Un Nouveau Manuscrit du 'grand mystique des galères,'" *Bulletin de la Société de l'histoire du protestantisme français* 124 (July–September 1978): 416–23; Émile G. Léonard, *L'Histoire générale du protestantisme* (Paris: Presses universitaires de France, 1964), 3: 61–64; Charles Read, "Un Confesseur de la R. P. R. sous Louis XIV: Elie Neau, 'Martyr sur les galères et dans les cachots de Marseille,'" *Bulletin de la Société de l'histoire du protestantisme français* 23 (1874): 529–44; Sheldon S. Cohen, "Elias Neau, 'Instructor to New York Slaves,'" *New-York Historical Society Quarterly* 55 (1971): 7–27; Frank J. Klingberg, *Anglican Humanitarianism in Colonial New York* (Philadelphia: Church Historical Society, 1940), 124–39.

13. Elias Neau, *An Account of the Sufferings of the French Protestants, Slaves on Board the French Kings Galleys* (London: Richard Parker, 1699), 2.

14. Butler, *Huguenots in America,* 162.

15. "Mémoire pour servir d'instruction à Monsieur le comte de Frontenac sur l'entreprise de la Nouvelle-York, 7 juin 1689," *Rapport de l'Archivist de la Province de Québec* 8 (1927–28): 12–16; quoted in J. F. Bosher, "Huguenot Merchants and the Protestant International in the Seventeenth Century," *William and Mary Quarterly* 52, no. 1 (January 1995): 89.

16. Böhme, *Aurora,* 368: 48.

17. Elias Neau, *Account of the Sufferings,* 8–9.

18. Ibid., 9–11.

19. Cotton Mather, *A Present from a farr country* (Boston: Green & Allen for Perry, 1698), 13–14.

20. Ibid., 17–18.

21. Ibid., 17–19.

22. Ibid., 13.

23. Ibid., 20–21.

24. Quoted in Butler, *Huguenots in America,* 165.

TEN   ❧   Being "at the Île of Rue"

EPIGRAPHS: Edward Howes, letter dated March 25, 1633, *Winthrop Papers,* vol. 3: *1631–1637* (Boston: Massachusetts Historical Society, 1943), 114–15. Edward Howes, letter dated January 22, 1627, *Winthrop Papers,* vol. 1: *1498–1628* (Boston: Massachusetts Historical Society, 1929), 374–75. John Winthrop, "Experiencia" (1616–18), written while mourning the death in childbirth of his second wife, Thomasine Clopton Winthrop (1583–1616), *Winthrop Papers,* 1: 191.

1. On the military and political significance of La Rochelle's offshore islands Ré and Oléron, see David Parker, *La Rochelle and the French Monarchy: Conflict and Order in Seventeenth-Century France* (London: Royal Historical Society, 1980), 14.

2. *Winthrop Papers,* 3: 114–15.

3. Robert C. Black III, *The Younger John Winthrop* (New York: Columbia University Press, 1966), 17–22; and Edmund S. Morgan, *The Puritan Dilemma: The Story of John Winthrop* (Boston: Little, Brown, 1958), 21–27. On Ireland as a "variation" on the English model and a precursor for American colonization in the seventeenth century, see Jack P. Greene, *Pursuits of Happiness: The Social Development of Early Modern British Colonies and the Formation of American Culture* (Chapel Hill: University of North Carolina Press, 1988), 101–23.

4. Black, *Younger John Winthrop,* 21–23.

5. Ibid., 124.

6. Charles Webster, *The Great Instauration: Science, Medicine, and Reform, 1626–1660* (London: Gerald Duckworth, 1975), 65.

7. Ibid., 66–67.

8. *Winthrop Papers,* 1: 278–79 (April 26, 1622).

9. Ibid.

10. Frances A. Yates, *The Rosicrucian Enlightenment* (Boulder, Colo.: Shambhala, 1978), 103–4.

11. Black, *Younger John Winthrop,* 26–7.

12. Ibid., 25–27.

13. *Winthrop Papers,* 1: 338, n. 35.

14. *Winthrop Papers,* 1: 337–38.

15. Owen Hannaway, *The Chemists and the Word: The Didactic Origins of Chemistry* (Baltimore: Johns Hopkins University Press, 1975), 43–4.

16. Ibid.

17. Ibid., 44.

18. *Winthrop Papers,* 1: 347–48.

19. Black, *Younger John Winthrop,* 28–31.

20. *Winthrop Papers,* 1: 352–53.

21. Black, *Younger John Winthrop,* 87–88, 113–14.

22. Webster, *Great Instauration,* 388–91.

23. Ibid., 390.

24. Ibid.

25. *Winthrop Papers,* 1: 359–60.

26. *Winthrop Papers,* 1: 374–75 (undated, but probably December 1627).

27. On the prolongation of life, see Webster, *Great Instauration,* 249–323.

28. *Winthrop Papers,* 1: 374–75 (January 22, 1627).

29. *Winthrop Papers,* 1: 374–75. For a useful discussion of the general analogy between Christ's passion, the redemption of postlapsarian mankind, and the transmutative action of the philosopher's stone on fallen matter, see Wayne Schumaker, *The Occult Sciences in the Renaissance: A Study in Intellectual Patterns* (Berkeley: University of California Press, 1972), 189–90.

30. *Winthrop Papers,* 3: 206.

31. Yates, *Rosicrucian Enlightenment,* 118–39, and Webster, *Great Instauration, 39.*

32. *Winthrop Papers,* 1: 374, n. 13; and "The Winthrop Papers," *North American Review* 105, no. 217 (October 1867): 608–13.

33. *The Wisdom of Solomon, trans. and ed.* David Winston (Garden City, N.Y.: Doubleday, 1979), 172–77, vv. 15–22. Winston argues the translation of "artificer" in the final line probably refers to a joiner, as a figure of the woodworker as metaphysical joiner of microcosm and macrocosm; as in Proverbs 8:30: "I was with him as one working as a joiner" (176).

34. David Winston, *Logos and Mystical Theology in Philo of Alexandria* (Cincinnati, Ohio: Hebrew Union College Press, 1985), 36.

35. I am grateful for Professor Janet Meisel's insights into the translation of this aphorism.

36. Winston, *Logos and Mystical Theology,* 14.

37. Ibid., 58.

38. Webster, *Great Instauration,* 45.

39. Yates, *Rosicrucian Enlightenment, fig. 24a, for an image of "Alchemy and Geometry."*

40. See similar pictographs of horoscopes in Hieronymus Cardanus (Jerome Cardan), *Libelle quinque* (Nuremburg, 1547), sig. 109v, 113v.

41. *Wisdom of Solomon,* trans. and ed. Winston, 177.

42. Edward Howes to John Winthrop Jr., January 22, 1627, *Winthrop Papers,* 1: 374–75.

43. *Winthrop Papers,* 1: 392–94.

44. *Winthrop Papers,* 1: 385 (April 7, 1628).

45. Black, *Younger John Winthrop,* 36–9.

46. Ibid., 38.

47. Romolo Quazza, *La guerra per la successione di Mantova e del Monferrato (1628–1631) da documenti inediti,* 2 vols., Pubblicazioni della Reale Accademia Virgiliana, 2d ser., Miscellanea, 5–6 (Mantua: G. Mondovì, 1926); see also *Winthrop Papers,* vol. 2: *1623–1630* (Boston: Massachusetts Historical Society, 1929), 73, n. 1.

48. *Winthrop Papers,* 2: 72–73 (to Emmanuel Downing, dated March 9, 1629), and 75–76 (to John Freeman, dated March 28, 1629).

49. *Winthrop Papers,* 2: 150–51.

50. For example, see *Winthrop Papers,* 2: 226–27 (Edward Howes to John Winthrop Jr., March 31, 1630).

51. Malcom Freiberg, ed., *Winthrop Papers,* vol. 6: *1650–1654* (Boston: Massachusetts Historical Society, 1992), 57–58 (August 26, 1650).

52. Ibid., 58.

53. *Winthrop Papers*, 3: 72.

54. Ibid.

55. *Winthrop Papers*, 3: 94

56. The inscription is reprinted in its entirety in *Winthrop Papers*, 3: 94–5, n. 2.

57. There is a huge bibliography by English ceramic historians on the relationship between the production of Bernard Palissy and his imitators in early seventeenth-century London, particularly concerning the "Palissy dishes": see Rhoda Edwards, "London Potters circa 1570–1710," *Journal of Ceramic History*, no. 6 (1974): 10, 121; Michael Archer, *Delftware: The Tin-glazed Earthenware of the British Isles: A Catalogue of the Collection in the Victoria and Albert Museum* (London: H.M. Stationery Office in Association with the Victoria and Albert Museum, 1997), 109–12; Louis L. Lipski, *Dated English Delftware: Tin-glazed Earthenware, 1600–1800,* ed. Michael Archer (London and Scranton, Pa.: Sotheby Publications, 1984), nos. 90–94, 99, 104–6, 110–13, 118–21, 125–26; Frank Britton, "Bernard Palissy and London Delftware," *English Ceramic Circle Transactions* 14, pt. 2 (1991): 172–73; Lionel Burman, "Motifs and Motivations: The Decoration of Some Seventeenth-Century London Delftwares—Part 2: Images and Emblems," *ibid.* 15, pt. 1 (1993): 105; Graham Slater, "English Delftware Copies of the Fécondité Pattern Dishes Attributed to Palissy," ibid. 17, no. 1 (1999): 47–67; and Leslie B Grigsby, "Dated English Delftware and Slipware in the Longridge Collection," *Antiques* 155, no. 6 (June 1999): 877–79.

58. Charles Dempsey, *Inventing the Renaissance Putto* (Chapel Hill: University of North Carolina Press, 2001), 95. For an illustration of the *Danaë* by Rosso, see Slater, "English Delftware Copies of the Fécondité Pattern Dishes," 48, fig. 3.

59. Grigsby, "Dated English Delftware and Slipware in the Longridge Collection," 879.

60. "The Lord created me at the beginning of his work, the first of his acts of old. / . . . when he marked out the foundations of the earth, / then I was there beside him, like a master workman; and I was daily his delight, rejoicing before him always, / rejoicing in his inhabited world and delighting in the sons of men. / . . . Happy is the man who listens to me, watching daily at my gates, waiting beside my doors." Proverbs 8:22, 29–31, 34.

61. Winston, *Logos and Mystical Theology in Philo of Alexandria*, 15–16, 20–21.

62. Theophrastus Paracelsus, *The Prophesies of Paracelsus: Occult Symbols, and Magic Figures with Esoteric Explanations,* trans. and ed. Paul M. Allen (Blauvelt, N.Y.: Rudolf Steiner Publications, 1973), 67.

63. Ibid.

64. For a discussion of the putto and *spiritello* and how they inform medieval and Renaissance concepts of body and spirit, see Dempsey, *Inventing the Renaissance Putto,* 86 et passim.

65. Paracelsus, *Prophesies of Paracelsus,* 86.

66. Robert Fludd, *Philosophia sacra et vere christiana seu meteorologia cosmica* (Frankfurt: Officina Bryana, 1626).

67. *Winthrop Papers,* 3: 96–98 (November 24, 1632).

68. Robert Fludd, *Medicina catholica* (Frankfurt: Willem Fitzer, 1629) and *Integrum morborum mysterium* (Frankfurt: Willem Fitzer, 1631) respectively; on their survival in Winthrop's library, see Roland Sterne Wilkinson, "The Alchemical Library of John Winthrop, Jr. (1606–1676) and His Descendants in Colonial America, Part IV: The Catalogue of Books," *Ambix* 13, no. 3 (October 1966): 155, nos. 89 and 90, in the New York Academy of Medicine.

69. This prayer and response are from Psalms 31:16 and 91:10–11.

70. For a brilliant exegesis of Philo's sources for this verse, which I have summarized here, see *Wisdom of Solomon,* ed. Winston, 175–76, verse 20.

71. Joscelyn Godwin, *Robert Fludd: Hermetic Philosopher and Surveyor of Two Worlds* (Boulder, Colo.: Shambhala, 1979), 56.

72. Job 6:4.

73. *Winthrop Papers,* 2: 91–92.

74. Ibid., 179 (Isaac Johnson to John Winthrop Sr. at Groton, December 17, 1629).

75. For the words quoted, see *Les Oeuvres de Maistre Bernard Palissy,* ed. B. Fillon and Louis Audiat (Niort: L. Clouzot, 1888), 2: 3, dedication of *Discours admirables* to Palissy's patron Antoine de Ponts in 1580; and see also the motto "Povrete Empeches les Bons" (fig. 14.34) in the frontispieces to both of Palissy's books. I have translated "les bons" as "happiness and safety."

76. Black, *Younger John Winthrop,* 86–87.

77. Karen Ordahl Kupperman, *Providence Island, 1630–1641: The Other Puritan Colony* (Cambridge: Cambridge University Press, 1993), 221–66.

78. *Winthrop Papers,* 3: 76 (April 3, 1632).

79. Ibid., 100 (November 28, 1632).

80. Ibid., 95 (November 23, 1632).

81. Quoted in Kupperman, *Providence Island,* 225. On Comenius and Harvard, see Samuel Eliot Morison, *Builders of the Bay Colony* (Boston: Houghton Mifflin, 1930), 273.

82. Pamela H. Smith, *The Business of Alchemy: Science and Culture in the Holy Roman Empire* (Princeton, N.J.: Princeton University Press, 1994), 231–40.

83. Ibid., 231–34.

84. *Oxford English Dictionary,* s.v. "parterre," definition 3.

85. Smith, *Business of Alchemy,* 232, fig. 25.

86. Ibid. 244.

87. *Winthrop Papers,* 3: 292 (September 3, 1636).

88. Robert Blair St. George, "Bawns and Beliefs: Architecture, Commerce, and Conversion in Early New England," *Winterthur Portfolio* 25, no. 4 (Winter 1990): 277.

89. Ibid., 273–74. Charles Estienne, *Maison Rustique, or, The Covntrie Farme,* compiled in the French tongue by Charles Steuens and Iohn Liebault . . . and translated into English by Richard Surflet . . . (London: Edm. Bollifant for Bonham Norton, 1600).

90. Ibid., 273.

91. *Winthrop Papers,* 3: 112(March 18, 1633); see also Howes's lament of "Rochell," 114–15.

92. The full original title page of the *Discours admirables* reads: *Discours Admirables, De La Nature Des Eavx Et Fonteines, Tant Naturelles Qu'Artificielles, des metaux, des sels & salines, des pierres, des terres, du feu & des emaux. Avec Plusieurs Autres Excellens secrets des choses naturelles. Plus Un Traite' De La Marne, Fort utile & necessaire, pour ceux qui se mellent de l'agriculture. Le Tout Dresse' Par Dialogues, Esquels sont introduits la theorique & la practique. Par M. Bernard Palissy, inventeur des rustiques figulines du Roy & de la Royne sa mere. A Treshaut, Et Trespuissant sieur le sire Anthoine de Ponts, Chevalier des ordres du Roy, Capitaine des cents gentils-hommes, et conseiller tres fidele de sa majeste. A Paris, Chez Martin le Jeune, a l'enseigne du Serpent, devant le college de Cambray. 1580. Avec Privilege Du Roy.* Winthrop's copy is currently in the collections of the New-York Society Library, and is listed as catalogue number 196 in Roland Sterne Wilkinson, "The Alchemical Library of John Winthrop, Jr. (1606–1676) and His Descendants in Colonial America, Part IV: The Catalogue of Books," *Ambix* 13, no. 3 (October 1966): 174. The history of this

volume and of the large segment of Winthrop the Younger's original alchemical library that de-scended through the Winthrop and Bayard families to the Society in December 1812 is told in Helen T. Farah, "The Winthrop Collection," New-York Society Library typescript LS K601IX, December 1965; Samuel Eliot Morison, "Statement on the Winthrop Collection," New-York Society Library typescript, Cambridge, Massachusetts, May 22, 1935; Herbert Greenberg, "Some Aspects of the Winthrop Library," New-York Society Library typescript, January 1935; id., "The Authenticity of the Library of John Winthrop the Younger," *American Literature* 8, no. 4 (January 1937): 448–52; Austin Baxter Keep, *History of the New-York Society Library* (Boston: Gregg Press, 1972), 266–69; and *The Minute Book of the Trustees of the New-York Society Library* 2: 150–51, entry for December 4, 1812.

ELEVEN ❧ The Geography of "Your Native Country"

1. Roland Sterne Wilkinson, "The Alchemical Library of John Winthrop, Jr. (1606–1676) and His Descendants in Colonial America, Part IV: The Catalogue of Books," *Ambix* 13, no. 3 (October 1966): 139–86; see esp. 174–75, cat. nos. 198–202, for the complete bibliographical anno-tation of each book and its current location.

2. Ibid., 150–51, 174–75.

3. Ronald Sterne Wilkinson, "The Alchemical Library of John Winthrop, Jr. (1606–1676) and His Descendants in Colonial America, Part I," *Ambix* 11, no. 1 (February 1963), 36–39.

4. Charles Webster, *From Paracelsus to Newton: Magic and the Making of Modern Science* (Cambridge: Cambridge University Press, 1982), 5; Wilkinson, "Alchemical Library of John Winthrop, Jr. . . . Part IV," 150, 182; these volumes are numbers 55, 251, and 247–49, respectively, in Wilkinson's catalogue. The volume by Severinus was originally in Dee's library and was also annotated in his hand.

5. Wilkinson, "Alchemical Library of John Winthrop, Jr. . . . Part IV," 182, cat. no. 247.

6. For indispensable insights into the symbiosis between monistic cosmology, manual expe-rience (as "praxis") and biblical exegesis in the mental and material world of early modern natu-ral philosophers, particularly for sixteenth- and seventeenth-century Paracelsians such as John Winthrop Jr., Edward Howes, and Bernard Palissy, see Owen Hannaway, *The Chemists and the Word: The Didactic Origins of Chemistry* (Baltimore: Johns Hopkins University Press, 1975), 1, 22–74; The full title of Croll's book is *Basilica Chymica, continens philosophicam propria laborum ex-perientia confirmatam descriptionem & usum remedediorum chymicorum selectissimorum e lumine gratiae et naturae desumptorum. In fine libri additus est eiusdem Autoris Tractatus novus de Signa-turis Rerum Internis* (Frankfort, 1609).

7. John Winthrop Jr. in London to John Winthrop in Groton, April 11, 1628, *Winthrop Papers,* vol. 1: *1498–1628* (Boston: Massachusetts Historical Society, 1929), 386–87.

8. Ibid., 389–90; John Winthrop in Groton to John Winthrop Jr. in London, April 15, 1628. On John Winthrop's use of his left hand, see 390, n. 3.

9. Ibid., 390.

10. Ibid., 390–91; John Winthrop Jr. in London to John Winthrop in Groton, April 18, 1628.

11. John Winthrop, *The History of New England from 1630 to 1649,* ed. James Savage (Boston: Phelps & Farnham, 1825–26), 2: 20.

12. Wilkinson, "Alchemical Library of John Winthrop, Jr . . . , Part I," 33.

13. Letter from Starkey to Winthrop dated August 2, 1648, in *Massachusetts Historical Society*

Collections, 5th ser. (Boston, 1871), 1: 150. In a letter of 1651 to Robert Boyle, Starkey used the word "key" (as in "the right key to this cabinet, which I have worked seven years to unlock") in a metaphorical sense; he offered Boyle the "key" to philosophical mercury and the philosophers' stone; letter quoted in William R. Newman, *Gehennical Fire: The Lives of George Starkey, an American Alchemist in the Scientific Revolution* (Cambridge, Mass.: Harvard University Press, 1994), 67.

14. Wilkinson, "Alchemical Library of John Winthrop, Jr. . . . Part IV," 183, cat. nos. 253 and 254.

15. For more on "Nicolas Flamel," see Lynn Thorndike, *A History of Magic and Experimental Science* (New York: Macmillan, 1923–58), 2: 165–66; *Hieroglyphicall Figures* is cat. no. 85 in Wilkinson, "Alchemical Library of John Winthrop, Jr. . . . Part IV," 155.

16. Newman, *Gehennical Fire,* 42–43.

17. Ibid., 42–44; see also Wilkinson, "Alchemical Library of John Winthrop, Jr. . . . Part I," 46–48.

18. Quoted in Robert C. Black III, *The Younger John Winthrop* (New York: Columbia University Press, 1966), 126.

19. See Jean de Léry, *History of a Voyage to the Land of Brazil, Otherwise Called America: Containing the Navigation and the Remarkable Things Seen on the Sea by the Author; the Behavior of Villegagnon in that Country; the Customs and Strange Ways of Life of the Various Savages; Together with the Description of Various Animals, Trees, Plants, and Other Singular Things Completely Unknown over Here,* trans. Janet Whatley (Berkeley: University of California Press, 1992), xx–xxi, xxxi.

20. George Lyman Kittredge, "Dr. Robert Child the Remonstrant," *Publications of the Colonial Society of Massachusetts: Transactions,* 1919: 124.

21. Joyce E. Chaplin, *Subject Matter: Technology, the Body and Science on the Anglo-American Frontier, 1500–1676* (Cambridge, Mass.: Harvard University Press, 2001), 20.

22. Cary Carson et al., "Impermanent Architecture in the Southern American Colonies," in Robert Blair St. George, ed., *Material Life in America, 1600–1860* (Boston: Northeastern University Press, 1988), 113–58.

23. Ivor Noël Hume, *Martin's Hundred* (1982; reprint, Charlottesville: University Press of Virginia, 1995), 101–10.

24. For an introduction to the scope and influence of alchemy in early modern European imperial courts, see Thorndike, *History of Magic and Experimental Science,* vol. 7; Rudolf Hirsch, "The Invention of Printing and the Diffusion of Alchemical and Chemical Knowledge," *Chymia* 3 (1950): 115–41; R. J. W. Evans, *Rudolf II and His World* (Oxford: Clarendon Press, 1973), 196–274; and Pamela Smith, *The Business of Alchemy: Science and Culture in the Holy Roman Empire* (Princeton, N.J.: Princeton University Press, 1994).

25. Julius F. Sachse, *The German Pietists of Provincial Pennsylvania, 1694–1708* (Philadelphia: P. C. Stockhausen, 1895); E. G. Alderfer, *The Ephrata Commune: An Early American Counterculture* (Pittsburgh: University of Pittsburgh Press, 1985); Walter C. Klein, *Johann Conrad Beissel, Mystic and Martinet, 1690–1768* (Philadelphia: University of Pennsylvania Press, 1942); James E. Ernst, *Ephrata: A History* ([*Yearbook of*] *the Pennsylvania German Folklore Society* 25 [1961]; Allentown, Pa.: Pennsylvania German Folklore Society, 1963); Gillian L. Gollin, *Moravians in Two Worlds* (New York: Columbia University Press, 1967); Jacob J. Sessler, *Communal Pietism Among Early American Moravians* (New York: Holt, 1933); Elizabeth W. Fisher, "'Prophesies and Rev-

elations': German Cabbalists in Early Pennsylvania," *Pennsylvania Magazine of History and Biography* 109 (1985): 299–333; Jon Butler, "Magic, Astrology, and the Early American Religious Heritage, 1600–1760," *American Historical Review* 84 (April 1979): 317–46; Ernest L. Lashlee, "Johannes Kelpius and His Woman in the Wilderness: A Chapter in the History of Colonial Pennsylvania Religious Thought," in *Glaube, Geist, Geschichte: Festschrift für Ernst Benz,* ed. Gerhard Müller and Winfried Zeller (Leiden: E. J. Brill, 1967), 327–38; Dennis McCort, "Johann Conrad Beissel, Colonial Mystic Poet," *German-American Studies* 8 (Fall, 1974): 1–26; and Bernard Bailyn, *The Peopling of British North America: An Introduction* (New York: Vintage Books, 1988), 123–31. The transaction in which Logan paid £2.2.9 for the alembic is recorded in the Account Book of Simon Edgell, George Vaux Papers, the American Philosophical Society, as discussed in Jay Robert Stiefel, "Simon Edgell (1687–1742): 'To a Puter Dish' and Grander Transactions of a London-trained Pewterer in Philadelphia," *Pewter Collectors Club of America, Inc.: The Bulletin* 12, no. 8 (Winter 2002): 353–88, and id., "Simon Edgell, Unalloyed," *Catalogue of Antiques and Fine Art* 4, no. 1 (Spring 2003): 170.

26. Hume, *Martin's Hundred,* 62–83, 185–298; John Noble Wilford, "Jamestown Fort, 'Birthplace' of America in 1607, Is Found," *New York Times,* September 13, 1996: A1, A12; and Beverly Straube, "European Ceramics in the New World: The Jamestown Example," in *Ceramics in America, 2001,* ed. Robert Hunter (Milwaukee: Chipstone Foundation, 2001; distributed by the University Press of New England), 49, fig. 4.

27. Judah Throckmorton to John Winthrop Jr. in Venice, April 17 1629, *Winthrop Papers,* vol. 2: *1623–1630* (Boston: Massachusetts Historical Society, 1929), 80.

28. Wilkinson, "Alchemical Library of John Winthrop, Jr. . . . Part 1," 42–43; Winthrop's copy of this volume is now at Yale.

29. *The Literary Diary of Ezra Stiles,* ed. Franklin Bowditch Dexter (New York: Scribner, 1901), 3: 264, 266; Edmund S. Morgan, *The Gentle Puritan: A Life of Ezra Stiles, 1727–1795* (New Haven, Conn.: Yale University Press, 1962), 130–57, 376–403. Smalt is a potassium glass colored blue by cobalt oxide and ground into a powdered pigment. See Jonathan L. Fairbanks, "Portrait Painting in Seventeenth-Century Boston: Its History, Methods, and Materials," in Jonathan L. Fairbanks and Robert F. Trent, eds., *New England Begins: The Seventeenth Century,* vol. 3: *Style* (Boston: Museum of Fine Arts, 1982), 451.

30. In the *Literary Diary,* 3: 266, Stiles identifies Erkelens as "being a Projector."

31. John Winthrop Jr. served as governor of Connecticut Colony in 1657, and again from 1659 until his death in 1676.

32. Stiles, *Literary Diary,* 3: 266. Transatlantic connections are explored in Charles Webster, *The Great Instauration: Science, Medicine and Reform, 1626–1660* (London: Gerald Duckworth, 1975); id., *From Paracelsus to Newton: Magic and the Making of Modern Science* (Cambridge: Cambridge University Press, 1982); Margaret C. Jacob, *The Radical Enlightenment: Pantheists, Freemasons, and Republicans* (London: Allen & Unwin, 1981); id., *The Cultural Meaning of the Scientific Revolution* (Philadelphia: Temple University Press, 1988); Frances A. Yates, *The Rosicrucian Enlightenment* (Boulder, Colo.: Shambhala, 1978), David D. Hall, *Worlds of Wonder, Days of Judgement: Popular Religious Belief in Early New England* (Cambridge, Mass.: Harvard University Press, 1989), 3–116; John L. Brooke, *The Refiner's Fire: The Making of Mormon Cosmology 1644–1844* (Cambridge: Cambridge University Press, 1994); and Newman, *Gehennical Fire,* 39–52.

33. Benjamin Tompson elegy, printed at Boston by John Foster, 1676. On Tompson, see

David D. Hall, *Worlds of Wonder, Days of Judgement: Popular Religious Belief in Early New England* (Cambridge, Mass.: Harvard University Press, 1990), 130, 236, 280; and Thomas Franklin Waters, *A Sketch of the Life of John Winthrop the Younger: Founder of Ipswich, Massachusetts in 1633* (Ipswich, Mass.: Ipswich Historical Society, 1899), 2: 77, n. 1.

34. Morgan, *Gentle Puritan,* 169.

35. Quoted in ibid., 174; see also 176.

36. Ibid., 171, 175; on the work of William Perkins, see Hall, *Worlds of Wonder,* 40, 50, 108, 273, 59, 198–204. Recent research argues that Edwards was closer to Stiles's natural-philosophical thought than previously imagined; see Avihu Zakai, *Jonathan Edwards's Philosophy of History: The Reenchantment of the World in the Age of Enlightenment* (Princeton, N.J.: Princeton University Press, 2003).

37. Quoted in Morgan, G*entle Puritan,* 175.

38. Ibid.

39. Webster, *Great Instauration,* 507.

40. Hall, *Worlds of Wonder,* 58–61, 198–201.

41. Morgan, *Gentle Puritan,* 173.

42. Webster, *Great Instauration,* 276–79.

43. Newman, *Gehennical Fire,* 1–3.

44. Quoted in ibid., 66.

45. Hillel Schwartz, *The French Prophets: The History of a Millenarian Group in Eighteenth-Century England* (Berkeley: University of California Press, 1980), 233–34.

46. Janice Knight, *Orthodoxies in Massachusetts: Rereading American Puritanism* (Cambridge, Mass.: Harvard University Press, 1994); see also Avihu Zakai, *Exile and Kingdom: History and Apocalypse in the Puritan Migration to America* (New York: Cambridge University Press, 1992).

47. John L. Brooke, *The Heart of the Commonwealth: Society and Political Culture in Worcester County, Massachusetts, 1713–1861* (New York: Cambridge University Press, 1989), 1–13; on the pluralism of frontier material culture, see id., "For Honour and Civil Worship to any Worthy Person': Burial, Baptism, and Community on the Massachusetts Near Frontier, 1730–1790," in Robert Blair St. George, ed., *Material Life in America, 1600–1860* (Boston : Northeastern University Press, 1988), 463–86; see also religious and cultural pluralism tied to demand for seasonal labor, in Daniel Vickers, *Farmers and Fishermen: Two Centuries of Work in Essex County, Massachusetts* (Chapel Hill: University of North Carolina Press, 1994).

48. Ezra Stiles, *A Discourse on Saving Knowledge* (Newport, R.I.: Solomon Southwick 1770), 42.

49. Books in quarto (also abbreviated 4to, or 4) usually measure about 9½″ × 12″. Inventories of Stiles's manuscripts taken between 1787 and 1793, when he wrote his will, are published in the appendix to Morgan, *Gentle Puritan,* 465–67.

50. Winthrop's appointment took place when the independent river towns and New Haven were united; he acquired the colony's royal charter from Charles II on April 23, 1662. Before then individual Connecticut settlements chose their own governors. Trumbull served as governor from 1769 to 1784; see Black, *Younger John Winthrop,* 206–31.

51. Schwartz, *French Prophets,* 243. The original Kabbala is thought to have been written in medieval Spain.

52. Ibid.

53. Letter from Stiles to Isaac Karigal, July 19, 1773, quoted in Morgan, *Gentle Puritan,* 144.

54. See Joscelyn Godwin, *Robert Fludd: Hermetic Philosopher and Surveyor of Two Worlds* (Boulder, Colo.: Shambhala, 1979), for reproductions of Fludd's renderings of the microcosm and macrocosm.

55. Ezra Stiles to Professor John Winthrop of Harvard (1714–79), one of the foremost American natural philosophers of the late eighteenth century, April 2, 1759, quoted in Morgan, *Gentle Puritan,* 153; and see also 151–57. Intellectual differences are evident; although a direct descendant of the adept, Professor Winthrop, a Newtonian, was unsympathetic to Stiles's Neoplatonic spiritualism. See also *Winthrop Papers,* 1: ix; and Perry Miller, "The End of the World," in *Errand into the Wilderness* (New York: Harper Torchbooks, 1956), 232–33.

56. Samuel King's portrait of Stiles is now at the Yale University Art Gallery (accession number 1955.3.1).

57. Ezra Stiles, *Literary Diary,* 2: August 1, [1771], as quoted in Josephine Setze, "Ezra Stiles of Yale," *Antiques* 72, no. 4 (October 1957): 349–50.

58. Ibid.

59. *Winthrop Papers,* vol. 3: *1631–1637* (Boston: Massachusetts Historical Society, 1943), 206.

60. Webster calls Sir Kenelm Digby a "rehabilitated Catholic" in *Great Instauration,* 303, but simply a Catholic without qualification on 503–4. Digby is called a "proselytizing Catholic" in Richard S. Dunn, *Puritans and Yankees: The Winthrop Dynasty of New England, 1630–1717* (Princeton, N.J.: Princeton University Press, 1962), 59. See also Bruce Jenacek, "Catholic Natural Philosophy and the Revification of Sir Kenelm Digby," in *Rethinking the Scientific Revolution,* ed. Margaret J. Osler (New York: Cambridge University Press, 2000), 89–118; and John Henry, "Atomism and Eschatology: Catholicism and Natural Philosophy in the Interregnum," *British Journal of the History of Science* 15, no. 51 (November 1982): 211–39.

61. Betty Jo Dobbs, "Studies in the Natural Philosophy of Sir Kenelm Digby," *Ambix,* 20, no. 3 (November 1973), pt. 2: 150–51.

62. See Digby's *Observations upon Religio Medici* (London: Printed by R.C. for Daniel Frere, 1643); and *Observations on the 22. Stanza in the 9th Canto of the 2d. Book of Spencers Faery Queen* (London: Printed for Daniel Frere, 1643).

63. *An Unhappy View of the Whole Behavior of my Lord Duke of Buckingham, at the French Island, called Isle of RHEE. Discovered by . . . an unfortunate commander in that untoward service* (London: Printed for R. Smith, 1648). The "Unfortunate commander" was named Colonel William Fleetwood.

64. See the *Articles of agreement made betweene the French King and those of Rochell, upon the rendition of the towne, the 24 of October last, 1628. According to the French coppies printed at Rochell and at Roan. Also a relation of a brave and resolute sea-fight, made by Sr. Kenelam Digby (on the Bay of Scandarone the 16 of June last past).* (London: Printed for N. Butler, 1628).

65. R. T. Petersson, *Sir Kenelm Digby: The Ornament of England, 1603–1665* (Cambridge, Mass.: Harvard University Press, 1956), 322–23; on the effect of Venetia's death on Digby's natural philosophy, see Jenacek, "Catholic Natural Philosophy and the Revification of Sir Kenelm Digby."

66. Ibid.

67 Dobbs, "Studies in the Natural Philosophy of Sir Kenelm Digby," pt. 2: 150. The patent was opposed by the local glass workers and their guild. The guild knew that Digby was the true "inventor" of the improved glass bottles and that Colnett was his operator and front man.

68. A narrative of these well-known events is in Maurice Ashley, *England in the Seventeenth Century* (New York: Penguin Books, 1972), 84–90.

69. *Aubrey's Brief Lives,* ed. Oliver Lawson Dick (London: Secker & Warburg, 1949), 98; see also Peterson, *Sir Kenelm Digby,* 212–22.

70. Beverley C. Southgate, *"Covetous of Truth": The Life and Work of Thomas White, 1593–1676* (Boston: Kluwer, 1993); Dorothea Krook, *John Sergeant and His Circle: A Study of Three Seventeenth-century English Aristotelians,* ed. Beverley C. Southgate (New York: E. J. Brill, 1993), ix–xv, 41–66.

71. Two editions of Digby's *Discourse, Concerning Infallibility in Religion* were published simultaneously in English in Paris and Amsterdam in 1652.

72. Krook, *John Sergeant and His Circle,* x–xi; and Petersson, *Sir Kenelm Digby,* 223–26.

73. Matthew Poole, *Nullity of the Romish Faith* (Oxford, 1666), 39, as quoted in Krook, *John Sergeant and His Circle,* xi.

74. On Cromwell's international Protestant alliance against France, see Jakob N. Bowman, *The Protestant Interest in Cromwell's Foreign Relations* (Heidelberg: Winter, 1900).

75. Ashley, *England in the Seventeenth Century,* 99–104. On Cromwell's Huguenot policy, see Bowman, *Protestant Interest,* 17–92.

76. Krook, *John Sergeant and His Circle,* xi; Holden quoted in Petersson, *Sir Kenelm Digby,* 224–25, also see 251–58.

77. Schwartz, *French Prophets,* 254–78.

78. Ernst Cassirer, *The Platonic Renaissance in England,* trans. James P. Pettegrove (New York: Gordian Press, 1970), 66–67.

79. Digby knew Bacon personally when both were at the court of James I. For an Aristotelian interpretation of Digby, see Krook, *John Sergeant and His Circle.*

80. Betty Jo Dobbs, "Studies in the Natural Philosophy of Sir Kenelm Digby," *Ambix 18,* no 1 (March 1971) [hereafter cited as Dobbs, pt. 1]: 13–14.

81. Webster, *Great Instauration,* 503–4. See also Jenacek, "Catholic Natural Philosophy and the Revification of Sir Kenelm Digby," and Henry, "Atomism and Eschatology."

82. Krook, *John Sergeant and His Circle,* see esp. Beverley Southgate's critique of Krook's insistence on Digby's Aristotelianism, "Editor's Introduction," xiii. See also T. Sorell, ed., *The Rise of Modern Philosophy: The Tension Between the New and Traditional Philosophies from Machiavelli to Leibniz* (New York: Oxford University Press, 1993); and Peter Galison, *Image and Logic: A Material Culture of Microphysics* (Chicago: University of Chicago Press, 1997).

83. See Southgate's "Editor's Introduction" in Krook, *John Sergeant and His Circle,* xi–xii.

84. Keith Hutchinson, "What Happened to Occult Qualities in the Scientific Revolution?" *Isis 73,* no. 267 (June 1982): 233–53; I am indebted to Elizabeth Hedrick for drawing this article to my attention.

85. Petersson, *Sir Kenelm Digby,* 241–45.

86. Ibid., 242–43.

87. Dobbs, pt. 1, 2; also E. W. Bligh, *Sir Kenelm Digby and his Venetia* (London: S. Low, Marston & Co., 1932); Thomas Longueville, *The Life of Sir Kenelm Digby by One of His Descendants* (London: Digby, Long & Co., 1896); H. M. Digby, *Sir Kenelm Digby and George Digby, Earl of Bristol* (London: Digby, Long & Co., 1912); John F. Fulton, "Sir Kenelm Digby," *Notes and Records of the Royal Society of London 15,* no. 1 (July 1960): 199–210; and Petersson, *Sir Kenelm Digby.* Digby wrote two autobiographical essays: *Private Memoirs of Sir Kenelm Digby, Gentleman of the Bedchamber of Charles I* (London: Saunders & Otley, 1827) and *Journal of a Voyage into the Mediterranean in 1628* (Westminster: Printed for the Camden Society, 1868). An analysis of

Digby's writings will appear in a forthcoming book by Elizabeth Hedrick. Professor Hedrick has generously shared three unpublished conference papers, "Science/Fiction in the Restoration: Sir Kenelm Digby and the Weapon-Salve"; "Gender, Matter, and the Latitudinarian Mind: The Case of Sir Kenelm Digby"; and "Prenatal Imprinting and the Female Imagination in the Seventeenth Century," which have helped form my discussion of the courtly and intellectual context of Digby's natural philosophy.

88. Two relatively recent studies in the history of science to consider the role of natural philosophers as courtiers are Mario Biagioli, *Galileo, Courtier: The Practice of Science in the Culture of Absolutism* (Chicago: University of Chicago Press, 1993); and Smith, *Business of Alchemy.*

89. See Robert Fludd, *Doctor Fludds answer unto M. Foster: or, The squeesing of Parson Fosters sponge, ordained by him for the wiping away of the weapon-salve. Where-in the sponge-bearers immodest carriage and behauiour towards its brethren is detected; the bitter flames of his slanderous reports, are by the sharpe vinegar of truth corrected and quite extinguished: and lastly, the virtuous validity of his sponge, in wiping away of the weapon-salve, is crushed out and cleane abolished . . .* (London: Nathaniel Butler, 1631); see also Allen G. Debus, "Robert Fludd and the Use of Gilbert's *De Magnete* in the Weapon Salve Controversy," *Journal of the History of Medicine and Allied Sciences* 19 (1964): 389–417.

90. Dobbs, pt. 1, 1–2; Hedrick, "Science/Fiction in the Restoration: Sir Kenelm Digby and the Weapon-Salve," 2–3.

91. Hedrick, "Science/Fiction in the Restoration," 3; and Dobbs, pt. 1, 6 n. 19.

92. Dobbs, pt. 1: 4 and n. 17.

93. Ibid., 5–6, 9.

94. Walter Pagel, *Paracelsus: An Introduction to Philosophical Medicine in the Era of the Renaissance* (Basel: Karger, 1982), 126–49.

95. The complete title is John Woodall, *The surgions Mate, or A Treatise Discovering faithfully and plainley the due contents of the Surgions Chest, the uses of the Instruments, the virtues and operations of the Medicines, the cures of the most frequent diseases at Sea: Namely Wounds, Apostumes, Ulcers, Fistulaes, Fractures, Dislocations, with the true manner of Amputation, the cure of the Scurvie, the Fluxes of the belly, of the Collica and Illiaca Passio, Tenasmus, and exitus Ani, the Callenture; With a brief Explanation of Sal, Sulphur, and Mercury; with certaine Characters, and tearmes of Arte. Published chiefly for the benefit of young Sea-Surgions, imployed in the East-India Companies Affaires* (London, 1617); see Dobbs, pt. 1: 7, 10.

96. On the importance of Buckingham's physical beauty to James I, see Roger Lockyer, *Buckingham: The Life and Political Career of George Villiers, First Duke of Buckingham, 1592–1628* (New York: Longman, 1981), 3–289.

97. Digby, *Private Memoirs of Sir Kenelm Digby.*

98. Dobbs, pt. 1: 6.

99. Hedrick, "Science/Fiction in the Restoration," 11–12.

100. Dobbs, pt. 1: 5.

101. Dobbs, pt. 1: 9; Pagel, *Paracelsus,* 117–21.

102. Digby, *Late Discourses,* 153–99, quoted in Dobbs, pt. 1: 11–12; see also Henry, "Atomism and Eschatology."

103. Cassirer, *Platonic Renaissance in England;* see also C. A. Patrides, ed., *The Cambridge Platonists* (Cambridge, Mass.: Harvard University Press, 1970); Frederick J. Powicke, *The Cambridge Platonists: A Study* (Hamden, Conn.: Archon Books, 1971); on the Platonic argument, see

Ben Lazare Mijuskovic, *The Achilles of Rationalist Arguments: The Simplicity, Unity, and Identity of Thought and Soul from the Cambridge Platonists to Kant: A Study in the History of an Argument* (The Hague: Martinus Nijhoff, 1974).

104. Ashley, *England in the Seventeenth Century*, 111–12.

105. Sir Kenelm Digby, *A Choice Collection of Rare Chymical Secrets and Experiments in Philosophy. As also Rare and unheard-of Medicines, Menstrums, and Alkahests; with the True Secret of Volatilizing the fixt Salt o Tartar. Collected And Experimented by the Honourable and truly Learned Sir Kenelm Digby, Kt. Chancellour to Her Majesty the Queen-Mother. Hitherto kept Secret since his Decease, but now Published for the good and benefit of the Publick, by George Hartman* (London: Printed for the Publisher, and are to be Sold by the Book-Selars of London, and at his own House in Hewes Court in Black-Fryers, 1682), 1–4. The other five occult writers mentioned were Agrippa, Villanova, Millius, Mayerus, and Isaac Holland.

106. On "simplicity" and its relation to Neoplatonism, see Mijuskovic, *Achilles of Rationalist Arguments*, 1–93.

107. Betty Jo Dobbs, "Studies in the Natural Philosophy of Sir Kenelm Digby, Part III: Digby's Experimental Alchemy—The Book of Secrets," *Ambix* 21, no. 1 (March 1974): 1–28. Digby's book of *Secrets* went through at least seven different editions in English, German, and Dutch; see also William Eamon, *Science and the Secrets of Nature: Books of Secrets in Medieval and Early Modern Culture* (Princeton, N.J.: Princeton University Press, 1994).

108. Webster, *Great Instauration*, 303.

109. The Harvard fire of 1764 destroyed the Digby gift of 1655, except for one volume: *John Cassiani Opera* (Antwerp, 1578); see *Collections of the Massachusetts Historical Society*, 3d ser., 10: 16 and 4th ser., 6: 116; Samuel Eliot Morison, *The Founding of Harvard College* (Cambridge, Mass.: Harvard University Press, 1935), 267–68; John Dunton, *The Life and Errors of John Dunton, Citizen of London; with the Lives and Characters of More Than a Thousand Contemporary Divines and Other Persons of Literary Eminence* (London: J. Nichols, 1818), 1: 115; and Petersson, *Sir Kenelm Digby*, 243.

110. *Collections of the Massachusetts Historical Society*, 3d ser., 10 (1849): 5–6.

111. Morison, *Builders of the Bay Colony*, 281.

112. Ibid., 281–82.

113. Quoted in Thomas Franklin Waters, *A Sketch of the Life of John Winthrop the Younger* (Ipswich, Mass.: Publications of the Ipswich Historical Society, 1899), 2: 44.

114. Morison, *Builders of the Bay Colony*, 281.

115. *Collections of the Massachusetts Historical Society*, 3d ser., 10 (1849): 15.

116. "Some Correspondence of John Winthrop, Jr., and Samuel Hartlib," ed. G. H. Turnbull, in *Proceedings of the Massachusetts Historical Society* 72, no. 1 (October 1957–December 1960): 46; letter from John Winthrop Jr. to Thomas Lake, April 15, 1661, in "Winthrop Papers, Part IV," *Collections of the Massachusetts Historical Society*, 5th ser., 8 (Boston: Massachusetts Historical Society, 1882): 73–74; Black, *Younger John Winthrop*, 54, 74–75, 119.

117. "Some Correspondence of John Winthrop, Jr., and Samuel Hartlib," 42–43.

118. Ibid., 54.

119. The full title of Winthrop's copy is *Enchiridion Physicae Restitutae, In quo verus Naturae concentus exponitur, plurimique antiquae Philosophiae errores, per canones & certas demonstrationes dilucide aperiuntur. Tractatus alter inscriptus, Arcanum Hermeticae Philosophiae opus, In quo occulta*

Naturae & Artis circa Lapidus Philosophorum materiam & operandi modum canonice & ordinate sunt manifesta. Utrumque opus eiusdem Authoris Anonymi. Spes Mea Est In Agno. Tertia editio emendata & aucta (Paris: Apud Nicolaum de Sercy, in Palatio, in Porticu Delphinaea, sub signo Fidei Coronatae, 1642). This volume is currently in the New York Academy of Medicine Library; see Roland Sterne Wilkinson, "The Alchemical Library of John Winthrop, Jr. (1606–1676), . . . Part IV," 153, cat. no. 73. Quotation from Jean d'Espagnet, *Enchyridion physicae restitutae, or The Summary of Physicks recovered, wherein the true harmony of nature is explained . . . (London: Printed by W. Bentley, 1651), 2–3.*

120. *Oxford English Dictionary,* s.v., "anagram," definition 2.

121. Edward Howes, quoted in *North American Review* 105, no. 217 (October 1867): 611–12.

T W E L V E   ❧   La Rochelle's Transatlantic Body

1. Mary Forth, John Jr.'s natural mother, died in childbirth in 1615; as did his father's second wife, Thomasine Clopton, in 1616.

2. *Winthrop Papers,* vol. 2: *1623–1630* (Boston: Massachusetts Historical Society, 1929), 58–59. Dating this undated letter ca. February 4, 1628, is discussed on 58, n. 3. A strong case has also been made for a date in late 1629. John Winthrop's letter of May 15, 1629, cited below, may have been written in direct response to this one.

3. Edmund S. Morgan writes that of all the arguments for emigration, the fates of La Rochelle and the Palatinate were "the most compelling . . . on his list"; see *The Puritan Dilemma: The Story of John Winthrop* (Boston: Little, Brown, 1958), 40. Despite the significance assigned to this event in the colonial historiography, it has not been studied closely from the transatlantic perspective.

4. *Winthrop Papers,* 2: 91–92. For the relationship between millennial thought, perceptions of corruption, and motives behind the Puritan migration to New England, see Avihu Zakai, *Exile and Kingdom: History and Apocalypse in the Puritan Migration to America* (New York: Cambridge University Press, 1992).

5. Morgan, *Puritan Dilemma,* 40. See also Zakai, *Exile and Kingdom.*

6. Paul S. Seaver, *Wallington's World: A Puritan Artisan in Seventeenth-Century London* (Stanford, Calif.: Stanford University Press, 1985), 104.

7. Ibid. Bradshaw's relation was written on October 30, 1628.

8. Quoted in ibid., 81.

9. On eucharistic piety, self-denial and the construction of the Christian body in the culture of late medieval religious women, see Caroline Walker Bynum, *Holy Feast and Holy Fast: The Religious Significance of Food to Medieval Women* (Berkeley: University of California Press, 1987), and id., *Fragmentation and Redemption: Essays on Gender and the Human Body* (New York: Zone Books, 1991).

10. *Winthrop Papers,* 2: 291.

11. Ibid., 288, 291.

12. Ibid., 288.

13. Ibid., 288–89.

14. Ibid., 289.

15. Ibid., 290.

16. Ibid., 292.

17. Ibid. On the Waldensian heresy, see Euan Cameron, *The Reformation of the Heretics: The Waldenses of the Alps, 1480–1580* (Oxford: Clarendon Press, 1984); and Alexis Muston, *The Israel of the Alps: A Complete History of the Waldenses and Their Colonies,* 2 vols. (London: Blackie & Son, 1875).

18. Seaver, *Wallington's World,* 144.

19. Ibid., 104, 143–44, 192.

20. Morgan, *Puritan Dilemma,* 15–21.

21. See S. L. Adams, "Foreign Policy and the Parliaments of 1621 and 1624," in Kevin Sharpe, ed., *Faction and Parliament: Essays on Early Stuart History* (Oxford: Clarendon Press, 1978), 152–53; on Louis XIII's campaigns against the Huguenots in 1620–29 and the rise of Richelieu beginning in 1621, see A. Lloyd Moote, *Louis XIII, the Just* (Berkeley: University of California Press, 1989), 116–36.

22. J. G. A. Pocock, "England," in Orest Ranum, ed., *National Consciousness: History and Political Culture in Early Modern Europe* (Baltimore: Johns Hopkins University Press, 1975), 103.

23. Daily transcripts of the Commons debates of 1628 are to be found in Robert C. Johnson, Mary Frear Keeler, Maija Jansson Cole, and William B. Bidwell, eds., *Commons Debates, 1628,* 4 vols. (New Haven, Conn.: Yale University Press, 1977–78). The debates on the Île de Ré and La Rochelle that occurred from June 3 to June 11, 1628, are located in vol. 4, 28 May–26 June 1628: 60–276; the Remonstrance of June 14, 1628, is transcribed in 4: 310–17.

24. See ibid., 4: 310. This number was announced in Parliament by Sir Edward Giles on June 14, 1628, when he asserted that of the 30,000 who had sailed with Buckingham: "There were 7,000 lost. When they returned home notice was taken how many came, and of those that returned sundry died [of "a great sickness amongst them"] as soon as they landed." Dr. Laud disputed this number and Buckingham's responsibility for all the deaths in his proposed reply to the Remonstrance presented to the king on June 17, 1628: "Nor was our loss of men such in that service as is voiced or near the number. Many indeed were lost since their return, for want of necessaries, which was not so taken to heart by them which should have supplied the necessaries of the state as was fitting." See Mary Frear Keeler, Maija Jansson Cole, and William B. Bidwell, *Proceedings in Parliament, 1628,* vol. 6: *Appendixes and Indexes* (New Haven, Conn.: Yale University Press, 1983), 54.

25. The first edition of William Fleetwood's *An Unhappy View of the Whole Behavior of my Lord Duke of Buckingham, at the French Island, called Isle of RHEE* was published in late 1627 (it does not mention Buckingham's assassination); I have used a slightly later edition here (London: Printed for R. Smith, 1648).

26. The *Oxford English Dictionary* definition of "effeminate" (1625) cites the K. Long translation of Barclay's *Argenis* (4.22.319): "But a soldier's death shall make amends for thy effeminate life." See also ca. 1430: "It is . . . the most perilous thyng A prince to been of his Condicion Effeminate"; 1555: "The sclenderesse of theyr capacitie and effeminate hartes"; 1609: "The soules of the effeminate shal be hungrie" (Douay Bible, Prov. 7:8); 1611: "His chiefest Consorts were effeminated persons, Ruffians and the like"; and 1619: "her effeminated king Basely captive, make him doe any thing." After the fact, but summary, is Gibbon's *Decline and Fall of the Roman Empire* (1776): "Rome was humbled beneath the effeminate luxury of Oriental despotism."

27. Fleetwood, *Unhappy View,* 2–9.

28. Ibid., 9–14. For a rare apology for the duke's performance at the Île de Ré, see the anonymous pamphlet: *A Continued Journall of All the Proceedings of the Duke of Buckingham his Grace, in The Isle of Ree since the last of July With the names of Those Noblemen as were Drowned and taken in going to releeve the Fort* (London: Thomas Walkley Printer, August 30, 1627).

29. N. R. N. Tyacke, "Puritanism, Arminianism and Counter-Revolution," in Conrad Russell, ed., *The Origins of the English Civil War* (London: Macmillan, 1980); see also Nicolas Tyacke, *Anti-Calvinists: The Rise of English Arminianism, 1590–1690* (Oxford: Oxford University Press, 1987).

30. In this context, "patent" is to be understood in the 1597 sense of "Abuses practiced by Monopolies and Patents of priviledge" (*Shorter Oxford English Dictionary*, s.v., ex. 2).

31. Johnson et al., eds., *Commons Debates, 1628*, 4: 130–31.

32. Ibid., 151.

33. Ibid., 313.

34. *Winthrop Papers, vol. 1: 1498–1628* (Boston: Massachusetts Historical Society, 1929), 195–96. On "heated speech" in colonial New England and perceptions of the physicality of the language of attack among seventeenth-century Calvinists, see Robert Blair St. George, "'Heated' Speech and Literacy in Seventeenth-Century New England," in David D. Hall and David Grayson Allen, eds., *Seventeenth-Century New England*, Colonial Society of Massachusetts Publications, 63 (Boston: The Society, 1984), 275–322.

35. Keeler et al., eds., *Proceedings in Parliament, 1628*, 6: 218.

36. On Buckingham and Parliament, see Kevin Sharpe, "The Earl of Arundal, His Circle and the Opposition to the Duke of Buckingham, 1618–1628," in id., ed., *Faction and Parliament*, 209–44; and Roger Lockyer, *Buckingham: The Life and Political Career of George Villiers, First Duke of Buckingham, 1592–1628* (New York: Longman, 1981), 89–124, 419–58.

37. Keeler et al., eds., *Proceedings in Parliament, 1628*, 6: 235. See also P. Clark, "Thomas Scott and the Growth of Urban Opposition to the Early Stuart Regime," *Historical Journal* 21, no. 1 (1978): 1–26.

38. Keeler et al., eds., *Proceedings in Parliament, 1628*, 6: 236.

39. On October 24, 1628; see the early translation: *Articles of Agreement Made Betweene the French King and those of Rochell, upon the Rendition of the Towne, the 24. of October last. 1628: According to the French Coppies Printed at Rochell and at Roan* (London: Printed for Nathaniell Butter, 1628).

40. On Eliot's role in the late 1620s and his relationship to Buckingham, see J. N. Ball, "Sir John Eliot and Parliament, 1624–1629," in Kevin Sharpe, ed., *Faction and Parliament*, 173–208; for a full-length biography of Eliot, see Harold Hulme, *The Life of Sir John Eliot, 1592–1632: Struggle for Parliamentary Freedom* (London: Allen & Unwin, 1957).

41. Johnson et al., eds., *Commons Debates, 1628*, 4: 60.

42. J. G. A. Pocock, *The Ancient Constitution and the Feudal Law: A Study of English Historical Thought in the Seventeenth Century* (New York: Norton, 1967), 30–69, 125–26.

43. The rhetorical term "true English heart," was used often by Eliot and other M.P.'s during the debates of 1628, as, for example, by Eliot on June 3; see Johnson et al., eds., *Commons Debates 1628*, 4: 62.

44. The most authoritative account of the beginnings of such historical thought and language is Pocock, *Ancient Constitution and the Feudal Law*, 1–90.

45. Bynum, *Holy Feast and Holy Fast*, 31–69.

46. Johnson et al., eds., *Commons Debates, 1628,* 4: 60–62; transcripts for June 3, 1628.

47. Ibid., 62.

48. Hugh Trevor-Roper, "Our First Whig Historian: Paul de Rapin-Thoyras," in id., *From Counter-Reformation to Glorious Revolution* (Chicago: University of Chicago Press, 1992), 250. I am indebted to Mauricio Tenorio for drawing this reference to my attention.

49. Pocock, *Ancient Constitution and the Feudal Law,* 6–7.

50. Ibid.

51. See Pocock, "The French Prelude to Modern Historiography," in id., *Ancient Constitution and the Feudal Law,* 16–27, 65.

52. Paul de Rapin-Thoyras, *The History of England: As Well Ecclesiastical as Civil,* 28 vols. (London: Printed for James and John Knapton, 1726–47).

53. For the influence of 1688 on English religious culture, see Nicolas Tyacke, *From Persecution to Toleration: The Glorious Revolution and Religion in England* (Oxford: Oxford University Press, 1991).

54. David Hume, *The History of England,* 6 vols. (London: Printed for A. Millar, 1754–62); Trevor-Roper, "Our First Whig Historian," 250, 264–65.

55. Ball, "Sir John Eliot and Parliament," 180–87.

56. Ibid., 198–99.

57. J. G. A. Pocock, "British History: A Plea for a New Subject," *Journal of Modern History* 47 (1975): 601–21; cf. Pocock's debate with Michael Hechter on 625–28; see also Pocock, "The Limits and Divisions of British History: In Search of the Unknown Subject," *American Historical Review* 87 (April 1982): 311–36.

58. Ernst H. Kantorowicz, *The King's Two Bodies: A Study in Medieval Political Theology* (Princeton, N.J.: Princeton University Press, 1957).

59. Johnson et al., eds., *Commons Debates, 1628,* 4: 311.

60. Ibid.

61. Ibid.

62. Ibid., 311–12.

63. Ibid., 312.

64. Ibid., 312–13.

65. Ibid., 313.

66. Ibid.

67. Ibid. 4: 188–89. Maynard was Buckingham's loyal creature until this speech of June 7, and as a result of his remarks about Machiavelli, he drew a strong rebuke from the duke, see 188, n. 55.

68. Ibid., see also 164.

69. Ibid., 315.

70. Cal Winslow, "Sussex Smugglers," and John G. Rule, "Wrecking and Coastal Plunder," in Douglas Hay et al., *Albion's Fatal Tree: Crime and Society in Eighteenth-Century England* (New York: Pantheon Books, 1975), 119–88.

71. Ibid.

72. Johnson et al., eds., *Commons Debates, 1628,* 4: 147.

73. Keeler et al., eds., *Proceedings in Parliament, 1628,* 6: 219–20.

74. Ibid., 314. In the original transcripts, "dispersed" is sometimes used interchangeably with "depressed" (see 314, n. 35). I have used "dispersed" in this context because this word—classically

associated with the Huguenot diaspora—approaches the original intention of the writers of the Remonstrance, who referred to La Rochelle in the text as exemplifying the destruction of "all the reformed churches in Christendom."

75. Ibid. The Commons appended to the end of the Remonstrance "A calendar or schedule of the shipping of this kingdom which have been taken by the enemy and lost at sea within the space of three years last past," naming the ships lost, as well as their tonnage and value, see 317ff.

76. Ibid.

77. Ibid., 315–16.

78. Ibid., 316–17.

79. Ibid., 317.

80. Geoffrey Keynes, *The Life of William Harvey* (Oxford: Clarendon Press, 1966), 146–47. The duke testified that the plaster contained London treacle and the juice of citrons (*Theriaca Londinensis* was prepared with thirty-two ingredients, including stag-horn and opium); and the potion was "plain posset with hartshorn in it."

81. Johnson et al., eds., *Commons Debates, 1628*, 4: 143–44. The "commission for a toleration" to which Coke refers derisively was presented by Sir John Savile on March 24, 1628.

82. Keynes, *Life of William Harvey*, 143–48.

83. Ibid., 152.

84. Ibid., 154–57, 178.

85. William Harvey, *Exercitatio anatomica de motu cordis et sanguinis in animalibus* (Frankfurt, 1628). I quote the dedication from William Harvey, *On the Motion of the Heart and Blood in Animals*, ed. Alexander Bowie and Mark Graubard (Chicago: Gateway Editions, 1962), 26–27. The first (Frankfurt) edition of *De motu cordis* was published in Latin by Willem Fitzer. Fitzer was the son-in-law of Johann Theodore de Bry, of the well-known Protestant publishing family, originally of Liège, who fled as refugees to Frankfurt and Oppenheim when Liège fell under Catholic control in the late sixteenth century. Johann Theodore de Bry was responsible for the publication of the important Paracelsian alchemical works of Robert Fludd and Michael Maier. He was the son of Theodore de Bry (d. 1598), made famous for the remarkable engravings that accompanied his publication of a series of volumes on sixteenth-century European voyages of discovery. Fitzer married Johann Theodore's daughter in 1625, and when his father-in-law died a year later, he became head of the family business. It is thought that Fludd, a friend and confident of Harvey's, recommended the de Bry–Fitzer press for *De motu cordis*. For more on the de Bry family, see Frances A. Yates, *The Rosicrucian Enlightenment* (Boulder, Colo.: Shambhala, 1978), 70–90; and Keynes, *Life of William Harvey*, 176.

86. Johnson et al., eds., *Commons Debates, 1628*, 4: 317.

87. The most important of these is Sir John Eliot, *The Monarchie of Man*, ed. A. B. Grosart, 2 vols. (London: Chiswick Press, 1879).

88. Ball, "Sir John Eliot and Parliament," 204–5.

89. Keeler et al., *Proceedings in Parliament, 1628*, 6: 52–57: "17 June 1628 Bishop Laud's proposed reply to the remonstrance presented to the King."

90. Johnson et al., eds., *Commons Debates, 1628*, 4: 139.

91. See *Oxford English Dictionary*, s.v., "effeminate" (1534), and n. 26 above.

92. *Winthrop Papers*, 1: 161, 163, 193.

93. Johnson et al., eds., *Commons Debates, 1628*, 4: 132 (June 5, 1628).

THIRTEEN   ❧   "Fraudulant father-Frenchmen"

1. On native English resistance to Huguenots, see Joseph P. Ward, *Metropolitan Communities: Trade Guilds, Identity, and Change in Early Modern London* (Stanford: Stanford University Press, 1997), 138–42; Tim Harris, *London Crowds in the Reign of Charles II: Propaganda and Politics from the Restoration until the Exclusion Crisis* (New York: Cambridge University Press, 1987); L. Williams, "Alien Immigrants in Relation to Industry and Society in Tudor England," *Proceedings of the Huguenot Society in London* 19 (1952–58): 146–69; E. S. de Beer, "The Revocation of the Edict of Nantes and French Public Opinion," ibid. 18 (1947–52): 292–310; Linda Colley, *Britons: Forging the Nation, 1707–1837* (New Haven, Conn.: Yale University Press, 1992), 85–100; M. R. Thorp, "The Anti-Huguenot Undercurrent in Late-Seventeenth-Century England," *Proceedings of the Huguenot Society in London* 22 (1970–76): 569–80; H. T. Dickinson, "The Tory Party's Attitude to Foreigners," *Bulletin of the Institute of Historical Research* 40 (1967): 153–65; M. Priestly, "Anglo-French Trade and the 'Unfavorable Balance' Controversy," *Economic History Review*, 2d ser., 4 (1951–52): 37–52; Richard M. Dunn, "The London Weavers' Riot of 1675," *Guildhall Studies in London History* 1, no. 1 (January 1973): 13–23; Robin D. Gwynn, *Huguenot Heritage: The History and Contribution of the Huguenots in Britain* (London: Routledge & Kegan Paul, 1985), 60–129; Catherine Swindlehurst, "'An unruly and presumptuous rabble': The Reaction of the Spitalfields Weaving Community to the Settlement of the Huguenots, 1660–90," in *From Strangers to Citizens: The Integration of Immigrant Communities in Britain, Ireland, and Colonial America, 1550–1750*, ed. Randolph Vigne and Charles Littleton (London: Huguenot Society of Great Britain and Ireland; Brighton: Sussex Academic Press, 2001), 366–74; and Joseph P. Ward, "Fictitious Shoemakers, Agitated Weavers and the Limits of Popular Xenophobia in Elizabethan London," in ibid., 80–87. Ward has questioned the standard xenophobia model of reception in the English trades, though his interpretation remains in the minority at present.

2. Count Lorenzo Magalotti, *Travels of Cosimo the Third, Grand Duke of Tuscany, through England, during the Reign of Charles the Second* (1669, London, 1821), 398.

3. This is not to say that the mid sixteenth century saw the first foreign weavers in England. Between 1337 and 1360, a substantial group of Flemish weavers had been invited to work at their trade in England and established an early industrial community at York. This instance, however, is in no way analogous to the depth, breadth, and duration of the influx of immigrants experienced in England as a result of the continental wars of religion in France and the Netherlands.

4. C. W. Chitty, "Aliens in England in the Sixteenth Century," *Race: A Journal of Race and Group Relations* 8, no. 2 (October 1966): 134–36.

5. On the new draperies, see N. J. Williams, "Two Documents Concerning the New Draperies," *Economic History Review*, 2d ser., 4, no. 3 (1952); and C. W. Chitty, "Aliens in England in the Sixteenth Century," *Race: A Journal of Race and Group Relations* 8, no. 2 (October 1966): 133–35.

6. R. H. Tawney and E. Power, eds., *Tudor Economic Documents* (London: Longmans, 1924), 3: 212; Ward, "Fictitious Shoemakers, Agitated Weavers," 81.

7. Warren C. Scoville, *The Persecution of the Huguenots and French Economic Development, 1680–1720* (Berkeley: University of California Press, 1960), 435–45.

8. In the sixteenth century when it was introduced into England from France and the Netherlands, "bays," or baize, was an unusually fine, soft, lightweight fabric, usually a woolen or "penistone," but sometimes a cotton or a woolen and linen mix, commonly used in the manu-

facture of clothing. "Says," on the other hand, were similarly light, but resembled serge. In the sixteenth century, says were occasionally composed of wool mixed with silk; by the seventeenth century, they were usually all wool.

9. See P. J. Bowden, *The Wool Trade in Tudor and Stuart England* (London: Macmillan, 1962).

10. Williams, "Two Documents Concerning the New Draperies"; and Chitty, "Aliens in England in the Sixteenth Century," 134.

11. Simonds D'Ewes, *A Complete Journal of the Votes, Speeches, and Debates both of the House of Lords and House of Commons throughout the whole reign of Queen Elizabeth* (London, 1708), 505–9.

12. John Strype, *Annals of the Reformation and Establishment of Religion* (1709; new ed., Oxford: Clarendon Press, 1824), vol. 4, no. 108: 234–36; also Chitty, "Aliens in England in the Sixteenth Century," 141–22.

13. On the centrality of the culture of politeness in early modern England and the movement to domesticate *politesse,* see Lawrence E. Klein, *Shaftesbury and the Culture of Politeness: Moral Discourse and Cultural Politics in Early Eighteenth-Century England* (Cambridge: Cambridge University Press, 1994).

14. On the London silk industry, see esp. Peter Thornton and Natalie Rothstein, "The Importance of the Huguenots in the London Silk Industry," *Proceedings of the Huguenot Society of London* 20 (1958–64): 60–88; and W. H. Manchee, "Some Huguenot Smugglers: The Impeachment of London Silk Merchants in 1698," *Proceedings of the Huguenot Society of London* 15 (1934–37): 406–27; on the revolution in style wrought by the "French bed" in England, see Tessa Murdoch, "Worthy of the Monarch: Immigrant Craftsmen and the Production of State Beds, 1660–1714," in *From Strangers to Citizens: The Integration of Immigrant Communities in Britain, Ireland, and Colonial America, 1550–1750,* ed. Randolph Vigne and Charles Littleton (London: Huguenot Society of Great Britain and Ireland; Brighton: Sussex Academic Press, 2001), 151–59.

15. Benno M. Forman, "Continental Furniture Craftsmen in London: 1511–1625," *Furniture History* 7 (1971): 95. The ordinance of 1483 was reconfirmed in the *Statutes* of 1523, 1524, and 1530.

16. Forman, "Continental Furniture Craftsmen in London," 97; for occupations of foreign tradesmen during the later seventeenth century, see W. Durrant Cooper, *List of Foreign Protestants and Aliens Resident in England, 1618–1688* (London: John Camden Hatten, 1862).

17. Victor Chinnery, *Oak Furniture The British Tradition: A History of Early Furniture in the British Isles and New England* (Woodbridge, Suffolk, UK: Baron Publishing, 1979), 125–6; see n. 29 below for full citation of the 1603 edition of Stow's *Survey of London.*

18. Peter Thornton, *Seventeenth-Century Interior Decoration in England, France, and Holland* (New Haven, Conn.: Yale University Press, 1978); see also Tessa Murdock et al., *The Quiet Conquest: The Huguenots, 1685–1985* (London: A. H. Jolly, 1985), 199–204, 289–312.

19. Robert Campbell, *The London Tradesman, 1747* (reprint, Newton Abbot, UK: David & Charles, 1973), 169–72.

20. Graham Parry, *The Golden Age Restor'd: The Culture of the Stuart Court, 1603–42* (New York: St. Martin's Press, 1981), 136–45, 215.

21. The classic text on Inigo Jones and the Stuarts remains Stephen Orgel and Roy Strong, *Inigo Jones: The Theatre of the Stuart Court* (Berkeley: University of California Press, 1973); see also Orgel, *The Jonsonian Masque* (Cambridge, Mass.: Harvard University Press, 1967); id., *The Illusion of Power* (Berkeley: University of California Press, 1975); and Parry, *Golden Age Restor'd,* 146–64.

22. Roger Lockyer, *Buckingham: The Life and Political Career of George Villiers, First Duke of Buckingham, 1592–1628* (New York: Longman, 1981), 53.

23. See Orgel and Strong, *Inigo Jones.*

24. Lockyer, *Buckingham,* 213–15; Chinnery, *Oak Furniture,* 431–34.

25. Parry, *Golden Age Restor'd,* 215.

26. For Buckingham's massive building program and the cycle of income and debt, see Lockyer, *Buckingham,* 53–76, 210–13.

27. For a general study of this phenomenon see Sharon Kettering, *Patrons, Brokers, and Clients in Seventeenth-Century France* (New York: Oxford University Press, 1986), esp. 21–29.

28. See Lawrence Klein, "The Third Earl of Shaftesbury and the Progress of Politeness," *Eighteenth-Century Studies* 18, no. 2 (Winter 1984–85): 186–214; and Lawrence E. Klein, *Shaftesbury and the Culture of Politeness.* See also, J. G. A. Pocock's formulation of the civic humanist tradition in terms of a tension between virtue and commerce in *The Machiavellian Moment: Florentine Political Thought and the Atlantic Republican Tradition* (Princeton, N.J.: Princeton University Press, 1975), 386–505; id., "The Varieties of Whiggism from Exclusion to Reform," in *Virtue, Commerce, and History* (Cambridge: Cambridge University Press, 1985); id., "Civic Humanism and Its Role in Anglo-American Thought," in *Politics, Language and Time* (New York: Atheneum, 1973), 80–103; and Norbert Elias, *The Civilizing Process: The History of Manners,* 2 vols. (New York: Pantheon Books, 1978, 1982); id., *The Court Society* (Oxford: Basil Blackwell, 1983); Marvin Becker, *Civility and Society in Western Europe, 1300–1600* (Bloomington: Indiana University Press, 1988); and Jürgen Habermas, *The Structural Transformation of the Public Sphere,* trans. Thomas Burger (Cambridge, Mass.: MIT Press, 1989). Richard L. Bushman explores general themes in the social history of American "polite" or "genteel" material culture in *The Refinement of America: Persons, Houses, Cities* (New York: Knopf, 1992), 30–99.

29. John Stow, *A Survey of London. Conteyning the originall, antiquity, increase, modern estate, and description of that city, written in the yeare 1598, by John Stow citizen of London. Since by the same author inceased, with divers rare notes of antiquity, and published in the yeare 1603. Also an Apologie (or defence) against the opinion of some men, concerning that citie, the greatnesse thereof* (London: John Windet, printer, 1603), 562–63.

30. Neil McKendrick et al., *The Birth of a Consumer Society* (Bloomington: Indiana University Press, 1982), 9–33; Joyce Appleby, *Economic Thought and Ideology in Seventeenth-Century England* (Princeton, N.J.: Princeton University Press, 1978); T. H. Breen, *The Marketplace of Revolution: How Consumer Politics Shaped American Independence* (N.Y.: Oxford, 2004); and Klein, "Third Earl of Shaftesbury and the Progress of Politeness," 187.

31. Robert F. Trent, "The Concept of Mannerism," in Jonathan L. Fairbanks and Robert F. Trent, eds., *New England Begins: The Seventeenth Century,* vol. 3: *Style* (Boston: Museum of Fine Arts, 1982), 375.

32. The most reliable general history of this period remains J. M. H. Salmon, *Society in Crisis: France in the Sixteenth Century* (New York: St. Martins Press, 1975).

33. For the most recent attempt at demographic synthesis, but one with estimates that are arguably very conservative, see Philip Benedict, *The Huguenot Population of France, 1600–1685: The Demographic Fate and Customs of a Religious Minority,* in *Transactions of the American Philosophical Society* 81, pt. 5 (1991), 3–5; see also Robin D. Gwynn, "The Arrival of Huguenot Refugees in England, 1680–1705," *Proceedings of the Huguenot Society of London* 21 (1969): 366–73; id., "The Distribution of Huguenot Refugees in England, 2: London and Its Environs," ibid. 22

(1976): 523 et passim; id., *Huguenot Heritage: The History and Contribution of the Huguenots in Britain* (Boston: Routledge & Kegan Paul, 1985), 35 et passim; Bernard Cottret, *Terre d'exil: L'Angleterre et ses réfugiés français et wallons, de la Réforme à la révocation de l'édit de Nantes, 1550–1700* (Paris: Aubier, 1985); and on the role of London, see Bertrand van Ruymbeke, "Le Refuge atlantique: La Diaspora huguenote et l'Atlantique anglo-americain" (paper delivered to the American Historical Association, January 1999).

34. J. Bulteel, *A Relation of the Troubles of the Three Foreign Churches in Kent* (London, 1645), 21–22; C. W. Chitty, "Aliens in England in the Seventeenth Century to 1660," *Race: A Journal of Race and Group Relations* 11, no. 2 (October 1969): 194–98.

35. Irene Scouloudi, "Alien Immigration Into and Alien Communities in London, 1558–1640," *Proceedings of the Huguenot Society of London* 16, no. 1 (1938): 35 et passim; Chitty, "Aliens in England in the Sixteenth Century," 136–37, 140. On the "urban graveyard effect," see Benedict, *Huguenot Population of France*, 46; evidence of the effect was also reported by Joyce Goodfriend, in "Huguenots in Colonial New York City: A Demographic Profile" (conference paper delivered at "Out of New Babylon: The Huguenots and Their Diaspora," Program in the Carolina Lowcountry and the Atlantic World, College of Charleston, May 14–17, 1997).

36. Benedict, *Huguenot Population of France*, 45, table 11.

37. For a discussion of *friperie* and the task of the *fripier* in early modern France, see Daniel Roche, *The Culture of Clothing: Dress and Fashion in the "Ancien Régime,"* trans. Jean Birrell (Cambridge: Cambridge University Press, 1994), 345–87.

38. For the phrase "declining minority," see Philip Benedict's *The Huguenot Population of France, 1600–1685: The Demographic Fate and Customs of a Religious Minority*, "Part 1: A Declining Minority," 7–79.

39. Forman, "Continental Furniture Craftsmen in London," 97.

40. Ibid., 96–97.

41. Quoted in ibid., 97.

42. *The Complete State Papers Domestic: Series One, 1547–1625* (Hassocks, U.K.: Harvester Press, 1977–81), James I, 1608–17, SP 14/41–14/94–pt. 9; Chitty, "Aliens in England in the Seventeenth Century to 1660," 190.

43. Edmund S. Morgan, *The Puritan Dilemma: The Story of John Winthrop* (Boston: Little, Brown, 1958), 21.

44. The disease metaphor may be found in a document dated 1654, quoted in Chitty, "Aliens in England in the Seventeenth Century to 1660," 190.

45. The literature on refugee gold- and silversmiths in England and its colonies is enormous and growing. For an introduction and bibliography, see Tessa Murdoch, comp., *The Quiet Conquest: The Huguenots, 1685–1985* (London: Museum of London, 1985), 229–42; see also Charles Oman, *English Engraved Silver, 1150–1900* (Boston: Faber & Faber, 1978); Philippa Glanville, *Silver in Tudor and Early Stuart England: A Social History and Catalogue of the National Collection, 1480–1660* (London: Victoria and Albert Museum, 1990); and, for a case study of the late sixteenth-century context for Huguenot silver and goldsmiths in London court circles, see Ellenor M. Alcorn, "'Some of the Kings of England Curiously Engraven': An Elizabethan Ewer and Basin in the Museum of Fine Arts, Boston," *Journal of the Museum of Fine Arts Boston* 5 (1993): 66–103.

46. Quoted in Chitty, "Aliens in England in the Seventeenth Century to 1660," 190.

47. Ibid.

48. Chitty, "Aliens in England in the Sixteenth Century," 135–36.

49. Klein, "Third Earl of Shaftesbury and the Progress of Politeness," 211, 213.

50. Ibid., 198.

51. Quoted in ibid., 199. Bushman also perceives "ambivalence" over the theatrical performance of politeness in American society, see *Refinement of America,* 181–203.

52. Klein, "Third Earl of Shaftesbury and the Progress of Politeness," 207. Note the convergence of Shaftesbury's Lockean critique of politesse, based on a call for "transparency," with a similarly anti-absolutist, anti-theatrical critique by the French philosophes of French fashion—and in particular clothing styles—during the 1770s; see Daniel Roche, *Culture of Clothing,* 516–19.

53. Arnold Hauser, *Mannerism: The Crisis of the Renaissance and the Origin of Modern Art* (Cambridge, Mass.: Harvard University Press, Belknap Press, 1986), 50.

FOURTEEN　❧　"The destruction that wasteth at noonday"

EPIGRAPH: Daniel Defoe, *A Journal of the Plague Year: being observations or memorials of the most remarkable occurrences, as well public as private, which happened in London during the last great visitation in 1665. Written by a Citizen who continued all the while in London. Never been made public before* (London, 1722), ed. Anthony Burgess and Christopher Bristow (London: Penguin Books, 1986), 34.

1. Ronald Paulson, Hogarth: *His Life, Art, and Times* (New Haven, Conn.: Published for the Paul Mellon Centre for Studies in British Art (London) by Yale University Press, 1971), 1: 80–81; Sean Shesgreen, *Hogarth and the Times-of-the-Day Tradition* (Ithaca, N.Y.: Cornell University Press, 1983), 105. On the Eglise des Grecs, see Robin D. Gwynn, "The Huguenots in Britain, the 'Protestant International' and the Defeat of Louis XIV," in *From Strangers to Citizens: The Integration of Immigrant Communities in Britain, Ireland, and Colonial America, 1550–1750,* ed. Randolph Vigne and Charles Littleton (London: Huguenot Society of Great Britain and Ireland; Brighton: Sussex Academic Press, 2001), 413. Unfortunately, unlike the excellent archive surviving for the French Church of London in Threadneedle Street, the oldest and earliest of England's forty-seven Huguenot churches in 1700, records for the Savoy Church and its annex, the Eglise des Grecs, were apparently lost in 1717.

2. Tessa Murdoch, comp., *The Quiet Conquest: The Huguenots, 1685–1985* (London: Museum of London, 1985), 193–98.

3. Ronald Paulson, *Hogarth's Graphic Works,* 3d rev. ed. (London: Print Room, 1989), 14–16; W. H. Manchee, "Hogarth and His Friendship with the Huguenots," *Proceedings of the Huguenot Society of London* 12 (1917–23): 134–38.

4. Now in the collection of Grimsthorpe and Drummond Castle. Hogarth completed the painting ca. 1736, and engraved and published the set two years later, on May 4, 1738. See Paulson, *Hogarth's Graphic Works,* 1: 179–80; 2: pl. 165; see also Murdoch, comp., *Quiet Conquest,* 5, 112, cat. no. 149.

5. Paulson, *Hogarth's Graphic Works,* 2: 178; Shesgreen, *Hogarth and the Times-of-the-Day Tradition,* 132–33.

6. On interiority of noonday demons in Roman mythology, see Charles Dempsey, *Inventing the Renaissance Putto* (Chapel Hill: University of North Carolina Press, 2001), 145; and Giorgio Agamben, *Stanze: La Parola e il fantasma nella cultura occidentale* (Turin: Einaudi, 1977), 1–14.

7. This metaphor is elucidated in Otto Mayr, *Authority, Liberty and Automatic Machinery in*

Early Modern Europe (Baltimore: Johns Hopkins University Press, 1989), esp. xv–xviii; William Hogarth, *The Analysis of Beauty* (1753), ed. Joseph Burke (Oxford: Clarendon Press, 1955), 86–87.

8. See Mayr, *Authority, Liberty and Automatic Machinery,* 98–101, for a summary of the early eighteenth century debate between Newton's spokesman, Samuel Clarke, a young courtly theologian, and the clockwork position argued by Gottfried Wilhelm Leibniz, historian and librarian for Georg Ludwig, elector of Hanover.

9. Hogarth, *Analysis of Beauty,* ed. Burke, 41–43.

10. Ibid., 22.

11. See Pierre Bourdieu, *La Distinction: Critique sociale du jugement* (Paris: Minuit, 1979). Many of these ideas appear with greater clarity and practical purpose in Bourdieu, *Outline of a Theory of Practice* (Cambridge: Cambridge University Press, 1977), 57, 178, 195 and passim; see also id., "What Makes a Social Class? On the Theoretical and Practical Existence of Groups," *Berkeley Journal of Sociology* 32 (1987): 1–17. Hogarth, *Analysis of Beauty,* ed. Burke, 85.

12. W. Jeffrey Bolster, *Black Jacks: African American Seamen in the Age of Sail* (Cambridge, Mass.: Harvard University Press, 1997). Hogarth writes of painting different races, including "dark brown, the mulatto;—black, the negro," in *Analysis of Beauty,* ed. Burke, 126.

13. Thomas Jefferson, *Notes on the State of Virginia* (Paris, 1784), in Adrienne Koch and William Peden, eds., *The Life and Selected Writings of Thomas Jefferson* (New York: Modern Library, 1944), 256–62.

14. For an introduction to the study of Robert Fludd with emphasis on the occult, see Serge Hutin, *Robert Fludd (1574–1637), Alchimiste et philosophe rosicrucien,* Collection Alchimie et alchimistes, no. 8 (Paris: Éditions de l'Omnium littéraire, 1971); Allen G. Debus, in *The English Paracelsians* (London: Oldbourne, 1965), 104–27; and id., "The Chemical Debates of the Seventeenth Century: The Reaction to Robert Fludd and Jean Baptiste van Helmont," in M. L. Righini Bonelli and William R. Shea, eds., *Reason, Experiment and Mysticism in the Scientific Revolution* (New York: Science History Publications, 1975), 19–47; "The Paracelsian Compromise in Elizabethan England," *Ambix* 8 (1960): 71–97; and "Renaissance Chemistry and the Work of Robert Fludd," *Ambix* 14 (1967): 42–59; see also Frances A. Yates, *The Rosicrucian Enlightenment* (Boulder, Colo.: Shambhala, 1978), 70–90; and id., *The Art of Memory* (Chicago: University of Chicago, 1966); and Joscelyn Godwin, *Robert Fludd: Hermetic Philosopher and Surveyor of Two Worlds* (Boulder, Colo.: Shambhala, 1979). For Flood in Winthrop's library, see Ronald Sterne Wilkinson, "The Alchemical Library of John Winthrop, Jr. (1606–1676) and His Descendants in Colonial America, Part IV: The Catalogue of Books," *Ambix* 13, no. 3 (October 1966), 156–57.

15. Hillel Schwartz, *The French Prophets: The History of a Millenarian Group in Eighteenth-Century England* (Berkeley: University of California Press, 1980), 216–92.

16. For a cogent analysis of Joachimism's great influence on reformed millennial experience, see John Martin, *Venice's Hidden Enemies: Italian Heretics in a Renaissance City* (Berkeley: University of California Press, 1993), 16, 98–99, 113–18.

17. William Hogarth, *The Analysis of Beauty: Written With a View of Fixing the Fluctuating Ideas of Taste* (London: Printed by J. Reeves for the Author: 1753), frontispiece.

18. Daniel Marot, *Oeuvres: Contenant plusiers pensséz utile aux architectes, peintres, sculpteurs, orfevres et jardiniers, et autres; le toutes en faveure de ceux qui s'appliquerent aux beaux arts* (The Hague: P. Husson, 1702).

19. Brock Jobe, "The Boston Furniture Industry, 1720–1740," in *Boston Furniture of the Eighteenth Century,* ed. Walter Muir Whitehill, Jonathan Fairbanks, and Brock Jobe (Boston: Colo-

nial Society of Massachusetts, 1974), 3–48 ; Benno M. Forman, "Delaware Valley 'Crookt Foot' and Slat-Back Chairs," *Winterthur Portfolio* 15, no. 1 (Spring 1980): 41–64; and Deborah Dependahl Waters, "Wares and Chairs: A Reappraisal of the Documents," in *Winterthur Portfolio* 13, *American Furniture and Its Makers,* ed. Ian M. G. Quimby (Chicago: University of Chicago Press: 1979), 161–73.

20. For an analysis of the analogy between parts of the human anatomy and furniture components in colonial America, see Laurel Thatcher Ulrich, "Furniture as Social History: Gender, Property, and Memory in the Decorative Arts," *American Furniture, 1995,* ed. Luke Beckerdite and William N. Hosley (Hanover, N.H.: University Press of New England, 1995): 42–52.

21. Hogarth, *Analysis of Beauty,* ed. Burke, 14, 70, 27.

22. Paulson, *Hogarth's Graphic Works,* 9 and figs. 66–81.

23. Hogarth observed in *Analysis of Beauty,* ed. Burke, 152: "our most common movements are seldom performed in such absolutely mean lines, as those of jointed dolls and puppets." For a classic study of mechanistic optics from Leonardo to Newton, with optical diagrams, see A. C. Crombie, "The Mechanistic Hypothesis and the Scientific Study of Vision," in *Science, Optics and Music in Medieval and Early Modern Thought* (London: Hambleton Press, 1990), 175–284, and figs. 1–38.

24. Robert Fludd, *Tomi secundi tractatus secundus: De praeternaturali utriusque mundi historia* (Frankfurt: Johann Theodore de Bry, 1621), 11.

25. As in definitions 6 and 8 for "wing" in the *Oxford English Dictionary;* or definition 2 for "winged": To summarize, two identical halves of a symmetrical artifact joined at center were called "wings" in seventeenth- and eighteenth-century parlance. For example, what we now commonly call "leaves" on the top of a hinged drop-leaf table might have been part of a "winged" table, and an iron hinge joined at its center with two symmetrical appendages might have been called a "winged" hinge.

26. C. H. Josten, "Robert Fludd's Theory of Geomancy and His Experiences at Avignon in the Winter of 1601 to 1602," *Journal of the Warburg and Courtauld Institutes* 27 (1964): 327.

27. Ibid.

28. Ibid.; see also Lynn Thorndike, *A History of Magic and Experimental Science* (New York: Macmillan, 1923–58), vol. 2, ch. 39; the detailed compendium of geomantic techniques reviewed in the treatises contained in *Fasciculus geomanticus in quo varia variorum opera geomantica continentur: opus maxime curiosum, a multis hactenus desideratum, nunc vero magno studio correctum & ex parte jam prima vice editum* (Verona, 1687, 1704); Robert Jaulin, *La Géomancie: Analyse formelle* (Paris: Mouton, 1966); and Nigel Permick, *The Ancient Science of Geomancy: Man in Harmony with the Earth* (London: Thames & Hudson, 1979).

29. The English translation was of Agrippa's *De incertitudine et vanitate omnium scientiarum et artium* first published in 1531.

30. Josten, "Robert Fludd's Theory of Geomancy," 328.

31. Godwin, *Robert Fludd,* 6–7.

32. Josten, "Robert Fludd's Theory of Geomancy," 331.

33. "Tractatus secundi, pars XI. De geomantia. in quartour libros divisa," in Robert Fludd, *Utriusque cosmi majoris scilicet et minoris metaphysica, physica atque technica historia in duo volumina secundum cosmi dfferentiam divisa . . . tomus primus De macrocosmi historia* (Oppenheim: Johann Theodore de Bry, 1617), 715–83; and "Tractatus primi. Sectionis II. De animae intellectualis scientia seu geomantia hominibus appropriata, quorum radii intellectuales extrinsecus, hoc est,

circa negotai mundana versates, & a centro dissipati in centrum recolliguntur," in Robert Fludd, *Tomi secundi tractatus primi sectio secunda, De technica microcosmi historia, in portiones VII* (Oppenheim: Johann Theodore de Bry, 1619), 37–46; see n. 28 above for the full citation of *Fasciculus geomanticus*. I use C. H. Josten's translation of major portions of these two texts; see "Robert Fludd's Theory of Geomancy," 328–31, hereafter, cited as Fludd, "Geomantia."

34. Fludd, "Geomantia," 328–29.

35. Ibid., 328–29.

36. Ibid., 329.

37. Ibid.

38. Ibid., 329.

39. Godwin, *Robert Fludd*, 6.

40. Fludd, "Geomantia," 329.

41. Ibid.

42. Allen G. Debus, "The Paracelsian Aerial Niter," *Isis* 55 (1964): 43–61, and id., "Robert Fludd and the Use of Gilbert's *De magnete* in the Weapon-Salve Controversy," *Journal of the History of Medicine and the Allied Sciences* 19 (1964): 389–417.

43. Fludd, "Geomantia," 329.

44. Ibid., 329.

45. Ibid.

46. Fludd, *Utriusque cosmi majoris*, 4–5.

47. Ibid., 7–8.

48. Fludd, "Geomantia," 329.

49. Robert Fludd, *De naturae simia seu technia macrocosmi historia* (Nature's Ape, or History of the Macrocosmic Arts) (Oppenheim: Johann Theodore de Bry, 1618; 2d ed., Frankfurt; id., 1624). On Thoth and De *naturae simia,* see W. H. Janson, "Apes and Ape Lore," *Studies of the Warburg Institute* 20 (1952): 305. On blacks as *simia,* see Winthrop P. Jordan, *White Over Black: American Attitudes toward the Negro, 1550–1812* (Chapel Hill: University of North Carolina Press, 1968), 29–32, 222–32.

50. Fludd, "Geomantia," 331.

51. Ibid., 330.

52. Sir Hugh Platt, *The Jewell House of Art and Nature: conteining diuers rare and profitable inuentions, together with sundry new experimentes in the art of husbandry, distillation, and moulding, faithfully and familiarly set downe, according to the auths owne experience, by Hugh Platte* (London: Printed by Peter Short, dwelling on Breadstreat hill, at the signe of the star, and are to be solde in Paules Church-yard, by William Ponsonby, 1594), 88.

53. Ibid.

54. Fludd, "Geomantia," 330.

55. William Eamon, *Science and the Secrets of Nature: Books of Secrets in Medieval and Early Modern Culture* (Princeton, N.J.: Princeton University Press, 1994), 315–16.

56. Fludd, "Geomantia," 330.

57. Ibid.

58. Ibid., 330–31.

59. Ibid., 331.

60. Ibid.

61. The complex biographical, aesthetic and political conflicts surrounding Hogarth's pro-

duction of "The Bathos" are discussed extensively in Paulson, *Hogarth: His Life, Art, and Times,* 2: 400–22.

62. Ibid., 413.

63. Ibid., 409.

64. Ibid., 409–11. While the print itself reads in the plate that it was "Published according to Act of Parliam't March 3'd 1764," it is probable that it was quickly altered after April 1 in response to the eclipse. A preliminary drawing exists for "Tail Piece" in which the dying sun and its chariot are conspicuously absent (ibid., 410, fig. 313a.). I assume that this and other subtle changes (including the placement of the sundial) were made in response to the eclipse.

65. Fludd, "Geomantia," 331.

66. The Eglise des Grecs was the first temple annex built in London after 1685, specifically for the overflow of refugees of the Revocation.

67. The full titles of the two source texts are: Robert Fludd, *Tomi secundi tractatus primi sectio secunda, De technica microcosmi historia, in portiones VII divisa* (Oppenheim: Johann Theodore de Bry, 1620), 55; and Clément Marot et Théodore de Bèze, *Les Psaumes mis en rime Francoise* (Paris: Par François Perrin pour Antoine Vincent, 1562).

68. On the dialogue in British Huguenot culture between "the wild and the walled [garden]," see Schwartz, *French Prophets,* 251–78.

69. Depending on the image, *porte* could mean "doorway" or "gateway," as well as "arch."

70. Fludd, *De naturae simia,* 160–61.

71. Yates, *Art of Memory,* 320–67.

72. On Hogarth's intense involvement with the London Grand Lodge, and his habitual use of masonic themes and debates in his art, see Paulson, *Hogarth's Graphic Works,* 52–54.

73. Jacobs locates French refugees at the center of the origins of European Freemasonry. After 1717, Jean Theophile Desaguliers is described as "the guiding force in British Freemasonry" (122); Margaret C. Jacobs, *The Radical Enlightenment: Pantheists, Freemasons and Republicans* (London: George Allen & Unwin, 1981), ch. 4.

74. Yates, *Art of Memory,* 304–5; Bernard Edward Jones, *Freemasons' Book of the Royal Arch* (London: G. G. Harrap, 1957).

75. See *sectio* 2, 48.

76. Ibid., quoted in Yates, *Art of Memory,* 327.

77. Ibid., 339–40.

78. *Philothei Iordani Bruni Nolani recens et completa Ars reminiscendi et in phantastico campo exarandi: ad plurimas in triginta sigillis inquirende, disponendi, atque retinendi implicitas novas rationes & artes introductiones* (London: J. Kingston and J. Charlewood, 1583).

79. Fludd was only nine when Bruno arrived in England in 1581 and thus could not have witnessed the lectures (Fludd entered in 1592, so some at St. John's College, Oxford, would have attended them). This was a period of the growth of skepticism in English learned culture; see Barbara J. Shapiro, *A Culture of Fact: England, 1550–1720* (Ithaca, N.Y.: Cornell University Press, 2000).

80. Yates, *Art of Memory,* 263, 340.

81. Ibid., 207–8.

82. Ibid., 206.

83. The relationship between trapezoids and circles has been established mathematically by the trapezoidal rule, a numerical method for evaluating the area between a curve and an axis by approximating the area with the areas of trapezoids.

84. Nigel Hiscock, *The Wise Master Builder: Platonic Geometry in Plans of Medieval Abbeys and Cathedrals* (Aldershot, UK: Ashgate, 2000), 274.

85. Nicolas Faucherre et al., *Les Fortifications du littoral: La Charente-Maritime* (Paris: Éditions Patrimoines et Médias, 1996), 160–82.

86. This was the case, for example, with the Blockhouse Church, erected in Fort Orange, New Netherlands, as a church and a "place of safety"; the cornerstone was laid on June 2, 1656. See Maud Esther Dilliard, *An Album of New Netherland* (New York: Bramhall House, 1963), fig. 49.

87. See, e.g., Edward Howes to John Winthrop Jr., March 26, 1632, in *Winthrop Papers*, vol. 3: *1631–1637* (Boston: Massachusetts Historical Society, 1943), 73–74.

88. Platt, *Jewell House*, 81.

89. This controversy is explained in Yates, *Art of Memory*, 266–86.

90. Platt, *Jewell House*, 85.

91. Ibid., 84–85.

92. Yates, *Art of Memory*, 285.

93. The second definition of "clog" in the *Oxford English Dictionary* (in use from the fifteenth through the seventeenth centuries) is: "A block or heavy piece of wood, or the like, attached to the leg or neck of a man or beast [usually with a chain], to impede motion or prevent escape."

94. Platt, *Jewell House*, 82–83.

95. Yates, *Art of Memory*, 305.

96. Ibid.

97. Ibid., 305–6.

98. Ibid., 328–29.

99. Jonathan L. Fairbanks and Robert F. Trent, eds., *New England Begins: The Seventeenth Century*, vol. 3: *Style* (Boston: Museum of Fine Arts, 1982), 530–32, entry 488; Trent's attribution of this group of artifacts to a joiner named John Emery of Newbury was retracted in Robert F. Trent, Peter Follansbee, and Alan Miller, "First Flowers of the Wilderness: Mannerist Furniture from a Northern Essex County, Massachusetts, Shop," in *American Furniture, 2001*, ed. Luke Beckerdite (Hanover, N.H.: University Press of New England, 2001), 1–12.

100. Fairbanks and Trent, eds., *New England Begins: The Seventeenth Century*, 3: 532.

101. Ibid. Trent et al. locate Parisian sources in "The Second School of Fountainbleau, ca. 1591–1600," see "First Flowers," 1, 52–53.

102. See Ulrich, "Furniture as Social History," 52–59; see also 53, fig 16, for a color photograph of the Hannah Barnard Cupboard.

103. A legal distinction was usually made between "dower" ("the part of or interest in the real estate of a deceased husband given by law to his widow during her life") and "dowry" ("the money, goods, or estate that a woman brings to her husband in marriage"). In most of colonial America, by law and custom, the husband returned the dowry to his wife's line in his will; see Benno M. Forman, "German Influences in Pennsylvania Furniture," in Scott T. Swank et al., *Arts of the Pennsylvania Germans* (New York: Norton, 1983), 140, n. 94.

104. Platt, *Jewell House*, 81.

105. Quoted in Yates, *Art of Memory*, 214.

106. See Leslie B. Grigsby, *English Slip-Decorated Earthenware at Williamsburg* (Williamsburg, Va.: Colonial Williamsburg Foundation, 1993), 28–37; Alison Grant, *North Devon Pottery:*

The Seventeenth Century (Exeter, UK: University of Exeter Press, 1983), 2–15, 35–116; and Linda Blanchard, ed., *Archaeology in Barnstaple, 1987–8* (Barnstaple, UK: North Devon District Council, 1988), 16–19. On the Windsor shops, see Joshua W. Lane and Donald P. White, "The Woodworkers of Windsor: A Connecticut Community of Craftsmen and their World, 1635–1715," *Catalogue of Antiques and Fine Art* 4, no. 2 (Early Summer 2003): 135–39; and Carol Sims, "Woodworkers of Windsor," *Antiques and the Arts Weekly* (Bee Publishing Co. Newtown, Conn.), May 23, 2003, 1, 40–41. For illustrations of Germanic examples, see Bernard Deneke, *Bauernmöbel: Ein Handbuch für Sammler und Liebhaber* (Munich: Keysersche Verlagsbuchhandlung, 1979), figs. 88, 89, 138, 146–49, 162, 212, 214; and Gisland M. Ritz, *Altegeschnitzte Bauernmöbel* (Munich: Verlag Georg D. W. Callwey, 1978), figs. 13, 15, 19, 48, 52, 74, 173, 222, 226, 229, 250.

107. Brock W. Jobe et al., *American Furniture with Related Decorative Arts, 1630–1830: The Milwaukee Art Museum and the Layton Art Collection* (New York: Hudson Hills Press, 1991), 37; the Peter Blin oral history is recounted in Jane Blinn, "Blinn Genealogical Manuscript," on deposit in the Connecticut Historical Society.

108. While Palissy was self-consciously Paracelsian, La Tour was a Caravaggist, a direct follower of Caravaggio's great Netherlandish disciples, Honthorst and Terbrugghen.

109. See Philip Conisbee et al., *Georges de La Tour and His World* (Washington, D.C.: National Gallery of Art, 1996), 13–148, 183–232; René Taveneaux, *Le Jansenisme en Lorraine 1640–1789* (Paris: Vrin, 1960); Alexander Sedgewick, *Jansenism in Seventeenth-Century France: Voices From the Wilderness* (Charlottesville: University Press of Virginia, 1977); and esp. Elizabeth Vickers, "The Iconography of Georges de La Tour," *Marsyas* 5 (1950): 105–17.

110. William Preston, *Illustrations of Masonry* (London, 1772; Alexandria, Va.: Cotton & Stewart, 1804), 45. The 1804 edition is one of the earliest from an American Press, after ten English editions.

111. On the relation between masonry and material culture in colonial Williamsburg, see F. Carey Howlett, "Admitted into the Mysteries: The Benjamin Bucktrout Masonic Master's Chair," *American Furniture, 1996*, ed. Luke Beckerdite (Hanover, N.H.: University of New England Press, 1996): 195–232.

112. Quoted in Yates, *Art of Memory*, 216.

113. Ibid.

114. Quoted in Ibid., 217.

115. Fludd, "Geomantia," 331.

116. John Foster's "Man of Signs" was titled "The Dominion of the Moon in Man's Body" when it appeared in *An Almanack of Coelestial Motions* (Boston: Printed by John Foster for John Usher, 1678); see Jonathan L. Fairbanks and Robert F. Trent, eds., *New England Begins: The Seventeenth Century, vol. 2: Mentality and Environment* (Boston: Museum of Fine Arts, 1982), 346–47, fig. 363. For more on Franklin's use of the image in *Poor Richard Improved*, see Frank H. Sommer, "German Language Books, Periodicals, and Manuscripts," in Scott T. Swank et al., *Arts of the Pennsylvania Germans* (New York: Norton, 1983), 276–77.

117. Wayne Shumaker, *The Occult Sciences in the Renaissance: A Study in Intellectual Patterns* (Berkeley: University of California Press, 1979), 110.

118. *Philo: The Embassy to Gaius,* trans. F. H. Colson (Cambridge, Mass.: Harvard University Press, 1962), 10.424–25.

119. Jacob, *Radical Enlightenment,* 120.

120. Godwin, *Robert Fludd*, 89.

121. For a discussion of the place of Jason's ship in the early history of Rosicrucianism in the Palatinate, see Yates, *Rosicrucian Enlightenment*, fig. 3 (a) and 10.

122. Julius S. Held, *Rembrandt and the Book of Tobit* (Northampton, Mass.: Gehenna Press, 1964).

123. See *The Book of Tobit*, trans. and ed. Frank Zimmermann (New York: Harper & Brothers, 1958), an edition that pays special attention to folkloric scholarship; see also Randolph Runyon, *Fowles/Irving/Barthes: Canonical Variations on an Apocryphal Theme* (Columbus: Published for Miami University by the Ohio State University Press, 1981), esp. 4–6.

124. *Book of Tobit*, trans. Zimmerman, 5:10–11.

125. Roland Mousnier, *The Institutions of France Under the Absolute Monarchy, 1598–1789: Society and State*, trans. Brian Pearce (Chicago: University of Chicago Press, 1979), 676; see also Sylvester Jenks, *A Short Review of the Book of Jansenius* (London [?]: n.p., 1710); *Philippe de Champaigne et Port-Royal: Musée national des Granges de Port-Royal, 29 avril–28 août 1995* (Paris: Réunion des musées nationaux, 1995); Richard M. Golden, *The Godly Rebellion: Parisian Curés and the Religious Fronde, 1652–1662* (Chapel Hill: University of North Carolina Press, 1981); Alexander Sedgwick, *The Travails of Conscience: The Arnauld Family and the Ancien Régime* (Cambridge, Mass.: Harvard University Press, 1998); and Jacques M. Gres-Gayer, *Le Jansénisme en Sorbonne, 1643–1656* (Paris: Klincksieck, 1996).

126. *Book of Tobit*, trans. Zimmerman, 6:1–10.

127. Ernest Jones, "The Symbolic Significance of Salt in Folklore and Superstition," in id., *Essays in Applied Psycho-analysis* (1923; London: Hogarth Press, 1951), 29 et passim.

128. Yates, *Art of Memory*, 326–27.

129. William Hogarth, *Anecdotes of William Hogarth Written by Himself: With Essays on His Life and Genius, and Criticisms on His Works, Selected from Walpole, Gilpin, J. Ireland, Lamb, Phillips and Others. To Which are Added a Catalogue of His Prints; Account of Their Variations, and Principal Copies; Lists of Paintings, Drawings, &c.* (London: J. B. Nichols & Son, 1833), 1–67.

130. Ibid., 2–3.

131. Ibid., 3.

132. Ibid.

133. Ibid., 3–4.

134. Ibid., 4.

135. Ibid., 13.

136. See how this ambivalence plays itself out poetically in the glazier Jacques-Louis Ménétra's "Epistle to My Mind," in id., *Journal of My Life*, ed. Daniel Roche, trans. Arthur Goldhammer (New York: Columbia University Press, 1986), 239–40.

137. Hogarth, *Anecdotes*, 48–49.

138. Ibid., 4–5.

139. Ibid., 76–77.

140. Ibid.

141. Ibid., 5–6.

142. Ibid., 36–37.

143. Ibid., 48.

144. Ibid., 46–47.

145. Ibid., 47.

146. Ibid., 8.

147. Ibid.

148. Ibid., pp. 9–10.

149. Ibid.

150. Ibid., 8–9.

151. Ibid., 11.

152. Ibid.

153. Ibid., 12.

154. Ibid.

155. Schwartz, *French Prophets*, 216–78.

156. See Lars Tharp, *Hogarth's China: Hogarth's Paintings and Eighteenth-Century Ceramics* (London: Merrell Holberton, 1997). This is a ceramic pitcher, probably redware of the Staffordshire type; similar ceramic pitchers appear in several of Hogarth's paintings and prints; see, e.g., 90, figs. 77–8; 103, fig. 88.

157. Paulson, *Hogarth: His Life, Art, and Times*, 2: 420–21. The final letter arrived shortly after Franklin sent word to Hogarth that the Library Company of Philadelphia intended to purchase a complete set of his engravings. An illustration of *Gin Lane* may be found in Paulson, *Hogarth's Graphic Works*, 370, fig. 186; the pitcher hangs in the middle ground to the right, over the establishment of "Kilman Distiller," a comment on Hogarth's distaste for the vice of drunkenness.

158. See E. Droz, *L'Imprimerie à La Rochelle*, vol. 1: *Barthélemy Berton, 1563–1573*, Travaux d'humanisme et Renaissance, 34 (Geneva: E. Droz, 1960), esp. 1: 26–9, et passim.

159. Berton's title page shows this emblematically as a block of matter in "mixed composition."

160. Pamela H. Smith, *The Business of Alchemy: Science and Culture in the Holy Roman Empire* (Princeton, N.J.: Princeton University Press, 1994), 89.

161. Ibid., 89–91.

FIFTEEN ❧ Hidden in Plain Sight

EPIGRAPH: *The Journal of John Fontaine: An Irish Huguenot Son in Spain and Virginia, 1710–1719*, ed. Edward Porter Alexander (Charlottesville: University Press of Virginia, 1972), 115.

1. These issues are explored in Richard Archer, "New England Mosaic: A Demographic Analysis for the Seventeenth Century," *William and Mary Quarterly* 47, no. 4 (October 1990): 477–502, and David Grayson Allen, *In English Ways: The Movement of Societies and the Transferal of English Local Law and Custom to Massachusetts Bay in the Seventeenth Century* (Chapel Hill: University of North Carolina Press, 1981), and Daniel Vickers, *Farmers and Fishermen: Two Centuries of Work in Essex County, Massachusetts, 1630–1850* (Chapel Hill: University of North Carolina Press, 1994); the pioneering study of the intense, specific localism of seventeenth-century transferal remains Sumner Chilton Powell, *Puritan Village: The Formation of a New England Town* (Middletown, Conn.: Wesleyan University Press, 1963); for the problem of pluralism and diffusion in seventeenth-century New England material culture, see Robert Blair St. George, *The Wrought Covenant: Source Material for the Study of Craftsmen and Community in Southeastern New England, 1620–1700* (Brockton, Mass.: Brockton Art Center / Fuller Memorial, 1979), and Jonathan L. Fairbanks and Robert F. Trent, eds., *New England Begins: The Seventeenth Century* (Boston: Museum of Fine Arts, 1982), esp. vol. 1, *Migration and Settlement*. The dissenting voice

in recent historiography comes from David Hackett Fischer, who maintains the primacy of East Anglian "hearth culture" transferred to colonial New England in *Albion's Seed: Four British Folkways in America* (New York: Oxford University Press, 1989), 13–205. Fischer's synchronic position has been aggressively challenged on both sides of the Atlantic; see Jack P. Greene, Virginia De John Anderson, James Horn, Barry Levy, Ned C. Landsman, and David Hackett Fischer, "Albion's Seed: Four British Folkways in America—A Symposium," *William and Mary Quarterly* 48, no. 2 (April 1991): 224–308.

2. On pluralism in early New York, see Thomas L. Purvis, "The National Origins of New Yorkers in 1790," *New York History* 67, no. 2 (April 1986): 133–50; Nan A. Rothschild, *New York City Neighborhoods: The Eighteenth Century* (New York: Academic Press, 1990); Joyce D. Goodfriend, *Before the Melting Pot: Society and Culture in Colonial New York City, 1664–1730* (Princeton, N.J.: Princeton University Press, 1992); and David S. Cohen, "How Dutch Were the Dutch of New Netherland?" *New York History* 62, no. 1 (January 1981): 43–50. On woodworking artisans, pluralism, and creolization, see Neil Duff Kamil, "Of American Kasten and the Mythology of 'Pure Dutchness': A Review Article," *American Furniture, 1993,* ed. Luke Beckerdite (Hanover, N.H.: University Press of New England, 1993): 275–82; Lonn Taylor and Dessa Bokides, *New Mexican Furniture, 1660–1940: The Origins, Survival, and Revival of Furniture Making in the Hispanic Southwest* (Santa Fe: Museum of New Mexico Press, 1987); and Lonn Taylor, "Hispanic Cabinetmakers and the Anglo-American Aesthetic," *Antiques* 136, no. 3 (September 1989): 554–67.

3. Elizabeth Paling Funk, "Netherlands' Popular Culture in the Knickerbocker Works of Washington Irving," in *New World Dutch Studies: Dutch Arts and Culture in Colonial America, 1609–1776,* ed. Roderic H. Blackburn and Nancy A. Kelley (Albany, N.Y.: Albany Institute of History and Art, 1987), 83–94; and Kamil, "Of American Kasten," 275–82.

4. Benno M. Forman, *American Seating Furniture, 1630–1730: An Interpretive Catalogue* (New York: Norton, 1988), 229–356; for a dissenting view, see Roger Gonzales and Daniel Putnam Brown Jr., "Boston and New York Leather Chairs: A Reappraisal," *American Furniture, 1996,* ed. Luke Beckerdite (Hanover, N.H.: University Press of New England, 1996): 175–94. Unfortunately, whereas Forman draws on painstaking archival research to support his artifactual analysis, Gonzales and Brown present virtually no documentary evidence to support their argument beyond willful assertions of the inherent righteousness of their very personal application of connoisseurship.

5. These inventories represent nearly the total of those known to survive in English from early New York City and Queens and Kings Counties on western Long Island and in northern Brooklyn. Inventories taken in English begin in 1664. The majority of original documents are currently on deposit in the New York State Archives in Albany, as well as in the Klapper Library, Queens College; the New-York Historical Society Library; and the H. F. DuPont Winterthur Museum, Joseph Downs Manuscript Collection.

6. R. W. Symonds, "The English Export Trade in Furniture to Colonial America, Part I," *Antiques* 27, no. 6 (June 1935): 216. The majority of such reports to Parliament (most authored by English merchants and the London guilds), appeared in the 1760s on the heels of the huge debt British taxpayers accumulated after the end of the Seven Years' War in 1763, prompting the Parliamentary Reform Acts; see John J. McCusker and Russel R. Menard, *The Economy of British America, 1607–1789: Needs and Opportunities for Study* (Chapel Hill: University of North Carolina Press, 1985), 190.

7. McCusker and Menard, *Economy of British America,* 92–93.

8. Ibid., 96–110.

9. Richard H. Randall Jr., "Boston Chairs," *Old-Time New England* 54, no. 1 (Summer 1963): 12–16; Brock Jobe, "The Boston Furniture Industry, 1720–1740," in *Boston Furniture of the Eighteenth Century,* ed. Walter Muir Whitehill (Boston: Colonial Society of Massachusetts, 1974), 40; Robert F. Trent, *Hearts and Crowns: Folk Chairs of the Connecticut Coast, 1720–1840: As Viewed in the Light of Henri Focillon's Introduction to "Art Populaire"* (New Haven, Conn.: New Haven Colony Historical Society, 1977), 32–35; see also the inventory of James Nappier of New York City, taken March 26, 1754, in which "6 Boston made leather chaires" are recorded, Joseph Downs Manuscript Collection, Winterthur Museum, acc. 53.190; and on March 28, 1701, Her Majesty's Custom's Clerks recorded that Benjamin Faneuil of New York City was to pay duty on "12 leather chairs [lately arrived on the sloop Rachell from] Boston where the above goods were made," in *An Account of Her Majesty's Revenue in the Province of New York, 1701–1709: The Customs Records of Early Colonial New York,* ed. Julius M. Block, Leo Hershkowitz, Kenneth Scott, and Constance D. Sherman (Ridgewood, N.J.: Gregg Press, 1966), 35. On the significance of talk among consumers about novel items available in the colonial marketplace in the process of anglicization beginning in the 1680s, see Timothy H. Breene, "An Empire of Goods: The Anglicization of Colonial America, 1690–1776," *Journal of British Studies* 25, no. 4 (October 1986): 470–99.

10. William Smith Jr., *The History of the Province of New-York,* vol. 1: *From the First Discovery to the Year 1732,* ed. Michael Kammen (Cambridge, Mass.: Harvard University Press, Belknap Press, 1972), 226; first edition published as William Smith, *The History of the Province of New-York From the First Discovery to the Year MDCCXXXII. To Which is annexed, A Description of the Country, with a short Account of the Inhabitants, their Trade, Religious and Political State, and the Constitution of the Courts of Justice in that Colony* (London: Printed for Thomas Wilcox, 1757).

11. Thomas Fitch Letterbook, microfilm M-1422, Joseph Downs Library, Winterthur Museum. The original letterbooks are now located in the American Antiquarian Society and the Massachusetts Historical Society respectively. For the Faneuil genealogy and the family's transatlantic trading and patronage network, see J. F. Bosher, "Huguenot Merchants and the Protestant International in the Seventeenth Century," *William and Mary Quarterly,* 3d ser., 52, no. 1 (January 1995): 84–92. For the Atlantic trading society of La Rochelle's mercantile community in Canada, see id., *The Canada Merchants, 1713–1763* (Oxford: Clarendon Press, 1987), 3–46, 109–90; and "The Imperial Environment of French Trade with Canada, 1660–1685," *English Historical Review* 108 (January 1993): 50–81.

12. Robert J. Gough, "The Myth of the 'Middle Colonies': An Analysis of Regionalization in Early America," *Pennsylvania Magazine of History and Biography* 103 (July 1983): 394–95. Gough borrows the term "human region" from Lewis Mumford.

13. Fitch Letterbook.

14. Ibid.

15. Population figures from Jack P. Greene, *Pursuits of Happiness: The Social Development of Early Modern British Colonies and the Formation of American Culture* (Chapel Hill: University of North Carolina Press, 1988), 178–80. The middle colonies was among the fastest-growing regions between 1660 and 1710 (in large part due to the "push factor" caused by the continental wars of religion). The concerns of the Board of Trade were focused initially on woolens manufactured on Long Island; see letters from Lord Cornbury to Secretary Hodges in 1705; Caleb Heathcote

to the Board of Trade on August 3, 1708; and Governor Hunter to the Board of Trade on November 12, 1715, in E. B. O'Callaghan, *The Documentary History of the State of New York,* 4 vols. (Albany, N.Y.: Weed, Parsons, & Comp., 1849–51), 1: 711–14.

16. See Neil Kamil, "Discursive Things: Language, Form, and Context in British America" (*American Historical Review,* forthcoming); for a detailed reconstruction of Faneuil's Saintongeais craft network in New York, see chapter 16.

17. For population figures based on census and tax records from 1695 and 1703, see Jon Butler, *The Huguenots in America: A Refugee People in New World Society* (Cambridge, Mass.: Harvard University Press, 1983), 151–2. The English made up 26.4 percent of New York's merchants in 1695; ethnicity was largely determined by surname alone in the study Butler quotes, hence the qualifier "arguably."

18. David Ormrod, "The Atlantic Economy and the `Protestant Capitalist International,' 1651–1775," *Historical Research* 66, no. 160 (June 1993): 197–207. See also Bosher, "Huguenot Merchants and the Protestant International in the Seventeenth Century," 77–100.

19. Fitch Letterbook.

20. Trent, "The Endicott Chairs," *Essex Institute Historical Collections* 114, no. 2 (April 1, 1978): 117–18.

21. Queens College, Klapper Library, Historical Documents Collection, Albany, II, fol. 2–84. When appraisers referred to condition, "old" was often accompanied by specific qualifiers such as "broken" or "much abused."

22. The armchair was sold at the Litchfield Auction Gallery in Litchfield, Connecticut, on January 6, 1991. The consignors reportedly purchased it from an unremembered "dealer in Greenwich, Connecticut about forty years ago." I am grateful to the Litchfield Auction Gallery for providing this information. On the Parisian "grand" chair, see Peter Thornton, "Upholstered Seat Furniture in Europe, Seventeenth and Eighteenth Centuries," in *Upholstery in America and Europe from the Seventeenth Century to World War I,* ed. Edward S. Cooke Jr. (New York: Norton, 1987), 33, fig. 8.

23. According to the *Oxford English Dictionary,* "escritoire" first appears in English in 1611. The migration pattern of the Cortelyou family is typical of the "old" (pre-Revocation) Huguenot diaspora, which usually made its way to New Amsterdam / New York by way of the Netherlands in the seventeenth century. Jacques Cortelyou was the first of the family to settle in New Amsterdam, where he was surveyor-general for the Dutch West India Company by 1660. It was in this capacity that Cortelyou executed his axiometric view of New Amsterdam in 1660, which served as the model for the well-known Castello Plan of 1670 (Biblioteca Medicea Laurenziana, Florence). For more on the Cortelyou and Castello plans, see Roderick H. Blackburn and Ruth Piwonka, *Remembrance of Patria: Dutch Arts and Culture in Colonial America 1609–1776* (Albany: Albany Institute of History and Art, 1988), 93. Cortelyou was born in Utrecht around 1625, according to Jasper Dankers's observations recorded in his *Journal of a Voyage to New York* (September 1679): "Jacques is a man advanced in years. He was born in Utrecht, but of French parents as we could readily discover from all his actions, looks, and language. He studied philosophy in his youth [at the University of Utrecht] and spoke Latin and good French. He was a mathematician and sworn land-surveyor. He had also formerly learned several sciences, and had some knowledge of medicine" (quoted in Maud Esther Dilliard, *Old Dutch Houses of Brooklyn* [New York: Richard R. Smith, 1945], n.p.). It was in this function as surveyor-general that, on February 16, 1660, Cortelyou laid out twenty-two house lots to establish the town of Bushwick

(Bos Wyck, or "Town in the Woods"). This was a Huguenot settlement, which began when fourteen refugees removed to Brooklyn from New Amsterdam (ibid.).

24. *Journal of John Fontaine*, 114–5. Fontaine's father was born in 1658, in Jenouille, Saintonge.

25. For an early map of Kings County roads, see Dilliard, *Old Dutch Houses of Brooklyn*, ix. For an analysis of Kings County and New York City kasten, see Peter M. Kenny, Frances Gruber Stafford, and Gilbert T. Vincent, *American Kasten: The Dutch-Style Cupboards of New York and New Jersey, 1650–1800* (New York: Metropolitan Museum of Art, 1991), 16–21; and cat. no. 8. For the story of the Flushing Remonstrance, see Henry D. Waller, *History of the Town of Flushing* (1899; West Jordan, Utah: Stemmons Publishing, 1988), 44; Haynes Trebor, *The Flushing Remonstrance* (Flushing, N.Y.: The Bowne House Historical Society, 1957), 3–4; and Neil D. Kamil, "'Like a house without a door and lock': Reflections on Religion, Popular Culture and Material Life in Early America: The Middle Colonies and the Upper South, 1650–1800," keynote address, in *Religion, Popular Culture and Material Life in the Middle Colonies and the Upper South, 1650–1800*, ed. Neil Duff Kamil and John J. McCusker, 34–36 (College Park, Md.: Maryland Colloquium on Early American History, 1990).

26. See John T. Kirk, *American Furniture and the British Tradition to 1830* (New York: Knopf, 1982), 235, fig. 752.

27. Peter Thornton, *Seventeenth-Century Interior Decoration in England, France and Holland* (New Haven, Conn.: Yale University Press, 1978), 180–82. The Huguenot settlement at Manakin, Virginia, located twenty miles above the fall line on the James River (or perhaps other Huguenot settlements in southeastern Virginia) is a second, less likely point of origin for this armchair. I am grateful to Luke Beckerdite for bringing this important example to my attention, and for sharing his insights into the role of the large population of French refugee artisans in the furniture production of both Virginia and South Carolina. For an introduction to the history of the Manakin settlement, see James L. Bugg, "Manakin Town in Virginia: Its Story and its People" (M.A. thesis, University of Virginia, 1950). For a photograph and discussion of the South Carolina chair's Huguenot influences, see Ronald Hurst and Jonathan Prown, *Southern Furniture 1680–1730: The Colonial Williamsburg Collection* (Williamsburg, Va.: Colonial Williamsburg Foundation, 1997), 52–54; see also John Bivins Jr., "The French Connection," *Journal of Early Southern Decorative Arts* 28, no. 1 (Summer 2002): 128–35.

28. Thornton, *Seventeenth-Century Interior Decoration*, 198–202. For an illustration of a British version of a sgabello, ca. 1626, see *Western Furniture 1350 to the Present Day in the Victoria and Albert Museum, London*, ed. Christopher Wilk (London: Philip Wilson, 1996), 52–53.

29. On the "double poire" see Forman, *American Seating Furniture*, 226.

30. The Van Cortlandt leather armchair was probably made for the original manor house around the time it was built, in 1697, by Stephanus Van Cortlandt (1643–1700). Stephanus died just three years later, when the chair passed to Philip Van Cortlandt (1683–1748). The chair might also have been made for Philip, since it could date as late as 1720. Upon Philip's death, it was willed to Pierre Van Cortlandt (1721–1814). With the death of Pierre, the armchair passed to Pierre Van Cortlandt II (1762–1843). It then descended to Pierre III. With the passing of Pierre's wife, Catherine Beck, in 1895, the chair was willed to her daughter, Catherine T. R. Van Cortlandt (1838–1921), who married John Rutherford Mathews (1835–1898). Finally, the chair passed to their daughter, Isabel Rutherford Mathews (May 1, 1878–July 24, 1909). When the Van Cortlandt Manor's furnishings were auctioned by Parke Bernet in New York on February 6–8, 1941, and March 7, 1942, the chair was one of the few items held out and it was sold privately to John

D. Rockefeller Jr., who displayed it in the Beekman Wing of Philipsburg Manor, Tarrytown, New York, the first of the properties that he purchased and had conserved for the present museum complex, Historic Hudson Valley. The Van Cortlandt Manor House was sold by Catherine Van Cortlandt Mason Browne, the last of the Van Cortlandt line to live in the ancestral home, in 1945. In 1953, Rockefeller purchased it for Sleepy Hollow Restorations (now Historic Hudson Valley), and in 1959, he returned the Van Cortlandt leather armchair to the second story hall, where it remains today. See Joseph T. Butler, *The Family Collections at Van Cortlandt Manor* (Tarrytown, N.Y.: Sleepy Hollow Restorations, 1967), 20, 42–3; "The Ancestral Record of the Family of Van Cortlandt" (holograph), Library, Historic Hudson Valley, Tarrytown, New York; and auction catalogues, Parke Bernet New York, February 6–8, 1941, and March 7, 1942. I am most grateful to Joseph T. Butler, director and curator emeritus of collections at Historic Hudson Valley, for his assistance with this genealogy.

31. The chair was in the Bybee Collection, Dallas, Texas, when it was nearly destroyed by fire in the 1970s. The remains of the scorched frame are now in storage at the Museum of Fine Arts, Boston.

32. This construction evidence should further discredit the tenacious argument that the New York leather chair was in fact produced either in Boston or, an even more remote possibility, the fledgling Piscataqua region of New Hampshire. The logic of the latter argument, first advanced by some dealers and antiquarians in the 1960s because a number of such chairs were supposedly "found" there, and now revived (along with the Boston thesis) on the basis of extremely tenuous physical evidence and no documentary evidence by Roger Gonzales and Daniel Putnam Brown Jr. (see n. 4 above), is particularly difficult to accept because of "Piscataqua's" close proximity to insurmountable competition from Boston, the region's indisputable entrepôt where a number of upholsterers plied their trade in an urban setting appropriate to their commercial and production needs, and where New Hampshire's elites went to purchase their leather chairs. Even a brief survey of the literature on seventeenth- and early eighteenth-century southeastern New Hampshire indicates that by no stretch of the imagination could an urban upholstery network such as ones in Boston and New York have been supported by the limited population and resources available there during this period. Finally, the Piscataqua leather chair "thesis" has failed even to attract notice, let alone support, in a plethora of the most recent research and publication on the early New Hampshire furniture industry. For the latter, see Brock Jobe, ed., *Portsmouth Furniture: Masterworks from the New Hampshire Seacoast* (Hanover, N.H.: University Press of New England, 1992); Gerald W. R. Ward, "Three Centuries of Life Along the Piscataqua River," *Antiques* 142, no. 1 (July 1992): 60–65; and Gerald W. R. Ward and Karin E. Cullity, "The Furniture," *Antiques* 142, no. 1 (July 1992): 94–103.

33. I. N. Phelps Stokes, *The Iconography of Manhattan Island, 1498–1909* (New York: R. H. Dodd, 1922), 4: 422. The historian Charles W. Baird argued that Jean was probably born in Saint-Lô, Normandy, because that was the ancestral seat of the family name Chevalier (Baird, *History of the Huguenot Emigration to America,* 2 vols. [New York: Dodd, Mead, 1885], 2: 280). However, I discovered many Chevaliers in the archives for Saintonge, where it was a common Huguenot name. Like many Huguenots from the northwest coast of France, Jean's branch of Le Chevaliers may have moved to the southwest during the civil wars. Strong evidence of a Saintongeais origin for the Le Chevaliers of New Amsterdam / New York, may be found in "*Recueil* de manuscrits sur les églises reformées de France reunie par les soins de Mr. Alexandre Crottet, ancien Pastur des églises Reformées de Pons, Gemozac et Mortagne en Saintonge," in *Huguenot*

Records, 1578–1787, reproduced by the South Carolina Historical Society in 1981 from records at the Charleston [S.C.] Library Society (SCHS-51-31-1). There were also numerous Jean Chevaliers recorded in the birth, marriage, death, and burial registers of Aunis in the seventeenth century, where they were located predominantly on the coast, particularly on the Île de Ré and in La Rochelle; see "Table des Baptemes faits a St. Martin isle de Re par M. Barbault, le pere, ministre en 1685, jusques et compris le mois de Septembre. Copiee sur le Registre de la dite Egise de 1685," in Notes et collections d'érudits, Archives préfectoraux de La Rochelle, files J. 102 and 103, handwritten manuscripts by J. Pandin de Lussaudiere, n.p. See also Edward Elbridge Salisbury, *Family Memorials: A Series of Genealogical and Biographical Monographs,* 2 vols. (privately printed, 1885), 2: 540–44. Salisbury also argues on the basis of the unique Chevalier coat of arms that Jean Le Chevalier Sr. probably came from Brittany, not Normandy, but he does admit that the family was fragmented early into separate branches, which moved to other areas in France. All the evidence suggests that the Le Chevaliers of New York originated in Normandy and that a branch moved to Saintonge. After the Revocation, Jean Le Chevalier's family moved to London. On April 9, 1687, they appeared on a list of refugees who were issued a warrant for naturalization at Whitehall. John Jr., the eldest child, would then have been about seventeen. There may have been a branch of this mobile family in Charleston during the late seventeenth and early eighteenth centuries as well. Joiner Pierre Le Chevalier's property is listed in *A Compleat Description of the Province of Carolina,* published by Edward Crisp and printed ca. 1711 (I thank Luke Beckerdite for this information).

34. Baird, *History of the Huguenot Emigration,* 2: 212. *New York Historical Manuscripts Dutch: The Register of Salomon Lachaire Notary Public of New Amsterdam, 1661, 1662,* trans. E. B. O'-Callachan, ed. Kenneth Scott and Kenneth Stryker-Rodda (Baltimore: Genealogical Publishing Co., 1978), xii, xvi. Salomon La Chair was baptized in Amsterdam's Walloon Church on January 30, 1628. For Jean Chevalier's City Hall contract, see Stokes, *Iconography of Manhattan Island,* 4: 305.

35. *New York Genealogical and Biographical Record* 15, no. 1 (January 1884): 36. Valenciennes entered the maelstrom of Reformation confessional conflict as early as the 1560s, when public singing of Marot's psalms and other "impious songs" was deemed threatening enough to warrant an official interdiction of similar heretical activities. See Donald R. Kelley, *The Beginning of Ideology: Consciousness and Society in the French Reformation* (Cambridge: Cambridge University Press, 1981), 99.

36. See Baird, *History of the Huguenot Emigration,* 2: 80. For Le Chevalier's involvement in the Eglise français, see *Collections of the Huguenot Society of America,* 1 (New York, 1886). For a longer discussion of the significance of Le Chevalier's dual church allegiances, see Kamil, "Of American Kasten," 278. For more on Joshua Delaplaine's artisanal activity, see J. Steward Johnson, "New York Cabinetmaking Prior to the Revolution" (M.A. thesis, University of Delaware, 1964), 23–24.

37. *New York State Calendar: English, 1664–1776,* 15 (Albany, N.Y.: Office of the Secretary of State, 1865–66), 247; *Collections of the New-York Historical Society* (New York: Printed for the Society, 1886), 58; John Chevalier vs. Duie Hungerford, Mayor's Court, June 11, 1700; and Albany I, fol. 1–11; and Queens College, Klapper Library, Historical Documents Collection, Mayor's Court Papers, 1. In an indenture dated June 1, 1700, the New York joiner Edward Burling agreed to "Give to his Said Apprentice a good Sett of Carpenters Tools & Shall learn him to write Read

& Cypher" (*Collections of the New-York Historical Society* [1886]: 585). On Jean Bouyer, see Morgan H. Seacord, *Biographical Sketches and Index of the Huguenot Settlers of New Rochelle, 1687–1776* (New Rochelle, N.Y.: Huguenot and Historical Association of New Rochelle, 1941), 15.

38. See payments by Thomas Weaver, Customs House, June 25– September 25, 1701, in *Account of Her Majesty's Revenue,* ed. Block et al., 34.

39. As a communicant in New York's first Trinity Church, the wealthiest and most politically powerful Anglican congregation in the city, Ellison's status was assured when he was awarded the prestigious contract to build its first pulpit. See *First Recorded Minutes Regarding the Building of Trinity Church in the City of New York: 1696–1697,* Trinity Church: Office of the Parish Archives, entry for October 5, 1696; and *Corporation of Trinity Church Minutes of the Vestry,* Trinity Church: Office of the Parish Archives, 1: 1697–1791, 221–22, 229. As of November 16, 1725, Ellison's outstanding debts totaled £8165.1.1½, and Jean Le Chevalier was among the debtors. See the inventory and "Book Debts from the Ledger of John Ellison, in the Hands of John Ellison, Jr." (also a joiner), Albany I, fol. 2–94, Queens College, Klapper Library, Historical Documents Collection; and the inventory of John Ellison Jr., October 6, 1730, New-York Historical Society Manuscript Division.

40. Fitch Letterbook. See also *Collections of the New-York Historical Society* (1886): 87. Richard Lott "upholsterer" became a freeman on September 30, 1707. The mayor's court referred to him as a "chairmaker" in a suit for nonpayment of debts (Richard Lott vs. Johannes Cuyler and John Cruger, October 21, 1707, Queens College, Klapper Library, Historical Documents Collection, Mayor's Court Papers.)

41. Fitch Letterbooks. On the notion of "unintended performance," see J. G. A. Pocock, *The Languages of Political Theory in Early Modern Europe* (Cambridge: Cambridge University Press, 1987), 31; and Peter Sahlins, "Fictions of a Catholic France: The Naturalization of Foreigners, 1685–1787," *Representations,* no. 47 (Summer 1994): 97.

42. By 1720, New York hardware merchants began stocking British upholstery materials in response to their declining availability from Boston merchants. Abraham Brock, lately a "merchant of Bristol," offered a tremendous quantity of textiles and yardgoods, woodworkers tools, a variety of hinges, latches, and standard upholstery materials including "7/8 of a gross of girth webb att 1:0:3," "41 bosses [probably boss-nails or metal studs] 0:3:5," and "3 Doz Tufting nails 0:3:5" (Inventory of Abraham Brock, May 4, 1720, Queens College, Klapper Library, Historical Documents Collection, fol. 2–37).

43. A. V. Phillips, *The Lott Family in America* (Ann Arbor, Mich.: Edward Brothers, 1942), 1–2; see also *Collections of the St. Nicholas Society of the City of New York: Genealogical Record* 4 (1934): 185. On patterns of Huguenot migration, see Warren C. Scoville, *The Persecution of the Huguenots and French Economic Development, 1680–1720* (Berkeley: University of California Press, 1960), 6. For example, George and Monwers Lott of New Utrecht were both carpenters active in the 1750s.

44. Archives départementales de la Charente-Maritime (hereafter ADCM), B 1325; 1350; 1417; 1492; 1568 and E suppl. 297; 317; 364; 800; 906; 907; 913; also E suppl. 317; 369; 1746–48.

45. On Suire's Saintongeais background, see Seacord, *Biographical Sketches and Index of the Huguenot Settlers of New Rochelle,* 50. Inventory of Jean Suire, Queens College, Klapper Library, Historical Documents Collection, Albany II, fol. 2–256.

46. Although the tools, materials and skills involved in saddlery, shoemaking, and leather

upholstery are related, Suire is unusual in having worked as a joiner and shoemaker. However, as we have seen, the Suires of La Rochelle ran a public house that shoemakers frequented with enough regularity to merit the attention of local police.

47. Some early Louisiana furniture was undoubtedly made by creole slaves and freedmen working in distinctive French regional idioms; see Jessie J. Poesch, *Early Furniture of Louisiana, 1750–1830* (New Orleans: Louisiana State Museum, 1972), 18–9, 33. New York artisans also exploited slave labor, a fact clearly evidenced by Jean Suire's "1 Negro about 8 yeares . . . 12:0:0" (Inventory of Jean Suire). On African-American artisans in early New York, see Shane White, *Somewhat More Independent: The End of Slavery in New York City, 1770–1810* (Athens: University of Georgia Press, 1991). On the church of Saint-Étienne, see *Inventaire général des monuments et des richesses artistiques de la France, Commission régionale de Poitou-Charentes, Charente-Maritime, Cantons Île de Ré* (Paris: Ministère de la culture, Direction du patrimoine, 1979), 153, 184–85.

48. Given this regional association, it is not surprising that the carved crest and front stretchers of the chair also recall italianate architectural models and designs carried into southwestern France from northern Italy during the late sixteenth century. As we have seen, elite elements of southwestern Protestant culture—including local Saintongeais nobility and such churchmen as the young Jean Calvin—made the pilgrimage south to seek patronage in northern Italy. Some varieties of London caned chairs also evidence this turning sequence.

49. In 1685, John Thomas of Hempstead, Queens County, owned "6 Cane Chars 3/0/0 [and] 6 Black Chars 1/4/0" (inventoried in order to signify a full "set" of twelve), but no leather chairs (inventory of John Thomas, 1685, Queens College, Klapper Library, Historical Documents Collection, Albany 1: 1–124).

50. Variants of the *cloture*'s carved floral panels also relate to coastal Connecticut carved and painted furniture. Compare particularly with carved work on case furniture traditionally associated with Blin and examples of painted furniture usually associated with Charles Guillam on the Connecticut shore, including the chest of drawers illustrated in figure 5.8 and, among many other examples, two painted chests in Winterthur Museum, illustrated in Dean A. Fales Jr., *American Painted Furniture, 1660–1880* (New York: Bonanza Books, 1986), 26–27, figs. 24–25. For evidence of these and other important Huguenot woodworking networks dispersed to the Long Island Sound region, see Robert F. Trent, "A Channel Islands Parallel for the Early Eighteenth-Century Connecticut Chests Attributed to Charles Guillam," *Studies in the Decorative Arts* 2, no. 1 (Fall 1994): 75–91; and Susan Prendergast Schoelwer, "Connecticut Sunflower Furniture: A Familiar Form Reconsidered," *Yale University Art Gallery Bulletin*, Spring 1989: 21–38; Schoelwer makes the case here that the sunflower is in fact a "Huguenot marigold." On Ezekial Carré, see Forman, *American Seating Furniture*, 226.

51. For the southwestern French backgrounds of the Durand and Coutant families, see Baird, *History of the Huguenot Emigration*, 2: 21, 61, 332, 1: 306. See also Jacqueline Calder, "Westchester County, New York Furniture," *Antiques* 121, no. 5 (May 1982): 1195–98; Benno M. Forman, "The Crown and York Chairs of Coastal Connecticut and the Work of the Durands of Milford," in *Pilgrim Century Furniture: An Historical Survey*, ed. Robert F. Trent (New York: Main Street / Universe Books, 1976), 158–65; Trent, *Hearts and Crowns*, 29–59; and Kathleen Eagen Johnson, "The Fiddleback Chair," in *Early American Furniture from Settlement to City: Aspects of Form, Style, and Regional Design from 1620 to 1830*, ed. Mary Jean Madigan and Susan Colgan (New York: Billboard Publications, 1983), 92–97. See also Trent, "Channel Islands Parallel," and Schoelwer, "Connecticut Sunflower Furniture."

52. What I call creolization is well documented as an art historical process in England and the Low Countries in Thornton, *Seventeenth-Century Interior Decoration.*

53. Forman, "Crown and York Chairs," 158, fig. 1. On Pierre Durand, see Baird, *History of the Huguenot Emigration,* 2: 332.

54. "The life of form" is borrowed from Henri Focillion's seminal essay of the same name, *La Vie des formes* (Paris: Presses universitaires de France, 1934). Forman, *American Seating Furniture,* 292–94.

55. Forman, *American Seating Furniture,* 292–94. In different examples using the same artifactual language, truncated columns, vases, twists, and other lapidary forms stacked symmetrically between and above the balusters are also commonly found. The Van Cortlandt leather armchair is exceptional in that it does not possess a slit under the crest rail. The term "french hollow" was never acknowledged by Forman, although he did carefully note this formal idiosyncrasy in relation to Boston models.

56. Ibid., 293–94.

57. Ibid., 293, caption for fig. 162. See esp. the London cane armchair illustrated in Peter M. Kenny, "Flat Gates, Draw Bars, Twists, and Urns: New York's Distinctive, Early Baroque Oval Tables with Falling Leaves," *American Furniture, 1994,* ed. Luke Beckerdite (Hanover, N.H.: University Press of New England, 1994): 120, fig. 25. The posts of this chair are nearly the same as the leather armchair illustrated in fig. 15.24. In a recent discussion of the London high-back Turkey-work chair illustrated in fig. 15.36, Margaret Swain argues that the slit in the chair's crest rail may have been to accommodate varying, pre-cut sizes of Turkey-work upholstery exclusively, and that "many" surviving New York chairs now covered in leather were probably originally Turkey-work (Margaret Swain, "The Turkey-work Chairs of Holyroodhouse," in *Upholstery in America and Europe,* ed. Cooke, 56–57). This theory is undermined by several chairs with this construction technique and original leather upholstery, including the "European" leather chair and a New York leather chair at the Van Alen House in Kinderhook, New York (Collections of the Columbia County Historical Society), as well as evidence that leather panels may also have been pre-cut. More likely, the slit was simply a sturdy, efficient, and economical way to upholster both Turkey-work and leather chairs. Two similar twist-turned and carved London cane chairs descended in the Wright family of Oyster Bay, Long Island and the Smith family of New York City and Setauket, Long Island. Both are illustrated in Dean F. Failey, *Long Island Is My Nation: The Decorative Arts and Craftsmen, 1640–1830* (Setauket, N.Y.: Society for the Preservation of Long Island Antiquities, 1976), 24, figs. 19, 20.

58. Forman, *American Seating Furniture,* 293, fig. 162. Daniel Marot's contribution to the Anglo-French and Dutch court style is discussed at length in Thornton, *Seventeenth-Century Interior Decoration,* 40–96.

59. *Inventaire général,* 153. There is a local tradition that the choir screen may have originally been made for the Jesuit chapel in Saintes, the principal Gallo-Roman city in Saintonge, but there is no evidence to support this assertion. It probably dates from 1629, but its present overall form is the result of restoration campaigns undertaken in 1845 and 1891, when the screen, which had been separated into three distinct sections during the eighteenth century, was reassembled.

60. Forman, *American Seating Furniture,* 152–53. This chair may have been made by Jean Le Chevalier's paternal grandfather, "Jan Cavelier," who framed and repaired the royal arms on New York's city hall in 1675, or by a contemporary New York joiner and carver. Most significantly, as

the subject of diffusion of motifs, a cherub with goat feet appears as a central motif in the design book of John Berger (working ca. 1718–32), a Boston Huguenot painter-stainer whose family originated in La Rochelle. See Robert A. Leath, "Jean Berger's Design Book: Huguenot Trades-men and the Dissemination of French Baroque Style," *American Furniture, 1994,* ed. Luke Beck-erdite (Hanover, N.H.: University Press of New England, 1994): 138, 145.

61. As quoted in Sahlins, "Fictions of a Catholic France," 85. State sponsored suppression of heresy did not end officially in France until the Edict of Toleration in November 1787.

62. The use of this method and language of assimilation is exemplified by Jon Butler in his otherwise excellent *The Huguenots in America: A Refugee People in New World Society* (Cam-bridge, Mass.: Harvard University Press, 1983); see pt. 2, "The Disappearance of the Huguenots in America," 69–198. For Butler's argument that "no significant stylistic differences separate the work of Huguenot from non-Huguenot silversmiths in the colonies," see 178–81. As quoted in Arthur Herman, "The Saumur Assembly, 1611: Huguenot Political Belief and Action in the Age of Marie de Medici," (Ph.D. diss., Johns Hopkins University, 1985), 36.

63. For a discussion of the interaction in social history methodology of folklore, linguistics, creolization, and pluralistic cultural convergence, see Charles Joyner, "A Single Southern Cul-ture: Cultural Interaction in the Old South," in *Black and White Cultural Interaction in the Ante-bellum South,* ed. Ted Ownby (Jackson: University Press of Mississippi, 1993), 11–17. For two classic formulations of this methodology, see Dell Hymes, *Foundations in Sociolinguistics: An Ethnographic Approach* (Philadelphia: University of Pennsylvania Press, 1974), and William Labov, *The Social Stratification of English In New York City* (New York: Center for Applied Lin-guistics, 1966), esp. 7–15.

64. Jack P. Greene, *Imperatives, Behaviors, and Identities: Essays in Early American Cultural History* (Charlottesville, Va.: University Press of Virginia, 1992), 9–11.

65. The term "French-turned" refers to an inward spiral turning brought to London by Huguenot turners. Spiral turning, when reduced to two dimensions, appears either as a series of serpentine lines or concentric circles; see R. W. Symonds, "Charles II Couches, Chairs and Stools 1660–1670," *Connoisseur* 93, no. 389 (January 1934): 19–20. The anthropologist Edward T. Hall suggests that, in general, "French handling of public and private space is sociopetal," whereas the English is "sociofugal" (Edward T. Hall, *The Hidden Dimension* [New York: Anchor Books, 1969]), 146–48.

66. Quentin Skinner, "Meaning and Understanding in the History of Ideas," *History and Theory* 8, no. 1 (1969): 48.

67. Christian Norberg-Schulz, *Intentions in Architecture* (Cambridge, Mass.: MIT Press, 1965), 29. Alfred Schutz, *Collected Papers,* vol. 1: *The Problem of Social Reality,* ed., Maurice Natanson (The Hague: Martinus Nijhoff, 1962), 229–30. Mary Douglas, *Risk and Blame: Essays in Cultural Theory* (London: Routledge, 1992), esp. 19: "In cognitive theory . . . the psyche is . . . primarily social. The social preoccupations of the person, infant or adult, would be like control gates through which all information has to pass. . . . News that is going to be accepted as true information has to be wearing a badge of loyalty to the particular political regime which the per-son supports; the rest is suspect, deliberately censored or unconsciously ignored."

68. Jean-François Nicéron, *La Perspective curieuse, ou, Magie artificielle des Effets merveilleux de l'optique . . . la catoptrique . . . ladioptrique . . .* (Paris: Pierre Billaine, 1638), quotations from the title page. I am grateful to Orest Ranum for bringing this important reference to my attention.

69. See the epigraph to this chapter.

70. In this context, perhaps the best evidence of the instability of convergence was the inability of New York's artisans to respond effectively to the more complex symbolic language that accompanied Boston's new-fashioned "crook'd back" chair with "horsebone feet"—the artifact that finally supplanted the Boston and New York plain leather chair after it first appeared in the city around 1722. This chair was defined by *both* its upholstery *and* its frame. For more on the Boston "crook'd back" chair, see Forman, *American Seating Furniture,* 296–356. For the classic text on the mechanically reproduced artifact, see Walter Benjamin, "The Work of Art in the Age of Mechanical Reproduction," in *Illuminations,* ed. Hannah Arendt (New York: Schocken Books, 1969), 217–52. See also Fredric Jameson, *Postmodernism, or, The Cultural Logic of Late Capitalism* (Durham, N.C.: Duke University Press, 1991), ix–xxii.

71. O'Callaghan, ed., *Documentary History of the State of New York,* 3: 259–62.

72. Ibid., 260.

73. Ibid., 262. The mayor's council met with Cornbury on March 4, 1708, and dismissed the charges "unanimously."

74. Meschinet de Richemond, "La Liberté de conscience dans la Marine à partir de 1685 d'apres les archives navales de Rochefort," *Bulletin de la Societé de l'Histoire du Protestantisme français* 51 (February 15, 1902): 88.

75. Charles W. Baird, *History of the Huguenot Emigration to America* (New York: Dodd, Mead, 1885), 2: 218–20; 220 n. 1.

76. Ibid., 209.

77. de Richemond, "Liberté de Conscience," 92.

78. Baird, *History of the Huguenot Emigration,* 1: 281.

SIXTEEN ❧ Fragments of Huguenot-Quaker Convergence in New York

1. Robert Fludd, *De naturae simia seu technia macrocosmi historia* (Nature's Ape, or History of the Macrocosmic Arts) (Oppenheim: Johann Theodore de Bry, 1618; 2d ed., Frankfurt; id., 1624), 718–20; I quote the English translation of the original Latin text by C. H. Josten, "Robert Fludd's Theory of Geomancy and His Experiences at Avignon in the Winter of 1601 to 1602," *Journal of the Warburg and Courtauld Institutes* 27 (1964): 332.

2. Joscelyn Godwin, *Robert Fludd: Hermetic Philosopher and Surveyor of Two Worlds* (Boulder, Colo.: Shambhala, 1979), 7.

3. Robert Fludd, *Of the Internal Principle of Terrestrial Astrology or Geomancy,* trans. Josten in "Robert Flood's Theory of Geomancy," 332.

4. Alfred Baudrillart, *Dictionnaire d'histoire et de géographie ecclésiastiques* (Paris: Letouzey & Ané, 1930), 5: col. 1134.

5. Fludd, *Of the Internal Principle,* 332.

6. Ibid.

7. Ibid., 332–33.

8. Ibid., 333.

9. Ibid.

10. Ibid.

11. Ibid., see also n. 19: "After 1590, the vice-legates were the actual governors of the papal estates at Avignon, while the office of legate, usually held by a relative of the pope, became purely nominal."

12. Ibid.

13. Ibid.

14. Ibid., 334.

15. Ibid.

16. Ibid.

17. On repetition and the task of Bourbon court historians, see Orest A. Ranum, *Artisans of Glory: Writers and Historical Thought in Seventeenth-Century France* (Chapel Hill: University of North Carolina Press, 1980).

18. Fludd, *Of the Internal Principle,* trans. Josten in "Robert Flood's Theory of Geomancy," 334.

19. Ibid. The translation of *petitor* as "seeker" seems appropriate and readable in this context.

20. Ibid., 334–35.

21. "John and Samuel Bowne Account Book, 1649–1703," New York Public Library, Main Branch, Manuscript Division, n.p., n.d. The next series of notations are from the year 1690.

22. "The Minutes of the Flushing Yearly Meeting, Later Called the New York Yearly Meeting, from its First Session in 1696 to 1702 Inclusive," 2, New York Friends Library; "copied from original by John Cox, Jr., and George W. Cocks, engrossed by James Close (1895–1898)."

23. On the renovation campaigns on the Flushing meetinghouse, see Henry Onderdonk Jr., *The Annals of Hempstead, 1643 to 1832; also, The Rise and Growth of the Society of Friends On Long Island and in New York, 1657 to 1826* (Hempstead, N.Y.: Lott Van de Water, 1878), 94–95; and Ann Gidley Lowry, *The Story of the Flushing Meeting House* (Flushing, N.Y.: Flushing Monthly Meeting of the Religious Society of Friends, 1969), 5–6, 19–26. New York was not deterred by the poverty that saved Massachusetts houses. The city's seventeenth-century sites are mostly hidden underground, buried in the wake of expansion.

24. See R. Peter Mooz, "Robert Feke," in *American Painting to 1776: A Reappraisal,* ed. Ian M. G. Quimby (Winterthur, Del.: Henry Francis du Pont Winterthur Museum, 1971), 181–92.

25. See "The Feake Family of Norfolk, London and Colonial America," *New York Genealogical and Biographical Record* 86, no. 3 (July 1955): 132–48.

26. "John and Samuel Bowne Account Book, 1649–1703."

27. Ibid., n.p., entry dated "3. day 3 mo 1696."

28. Ibid., "19th: of ye: 2d: mo: 1680"; see also other references to Clay in 1680, though of unspecified date and unpaginated.

29. Mayor's Court Papers, 1, September 9, 1732, Queens College, Klapper Library, Manuscript Division. Blake pleaded *non assumpsit* to the charge. "John Blake, Shipwright," was declared a freeman of the City of New York on December 9, 1718; see *Collections of the New-York Historical Society* (1886): 98. On March 24, 1732, Blake sued Zebediah Hunt for £6.10s. owed (and £10 damages) on "1 main mast 1 foremast and 1 boom," see Mayor's Court Papers, 1, March 24, 1732. On Blake's Irish descent, see "Blake Family," vertical file in the New York Public Library, Genealogy Division, and Samuel W. Eager, *A History of Orange County, New York* (New York, 1846), on the Blakes who were early settlers of Neeleytown.

30. "John and Samuel Bowne Account Book," n.p., under "31th: 11th mth of 1680." Frames of the few surviving early western Long Island houses were commonly made of hard pine, whereas the framed houses of Massachusetts Bay were usually oak. See Abbott L. Cummings, James Sexton, and Christopher Nevins, "A Walking Tour of Ogdon House, Fairfield, Connecticut," in *The Impact of New Netherlands upon the Colonial Long Island Basin: Report of a Yale-*

Smithsonian Seminar . . . May 3–5, 1990 (New Haven, Conn., and Washington, D.C.: The Yale and Smithsonian Seminar on Material Culture, 1993), ed. Joshua W. Lane, 27; and Abbott Lowell Cummings, *The Framed Houses of Massachusetts Bay, 1625–1725* (Cambridge, Mass.: Harvard University Press, 1979). Hard pine was often used as a secondary wood in colonial New Amsterdam / New York furniture as well.

31. "John and Samuel Bowne Account Book," n.p., found under "3d: of ye 6th month 1684."

32. See Van Santvoord Merle-Smith, The Village of *Oyster Bay: Its Founding and Growth from 1653 to 1700* (New York: Doubleday, 1953); Dean F. Failey, *Long Island Is my Nation: The Decorative Arts and Craftsmen, 1640–1830* (Setauket, N.Y.: Society for the Preservation of Long Island Antiquities, 1976), 291–92; original woodwork recovered from the west room of the Oyster Bay house (ca. 1667) of Job Wright, possibly Peter's son, has survived in the collections of Winterthur Museum. The room displays very typical southeastern New England framed construction. The progenitor of the Wright Family of Oyster Bay was Peter Wright, a New England Quaker who immigrated in 1653. Many Wrights were woodworkers.

33. On the Andrews Family of Flushing and New York City, see Mary Powell Bunker, *Long Island Genealogies: Being Kindred Descendants of Thomas Powell of Bethpage, Long Island, 1688* (Baltimore: Genealogical Publishing Company, 1976), 170–71; and Charles F. Cochran, *From Seven Generations of the Ancestry of Captain Abram Piatt Andrew* (New York: privately printed, n.d.), see genealogical chart. Cochran raised the possibility that the Long Island Andrews were lowland Scots. There is no dispute from any quarter that the family was "British."

34. Onderdonk, *Annals of Hempstead,* 96.

35. *Massachusetts Historical Society Collections,* 3d ser., 10 (1849): 27–28; similarly, on December 10, 1675, Williams wrote Winthrop: "You have always bene noted for tendernes toward mens soules, especially for conscience sake to God. You have always bene noted for tendernes toward the bodjes & infirmities of poor mortels." (ibid., 4th ser., 6 (1863): 305–6).

36. Bunker, *Long Island Genealogies,* 170–71.

37. Collections of the *New-York Historical Society: Burghers and Freemen, 1675–1866; Apprentices, 1694–1707* (1885): 92.

38. The probate inventory of "Germanicus Andrew, Upholsterer of New York City" was appraised by Lancaster Symms and Edward Pennant on May 29, 1718: Queens College, Albany II, folder 2–7.

39. See Queens College, Klapper Library, Archival Division, Mayor's Court Papers, 1: December 13, 1718, Joseph Howard vs. Edward Burling; March 19, 1727, Edward Burling vs. Barent Deforeest (De Forest); May 1, 1727, Edward Burling vs. Barent Defreest (De Forest).

"Anthony Chishull, Upholsterer," named freeman January 28, 1702, *Collections of the New-York Historical Society* (1886): 76; see also Philadelphia Wills, Henry Francis du Pont Winterthur Museum Library, Joseph Downs Manuscript Collection, 73/1702 (made Jamaica, W.I., May 31, 1702; entered at New York City August 10, 1702); the geographic mobility of this upholsterer may be gleaned from the following excerpt from his will: "I give and bequeath unto my loving brother John Chiswell in London and [my wife Ann] Chiswell in New York all my real & personall Estate of what nature and quality or condition soever whereof I now posses'd or any way Invested in England New York Pennsylvania or Elsewhere." (I am grateful to Ellen Rosenthal for bringing the latter reference to my attention.) "Thomas Wenman, Upholsterer"; "John Schultz, Upholsterer," named freemen, *Collections of the New-York Historical Society* (1885): 99, 136; on Wileman, see *New York Gazette,* no. 278, February 16–23, 1730; Vestry Minutes of Trinity Church in

New York, Trinity Church Archives, May 1, 1711, July [?], 1719, July 9, 1727, May 10, 1732, and August 23, 749.

Chiswell, who settled in New York in 1701—by way of London and Philadelphia—died just one year later, while trading on the island of Jamaica. Thomas Wenman and John Schultz appear in the records once only, when named freemen of the city, on November 10, 1719, and June 27, 1738, respectively. After that both men simply disappear from the records. This in itself was unusual for active upholsterers. As high-level artisans, merchants, middlemen, and designers, upholsterers were recorded in transactions more frequently than other craftsmen, and they commonly appear in the accounts of both producers and consumers. Since upholsterers' customers were elite, the survival rate for documentation is also unusually high.

Henry Wileman had a somewhat longer, albeit checkered, career. Early in his working life, Wileman was an active member of Trinity Church (Anglican), where the vestry minutes recorded his donation of £1.10s toward a new church steeple in 1711. Wileman was elected a vestryman of Trinity in 1719. In 1727, he purchased a patent for "whole" pew number 108, toward the back of the opulent new building, but still potent proof of Wileman's success and high social aspirations. After this, there is no mention of Wileman the upholsterer, and it would appear that he diversified unsuccessfully into mercantile ventures and land speculation. He may also served as an attorney for other artisans. Three times between 1718 and 1727, one "Mr. Wileman" was recorded as an attorney in the mayor's court, where he represented Edward Burling, a New York Quaker joiner with Flushing family ties and strong connections to the city's Huguenot community (more will be said about him below). However, on May 10, 1732, the Trinity vestry minutes reported that "Mr. Henry Wileman late of this city but now residing in the Country," had petitioned to be relieved of payment for the pew he purchased so proudly in 1727 if he agreed to relinquish his claim to the patent. On the same day, the vestry agreed to arrange all the details of this settlement. On August 23, 1749, the next time Wileman's name was mentioned, it was merely to record his death, although the vestry had distanced itself by then and was uncertain of the exact date.

40. Letter of June 15, 1730, from Thomas Fitch to Madame Renaudet, Thomas Fitch Letter Book, Henry Francis du Pont Winterthur Museum Library, Joseph Downs Manuscript Collection (M-1422).

41. This process of artisanal convergence between Huguenots and Quakers was already under way in the London refugee ghetto of Spitalfields and the other eastern out parishes; see Catherine Swindlehurst, "'An unruly and presumptuous rabble': The Reaction of the Spitalfields Weaving Community to the Settlement of the Huguenots, 1660–90," in *From Strangers to Citizens: The Integration of Immigrant Communities in Britain, Ireland, and Colonial America, 1550–1750,* ed. Randolph Vigne and Charles Littleton (London: Huguenot Society of Great Britain and Ireland; Brighton: Sussex Academic Press, 2001), 369.

42. Louis Effingham, *The De Forest, Dommerich, Hall and Allied Families* (New York: privately published, 1924), 26.

43. *Collections of the New-York Historical Society* (1886): 21.

44. "New York Marriages, from the Friends' Records of Philadelphia," *New York Genealogical and Biographical Record* 3, no. 1 (January 1872): 51. The name Caspar Huet is spelled in a francophone manner, but it does not appear in any other context, so it is difficult to draw conclusions as to his ethnicity. Huet may also represent a phonetic spelling of Hewett. On the other hand, several of the twenty witnesses had strong Huguenot connections. For example, John Delavall

was probably a member of the De la Cheval family of Marennes, Saintonge, where most were active in the shoemaking trades. The De la Chevals were closely allied with the DuBois family, also from Marennes, who had early connections with the Cressons and Delaplaines in Staten Island and Esopus (later Kingston); see Charles W. Baird, *History of the Huguenot Emigration to America* (New York: Dodd, Mead, 1885), 2: 28, n. 2.

45. John E. Stillwell, Historical and Genealogical *Miscellany: Data Relating to the Settlers and Settlement of New York and New Jersey* (Baltimore: Genealogical Publishing Co., 1970), 1: 150–56; Baird, *History of the Huguenot Emigration to America*, 1: 186–200; James Riker, *Harlem: Its Origins and Early Annals* (Upper Saddle River, N.J.: Literature House, 1970), 301; *New York Genealogical and Biographical Record*, 12 no. 4 (October 1881): 188. For the ethnicity of individuals in 1706 Staten Island census, see Field Horne, "The Social Historical Context of the Voorlezer's House at Richmondtown, Staten Island, New York" (on file at Richmondtown Restoration, Staten Island Historical Society, 1986), 135–52. On the Waldenses of seventeenth-century Staten Island, see John Romeyn Brodhead, *History of the State of New York,* 2 vols. (New York: Harper, 1853–71), 1: 631–32, 692.

46. Horne, "Social Historical Context of the Voorlezer's House," 140. At his death in 1714, for example, the inventory of Mark du Sauchoy's possessions on his Richmondtown farm recorded 1,000 sheaves of flax worth £3.5s.; 20 bushels of flax seed (£1.10s.); a "break for flax" (5s. 9d.), and a "hatchill" (£1.3s.). Du Sauchoy's father, who came to New Netherlands from Picardy in 1657, typifies the northern French origin of numerous pre-1664 refugees.

47. Sung Bok Kim, *Landlord and Tenant in Colonial New York: Manorial Society, 1664–1775* (Chapel Hill: University of North Carolina Press, 1978), frontispiece, 37–71, 284–351; see also the map and reconstruction of "Dutch and English Land Grants, 1629–1708," in Roderick H. Blackburn and Ruth Piwonka, *Remembrance of Patria: Dutch Arts and Culture in Colonial America, 1609–1776* (Albany, N.Y.: Albany Institute of History and Art, 1988), 64–65, esp. nos. 22, 24.

48. When the new fighting erupted in 1663, Pierre Cresson joined an expedition of soldiers from Staten Island that successfully defended Wiltwyck. In this military capacity, Cresson may have encountered Underhill, himself involved in similar land-grabbing expeditions not far away.

49. Baird, *History of the Huguenot Emigration to America*, 1: 190–200; ibid., 65, no. 24. The original recipients of the New Paltz land grant in 1677 were Louis DuBois, Abraham Hasbrouck, Andreis LeFebre, Jean Hasbrouck, Peter Deyo, Lewis Bevier, Antoine Crispel, Abraham DuBois, Hugo Frere, Isaac DuBois, and Simon LeFevre. The DuBois family of New Paltz originated in Marennes, Saintonge, see ibid., 2: 28, n. 2.

50. See Peter M. Kenny, "Flat Gates, Draw Bars, Twists, and Urns: New York's Distinctive, Early Baroque Oval Tables with Falling Leaves," *American Furniture, 1994,* ed. Luke Beckerdite (Hanover, N.H.: University Press of New England / Chipstone Foundation, 1994): 106–35.

51. The four staircases in Saint-Martin-de-Ré are in the Arsenal of the Citadel (1681–85; the best documented), Les Glandiers (ca. 1695), La Croix-Blanche, and no. 11, quai Job-Foran, a private house (both late 1600s–early 1700s?); see *Inventaire général des monuments et des richesses artistiques de la France, Commission régionale de Poitou-Charentes, Charente-Maritime, Cantons Île de Ré* (Paris: Ministère de la culture, Direction du patrimoine, 1979), 292–304, 312–41, 433–506, 437–535.

52. See Guillaume Janneau, *Pour discerner les styles dans le mobilier—Les Arts decoratifs: Les Meubles de l'art antique au style Louis XIV* (Paris: Librairie d'Art R. Ducher, 1929), 30–31, figs. 28–31.

53. *Collections of the New-York Historical Society* (1892): 450; see also J. Stewart Johnson, "New York Cabinetmaking Prior to the Revolution"(M.A. thesis, University of Delaware, 1964), 25. This master's thesis contains the most complete transcription to date of Joshua Delaplaine's account books. The exact date of Joshua's death is uncertain, although his will was dated October 2, 1771.

54. Thomas Story, *A Journal of the Life of Thomas Story: Containing, an account of his remarkable convincement of, and embracing the principle of truth, as held by the people called Quakers; and also, of his travels and labours in the service of the Gospel: with many other occurences and observations* (Newcastle upon Tyne: Isaac Thompson, 1747), 249.

55. Jon Butler, "Thinking About Dutch-English Religious Interaction in New York and Connecticut," in *Impact of New Netherlands upon the Colonial Long Island Basin,* ed. Lane, 53.

56. The Burling-Delaplaine accounts for 1721–27 are transcribed in full in Johnson, "New York Cabinetmaking Prior to the Revolution," appendix E.

57. Ibid.

58. Ibid., appendix F.

59. *New York Gazette,* August 26–September 2, 1728, and August 23–30, 1731.

60. Denis J. Maika, "Slaves and Slaveholding in New York's Philipse Family, 1660–1750" (on file at Historic Hudson Valley Library, Tarrytown, New York, September 1997), 1–53.

61. Mayor's common council minutes, May 5, 1736, Municipal Archives file 369. On the maritime and mercantile social geography of the East Ward during the early eighteenth century, see Thomas J. Archdeacon, *New York City, 1664–1710: Conquest and Change* (Ithaca, N.Y.: Cornell University Press, 1976), 92–93.

62. An illustration of the face-grain plug technique used on New York Colony furniture may be found in Peter M. Kenny, "New York's Distinctive, Early Baroque Oval Tables with Falling Leaves," 128, fig. 33. Variations of the concealed or invisible pin appear in canoes built in the Dutch East Indies. The words "pin" and "deck" (under which the pins were concealed) were Dutch words unknown in Indonesia before they were adopted by the Moluccan language to describe this construction method on local cora-cora, or war vessels, so it is logical to assume the joint was a Dutch innovation in the colonized culture; see Paul Michael Taylor, "New Netherlands and the Netherlands East Indies," in *Impact of New Netherlands upon the Colonial Long Island Basin,* ed. Lane, 62–63.

63. John Gardner, "The Dutch Influence on Colonial American Small Craft," in *Impact of New Netherlands upon the Colonial Long Island Basin,* ed. Lane, 75.

64. For Burling's genealogy and transatlantic Quaker associations, see Lawrence Buckley Thomas, *The Thomas Book: Giving the Genealogies of Sir Rhys ap Thomas, K.G., the Thomas Family Descended from Him, and of Some Allied Families* (New York: Henry T. Thomas Co., 1896), n.p.; "Records of the Society of Friends of the City of New York and Vicinity: 1640–1800," *New York Genealogical and Biographical Record* 3, no. 4 (October 1872): 111–12; and William A. Eardeley, "Notes on Flushing Quaker Families" (Long Island Historical Society, MS, file 234), n.p.

65. "John and Samuel Bowne Account Book," 29, 1st mo, 1681.

66. Ibid., 1681 and 1687.

67. Ibid.; see also *Collections of the New-York Historical Society* (1886): 52.

68. See J. W. Wallace, *Address at the 200th Anniversary of the Birth of William Bradford* (Albany, N.Y., 1863).

69. Onderdonk, *Annals of Hempstead,* 12–14.

70. William Penn, *A Brief Account of the Province of Pennsylvania, Lately Granted by the King, Under the Great Seal of England, To William Penn* (London: Benjamin Clark, 1681); and William Penn, *A Brief Account of the Province of East-Jersey in America, Published by the Present Proprietors Thereof, viz, William Penn et al, For Information of all such Persons who may be Inclined to Settle Themselves, Families and Servants in that Country* (London: Benjamin Clark, 1682).

71. "John and Samuel Bowne Account Book," n.d. (ca. 1690), n.p., records land transactions valued at £50 involving a transfer of ownership in Philadelphia and Chester County to Bowne's son Samuel. Bowne knew Penn well enough by 1683 to record Penn's debt for £13.10s. "for cyder & hay"; and his account book also notes (by Samuel) for "the 7 mo/ 1700: then dis-borsed at [Jamaica, Long Island,] on ye account of entertainment for William penn & other friends: 1= 10: 00." See John Bowne Account Book, entries for "1683," and "7 mo/ 1700."

72. John Bowne Account Book, entry by Samuel Bowne, "11 of ye 2nd mo 96."

73. William Wade Hinshaw, *The Encyclopedia of American Quaker Genealogy: New York City and Long Island* (Ann Arbor, Mich.: Edwards Brothers, 1940), 3: 117; Floyd Ferris, *The Jeffrey Ferris Family Genealogy* (Ithaca, N.Y.: privately published, 1963), 5–6; and Henry R. Stiles, *The History of Ancient Wethersfield,* 2 vols. (Somersworth, N.H.: New Hampshire Publishing Co., 1904), 2: 320.

74. Story, *Journal,* 221.

75. Ibid., 256–57.

76. The Townsends, a large Quaker family of woodworking artisans, often attended these meetings to hear Story and his friends speak. They followed much the same pattern of land acquisition as the Ferrises, but began their penetration of the Sound region from Oyster Bay rather than Flushing. As a result, most of their landholdings were in Oyster Bay and Newport, not Westchester. Oyster Bay remained mostly a mix of Quaker migrants who converged on the new town from Flushing and Wethersfield. There were many exceptions, however. When Daniel Townsend, a carpenter, died in his hometown of Oyster Bay in 1732, he was credited with several land grants in what was then called Westchester County. We also know the Feke family had interests in both Flushing and Oyster Bay, as well as Westchester Town and Newport. For a nearly complete list of the woodworking Townsends of Oyster Bay, ca. 1660–1776, see Failey, *Long Island Is My Nation,* 260. I would add to that list the probable father of Daniel Townsend (d. 1732), also named Daniel Townsend, a carpenter and turner of "Cedar Swamp" (Oyster Bay), who died in 1722, when his probate inventory was taken; see his inventory on file at the New-York Historical Society, taken on May 2, 1722.

77. Lloyd Ultan, *The Bronx in the Frontier Era: From the Beginning to 1696* (The Bronx, N.Y.: Bronx County Historical Society, 1993), 70–80, 127–28, 150–56; David William Voorhees, "Jacob Leisler and the Huguenot Network in the English Atlantic World," in *From Strangers to Citizens: The Integration of Immigrant Communities in Britain, Ireland, and Colonial America, 1550–1750,* ed. Randolph Vigne and Charles Littleton (London: Huguenot Society of Great Britain and Ireland; Brighton: Sussex Academic Press, 2001), 322–25.

78. On the specifics of this "land grab" for the lower Hudson Valley and the pressures English settlers placed on New Amsterdam between 1654 and 1664, see Ultan, *Bronx in the Frontier Era,* 64.

79. *Collections of the New-York Historical Society* (1886): 585.

80. Ibid., 612–13, and 107.

81. Ibid., 614.

82. Quaker records for the Flushing meeting note that Bejamin Burling was born "6 day 12 mo 1689–90" and died "at New York 21 day 10 mo 1709".

83. James Burling was listed as a "New York merchant" on April 13, 1753, when he purchased £58.14.10 worth of molasses; see Holmes Account Book, Winterthur Museum, Joseph Downs Manuscript Collection (no. 71 x 71 w). He was called an "attorney" on September 28, 1737; see Trinity Church Vestry Minutes, 1: 189.

84. Failey, *Long Island Is my Nation,* 92, fig. 110.

85. *Collections of the New-York Historical Society* (1886): 620.

86. Effingham, *De Forest, Dommerich, Hall and Allied Families,* 236; see also Carl Boyer, ed., *Ship Passenger Lists, New York and New Jersey, 1600–1825* (Newhall, Calif.: privately published, 1978), 236. Both sources say Vincent Tillou died sometime before September 27, 1709.

87. Two artisans named John Vincent were listed in the 1710 probate inventory of the New York merchant Ouzeel Van Swieten. One John Vincent was called a "leather dresser of New York City," the other a "cooper." The pair were probably father and son. The John Vincents were named creditors of Van Swieten's estate for £13.17.½ in leather goods, and £118.14.½ for cooperage. It is reasonable to assume that John Vincent the cooper was the father, for he appears as such in New York's records as early as 1676, when he was taxed £100 pounds. Queens College, Albany 2: 2–284, July 19, 1710; see also New York City Tax List for 1676, in *New York Genealogical and Biographical Record* 2, no. 1 (January 1871): 37.

88. *Collections of the New-York Historical Society* (1885): 63.

89. Inventory at New-York Historical Society, taken July 1, 1734.

90. *New York Gazette,* no. 386 (March 13–20, 1732).

91. On enslaved African-American artisans working as skilled labor in the maritime trades in Philadelphia, Richmond, and Charleston during the early eighteenth century, see Gary B. Nash, *Forging Freedom: The Formation of Philadelphia's Black Community, 1720–1840* (Cambridge, Mass.: Harvard University Press, 1988), 8–37; and id., "Slaves and Slave Owners in Colonial Philadelphia," in *African Americans in Pennsylvania: Shifting Historical Perspectives,* ed. Joe William Trotter Jr. and Eric Ledell Smith (University Park: Pennsylvania State University Press, 1997), 56–60; James Sidbury, *Ploughshares into Swords: Race, Rebellion, and Identity in Gabriel's Virginia, 1730–1810* (Cambridge: Cambridge University Press, 1997), 152–219; Philip D. Morgan, "Black Life in Eighteenth-Century Charleston," *Perspectives in American History,* n.s., 1 (1984): 188–206; and Morgan, "British Encounters with Africans and African-Americans," in *Strangers Within the Realm: Cultural Margins of the First British Empire,* ed. Bernard Bailyn and Philip D. Morgan (Chapel Hill: University of North Carolina Press, 1991), 176–78. On the intricate practice and system of rates for hiring skilled slave artisans, an important business in Richmond, see Sidbury, *Ploughshares into Swords,* 187–201.

92. Quoted in Morgan, "Black Life in Eighteenth-Century Charleston," 205. On Huguenot dominance in the woodworking trades of early eighteenth-century Charleston, see Luke Beckerdite, "Religion, Artisanry, and Cultural Identity: The Huguenot Experience in South Carolina, 1680–1725," *American Furniture, 1997,* ed. id. (Hanover, N.H.: University Press of New England, 1997): 197–227; this includes an appendix listing refugee joiners in the Low Country and their presumed origins in France.

93. On hiring large gangs of unskilled slave labor for urban civic projects, and the value of protecting skilled slave labor for the lucrative hiring business, see Sidbury, *Ploughshares into Swords,* 160–76, 187–201.

94. On the slave community at Philips's mill in Tarrytown and the boatman Diamond's duties, see Maika, "Slaves and Slaveholding in New York's Philipse Family," 1–53.

95. Queens College, Mayor's Common Council, Municipal Archives, May 5, 1735, file 369. One of the Van Zandts was undoubtedly Johannes Van Zandt (Jean Vincent), a blockmaker who was declared a freeman of the city on June 16, 1730. He may have been Wynant's brother, son, or nephew; see *Collections of the New-York Historical Society* (1886): 114.

96. Queens College, MCC, Municipal Archives, May 5, 1736, file 369.

97. Simon Bresteade, "carpenter," came from a family of coopers, blockmakers, and turners that arrived in New Amsterdam via Holland in 1636. Simon was named a freeman of the city on August 23, 1698, see *Collections of the New-York Historical Society* (1885): 64. On the family's Danish origins, see John O. Evjen, *Scandinavian Immigrants in New York, 1630–1674* (Minneapolis: K. C. Halter, 1916), 218–20; and New York Public Library, Genealogical Division, A.V. 154 (pamphlet file): Van Bresteede Family.

98. *Collections of the New-York Historical Society* (1909): 117.

99. Ibid.

100. *Collections of the New-York Historical Society* (1909): 114–15; Johnson, "New York Cabinetmaking," 25.

101. *Collections of the New-York Historical Society* (1885): 118.

102. A tamarind is the pod of the tropical tree *Tamarindus indica,* which grew in the West Indies; its seeds were contained in a juicy pulp consumed by the colonists in beverages and foods.

103. Quoted in full in Johnson, "New York Cabinetmaking," appendix D.

104. *Collections of the New-York Historical Society* (1909): 176.

105. Minutes of the Vestry of Trinity Church, 1: 224, February 1, 1743. The original document containing Jandine's design is missing from the Trinity archives. Janine was declared a freeman carpenter on October 26, 1728, see *Collections of the New-York Historical Society* (1886): 112.

106. Queens College, Klapper Library, Manuscript Division, Mayor's Court Papers, 1: October 5, 1728; January 31, 1729.

107. Ibid., January 18, 1728; January 27, 1728. Bomier raised the £20 pound bond and was released on January 27.

108. *Collections of the New-York Historical Society* (1909): 114–15.

109. On the numerous Lawrence-Burling-Bowne family connections, see "Thomas Genealogical Notes" (New York Genealogical and Biographical Society, MS, file GT 3664), 111–12; see also *New York Genealogical and Biographical Record* 3, no. 3 (July 1872): 121–31.

110. *Collections of the New-York Historical Society* (1886): 106; moreover, a fashionable tall clock, made in New York City or Flushing, with a rare veneered case, is signed "Joseph Lawrence" on the face. The works are presumed not to be original to the case, though they are of the period and may be of New York manufacture; see Failey, *Long Island Is My Nation,* fig. 46.

111. *New York Gazette,* no. 477 (December 9–17, 1734).

112. Wilson V. Ledley, "New Netherland Families" (New York Public Library, typescript, November 1, 1958, micro *ZI-64), n.p.; Horne, " Social Historical Context of the Voorlezer's House," 140.

113. *Collections of the New-York Historical Society* (1886): 95.

114. Queens College, Klapper Library, Manuscript Division, Mayor's Court Papers, 1: April 19, 1719, Bailpiece, Christopher Rousby vs. James McGrath. The inventory of James McGrath of Flushing was appraised by Adam Lawrence on December 4, 1726. In addition to a number of

woodworker's tools, including "1 Iron Square . . . 1 Drawin Knife . . . 1 auger . . . 1 hammer . . . 1 tennent saw . . . [and] 1 Hand saw," McGrath owned several articles of furniture that must have been purchased in the city, including "1 Dressing glass 1/ 0/ 0 and 10 Cain chears 5/ 0/ 0," both imported items. See *New-York Historical Society Inventories*.

115. *Collections of the New-York Historical Society* (1886): 95.

116. *New York Gazette*, no. 518 (September 22–29, 1735).

117. See Robert F. Trent, "A Channel Islands Parallel for the Early Eighteenth-Century Connecticut Chests Attributed to Charles Guillam," *Studies in the Decorative Arts* 2, no. 1 (Fall 1994): 75–91.

118. See J. Franklin Jameson, *Narratives of New Netherland, 1609–1664* (New York: Barnes and Noble, 1909), 430; Archdeacon, *New York City, 1664–1710*, 39.

119. Baird, *History of the Huguenot Emigration to America*, 1: 282–83; Boyer, ed., *Ship Passenger Lists*, 226.

120. *Collections of the New-York Historical Society* (1909): 134; see also Johnson, "New York Cabinetmaking Prior to the Revolution," 25–26.

121. Onderdonk, *Annals of Hempstead*, 60.

122. Boyer, ed., *Ship Passenger Lists*, 231–32.

123. Onderdonk, *Annals of Hempstead*, 60; Jack L. Lindsey et al., *Worldly Goods: The Arts of Early Pennsylvania, 1680–1758* (Philadelphia: Philadelphia Museum of Art, 1999), 149–53. See 149, fig. 197, for a Chester County, Pennsylvania, table that may be compared generally with the table depicted here in figure 16.8.

124. Ibid.

125. Effingham, *De Forest, Dommerich, Hall and Allied Families*, 26.

126. Cummings, *Framed Houses of Massachusetts Bay;* see English and New England examples of beam and supporting post in figs. 215–17; brackets in figs. 17, 184, 185.

127. Failey, *Long Island Is My Nation*, 9–6, 9–7, and 23, fig. 17, for Bowne House chair; the two earliest survivals from this group may be seen in Robert Bishop, *Centuries and Styles of the American Chair, 1640–1970* (New York: Dutton, 1972), 26, figs. 15–16; see also Benno M. Forman, *American Seating Furniture*, 128–31.

128. This chair was de-accessioned from Historic Deerfield in 1982 when the curators were unable to determine its geographic origin. They speculated on New France (use of birch; absence of a lower rear stretcher), England, and mid-Atlantic America. In any case, the chair was not from the Connecticut Valley, the museum's collecting interest. Yet birch was commonly used by New York's joiners during the early period. Unlike most American joined chairs, some New York and New Jersey chairs survive with pine seats and backs. This, then, is a hybrid of Long Island Sound styles and practices made in the rural workshop of a general woodworker: the carved "crenelated" back panel adapts standard New Haven Colony practice, where the molding around the seat is also common, as in the Old Plymouth Colony west to Rhode Island, and on New York chairs (fig. 15.40); the back panel is feathered with a block plane, like rural Dutch furniture and New York and Rhode Island furniture made in the Netherlandish tradition; the ogee molding strip with its high step on the seat is common on Long Island, Hudson Valley, and New Jersey woodwork; the unusual carved volutes on the crest relate to imported cosmopolitan cane and leather chairs, but above all they are perfect miniatures of the idiosyncratic carved arms on the documented Huntington chair in fig. 16.14. The stretcher arrangement below the seat is found on all Continental but especially French chairs. Such chairs were acceptable to clients familiar

with British regional chair-making traditions and were also to be found in provincial French, German, and Dutch households. Evidence around the unusual concave seat, which harkens back to the rustic Italian sgabello, shows that it was originally upholstered, with the ogee molding at the back serving as a cushion stop.

Philip Zea, former curator (now Director) at Historic Deerfield (letter to the author, December 21, 1982), assessed its deliberations, adding: "I felt that it was Mid-Atlantic"; Dr. Bernard D. Cotton, head of the Regional Furniture Society in England (letter to the author, November 30, 1997), argued against Canada and England and for a hybrid from the shop of a rural general woodworker, but he also perceived a strong resemblance to the upright proportions of joined "chairs from Lowland Scotland and the Isle of Man (which were also Scottish in origin)," a tradition well documented in early New Jersey joined chairs; and Simon Honig, curator of the Openluchtmuseum, in Arnhem, the Netherlands, observed (letter to the author, September 24, 1997):

> the armchair is of the same type as some chairs in our collection. These chairs are all from the province [of] Limburg [Holland]. . . . In the adjoining parts of Belgium and Germany are stylistic similarities. . . . I think the original form of the chair goes back to the 16th century in the greater part of Europe, and there are relicts in the 18th century. In Limburg such relicts remain until the end of the 19th century. But in books about English furniture one can see nearly the same models. All children of the same family.

129. John and Samuel Bowne Account Book, "4d 4m 1696; and 10d 3mo 1701."

130. Story, *Journal,* 32–33.

131. Fludd, *Of the Internal Principle,* trans. Josten in "Robert Flood's Theory of Geomancy," 334–35.

132. Story, *Journal,* 32–33, 260.

133. John and Samuel Bowne Account Book, "24 day 1mo 96; 28d 3m 1696; 3 mo 1700; and 3d 3m 1696."

134. Well-situated land by a waterway was often used as an inducement to settle blacksmiths in the towns. For example, on April 5, 1720, the town of Hempstead, Long Island, assigned John Rider, of Flushing, "about three-quarters of an acre of land joining near Matthew Gerritsen's bay, joining to Nicholl's line, which comes where Elias Baily did formerly live, for to set up a smith's shop on, and to do smith work for the neighbors there adjoining as they do want it." Elias Baily was an Anglo-Huguenot from a family that included Long Island, Westchester, and New York City French-Quaker craftsmen. See Onderdonk, *Annals of Hempstead,* 69; on the Baily (Bailly, Bailey) family of Lorraine, Aunis, England, and New York, see Grenville C. Mackensie, "Early Records of the Bailey Family of Westchester County" (New York Public Library, MS, vertical file); and Hubert Élie, *De quelques familles immigrées en Lorraine* (Nancy: Berger-Levrault, 1957). Nicholas Baily was called a "cabinetmaker" and declared a freeman on June 19, 1739, *Collections of the New-York Historical Society* (1885): 139.

135. John and Samuel Bowne Account Book, see Samuel Bowne accounts with James Clement from "12 mo 1697" to "9 mo 1701." On Clement's legal skills, see Onderdonk, *Annals of Hempstead,* 14.

136. Ibid., "3 day 3 month 1696"; same page, n.d., probably same as previous; and "10th 2 mo [1696]." See also Onderdonk, *Annals of Hempstead,* 94–95. The meaning of this notation is unclear. Did it refer to an act that finalized the 1692 purchase once the building was complete and put into service as the site of the *Yearly* Meeting? Or does it refer to a new transaction in New

York. This is not easy to know. The Yearly Meeting was in the process of changing its name from the Flushing to New York Meeting between 1696 and 1702. However, the meetinghouse in Flushing remained the official site of the New York Yearly Meeting thereafter, so it stands to reason the 1692 purchase was recorded in 1696. Available evidence seems to point to these two references referring only to the meetinghouse in Flushing. If the building campaign of 1696–1701 overlapped in time with the acquisition of new property for a meetinghouse in New York (1696), it is prudent to wonder whether this work was actually performed on a purported meetinghouse in New York and not Flushing. Since none of the work done during this period refers to New York in any way (such as shipment of wood "to New York"), and all the artisans were native Flushing Quakers, and not New Yorkers, the weight of the evidence points strongly to the work being done on the interior of the Flushing meetinghouse. Recall that the contract with John Feke said the work was expected to be ready for interior finishing in late 1693—one year after the acquisition of the land. We know that the building was only minimally ready by 1694. John Bowne died in 1694, arguably causing delay. It is reasonable to assume that much interior finishing was still to be done ca. 1696–1701 in Flushing.

137. Thomas Dickenson, "James Clement of Flushing and His Children" (New York Genealogical and Biographical Society, MS, April 25, 1963, file 9699),1–3.

138. Ibid.

139. Baird, *History of the Huguenot Emigration to America*, 1: 182, and *New York Genealogical and Biographical Record* 14, no. 2 (April 1883): 184, cite the arrival in New Netherlands of Bastiaen Clement on board the ship *Faith*, from Doornick, in February 1659.

140. Teunis G. Bergen, Register in Alphabetical Order of the *Early Settlers of King's County, Long Island, New York from Its First Settlement by Europeans to 1700* (New York: S. W. Green's Son, 1881), 63–64.

141. Cummings, *Framed Houses of Massachusetts Bay,* 197; Robert A. Leath, "John Berger's Design Book: Huguenot Tradesmen and the Dissemination of the French Baroque Style," *American Furniture, 1994,* ed. Luke Beckerdite (Hanover, N.H.: University Press of New England, 1994): 136–61.

142. *Massachusetts Archives,* 129: 237; petition dated October 7, 1688; Baird, *History of the Huguenot Emigration to America,* 2: 205–8, see esp. 207–8, n. 1. Another branch of this Huguenot family migrated first to the Palatinate (where they stayed perhaps two generations) and then migrated later to Pennsylvania, where many pietistic Huguenots spoke French and German and lived in the Germanic counties. One "Clemens, Gerhard—w. 2 sons" was named on "the Board of Trade List of [the] First Party of Palatines in London, [on] May 3, 1709"; see Walter Allen Knittle, *Early Eighteenth-Century Palatine Emigration* (Baltimore: Genealogical Publishing Co., 1965), 245. This Gerhard was undoubtedly the progenitor of the Clemens family of Montgomery County, Pennsylvania. See *The Account Book of the Clemens Family of Lower Salford Township, Montgomery County, Pennsylvania, 1749–1857,* trans. Raymond E. Hollenback, ed. Alan G. Keyser (Breinigsville, Pa.: Pennsylvania German Society, 1975); Scott T. Swank, "Proxemic Patterns," in id., et al., *Arts of the Pennsylvania Germans* (New York: Norton, 1983), 40–42; and Beatrice B. Garvan and Charles F. Hummel, *The Pennsylvania Germans: A Celebration of their Arts, 1683–1850* (Philadelphia: Philadelphia Museum of Art, 1982), 151–55.

143. Dickenson, "James Clement of Flushing and His Children," 4–11.

144. Ibid.

145. Ibid., 4–5; see also Henry Onderdonk Jr., *Queens County in Olden Times* (Jamaica, N.Y.: Charles Welling 1865), 17.

146. John and Samuel Bowne Account Book, October 20, 1676, n.p.; on the James Clement farm in Bayside, see E. B. O'Callaghan, *The Documentary History of the State of New York,* 4 vols. (Albany, N.Y.: Weed, Parsons, & Comp., 1849–51), 2: 460, and *Collections of the New-York Historical Society,* 1892, Abstracts of Wills (1665–1707), 1: 468.

147. Hinshaw, *Encyclopedia of American Quaker Genealogy,* 3: 72.

148. Onderdonk, *Annals of Hempstead,* 94.

149. Dickenson, "James Clement of Flushing and His Children," 4–6.

150. Schwartz, *French Prophets,* 155–90; Swindlehurst, "'An unruly and presumptuous rabble,'" 367.

151. See François Lebrun, "The Two Reformations: Communal Devotion and Personal Piety," in *A History of Private Life: Passions of the Renaissance,* ed. Roger Chartier, trans. Arthur Goldhammer (Cambridge, Mass.: Harvard University Press, 1989), 3: 68–109.

152. O'Callaghan, ed., *Documentary History of New York,* 1: 661–65.

153. Sarah was the widow of John Hinchman, a magistrate (or *schepen*) of the town in 1673; see John Romeyn Brodhead, *Documents Relative to the Colonial History of the State of New-York Procured in Holland, England and France,* (Albany: Weed, Parsons, 1858), 2: 591.

154. *Collections of the New-York Historical Society,* 1902, Unrecorded Wills Prior to 1790, 11: 41; Dickerson, "James Clement of Flushing and His Children," 7–9.

155. Thomas Dickenson, "James Clement of Flushing and His Children," 9–10.

156. O'Callaghan, ed., *Documentary History of New York,* 1: 661–5.

157. Boyer, ed., *Ship Passenger Lists,* 142.

158. After his first appearance in the Flushing census of 1698, John Clement appears as "John Clemans of Flushing" in a minor land transaction of 1712, in which he sold ten acres of land to Joseph Ludlow of Jamaica for £30; as holding a bond in a will of the Saintongeais Huguenot John Dumaresque (De Marais, Demarest) of New York; and on April 28, 1730, as the only non-Quaker witness to the will of Hugh Coperthwait of Flushing, in which a boundary to John Clement's land was mentioned; after this last reference of 1730, John Clement disappears and may have removed from Flushing. In his will (1725), James Clement makes a large bequest of £60 to a "brother Clement." It remains unclear whether this mysterious brother was Quaker, an unnamed son—that is, one of his sons' brothers—or perhaps this John of Flushing, or Jan of New Utrecht. See Dickenson, "James Clement of Flushing and His Children," 4, 10–11.

159. Bownas's account of the controversy is quoted in full in Onderdonk, *Annals of Hempstead,* 12–14; the two quotations are from 12.

160. Ibid.

161. Ibid.

162. Ibid., 12–13.

163. Ibid., 13.

164. Ibid.

165. See *Oxford English Dictionary,* s.v. The term "bill" here refers to an indictment by a grand jury.

166. Onderdonk, *Annals of Hempstead,* 13.

167. Ibid., 14.

168. Ibid., 14.

169. Ibid.

170. Ibid.

171. Story, *Journal*, 222, 243, 256, 369.

172. Ibid., 370.

173. Samuel Clement's date of birth is surmised to be 1686 in Dickenson, "James Clement of Flushing and His Children," 11–12; Samuel Clement was the appraiser of the probate inventory of Samuel Lawrence of Flushing, taken on June 25, 1760, the latest date at which he can be documented as alive, see New-York Historical Society inventory taken June 25, 1760. Samuel Clement received a bequest of £40 but no property in James Clement's will of 1725.

174. See Failey, *Long Island Is My Nation*, 272.

175. By undocumented tradition, Samuel Clement married Sarah Jackson (b. December 11, 1697) of Flushing; see Dickenson, "James Clement of Flushing and His Children," 46–52. Sarah Jackson was the daughter of James Jackson of Flushing (d. 1735), who appeared in an advertisement in the *New York Gazette*, no. 404 (July 16–23, 1733). The Jackson family had strong ties to Hempstead, where they were among the town's largest landowners and ratepayers; see Onderdonk, *Annals of Hempstead*, 56. Was Sarah Jackson a relation of the carpenter and joiner Patrick Jackson (working in New York City in 1725), or the coopers John and William Jackson (working in New York City in 1722)? If so, it is possible that James Clement trained Patrick Jackson as an apprentice alongside his son Samuel.

176. *New-York Historical Society Inventories*, June 25, 1760. Samuel Clement's signature on this inventory precisely matches the one in the inscription of 1726. The high chest and dressing table were acquired by the New York City dealers Ginzburg and Levy directly from the Lawrence family of Flushing and resold to the Henry Francis du Pont Winterthur Museum in 1957; see Winterthur's registrar's files M57.511 and M57.512.

177. See Benno M. Forman, "The Chest of Drawers in America, 1635–1730: The Origin of the Joined Chest of Drawers," *Winterthur Portfolio* 20, no. 1 (Spring 1985): 1–30; and Robert F. Trent, "The Chest of Drawers in America, 1635–1730: A Postscript," ibid.: 31–48.

178. See Neil D. Kamil, "Of American Kasten and the Mythology of 'Pure Dutchness': A Review Article," *American Furniture, 1993*, ed. Luke Beckerdite (Hanover, N.H.: University Press of New England, 1993): 275–82; Simon Schama, *The Embarrassment of Riches: An Interpretation of Dutch Culture in the Golden Age* (New York: Knopf, 1987), ch. 6: "Housewives and Hussies: Homeliness and Worldliness." For a discussion of matrilineal furniture, the feminine sphere and maintenance of the woman's portion in early New England households, see Laurel Thatcher Ulrich, "Furniture as Social History: Gender, Property, and Memory in the Decorative Arts," *American Furniture, 1995*, ed. Luke Beckerdite and William N. Hosley (Hanover, N.H.: University Press of New England, 1995): 53–59.

179. In eighteenth-century male and female "recipes" for the Clemens family of Montgomery County, Pennsylvania—the family paradigm for material goods given newly married children to set up independent households by relatives—*both* male and female children were expected to receive some variant of the chest of drawers. For males, this was sometimes included in a desk, which might have four or five drawers underneath the fall board, to be used for apparel and other personal possessions; see *Account Book of the Clemens Family*, ed. Keyser, 10 et passim; and Swank, "Proxemic Patterns," 40–42.

180. Could this also be the high chest of drawers in the Bowne house, and descended in the Bowne family (illustrated in Failey, *Long Island Is My Nation,* fig. 41)? By tradition, this particular artifact came into the family in 1691, the date John Bowne's daughter Hannah married Benjamin Field. Furniture historians have assumed that this date was early, but it bears reexamination.

181. On kasten, see Peter M. Kenny, Frances Gruber Safford, and Gilbert T. Vincent, *American Kasten: The Dutch-Style Cupboards of New York and New Jersey, 1650–1800* (New York: Metropolitan Museum of Art, 1991), and Kamil, "Of American Kasten," 275–82; on the British-American chest of drawers as a new system of organization, see Gerald W. R. Ward, *American Case Furniture in the Mabel Brady Garvan and Other Collections at Yale University* (New Haven, Conn.: Yale University Art Gallery, 1988), 10–12; John Bowne Account Book, [ ] 1685: William [Denears] acount [*sic*]; on the de Nyse family and spellings of the surname, see Charlotte Rebecca Woglom Bangs, *Our Ancestors* (Brooklyn, N.Y.: Press of Kings County Journal, 1896), New York Public Library, Genealogical Division (file for the De Nyse family).

182. For examples of kasten with endgrain pins exposed at the front, see Kenny et al., *American Kasten,* figs. 1, 16, 17, 19, 22, 25, 26, and cat. nos. 6, 8–13, 16; for a photograph of a high chest of drawers with endgrain pins exposed attributed to James or Samuel Clement, see Failey, *Long Island Is My Nation,* fig. 17A.

183. In George Fox, *Gospel-Truth Demonstrated* (1706), 1059.

184. See Christopher Hill, *The World Turned Upside Down: Radical Ideas During the English Revolution* (New York: Viking, 1973), 260.

185. Margaret C. Jacob, *The Radical Enlightenment: Pantheists, Freemasons and Republicans* (London: George Allen & Unwin, 1981), 172, 32.

186. Story, *Journal,* iv. This quotation is from the last lines of the introduction to Thomas Story's posthumously published journal, which was written by James Wilson and John Wilson, "well-wishing friends."

187. Ibid., 362.

188. Ibid., 15–16.

189. See Roger Chartier, "The Practical Impact of Writing," and Jacques Revel, "The Uses of Civility," in *A History of Private Life: Passions of the Renaissance,* ed. Roger Chartier, trans. Arthur Goldhammer (Cambridge, Mass.: Harvard University Press, 1989), 3: 111–60, 173–82. David P. Becher, *The Practice of Writing: The Hofer Collection of Writing Manuals, 1514–1800* (Cambridge, Mass.: Harvard College Library, 1997), 52.

190. See Randall Herbert Balmar, *A Perfect Babel of Confusion: Dutch Religion and English Culture in the Middle Colonies* (New York: Oxford University Press, 1989).

191. Figures compiled by Jaap Jacobs; see his "Between Repression and Approval: Connivance and Tolerance in the Dutch Republic and New Netherland," *De Halve Maen: Magazine of the Dutch Colonial Period in America* 71, no. 3 (1998): 51–58.

192. Figures on Utrecht compiled by Benjamin Kaplan and delivered in a paper at the Brandeis University European History Colloquium, Spring 1991; see Benjamin J. Kaplan, *Calvinists and Libertines: Confession and Community in Utrecht, 1578–1620* (New York: Oxford University Press, 1995), for his argument.

193. Alastair Duke, Gillian Lewis, and Andrew Pettegree, trans. and eds., *Calvinism in Europe, 1540–1610: A Collection of Documents* (Manchester, UK: Manchester University Press, 1992), 196–99.

194. Herbert F. Ricard, ed., *Journal of John Bowne, 1650–1694* (New Orleans: Polyanthos, 1975), vii. Kieft was governor and director-general of New Netherlands from 1637 to 1646.

195. Jacobs, "Between Repression and Approval."

196. Onderdonk, *Annals of Hempstead,* 5.

197. Ibid.

198. Ibid., 6.

199. Ibid., 6–7.

200. Ibid., 18.

201. Charles U. Powell, "The Quakers in Flushing, 1657–1937," *North Shore Daily Journal* (Flushing, N.Y.), July 3, 1937.

202. Quoted in "The Winthrop Papers," *North American Review* 105, no. 217 (October 1867): 617–18.

203. Letter from John Underhill to John Winthrop Jr., April 12, 1656, *Massachusetts Historical Society Collections,* 4th ser., 2: (1859): 183.

204. On John Winthrop, Jr.'s relationship with Stuyvesant, see Robert C. Black, *The Younger John Winthrop,* 154–277.

205. Ibid., 184–6.

206. Quoted in "Winthrop Papers," 619.

207. Ian K. Steele, *Warpaths: Invasions of North America* (New York: Oxford University Press, 1994), 91.

208. Richard C. Black III, *The Younger John Winthrop* (New York: Columbia University Press, 1966), 94.

209. Failey, *Long Island Is my Nation,* 156.

210. Francis Jennings, *The Invasion of America: Indians, Colonialism, and the Cant of Conquest* (New York: Norton, 1976), 177–227; Jay Gitlin, "Cultural Geography of the Dutch in the Long Island Basin," in *Impact of New Netherlands upon the Colonial Long Island Basin,* ed. Lane, 7; Jonathan L. Fairbanks and Robert F. Trent, eds., *New England Begins: The Seventeenth Century, vol. 1: Migration and Settlement* (Boston : Museum of Fine Arts, 1982), 75.

211. Steele, *Warpaths,* 91–93.

212. Ibid., 116.

213. Myron H. Luke, "Captain John Underhill and Long Island," *Nassau County Historical Society Journal,* Winter 1964, 1–10; an English portrait of Underhill (ca. 1620–29), in military pose, is currently in the collections of the Society of the Preservation of Long Island Antiquities, and is illustrated in Failey, *Long Island Is My Nation,* 14, fig. 4.

214. Quoted in "Winthrop Papers," 618–19.

215. Jaap Jacobs, "The Hartford Treaty: A European Perspective on a New World Conflict," *De Halve Maen: Magazine of the Dutch Colonial Period in America* 68 (1995): 74–79; Jameson, *Narratives of New Netherland,* 427–31; and Black, *Younger John Winthrop,* 164–66, 390.

216. Black, *Younger John Winthrop,* 204–5; Mario Biagioli, *Galileo, Courtier: The Practice of Science in the Age of Absolutism* (Chicago: University of Chicago Press, 1993), 2–54; and id., "Galileo the Emblem Maker," *Isis* 81, no. 307 (June 1990): 230–58.

217. Black, *Younger John Winthrop,* 206–31, 268–69; see also "The Journal Kept by the Commissioners Cornelis van Ruyven, Burgomaster van Cortlandt and Mr. John Laurence, Burgher and Inhabitant of the Town of New Amsterdam, During their Journey to Hartford," October 15–26, 1663, in Jameson, *Narratives of New Netherland,* 427–45; and on the experience of pidgin

dialects in the Long Island Sound region, see John Demos, "Searching for Abbottsij Van Cummingshuysen, House Carpenter in Two Worlds," in *Impact of New Netherland upon the Colonial Long Island Basin,* ed. Lane, 13–19.

218. Black, *Younger Winthrop,* 264–77.

219. Jacobs, "Between Repression and Approval."

220. Quoted in Henry D. Waller, *History of the Town of Flushing* (Flushing, N.Y., 1899), 44.

221. E. B. O'Callaghan and B. Fernow, eds., *Documents Relative to the Colonial History of the State of New York* (Albany, N.Y., 1853–83), 1: 110–11.

222. For more on this painting, see Blackburn and Piwonka, *Remembrance of Patria,* 46, fig. 4.

223. Ricard, ed., *Journal of John Bowne,* appendix; see also, Haynes Trebor, *The Flushing Remonstrance* (Flushing, N.Y., 1957), 3–4.

224. Ricard, ed., *Journal of John Bowne,* 33–34. Ricard's edited transcription is heroic, because the orthography displayed by Bowne is strange even by seventeenth-century standards. The original, preserved in the manuscript room of the New-York Historical Society, is almost indecipherable; the original manuscript pages quoted are fol. 63 and fol. 63 verso.

225. Another precedent for Samuel Clement's inscription on the high chest in 1726.

226. Ricard, ed., *Journal of John Bowne,* 69, n. 123.

227. Ibid., 70–71, n. 124.

228. On the extent of ecumenical pietism in colonial America, see John B. Frantz, "The Awakening of Religion Among the German Settlers in the Middle Colonies," *William and Mary Quarterly,* 33 (1976): 274–87.

229. John Bossy, *Christianity in the West, 1400–1700* (Oxford: Oxford University Press, 1985), 109–14.

230. Ibid., 111–12.

231. H. Gelin, "Inscriptions huguenotes (Poitou, Aunis, Saintonge, etc.)," *Bulletin de la Société de l'histoire du protestantisme français* 42, no. 11 (1893): 565–88; and pt. 2 ("Suite"), ibid., no. 12 (1893): 658–60.

232. Ibid., pt. 1, 588.

233. Ibid., 568.

234. Ibid., 569.

235. Thomas Roberts, a Huguenot "wine cooper" named a freeman of New York City in 1698, who was witness to the indenture of the Huguenot Pierre Traviere to the Rochelais master cooper Pierre Chaigneau, was probably descended from the same family. See *Collections of the New-York Historical Society* (1886): 67, 77; Mayor's Court Papers, 1: December 10, 1706; Pierre (or Peter) Chaigneau was a refugee from La Rochelle who immigrated to New York via England in 1691. He was naturalized in London on March 21, 1688, and was made a freeman of New York City on May 29, 1691, see Baird, *History of the Huguenot Emigration to America,* 1: 288.

236. Gelin, "Inscriptions huguenotes," pt. 1, 585.

237. Ibid.; on La Rochelle's surviving *inscriptions lapidaires,* I have benefited from personal communications with the late local antiquarian, Father Bernard Coutant.

238. Gelin, "Inscriptions huguenotes," 586. I translate *lobiet* here as *l'aubier,* or sapwood. But *lobiet* may also suggest a play on *obier,* a wild rose or guelder rose. The Rosicrucians, as well as many pietist groups, used the thorned, sweet-smelling rose to represent the emergence of the Holy Spirit out of pain and suffering.

239. For a brief biographical sketch and the publication in toto of the single surviving copy

of this important design book, now in the collections of the Historic Charleston Foundation, see Robert A. Leath, "Jean Berger's Design Book: Huguenot Tradesmen and the Dissemination of the French Baroque Style," *American Furniture, 1994,* ed. Luke Beckerdite (Hanover, N.H.: University Press of New England, 1994): 136–61.

240. Orest Ranum, "The Refuges of Intimacy," in Philippe Ariès and Georges Duby, eds., *A History of Private Life,* vol. 3: *Passions of the Renaissance,* trans. Arthur Goldhammer, ed. Roger Chartier (Cambridge, Mass.: Harvard University Press, Belknap Press, 1987–91): 231–33.

241. Gelin, "Inscriptions huguenotes," pt. 1, 572–74, for other examples.

242. Ibid., 573.

243. Ibid, 574–55; for more on the Rabaine d'Usson family, see Alexandre Crottet, *Histoire des églises réformées de Pons, Gemozac et Mortagne en Saintonge, précédée d'une notice étendue sur l'établissement de la réforme dans cette province, l'Aunis et l'Angoumois* (Bordeaux: A. Castillon, 1841), 85. For an illustration of the Château d'Usson, moved from its original location in 1884, see Louis Papy, *Aunis et Saintonge* (Grenoble: B. Arthaud, 1937), 54.

244. Jacques-Louis Ménétra, *Journal of My Life,* ed. Daniel Roche, trans. Arthur Goldhammer (New York: Columbia University Press, 1986), 239–40; from the coda, "Epistle to My Mind."

245. For the religious dimensions of Leisler's rebellion and its aftermath, see Randall Balmer, "Traitors and Papists: The Religious Dimensions of Leisler's Rebellion," *New York History* 70 (1989): 341–72; Donna Merwick, "Being Dutch: An Interpretation of Why Jacob Leisler Died," *New York History* 70 (1989): 376–86; Adrian Howe, "The Bayard Treason Trial: Dramatizing Anglo-Dutch Politics in Early Eighteenth-Century New York City," *William and Mary Quarterly* 47 (1990): 62–63, 85–89; David William Vorhees, "'In Behalf of the true Protestant Religion': The Glorious Revolution in New York" (Ph.D. diss., New York University, 1988).

246. On the Anglicans, see John Webb Pratt, *Religion, Politics, and Diversity: The Church-State Theme in New York History* (Ithaca, N.Y.: Cornell University Press, 1967), 49–77; Milton M. Klein, "Church, State, and Education: Testing the Issues in Colonial New York," *New York History* 45 (1964): 291–303; and Robert J. Gough, "The Myth of the 'Middle Colonies': An Analysis of Regionalization in Early America," *Pennsylvania Magazine of History and Biography,* 408–9. For the classic formulation of the conflict between sacerdotalism and lay piety as an animating force in the reformation, see Steven E. Ozment, *The Reformation in the Cities: The Appeal of Protestantism in Sixteenth-Century Germany and Switzerland* (New Haven, Conn.: Yale University Press, 1975); and for New England, see David D. Hall, *The Faithful Shepherd: A History of the New England Ministry in the Seventeenth Century* (Chapel Hill: University of North Carolina Press, 1972).

247. Quoted in Frantz, "Awakening of Religion," 273.

248. Ibid., 283. It is important to remember that although Muhlenberg was sent by the pietistic Lutheran Halle Missionary Society to Pennsylvania and has always been associated with German pietism in that colony, he also served the Lutheran congregation in New York City for a time and traveled as an itinerant throughout the Hudson, Mohawk, Delaware, and Susquehanna river valleys during the 1740s. Communication between disparate German sects from New York to Georgia—including both pietists and non-pietists (such as the Mennonites, Amish, and Schwenkfelders)—cannot be overestimated as an important factor in understanding their common history.

249. Story, *Journal,* 220.

250. Ibid., 221.

251. Ibid.

252. Bossy, *Christianity in the West,* 113.

253. Story, *Journal, 22.*

254. Quoted in Carlo Ginzburg, *The Cheese and the Worms: The Cosmos of a Sixteenth-Century Miller,* trans. John and Anne Tedeschi (Baltimore: Johns Hopkins University Press, 1980), 55–56.

255. Ibid., 127.

256. Ibid., 9–10.

257. Quoted in Hill, *World Turned Upside Down,* 186.

258. Bossy, *Christianity in the West,* 113.

259. See Ginzburg, *Cheese and the Worms,* 76–81; O'Callaghan, ed., *Documentary History of the State of New York,* 3: 106; and for the artisanal context, see Failey, *Long Island Is My Nation,* 13.

260. Barry Levy, *Quakers and the American Family: British Settlement in the Delaware Valley* (New York: Oxford University Press, 1988), 25–52.

261. Ibid., 85.

262. Fernand Braudel, *The Mediterranean and the Mediterranean World in the Age of Philip II,* Siân Reynolds, trans. (New York: Harper Colophon, 1976), 2: 665. Braudel was referring here to the social, cultural and political organization of the pluralistic Ottoman Empire, during the late fifteenth and sixteenth centuries.

263. Richard Bauman, *Let Your Words Be Few: Symbolism of Speaking and Silence Among Seventeenth-Century Quakers* (Prospect Heights, Ill.: Waveland Press, 1990), 1–19.

264. Ibid., 21.

265. Ibid., 24.

266. Euan Cameron, *The Reformation of the Heretics: The Waldenses of the Alps, 1580–1580* (Oxford: Clarendon Press, 1984), 224.

267. Bauman, *Let Your Words Be Few,* 24.

268. Ibid., 3–4.

269. Ibid., 4.

270. Ibid.

271. Fludd, *Of the Internal Principle,* 334–35. Fludd refers here to Charles de Lorraine (1571–1640), the fourth duc de Guise since 1588; and his brother, François Alexandre Paris de Lorraine, chevalier de Guise (1589–1614), knight of Malta, see Josten, "Robert Fludd's Theory of Geomancy," 335, nn. 34–35.

272. Bossy, *Christianity in the West,* 113.

273. Ibid., 113–14.

274. Walter J. Ong, *Orality and Literacy: The Technologizing of the Word* (London: Methuen, 1982), 121; on Bossy's use of Ong, "the most interesting of the more theoretical approaches," see *Christianity in the West,* 179.

275. Benjamin Franklin, *Autobiography,* ed. J. A. Leo Lemay and P. M. Zell (New York: Norton, 1986), 22–23.

276. Benjamin W. Labaree, "Colonial Trade and Shipping Between Connecticut and New Netherlands," in *Impact of New Netherlands upon the Colonial Long Island Basin,* ed. Lane, 66.

277. See esp. Carlo Ginzburg, *Clues, Myths and the Historical Method,* trans. John Tedeschi and Anne Tedeschi (Baltimore: Johns Hopkins University Press, 1989); see also John Martin, "Journeys to the World of the Dead," *Journal of Social History* 25, no. 3 (Spring 1992): 616–19, a

useful review of Ginzburg's methodologies and influences, as well as a good summary of the interdisciplinary literature of pluralistic convergence; and Natalie Zemon Davis, "The Sacred and the Body Social in Lyon," *Past and Present* 90 (1981): 68–69.

278. Quoted in Pamela H. Smith, *The Business of Alchemy: Science and Culture in the Holy Roman Empire* (Princeton, N.J.: Princeton University Press, 1994), 52.

279. J. Franklin Jameson, "Narrative of Father Jogues, Reported by Father Buteux, 1645," in id., *Narratives of New Netherland,* 252.

280. This refers to the Hundred Associates, also known as the Company of New France, which controlled the monopoly for New France from 1627 to 1663.

281. Aloysius Gonzaga (1568–1591), also San Luigi di Gonzaga. Gonzaga had been beatified as a Jesuit saint in Jogues's lifetime (in 1621), and was canonized in 1726.

282. Jameson, *Narratives of New Netherland,* 253.

283. Ibid., 252.

SEVENTEEN ❧ Reflections on a Three-Legged Chair

1. On the relation of Leddell's transatlantic life and metalwork, with particular emphasis on origins of his propagandistic religious and political imagery, see Janine E. Skerry and Jeanne Sloane, "Images of Politics and Religion on Silver Engraved by Joseph Leddel," *Antiques* 141. no. 3 (March 1992): 490–99; for discussions of the Leddel sundial, see Donald L. Fennimore, "The Sundial in America," ibid. 142, no. 2 (August 1992): 196–203, and id., *Metalwork in Early America: Copper and Its Alloys from the Winterthur Collection* (Winterthur, Del.: Henry Francis du Pont Winterthur Museum, 1996), 294–95.

2. Martha Gandy Fales and Robert L. Raley, "Christopher Colles, Engineer and Architect," *Winterthur Newsletter* 5, no. 7 (September 25, 1959): 1; Fennimore, *Metalwork in Early America,* 290; the four known Christopher Colles sundials are in the collections of the Smithsonian Institution, Washington D.C.; the New-York Historical Society, New York City; and Van Cortlandt Manor, Historic Hudson Valley, Tarrytown, N.Y. (with a history of ownership in the Van Cortlandt family); the fourth was found on Long Island and is currently in a private collection. Of the four, only the latter sundial (fig. 17.2) retains its original iron gnomon with a copper laminate arm. See also the brass and copper hydrometer, used to measure the density of liquids (especially spirits such as rum), "Invented and Made by Christopher Colles. New-York," currently in the Henry Francis du Pont Winterthur Museum, Winterthur, Delaware, in Fennimore, *Metalwork in Early America,* fig. 187, 290.

3. The term *fugio* connotes "disappear" as well as "fly."

4. For sundial placement, see Fennimore, *Metalwork in Early America,* 294.

5. Skerry and Sloane, "Images of Politics and Religion on Silver Engraved by Joseph Leddel," 490–99; and *The Collection of Mr. and Mrs. Eddy Nicholson* (New York: Christie's, January 27–28, 1995), lot 621, 40–43.

6. On perceptions of Huguenot monarchomachs, see Quentin Skinner, *The Foundations of Modern Political Thought: The Age of Reformation* (Cambridge: Cambridge University Press, 1978), 2: 301.

7. For a nineteenth-century example of just such a construction, see Marco Sioli, "Huguenot Traditions in the Mountains of Kentucky: Daniel Trabue's Memories," *Journal of American History* 84, no. 4 (March 1998): 1313–33.

8. For the French tradition that informed Leddell's understanding of emblematic structures, see David Russell, *Emblematic Structures in Renaissance French Culture* (Toronto: University of Toronto Press, 1995), 111–91.

9. Archibald Kennedy, *An Essay on the Government of the Colonies* (New York, 1752), 3; for the political context in the 1750s, see Alan Tully, *Forming American Politics: Ideals, Interests, and Institutions in Colonial New York and Pennsylvania* (Baltimore: Johns Hopkins University Press, 1994). For more on Kennedy, see Cathy Matson, *Merchants and Empire: Trading in Colonial New York* (Baltimore: Johns Hopkins University Press, 1998), 225, 254, 292.

10. Kennedy, *Essay on the Government of the Colonies*, 3.

11. Ibid., 22.

12. William Smith, *Opinion Humbly Offered to the General Assembly of New York: Mr. Smith's Opinion, relating to Courts of Equity within the Colony of New-York* (New York, 1734), 2. While adopting his well-known tactics, Kennedy does not invoke Coke's name per se, although, as in Smith's case, this was a commonplace of New York political discourse during the 1750s. When Coke was named outright by pamphleteers, it was usually in support of assembly rights and in close association with his role as Parliament's legal historian in the Commons debates of 1627–28.

13. Kennedy, *Essay on the Government of the Colonies*, 20.

14. Ibid., 22.

15. Ibid., 20.

16. Ibid.

17. Ibid.

Index